CLASSIC TRACKS
BACK TO BACK SINGLES

Thunder Bay Press

An imprint of the Advantage Publishers Group
10350 Barnes Canyon Road, San Diego, CA 92121
www.thunderbaybooks.com

Volume copyright © 2008 by Outline Press Ltd.
Text © 2008 by Outline Press Ltd.

ISBN–13: 978–1–59223–872–9
ISBN–10: 1–59223–872–6

The Library of Congress has cataloged the original Thunder Bay edition as follows:

Singles : six decades of hot hits & classic cuts / [edited by] Tony Bacon.
        p. cm.
    ISBN-13: 978-1-59223-651-0
    ISBN-10: 1-59223-651-0
    1. Popular music--Discography. 2. Popular music--Biography. 3. Sound
recording industry. I. Bacon, Tony, 1954-

    ML156.4.P6S58 2006
    781.6409'045--dc22

                                                            2006051104

WITH CONTRIBUTIONS FROM

JOHNNY BLACK
MARK BREND
TONY BURTON
SEAN EGAN
JOEL MCIVER
JOHN MORRISH
TAMARA PALMER
THOMAS JEROME SEABROOK

COMMISSIONING EDITOR: **THOMAS JEROME SEABROOK**
EDITOR: **TONY BACON**
DESIGN: **BALLEY DESIGN LIMITED**

Printed by Colorprint Offset Ltd. (Hong Kong)

1 2 3 4 5 12 11 10 09 08

CLASSIC TRACKS BACK TO BACK SINGLES

Introduction

Classic Tracks Back To Back: Singles profiles more than 750 of the most important records from the 1950s to the present day.

The book opens in the rock'n'roll era with such undisputed classics as '(We're Gonna) Rock Around The Clock' by Bill Haley & His Comets **6**, 'Maybellene' by Chuck Berry **14**, and 'Jailhouse Rock' by Elvis Presley **30**.

The three-minute pop single was arguably at its most influential in the 1960s. Phil Spector upped the ante in 1963 with his productions of hits by The Crystals and The Ronettes **60**. Spector's 'Wall Of Sound' was the primary inspiration behind The Beach Boys' 'Good Vibrations' **82**, either side of which came Bob Dylan's six-minute epic 'Like A Rolling Stone' **78** and The Beatles' classic double A-side 'Penny Lane' / 'Strawberry Fields Forever' **88**. The 1960s were awash, too, with great soul singles, from 'Stand By Me' by Ben E. King **48** and 'Reach Out I'll Be There' by The Four Tops **86** to 'Respect' by Aretha Franklin **99** and Otis Redding's '(Sittin' On) The Dock Of The Bay' **107**.

In the 1970s, what constituted a popular-music single became harder and harder to quantify. It could mean anything from pensive piano balladry, in the form of John Lennon's 'Imagine' **126** to the R&B-funk of Stevie Wonder's 'Superstition' **137**; from epic, operatic rock – Queen's 'Bohemian Rhapsody' **152** – to punchy disco-pop, such as The Bee Gees' 'Stayin' Alive' **172**.

The 1980s were similarly eclectic. Synth pop, typified by 'Don't You Want Me' by The Human League **193**, set the mood, while rap made its first mark on the charts in the form of 'The Message' by Grandmaster Flash & The Furious Five **198**. The decade's biggest stars were solo artists rather than bands. Chief among them were Michael Jackson ('Billie Jean' **208**), Prince ('Kiss' **222**), and Madonna ('Like A Prayer' **235**).

The 1990s began with a sequence of record-breaking hits that seemed to cling on to the Number 1 spot for an eternity, notably '(Everything I Do) I Do It For You' by Brian Adams **249** and Whitney Houston's 'I Will Always Love You' **252**. Pure, unabashed pop made a triumphant return later in the decade in the form of 'Wannabe' by The Spice Girls **271** and '… Baby One More Time' by Britney Spears **280**.

R&B and hip-hop came to dominate the charts at the turn of the millennium, typified by Eminem's 'My Name' Is' **286** and 'Independent Women Part 1' by Destiny's Child **291**, and subsequently by such crossover hits as 'Hey Ya!' by OutKast **304** and 'Crazy' by Gnarls Barkley **316** – the first record to top the British singles chart on the strength of internet downloads alone.

A-Z listing of featured artists

1954

(We're Gonna) Rock Around The Clock
Bill Haley & His Comets

Released May 1954
Decca *9-29124* (U.S. #1) / Brunswick *05317* (U.K. #1)

The first rock'n'roll record to top the U.S. singles chart was, officially, a foxtrot. That's how Decca Records listed 'Rock Around The Clock' when it was released on May 13, 1954, tucked away discreetly on the B-side of 'Thirteen Women,' which Decca considered a more commercial waxing.

Clearly, the music business in 1955 had no more of an inkling that a new music was about to change the world than it would when The Beatles emerged in 1962, when punk arrived in 1976, or when Nirvana's grunge turned the '90s on its head. And that's enormously encouraging, because it means that despite the collective wisdom of the men in suits, despite their vast marketing budgets and their intensive audience research, the music belongs not to them but to the fans. Fans inject a healthy drop of unpredictability into the comforting formulas and tidy equations that the music industry lives by, and that is what made the triumph of 'Rock Around The Clock' so glorious.

It's like a classic detective story where all the clues are there for everyone to see – but they never come together until all is revealed at the end. In retrospect, it's obvious to us that Decca, RCA, and the other 1950s music-industry giants should have seen it coming. The electric guitar had been around since the 1930s, the term rock'n'roll was widely used as a musical description by the end of the '40s, and the spread of radio meant that white kids were increasingly exposed to black music.

Chuck Berry had been wowing live audiences with his guitar-fueled, countrified rhythm & blues since 1953, and on April 24, 1954, music trade magazine *Billboard* spelled out the future under the headline, 'Teenagers Demand Music With A Beat.' As Bill Haley himself said later: "The musical world was starved for something new. The days of the solo vocalist and the big bands had gone. About the only thing that was making noise was progressive jazz, but this was just above the heads of the average listener."

We should not judge Decca too harshly. Even if they had seen the signs, Haley was not the likeliest candidate to lead a teenage revolution. For much of his career he was billed as 'Yodeling Bill Haley – singing cowboy' and by 1954 he was already on the wrong side of 30. Nevertheless, he was ideally placed to fuse his western swing with the black roots of gospel and blues in a way that would take rock'n'roll to a mass audience. 'Rock Around The Clock' was not his priority on April 12, 1954, when Haley began a recording session in Decca's Pythian Temple Studio, a converted ballroom in New York City. The session's producer, Milt Gabler, said: "You could blow there, because there was this big, high ceiling. We had drapes hanging from the balconies, and a live wooden floor." Having worked with rhythm & blues pioneer Louis Jordan, Gabler knew how to achieve a dynamic, contemporary sound, and spent two-and-a-half hours to get a good take of 'Thirteen Women,' leaving just 30 minutes for the B-side.

'Rock Around The Clock,' written by James Myers and Max Freedman in 1952, had been recorded by Sonny Dae & His Knights as a jump jazz item, but when Haley heard it, he knew it was perfect for an idea he'd had for some while. "I felt that if I could take, say, a Dixieland tune and drop the first and third beats, and accentuate the second and fourth, and add a beat, the listeners could clap as well as dance; this would be what they were after." Unfortunately there was bad blood between

Myers and Dave Miller, head of Essex Records, to which Haley was contracted at the time. "Every time Miller would see it, he'd tear it up and throw it away," Haley recalled. "So I never could record it."

Haley's move to Decca cleared the way for recording the song, which the band re-fashioned at a rehearsal in his basement the night before the studio session. The saxophone player with Haley's group, The Comets, was Joey D'Ambrosia, who remembered: "First we listened to Sonny Dae's recording. Then we decided the record would have more bounce if we added staccato riffs throughout the song. The voicing on the riffs was three parts – sax, lead guitar, and steel [guitar]." Guitarist Danny Cedrone was uncertain about playing a guitar solo until bassist Marshall Lytle suggested he should simply re-use the one he'd played on Haley's earlier recording of 'Rock The Joint.'

Only one of The Comets, pianist Johnny Grandy, could read music, so once they were in the Pythian Temple, Gabler's years of studio experience came into play. To add zest to the backings, he would hum standard rhythm & blues riffs that the band copied by ear. It was also Gabler who told steel guitarist Billy Williamson to "take the steel bar and hit it across the strings of the guitar and make it arc. It'd make 'POW! POW!' I'd say, 'Give me some of those lightning flashes, Billy!'" Gabler also put three mikes on the drums to achieve a fuller sound and added

plenty of reverb to the track. For the final master he combined two tracks, one where Haley's voice had been drowned out by the musicians, and another on which the voice was clear.

The initial release of 'Rock Around The Clock' stiffed in the U.S., and it was not until March 1955, when it was used as the theme tune for the film *Blackboard Jungle*, that the song took off. "Kids started dancing in the aisles," explained Marshall Lytle. "Then it took the world by storm." It entered the U.S. Top 40 on May 14, 1955, and hit Number 1 on June 29. On November 25 it repeated the trick in the U.K. and became Britain's first million-selling single. Haley's subsequent U.K. tour inspired London schoolboy Cliff Richard to become Britain's first homegrown rock'n'roller, and Paul McCartney still vividly remembers seeing Haley's group at the Liverpool Odeon. "The lights went down and you had 'One, two, three o'clock, four o'clock – rock!' Bingo! There they were."

By the time Elvis Presley followed Haley to the U.S. Number 1 spot with 'Heartbreak Hotel' on April 21, 1956, it was clear that rock'n'roll was not just the most significant new musical form of the decade but a unifying force for youth of every color and creed. 'Rock Around The Clock' has by now notched up over 25 million sales worldwide, and while it was certainly not the first rock'n'roll record and arguably not the greatest, it was undeniably the one that changed everything.

FORTY-FIVE REVOLUTIONS PER MINUTE

RCA introduced the 45 rpm seven-inch vinyl disc in March 1949, probably as a panic response to the launch of a 33-1/3 rpm long-playing disc by its rival, CBS. RCA certainly rushed the little disc into production. The head of CBS had given RCA boss David Sarnoff a sneak preview of the LP only three weeks before its official launch in June 1948, hoping that RCA would start transferring its catalogue of recordings to the new medium. Instead, stung by CBS's coup, Sarnoff launched his own vinyl record.

CBS had taken the 33-1/3 speed from movie work, where it had provided a sound disc that ran as long as a standard reel of film. Using the new speed, the new vinyl, a narrower groove, and a smaller needle, the LP achieved a practical running time of 22 minutes, later extended to 30.

CBS's disc was developed by trial and error, but RCA developed the 45 using complex mathematics. Its engineers discovered that optimum sound quality came when the outside diameter of the playing area was twice that of the inner groove; that's why seven-inch records have a three-and-a-half-inch label. The 45 rpm speed gave the right frequency range and low distortion, resulting in a record with better fidelity at the end of a side than the LP.

One other factor was important: the duration of the 45 was identical to that of the old 78 shellac record, meaning RCA could simply transfer existing recordings to the new medium. In any case, the company had analyzed its catalogue and discovered that 96 per cent of its 'musical units' – songs or classical movements – were less than five minutes long. RCA thought that would answer any criticisms of the short playing time.

Singles were also cheaper to produce and sell. Not only did they use less vinyl, but they carried only two songs, meaning their musical content was much cheaper. The four-minute time limit proved absurd for classical music, but RCA coupled the discs with a new 'autochanger' record player that would play them one after the other (up to a claimed maximum of 50 minutes). The discs had a raised inner shoulder designed to protect the playing surface when they were stacked.

Early publicity for the seven-inch format made much of its convenience. The record player was smaller, and the discs would fit on shelves: 150 singles would supposedly fit into one foot of shelf space. At launch, records were issued in color-coded vinyl: black for popular music, but red for classical, green for country, yellow for children's music, and so on. This did not last long, although colored vinyl did not pose a technical problem and was revived many times in the single's long life.

The first single was a marketing tool, the 'Whirl-Away Demonstration Record,' sent to dealers early in 1949, but by the time of the official launch, RCA had 76 albums (packages of singles) and 104 singles available. It soon became apparent that the LP was a better format for classical music, and RCA even considered abandoning its 45 rpm single.

In the event, it was saved by the teenage pop market, which liked the new format because it was cheap, unbreakable, and convenient. The jukebox industry liked it too. By 1951, the other major record companies had adopted the 45 for pop, although the old 78 did survive in parallel for a while, and RCA had gone over to the LP for classical music.

Throughout the life of the 45 rpm single, manufacturing techniques stayed the same. First the disc is cut on a lathe on a blank acetate disc. That is then 'silvered,' meaning coated with a thin layer of metal, and the acetate peeled away as the first stage of creating a metal 'stamper,' with a raised track matching the original groove.

A 'pancake' of vinyl, heated to make it soft, is then placed between two stampers (for A and B sides) in a press, and the record stamped out. The record's labels are added in the same process. Excess vinyl is then cut away, leaving the single record. Although its origins are considerably more hi-tech, a CD is manufactured in much the same way, but covered with a flat protective covering.

Although it is no longer a mass-market product, the seven-inch vinyl single is still going strong as a promotional device and a magnet for collectors.

That's All Right
Elvis Presley

Released July 1954
Sun *209* (U.S.) / Not issued U.K.

Elvis Aaron Presley had visited Sam Phillips's Memphis Recording Services a couple of times in 1953 and '54 to cut a pair of double-sided acetates for his mother at $3.98 a throw. Phillips wasn't especially impressed but remarked: "We might call you sometime." That call finally came, and on Monday July 5, 1954, Elvis entered the home of Sun records on 706 Union Avenue, Memphis, Tennessee, for his first commercial recording session.

At first it was intended simply as an audition, and the recording of 'That's All Right' came about quite by accident. With Scotty Moore on guitar and Bill Black on stand-up bass, the ensemble kicked off with a rendition of 'Harbor Lights' before trying around a dozen takes of 'I Love You Because.' It was during a break in proceedings that Elvis launched into Arthur 'Big Boy' Crudup's blues 'That's All Right.' While Elvis jumped around and acted the fool, Moore and Black grabbed their instruments and joined in. The combination of Black's slapping bass and Moore's country licks was a shotgun marriage of country & western and rhythm & blues, now known as rockabilly.

It was a raw, authentic sound, but Presley's naive enthusiasm quickly evolved into quiet confidence as they made take after take, and Phillips soon realized that something new and exciting was happening. He'd finally found what he'd been looking for: a white boy who could sing the blues. As we now know, it was a defining moment in musical history, and the foundation stone of rock'n'roll was laid on that day. Asked a couple

of years later about his music, the king replied: "The colored folk been singing it and playing it just the way I'm doin' now, man, for more years than I know. Nobody paid it no mind till I goosed it up."

Rose-Marie
Slim Whitman

Released April 1954
Imperial *8236* (U.S. #22) / London *HL 8061* (U.K. #1)

Cowboy yodeler Slim Whitman was discovered by Colonel Tom Parker, who later managed Elvis Presley. Whitman refused to sing about drinkin' or cheatin', in effect putting about half of all country songs out of his reach. Nevertheless, he done good: his first U.S. Top 10 came in 1951 with 'Indian Love Call,' drawn from the 1924 musical *Rose-Marie*.

The same musical's title song became his biggest international hit, spending a staggering 11 weeks at Number 1 in Britain, a record that would be unbroken until 1991. Movie mavens will know that it's Whitman's distinctive tenor-falsetto styling on 'Indian Love Call' that causes alien brains to explode in the 1996 sci-fi spoof *Mars Attacks*.

Shake Rattle And Roll
Joe Turner

Released April 1954
Atlantic *1026* (U.S. #22) / Not issued U.K.

Atlantic Records was formed in 1947 by Ahmet Ertegun, the son of Turkey's Ambassador to Washington, with a $10,000 loan from his dentist. The label became one of the prime outlets for 1950s rhythm & blues. Ertegun was in the business not so much to make money but more for the joy of the music. He said: "I wanted to make records like the records I loved, which were real blues records." By 1954 Atlantic was having great success with Ruth Brown, The Clovers, Ray Charles, and Kansas City-born blues shouter 'Big' Joe Turner, a former vocalist with Count Basie. Featuring Ertegun and Wexler on backing vocals, 'Shake Rattle And Roll' was especially written by Atlantic songwriter Jesse Stone under the pseudonym 'Charles E. Calhoun' and recorded at Atlantic's makeshift office-cum-studio on West 56th Street on February 9th, 1954. It reached Number 1 on *Billboard's* rhythm & blues chart. (What had been called 'Race' music became 'Rhythm & Blues' when Atlantic's Jerry Wexler renamed the relevant *Billboard* chart in 1949 – R&B records were still excluded from the main 'pop' chart.) Turner, meanwhile, made plenty of money for Atlantic but, despite all his hits, didn't make much himself and died penniless in 1987. Ertegun, one of the most respected men in the business, quietly paid for the funeral and settled the mortgage on Turner's widow's home.

Hey Senorita / Earth Angel (Will You Be Mine)
The Penguins

Released October 1954
DooTone *348* (U.S. #8) / Not issued U.K.

Music critics sometimes sarcastically describe records as "sounding as if they were recorded in a garage." Well, this one was. Producer Walter Williams remembered the session: "Every time the dog barked next door, I'd have to go out and shut him up, and then we'd do another take." This was the only U.S. Top 40 hit for The Penguins, a simple but elegant recording now judged by many to be one of the finest examples of what would become known as doo-wop. The group, whose name came from the picture of Willie the Penguin seen on packs of Kool cigarettes, was signed up on the strength of Curtis Williams's song 'Hey Senorita.' It was released as the A-side, but DJs soon flipped it for 'Earth Angel.' Legal complications added other names to the credits on the record, first issued as solely a Curtis Williams composition.

Once 'Earth Angel' got on the radio, the huge demand for the record nearly bankrupted DooTone. Williams again: "The record started selling so quickly, I ran out of paper for the label. That's why 'Earth Angel' was pressed on so many different colored labels." There were a number of covers by other artists, a common occurrence at the time, most notably by The Crew Cuts, a squeaky-clean white vocal group from Canada. Their version got higher up the U.S. charts and was the hit in Britain, but hindsight tells us now that the original by The Penguins – despite the cheap and amateurish production – is one of the great doo-wop records of all time.

Mr. Sandman
The Chordettes

Released October 1954
Cadence *1247* (U.S. #1) / Columbia *DB 3553* (U.K. #1)

Big-band leader Vaughn Monroe tucked away songwriter Pat Ballard's snappy 'Mr. Sandman' on the B-side of his minor 1954 hit 'They Were Doing The Mambo.' Luckily, Archie Bleyer of Cadence Records rescued the song with a recording by The Chordettes, a girl group from Sheboygan, Michigan. Bleyer's sparkling arrangement and the girls' energetic, jazzy harmonizing rocketed it past a competing version by The Four Aces to nab the U.S. Number 1 slot on November 27, 1954, for the first of seven weeks. By the time it entered the U.K. chart in January 1955 it was up against no fewer than three other versions but still destroyed the competition. In retrospect it's clear that The Chordettes were the stylistic bridge between the barbershop harmony vocalizing of predecessors such as The Andrews Sisters and the rhythm & blues pop of The Shirelles, which would spark the girl-group craze of the early 1960s.

Pledging My Love
Johnny Ace

Released December 1954
Duke *136* (U.S. #17) / Not issued U.K.

John Marshall Alexander was signed to Duke Records in 1952 and his first hit, as Johnny Ace With The Beale Streeters, was 'My Song,' which topped Billboard's rhythm & blues chart for nine weeks. Ace was just

another sweet-voiced R&B singer with a sensitive baritone but earned eternal fame as the first rock'n'roll casualty. Drunk on vodka on Christmas Eve 1954, he shot himself – allegedly in a game of Russian roulette – backstage at a 'Negro Christmas Party' at the City Auditorium in Houston, Texas.

His posthumous hit 'Pledging My Love,' recorded in Houston on January 17, 1954, was co-written by Duke owner Don Robey and featured backup by Johnny 'Hand Jive' Otis & His Orchestra. There was a competing chart version by Teresa Brewer on Coral. The song has been much covered over the years, and in a bizarre coincidence was on the B-side of 'Way Down,' Elvis Presley's single at the time of his death.

White Christmas
Bing Crosby

Released October 1942
Decca *18429* (U.S.) / Brunswick *03384* (U.K) / Numerous chart entries

With a boost in popularity during 1954 thanks to its inclusion as the theme song of a Bing Crosby movie, it's no surprise that 'White Christmas' peaked at Number 13 in the U.S. *Billboard* chart that December. In fact, it had charted virtually every year since its first release in 1942 – and for some reason nearly always around December.

Indeed, until recently, Crosby's version of 'White Christmas' was the biggest selling single record of all time, having sold over 30 million copies over many, many years. It was Elton John who finally beat the record, with his version of 'Candle In The Wind,' specially recorded to mark the funeral of Diana, Princess Of Wales, and selling 33 million copies in just a few months.

Crosby was without doubt the biggest star of the first half of the 20th century, arriving when radio was entering its golden era and beginning his recording career just as the electric microphone was introduced, allowing for a close-up 'crooning' style of singing. He became America's greatest ever radio star, and appeared in over 50 Hollywood movies, including the famous *Road* series with his lifetime friend Bob Hope.

'White Christmas' was written by Irving Berlin for the 1942 Crosby movie Holiday Inn. For those who complain that "they don't write songs like they used to" and maintain that modern songwriters lack the requisite skills, it's interesting to note that Berlin could not read music and could only play the piano in one key, and only on the black notes. Recalling the day he first presented the song to the relaxed crooner, Berlin said: "When he read the song he just took his pipe out of his mouth and said to me, 'You don't have to worry about this one, Irving.'"

Crosby premiered the song on his radio show on Christmas Day 1941 and went into the studio to record it the following summer. It was May 29, 1942, and there was a 90-degree heatwave in Los Angeles. The air-conditioning had broken down, so Crosby stripped to the waist in the summer heat to sing: "I'm dreaming of a white Christmas." When the original masters of this 1942 recording wore out, Crosby made a new version, in March 1947, but the singer, the engineers, the John Scott Trotter Orchestra, and the Ken Darby Singers kept as close as possible to their original. No doubt it will still be selling strongly in 2042.

1955

Maybellene
Chuck Berry

Released July 1955
Chess *1604* (U.S. #5) / London *REU 1053* (U.K.)

Tutti-Frutti
Little Richard

Released October 1955
Specialty *561* (U.S. #7) / London *HLO 8366* (U.K. B-side)

When the saxman in boogie pianist Johnnie Johnson's band dropped out of a lucrative 1952 New Year's Eve gig at the last minute, Johnson hastily called in untried guitarist Chuck Berry as a stopgap replacement. That night, as Johnson remembered it later, Berry played a country song called 'Ida Red.' "The audience went crazy," said Johnson. "We had to play that song again, maybe two or three times." Some experts have pinpointed that moment as the beginning of rock'n'roll because, 17 months later, Berry re-worked 'Ida Red' and released it on Chicago-based Chess Records as 'Maybellene.' Chuck didn't know it, but the label's boss, Leonard Chess, arranged a payola kickback for DJ Alan Freed: the DJ would be credited as co-composer if he played the song regularly on his influential radio show, and if the record was a hit, Freed would earn massive royalties. With Freed's enthusiastic support, 'Maybellene' soared to Number 1 in the *Billboard* R&B chart and Number 5 on the pop chart, kick-starting the rock'n'roll revolution.

Down in J&M Studios, New Orleans, on September 14, 1955, barely a month after Berry started the commotion, the bizarrely pompadoured singer-pianist Richard Penniman recorded a cleaned-up version of a

filthy ditty with which he'd wowed club audiences for years. As he recalled: "It used to crack the crowds up when I sang it in the clubs, with those risqué lyrics, 'Tutti-Frutti good booty / If it don't fit, don't force it / You can grease it, make it easy.' I never thought it would be a hit."

Luckily his producer, Bumps Blackwell, knew better. Blackwell had aspiring local songwriter Dorothy La Bostrie come up with acceptable lyrics and, at the end of a fruitless session, captured Penniman's frantically cranked-up rendition of the song – complete with an improvised opening scream of "Awopbopaloobopalopbamboom." It was the scream that sold the track to Art Rupe, owner of Specialty Records, who later revealed: "The reason I picked it wasn't solely for the tempo. It was because of the wild intro; it was different, you know? Be Bop A Lop Bop! All that in front. You didn't hear things like that much on a record."

America's record-trade bible *Billboard* reviewed 'Tutti-Frutti' favorably as a "cleverly styled novelty with nonsense words" and on January 28, 1956, it entered the Top 40 singles chart, only to stall disappointingly at Number 17. "The white radio stations wouldn't play Richard's version," explained Blackwell. This was largely because, in a classic example of a white artist profiting from a black artist's inspiration, clean-cut teen crooner Pat Boone had rapidly knocked up an insipid cover version, which hogged the airplay and soared to Number 12. In the long run, of course, innovators like Chuck Berry and Little Richard would be recognized as the founding fathers of rock'n'roll. Indeed, the writing was already clearly on the wall in December 1955 when, at a copyright organization's awards dinner in New York City, 11 of the 23 prizes went to black-originated R&B songs, including Berry's 'Maybellene' and Johnny Ace's 'Pledging My Love.'

Cherry Pink And Apple Blossom White
Perez Prado

Released February 1955
RCA *5965* (U.S. #1) / HMV *B 10833* (U.K. #1)

In 1955 the mambo was an international outrage and 'king of the mambo' Perez Prado, with his goatee and lacquered pompadour, was just about the hippest thing on two legs. By adding swing jazz stylings to hot Latin music, Prado ruled the mambo roost in a world where the President of the Philippines declared it a 'national calamity' and church leaders threatened to deny absolution for anyone caught dancing it. 'Cherry Pink,' featuring sensational trumpet virtuosity from Billy Regis, was the biggest hit of the craze, spending ten weeks at Number 1 in the U.S. and inspiring countless cover versions worldwide. Technically, however, it's a cha-cha.

Unchained Melody
Les Baxter, His Chorus & Orchestra

Released March 1955
Capitol *3055* (U.S. #1) / Not issued U.K.

Before the proliferation of record players, sales of sheet music were more significant to the music business than sales of discs. Consequently, great songs rather than artists were regarded as the real money-spinners, and no song illustrates this better than the haunting evergreen 'Unchained Melody,' composed by Alex North and Hy Zaret.

It was first recorded by Al Hibbler for the soundtrack of the otherwise forgettable movie *Unchained*, but Les Baxter's version won the U.S. chart battle, peaking at Number 1, while a Roy Hamilton interpretation topped the rhythm & blues chart. Jimmy Young – who later became a BBC radio DJ – took it to Number 1 in the U.K. against fierce competition from no fewer than 13 other versions. The Righteous Brothers, Leo Sayer, and Will Young are just three artists among many for whom 'Unchained Melody' has delivered chart success in every decade since.

Pickin' A Chicken
Eve Boswell

Released December 1955
Not issued U.S. / Parlophone *R 4082* (U.K. #9)

Rarely, if ever, does Hungarian-born popular vocalist Eve Boswell's biggest hit, the cheerfully robust 'Pickin' A Chicken,' appear in lists of all-time great singles, but its significance is undeniable.

A young producer, George Martin, had joined EMI in 1950, working at EMI's studios on Abbey Road in north-west London on classical and light popular recordings. His gifts as a producer and arranger were quickly recognized so, five years later, he became Britain's youngest-ever record company head, at EMI subsidiary Parlophone. Impressive perhaps, but Parlophone was then regarded as EMI's Cinderella, a poor relation of the parent company. Nevertheless, when his production of 'Pickin' A Chicken' entered the U.K. pop singles chart on the last day of 1955, it signaled the start of a new era for the label. Martin soon secured more hits, mainly with imaginative and innovative novelty material by Bernard Cribbins, Peter Sellers, and others, but he was also instrumental in bringing rock'n'roll to the label with young vocalist Jim Dale.

By the early 1960s Martin was actively scouting for a young act that could push Parlophone to the top of the pile, and he found it when he signed The Beatles on June 4, 1962. Although Beatles productions dominated public perception of his work, he continued to make memorable

hits for dozens of other acts, from the atmospheric 'Sun Arise' for Rolf Harris in late 1962 to Elton John's record-shattering 1997 re-interpretation of 'Candle In The Wind.' With no fewer than 30 Number 1 hit singles to his credit, Martin is one of the most successful producers of all time.

Hummingbird
Les Paul & Mary Ford

Released June 1955
Capitol *3165* (U.S. #7) / Philips *PB 498* (U.K.)

Les Paul's importance to rock guitar playing is hard to overstate. The Gibson guitar company's first solidbody electric guitar was its Les Paul Model in 1952, and his innovations in guitar design, multi-track recording, and tape speed manipulation created some of the most distinctive sounds ever put on disc. Beyond all this, however, Paul and his vocalist wife Mary Ford were able to make these new sounds accessible to the general public in a string of huge hit singles. 'Hummingbird' wasn't their biggest hit, but it finds Paul in sparkling form, brilliantly decorating Mary's elegant reading of the main melody.

Rock Island Line
The Lonnie Donegan Skiffle Group

Released November 1955
London *1650* (U.S. #8) / Decca *F 10647* (U.K. #8)

Hard though it may be to grasp today, the skiffle craze of the mid 1950s rivaled rock'n'roll as the favored sound of Britain's youth. It was simple, energetic music made with improvised and cheap musical instruments that thrived in a time of post-war austerity. Many British rock heroes of the 1960s – including John Lennon, Brian Jones, and Van Morrison – cut their musical teeth in skiffle bands, bashing out three chords on cheap acoustic guitars. Lonnie Donegan, skiffle's undisputed king, was their hero, and 'Rock Island Line,' his debut single, was skiffle's biggest hit.

The origins of skiffle lie in an earlier British music trend, the 'trad' jazz revival of the late 1940s and early 1950s, which nurtured a particular fondness for New Orleans jazz. Many of London's trad jazz bands introduced stripped-down, high-energy reworkings of old jazz, folk, blues, and jug tunes into their live sets, to which the term 'skiffle' was attached. In October 1954 popular trad jazzers The Chris Barber Band recorded an album called *New Orleans Joys*, which encapsulated the characteristics of the trad revival. The bulk of the album was given over to the band's songs, but its banjoist and guitarist, Lonnie Donegan, was allowed two solo spots that represented the skiffle section of the band's live set. One of these was a primitive rendering of an old Huddie Ledbetter song, 'Rock Island Line.'

A full year after the album was first released, and after several singles had already been taken from it, Decca put out 'Rock Island Line' as a single (initially in 78 rpm form), originally credited to The Lonnie Donegan Skiffle Group. By January 1956 it was riding high in the British singles chart, establishing skiffle as a phenomenon in its own right, not just a sideshow to the trad-jazz movement. A shade under two-and-a-half-minutes long, with a lyric about negotiating railway tolls in New Orleans that would have meant precisely nothing to a British teenager, 'Rock Island Line' is one of the most primitive hit records ever. Donegan leads with three briskly strummed acoustic guitar chords and a yelping, hollering vocal, Chris Barber plucks a stand-up bass, and Beryl Bryden provides rhythmic accompaniment on a washboard. And that's it.

It was this simplicity that was the appeal of skiffle – like punk rock 20 years later, anyone could do it. But the craze was shortlived. Rock'n'roll was more glamorous, and by 1958 the callow, gauche teenagers who had imitated Donegan with cheap acoustics were trading up to cheap electric guitars and switching allegiance to rockers like Cliff Richard and Buddy Holly. Donegan, however, outlasted the craze he started. Unlike most other skiffle artists, he had hits in the U.S. and enjoyed British chart success into the 1960s. At his commercial peak – roughly early 1956 to mid 1958 – he was, in Britain, as big a star as Elvis and Little Richard. He died in 2002, not long after recording a final album with the help of many of the generation of rock stars he inspired.

Only You (And You Alone)
The Platters

Released July 1955
Mercury *70633* (U.S. #5) / Mercury *MT 117* (U.K. #18)

The Platters' deliciously smooth, rich vocal textures on 'Only You' owed something to swing-era outfits like The Mills Brothers and The Ink Spots, but it made them the first black combo of the rhythm & blues years to earn mainstream success with a song that was neither a novelty number nor a jump jive track. It was written by their manager, Buck Ram, and they'd first recorded it, complete with a whistling solo, for Federal Records in 1954. The superior Mercury version, with its gently insistent rock'n'roll beat and Tony Williams's ingenious vocal stutter, made them international stars and set them off on a run of twenty-three U.S. hits.

1955

Darling, Je Vous Aime Beaucoup
Nat 'King' Cole

Released February 1955
Capitol *3027* (U.S. #7) / Not issued U.K.

The son of a Baptist Minister, Cole was the most successful black American of the post-war period. After years of success as a jazz pianist, he decided in 1946 to stake his future on his voice, rather than his fingers. This delightful piece of *franglais* – complete with heavily backing choir – was recorded on the 24th of August 1953, but not issued until 18 months later. It was originally a hit for the American-born cabaret star The Incomparable Hildegarde in 1943, having been written for her by her manager, Anna Sosenko. Cole's version featured as the closing song in the 1955 biographical movie *The Nat 'King' Cole Story*, and on his 1956 album *Ballads Of The Day*.

Love And Marriage
Frank Sinatra

Released October 1955
Capitol *3260* (U.S. #5) / Capitol *CL 14503* (U.K. #3)

Born in Hoboken, New Jersey, on December 12, 1915, Francis Albert Sinatra was probably the finest vocal interpreter of 20th-century popular song. 'Love And Marriage' was specially written by Jimmy Van Heusen and Sammy Cahn for an NBC-TV musical version of Thornton Wilder's play *Our Town*, which starred Sinatra together with Paul Newman and Eva Marie Saint. He recorded it under the guiding baton of Nelson Riddle on August 15, 1955, at KHJ Studio in Hollywood and released it as a single, between his albums *In The Wee Small Hours* and the classic *Songs For Swingin' Lovers*. Cahn was one of the greatest American wordsmiths – Sinatra recorded 87 of his songs. Speaking of Sinatra's vocal interpretations, Cahn said: "He moved into a lyric like it was his house." One of the most telling comments on Sinatra's talent came from his own idol, Bing Crosby, who remarked: "Frank Sinatra is the kind of singer who comes along once in a lifetime. But why did it have to be in my lifetime?"

Heartbreak Hotel
Elvis Presley

Released January 1956
RCA *47-6420* (U.S. #1) / HMV *POP 182* (U.K. #2)

Hound Dog
Elvis Presley
Released July 1956
RCA *47-6604* (U.S. #1) / HMV *POP 249* (U.K. #2)

Blue Suede Shoes
Carl Perkins
Released January 1956
Sun *234* (U.S. #2) / London *HLU 8271* (U.K. #10)

Chuck Berry found mainstream success with 'Maybellene' in 1955 by marrying white country to black rhythm & blues, but white-trash teenager Elvis Presley had set off down the same route on July 5, 1954, when he covered bluesman Arthur 'Big Boy' Crudup's 'That's All Right' for Sun Records of Memphis. Elvis, however, didn't make much of an impact on the charts until April 21, 1956, when 'Heartbreak Hotel' hit Number 1.

The song was sparked to life by a *Miami Herald* story about an unidentified middle-aged man who had committed suicide leaving a note that said only "I walk a lonely street." Inspired by this grim tale, songwriter Mae Axton wrote 'Heartbreak Hotel' with Presley in mind. Having lately been bought from the independent Sun Records for an unprecedented $40,000 by the multi-national RCA, Presley was at a make or break point in his career. It was vital that his first recording session for RCA in their Nashville studios should go well. The company was providing a state-of-the-art recording environment and some of the

finest session players available, but they also wanted top-notch material and a great performance from their young rising star.

As well as Presley's Sun sidemen, guitarist Scotty Moore, bassist Bill Black, and drummer D J Fontana, the session was enhanced with the estimable Chet Atkins on rhythm guitar, the nimble-fingered Floyd Cramer on piano, and members of the top-rated gospel group The Jordanaires handling back-up vocals. Elvis rose to the occasion with a smoldering echo-drenched vocal that made the most of the song's melodramatic lyric – but it didn't exactly fly off the shelves when it was released in late January. It wasn't until April 3, when Presley sang it on NBC-TV's *Milton Berle Show*, with an audience estimated at a quarter of the entire U.S. population, that 'Heartbreak Hotel' finally took off.

Three weeks later it was at Number 1 and rock'n'roll was clearly becoming not just the most significant new musical form of the decade but a rallying point for youth of whatever color or creed. Not one but three Beatles – John Lennon, Paul McCartney, and George Harrison – subsequently cited 'Heartbreak Hotel' as a profound inspiration, and Bob Dylan said: "When I first heard Elvis's voice I just knew that I wasn't going to work for anybody; and nobody was going to be my boss. ... Hearing him for the first time was like busting out of jail."

Big Mama Thornton recorded the original version of 'Hound Dog' on August 13, 1952. Written by Jerry Leiber and Mike Stoller, who would become the most successful songwriting and production team of the 1950s, the song was released in at least six versions and a couple of parodies before Elvis turned it into a massive international smash.

It was in late March 1956, during a week-long engagement at the Frontier Hotel in Las Vegas, that Elvis dropped into the lounge to watch Freddie Bell & The Bellboys. He enjoyed their humorous treatment of 'Hound Dog' so much that he decided to include it in his own act. Presley's guitarist Scotty Moore recalled: "We stole it straight from them. He already knew it, knew the song, but when we seen those guys do it, he said, 'There's a natural.' We never did it in Las Vegas, but we were just looking on it as comic relief, if you will, just another number to do onstage."

Moore's recollection is confirmed by the fact that Presley performed the song twice on national TV shows before finally recording it, somewhat reluctantly, in July. Steve Allen, host of one of the shows on which Presley performed the song, reckoned: "It was television that made Elvis's success possible. What his millions of young fans responded to was obviously not his voice but Elvis himself. His face, his body, his gyrations, his cute country-boy persona."

Not everyone responded so favorably. U.S. Congressman Emanuel Celler, for one, was horrified. "Rock'n'roll has its place among the colored people," he ranted. "The bad taste exemplified by Elvis Presley Hound Dog music, with his animal gyrations, which are certainly most distasteful to me, are violative of all that I know to be in good taste." Nevertheless, what Leiber & Stoller had knocked up in nine minutes as a country-blues for Big Mama went on, thanks to Presley's supercharged rendition, to top the U.S. chart for 11 solid weeks.

Sun Records owner Sam Phillips later told of how, during the anxious weeks before Presley's 'Heartbreak Hotel' took off, RCA's A&R guru Steve Sholes began seriously wondering if he'd bought the wrong artist from Sun. Carl Perkins's version of 'Blue Suede Shoes' was looking like a much better bet for massive success. Perkins wrote it at a relatively slow tempo, but Phillips encouraged him to speed it up for the record and changed the lyric slightly but significantly. "When he said, 'Go, man,

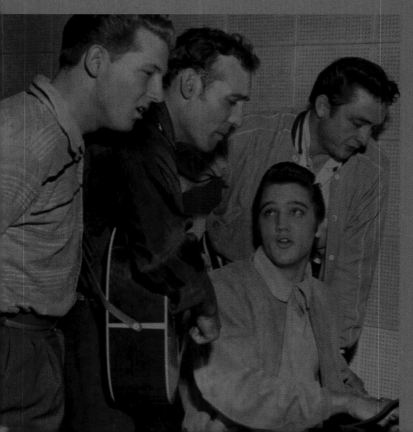

go,' the only contribution I made was 'Go, cat, go.' It takes it completely out of the country category – that one word."

Even so, Perkins's lively and spirited version isn't exactly rock'n'roll, and some observers have gone so far as to declare it a pioneering example of folk-rock – a genre more usually associated with the mid 1960s. Whatever it was, the song proved to have such a wide appeal that, after entering the U.S. pop Top 40 on March 10, 1956, it quickly started to appear in the country and rhythm & blues charts as well.

RCA's Sholes, meanwhile, had arranged for Presley to cover 'Blue Suede Shoes' as insurance against the possible failure of 'Heartbreak Hotel.' This, along with other versions by Boyd Bennett, Sid King, and Pee Wee King, meant that Perkins was up against some stiff competition, but the real disaster struck on March 22. On the way to an appearance on a Perry Como show that would almost certainly have boosted 'Blue Suede Shoes' to Number 1, Perkins was hospitalized by a horrific car crash that killed his brother Jay.

Despite Elvis promptly promoting his version with several TV appearances, he could only take it to Number 20, while the Perkins original went on to score Top 3 positions in the pop, country, and R&B charts, an unprecedented crossover feat at the time.

1956

I Walk The Line
Johnny Cash

Released May 1956
Sun *241* (U.S. #17) / London *HL 8358* (U.K.)

Johnny Cash was the legendary Man In Black, the first 'outlaw' of country, and a member of the famous Million Dollar Quartet (Cash, Presley, Lewis, and Perkins). He auditioned for Sam Phillips at Sun Records in 1955 as part of The Tennessee Three, playing gospel. Phillips pointed out that they'd need to sing country if they wanted to succeed. Taking this on board, Cash swiftly delivered his own compositions 'Cry Cry Cry' and 'Folsom Prison Blues.' Their third single, 'I Walk The Line', released in May 1956, was the first to cross over to the pop charts. Cash had begun writing the song some years earlier when he first learned to play guitar in 1950 while stationed in Germany with the U.S. Air Force. He originally performed it as a slow ballad on the *Louisiana Hayride* TV show, but Phillips suggested speeding it up somewhat for the recording, and Cash's distinctive growl combined with some subtly clever key changes assured success. Cash stayed with Sun for three years before departing to Columbia and ultimately became an American icon. He continued to record and perform until his death in 2003, making some of his best recordings towards the end of his life, in particular the stunning, intense rendition of a Nine Inch Nails song, 'Hurt.'

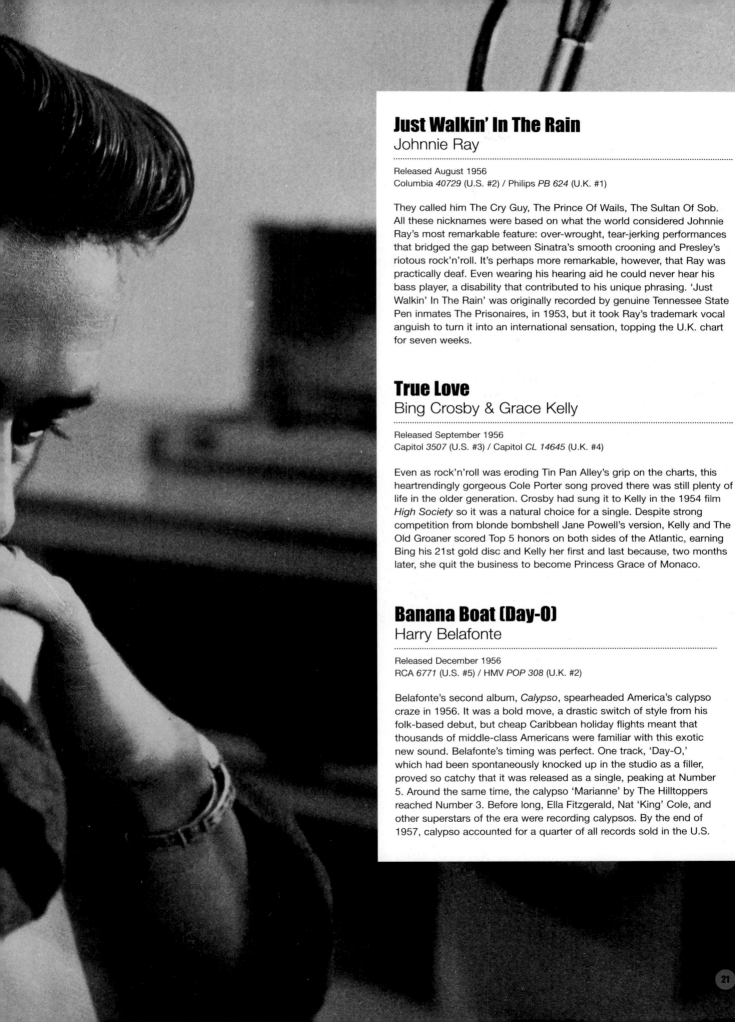

Just Walkin' In The Rain
Johnnie Ray

Released August 1956
Columbia *40729* (U.S. #2) / Philips *PB 624* (U.K. #1)

They called him The Cry Guy, The Prince Of Wails, The Sultan Of Sob. All these nicknames were based on what the world considered Johnnie Ray's most remarkable feature: over-wrought, tear-jerking performances that bridged the gap between Sinatra's smooth crooning and Presley's riotous rock'n'roll. It's perhaps more remarkable, however, that Ray was practically deaf. Even wearing his hearing aid he could never hear his bass player, a disability that contributed to his unique phrasing. 'Just Walkin' In The Rain' was originally recorded by genuine Tennessee State Pen inmates The Prisonaires, in 1953, but it took Ray's trademark vocal anguish to turn it into an international sensation, topping the U.K. chart for seven weeks.

True Love
Bing Crosby & Grace Kelly

Released September 1956
Capitol *3507* (U.S. #3) / Capitol *CL 14645* (U.K. #4)

Even as rock'n'roll was eroding Tin Pan Alley's grip on the charts, this heartrendingly gorgeous Cole Porter song proved there was still plenty of life in the older generation. Crosby had sung it to Kelly in the 1954 film *High Society* so it was a natural choice for a single. Despite strong competition from blonde bombshell Jane Powell's version, Kelly and The Old Groaner scored Top 5 honors on both sides of the Atlantic, earning Bing his 21st gold disc and Kelly her first and last because, two months later, she quit the business to become Princess Grace of Monaco.

Banana Boat (Day-O)
Harry Belafonte

Released December 1956
RCA *6771* (U.S. #5) / HMV *POP 308* (U.K. #2)

Belafonte's second album, *Calypso*, spearheaded America's calypso craze in 1956. It was a bold move, a drastic switch of style from his folk-based debut, but cheap Caribbean holiday flights meant that thousands of middle-class Americans were familiar with this exotic new sound. Belafonte's timing was perfect. One track, 'Day-O,' which had been spontaneously knocked up in the studio as a filler, proved so catchy that it was released as a single, peaking at Number 5. Around the same time, the calypso 'Marianne' by The Hilltoppers reached Number 3. Before long, Ella Fitzgerald, Nat 'King' Cole, and other superstars of the era were recording calypsos. By the end of 1957, calypso accounted for a quarter of all records sold in the U.S.

Be-Bop-A-Lula
Gene Vincent & His Blue Caps

Released June 1956
Capitol *3450* (U.S. #7) / Capitol *CL 14599* (U.K. #16)

Long Tall Sally
Little Richard
Released March 1956
Speciality *572* (U.S. #6) / London *HLO 8366* (U.K. #3)

Blueberry Hill
Fats Domino
Released September 1956
Imperial *5407* (U.S. #2) / London *HLU 8330* (U.K. #6)

THE CAPITOL TOWER · HOLLYWOOD, CALIFORNIA, U.S.A.

The golden age of rock'n'roll is generally acknowledged as the period from July 1955 when 'Rock Around The Clock' hit Number 1 until Buddy Holly's death on February 3, 1959 – "the day the music died." By that time, Jerry Lee Lewis's career was in tatters, Little Richard had found religion, Chuck Berry had written his best tunes, Bill Haley was well past his sell-by date, and Elvis had joined the army. The classic year for the genre was 1956, awash with hits such as 'Blue Suede Shoes,' 'Hound Dog,' 'Tutti-Frutti,' 'See You Later Alligator,' 'Roll Over Beethoven,' and a few others that deserve a special mention.

Through the mists of time, the pedigree of 'Be-Bop-A-Lula' is difficult to see clearly. We'll stick with the legend that states that young Mr. Vincent (born Vincent Eugene Craddock) bought the song for $25 from a fellow marine while in naval hospital recovering from a motorcycle accident. He played it to 'Sheriff' Tex Davis, a DJ at WCMS, who saw some potential and coupled him with Cliff Gallup's band, and made a demo recording at the radio station.

That demo was then dispatched to Ken Nelson at Capitol Records, which was eagerly searching for its own Elvis. For his pains, Davis cut himself in as co-writer and would make off with half the royalties of what became a huge hit and a legendary recording. Capitol soon gave a positive reply, and a formal recording session was arranged at Owen Bradley's Nashville studios for May 4, 1956.

Mort Thomasson was the studio engineer responsible for the massive echo treatment on the session, when Gallup's band were officially renamed as The Blue Caps. Thomasson recalled that Vincent and his band "looked like a motorcycle gang." Unsure of their musical expertise, producer Ken Nelson had some session musicians on standby, but it quickly became apparent they wouldn't be needed. According to Thomasson: "They started playing and all hell broke loose – they didn't know nothing except to play loud and fast." Legend has it that Elvis's mum thought it was her own son when she first heard the recording on the radio.

It was a teenage girl, Enotris Johnson, who originally brought the rough lyrical idea for Little Richard's second hit to producer Robert 'Bumps' Blackwell at Specialty Records. (She also contributed to Richard's 1957 hit 'Jenny Jenny.') Many white American radio stations had refused to play 'Tutti-Frutti,' the first hit by this bizarre, black, camp figure who wore heavy make-up, loud clothes, and had his hair in a huge pompadour.

In an effort to beat Pat Boone, who'd had the bigger hit with 'Tutti Frutti,' when it came to Richard's second single, 'Long Tall Sally' (originally titled 'The Thing,' then 'Bald Headed Sally'), Blackwell encouraged him to sing the song at breakneck speed so that Boone wouldn't be able to catch the lyrics.

Boone covered the song nevertheless, but this time Richard beat him up the charts. The Beatles covered 'Long Tall Sally' and McCartney himself wrote an undisguised Little Richard-style screamer, 'I'm Down,' as the B-side of The Beatles' 1965 single 'Help!'

New Orleans-born pianist Antoine Domino was earning $3 a week playing in honky-tonks when he was spotted by Imperial Records producer Dave Bartholomew in 1949. Although not strictly a rock'n'roll artist, Fats had 60 Billboard Top 100 hits in less than ten years. But he nearly didn't record 'Blueberry Hill,' his biggest hit, at all.

Bartholomew was set against recording a song that had already been a hit several times, but fortunately for posterity Fats won the day. The song was written in 1940 for yodeling cowboy Gene Autry – who with his trusty horse Champion seemed to make his Westerns at the rate of about one per week – and was featured in Autry's 1941 movie *The Singing Hill*.

By that time the tune had already been a Number 1 hit for Glenn Miller. According to lyricist Larry Stock, a major publisher at first turned down his song because "blueberries don't grow on hills." Stock assured them they did, and since then it has been recorded by any number of artists, although there's little doubt that Fats made the definitive version.

I Put A Spell On You
Screamin' Jay Hawkins

Released November 1956
Okeh *7072* (U.S.) / Fontana *H 107* (U.K.)

Originally conceived as a simple ballad, 'I Put A Spell On You' became one of the most striking and unusual singles of the late 1950s. It is also one of the more notable banned records of the rock'n'roll era. Radio stations across the U.S. and abroad objected to Hawkins's suggestive, animalistic vocal performance and would only play a significantly edited version. Perhaps because of this, the single failed to chart on its release, but it has since become a cult classic, not to mention a favorite of compilers of scary-movie soundtracks.

This best-known version of 'I Put A Spell On You' is not, in fact, the original. Hawkins first wrote and recorded it in a more serene setting in 1949 but was encouraged by producer Arnold Maxon to update the song, with a performance more in keeping with its title. Legend has it that Hawkins and his band were drunk as skunks while recording the song, which goes some way to explain the opening half-minute of groaning and grunting. Hawkins's visceral baritone is offset effectively by a chorus of cooing backing vocalists and a spacious, bass-led arrangement.

Hawkins recorded a number of similarly maniacal follow-ups in subsequent years, although none is so well known as 'Spell' (since covered by everyone from Nina Simone to Marilyn Manson).

I'm Not A Juvenile Delinquent
Frankie Lymon & The Teenagers

Released November 1956
Gee *1026* (U.S.) / Columbia *DB 3878* (U.K. #12)

Diana
Paul Anka

Released May 1957
ABC-Paramount *9831* (U.S. #1) / Columbia *DB 3980* (U.K. #1)

Lymon's best-remembered hit is 'Why Do Fools Fall In Love,' but 'Delinquent' was easily his weirdest. With rock'n'rollers coming in for more than their share of harsh adult censure, this single was designed as a teenage counterblast. The harsh reality, however, was that fresh-faced Frankie was pimping and doing drugs on the streets of Harlem before he was 16, making him precisely what his heartfelt denial claimed he wasn't. His record label, Gee, was part-owned by Morris Levy, probably the most notorious gangster in the music business of the time. Levy used his muscle to have himself credited as the song's composer, although it was in fact written by Bobby Spencer of The Cadillacs, who would write Millie's ska novelty hit 'My Boy Lollipop.' Lymon died of a heroin overdose at the age of just 25 on April 30, 1968. Levy, meanwhile, landed ten years on extortion charges in 1988.

Unfair adult perceptions of teenage immaturity also fueled Paul Anka's lovelorn 'Diana,' the true tale of his 15-year-old lust for 20-year-old babysitter Diana Ayoub. Anka, however, was a clean-living boy signed to a reputable company, so when 'Diana' went on to sell over nine million copies worldwide and became one of the bestselling singles of all time, he was in clover. Somehow, Ayoub found the now-wealthy singer more appealing, but Anka himself was no longer smitten. In 1963, as all good rock stars should, he married a leggy blonde model in Paris, France.

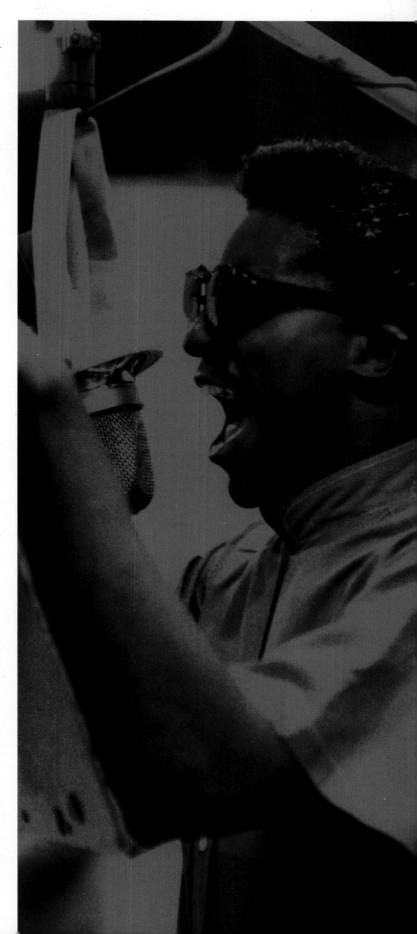

Who Do You Love
Bo Diddley

Released March 1957
Checker *842* (U.S.) / Not issued U.K.

Hey! Bo Diddley
Bo Diddley

Released October 1957
Checker *860* (U.S.) / Not issued U.K.

Bo Diddley stands among the most influential early rock'n'roll performers, despite his failure to achieve the commercial success of many of his peers. After turning his back on a potentially lucrative boxing career, he signed to Checker Records in 1955 and immediately began to pile up an impressive body of work, characterized by insistent tremolo-laden guitar licks not entirely dissimilar to those of Chuck Berry.

'Who Do You Love' is set apart from a lot of Diddley's contemporary material by its shuffling drum pattern, while the call-and-response of the title's question and the instrumental answer stick in the brain long after the song has finished. It features some of Diddley's strongest and most surreal lyrics, taking in cobra snake neckties and a chimney "made out of human skull." Like many of his songs, it has been regularly covered in subsequent years, by artists including The Doors and Tom Rush. 'Hey! Bo Diddley' was just one of a number of his self-referential songs, which in a way predate a similar, widespread trend in modern rap lyrics. He began his career with the single 'Bo Diddley' in 1955 and soon followed it with titles like 'Diddley Daddy,' 'Bo's Guitar,' and 'Diddling.' It wasn't all self-love, however: another early single, 'Bring It To Jerome,' was named for one of his regular musical foils, bassist and maracas-shaker Jerome Green.

That'll Be The Day
The Crickets

Released May 1957
Brunswick *55009* (U.S. #1) / Coral *Q 72279* (U.K. #1)

Oh Boy! / Not Fade Away
The Crickets

Released October 1957
Brunswick *55035* (U.S. #10) / Coral *Q 72298* (U.K. #3)

A new John Wayne movie, *The Searchers*, opened at The State Theatre in Lubbock, Texas, on May 31, 1956. During its run, two local teenagers, Buddy Holly and Jerry Allison, were so taken by Wayne's catch-phrase, "That'll be the day," that they borrowed it for a song title. Two months later, having just recorded it for Decca in Nashville, Allison was crushed when the producer rubbished it as "the worst song I've ever heard in my life." Nevertheless, they persevered, investing $60 to re-record it as a demo on February 27, 1957 in Clovis, New Mexico.

Bob Thiele, a legendarily discerning A&R boss at Brunswick/Coral Records, signed them up and decided to release the demo as a single, credited to The Crickets to avoid breaching the terms of Holly's Decca contract. When Brunswick's version, pegged by *Billboard* as "medium-beat rockabilly," started to take off, Decca unearthed their version of the worst song their producer had ever heard and released it, but it was The Crickets who rocketed to Number 1 in the U.S. and U.K., where it became the first song John Lennon ever learned to play.

So prolific was Holly at this time that The Crickets' next release, 'Oh Boy,' featured a killer B-side, 'Not Fade Away,' which integrated Bo Diddley's famed hambone riff into a more accessible rock'n'roll song format. It would eventually provide the first Top 10 hit for The Rolling Stones in 1964, a debut single for Rush in 1973, and made regular appearances at Grateful Dead gigs.

Great Balls Of Fire

Jerry Lee Lewis & His Pumping Piano

Released November 1957
Sun *281* (U.S. #2) / London *HLS 8529* (U.K. #1)

There are many who believe that Jerry Lee Lewis was the true king of rock'n'roll. He certainly leads an uncompromising life, in contrast to the always demurring and polite Elvis Presley. Lewis began playing piano at age nine. His parents mortgaged their house to buy his first instrument, and legend has it that they lost their home when they couldn't meet the repayments. Expelled from preacher training college for playing hymns boogie-woogie style, he had been resident pianist at a number of brothels, and declared himself 'the greatest' long before Muhammad Ali.

Lewis had been married twice before he arrived at Sun Records for an audition in 1956, a trip financed by the sale of 33 dozen eggs. His second Sun release, 'Whole Lot Of Shakin' Goin' On,' was banned by many U.S. radio stations as obscene but sold a reputed six million copies across America.

He was something of a wild inferno both onstage and off. Kicking over his piano stool was at first an accident, but he soon incorporated it into his act. Before too long he was demanding to close the show on any tour on which he appeared, but on one memorable outing with Chuck Berry, he was forced to open the show. Setting fire to his piano as he departed, he remarked: "I'd like to see any son of a bitch try to follow that!"

Lewis's greatest song was his third Sun single, 'Great Balls Of Fire,' which sold a million copies in its first ten days of release, but was held at Number 2 on the U.S. chart by 'At The Hop' by Danny & The Juniors. 'Great Balls Of Fire' was written by Otis Blackwell and the aptly named Jack Hammer, whose sole contribution amounted to the title itself. Blackwell wrote a number of key rock'n'roll anthems including 'All Shook Up,' 'Don't Be Cruel,' and 'Return To Sender' for Elvis, 'Handy Man' for Jimmy Jones, and 'Fever' for Little Willie John.

Jerry Lee's career plummeted in the wake of bad publicity following the revelation that he had married his 13-year-old cousin Myra. Although such marriages weren't uncommon in the American South, Lewis was on tour in Britain when the news broke, and the U.K. papers voiced their outrage. A 37-date tour was canceled after just three engagements, and Lewis returned to the U.S., his career in shreds. It took the best part of ten years for him to get back on track.

Relentlessly living up to the sex and drugs and rock'n'roll lifestyle, Lewis has been on the critical list on a number of occasions. Following emergency surgery for a ruptured stomach ulcer in 1981, he was given a 50-50 chance of survival. On leaving hospital his immediate response was to buy a new customized Cadillac, a big cigar, and a bottle of his favorite whiskey, claiming: "As long as they gimme a piano I'll be out there. They try to take that away, I'm gonna kick some ass."

Peggy Sue
Buddy Holly

Released September 1957
Coral *61885* (U.S. #3) / Coral Q *72293* (U.K. #6)

Can a song change the course of events in the real world? Of course it can. This Holly classic started life as 'Cindy Lou' in honor of Buddy's niece, but Crickets' drummer Jerry Allison, who had recently broken up with his girlfriend, Peggy Sue Gerron, suggested the name-change as a way of getting back into her good books.

Probably the best-remembered song in Holly's catalogue, 'Peggy Sue' was recorded on July 1, 1957, at producer Norman Petty's studio in Clovis, New Mexico. When the session kicked off, the backing had a calypso feel, not unlike Harry Belafonte's then-popular 'Banana Boat (Day-O),' but it just wasn't working.

When Allison was asked to play a consistently rolling paradiddle, which he did on a snare drum with the snares turned off, the song took on a dynamic rock'n'roll aspect, which Holly intensified by playing his rhythm guitar part entirely with speedy downstrokes. The result was a song of unusually propulsive, throbbing intensity that soared to Number 3 in the U.S. and Number 6 in Britain.

It also had the desired effect of bringing Allison and Peggy Sue together again – so effectively that they eloped on July 22, 1958, to Honey Grove, Texas, and got married. That might have been the end of it had Holly's father not suggested that there might be some mileage in writing a sequel. Buddy agreed and recorded 'Peggy Sue Got Married' on December 5 in his New York City apartment. Released as a single after Holly's tragic death, it reached Number 13 in Britain.

I'm Walking / A Teenager's Romance
Ricky Nelson

Released April 1957
Verve *10047* (U.S. #2) / HMV *POP 355* (U.K.)

Ricky Nelson was the first teen pop star created by a television series. Many would follow in his footsteps, notably The Monkees in the 1960s and David Cassidy in the '70s. Nelson had played himself in his parents' radio and TV sitcom *The Adventures Of Ozzie And Harriet* since 1949. Spotted there by famed jazz guitarist and Verve A&R chief Barney Kessel, he was wheeled in for a recording session where Kessel suggested a cover of Fats Domino's recent hit 'I'm Walking' coupled with the custom-written throwaway 'A Teenager's Romance.'

Nelson's version of 'I'm Walking' got national TV exposure when he performed it on the family show and swiftly flew up the charts. When the song peaked, radio stations began playing the other side, which rose even higher. Nelson recorded one further single for Verve, but the lack of a binding contract coupled with the company's reluctance to cough up royalties resulted in a move to Imperial. Nelson's career really took off and he enjoyed an impressive run of hits until 1964.

At The Hop
Danny & The Juniors

Released November 1957
ABC-Paramount *9871* (U.S. #1) / HMV *POP 436* (U.K. #3)

Danny Rapp first put together his Philadelphia high-school group in 1955 as The Juvenairs. Philly was the home of America's most influential television show of the period, *American Bandstand*, which Dick Clark began hosting for WFIL-TV in 1956. Clark became an extremely powerful man in American popular music, although he skillfully managed to avoid the payola scandal of the early 1960s that ruined DJ Alan Freed. Producer Arthur Singer took a song called 'Do The Bop' to Clark, who suggested a change of title since the bop dance craze was on the wane. Duly re-titled, 'At The Hop' sold 7,000 copies in Philadelphia when first released by Danny & The Juniors on Singer's local Singular label and was soon picked up for national distribution by ABC-Paramount. The final piece of the puzzle fell into place when another group failed to turn up for *Bandstand* and Danny & the Juniors hopped in at the last moment.

Mr. Lee
The Bobbettes

Released June 1957
Atlantic *1144* (U.S. #6) / London *HLE 8477* (U.K.)

Maybe
The Chantels

Released December 1957
End *1005* (U.S. #15) / London *HLU 8561* (U.K.)

The Shirelles, who ascended to the U.S. Number 1 slot in 1961 with Carole King's 'Will You Love Me Tomorrow,' are now usually thought of as the starters of the girl-group sound. So where does that leave New York's Bobbettes, who made their U.S. Top 40 chart debut with 'Mr. Lee' on August 12, 1957? As the first all-female doo-wop group to hit Number 1 on the rhythm & blues chart, they surely deserve some kind of recognition.

They were followed almost immediately by another all-female quintet, The Chantels, who recorded 'Maybe' in a disused Manhattan church to take advantage of the building's superb acoustics. It worked, and 'Maybe' hit Number 15 on the national charts and Number 2 on the R&B chart. The Shirelles paved the way, but only after The Bobbettes and The Chantels had blazed the trail.

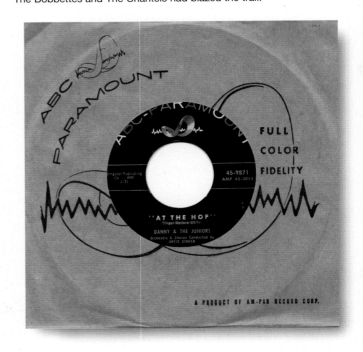

CHARTING THE BESTSELLING SINGLES

Record charts have been around for more than 60 years and are always a source of fascination for music fans, but they exist primarily as a tool for the music industry. *Billboard* began life as a magazine for the advertisement-hoarding industry and then turned to show business in the broadest sense, including circuses and carnivals. In the 1930s, however, it started to concentrate on music, encouraged by jukebox manufacturers, who became important advertisers.

In 1936, *Billboard* introduced the ancestor of the modern pop chart when it created a list of the songs most commonly played on three major radio stations. Earlier in the century, the music publishers who were *Billboard*'s customers had been ambivalent about radio, fearing it would destroy home performance and the associated sheet-music market. But they were already earning money from so-called 'mechanicals,' meaning fees for the reproduction of songs on player-pianos, cylinders, records, and jukeboxes, and from public performances. They soon realized that radio had huge potential for promoting both sheet music and record sales.

As a result, the music publishers changed from opposing the playing of their songs on radio to promoting the idea, through a network of 'pluggers' who were paid according to the number of plays their songs achieved. The new chart assisted those pluggers as well as the record shops, which could now stock the popular discs of the day.

By 1940, however, the magazine realized that records were now the most important means of selling publishers' wares. So in July that year *Billboard* introduced its Music Popularity Chart. This brought together existing charts of 'Records most popular on music machines' (jukeboxes, in other words), 'Sheet Music Best Sellers,' an alphabetical list of 'Songs With Most Radio Plugs,' and a new chart of 'Best selling retail records' based on a survey of stores around the U.S. The various charts reflected the way the interest of the readership continued to be

split between sheet music and records. In 1945, *Billboard* introduced its Honor Roll Of Hits, which combined both elements in an attempt to discover "the nation's top 10 tunes." The record sales chart dominated, however, and in 1958 it formed the basis of the celebrated Hot 100 singles chart, although that has always combined record sales with radio airplay. Over the years, the number of charts expanded, to reflect different genres. Most importantly, the first chart of black music, the Harlem Hit Parade, based on sales in that New York district, was introduced in 1942. In 1945 its name was changed to Race Records, finally becoming Rhythm & Blues in 1949. It would retain that name until the late 1960s. Country, meanwhile, made its *Billboard* debut in a jukebox chart of 'Folk Records' in 1944. The magazine currently features charts for R&B, country, Latin, Christian, dance, rock, adult contemporary, international, and others, including digital and cell-phone downloads.

Billboard charts were never the only charts. *Cash Box*, another American trade magazine, offered its own versions, which had a slightly different methodology and consequently gave different results. The trades produced geographical charts, but there were also local charts, compiled by small record stores or based on radio-station plays. These often showed quite different patterns of popularity than the national charts and allowed artists to claim local hits. For instance, the first Beach Boys single, 'Surfin',' reached Number 2 in the Los Angeles area when originally released on the tiny Candix label and enabled them to secure a deal with Capitol, a major label.

In the U.K., charts began with the *New Musical Express*'s Top Twelve, in 1952. A survey of only 20 shops at the beginning, it became the Top Twenty in 1954, and spawned imitators from *Melody Maker*, *Record Mirror*, and *Disc*. For the trade market, *Record Retailer* started a Top 50 in 1960. The BBC's chart began as a combination of the charts published by the consumer magazines, but from 1969 it employed the British Market Research Bureau to compile what is now the pre-eminent chart in Britain.

Jailhouse Rock
Elvis Presley

Released September 1957
RCA *47-7035* (U.S. #1) / RCA *1028* (U.K. #1)

Jerry Leiber and Mike Stoller were commissioned to write two songs for Presley's second movie, *Loving You* (1957). Later that year, they gravitated to writing and producing the entire score for his next movie, *Jailhouse Rock*, and for a brief period their names became synonymous with that of the king.

Although *Jailhouse Rock* is considered by many as the high water mark of Presley's generally disappointing movie career, Jerry Leiber, tasked with writing the words of the songs that would accompany the movie's action, was not impressed by the script. However, Leiber had got used to looking for a nugget within Presley's film vehicles that would allow him to do something exciting. Sometimes this involved turning a scenario on its head.

Leiber found a scene where a song was prescribed and which he thought ridiculously feeble for a prison setting, so instead he delivered 'Jailhouse Rock,' fully expecting the producers to reject it. Instead he was rewarded with such a positive response that the song became the title track of the movie.

To partner Stoller's melody, Leiber provided a lyric depicting a prison playing host to a wild party. There was even a slight hint of homosexual activity in the couplet: "Number 47 said to number 3 / You're the cutest jailbird I ever did see." Presley meanwhile contributed a typically committed vocal to a stop-start backing, where the walking bassline was a highpoint. In the relevant sequence of the movie Presley provided some accompanying choreography – shimmying in prison stripes and sliding down a pole – that has become indelibly associated with the song.

LEIBER & STOLLER: IS THAT ALL THERE IS?

Jerry Leiber and Mike Stoller were the first important non-performing songwriters of the rock era. Leiber has always provided lyrics and Stoller the melodies to their songs. Precociously gifted, they were still in their teens when their compositions were recorded by Jimmy Witherspoon and The Robins. By 1952, Stoller had become bored with generic blues and insisted on a more specific melody for 'Kansas City,' originally recorded by Little Willie Littlefield as 'K.C. Lovin' but which would go on to be covered by more than a hundred artists, including Wilbert Harrison (who hit the top in the U.S. with the song in 1959), Little Richard, and The Beatles.

Leiber & Stoller's lives were changed by accident. Their song 'Hound Dog' – a 12-bar diatribe against a feckless man – had been a hit on the rhythm & blues charts in 1953 for Big Mama Thornton. In 1956 it was covered by a white singer they'd never heard of – one Elvis Presley. The pair found Presley's bowdlerized version laughable, but did not object to the fame and the money that his transatlantic smash earned them. They would provide Presley with many songs over the next few years, including some of his best known: 'Loving You,' 'Jailhouse Rock,' 'Trouble,' 'King Creole,' and 'Baby I Don't Care.' They got on well with Presley but the relationship foundered in a business wrangle with his manager Tom Parker.

The pair's stream of records for black vocal group The Coasters, meanwhile, saw them employing narratives, comic-book imagery, and funny voices to create records unique for the era, including 'Searchin',' 'Young Blood,' 'Yakety Yak,' 'Charlie Brown,' 'Along Came Jones,' and 'Poison Ivy.' Another song intended for The Coasters was 'Love Potion No. 9,' but instead it was given as a favor to a similar group, The Clovers.

They didn't write much for The Drifters, but 'There Goes My Baby' was not only a U.S. Number 2 but also massively influential for two things never heard before on a rhythm & blues or rock recording: classical strings and Latin rhythms. They also hit big with ex-Drifters vocalist Ben E. King in 1961. But their productivity declined when they set up their own Red Bird label in 1963, leaving them burdened by administration.

After selling the label three years later they were never the same force again, but remained in demand as producers and songwriters. 'Is That All There Is' was a spoken-word hit for Peggy Lee influenced by Kurt Weill and Bertolt Brecht. 'Pearl's A Singer' saw them rewrite an old song for Elkie Brooks to create a 1977 Top 10 U.K. hit. In 1995, delivering 'The Girls I Never Kissed' to Frank Sinatra, they provided material to just about the only major artist who had never recorded one of their songs.

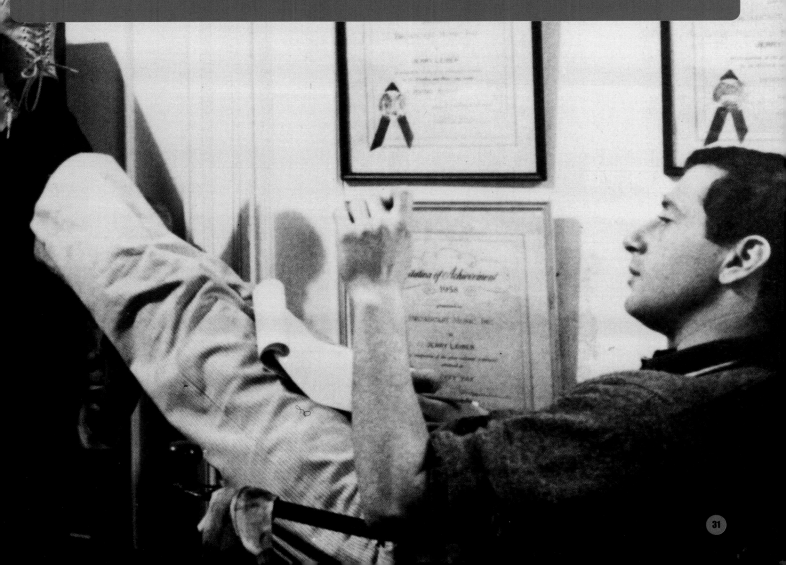

Catch A Falling Star / Magic Moments
Perry Como

Released January 1958
RCA 7128 (U.S. #1) / RCA 1036 (U.K. #1)

This was a double-sided hit, and while 'Catch A Falling Star' was the chart-topper in America, in Britain it was 'Magic Moments' that spent eight weeks at the top. Former barber and king of laidback, Pierino Como had been singing with bands since 1933 and signed with RCA in '43. 'Magic Moments' is of particular significance since it was one of the first hits written by Burt Bacharach and Hal David. In fact their very first hit, 'The Story Of My Life,' a U.S. hit for Marty Robbins, was a U.K. Number 1 for Michael Holliday the week before 'Magic Moments.' Meanwhile, 'Catch A Falling Star' won the first ever official Gold Disc for sales of one million copies and a Grammy for Best Male Vocal Performance. (RCA first dreamed up the Gold Disc idea as a gimmick, in 1940, awarding one to Glenn Miller for 'Chattanooga Choo Choo.') Como enjoyed something of a revival in the early 1970s covering contemporary material such as Don McLean's 'And I Love You So,' by which time he'd racked up an impressive 150 U.S. chart entries.

Tom Hark
Elias & His Zigzag Jive Flutes

Released March 1958
Not issued U.S. / Columbia DB 4109 (U.K.)

The influence on pop of black American music – jazz, blues, rhythm & blues – is well documented. Caribbean calypso and South American cha-cha also had a big effect on the 1950s charts, but the influence of Africa itself is often overlooked. The Weavers, for example, had taken the Zulu folk song 'Wimoweh' into the U.S. charts in 1952. 'Tom Hark' was a much more authentic proposition: Elias and his Flutes were a proper kwela band made up of buskers from the streets of Johannesburg, South Africa, and led by penny-whistle virtuoso Big Voice Jack Lerole. Remarkably, such effervescent, high-pitched, rhythmically-driven music would not gain international acclaim until Paul Simon included kwela musicians on his 1986 album *Graceland*.

Witch Doctor
David Seville

Released March 1958
Liberty 55132 (U.S. #1) / London HLU 8619 (U.K. #11)

The Purple People Eater
Sheb Wooley

Released May 1958
MGM 12651 (U.S. #1) / MGM 981 (U.K. #12)

Les Paul had been doing it with his guitar for years, but when David Seville decided to use the studio's tape recorder to speed up his vocals, he unwittingly established a new musical sub-genre. Seville's humorous song, with its unforgettable hook, "Oo-ee-ooh-ah-ah ting-tang walla-walla-bing-bang," used the speeding-up technique to create the weird voice of 'Witch Doctor' and land him a Number 1 smash. Before long, singing cowboy Sheb Wooley rehashed the idea for the alien voices in his Number 1, 'The Purple People Eater,' and The Chipmunks, another Seville creation, topped the chart in December. The U.K.'s singing piglet puppets, Pinky & Perky, also found success with the technique, which remains a staple of novelty discs even now.

Return To Me
Dean Martin

Released March 1958
Capitol 3894 (U.S. #4) / Capitol CL 14844 (U.K. #2)

Former shoeshine boy, casino croupier, and amateur boxer Dino Paul Crocetti first found gainful employment as a singer in 1941. Five years later he teamed up with comedian Jerry Lewis for one of the most successful entertainment partnerships in U.S. history. In 1957 the pair broke up somewhat acrimoniously and Martin stepped out alone, introducing his new 'drunk' persona. Many thought he wouldn't make it on his own, but he proved them all wrong with a highly successful film and recording career. 'Return To Me' was co-written by bandleader Guy Lombardo's brother Carmen in 1957 and first recorded by Guy's Orchestra with vocals by Don Rodney, but became Martin's first hit after the split with Lewis. Dean Martin was Elvis Presley's favorite vocalist, and according to author Peter Guralnick, Elvis purchased a copy of this very record the week before he enlisted in the U.S. Army.

All I Have To Do Is Dream / Claudette
The Everly Brothers

Released April 1958
Cadence 1348 (U.S. #1) / London HLA 8618 (U.K. #1)

The Everly Brothers were one of the pivotal acts in popular music history. Don Everly (born 1937) and Phil Everly (1939) grew up in a musical family and made their first performance on their parents' radio show when Don was eight and Phil just six. Their close-harmony country-rock became an enormous influence on the wave of artists who found fame in the 1960s. A teenage Paul McCartney bought all the Everlys singles as soon as they were released, and Bob Dylan was a staunch Everlys fan. Dylan said: "We owe those guys everything. They started it all."

They got their record deal through an introduction by family friend and Nashville heavyweight Chet Atkins, coupling the duo with husband-and-wife songwriting team Felice and Boudleaux Bryant. The combination was to become one of the most successful in pop music history. The Bryants were by no means teenagers – Boudleaux was born in 1920, Felice in 1925. The couple met and married in 1945, at which point

Boudleaux began putting music to Felice's poems, and one of Nashville's most successful songwriting partnerships was born. The first song the Bryants presented to the Everlys was 'Bye Bye Love,' one that had already been given the thumbs-down by everyone in Nashville, including Elvis Presley.

Although the Everlys had been signed as a country act, Atkins gave them more of a rock'n'roll sound coupled with those close-harmony vocals. This combination proved to be the perfect vehicle for the brothers, and 'Bye Bye Love' became a huge international hit. The Bryants followed up with a string of gems including 'Wake Up Little Susie' and 'All I Have To Do Is Dream,' which Boudleaux claims was written in 15 minutes. 'Dream' became the duo's best loved song and their biggest seller, topping the charts on both sides of the Atlantic. It was also a double-sided hit, marking Roy Orbison's arrival as a hit songwriter with 'Claudette,' written for his wife. Orbison had recorded the song a couple of years previously while at Sun Records but it had not been released.

Fever
Peggy Lee

Released July 1958
Capitol *3998* (U.S. #8) / Capitol *CL 14902* (U.K. #5)

'Fever' was Peggy Lee's crowning achievement – almost two decades into her singing career – and remains one of the definitive moments in late-1950s swing. Lee was notable during the decade as one of the few female singers who contributed to her own material. She co-wrote 'Mañana (Is Soon Enough For Me),' which was later a hit for Dean Martin, and 'He's A Tramp,' as featured in Disney's *Lady And The Tramp*.

'Fever,' however, was not one of Lee's own compositions. It was written in 1956 by Eddie Cooley and Otis Blackwell, although at the time Blackwell took the more 'white sounding' name of his stepfather, John Davenport, most likely to avoid any potential racial prejudice. His other writing credits – as Davenport – include the Elvis Presley hits 'All Shook Up' and 'Don't Be Cruel,' and Jerry Lee Lewis's 'Great Balls Of Fire.'

'Fever' was a hit first for Little Willie John in a more straightforward rock'n'roll setting. Lee made the song her own by adapting the lyrics, suggesting the slower, jazzier arrangement, and offering up a typically sultry vocal performance. None of the subsequent cover versions – by artists including Madonna and Ella Fitzgerald – have come close to Lee's.

Tom Dooley
The Kingston Trio

Released August 1958
Capitol *4049* (U.S. #1) / Capitol *CL 14951* (U.K. #5)

This deftly modernized Blue Ridge Mountains ballad was based on the exploits of Tom Dula, hanged for murder in 1868, and it changed America's folk-music scene forever. What had been a determinedly purist, avowedly non-commercial, left-wing liberal ferment was suddenly represented at Number 1 in the pop charts by The Kingston Trio. Few denied their artistry, but to be this successful approached heresy. Because of The Kingston Trio, the next generation of folkies, including Joan Baez and Bob Dylan, and folk-rockers like The Byrds and The Band, knew that their music could resound beyond the basket-houses of Cambridge, Massachusetts, and New York City's Greenwich Village. Folk music was now, officially, big business.

Smoke Gets In Your Eyes
The Platters

Released November 1958
Mercury *71383* (U.S. #1) / Mercury *AMT 1016* (U.K. #1)

This timelessly beautiful Otto Harbach-Jerome Kern standard first became a Number 1 hit for Paul Whiteman's Orchestra back in 1934. It would score again for Bryan Ferry in 1974 and John Alford in 1996, but few would dispute that The Platters created the definitive recording.

The group had chosen the song against the advice of Mercury Records boss Art Talmadge, who thought they needed contemporary material, and they faced an injunction from Jerome Kern's widow who tried to prevent them releasing it. But in the end, quality won out and The Platters' immaculately serene rendition scored a Number 1 on both sides of the Atlantic.

Rumble
Link Wray & His Ray Men

Released April 1958
Cadence *1347* (U.S. #16) / London *HLA 8623* (U.K.)

One of the great debut singles of the 1950s, 'Rumble' inaugurated a pioneering guitar style that went on to influence everything from blues-rock to heavy metal. If anybody can lay claim to inventing the power chord – that distorted beast so prevalent in rhythm guitar playing ever since – then it's Link Wray. No less an authority than Pete Towshend of The Who admitted: "If it hadn't been for Link Wray and 'Rumble' I would never have picked up a guitar."

'Rumble' is dominated by Wray's dirty, thick guitar chords, which gradually deteriorate into a soup of tremolo effects as the song moves to its conclusion, underpinned by the unfussy playing of his drumming brother Doug and bassist Shorty Horton. 'Rumble' reached Number 16 in the U.S. chart on its release but ended up as the trio's only recording for the Cadence label.

The song's title, inspired by the fight scenes in *West Side Story*, was taken by many to be an incitement to teenage violence. Bowing to pressure, Cadence boss Archie Bleyer asked the group to clean up its act and work with The Everly Brothers' producers in Nashville. Wray refused and moved to Epic Records, but he would never again record anything that matched the power of 'Rumble.'

Although his career dwindled through the next three decades, Wray enjoyed a resurgence of interest after 'Rumble' was included in the beyond-cool soundtrack to Quentin Tarantino's *Pulp Fiction* movie, but even then found himself overshadowed by another guitar instrumental used in the same film, Dick Dale's surf classic 'Miserlou.'

Johnny B. Goode
Chuck Berry

Released April 1958
Chess *1691* (U.S. #8) / London American *HLM 8629* (U.K.)

Chuck Berry's songs have been an unparalleled influence upon pop musicians of the last 45 years. While Bill Haley and Elvis changed the music, it was artists such as Berry and Buddy Holly who inspired the beat bands of the 1960s to write their own songs.

Berry was once called "the folk poet of the 1950s" but there have been some recent attempts to show that at least some of the classic songs credited to him were partially written by his pianist, Johnnie Johnson. However, a 2002 judgment dismissed any claim that Johnson might have had, principally because he waited some 35 years to stake his claim in the construction of these seminal tunes, over 30 of which Johnson claimed that he and Berry had created together.

'Johnny B. Goode' was recorded on February 28, 1958, and was allegedly written by Berry in honor of Johnson, although it was mostly about himself. In his autobiography Berry says: "I'd guess my mother has as much right to be declared the source of 'Johnny B. Goode' as any other contender in that she was the one that repeatedly commented that I would be a millionaire someday." 'Goode' was a reference to Goode Street, the street on which Berry grew up. The song has

become the most covered in Berry's extensive catalogue – and could well be one of the first songs from our planet that alien beings will hear. It was dispatched on copper disc upon the Voyager probe launched into outer space in 1977. Remarkably, Berry only ever had one Number 1 record throughout his career, the abysmal 'My Ding-A-Ling,' a transatlantic chart-topper in 1972 filled with double entendres that, purely from a historical perspective, somewhat detracts from the man's unique contribution to popular music.

Summertime Blues
Eddie Cochran

Released June 1958
Liberty *55144* (U.S. #8) / London *HLU 8702* (U.K. #18)

Cochran is not often remembered as one of the great stars of rock'n'roll, mainly because of his brief career, but nonetheless he left us with some classic songs of the genre. Following a couple of hillbilly singles in 1955, he teamed with songwriter Jerry Capehart and together they wrote most of his biggest hits. Like many of the best songs of the rock'n'roll era, 'Summertime Blues' was a success thanks to its simplicity and honesty. Together with his other major hit, 'C'mon Everybody,' it celebrated teenage life – the parties, the music, the cars, and the rebellion against increasingly uncomprehending parents.

Cochran and Capehart had been working on 'Summertime Blues' for some time before recording the song in May 1958. It was originally intended only as a B-side to an A composed by Sharon Sheeley, 'Love Again.' Sheeley, a teenage songwriter, later became Cochran's girlfriend and had just written Ricky Nelson's American Number 1, 'Poor Little Fool.' She and Cochran wrote another of his best songs, 'Somethin' Else,' later covered by Tom Petty, Showaddywaddy, and The Sex Pistols. However, it was in 'Summertime Blues' that Cochran found his trademark style, and as an A-side it became his biggest hit, reaching the Top 20 in both America and Britain and turning Cochran into an overnight star.

Move It
Cliff Richard

Released August 1958
Not issued U.S. / Columbia *DB 4178* (U.K. #2)

Rock'n'roll was an exclusively American phenomenon until September 12, 1958, when Cliff Richard entered the U.K. charts with 'Move It.'

A former member of the Dick Teague Skiffle Group, Cliff had switched to rock'n'roll after hearing Elvis Presley. By the middle of 1958, he and his band The Drifters (later renamed The Shadows) were playing regularly at London's hip 2Is coffee bar. They were snapped up by EMI Records, on the prowl for homegrown rock'n'roll talent. Their first single was to be 'Schoolboy Crush,' but they had no B-side until Cliff's guitarist Ian Samwell, infuriated by a smug feature in U.K. music weekly *Melody Maker* predicting the imminent demise of rock'n'roll, poured his righteous rage into a song, 'Move It.'

Samwell started by trying to imitate a Chuck Berry-style riff. "I came up with this little introduction," he said, "and then the words just popped into my head – 'C'mon pretty baby, let's a-move it and a-groove it' –

deliberately making it as American as possible. Remember, people in Britain simply didn't call each other 'baby' back then, and moving it and grooving it was considered positively obscene."

Released as the B-side of 'Schoolboy Crush' on EMI's Columbia label, the song was only switched over when TV producer Jack Good refused to allow Cliff to sing the A-side on his show, *Oh Boy!*. Good wanted 'Move It' or nothing – and the British public agreed with him, sending the single to Number 2. After Cliff, the floodgates opened, and by the mid 1960s British rock ruled the world.

To Know Him Is To Love Him
The Teddy Bears

Released September 1958
Dore *503* (U.S. #1) / London *HLN 8733* (U.K. #2)

Phil Spector bought his first guitar after hearing British skiffle star Lonnie Donegan sing the old Huddie Ledbetter song 'Rock Island Line' and started his first band, The Sleepwalkers, at Hollywood's Fairfax High. He was barely 18 when he composed 'To Know Him Is To Love Him' for his next combo, The Teddy Bears. The song was somewhat morbidly inspired by the inscription on his father's tombstone and became a hit right out of the box, securing the top spot on December 1, 1958. The group never had another hit, but Spector moved into production, created the Wall Of Sound, and masterminded the careers of The Ronettes, The Crystals, and many more.

Lonely Teardrops
Jackie Wilson

Released November 1958
Brunswick *55105* (U.S. #7) / Coral *Q 72347* (U.K.)

Night
Jackie Wilson

Released February 1960
Brunswick *55166* (U.S. #4) / Not issued U.K.

Jackie Wilson was based in Detroit but his first success came in Britain when the vibrant 'Reet Petite,' written by Motown founder Berry Gordy, reached Number 6 there late in 1957. However, Wilson's follow-ups didn't click with the Brits, but his luck held when another Gordy composition, the calypso-doowop-gospel styled 'Lonely Teardrops,' secured his first U.S. Top 10 placing.

In his autobiography, *To Be Loved*, Gordy recounted the song's origins. "I created a story about a guy crying, begging a lost love to come back. I started with 'My eyes are crying lonely teardrops.' I liked it, but not exactly. Too common. I changed 'My eyes are crying' to 'My heart is crying.' I liked it."

So did the American public, who bought over a million copies, keeping it at Number 1 in the R&B chart for seven weeks. After that, Wilson could do no wrong, notching up a further 20 hits by the end of the 1960s. The biggest of these was 'Night,' peaking at Number 4 in April 1960. Given that the U.K. had dried up on Wilson, it might seem curious that 'Night,' an obviously commercial proposition, was never released there. The reason? Wilson's U.K. label, Coral, apparently reasoned that the British

public might disapprove of a pop song based on the aria 'My Heart At Thy Sweet Voice' from the Saint-Saens' opera *Samson & Delilah*. Wilson's luck hadn't quite run out, however, because when his American hits dried up in 1968, Britain came on stream again, giving him major triumphs with 'Higher And Higher' and 'I Get The Sweetest Feeling.'

Donna / La Bamba
Ritchie Valens

Released November 1958
Del-Fi *4110* (U.S. #2) / London *HL 8803* (U.K. #29)

It Doesn't Matter Anymore
Buddy Holly

Released January 1959
Coral *62074* (U.S. #13) / Coral *Q 72360* (U.K. #1)

As with Bill Haley's 'Rock Around The Clock' and Cliff Richard's 'Move It,' Richie Valens's seminal rocker 'La Bamba' was tucked away on a B-side. The A-side was a nicely crafted affirmation of undying love for his girlfriend Donna Ludwig and did well, reaching Number 2 in the *Billboard* chart, but it was ultimately eclipsed by a rocked-up Mexican folk tune.

Valens was reluctant even to record 'La Bamba,' fearing that the all-important white audience wouldn't understand the lyrics, which were entirely in Spanish. Underpinned by the throb of an unusual and relatively new instrument, the electric bass, 'La Bamba' thrashed along with a rock'n'roll spirit – and one that inspired songwriter Bert Berns to re-shape it, with English lyrics, as 'Twist And Shout.' A significant hit for The Isley Brothers and The Beatles, Berns's song became a staple live number for virtually every 1960s beat group. 'La Bamba' itself would hit Number 1 as the title song for a 1987 Valens biopic.

Buddy Holly was so struck by the Paul Anka-composed 'It Doesn't Matter Anymore' that he recorded it on the day he first heard it, October 21, 1958. It would bring him his first British chart topper but, tragically, he and Valens both died in a plane crash on February 3, 1959, so neither saw the fruits of their final works. The following day, delivery boy Don McLean cut open a bundle of newspapers in New Rochelle, New York, and was heartbroken to read of Holly's death. Years later, in 'American Pie,' he would immortalize that crash as "the day the music died."

There Goes My Baby
The Drifters

Released April 1959
Atlantic *2025* (U.S. #2) / London *HLE 8892* (U.K.)

Shout
The Isley Brothers

Released August 1959
RCA *7588* (U.S.) / RCA *1149* (U.K.)

The Drifters' first hit had Ben E. King on lead vocals and Jerry Leiber and Mike Stoller as producers, and was a landmark in the development of popular music. King composed 'There Goes My Baby' and brought it to a session, but lead vocalist Charlie Thomas wasn't getting it. So King stepped up to the mic and delivered an impeccable performance.

Leiber & Stoller, keen not to simply replicate the hit-making formula they had used with The Coasters, saw The Drifters as a more sophisticated project and introduced a swaying Brazilian baion rhythm and an elegantly swirling string section. As Carole King later observed: "It had the guts of R&B and the 'head' of classical music." Rhythm & blues was now firmly on the road to becoming soul.

'Shout' by The Isley Brothers was a much less sophisticated proposition but proved equally important in shaping the future of R&B. During a rousing rendition of Jackie Wilson's 'Lonely Teardrops' in Washington, D.C., one of the Isleys threw in the line: "You know you make me want to shout." The crowd shouted back so enthusiastically that they decided to build that line into a blockbuster audience-response song.

When Ernie Maresca secured a Top 10 smash in April 1962 with 'Shout! Shout! (Knock Yourself Out)' the Isleys saw an opportunity to revive Bert Berns's composition 'Twist And Shout,' which had been a minor hit for The Top Notes during the early-1960s twist craze. By the time The Beatles took it to a U.S. Number 2 in 1964, the merger of rock'n'roll and R&B was official.

above > Clockwise from top left: Zeke Carey, Terry Johnson, Nate Nelson, Jake Carey, and Paul Wilson of The Flamingos c. 1960.
left > Left to right: Ben E. King, Charlie Thomas, Dock Green, and Elsbearry Hobbs of The Drifters.

I Only Have Eyes For You
The Flamingos

Released April 1959
End *1046* (U.S. #11) / Top Rank *JAR 263* (U.K.)

'I Only Have Eyes For You' remains one of the most memorable hits of the doo-wop era and, like much of The Flamingos' catalogue, was a clear influence on the Motown Sound of the 1960s.

The Flamingos formed around cousins Jake and Zeke Carey, who in 1950 relocated from Baltimore to Chicago, where they met fellow choristers Paul Wilson and Johnny Carter, and later lead vocalist Sollie McElroy. After recording several unsuccessful singles for the Chance label, the group signed to Checker, scoring their first hits in 1956 with 'I'll Be Home' and 'A Kiss From Your Lips.' That year they also starred in the *Rock, Rock, Rock* movie and performed with Bill Haley and The Platters as part of the first racially-integrated rock'n'roll tour.

By this stage, as well as being tremendous vocalists, The Flamingos had become accomplished musicians and honed their onstage dance routines in the manner of 1960s groups like The Temptations. Their success was soon put on hold, however: there were contractual wrangles with Checker, and Jake Carey and Johnny Carter were called up for military service. Carey returned to the group in 1958, but Carter made a clean break and joined another vocal group, The Dells.

In late 1958 The Flamingos signed to End Records and hit their commercial and artistic peak, first with 'Lovers Never Say Goodbye' and then 'I Only Have Eyes For You.' Originally recorded by bandleader Eddy Duchin in 1934, the song soared into the upper reaches of the chart on the strength of its warm, ethereal backing vocals, the gently nagging, piano-led arrangement, and, most importantly, McElroy's lilting lead vocal about a love that "must be a kind of blind love."

Peter Gunn
Duane Eddy

Released March 1959
Jamie *1122* (U.S. B-side; A #27) / London *HLW 8879* (U.K #6)

Duane Eddy began playing guitar when he was five years old, had his first hit in 1958 with 'Rebel Rouser,' and became one of the most successful instrumental artists in pop history. His famous 'twangy' guitar sound was inspired by Bill Justis's 1957 hit 'Raunchy.' Eddy's sound came from his habit of playing lead on the bass strings of his Gretsch guitar, aided by the studio expertise of producer Lee Hazlewood, including a novel 'drainpipe' echo chamber.

'Peter Gunn' was written by Henry Mancini for the late-1950s American TV detective series of the same name and was originally a U.S. hit for the Ray Anthony Orchestra. Eddy's recording was originally released in the U.S. as the B-side of his 1959 Top 30 hit 'Yep!', although in Britain it was flipped and 'Peter Gunn' became his first Top 10 hit. Eddy recorded most of his hits with Lee Hazlewood's band, including top-notch session musicians Larry Knechtel (organ, bass) and Jim Horn (saxophone), later full-time members of Phil Spector's so-called Wrecking Crew. 'Peter Gunn' was reissued in America as an A-side and made number 27 in 1960. Eddy was invited to record the tune again in 1986 with London studio band Art Of Noise when it reached number 8. Shortly after this he recorded a comeback album produced by ELO leader Jeff Lynne and with guest appearances by Eddy fans Ry Cooder, Paul McCartney, and George Harrison.

Quiet Village
Martin Denny

Released early 1959
Liberty *55162* (U.S. #4) / London *HLU 8860* (U.K.)

Denny's instrumental hit is the best known 'exotica' record, a genre that resists easy definition. It imagines what Polynesian, Afro-Caribbean, and Hawaiian music might sound like, and caught the attention of a newly-affluent American middle-class beginning to warm to the idea of foreign travel. But it was not in any sense the real music of those cultures. Its 'exotic' credentials depended to a great extent on its packaging, with jackets featuring a dusky bikini-clad beauty in an appropriate setting; the music itself owed more to jazz, swing, and easy listening.

It all started in 1951 when musician, composer, and arranger Les Baxter recorded an album on Capitol, *Le Sacre Du Sauvage (Ritual Of The Savage)*. It included 'Quiet Village,' which in Denny's hands a few years later became an engagingly insistent piano-led instrumental. Denny was a former child prodigy already into his 40s when he moved to Hawaii in 1954. There he formed a piano-and-vibes group that included percussionist Augie Colon. The band usually played in the open air and became accustomed to performing to a background chorus of croaking bullfrogs and screeching birds. As a joke, Colon began imitating the bird calls onstage, a ruse that fitted well with the band's ersatz tropical style. Throwing in a few Southern Pacific and Eastern percussion instruments, Denny arrived at the sound heard on 'Quiet Village.' He recorded the song in mono in 1956, to little success, but when he tried again with a stereo version in 1959 he scored a major hit.

Mack The Knife
Bobby Darin

Released August 1959
Atco *6147* (U.S. #1) / London *HLK 8939* (U.K #1)

'Mack The Knife,' or 'Moritat' as it was originally entitled, was written by Kurt Weill and Bertolt Brecht for their 1928 *Threepenny Opera*, itself based upon the first opera in English, *The Beggar's Opera*, written by John Gay in the early 18th century. *The Threepenny Opera* was first performed on Broadway in 1933 but was revived in 1955, after which the song became a hit for Dick Hyman. Louis Armstrong released the first version with the title 'Mack The Knife' in 1956.

Bobby Darin signed to Decca Records shortly before his 20th birthday and recorded four singles without success before switching to Atlantic's Atco label. Producer Ahmet Ertegun recalled: "I thought he was a fantastic artist, and just needed to be recorded properly." Under Ertegun's supervision Darin recorded his first hit, 'Splish Splash,' a novelty song that he had written in 15 minutes. But Darin wasn't satisfied to be a fly-by-night pop star and yearned respect as a 'real singer,' which explains his switch in 1959 to covering standards with Sinatra-like swinging arrangements.

Since 'Mack' had been a hit so many times before, Darin didn't consider it as a single, but when his label decided to release the song, Darin informed Dick Clark that he would perform it on Clark's influential TV show *American Bandstand*. The producer allegedly commented: "If he wants to turn his career into chopped liver, so be it." In fact it was probably the smartest career move that Darin ever made. While his version became the sixth to hit the U.S. charts it was also the most successful: his only American Number 1, and the biggest hit of the year, spending nine weeks at the top and winning two Grammy awards.

1959

What'd I Say (Part 1) / What'd I Say (Part 2)
Ray Charles

Released June 1959
Atlantic *2031* (U.S. #6) / London *HLE 8917* (U.K.)

'What'd I Say' was the record that introduced the world to the genius of Ray Charles and remains one of his finest individual achievements. It was considered so long at six-and-a-half minutes that it had to be spread over two sides of a single, which explains the addition of 'Part 1' and 'Part 2' to the title.

Charles studied composition at the St. Augustine School For The Deaf And The Blind, moved to Seattle, and made his recording debut with 'Confession Blues' in 1949 as part of The Maxim Trio. He spent the next few years honing his sound on a series of singles for the Downbeat, Swingtime, and Atlantic labels, gradually developing his celebrated amalgam of blues and gospel that in essence became a template for 1960s soul. By the mid 1950s he was making regular use of a horn quintet on such epochal recordings as 'I've Got A Woman' and 'Hallelujah I Love Her So,' lending the songs a raucous, euphoric backdrop.

The story goes that 'What'd I Say' began at a live performance early in 1959. By the end of a long show, Charles found himself short of material. Undeterred, he started to improvise – first with a series of 12-bar blues-based runs on the electric piano and then by starting a call-and-response with his female backing singers, The Raelettes.

On February 18th, 1959, Charles went to New York City to cut the song with Atlantic engineer Tom Dowd. 'What'd I Say' begins, as it had on that night of inspiration a few weeks earlier, with Charles's electric piano. Bassist Milton Garrard and drummer Milt Turner soon join in, and the three of them take time to feel their way around the song's simple but captivating structure. The riffs and licks Charles plays might sound traditional to modern ears, but it's no exaggeration to suggest that, at the time, he was in the midst of formulating a blueprint for R&B-soul keyboard playing.

Charles's vocal doesn't arrive until just over a minute and a half into the track – all the more remarkable given that many pop records of the time were not much longer than that. He leads the band through a half dozen verses of suggestive couplets about a girl in a red dress who can "do the Birdland all night long," and is eventually joined by the now-mandatory horn section before the song comes to what seems like a sudden stop after four-and-a-half minutes. The Raelettes then make an appearance, first to plead with Charles to continue, and then, when he agrees, to trade moans and groans with him to the song's close.

All this added up not only to a landmark record but also to a great pile of controversy. 'What'd I Say' was one of the most sexually charged single releases of the time, but that didn't stop it climbing to Number 6 on the U.S. pop chart and to the top of the R&B chart. After the furore died down, the recording inspired numerous covers by artists including Roy Orbison and Elvis Presley (in his 1964 movie *Viva Las Vegas*).

Venus
Frankie Avalon

Released February 1959
Chancellor *1031* (U.S. #1) / HMV *POP 603* (U.K #16)

A song with the title 'Venus' topped the American charts on three separate occasions. The first was composed by songwriter Ed Marshall, who presented it to Frankie Avalon after popping round to the singer's Philadelphia home one afternoon. Avalon liked it, was sure it was a hit, but was worried when he heard that Marshall had just hotfooted it from Al Martino's place. Martino thought it was more likely just an album cut, but Avalon wasn't taking any chances and recorded the song within three days. Avalon had a further U.S. Number 1, but was robbed in Britain when the second, 'Why,' was covered by Anthony Newley and hit the top there.

'Venus' version two was composed by Robbie van Leeuwen and reached Number 1 for Dutch group Shocking Blue in 1969. Covered by British trio Bananarama, it topped the charts yet again in 1986 – and can be credited with yet another chart-topping appearance when it formed the basis of the 'Stars On 45' medley, a Number 1 in 1981.

Puppy Love
Dolly Parton

Released early 1959
Goldband *45-8213* (U.S.) / Not issued U.K.

One of 12 children brought up in poverty, Parton began making up songs as a child, and by her early teens was an accomplished singer and regular performer on local radio and television in Knoxville, Tennessee. It was her uncle Bill Owens who gave her a guitar when she was seven years old. He also offered some songwriting assistance for her first recording, 'Puppy Love' / 'Girl Left Alone,' taped at Goldband Records in Lake Charles, Louisiana, in 1959 when Parton was just 13.

Studio owner Eddie Shuler remembers that little Dolly had to use the highest stool in the studio to get close enough to the microphone. (The original tape of this recording now resides at the Country Music Hall Of Fame in Nashville.)

It would be another five years before Parton recorded again, but it must have been something she was particularly looking forward to. The day after she graduated from High School in 1964, she packed her bags, took the first Greyhound to Nashville, and never looked back.

A Teenager In Love
Dion & The Belmonts

Released April 1959
Laurie *3027* (U.S. #5) / London *HLU 8874* (U.K. #28)

Dion DiMucci and his Belmonts – Freddy Milano, Angelo D'Aleo, and Carlo Mastrangelo – were one of many groups of Bronx-based Italian-American teenagers singing doo-wop in the late 1950s. 'Teenager In Love' was the biggest of their several hit singles, a record that ably demonstrates the group's gift for imbuing standard teen-pop fluff with a sense of yearning for transcendence. This was largely due to Dion himself, a blue-eyed-soul singer a decade before the term was coined. Marty Wilde covered the song for the British market and grabbed a bigger slice of the U.K. sales, but his pale imitation serves only to underline Dion's status as one of rock's great voices.

Tiger
Fabian

Released June 1959
Chancellor *1037* (U.S. #3) / HMV *POP 643* (U.K.)

From the 'blink and you'll miss them' brigade, Fabian saw 'Tiger' become the biggest of his eight American Top 40 hits in a 13-month whirlwind career. Originally hired purely on the basis of his good looks, Fabian Forte was just 15 years old when he recorded his debut, a Doc Pomus and Mort Shuman song with the unlikely title 'I'm A Man.' The songwriting duo also delivered his second hit, 'Turn Me Loose,' which Fabian debuted on the TV show *American Bandstand* in March 1959.

'Tiger' was a U.S. Number 3, with the unforgettable line "Hey, lumpa sugar, you look kinda sweet," before his movie debut in *Hound Dog Man*, the title song of which was his only British hit. A reviewer noted that in the movie "Fabian is surprisingly good" but then added: "Of course, he also sings." Three more hits followed with diminishing returns, but by April 1960 Fabian had become embroiled in the payola scandal, and when it was revealed that his recordings had been "significantly doctored" to improve his voice, his career was over.

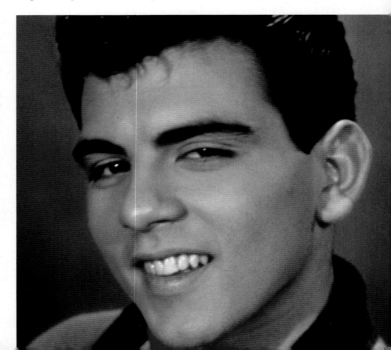

ALAN FREED AND THE PAYOLA SCANDAL

Payola is as old as the music industry. It means the payment of incentives to people to sing your songs or play your records. In the sheet-music days, pluggers handed out cash to performers to promote the songs they were trying to sell. Later, they would hand out gifts to early DJs to play the tunes they had for sale. By the time the 'payola' scandal broke in the U.S. in the late 1950s, the practice was well established and no one seemed to be unduly concerned. But people were annoyed and scared by rock'n'roll music, which had been championed on radio, and in particular by New York City DJ Alan Freed. Ostensibly a campaign against corruption, the payola scandal was also a way of attacking rock and its promoters.

Freed had begun his career as a classical music DJ in Cleveland, Ohio. In 1951 he was encouraged to change to playing rhythm & blues, which he began to call "rock'n'roll" to distance it from its black origins. While his claims to have invented the term were an exaggeration, Freed enthusiastically promoted the music it described. In 1954, having outgrown Cleveland, Freed moved to New York where he was recognized as the most influential DJ in the country. Calling himself Moondog, howling into the microphone, and speaking in a deep, gravelly voice, he won over a huge audience both by his musical choices and his on-air personality. He enraged the conventional morality of the day by organizing concerts that attracted a mixed-race crowd and by playing the original versions of songs by black artists rather than innocuous white cover versions.

The payola scandal began when a congressional committee that had been investigating quiz-show rigging in television turned its attentions to practices in the record and radio industries. Payola was seen as another symptom of a corrupt society. But it was not a crime; it was just unpopular within the record and music-publishing industries, mainly among those who thought that rock'n'roll was only being played because DJs had been bribed. It was certainly the case that payola had made DJs more receptive to the output of the small independent labels who championed the new music.

The committee began hearings in February 1960, and immediately the major record companies and radio stations disowned the practice, which was being viewed as 'unfair competition.' Employees were immediately required to sign affidavits to say they had never taken payola. Alan Freed refused and was sacked by WABC Radio. In the committee's hearings, he admitted that he had been on the payroll of several record companies, but had never taken "a dime" to play a record. "I'd be a fool to," he said. "I'd be giving up control of my program." His argument was that he was paid to advise record companies on the music that would sell well, rather than helping sell the music they had made. Either way, it brought him a handsome income. He had also benefited from another common practice of the era and was credited as co-composer of some 15 songs, including Chuck Berry's 'Maybellene' and 'Sincerely' by The Moonglows.

Nonetheless, despite cooperating with the committee, Freed was charged – not for payola, which did not become an offence until later in 1960, but for the New York State offence of 'commercial bribery.' His crime was to take inducements without informing his employer. After a plea bargain, he was fined $500 and given a suspended six-month jail sentence. However, by this time, partly as a result of his heavy drinking, his career was on the skids. An indictment for tax evasion during the payola years arrived in 1964, by which time he was out of work and broke. Within a year, at age 43, he was dead.

Wonderful World
Sam Cooke

Released May 1960
Keen *8-2112* (U.S. #12) / HMV *POP 754* (U.K. #27)

Cooke was 'the man who invented soul music' and an influence on so many others – Marvin Gaye, Otis Redding, Al Green, the list is almost endless. But this extremely talented singer, writer, arranger, and producer would surely have produced even greater work had he not died in somewhat mysterious circumstances at the tragically young age of 29 in 1964.

At first he recorded gospel music for Art Rupe's Specialty label, but the two fell out when Cooke and producer Bumps Blackwell recorded the poppy 'You Send Me' in 1957. Rupe, in a magnanimous but costly decision, allowed Cooke and Blackwell to depart, with the song and Cooke's contract, to Keen Records – and watched as 'You Send Me' shot to Number 1.

While with Keen, Cooke's songs just got better and better. Among the other classic sides he recorded for the label were 'Only Sixteen' and 'Wonderful World,' recorded at his last session for the label in Los Angeles on March 2, 1959. 'Wonderful World' became one of his best loved and most covered songs. Surprisingly, this inspired slice of pop songwriting was looked upon as something of a throwaway at the time and wasn't released until over a year later, by which time Cooke had moved on to RCA. The song was originally written by Lou Adler and Herb Alpert, but Cooke added the finishing lyrical touches, and the trio used the songwriting pseudonym 'Barbara Campbell.' It became a huge hit in Britain in 1986, reissued in conjunction with a TV advertisement for jeans.

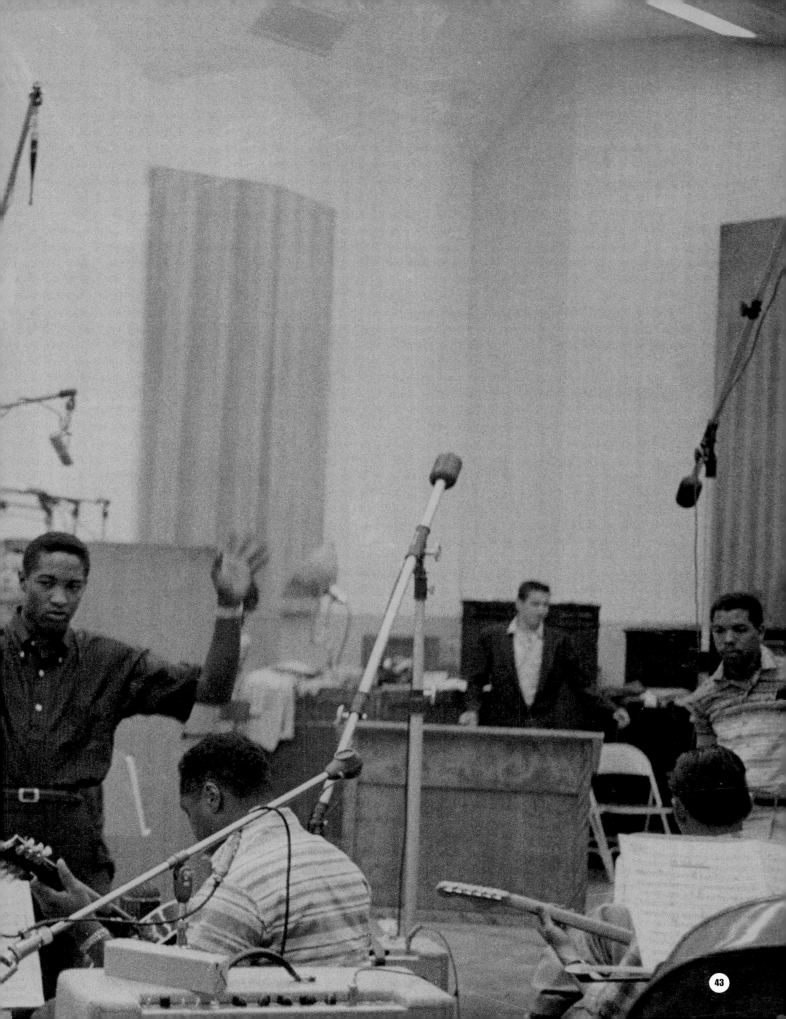

Cause I Love You
Carla & Rufus

Released August 1960
Satellite *102* (U.S.) / Not issued U.K.

Way back in the 1930s, Rufus Thomas was a comedian working with a traveling revue, The Rabbit Foot Minstrels. He made his first recording, 'I'll Be A Good Boy,' in 1949, but his rise to fame coincided with a stint as a DJ on the Memphis-based WDIA, one of the era's few black-owned stations. While at WDIA he launched his first hit, 'Bear Cat' (1953), an answer song to Big Mama Thornton's 'Hound Dog' and, more significantly, the first national chart hit for Sun Records.

Come 1959, Rufus and his daughter Carla proved significant in launching another vitally important Memphis label, Stax Records. ''Cause I Love You,' based largely on the New Orleans-style rhythm of Jessie Hill's 'Ooh Poo Pah Doo,' was the first track recorded in a converted theatre at 926 East McLemore, the brand new studio of country-music based Satellite Records. When the song broke out locally, Satellite owner Jim Stewart realized that his label's future lay with rhythm & blues. "It was like a blind man who suddenly gained his sight," he later explained. The success of the duet, which also featured 16-year-old Booker T. Jones on saxophone, convinced Atlantic Records producer Jerry Wexler to invest a $5,000 advance to secure a five-year option on the pair which, in turn, led to the re-launching of Satellite as Stax.

Stax went on to become the world's coolest soul and rhythm & blues label, while Rufus's raw but upbeat vocals and starkly simple proto-funk grooves made him almost as big a star as Carla, who was rarely out of the U.S. R&B charts for the rest of the decade.

Bye Bye Baby
Mary Wells

Released December 1960
Motown *1003* (U.S.) / Not issued U.K.

Former Ford Motor Company employee Berry Gordy was the man behind Motown Records, a business he would build up from an $800 loan in 1959 to one of the most successful black-run corporations in America, selling out 29 years later in 1988 for $61 million. (Gordy wisely held on to the valuable Jobete song catalogue, later selling a 50 per cent share in the company for a whopping $132 million.) Along the way he brought us such artists as The Supremes, featuring Diana Ross, Smokey Robinson, The Four Tops, Stevie Wonder, The Temptations, The Jackson 5, featuring 12-year-old Michael Jackson, and Marvin Gaye.

One of Gordy's first major artists was Mary Wells. She has been somewhat forgotten in the mists of time, despite giving Motown many early hits. Gordy originally got started in the music business writing hits for Jackie Wilson, and 17-year-old Mary Wells had Wilson in mind for her song 'Bye Bye Baby,' which she took to Gordy. Now with his own company to run, Gordy immediately suggested she record the song herself.It was not a major pop hit, but Wells went on to provide Motown with eleven Top 40 hits between 1961 and 1964, culminating in her international hit 'My Guy,' penned by Smokey Robinson. Ironically, 'My Guy' came out just as she was preparing to join 20th Century Fox for a large advance with talk of movie projects, but nothing ever came of the plans, and her Motown hits remain her greatest successes.

Stuck On You
Elvis Presley

Released March 1960
RCA *47-7740* (U.S. #1) / RCA *1187* (U.K. #3)

'Stuck On You' is far from Elvis's greatest recording, but as his first release after his Army service it assumed huge significance, racking up 1,250,000 advance sales before its title had even been announced. It was also the first stereo single to hit Number 1 in the U.S. and the first in RCA's new policy of releasing all singles in stereo. Domenico Modugno's 1958 Number 1, 'Volaré,' sparked a lasting taste for classy Italian songs, which Presley plugged into with 'It's Now Or Never,' based on the 1901 composition 'O Sole Mio.' There had already been successful versions of the song, but it still became Presley's biggest seller ever – 20 million copies and counting – and opened the door to the adult market for many upwardly mobile rock'n'rollers.

Three Steps to Heaven
Eddie Cochran

Released May 1960
Liberty *55242* (U.S.) / London *HLG 9115* (U.K. #1)

Cochran recorded this on January 8, 1960, at Gold Star studios in Hollywood, California, during his last recording session, alongside 'Cherished Memories' and 'Cut Across Shorty.' Cochran then flew to the U.K. to headline a tour with Gene Vincent. Following a final concert at the Bristol Hippodrome on April 16, Cochran, his girlfriend Sharon Sheeley, and Vincent hired a taxi to return to London. In the early hours of the morning near Chippenham, Wlitshire, the taxi hit a lamp-post. Cochran was thrown through the windshield and died later in hospital, while Vincent, Sheeley, and the taxi driver were seriously injured. In an ironic conclusion to Cochran's sadly short career, 'Three Steps To Heaven' became a posthumous Number 1 in Britain in June 1960, but surprisingly was not a hit in America. The song was later covered by British rock'n'roll revival band Showaddywaddy, becoming a Number 2 U.K. hit in 1975.

above > Clockwise from top left: Otis Redding, Stax Records owner Jim Stewart, Rufus Thomas, Booker T, and Carla Thomas, pictured at the Stax headquarters in Memphis, Tennessee, in the mid 1960s.

My Old Man's A Dustman
Lonnie Donegan

Released March 1960
Not issued U.S. / Pye *7N 15256* (U.K. #1)

Tie Me Kangaroo Down Sport
Rolf Harris
Released May 1960
Epic *9596* (U.S. #3) / Columbia *DB 4483* (U.K. #9)

Itsy Bitsy Teeny Weeny Yellow Polka Dot Bikini
Brian Hyland
Released June 1960
Kapp *342* (U.S. #1) / London *HLR 9161* (U.K. #8)

Lonnie Donegan was not content merely to be Britain's king of skiffle in the 1950s, but carved out a new career for himself as a fresh decade dawned by tapping into a rich vein of cockney music-hall humor. Despite the handicap of having been born in Scotland, he convincingly portrayed a London barrow-boy stereotype in 'My Old Man's A Dustman,' his biggest U.K. hit, while 'Does Your Chewing Gum Lose Its Flavour' restored him to the American charts where he'd last been seen in 1956. Similar Brit humor was adopted by beat-boom bands such as The Small Faces and The Kinks and remains present in post-millennium groups inlcuding The Arctic Monkeys.

Shortly after Donegan's 'Dustman' and on the other side of the globe, all-round entertainer Rolf Harris hit the Australian top spot by parodying Aussie idiosyncrasies in 'Tie Me Kangaroo Down Sport,' which (and this is true) he adapted from a Harry Belafonte calypso with the lyric: "Tie me donkey down there, let him bray let him bray." Storming out of Australia into the British and American Top 10s, Harris embarked on a diverse career that thrives to this day.

Brooklyn schoolboy Brian Hyland's entry into the 1960 novelty-hit stakes came with 'Itsy Bitsy Teeny Weeny Yellow Polka Dot Bikini,' a cutely catchy ditty composed by Paul Vance after watching his two-year-old daughter playing on the beach. Fortunately, Hyland was able to transcend his novelty status and scored subsequent hits including 'Ginny Come Lately' and 'Sealed With A Kiss,' which established him as a class act.

Only The Lonely (Know How I Feel)
Roy Orbison

Released May 1960
Monument *421* (U.S. #2) / London *HLU 9149* (U.K. #1)

It is one of the great mysteries of popular music. The "ooh-eeh-ooh-ah-ah" gibberish in David Seville's 'Witch Doctor' is rib-ticklingly funny. But somehow when 'Only The Lonely' opens up with the equally nonsensical "Dum dum dum dummy doo wah, woh yeah yeah woh-woh, oh-woh-woh-woh-woh-oh-ooh-wah-ah-ah" every syllable sounds like a ripple of sorrow. Orbison's astonishing voice, swooping and soaring, tear-stained yet unbroken, was a major factor, and although 'Only The Lonely' fell just short of the U.S. Number 1 position it went all the way in the U.K. and transformed Orbison, a struggling rock'n'roll hopeful, into The Big O, master of the heart-stopping ballad.

Walk – Don't Run
The Ventures

Released May 1960
Dolton *25* (U.S. #2) / Top Rank *JAR 417* (U.K. #8)

Apache
The Shadows

Released July 1960
ABC-Paramount *10138* (U.S.) / Columbia *DB 4484* (U.K. #1)

The Ventures didn't invent rock guitar instrumentals – Link Wray and Duane Eddy pioneered that field years earlier. Nor did they invent surf music – Dick Dale & The Del-Tones did that during their late 1950s residency at the Rendezvous Ballroom in Balboa, California. Nevertheless it's hard to deny that their restlessly churning 'Walk – Don't

Run,' which peaked at Number 2 in August 1960, sparked America's early-1960s surf instrumental craze. In its wake came The Chantays with 'Pipeline,' The Surfaris with 'Wipe Out,' and many more.

'Walk – Don't Run' started life as a smooth, jazzy confection by guitarist Johnny Smith in 1954, which The Ventures discovered in a 1957 version on a Chet Atkins album, *Hi-Fi In Focus*. By the time they had stripped it back to a minimalist rock'n'roll chord sequence overlaid by a single-note melody line, it was virtually a new song. Johnny Smith himself later told the band that if they hadn't named it 'Walk – Don't Run' he wouldn't have recognized it.

Meanwhile, over in Britain, Cliff Richard's backing group The Shadows were about to score their first Number 1 with 'Apache,' a titanic tower of twang underpinned by pounding war drums, the first of more than 30 chart hits for the group over the next two decades. No other instrumental outfit came close to matching The Shadows' consistency and longevity, and their leader, Hank B. Marvin, is one of the most influential rock guitarists of all time, cited as a primary influence by Eric Clapton, Mark Knopfler, Neil Young, and dozens of other top axemen.

Shakin' All Over
Johnny Kidd & The Pirates

Released June 1960
APT-ABC *25040* (U.S.) / HMV *POP 753* (U.K. #1)

There wasn't much of any lasting quality that emerged from British recording studios in the early 1960s, but 'Shakin' All Over' was a notable exception. The song, written by Kidd (a.k.a. Frederick Heath) and his manager Gus Robinson, was allegedly thrown together in about half an hour the night before it was recorded at EMI's Abbey Road studios on May 13, 1960. The group were scheduled to record a cover of 'Yes Sir, That's My Baby' and needed a B-side. 'Shakin'' was recorded in one take. To the record company executives it was obvious that this should be the A-side, much to Kidd's surprise and joy. Clem Cattini was the

drummer with Kidd's band. He later played on dozens of 1960s hits by The Tornados, The Kinks, Donovan, and T.Rex, and claims to have played on 45 Number 1 hits. Johnny Kidd's chart career ground to a halt in 1964 when a new wave of beat groups arrived. Cattini recalled that Walter Ridley, who was credited with this production, "didn't know anything about rock'n'roll," and was apparently not even at the session, in fact produced by Ridley's assistant, Peter Sullivan.

The Twist
Chubby Checker

Released June 1960
Parkway *811* (U.S. #1) / Columbia *DB 4503* (U.K.)

In 1958, Detroit-based rhythm & blues singer Hank Ballard was watching his band improvising some dance steps as they played and he decided to write a song based on their moves. He called it 'The Twist' but his label, King Records, didn't think it was good enough to release as a single, so it was relegated to the B-side of a ballad, 'Teardrops On Your Letter.' Kids who came to see Ballard started picking up on 'The Twist,' and by the summer of 1960 the influential TV presenter Dick Clark noticed dancers twisting on his show, *American Bandstand*.

A shrewd operator, Clark arranged for Chubby Checker to cover Ballard's song, duplicating the original so precisely that when Ballard heard it on the radio he thought it was his own recording. Boosted by appearances on *Bandstand*, Chubby's version hit Number 1 on September 19, 1960, returning to the top more than a year later when the dance caught on among older music fans.

Chubby's follow-up, 'Let's Twist Again,' spread the fever to Europe, hotly pursued by a flood of twist-related releases, from Joey Dee's 'Peppermint Twist' to Sam Cooke's 'Twistin' The Night Away' and The Isley Brothers' 'Twist And Shout.' It became evident on November 14, 1961, that Ballard's B-side had penetrated the highest echelons of society when the U.S. Presidential Press Secretary, Pierre Salinger, officially denied that anyone had danced the twist during a recent party in the White House. The shake, the hully-gully, and the watusi were just around the corner – but let's not mention the funky chicken.

Oh Carolina / I Met A Man
The Folkes Brothers

Released late 1960
Buster Wild Bells *ZSP 52833* (Jamaica) / Blue Beat *BB 30* (U.K.)

This is arguably the most significant recording in Jamaican musical history and is often touted as the first ska record. The Folkes Brothers made just this one record, produced by vocalist and DJ Prince Buster in 1960. He'd been fascinated by the Rastafarian drumming of Count Ossie (Oswald Williams), which he incorporated into the single alongside featured teenage brothers John, Mico, and Junior Folkes on vocals. Buster supplied clapping and imitation horn sounds, and the whole thing was recorded with one microphone. Written by John Folkes in 1958, the track was released on the Blue Beat label in Britain in 1960, where it later became a club favorite. However, when Shaggy made 'Oh Carolina' internationally famous some 33 years later and the cash started rolling in, it prompted a number of lawsuits, and Prince Buster claimed that he had written the song. In a November 1994 decision, the British High Court decided otherwise, thus guaranteeing John Folkes a happy retirement. Mr. Folkes himself denies the ska tag and calls this a "heritage folk song."

Spanish Harlem
Ben E. King

Released January 1961
Atco *6185* (U.S. #10) / London *HLK 9258* (U.K.)

Stand By Me
Ben E. King

Released May 1961
Atco *6194* (U.S. #4) / London *HLK 9358* (U.K. #27)

Legendary producers Jerry Leiber and Mike Stoller had been working for Atlantic Records since 1956 writing and producing a slew of hits for The Coasters and The Drifters. They also wrote some of Elvis Presley's biggest hits including 'Hound Dog' and 'Jailhouse Rock.'

When lead vocalist Ben E. King left The Drifters in 1960, he recorded four songs in a remarkable three-hour session on October 27, including 'Spanish Harlem' and 'Stand By Me.' Phil Spector was also in the studio that day: he had written 'Spanish Harlem' with Leiber after pestering him for ages about writing a song together. 'Stand By Me' was put together in the studio and inspired by several gospel songs, including an early Sam Cooke record. King had suggested recording a version with The Drifters, but they weren't interested. Arriving at the session early, he sang what he had – some lyrics and a few bars of music – and worked with Leiber to complete the song. When Mike Stoller arrived, he came up with the defining bassline, and a classic was born.

'Stand By Me' was not a major British hit the first time around, but topped the U.K. chart in 1987 after appearing in a movie of the same name and a jeans commercial. Muhammad Ali, when he was still Cassius Clay, made a recording of 'Stand By Me,' on the B-side of his 1963 single, 'I Am The Greatest.' John Lennon had a hit with the song in 1975, taken from his *Rock'N'Roll* album in which, coincidentally, Phil Spector was involved.

Crazy
Patsy Cline

Released October 1961
Decca *31317* (U.S. #9) / Brunswick *05861* (U.K.)

'Crazy' was written by up-and-coming songwriter Willie Nelson and recorded under unusual circumstances. Two months before the session, Cline had been in a near-fatal automobile accident. Consequently she recorded the song while still on crutches and had problems sustaining notes because her ribs hurt when she tried to hold her breath.

She also had some difficulty grasping the song, and in an unusual move for the time producer Owen Bradley suggested that the backing track should be recorded first, and then Cline could return at a later date to record her vocal. This of course became normal practice, but back in the early 1960s it was more common to record several versions of a song 'live' in the studio with band or orchestra and then release the best take. The 'Crazy' session featured Nashville session legend Floyd Cramer on piano and The Jordanaires, most famous for their work with Elvis, on backing vocals.

Cline had been presented with two new Willie Nelson songs by fellow country artist Billy Walker. The other one was 'Funny How Time Slips Away' and was Cline's preference. However, fate stepped in when Walker refused to let her have it. She settled for 'Crazy,' and a classic recording was born.

According to Bradley, when she did indeed return to the studio a few days later to record her vocal, she nailed it on the first take. 'Crazy' was not a hit in Britain at the time but became a surprise chart entry there in 1990. It has the additional honor of being the most played jukebox hit of all time.

DANCING THE JUKEBOXE JIVE

The idea of a machine that would play music in return for small change is almost as old as recorded music itself. Thomas Edison's cylinder-based phonograph was patented in 1877, and only 12 years later a coin-operated version of the machine was first demonstrated, in a restaurant in San Francisco.

The 'nickel-in-the-slot phonograph,' so called because it charged 5¢ a play, was an immediate and astonishing success. Its inventor, Louis Glass, told a convention of phonograph operators that in the first six months of operation, his first 15 machines took $4,000, worth something like $80,000 today. Glass's machines bore little resemblance to later jukeboxes: they only played one record, which would be changed every day or two, and with no amplification, only four customers could listen at one time, through crude acoustic earphones. (Interestingly, a Brit, Charles Adam Randall patented an 'automatic parlophone' in London a year earlier, but there is no evidence it was ever built.)

The early machines tended to be electrically driven, either by battery or the early AC power supply. Reliable spring-driven machines came later and were a boon because they could be used in areas without electric power. The modern jukebox began to take shape at the turn of the 20th century with the arrival of the Automatic Entertainer, which offered 24 selections, on disc, played through a 40-inch acoustic horn on the top.

The year 1925 saw the first electrically-recorded 78 rpm discs, but record players remained purely acoustic for several more years. Because a large acoustic horn could fill a domestic living room, manufacturers thought that electrical amplification was unnecessary. Jukeboxes, however, were installed in noisy public spaces and needed much more volume, especially for dancing. The turning point came with the National Automatic Selective Phonograph of 1927. This electrically-amplified machine could select from 20 songs on 10 records. It is usually recognized as the first real jukebox and was made by the forerunner of the Automatic Musical Instrument company, one of the most celebrated names in the business. Another famous company, Wurlitzer, launched its first real jukebox in 1933.

Jukeboxes only began to acquire their classic look in the late 1930s, when J.P. Seeburg introduced colorful plastics. The last of the 'big four' manufacturers, Rock-Ola, entered the market in 1939. Its name is often associated with rock'n'roll, but that's entirely accidental. It was owned by a man called David Rockola.

In the late 1940s and early 1950s, great efforts went into increasing the available selections on the machines. The 200-selection machine was introduced by Seeburg in 1955. That marked a high-point for the conventional machine. In the 1950s, Seeburg had introduced the first jukebox that played 45s, although in poor black areas the old 78 standard lived on as late as 1958, not least because operators had moved the redundant machines to those neighborhoods. Some see the jukebox as the savior of the 45 single in the 'war of the speeds' in the early 1950s. (No jukebox ever played 12-inch 33 rpm albums.) The dominance of jukebox sales as an outlet for 45 rpm production also ensured that jukebox hits did well in the charts.

The word 'jukebox' is first recorded in 1939, in a *Time* magazine article on Glenn Miller, who attributed his success to his popularity on the machines. 'Jukes' or 'juke-joints' were roadhouses or bars frequented by black plantation workers in the Southern states of the U.S., while 'to juke' meant to dance. The word is believed to come from a West African

term meaning 'disorderly' or 'wicked.' The early coin-operated phonographs were too expensive for the black bars, but by the 1930s they had become established as a cheap replacement for live musicians.

In the 1940s and 1950s, when radio was effectively off-limits to black artists, jukeboxes were a key part of the burgeoning rhythm & blues scene. Independent operators would take their records direct to the juke joints and even provide the owners with coins so they could promote their records. There was thus a close connection between record makers and listeners; many in the early independent rock'n'roll record companies began in the jukebox business.

In the 1950s, jukeboxes led the youth trend taking rhythm & blues and then rock'n'roll music out of the purely black marketplace, by enabling white listeners to hear the authentic originals rather than the white cover versions that were so prominent on radio. Jukeboxes have always catered to a wide range of tastes, however. A poll of jukebox operators in 1996 declared that the 'number 1 jukebox single of all time' was Patsy Cline's 'Crazy.'

After the glory days, later innovations were less far-reaching, including stereo and CD operation. Today the jukebox is still going strong, in digital versions that hold some 5,000 songs on hard disk while allowing customers to download their choices from a catalogue of at least 150,000 songs held on a central server. They won't be getting those for a nickel, however. Many of the new machines accept credit cards.

Runaway
Del Shannon

Released March 1961
Big Top *3067* (U.S. #1) / London *HLX 9317* (U.K. #1)

Sharp good looks, a strong voice, and songwriting ability put Del Shannon into the charts in 1961 and kept him there until the middle of the decade. 'Runaway' was Shannon's first hit, and his biggest. It is a true pop classic: engagingly catchy without being trite, and unusual yet accessible.

The first thing that set 'Runaway' apart is the way Shannon uses his falsetto so effectively and prominently. Then there's the song's unusual structure, which abandoned conventional verse-chorus repeats. And there's the instrumental break played by Shannon's keyboard player, Max Crook, on an instrument he dubbed the Musitron, which was in fact a modified Clavioline, a small, three-octave electronic keyboard invented in France in 1947.

Although we hear 'Runaway' as a flawless pop capsule, the session at which it was recorded was fraught. The producer was concerned about the song's unconventional shape, and after it was recorded he speeded up the tapes to make them sound more commercial (and, some say, to disguise Shannon's wayward pitching).

The released record, originally recorded in A minor, is pitched somewhere just below B flat minor. Yet for all this, 'Runaway' became one of those records that transcends its time and origins. It was a massive international hit, and still sounds good today.

Although Shannon never scored as big a hit again after 'Runaway,' he remained a major worldwide star for several years. By the end of the decade he had drifted into management, production, and cabaret work, punctuated with occasional comebacks. Reputedly depressed at his inability to re-launch his pop career, he took his own life in February 1990.

Are You Sure
The Allisons

Released February 1961
London *1977* (U.S.) / Fontana *H 294* (U.K. #2)

The Eurovision Song Contest was established in 1956 but, although it boosted sales and built careers in Europe, Britain still hadn't won the competition by 1961. The Allisons were Bob and John, and with their optimistic, self-composed Everly Brothers soundalike 'Are You Sure' seemed to be serious contenders. But they returned from the Contest in France mere runners-up, and headed smack into a press storm over revelations that – gasp! – they were not brothers. In fact they were Colin Day and Brian Alford. Nonetheless, the publicity helped them all the way to Number 2 in Britain where they were held off the top spot by – who else? – The Everly Brothers, with 'Walk Right Back.'

Blue Moon
The Marcels

Released February 1961
Colpix *186* (U.S. #1) / Pye *7N 25073* (U.K. #1)

Pity The Collegians, whose vocal arrangements on their 1957 doo-wop classic 'Zoom Zoom Zoom' provided the inspiration for The Marcels' dramatic restructuring of the 1934 Rogers & Hart standard 'Blue Moon.' Despite the blatant plagiarism, rarely have the opening seconds of any record been as arresting as Fred Johnson's tongue-twisting bass vocal that introduces the Pittsburgh vocal quintet's greatest moment. Not only did 'Blue Moon' top the charts on both sides of the Atlantic and start a doo-wop revival, it inspired two tribute hits, Johnny Cymbal's 'Mr. Bassman' and Barry Mann's 'Who Put The Bomp,' both saluting Johnson's vocal prowess.

Halfway To Paradise
Billy Fury

Released April 1961
Not issued U.S. / Decca *F 11349* (U.K. #3)

Ronald Wycherley was signed up to the stable of the famous U.K. impresario Larry Parnes, affectionately known by the British press as 'Mr. Parnes, Shillings, and Pence.' Parnes renamed the boy Billy Fury and reckoned he was "the most important rock'n'roll singer Britain ever produced." This is not particularly apparent on 'Halfway To Paradise,' one of several Fury hits that made the Top 3 in Britain, although he never managed a number 1. (To hear Fury at his rock'n'roll best, check out his 1960 album *The Sound Of Fury*.) 'Halfway To Paradise' was a cover of a U.S. Number 39 hit by Tony Orlando (who would later find international fame fronting Dawn on such ditties as 'Tie A Yellow Ribbon Round The Ole Oak Tree'). Renowned U.K. session guitarist Big Jim Sullivan played on 'Paradise,' one of the first hit compositions of Gerry Goffin and Carole King.

Quarter To Three
U.S. Bonds

Released May 1961
Legrand *1008* (U.S. #1) / Top Rank *JAR 575* (U.K. #7)

Following his first hit, 'New Orleans,' Gary 'U.S.' Bonds threw a party and invited label-mates The Church Street Five. They weren't as merry as Bonds because their saxophone-based instrumental, 'A Night With Daddy G,' had flopped. Astutely, their leader, Gene Barge (a.k.a. Daddy G), asked Gary if he'd write some lyrics for the track, and the inebriated vocalist rattled off 'Quarter To Three' in ten minutes. They recorded it that night and by June 26 it was Number 1 in *Billboard*. Bonds never again hit the top, but he did bank a substantial out-of-court settlement when he sued Chubby Checker in 1963 because Chubby's 'Dancin' Party' bore uncanny resemblances to 'Quarter To Three.'

Take Five
Dave Brubeck Quartet

Released September 1961
Columbia *31769* (U.S. #25) / Fontana *H 339* (U.K. #6)

It isn't often that a jazz artist has a hit single, but pianist Dave Brubeck and his Quartet managed several in the early 1960s, of which 'Take Five' was the biggest. Composed by Quartet saxophonist Paul Desmond, 'Take Five' gains much of its distinctive flavor from its 5/4 time and is one of many Brubeck songs in unconventional time signatures (unconventional meaning anything other than 4/4, 3/4, or 6/8). Although Brubeck is sometimes disdained by jazz purists – mainly because he enjoyed this crossover pop success – the pianist has been one of the genre's most productive artists. Now in his 80s, he still composes, performs, and records.

Runaround Sue
Dion

Released September 1961
Laurie *3110* (U.S. #1) / Top Rank *JAR 586* (U.K. #11)

The Wanderer
Dion

Released December 1961
Laurie *3115* (U.S. #2) / HMV *POP 971* (U.K. #10)

Dion split from his backing group The Belmonts in 1960 and went on to achieve even greater chart success as a solo act. 'Runaround Sue' and 'The Wanderer' were the two biggest hits in this stage of a career that continues to this day. In the first song he is the wounded lover; in the second all macho swagger and braggadocio. His voice is flexible enough to serve him perfectly in both roles. Heroin addiction would later derail his career for a while, but he reinvented himself first as an acoustic singer-songwriter, then a gospel act, then a street-smart New York hipster, unique among 1950s rockers in his ability to remain artistically vibrant through the decades. "Nobody is hipper than Dion," Lou Reed once said – and he was right.

There's No Other (Like My Baby)
The Crystals

Released October 1961
Philles *100* (U.S. #20) / Parlophone *R 4867* (U.K.)

In the three years after Phil Spector wrote and performed on his first hit, 'To Know Him Is To Love Him' by The Teddy Bears, he learned the crafts of record production and musical arrangement as he worked on classic singles for Ben E. King, Gene Pitney, and others. As the first release on his newly formed Philles label, 'There's No Other' ignited the fire that Spector had started as a Teddy Bear. The Crystals had six consecutive hits and established Philles as a major chart force. Two years later they were the group with which Spector perfected his awesome Wall Of Sound production technique, which can be heard on such landmark singles as 'Da Doo Ron Ron' and 'Then He Kissed Me.'

Telstar
The Tornados

Released August 1962
London *9561* (U.S. #1) / Decca *F 11494* (U.K. #1)

The early 1960s were a golden age for instrumental rock, with artists like The Shadows, Duane Eddy, and The Ventures all thriving. But their best efforts were eclipsed by 'Telstar,' a record credited to The Tornados but which was more the work of its composer and producer, Joe Meek.

The story of 'Telstar' starts in July 1962 when the Telstar 1 satellite was rocketed into orbit. It provided the first transatlantic television broadcast, and hundreds of thousands of viewers huddled around their televisions, captivated when the ghostly, indistinct image of a man sitting at a desk finally appeared on the screen. Joe Meek was one of them.

Meek was already fascinated with the idea of space travel and loved electronic gadgetry. Those two passions meant he could not miss the Telstar broadcast; later, dwelling on the night's events, he was struck with a tune. He then began his idiosyncratic method of composing, which involved singing a very vague approximation of his tune over a backing track that he'd already recorded for another song. One of Meek's associates, Dave Adams, was charged with deciphering the music encrypted in Meek's wailing, and gradually the 'Telstar' melody emerged.

A few days later The Tornados came to Meek's unique home studio and began work on the song. The band were part of Meek's stable of artists, worked as an instrumental rock group, and backed British rock'n'roll star Billy Fury. They labored with Meek for a day and a half, and by the end had a backing track recorded, but the melody line was yet to be added. The Tornados then had to leave for an engagement with Fury, so Meek worked on with another collaborator, Geoff Goddard, who had co-written

an earlier Meek-produced hit, 'Johnny Remember Me,' for John Leyton. Meek sat Goddard down at a Clavioline, a small electronic keyboard, to lay down the melody line. Between them, the two strange friends – united in their belief that Buddy Holly spoke to them from beyond the grave – completed the record.

The end result was the most radical British rock'n'roll single yet recorded, distinguished by a simple, rousing tune – Goddard's Clavioline part – and Meek's peculiar production. The record is peppered with Meek's homespun ingenuity: electronic static for an intro; harp-like arpeggios performed on a piano with tacks stuck in the hammers; swathes of echo and reverb. Yet for all its oddness, it is an immediately accessible pop record.

'Telstar' went on to become one of the biggest hits of 1962, not only topping the charts in Britain but also in the U.S. – the first British rock record to do so. It sold more than five million copies worldwide on first release, remained in Decca's catalogue continually until the mid 1980s, and is still the best-selling rock instrumental single ever.

JOE MEEK: THE ORIGINAL INDEPENDENT PRODUCER

The producer and songwriter Joe Meek was an unlikely candidate for pop success. From a very early age he didn't fit in. His mother had wanted a girl, and it is said that Meek wore dresses until he went to school. As he grew up he became sensitive and often bad tempered. Although well built, he avoided sports and other typically boisterous boyhood activities in favor of the solitude of a garden shed. Here his fascination with sound and electronics was born as he dismantled old radios and gramophones.

As a young man, Meek found his way to London and worked his way through a series of jobs in recording studios. These rarely lasted very long as Meek usually quarreled with his employers over some sleight, real or imagined. But he seemed to have a knack, and was involved in the making of several big hits of the time, including Lonnie Donegan's 'Cumberland Gap' and Frankie Vaughan's 'Green Door.'

Despite this success, Meek was frustrated with the unwritten rules and established hierarchy of the music business of the 1950s, and he yearned for independence. He eventually found this in his home studio, in a rented flat above a leather goods shop in Holloway Road, north London. Here he wrote and recorded dozens of songs for his roster of artists, making finished masters that he then hawked around to major labels under the aegis of RGM Productions (named for the initials of his given name, Robert George Meek). Although commonplace now, independent production companies were unknown at the time.

Many of the recordings Meek made were indifferent, some simply awful. But a few were touched with a true, strange greatness. The classic death disc, 'Johnny Remember Me' by John Leyton (1961), has ghostly female voices singing from a deep well of reverb, representing the dead heroine's pleas from beyond the grave. 'Have I The Right' by The Honeycombs (1964) features bass drum augmented by the band stamping on the stairs at Holloway Road. Both were British Number 1 hits.

But 'Telstar' was Meek's greatest triumph, although it also contributed to his downfall. A French composer, Jean Ledrut, claimed that Meek had stolen the tune from a piece of film music Ledrut had written in 1960. He sued, and Meek's royalties for 'Telstar' were frozen while the case meandered through the French courts. Eventually Meek got his money, but the anxiety further damaged what was already a fragile state of mind.

Although Meek had hits after 'Telstar,' eventually his career faltered. Always unstable and prone to fits of temper, he became increasingly paranoid, believing that his competitors, among them Phil Spector, were bugging his studio to learn his tricks. He took pills to stay awake as he worked too hard, which increased his jumpiness. A gay man at a time when homosexuality was illegal, he was arrested for importuning, and was terrified that his family would find out. His interest in the occult became an obsession. Then, on February 3, 1967, Meek argued with his landlady and shot her dead, before reloading and blowing his own head off. He was 38 years old. It was eight years to the day since his hero, Buddy Holly, had died.

Shout – Part 1
Joey Dee & The Starliters

Released March 1962
Roulette *4416* (U.S. #6) / Columbia *DB 4842* (U.K.)

This is one of the all-time rhythm & blues classics, and had been a hit for The Isley Brothers, who recorded their original in July 1959. The two records indicate the segregation that still existed between R&B and pop in the U.S. – the Isleys' recording was a great production by Hugo Peretti and Luigi Creatore, yet due to the lack of radio exposure it made only Number 47 on the pop charts.

Joey Dee & The Starliters were the house band at New York City's Peppermint Lounge in 1960, which led to a contract with Roulette Records. They recorded the cash-in 'Peppermint Twist,' an American Number 1 in early 1962, directly following Chubby Checker's 'The Twist.' The group gave the twist another shot with their second single, 'Hey, Let's Twist,' before trying something different with their Isleys cover.

If I Had A Hammer (The Hammer Song)
Peter Paul & Mary

Released August 1962
Warner *WB 5296* (U.S. #10) / Warner *WB 74 51911* (U.K.)

This Greenwich Village trio were brought together by Bob Dylan's manager Albert Grossman to capitalize on America's lucrative early-1960s folk-music market. They scored their first hit with 'Lemon Tree,' a late entry in the calypso stakes, but really made their mark when their Grammy-winning performance of folk doyen Pete Seeger's 'The Hammer Song' got to Number 10. An even more successful version by Trini Lopez peaked at Number 3 just over a year later, and it went on to achieve a status many great songwriters only dream of: most people think it is a traditional song.

Green Onions
Booker T. & The M.G.s

Released August 1962
Stax *127* (U.S. #3) / London *HLK 9595* (U.K.)

Booker T. and the M.G.s were the house band for Stax Records, soul's biggest hit factory after Motown, and as such were one of the most listened-to bands of the 1960s: they played on hits by the likes of Otis Redding, Wilson Pickett, and Sam & Dave, to name just a few. The four-piece of organist Booker T. Jones, guitarist Steve Cropper, drummer Al Jackson, and bassist Donald 'Duck' Dunn also recorded a series of instrumental hits under their own name – it stands for Memphis Group.

'Green Onions,' a mid-paced organ groove punctuated by Cropper's clipped, brash guitar chords, set a million toes a-tapping. But the song was a musical accident, a simple warm-up jam committed to tape while the band were waiting in vain for a singer to turn up for a session. It was first released as the B-side to 'Behave Yourself,' a coupling ignored until the sides were flipped. Originally a U.S. hit in 1962, it remained an underground favorite on the British mod scene through the 1960s. With the resurgence of that movement in the late 1970s, 'Green Onions' then made a belated appearance in the U.K. charts.

Monster Mash
Bobby 'Boris' Pickett & The Crypt-Kickers

Released September 1962
Garpax *44167* (U.S. #1) / London *HLU 9597* (U.K.)

This classic novelty hit tapped into an early-1960s revival of the great monster movies – *Dracula*, *Frankenstein*, and so on – and has become a perennial Halloween favorite. The song's title was inspired by the mashed potato dance, a close relative of the twist.

The song itself was the work of an aspiring actor, Bobby Pickett, who performed the spoken vocal in the style of horror movie star Boris Karloff. His backing group included noted session player Leon Russell. Pickett followed up two months later with the less successful festive-themed 'Monster's Holiday.' In 2005 he recorded 'Climate Mash' as a protest against the U.S. Government's failure to respond adequately to the threat of global warming. 'Monster Mash' only became a hit in Britain in 1973.

The Lonely Bull (El Solo Torro)
The Tijuana Brass Featuring Herb Alpert

Released October 1962
A&M *703* (U.S. #6) / Stateside *SS 138* (U.K. #22)

Herb Alpert's Tijuana Brass was something of a phenomenon on the American album charts during the 1960s, clocking up several years' worth of chart action and five Number 1 LPs, quite a remarkable achievement in the golden age of pop.

Alpert originally recorded 'The Lonely Bull' in his garage as 'Twinkle Star' in 1962 and said that he was inspired by a trip to Tijuana, Mexico, where he experienced his first bullfight. He incorporated the sound of live bullfight effects, but still couldn't find a record company interested in releasing the track, so he set up his own A&M Records with Jerry Moss. The Tijuana Brass was an instant success. At first Alpert shipped copies of the record out of his garage, and the single soon sold 700,000 copies. In 1990 Alpert and Moss cashed in their chips, selling their A&M label to Polygram for a cool $500 million.

Zip-A-Dee Doo-Dah
Bob B. Soxx & The Blue Jeans

Released November 1962
Philles *107* (U.S. #8) / London *HLU 9646* (U.K.)

This children's song, written in 1945 by Ray Gilbert and Allie Wrubel for the Disney movie *Song Of The South*, was recorded by Phil Spector on August 24, 1962, and was among the first sessions where the producer achieved the huge sound he had been looking for. Not surprising: there were two guitarists, three bass players (including legendary session player Carole Kaye), two pianists, a drummer, and a percussionist. The studio was Gold Star in Los Angeles, and from this point until Tina Turner's 'River Deep' in 1966 Spector would record everything there. Spector rehearsed the band for three hours until he finally got what he wanted, recording the track in one take and adding the vocals of Bobby Sheen, Darlene Love, and Fanita James.

It Might As Well Rain Until September
Carole King

Released July 1962
Dimension *2000* (U.S. #22) / London *HLU 9591* (U.K. #3)

In 1961 Carole King was a staff songwriter for New York City publishers Aldon Music, and together with her lyricist Gerry Goffin composed two U.S. Number 1s, The Shirelles' 'Will You Love Me Tomorrow' and Bobby Vee's 'Take Good Care Of My Baby.' When King presented Aldon supremo Don Kirshner with a new demo for Vee, 'It Might As Well Rain Until September,' Kirshner decided it was good enough to release as it stood, under King's name. It did well in America and even better in the U.K., but almost a decade passed before King charted again, with 'It's Too Late,' which established her as the brand leader for the rising generation of female singer-songwriters.

She Loves You
The Beatles

Released August 1963
Swan *4152* (U.S. #1) / Parlophone *R 5055* (U.K. #1)

I Want To Hold Your Hand
The Beatles

Released November 1963
Capitol *5112* (U.S. #1) / Parlophone *R 5084* (U.K. #1)

Paul McCartney made it sound so simple. "We just sat up in one of our hotel rooms for a few hours and wrote it." That's how he explained the phenomenon that was 'She Loves You.' To be more precise, the room was in Turk's Hotel, Newcastle Upon Tyne, a shipbuilding town in the north-east of England, where he found himself immediately after a gig at the Majestic Ballroom. "I got the idea for doing one of those answer-type songs where someone says, 'She loves you,' and the other person says, 'Yes' or 'Yeah, Yeah.' John and I thought it was a stupid thing – and it really was, when you think about it."

Stupid or not, 'She Loves You' fairly exploded out of its grooves from the second the needle hit the vinyl. Banging straight into the chorus, dispensing with the formality of an opening verse, gave the song instant impact, but repeated plays revealed plenty of delicious subtleties, including those weird 'Yeah, yeah, yeah' vocal harmonies. Producer George Martin explained they were "a major sixth with George Harrison doing the sixth, and the other two the third and fifth. It was just the way Glenn Miller wrote for the saxophone."

It became their second U.K. Number 1 on September 12, 1963, at which point The Beatles were a household name in Britain but virtually unknown in America. Capitol Records, the customary home for Parlophone product in the U.S., was steadfastly refusing to release Beatles records, so 'She Loves You' appeared there later that month on the Swan label – to massive public indifference. Beatles manager Brian Epstein was quite used to this sort of reaction in America. It had been the same when they'd put out 'Please Please Me' and 'From Me To You' on Vee-Jay Records.

Back in Britain, meanwhile, there was no stopping them. After four triumphant weeks, 'She Loves You' slipped off the top, on October 10, only to re-appear at Number 1 on November 28 for another two weeks before being replaced by their next release, 'I Want To Hold Your Hand,' which hogged the summit for five solid weeks. The Beatles had become the first artists ever to replace themselves at the top of the U.K. singles chart.

Finally, Capitol in America began to waver. Maybe The Beatles did have something to offer after all. On December 26 they rush-released 'I Want To Hold Your Hand' and eight days later America had its first glimpse of Beatlemania when they were featured on TV's *Jack Paar Show*. On February 1, 'I Want To Hold Your Hand' was Number 1 in America, until, in a bizarre reversal of the British situation, it was replaced at the top by 'She Loves You' on March 21. Then, incredibly, on April 4, 'Can't Buy Me Love' made it three in a row – an unprecedented achievement in chart history. America was now, officially, a suburb of Liverpool.

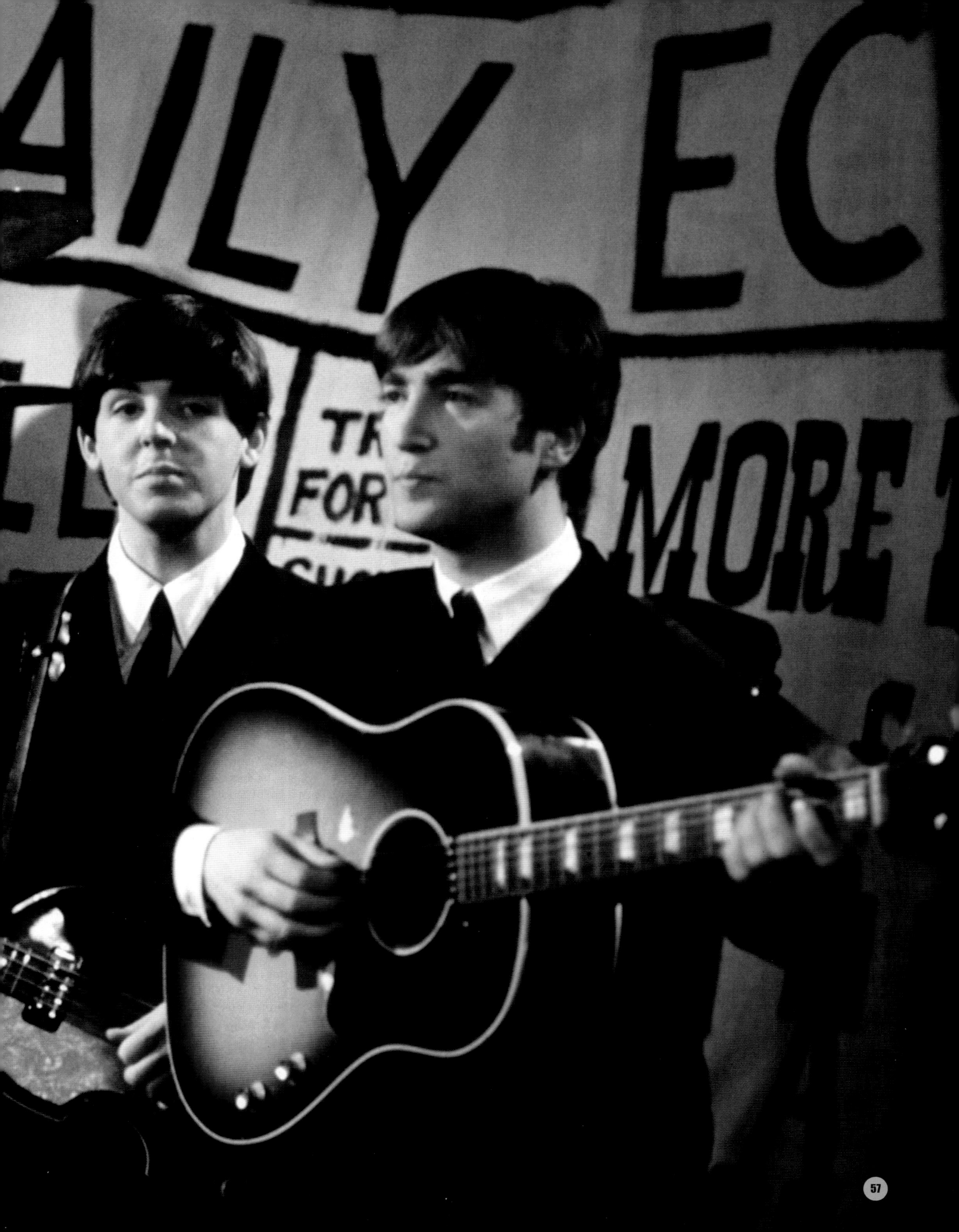
FOR
MORE

Summer Holiday
Cliff Richard & The Shadows

Released February 1963
Not issued U.S. / Columbia *DB 4977* (U.K. #1)

Diamonds
Jet Harris & Tony Meehan

Released January 1963
London *4589* (U.S.) / Decca *F 11563* (U.K. #1)

Before the arrival of The Beatles, Cliff Richard and his backing group The Shadows dominated the U.K. charts. By the early 1960s Cliff, like his American rival Elvis, had moved into the movie business, though on a somewhat smaller scale. 'Summer Holiday,' the theme song of his 1963 movie, became his seventh British Number 1, although those chart-toppers would become less frequent with the arrival of The Beatles and the rest. Cliff did perform the song in America on the Ed Sullivan TV show in April, but it was not released in the States, and consequently a cover appeared by one Jimmy Griffin, later to find success in the 1970s as a member of Bread.

Tony Meehan (drums) and Jet Harris (bass) left The Shadows in 1961 and 1962 respectively, and although at first they did not intend to work together, Meehan saw Harris at Decca Records where Meehan was now working in A&R. Their big hit 'Diamonds' (with Harris playing lead bass) was composed by Jerry Lordan, who had already delivered three massive hits for The Shadows: 'Apache' (on which both Harris and Meehan had performed), 'Wonderful Land,' and 'Atlantis.' In one of those musical twists of fate, The Shadows' British chart-topper 'Dance On!' was replaced by Harris & Meehan's 'Diamonds' in January 1963. Following a couple of further hits, the duo's career was curtailed when Harris was injured in an automobile accident. Cliff Richard, Britain's most consistently successful chart artist, has had only had a handful of U.S. hits, but it seems remarkable that The Shadows, hugely popular in Europe and the rest of the world, have had none whatsoever.

Sweets For My Sweet
The Searchers

Released June 1963
Mercury *72172* (U.S.) / Pye *7N 15533* (U.K. #1)

The Searchers paid their dues on the same Continental circuit as The Beatles, performing at the Star Club in the notorious Reeperbahn district of Hamburg, Germany. Reckoned as second only to the Fab Four on Merseyside in terms of musicianship and local popularity, and named for the same John Wayne movie in which the big man's repetition of the phrase "That'll be the day" inspired the Buddy Holly classic, they were duly signed to Pye Records in 1963. Their first record was this cover of a Drifters U.S. hit from 1961 that took them straight to the top of the U.K. charts. The group delivered a string of Top 10 hits, including 'When You Walk In The Room' and 'Needles And Pins,' under the guidance of writer-producer Tony Hatch, and it was Hatch himself who wrote the group's second hit, 'Sugar And Spice.' While the group were highly competent musically, their sound never progressed and their chart career was cut short by a lack of original material.

You'll Never Walk Alone
Gerry & The Pacemakers

Released September 1963
Laurie *3218* (U.S.) / Columbia *DB 7126* (U.K. #1)

When Gerry & The Pacemakers became the first Liverpool group to reach Number 1 in Britain, with 'How Do You Do It,' it seemed as if they might outshine The Beatles as Liverpool's biggest pop band. And their powerful cover of 'You'll Never Walk Alone,' the 1945 Rodgers & Hammerstein classic, became their third consecutive U.K. Number 1 single at a time when The Beatles had only managed two.

That also gave them three Number 1s with their first three singles, a feat unequalled in Britain until another Liverpool band, Frankie Goes To Hollywood, did the same in 1984. Remarkably, Gerry took 'You'll Never Walk Alone' to Number 1 again, as lead vocalist of The Crowd in 1985, to raise funds for victims of a fire at Bradford soccer stadium that claimed the lives of 56 football fans.

I Wanna Be Your Man
The Rolling Stones

Released November 1963
London *9641* (U.S.) / Decca *F 11764* (U.K. #12)

John Lennon and Paul McCartney offered The Rolling Stones a helping hand by giving them 'I Wanna Be Your Man' before recording it themselves. Lennon and McCartney later offered different accounts of how the song was handed over to the Stones. Did they play an incomplete version to Jagger in a club where the Stones were performing and finish it off for him right there? Or did the two soon-to-be-pop-superpowers meet in a taxi cab in London? However they got hold of it, the Stones managed to inject some of their patented bad-boy attitude into what – in the hands of The Beatles, with Ringo singing – was a pretty tame song. It became the Stones' second U.K. hit after their cover of Chuck Berry's 'Come On.'

SEVEN INCHES OF EXTENDED PLAY

Within months of RCA having introduced its new 45 rpm seven-inch single back in the late 1940s, it must have been apparent that the short playing time was a problem. The result was the 'extended play' or EP record, a triumph in the art of getting quite a lot into a small space.

Introduced in late 1951, the seven-inch EP boasted two songs and a running time of just over seven minutes on each side. The extra time was achieved by compressing the music to reduce its dynamic range and cutting the disc at a low level so that the grooves could be closer together. The result was a reduction in fidelity and volume, but it proved acceptable to most listeners.

In the early 1950s the standard pop LP was a ten-inch disc holding about eight songs. Two EPs, packaged together in a similar pictorial sleeve, made a satisfactory alternative. RCA, committed to its own 45 rpm seven-inch format, initially produced just EPs and singles for its own artists. But other companies hedged their bets, sometimes releasing one set of songs as an LP, twin EPs, or multiple singles.

When the 12-inch LP became standard in pop music, midway through the 1950s, the idea of the EP as a replacement for LPs fell by the wayside. From that point on, EPs became a sampler of the LP for those who could not afford the real thing, which was certainly the case for young pop fans. They had already embraced the 45 format, and the fact that EPs came in a sleeve with a picture of their idol on the front only enhanced the appeal of these records.

Elvis Presley was one of the first artists to exploit the EP, to the extent that some thought that EPs were named for his initials. RCA issued an EP of four tracks from his LP, at the same time and in the same sleeve (later imitated by The Clash for *London Calling*). The EP went to DJs, who immediately began playing its opening track, 'Blue Suede Shoes,' giving Elvis his third hit and keeping Carl Perkins's original off the top of the chart. There was also an eight-song double-EP pack.

Eight further Elvis EPs were released in his first year with RCA. The format proved especially suitable for the soundtrack to his first film, *Love Me Tender*, since that only included four songs. Other artists and labels

followed up, and *Billboard* magazine introduced an EP chart in 1957, although it only ran for three years, by which time the format was starting to fade in the U.S. Some indication of its early demise was that while The Beatles released hundreds of EPs in markets around the world, only two official Capitol releases made it on to the U.S. market. Similarly, The Monkees issued only two EPs, and those just for jukebox owners.

In less affluent Britain, however, the EP had a much longer life. It was a cheap alternative to the LP: most of The Beatles' many British EPs served that function. EPs of original material were rarer. The Beatles' *Long Tall Sally* EP of June 1964 was one example, as was The Who's *Ready Steady Who* of 1965.

Sometimes, it was a way of cashing in on artists who had achieved a hit or two and who weren't expected to have any more. The EP might contain just two hits and two B-sides. One further function was to launch a new act, test its market potential, or cash in quickly on chart success. In January 1964, after The Rolling Stones had gained two modest hits, Decca released an EP of cover versions while they were in the studios recording their first album. Other important Stones EPs included *Five By Five* and *Got Live If You Want It*, containing bluesy material that appealed to a more dedicated audience than their singles. Many 1960s EPs have since become hugely collectable, not least because of their attractive packaging.

Perhaps the artistic high-point of the whole EP story was The Beatles' *Magical Mystery Tour* of 1967. A double EP reminiscent of the earliest EP albums, it contained six songs in elaborate packaging, including a 32-page full-color booklet. EPs had a second coming during Britain's punk-rock era. They made good commercial sense. Many of the innumerable bands launched in that shortlived era only had a couple of good songs in them. The EPs also allowed small or homemade labels to showcase several of their artists. Later, the format mutated into the maxi-single, usually on 12-inch vinyl running at 45 rpm.

Today, the EP continues to have a nominal existence through short CDs or on 12-inch vinyl and has been favored by acts including My Bloody Valentine, Belle & Sebastian, and Radiohead. Indeed, Radiohead's first commercial release, *Drill*, was an EP on CD and 12-inch vinyl. When the original format surfaces today, it is usually as a promotional stunt. Early in 2006, Paul Weller released his *As Is Now* album on two CDs. At the same time, he issued four tracks from it as a 45 rpm EP on seven-inch vinyl, for one week only.

left > The Rolling Stones' *5x5 EP*, featuring five songs recorded at Chess Studios during the group's first trip to the U.S., and The Beatles' *Magical Mystery Tour*, which includes the much loved 'I Am The Walrus.'

Da Doo Ron Ron
(When He Walked Me Home)
The Crystals

Released April 1963
Philles *112* (U.S. #3) / London *HLU 9732* (U.K. #5)

Be My Baby
The Ronettes

Released August 1963
Philles *116* (U.S. #2) / London *HLU 9793* (U.K. #4)

There are those who maintain that Gene Pitney's 1961 single 'Every Breath I Take' was Phil Spector's first fully-realized Wall Of Sound production, but the cavernous depths from which The Crystals 'Da Doo Ron Ron' seems to emerge is the record that introduced America to The Wall. Spector once explained: "I was looking for a sound so strong that if the material was not the greatest, the sound would carry the record."

To achieve that sound, Spector began by putting together a hand-picked session-player elite featuring guitarists Glen Campbell, Sonny Bono, and Barney Kessel, pianist Leon Russell, and drummer Hal Blaine, to name just a few. He would augment this basic core with additional players, often cramming 30 or more musicians into a tiny studio at Gold Star in Hollywood, California, and then opening up the echo chambers to their fullest extent. While most producers were seeking a clean, clearly defined sound with lots of separation between instruments, Spector was creating a huge swirling sonic soup.

'Da Doo Ron Ron' thundered into the U.S. Top 40 on May 11, 1963, peaking at Number 3, but in purely sonic terms it was dwarfed by the signature drum lick that opened 'Be My Baby' and the swoon-inducing orchestral parts that soared through its gargantuan soundscape. Beach Boys genius Brian Wilson would later admit that 'Be My Baby' was "where I learned how to produce records." After Phil Spector, the sound of a record could be every bit as important as its melody, lyric, or performance.

PHIL SPECTOR AND HIS WALL OF SOUND

Phil Spector first appeared on the scene in 1958 with his Number 1 composition for The Teddy Bears, 'To Know Him Is To Love Him.' He then spent two years learning about record production under the expert guidance of Jerry Leiber and Mike Stoller. Spector was present at most of their sessions between 1959 and 1961, although he would later make some wild claims about his input, hotly denied by the duo. He set up his Philles label in late 1961, and the acclaimed recordings he made between 1963 and 1966 were all taped at Gold Star studios in Los Angeles.

To create his famous Wall Of Sound, Spector used a regular team of local session musicians, who became known as The Wrecking Crew. Despite the advent of stereo and multi-track facilities, he insisted on releasing his records in mono: that way, he argued, they would sound the same way on radio and record as he heard them in the studio. Using multiple combinations of instruments and rehearsing his musicians for hours, and sometimes days on end, he would then record everyone as an ensemble. This resulted in considerable leakage of sound between microphones but it gave his three-minute slices of magic their unique sound. Spector called these anthems of the generation his "little symphonies for the kids."

After an early incident when DJs flipped one of his records, he began putting somewhat second-rate instrumentals on his B-sides to ensure this would never happen again. Spector used the best writers he could find to compose his material, beginning with Jeff Barry and Ellie Greenwich, with whom he wrote 'Da Doo Ron Ron' and 'Then He Kissed Me' for The Crystals and 'Be My Baby' and 'Baby I Love You' for The Ronettes. He later teamed up with Barry Mann and Cynthia Weil for further hits, including the classic Righteous Brothers' 1964 smash 'You've Lost That Lovin' Feelin'.'

His masterwork was Ike & Tina Turner's 'River Deep, Mountain High,' a monster of a record that featured over 20 musicians in the cramped studio and an additional 20 background vocalists. Hailed as a work of genius in Britain, it was virtually ignored by American radio and the song only reached Number 88. This rejection so enraged Spector that he closed down his Philles label and went into semi-retirement. He returned at the end of the 1960s to salvage The Beatles' album *Let It Be* (or, if you ask Paul McCartney and many others, to ruin it) and produced albums for John Lennon (*Imagine*) and George Harrison (*All Things Must Pass*).

Puff (The Magic Dragon)
Peter Paul & Mary

Released February 1963
Warner 5348 (U.S. #2) / Warner WB 95 (U.K.)

Peter Paul & Mary were the most popular folk-based group of the 1960s, scoring ten albums in the American Top 20 between 1962 and 1970. They mixed children's songs, comedy, and folk material, and were partially responsible for Bob Dylan's first popularity thanks to their hit recordings of his songs 'Blowin' In The Wind' and 'Don't Think Twice It's All Right' in 1963. Following the trio's first two hits in 1962, 'Lemon Tree' and 'If I Had A Hammer,' they reached Number 2 on the U.S. chart with 'Puff The Magic Dragon,' which became a children's favorite, despite some rumored drug connotations. It was based on a poem written by Leonard Lipton in 1959. Group member Paul Stookey said later: "Puff never was anything except a song about the innocence of childhood and the sadness of the passing of that kind of innocence that we all feel."

Ring Of Fire
Johnny Cash

Released May 1963
Columbia 42788 (U.S. #17) / CBS AAG 159 (U.K.)

'Ring Of Fire' was the single that cemented Cash's reputation as the outsider anti-hero of country music. Like many of his hits of the time, it spent several weeks atop the country chart, but also reached Number 17 on the U.S. pop chart, making it Cash's biggest mainstream success since 'Ballad Of A Teenage Queen' and 'Guess Things Happen That Way,' which both made the Top 20 in 1958. With its jaunty rhythm offset by that memorably ominous vocal delivery, the song has all the hallmarks of classic Cash, even if its toughest critics find the breezy Mariachi trumpet break to be at odds with lyrics about falling "down, down, down."

Unlike many of his other most famous recordings, 'Ring Of Fire' was not one of Cash's own compositions. It was written for him by his future wife June Carter – a big country music star in her own right as part of the second incarnation of The Carter Family – and singer-songwriter Merle Kilgore. Carter and Kilgore most likely had Cash in mind when they wrote the song, however: it sounds today as well-suited to the Man In Black as any of his self-penned hits, from 'I Walk The Line' to 'Folsom Prison Blues.'

Surfin' U.S.A.
The Beach Boys

Released March 1963
Capitol 4932 (U.S. #3) / Capitol CL 15305 (U.K. #24)

Given their shaky start, it's a miracle The Beach Boys survived. Their sparky 1961 debut single, 'Surfin',' wiped out at Number 75 and earned them so little money that guitarist Al Jardine quit to study dentistry. Although the follow-up, 'Surfin' Safari,' took them into the Top 20, their third single, 'Ten Little Indians,' couldn't struggle beyond Number 49.

Things looked very promising when a fourth release, 'Surfin' U.S.A.,' soared to Number 3. Then, when Jan & Dean hit Number 1 two weeks later with 'Surf City,' written by head Beach Boy Brian Wilson, the group

began to look like the biggest new musical force in America. Ultimately, though, 'Surfin' U.S.A.' plunged them into an embarrassing and costly fracas when Chuck Berry sued because the song was almost identical to his 1958 hit 'Sweet Little Sixteen.' (Evidently Chuck had forgotten that 'Maybellene,' which made him a star, was little more than a re-write of Bob Wills's 'Ida Red.')

Despite their ups and downs, The Beach Boys persevered and, by the end of 1963, they were the biggest group in America. And then The Beatles showed up. "They eclipsed a lot of what we'd worked for," said Brian Wilson. "I just couldn't handle the fact that there were these four guys from England coming over here to America to invade our territory."

Wilson hit back with the brilliantly arranged and masterfully performed teen epic 'I Get Around,' delivering The Beach Boys their first U.S. Number 1 and serving notice on The Beatles that America's surf kings were here to stay. The most exciting chart battle of the decade was on.

Can't Get Used To Losing You
Andy Williams

Released March 1963
Columbia 42674 (U.S. #2) / CBS AAG 138 (U.K. #2)

Certain M.O.R. songs transcend the schmaltz of that genre, and this hauntingly restless Doc Pomus-Mort Schuman composition is one of the best. It was Williams's 14th chart entry, peaking at Number 2 on both sides of the Atlantic, but more significantly it made Williams hip with a younger audience. A ska-punk treatment of the song by The Beat restored it to the U.K. Top 3 in 1983, and when Enya's debut single, 'Orinoco Flow,' hit the British Number 1 spot in 1988 it was impossible not to notice the resemblance between her synthesized string arrangement and the pizzicato violins that drive 'Can't Get Used To Losing You.'

Fingertips – Pt. 2
Little Stevie Wonder

Released June 1963
Tamla 54080 (U.S. #1) / Oriole CBA 1853 (U.K.)

The marketing of Steveland Morris Judkins was highly imaginative. Having signed the precociously gifted multi-instrumentalist in 1962, Motown Records had to work out how to present him to the world. First, he needed a name. He was just five feet tall, so 'Little' linked him nicely to Little Richard, Little Walter, and other rhythm & blues greats. Stevie was an appropriately diminutive connection to his given name, and Wonder had the edge over Judkins.

After his first album, Motown wanted to capitalize on the energy of his live shows, so they released Little Stevie Wonder – The 12-year-old

Genius. Stevie was now 13, but Motown wasn't about to let mere facts get in the way of a great title. Better yet, Stevie was blind, black, and soulful, so the word Genius slyly implied a younger version of Ray Charles, widely known as The Genius.

All of this, however, would count for nothing if Stevie couldn't live up to Motown's carefully contrived hype. 'Fingertips – Pt. 2,' a hand-clappin', foot-stompin', harmonica-based call-and-response riot, recorded live in Chicago, proved beyond a shadow of a doubt that he could. "It was the first time he had ever performed it," remembered Motown producer Hank Cosby, who had written the music but left the words to Stevie. "As he was singing, half the song was ad-libbed right there."

On August 24, 1963, the single and album made Stevie the first artist ever to top America's three key charts – pop singles, rhythm & blues singles, and LPs – all in the same week. Enough said.

Blue Velvet
Bobby Vinton

Released August 1963
Epic *9614* (U.S. #1) / Columbia *DB 7110* (U.K.)

Vinton was yet another student of the Dick Clark college of pop stars and one of a whole string of Bobbys who appeared on the American pop scene at the time, alongside Vee, Rydell, and Darin. He may well have inspired the 1962 Marcie Blane-Susan Maughan hit 'Bobby's Girl,' but this particular Bobby was the most successful chart act with a run of U.S. hits from 1962 to 1975, although in Britain he was much less popular and only had three hits.

'Blue Velvet' was originally recorded by Tony Bennett and The Percy Faith Orchestra back in 1951, but Vinton's U.S. chart-topper is now considered to be the definitive version. It wasn't a hit in Britain, though, until 1990, when it was used in a TV advertisement for a face cream. The recording also featured in David Lynch's critically acclaimed 1986 movie of the same name.

Louie Louie
The Kingsmen

Released September 1963
Wand *143* (U.S. #2) / Pye *7N 25231* (U.K. #26)

An undisputed triumph of style over substance, 'Louie Louie' provided a blueprint for every garage-rock band that followed. Originally by Richard Berry, the song was given a new lease on life by The Kingsmen's loose, lugubrious arrangement, in particular the stuttering third beat. This offbeat, now commonplace, was unusual at the time and apparently arose when frontman Jack Ely muddled the rhythm while teaching the song to the rest of the band.

Another important part of the appeal of 'Louie Louie' is its primitive sound. It was The Kingsmen's second single, recorded in a budget studio for less than $50 with just three microphones. One was on the bass drum, one was overhead – which vocalist Jack Ely strained on tiptoe to reach and which was also charged with picking up the rest of the band – and one was in front of Mike Mitchell's guitar amp and switched on only for his solo.

'Louie Louie' failed to make much of an impression on its first release on the Jerden label in June 1963 but started to climb up the charts after a reissue three months later on Wand. By the beginning of 1964 it had climbed to Number 2 on the U.S. singles chart and peaked at Number 26 in Britain.

The success rather went to the group's heads, particularly drummer Lynn Easton, who took the copyright on the group's name and insisted he take over on vocals. Two members left the band – a dissatisfied Ely, whose raunchy warble was another key ingredient in the song's success, along with bassist Bob Nordby – and The Kingsmen were never the same again.

Dominique
The Singing Nun (Soeur Sourire)

Released November 1963
Philips *40152* (U.S. #1) / Philips *BF 1293* (U.K. #7)

The Singing Nun must rate as one of the most unusual acts ever to grace the charts. Aside from qualifying as a one-hit wonder, she was the first artist with a simultaneous Number 1 single and album on the American charts. She even won a Grammy award, for Best Gospel Or Other Religious Recording. Born Jeanine Deckers in Belgium in 1933, she became a Dominican nun and adopted the name Sister Luc-Gabrielle in the 1950s.

In 1961, accompanied by her Mother Superior, she visited Philips Records headquarters in Brussels. Could the company arrange to record her and manufacture a few hundred records to be given as gifts to the other nuns?

Philips agreed to a private recording, but when the company's executives heard the material, they offered her a contract, with all proceeds going to the Dominican order. They also suggested she be known on record as Soeur Sourire (Sister Smile). Following large sales throughout Europe, her recordings were released in Britain and America, where she was billed as The Singing Nun.

'Dominique,' sung mostly in French, was written as a tribute to St Dominic, founder of her Catholic order. The Singing Nun's album spent a remarkable ten weeks at Number 1 in America and was replaced in early 1964 by the arrival of The Beatles' first U.S. collection, *Meet The Beatles*. It was the beginning of a new era, and it's unlikely that the she would have been so successful had she arrived after 1963.

Jeanine Deckers continued with missionary work throughout her life but was later hounded by the Belgian tax authorities for back-taxes relating to her income as Soeur Sourire. In 1985, in despair over her tax difficulties, she took her own life in a suicide pact with a close friend.

House Of The Rising Sun
The Animals

Released June 1964
MGM *13264* (U.S. #1) / Columbia *DB 7301* (U.K. #1)

Maybe this 1964 recording really did make Bob Dylan decide to put down his acoustic guitar and pick up an electric, to the disgust of many of his folk fans. The Animals started as The Alan Price Combo, a rhythm & blues band from a working-class neighborhood of Newcastle Upon Tyne in north-east England. Relocating to London, they became The Animals and were coupled with up-and-coming record producer Mickie Most, on EMI's Columbia label.

Most used to fly to the U.S. every couple of weeks to pick up the latest songs from the leading Brill Building songwriters, and was keen for the group to record the poppy 'Can't You Hear My Heartbeat' (later a hit for Herman's Hermits). The Animals refused, though, insisting instead on taping 'House Of The Rising Sun,' a traditional folk blues of uncertain heritage that was first recorded in the 1920s.

The Animals began their session for the song one morning at 8:00am. Following just one run-through, it was promptly taped and the work was over by 8:30. Total recording cost? Just £4/10/- (£4.50, about $12.50 at the time). With the song in the can, Most was now convinced that it would be a hit, despite its lyric about a brothel and its four-and-a-half-minute length at a time when most singles clocked in at about two-and-

a-half. EMI weren't so easily convinced, but following the Top 30 appearance of The Animals' debut, 'Baby Let Me Take You Home,' Most persuaded them to release the powerful performance. In America, where radio play for such a lengthy song was impossible, MGM released an edited version.

In the wake of the song's success there was considerable disagreement within the group as to who had arranged this traditional number. The only name that appeared on the label credit was that of Alan Price, although all The Animals had contributed, notably Hilton Valentine, who provided the distinctive guitar riff. The rest of the group, somewhat naive in the ways of the music industry, were informed that there wasn't enough room on the label for all of their names – a pretty lame excuse.

Because
Dave Clark Five

Released July 1964
Epic *9704* (U.S. #3) / Not issued U.K.

British drummer Dave Clark was an astute businessman from the very beginning. He managed the group himself, and it was Clark who arranged and produced the group's hits, leasing the masters to EMI's Columbia label in the U.K. (and Epic in the U.S.). and setting up his own music-publishing company to oversee royalties. With full control over all aspects of his career, and negotiating an unusually high royalty deal with record companies, Clark was a millionaire by his early 20s and invested his money wisely. In America, the group rivaled The Beatles, enjoying sixteen Top 30 hits between 1964 and 1967. Following their massive success with 'Glad All Over,' 'Bits And Pieces,' and 'Do You Love Me,' this ballad – written by Dave Clark and keyboardist Mike Smith – was an American-only release and became their biggest U.S. hit so far.

A Hard Day's Night
The Beatles

Released July 1964
Capitol *5222* (U.S. #1) / Parlophone *R 5160* (U.K. #1)

The Beatles first arrived on American soil on February 3, 1964, and immediately took the country by storm. By the time they released this single they had already scored eleven Top 40 hits and four Number 1s in America in just four months. This notched up their fifth Number 1, on both sides of the Atlantic. At this point in their career the group could probably have recorded the weather report put to music and still have a chart-topper – but of course they delivered yet another gem.

It was the title track of their debut movie and accompanying album, which was their first to contain entirely original material (although on the abbreviated and rearranged U.S. edition, two tracks were instrumentals, performed by The George Martin Orchestra). The title was a Ringo-ism, uttered after a long day's filming, and the song was created literally overnight. While making the film, loosely based around a 'typical' day in the life of the group, producer Walter Shenson mentioned to John Lennon that it would be great to have a song called 'A Hard Day's Night' to play over the credits. Lennon said he'd think about it, and at 8:30 the following morning, he and Paul McCartney turned up and sang Shenson the finished article. They recorded it at Abbey Road studios on April 16, 1964. It is especially notable for George Harrison's strident opening chord, the subject of much debate among guitarists ever since, and for winning The Beatles their first Grammy award, for Best Vocal Performance By A Vocal Group.

You Really Got Me
The Kinks

Released August 1964
Reprise *0306* (U.S. #7) / Pye *7N 15673* (U.K. #1)

One of the landmark hits of the British Invasion, 'You Really Got Me' is cited by many commentators as the birthplace of heavy rock – an argument given further credence 14 years later when a cover of the song launched the metal quartet Van Halen.

With its simple two-chord riff and snarling vocal, the third single from The Kinks is a world apart from the gentler, psychedelic material that singer-songwriter Ray Davies would devise in subsequent years. Nonetheless, it proved to be the making of the group, topping the U.K. singles chart and climbing into the U.S. Top 10 a month later – no mean feat for a fledgling British quartet that had only formed a year earlier. The record's defining aspect is the dirty, distorted guitar sound, provided by Ray Davies's 17-year-old brother Dave (and not, despite persistent rumors to the contrary, by future Led Zeppelin axeman Jimmy Page).

Dave achieved this revolutionary sound by cutting slits in the speaker of his Elpico amplifier, and used it not just for the main power-chord riff but also during his juddering, ferocious guitar solo that, like the song itself, is reminiscent of The Kingsmen's lo-fi 1963 classic 'Louie Louie.'

The Kinks went on to become one of the most internationally successful British groups of the next decade, later inspiring not just heavy rock but also the mid-1990s Britpop scene.

Time Is On My Side
The Rolling Stones

Released September 1964
London *9708* (U.S. #6) / Not issued U.K.

Little Red Rooster
The Rolling Stones

Released November 1964
Not issued U.S. / Decca *F 12014* (U.K. #1)

'Time Is On My Side' was a powerfully soulful cut squirreled away on the B-side of 'Baby Don't Come On With Me,' a 1963 single by trombone virtuoso Kai Winding with the song credited to Norman Meade. It remained a humble B-side when Irma Thomas released her version the following year, but the Stones spotted its potential to be something bigger.

At London's Regent Sound studio in June 1964 they recorded the slow, smoldering version, complete with gospel-style organ, that delivered their first U.S. Top 10 entry – and still crediting Meade as composer. Just as they knew nothing of the Kai Winding original, they had no idea that 'Norman Meade' was really acclaimed American songsmith, producer, and arranger Jerry Ragavoy. The Stones didn't release 'Time' in the U.K., probably because they felt that it didn't suit the wild-men-of-rock image they had cultivated at home. As Stones guitarist Keith Richards said: "In America we were basically known for heavy, slow-ish ballads. 'Time Is On My Side,' 'Tell Me,' 'Heart Of Stone.'"

But this doesn't explain why, towards the end of 1964, they similarly failed to release in America their chart-topping British version of the Willie Dixon composition 'Little Red Rooster.' It was, after all, heavy and slow-ish – just what their Stateside fans were lapping up. But the group's reasoning was probably right. They'd picked up on the song from the Sam Cooke version, which had already done well enough in the U.S. charts (Number 11) to significantly reduce the sales potential of their own attempt.

Here I Go Again
The Hollies

Released May 1964
Imperial *66044* (U.S.) / Parlophone *R 5137* (U.K. #4)

As Merseybeat gathered momentum, Britain's record companies began looking beyond Liverpool for talent. The Hollies from nearby Manchester were among the first beneficiaries of that policy. After four chart entries, each bigger than the last, they consolidated their success with their vibrant performance of 'Here I Go Again,' confirming them as the U.K.'s best vocal harmony group. Even so, they didn't secure a Number 1 until the unstoppable 'I'm Alive' did the trick on June 24, 1965, prompting Hollie and working-class lad Graham Nash to declare that they had escaped the cycle of "work 40 years, get a gold watch, and then die." He concluded: "Music saved our ass."

DICK CLARK: THE AMERICAN BANDSTAND MAN

Dick Clark is one of the most important figures in the early development of rock'n'roll and its transformation into the innocuous pop of the early 1960s. Clark was a radio DJ in Philadelphia in 1956 when he was invited to take over a local pop-music TV show after its original host had been arrested for drunken driving.

The format of *Bandstand* was simple. Records were played, clean-cut well-dressed and impeccably-behaved teenagers danced, and the stars of the day made brief personal appearances, though there was no live playing. In August 1957, following phenomenal local success, the show went national, appearing on ABC-TV for 90 minutes every weekday afternoon, just as teenagers were coming home from school.

The renamed *American Bandstand* gave early national exposure to many important artists, including Chuck Berry, Jerry Lee Lewis, Buddy Holly, and Chubby Checker. It was racially integrated, with a modest number of black teenagers dancing alongside their white peers and even, on occasions, interviewed on air. The show made Philadelphia the most important market for the music industry, with particular benefits to local labels such as Cameo-Parkway, Swan, and Chancellor. Clark had financial involvement in them all, as well as 30 more companies involved in publishing, distribution, artist management, and record manufacture.

This cozy relationship inevitably drew the attention of the payola investigation, which looked into the practice of record companies buying airtime. But while the scandal ended the career of the more threatening Alan Freed, it did no great harm to that of Clark, although he was forced to give up his music-business interests.

In a public hearing, he told the congressional investigation into payola that he had merely been trying to secure his financial future. Indeed, he always maintained that his interest in rock'n'roll had been primarily commercial: his own tastes ran more to big-band music. Backed by his employers and respectful to the committee, Clark walked away with his reputation effectively intact, despite admitting he had received jewelry and a fur stole from a record-company executive.

A clean-cut, avuncular figure, 27 years old when his TV series went national, Clark successfully moderated the element of threat in rock'n'roll music, paving the way for the bland teen-idol period of the early 1960s. He would host *American Bandstand* until 1989, by which time his broadcasting career had moved on to quiz-shows, variety, and production.

That year he told *Rolling Stone* magazine that he had learned an important lesson from the payola hearings: "Protect your ass at all times."

Walk On By
Dionne Warwick

Released April 1964
Scepter *1274* (U.S. #6) / Pye *7N 25241* (U.K. #9)

Florence Greenberg, head of Scepter Records, thought so little of 'Walk On By' that she relegated it to a B-side. DJ Murray The K disagreed with the decision to put 'Any Old Time Of The Day' on the A-side and began playing the flip, creating the momentum that would take 'Walk On By' into the U.S. Top 10. The record scored similarly in Britain.

Without wishing to beat the unfortunate Greenberg over the head, it's certainly difficult to understand her initial decision. 'Walk On By' is perhaps the greatest ever collaboration between composers Bacharach & David and vocalist Dionne Warwick.

Subtle piano and chinka-chinka guitars form the opening before Warwick, always close to sobbing, begins gently enunciating a lyric in which the narrator tells her ex that, should he come across her, he should ignore the devastation he has wreaked by leaving her. As she sings that self-flagellating title refrain, it is counterpointed by flugelhorn.

The end of each verse in which the title refrain is set is followed by a rumbling piano run, to stunning effect, and the instrumental break is given over to the velvet strings heard briefly in the second verse.

There have been many cover versions of the song, the most noteworthy probably Isaac Hayes's 12-minute vamp and The Stranglers' more

aggressive rendition. The definitive performance remains Warwick's original, a recording that possesses utter class and utter soulfulness, a difficult balance for many – including, often, Bacharach & David.

THE COCKTAIL-LOUNGE CLASS OF BACHARACH & DAVID

It was perfectly appropriate that Burt Bacharach, a classically trained musician, should meet professional lyricist Hal David in the Brill Building, where so many pop songwriting partnerships flourished. They immediately had hits together – with 'The Story Of My Life,' recorded by Marty Robbins, and Perry Como's jaunty 'Magic Moments,' both in 1957 – but did not immediately become exclusive partners. That happened around the time they began writing a string of hits for Dionne Warwick.

The gifted black vocalist was originally hired merely to sing the duo's demos, but they soon gave Warwick her own career, starting with the seething 'Don't Make Me Over' (1963) and continuing through the dramatic 'Anyone Who Had a Heart,' the masochistic 'Walk On By,' the blissful 'I Say a Little Prayer,' and the deceptively pretty tale of crushed ambition, 'Do You Know the Way to San Jose?' These songs – like so many of Bacharach & David's – were notable for their lyrical maturity, musical sophistication, and often an ability to convey a convincing female perspective.

Gene Pitney and Jackie DeShannon – good songwriters themselves – benefited from the magic touch of Bacharach & David, Pitney with 'True Love Never Runs Smooth' and 'Twenty Four Hours From Tulsa' and DeShannon with 'What The World Needs Now Is Love.' That magic touch ensured the duo were hired to work on movies, devising the title themes to *What's New Pussycat?* – its nonsensical lyric sung with ludicrous enthusiasm by Tom Jones – and *Alfie*. The latter is Bacharach's

favorite of his own songs, but Cilla Black's impassioned version was rejected by the producers of the movie while still managing to go Top 10 in the U.K. charts. Herb Alpert recorded Bacharach & David's theme for the spoof Bond flick *Casino Royale*, but their biggest movie-related triumph was 'Raindrops Keep Falling On My Head.' Although this euphoric creation seemed lost in the sometimes gritty post-modernist western *Butch Cassidy And The Sundance Kid*, it had enough feel-good quality to ensure that B.J. Thomas's single became a U.S. Number 1. Sacha Distel had the biggest of three simultaneous U.K. hit versions.

Casino Royale also saw the unveiling of the duo's 'The Look Of Love,' sung by Dusty Springfield, the first song they gave to her after she had hit big with Bacharach & David material by issuing her own takes on the original versions of 'Wishin' And Hopin'' and 'I Just Don't Know What To Do With Myself.' Herb Alpert meanwhile achieved a U.S. Number 1 with the pair's 'This Guy's In Love With You,' and The Carpenters inaugurated their chart career with 'Close To You.'

Bacharach & David's partnership and friendship was frayed in the early 1970s as their work for the soundtrack to *Lost Horizon* was poorly received and then pulled apart by publishing-related lawsuits. Some have suggested that their compositions too often stray uncomfortably close to cocktail-lounge music in pursuit of class – Warwick's excepted, there was little grit in their songs – but there is no doubting that Bacharach & David brought a genuine sophistication to post-Elvis popular music.

Where Did Our Love Go
The Supremes

Released June 1964
Motown *1060* (U.S. #1) / Stateside *SS 327* (U.K. #3)

Baby Love
The Supremes

Released September 1964
Motown *1066* (U.S. #1) / Stateside *SS 350* (U.K. #1)

With these two singles, The Supremes began a remarkable run of Number 1 hit singles that made them the most successful girl group of the 1960s and the most bankable stars on the Motown books.

Surprisingly, however, their career didn't have a particularly auspicious start. None of the trio's first half-dozen singles made it beyond the lower reaches of the U.S. Top 100, but Motown boss Berry Gordy kept his faith in The Supremes, and in late 1963 allocated them to crack songwriting and production team Holland-Dozier-Holland as a special project.

The effect was almost instantaneous: in less than a year came a pair of landmark singles that shot The Supremes to the top of the pop firmament. 'Where Did Our Love Go' was originally offered to, and rejected by, The Marvelettes, and even The Supremes themselves, still bereft of a genuine hit, were unsure about the song. But along with 'Baby Love' it was cast from the classic Motown pop-soul mold: each is led by bright drums, strident bass, and tinkly keys. And in front of that perfect backdrop sit a pair of sumptuous Diana Ross vocals, backed with restraint and elegance by Florence Ballard and Mary Wilson. The producers had in fact argued over whether Ross or Wilson should take the lead vocal.

Not only did The Supremes sound brilliant but also they looked and acted the part, putting their peers to shame in almost every area. It's a measure of how hot The Supremes – and Holland-Dozier-Holland – were at this point in their careers when you consider the B-sides: they too are nearly faultless, particularly 'Ask Any Girl' on the flip of 'Baby Love.'

Oh Pretty Woman
Roy Orbison & The Candy Men

Released August 1964
Monument *851* (U.S. #1) / London *HLU 9919* (U.K. #1)

Many of Roy Orbison's hits seemed to be tales of woe and heartbreak with unhappy endings – although Roy concluded: "On balance, I'd say it was at least 50-50." This was probably his most upbeat song. Orbison, who adopted his trademark dark glasses one night after mislaying his regular reading specs, had bought himself out of his Sun Records contract after writing 'Claudette' for The Everly Brothers. He then recorded 'Only The Lonely' himself, after it had been turned down by Elvis and the Everlys, and it became his first major hit.

Looking for a follow-up to his June 1964 U.K. Number 1 'It's Over,' Orbison and his writing partner Bill Dees were dabbling in the studio when his wife Claudette announced that she was going shopping. Orbison: "I said, 'Do you have any money?' And Bill Dees said, 'Pretty woman never needs any money!' Then he said, 'Would that make a great song title?' I said, 'No, but 'Pretty Woman' would.' So I started playing guitar, and he was slapping the table for drums, and by the time she got back – which was about 40 minutes later – we had the song."

Orbison's life was filled with tragedy. Claudette was killed in a motorcycle accident in 1966, and two of his three children died in a house fire in 1968. Some 20 years later, when he was on the verge of a major comeback after renewed success with the Traveling Wilburys, and with a new album ready for release, he died of a heart attack, on December 6, 1988. We should be thankful that his voice and his music, at least, are still with us.

Dancing In The Street
Martha & The Vandellas

Released August 1964
Gordy *7033* (U.S. #2) / Stateside *SS 345* (U.K. #28)

Surely in the Top 5 all-time Motown classics, this is the song from which Keith Richards claims he stole the idea for his 'Satisfaction' riff. Martha Reeves and her Vandellas always played second fiddle to The Supremes in the corridors of Motown, but they still got a fair slice of the action with some classic songs, including 'Heat Wave,' 'Nowhere To Run,' and 'Jimmy Mack.'

'Dancing In The Street' was originally slated for Kim Weston, but Martha Reeves – who was working part-time as a secretary for the company – got lucky and recorded what was supposed to be the demo. There was no contest. This was the Motown sound at its very best, with the tambourine mixed so far upfront it cracked like a whip. Motown boss Berry Gordy reckoned: "My goal to hook people in the first 20 seconds was never accomplished better. The intro was a hit before Martha even opened her mouth."

Downtown
Petula Clark

Released October 1964
Warner *5494* (U.S.) / Pye *7N 15722* (U.K.)

Petula Clark was one of Europe's most popular *chanteuse* of the 1960s. Born in Epsom, Surrey in 1932, she was encouraged to sing from an early age. By 1943 she had her own radio show and during the 1940s and 1950s appeared in over 20 movies. She began recording in 1949 and was a regular chart visitor until 1972. Enter Tony Hatch, one of the U.K.'s big backroom boys of 1960s pop. As A&R manager for Pye Records in Britain he delivered hits for Emile Ford and Mark Wynter as well as writing material for American acts Bobby Rydell, Connie Francis, and Pat Boone, and arranging for Lonnie Donegan. In 1963 he traveled to Liverpool and signed The Searchers, producing all their material and writing their second big hit, 'Sugar And Spice' under the pseudonym 'Fred Nightingale.'

By this time Hatch was writing and producing for Ms. Clark. He was inspired to write 'Downtown' during a 1964 trip to New York City and his first walk down Broadway. He originally wrote the song with The Drifters in mind, but when he played the melody to Clark she told him that if he could come up with a set of lyrics to match the quality of the melody and his title 'Downtown,' she would record it.

According to Hatch, he was still writing the lyrics half an hour before it was recorded. Remarkably, 'Downtown' won a Grammy award as 'Best Rock'n'Roll Recording' and in 2003 the record won a prestigious Grammy Hall Of Fame Award. Such awards are given only to "recordings of lasting qualitative or historical significance that are at least 25 years old."

Leader Of The Pack
The Shangri Las

Released October 1964
Red Bird *10-014* (U.S. #1) / Red Bird *RB 10014* (U.K. #11)

This is a wrought-up teen drama telling the story of a girl's love for a motorbikin' boy from the wrong side of down. Spoken word sections and dramatic piano flourishes lead into impassioned call-and-response vocals before the record peaks with revving engines and screeching tires, signaling the tragic end of the bad boy with the heart of gold.

Those engine noises and tire squeals reputedly came from producer George 'Shadow' Morton's Harley Davidson, which he drove into the studio. But that might just be another example of the self-mythologizing that Morton revelled in. An enigmatic figure, he later worked with artists as diverse as Vanilla Fudge, Janis Ian, and The New York Dolls, before drug addiction drove him into obscurity. Which is where – fittingly, perhaps, given his self-cultivated aura of mystery – he remains.

The Shangri-Las had several other hits under Morton's guidance, all carefully constructed mini-operas high on kitsch but nonetheless strangely affecting. Whether the group were the embodiment of sassy street-girl cool or mere puppets in Morton's hands is difficult to assess. But it hardly matters. Between them, Morton and The Shangri-Las constructed a unique pop legacy.

THE ORIGINAL PORTABLE MUSIC PLAYER

Transistor radios are always associated with pop music, but their impact was slow in coming. To begin with, their relatively high price placed them well out of the reach of teenagers. True portable radios only became possible with the arrival of the transistor, invented by Bell Laboratories in 1947. Initially the new technology was used only in hearing aids, but in the early 1950s hobbyists began to experiment by using them in radios, which until then had depended on heavy, expensive, power-guzzling tubes.

Texas Instruments, one of the first companies to manufacture transistors, went looking for a partner to make a radio it had designed, but most manufacturers saw no point in undercutting their existing products. A small company in Indianapolis, known as IDEA, decided to go ahead. These were the Cold War years, and IDEA's president apparently believed that a battery radio would become an essential of life in the event of a nuclear attack.

The result was a small radio known as the Regency TR-1. It appeared on the market in November 1954, priced at $49.95 (£18), equivalent to some $350 (£200) today. Batteries were extra. It used only four transistors, and its performance was poor. A much better eight-transistor radio was produced by Raytheon in February 1955, at $80. This American manufacturing activity was a false dawn, however. In August 1955 a Japanese company called Totsuko (later Sony) produced its first transistor radio, the TR-55. Its real breakthrough came with the TR-63, the first 'pocketable' radio. In truth, it was slightly too large for a normal shirt pocket, so Sony ordered a batch of special shirts with enlarged pockets, to be worn by its sales force.

At first both Japanese and American-built transistor radios were expensive. Only in the 1960s, when U.S. prices dropped below $20, they did become readily available to the teenagers with whom they are always associated. Previously, radios had been large objects in the family living room, which meant that young people's music was subject to parental scrutiny, criticism, and mockery. Now it became possible for the young to listen to music away from their parents, which created a whole new market. It was a turning point in the development of pop music and the music industry.

You've Lost That Lovin' Feelin'
The Righteous Brothers

....

Released December 1964
Philles *124* (U.S. #1) / London *HLU 9943* (U.K. #1)

'You've Lost That Lovin' Feelin" is officially the most broadcast record of the 20th century in America (at least according to the BMI performing rights organization). But, perhaps more importantly, it is also a record of incredible sophistication and innovation – attributes that aren't always reflected in the amount of radio plays a single receives.

The Righteous Brothers were a West Coast vocal duo consisting of the unrelated Bill Medley and Bobby Hatfield. Medley was an able songwriter himself, penning 'Little Latin Lupe Lu,' covered by Mitch Ryder in 1966. Nonetheless, it was frustration at their own chart failure that prompted The Righteous Bothers in the early 1960s to seek out legendary producer and idol-maker Phil Spector, a trek that so many other would-be stars would make. Spector recognized great raw material in the duo, in particular the magical combination of Medley's deep baritone and Hatfield's skilful tenor and falsetto lines.

Spector approached songwriters Barry Mann and Cynthia Weil, with whom he'd already had some success with The Paris Sisters and The Crystals. The husband-and-wife team decided that Medley and Hatfield's voices would be suited to a ballad and set about writing one, inspired by a favorite song of the moment, 'Baby I Need Your Loving' by the Four Tops, written by Holland-Dozier-Holland. Mann & Weil played two verses and the chorus to Spector over the telephone. The producer was extremely enthusiastic. How could he not be? The song contained one of the great opening lines of all time, written by Mann, who did not usually provide the lyrics: "You never close your eyes any more when I kiss your lips."

The pair finished the song with Spector. His contributions were valuable: Spector came up with the idea for the descending refrain at the end of each chorus, "Gone, gone, gone – whoa-oh-ohhh," and for the Latin-style riff leading into the bridge, which made it highly distinctive for the time.

The finished record was revolutionary. Part of this was deliberate: it was nearly four minutes long, usually a real obstacle to radio airplay in those days. Mostly it was accidental: the artists and writers would find themselves credited with inventing a new genre, blue-eyed soul. While they took their initial creative cue from The Four Tops, Mann & Weil never imagined they would help bridge the gap between white and black musical styles.

Despite all this, the record did not mark the start of an especially fruitful relationship between composers and artist. Although Mann & Weil did provide another U.S. Number 1 for The Righteous Brothers in 1966, with '(You're My) Soul And Inspiration,' that song is far behind 'Unchained Melody' among the Brothers' best remembered records. Both writers and artists, however, would reap the financial dividends of 'Lovin' Feelin'' for some time to come and enjoy the record's artistic glory forever.

left > Barry Mann and Cynthia Weil, captured in the midst of composing one of their many hit songs.
right > The Brill Building in New York City, where many of the duo's songwriting peers were based.

BARRY MANN & CYNTHIA WEIL: NEW YORK SONGWRITING

Budding New York songwriters Cynthia Weil and Barry Mann met when Weil deliberately engineered a meeting at the offices of Aldon Music Publishing for reasons more romantic than professional. Weil was a writer from a Broadway tradition. Mann had turned to songwriting almost in desperation after dropping out of an architecture course. He had dabbled with performing, scoring a Top 10 hit in 1961 with 'Who Put The Bomp (In The Bomp, Bomp, Bomp).' Vinny Monty's 'Painting The Town With Teardrops' was the first song Mann & Weil wrote together and their first collaboration successfully placed with an artist, while 'Bless You' by Tony Orlando was the duo's first hit, in 1961, the same year they married.

Mann handed over all the lyric writing to Weil, and the two settled on a technique of melody-first from which they almost never deviated. They loved the atmosphere at Aldon Music on New York City's Broadway, writing nearly half of their songs in one of the spartan cubicles there and often overhearing the works-in-progress of other Aldon writers such as Neil Sedaka & Howard Greenfield and fellow man-and-wife team Gerry Goffin & Carole King. This is often referred to as the Brill Building scene, although Aldon was in offices a block away from the Brill Building, which was at 1619 Broadway.

Phil Spector was one of the first to spot their abilities and they repaid his faith with a couple of early-1960s hits for his girl group The Crystals, 'Uptown' and 'He's Sure The Boy I Love.' The former was a pointer to the quietly revolutionary lyrics that Weil would write, its proletarian tableau depicting a man taking solace from his lack of fulfillment and power at work through the joy of his domestic life. Spector declined to release 'On Broadway,' another song the pair had provided for The Crystals, so they approached Leiber & Stoller and their four-way rewrite became a hit for The Drifters in 1963. Evidently Spector had no hard feelings: in 1964 Mann, Weil, and Spector collaborated on the phenomenally successful Righteous Brothers hit 'You've Lost That Lovin' Feelin'.'

Weil was now in her stride as a social commenter as the pair provided The Animals with the angry-young-man anthem 'We've Gotta Get Out Of This Place' and Paul Revere & The Raiders with the anti-drugs diatribe 'Kicks.' However, their anti-segregationist song 'Only In America,' designed for The Drifters, was considered too controversial for radio airplay, and so they censored themselves for a version that became a patriotic chart success for Jay & The Americans. As if to prove that not all issues are black and white, they wrote the reflective 'Shades Of Gray,' recorded by The Monkees.

The golden age of the Brill Building sputtered to an end towards the close of the 1960s, but Mann & Weil's own success continued into the 1970s, with Elvis Presley covering 'I Just Can't Help Believing' and Dolly Parton recording 'Here You Come Again.' The next decade saw them branching out into soundtracks, including the animated movies *An American Tail* (1986) and *Muppet Treasure Island* (1996). This remarkable team entered the 21st century proving they still had chart appeal by working with Hanson.

WHEN JACKIE DESHANNON WALKS IN THE ROOM

Jackie DeShannon seemed destined for stardom as a recording artist. Not only could she write songs, but she was a powerful singer possessed of a quite incandescent beauty. For reasons that remain unfathomable, she secured only a couple of significant hits as an artist, one of which was by another writer. But she has had a very successful career as a freelance songwriter and contributed some memorable compositions to the rock canon.

Born in Kentucky, DeShannon was a singer from the start of her career, but at the same time she was placing songs with artists, often co-written with her friend Sharon Sheeley. Among these early works were two U.S. hits for Brenda Lee – 'Dum Dum,' Number 4 in 1961, and 'Heart In Hand,' Number 15 in 1962 – and '(He's) The Great Impostor,' which reached Number 30 in 1961 for The Fleetwoods.

Over in Britain, The Searchers had two hits in 1964 with songs associated with DeShannon: 'Needles And Pins,' which she had recorded, although it was written by Sonny Bono and Jack Nitzsche, and her own composition 'When You Walk In The Room.' Both of the Searchers recordings feature 12-string guitar riffs and a chiming ambience more commonly associated with folk rather than rock. DeShannon imported a little of folk's intellectual gravitas, too: not many songs of the era featured the word "nonchalant," but there it is in 'When You Walk In The Room.'

DeShannon was responsible for Marianne Faithfull's 'Come And Stay With Me,' a U.K. Number 4 and U.S. Number 26 in 1965. Her links to the British scene did not end there. A pre-Led Zeppelin Jimmy Page collaborated with her on several songs, and a Page B-side, 'Keep Movin',' featured her vocals. It has been rumored that the Led Zeppelin song 'Tangerine' was written about DeShannon.

Also in 1965, DeShannon scored her first major hit as an artist when she took 'What The World Needs Now Is Love,' an idealistic Bacharach & David song that Dionne Warwick had rejected, into the U.S. Top 10. The same year saw the appearance of The Byrds' debut album, which contained an excellent DeShannon song, 'Don't Doubt Yourself Babe,' a thank-you for the support she'd shown the band. DeShannon also wrote the erotically-charged theme song for the movie *Splendor In The Grass*.

She achieved her biggest solo hit in 1969 with 'Put A Little Love In Your Heart,' a song DeShannon wrote with Jimmy Holiday and her brother Randy Myers, full of hippie-inflected idealism and almost a bookend to 'What The World Needs Now Is Love,' but with some funky undertones. It went to Number 4. The same team was responsible for the U.S. Top 40 song 'Love Will Find A Way' later that year, marking DeShannon's last hit as an artist. Although she made several singer-songwriter albums in the 1970s, her performing career ground to a halt for two decades thanks to a lack of artistic control. However, as if to prove the utter unpredictability of fate, she found herself with a transatlantic smash in 1981 when gravel-throated singer Kim Carnes unexpectedly covered the smoky, atmospheric 'Bette Davis Eyes' that DeShannon had written with Donna Weiss.

(I Can't Get No) Satisfaction
The Rolling Stones

Released May 1965
London *9766* (U.S. #1)/ Decca *F 12220* (U.K. #1)

As Tears Go By
Marianne Faithfull

Released July 1964
London *9697* (U.S. #22)/ Decca *F 11923* (U.K. #9)

The Rolling Stones started out by reinventing Chicago electric blues for a British teen audience, but their far-sighted manager, Andrew Loog Oldham, realized that the key to longevity lay in persuading the band to write their own material. The story goes that he locked an initially reluctant Mick Jagger and Keith Richards into a room to compose their first songs, which they later dismissed as commercial pap. But after these inauspicious beginnings, the two rapidly matured into a hit-making machine to rival Lennon & McCartney.

One of the first Jagger-Richards songs the world heard was 'As Tears Go By,' as performed by Marianne Faithfull. A poignant folk ballad perfectly suited to Faithfull's fragile voice, it was a big American and British hit a year before the Stones released their own version (which became a U.S. hit single) and a year before the group really got into their stride recording their own material. Around the same time that Faithfull made her chart debut with 'As Tears Go By,' in summer 1964, they scored a minor U.S. hit with the self-penned 'Tell Me (You're Coming Back)' but followed it with a couple of covers, 'Time Is On My Side' and 'It's All Over Now.' It wasn't until 1965 and 'The Last Time' that the famous run of big Jagger-Richards hits started. 'Satisfaction,' perhaps the most famous of them all, went to the top in the middle of the year.

Although it has come to be considered as a 'rock' archetype, 'Satisfaction' is a record crammed with pop hooks: Richards's simple fuzz guitar riff, Charlie Watts's drum break before the chorus, and the shouting frustration of the chorus itself. Jagger and Richards chanting "I can't get no! Satisfaction!" seemed to embody the anger of teenagers kicking against the constraints of the staid adult world, just at a time when they were becoming a real social force. Soul legend Otis Redding scored a minor hit with his cover of the song in 1966, a version which the Stones themselves professed to prefer to their own. For most of us, however, it's their original that satisfies the most.

Faithfull went on to have a number of wistful folk-pop hits during the next few years before drug addiction sent her into what seemed like an irreversible tailspin in the early 1970s. To her considerable credit, she re-emerged at the very end of that decade, her voice transformed to a husky growl, with a classic rendition of 'The Ballad Of Lucy Jordan.' This heralded a second phase of her career that continues still. These days, Faithfull is the grande dame of rock chicks, releasing occasional albums assisted by a host of younger, mainly male, musicians. The Stones, of course, just never stopped rolling. The hits, mostly written by Jagger-Richards, keep coming, and the band remain the biggest live draw in rock.

Yesterday
The Beatles

Released September 1965
Capitol *5498* (U.S. #1) / Not issued U.K.

'Yesterday' is perhaps the best known song in The Beatles' extensive canon of popular music standards. It stands among the most performed and covered songs of all time and was the most played record on U.S. radio for eight consecutive years, from 1965 to 1972. It is one of Paul McCartney's finest moments. It topped the U.S. chart, but its release as a U.K. single was blocked by the other three Beatles, who didn't think much of it. This might have had something to do with the fact that 'Yesterday' was the first Beatles song to feature only its author and none of the other members of the band. McCartney is backed by a string quartet, scored by producer George Martin.

McCartney maintains that 'Yesterday' arrived, near enough fully formed, in a dream, and that he leapt out of bed on the morning in question to play it straight into a tape recorder, lest he forget it. Amazed at its effortless birth, he was sure he must have unconsciously plagiarized another writer's work, and spent the next month playing the song to various music-industry figures, expecting that eventually somebody would identify it. Nobody did – although some have since suggested a likeness to Ray Charles's 'Georgia On My Mind' – so McCartney polished off the lyric, dropping the working title of 'Scrambled Eggs,'

and recorded the song during the *Help!* sessions. 'Yesterday' was the eighth of 19 American Number 1 hits for The Beatles and has since been recorded by over 3,000 artists, from Frank Sinatra to Boyz II Men.

I Got You Babe
Sonny & Cher

Released July 1965
Atco *6359* (U.S. #1) / Atlantic *AT 4035* (U.K. #1)

Salvatore 'Sonny' Bono had been hustling his songs in Los Angeles for some years before he met 16-year-old Cherilyn Sarkisian in 1963. Sonny was an assistant to producer Phil Spector while Cher began working as a back-up singer on Spector sessions, and the two became lovers. After much persuasion from Sonny, she was allowed to record one single for Spector in 1964, a cash-in on The Beatles' success, 'Ringo I Love You,' on which she was credited as Bonnie Jo Mason. Sonny had already enjoyed some songwriting success with Spector's studio arranger, Jack Nitzsche. The pair had written 'Needles And Pins' for Jackie DeShannon, and this became an international hit for British group The Searchers.

When Spector refused to entertain the idea of recording further material with Sonny's girlfriend, the couple left and recorded a couple of unsuccessful singles as Caesar & Cleo for Reprise. They mostly sang duets: although Sonny wanted to record Cher alone, she was nervous behind the microphone and insisted that Sonny join her. Reprise had neglected to sign the duo to a binding contract and Atlantic, who stepped in with a better offer, were rewarded when Bono came up with the hippie-lovers duet, 'I Got You Babe.' It was recorded at Gold Star studio in Los Angeles, home of Spector's hits and using the same session musicians. Atlantic originally scheduled the B-side, 'It's Gonna Rain,' for release, so Bono, a former promotions man, had to outsmart his own record company. He quickly arranged some heavy airplay for 'I Got You Babe' and Atlantic were forced to change their plans.

Mr Tambourine Man
The Byrds

Released June 1965
Columbia *43271* (U.S. #1) / CBS *201765* (U.K. #1)

Turn! Turn! Turn! (To Everything There Is A Season)
The Byrds
Released October 1965
Columbia *43424* (U.S. #1) / CBS *202008* (U.K. #26)

Eight Miles High
The Byrds
Released April 1966
Columbia *43578* (U.S. #14) / CBS *202067* (U.K. #24)

Although more credit tends to go to The Beatles, The Beach Boys, and the Stones, The Byrds were one of the most influential and consistent bands of the 1960s. Almost permanently blighted by in-fighting and factionalism, Roger McGuinn and his ever-changing cast of colleagues all but invented folk-rock, psychedelic-rock, and country-rock, were the single most important factor in bringing Bob Dylan to the attention of the rock audience, and remain one of the few bands to have a guitar sound named after them – the jangle of a picked 12-string Rickenbacker will forever be termed 'Byrdsian' by rock writers.

The band's breakthrough hit was 'Mr Tambourine Man.' Dylan's original was a multi-versed acoustic meander through typically elliptical wordplay. The Byrds stripped the song back to one verse and a few chorus repeats, in doing so introducing folk to Merseybeat and creating folk-rock, and opening a door into the charts for artists like Simon & Garfunkel and The Mamas & The Papas. McGuinn, with his heavily-compressed Rickenbacker guitar, was the only member of the band to play on the record; other instrumental duties were taken by tightly drilled sessionmen. But the serene, uplifting three-part harmonies of the chorus were the work of band members McGuinn, Gene Clark, and David Crosby. (The other two original members were bassist Chris Hillman and drummer Michael Clarke.)

'Turn! Turn! Turn!,' with lyrics lifted from the Old Testament book of Ecclesiastes, was another folk-rock classic and another big hit. This time it was the turn of traditional folkie and activist Pete Seeger to have his song reinvented. But by the time of 'Eight Miles High,' which came a year after the band's breakthrough, The Byrds were already moving on from folk-rock. A band composition of considerable sophistication, it boasts one of the most avant-garde guitar solos ever to make the charts. McGuinn's apparently free-form freak-out was, he said, carefully constructed and inspired by the playing of jazz saxophonist John Coltrane.

'Eight Miles High' aroused considerable controversy for the supposed drug references in the lyrics. In those days, the merest mention of the word 'high' was enough to have the moral guardians of the popular press in a frenzy of disapproval. To this day, McGuinn and other surviving band members insist the song is about nothing more than the band's flight to Britain for a tour.

After 'Eight Miles High,' various Byrds began to leave, although the band continued to record in various configurations into the 1970s. Later incarnations rarely troubled the singles charts, although their albums are now revered, particularly *Sweetheart Of The Rodeo*, one of the first country-rock records. Meanwhile David Crosby, who left the band in 1967, went on to form the massively successful Crosby Stills Nash & (sometimes) Young.

Wooly Bully
Sam The Sham & The Pharaohs

Released April 1965
MGM *13322* (U.S. #2) / MGM *1269* (U.K. #11)

'Wooly Bully' opens with a joyous cry to "dance rock'n'roll" and is – like its near namesake, 'Louie Louie' by The Kingsmen – an irresistibly primitive slice of 1960s garage rock. It was a multi-million-selling international hit, despite being banned by numerous radio stations who couldn't follow the unintelligible vocal and were worried that flamboyant Texan frontman Domingo 'Sam' Samudio might be singing something risqué. Sam and his cronies followed it with a number of other U.S. chart hits – mostly novelty songs like 'The Hair On My Chinny Chin Chin' – but none sticks in the memory like 'Wooly Bully.'

The Sounds Of Silence
Simon & Garfunkel

Released November 1965
Columbia *43396* (U.S. #1) / CBS *201977* (U.K.)

On February 19, 1964, Paul Simon was in his bathroom with the water running and the light off. Why? "Because the bathroom had tiles, so it was a slight echo chamber," he said. "I'd turn on the faucet so that water would run – I like that sound, it's very soothing to me – and I'd play. In the dark." The song he completed that day, which he'd started three months earlier, was 'The Sounds Of Silence.' It was a haunting rumination on man's inability to communicate with man, and it found its way onto aspiring folk duo Simon & Garfunkel's debut album, *Wednesday Morning, 3AM*. But when that record didn't sell, Art Garfunkel went back to university and Simon went to live and work in Europe.

However, one Boston radio station doggedly playlisted 'The Sounds Of Silence,' drumming up so much audience response that Columbia Records producer Tom Wilson was assigned to upgrade the song from a simple folksy acoustic duet to fully fledged electric folk-rock. Wilson was then working with Bob Dylan on his new electric music so, naturally, he used Dylan's musicians to overdub electric guitar and drums onto the track. Listen closely and you'll hear them trying to keep in time with the duo's original idiosyncrasies.

On December 4, 1965, Wilson's studio-augmented version of 'The Sounds Of Silence' entered the U.S. Top 40, and by the time it hit Number 1 on New Year's Day, Simon & Garfunkel were back in business, set to become the biggest popular music duo of the 1960s.

My Generation
The Who

Released October 1965
Decca *31877* (U.S.) / Brunswick *05944* (U.K. #2)

In 1965, Who guitarist and songwriter Pete Townshend had recently come into the possession of a Packard hearse. Parked outside his home in London's Chesham Place, it was spotted one day by the Queen Mother, who was immediately adjacent in Buckingham Palace. "Her husband had been buried in a similar vehicle and it reminded her of him," Townshend said later. With one imperious wave of an over-privileged arm, the car was towed away.

That and another incident, when a posh lady made a snooty comment when he was out driving a different car, inspired Townshend to pen a composition that constituted an explosion of frustration with the sorry lot of the young and non-posh in grey, drizzly, rigidly hierarchal 1960s Britain. Each verse culminated in the line "Hope I die before I get old!" This was true jaw-socking bluntness in those times of socially decorous entertainers.

While the song started out as a slow blues, Townshend's colleagues eventually settled on an arrangement that was entirely sympathetic with the snarling lyric. The rhythm section of John Entwistle (bass) and Keith Moon (drums) provided a relentless, charging, bruising ambience. Singer Roger Daltrey stutters the lyric like a buffoon, alluding to a physical effect of purple hearts, the mod constituency's drug of choice. Entwistle meanwhile contributes the first ever bass solo on a pop record. It somehow spoils the perfection of 'My Generation' that it didn't go to Number 1 in any of the four competing U.K. pop charts of the day. But make no mistake: on this record, The Who were the mouthpiece for millions.

California Dreamin'
The Mamas & The Papas

Released December 1965
Dunhill *4020* (U.S. #4) / RCA *1503* (U.K. #23)

The Mamas & The Papas were leaders of the West Coast folk-rock movement of the middle 1960s, part of a social circle that included Scott McKenzie, Barry McGuire, Lovin' Spoonful leader John Sebastian, and Roger McGuinn of The Byrds. They had sprung from the Greenwich Village folk scene over in New York City, as John Phillips, his wife Michelle, Cass Elliot, and Denny Doherty worked their way through a number of folk groups, including The Smoothies, The Journeymen, and The Mugwumps, before joining forces to form The New Journeymen. The group then relocated to Los Angeles where they lived in the house of their friend Barry McGuire, who had recently enjoyed a worldwide hit with his apocalyptic 'Eve Of Destruction.'

McGuire decided to use the group as backing singers on his album *This Precious Time* – at which point they called themselves The Magic Circle – and among the songs he recorded was John and Michelle's 'California Dreamin'.' When Dunhill Records owner Lou Adler heard the album, and particularly that song, he was so impressed that he signed The Magic Circle. The group was re-christened The Mamas & The Papas, and their first single release was their own interpretation of 'California Dreamin'' using McGuire's backing track. The only difference was that McGuire's gruff voice was erased from the tape and The Mamas & The Papas recorded a new set of lead vocals. It became a huge international hit in 1966 and was one of the songs responsible for ushering in the hippie era.

It's Not Unusual

Tom Jones

Released January 1965
Parrot *9737* (U.S. #10) / Decca *F 12062* (U.K. #1)

Tom Jones (born Thomas Woodward) was discovered in 1964 by Gordon Mills, singing at the Top Hat Club in Merthyr Tydfil, Wales. Performing as the frontman of Tommy Scott & The Senators, he was hailed as "the twisting vocalist from Pontypridd." Mills had co-written 'It's Not Unusual' for barefoot songbird Sandie Shaw, intended as a follow-up to her recent Number 1, '(There's) Always Something There To Remind Me.' Mills used Jones and his band to record a demo of the song, and the singer tried to persuade him to hand it over, but Mills was adamant that it would go to Shaw. However, when Jones persisted, Mills finally said, "I'll tell you what, if Sandie Shaw turns it down, I'll let you have it." Fortunately for Jones that's exactly what happened, and he went into the studio to make a proper recording. Apparently he was so enthusiastic about the song that his vocal completely drowned out the studio musicians, and a few days later a third recording had to be made, this time with a louder horn section and with Jones singing in the tape-storage closet. It was definitely third time lucky, and his vigorous interpretation was soon rewarded when 'It's Not Unusual' flew to Number 1 on the British charts.

Stop! In The Name Of Love

The Supremes

Released February 1965
Motown *1074* (U.S. #1) / Tamla Motown *TMG 501* (U.K. #7)

The Supremes were Motown's most successful act of the 1960s, with no fewer than 12 American Number 1s between 1964 and the departure of lead singer Diana Ross at the end of 1969. No other American act achieved so many Number 1s during the 1960s. It was a phenomenal achievement for the trio of women who, before their smash hit 'Where

Did Our Love Go,' were known around the corridors of Motown as the 'no-hit' Supremes. 'Stop!' was the fourth in a series of five consecutive American chart-toppers for the group, all written by Holland-Dozier-Holland, and the first single released on the custom Tamla Motown label in Britain. Lamont Dozier recalled that the title sprang from an argument with his girlfriend. She was about to walk out the door and the phrase "stop in the name of the law" came into his head. Dozier said: "I just changed it slightly to 'stop in the name of love' and there was my song."

I Can't Help Myself

The Four Tops

Released May 1965
Motown *1076* (U.S. #1) / Tamla Motown *TMG 515* (U.K. #23)

When Motown songwriter Lamont Dozier was a child, his grandmother ran a beauty parlor from home. Her flirtatious husband would call out greetings to the arriving customers: 'Hi sugar pie,' and 'Hi, honey bunch.' The young Dozier's brain evidently filed away the scene. In 1965, as he attempted to write with the brothers Holland their second hit for The Four Tops following 'Baby I Need Your Loving,' he incorporated the phrases into the chorus of this brisk-paced song of romantic devotion. The trio's next effort for the Tops was so similar that many erroneously thought that the same backing track was employed. Its title? 'The Same Old Song.'

Papa's Got A Brand New Bag Part 1

James Brown

Released July 1965
King *5999* (U.S. #8) / London *HL 9990* (U.K. #25)

I Got You (I Feel Good)

James Brown

Released November 1965
King *6015* (U.S. #3) / Pye International *7N 25350* (U.K. #29)

Just as Motown was becoming slick and sophisticated and Bob Dylan was writing the most complex lyrics ever heard in popular music, James Brown re-invented square one. The razor-sharp guitar rhythms and shattering horn riffs of 'Papa's Got A Brand New Bag' were simultaneously primitive and brand spanking new. He recorded it on February 1, 1965, and claimed: "When I saw the speakers jumping, vibrating in a certain way, I knew that was it – deliverance. What I started on 'Out Of Sight' I took all the way on 'Papa's Got A Brand New Bag.'"

The lyrics seemed largely gibberish, but for sheer, unbridled energy nothing else came close in the mid 1960s. Brown had been scoring hits since the late 1950s, but 'Brand New Bag' wrote his name large on the map. Now recognized as the template for funk, it reached Number 1 in the American R&B chart, Number 8 on the pop chart, and collected a Grammy as the year's Best Rhythm & Blues Recording.

The follow-up, 'I Got You,' was a barely-disguised re-write of Brown's earlier composition, 'I Found You,' which had flopped when recorded by his girlfriend, Yvonne Fair, in 1962. Mick Jagger said at the time that it was "a good record" but rightly qualified his praise by observing that it didn't compare with 'Brand New Bag.' Nevertheless, using the success of 'Bag' as a springboard, 'I Got You' went on to become Brown's biggest-ever hit, peaking at Number 3 in the U.S. pop chart.

In The Midnight Hour
Wilson Pickett

Released July 1965
Atlantic 2289 (U.S. #21) / Atlantic AT 4036 (U.K. #12)

Atlantic tagged their new signing as 'the Wicked Pickett' in 1965. He had already recorded for a couple of labels before landing at the company, notably as a member of The Falcons, singing lead on their 1962 R&B hit 'I Found A Love.' It was another Falcons member, 'Sir' Mack Rice, who would later deliver one of Wilson's other memorable hits, 'Mustang Sally.'

Following a couple of flops for Atlantic recorded in New York City, Pickett found himself coupled with Booker T. & The MGs and the Memphis Horns at Stax studios. Producer Jerry Wexler had decided to try cooking up a Memphis soul stew for the singer. This combination would usher in a looser, funky soul sound that became the hallmark of Stax and Atlantic's soul sides during the mid 1960s.

MGs guitarist Steve Cropper did his homework when he heard Pickett was coming to town. Checking out some earlier records, he noticed that Pickett had a habitual routine of repeating phrases such as: "See my Jesus in the midnight hour." Cropper said: "He'd start preaching this 'midnight hour' thing on the fade-outs." When Pickett arrived in town, he and Cropper retired to the Lorraine Hotel where they found an immediate empathy and quickly wrote a couple of songs, including the one that would become his theme song, 'In The Midnight Hour.' When it came to recording and the band couldn't quite get the right groove, Wexler danced the jerk around the studio, much to the musicians' amusement, and a classic soul anthem was swiftly in the can.

Respect
Otis Redding

Released August 1965
Volt 128 (U.S. #35) / Atlantic AT 4039 (U.K.)

R&B of the 1950s turned into soul in the 1960s through Sam Cooke and James Brown and two of the major labels most associated with the music, Stax and Atlantic. Otis Redding began his career in the early 1960s and had his first R&B hit in 1963 with his own composition, 'These Arms Of Mine,' on the Stax subsiadiary label, Volt. Redding soon became Stax's biggest artist and was one of the Southern States' best soul singers.

He was a great interpreter of covers but often wrote his own material, notably 'Respect,' which together with 'I've Been Loving You Too Long' and his cover of the Temptations 'My Girl' were his first three pop hits of 1965, all appearing on his classic album Otis Blue. Remarkably, all three were recorded on the very same day and the entire album was cut during a single weekend between tour dates.

'Respect' may well have been written that very weekend. MGs drummer Al Jackson recalled the song's inspiration. Redding had apparently been complaining about a recent grueling tour, and Jackson said to him: "What are you griping about? You're on the road all the time. All you can look for is a little respect when you come home."

Famously, 'Respect' was later covered by Aretha Franklin, who created a powerful new arrangement and turned a song written by a man into a feminist anthem. Upon hearing Franklin's completely re-worked version, recorded a couple of years after his original, Redding is reported to have said: "That little girl done took my song away!"

The Carnival Is Over
The Seekers

Released October 1965
Capitol 5531 (U.S.) / Columbia DB 7711 (U.K. #1)

The Seekers were an Australian quartet fronted by vocalist Judith Durham who played a crossbreed of folk and white gospel. Like many antipodeans, they traveled to London, England, to find fame and fortune. At first they were signed by EMI to their mail-order division, World Record Club, before being transferred to the company's Columbia label. They were managed by Tom Springfield, brother of Dusty and former member of British folk trio The Springfields, who composed many of the group's hits, including the first three: 'I'll Never Find Another You,' 'A World Of Our Own,' and 'The Carnival Is Over.' The latter song was based on an old Russian folk-song, a pedigree it shared with at least two other major hits, Mary Hopkin's 'Those Were The Days' and Kenny Ball's 'Midnight In Moscow.' It tells the story of a 17th century Cossack rebel leader named Stenka Razin. (Pete Seeger had used the same melody in 1950 for a song he called 'River Of My People.') It became the group's second British Number 1 but was not a hit in America. When they split up in 1968, guitarist Keith Potger managed the successful New Seekers.

Uptight (Everything's Alright)
Stevie Wonder

Released November 1965
Tamla 54124 (U.S. #3) / Tamla Motown TMG 545 (U.K. #14)

The word 'genius' has been much overused in the music business, but one man who undoubtedly deserves the title is Stevie Wonder. Here is a musician who writes all his own material, plays virtually most of the instruments on his records – harmonica, guitars, drums, and keyboards – and is in possession of a marvelous voice. As if that weren't enough, he arranges and produces his own records.

Kicking off a chart career with a Number 1 single and album is always going to be hard to follow, especially when you're 13 years old, as 'Little' Stevie Wonder was when 'Fingertips' hit the top of the American charts. It took him over two years to find his voice, but during that period he was constantly hanging around the Motown studios, learning all the tricks as an apprentice in America's top hit factory of the era. Wonder had formed a songwriting partnership with Henry Cosby and Sylvia Moy that was to produce many of his 1960s hits, including 'I Was Made To Love Her,' 'I'm Wondering,' 'My Cherie Amour,' and 'Uptight,' his second hit as plain Stevie Wonder. 'Uptight' was inspired by 'Satisfaction' by The Rolling Stones (which itself was inspired by Motown's own 'Dancing In The Street') and featured some ferocious drumming by Benny Benjamin, backbone of the Motown house band, The Funk Brothers. Showcasing the by now familiar Motown sound, it reached Number 1 on the R&B chart and Number 3 in the pop chart, forming a solid foundation stone for what would be a remarkable career.

Like A Rolling Stone
Bob Dylan

Released July 1965
Columbia *43346* (U.S. #2) / CBS *201811* (U.K. #4)

In 1964 there had been no reason to think that Bob Dylan was doing anything other than purveying the sound he wanted to. His format was one man, one guitar, and a head full of grievances about the conduct of his supposed elders and betters. It made his reputation and led some to call him the Voice Of A Generation. Others who had known him longer knew better. The kids with whom Dylan had played in amateur bands back in Hibbing, Minnesota, where he grew up knew that he was a rock'n'roll kid. Even his high-school teachers – had they been interested in such things – would have been able to put right the folkies who thought Dylan was loyal to their cause. In his high-school yearbook, Dylan – then Robert Zimmerman – had written that his ambition was to "join Little Richard."

Dylan must have been gratified to be lauded by critics, to play to adoring audiences, and to see several of his zeitgeist-encapsulating songs such as 'Blowin' In The Wind' recorded in lucrative covers. But he wasn't satisfied. The trouble was, it wasn't that easy for Dylan to do what he now wanted to do. It is difficult to convey to today's audience the extent of the division between rock-pop and folk that existed in the early to mid 1960s. There was something like a Berlin Wall between the genres. Dylan's folk fans considered their music as having intellectual weight and socio-political import and viewed rock'n'roll and pop as adolescent trash. His own audience could very well turn against him if he made a record that displayed his true tastes. And there might not be a new audience there to take up the slack: the idea that the kids buying 'A Hard Day's Night' or 'It's All Over Now' might be able to relate to a man who penned such literate songs as 'To Ramona' was not necessarily a plausible one.

However, emboldened by The Animals' stunning, shimmering electric hit arrangement of 'The House Of The Rising Sun' – a standard he had included on his debut album – Dylan booked into Columbia Studio A in New York City in January 1965 with a full band. This was not the type of band that had accompanied folk-scene contemporaries such as Fred Neil or Tim Hardin. Dylan instructed these people to play rhythm & blues and rock'n'roll. They did not appear on all the tracks of the resulting album, *Bringing It All Back Home* (March '65), which was divided neatly down the middle: the first side featured tracks with band accompaniment, the second Dylan's familiar voice-guitar-harmonica format. Nonetheless, it was one of the rock tracks – the hip-talking Chuck Berry update 'Subterranean Homesick Blues' – that became a Top 10 hit for Dylan in Britain when he toured there in the spring.

Dylan took a band to the Newport Folk Festival in July 1965, where he was booed by parts of the audience – perhaps because he had seemingly turned his back on folk in favor of rock music, or maybe just because the sound was too loud. Folkies were beginning to perceive him as a mercenary betrayer of the folk idiom. It soon didn't matter. It was at this juncture that a new Los Angeles group called The Byrds took an electric version of his song 'Mr. Tambourine Man' to Number 1 on both sides of the Atlantic. The week before Newport saw the release of Dylan's new single, 'Like A Rolling Stone.' Its subsequent success proved he had access to pop's mass market, not just through cover versions by the likes of The Byrds; its extraordinary grittiness and length proved that he did not have to compromise his art one jot to reach that mass market. Many consider it the finest single ever made.

The song had started out as what Dylan described as "this long piece of vomit." Certainly on the finished record Dylan seemed to be throwing up all the bile and hatred in his system, spitting out his satisfaction at the downfall of an over-privileged character who had wronged him. While Dylan had clearly labored hard in writing the lyric and editing it down, the recording process was extremely quick. Al Kooper – a guitarist who bluffed his way into playing organ on the record – has even said that the first complete take was the one used.

Kooper had never played organ before and Dylan strummed his electric guitar like it was an acoustic, but this rawness only added to the song's gritty ambience. The lyrics were as poetic and dazzling as Dylan's always were, but were also utterly street-level. The record proved that, just like a film or novel, popular music could be a window on real life. Dylan's vocal performance was mesmerizing, raising goosebumps on your flesh as he capped every malice-dripping verse with the accusatory refrain "How does it *feel*?" Just to drive home the point that pop-rock had never heard anything like it, the record ran to six minutes, double the standard single length for the time. Now we think nothing of it, but it's astonishing that such an all-round revolutionary release should become a smash.

The Berlin Wall that divided folk and rock was destroyed by 'Like A Rolling Stone.' With one release, Dylan had proved that moon-in-June conventions did not have to inform the lyrics of records aimed at the hit parade. Giants like The Beatles, the Stones, The Beach Boys, and the countless pop minnows who copied the moves of those giants were suddenly liberated. The financial and artistic success of 'Like A Rolling Stone' had effectively given them permission to write about anything they wanted to, in whatever format they chose, and to ignore misgivings about controversy or of rendering themselves uncommercial. 'Like A Rolling Stone' had no less an effect than to turn rock'n'roll into rock, causing a kids' medium to grow up overnight and to be seen as just as valid and important as any other art form.

The Sun Ain't Gonna Shine (Anymore)
The Walker Brothers

Released February 1966
Smash *2032* (U.S. #13) / Phillips *BF 1473* (U.K. #1)

Americans Scott Engel, John Maus, and Gary Leeds – a.k.a. The Walker Brothers – relocated to Britain in 1965 to launch a pop career that engendered hysteria on a level with Beatlemania in their adopted homeland, although in America the response was more muted. Tall and handsome to a man, they released a string of epic, orchestrated ballads powered by Engel's resonant baritone, ensuring the band were chart regulars from 1965 until 1967. Engel was always the musical focus of the group, although Maus occasionally took lead vocals. Leeds, nominally the band's drummer, didn't do much, as most of the music on the band's records was cut by session players. 'The Sun Ain't Gonna Shine' was one of their two British chart-toppers and one of just two of their singles that also charted well in America.

After the band split, only Engel – as Scott Walker – was able to sustain a career in music, albeit an unusual one. For several years in the late 1960s and early 1970s he vacillated between two extremes. On one hand there were dark, existential solo albums full of Jacques Brel covers and his own compositions; on the other, mainstream readings of MOR standards, a TV series, and cabaret appearances. He surprised everyone – maybe even himself – by regrouping with Maus and Leeds in the mid 1970s and returning to the British charts with a version of Tom Rush's 'No Regrets.'

These Boots Are Made For Walkin'
Nancy Sinatra

Released January 1966
Reprise *0432* (U.S. #1) / Reprise *R 20432* (U.K. #1)

Somethin' Stupid
Nancy Sinatra & Frank Sinatra

Released March 1967
Reprise *0561* (U.S. #1) / Reprise *RS 23166* (U.K. #1)

Although often compared, unfairly, to her legendary father, Nancy Sinatra recorded a number of seminal hits in the late 1960s, most of them in collaboration with the cult singer-songwriter Lee Hazlewood. 'These Boots Are Made For Walkin" was her breakthrough release, and topped the charts on both sides of the Atlantic. Hazlewood apparently instructed his young protégé to sing the song as if she was a young girl giving the brush-off to a middle-aged man. This gives her vocal a detached insolence perfectly in keeping with the lazy cool of the backing track. Hazlewood called in The Wrecking Crew to record 'Boots' and their playing is exemplary, particularly Hal Blaine's deft, uncluttered drumming and the neat combination of Carol Kaye on electric bass and Ray Pohlman on stand-up acoustic bass.

Sinatra followed 'Boots' with several more Hazlewood-penned hits and the James Bond theme 'You Only Live Twice' before recording the duet for which she is best known. 'Somethin' Stupid' set her sweet, youthful voice against her father's older, knowing croon, and provided him with his first ever Gold-certified single in America. After that, Nancy resumed her work with Hazlewood, recording two further classic singles in 1968, both of which feature on their collaborative album *Nancy & Lee*. 'You've Lost That Lovin' Feelin" is perhaps the only subsequent version to do justice to the timeless original by The Righteous Brothers, while 'Some Velvet Morning' was recently named by the U.K.'s *Daily Telegraph* newspaper as the greatest duet of all time.

When A Man Loves A Woman
Percy Sledge

Released April 1966
Atlantic *2326* (U.S. #1) / Atlantic *584 001* (U.K. #4)

This classic love song began life as an on-stage jam when Sledge was depressed at the loss of a girlfriend, and originally it had the working title 'Why Did You Leave Me?' Sledge and his musicians worked to improve it for several months before coming up with the new title, but due to the basic facilities in the studio, the major part of the song had to be recorded in mono in one take, with the horns and background vocals recorded at one later overdubbing session. The finished recording was down on tape just before Christmas 1965, but the musicians weren't particularly impressed with the result, especially since Sledge was decidedly off key. The overdubbed horn section was also painfully out of tune, but producer Quinn Ivy felt the recording had a certain something, and a copy was sent to Jerry Wexler at Atlantic Records. He agreed, but insisted that a new recording be made, this time in tune, at Atlantic's expense. Several weeks and a lot of dollars were spent to create a totally new version of the song, but due to a mix-up, Atlantic released the first version, out-of-tune horns and all.

Mr, Sledge had come up with the original idea for the song but he somewhat unwisely waved goodbye to a fortune by giving writing credit to organist Arthur Wright and bassist Cameron Lewis. The song generated millions of dollars in royalties over the years, although poor Percy probably saw very little of it.

River Deep – Mountain High
Ike & Tina Turner

Released May 1966
Philles *131* (U.S.) / London *HL 10046* (U.K. #3)

By 1966, the marriage of Ellie Greenwich and Jeff Barry had come to an end. Amongst many other hits, their joint songwriting credits included 'Baby I Love You,' 'Be My Baby,' 'Chapel Of Love,' 'Da Doo Ron Ron,' 'Do Wah Diddy Diddy,' and 'Leader Of The Pack.' Professional separation seemed to be inevitable too. To this day, Greenwich is unsure if producer Phil Spector, with whom they'd had considerable success, knew that the two were no longer involved when he contacted them about collaborating on new material. They agreed, and proceeded to stitch together three song fragments that each of them had devised, creating in the process an almost orgasmic hymn of romantic devotion.

Naturally there were variations in tempo and melody in such a process, and Spector appropriately applied an operatic tone when he came to record it with Tina Turner. (The brandname established with her husband was retained, but Ike does not appear on the record.) As if trying to claw back his status after recent flops, Spector poured everything – including a then mind-boggling $22,000 – into a track of extraordinary grandiosity.

While the record went Top 3 in the U.K. it flopped in the States, and a devastated Spector retired, albeit temporarily. Today the recording enjoys a legendary reputation at odds with its original chart placing, and is much covered and revered as the apotheosis of the Spector Wall Of Sound.

Mellow Yellow
Donovan

Released November 1966
Epic *10098* (U.S. #2) / Pye *7N 17267* (U.K. #8)

Irish singer Donovan had suffered during the early part of his career after he was labeled a 'Dylan copyist,' but when top producer Mickie Most took over, his folk ditties were transformed into pop hits. Their first effort together, 'Sunshine Superman,' hit number 1 on the U.S. charts. But

U.K. contractual disputes meant that 'Superman' and this follow-up were released in America many months before they came out in Britain.

Donovan was part of The Beatles' inner circle, and fab-four links to his music were numerous. 'Sunshine Superman' had originally been titled 'For John And Paul,' while 'Mellow Yellow' featured background whispering by Paul McCartney. Donovan featured as a background vocalist on the group's 'Yellow Submarine' and supplied its author with a couple of lines for the song when McCartney got stuck. He also appeared on the worldwide live-by-satellite performance of 'All You Need Is Love' in August 1967, and his hit of the same year, 'Jennifer Juniper,' was written for Jenny Boyd, younger sister of George Harrison's wife Patti. The lyric of 'Mellow Yellow' mentioned an "electrical banana," and in the U.S. Country Joe McDonald allegedly started a rumor that you could get high by smoking dried banana skins, which gave the song a whole new meaning – one which Donovan has always refuted.

I'm A Believer
The Monkees

Released November 1966
Colgems *1002* (U.S. #1) / RCA *1560* (U.K. #1)

Last Train To Clarksville
The Monkees

Released August 1966
Colgems *1001* (U.S. #1) / RCA *1547* (U.K. #23)

American TV producers Bob Rafelson and Bert Schneider had a great idea: why not make a series about a zany pop quartet that combined the attributes of The Beatles and The Marx Brothers? After considering The Lovin' Spoonful, they opted instead to advertise in the movie biz bible *Variety*. From over 400 auditioners they selected four personable young men – Michael Nesmith, Peter Tork, Mickey Dolenz, and Davy Jones – blessed with varying degrees of musical and acting talent. Screen Gems bought the idea, and music publishing mogul Don Kirshner was drafted in to find songs for the show. The reliable duo of Tommy Boyce and Bobby Hart (who also composed *The Monkees* theme) came up with the lively 'Last Train To Clarksville,' apparently inspired by a mis-hearing of the lyrics to The Beatles' 'Paperback Writer.' With Monkees' vocals dubbed on top of a backing track played by top New York sessioneers, the song was virtually guaranteed its Number 1 placing on November 5, 1966, amongst all the publicity generated by the TV show.

Their next single, 'I'm A Believer,' did even better. Written by aspiring young songsmith Neil Diamond, this was a marginally more rock-oriented track with a hint of blue-eyed gospel. The success of 'Clarksville' was largely limited to America, but with the TV series now being broadcast overseas, *Billboard* magazine was able to report on March 11, 1967, that Europe too was now "gripped by Monkeesteria." It was a blatantly patriotic attempt to bestow a whiff of Beatlemania on America's young pretenders, but it was also true.

Good Vibrations
The Beach Boys

....

Released October 1966
Capitol *5676* (U.S. #1) / Capitol *CL 15475* (U.K. #1)

Brian Wilson picked up the phone and called long-distance from Western Recorders studio, Los Angeles, to his brother Carl. It was Monday August 15, 1966. That night, The Beach Boys were playing half way across America in the Municipal Auditorium at Minot, North Dakota. "The first time I ever heard the music to 'Good Vibrations,'" remembered Carl many years later, "I came back to my hotel room and the phone rang, and it was Brian. He called from the recording studio and played this really bizarre-sounding music over the phone."

At this point in their career, The Beach Boys were a group divided into two distinct entities. Their emotionally unstable creative genius, Brian, had withdrawn from live performances and spent his time working on new music for the group in a string of Los Angeles studios. The other five members maintained the public face of The Beach Boys. They did the touring, the radio and TV appearances, and the promotional visits to record stores, while Brian remained cocooned in L.A. with The Wrecking Crew, an elite cadre of America's top session players.

Wrecking Crew bassist Carol Kaye was in Hollywood's Gold Star Studios on February 18, 1966. when Brian supervised recording of the first track for 'Good Vibrations.' She recalled: "He'd come in and play piano to give us the feel for the tune, then go in the booth. Brian would give us instructions from the booth where he'd experiment with sounds. I never knew Brian was a bass player until much later; he never played bass in front of me." Kaye also noted that The Wrecking Crew were routinely expected to create musical parts for the other artists they worked with, but Brian usually had their contributions already written for them. "He'd let the rhythm guitars and drums play what they want, with direction from the booth sometimes, but it was all Brian in the production," she said. "We were in awe of Brian."

Brian once defined 'Good Vibrations' as a pocket symphony and justified that description by explaining that within its three minutes and thirty-five seconds he oversaw "a lot of riff changes … it had a lot of movements. … Changes, changes, changes. Building harmonies here, drop this voice out, this comes in, bring the echo chamber in … bring the cello up a little louder here … a series of intricate harmonies and mood changes."

As well as controlling every musical note in 'Good Vibrations,' Wilson took one vital step further. He was one of the first rock musicians to use the unique characteristics of individual studios to enhance his musical vision. As one example, he explained how "we recorded the 'Ah I love the colorful clothes she wears' sections at Gold Star, and the 'I'm pickin' up good vibrations' at Columbia."

Although he did work on other songs at this time, Brian's top priority was 'Good Vibrations' through the spring and summer of 1966. To those around him, however, his working methods seemed outlandish. "They were in the studio and they had an idea of what they wanted, but they didn't know how to find it right off," recalled country music star and former L.A. session player Glen Campbell. "And, gosh, Brian, he'd be in there doing that theremin line for 'Good Vibrations,' tryin' to get that thing right. I think it cost him $105 a man just to sit there trying to do that for three hours." Brian had previously used an electro-theremin – a primitive electronic instrument – on the *Pet Sounds* track 'I Just Wasn't Made For These Times' but it came into sharp relief on 'Good Vibrations,' providing the high-pitched ethereal howl of 'oo-wee-ooh' that adds a spine-tingling touch to the already catchy chorus.

Brian remained completely on top of the music during these complex sessions but the one thing he did lose sight of was the world outside 'Good Vibrations.' Come May of 1966, the other Beach Boys and the executives at Capitol Records were becoming increasingly concerned about the disproportionate amount of time and money he was investing into just one song – a song none of them had even heard yet. Capitol's anxiety was grounded in good, solid business practice. "In those days," admitted Brian, "you could record a single for $1,500. 'Good Vibrations' cost about $15,000." No record in the history of popular music had ever cost so much or taken this long, and Capitol execs were well aware of the prodigious amounts of dope being consumed during the studio sessions.

The Beach Boys, however, were more concerned about their working relationship with Brian. He had established, on the *Pet Sounds* album, his pattern of creating tracks without them, merely calling them in at the last minute to add their vocals. With 'Good Vibrations,' it was beginning to look as if that call might never come. Did he really need them at all? They need not have worried. Just nine days after the long-distance conversation with Carl in North Dakota, Brian invited the others to join him in Sunset Sound. As lead vocalist Mike Love remembered: "It was kind of a cliffhanger. Brian said, 'We need some words,' and I said, 'Well, OK. Let's see.'" Ten minutes before the session started, Mike was barreling down Hollywood freeway dictating lyrics.

It was an intense day, during which Love recalls 25 to 30 overdubs being applied to just one small section. But, working to Brian's guide vocal, they made substantial progress and, on September 21, 1966, at Columbia Studio A, Brian finally completed 'Good Vibrations.' He remembered: "When I dubbed it down, made the final mix, it was a feeling of power. It was a rush, a feeling of exaltation. I remember saying, 'Oh, my God.'"

Released on October 10, 'Good Vibrations' reached Number 1 in the U.S. and U.K. and went on to become the first million-selling Beach Boys single. It was nominated for the music industry's highest honor, a Best Contemporary Rock'n'Roll Recording Grammy but, astonishingly, the expert Grammy judges decided it wasn't quite as good as 'Winchester Cathedral' by The New Vaudeville Band. Time, however, has rectified that mind-boggling decision and 'Good Vibrations' is now acknowledged not just as an all-time classic single but as a recording that changed the course of popular music.

major labels who wanted to distribute the single nationally. The band signed with Cameo-Parkway, allegedly because their label was ?'s favorite color, orange. '96 Tears' eventually climbed all the way to the top of the national charts, followed by several lesser hits, before changing times rendered the band's primitive rock obsolete. ? has resurfaced periodically since then, recording, gigging, and claiming to hail from Mars.

The Shadows Of Knight added another twist to the cultural exchange that first saw the Stones and The Yardbirds reinterpreting Chicago electric blues. They delved into the same influences, but through the British bands' interpretations rather than the American originals. Their albums were peppered with revved-up blues standards, but their breakthrough single was a reasonably faithful cover of Them's 'Gloria.'

Thanks to the inclusion of the psychedelic pop classic 'I Had Too Much To Dream (Last Night)' on the later *Nuggets* compilation, The Electric Prunes are remembered as typical 1960s garage punks. In fact, the band – or at least, the name – enjoyed a curious, varied career that stretched to five albums. At first most Prunes material, including 'Too Much To Dream,' was provided by the commercial songwriting team of Annette Tucker and Nancie Mantz. In the hands of the band and their producer, Dave Hassinger, who had engineered some Rolling Stones sessions in the mid 1960s, this raw material was lent a measure of sonic adventure by experiments with reverb, backwards guitar, and other effects that fitted well with the 1960s penchant for pop weirdness.

A similar follow-up hit, 'Get Me To The World On Time,' and an album including both singles marked this first phase in the band's history. A second album, *Underground*, saw the band briefly wresting control of their destiny, writing their own material as they continued with the odd noises. But the hits stopped, and The Electric Prunes fell into the hands of composer David Axelrod. This proved to be an ill-starred marriage that led to the gradual disintegration of the band. Eventually it became little more than a name-badge to put on recordings made by other people. A religious concept album in Latin ensued, and by the time of the appositely-titled *Just Good Old Rock'n'Roll*, the final album to bear the Prunes' name, no original members remained.

96 Tears
? & The Mysterians

....

Released February 1966
Cameo *428* (U.S. #1) / Cameo Parkway *C 428* (U.K. #37)

Gloria
The Shadows Of Knight
Released January 1966
Dunwich *116* (U.S. #10) / Atlantic *AT 4085* (U.K.)

I Had Too Much To Dream (Last Night)
The Electric Prunes
Released November 1966
Reprise *0532* (U.S. #11) / Reprise *RS 20532* (U.K.)

The youth of America responded to the Beatles and Stones-led British invasion of 1964 with a musical mobilization on a vast scale. Across the land, in garages, bars, schools, and youth clubs, countless teenagers tore through 'Louie Louie' with more enthusiasm than expertise. For most of these garage bands, a locally released independent single was the absolute peak of their achievements. Yet a few went beyond that, scoring national, even international hits, touring, and even making albums.

The Mysterians were fronted by ?, previously one Rudy Martinez, who had legally changed his name to ? (and not 'Question Mark'). He permanently wore shades. The group's debut hit was driven by a two-chord organ riff, over which ? wailed about "too many teardrops for one heart to cry." It was first recorded for a small label, Pa-Go-Go, and became a regional hit, in the process attracting the attention of several

Wild Thing
The Troggs

....

Released April 1966
Fontana *1548* (U.S. #1) / Fontana *TF 689* (U.K. #2)

The Troggs seemed like an unlikely proposition for international pop stardom. They hailed from unfashionable Andover in the south-west of England and were fronted by a bricklayer-turned-singer, Reg Ball, who with comic audacity had been renamed Reg Presley. Yet they scored an impressive run of pop-rock hits in the 1960s, all basic in the extreme, and 'Wild Thing' was the first.

In many ways it is an eccentric record – replete with an incongruous ocarina solo and pauses that defiantly fall out of step with the song's rhythmic pulse – but it caught the imagination of millions. Including Jimi Hendrix, who later fashioned a greedy, unsubtle version of his own. Hendrix and the rest of us might never have heard the song if The Troggs hadn't come across it in the office of their manager Larry Page in the form of a demo by writer Chip Taylor. Looking for something unusual to kick-start their career, they felt it was worth a shot. If nothing else, the story of how 'Wild Thing' was recorded tells a story about how singles were sometimes made in those far-off, simple times. Presley recalled that producer Larry Page was recording an orchestral session. "He said we had to be up there waiting outside the studio in case there was any time left at the end. As it turned out there was 45 minutes to get our gear in, get a sound, record it, and get out. And we did the B-side as well."

Somebody Help Me
The Spencer Davis Group

Released March 1966
Atco *6416* (U.S.) / Fontana *TF 679* (U.K. #1)

The Spencer Davis Group were named after their guitarist, but are more associated with two entirely different names, Jackie Edwards and Stevie Winwood. The latter was the band's bizarrely gravel-throated teenage singer-keyboardist, while the former was not a member of the Group at all but a Jamaican songwriter who composed a couple of their early hits. The first hit Edwards provided for them, 'Keep On Running,' is the best known but this follow-up was another good record, even if it rather shamelessly adhered to the template of its predecessor in its grittily impassioned singing and identikit guitar licks.

Kicks
Paul Revere & The Raiders Featuring Mark Lindsay

Released March 1966
Columbia *43556* (U.S. #4) / CBS *202205* (U.K.)

The name of Paul Revere & The Raiders doesn't resonate so much today – especially in the U.K. where they failed to register on charts or public radar – but the group secured a dozen *Billboard* Top 40 placings in the U.S. during the 1960s. Mostly their records were infectious and earthy enough to sideline their gimmicky revolutionary war costumes – even if they did seem to be inordinately and permanently angry at girls. The denunciatory tone of this particular number was more understandable: it was written by Barry Mann & Cynthia Weil as a wake-up-call to a friend who was destroying himself with drugs.

Paperback Writer / Rain
The Beatles

Released June 1966
Capitol *5651* (U.S. #1) / Parlophone *R 5452* (U.K. #1)

This single marked the point at which The Beatles moved from pop group to rock band. The a cappella fronted A-side was recorded during sessions for *Revolver* in mid-April 1966 and featured a heavier guitar sound from the group. The B-side, 'Rain,' had plenty of studio trickery with some of The Beatles' earliest experimentation with backwards tapes and vocals and what Ringo considers his best ever performance. After much interference with their releases, from here on Beatles singles were duplicated on both sides of the Atlantic, with the same A and B-sides.

The Beatles popularity in America was marred that summer following John Lennon's comment in an interview with the London *Evening Standard* that "we're more popular than Jesus right now." Though this remark went unnoticed in Britain, all hell broke loose in America with

public burnings of the group's records – even the Ku Klux Klan got in on the action. The Beatles were about to retreat permanently into the studio and played their last live gig at Candlestick Park in San Francisco (with the exception of the famous rooftop 'concert' in 1969). These final live performances must have been excruciating for Lennon, who had already recorded *Revolver*'s otherworldly 'Tomorrow Never Knows' yet still had to go on stage singing "she loves you, yeah, yeah, yeah."

Sunny Afternoon
The Kinks

Released June 1966
Reprise *0497* (U.S. #14) / Pye *7N 17125* (U.K. #1)

The Kinks virtually invented heavy rock with 'You Really Got Me' in 1964 but had proved themselves equally able at affecting ballads with the lovely, melancholic 'Tired Of Waiting For You,' a talent consolidated by 'Set Me Free,' 'See My Friend,' and then in summer 1966 'Sunny Afternoon.'

Kinks supremo Ray Davies wrote the song while recuperating from a nervous breakdown. The lugubrious, descending introduction marks it out as one of those numbers recognizable from its first notes, while the opening line – "The taxman's taken all my dough" – was a real grabber.

Ray's colleagues provide deft backing and sweetly cooing harmonies, but it is his own lead voice that really lifts this track into the ranks of the immortal. His tale of a man broken financially and romantically is sung to exquisite effect in a voice that drifts between conventional pop and the vaudeville stylings of a Jimmy Durante or an Al Jolson. The breadth of The Kinks' talents are displayed on the B-side, which offers up the smoldering hard-rock of 'I'm Not Like Everybody Else.'

I Feel Free
Cream

Released December 1966
Atco *6462* (U.S.) / Reaction *591 011* (U.K. #11)

When guitarist Eric Clapton, bassist Jack Bruce, and drummer Ginger Baker formed a new band in summer 1966 they were aware that they were pooling talents considered significant, to say the least. Suitably boastful, they titled themselves Cream because of this fact. As if that wasn't enough, they proceeded to explore a musical style that was quite new. Their super-amplified blues shot through with virtuoso playing swiftly made them one of the biggest and most important groups of the era, as they helped to prove that rock could be about more than pretty melodies and banal lyrics and could contain the improvisation and virtuosity that jazz, for instance, took for granted.

Singles were not really their forte. Cream's style thrived more on albums and especially the live concert. But at the same time they did not disdain singles in the same way that Led Zeppelin soon would. 'I Feel Free' is like much of their studio work in that it exhibits a discipline usually lacking from their live sets, which typically included very long drum and guitar solos. With a melody from Bruce and a lyric supplied by non-band-member Pete Brown, it featured a pretty 'bomp bomp' vocal riff, a hummed vocal counter riff, and a concise pop melody. Clapton's powerful lead guitar work meanwhile hints at the group's 'other' identity, and the delicious way that the anguished, double-time verses contrast with the whimsy of the rest of the composition point to heavier inclinations held in check.

Reach Out I'll Be There
The Four Tops

Released August 1966
Motown *1098* (U.S. #1) / Tamla Motown *TMG 579* (U.K. #1)

By the fall of 1966, writers Holland-Dozier-Holland had secured five *Billboard* hits for black vocal outfit The Four Tops. While these included the chart-topper 'I Can't Help Myself,' the fact that the last two had stalled in the lower reaches of the Top 20 indicated that they might be losing their touch with the group. Perhaps this was partly the reason that, at a Motown quality-control meeting, a company employee insisted that 'Reach Out' would not sell. "Too different," was his conclusion. However, this was the very quality that Motown boss Berry Gordy liked about it, causing him to take the executive decision to release it.

Certainly the record was singular in its grandiosity. The kids would no doubt be able to empathize with the customarily passionate vocal from Levi Stubbs, but the singing was also tinged with an epic pathos they might find risible. Meanwhile, what were they to make of the flute, oboe, and exotic percussion of the instrumentation? Just because Lamont Dozier and Brian Holland were weaned on a mixture of gospel and classical music, it didn't mean that young Americans would want to know about a fusion of those styles.

As it turned out, they very much did want to know about it. And so did British kids – they, like their American counterparts, sent it to the top. "We just wanted to keep striving for something different to make people listen to Holland-Dozier-Holland," Brian Holland said later. "It was a gem of a song."

HOLLAND-DOZIER-HOLLAND: THE MOTOWN HIT MACHINE

In 1963, Freddie Gorman made it clear to his Motown songwriting colleagues Brian Holland and Lamont Dozier that his job as a postman was making it too difficult to continue writing with them. Holland's brother Eddie – hitherto a recording artist – was drafted in to take up the slack, and one of the most famous publishing credits of all time was born.

Each of the team's members would give you a different story about why the names are credited in the order Holland-Dozier-Holland (often abbreviated to H-D-H) but they all agreed on the way they worked as a unit. Brian and Lamont would come up with the initial idea or title and write a melody, which would then be passed on to Eddie, who would devise a lyric. Regardless of contribution, credit and royalties would be divided up in exact thirds. It was a streamlined process that yielded the trio, and their label, record sales estimated at 73 million over five years. And as if to prove that factory methods do not necessarily equate with philistinism, they produced classic song after classic song.

'Come And Get These Memories' was the first song credited to the trio, although Lamont had written most if it already. He has said that their first true collaboration was either Mary Wells's 'You Lost The Sweetest Boy' or The Marvellettes' 'Locking Up My Heart' – both *Billboard* Top 50 entries in 1963. That same year they gave Martha & The Vandellas a brace of Top 10 U.S. singles, 'Heat Wave' and 'Quicksand,' as well as

one for Smokey Robinson's Miracles in the gimmicky 'Mickey's Monkey.' In 1964 H-D-H secured their first Number 1, for female vocal trio The Supremes, in the shape of 'Where Did Our Love Go?' A song of almost nursery-rhyme simplicity, it was ridiculed by the group as a Marvellettes cast-off, but their attitude changed when it topped the chart. An astonishing nine further *Billboard* chart-toppers followed, including 'Baby Love,' 'Come See About Me,' 'Stop! In The Name of Love,' 'Back In My Arms Again,' 'You Can't Hurry Love,' and 'You Keep Me Hangin' On.'

Vocal quartet The Four Tops were also granted the H-D-H magic touch, starting with 'Baby I Need Your Loving' and continuing through 'I Can't Help Myself' and its soundalike but still superb 'It's The Same Old Song.' The songwriters moved into epic territory with the Tops for the ornate 'Reach Out I'll Be There,' a 1966 transatlantic Number 1, and 'Standing In The Shadows Of Love.' Marvin Gaye didn't use them quite so often, but they did give him 'How Sweet It Is To Be Loved By You' – which is probably better known now in its 1975 cover version by James Taylor, a hit ten years after Gaye charted with the song.

While Holland-Dozier-Holland continued to have big hits on their own labels after parting company with Motown in the late 1960s following a financial dispute, neither they nor Motown were ever quite the same force again.

Penny Lane / Strawberry Fields Forever
The Beatles

Released February 1967
Capitol *5810* (U.S. #1) / Parlophone *R 5570* (U.K. #2)

The Beatles' finest and most accomplished single, this double A-side release provides a perfect summation of the two sides of the group. Both songs were conceived as evocations of their authors' childhoods and are named for parts of their hometown of Liverpool, England. But while Paul McCartney's 'Penny Lane' is a breezy, immaculately recorded singalong, John Lennon's flipside, 'Strawberry Fields Forever,' is ominous and hypnotic, and more concerned with mood than melody.

'Penny Lane' and 'Strawberry Fields Forever' were the first new Beatles songs released since *Revolver*, which had been issued six months earlier in August 1966. This constituted the longest pause between releases of the group's career, although they had managed to plug a gap in the Christmas market with the thoroughly unnecessary compilation *A Collection Of Beatles Oldies*. These two songs, though, were anything but oldies: intended originally as part of the *Sgt. Pepper* album, they showcase the group's growing mastery of the recording studio and Lennon & McCartney's apparently effortless affinity for song.

Of the pair, 'Strawberry Fields Forever' was recorded first, beginning on November 24, 1966, at Abbey Road Studio 2. The Beatles hadn't convened in a recording studio since June, having spent the summer on their final concert tour and the intervening months working on individual projects: Lennon took an acting role in *Help!*-director Richard Lester's *How I Won The War*; McCartney composed the score to *The Family Way*; George Harrison traveled to India to study the sitar; and Ringo Starr did nothing of importance.

As such, initial work on 'Strawberry Fields' was filled with false starts and regularly interrupted by other projects, whether it be the recording of the fan-club-only single 'Pantomime: Everywhere It's Christmas' or Lennon's appearance on the TV comedy show *Not Only . . . But Also* alongside legendary funny-men Peter Cook and Dudley Moore.

By the end of November, The Beatles had completed seven takes of 'Strawberry Fields' with Lennon on acoustic guitar and vocals, Harrison playing an electric slide-guitar part, Starr on drums, and McCartney on bass and Mellotron. A forerunner of the sampler, the Mellotron was a keyboard instrument containing tape loops of brass, string, and woodwind sounds, each triggered by different keys. McCartney played the song's distinctive introductory bars on the instrument.

Lennon, though, was unhappy with these recordings but, equally, was unsure as to what needed to be done to improve them. After a week's contemplation (during which time work commenced on McCartney's 'When I'm Sixty-Four') he enlisted George Martin to score 'Strawberry Fields' for trumpets and cellos. The Beatles recorded a new, faster version of the song on December 8 and 9, with a much more complex arrangement that included backwards cymbals and an Indian instrument, the surmandal, on which Harrison plays the unusual scale that links the later choruses back to the verse. The brass and string parts were added a week later, and 'Strawberry Fields Forever' was completed.

Or so everyone thought. After a further week of mulling over the song, Lennon decided he liked the first minute of the slower, sparser version, but also the remaining couple of minutes of the busier, orchestrated rendition. He called George Martin and engineer Geoff Emerick back to the song, asking them to create a composite mix of the two. This wasn't entirely straightforward, particularly as the two versions were recorded in different keys. But by speeding up the first and slowing down the second, Martin was able to create a seamless edit at about the one-minute mark. And with that, 'Strawberry Fields' was finally finished.

Lyrically, 'Strawberry Fields Forever' finds John Lennon at his most oblique and unsure of himself. Like the hazy, spellbinding music, the words bear the hallmarks of a mind opened up but also thrown into confusion by LSD. In recalling childhood memories of the Strawberry Fields park, located just around the corner from where he was brought up, Lennon uses the narrative device of a young girl, wandering and wondering absentmindedly. Lines about how "no one I think is in my tree" are intentionally stuttering and contradictory, and ultimately reveal little more than that "living is easy with eyes closed."

While 'Strawberry Fields' has the sound and feel of a memory about to slip away, 'Penny Lane' displays a much more definite, detailed recall. It does possess a certain wistfulness but paints a much more cheerful picture: in five neatly constructed verses, McCartney reminisces about barbers and bankers and children laughing, under a blanket of "blue suburban skies." Musically, 'Penny Lane' is clearly inspired by Brian Wilson's widescreen production of The Beach Boys' *Pet Sounds* album. Driven by jolly, staccato piano and the by now de rigueur walking bassline,

the song grows over its tight three minutes with the addition of several other keyboard parts, rousing trumpets, flugelhorn, and – in the most explicit indicator of The Beach Boys' influence – a melancholy flute.

The recording of 'Penny Lane' was much more straightforward than that of 'Strawberry Fields Forever.' McCartney taped the basic tracks alone four days after Christmas before inviting the other Beatles to add to it in the first week of 1967. While it might not outwardly display the technical wizardry of 'Strawberry Fields,' 'Penny Lane' is in fact packed with clever studio tricks.

Most notable are the various piano parts, which were recorded at different speeds and then synchronized together to create unusual overtones. During the second week of January, a whole host of additional instruments were overdubbed by guest musicians, including flute, oboe, cor anglais, and double bass. McCartney decided on the final finishing touch – a piccolo-trumpet solo – after watching a performance of Bach's *Brandenburg Concerto Number Two in F Major* on BBC television.

With 'Penny Lane' completed, The Beatles continued work on what would become *Sgt. Pepper*, turning next to 'A Day In The Life.' By this stage, however, the group's label was in need of a new Beatles single. With only three tracks completed since November (the other one was 'When I'm Sixty-Four'), they opted for a double A-side, consisting of 'Penny Lane' and 'Strawberry Fields Forever,' thus disqualifying both from inclusion on any as-yet unfinished new album. George Martin has always considered this to be a huge mistake, claiming – quite rightly – that *Sgt. Pepper* would have been a much stronger album with the inclusion of these two songs.

At the end of January, as had become customary The Beatles shot a short promo film for each side of the single, with the Swedish director Peter Goldmann. (They had been doing this since late 1965, in part to avoid having to turn up to perform on *Top Of The Pops* and other TV music shows.) The single itself was released in mid February and quickly climbed to Number 1 on the U.S. singles chart. In the U.K., however, it was held off the top spot by Engelbert Humperdinck's 'Release Me.'

Happy Together
The Turtles

Released February 1967
White Whale *244* (U.S. #1) / London *HL 10115* (U.K. #12)

This whimsical pop classic was turned down by a number of artists, including The Vogues and Gary Lewis & The Playboys, before The Turtles took it to Number 1. It replaced The Beatles' glorious double A-side 'Penny Lane' / 'Strawberry Fields Forever' at the top of the U.S. singles chart – rather fittingly, as The Turtles had been inspired to move away from their earlier folk-rock material towards the richer sound of 'Happy Together' by the fab four's recent experimental offerings.

Silence Is Golden
The Tremeloes

Released April 1967
Epic *10184* (U.S. #11) / CBS *2723* (U.K. #1)

With their erstwhile leader, Brian Poole, The Tremeloes had the distinction of signing to Decca instead of The Beatles; the two bands had auditioned on the same day. A solid run of beat-pop chart singles followed, until 1966 when Poole left for a solo career, eventually returning to his family butchers business. His former backing band did better without him, having hits into the 1970s. 'Silence Is Golden,' an old Four Seasons B-side, was the biggest. It's a finely executed slice of gentle, mid-paced harmony pop that gave the band a British chart-topper, although the musical sweetness disguised a darker lyric: "Talking is cheap, people follow like sheep / Even though there is nowhere to go," sang lead vocalist Len 'Chip' Hawkes. Within a few years, changing tastes meant there was nowhere for The Tremeloes to go. Tiring of their pop image, they alienated their fans by disowning their back catalogue and 'going progressive.' When this stunt failed, the band quickly reclaimed their old hits again and took them out on to the cabaret circuit, where a version of the band performs 'Silence Is Golden' to this day.

Born Under A Bad Sign
Albert King

Released May 1967
Stax *217* (U.S.) / Stax *601 015* (U.K.)

Like his contemporaries Freddy and B.B. King, blues guitarist Albert King was a crucial influence on many rock guitarists, including Eric Clapton, Jimi Hendrix, and Stevie Ray Vaughan. Though he began recording in 1953, King didn't find any real success until he joined Stax Records in 1966 and was coupled with Booker T. & The MGs, creating a blues sound coated with Memphis soul. MGs guitarist Steve Cropper recalled that King could neither read nor write, and it was difficult to persuade him to record songs with which he was unfamiliar. Among the sides he recorded at Stax were 'Laundromat Blues,' 'Crosscut Saw,' and 'Born Under A Bad Sign,' specially written for King by Booker T. Jones and singer William Bell, and later notably covered by Clapton's band Cream. King had a unique playing style, often using his left-handed Flying V guitar strung 'upside down' and with his unorthodox tuning that resulted from his first attempts to play on a homemade guitar.

Light My Fire
The Doors

Released June 1967
Elektra *45615* (U.S. #1) / Elektra *EKSN 45014* (U.K.)

It is Jim Morrison's beauty, akin to that of Michelangelo's David, that has become the image most associated with The Doors. Consequently, many are under the impression that it was he who wrote this, the band's most famous song. Others assume it was written by keyboardist Ray Manzarek, the musical star of the record. In fact it was guitarist Robbie Krieger who came up with the number after a meeting during the group's early days when Morrison encouraged his colleagues to compensate for the paucity of their original material.

Knowing of Morrison's "very heavy" lyrical tastes, as Kreiger described them, the guitarist decided to write a song that would incorporate one of the four elements. Morrison loved the smoldering sensuality of the creation, tweaking the lyric only a little. The group worked up the song and emerged at the end with a six-and-a-half-minute epic featuring lengthy instrumental passages, with Manzarek's manic organ runs particularly prominent, alternating with a somber yet desirous vocal.

Those lengthy instrumental passages were mostly jettisoned for the edit of the song that was considered necessary for a single release. Even in chopped form, the song sounded like little else in mainstream rock, particularly with its blatant drug reference in the line "We couldn't get much higher," recitation of which got them banned from the influential *Ed Sullivan* TV show forever. The record still spent three weeks at the top of the U.S. chart. José Feliciano's 1968 cover was at first the more popular version in Britain, where The Doors' original would have to wait until 1991 to go Top 10.

Purple Haze
The Jimi Hendrix Experience

Released March 1967
Reprise *0597* (U.S.) / Track *604 001* (U.K. #3)

This was the first self-composed single by The Jimi Hendrix Experience, full of quality and epoch-marking innovation, and yet when manager Chas Chandler had signed the guitarist months previously, he had no idea whether Hendrix could write songs or not.

Chandler had bridged the gap between Hendrix the dazzling guitarist and Hendrix the proficient songwriter – he'd only composed scraps and generic exercises before – by getting him to record his live staple 'Hey Joe,' and a very good record it made too. But 'Purple Haze' was the fundamentally important single that proved he was not some kind of 'guitar Elvis' – an iconic figure but still a mere interpreter – but really had become a significant artistic force.

It's difficult to convey just how barrier-smashing 'Purple Haze' was in the first quarter of 1967. So it is fitting that this utterly alien-sounding record was partly inspired by a science fiction story, namely *Night Of Light* by Philip José Farmer, in which the phrase "purple haze" is used to describe the disorienting effects of sunspot activity on a planet called Dante's Joy.

The lyric was appropriately surreal, its discussion of the hazy state capped by bizarre interrogatives like "Is this tomorrow or just the end of time?" and, deliciously, "'Scuse me while I kiss the sky." The music was even more arresting in its freshness, propelled by a ferocious guitar riff that made even 'You Really Got Me' sound tame and yet somehow always retaining a melodic commerciality.

White Rabbit
Jefferson Airplane

Released June 1967
RCA *9248* (U.S. #8) / RCA *1631* (U.K.)

With a lyric inspired by *Alice In Wonderland,* the disquietingly catchy 'White Rabbit' was one of the defining singles of late-1960s U.S. psychedelic rock. Jefferson Airplane had formed in 1965; their debut album of the following year failed to chart, but like many of their contemporaries the group benefited from an appearance at the 1967 Monterey International Pop Festival.

The arrival of vocalist and songwriter Grace Slick gave the group a stronger focus. Her rich, powerful vocal belied a sweet, almost childlike image. Slick also contributed the two songs that made Jefferson Airplane the first truly internationally successful West Coast psychedelic rock group: the rousing 'Somebody To Love' and its insidious follow-up, 'White Rabbit.'

While the words to 'White Rabbit' are clearly from Lewis Carroll's *Alice In Wonderland*, the music came to Slick, according to later interviews, after a day spent listening again and again to Miles Davis's *Sketches Of Spain* while under the influence of LSD. There is also a suggestion of Ravel's *Bolero* in the insistent, militaristic rhythms and the way the song gradually builds to its menacing peak, over which Slick implores the listener, somewhat amusingly, to "remember what the dormouse said."

As well as its obvious musical charm, 'White Rabbit' was aided in its ascent up the *Billboard* singles chart by a memorable performance of the song on the *Ed Sullivan* TV show. The group was filmed using then cutting-edge chroma key technology (also known as 'blue screen') that gave the song a suitably hallucinatory visual backdrop.

Heroes And Villains
The Beach Boys

Released July 1967
Brother *1001* (U.S. #12) / Capitol *CL 15510* (U.K. #8)

Although it was never completed to bandleader Brian Wilson's satisfaction, 'Heroes And Villains' remains one of The Beach Boys most accomplished singles. A second pocket symphony in the vein of 'Good Vibrations,' the single version is significantly shorter and less complex than Wilson had in mind.

In fact Wilson handed it over to Capitol as a compromise as sessions for the (ultimately abandoned) *Smile* album ran over time. Nonetheless, its rousing verses and elegant chorus – not to mention the sublime middle eight – are vastly superior to most of the popular music of the time.

Four decades later, a longer, more extravagant 'Heroes And Villains' was included on a newly re-recorded version of Smile, put together by Wilson, original lyricist Van Dyke Parkes, and Darian Sahanaja of the Beach Boys-inspired group The Wondermints.

A Whiter Shade Of Pale
Procol Harum

Released May 1967
Deram *7507* (U.S. #5) / Deram *DM 126* (U.K. #1)

With its haunting, Bach-derived melody and impenetrable lyrics, 'A Whiter Shade Of Pale' is one of the all-time great debut singles. It was also one of the few things that Beatles John Lennon and Paul McCartney could agree upon in 1967: the former is said to have listened to it on endless repeat during long limo rides, while the latter has since named it one of his favorite songs of the 1960s.

Before fronting Procol Harum, Gary Brooker led The Paramounts, an R&B covers band who had a minor U.K. hit in 1963 with a version of The Coasters' 'Poison Ivy.' By 1966 the group had dissolved, and Brooker began writing songs with lyricist Keith Reid.

Reid and Brooker originally saw themselves as a professional songwriting partnership in the manner of the classic Brill Building teams of the time, but after struggling to find artists to record their songs they decided there was nothing else for it but to put together a band of their own. Reid remained with Procol Harum (named for their manager's cat) as a 'non-musical' member, contributing the lyrics to each of the group's 11 studio albums.

Procol Harum recorded 'A Whiter Shade Of Pale' in 1967 with producer Denny Cordell, who worked with The Moody Blues, The Move, and Joe Cocker. Musically, the song's main chord progression and melody bears a resemblance to a section of Johann Sebastian Bach's *Suite No. 3 in D Major*, more commonly known as *Air On A G String*. Reid and Brooker have always been listed as the song's composers, but at the time of writing the group's keyboardist, Matthew Fisher, had instigated legal action against the pair, claiming to have come up with the distinctive organ riff himself.

Lyrically, the single is a maze of confusing couplets about skipping "the light fandango," vestal virgins, turning cartwheels, and ghostly faces. Neither Reid nor Brooker has ever explained what the words mean, prompting years of over-eager analysis, particularly in the current age of nitpicking everything to the nth degree on the internet. Ultimately, it's probably no more or less than a love song packed full of intentionally bewildering nautical metaphors.

Whatever it meant then or means now, 'A Whiter Shade Of Pale' struck a chord with listeners across the world in 1967, topping the U.K. singles chart for six weeks during the Summer of Love and peaking at Number 5 in America. Coupled with the similar success of 'Nights In White Satin' by The Moody Blues, the single marked out the Deram label as the home of British progressive rock. It ended up as Procol Harum's only release for Deram, however, as by the fall of the same year they had moved to Regal Zonophone in Britain and A&M in the States. Although the follow-up single, 'Homburg,' gave them a second international hit, Procol Harum would never again match the success of their debut.

Brown Eyed Girl
Van Morrison

Released June 1967
Bang *545* (U.S. #10) / London *HLZ 10150* (U.K.)

In April 2005 the White House revealed that 'Brown Eyed Girl' was one of George W. Bush's favorite songs, featuring on his iPod selection. Quite how this will affect the song's popularity is unknown, although Irish singer Van Morrison's response was: "I would have preferred it if it was a new song."

Following a particularly grueling American tour in 1966, Morrison left Them and accepted a one-way-ticket to New York City and a solo contract from Bert Berns's Bang Records. Berns had produced Them in London – 'Here Comes The Night' was a Berns composition – and was a major player in 1960s pop music as a producer, publisher, and songwriter.

Of course, Berns wanted Morrison to record hits, which was not at all what Morrison had in mind, and most of his material for Bang was about as uncommercial as it gets. However, one song that emerged from the sessions turned into a big hit in America. Morrison's original title was 'Brown Skinned Girl.' Beginning life as a "calypso thing" it somehow got changed along the way. None too happy at this 'commercial' turn of events, Morrison returned to Belfast before he had completed his vocals for the song, and consequently Jeff Barry (writer of dozens of hits with Ellie Greenwich) had to overdub the "sha la la" chorus at the end of the record. (The line "making love in the green grass" was edited out of the third verse for radio purposes.)

While it was never a hit in the U.K., 'Brown Eyed Girl' has since become something of a classic summer anthem, and despite Morrison's anger over his contractual circumstances in 1967 (yes – he was a grumpy young man too), this was the song that launched his solo career.

Itchycoo Park
The Small Faces

Released July 1967
Immediate *501* (U.S. #16) / Immediate *IM 057* (U.K. #3)

Together with The Who, The Small Faces were one of the most popular groups with the British mod movement of the middle 1960s. Like The Who they began as an R&B outfit, but as their career progressed, and with unlimited studio time at their disposal, they ventured into broader musical areas. Prior to joining erstwhile Rolling Stones manager Andrew Loog Oldham's Immediate label in 1967, they had recorded a string of hits for Decca. Oldham allegedly paid former manager Don Arden £25,000 for this transaction (about $60,000 at the time), which was delivered in cash in a brown paper bag

The group's first single for Immediate, 'Here Come The Nice,' was released in May 1967 and rose to Number 12 in Britain, quickly followed by 'Itchycoo Park,' a song with a surrealistic lyric that contained a number of relatively undisguised drug references. The BBC gramophone committee, charged with banning unsuitable records from the corporation's airwaves, seemed to be gloriously unaware of this, and were probably more used to stimulants of the liquid variety, although they had earlier objected to a number of The Small Faces' Decca singles because of sexual innuendo.

'Itchycoo Park' rose to Number 3 in Britain and became the group's sole American hit. According to drummer Kenny Jones: "Itchycoo Park wasn't really a park, it was an overgrown bombsite full of stinging nettles in Ilford [east London] which ran down to the railway lines." The recording was particularly notable for its use of phasing, a technical effect that produced a strange 'whooshing' sound. While their two psychedelic singles are undeniably good, The Small Faces were in fact one of Britain's most accomplished R&B bands and Marriott one of the country's finest R&B vocalists, as he would prove on their next and perhaps best single, 'Tin Soldier.'

Hole In My Shoe
Traffic

Released August 1967
United Artists *50218* (U.S.) / Island *WIP 6017* (U.K. #2)

Considering that Stevie Winwood left The Spencer Davis Group to participate in a band with a little more musical gravitas, it's ironic that Traffic are now remembered mostly by the record, written by the frequently-fired band member Dave Mason. Despite its Eastern ambience, backwards effects, and hallucinogenic lyric, it boasted the type of sing-song melody that made it attractive to children. To underline its lightweight aura, it became even better known when Neil – a hippie character from the TV comedy series *The Young Ones* – took a not entirely serious rendition to Number 2 in Britain in 1984.

Nights In White Satin
The Moody Blues

Released November 1967
Deram *85023* (U.S. #2) / Deram *DM 161* (U.K. #9)

When Justin Hayward and John Lodge joined The Moody Blues in 1966, they joined an R&B group that had already enjoyed their moment of fame with the 1965 Number 1 'Go Now' and were back to playing gigs for small change. With two new songwriting members, the group decided they had little to lose by changing their image and created a sequence of songs based around a normal day, in which Hayward's 'Nights In White Satin' formed an integral part.

At this point Decca approached the group and suggested they record a rock version of Dvorak's *New World Symphony*. This wasn't exactly what they had in mind, but it certainly suited their purposes. Demanding a week 'alone' in the studio, the Moodys proceeded to record their new material and the result was *Days Of Future Passed*, a song suite interwoven with orchestral links written by Peter Knight.

Presenting the finished product to Decca's executives, the group was met with a stunned silence. It certainly wasn't Dvorak, but since a good deal of money had been spent making the album, it proved to be something of a fait accompli. While the album took some time to find an audience, its high point, 'Nights In White Satin,' was the song that finally began to attract attention.

Of the group's breakthrough song, Hayward said: "I knew when I wrote it that it was like nothing I'd ever done before. I was just a 19-year-old kid … and there's actually a lot of wisdom there that I never noticed at the time." 'Nights In White Satin' remains their best-loved and most successful song. It made its mark on the British Top 20 on three separate occasions but did not reach the U.S. charts until 1972.

I Can See For Miles
The Who

Released October 1967
Decca *32206* (U.S. #9) / Track *604 011* (U.K. #10)

"To me it was the ultimate Who record," Pete Townshend once pronounced of this psychedelic hard-rock single. It certainly sounds like it was intended that way. Despite the sparse instrumentation there is a grandness about the sound and the vaguely science-fiction-like lyric. Keith Moon's drums sound absolutely gigantic and Townshend's fretboard slashings are epic. It was almost a running joke that, despite their massive significance, The Who never had a Number 1 U.K. or U.S. single. That joke turned sour here, with Townshend bitter at the record's modest chart achievements. "I spat on the British record buyer," he said.

Pictures Of Matchstick Men
The Status Quo

Released November 1967
Cadet Concept *7001* (U.S. #12) / Pye *7N 17449* (U.K. #7)

A clever pastiche of the British psychedelic rock of the time, 'Pictures Of Matchstick Men' would give Status Quo their only U.S. hit (next year), although the group was a mainstay on the U.K. charts for the rest of the century. Driven by wah-wah guitar, organ, and crashing drums, the single was The Status Quo's first for the Pye label in Britain. After several similarly trippy releases, the group dropped the definite article from its name and turned to a more simplistic style based on 12-bar blues, with which they stuck doggedly for the next three decades. Despite an often unfashionable sound – and image – Status Quo continued to score hit after hit in the U.K., including 'Rockin' All Over The World' (1977) and 'In The Army Now' (1986).

Arnold Layne
Pink Floyd

Released March 1967
Tower *333* (U.S.) / Columbia *DB 8156* (U.K. #20)

See Emily Play
Pink Floyd

Released June 1967
Tower *356* (U.S.) / Columbia *DB 8214* (U.K. #6)

Pink Floyd's debut single, 'Arnold Layne,' was written by their guitarist-vocalist Syd Barrett and banned by British radio, never rising above Number 20 in the charts.

Nonetheless, its influence was significant. The young Phil Collins was a big fan of the song, and Cream's bassist Jack Bruce recalled it as "the first truly English song about English life with a tremendous lyric. It certainly unlocked doors and made things possible."

Given that Arnold is a thief specializing in stealing ladies' lingerie from washing lines, it should be stressed that what the song made possible was not knicker nicking but a homegrown approach to psychedelia that would ultimately free British bands from merely imitating the American pioneers.

With the eerie sounds of their second single, 'See Emily Play,' the Floyd took psychedelia to the masses, peaking at Number 6 in the British chart. Mind-blowing though the record sounded back then, Floyd keyboardist Rick

Wright insisted in retrospect that much of its groundbreaking sonic landscape was achieved by a relatively simple means. "That 'Hawaiian' bit at the end of each verse," he noted, "was just Syd using a bottleneck through echo."

Tragically, Barrett would become one of rock's first acid casualties. His chemically-enhanced musical vision powered the band through their innovative first album, but as his friend (and replacement) David Gilmour recalled, Barrett was already burning out when Gilmour visited him in London's Sound Techniques on May 23, 1967. "I went down to the studio," said Gilmour, "and he didn't even recognize me – and that was the day they were making 'See Emily Play.'"

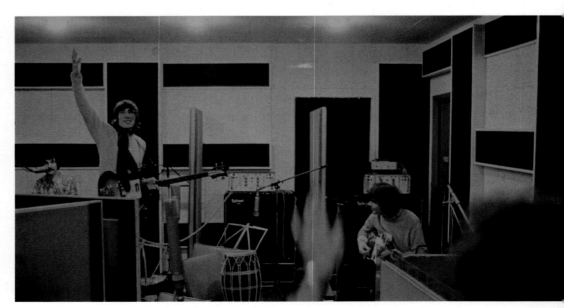

PIRATES INVADE THE BRITISH AIRWAVES

On radio, the Summer of Love was marred by storm clouds and downpours. Those hot, heady months coincided with a transition in British broadcasting, which meant that sometimes, when you tuned to your favorite station, all you got was static. Indeed, the only way you could be sure to hear the pop hits of the day was by turning the dial on your transistor radio to 'the great 208,' Radio Luxembourg. That commercial station had been broadcasting popular music around Europe for decades with short, fast-moving shows sponsored by eager advertisers. Since the 1950s Luxembourg had actively courted the youth audience and was well established amongst British teenagers as the best place to hear rock'n'roll.

The BBC, on the other hand, was slow to respond to the new music and teen culture. Since the late 1940s it had operated three main radio stations: the Home Service, which broadcast news and current affairs; the Third Programme, for classical music; and the Light Programme, on which pop competed for air time with easy listening and comedy. This restrictive set-up was constrained even further by an archaic agreement that meant the Light could only play up to five hours of commercial recordings a day. This led to a strange position where current hit records were often performed live, rather than the single being played. What is more, most of these live performances were dire cover versions by BBC musicians rather than performances by the original artists playing their own songs.

With the staid BBC marginalizing itself, and no British commercial radio, Luxembourg's pre-eminence in pop broadcasting was unchallenged. Until 1964, that is, with the launch of the first pirate radio stations. The maritime allusion in the name was appropriate: these stations broadcast into the British mainland from high-powered transmitters fitted into battered old merchant ships moored just outside British territorial waters – and therefore just out of reach of the law. Unhampered by arcane regulations, these stations played an almost constant stream of rock and pop – chart hits and underground sounds – interrupted only by the advertisements that funded the stations and the DJs' quick-fire patter. They became immensely popular with British youth.

The first pirate to take to the seas was Radio Caroline, which by 1966 was boasting more than six million listeners. Radio London was even more successful, with nearly eight-and-a-half-million tuning in. There were others, too: Radio City, Radio Essex, Radio Scotland, even the shortlived Radio Sutch, the vehicle of novelty rock'n'roller and relentless self-publicist Screaming Lord Sutch.

It wasn't just the open broadcast policies that attracted millions to the pirates. The stations were illegal – loathed by the broadcast establishment and the subject of much hand-wringing in the British

parliament. The music business itself was forced into a position of awkward ambivalence: it appreciated the massive exposure that the pirates gave to new records, but resented the fact that they didn't pay airplay royalties. So in tuning the dial to Caroline or London, you were guaranteed not only some great music, but also a frisson of outlaw excitement – an irresistible combination for any rebelliously-minded teenager. But it couldn't go on.

At the very peak of pirate radio's success, a new bill was going through parliament that would extend the arm of the law sufficiently to ensure that the pirate ships were within its reach. At the same time, plans were set in motion to revamp BBC radio. The plans involved creating both a national pop station, which became Radio One, and local BBC stations. The first of these measures came into effect at the height of the Summer of Love with the passing of the Marine Offences Act on August 15, 1967. Radio London broadcast its last record that same day, The Beatles' 'A Day In The Life.' Thousands of fans gathered outside a London railway station to welcome the station's DJs as they returned home from their doomed vessel. Caroline kept going, denying the law, until 1968, until it too bowed to the inevitable.

Six weeks or so after the passing of the act, the BBC launched its new pop station. For much of that intervening period the corporation had been frantically interviewing dozens of applicants for jobs on the new station, most of them recently disembarked from the pirate ships plus a few who'd come over from Luxembourg. So when the station was launched, the DJs in that first roster were names already familiar to Britain's teenagers, including Tony Blackburn (who had worked on radios Caroline, London, and Luxembourg) and John Peel (Radio London).

The momentous day of the launch came on September 30 when, at 5:30am, the Light Programme opened for the last time. It broadcast for a mere one and a half hours, before a new specially-written Radio One theme tune was played, 'Theme One' by The George Martin Orchestra. Then, at 7:00am, Tony Blackburn opened the first ever show on Radio One, playing 'Flowers In The Rain' by The Move.

Release Me (And Let Me Love Again)
Engelbert Humperdinck

Released January 1967
Parrot 40011 (U.S. #4) / Decca F 12541 (U.K. #1)

Raised in Leicester, England, Gerry Dorsey recorded his first single, 'Mr. Music Man,' for Decca in 1958, and then found himself going nowhere fast. By 1966 he and his wife were living in poverty in a small apartment, but it was a long-time friendship with Gordon Mills that was to be his salvation. Mills had successfully guided Tom Jones to superstardom.

With Jones's career doing nicely, Mills decided to assist his old friend Dorsey. The first matter of business was to kill off 'Gerry Dorsey' and come up with a new name. They settled on the unlikely Engelbert Humperdinck, a name borrowed from an old German composer. It was a mouthful – but certainly likely to attract attention. (Later on, when Mills signed Ray O'Sullivan and changed his first name to Gilbert, Humperdinck had the audacity to remark that it was "a ridiculous name.")

'Release Me' was Engelbert's third single under Mills's guidance. It was written in 1946 and became a country standard, earning hits on the Country charts for Jimmy Heap, Ray Price, and Kitty Wells in 1954, as well as a Number 8 *Billboard* pop hit for Esther Phillips in 1962. Engelbert's version hit home in Britain after the singer performed it on the highly popular nationally televised entertainment show *Sunday Night At The London Palladium*. The record famously kept The Beatles' classic double-A-side 'Penny Lane' / 'Strawberry Fields Forever' from reaching Number 1 in Britain. During some of Engelbert's early shows in 1967, where new acts with major hits would play so-called package tours, among his unlikely fellow travelers was The Jimi Hendrix Experience.

For What It's Worth (Stop, Hey What's That Sound)
Buffalo Springfield

Released January 1967
Atco 6459 (U.S. #7) / Atlantic 584 077 (U.K.)

Neil Young is the most celebrated ex-member of Buffalo Springfield, but it was Stephen Stills who wrote this one iconic song of the group's (admittedly brief) career. It sprang out of the civil war in miniature that Stills was witnessing on Los Angeles's Sunset Strip at the time. A couple of clubs, Pandora's Box and the Whisky A Go Go, became beacons to some particularly troublesome youngsters. Not that they were causing trouble in the conventional sense – violence was hardly the currency when Love & Peace was the vibe and grass the stimulant of choice – but young and old seemed at their farthest apart during the late 1960s. White L.A.P.D. cops, many from the deep South, found the sight of teens and 20-somethings with hair hanging to their shoulders, swathed in outlandish clothes and brandishing joints, akin to an invasion from another planet. Soon, batons were whistling through the air. Stills had recently returned from Latin America and was horrified at how similar the tensions in that region on the brink of revolution were to those in a developed democracy. He concocted this brooding creation about what he saw, flecked with eerie, ringing guitar harmonics and, despite the song's ambivalence, boasting an ominous, unforgettable chorus that sounded like a generational call to arms: "Stop, hey, what's that sound? / Everybody look – what's going down?"

The Guns Of Navarone
The Skatalites

Released April 1967
Not issued U.S. / Island WI 168 (U.K. #36)

Nothing could be further removed from ska, the Jamaican predecessor of reggae, than a World War II movie starring the very proper David Niven. But then it's unlikely that much thought went into this jaunty instrumental recording of the theme to *The Guns Of Navarone* in the first place: it was simply one of hundreds laid down by the loose aggregation of musicians who played under the Skatalites banner in the mid 1960s. By the time the record climbed the charts in the U.K. the band had ceased to exist, mainly because leader Don Drummond had been convicted of killing his wife in 1965.

San Francisco (Be Sure To Wear Flowers In Your Hair)
Scott McKenzie

Released May 1967
Ode 103 (U.S. #4) / CBS 2816 (U.K. #1)

The definitive flower-power anthem, 'San Francisco' gave its singer Scott McKenzie a brief moment of fame in the hippie summer of 1967. The folk-rock movement was big business at the time and The Mamas & The Papas were the movement's key figures, so it's no surprise to discover that Mamas & Papas leader John Phillips wrote this song. He did so at McKenzie's suggestion, as a song for all the hippies attending the 1967 Monterey Pop Festival. According to McKenzie, Phillips wrote the song within 20 minutes. Phillips and his manager Lou Adler were the principal arrangers of the Festival, and the blanket airplay that 'San Francisco' received on the West Coast leading up to the concert was nothing short of free advertising. In contemporary interviews, McKenzie was very sincere about his flower-power philosophy. He certainly did wear flowers in his hair during the recording of the song.

Can't Take My Eyes Off You
Frankie Valli

Released May 1967
Philips 40446 (U.S. #2) / Philips BF 1580 (U.K.)

The Four Seasons had been cranking out hits for three years before frontman Frankie Valli started a solo career in parallel with the Seasons in 1965. He began with 'The Sun Ain't Gonna Shine (Anymore),' which flopped for him but became familiar through The Walker Brothers' version. That had been composed by the Seasons' writing team of Bob Crewe and Bob Gaudio, who also supplied Valli's major solo success with 'Can't Take My Eyes Off You.' The success seemed somehow pointless: it sounded like cocktail-lounge music compared to The Four Seasons' much-loved recipe of pop gems garnished with operatically intense vocals.

You Keep Me Hangin' On
Vanilla Fudge

Released June 1967
Atco *6495* (U.S. #6) / Atlantic *584 123* (U.K. #18)

Previously known as The Pigeons, Vanilla Fudge played what they called "psychedelic-symphonic rock" and their initial idea was to play slowed-down and lengthy re-arrangements of recent hits. This version of the 1966 Supremes Number 1 was their only major hit and quite impressed co-writer Brian Holland, who said: "They did a brilliant re-adaptation – I was happy to hear it like that." The Fudge's version only managed to reach Number 67 on its first release in 1967 but when reissued the following year made Number 6. (Kim Wilde would take the song to Number 1 in America in 1987.) In 1968 Jeff Beck had plans to form a group with Rod Stewart and two Fudge members, bassist Tim Bogert and drummer Carmine Appice, but the plans were put on hold, only to be resurrected in 1973 and leading to the creation of Beck Bogert & Appice.

The Letter
The Box Tops

Released August 1967
Mala *565* (U.S. #1) / Stateside *SS 2044* (U.K. #5)

Chips Moman, who had been instrumental in the success of the legendary soul label Stax, ran American Sound Studios in Memphis, a hotbed of hit-making in the 1960s with a core group of elite session musicians. Among the many hits recorded at American were Dusty Springfield's 'Son Of A Preacher Man,' Presley's 'In The Ghetto' and 'Suspicious Minds,' and hits by Neil Diamond, B.J. Thomas, and this gem by The Box Tops, a local group who got their name at the session itself. Written by Wayne Carson Thompson, composer of 'Always On My Mind,' this must be one of the shortest records to top the charts, clocking in at under two minutes. Moman said that between 1967 and 1971 over 100 hits were recorded at his studio and claimed that during one particular week there were 28 hits on the *Billboard* Hot 100 that had all been recorded at American – and all featured the same musicians.

Soul Man
Sam & Dave

Released August 1967
Stax *231* (U.S. #2) / Stax *601 023* (U.K. #24)

It's a well known rule of rock music that every anthem intended to celebrate rock'n'roll somehow manages to end up bereft of the musical qualities it is aimed to convey. However, 'Soul Man' perfectly conveyed the rousing passion, delightful brass work, and instant singlalongability of the best soul music. And it was not surprising, considering that the song was written by Isaac Hayes and Dave Porter and featured the impeccable backing of Booker T. & The MGs. On the other hand, the theory is probably blown to pieces by the fact that The Blues Brothers reputedly sold more copies of the song with their anodyne cover of 1979.

What A Wonderful World
Louis Armstrong

Released November 1967
ABC-Paramount *10982* (U.S.) / HMV *POP 1615* (U.K. #1)

If this was the only recording you ever heard by Louis Daniel Armstrong you could be forgiven for not realizing that he was one of the most important and influential musicians of the 20th century. At 66 years of age he became the oldest person to top the U.K. charts when 'What A Wonderful World' hit Number 1 early in 1968. (Of course, there's every possibility that Cliff Richard might beat this record – any time after June 2007.) There are many scholars who believe that popular music as we know it might not have existed without the pioneering vocal techniques of Louis Armstrong back in the 1920s.

Armstrong was no stranger to the charts, although his forays became somewhat more limited in the age of rock'n'roll. Some might describe 'Wonderful World' as a sentimental load of old bunkum, but it was especially written for Louis, and he loved it. A chart-topper in Britain, it comes as something of a surprise to discover that the 45 was not a hit on first release in America. This may have had something to do with the stringent Top 40 radio formatting that would have excluded such a middle-of-the-road performance, but the main reason was the fact that ABC Records chief Larry Newton hated the record and refused to have it promoted. It finally charted in the States after featuring in the 1987 movie *Good Morning Vietnam*, peaking at Number 32.

above > Aretha Franklin takes a break during a January 1969 recording session at Muscle Shoals Sound Studios in Alabama with arranger Arif Mardin (left) and engineer Tom Dowd (right).

Respect
Aretha Franklin

Released March 1967
Atlantic *2403* (U.S. #1) / Atlantic *584 115* (U.K. #10)

I Say A Little Prayer
Aretha Franklin

Released July 1968
Atlantic *2546* (U.S. #6) / Atlantic *584 206* (U.K. #4)

Aretha Franklin – or The Queen Of Atlantic Soul as she became known – scored a peerless run of hits during the mid to late 1960s. She made her first recordings as a gospel singer during the late 1950s before being signed by John Hammond to Columbia Records at the age of 18, in 1960. Hammond's attempts to push her as a blues singer failed, and she left the left the label six years later without a Top 30 hit to her name.

Franklin's fortunes changed in late 1966 when she found herself a new home at Atlantic Records and a behind-the-boards team that couldn't possibly fail: producer Jerry Wexler, who had worked with Wilson Pickett, Rufus Thomas, and Solomon Burke; engineer Tom Dowd, whose previous clients included everyone from John Coltrane to The Drifters; and arranger Arif Mardin, who went on to work with The Bee Gees and Dusty Springfield among others.

The remarkable metamorphosis in Franklin's sound – and her commercial appeal – was apparent from the outset with her first single for Atlantic, the U.S. Top 10 hit 'I Never Loved A Man (The Way I Love You).' That song was almost immediately overshadowed by its follow-up, however, a staggering rendition of Otis Redding's 'Respect.' Redding's 1965 original is still considered among the best Southern blues-soul records of the era, but Franklin took the song much further. She cut her version of 'Respect' on Valentines Day 1967 with her sisters Carolyn and Erma on backing vocals. Drummer Gene Chrisman, bassist Tommy Cogbill, pianist Dewey Oldham, and a trio of saxophonists provided the perfect musical backdrop, but the real masterstroke was Franklin's adaptation of the lyric for the unforgettable "R-E-S-P-E-C-T" refrain. The 45 shot to the top of the U.S. charts and into the U.K. Top 10.

Franklin then embarked on a mazy run of great singles, including 'Baby I Love You,' 'A Natural Woman (You Make Me Feel Like),' and 'Chain Of Fools.' The pick of the bunch, however, was 'I Say A Little Prayer.' Like 'Respect' it had already been a hit for another artist, Dionne Warwick, in the summer of 1967. But again, Franklin recorded the definitive version. Warwick's reading of the Burt Bacharach-Hal David song is fast and breezy, and indeed Bacharach considered it to be too fast – which explains why, as producer of the Franklin version, he gave the song a slower tempo and a jazz-soul arrangement, stripping it back to piano, bass, drums, and acoustic guitar. The vocal delivery is, as ever, flawless. 'I Say A Little Prayer' was twinned with the upbeat 'The House That Jack Built' as a double A-side single on its release in the U.S., while in the U.K. it was backed with 'See Saw.'

Time Of The Season
The Zombies

Released April 1968
Date *1628* (U.S. #3) / CBS *3380* (U.K.)

The Zombies burst to public prominence in 1964 with the transatlantic success of 'She's Not There,' but later their musical sophistication and silky electric organ runs seemed to fall out of favor with the record-buying public. By the time they came to cut this track to round off their album *Odessey And Oracle* they had tired of the commercial freefall and decided to split. 'Time Of The Season' saw The Zombies displaying unusual sensuality, with smooth but urgent instrumentation and singer Colin Blunstone asking to "give it to me easy." The words were completed by composer-keyboardist Rod Argent on the morning that the band came to rehearse the song for the first time and he had to send his colleagues down the pub while he added the final touches.

The recording session was conducted in an extremely fractious atmosphere. Thoughts were on the future, not on completing this contractual obligation. "The language was as extreme as you can imagine," said Blunstone. But perhaps this was as nothing compared to the language employed by people in and around The Zombies when the record was released later in the States, after the band's dissolution, and proceeded to march into the Top 3. Argent had already set up his own band and refused point blank to reform The Zombies and take advantage of the success, feeling it would be a step backwards. Bizarrely, while Argent stuck to his principles, a fake Zombies began playing gigs to fill the gap in the market.

Jumpin' Jack Flash
The Rolling Stones

Released May 1968
London *908* (U.S. #3) / Decca *F 12782* (U.K. #1)

'Jumpin' Jack Flash' is one of the Stones' greatest performances on record and marked a decisive return to form for the group in 1968 following a lengthy period in the musical wilderness. Its arrival highlighted a period of transition for the group: it was the first Stones recording produced by Jimmy Miller, but one of the last to feature founding member Brian Jones. The year before had been marred by a series of drug busts and, amid these legal problems, the Stones, like just about everybody else, had been attempting to compete with The Beatles' landmark *Sgt. Pepper* album. This resulted in *Their Satanic Majesties Request*, a pseudo-psychedelic mess with an expensive three-dimensional jacket illustration, put together while three Stones – Jagger, Richards, and Jones – were in and out of court and prison.

According to bass guitarist Bill Wyman, 'Jumpin' Jack Flash' was based upon a piano riff that he came up with after arriving early at rehearsals one day. Together with Charlie Watts and Brian Jones, he expanded the idea until Jagger and Richards arrived and exclaimed: "Keep playing that, and don't forget it – it sounds great!" The song soon came together, and Jagger wrote one of his most savage sets of lyrics, including the line: "I was raised by a toothless, bearded hag." Quite what his mother thought about this is unknown. Keith Richards has confirmed in interviews that 'Flash,' his favorite Stones song, was Wyman's idea. But the bassist never received a writer's credit for his efforts. He magnanimously admitted that he didn't worry about it at the time

because "the song only contributed to the band's continued success." However, in retrospect, he probably wishes he'd put his foot down and claimed his share of the royalties of one of the Stones' greatest songs.

Fire
The Crazy World Of Arthur Brown

Released June 1968
Atlantic *2556* (U.S. #2) / Track *604022* (U.K. #1)

Opening with a cry of "I am the God of hellfire," this was one of the more unlikely British Number 1 hits of the 1960s. The crazed vocal is matched by an insistent, apocalyptic Hammond organ and sharp bursts of trumpet. Although Brown was never able to repeat its success, this single was more than enough to earn him a place in pop history. He became notorious for his onstage antics, which included (seemingly) setting his head on fire and performing naked. Such behavior inspired countless other shock-rockers, from Alice Cooper to Marilyn Manson.

Hey Jude / Revolution
The Beatles

Released August 1968
Apple *2276* (U.S. #1) / Apple *R 5722* (U.K. #1)

Clocking in at over seven minutes, 'Hey Jude' became the first release on The Beatles' new Apple label. It is one of Paul McCartney's more soulful compositions – which explains a cover version by Wilson Pickett featuring Duane Allman on guitar – and was the group's first recording outside EMI's Abbey Road. Work on it did begin at EMI's studios until the group discovered that London's Trident studios had an 8-track recorder, whereas Abbey Road only had 4-track at the time. When EMI

heard about this they demanded the recording continue at Abbey Road, but because the machine at Trident was faulty, this proved impossible.

McCartney had written the song with John Lennon's son Julian in mind as he drove down to Lennon's home. The recording was made during sessions for the double *'White Album,'* during which George Harrison was playing answering phrases to McCartney's lines, something that annoyed the composer, who wanted to keep it simple. McCartney later recalled saying: "George, do us a favor, man. Don't play that. We'll have a solo later or something. But don't answer every phrase; it's going to get boring very soon."

'Revolution' was taped a couple of weeks before 'Hey Jude' and remains one of the band's most powerful recordings. Lennon had hoped his song would be the A-side, but as so often happened McCartney had come up with something better – and 'Hey Jude' was one of Lennon's favorite McCartney songs. The double-headed single became their most successful American 45, spending nine weeks at Number 1.

Abraham, Martin And John
Dion

Released October 1968
Laurie *3464* (U.S. #4) / London *HLP 10229* (U.K.)

Five years after his last chart entry, Dion returned, artistically rejuvenated, with this hymn to Abraham Lincoln, Martin Luther King, John F Kennedy (and Bobby Kennedy too, although he didn't make it into the title). The rock'n'roll and doo-wop styles of the Dion of old were replaced by an easy, mid-paced folk-rock groove, over which Dion's voice swoops and glides with characteristic grace. Dion hasn't had a hit since this, but he still records well-received albums. In 1970 Marvin Gaye slowed the song down and took it into the charts again.

Eloise
Barry Ryan

Released October 1968
Not issued U.S. / MGM *1442* (U.K. #2)

Paul and Barry Ryan were sons of Marion Ryan, who had scored a British hit single in 1958. As a duo the brothers had eight minor British hits of their own between 1965 and '67, before Paul volunteered for a backseat role, writing for his brother. The rearranged partnership scored a spectacular success with their first single, 'Eloise,' easily the Ryan family's biggest hit. An orchestral epic that sprawled well past the regulation three minutes, it pushed Ryan to the very edge of his rather limited vocal range and beyond, and the song ends with a fade-out over which the singer breaks down into near hysterics. British punks The Damned scored their biggest hit with a cover version in 1986.

Wichita Lineman
Glen Campbell

Released November 1968
Capitol *2302* (U.S. #3) / Ember *EMBS 261* (U.K. #7)

After scoring a Top 30 hit with 'By The Time I Get To Phoenix,' Glen Campbell contacted the song's composer, Jimmy Webb, with a request for a follow-up, suggesting that it too should have a place-name in the title. From such an apparently mercenary prompt came the second installment of a trilogy that, with another single, 'Galveston,' marked collectively one of the more haunting and subtle musical creations of the 1960s. The lonesome plight of the narrator, a telegraph-pole repairman, is underlined by Webb's organ work in a somehow vast and yet empty soundscape, alongside the memorable line: "And I need you more than want you / And I want you for all time."

JIMMY WEBB: PLAYING CHECKERS BY THE TREES

Songwriter Jimmy Webb was born in Elk City, Oklahoma, in 1946, the son of a minister. As a young man he worked for Jobete, Motown's music publishing company, and the first song of his to be recorded was a track on a Supremes Christmas album. His first hit was 'Up – Up And Away' a Top 10 hit for The 5th Dimension in the U.S., and The Johnny Mann Singers in Britain. The song is destined to be cued every time a TV show runs something about Superman.

That same year, Glen Campbell covered Webb's song 'By The Time I Get To Phoenix' and it made the U.S. Top 30. The cleft-jawed, wholesome artist was a simple man, as happy to record characterless versions of 'Dock Of The Bay' as sophisticated fare like 'Phoenix,' but Webb wasn't going to agonize about Campbell being little more than a cipher in the process. Among the other Webb songs Campbell released are 'Wichita Lineman and 'Galveston,' which, with 'Phoenix,' form a triumvirate of exquisite bleakness. (Campbell has said Webb told him all three were about the same character.)

The Association turned down a Webb song called 'Macarthur Park' and, in a bizarre move, Webb decided to ask his friend, the hard-drinking actor Richard Harris, to become a recording artist for this ornate and often effete extravaganza, boasting such risible lines as: "Someone left

the cake out in the rain / I don't think that I can take it / 'Cos it took so long to bake it / And I'll never have that recipe again." Yet the record often has a vast sweep and even majesty – one writer compared it to Gershwin's *Rhapsody In Blue* – and it was certainly an achievement to take a seven-minutes-plus record into the Top 3 in both the U.K. and U.S. charts in 1968. It should also be noted that at this point Webb was just 21 years old.

Webb has cited his song 'The Moon Is A Harsh Mistress,' recorded by several artists including Judy Collins and Joe Cocker, as a personal favorite, despite its harrowing subject matter: it concerns a manipulative married woman with whom the narrator embarks on an affair. His song 'Highwayman' was recorded by The Highwaymen – an illustrious line-up of Waylon Jennings, Willie Nelson, Johnny Cash, and Kris Kristofferson. Webb's creation was superbly appropriate to these peddlers of mythical outlaw tales and was a U.S. Country Number 1 in 1985. Meanwhile, Linda Ronstadt had a U.S. Adult Contemporary hit in 1990 with Webb's 'Adios.'

Webb's music became less orientated towards the hit parade as he turned his attention with increasing frequency to film, theatre, and TV scores and themes, but his imaginative and never simple music has regularly pointed to new possibilities for rock and pop.

Mrs. Robinson
Simon & Garfunkel

Released April 1968
Columbia *44511* (U.S. #1) / CBS *3443* (U.K. #4)

Although The Lovin' Spoonful had written two soundtracks by the time director Mike Nichols used Simon & Garfunkel's music as part of the score for *The Graduate*, it was the phenomenal commercial success of the resulting album that really kicked off the whole pop soundtrack industry. Previously, the idea of getting 'kids' who weren't classically trained to provide the mood-setting music for motion pictures was considered absurd.

Ironically, that soundtrack album was almost worthless. Nichols merely used previously-released Simon & Garfunkel records, with the exception of one new Paul Simon song, 'Mrs. Robinson.' And while the song is generally considered as great as any of the duo's other hits, the version you'll probably hear on the radio is not the one featured in the movie, which is a prototype version barely longer than a minute. Simon fleshed out the song for inclusion on *Bookends*, the Simon & Garfunkel album released simultaneously with *The Graduate* soundtrack.

The song began life as an instrumental for which Simon could not find words. Art Garfunkel suggested inserting the name of the film's main female character, and Simon developed that to include a memorable verse employing baseball star Joe DiMaggio as a symbol of America's turmoil. Another memorable feature of the hit version is the twining acoustic guitar figure that introduces the record and recurs pleasantly throughout. 'Mrs. Robinson' later served to break The Lemonheads when they released a power-pop version of the song in 1992.

Sunshine Of Your Love
Cream

Released February 1968
Atco *6544* (U.S. #5) / Polydor *56 286* (U.K. #25)

Cream and The Jimi Hendrix Experience were similar in that they were power trios with blues leanings and each had virtuoso musicians, so it's appropriate that 'Sunshine Of Your Love' was not only inspired by Hendrix, but influenced him too.

Cream bassist Jack Bruce devised the song's Kalashnikov riff specifically as a tribute to the guitarist after seeing the Experience in concert in London in 1967. Lyricist Pete Brown and guitarist Eric Clapton also got composer credits on this roaring anthem to romance. When Cream announced their split in 1969, Hendrix hijacked his appearance on Lulu's TV show to perform a tribute to them. He played 'Sunshine Of Your Love.'

Born To Be Wild
Steppenwolf

Released June 1968
Dunhill-ABC *4138* (U.S. #2) / Stateside *SS 8017* (U.K. #30)

Steppenwolf's frontman John Kay would never have made a biker. Always afflicted by bad eyesight, he was registered blind while still a young man. This didn't stop him from composing a song that became the anthem of leather-clad Harley Davidson owners all over America's highways. While Steppenwolf went on to enjoy a long career and a dozen further U.S. hits, most notably 'Magic Carpet Ride,' this staple of gold radio remains the one song of theirs that most people know. No disgrace in that, for 'Born To Be Wild' is a great record. It also gave a name to a new genre.

The song was written by Mars Bonfire, a.k.a. Dennis Edmonton, brother of Steppenwolf's drummer and a member of Sparrow. Edmonton found inspiration in a motorcycle poster bearing the legend Born To Ride. When he used the phrase "heavy metal thunder" to describe the roar of a motorcycle, his words passed into the language, so applicable did they seem to the menacing and distorted sounds then in vogue. The song portrays the motorcycle as transport for the man who refuses to be tied by straight society's chains. Kay's hedonistic vocal is given a smooth if throbbing ride by a bed of growling guitar and waves of organ. The song's anti-establishment credentials were cemented by its inclusion in the movie *Easy Rider* in 1969.

On The Road Again
Canned Heat

Released July 1968
Liberty *56038* (U.S. #16) / Liberty *LBS 15090* (U.K. #8)

On first hearing, 'On The Road Again' sounds like a simple collection of blues mannerisms. With repeated listens, however, the constituents come to seem collectively not a bag of clichés but a validation of the form. There's the 12-bar progression as old as the hills, the guitar and harp riff, the chugging melody that is almost not a melody at all but a sustained groove, and the blues lyrics' staple phrase, "One morning down the road I'm gone." Folky solo artist Katie Melua recorded a most unlikely cover version in 2005.

Suzie Q. (Part 1) / Suzie Q. (Part 2)
Creedence Clearwater Revival

Released September 1968
Fantasy *616* (U.S. #11) / Not issued U.K.

'Suzie Q' was the only Creedence hit not composed by John Fogerty; nonetheless, this four-man group's success was clearly down to one person. Sole writer, arranger, and producer of all the band's hits except this cover of a Dale Hawkins song, Fogerty had the voice and the guitar style that became the CCR trademark.

This is underlined by the sound of his later, more infrequent solo recordings, and the fact that the band's final studio album *Mardi Gras* was a relative flop. Known as 'Fogerty's Revenge,' it had songwriting duties split equally among the band. Rock critic Jon Landau described it as "the worst album by a major group that I have ever heard." This was a sad end for the band that had a string of nine million-selling singles in America in just 29 months.

They formed as The Blue Velvets in San Francisco in 1959, nowhere near the Mississippi delta that Fogerty liked to sing about so much. They became The Golliwogs on signing to Fantasy in 1964. Several hitless years followed until the end of 1967 when they became Creedence Clearwater Revival. Beginning with a mixture of covers and originals, Fogerty soon moved into top songwriting gear and delivered 'Proud Mary,' followed by 'Bad Moon Rising,' 'Green River,' 'Down On The Corner,' and a further five million-sellers (not to mention some great B-sides and album tracks). Creedence were the most successful band of the period, whether you measure them by sales or as a concert attraction. The only surprise was that in America their 45s always stranded at Number 2; they never enjoyed a U.S. Number 1 single.

Following the demise of the band in 1972, Fogerty discovered that not only had contractual obligations virtually robbed him of his songs, but also he was obliged to deliver a further eight albums to Fantasy. He refused to work under these conditions, and many years of legal battles and recriminations ensued between him and Fantasy boss Saul Zaentz.

Fogerty even refused to perform any of his Creedence hits for over 20 years because most of the money went to Zaentz. Finally, in the mid 1990s, he was able to sort out his legal difficulties and regained control of his songs – although the seemingly endless re-issues of Creedence material in the intervening years must surely have cost him several million dollars in lost earnings.

All Along The Watchtower
The Jimi Hendrix Experience

Released September 1968
Reprise *0767* (U.S. #20) / Track *604 025* (U.K. #5)

In Hendrix's pre-fame days his friends and acquaintances were amazed by his obsession with Bob Dylan. In an era when the idea of 'crossover' was little known, it seemed remarkable that a black kid should be so into a white artist. However, Hendrix was not interested in sociological ghettos. He loved Dylan's dazzling song-words – and he didn't do a bad pastiche in his own song, 'The Wind Cries Mary,' with lines such as: "After all the jacks are in their boxes / And the clowns have all gone to bed."

When Dylan returned to music after sitting out 1967 following his motorcycle accident, it was with the acoustic-flavored album *John Wesley Harding*, whose stand-out track 'All Along The Watchtower' summed up the record's tone of vague foreboding, right down to the way the song apparently ended on a cliff-hanger: "Two riders were approaching / The wind began to howl."

By the time The Jimi Hendrix Experience knuckled down to recording a version of the song at Olympic studios in London, covering Dylan songs was a lucrative tradition. But Hendrix was breaking the mold a little, because he was already successful as an artist with his own songs. He broke the mold of the song itself, too. Where Dylan's original was a finely detailed, sepia-toned sketch, Hendrix used big, bold brush strokes – power chords, castanets, and surround-sound production techniques – to create a dazzling alternative version. Dylan was so impressed that he started playing it like the Experience in concert.

Albatross
Fleetwood Mac

Released November 1968
Epic *10436* (U.S.) / Blue Horizon *57 3145* (U.K. #1)

Upon its release, 'Albatross' had few friends. "Peter Green's Fleetwood Mac are already too commercial and have lost their original guts," fulminated BBC Radio One DJ Mike Raven. His colleague John Peel played the B-side instead, while the BBC's *Top Of The Pops* TV chart show initially wouldn't give 'Albatross' a break.

It's not difficult to understand their surprise. Fleetwood Mac's eponymous first album was stuffed to the gills with 12-bar blues. They had quickly moved beyond covers, but tracks like the slinky 'Black Magic Woman' were still informed by the gritty spirit of the blues. By comparison the instrumental 'Albatross' sounded like background music for a wildlife documentary – for which purpose it has often been used subsequently. This tranquil meld of languorous guitar work and subtle cymbal washes was inspired by a combination of a 1950s oldie called 'Sleepwalk' by Santo & Johnny, the Coleridge poem *The Rime Of The Ancient Mariner*, which features an albatross that brings a curse down on sailors who kill it, and a group of notes from an Eric Clapton solo, although played more slowly.

The U.K. public did get a chance to hear 'Albatross' when *Top Of The Pops* needed something to play over the end credits nearly a month after the record's release, and as many as 60,000 orders were placed for the single in the next 24 hours. By Christmas it was Number 1 in Britain. No less than The Beatles were fans, borrowing its guitar work for *Abbey Road*'s 'Sun King.'

I Heard It Through The Grapevine
Marvin Gaye

Released November 1968
Tamla *54176* (U.S. #1) / Tamla Motown *TMG 686* (U.K. #1)

'Grapevine' was one of the greatest Motown singles, but it was recorded by a number of the label's other acts before Marvin Gaye released the definitive version. Written in 1967 by Norman Whitfield and Barrett Strong, the song had something of an uneasy gestation. Whitfield recorded it twice, with Smokey Robinson & The Miracles and The Isley Brothers, but neither version made it past Motown's stringent quality-control committee, which met on Fridays to decide if new songs were fit for release. Undeterred, Whitfield presented the song to Gaye, and spent most of April and May 1967 working on a new recording of the song with him.

This time, he gave 'Grapevine' a slower, spookier arrangement, built around voodoo drums, tense electric piano, and a nightmarish string arrangement, much more in keeping with its lyrical theme, the sudden realization of a romantic betrayal. As on many of the great Motown records of the 1960s, the bulk of the instrumentation was provided by the label's peerless house band, The Funk Brothers. Gaye's wounded vocal is pitched just outside his normal register, giving it a suitably raw edge. Set against him are the sweet, soothing tones of The Andantes: Jackie Hicks, Marlene Barrow, and Louvain Demps.

It seems inconceivable now, but this version too failed to impress when first aired at a quality-control meeting. Motown head Berry Gordy was by now sick of the song, but Whitfield persevered, taking it next to Gladys Knight & The Pips. Their version recast the song – somewhat dubiously – as an upbeat, pop-gospel number, in the manner of Aretha Franklin's recent U.S. hit 'Respect.' It climbed to Number 2 on the *Billboard* Hot 100 at the tail end of 1967 and spent six weeks on top of the R&B chart.

Despite turning 'Grapevine' into a big hit, Whitfield still felt that Gaye's tortured reading of the song better captured its mood and throughout 1968 continued to pressure Gordy to release it. The Motown boss eventually relented, agreeing to its inclusion on Gaye's *In The Groove* album but not to its issue as a single. He thought that, having recently been a hit for Knight, it was unlikely that it would do so well so soon for Gaye. But when the album was sent out to radio stations, 'Grapevine' was the most played and most requested song, forcing Gordy to release it against his better judgment. Lo and behold, it was an instant smash hit, spending seven weeks on top of the *Billboard* pop singles chart in December 1968 and January 1969, and reached Number 1 in Britain too. It was, until the release of The Jackson 5's 'I'll Be There' in 1970, the most successful Motown single ever.

With what remains the definitive reading in the can and at the top of the charts, Whitfield still found it necessary to cut the song again, with both The Temptations, in 1969, and The Undisputed Truth, in 1971. Neither comes close to Gaye's version, however, and nor do the many subsequent covers by artists as diverse as Credence Clearwater Revival and The Slits.

I'm Gonna Make You Love Me
Diana Ross & The Supremes & The Temptations

Released November 1968
Motown *1137* (U.S. #2) / Tamla Motown *TMG 685* (U.K. #3)

In 1968 Motown hit upon the financially lucrative idea of teaming up The Supremes, whose fans were mostly white, with The Temptations, who had a largely black following. This came as a welcome reunion for the two groups, who both hailed from Detroit and had worked together regularly, pre-fame, in the early 1960s. 'I'm Gonna Make You Love Me' was originally a hit on Mercury Records in 1967 for Dee Dee Warwick (little sister of Dionne) and as such marked one of the first occasions that Motown put out a record not written by one of the label's own songwriting stable. It was the biggest of several hits for the Supremes-Temptations pairing and was only stopped from hitting the Number 1 spot in the U.S. by Marvin Gaye's colossal 'I Heard It Through The Grapevine.' In 1970 The Supremes repeated the trick alongside The Four Tops, with whom they dueted on 'River Deep – Mountain High.'

(Sittin' On) The Dock Of The Bay
Otis Redding

Released January 1968
Volt *157* (U.S. #1) / Stax *601 031* (U.K. #3)

On December 6, 1967, Otis Redding began a two-day recording session at Stax Records in Memphis, Tennessee, which was intended to launch an ambitious new phase of his career. Earlier hits such as 'Respect' and 'Fa-Fa-Fa-Fa-Fa (Sad Song)' had established him alongside Wilson Pickett as America's premier hard R&B vocalist, but 'Dock Of The Bay' was planned as the first of his new black folk songs. "Otis and I spent a lot of time talking about his image," said Al Bell, then vice president of Stax Records. "We started moving him into some kind of black folk-singer image, which might advance him to where we would get more than just Southern black radio play."

The idea for the song had come to Otis while he was staying on a houseboat in Sausalito, California. "When he brought it to Memphis," remembered Stax house-band guitarist Steve Cropper, "it had this little intro and about one verse. He said, 'What do you think of this?' And I said, 'It's great.'" Much as he liked it, Cropper had reservations. "It had no R&B in it whatsoever. I thought it might even be detrimental." Redding remained adamant that the song would be a big hit. But before it could be released he died when his plane crashed into the icy waters of Lake Monoma in Wisconsin. Three months later, 'Dock Of The Bay' became America's first posthumous Number 1 single, proving Redding right and going on to win two Grammys.

1968

I've Gotta Get A Message To You
The Bee Gees

Released August 1968
Atco *6603* (U.S. #8) / Polydor *56 273* (U.K. #1)

Barry, Robin, and Maurice Gibb have one of the richest back-catalogues in pop music history. Their songs are regularly recorded by new artists and appreciated by new generations, and seem set to do so for many years to come. They have certainly had a see-saw career, with more comebacks than Frank Sinatra. From reaching the mountain-top after the *Saturday Night Fever* movie in the late 1970s they found themselves virtually ostracized in the disco backlash that followed. American radio stations even promoted 'No Bee Gees' weekends.

Following their first string of hits, including 'New York Mining Disaster 1941,' 'To Love Somebody,' '(The Night The Lights Went Out In) Massachusetts,' and 'Words,' and shortly after 'I've Gotta Get A Message To You,' the egos began to clash. Perhaps this was the price of fame at such an early age – Barry was 21, twins Robin and Maurice just 19 – and the brothers parted temporarily. Robin was 'persuaded' to pursue a solo career. Barry and Maurice continued as a duo, but the magic was gone, and the three soon realized that their greatest strength lay in writing and performing together. By this time, however, their popularity had waned, and there followed some lean years in the early 1970s, culminating in the rejection of an entire album of material by their record company in 1974.

'I've Gotta Get A Message' was a somewhat unusual song, about a man awaiting his execution, and was recorded the same day it was written. In a contemporary interview, Robin Gibb explained that the song was about someone who has "killed a man who's been carrying on with his wife, and he wants to get a message to her before he dies." That the subject bordered on the distasteful did not seem to bother the record-buying public, and the single became the group's second British Number 1.

Dream A Little Dream Of Me
Mama Cass With The Mamas & The Papas

Released July 1968
Dunhill *4145* (U.S. #12) / RCA *1726* (U.K. #11)

Recorded in the midst of the demise of The Mamas And The Papas, 'Dream A Little Dream Of Me' originally featured on the group's fourth and final album but was re-credited by the Dunhill label as the debut single release of its new solo star. Arranged and produced by the group's manager, Lou Adler, the song is remembered for its lilting vocal melody, but it also bears the influence of musique concrète. Cass's voice emerges from a collage of disparate sounds – bass and flute alongside crashing waves and radio tuning – before it is eventually whisked away, and up the charts, by what sounds like a Hawaiian bar band.

Everyday People
Sly & The Family Stone

Released November 1968
Epic *10407* (U.S. #1) / Direction *58 3938* (U.K. #36)

'Everyday People' was the first of three U.S. Number 1 hits for Sly and delivered on the promise of the same year's 'Dance To The Music,' showcasing a sound that mixed evangelical soul with psychedelic funk. As well as spending four weeks atop the *Billboard* singles chart, 'Everyday People' inspired a whole host of other musicians, particularly Motown producer Norman Whitfield, who would give The Temptations' *Cloud Nine* a similarly widescreen, genre-bending sheen. The success of the single helped cement Sly & The Family Stone's position as the first hit act with a fully racially-integrated line-up, while the group's Larry Graham maintained that it features the first example of 'slap bass' playing on a record.

Son-Of-A Preacher Man
Dusty Springfield

Released November 1968
Atlantic *2580* (U.S. #10) / Philips *BF 1730* (U.K. #9)

It was Dusty's recording of one of Carole King's songs, 'Some Of Your Lovin',' that attracted the attention of legendary producer and founder of Atlantic Records, Ahmet Ertegun, and since her U.S contract with Philips had expired he was eager to sign her. Ertegun arranged for her to record at American Studios in Memphis, and Dusty was put together with production godfathers Arif Mardin, Jerry Wexler, and Tom Dowd to record what is without doubt her finest album, *Dusty In Memphis*.

'Son-Of-A Preacher Man' was first offered to Aretha Franklin, but the Queen of Soul apparently turned it down on the grounds of the somewhat risqué lyrics. Ms. Franklin was herself the daughter of a preacher man. After Dusty's version had become a hit, Franklin later changed her mind and recorded the song.

The sessions in Memphis weren't without problems. When Wexler first met Dusty to present the material that he had gathered for her to record, she turned down everything and promptly returned to London. This was not unusual for the often moody vocalist, and having gathered her thoughts she returned some weeks later in a more enthusiastic frame of mind. Dusty was also used to performing her vocals after the musicians had cut the finished instrumental tracks, though this was not the system at American Studios, where vocalists and musicians normally worked together. Dusty stood her ground, and while she was present at the Memphis sessions, she recorded her vocals later at Atlantic's studio in New York City.

Hooked On A Feeling
B.J. Thomas

Released November 1968
Scepter *12230* (U.S. #5) / Pye International *7N 25481* (U.K.)

Thomas was a highly successful artist in America with a string of hits between 1966 and 1977, most of which were recorded at American Studios in Memphis and produced by Chips Moman. It was a hotbed of activity, particularly in the late 1960s, and there was plenty of songwriting talent around to deliver hit material.

'Hooked' was written by Mark James, who composed Elvis Presley's 'Suspicious Minds,' and features an appealing guitar-sitar sound, becoming a U.S. Number 5 for Thomas early in 1969. Though not a hit in Britain, it was revived there in 1971 by eccentric pop personality Jonathan King, who introduced the "ooga-choogas" later used by Swedish outfit Blue Swede who covered the song in 1974 and were rewarded with a surprise American Number 1. (The same week that Blue Swede reached the top, Abba won the Eurovision Song Contest in Britain, marking a great seven days for Swedish pop.) That might have been the end of the story, but the song enjoyed a revival many years later when it featured in the popular TV series *Ally McBeal* for some notorious 'dancing baby' sequences.

Je T'aime … Moi Non Plus
Jane Birkin & Serge Gainsbourg

Released July 1969
Fontana *TF 1042* (U.S.) / Major Minor *MM 645* (U.K. #1)

While it may sound as if Jane Birkin and Serge Gainsbourg are having a fairly good time in the studio recording this song, in fact they were in separate booths, and the decadent piece wasn't recorded in France, either, but in a studio in central London. Gainsbourg had originally recorded this erotic little number with his previous beau, Brigitte Bardot, a couple of years before, and that recording was reputed to be the real thing. However, after some persuasion from Bardot's husband, the 'session' remained unreleased. In the meantime Gainsbourg met Jane Birkin while making a movie in France, and once they became lovers it didn't take him long to persuade her to record the song anew with him.

Released in Britain on the Fontana label it was, not surprisingly, immediately banned by the BBC. A breathless Birkin (who definitely hadn't just dashed back from the drugstore with a pack of Gitanes for Serge) was serenaded by muttered sweet-nothings from Gainsbourg that few in Britain understood, though they certainly got the picture. The ensuing publicity helped the record sell quickly, and before long it had reached Number 2. At this point, Fontana suddenly woke up to the record's risqué content and swiftly removed it from their catalogue. Following Fontana's withdrawal … an independent label, Major Minor, took over the rights and the record returned to the charts, this time going all the way to Number 1 in Britain. In America, where airplay was even more restricted, the recording appropriately rose no higher than number soixante-neuf (69).

Saved By The Bell
Robin Gibb

Released July 1969
Atco *6698* (U.S.) / Polydor *56337* (U.K. #2)

In February 1969 The Bee Gees were two years into their first run of hits when Robin Gibb split from his brothers Maurice and Barry over a dispute about which song should be the band's next single. Polite sniping in the music press ensued, while Robin Gibb quickly plunged into life as a solo artist, taking this self-penned ballad to the upper reaches of the British and German singles charts.

The record is notable not only as an example of just how epic a pop song could get with an orchestra behind it, but also for the first use of an electronic drum machine on a hit record. You can clearly hear the primitive device chugging away under Gibb's trademark vibrato and the lush strings. It was a quietly revolutionary moment that passed unnoticed at the time, but by the 1980s the drum machine would be an accepted and significant part of the pop musician's musical palette.

After this strong start, Gibb's career faltered. He released an intriguing and highly original solo album, *Robin's Reign*, that failed commercially, although it has since attracted a cult following. Another was recorded and left unreleased, but has since leaked onto the internet. In 1971 Gibb rejoined his brothers in The Bee Gees for a few years in the commercial doldrums before disco gave them a new lease on life.

In The Year 2525 (Exordium & Terminus)
Zager & Evans

Released June 1969
RCA *0174* (U.S. #1) / RCA *1860* (U.K. #1)

In 1968, Denny Zager and Rick Evans were a folk-rock duo scratching a living in the finest motel lounges of Lincoln, Nebraska. "We were looking for up-tempo material," recalled Zager some years later, "because most of the stuff we did was ballads." Serendipitously, Evans had spent an entire 30 minutes knocking up the apocalyptic sci-fi epic 'In The Year 2525' four years earlier, but his previous band, The Eccentrics, wouldn't record it. Released on local label Truth Records in 1968, it attracted the attention of RCA, who sold a million copies within two months and four million overall. "We tried everything to come up with that second hit," said Zager, "but it never happened."

Marrakesh Express
Crosby Stills & Nash

Released July 1969
Atlantic *2652* (U.S. #28) / Atlantic *584 283* (U.K. #17)

He Ain't Heavy, He's My Brother
The Hollies

Released September 1969
Epic *10532* (U.S. #7) / Parlophone *R 5806* (U.K. #3)

Graham Nash left The Hollies in December 1968 in disagreement over the proposed recording of a collection of Dylan covers (which they later recorded as *Hollies Sing Dylan*) and their alleged rejection of his own song 'Marrakesh Express.' Nash had made a number of new friends in America, more in keeping with his own musical ambitions. David Crosby had been a fan of Nash's harmony vocals for some time, and in June 1968, while The Hollies were touring America, he had taken Nash to meet Stephen Stills.

Crosby and Stills sang a new Stills composition, 'You Don't Have To Cry,' to Nash, and after just two listens the Hollie instinctively added a third harmony. Apparently the three then looked at each other in disbelief. Nash described the moment as "nothing short of musical magic." Purely by accident they had discovered a unique harmony sound that became the hallmark of Crosby Stills & Nash, initially heard by many music fans on CSN's first hit, 'Marrakesh Express.'

Nash was replaced in The Hollies by former Escorts and Swinging Blue Jeans guitarist Terry Sylvester, and the group's chart success continued, despite Nash's departure. 'He Ain't Heavy, He's My Brother' hit in 1969, featuring Elton John on piano. The song was also a U.S chart entry for Neil Diamond, in 1970, and eventually made number 1 for The Hollies in Britain in 1988 after featuring in a TV advertisement for beer.

I Want You Back
The Jackson 5

Released November 1969
Motown *1157* (U.S. #1) / Tamla Motown *TMG 724* (U.K. #2)

The fact has now been obscured by the headline-guzzling train-wreck of Michael Jackson's private life and the multi-platinum success of his solo career, but the names of Jermaine, Jackie, Michael, Marlon, and Tito Jackson once collectively tripped off the tongue of young record purchasers worldwide. The Jackson 5 were a phenomenon: their first four singles went to the top of the U.S. chart and they spawned their own cartoon series.

It was a phenomenon that was very important to Motown. The label had just lost Holland-Dozier-Holland in a dispute about royalty rates. While no one songwriting team is bigger than a label, Motown supremo Berry Gordy was clearly stung by their defection, and gained an injunction preventing them from working elsewhere. He pointedly depersonalized the songwriting and production credits on this Jackson 5 debut – "The Corporation," read the label – lest these workers also became too big for their boots.

In fact Deke Richards, Fonce Mizel, and Freddie Perren were the creative team behind 'I Want You Back,' originally written for Gladys Knight & The Pips. Gordy, once a songwriter himself, wasn't satisfied with lyric or arrangement. The words were overhauled and the key lowered. The result was a passionate declaration of regret at a fractured relationship, plainly absurd from such children. But listeners ceased to think about that once they heard the utter commitment in main lead-singer Michael's voice and witnessed the preternaturally slick dance routines of the combo on TV.

Honky Tonk Women
Rolling Stones

Released July 1969
London *910* (U.S. #1) / Decca *F 12952* (U.K. #1)

When Keith Richards discovered Ry Cooder's open-G guitar tuning it opened up a whole new box of tricks for the Stones guitarist, first demonstrated here. As well as being Mick Taylor's first performance with the band, it was in fact his audition. Brian Jones, though officially not yet out of the band, was not present on June 1, 1969, when former John Mayall guitarist Taylor arrived. The band listened to some playbacks, did some mixing, and then at around 11:00pm began recording.

After a few rehearsals, producer Jimmy Miller sat at the drums and demonstrated to Charlie Watts what he thought would be a suitable rhythm. By 4:00am the following day the track was complete (Miller added the distinctive cowbell). Jones officially left the group shortly afterwards – and was was found dead in his swimming pool only a month later.

The B-side, 'You Can't Always Get What You Want,' was one of the group's most unusual tracks, featuring the London Bach Choir and an orchestration by former Phil Spector arranger Jack Nitzsche, alongside keyboards played by Al Kooper. This would be the Stones' last single for Decca before they signed a new custom deal with Atlantic. The degree of animosity between the Stones and Decca is best revealed by their parting of the ways when their contract expired in 1970: with one final single owing to the company, they delivered the un-releasable 'Cocksucker Blues.'

Whole Lotta Love
Led Zeppelin

Released November 1969
Atlantic *45-2690* (U.S. #4) / Not issued U.K.

Had this book been restricted to singles released only in an artist's home territory then Led Zeppelin would not feature in it at all. In an era when a band could gain kudos by spurning singles – which at the time were beginning to be seen by rock's maturing audience as kid's fodder – they made sure that no Zeppelin 45 ever came out in Britain.

Vocalist Robert Plant had learned the song after seeing The Small Faces play in his native Midlands. Their 'You Need Loving' was a rip-off of bluesman Willie Dixon's lustful song 'You Need Love.' When Zeppelin guitarist Jimmy Page presented Plant with a brilliant, instantly memorable guitar riff, the singer lashed the Dixon-Small Faces song onto it – although it wasn't until 1985 that Dixon's daughter brought the steal to his attention.

Whatever the moral dubiousness of Zeppelin's plagiarism, it can't be doubted that they added profoundly to what they appropriated: not just through Page's riff but the characteristic collective muscle and swagger with which they rendered the song. Radio stations began playing a version that omitted the lengthy instrumental middle section (and Plant's vaguely embarrassing orgasm sounds) and Atlantic Records promptly created their own radio-edit version. Almost as if God were mocking Zeppelin for their hold-out on U.K. singles, the song would achieve a bizarre afterlife as the theme tune to Britain's *Top Of The Pops* TV chart show.

Israelites
Desmond Dekker & The Aces

Released February 1969
Uni *55129* (U.S. #9) / Pyramid *PYR 6058* (U.K. #1)

Leslie Kong, one of the great early reggae producers, was a Chinese-Jamaican ice-cream café proprietor turned record producer. Desmond Dekker composed 'Poor Me Israelite' while out walking in the park one afternoon. Overhearing a couple arguing about money, an opening line came into his mind, "Get up in the morning slaving for bread," and by the time he'd walked home he had the whole song worked out.

The song was originally released in Jamaica in 1968 as 'Poor Me Israelite' and was only a small local hit, but it attracted some dance-floor attention in Britain. Graeme Goodall released the record there on his Pyramid Records, but was told by the BBC after just one broadcast that the record was too badly produced for further radio plays. So Goodall had the tapes sent over from Jamaica and remixed the track, shortening the title to 'Israelites.' The BBC then agreed to play the new version and it immediately took off.

It hit the British charts in March 1969 and launched a big wave of reggae popularity. The music was adopted by skinheads, who wore braces (suspenders) and boots and liked to look for some 'bovver,' or trouble. Dekker remains one of the most popular Jamaican artists of all time in Britain, and a re-recording of the song went Top 10 again there in 1975.

One of the most popular reggae tracks of all time, the song is in fact a blues, a cry of despair for survival, and was the first truly international reggae hit. (Johnny Nash's hits of the previous year were in the rock-steady style, and while they were recorded in Jamaica, Nash was from Texas.)

The Boxer
Simon & Garfunkel

Released April 1969
Columbia *44785* (U.S. #7) / CBS *4162* (U.K. #6)

They say the devil has all the best songs but, just occasionally, inspiration can come from a more elevated plane. Paul Simon has claimed that much of the lyric of 'The Boxer' came about because "I was reading the Bible around that time. That's where phrases such as 'workman's wages' came from, and 'seeking out the poorer quarters.'"

Simon & Garfunkel had enjoyed hits since 1965, but the runaway success of the infectiously upbeat 'Mrs. Robinson,' boosted by its use in the 1968 movie *The Graduate*, had brought them unprecedented levels of fame. 'The Boxer,' with its rippling guitar and melancholic lyric, was an unlikely follow-up but is arguably their quintessential musical statement. The elegant synthesizer solo and the dramatic percussive slaps are remarkably innovative touches in an arrangement that evolves like a flower opening in a stop-motion film, each new element blending in unobtrusively as the verses rise and fall around the "lie-la-lie" vocal hook.

This was remarkably cerebral pop, far too metaphysically inclined to have any hope of matching the success of 'Mrs. Robinson,' but then that's exactly what Paul Simon intended. "I think the song was about me," he said. "Everybody's beating me up, and I'm telling you now I'm going to go away if you don't stop." It didn't even make the Top 5 in

Billboard, floundering at Number 7. A year later, the melodramatic gospel schmaltz of 'Bridge Over Troubled Water' would restore them to Number 1, becoming their signature song and, regrettably, eclipsing 'The Boxer.'

Aquarius–Let The Sunshine In (The Flesh Failures)
The 5th Dimension

Released February 1969
Soul City *772* (U.S. #1) / Liberty *LBF 15193* (U.K. #11)

This vocal quintet based in Los Angeles had their first major hit a couple of years earlier with 'Up – Up And Away,' giving songwriter Jimmy Webb his first Top 10 single and enough royalties to purchase his first piano. The group also helped to popularize the songs of contemporary writer Laura Nyro. Their biggest worldwide hit was this medley of two songs from the hippie musical *Hair* which had opened on Broadway in 1968. Notorious for its explicit language and on-stage nudity, *Hair* also supplied hits for Oliver with 'Good Morning Starshine' and Nina Simone performing 'Ain't Got No – I Got Life.' Husband-and-wife Dimension members Marilyn McCoo and Billy Davis Jr. had a 1977 Number 1 with 'You Don't Have To Be A Star (To Be In My Show).'

Get Back
The Beatles With Billy Preston

Released April 1969
Apple *2490* (U.S. #1) / Apple *R 5777* (U.K. #1)

This song, which briefly gave its name to the project in which The Beatles attempted to return to the days of no overdubs, marked a couple of rarities. One was the unique co-credit given to elegant keyboardist Billy Preston. The other was a switching of roles by Lennon and Harrison. While Lennon's lead guitar work was rather watery, Harrison's brilliant rhythm guitar gave the track a rock solid, razor sharp groove that helped to prove the intended point that, ornate masterpieces like *Sgt. Pepper* notwithstanding, The Beatles were still at heart a fabulous rock'n'roll band.

Space Oddity
David Bowie

Released July 1969
Mercury *72949* (U.S.) / Philips *BF 1801* (U.K. #5)

Released to coincide with Neil Armstrong's giant leap for mankind, 'Space Oddity' gave David Bowie his first U.K. hit single, launching a career that continues into the 21st century. The lead track from his second album, 'Space Oddity' was Bowie's first release for Philips/Mercury following several years of unsuccessful recordings for the Deram label. George Martin turned down the opportunity to produce the single, as did Tony Visconti (who went on to make numerous albums with Bowie). Visconti considered 'Space Oddity' to be too gimmicky and handed it over to his assistant, Gus Dudgeon, who cut the single with Bowie on June 20, 1969, at Trident Studios in London, England. It was rush-released just three weeks later, in time for the Apollo 11 moon landing.

'Space Oddity' is one of Bowie's finest narrative songs, spinning a tale over its five minutes about an astronaut, Major Tom, who gets lost – perhaps intentionally – on an intergalactic mission. Driven by Bowie's acoustic guitar, the song leaps from slow, atmospheric verses through soaring choruses and several instrumental breaks. The other musicians include noted session bassist Herbie Flowers and keyboardist Rick Wakeman, who went on to join the progressive rock group Yes. Bowie plays a Stylophone on the song, a tiny, oscillating keyboard sold mostly as a children's toy. Bowie and the single benefited from his appearance in press ads for the instrument around the time of the release of 'Oddity.'

What really helped push the single up the U.K. charts, however, was the BBC's decision to use the song during its coverage of the moon landing. 'Space Oddity' remained a favorite both of its author and his audience. The single returned to the British charts in 1975, to make Number 1, and in the U.S. two years earlier had reached Number 15. Bowie returned to the Major Tom character for his 1980 U.K. Number 1 hit 'Ashes To Ashes' and on the 1995 single, 'Hello Spaceboy.'

Something In The Air
Thunderclap Newman

Released May 1969
Track 2656 (U.S. #37) / Track 604 031 (U.K. #1)

This trio escaped the one-hit wonder tag by earning a week at Number 46 for the follow-up to this British chart-topper in the summer of 1969. They had got to know Pete Townshend after vocalist Speedy Keen's composition 'Armenia City In The Sky' opened The Who's Sell Out album in 1968. Townshend produced and played bass guitar as 'Bijou Drains' on 'Something In The Air,' originally titled 'Revolution.' But as John Lennon had already done that, Townshend gave the song its new title, and his involvement generated the necessary publicity to send it all the way to Number 1 in Britain, complete with magical piano interludes by Andy Newman.

A Boy Named Sue
Johnny Cash

Released July 1969
Columbia 44944 (U.S. #2) / CBS 4460 (U.K. #4)

That 'A Boy Named Sue' sounds unlike anything else in Johnny Cash's generally brooding canon is down to the fact that it was written by Shel Silverstein, the gifted but comedy-inclined composer of, among others, 'The Cover Of Rolling Stone' and 'Freakin' At The Freakers Ball.' His 'Boy Named Sue' is the tale of a man who grows up mean because of the ridicule inspired by his feminine name – which doesn't make sense. Why doesn't he just change it? But it provides some good laughs. Cash recorded it at San Quentin prison and does a remarkable job, considering that he was reading the unfamiliar lyric from a sheet of paper.

Sugar Sugar
The Archies

Released July 1969
Calendar 1008 (U.S. #1) / RCA 1872 (U.K. #1)

Music publishing mogul Don Kirshner, who masterminded the songs for The Monkees, was somewhat embittered when that manufactured quartet deprived him of a share of their profit by deciding to write their own songs. Reasoning that cartoons don't have egos, he invented The Archies, an animated TV series based on a popular comic book, and supplied songs for that instead. A guaranteed party floor-filler, 'Sugar Sugar,' written by Jeff Barry and Andy Kim, was performed by top-notch studio sessioneers, including vocalist Ron Dante, who around the same time was in the U.S. Top 10 singing lead on 'Tracy' by The Cuff Links. 'Sugar Sugar,' the best-selling single of 1969, remains the definitive bubblegum hit.

Everybody's Talkin'
Nilsson

Released August 1969
RCA 0161 (U.S. #6) / RCA 1876 (U.K. #23)

Nilsson had spent many years as a successful songwriter, with his compositions covered by the likes of Three Dog Night, The Yardbirds, and The Monkees, so it was somewhat ironic that his debut hit was written by someone else. The reclusive folk-rock innovator Fred Neil composed 'Everybody's Talkin'' and was the first to record it. Neil retired from music in the early 1970s, funded for the rest of his life by the proceeds from the song, which has been much covered.

An insouciant shrug-of-the-shoulders of a record, Nilsson's version was taken at a faster pace than Neil's original, and had more pop appeal. It was chosen for inclusion on the soundtrack of the Dustin Hoffman movie Midnight Cowboy, which helped the single into both the U.S. and U.K. charts. It has remained lodged in pop's collective consciousness ever since and in the U.S. it remains one of the most-played singles on oldies radio. A few year's later, Nilsson scored a second big hit with a cover version, 'Without You,' written by two members of British band Badfinger.

Is That All There Is?
Peggy Lee

Released September 1969
Capitol *2602* (U.S. #11) / Capitol *CL 15614* (U.K.)

Written by Jerry Leiber and Mike Stoller, this magnificent single proved that they and the song's vocalist, Peggy Lee, could still cut it, well after their 1950s heyday. Although Lee had recently recorded well-chosen covers of songs by such contemporary songwriters as Jimmy Webb and Carole King, 'Is That All There Is?' is far removed from the rock-orientated sounds of the time. Against a backdrop of delicate piano and whimsical orchestrations, arranged and conducted by Randy Newman, Lee offers a suitably lugubrious vocal performance that ponders whether there is any more to life. If there isn't, she concludes, we should "break out the booze and have a ball." It was the only one of her recordings to win her a Grammy, for Best Contemporary Vocal Performance, although in 1995 she was given a Lifetime Achievement Award.

Suspicious Minds
Elvis Presley

Released August 1969
RCA *47 9764* (U.S. #1) / RCA *1900* (U.K. #2)

Aside from his early recordings at RCA's Nashville studios, the few weeks that Presley spent at the American Sound Studios in Memphis during January and February 1969 must rate as the most rewarding and productive of his career. It was the first time Elvis had recorded in a Memphis studio since his pre-RCA days at Sun in 1955.

'Suspicious Minds' was recorded between 4:00 and 7:00am on the last day of the first ten-day session and was considered the song with the biggest hit potential. The basic track took just four takes, although it was many months until the song was released, mainly due to a lengthy dispute over the publishing royalties. As was the custom with the Presley organization, Freddie Bienstock, who looked after Elvis Presley Music, demanded a cut of the publishing rights, but there was no way that songwriter Mark James was going to agree to a royalty split.

It was a lengthy conflict, and consequently 'Suspicious Minds' didn't appear on the original *From Elvis In Memphis* album. Under normal circumstances the song might never have been released at all. However, all were agreed that the recording was the highlight of the sessions, and once Elvis began performing it at his summer appearances at the Las Vegas Hilton, it was finally released in August 1969. Following the Number 3 success of 'In The Ghetto' (recorded in Memphis two days before 'Suspicious Minds') Elvis was on a roll, and the record became his first American Number 1 record for seven years, and the last in his lifetime. In a 2002 poll by the *New Musical Express*, readers voted it the best Elvis song of all time.

My Way
Frank Sinatra

Released March 1969
Reprise *0817* (U.S. #27) / Reprise *RS 20817* (U.K. #5)

Although Frank Sinatra's years with Capitol during the 1950s were the most productive and successful of his career, in 1961 he established his own record label, Reprise, and enjoyed continuing chart success throughout the decade. However, 'My Way' would be his last American hit single for 11 years and preceded the first of his endless retirements. With this in mind, Sinatra had long been trying to persuade Paul Anka to compose an appropriate song, and Anka came up with the goods while on holiday in France. There he heard the song 'Comme d'Habitude' by Claude François and, recognizing the potential in the melody, he bought the rights and composed a new English lyric with Sinatra in mind.

Recorded December 30, 1968, in Hollywood, 'My Way' was released the following spring and soon became a big hit in Britain, although in America it only reached Number 27. Though latter-day Sinatra fans often cite 'My Way' as their favorite, Ol' Blue Eyes himself grew to hate the song that became his signature tune. It was infamously covered by Sid Vicious and The Sex Pistols in 1978, but David Bowie had tried his hand at a translation of the French original before Anka. Bowie wrote his version in 1968 and titled it 'Even A Fool Learns To Love,' but it was never released and may not even have been recorded, although Bowie's lyrics have become available on various internet sites.

Funky Drummer (Part 1)
James Brown

....

Released February 1970
King *6290* (U.S.) / Not issued U.K.

Get Up (I Feel Like Being Like A) Sex Machine (Part 1)
James Brown

....

Released July 1970
King *6318* (U.S. #15) / Polydor *2001 071* (U.K. #32)

James Brown's recorded output in the 1960s and 1970s was prodigious by anybody's standards. In 1969 alone he released 15 singles and five albums, including the landmark 'Say It Loud – I'm Black And I'm Proud.' While he wasn't quite so prolific in 1970, the year did throw up a pair of epochal singles, both among the most important recordings of his career.

Cut on November 20th, 1969, in Cincinnati, Ohio, 'Funky Drummer' was one of Brown's last recordings with his backing group The Famous Flames. While the song itself isn't as instantly memorable as some of his earlier hits, the drum break – played by Clyde Stubblefield – has become one of the most sampled beats in hip-hop and electronic music. Everyone from Public Enemy to TLC and The Beastie Boys to Vanilla Ice has built a rhythm track out of Stubblefield's funky drumming.

By the summer of 1970 Brown had disbanded The Famous Flames and put together a new group, The JB's, with a membership that included future funk legend Bootsy Collins. The new group's first release was the breathtaking 'Get Up (I Feel Like Being Like A) Sex Machine,' driven by Collins's extraordinary bass playing and his brother Catfish's slick guitar licks. Both Collins brothers were also integral members of George Clinton's groups Parliament and Funkadelic. 'Sex Machine' provided Brown with his first U.K. hit since 'It's A Man's Man's Man's World' back in 1966, and the disc paved the way for almost every funk record of the 1970s.

Give Me Just A Little More Time
Chairmen Of The Board

Released January 1970
Invictus 9074 (U.S. #3) / Invictus INV 501 (U.K. #3)

Band Of Gold
Freda Payne

Released April 1970
Invictus 9075 (U.S. #3) / Invictus INV 502 (U.K. #1)

Holland-Dozier-Holland, the songwriting and production engine that powered Motown's hit factory, fell out spectacularly with Motown boss Berry Gordy as the 1960s ended. Unhappy with their share of the royalties from their dozens of hits, they quit Motown and started their own label, Invictus. The launch of this new venture was stalled, though, by a lengthy legal battle that put the team out of action for the best part of two years when they were at the top of their game.

The Chairmen Of The Board, formed to be a new Four Tops for Invictus, helped Invictus off to a flying start with 'Give Me Just A Little More Time,' which peaked at Number 3 in Billboard. It still stands as the band's defining moment, featuring an extraordinarily powerful virtuoso vocal performance by 'General' Norman Johnson who, fittingly, first found fame as the vocalist on The Showmen's 1961 rock'n'roll anthem, 'It Will Stand.'

By no means an overnight success, Freda Payne was a seasoned vocalist who had sung jazz with both Duke Ellington and Quincy Jones and appeared on Broadway before renewing an old friendship with Brian Holland in 1969 and signing up with Invictus. This was one of the first songs she recorded for the label, although Payne wasn't keen on the lyrical content of this honeymoon melodrama, essentially a story of non-consummation of wedding vows – an unusual subject for a pop single. She needn't have worried: 'Band Of Gold' swiftly became a major international hit, proving that HDH had not lost their magic touch in the intervening years.

All of which brings us to the most interesting revelation about 'Band Of Gold.' At the time, HDH were still under a Motown restraining order and could therefore not write for other labels. While 'Band Of Gold' had songwriting credits to Ronald Dunbar and Edith Wayne, there were always industry suspicions that HDH were the real authors, an accusation rigorously denied at the time. In recent years, however, with the Motown lawsuits long forgotten, the trio have finally admitted that they did indeed write the song, and that company employees Dunbar and Wayne's names were used as a cover.

War
Edwin Starr

Released June 1970
Gordy 7101 (U.S. #1) / Tamla Motown TMG 754 (U.K. #3)

In the early 1970s, Motown Records was in a period of transition. It had recently lost the prolific writing and production team of Holland-Dozier-Holland, and somehow the label had to fill the void. For Norman Whitfield, a successful Motown house producer since the early 1960s, HDH's departure precipitated a golden age. Inspired by Sly & The Family Stone's psychedelic soul innovations, Whitfield helmed extraordinarily ambitious singles such as The Temptations' 'Cloud Nine' and Marvin Gaye's 'I Heard It Through The Grapevine.'

'War' was produced and written by Whitfield, establishing a curious new hybrid: the psychedelic-soul freak-out protest song, and all built around the ever-reliable 'Louie Louie' riff. "None of us thought after we cut it that it would be such a big hit," Starr admitted in 1971. "And, although it sounds a real complicated thing on the single, it wasn't as hard as that to get together." Originally recorded as an album track by The Temptations, 'War' had prompted hundreds of letters from students asking the Temps to release it as a single, but they were already committed to another Whitfield production, 'Ball Of Confusion.'

Now that he was alerted to the song's commercial potential, Whitfield was unwilling to let 'War' languish as just another album track, and he offered it to Starr, whose powerhouse performance rocketed the song to Number 1 and justly earned a Grammy for Best Male R&B Vocal Performance. The song has a wider significance, too: along with Marvin Gaye's 'What's Going On' it marked Motown's emergence as a politically active label.

Ain't No Mountain High Enough
Diana Ross

Released July 1970
Motown 1169 (U.S. #1) / Tamla Motown TMG 751 (U.K. #6)

Berry Gordy had been fine-tuning his plans for Diana Ross's solo career for some years before her departure from The Supremes at the end of 1969. The group's final single with Ross, 'Someday We'll Be Together Again,' was intended to be her solo debut, but ultimately it was decided that it would be more appropriate as a Supremes swansong, and it topped the U.S. charts at the turn of the decade. Now, the most important task was to find a song to launch Ross as a solo artist.

After an unsuccessful attempt to produce some hits with outside producer Bones Howe, responsible for Number 1s by The Association and The 5th Dimension, Gordy put Ross together with one of Motown's own teams, Nickolas Ashford and Valerie Simpson. Among the songs they recorded with her was this completely rearranged version of 'Ain't No Mountain,' a song they had recorded with Marvin Gaye & Tammi Terrell in 1967.

For Ross's version they added some newly-composed spoken segments, but the only problem was that the result was six minutes long, and Gordy had no intention of releasing it as a single. That changed when U.S. radio DJs began to feature the song, forcing Motown to release an edited version, which soared to the top of the charts in September 1970 and became Ross's first major solo triumph.

Bridge Over Troubled Water
Simon & Garfunkel

Released February 1970
Columbia *45079* (U.S. #1) / CBS *4790* (U.K. #1)

Bridge Over Troubled Water was an apt title for what would be Simon & Garfunkel's last studio album together: they certainly went through some extremely troubled times making the record. During much of the recording Art Garfunkel was absent from the studio, busy filming *Catch 22* in which he starred. Paul Simon spent a good deal of time working alone, writing and recording the songs, some of which were aimed directly at the absent Garfunkel. For example, 'Why Don't You Write Me' and 'The Only Living Boy In New York' addressed 'Tom' – Garfunkel had been 'Tom' in their earlier incarnation, Tom & Jerry – and referred to Garfunkel's frequent trips to Mexico for the filming.

'Bridge Over Troubled Water' was one of the few songs on the album where the duo spent much time working together. Simon, who originally envisaged the song as a gospel hymn, wrote it on guitar, recording a demo that he played to Garfunkel. (This demo eventually surfaced on Simon's *1964/1993* boxed set.) It was only later that the song turned into a tour de force, highlighting Garfunkel's angelic voice and the piano of Larry Knechtel, in a grandiose arrangement inspired by Phil Spector's production of 'Ol' Man River' for The Righteous Brothers.

At first there were only two verses, but Garfunkel felt that the song needed a third and persuaded Simon to write one. In later years, perfectionist Simon regretted these events, feeling that the final verse was not as good as the first two. Talking in a 1972 interview, he said: "[Garfunkel] didn't want to sing it himself – he felt I should have done it, and many times I think I'm sorry I didn't do it." About the album itself, Simon recalled: "On several tracks there's no Artie at all – it's a Simon & Garfunkel record, but there are many songs where you don't hear Simon & Garfunkel singing together."

There was much bickering in the studio, and Garfunkel's refusal to record a song Simon had written, 'Cuba Si, Nixon No,' coupled with Simon's refusal to complete 'Feuilles-O' (which later appeared on Garfunkel's debut solo album) reduced the *Troubled Water* album to 11 tracks, marking the end for the duo who then went their separate ways.

Surprisingly, and considering the amount of effort put into the recording, neither Simon nor Garfunkel thought 'Bridge Over Troubled Water' was a potential hit single. However, when the album was completed, Columbia Records chief Clive Davis decided it should be both the first single and the title of the album.

Upon release, the single went straight to Number 1 on the U.S. charts. Massive radio exposure helped lift the album to the top spot seven days later, while the title song won the Grammy for Song Of The Year.

AIRING THE HITS: THE TOP 40 RADIO FORMAT

AM, which stands for Amplitude Modulation, is the original and simplest form of radio. Although it has now largely been supplanted by FM (Frequency Modulation) and digital radio, which provide better sound and less interference, AM was the home of music radio through most of the 20th century and in the golden era of rock and pop.

Before television, radio in America was dominated by national stations providing live music, drama, comedy, serials, and news. When television arrived, most of these forms of programming migrated to the new medium, leaving radio with music but a limited income. While the national stations declined, local stations made the most of their modest budgets by playing records, chosen by DJs (disc jockeys) and catering to local and specialized tastes, notably country and rhythm & blues.

These DJs rapidly developed vivid on-air personalities, and because of the quirks of AM transmission (especially late at night) developed audiences far outside their local areas. In the world of rock'n'roll, they included Alan Freed, most famously, but also Danny 'Cat Man' Stiles, Tommy 'Dr. Jive' Smalls, Douglas 'Jocko' Henderson, George 'Hound Dog' Lorenz, Ken 'Jack The Cat' Elliott, and others. What many of the white DJs had in common was that they did their best to sound black, using jive talk and black slang to accompany the black music they were playing.

Perhaps the most celebrated was Wolfman Jack, real name Bob Smith, who began broadcasting from a station just across the border in Mexico in 1962. Because the station was not subject to U.S. broadcast power restrictions, it had a huge reach across the U.S., and the Wolfman, with his gravel voice, howls, and innuendo, became a cult. He did not reveal his true identity until 1973, when he appeared in a pivotal scene in the George Lucas film *American Graffiti*.

As time went by, many of the local stations were bought by regional operators and formed into chains, which began to develop a new format called Top 40. There had long been weekly chart shows, but in the 1950s a chain owner called Todd Storz took things much further. Observing the way jukebox customers chose the same songs repeatedly, he limited the music output of his stations to just the top 40 songs sold in local stores, and then arranged for the top 10 records to be played more frequently than the others. This was called 'rotation.' The idea was that the casual listener would never have to wait more than a few minutes for one of the major hits of the day.

But there was more to the Top 40 concept than that. News bulletins and commercials now appeared at fixed times, and jingles, DJ patter, and audience competitions and promotions were introduced. The idea, above all, was to avoid any sort of silence, known as 'dead air' in radio jargon.

Although the DJs' personalities were still an essential part of the mix, they now had to squeeze themselves into a rigid format, and had lost the ability to express their own musical tastes. Those who were primarily motivated by music moved on to FM. Escapees from AM included Murray 'The K' Kaufman, who had become famous as 'the fifth Beatle' when he attached himself to the band on their first tour of the States. A new, album-based type of music programming, known as freeform or progressive rock, began to blossom on FM in the mid 1960s.

Both Top 40 and AM radio continue to thrive today, however. *American Top 40* is a nationally syndicated chart show, launched in 1970 by Casey Kasem (the voice of Shaggy in the Scooby-Doo cartoons) and continuing to this day. Unlike classic Top 40 radio, it uses a countdown format and includes snippets of biographical information about the featured artists, as well as requests and audience queries. While AM radio is now primarily the home of U.S. talk radio it still hosts some music stations in the States and elsewhere in the world.

Mama Told Me (Not To Come)
Three Dog Night

Released May 1970
Dunhill/ABC *4239* (U.S. #1) / Stateside *SS 8052* (U.K. #3)

As strange as it might seem to think it today, from 1969 to 1975 Three Dog Night were one of the most successful bands in the U.S. During that period the group – essentially a vocal trio – had twenty-one Top-40 *Billboard* chart entries, with three chart-toppers among them. The group's biggest hits were all covers, but they were no bland copyists. Not only did they devise interesting arrangements but also they covered songs by people not normally associated with the charts, including Laura Nyro and, in this case, Randy Newman. In its depiction of a youth horrified by the decadent goings-on at a party, the song could not have been more out of tune with the supposedly liberated spirit of the times.

All Right Now
Free

Released May 1970
A&M *1206* (U.S. #4) / Island *WIP 6082* (U.K. #2)

By 1970, Free had two albums behind them but seemed little more than a group following uncertainly in the footsteps of Peter Green's Fleetwood Mac and their bluesy hard rock. It was precisely because the band realized there were limits to 12-bar laments, however authentic, that led to this song's creation.

A gig in Durham, England, had seen the band leaving the stage to the sound of their own footsteps. "It was obvious that we needed an up-tempo number, a rocker to close our shows," drummer Simon Kirke said later. Bassist Andy Fraser began dancing around the dressing room singing the phrase "all right now" and proceeded to write the song on the spot. The process took him ten minutes. The lyric was a sparkling tale of flirtation leading to sexual congress, driven home by one of the all-time great rockin' guitar riffs.

The band then applied their considerable skills of extemporization to the raw material, ending up with a track lasting over five minutes as the finale of their third album, *Fire And Water*. Ironically, after all that work, the song had to be edited for single release. While such measures are usually considered sacrilege, the song was given greater punch and power after the shortening of its lengthy instrumental section. 'All Right Now' was one of two great singles kept from the top of the British charts by the (admittedly fine) Mungo Jerry song 'In The Summertime.' The other one was T. Rex's 'Ride A White Swan.'

Lola
The Kinks

Released June 1970
Reprise *0930* (U.S. #9) / Pye *7N 17961* (U.K. #2)

Like many successful groups of the 1960s, The Kinks ran out of steam a little as the new decade arrived, not least due to Ray Davies's predilection for writing a series of concept albums. This was the last of a lengthy run of hits in America, and with the exception of the follow-up, 'Apeman,'

their last ever U.K. Top 10 hit. The group did, however, enjoy a second round of success in the States in the late 1970s, and hit Number 13 in Britain in 1983 with 'Come Dancing.'

The Kinks had been one of Britain's most successful pop groups of the 1960s. When leader Ray Davies found his songwriting feet, he created some of the best typically British popular music of the era. He produced a classic series of cleverly written songs, including 'Dead End Street,' 'Sunny Afternoon,' 'Dedicated Follower Of Fashion,' and 'Waterloo Sunset' (originally titled 'Liverpool Sunset' but changed when The Beatles released 'Penny Lane' / 'Strawberry Fields'). Davies continues to be recognized as one of the most intuitive pop writers of the period.

The inspiration for 'Lola' came to Davies from a male colleague who thought he was on to a good thing in a dingy London nightclub. As the night wore on, his dancing partner's chin-stubble became increasingly apparent, leading to the song's clever punchline: "I'm glad I'm a man … and so's Lola."

The single was banned in Australia for its sexual imagery, and was about to be banned by the BBC in Britain: the lyric mentioned Coca-Cola, and product advertising was not allowed on the Corporation's airwaves. Davies was in the U.S. when this news arrived and made a swift 24-hour trip back to London to replace the offending line with "cherry-cola."

My Sweet Lord
George Harrison

Released November 1970
Apple *2995* (U.S. #1) / Apple *R 5884* (U.K. #1)

Many fans were surprised when George Harrison became the first ex-Beatle to hit the top of the singles chart following the group's demise at the beginning of 1970. His songwriting talents had always been overshadowed by those of Lennon and McCartney – and Harrison can't have been particularly happy when Frank Sinatra repeatedly introduced 'Something' as "the best song Lennon & McCartney have written."

While a judge would later decide otherwise, Harrison said that 'My Sweet Lord' was inspired by The Edwin Hawkins Singers' 1969 hit 'Oh Happy Day.' He originally gave the song to Billy Preston with the intention that Preston should release it as a single. However, having recorded his own version together with producer Phil Spector, he earmarked it as the debut single from his triple album *All Things Must Pass*, and the Preston single was withdrawn.

After 'My Sweet Lord' had topped charts around the world and sold in excess of five million copies, it became apparent that the melody was not unlike The Chiffons' 1963 hit, 'He's So Fine,' written by Ronnie Mack. A protracted lawsuit began, which George Harrison eventually lost some five years later, although he always maintained that the similarity was purely coincidental. An American district court judge agreed that Harrison's so called 'plagiarism' might well have been sub-conscious, but still awarded in favor of the plaintive to the tune of $587,000.

Harrison topped the *Billboard* Hot 100 on two further occasions over the years – with 'Give Me Love' in 1973 and 'Got My Mind Set On You' in 1987 – but neither single matched the enduring popularity of 'My Sweet Lord.' After his death in November 2001 this, his most successful solo recording, returned to the top of the U.K. charts in January 2002.

Paranoid
Black Sabbath

Released August 1970
Warner Bros. *7437* (U.S.) / Vertigo *6059 010* (U.K. #4)

'Paranoid' is the Black Sabbath song that even people who normally detest the group actually like. Part of the reason for this is because it doesn't sound like them at all, but rather their contemporaries in the heavy-metal world, Deep Purple.

Throughout their career, Sabbath have played the slow, grinding, menacing music they had pioneered on their eponymous 1970 debut and that arguably gave them the right to claim the title of founders of the HM genre. (Led Zeppelin fans may think otherwise.) On 'Paranoid' the group retained their gloomy subject matter but speeded up the tempo to create that most unlikely of beasts, a Sabbath smash hit: not only did it achieve a U.K. Top 5 in 1970 but a decade later climbed to Number 14.

Perhaps the uncharacteristic Purple-like speed happened because the group didn't agonize much about the track. With work almost completed on their second album, producer Roger Bain pointed out that an extra three or four minutes of material was needed to round it off. Guitarist Tony Iommi devised a riff, singer Ozzy Osbourne a melody, and bassist 'Geezer' Butler a lyric, the latter prompted by the fact that people kept accusing him of being paranoid. Within ten minutes the band had on their hands a creation that would ensure they achieved what most heavy metal men never managed: a hit single primed for the pop-loving masses.

Your Song
Elton John

Released November 1970
UNI *55265* (U.S. #8) / DJM *DJS 233* (U.K. #7)

Reginald Kenneth Dwight became Elton John in December 1967 when he left his group Bluesology. By that time he'd begun writing with lyricist Bernie Taupin after joining up through an ad for talent in *New Musical Express* placed by Liberty Records.

It's important to appreciate the importance of Taupin in John's career, as he pointed out in a 1970 interview: "Without Bernie, there'd be no songs. I get very annoyed when people ignore him." The duo were signed to a writing deal by Dick James, whose impressive publishing empire included administration of The Beatles' catalogue. Taupin received £10 per week, John £15 (about $25/$35). Soon afterwards Elton John was signed as a recording artist.

DJM released three albums, *Empty Sky*, *Elton John*, and *Tumbleweed Connection*, and five singles, before his breakthrough hit, 'Your Song,' was released towards the end of 1970. Between the recording of this song and its release, John continued to supplement his income by recording cover versions of current hits for Hallmark on the budget label's *Top Of The Pops* series. He can be heard performing such 1970 hits as 'Spirit In The Sky,' 'Young Gifted And Black,' and 'In The Summertime.' In more recent years these ancient recordings have resurfaced, collected on the album *Reg Dwight's Piano Goes Pop*.

'Your Song,' which Taupin now calls "wonderfully naive," was released to coincide with John's second visit to America. Taupin wrote the lyrics over a scrambled-egg breakfast at John's mother's house in north-west London when he was just 17 years old.

Spirit In The Sky
Norman Greenbaum

Released February 1970
Reprise 0885 (U.S. #3) / Reprise RS 20885 (U.K. #1)

No one can have been more surprised than American singer Norman Greenbaum when his quasi-religious 'Spirit In The Sky' reached Number 1 in Britain in 1970. One of the all-time one-hit-wonders, Greenbaum made a few albums for Warner Brothers in the States that produced nothing of note and he swiftly disappeared into the annals of pop history. He had in fact visited the U.S. charts on one previous occasion as a member of Dr West's Medicine Show & Junk Band, in 1966, with the unlikely titled 'Eggplant That Ate Chicago' that reached Number 52.

Greenbaum's 'Spirit In The Sky' came about when he felt inclined to write a gospel-tinged song, influenced by country singer Porter Wagoner. Greenbaum noted that Wagoner always ended his television show with a gospel number, one of which was a song about a preacher. So it was that Greenbaum wrote his own religious rock song. Recorded in the autumn of 1969, the single had a distinctive fuzz-guitar intro and unusual lyrics. While Greenbaum's chart career may have been short, his song has continued to pay the bills. Dr & The Medics took their cover version to Number 1 in Britain in 1986, while the original version has appeared on dozens of oldies compilation albums, in several movies, and on numerous television advertisements.

(They Long To Be) Close To You
The Carpenters

Released May 1970
A&M 1183 (U.S. #1) / A&M AMS 800 (U.K. #6)

When 'Close To You' was first recorded way back in 1963 by television's Dr. Kildare, alias Richard Chamberlain, it failed to make any impression

on the charts. But The Carpenters were lucky that the song hadn't been a hit. In 1964, Dusty Springfield made a recording that was scheduled as a follow-up to her Bacharach & David U.K. hit 'I Just Don't Know What To Do With Myself.' However, it was left on the shelf and didn't appear until her 1967 album Where Am I Going?

Brother and sister duo Richard and Karen Carpenter were one of the most popular easy-listening acts of the 1970s, with their distinctive vocal sound and a combination of original material and contemporary covers. Composer Burt Bacharach had earlier suggested that Herb Alpert record 'Close To You' after

Alpert's success with another Bacharach & David song, 'This Guy's In Love With You,' but Alpert thought the lyric was too sugary. He passed it on to Richard Carpenter, who didn't like the song much either but

eventually agreed to record it, although there was a considerable difference of opinion regarding the record's potential. Lyricist Hal David wasn't impressed at all, and recalled: "When A&M sent over the [Carpenters] record I didn't think it was a hit. Not that Karen Carpenter didn't sound great – I just thought it didn't have what it took to really catch on. It shows that nobody, myself included, knows a hit until it becomes a hit."

In The Summertime
Mungo Jerry

Released May 1970
Janus 125 (U.S. #3) / Dawn DNX 2502 (U.K. #1)

Some 35 years down the line, 'In The Summertime' has become one of the best-loved summer anthems of all time. You only need to write one hit like this and you're set for life, as Ray Dorset has discovered. Looking back to 1970, Mungo Jerry frontman Dorset recalled that his music then was "a hobby that became a job, but I never imagined music would become my career." The former Good Earth Band played their first gig as Mungo Jerry at the Hollywood Pop Festival in Newcastle-under-Lyme, England, in May 1970, and their good-time blend of skiffle and jug-band blues stole the show.

In what looks retrospectively like a wise decision, the group had apparently turned down an £8 ($20) gig that weekend to appear at the festival. The following week 'In The Summertime' shot to the top, where it remained for seven weeks, and it soon topped charts around the world, shifting several million copies in the process and becoming the group's only U.S. hit. Dorset and his bank manager must have been thrilled when Shaggy took up a new version of the song up the charts in 1995. Shaggy's album on which the song appeared, Boombastic, was a multi-million seller. Let's face it: in Ray Dorset's household it must be summertime all year round.

Black Magic Woman
Santana

Released October 1970
Columbia 45270 (U.S. #4) / CBS 5325 (U.K.)

Santana were originally signed to Columbia in 1969, and it was label boss Clive Davis who also engineered an impressive comeback 30 years later with the multi-platinum Supernatural. Mexico-born Carlos Santana is one of the world's most distinctive guitarists, and his band had their major breakthrough in 1969 at the Woodstock festival, where their Latin-rock fusion 'Soul Sacrifice' was one of the event's highlights. The movie and soundtrack album arrived the following summer, just in time for their second album Abraxas, which is still considered their finest collection.

One of the major hits from the album, 'Black Magic Woman,' was not a Santana original but had been composed by Peter Green, a minor U.K. hit for his band Fleetwood Mac in April 1968. Santana recorded the song at the urging of the group's keyboard player and vocalist Greg Rolie, although he said it took about a year to persuade them. Abraxas, a million-selling Number 1 album in America, also gave the group a U.S. hit with 'Oye Como Va,' while another track, 'Samba Pa Ti,' became their first British hit in 1974.

What's Going On
Marvin Gaye

Released January 1971
Tamla *54201* (U.S. #2) / Tamla Motown *TMG 775* (U.K.)

Among the finest of the many classic Motown singles of the 1960s and early 1970s, 'What's Going On' signposted Marvin Gaye's move from a merely great pop singer to a serious musical artist. In the late 1960s, Gaye had released the biggest hits of his career to date, including 'I Heard It

Through The Grapevine' and 'Too Busy Thinking About My Baby,' but increasingly felt that he wanted to make music in a more spiritual, socially conscious vein. He was also deeply affected by the death of his singing partner, Tammi Terrell, from a brain tumor in March 1970, aged just 24. The melancholy tone of the U.K. single he released next, 'Abraham, Martin, And John,' gave some indication of where Gaye would soon be headed.

The initial idea for 'What's Going On' came from The Four Tops' Obie Benson, who worked on it with Motown songwriter Al Cleveland before bringing it to Gaye. At this point Gaye was in such a state of depression that he considered retiring, but Benson and Cleveland convinced him to record the song himself rather than produce it for another group, The Originals, as Gaye had originally intended.

With David Van DePitte on production duties, Gaye and various members of Motown house band The Funk Brothers recorded the basic tracks of 'What's Going On' (and its eventual B-side, 'God Is Love') at Hitsville U.S.A. Studio A on June 1st, 1970. Gaye returned to the studio during the second week of July to add various vocal parts, while the strings were taped in September.

'What's Going On' introduced a new vocal style for both Gaye and Motown. Although the label had been using a primitive form of multi-tracking since the mid 1960s – particularly to add power to vocal tracks, as on The Supremes' 'You Keep Me Hanging On' – Gaye took the process a step further. Singing in a softer, more soulful voice than on his earlier hits, he added his own backing harmonies to each of his vocal parts, resulting in the subtle, graceful sound that became a hallmark of his later releases. He added to the song's sense of spiritual dislocation by including background sounds of partygoers, utterly at odds with his own lament about the state of the world.

While Gaye was certain he had created his masterpiece, Motown head Berry Gordy was not so sure and was initially reluctant to release it. Gaye countered by refusing to record any more music for Motown. When Gordy eventually relented, in early 1971, the song began its swift climb up the Billboard singles chart, prompting the label head to order a whole album of similar material. That album is, of course, *What's Going On*, generally recognized as both Motown and Gaye's finest artistic statement, and one of the landmark recordings of the early 1970s. Surprisingly, however, given the earlier success of Gaye's hits like 'I Heard It Through The Grapevine,' neither single nor album charted in Britain.

Tired Of Being Alone
Al Green

Released May 1971
Hi *2194* (U.S. #11) / London *HLU 10337* (U.K. #4)

Let's Stay Together
Al Green

Released November 1971
Hi *2202* (U.S. #1) / London *HLU 10348* (U.K. #7)

Having languished in obscurity for years as a sub-Sam & Dave soul shouter, Al Green finally achieved mainstream success with his own composition, 'Tired Of Being Alone,' a laidback Southern soul groove telling the story of his unhappy romance with singer Laura Lee. "This lady used to leave me all the time," he revealed. "She was the busiest woman I'd ever seen. Always had something to do – her nails, hair, shopping. Consequently, I was alone a lot, and that's why I wrote that song."

Producer Willie Mitchell, who started out as a Hi Records artist in the early 1960s, was vital in changing Green's direction and, between them, the pair established Hi as second in the Southern soul stakes only to Stax, with whom they shared many session players. 'Tired Of Being Alone' entered *Billboard*'s U.S. Top 40 chart on August 21, 1971, and peaked at Number 11. It did even better in the U.K. where it soared to Number 4 in October, the same month that it earned a gold disc in the States.

Having scored a major hit, Green was keen to try his luck with another up-tempo hard-soul workout, but Mitchell prevailed on him to remain in the smooth soul vein and the result was the sublime 'Let's Stay Together,' which gave Green his only U.S. Number 1, on February 12, 1972, and established Willie Mitchell's Hi Records sound as the new benchmark in soul: finely tuned percussion, laidback rhythm, and tough but understated brass stabs.

Imagine
John Lennon Plastic Ono Band

Released October 1971
Apple *1840* (U.S. #3) / Apple *R 6009* (U.K. #1)

'Imagine' is the record that saved John Lennon's post-Beatles reputation. There is much talk of Lennon writing songs with an edge that was profoundly lacking in Paul McCartney's solo material. Yet if this song was removed when assessing the quality of Lennon's post-Beatles career, there would be a remarkably threadbare catalogue left behind and – notwithstanding his five-year sabbatical and early demise – precious few truly top quality songs, let alone iconic ones.

Lennon once described his *Imagine* album as a sugar-coated version of the preceding LP, the confessional and raw *Plastic Ono Band*. The title track, 'Imagine,' was certainly a sweetened variant of the political songwriting that Lennon engaged in before and after. This is not just due to the pretty, stately melody and Lennon's simple but hypnotic piano playing. 'Power To The People' (1971) and the *Sometime In New York City* album (1972) had the sort of agitprop lyrics loved by people with posters of Che Guevara on their walls. 'Imagine' was a song geared to such people's utopian ideals but designed to be palatable to the masses. So palatable, apparently, as to be opaque for some. How else to explain the British Conservative party using it at an annual conference during their most right-wing phase in modern history?

Many have pointed to the easy sentimentality and platitudinous nature of lines such as: "Imagine all the people living life in peace." Easy for some, perhaps, but they marked the culmination of a difficult journey that Lennon had taken from his time as a surprisingly violent young man – including violence against women and, allegedly, ex-Beatle colleague Stuart Sutcliffe – into his later years as a pacifist and feminist. However, he could have done more to stifle qualms about the apparent hypocrisy in the line "Imagine no possessions / I wonder if you can?" simply by changing that 'you' to 'we.' Despite that wrinkle, the end result was quite remarkable: a song that almost instantly achieved status as a mass rallying cry among such similarly gentle, abstract left-wing anthems as 'We Shall Overcome' and 'Blowin' In The Wind.'

There can be little doubt that the impact of 'Imagine' on the popular consciousness was increased by Lennon's murder, manifested since by its regularly topping public polls to find the greatest song of the 20th century or of all time. There is a poetic act of defiance involved in voting for it, a display of confidence in the utopianism of the lyric and a mark against the type of evil that led to his death. Nonetheless, 'Imagine' did have a significant resonance when Lennon was still with us.

It went unreleased as a single in Britain until 1975 – amazingly, there were no contemporaneous 45s issued from the *Imagine* album in Lennon's homeland – and effortlessly sailed to Number 6 there despite the fact that Lennon was now on the cusp of his half-decade withdrawal from the music business. Following his death in December 1980 it went all the way to a U.K. Number 1.

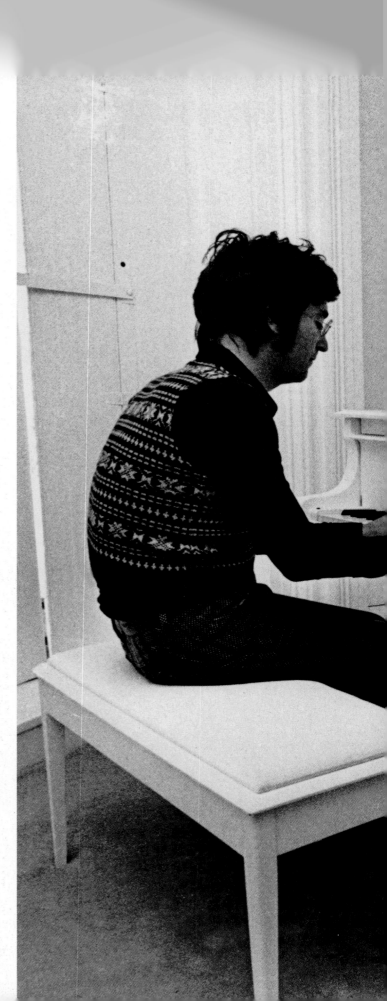

Layla
Derek & The Dominos

Released March 1971
Atco *6809* (U.S. #10) / Polydor *2001 148* (U.K. #7)

Eric Clapton wrote this song for George Harrison's wife, Pattie Boyd, whom Clapton had "fallen madly in love with." Ms. Boyd is one of the most famously serenaded women in rock history, with Harrison's 'Something' and Clapton's later 'Wonderful Tonight' also to her credit. By the time of 'Wonderful Tonight' Clapton had successfully won Pattie's heart and married her.

Following his stints with Cream and Blind Faith, Clapton was anxious to escape his guitar-hero image and disappear into the background. He toured America with Delaney & Bonnie And Friends before stealing the backbone of Delaney's band and retiring to Criteria Studios in Miami, Florida, to record his next project, as Derek & The Dominos. He deliberately intended this to be a low-profile affair, fronting the band as 'Derek' and refusing to have his name on the resulting album.

Tom Dowd was hired to co-produce the sessions, and it so happened that Dowd was currently engaged in producing an album for The Allman Brothers. Guitarist Duane Allman swiftly became friends with Clapton and joined the Dominos sessions to play slide guitar. The full version of 'Layla' was recorded in two distinctively separate sessions.

The first, with one of the all-time great power-guitar riffs, was written by Clapton and recorded in September 1970, while the instrumental second part was written by drummer Jim Gordon and recorded in October. The two sections were then spliced together at the mixing stage. The song became the title track of the Dominos album, released in December, and was first issued as a single early in 1971 but did not chart until 1972.

Won't Get Fooled Again
The Who

Released June 1971
Decca *32846* (U.S. #15) / Track *2094 009* (U.K. #9)

Rescued from the abandoned *Lifehouse* project, Townshend's planned successor to *Tommy*, 'Won't Get Fooled Again' was a stunning climax to what was undoubtedly The Who's best studio album. Following a false start at New York City's Record Plant studio in March 1971, where drummer Keith Moon's drug intake seriously alarmed the rest of the group, recording was switched to Britain and supervised by Glyn Johns. Townshend had been experimenting at home with an early synthesizer and came up with the sequence that formed the basis of the song.

Recorded in the main hall of Mick Jagger's house Stargroves in April using the Rolling Stones mobile studio, the song is not, as many assume, a revolutionary anthem. According to Townshend, it was "a song against the revolution. The first verse sounds like a revolution song and the second like somebody getting tired of it." With The Who playing at their very best, this eight-and-a-half-minute epic, hacked down to under four as a single, was cleverly programmed as the last track on side two of *Who's Next*. Other songs from *Lifehouse* including 'Let's See Action,' 'Relay,' and 'Join Together' were released as singles in the following years, while the entire project eventually came to fruition nearly 30 years later.

Get It On
T. Rex

Released July 1971
Reprise *1032* (U.S. #10) / Fly *BUG 10* (U.K. #1)

'Get It On' is the best known and most successful single by one of the leading lights of the British early-1970s glam-rock scene. In the U.S. it was given a slightly elongated title, 'Bang A Gong (Get It On),' in part to distinguish it from a similarly titled single by the jazz-rock outfit Chase, but also so as not to offend American listeners' delicate sensibilities. It was the group's only American Top 40 hit.

Marc Bolan formed the original, folk-rock Tyrannosaurus Rex in late 1967. The duo's long-winded debut album, *My People Were Fair And Had Sky In Their Hair But Now They're Content To Wear Stars In Their Brows*, marked the start of a career-long association with producer Tony Visconti, who also worked on a number of key David Bowie albums. By the dawn of the 1970s Bolan had abbreviated the Tyrannosaurus in the group's name, switched to electric guitar, and brought in three new backing musicians to replace original percussionist Steve Took.

These changes resulted in 'Ride A White Swan' and 'Hot Love,' both becoming unexpected U.K. hits and the second reaching Number 1. With T. Rex now a full-on touring machine, Visconti was forced to record *Electric Warrior*, the group's defining fifth LP, on the run at various British and American studios. The album was preceded by the release of 'Get It On,' an exultant piece of dirty blues with a guitar riff later 'borrowed' wholesale by the 1990s retro rock act Oasis. It came third in a run of ten consecutive U.K. Top 5 chart entries for T. Rex, including such later gems as '20th Century Boy' and 'Metal Guru.'

Maggie May
Rod Stewart

Released July 1971
Mercury *73224* (U.S. #1) / Mercury *6052 097* (U.K. #1)

Rod Stewart has an anonymous Cleveland DJ to thank for superstardom. In 1971, a rendition of Tim Hardin's 'Reason To Believe' was chosen as the single to promote Stewart's third solo album, the magnificent *Every Picture Tells A Story*. The DJ preferred the flip and began playing it. 'Reason to Believe' was quite lovely, but you could see his point.

'Maggie May' was a composition by Stewart and a guitarist, Martin Quittenton, who had worked on Stewart's first two albums. The two wrote the song when Quittenton was staying at Stewart's house for the purpose of playing on the third LP. Quittenton devised the famous 12-string acoustic guitar intro on the subway on his way to the studio one day.

While 'Maggie May' was, like most Stewart music of the time, essentially rustic, it was a quite extraordinary extravaganza. Its close to six minutes of playing time takes in the coming-of-age tale of a boy who falls for and is then spurned by an older woman and features not only great backing and the usual fine, raspy singing from Stewart but some exquisite moments, those little crescendos of brilliance or spontaneity that make repeated listening a pleasure. This is especially so of the concluding verse, in which the narrator juggles his options – school, or careers as a pool player or (he wishes) a singer – while a celeste ratchets up the poignancy behind him. The single became a Number 1 in Britain and America, and the parent album simultaneously proceeded to replicate that transatlantic chart-topping feat, a history-making first.

I'd Like To Teach The World To Sing
The New Seekers

Released December 1971
Elektra *45762* (U.S. #7) / Polydor *2058 184* (U.K. #1)

The New Seekers were assembled in 1969, logically enough by a former member of The Seekers, Keith Potger. At first performing with the group, he soon withdrew into a management role, selecting their material. In 1970 they were hired by American Coca-Cola executive Bill Backer to record a number of advertising jingles for the company. Arriving in Britain, Backer had come up with the line: "I'd like to buy the world a coke and keep it company." Together with Roger Cook and Billy Davis, who had written hits with Berry Gordy, they put together the new lyric the night before the session. The tune was based on a melody by Cook and Roger Greenaway, entitled 'True Love And Apple Pie,' and the result became perhaps the most successful advertising jingle of all time.

The TV advertising campaign began in 1971, and featured a crowd of youngsters on a hilltop miming to The New Seekers' vocals. The tune was so successful that listeners phoned U.S. stations asking where they could buy the record. At this point Backer arranged for Cook and Greenaway to rewrite the lyric, and since The New Seekers were unavailable, recorded it with a group appropriately named The Hilltop Singers. Shortly afterwards, The New Seekers rushed into a New York studio to record the new lyrics over their original version. New Seekers vocalist Lyn Paul said: "I remember thinking I wasn't very keen on it. How wrong can you be?" Both versions made the U.S. Top 20, although The New Seekers climbed higher, and in Britain their version reached Number 1. Brit-pop band Oasis later hijacked part of the melody for their 1994 single 'Shakermaker,' which resulted in an expensive plagiarism case.

Ain't No Sunshine
Bill Withers

Released June 1971
Sussex *219* (U.S. #3) / A&M *AMS 858* (U.K.)

Bill Withers began writing songs because, as he recalled, "I figured if I was going to be a singer, I'd have to have some tunes." As he hawked his material around the Los Angeles labels, a chance meeting with Booker T. Jones got him a deal with the small Sussex label. His debut album, *Just As I Am*, was produced by Jones, and the musicians included three members of the world's greatest house-band: the impressive studio line-up of Booker T. & The MGs minus guitarist Steve Cropper and supplemented by Stephen Stills.

Among the songs recorded was 'Ain't No Sunshine,' a concise performance at just over two minutes. The lengthy repetition of "I know, I know..." was a result of Withers forgetting the words, but it sounded so good it was left in. 'Sunshine' was at first released as the B-side of 'Harlem,' but DJs soon found the gem on the other side and the song rose to Number 3 on the U.S. charts in the fall of 1971 and won Withers a Grammy award for Best Rhythm & Blues Song. It was not a hit in Britain, where the song was covered by a young Michael Jackson, reaching Number 8 a year later.

Riders On The Storm
The Doors

Released June 1971
Elektra *45738* (U.S. #14) / Elektra *K 12021* (U.K. #22)

'Riders On The Storm' seemed to mark a return to form for The Doors after a couple of years of lesser recordings. Sadly, however, it became the group's swan song, as vocalist Jim Morrison died just as the single began to climb up the charts.

The recording is driven by session player Jerry Scheff's walking bassline and Ray Manzarek's energetic electric piano, and has a more mature, blues-derived sound compared to The Doors earlier work. The group arrived at this refined sound alongside Bruce Botnick, who was promoted from his usual role of engineer to produce the album *L.A. Woman* after Paul Rothchild dropped out, unhappy with the group's apparent direction. Far from being what Rothchild considered "cocktail music," however, the resulting album was one of The Doors' finest, second only perhaps to their eponymous 1967 debut.

'Riders On The Storm' was the second single release from *L.A. Woman* and followed 'Love Her Madly' into the upper reaches of the U.S. *Billboard* chart. Like the earlier Doors classic, 'Light My Fire,' the rambling album cut – which stretched beyond the seven-minute mark – had to be edited down for the singles market but lost little of its mesmeric, foreboding charm. Featuring one of Morrison's strongest vocal performances, it was already on its way to becoming a hit when the singer died suddenly of a drug-induced heart attack at his home in Paris, France, on July 3, 1971.

Theme From Shaft
Isaac Hayes

Released September 1971
Enterprise *9038* (U.S. #1) / Stax *2025 069* (U.K. #4)

When Isaac Hayes was asked to provide music for the ground-breaking blaxploitation movie *Shaft*, the former Stax Records songwriter simply dug up a track he had knocked up a year earlier. "I pulled it out," he explains, "and told Skip, my guitarist, 'Man, put the wah-wah on this.'" The resulting combo of sharp-edged wah-wah guitar and rapidly clattering hi-hat not only won an Academy Award for Best Song and a Best Instrumental Arrangement Grammy, but 'Shaft' went to Number 1 in *Billboard* and established the blueprint for an influential new funky stew. Hayes, who later found even greater fame as Chef in the cult TV series *South Park*, was inducted into the Rock & Roll Hall Of Fame in 2002.

Family Affair
Sly & The Family Stone

Released October 1971
Epic *10805* (U.S. #1) / Epic *EPC 7632* (U.K. #15)

'Family Affair' is the work of a musical genius on the verge of a meltdown. It was the third and last of the group's U.S. Number 1 hits, and the Family Stone – not to mention Sly Stone himself – began to

disintegrate soon afterwards. The group marked the end of the first phase of their career – which culminated in the chart-topping 'Thank You (Fallettinme Be Mice Elf Again)' – with a *Greatest Hits* compilation in late 1970. Sly spent much of the next year pulling together his masterpiece, the *There's A Riot Goin' On* album, in something of a drugged haze, re-recording some of the tracks so many times that the tapes began to warp.

'Family Affair' was the first fruit of the lengthy, disorganized *Riot* sessions. Although it didn't exactly prepare the group's fans for what was to come on the full-length vinyl, it does have a markedly hazier sound compared to the Family Stone's earlier hits. It was the first ever Number 1 hit to be underpinned by a programmed drum track, for which Stone used a Maestro Rhythm King machine. He also played the bass himself – Larry Graham was still in the group at this point, but his parts were wiped by the paranoid bandleader. The other instruments were played by session men, with Billy Preston contributing Rhodes electric piano and Bobby Womack adding wah-wah-laden guitar. Sly shares the vocal with his sister, Rose, the only other member of the Family Stone to feature on the single.

Have You Seen Her
The Chi-Lites

Released October 1971
Brunswick *55462* (U.S. #3) / MCA *MU 1146* (U.K. #3)

Like Detroit, Memphis, and Philadelphia, Chicago too was a hotbed of R&B and soul music, home to such artists as Curtis Mayfield, Jackie Wilson, Jerry Butler, The Delfonics, and Gene Chandler. The Chi-Lites were formed in 1959, led by vocalist-writer Eugene Record, and while their chart debut was the funky '(For God's Sake) Give More Power To The People,' they staked out a place with a string of smooth-soul plaintive ballads including 'The Coldest Days Of My Life,' 'Oh Girl' (a U.S Number 1), and 'Have You Seen Her,' co-written by another of the Windy City's finest, Barbara Acklin, and later updated by M.C. Hammer. The Chi-lites' chart career in Britain lasted beyond its 1973 American conclusion, with 'Have You Seen Her' again scaling the U.K. Top 10 in 1975, together with a number of non-U.S. pop hits including 'Homely Girl' (later covered by UB40), 'Too Good To Be Forgotten,' and 'It's Time For Love.'

A Horse With No Name
America

Released December 1971
Warner Bros. *7555* (U.S. #1) / Warner Bros. *K 16128* (U.K. #3)

This was so much in the contemporarily popular style of Crosby Stills Nash & Young that on first hearing many listeners thought that this was indeed Neil Young – and coincidentally it replaced Young's 'Heart Of Gold' at Number 1 in the U.S. Though American, these three sons of U.K.-based Air Force officers got together in England where they recorded their first album. The record included this track, which became a hit in Britain before a U.S. release saw it topping the American charts in March 1972. Their debut album spent five weeks at the top of the *Billboard* album charts and the group won the Grammy for Best New Artist. Riding on the popular early-1970s singer-songwriter wave, America followed up with several appealing acoustic-based hits, including 'I Need You' and 'Ventura Highway.' Their later recordings were overseen by former Beatles producer George Martin, resulting in a second American Number 1 with 'Sister Golden Hair' in 1975.

Without You
Nilsson

Released December 1971
RCA *0604* (U.S. #1) / RCA *2165* (U.K. #1)

Few songs have a history as sad as this sweet ballad. Its compositional division was unusually neat: Badfinger's Pete Ham supplied the lilting verses while his fellow guitarist Tom Evans provided the soaring chorus ("I can't live, if living is without you").

Originally it was just a track on the band's second album, but hard-boozing rocker Nilsson surprised the group by releasing an incongruously delicate version that went Top 5 in the States at the same time as Badfinger's own 'Day After Day.' The millionaire status one would expect for the composers never materialized: legal wrangles prevented them receiving their due. Both musicians eventually committed suicide.

Morning Has Broken
Cat Stevens

Released December 1971
A&M *1335* (U.S. #6) / Island *WIP 6121* (U.K. #9)

Before embracing Islam in 1979 and changing his name to Yusuf Islam, Cat Stevens enjoyed two successful musical careers. The first was as a pop star in the late 1960s with the hits 'Matthew And Son,' 'I Love My Dog,' and 'I'm Gonna Get Me A Gun.'

Following a year in recuperation from tuberculosis he returned as Britain's premier singer-songwriter, recording a string of million-selling albums and hits including 'Lady D'Arbanville,' 'Father And Son,' 'Moonshadow,' and 'Morning Has Broken.' 'Father And Son' was one of a number of songs that Stevens wrote for a proposed musical, *Revolussia*, about the Russian Tsarist dynasty, telling the story of a peasant farmer's son who goes off to join the revolution.

Most of Stevens's hits were self-composed, but 'Morning Has Broken' was an old English hymn, written by Eleanor Farjean and often sung at morning assemblies in British schools. Stevens had rediscovered the song in the religious section of a London bookstore and recorded it in March 1971 for his *Teaser And The Firecat* album.

Keyboard virtuoso Rick Wakeman played piano and assisted Stevens with the arrangement, and according to later interviews never received his session fee for the job. Wakeman recalled that when the song became a hit and the record company had difficulty in finding a pianist to appear on British TV chart show *Top Of The Pops*, the musician's reply on being contacted was: "Tough!" An exchange of correspondence in *Q* magazine finally resolved the situation almost 30 years later, and Wakeman duly received a check for £9.50 (about $15) from Yusuf Islam to settle his long-overdue session fee.

American Pie
Don McLean

Released November 1971
United Artists *50856* (U.S. #1) / United Artists *UP 35325* (U.K. #2)

Don McLean was by no means a one-hit wonder, but his international hit 'American Pie' has certainly overshadowed the rest of his work. McLean himself has often complained that its huge success has meant that a lot of his other songs have been largely overlooked.

A folk singer since 1963, McLean began to attract attention when he became 'The Hudson River Troubadour' in 1968, a job given to him by the New York State Council on the Arts. This entailed playing to Hudson River communities up to three times a day for a month and brought him to the attention of folk singer Pete Seeger, who later called McLean "the finest singer and songwriter I have met since Bob Dylan." American record companies didn't necessarily share this opinion.

While McLean's popularity among folk audiences was increasing, 34 record companies turned down his demo tapes before he finally got a deal with the small Mediarts label, who released his debut album *Tapestry* in 1970. The record didn't sell particularly well, but McLean kept touring and performing, and during this period he began writing 'American Pie.' It was at this point that the large United Artists company bought Mediarts.

Over the years, much has been read into the lyrical content of the song, which takes as its starting point the death of Buddy Holly in 1959, "the day the music died." It was Holly who had inspired McLean to pick up a guitar in the first place. "I was in love with Buddy Holly and his music," he recalled, "and I remember sadly that by 1964 you didn't hear anything about Buddy Holly. He was completely forgotten. But I didn't forget him. I think this song helped make people aware that Buddy's legitimate musical contribution had been overlooked."

It is generally assumed to be a nostalgic look at the growth of popular contemporary music in the 1960s, but according to McLean the theme of this eight-and-a-half-minute epic was that "commercialism is the death of inspiration." This negative trend was perhaps reflected in McLean's own difficulty in obtaining a record contract. One positive outcome of the song's success was a renaissance for the recordings of Buddy Holly.

Because of its length, 'American Pie' was split into two parts on the single, but most U.S. radio stations soon featured the entire song, and it became one of the most-played records of the time, swiftly rising to Number 1. McLean's follow-up, 'Vincent,' a tribute to painter Vincent Van Gogh, did nearly as well, reaching Number 1 in Britain where 'Pie' had stalled at 2.

However, the huge success of 'American Pie' had taken McLean somewhat by surprise, and contrary to his record company's wishes, he didn't see himself as a hit songwriter, preferring to return to his folk roots. Consequently, record-buyers generally overlooked his later recordings, and apart from a brief return in 1980 with a cover of Roy Orbison's 'Crying' – a British Number 1 which his American record company had rejected in 1978 – McLean's chart success has been limited.

Me And Bobby McGee
Janis Joplin

Released January 1971
Columbia *45314* (U.S. #1) / CBS *7019* (U.K.)

Part-time helicopter pilot, part-time recording studio janitor, and full-time aspiring songwriter Kris Kristofferson picked up his phone one day to hear a Mr. Fred Foster saying: "I've got a song title for you." Foster owned the Nashville building where Felice and Boudleaux Bryant, composers of quality hits for The Everly Brothers and others, worked alongside their secretary, Bobbie McFee. Foster evidently liked the sound of the name and suggested that Kristofferson should write a song called 'Me And Bobbie McFee.'

It took Kristofferson three months, and he tinkered a little with the title, but not everyone immediately recognized it as a classic. "Some of my songwriting friends wanted me to take the line 'Freedom's just another word for nothing left to lose' out of the song," he recalled. "They said, 'You got these great concrete images and then you change to this philosophical statement in the chorus.'"

When Johnny Cash heard it, however, he knew better. First he convinced Roger Miller to record it, then he offered Kristofferson a slot at the 1969 Newport Folk Festival, which got his career off and running. Come 1970, Kristofferson was a successful Columbia Records artist and, on the night of October 3, his girlfriend, Janis Joplin, recorded what is now recognized as the definitive version of the song in one brilliant take. The following day she died of a heroin overdose. It hit Number 1 in *Billboard* on March 20, 1971, and still regularly appears in critics' polls of all-time great songs.

You've Got A Friend
James Taylor

Released June 1971
Warner Bros. *7498* (U.S. #1) / Warner Bros. *WB 16085* (U.K. #4)

When Carole King moved over to the West Coast at the turn of the 1970s she ended up quite spectacularly in the right place at the right time. As her generation entered a new decade, exhaustion at the ceaseless concern with the problems of others that had characterized the 1960s began to set in. Introspection became the order of the day. Musically, this was manifested in the singer-songwriter movement.

Not entirely as expected, King, a New Yorker and Brill Building pop merchant, became the queen of the laidback and mainly acoustic songs of Pacific adult reflection that characterized the genre. Her breakthrough album *Tapestry* – at one point the second biggest-selling album of all time – featured a song that perfectly encapsulated that style, 'You've Got A Friend.' It was a mature song about friendship, sounding like it was meant as a comforting message from one divorced woman (which King now was) to another – although there was a token 'baby' at the close.

James Taylor brought forward the romantic element of this almost gender-neutral song when he decided to cover it. Taylor knew it well: he had played acoustic guitar on King's version. King returned the favor by contributing backing vocals to his own recording, which was more guitar-heavy, with some subtle conga work. The result was Taylor's sole U.S. Number 1 – and a not unpleasant reminder for King of the days when she used to provide hits for others.

TAKE GOOD CARE OF CAROLE KING

Carole King enjoys a rare distinction. She is one of the few non-performing composers to have reinvented herself as an artist. Once synonymous with Brill Building pop through her songwriting partnership with husband Gerry Goffin, she subsequently stepped triumphantly into the spotlight herself with the album *Tapestry*, a record that seemed to reside in every home during the early 1970s.

Goffin & King were almost a mirror image of their friends and fellow Aldon Music writers Barry Mann & Cynthia Weil. Whereas Mann & Weil had a man who wrote melodies and a woman who gave them lyrics, Goffin & King had the reverse operational procedure. In fact, this produced one of the more intriguing head-scratchers of rock history: when the pair achieved their first success by providing The Shirelles with a U.S. chart-topper in 1961 with 'Will You Love Me Tomorrow' – a will-he-still-respect-me-in-the-morning rumination with a beautiful pizzicato string arrangement – many were amazed that Goffin could write with such sensitivity from a female perspective.

Before embarking on that career as a freelance writer, King had tried it as a solo without success – and one of her discs, 'Oh Neil,' was an answer-song to 'Oh Carol,' which Neil Sedaka had written for her. A selection of her collaborations with Goffin constitutes an almost ridiculously familiar litany of catchy and memorable songs: 'Crying In The Rain' (The Everly Brothers); 'Don't Bring Me Down' (The Animals);

'I'm Into Something Good' (Herman's Hermits); 'The Loco-Motion' (Little Eva); 'One Fine Day' (The Chiffons); 'Pleasant Valley Sunday' (The Monkees); 'Take Good Care Of My Baby' (Bobby Vee); 'Up On The Roof' (The Drifters); and 'A Natural Woman (You Make Me Feel Like)' (Aretha Franklin). 'The Loco-Motion' was a U.S. Top 3 in three successive decades: Grand Funk and Kylie Minogue successfully resurrecting it in the 1970s and '80s. Meanwhile, 'Chains' by The Cookies only made a U.S. Number 17 but was later covered by The Beatles on their first album, a lucrative occurrence for Goffin & King.

King had secured a solo hit in '62 with 'It Might As Well Rain Until September' but her career as a recording artist did not take off until she and Goffin parted company in the late 1960s, following which she formed part of a trio called The City. Now forgotten, they put out an album containing 'Hi-De-Ho,' a hit for Blood Sweat & Tears, and 'I Wasn't Born To Follow,' which became not only a highlight of The Byrds' *Notorious Byrd Brothers* album but also a key song in the movie *Easy Rider*.

In 1971, James Taylor had a transatlantic hit with King's song 'You've Got A Friend.' It had been Taylor who encouraged her to record solo material, and phenomenal success ensued from that suggestion. From that point on King's career was really as an albums artist, although it included a U.S. Number 1 single in 'It's Too Late.' *Tapestry* was the longest charting album of all time by a female artist.

below > Carole King, producer Lou Adler (center), and James Taylor (right), pictured during sessions for King's hugely successful *Tapestry* album at A&M studios in 1970.

Heart Of Gold
Neil Young

Released February 1972
Reprise 1065 (U.S. #1) / K 14140 (U.K. #10)

Neil Young's only U.S. Number 1 hit single remains a classic of the early 1970s singer-songwriter genre. Ever contrary, however, its author spent the ensuing years – until he began to mellow slightly in the 1990s – doggedly making anything but a follow-up.

Young was a member of the seminal country-rock group Buffalo Springfield and also part of a 'supergroup' alongside David Crosby, Stephen Stills, and Graham Nash before his solo career began to take off. His first truly great album was his third full-length effort, *After The Gold Rush*, which yielded the minor hit 'Only Love Can Break Your Heart.' The follow-up was *Harvest*, from which 'Heart Of Gold' was taken, and this album was a strange assortment of disparate recordings made with different musicians, ranging from the heavily orchestrated 'A Man Needs A Maid' to the hard rock 'Words (Between The Lines Of Age).'

Stuck slap-bang in the middle of this, like the proverbial diamond in the rough, is this sweet, country-tinged single. 'Heart Of Gold' is driven by Young's strident acoustic guitar and the drumming of noted session player Kenny Buttrey (whose other credits include Bob Dylan's *Blonde On Blonde* album). Added color is provided by steel guitarist Ben Keith and backing vocals from Linda Ronstadt and James Taylor.

Topped off by one of Young's most haunting, memorable melodies, sung in his usual broken voice, the single became his biggest hit in Britain and the U.S. but served only to make him determined not to record anything else with such a mainstream sheen. As he wrote in the sleevenotes to his *Decade* anthology: "This song put me in the middle of the road. Traveling there soon became a bore so I headed for the ditch. A rougher ride, but I met more interesting people there."

Take It Easy
The Eagles

Released May 1972
Asylum 11005 (U.S. #12) / Asylum AYM 505 (U.K.)

Ironically, 'Take Is Easy' – the record that broke The Eagles – is really more of a Jackson Browne song. He penned the bulk of this number, including that unforgettable opener about running down the road trying to loosen his load with seven women on his mind: "Four that wanna own me / Two that wanna stone me / One says she's a friend of mine."

At the time Browne was living in the apartment below that of Glenn Frey, whose band The Eagles were just out of the blocks. Browne's somewhat anxious and self-deprecating verses were balanced out by a new verse from Frey in which he boasts about a woman noticeably taking an interest in him. Few probably noticed the 'join,' distracted by the streamlined and feel-good vibe of this perfect highway-cruising music.

A George Jones fan would probably not consider the record to be anything other than straightahead rock, but there was a noticeable 'twanginess' to it that would have surprised the average rock-radio listener. It is possibly The Eagles' greatest achievement that pretty soon the surprise at such rural inflections on the pop charts would be something that people didn't even think about – indicated by the fact that *Their Greatest Hits 1971-1975* would become the biggest-selling album of the 20th century. Up to the late 1960s, rock was so associated with radicalism and country with conservatism that country-rock was a tag that made as much sense as communist-fascism.

Listen To The Music
The Doobie Brothers

Released August 1972
Warners 7619 (U.S. #11) / Warners K 16208 (U.K. #29)

The Doobies' second album *Toulouse Street* adhered to their previous formula of soft boogie but intensified the punch, in part thanks to their recruitment of a second drummer. The LP led off with 'Listen To The Music.' The riff had been used on 'Feelin' Down Farther,' a track on the group's debut album, but was transferred here to acoustic guitar, now strapped to a lyric celebrating the soothing qualities of music and given a little gimmick with a dash of a whoosing 'phased' sound effect. A version that edited out the virtuosity was released as a single (two years later in Britain) and lucratively established the band as competitors to soft rock acts such as The Eagles.

You're So Vain
Carly Simon

Released November 1972
Elektra 45824 (U.S. #1) / Elektra K 12077 (U.K. #3)

Along with Carole King, Carly Simon was in the vanguard of a new generation of female singer-songwriters that emerged in the early 1970s: confessional, literate, mature, yet pop-savvy. She had been seen in the charts before 'You're So Vain' but it was this single that really established her reputation. It had an irresistible chorus paired with a lyric that shines an unforgiving light on the self-obsession of celebrity, and became a huge international hit.

The frank tone of the words seemed to leave little doubt that the song was autobiographical, but who was she singing about? Was it Mick Jagger? Or Warren Beatty? Or Kris Kristofferson, maybe? Rumors abounded, while Simon herself kept teasingly quiet, dropping the odd hint and red herring. More than 30 years later she still won't say. One person she said it definitely wasn't about, though, was fellow singer-songwriter James Taylor, whom she married one month before the song hit number 1 in America.

The First Time Ever I Saw Your Face
Roberta Flack

Released February 1972
Atlantic *2864* (U.S. #1) / Atlantic *K 10161* (U.K. #14)

Scottish-born folk artist Ewan MacColl composed this song for his wife Peggy Seeger (half-sister of the folk singer Pete) in 1957. Peggy was performing in a play in the U.S. at the time, and legend has it that MacColl, who'd written this eulogy of undying love in under an hour, sang it to his wife down the telephone. MacColl was probably just as surprised as Roberta Flack when his song went to Number 1 in America some 15 years after it had been composed.

Recorded in 1969, the song became a hit in 1972 after it had featured in the Clint Eastwood movie *Play Misty For Me*. In the wake of Flack's success with the song came a number of sugary cover versions by artists such as Engelbert Humperdinck, Andy Williams, and Mantovani. MacColl is on record as particularly hating Elvis Presley's version. 'The First Time Ever I Saw Your Face' won two Grammy awards, for Song Of The Year and Record Of The Year, awards Ms. Flack was to win again the following year for her next big hit, 'Killing Me Softly With His Song.'

Puppy Love
Donny Osmond

Released February 1972
MGM *14367* (U.S. #3) / MGM *2006 104* (U.K. #1)

Behind the lightweight image of The Osmonds there was real musical talent. They all played instruments and wrote some of their own material. In fact, the family would probably be outraged that this single – a Donny solo 45 that was a syrupy cover of an old Paul Anka song – is the sole representation in this book of the Osmonds phenomenon of the early 1970s. It became the best known song associated with any of them, and thus marked the point at which they took an irrevocable step, after which they would be remembered not as purveyors of classy rock songs like 'Crazy Horses' but of fodder for teenyboppers.

Amazing Grace
The Pipes & Drums & Military Band Of The Royal Scots Dragoon Guards

Released March 1972
RCA *0709* (U.S. #11) / RCA *2191* (U.K. #1)

Perhaps the most surprising thing about this British Number 1 is that it also made the U.S Top 20. While bagpipes arouse some nationalistic emotions in Britain (or more specifically, in Scotland) they are not often heard on American Top 40 radio. The song was composed in 1779 by the Reverend John Newton and had already been a transatlantic hit in a stunning a cappella version by Judy Collins that spent 67 weeks lingering in the U.K charts between 1970 and 1972. Formed in 1678, The Royal Scots Dragoon Guards can take pride in being the oldest established act ever to hit the charts. Those 294 years it took them to get a hit will certainly take some beating. Unfortunately, they won't be having any more hits since they were amalgamated into another unit in 1994. Younger readers will be familiar with this tune because it forms the basis of All Saints' late-1990s hit 'Never Ever.'

My Ding-A-Ling
Chuck Berry

Released August 1972
Chess *2131* (U.S. #1) / Chess *6145 019* (U.K. #1)

Chuck Berry might have written some of the greatest and most covered entries in the rock canon, but his biggest hit as a performer was with this novelty song. 'My Ding A Ling' was edited from a longer live recording made in the distinctly un-rock'n'roll setting of Coventry, England, and is a faintly sinister combination of infantile singalong and risqué lyric. Who could resist one of the founding fathers of rock'n'roll inviting us to play with his 'ding-a-ling'? Hardly anyone, it seems, as the song topped the U.K. and U.S. charts and went gold, giving Berry an unexpected second commercial wind well into the middle years of his career. A second transatlantic Top 30 hit, 'Reelin' & Rockin',' taken from the same live recording, followed in early 1973.

In A Broken Dream
Python Lee Jackson

Released September 1972
GNP Crescendo *449* (U.S) / Youngblood *YB 1002* (U.K. #3)

If the vocalist on this song sounds naggingly familiar, that's because it is none other than Rod Stewart. Back in 1968, British DJ John Peel signed Australian band Python Lee Jackson to his Dandelion label and asked his friend Rod Stewart to record a guide vocal for them. The track remained unreleased because the band's singer, Dave Bentley, never got around to recording his own vocal. The producer of the session, Miki Dallon, bought the tapes from Peel, sensing their worth, and released the song as a single on his own Youngblood label in 1970. It was ignored, but two years later Stewart was a major international star – enough to push a re-released 'In A Broken Dream' high up the U.K. charts.

The Cover Of Rolling Stone
Dr. Hook & The Medicine Show

Released November 1972
Columbia *45732* (U.S. #6) / CBS *1037* (U.K.)

Written by band manager Shel Silverstein, the song documents the frustration of a generically stoned and decadent rock group who fail to ever make the prestigious appearance on the front of the rock journal. Its non-appearance on the U.K. chart was due to the BBC refusing to play a track they considered to be advertising (despite Dr. Hook playfully recording a special promo version, 'The Cover Of Radio Times,' referring to the BBC's listings magazine). Ironically, Dr. Hook did appear on the cover of *Rolling Stone* in March 1973, after the single became a hit. When the band dropped 'Medicine Show' from their name and no longer recorded Silverstein songs, they became purveyors of the type of soporific weepie that Silverstein had intended to parody with their debut, 'Sylvia's Mother.'

Rockin' Robin
Michael Jackson

Released March 1972
Motown *1197* (U.S. #2) / Tamla Motown *TMG 816* (U.K. #3)

He would become the biggest-selling solo artist of all time, but Michael Jackson was already something of a chart veteran when he first struck out on his own, at the age of just 13, in late 1971. His second solo single – following the international hit ballad 'Got To Be There' – was 'Rockin' Robin,' a classic of 1970s Motown.

Most of Jackson's full-length debut album, *Got To Be There*, was overseen by The Corporation, the team of Motown writers, arrangers, and producers that included the label's founder, Berry Gordy. 'Rockin' Robin,' however, was the work of a relatively unknown duo, Mel Larson and Jerry Marcellino, who took Bobby Day's 1958 novelty hit and turned it into a bright, funky, pop smash.

While Michael continued to record and perform with The Jackson 5 throughout the 1970s, the future King Of Pop scored three further hits in 1972, including his first solo U.S. Number 1, 'Ben.'

Papa Was A Rollin' Stone
The Temptations

Released October 1972
Gordy *7121* (U.S. #1) / Tamla Motown *TMG 839* (U.K. #14)

During Motown's 1960s domination of the black-music market, The Temptations were the main male rivals to The Four Tops, their hits stretching from 1964 until 1985, by which time the Tops had long since left the company.

During the early part of the Temps' career, the hits were supplied by Smokey Robinson, one of Motown's most prolific and respected writers, but by 1966 their recordings fell under the guiding hands of rising writer-producer Norman Whitfield. After Whitfield teamed up with co-writer Barrett Strong in 1967, the duo delivered some classic hits for the group. 'Cloud Nine' was the first of a string of psychedelic-soul songs with politically aware lyrics by Whitfield and Strong, who followed through with 'I Can't Get Next To You,' 'Psychedelic Shack,' and 'Ball Of Confusion (That's What The World Is Today).'

Whitfield's funk masterpiece is without doubt his 1972 creation, 'Papa Was A Rollin' Stone.' Clocking in at almost seven minutes, the song runs for almost two minutes before the vocals begin.

Dennis Edwards, lead vocalist on the song, was far from happy at the recording session. He recalled: "It upset me. I kept asking: When do I come in, when do I come in? I got so mad that I sang [the song's opening lines]: 'It was the third of September / That day I'll always remember' very tightly, not my usual style. But Norman was real good at psyching us up, and I realized it was the attitude he wanted. I was wrong about that record – I'm glad I was wrong."

The end result is best described as a soul symphony, the fine vocal arrangement combining with Whitfield's subtle production to make it one of The Temptations' most successful records – and even the era-identifying wah-wah guitars have failed to date this remarkable recording.

Superstition
Stevie Wonder

Released October 1972
Tamla *54226* (U.S. #1) / Tamla Motown *TMG 841* (U.K. #11)

'Superstition' is an R&B-funk classic that captures Stevie Wonder in the midst of his prolific early-20s. It was his first U.S. Number 1 for almost a decade, following his 1963 breakthrough hit 'Fingertips (Part 2).' He had spent the 1960s as a fairly typical – albeit highly talented – Motown star, chalking up hits like 'I Was Made To Love Her' and 'My Cherie Amour.' After his initial contract with the label expired on his 21st birthday, in May 1971, he was at first reluctant to sign again: like Marvin Gaye, he was dissatisfied at the lack of creative control the label offered him. By the end of the year, however, he had convinced Motown head Berry Gordy of his abilities and was given permission to write, arrange, record, and produce the subsequent *Music Of My Mind* LP himself.

Music Of My Mind was the first of five classic albums recorded by Wonder in an intensive five-year period that demonstrated his abilities as one of the most dazzlingly inventive musicians and songwriters of the 1970s. Soon after, he started work on *Talking Book*, for which one of his principal collaborators was guitarist Jeff Beck. 'Superstition' arose while the pair were jamming in the studio. Beck came up with the drum groove, Wonder the distinctive clavinet riff. Wonder originally offered the song to Beck, but saw so much promise in the guitar man's version that he decided to issue it as a single himself, much to the annoyance of Beck's label.

'Superstition' has a blend of funk, rock, and R&B that opened up Wonder's appeal to a white audience, and with the single on top of the *Billboard* Hot 100 he received an invitation to tour with and regularly jam onstage alongside The Rolling Stones. A host of other great singles followed over the next few years, but the double-Grammy-winning 'Superstition' remains the pick of the bunch.

Superfly
Curtis Mayfield

Released November 1972
Curtom *1978* (U.S. #8) / Buddah *2011 156* (U.K.)

During the racially explosive 1960s, Curtis Mayfield, as a member of The Impressions, delivered some of the finest musical social-commentaries of the age, including his compositions 'People Get Ready,' 'Keep On Pushing,' and 'Choice Of Colors.' What is more, these were songs filled with optimism. He continued on the same path after leaving The Impressions in 1970, and his solo debut album included his later U.K. hit 'Move On Up,' which inexplicably was not released as a single in America.

Following the success of *Shaft* and its accompanying soundtrack by Isaac Hayes there was a rash of what we now call blaxploitation movies. *Superfly* may not have been the best of these – it concerned the morally questionable and not particularly original story of a Harlem dealer out one last coup – but it certainly fielded the finest soundtrack.

Rather than glorifying the *Superfly* story, Mayfield, who felt the movie was something of an infomercial for cocaine, chose to deliver a series of anti-drug messages that were beautifully arranged and orchestrated, in stark contrast to the on-screen activities. 'Freddie's Dead,' which did not in fact appear in the movie, was a bigger hit, while the title track rose to Number 8 in America and the soundtrack LP spent four weeks at Number 1. The cornerstone blaxploitation soundtrack, regardless of the movie it was made to enhance, *Superfly* is a classic album that stands as Mayfield's finest creation.

Virginia Plain
Roxy Music

Released August 1972
Reprise *1124* (U.S.) / Island *WIP 6144* (U.K. #4)

Roxy Music's debut single sounded like nothing else in 1972, and still doesn't, despite a host of imitators. In their formative years, the group was often lumped in with the British glam-rock scene of the time, but it was evident from the opening bars of 'Virginia Plain' that Roxy had a much more cultured, intellectual sound than that of the bulk of their contemporaries.

The single opens with frontman Bryan Ferry frantically stabbing at his piano and Phil Manzanera beating ugly sounds from his fuzz-toned guitar. Drummer Paul Thompson and bassist Rik Kenton (who was only in the band for six months, and as such appeared only on this single) give the song a firm rhythmic foundation before Ferry introduces his unusual warbling croon, giving voice to a lyric that's part Lou Reed street hustle and part F. Scott Fitzgerald glitz and glamor. What pushes the song even further from the standard fare of the time are the contributions of the group's other two members: Andy Mackay flits between saxophone and oboe, while sound-manipulator and keyboardist Eno coaxes all manner of unearthly sounds from his banks of high-tech machinery.

Roxy Music benefited from a visual appeal to match their ambitious sound, particularly in the case of Ferry, the dapper fop, and the ever-eccentric Eno, who spent much of the period dressed like a futuristic peacock. Although it would take some time for significant American success to arrive, 'Virginia Plain' gave the group a debut hit in the U.K., where their first LP *Roxy Music* also reached the Top 10. They followed it early in 1973 with 'Pjamarama' and a second, equally successful album, *For Your Pleasure*.

right > Roxy Music performing on the BBC TV show *Full House* on November 25th, 1972. Left to right: Phil Manzanera, Eno, Andy Mackay, Rik Kenton, Bryan Ferry, and Paul Thompson (hidden behind a cymbal).

Rock And Roll (Part 1) / Rock And Roll (Part 2)
Gary Glitter

Released March 1972
Bell *45237* (U.S. #7) / Bell *1216* (U.K. #2)

Paul Gadd had leapt on every passing bandwagon during the 1960s before finally finding a place for his over-the-top showmanship as British glam-rock icon Gary Glitter (other names under consideration were Stanley Sparkle, Terry Tinsel, and Vicky Vomit). Between 1960 and 1971 he'd recorded unsuccessfully for Decca, Parlophone, and MCA and worked as a warm-up act on British television's *Ready Steady Go!* pop show. In 1971 he teamed up with producer Mike Leander, with whom he'd been associated since 1961, and created a 15-minute stomp-and-shout piece of nonsense, edited down to a two-part single as 'Rock And Roll (Parts 1 & 2).'

It was the mostly instrumental 'Part 2' that hit the charts after some three months on release, assisted by Gary's performance in glitter suits, ludicrously tight trousers, and platform boots, all the while displaying his hairy chest and wearing a permanently astonished expression. A stream of similar follow-ups included three British Number 1s, although this would be his only sizeable hit in the U.S, where 'Part 2' was used widely as a sports anthem. The one time 'Leader Of The Gang' has since fallen out of favor following his conviction in the U.K. for possession of child pornography in 1999 and subsequent imprisonment in Vietnam on charges of sexual abuse of minors in 2006.

Tumbling Dice
The Rolling Stones

Released April 1972
Rolling Stones *19103* (U.S. #7, U.K. #5)

By 1972, The Rolling Stones were past masters at the classic single. Which is why many were bewildered when they unleashed 'Tumbling Dice,' a seemingly lethargic, slovenly, almost tuneless recording with indecipherable lyrics. On first hearing, everything sounds inadequate, particularly as it lurches through three different tempos in its opening bars and mixes different elements like female backing coos and guitar lines that fall in and out of focus. That the track marched into the upper reaches of the world's charts was ascribed by many to the goodwill that the group's back-catalogue had engendered in the buying public.

When the song's parent album, *Exile On Main Street*, emerged the following month, the single begun to make a bit more sense. It was certainly representative of that long player's exhausted, sluggish, and frayed timbre. This was due to the fact that part of the album (not all, as has often been assumed) was recorded in stultifying conditions in the basement of Keith Richards's rented French mansion Nellcote – and then sometimes overdubbed in his crowded, clattering kitchen. 'Dice' started life as 'Good Time Women' in 1970 at Jagger's English house. It was re-recorded at Nellcote in the summer of 1971, with a new lyric and a drunken ambience that – irony of ironies given later personnel changes – was reminiscent of the style of Stones wannabes The Faces. 'Tumbling Dice' began to make further sense as the fans realized that, like the album, its scuffed, inchoate nature assumed a real charm once the listener got used to such unprofessional methods.

School's Out
Alice Cooper

Released May 1972
Warner Bros. *7596* (U.S. #7) / Warner Bros. *K 16188* (U.K. #1)

For a brief period, Alice Cooper (then a band, not a person) were considered to be as scandalous as Elvis or The Sex Pistols at the height of their respective notoriety. One reason was the genuinely disturbing streaked mascaraed face of their frontman. Another was the group's macabre stage shows, involving guillotines and snakes. And another was this record. Although its anti-education sentiment now sounds dated, at the time it still bothered a generation who had been in power before the 1960s became permissive and who were not yet retired.

Cooper frontman Vince Furnier was inspired to write the lyric of 'School's Out' when he saw an old movie in which a character called Mugs whacked someone around the head while enunciating the phrase. The cartoon-like nature of this bad boy's anthem is illustrated by the line at the end of a litany of boasts about their rebellious acts: "We can't even think of a word that rhymes!" Guitarist Glen Buxton provided a fine dirty-guitar riff while producer Bob Ezrin kept the metal this side of pop.

Despite the quality of the record, it was a surprise when its commercial success and scandal-mongering carried over to Britain (where moral guardian Mary Whitehouse wanted it banned). "We got no class / And we got no principles" was a pun that made no sense in the U.K., where heads of schools were not principals but headmasters or headmistresses. And the phrase "school's out" is not part of the lexicon in Britain, where schools instead "break up."

Silver Machine
Hawkwind

Released June 1972
United Artists *50949* (U.S.) / United Artists *UP 35381* (U.K. #3)

If ever a band was known for just one song, it's Hawkwind. Yet while they have rarely troubled the chart compilers since the release of 'Silver Machine,' the group has enjoyed a successful career for three decades, courtesy of a fanatical following for their virtually unique 'space rock.'

'Silver Machine' was a co-write between Dave Brock and Bob Calvert, who had joined the group in the month that the song was recorded at a Greasy Truckers party at London's Roundhouse in February 1972. It posits the titular spacecraft as a girl-pulling device on the level of a Porsche.

Hawkwind had begun life as Group X in 1969, springing from the thriving hippie community then in Notting Hill Gate, west London. Yet it was the distinctly un-hippie Lemmy who sang the vocal on 'Silver Machine.' Calvert, poet-in-residence and sometime vocalist, had been sectioned under mental health legislation for 28 days and the band, who found his BBC English vocal style laughable, took advantage of this by wiping his singing and having the future Motorhead frontman replace it.

It was the prevailing tradition (in the U.K., at least) rather than hippie idealism that led the band to not include the track on their next album, although the full Roundhouse version – with Calvert on vocals and running to eight minutes – appeared on the contemporaneous various-artists triple LP *Glastonbury Fayre*.

Hocus Pocus
Focus

Released October 1972
Sire *704* (U.S. #9) / Polydor *2001 211* (U.K #20)

Focus was one of a handful of Dutch groups including Shocking Blue and Golden Earring who found chart success on both sides of the Atlantic in the early 1970s. Featuring Jan Akkerman on guitar and Thijs van Leer on flute, keyboards, and vocals, the mostly instrumental group had classical leanings, with flavors of The Nice and Jethro Tull. 'Hocus Pocus' was recorded in London with British blues producer Mike Vernon as something of a joke that came about during a studio jam session. On the spur of the moment, not wishing to be outdone by the rest of the band's improvisation, Leer decided to yodel, something he claimed he had never done before. Vernon recalled: "It used to look more painful than it was in reality – he was bright red by the time he'd finished yodeling the high bit." This edited version of the six-and-a-half-minute original recorded in 1971 became a hit when a later single, 'Sylvia,' climbed the British charts early in 1973. The U.S. version of 'Hocus Pocus' was a completely different mix.

The Jean Genie
David Bowie

Released November 1972
RCA *0838* (U.S.) / RCA *2302* (U.K. #2)

This playfully androgynous hit cemented David Bowie's position among the leading lights of British music and capped a remarkable 12 months for its author. In the final weeks of 1971 he issued the slow-burning *Hunky Dory* LP and its resplendent single, 'Changes,' quickly following them both with the landmark concept album *The Rise And Fall Of Ziggy Stardust And The Spiders From Mars*. For that album he 'became' the title character, blurring – or perhaps erasing – the line between the performer and his songs.

Like the album *Aladdin Sane* that it trailed, 'The Jean Genie' is a more robust, refined take on the *Ziggy Stardust* material. Bowie's backing trio – still trading as The Spiders From Mars – had by now achieved an incredible synchronicity with their leader and, noting this, producer Ken Scott refrained from any unnecessary sonic bells and whistles, limiting his contribution to capturing a great band and song. The single is

propelled forward by Mick Ronson's corrosive lead guitar and Trevor Bolder's swaggering bass, underpinned by Mick Woodmansey's tight, uncluttered drumming. Bowie himself contributes intermittent harmonica as well as a fervent vocal, pleading with the Jean Genie to "let yourself go!"

'The Jean Genie' was Bowie's highest charting single so far in the U.K., arriving just as glam-rock began to dominate the airwaves there. As it hung around on the charts in the early months of 1973, it was joined by significant hits for artists including T. Rex, The Sweet, and Slade. While most of

his peers' careers would fall into decline by the mid 1970s, Bowie's went from strength to strength as he recorded a series of diverse, innovative albums throughout the decade and beyond.

Whiskey In The Jar
Thin Lizzy

Released November 1972
London *20076* (U.S.) / Decca F *13355* (U.K. #6)

Irish rockers Thin Lizzy scored their debut hit with this reworking of a traditional folk song. At the time the band was a three-piece fronted by bassist and singer Phil Lynott, whose gruff but tender tones give the single much of its appeal. But the record's dominant feature is a melodic electric guitar refrain and a ringing solo by Eric Bell. He left Thin Lizzy shortly after 'Whiskey' charted in Britain, complaining that the band was becoming too commercial. Lynott, meanwhile, waited three years before returning to the singles charts with his reconfigured group and 'The Boys Are Back In Town,' with Bell replaced by not one, but two lead guitarists.

Walk On The Wild Side
Lou Reed

Released November 1972
RCA *0887* (U.S. #16) / RCA *2303* (U.K. #10)

The history of popular music is overflowing with records that might have become big hits were it not for their 'obscene' lyrics and the ensuing radio ban. But 'Walk On The Wild Side' managed to slip through the censors' nets, despite its reference to "giving head," and became Lou Reed's greatest solo success.

Few expected much of a solo career from Reed after he left The Velvet Underground in 1970. His former group had yet to gain the recognition it holds today, and Reed himself seemed unlikely to buck that trend by setting out on his own. One of his few fans at the time, however, was David Bowie, the rising star of British glam-rock, who helped Reed get a deal with RCA. (Bowie gave another of his cult heroes, Iggy Pop, a similar leg-up the following year.)

Bowie and his guitarist, Mick Ronson, then produced Reed's second solo album, *Transformer*. Cleaner and more melodic than any of Reed's earlier work, the album contains some of his best-loved solo work, including 'Perfect Day' and 'Satellite Of Love.' Even more memorable is 'Walk On The Wild Side.' Pretty much everything about the song is exactly right, from Herbie Flowers's lugubrious bass to the "colored girls" cooing backing vocals and, of course, Reed's straight-talking lyric, which didn't deviate much from the subject matter of his Velvet Underground output – drugs, gender confusion, and so on – but was well served by a refined, calmer setting.

All Because Of You
Geordie

Released March 1973
MGM *14539* (U.S.) / EMI *2008* (U.K. #6)

Geordie would be remembered simply as glam-rock also-rans if it wasn't for the presence of one Brian Johnson on lead vocals. After his first band's 15 minutes of fame, Johnson re-emerged in 1980 as the replacement for Bon Scott, recently-deceased vocalist of AC/DC. The Australian metal monsters became one of a very few big bands not only to survive the death of a totemic member but also to get even bigger afterwards. "Just look at me now I'm shouting," pronounced Johnson on this, the biggest of Geordie's four minor U.K. hits. Over 30 years later he is still shouting, his gritty tones having graced some of rock's best-selling albums.

I Wish It Could Be Christmas Everyday
Wizzard

Released November 1973
Not issued U.S. / Harvest *HAR 5079* (U.K. #3)

Merry Xmas Everybody
Slade

Released December 1973
Warner Bros. *7759* (U.S.) / Polydor *2058 422* (U.K. #1)

This year saw two of the kings of British glam-rock tussling for the top of the charts with Christmas records. By now, Wizzard's frontman Roy Wood was on his third noteworthy band. He had made his name with pop-psychedelic outfit The Move and helped form the Electric Light Orchestra. With Wizzard he married grandiose Spector-pop to an image that brought to mind a simian antecedent of Ziggy Stardust.

Blockbuster
The Sweet

Released January 1973
RCA *45361* (U.S.) / RCA *2305* (U.K. #1)

Someone once described the British glam-rock bands of the 1970s as "bricklayers in leotards." Never was this description more apt than in the case of The Sweet, four out-of-condition, beer-drinking journeymen done up in sequins, satin, and make-up. Although the band had been doing the rounds as Sweetshop in the 1960s, it wasn't until 1971 and with their newly truncated name that they started to get some chart action with their hybrid of bubblegum pop and heavy metal. A string of 15 British hit singles lasted through most of the decade, many penned by glam-rock's songwriting maestros, Nicky Chinn and Mike Chapman.

Some British glam acts found that their style just didn't translate into American, but The Sweet were an exception, becoming a big live draw and chart act there. The truth was, leaving aside the comically garish presentation, the band's records were well-crafted, catchy pop-rock that sat well on U.S. playlists, not a million miles from Alice Cooper or even very early Aerosmith.

'Blockbuster' was the band's biggest U.K. hit and a conundrum for those whose musical judgments were too influenced by notions of what was and wasn't critically acceptable, and who would otherwise dismiss The Sweet as pop lightweights. The song was based on an old blues riff, the same one that the ultra-hip David Bowie had pinched for 'The Jean Genie' just a few months earlier.

Slade, meanwhile, were the biggest band of the British glam-rock era, notching up an impressive seventeen Top-20 singles in a five-year stretch in the 1970s, plus a few more during their second coming in the 1980s. Among the best of these was 'Cum On Feel The Noize,' with its deliberately misspelled title (a Slade trademark) and shout-along chorus reinforcing the band's cartoon yob image. But where close rivals like The Sweet gamely tapped into the international language of rock androgyny and saw chart action outside their homeland, Slade, with their soccer-terrace rock, remained a peculiarly British phenomenon.

The title of Wood's creation is the almost verbatim sentiment expressed by children, and indeed many adults, as they bask in spiritual mellowness (and gifts) each Yuletide. But that didn't make the record any less a stroke of quasi-genius. Wood insisted that a kids' choir was transported from his native Birmingham for chorus work on the recording session.

Slade's record started life as a psychedelic leftover from the 1960s called 'Ride Yourself A Rocking Chair,' the tune of which was cannibalized when bassist Jim Lea's grandmother lamented the fact that nobody wrote Christmas songs any more. No doubt granny Lea was pleased at the sudden plenitude of Christmas records – and the fact that it was Slade who won the battle for Number 1.However, both Wizzard and Slade emerged in artistic triumph, each having managed to create a song that perfectly captured the tearfully happy atmosphere of the holiday season.

above left > The Sweet performing on *Top Of The Pops* in 1973.
below left > Slade on the same show.
right > Wizzard frontman Ron Wood.

TOP OF THE POPS: THE BRITISH CHARTS ON TV

Nothing has had more influence over single sales in the U.K. than the BBC's long-running television show, *Top Of The Pops*. Over 2,000 editions of the chart program aired between 1964 and 2006, but it was not considered very promising when it began. It was first shown on January 1, 1964, commissioned for a run of just six shows. Nonetheless, it was a hit from the start, thanks to a tight format that has been imitated in numerous countries across the world. Each show includes a rundown of the week's bestselling records, in reverse order, and ends with the current Number 1. In between, there are live appearances by acts, miming to their records with different degrees of accuracy and enthusiasm, and filmed sequences. In the heyday of the show, various troupes of dancers – of which the most famous was Pan's People – would perform choreographed sequences to accompany records by acts who were not available to appear and had not supplied films.

Thanks to its huge family audience – for many years the show was a fixture in the main BBC-1 evening schedule – *Top Of The Pops* succeeded in attracting the big names right from the beginning. The very first edition, broadcast from a converted church hall in Manchester, opened with The Rolling Stones performing 'I Wanna Be Your Man' and continued with Dusty Springfield, The Dave Clark Five, The Hollies, and The Swinging Blue Jeans. There were filmed items from Cliff Richard & The Shadows, Freddie & The Dreamers, and, in the Number 1 slot, The Beatles with 'I Want To Hold Your Hand.'

In 1967, the program moved to the BBC's London studios, and DJs from the broadcaster's new pop channel, Radio One, took over presentation duties. The format remained the same, however, and it proved remarkably accommodating to successive generations of artists. Even at the height of rock's album-led self-importance, *TOTP* retained its central role in the teenage market.

While some artists refused to appear because of the show's insistence on miming, others turned up but mocked the process: Les Gray of Mud once brought a ventriloquist's dummy on stage to 'sing' his lead vocal. However, an attempt in 1991 to introduce live vocals over pre-recorded backing tracks proved shortlived, thanks to atrocious performances. Nirvana's only appearance on the show, performing 'Smells Like Teen Spirit,' was during this era. Kurt Cobain sang in a low, mournful voice that he later claimed was a homage to Morrissey.

Over the years, the BBC extended the *Top Of The Pops* brand to take in various spin-off programs, a magazine, and separate programing for BBC Prime, the Beeb's satellite channel for Europe, Africa, and the Middle East. But as sales of singles fell, the show began to decline in popularity. After 40 years, it was moved in 2004 to BBC-2, the Corporation's second TV channel. Two years later, with a sad inevitability, it was announced that *Top Of The Pops* would be broadcast for the very last time on 30th July, 2006.

Frankenstein
The Edgar Winter Group

Released February 1973
Epic *10967* (U.S. #1) / Epic *EPC 1440* (U.K. #18)

Keyboardist Edgar Winter had played with his guitarist brother Johnny and in his own brass-based outfit White Trash before forming The Edgar Winter Group in 1972, kicking off with his debut Epic album *They Only Come Out At Night*. 'Frankenstein' was one of the greatest all-time rock instrumentals, featuring some nifty ARP synthesizer effects, and began life as a lengthy on-stage jam entitled 'The Double Drum Solo.' In the studio it was just as lengthy, and Winter and producer Rick Derringer spent hours chopping and editing down the master tape to an acceptable length. In fact it became something of a monster – which explains its final title. At first it was released as the B-side to the album's first single, 'Hangin' Around,' but was soon flipped by radio DJs and began a three-month climb to the summit of the U.S. charts.

Reelin' In The Years
Steely Dan

Released March 1973
ABC *11352* (U.S. #11) / Probe *PRO 587* (U.K.)

Led Zeppelin's Jimmy Page has said his all-time favorite guitar solo is the astonishingly euphoric confection of arpeggiated triads, multi-bends, pull-offs, slides, and hammer-ons immaculately executed by Elliott Randall on 'Reelin' In The Years.' And when Eric Clapton first heard it, he was so blown away that he wanted to meet the man responsible. Steely Dan was a pair of jobbing musos based in New York, Donald Fagen and Walter Becker. They fashioned a peerless catalogue of rock classics by the simple expedient of writing great songs, hiring only the finest session players to play them, and then testing these hapless virtuosi to distraction with endless re-takes in pursuit of perfection.

Famously, Becker & Fagen were huge jazz fans, but their working methods would obliterate the spontaneity essential to the creation of good jazz. Fagen countered that songs like 'Reelin' In The Years' were "composed and then improvised on." Randall seemed to confirm this, reporting that on his first day in the studio they simply asked him to pull off a solo that their regular guitarist hadn't managed in two days. However, the song is much more than a tune and some words hung around a killer solo. Fagen perfectly nails a near-impossible stream of inscrutable lyrics, the rhythm section is permafrost solid, and the whole construction is architecturally brilliant. Mind you, it must break Clapton and Page's hearts to learn that, in Randall's opinion, "The first solo I did on 'Reelin' In The Years' should have been the keeper. Unfortunately the record button wasn't on."

Yesterday Once More
The Carpenters

Released May 1973
A&M *1446* (U.S. #2) / A&M *AMS 7073* (U.K. #2)

This was just one of an impressive twenty American Top 40 hits that The Carpenters scored between 1970 and 1981, ten of which made the Top 3. At the height of their popularity in 1973 they shrewdly took advantage of a nostalgia boom by recording a medley of 1960s hits on their album *Now & Then*. They had been doing the same thing during recent concerts to a very favorable response. The medley was cleverly linked together like a '60s U.S. radio show with a DJ adding inserts. Richard Carpenter recalled: "The 'oldies' were enjoying a resurgence in popularity during the early 1970s, much to the delight of Karen and me. I thought it would be nice to write a song about this and use the piece to bookend the [album's] oldies medley." The result was 'Yesterday Once More.'

Smoke On The Water
Deep Purple

Released May 1973
Warner *7710* (U.S. #4) / Purple *PUR 132* (U.K. #21)

'Smoke On The Water' was famously recorded in Montreux, Switzerland, following a fire at the Montreux Casino where Deep Purple were intending to tape their new album on the Rolling Stones mobile studio. The song was inspired by the sight of smoke from the fire drifting over Lake Geneva. Purple bassist Roger Glover came up with the title, and the lyric of this self-explanatory tale was completed by vocalist Ian Gillan. The track was cut when the band relocated to the Grand Hotel, closed for the winter season, and recorded in a hotel corridor with mattresses brought in for soundproofing.

Guitarist Ritchie Blackmore recalled that they were recording at such a high volume that "we were waking up the neighbors about five miles away." Police arrived en masse to put a stop to the session, but the group didn't let them in until they had finished the track to their satisfaction. Organist Jon Lord remembered the song's working title was 'Durh Durh Durh,' unsurprising given its guitar riff, probably the most famous in rock history. But the huge success of the song came as something of a surprise to the band.

Deep Purple had specifically written another track, 'Never Before,' as a likely single, and Gillan said he thought it was "the most commercial thing we'd ever done." However, it only reached Number 35 in the U.K. charts. Gillan also claimed that 'Smoke' was only recorded as a last-minute filler when they discovered they were a little short of material. Even with the finished recording in the can, the group didn't think it was anything out of the ordinary until U.S. radio DJs started highlighting the track. It became an American hit in 1973, with a live-in-Japan version on the B-side, but was not released as a single in Britain until 1977, by which time the legendary Mark 2 Deep Purple line-up had long since disbanded.

Let's Get It On
Marvin Gaye

Released June 1973
Tamla *54234* (U.S. #1) / Tamla Motown *TMG 868* (U.K. #31)

Following Marvin Gaye's stream-of-social-consciousness album, *What's Going On,* and his blaxploitation movie soundtrack *Trouble Man*, he returned to the subject closest to his heart for 'Let's Get It On.' This celebration of sex was inspired by his new love, Janis Hunter, the woman who would become wife number two. Co-writer Ed Townsend's original framework for the song had been about "getting on with life," but Gaye cut to the basics, leaving no doubt what he was talking about. The song spent two weeks atop the U.S. charts – showing how much had changed in just two years since Marc Bolan's 'Get It On' was considered too risqué a title for the American market and modified to 'Bang A Gong.'

Shortly afterwards Gaye made an album of duets with Diana Ross, and his career for the remainder of his lifetime was troubled, to say the least. He married Ms. Hunter in 1977, but the following year a slight disagreement with the I.R.S. over several million dollars in back taxes resulted in a particularly acrimonious divorce, which in turn led to Gaye's 1979 double album, *Here, My Dear*. This was literally presented to his departing wife as part of their divorce settlement. There then followed a severe drug problem for Gaye, and he eventually left Motown in 1981. Retreating to Ostend, Belgium, of all places (partly to avoid the I.R.S.), he managed to resurrect his career and return to the world's charts with the equally explicit 'Sexual Healing' in 1982.

While his career fluctuated between soul perfection (*What's Going On*) and willful self-indulgence (*Here, My Dear*), there's no doubt that Gaye possessed one of the finest voices in popular music. Sadly, his troubled life reached a bizarre conclusion when he was shot dead by his own father on April 1, 1984.

Knockin' On Heaven's Door
Bob Dylan

Released August 1973
Columbia *45913* (U.S. #12) / CBS *1762* (U.K. #14)

Following the release of *New Morning* (1970) the only official new Bob Dylan album in the next four years was his soundtrack to the Sam Peckinpah movie *Pat Garrett & Billy The Kid*. Dylan had a small but telling role as the eccentric Alias. He had also been approached to write a score, and was triumphant in this capacity. 'Knockin' On Heaven's Door,' a dark but beautiful composition for a death scene, not only obtained the producers more publicity than they may have hoped for, but also reassured Dylan fans despairing at his prolonged absence that his talent remained very much intact.

Rock On
David Essex

Released August 1973
Columbia *45940* (U.S. #5) / CBS *1693* (U.K. #3)

David Essex made many records following this inaugural 1973 hit but none has sounded like this echo-drenched and vaguely menacing creation. Essex wrote the song for the movie *That'll Be The Day*, in which he starred, but it was turned down by the producers on the grounds that its strangeness did not fit the film's 1950s retro tone, despite namechecking the likes of James Dean and 'Blue Suede Shoes.' Essex recorded it and gained a solo record that went Top 5 in the U.K. and U.S., surely one of the most skeletal and spooky concoctions to do so.

Hello It's Me
Todd Rundgren

Released September 1973
Bearsville *0009* (U.S. #5) / Bearsville *K 15513* (U.K.)

Rundgren had originally recorded this song with his 1960s power-pop band The Nazz, but re-worked it as a solo vehicle for his album *Something/Anything?*. Rundgren described his song as "just a dense arrangement of simple parts," built around a chord sequence lifted from jazz organist Jimmy Smith's version of 'When Johnny Comes Marching Home.'

It brought him his biggest chart success, but the ease with which he could knock off hits like this and 'I Saw The Light' soon led him to reject commercial music. After it peaked at Number 5 in *Billboard*, Rundgren refused to release anything else from the album and pursued cultish credibility instead.

Seasons In The Sun
Terry Jacks

Released December 1973
Bell *45432* (U.S. #1) / Bell *1344* (U.K. #1)

Hated and loved in equal intensity due to its unashamed sentimentality, this song is about a dying man saying his goodbyes to friend, father, and wife, with a pseudo-profound chorus kiss-off: "The hills that we climbed / Were just seasons out of time." The lyrics were an English translation by Rod McKuen of a Jacques Brel song, and the result was originally recorded by The Kingston Trio. Jacks had been upset by a friend's death and decided to put out his rendition on his own label, with huge success. It was not too much of a surprise when boy-band Westlife later recorded a U.K. chart-topping take of the song, but the version by grunge-meisters Nirvana amazed many fans. It turned out that the Terry Jacks single had been the first record Kurt Cobain ever bought.

Jungle Boogie
Kool & The Gang

Released November 1973
De-Lite *559* (U.S. #4) / Polydor *2001 500* (U.K.)

For those wishing to get down on the early-1970s pre-disco dancefloors there were no better records than those made by Kool & The Gang. The group delivered a string of strutting classics including 'Funky Stuff,' 'Jungle Boogie,' 'Hollywood Swingin',' and 'Spirit Of The Boogie,' horn-and-chant driven workouts that were an inspiration to many in the disco age. Surely K.C. & The Sunshine Band would never have existed without the groundwork of Kool & The Gang? The group would have even greater success some five years later with glossy, commercial, watered-down funk such as 'Celebration' and 'Ladies Night,' but these early sides were the genuine article. (U.K.-label sales suffered as the group's British company was slow to get records to market, allowing imports to sell instead.) 'Jungle Boogie' was the biggest of the Gang's early hits, and would feature in John Travolta's comeback movie *Pulp Fiction*. Now, blow that whistle and get down with the genies!

Tiger Feet
Mud

Released January 1974
Not issued U.S. / RAK *166* (U.K. #1)

British quartet Mud were merely a jobbing covers band when songwriters Nicky Chinn and Mike Chapman took them under their wing. At first the group were mere puppets, but at least they were afforded the privilege of playing on their own records after the first couple of releases. The decision was vindicated by their contributions to this U.K. Number 1 of early 1974.

While the bedrock of the record was the songwriting team's soccer-terrace chant melody and a lyric that reveled in its own meaninglessness and stupidity, the quite thunderous rhythm section and the sublime twin-guitar runs after each chorus, provided by Mud, contributed hugely to what is surely the quintessential Chinnichap glam-rock anthem.

Devil Gate Drive
Suzi Quatro

Released February 1974
Not issued U.S. / RAK *167* (U.K. #1)

Another major beneficiary of the Chinnichap midas touch was the American singer-bassist Suzi Quatro, who burst onto the U.K. singles chart in 1973 with a Number 1 hit, 'Can The Can,' penned by the songwriting duo. In the late 1960s Quatro had been a member of garage-rock girl group The Pleasure Seekers – which later became Cradle – alongside her sisters, Arlene, Patti, and Nancy. She moved to London in 1971 after being discovered by 1960s pop producer and RAK label boss Mickie Most. After 'Can The Can,' 'Devil Gate Drive' gave her a second U.K. chart-topper, and was one of 11 British Top 40 hits. While her records had little impact in the U.S., she did achieve a brief period of fame there in the late 1970s as a semi-regular guest star on *Happy Days*, and was a clear influence on later female rockers, among them Joan Jett.

A BALLROOM BLITZ WITH CHINN & CHAPMAN

Nicky Chinn and Mike Chapman were the premier songwriters and star-makers in Britain between 1973 and 1975 and became indelibly associated with a genre that came to be known as glam-rock. They had nothing to do with the glitter and sequins that adorned some of the acts for whom they wrote, but glam was also about a sound, and for this they certainly were responsible – although a nod should be given to Slade, one of the bands they didn't handle. Glam songs almost always sounded like anthems, shot though with the distinctly British flavor of a soccer-crowd singalong, with chanted vocals and thumping percussion. When the glam craze ended, the pair moved on effortlessly to other musical styles, with similar success.

Chinn was British, Chapman Australian, and they met in London in 1970. Chinn was a non-musician embarking on a career as a lyricist; guitarist Chapman was a member of a struggling band, Tangerine Peel. They had

a comfort zone thanks to the wealth of Chinn's family – Chinn financed their early demos – and they set about devising songs informed by what Chinn described as an "essential commerciality. Very, very pop indeed."

Early hits included an Archies-flavored jingle-pop number 'Funny Funny' (U.K. Top 20 for Sweet in 1971) and the downbeat and folk-ish 'Tom Tom Turnaround' (U.K. Number 6 for New World around the same time). Chinn & Chapman provided further hits for Sweet in 'Little Willy,' 'Co-Co,' and 'Poppa Joe,' but when they took the band into a more raucous style with the crunching 'Hellraiser,' 'Ballroom Blitz,' and 'Blockbuster' they began – unknowingly – to define an era in Britain.

The duo developed a formula of nonsensical but undeniably catchy and galvanizing rock'n'roll records, with lyrics chosen more for alliteration than linear coherency, which they gave to Mud ('Crazy,' 'Dyna-Mite,' and the titanic 'Tiger Feet' among them), Suzi Quatro ('Can The Can,' '48 Crash,' 'Devil Gate Drive') and Arrows ('A Touch Too Much').

Chinn & Chapman – or 'Chinnichap' as they became known collectively – came up with an Elvis-alike ballad, 'Lonely This Christmas,' which not only was a U.K. Yuletide Number 1 for Mud in 1974 but also proved they could write beyond the glam template. This versatility came in handy as glam started to fade in '74. Chinnichap were by now working on the start of a succession of fine hits for Smokie, boasting mellow tones and sophisticated words far removed from their earlier creations.

In the late 1970s, having racked up five U.K. chart-toppers as writers, the pair relocated to the States, a market that had proved largely immune both to glam and their songs. They secured U.S. chart placings with Huey Lewis, Tina Turner, and Exile, but before long the pair's partnership and friendship was ending. Chapman moved with great success into record production. Chinn experimented with different songwriting partners but, finding he wasn't enjoying the work as much as he had with Chapman, retired to tend a back catalogue that has continued to be lucrative, testament to the success of that "very, very pop indeed" sensibility.

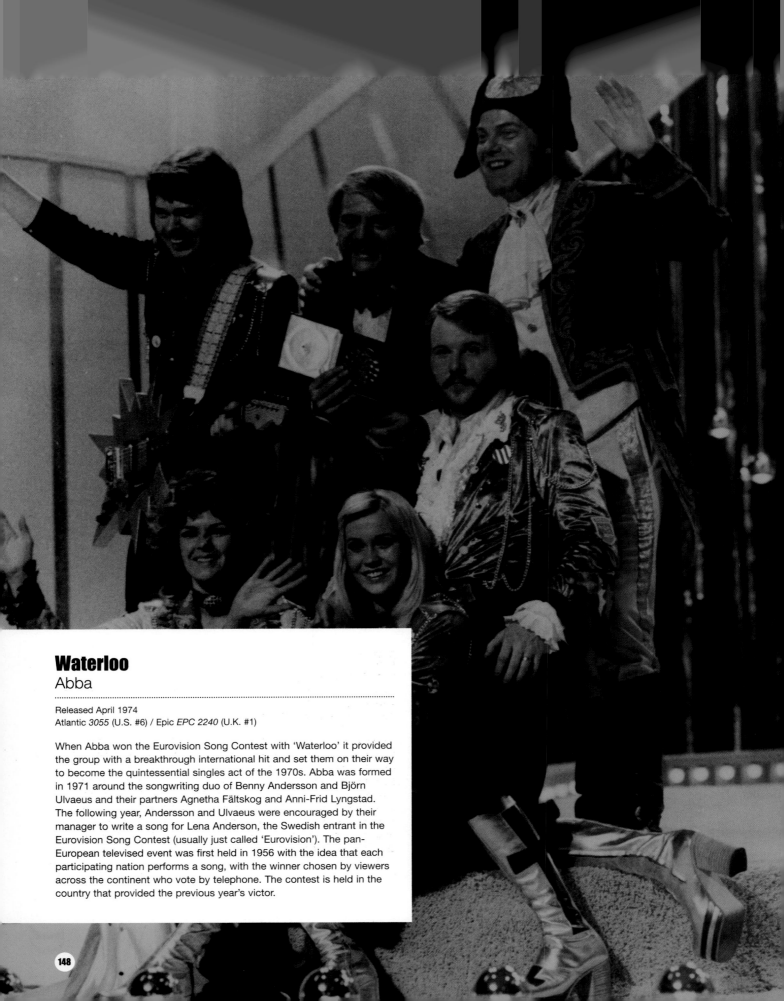

Waterloo
Abba

Released April 1974
Atlantic *3055* (U.S. #6) / Epic *EPC 2240* (U.K. #1)

When Abba won the Eurovision Song Contest with 'Waterloo' it provided the group with a breakthrough international hit and set them on their way to become the quintessential singles act of the 1970s. Abba was formed in 1971 around the songwriting duo of Benny Andersson and Björn Ulvaeus and their partners Agnetha Fältskog and Anni-Frid Lyngstad. The following year, Andersson and Ulvaeus were encouraged by their manager to write a song for Lena Anderson, the Swedish entrant in the Eurovision Song Contest (usually just called 'Eurovision'). The pan-European televised event was first held in 1956 with the idea that each participating nation performs a song, with the winner chosen by viewers across the continent who vote by telephone. The contest is held in the country that provided the previous year's victor.

Having caught the Eurovision bug, Andersson and Ulvaeus entered Abba into the 1973 contest. Their song, 'Ring Ring,' failed to make it beyond the preliminary stages of the competition but gave a glimpse of what was to follow. It demonstrated for the first time the potent combination of Andersson and Ulvaeus's knack for a catchy tune, Fältskog and Lyngstad's sugary-sweet voices, and the Phil Spector-influenced production talents of Michael B. Tretow.

The following year found Abba (and Tretow) determined to win Eurovision and to use it as a launch-pad for international stardom. For 1974's performance the group wrote and performed 'Waterloo,' an inspired blend of the proto-disco-pop of 'Ring Ring' and the glam-rock sound that currently dominated the British charts. 'Waterloo' stole the show at the 1974 contest, becoming such a favorite that in 2005 it was named as the greatest song in the history of the competition. More importantly for Abba, however, it topped the U.K. singles chart and reached the U.S. Top 10, laying the foundations for a career that would yield such classic hits as 'The Winner Takes It All,' 'Take A Chance On Me,' and 'Dancing Queen.'

This Town Ain't Big Enough For Both Of Us
Sparks

Released April 1974
Island *001* (U.S.) / Island *WIP 6193* (U.K. #2)

'This Town Ain't Big Enough For Both Of Us' is one of the most memorably off-the-wall singles of the glam-rock era. It introduced the eccentric Mael brothers to the pop world – wild-eyed vocalist Russel and Hitler-mustached keyboardist Ron – and packed more into its three minutes than a lot of bands managed in their entire careers. The Maels

formed the first incarnation of Sparks (at first known as Halfnelson) in the late 1960s in America and recorded two albums for Todd Rundgren's Bearsville label. Neither was a success, prompting the brothers to dismantle the band and move to London, England. Recruiting a new set of British musicians, they set about recording a third album, *Kimono My House*, with producer Muff Winwood, elder brother of Traffic frontman Steve.

'This Town Ain't Big Enough For Both Of Us' was the first single to be drawn from the album, and the debut release of Sparks Mark 2. It fades in over a backdrop of pulsating, hypnotic keyboards, as Russel intones the beginnings of a lyric about "stampeding rhinos, elephants, and tacky tigers." The words grow more bizarre as the song progresses – "You are a khaki-colored bombardier, it's Hiroshima that you're nearing" – but are matched by the ever-changing music, which evokes nothing much else except perhaps Queen with attention deficit disorder. Indeed, in some ways 'This Town' is a punchier prototype for 'Bohemian Rhapsody,' particularly given its numerous key and time-changes and the pseudo-operatic vocals. Sparks's single was a huge hit in the U.K. during the summer of 1974, and while there were a few respectable follow-ups, such as 'Amateur Hour' from the same year, Sparks were never able to match its success.

When Will I See You Again
The Three Degrees

Released June 1974
Philadelphia *3550* (U.S. #2) / Philadelphia *PIR 2155* (U.K. #1)

Although they did not quite live up to the billing, The Three Degrees had a good try at taking on the mantle of top female pop-soul vocal group, worn so elegantly and for so long by The Supremes. In fact, The Three Degrees had a history almost as long as their Motown rivals: they had formed in the early 1960s, but by the time 'When Will I See You Again' went platinum in 1974, none of the original line-up remained. The group was said to be a favorite of Prince Charles, a fact confirmed when he booked them to play at his 30th birthday party at Buckingham Palace. Later, they were guests at his wedding to Princess Diana, although she preferred Status Quo. (British pop act Brother Beyond had a minor hit with a cover of 'When Will I See you Again' in 1989.)

Emma
Hot Chocolate

Released March 1974
Big Tree *16031* (U.S. #8) / RAK *168* (U.K. #3)

The ominous two-chord riff that underpins 'Emma' is the perfect foundation for a lyric telling the story of a young woman who takes her own life, disillusioned after a failed search for fame and fortune. It features one of pop's most memorable fade-outs, with lead singer Errol Brown screaming the title over a descending five-note guitar riff. Hot Chocolate had a knack for that sort of thing, and their polished pop-rock served them well. Between 1970 and 1984 they had at least one British chart single every year, and a few U.S. hits too. 'Emma' was the first to chart in both countries, reaching its U.S. peak a year after it hit in Britain.

The Air That I Breathe
The Hollies

Released January 1974
Epic *11100* (U.S. #6) / Polydor *2058 435* (U.K. #2)

This hit marked the end of the road for The Hollies as a regular chart force. With a string of chart singles dating back to 1963 – all produced by George Martin's former Parlophone deputy Ron Richards – they were one of Britain's most consistently successful singles groups, with twenty-six Top-30 hits between 1963 and 1974. But an unexpected return to Number 1 in Britain in 1988 with 'He Ain't Heavy, He's My Brother' ensured that their U.K. Number 1s spanned an impressive 23 years. In America they enjoyed some of their biggest hits in the early 1970s. 'He Ain't Heavy' reached Number 7 in 1970, while the Creedence-like 'Long Cool Woman In A Black Dress' was their biggest ever U.S. hit, making Number 2 in August 1972.

Following the departure of Graham Nash and the break-up of the group's songwriting team of Nash, Tony Hicks, and Allan Clarke, The Hollies had used mostly contemporary pop writers such as Roger Cook, Roger Greenaway, and Tony Macaulay. Clarke wrote 'Long Cool Woman' with Cook and Greenaway. The group found 'The Air That I Breathe' on *Star Spangled Banner*, a 1973 solo album by Phil Everly, and the song was written by Albert Hammond and Mike Hazelwood. Hammond would become one of the world's most successful songwriters over the next 20 years. 'Air' had originally appearing on Hammond's own album, *It Never Rains In Southern California*, in 1972, and would become a U.K Top 10 hit again in 1998 when it was covered by Simply Red.

Sweet Home Alabama
Lynyrd Skynyrd

Released July 1974
MCA *40258* (U.S. #8) / MCA *160* (U.K.)

Lynyrd Skynyrd wrote this breakthrough hit, at least in part, in response to Neil Young's scathing 'Southern Man.' Young's song, included on his third solo album, *After The Gold Rush* (1970), was an attack on what he perceived as prevalent racist attitudes in the Southern United States. He warmed to the theme further on 'Alabama,' which featured on the subsequent *Harvest* (1972). Lynyrd Skynyrd frontman Ronnie Van Zant wrote 'Sweet Home Alabama' shortly thereafter. It was included on the group's sophomore album, *Second Helping*, and as a single.

While 'Sweet Home' does mention Young by name – "I hope Neil Young will remember / Southern Man don't need him around anyhow" – its role at the center of a supposed feud between the two parties is often exaggerated. Young and Van Zant might not have agreed about the politics of the South, but they were still mutual fans of each other's work. Young has even covered 'Sweet Home Alabama' live on a number of occasions. Speaking in 1992, he decided that "they didn't really put me down. [Not] in a way that matters. Shit, I think 'Sweet Home Alabama' is a great song."

Lynyrd Skynyrd had a further hit later in 1974 with the rock staple 'Free Bird' and continued to tour and record successfully until October 1977, when Van Zant and fellow band-members Steve and Cassie Gaines were killed in a plane crash.

You Are So Beautiful
Joe Cocker

Released December 1974
A&M *1641* (U.S. #5) / Fly *BUG 57* (U.K.)

With a voice that sounded as if he gargled gravel for breakfast, Joe Cocker has had something of a see-saw career. Born in Sheffield, England, Cocker enjoyed a breakthrough at home with his cover of The Beatles' 'With A Little Help From My Friends' in 1968 and went on to extensive American success with his 1970 tour and album *Mad Dogs And Englishmen*. Tour exhaustion put Cocker out of action for a period during which he was temporarily refused entrance to the U.S. following an Australian drugs charge. He had his biggest American success of the 1970s with this somewhat out-of-character but eloquently simple love song, composed by Billy Preston and Bruce Fisher. The song had originally appeared on Preston's 1974 album *The Kids & Me*. After Cocker had a Number 5 U.S. hit with his interpretation, he would have to wait another seven years for a Top 40 hit on either side of the Atlantic, when he topped the American charts with 'Up Where We Belong' in a duet with Jennifer Warnes.

You're The First, The Last, My Everything
Barry White

Released October 1974
20th Century *2133* (U.S. #2, U.K. #1)

An unlikely sex symbol, and sadly with us no more, Barry White weighed in at 300 pounds, sported a goatee beard, and had long curly hair. But of course, he didn't always have that voice. Unlikely as it now seems, White recalled: "Until I was 14 years old I had a sound not unlike the high-pitched voice of Michael Jackson." However, when he reached puberty his voice broke overnight, "like a drop off the Empire State Building," as he put it. "I woke up, and spoke to my mother – and scared us both to death."

White's highly orchestrated recordings, often accompanied by long erotic monologues, gave him a string of Top 10 hits during the 1970s as well as success with his Love Unlimited trio and The Love Unlimited Orchestra. Of the transatlantic hits he racked up between 1973 and 1979, 'You're The First' was the most successful, reaching Number 1 in Britain and Number 2 in America. White, and this song in particular, enjoyed something of a renaissance in 2000 when featured in the hit TV series *Ally McBeal*. The Man was back, and even made a cameo appearance on the show.

Apart from creating music, Mr. White was much in demand for his advice with regard to the intricacies of relationships, and particularly the creation of seductive circumstances. White advised that to get in the mood, a romantic song is a must (preferably one of his), saying that a red-hot evening should include a candlelit dinner and plenty of time. He suggested that at the end of a relationship one should "get back out there A.S.A.P. and find someone else to love."

In a bizarre turn of events, marine center officials in Britain hoped that White's seductive songs would do for sharks what they have done for countless humans. Staff at the Great Yarmouth Sea Life Centre played his music to their sharks in an effort to spice up their sex life, and this practice has now spread to other marine establishments around the country. Perhaps they should reconfigure the song as 'You're The First, The Last, My Every Fin'?

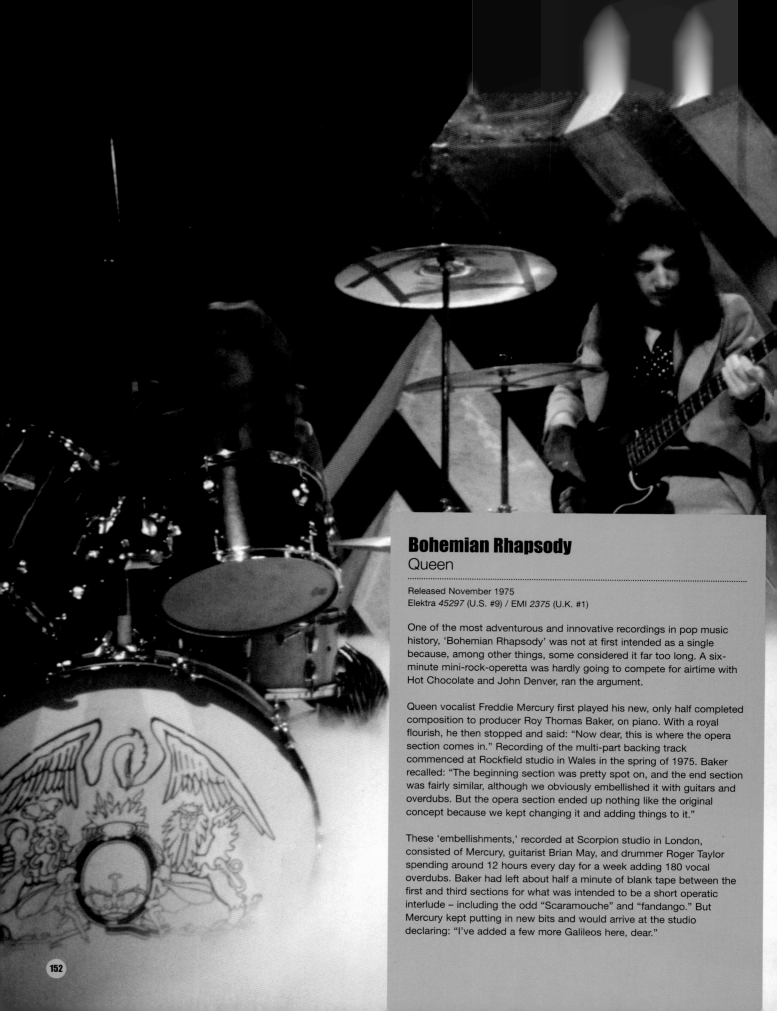

Bohemian Rhapsody
Queen

Released November 1975
Elektra *45297* (U.S. #9) / EMI *2375* (U.K. #1)

One of the most adventurous and innovative recordings in pop music history, 'Bohemian Rhapsody' was not at first intended as a single because, among other things, some considered it far too long. A six-minute mini-rock-operetta was hardly going to compete for airtime with Hot Chocolate and John Denver, ran the argument.

Queen vocalist Freddie Mercury first played his new, only half completed composition to producer Roy Thomas Baker, on piano. With a royal flourish, he then stopped and said: "Now dear, this is where the opera section comes in." Recording of the multi-part backing track commenced at Rockfield studio in Wales in the spring of 1975. Baker recalled: "The beginning section was pretty spot on, and the end section was fairly similar, although we obviously embellished it with guitars and overdubs. But the opera section ended up nothing like the original concept because we kept changing it and adding things to it."

These 'embellishments,' recorded at Scorpion studio in London, consisted of Mercury, guitarist Brian May, and drummer Roger Taylor spending around 12 hours every day for a week adding 180 vocal overdubs. Baker had left about half a minute of blank tape between the first and third sections for what was intended to be a short operatic interlude – including the odd "Scaramouche" and "fandango." But Mercury kept putting in new bits and would arrive at the studio declaring: "I've added a few more Galileos here, dear."

There were so many edits on the tape that Baker remembered it looking "like a zebra-crossing whizzing by." Mercury: "That middle section got longer and longer and longer. ...We were all in hysterics when it was being recorded. ...We had to sit there going, 'No, no, no, no, no, no, no, no!' about 150 times." This wasn't the only problem. Even using 24-track technology, the many overdubs meant the engineers had to employ tricks such as track 'bouncing' to accommodate the increasing number of vocals, and even a number of complete tape-to-tape transfers. Baker said the making of the song "was basically one continuous track bounce."

There is an oft-repeated myth that by this time the master tape was "almost transparent," but when the tapes were recently retrieved for conversion to surround-sound, the "transparent" claim was proved untrue. The tape also exhibited no physical edits, which would indicate that the original master tape must have been transferred at some stage. (The conversion did reveal that there were three alternative takes for the lead vocals.) Baker reckoned that the total recording time was about three weeks, including two days for the basic backing track, seven days for all the vocal overdubs, a few more for guitar overdubs, and two days of mixing. For most acts, this was enough time to record an entire album, and the total cost was astronomical.

Since their third album, *Sheer Heart Attack*, the band had fallen out with their previous management, Trident, and signed a new deal with Elton John's manager John Reid in time for *A Night At The Opera*, named after a Marx Brothers movie that the group had watched during work at Rockfield. In one of his first directives as the group's manager, Reid insisted that EMI release 'Bohemian Rhapsody' as a single, although both Queen and EMI thought radio DJs would not be interested. According to Reid, Elton John told Queen that they were crazy even to consider releasing a single of such length. This seems odd, however, since three of Elton's own recent singles were just as lengthy. Baker recalled that he was ready for this argument and noted that songs of equal length such as Richard Harris's 'MacArthur Park' and 'Eloise' by Barry Ryan, both issued in 1968, had been readily played by the BBC in Britain. Surely it was the quality of the product that mattered?

Queen rather cleverly circumvented EMI's reluctance by giving a copy of the completed track to London's Capital Radio DJ Kenny Everett, a friend of Mercury's. With a nod and a wink, they gave Everett strict instructions not to play the record. That certainly did the trick: Everett played it 14 times in two days on his weekend radio show, claiming on-air that his "finger had slipped." With this amount of exposure, a Number 1 record was pretty much guaranteed, and EMI were persuaded.

Realizing that live performance of the song was going to be tricky, the group decided to make a promotional video that could be screened to promote the single. Roger Taylor said: "We only did it because we had to be in Liverpool and couldn't do [TV singles show] *Top Of The Pops*." The ground-breaking video has often been described as the first of its kind, but the idea of promo clips dates back at least to the 1960s and had been used by The Beatles after they ceased touring. Brian May said: "Everyone thought the film was a huge production. But it was really easy to do, and since then we've spent a lot of time on films which probably aren't as good, and certainly didn't get the exposure."

What is true is that this innovative clip cost a meager £4,500 (about $10,000 at the time) and was screened for nine consecutive weeks on *Top Of The Pops* while the song was Number 1. It ushered in the age of video clips and, ultimately, the arrival of MTV. Ironically, Queen would later criticize the importance of video presentation versus musical content in their 1984 hit 'Radio Ga Ga.'

So what was 'Bohemian Rhapsody' all about? Mercury was never particularly forthcoming. Roger Taylor said: "Freddie had the whole song mapped out in his head. Don't ask me to explain what it's about because I haven't got a fucking clue. It's the vibe that's important." According to Kenny Everett, Mercury told him it was "random rhyming nonsense."

Does it really matter? From the opening 15 seconds of a cappella voices to the closing gong, this was Queen's finest moment on record. Their greatest performance on stage was the 17-minute medley of hits they delivered in front of millions worldwide at Live Aid ten years later in the summer of 1985. In his usual no-nonsense vocabulary, Live Aid organizer Bob Geldof secured the services of Freddie Mercury and his band by phoning their manager and saying: "Tell the old faggot it's gonna be the biggest thing that ever happened." Showman Freddie Mercury could hardly turn down an offer like that, and the group didn't disappoint. Following the show, Geldof said: "Queen were absolutely the best band of the day."

'Bo-Rap' topped the U.K. charts for nine weeks from November 1975 and a further five from December 1991, following Mercury's death. Reigning over the new year on both occasions meant that the song gained the unique distiction of being Number 1 in four separate years.

The original Number 9 placing in America was eclipsed by a 1992 Number 2 in the wake of the song's central role in the hilarious head-banging scene from the movie *Wayne's World*. Strangely, the Abba song that followed Queen to Number 1 in early 1976 may have gained some subliminal promotion since its title, 'Mamma Mia,' also appeared in the Queen hit.

Many commentators at the time thought that 'Bohemian Rhapsody' was symptomatic of the excess of 1970s progressive rock, but time and wisdom have drawn different conclusions. It is the third biggest selling single of all time in Britain, and in a 2002 survey undertaken by the *Guinness Book Of British Hit Singles* to discover the U.K. public's favorite all-time 45, 'Bohemian Rhapsody' was the runaway Number 1 choice.

Autobahn
Kraftwerk

Released February 1975
Vertigo *203* (U.S. #25) / Vertigo *6147 012* (U.K. #11)

With the benefit of hindsight, we can recognize the German synthesizer band Kraftwerk as true pioneers of pop. The band's influence has spread through hip-hop, techno, and the New Romantic movement, and bled into virtually all mainstream rock and pop. Many are the hits by artists as diverse as Madonna, New Order, and Afrika Bambaataa, to name just a few, that simply wouldn't have been made if it wasn't for the impeccably drawn sonic blueprint that emerged from Kraftwerk's Kling Klang studio more than 30 years ago.

The album *Autobahn,* which included a lengthy version of the title track from which the single was edited, was Kraftwerk's fourth, and the first to be issued in America. Until that point the band were thought of as little more than marginal German eccentrics, and even after 'Autobahn,' their breakthrough single, it was a while before their importance was understood. The mix of precision electronic rhythms, pulsing synthesizers, and deadpan vocals simply had not been heard before. Even though 'Autobahn' the single and then the album were big international hits, for some time afterwards many considered Kraftwerk as little more than a novelty act.

The song is a hymn to the straight-line speed and efficiency of the German freeway network, itself an apposite image of the new music of Kraftwerk (the group's name means 'power station'). Sounds surge into the mix and hit a crescendo before fading out again, evoking a sleek Mercedes passing at 100 mph, while a detached voice intones: "Wir fahr'n fahr'n fahr'n auf der Autobahn." To some ears, this sounded like "Fun, fun, fun on the Autobahn," leading a handful of critics to conclude that Kraftwerk were engaged in some Teutonic spoof of The Beach Boys. They weren't, of course: they were just being themselves. And although there have been many imitators, still no one else sounds quite like Kraftwerk.

Roadrunner
Jonathan Richman & The Modern Lovers

Released June 1975
Beserkley *5701* (U.S.) / United Artists *36006* (U.K. #11)

This classic of proto-punk garage rock took the long route to success. It was recorded in 1973, not issued as a single until 1975 in Britain and '76 in America, and did not chart until 1977. It was produced by former Velvet Underground member John Cale and featured guitarist Jerry Harrison, who had joined Talking Heads by the time 'Roadrunner' reached the U.K. singles chart. Opening with a cry of "one-two-three-four-five-six!" the song is a frenetic, two-chord paean to driving down the highway while listening to the radio. It remains Richman's defining moment, although more people may be aware of him – probably without realizing – for his musical role in the 1998 comedy movie *There's Something About Mary*.

No Regrets
The Walker Brothers

Released October 1975
Not issued U.S. / GTO *GT 42* (U.K. #7)

They were teen-idol balladeers of the 1960s, but when they reformed unexpectedly in 1975, The Walker Brothers adopted a more mature, country-rock sound. They immediately reaped rewards from the change of direction with a hit version of Tom Rush's classic break-up song, 'No Regrets.'

Rush had originally recorded the song with an acoustic arrangement on his 1968 album, *Circle Game*, and he came back to it in 1974, recasting it with sweeping strings and a searing guitar solo for his *Ladies Love Outlaws* album. It was this that caught the ears of the reformed Walkers, and they copied the arrangement virtually note-for-note: same string part, same guitar solo. 'No Regrets' was given title billing for the band's first comeback album and was released as a single, briefly competing for airtime with a single of Rush's version in the arrangement the Walkers had covered.

Scott, John, and Garry – who weren't brothers at all – won the battle for a chart place, but Rush earned his composer's royalties and reasoned that imitation was the sincerest form of flattery. Another twist in the tale came in 1982 when Midge Ure had a hit with yet another version of the song. Although Ure made heavy use of drum machines and synthesizers it was clear that his version still owed much to The Walker Brothers cut, and thereby to the Tom Rush take.

Lady Marmalade (Voulez-Vous Coucher Avec Moi Ce Soir?)
LaBelle

Released January 1975
Epic *50048* (U.S. #1) / Epic *EPC 2852* (U.K. #17)

'Lady Marmalade' was released a mighty 13 years after Patti 'Patricia Holt' LaBelle and her band had scored their first hit, and made it to Number 1 on the U.S. Billboard charts, staying around for months and refusing to budge either from the listings or from the brain of anyone who heard it. Damn, those girls were funky, with their coy invitations of "Voulez-vous coucher avec moi ce soir?" and what sounded like some sort of sexual voodoo chant in the immortal verse "Itchi gitchi ya ya da da / Itchi gitchi ya ya here / Mocha-choca-lata ya ya / Creole Lady Marmalade!" Musically, it's pure fatback funk, with a huge bass and piano part playing that awe-inspiring backing lick in full, those vocal improvisations and interjections from the singers lending a grind that seems positively rude.

The trio's outlandish image made the impact of the song all the more forceful: they wore silver Funkadelic-like apparel and came up with futuristic soundbites that could have come straight from the sci-fi-meets-Black-Panther world of George Clinton and Bootsy Collins. Little wonder that the song has been covered with varying degrees of success by modern acts such as All Saints and a collective of high-stepping R&B females, Christina Aguilera, Lil' Kim, Mya, & Pink. 'Lady Marmalade' remains one of the finest moments of the classic girl-group era – and, remarkably, it's not even a love song. Patti LaBelle herself couldn't match its success, and she slipped into AOR blandness in the 1980s, in the following decade espousing causes such as diabetes awareness. But as career highs go, this is one to cherish.

Bye Bye Baby
The Bay City Rollers

Released March 1975
Arista *0120* (U.S.) / Bell *1409* (U.K. #1)

'Bye Bye Baby' was the start of a new era for The Bay City Rollers. With five U.K. Top 10 hits under their belt, they decided that the time was ripe to play on their own records, instead of giving way again to the sessioneers who had fulfilled that function, and to write their own singles. It took a little longer to achieve the latter objective than the former – and even that was shortlived – but 'Bye Bye Baby,' as the band's first U.K. Number 1, constituted a vindication of sorts.

The song was an old Four Seasons number, although the Rollers knew it from a version by British harmony group The Symbols, who had secured the only U.K. hit for the song so far. The Rollers could not hope to match Frankie Valli's vocal gymnastics or the musicianship of the original, but their rendition was pleasant enough. That could be said about their entire catalogue, and hardly seemed to explain the global domination that briefly followed. America succumbed later in 1975 when 'Saturday Night' became a chart-topper there, following the Stateside failure of 'Bye Bye Baby.' The group's trick seemed to be their ability to hold teens and pre-teens in their thrall thanks to a set of genuinely personable natures. They were not, as has been erroneously alleged, precursors of the boy-band genre: the Rollers were musicians, not a vocal group.

However, none of the retrospective credibility that has been afforded Abba will go to them, for The Bay City Rollers were, quite simply, the definition of lightweight.

Jive Talkin'
The Bee Gees

Released May 1975
RSO *510* (U.S. #1) / RSO *2090 160* (U.K. #5)

Following their first string of 1960s hits, The Bee Gees saw their popularity slowly declining. There followed some lean years in the early 1970s culminating in the rejection of an entire album of material by their record company in 1974. That unreleased album, *A Kick In The Head Is Worth Eight In The Pants*, was the group's turning point – and a kick in the pants was exactly what they needed, and got, when their manager, Robert Stigwood, connected them with veteran producer Arif Mardin. The trio's songwriting magic returned for *Main Course*, the 1975 album that marked a dramatic return by the group who many thought were past their best.

'Jive Talkin'' was originally inspired by a daily trip that the brothers Gibb took over a metal bridge to and from the studio. The metallic rhythm that the bridge produced inspired an idea that began as "Drive talking…" but quickly evolved into the more famous title. Upon presenting their new song to Mardin, the group were surprised to discover what it actually meant. They'd been thinking in terms of dancing, whereas Mardin was quick to point out that in the context of the song it was black slang for talking rubbish. This didn't worry the group, who quickly changed their original lyric "you dance with your eyes" into "you're telling me lies." They were swiftly rewarded with their second U.S. Number 1 and repeated the success with 'You Should Be Dancing' in 1976. Little did they know that in a couple of years the whole world would be dancing to their new R&B music.

I'm Not In Love
10cc

Released May 1975
Mercury *73678* (U.S. #2) / Mercury *6008 014* (U.K. #1)

It was always easy to admire 10cc but difficult to love them. After all, few people love a smart-ass. Or to put it more scientifically, 10cc had unquestionable musical and production abilities, but their songs were so self-conscious and post-modern that it seemed as though they were above all this. By 1975, the quartet had racked up five Top 10 U.K. hits, including the rip-roaring 'Rubber Bullets' but also 'Donna,' a pastiche of a 1950s oldie that was so knowing as to be somehow insufferable, and considered by many to be part of the problem. Depending on your taste, 'I'm Not In Love' either rectified a deficiency of soullessness, or confirmed it.

The song started life with 10cc guitarist Eric Stewart, whose girlfriend of the time complained to him that he didn't tell her he loved her often enough. His response was not so cruel as the song title – he replied that it was meaningless if he said so every day – but the idea for a song was born. The group piled on vocal harmony after vocal harmony and had a slightly speech-impaired studio receptionist intone "big boys don't cwy" in an interlude. One highly unusually effect came from the fact that the recording has no drums. Once the record was complete, the band lay on the studio floor in the dark listening to the creamy result. The single, edited down from the LP version, was massively popular, even among those cynical enough to perceive it as sheer form and artifice.

That's The Way (I Like It)
K.C. & The Sunshine Band

Released June 1975
T.K. *1015* (U.S. #1) / Jayboy *BOY 99* (U.K. #4)

K.C. was Harry Wayne Casey, and as a commercial disco artist he understood the value of repetition just as well as his punk contemporaries The Ramones. The title of 'That's The Way I Like It' is repeated 17 times during the course of the song, with the truncated phrase "that's the way" turning up another eight times. But it wasn't just endless chorus repeats that gave K.C. and his Sunshine Band this smash hit – it was the memorable tune, the eminently danceable groove, and the stabbing horn interjections. Together they made a record still guaranteed to send even the most reluctant and ungainly of dancers onto the floor. It was a formula that served the band well and gave them many more hits. One of the last was 'Give It Up,' where the title was repeated 22 times.

Rhinestone Cowboy
Glen Campbell

Released June 1975
Capitol *4095* (U.S. #1) / Capitol *CL 15824* (U.K. #4)

This is a masterpiece of songwriting economy, performed with great gusto by one of the most popular country singers of the 1960s and '70s. 'Rhinestone Cowboy' tells the maudlin tale of a Broadway entertainer who has "been walkin' these streets so long / Singin' the same old song" and knows at heart that he is never destined for glory. But the show must go on, and as the song continues, the melody expertly ascends, mirroring the chest-beating optimism of the pay-off line: "But I'm gonna be where the lights are shinin' on me." It has become the song that Campbell is most associated with and, although it was not his own composition, he clearly empathized with its lyrical content, even going so far as to title his 1994 autobiography *Rhinestone Cowboy*.

It Only Takes A Minute
Tavares

Released July 1975
Capitol *4111* (U.S. #10) / Capitol *CL 15832* (U.K.)

Like the Jacksons, the Osmonds, and the Isleys, Tavares were a family R&B group, this one consisting of five brothers from New Bedford, Massachusetts. Originally called Chubby & The Turnpikes, they reverted to the family name before signing to Capitol in 1973. The first album was produced by Johnny Bristol and the group then teamed up with writer-producers Dennis Lambert and Brian Potter, who had recently enjoyed major success with the post-Motown Four Tops. 'It Only Takes A Minute' was an R&B Number 1 and their biggest of eight Top-40 pop hits in America, reaching Number 10 on the regular chart. It was not a hit at the time in Britain, despite heavy disco play, and the following year was covered there by Jonathan King, man of many hats, under the guise One Hundred Ton And A Feather, making Number 9. Tavares's most enduring hit in the U.K. was 'Heaven Must Be Missing An Angel,' a Number 4 in 1976 and Number 12 when remixed in 1986.

Sailing
Rod Stewart

Released August 1975
Warner Bros. *WB 8146* (U.S.) / Warner Bros. *K 16600* (U.K. #1)

For his first Warner Brothers album, *Atlantic Crossing*, Rod Stewart had engaged renowned R&B producer Tom Dowd to record with the famous Muscle Shoals rhythm section in Alabama. When Stewart was introduced to the musicians, he was convinced Dowd was playing a joke on him, exclaiming: "That can't be the Muscle Shoals rhythm section, they're all white!" It wasn't until he heard the band play that he was convinced. 'Sailing' was written by Gavin Sutherland of British group The Sutherland Brothers, who had released it as a single without success. Stewart made the song his own and its singalong chorus soon made it popular with soccer crowds throughout Britain, where it remains a firm favorite. Stewart said: 'I recorded it in Alabama, a partially 'dry' state. I was asked to sing live at 10:30 in the morning with no lubrication for the vocal chords on hand – get my drift?" A U.K. Number 1 in 1975, it returned  to the Top 3 the following year when featured in a BBC documentary series about the aircraft carrier Ark Royal. Surprisingly, 'Sailing' flopped in the States, only making Number 58, although the following year Stewart would enjoy a U.S. Number 1 with 'Tonight's The Night.'

You Sexy Thing
Hot Chocolate

Released November 1975
Big Tree *16047* (U.S. #3) / *RAK 221* (U.K. #2)

An ardent chorus, a chattering conga pattern, and a memorable six-note guitar riff are just a few of the hooks in Hot Chocolate's biggest hit. Lead singer Errol Brown was just the man for the mildly suggestive lyrics, too. Smooth, snake-hipped, and usually dressed in a silk shirt unbuttoned almost to the waist, Brown had a carefully cultivated ladies-man image that was a major factor in the band's success. A little dangerous, maybe, but not really bad. "Oh touch me, you sexy thing," he screamed as the song seductively slinked to a close – and millions wished they could. Panties were thrown, singles were bought, and 'You Sexy Thing' became a huge U.S. and U.K. hit, charting again in Britain in the 1980s and 1990s.

No Woman, No Cry
Bob Marley & The Wailers

Released August 1975
Island *037* (U.S.) / Island *WIP 6244* (U.K. #8)

Eternally misinterpreted as meaning "you're better off without a woman" when in fact the title means the much more sympathetic "woman, please don't cry," this song was the first British hit for Bob Marley & The Wailers. It is one of the few songs best known as a live version, and was edited down from the take on the band's *Live!* LP (although the original version on the *Natty Dread* album, also released in '75, is worth checking out). While Marley is usually assumed to have written the song, the credit was given to Vincent Ford, a friend of Bob's who ran a soup kitchen in Kingston, Jamaica. Revenue from the song kept Ford's charitable operation running for years.

In 'No Woman, No Cry' Marley demonstrates his mastery of storytelling, laying down his sentiments of political despair and encouragement within a format that is almost a hymn. Over an organ backing simultaneously hypnotic and stirring, he sings: "I remember when we used to sit / In the government yard in Trenchtown / Observing the hypocrites / As they would mingle with the good people we meet." His backing singers gently raise their voices in angelic harmony, before the song takes off half way through and evolves into a funkier, almost gospel invocation of "everything's gonna be all right" that, you can safely assume, everyone in the world can sing. It's remarkably effective, and a perfect route into the otherwise more challenging Marley canon.

Born To Run
Bruce Springsteen

Released September 1975
Columbia *10209* (U.S. #23) / CBS *3661* (U.K.)

This was probably the most important recording in Springsteen's career. It was make or break time for the future Boss after his first two albums had sold poorly. He later described 'Born To Run' as "my shot at the title. A 24-year-old kid aimin' at 'the greatest rock'n'roll record ever.'" He re-wrote and re-wrote the song over a period of about six months, filling up 50 pages in his notebook until he was satisfied with the lyric.

It took a further three months to complete the recording of this one song, which cost $10,000. The original take was overdubbed with everything imaginable, including female back-up vocals and a string arrangement, by which time Springsteen had completely lost the plot. He recalled: "I was striving for something very specific that I didn't know how to get." Fortunately, Jon Landau did. He was brought on board in an advisory capacity and boiled down all the overdubs to the basic ingredients that had featured on the original version.

Landau had witnessed Springsteen's first live performance of the song on May 9, 1974, in Cambridge, Massachusetts, and wrote a review ("I saw the future of rock'n'roll") that has since become famous. Even when completed, 'Born To Run' had a lukewarm reception at Columbia Records, so manager Mike Appel sent cassettes to a number of radio jocks – and Columbia was furious. Appel said: "People were coming into the stores – in Cleveland, Dallas, Boston, all over – looking for the new Springsteen album, which didn't exist. All we'd cut to that point was a single that hadn't been released." All the hype eventually paid off and secured cover stories on Springsteen in *Newsweek* and *Time* during the same week. In the U.K. that hype was detrimental, and 'Born To Run' wasn't a hit until a live version finally made the charts in 1987.

The Boys Are Back In Town
Thin Lizzy

Released April 1976
Mercury *73786* (U.S. #12) / Vertigo *6059 139* (U.K. #8)

'The Boys Are Back In Town' was the apotheosis of Thin Lizzy's tandem guitar attack. The riff following the fist-punching choruses saw Brian Robertson and Scott Gorham playing in harmony what sounded like a speeded-up, dirtied-down version of Woody Woodpecker's laugh. It made for one of the most unforgettable licks in rock history.

Also memorable was the opening guitar lick, which, ingeniously, was adapted from the horn chart in a lesser-known Bruce Springsteen song called 'Kitty's Back.' There is still a trace of Springsteen about the song's blue-collar ambience and anthemic properties. The lyrics by Lizzy bassist and frontman Phil Lynott started out with "G.I. Joe's back in town" before he decided to jettison the idea of a returning Vietnam vet for a song based on a disreputable Manchester mob, the Quality Street Gang. The words possess a cartoon quality and at least appear to make sense ("If that chick don't wanna know, forget her!") but any misgivings about the song are swept aside by a chorus so infectious as to be ludicrous, even though it does consist merely of the title phrase repeated over and over by a voice performing a call-and-response with itself in each speaker.

Jon Bon Jovi has admitted that he based his band's entire style on Lizzy. Their continuing impact is underlined by the fact that Dan Hawkins, guitarist with The Darkness, is rarely seen in public without a Lizzy T-shirt.

Devil Woman
Cliff Richard

Released April 1976
Rocket *40574* (U.S. #6) / EMI *2458* (U.K. #9)

The perpetual bachelor boy was already 20 years into his career and looking a bit tired when he emerged rejuvenated with 'Devil Woman.' Hailed at the time as a return to Cliff's rock'n'roll roots and considered in questionable taste by his Christian fans, 'Devil Woman' in fact sounds pretty tame. But it is perfectly executed mature pop and set the tone for a run of late-1970s / early-1980s chart hits, including 'We Don't Talk Anymore' and 'Wired For Sound.' Most of Cliff's dozens of U.K. hit singles have missed the mark in America, but 'Devil Woman' charted very respectably there.

A Little Bit More
Dr. Hook

Released June 1976
Capitol *4280* (U.S. #11) / Capitol *CL 15871* (U.K. #2)

Formed in 1968 as Dr. Hook & The Medicine Show, this country-pop outfit featured two lead singers, Ray Sawyer (the one with the eye-patch, added after he lost an eye in an automobile accident) and Dennis Locorriere. Their first success came with songs written by *Playboy* cartoonist Shel Silverstein. 'Sylvia's Mother' was a worldwide hit after Columbia chief Clive Davis put the company's promotional muscle

behind it, followed by 'The Cover Of Rolling Stone.' Legal problems and the departure of Davis from Columbia led to a switch to Capitol and decidedly more middle-of-the-road country material recorded in Nashville – and to far greater success, particularly internationally. 'A Little Bit More,' composed by the unlikely-named Bobby Gosh, was co-produced by Waylon Jennings and gave Dr. Hook a worldwide hit, leading to a new wave of success that culminated in 1979 with a U.K. Number 1 for 'When You're In Love With A Beautiful Woman.'

Let's Stick Together
Bryan Ferry

Released June 1976
Atlantic *3351* (U.S.) / Island *WIP 6307* (U.K. #4)

Roxy Music's distinctive vocalist Bryan Ferry began his parallel solo career after the band's second album in 1973. For his early projects he stuck to covers while keeping original material for the Roxy albums, and he wrote or co-wrote nearly all of Roxy Music's hits. His first U.K. solo hit in October 1973 was a cover of Bob Dylan's 'A Hard Rain's A-Gonna Fall' and he followed through the following year with remakes of Dobie Gray's 'The In Crowd' and The Platters' 'Smoke Gets In Your Eyes' before his biggest solo success in 1976 with 'Let's Stick Together.' None of these were hits in America, and indeed neither Roxy Music nor Ferry on his own have enjoyed much U.S. chart action.

For his solo career, Ferry adopted a suave dinner-jacket-and-bow-tie image, something like a modern day crooner, in contrast to his more bohemian appearance in Roxy Music. His third solo album, bearing the same title as this hit, was simply a hotchpotch of B-sides and a couple of current singles of which this, a full-throttle three minutes with an

effective saxophone lead, was the standout track. While the song was perhaps best known as 'Let's *Work* Together,' a hit for blues band Canned Heat in 1970, writer Wilbert Harrison had originally recorded it in 1962 as 'Let's Stick Together' before later re-recording it in 1969 as 'Let's Work Together.' Ferry made a second chart appearance in Britain in 1988 with the song, given considerably more punch in a remix by Bob Clearmountain.

Harvest For The World
The Isley Brothers

Released June 1976
T-Neck *2260* (U.S.) / Epic *EPC 4369* (U.K. #10)

Although only a minor hit in the U.S., the international success of 'Harvest' provided evidence of how soul-folk fusion, pioneered by Otis Redding's 'Dock Of The Bay' in 1968, was coming of age in the mid 1970s. The Isleys had weathered pop's changing fashions from their early-1960s R&B successes, through a rock-oriented approach as the decade ended, to their generally folkier leanings on 1973's *3+3* album. Now they were delivering an ecological message through an artful blend of strummy guitars, keyboards, and handclaps. Enduringly popular, 'Harvest' has been covered by artists as diverse as Power Station (1985), The Christians (1988), and Kirsty MacColl (1999).

If You Leave Me Now
Chicago

Released July 1976
Columbia *10390* (U.S. #1) / CBS *4603* (U.K. #1)

Like the similarly brass-driven Blood Sweat & Tears (with whom they shared a producer), Chicago signed to Columbia in 1969. The group elongated their name to Chicago Transit Authority after threatened legal action by the mayor of the Windy City. At first they scored only in Britain, with 'I'm A Man' and '25 Or 6 To 4' in 1970, but soon racked up a wall full of platinum albums Stateside and over a dozen hit singles before a mid-1970s switch to AOR ballads.

'If You Leave Me Now' gave them their first Number 1 on both sides of the Atlantic. Written and sung by bass guitarist Peter Cetera, the song featured fine acoustic guitar solos played by producer James Guercio. They continued in similar style, later enjoying further ballad success, with 'Hard To Say I'm Sorry' and 'You're The Inspiration' in the early 1980s, both composed by Cetera together with the group's later producer David Foster, before Cetera's departure for a solo career in 1985.

(Don't Fear) The Reaper
Blue Öyster Cult

Released July 1976
Columbia *10384* (U.S. #12) / CBS *6333* (U.K. #16)

Considering the lawsuits that heavy metal bands have attracted from parents of distressed or dead teenagers for their alleged backwards messages and gloomy lyrics, it is surprising that Blue Öyster Cult's signature song has not thus far led to the same. Buck Dharma, the Cult guitarist who wrote it, denies that it celebrates suicide, claiming its subject is a love that transcends the physical. The musical backing is

suitably epic and stately, and boasts a typical Öyster airbrushed polish. It's intelligent heavy metal – even if the song is not quite as disquieting or magisterial as it's clearly intended to be.

More Than A Feeling
Boston

Released September 1976
Epic *50266* (U.S. #5) / Epic *EPC 4658* (U.K. #22)

Boston marked a phenomenon that really only became possible in the 1970s: a faceless band. Hitherto, record consumers would not tolerate pop or rock bands with whom they could not associate a face, so bound up was popular music with good looks – or at least with image. By the '70s, the audience for rock had grown with the medium. To record purchasers older than teens, the only requisite was good music. This makes it all the more interesting that Boston was the kind of band disdained by punk, a movement that was shifting onto the public radar in Britain just as Boston secured a transatlantic hit with this, their debut.

The boast of punk was that it was liberating for performers, especially females, because nobody cared what they looked like, but Boston were ahead of them on that score. Also ironic is that, although Boston have always suffered from a 'corporate' image, they in fact have always supported and aligned themselves with left and liberal causes. The group is essentially Tom Scholz, the one mainstay of the group and the mastermind behind their multi-tracked extravaganzas.

Scholz touched all bases in this song: a crunching guitar riff, soaring melody, a lyric of music-inspired nostalgia, and an airbrushed, widescreen production. The result was FM immortality. Its parent album became one of history's all-time biggest sellers.

Livin' Thing
Electric Light Orchestra

Released October 1976
United Artists/Jet *888* (U.S. #13) / Jet *UP 36184* (U.K. #4)

The Electric Light Orchestra was originally conceived as "a band with strings" in the late 1960s by Birmingham musicians Roy Wood and Jeff Lynne. By 1976, Wood was long gone and Lynne was the sole writer, singer, guitarist, and producer of all ELO's material. 'Livin' Thing' was the first of three hit singles on both sides of the Atlantic from *A New World Record*, ELO's first million-selling U.S. album.

One of Lynne's major problems was recording all his string overdubs with studio orchestras, particularly in Britain where archaic Musicians' Union rules continued to frustrate him. Lynne recalled: "We'd be coming to the end of a song and the clock would be going just over the minute, and they'd just stop. Unless you booked them for another three hours to play this extra minute, they were gone."

Lynne eventually discovered Musicland studios in Munich, Germany, and took his business there. "Orchestras in Munich were totally different," he concluded. "They'd all crowd into the control room and go, 'Wow, that's good! Let's try it again. Maybe we can make it better.'" (The Beautiful South had a U.K. hit with a re-make of 'Livin' Thing' in 2004.)

December 1963 (Oh What A Night)
The 4 Seasons

Released January 1976
Warner Bros./Curb *8168* (U.S. #1) / Warner Bros/Curb *K 16688* (U.K. #1)

The Seasons were one of America's most successful vocal acts of the 1960s, with twenty-seven U.S. Top-40 hits between 1962 and 1968, including four Number 1s, but were not nearly so popular in the U.K., with only nine Top-40 hits there in the same period, the biggest of which were 'Sherry,' Let's Hang On,' and 'Rag Doll.' It was a slightly reformatted group that returned in the 1970s, although the main ingredients were still on board: vocalist Frankie Valli and writer-producer Bob Gaudio.

This song was originally written about the repeal of prohibition in America in December 1933, an unlikely subject for a pop song, which was why the story was updated to 1963. The Seasons had a couple more hits during this revival, but it was Valli who made the most of the opportunity, enjoying two solo U.S. Number 1s with 'My Eyes Adored You' and 1978's Barry Gibb-composed theme for the *Grease* movie.

Save Your Kisses For Me
Brotherhood Of Man

Released March 1976
Pye *71066* (U.S. #27) / Pye *7N 45569* (U.K. #1)

The group was originally formed by Tony Hiller as a studio session outfit in 1969 and had a transatlantic hit with 'United We Stand,' something of a gay anthem. The name was then resurrected for an entirely new group in 1976 to front this composition at the Eurovision Song Contest. The song was an odds-on favorite and won the contest by a large margin. Unsurprisingly, the victorious Brotherhood, with their popular two-boy two-girl line-up, were labeled as Abba copyists, and scored in Britain and Europe with a number of further Abba-flavored concoctions, including the U.K. Number 1s 'Angelo' and 'Figaro.' Ironically, justice was seen to be done when Abba's own 'Fernando,' a definitively superior product, replaced 'Save Your Kisses' as Britain's Number 1.

Play That Funky Music
Wild Cherry

Released June 1976
Epic *50225* (U.S. #1) / Epic *EPC 4593* (U.K. #7)

In the mid 1970s Wild Cherry was just another heavy rock band that suddenly found itself playing to disco audiences who were demanding a different beat. This track was inspired by a cry of, "Play that funky music, white boy," from the audience. Guitarist-vocalist Robert Parissi rose to the challenge and wrote the song, initially slated as the B-side of their cover of The Commodores' 'I Feel Sanctified.' Their record company decided otherwise, and rightly so: it's a decidedly funky track that stands up well today and ain't half bad for a bunch of white boys. The group got its name from the flavor of a box of cough drops, but despite a few other minor U.S. hits, this was their only big international success. The song was covered in 1991 by Robert Van Winkle, alias Vanilla Ice, as a follow-up to his chart-topping 'Ice Ice Baby.'

Dancing Queen
Abba

Released August 1976
Atlantic *3372* (U.S. #1) / Epic *EPC 4499* (U.K. #1)

There are a couple of myths that have endured about Abba. One is that they bowed out at their artistic and commercial peak. In fact, the recordings at the end of their career had begun to pall, with unlovely and lazy synthesized arrangements replacing their organic if ultra-slick instrumentation. This decay seemed to be reflected by chart positions: it's shocking to realize that, come the end, their singles were stalling outside the Top 30 in the U.K., always one of their most lucrative territories.

Similarly foggy memory surrounds success at the beginning of their career. Contrary to the recollections of many, it was not all plain sailing once the immortal 'Waterloo' had won the 1974 Eurovision Song Contest. It was only with the sensual 'S.O.S.' well over a year later that the group began to claw their way back to respectable chart positions. While the following 'Mamma Mia' and 'Fernando' were both U.K. chart-toppers, it was with 'Dancing Queen' that they really secured more than a foothold in rock history. Alongside 'Waterloo' it has become their signature song. America occasionally allowed the group into its Top 10 but was always uneven in its affections for the Swedish singers. But for 'Dancing Queen' the nation succumbed unequivocally, granting Abba their sole Stateside Number 1.

A mini-myth surrounds this song itself. Because Abba performed it two months before its official release at a gala to celebrate the nuptials of the king of Sweden, many assumed that it was written specifically for the occasion. In fact, it started life in August 1975 as a track provisionally titled 'Boogaloo,' which authors Björn Ulvaeus and Benny Andersson had vague visions of giving a 'dance' feel. Their session musicians – and how strange it is to contemplate that Abba was never a self-contained entity but a vocal group with a resident guitarist and keyboardist – achieved the result with a self-conscious cross of disco smash 'Rock Your Baby' by George McCrae and a Dr. John album. Only then was the lyric added, and with subject matter concerning a 17-year-old queen of the disco, the song was destined to endear itself to dancefloor-addicted teenagers everywhere.

One half of Abba's female vocal pairing, Agnetha Fältskog, has said that the group knew instantly that the song was going to be "massive," but the track did not gain an immediate release. It's a testament to how strong were the act's compositions at this point that they were able to put 'Dancing Queen' on the back burner and instead release as a single 'Fernando' – and a testament to their pop craftsmanship that 'Fernando' became a smash despite its almost surreally unlikely subject matter of Latin American revolutionaries. When 'Dancing Queen' was issued it did indeed become the "massive" hit foreseen by Fältskog – and seemed to know it was destined for immortality by giddily announcing its arrival with surely the most famous piano glissando in pop history.

Blitzkrieg Bop
The Ramones

Released May 1976
Sire *725* (U.S.) / Sire *6078 601* (U.K.)

New Rose
The Damned

Released October 1976
Not issued U.S. / Stiff *BUY 6* (U.K.)

Some earlier bands such as The Stooges may have displayed many of the characteristics later associated with punk, but The Ramones were the first punk-rock band, and 'Blitzkrieg Bop' was the first punk-rock single. Formed in 1974, 'da brudders' Joey, Johnny, Dee Dee, and Tommy donned ripped drainpipe jeans, battered sneakers, and biker jackets, adopted the surname Ramone, and started playing to initially hostile audiences in the clubs of New York City.

Although The Ramones took their musical cues from the past, they used them to create the future. Rock'n'roll, surf, Phil Spector, and 1960s garage-rock were the inspirations. The music was stripped back to the barest of essentials: no drum fills, no guitar solos, just short, fast, four-chord songs with catchy tunes and the dumbest of lyrics. Today, it doesn't seem like the recipe for a revolution, such is the extent to which The Ramones' aesthetic has become common currency. But in an era gorged on musical excess, it was indeed revolutionary.

The band signed to Sire Records in late 1975 and recorded their debut album for under $6,000 (about £3,300) early the following year, from which 'Blitzkrieg Bop' was lifted as a single. Opening with a refrain of "Hey, ho, let's go!" shouted (not sung) over brutalized tom toms, it was a wake-up call for a generation. Not that everyone instantly opened their eyes. 'Blitzkrieg Bop' was not a hit, nor did it get a great deal of airplay, and in an era when conspicuous musicianship was revered, most critics and many rock fans were simply baffled by the starved pop minimalism.

STIFF: THE WORLD'S MOST FLEXIBLE RECORD LABEL

The rise of 'New Rose' by The Damned helped establish one of the key British independent labels of the punk era, Stiff Records, and its in-house producer, Nick Lowe. The label was founded in 1976 by Dave Robinson and Jake Riviera, ex-managers of pub-rock groups Brinsley Schwarz and Dr. Feelgood respectively. Lowe had been the bassist and vocalist in the former group, and released the first Stiff single, 'So It Goes.' He then took on the role of producer of much of the label's initial output, most notably the landmark punk single 'New Rose' by The Damned. He was at the helm of all Elvis Costello's 1970s work, including the singles 'Less Than Zero' and 'Watching The Detectives.' He also continued his own recording career, which included the formation of Rockpile with Dave Edmunds. Because they were signed to different labels, only one of the albums the duo recorded together was credited to Rockpile; the rest masqueraded as solo albums by Lowe and by Edmunds.

Although the label's output was more diverse than is often thought, stretching way beyond three-chord punk-rock, for the first couple of years their releases were very much of a type. The regular deployment of Lowe as producer was integral to this, as was the series of iconic jackets designed by graphic artist Barney Bubbles. Stiff also maintained a relentless – and often somewhat controversial – marketing strategy, which included arranging for Costello to be "arrested for busking" outside CBS Records (who later signed him to a lucrative long-term contract).

As was the case with almost everything punk, Stiff didn't last long in its original incarnation. Riviera left to form the shortlived Radar Records in early 1978, taking Costello and Lowe with him. Robinson responded by diversifying the Stiff roster further, and in the process scoring greater commercial success with artists including Ian Dury & The Blockheads, Madness, and Kirsty MacColl.

The criticism leveled at The Ramones in the early days was that they "couldn't play," and if musicianship is about nothing more than deft fingerwork, then that was true. But what The Ramones could do was drill straight to the very heart of what made rock'n'roll so exciting in the first place.

They first played in Britain in July 1976, galvanizing the nascent London punk scene. In the audience to see them were members not only of The Clash and The Sex Pistols but also the band that would release the official first British punk single, The Damned. Like The Ramones, The Damned played loud, fast, and basic, and like their American counterparts they too had a well-tuned pop sensibility, all heard on their debut single, 'New Rose.' Released on British independent label Stiff, 'New Rose' was an attention-grabber from the moment the band's singer – Bela Lugosi lookalike Dave Vanian – posed the question: "Is she really going out with him?" before standing back for a flurry of drums and some quick-fire chord changes. Like 'Blitzkrieg Bop' it was all over in two minutes.

At odds with their reputations for brevity, both The Ramones and The Damned forged enduring careers. The Ramones toured and recorded relentlessly for another 20 years, while The Damned still appear in one configuration or another. But any quibbles about failing to grow old gracefully should be set aside in the face of these two masterful distillations of the very essence of rock'n'roll

Anarchy In The U.K.
The Sex Pistols

Released November 1976
Not issued U.S. / EMI *2566* (U.K. #38)

The music of The Sex Pistols was driven by the singular dissatisfaction of the young in mid-1970s Britain. The economy was stagnant and the national atmosphere was one of conflict and discontent, epitomized by the labor strikes that seemed to erupt every single day. Combine that with the perpetually drizzly weather that has always afflicted the country and things seemed to assume a permanent grayness. It was even grimmer for the kids. Clearly the stars of the 1960s had all long passed their peak, their somnambulant albums reeking of the blunted artistic ambition engendered by success, their gigs reeking of self-regard in the form of interminable extemporization.

It was their contempt for their dreary culture and moribund music scene that underpinned the Pistols' music. Singer Johnny Rotten was the last to join the band. While primarily invited into the fold because the group liked his short hair and distressed clothes sense (both then rare), his diseased, wheezy voice was quite unusual too. By astonishing fortuitousness, this young man, picked for reasons of surface flash, transpired to have a unique ability for writing lyrics, steeped in disgust at both himself and the world, that was the missing piece in their brand of alt rock, whose reference points were The Velvet Underground, The Stooges, and The New York Dolls. The Pistols were soon outraging London and then the country with music that was as snotty and sneering as their demeanor, and they were already semi-mythical before they released this, their first record, the only one ever to be issued by the group's original line-up.

Such was the myth – they inspired concert violence, wore swastikas, and had a reputation for studied musical incompetence – that when this debut did appear, it came as a surprise to those who had not seen them live. It was relatively conventional. Rotten's lyric may have started with the chilling conversational gambit, "I am an anti-Christ!" and ended with the equally disturbing, "Destro-o-oy!" and his menacing vocal certainly gave it a demented kink. But otherwise it was all comparatively familiar, highly competent hard-rock, complete with two nifty guitar breaks. The band had labored hard and agonized long over the record, the ultimate product of sessions stretching from July to October 1976 supervised by two different producers, Dave Goodman and Chris Thomas. Despite the joint group composing credit, the song was a collaboration between Rotten and bassist Glen Matlock. Matlock had devised the melody after guitarist Steve Jones had suggested the band needed an anthem. Rotten wrote the lyric following a pub conversation in which band friend and sleeve designer Jamie Reed contributed several ideas.

The record eventually made Number 38 on the British chart. Rotten has said that had it not been for their scandal-making, record-deal-ending appearance on tea-time TV that December, it would have made the top spot. While that does seem unlikely, it is exactly what happened (in some charts) to their controversial follow-up, 'God Save The Queen.'

God Save The Queen
Sex Pistols

Released May 1977
Not issued U.S. / Virgin *VS 181* (U.K. #2)

By early 1977 The Sex Pistols and their media-manipulating manager Malcolm McLaren had managed to relieve two major record companies of considerable amounts of money for agreeing not to release their records.

It was EMI who first signed up Johnny Rotten and his sneering crew in October 1976, releasing their first single, 'Anarchy In The UK.' The relationship didn't last long, and following a scandalous appearance on an early-evening British television show and other acts of public disorder, EMI dumped the group alleging "adverse publicity," deleting 'Anarchy' after sales of 55,000, and letting the band keep the £40,000 advance (about $70,000 at the time).

McLaren next cut a deal with A&M. 'God Save The Queen' – originally entitled 'No Future' – was to be their next single, and with the track's title in mind and Queen Elizabeth's Silver Jubilee celebrations fast approaching, an official signing ceremony was staged outside Buckingham Palace on the March 10th 1977. Just six days later the A&M contract was also terminated, making this possibly the shortest recording contract in pop-music history.

This was the result of a riotous party at A&M's headquarters to celebrate the signing, at which the company's employees were so disgusted by the group's behaviour that they were dropped before any product was released. The Pistols and McLaren received another golden handshake, this time a princely £75,000 (about $132,000) for doing absolutely nothing. By this time, however, A&M had already pressed 25,000 copies of the single, which had to be destroyed, although some remain in circulation and are among the most collectable of rarities. (An A&M copy of 'God Save The Queen' was sold for £2,820 – about $4,085 – at a Sotheby's auction in 2001.)

Now desperate to get the single out in time for the Jubilee in June, McLaren then signed with Richard Branson's Virgin for further £15,000 (about $26,000), and 'God Save The Queen' was officially released on May 27th. While this controversial single received minimum radio play, the wave of publicity surrounding the group made sure that it sold 150,000 copies in five days, reaching Number 2 on the officially recognized BBC/British Market Research Bureau chart, although it's always been alleged that the British Phonographic Industry managed to rig its own chart so that they would not suffer the embarrassment of having 'God Save The Queen' at Number 1 in Jubilee week.

left > The Sex Pistols and Malcolm McLaren sign a short-lived deal with A&M outside Buckingham Palace, London.
below > The group onstage in the U.S. in January 1978.

White Riot
The Clash

Released March 1977
Not issued U.S. / CBS *5058* (U.K. #38)

In August 1976, Clash frontman Joe Strummer, bassist Paul Simonon, and manager Bernard Rhodes attended the annual festival in west London's Notting Hill Gate. Always a lively affair, in this instance the carnival became literally incendiary as black youths – who had long accused the city's police of racial harassment – erupted into spontaneous violence. Strummer and Simonon enjoyed the civil disobedience enough to pitch in themselves, but the experience was of more importance because it provided the nascent group with its first signature song. Written by Strummer and lead guitarist Mick Jones, 'White Riot' proposed that the Caucausian working class youth should express their dissatisfaction in a similar fashion, with a "White riot / A riot of my own!"

Overlaid with the sound of stomping boots, breaking glass, and police sirens, 'White Riot' was the first single recorded by The Clash for CBS under the terms of a £100,000 deal (about $175,000) that some saw as a betrayal of the very principles of U.K. punk. Others were amazed that such a growling, brutal song could become a semi-hit – especially with little radio play or promotion. But as it climbed into the British Top 40, 'White Riot' proved that punk had become the street-level voice-of-real-youth.

Do Anything You Wanna Do
Eddie & The Hot Rods

Released August 1977
Island *IS 093* (U.S.) / Island *WIP 6401* (U.K. #9)

A hymn to the perpetual adolescent struggle for freedom, 'Do Anything You Wanna Do' is a perfect marriage of lyrics and music. The simplistic yearning of lines such as "Searching for adventure / It's the kind of life to find" sound like profound spiritual truths when pitted against a wall of ringing Telecaster chords. Eddie & The Hot Rods had the misfortune to fall between two British styles of the time – too fast and basic for pub rock, and just a little too old for punk. But they made a series of strong singles, of which 'Do Anything' was the biggest and best. The band's ambiguous status was underlined when, at the height of punk, they appeared on the *Top of The Pops* TV singles show to promote the single. Singer Barrie Masters unwittingly committed the ultimate fashion crime of the time – he wore white flares.

Marquee Moon
Television

Released March 1977
Not issued U.S. / Elektra *K 12252* (U.K. #30)

Blank Generation
Richard Hell & The Voidoids
Released September 1977
Sire *SRE1003* (U.S.A.) / Sire *6078608* (U.K.)

Psycho Killer
Talking Heads
Released December 1977
Sire *1013* (U.S.A.) / Sire *6078610* (U.K.)

Less than a year after The Ramones lit the fuse under a stagnant rock scene, New York punk had evolved into something more arch and intellectual, characterized by angular, spidery guitars and obtuse, diffident lyrics.

First out of the blocks was Television, who had formed from the ashes of The Neon Boys in 1973. The group's first single for Elektra, 'Marquee Moon,' seemingly broke all the rules of the fledgling punk movement: it has key changes and guitar solos, and runs to almost eleven minutes. While that might sound like a recipe for progressive rock – anathema to any punk worth his salt – Television did, nonetheless, share a visceral urgency with their punk peers, and in Tom Verlaine they had one of the great atonal singers.

Before rounding up the Voidoids, Richard Hell was the bassist in an early incarnation of Television, and co-wrote 'Chinese Rocks' with former New York Doll Johnny Thunders for the latter's new group The Heartbreakers. The Voidoids second single – following '(I Could Live With You In) Another World' – 'Blank Generation' is pitched somewhere between the sound of Hell's previous bands: more raw and primal than Verlaine's bunch, but still knowingly playful.

Although both retain ever-growing cult followings, Richard Hell and Television found their careers waning by the end of the 1970s. Talking Heads, meanwhile, were only just getting started in 1977, and would remain active – and dazzlingly creative – well into the 1980s. 'Psycho Killer' is one of several early gems that, in David Byrne's "fa-fa-fa-fa-fa-fa-fa-fa-fa-fa" breakdown, contains the greatest pop stutter since The Who's 'My Generation.'

Hotel California
The Eagles

Released February 1977
Asylum *45386* (U.S. #1) / Asylum *K 13079* (U.K. #8)

A lot had happened to The Eagles in the years since their 1972 debut single 'Take It Easy,' during which time they had become one of the biggest acts on the planet, notching up six U.S. Top 10 hits (including three Number 1s) in the process, and turned into a symbol for some for everything that was 'wrong' in music. Punks didn't consider them quite the sell-out acts that Rod Stewart and The Rolling Stones had become in their eyes, but The Eagles were frequently cited by the new wave as representatives of a self-satisfied rock elite who had jettisoned grit in favor of soporific tempos, vapid production techniques, and self-satisfied lyrics.

Added to the alleged crimes of The Eagles was the fact that their success made them the de facto leaders of the country-rock genre, whose roots in Californian cocaine culture and Me Generation ethics were anathema to those who held that contemporary popular music should exhibit a concern for the issues of the day. "It's our job to get people off," Eagles drummer Don Henley had shrugged in a 1975 interview, "not to get them crazy and militant." The same interview had seen him splutter: "I hate those stupid labels! I hate when people call us a country-rock band, because they are so full of it. We can do anything!"

Hotel California was the album that saw The Eagles move away from country rock and start to embrace social commentary. The former may have had something to do with a change of personnel, with Bernie Leadon replaced on guitar by Joe Walsh. The album's title track sets the sunny State as a metaphor for the condition of America. A traveler checks into the Hotel California and finds himself in a decadent nightmare. The lyrics are brilliantly constructed and in places genuinely spooky, as in the line "You can check out any time you like but you can never leave." Musically, the crux of the record is its stunning guitar finale. Played by Don Felder and Joe Walsh alternately and then in tandem, the guitars twine, snake, yowl, and cool across the space of two endlessly fascinating minutes. Inexplicably, many DJs opted to fade the record at this point.

'Hotel California' is what 'Stairway To Heaven' is to Led Zeppelin, and 'Bohemian Rhapsody' to Queen: the grand statement of their career, an opus whose self-consciousness generates a degree of ridicule and accusations of pompousness, but at the same time underlines an intense dedication to craft that lifts the recording to the stature, quite simply, of a classic piece of work.

American Girl
Tom Petty & The Heartbreakers

Released May 1977
Shelter *62007* (U.S.) / Shelter *WIP 6403* (U.K. #40)

The Byrd's Roger McGuinn once heard this song on the radio and sat trying to remember when he'd recorded it. Petty certainly had captured McGuinn's jangling guitar and quavering vocal style, but it would be unfair to dismiss the song as a Byrds pastiche. While it was probably inspired by the patriotic ambience of the year of the bicentennial – it was recorded on July 4, 1976 – there is more to the lyric than the rousing celebration of American womanhood that it at first appears to be. Petty, however, denies an urban myth that the song is about a student's suicide.

Dreams
Fleetwood Mac

Released April 1977
Warner Bros. *8371* (U.S. #1) / Warner Bros. *K 16969* (U.K. #24)

Fleetwood Mac's only American Number 1 single was written on a black velvet bed in Sly Stone's cocaine pit. The group was formerly a successful Brit-blues combo but had long since relocated to California, now re-energized by the incorporation of two estimable and romantically entwined young songwriters, Lindsey Buckingham and Stevie Nicks. The Mac's eponymous 1975 album had restored the ailing band to the top spot in the *Billboard* album chart. 'Dreams' arrived while they were squirreled away in the Record Plant in Sausalito, California, recording what would become the mega-platinum follow-up album, *Rumours*.

One afternoon while the rest of the band was busy in the main studio, Nicks lugged her Fender Rhodes piano into a smaller studio, favored by Sly of Sly & The Family Stone, and settled down on a bed in a sunken pit that, according to Mac founder-member Mick Fleetwood, "was usually occupied by people we didn't know, tapping razors on mirrors." Seated Indian-style on the bed, Nicks recalled how she simply "found a drum pattern, switched my little cassette player on, and wrote 'Dreams' in about ten minutes."

According to Fleetwood Mac's other female songwriter, Christine McVie, the ten-minute wonder song consisted of "just three chords and one note in the left hand," and it had to be dramatically refashioned into three distinct sections by Buckingham before it came to life. Sadly, this professional camaraderie masked the fact that the song was about the agonizing break-up of Nicks's romance with Buckingham following her dalliance with Don Henley of The Eagles.

Mull Of Kintyre / Girls' School
Wings

Released November 1977
Capitol *4504* (U.S.) / Capitol *R 6018* (U.K. #1)

A mull in Scotland is a promontory, and the Mull of Kintyre is at the south-western tip of the Kintyre peninsula – a few miles from Paul McCartney's Scottish farm where this song was recorded using a mobile studio in a barn. It was a deliberate attempt to write a modern Scottish anthem, and McCartney, who hired seven pipers and ten drummers from the Campbell Town Pipe Band to assist him, described it as a cross between 'Sailing' and 'Amazing Grace.' He thought 'Mull' was something of a throwaway but was proved quite wrong when it became the biggest-selling record of all time in Britain, spending nine weeks at Number 1, selling over two million copies, and beating the previous record holder – his own 'She Loves You' for The Beatles. It was McCartney's first British post-Beatles Number 1 (although in America he'd already had five chart-toppers: 'Uncle Albert,' 'My Love,' 'Band On The Run,' 'Listen To What The Man Said,' and 'Silly Love Songs'). 'Mull' was part of a double A-side in Britain but didn't hit in America, where 'Girls' School,' the B-side, made the running and reached a modest Number 33. 'Mull Of Kintyre' was co-written with fellow Wings member Denny Laine, who later sold his rights back to McCartney when he was declared bankrupt.

I Feel Love
Donna Summer

Released July 1977
Casablanca *884* (U.S. #6) / GTO *GT 100* (U.K. #1)

The first British Number 1 hit to be constructed entirely from synthesized electronic sounds, 'I Feel Love' is a landmark in the evolution of the pop single. It was the brainchild of production duo Giorgio Moroder and Pete Bellotte, setting Summer's euphoric vocal against a futuristic backdrop of unrelenting programmed bass and drums.

Donna Summer stood among the most popular performers of the disco era, achieving a level of success exceeded only by The Bee Gees. Like them, she began her career before the disco boom and continued to score hits beyond it. Born Donna Andrea Gaines in Boston, Massachusetts, Summer moved to Germany as a teenager in the late 1960s and performed there in the musicals *Hair* and *Godspell*. She spent the early 1970s working on the fringes of the music industry before meeting Moroder and Bellotte, who produced her first European hit, 'The Hostage,' in 1974.

Summer, Moroder, and Bellotte developed a signature sound over the next couple of years. The sultry, funky 'Love To Love You Baby' (1976) gave Summer her first U.S. hit, despite radio bans brought on by her suggestive heavy breathing. Her album of the same name included a dazzlingly exploratory 17-minute version of the title track. Summer was unusual among disco artists in that she focused just as much on albums as singles, notably the conceptual set *Four Seasons Of Love*. She latched onto the trend for issuing lengthy mixes on 12-inch vinyl – aimed mostly at dance clubs – alongside shorter versions, edited down for the singles market.

By 1977 Summer and her producers had begun to tire of the lush string arrangements and rich production jobs that had come to characterize disco (and which they had helped to popularize). Trailing the release of her fifth full-length album, *I Remember Yesterday*, 'I Feel Love' introduced a sleeker, sparser, ultra-modern sound driven by squelching, programmed bass and loops of overlapping electronic drums, with the sweeping strings of old replaced by a single droning synthesizer.

One of the most important electronic recordings of the 1970s, 'I Feel Love' showed that a huge international hit could be achieved without having to use conventional instrumentation or backing musicians, and effectively drew up the blueprint for much of the techno and house music of the 1980s and 1990s. While other records could claim to be more innovative – 'Trans Europe Express' by Kraftwerk, perhaps, or Brian Eno's album *Another Green World* – none had the commercial clout of 'I Feel Love.' The most crucial element in its mainstream success, however, is the exultant vocal melody, which gives a much-needed human counterpoint to the harsh, robotic backing track.

'I Feel Love' gave Donna Summer her first Number 1 hit in the U.K. and was the first of her singles to reach the U.S. Top 10 since 'Love To Love You Baby.' Her star continued to rise for the remainder of the 1970s, earning her the title The Queen Of Disco. In 1978 and '79 she released four chart-topping singles in the U.S. – 'MacArthur Park,' 'Hot Stuff,' 'Bad Girls,' and 'No More Tears (Enough Is Enough)' – but 'I Feel Love' remains her most important recording.

12-INCH SINGLES: ACCOMMODATING THE MEGAMIX

The 12-inch single was introduced out of musical necessity and economic acumen. For the previous three decades there had been few challengers to the 7-inch 45rpm disc, which had been in use since 1949. The 7-inch had been devised to hold up to five minutes of music, which was more than ample at the point of its introduction, when the average popular song tended to last around two minutes. In the 1950s, with the arrival of the EP (extended play), the discs could hold up to seven minutes per side.

The extended-play format was achieved by cutting thinner, tighter grooves into the vinyl. This lowered the signal-to-noise ratio, resulting in a decrease in sound quality and volume. It didn't seem to matter a great deal to the record-buying public of the 1950s, but in subsequent decades there was a marked increase in the quality of record production and home stereo equipment. As a result, listeners expected a better quality of sound. The arrival of disco music in the mid 1970s made the need for a new format even more pressing. Record makers had begun to produce extended mixes of songs, aimed predominantly at club DJs. Thus a new format was required, one that could accommodate longer songs without any noticeable depreciation in fidelity and volume.

There was no real point in attempting to enhance the 7-inch single as, by this point, there was little difference in the production costs of that or a 12-inch disc. A 12-inch 45rpm single would be able to hold more music and, just as crucially, reproduce it at a higher fidelity, because it allowed for wider, deeper grooves to be cut. From an economic standpoint, a 12-inch record looked like a bigger, better product and could thus be marketed and priced as such. It also allowed record labels to sell two different versions of a single – the conventional 7-inch pop single and a 12-inch version, sometimes referred to as a 'maxi single,' which was labeled as containing extended club mixes. The idea was that the devoted fan would have to buy both.

The first commercially released 12-inch single was Walter Gibbons's remix of 'Ten Percent' by the Philadelphia-based disco act Double Exposure. The format quickly grew in popularity, notably with releases by disco acts such as Boney M and Donna Summer. It became a staple of independent record labels during the 1980s, notably Factory Records, which in 1983 issued the biggest-selling 12-inch single of all time, 'Blue Monday' by New Order.

"Heroes"
David Bowie

Released October 1977
RCA *11211* (U.S.) / RCA *PB 1121* (U.K. #24)

Although it wasn't a major chart success, '"Heroes"' has come to be recognized as perhaps the finest moment in the career of one of the stalwarts of British music. It was the title track from Bowie's second album of 1977 and arrived in the midst of the most experimental period of his career. After going through a series of stylistic changes that took him from proto-metal to glam-rock to plastic soul in the earlier 1970s, Bowie moved to Berlin, Germany, in 1976 and made three albums there – *Low*, *"Heroes,"* and *Lodger* – with his regular producer Tony Visconti and the pioneering electronic musician Brian Eno.

These albums contain some of Bowie's best and most adventurous work, but much of it finds him at his least commercial. '"Heroes"' is the one song from this period that stands up as a classic pop song. Bowie was inspired to write the lyric after catching sight of Visconti and backing singer Antonia Maass canoodling by a wall. It was given a suitably widescreen backing, dominated by Robert Fripp's searing lead guitar

parts, which were played through Eno's EMS synthesizer. Fripp flew in from the U.S. to record all of his parts for *"Heroes"* in one brief session.

The most striking aspect of the song is Bowie's vocal. Easily the most powerful of his career, it begins in a soft, conversational tone but gradually rises and by the song's close has become a passionate cry. The ever-inventive Visconti captured Bowie's vocal in one pass by setting up three microphones in the studio at different distances from the singer. Each had a 'noise gate' attached so that it would only switch on when Bowie reached a certain level of volume. For the opening verses his voice was picked up only by the first, closest mike, lending it a gentle intimacy, but the full-throated pleas of the latter part of the song were captured by all three microphones, allowing the sound to swirl and echo in the distance.

Surprisingly, given its anthemic qualities, '"Heroes"' failed to match the chart success of earlier Bowie singles like 'Space Oddity' or 'The Jean Genie.' It was a hit across Europe, in part because it was also issued in German and French-language versions (as '"Helden"' and '"Héros"' respectively). Despite its continual use in advertising and at sporting events, the single has lost none of its original power and remains constant at the top end of many a list of the Greatest Singles Of All Time.

below > David Bowie (right) at Hansa By The Wall studios in Berlin, Germany, where he recorded "Heroes" with former King Crimson guitarist Robert Fripp (left) and sonic alchemist Brian Eno (center).

Stayin' Alive
The Bee Gees

Released December 1977
RSO 885 (U.S. #1) / RSO 2090 267 (U.K. #4)

How Deep Is Your Love
The Bee Gees
Released September 1977
RSO 882 (U.S. #1) / RSO 2090 259 (U.K. #3)

Night Fever
The Bee Gees
Released January 1978
RSO 889 (U.S. #1) / RSO 002 (U.K. #1)

More Than A Woman
Tavares
Released April 1978
Capitol 4500 (U.S. #32) / Capitol CL 15977 (U.K. #7)

On December 24, 1977, 'How Deep Is Your Love' became the first of six consecutive singles on RSO Records to hit the U.S. Number 1 slot, giving rock, theatre, and movie mogul Robert Stigwood's label a resounding five months' domination of the American chart. 'How Deep Is Your Love' was followed to the top by Player's 'Baby Come Back,' The Bee Gees' 'Stayin' Alive,' Andy Gibb's 'Love Is Thicker Than Water,' The Bee Gees yet again with 'Night Fever,' and finally 'If I Can't Have You' by Yvonne Elliman.

Tidy as it would be to explain away this phenomenal achievement as simply the magic of The Bee Gees, the reality is a much more complex tale involving the brothers Gibb, their canny manager, the emergence of a new dance craze, and a low-budget teen movie starring an unknown but charismatic young hopeful.

In the summer of 1976 on both sides of the Atlantic punk rock was beginning to emerge as a powerful new musical force. Meanwhile, the hopelessly old-fangled Bee Gees were ensconced in the Chateau

D'Herouville outside Paris, France, working on their next album. Stigwood, their manager, was in New York City where his gaze fell upon a feature by Nik Cohn in *New York* magazine. Cohn eloquently described the music, attitudes, and fashions that surrounded the emerging culture of the Big Apple's discotheques. Stigwood immediately saw an opportunity to make a killing with a movie about disco-obsessed teens. His clients The Bee Gees had already scored chart-toppers with dance-oriented material, including 'Jive Talkin'' and 'You Should Be Dancing,' so he made a transatlantic call to Barry Gibb.

"All of those songs in *Saturday Night Fever* were for our own album," Barry remembered later. "They weren't for Fever at all. Robert just happened to hear those four or five songs and said he wanted them for the movie." His brother Maurice recalled Stigwood telling them precious little about the project. "All we knew was that it was about this guy who works in a paint shop, blows his wages every Saturday night, and wins a dance competition."

Stigwood's name is familiar to most serious music fans, but few know very much more about this powerful entertainment entrepreneur. Ruddy faced and notoriously stubborn, Stiggy had arrived in London from Australia in 1959 as a backpacker with just £3 ($8) in his pocket. After an unsuccessful attempt to be a pop singer, he switched to artist management, guiding British teen idol John Leyton. By 1967 Stigwood was working with Beatles manager Brian Epstein and learned enough to build The Bee Gees up to the point where they became significant rivals to the Liverpool group. An astute talent-spotter, Stigwood secured a roster of very successful acts, including Cream, and was a millionaire by the age of 30. When he quit Britain in the early 1970s to avoid punitive taxation, he was already one of the most powerful men in the music business.

During the first week of December 1977, American cinema audiences were treated to a 30-second trailer for *Saturday Night Fever*. It was largely unmemorable, consisting mainly of the feet of the movie's unknown leading man, John Travolta, striding down a New York street – but pounding away behind those feet was 'Stayin' Alive,' a song that had started life as a few lines scrawled by Robin Gibb on his Concorde ticket. It was 'Stayin' Alive' that brought the trailer vibrantly to life. When Stigwood first heard 'Stayin' Alive' he was adamant that the Gibbs should change the title to 'Saturday Night' but Barry refused. "We said, 'There are so many songs out there called 'Saturday Night.' It's corny. It's a terrible title.'"

The movie premiered in New York City on December 14, 1977, and 'How Deep Is Your Love,' which Barry Gibb confidently predicted would flop in the face of the rising tide of punk, was at Number 1 before Christmas, initiating a run of *Saturday Night Fever*-related chart successes that broke all previous records. Aside from the chart-toppers by The Bee Gees and Yvonne Elliman already mentioned, the movie was also responsible for the success of 'Boogie Shoes' by K.C. & The Sunshine Band (U.S. Number 35) and 'Disco Inferno' by The Trammps (Number 11).

A peculiarity of the *Fever* soundtrack was that it included two versions of 'More Than A Woman,' one by The Bee Gees and one by Tavares. When the Tavares version came out as a single in America it floundered at Number 32, probably because it was already available on the album and as the B-side of The Bee Gees' 'Night Fever.' However, on May 6, 1978, it entered the U.K. charts, where it peaked at Number 7, reviving Tavares's flagging fortunes on the international stage.

By the end of the 1970s, the *Saturday Night Fever* soundtrack had sold 25 million copies, and the movie, made for just $7 million, has since grossed well over $300 million, transforming Stigwood, in his own words,

"from a minor millionaire into a minor billionaire." In the early 1990s he left his 26-acre estate in Bermuda and returned to live on his 55-acre Barton Manor on the Isle Of Wight in southern England. A recent estimate of his personal fortune put it at £170 million and rising.

Despite the large sums of money that *Saturday Night Fever* deposited into the Bee Gee coffers, it continues to irritate them that the movie's astonishing impact radically altered perceptions of their music. "We were being called blue-eyed soul," Maurice said shortly before his unexpected death in 2003, "but when the film came out we were the kings of disco. 'How Deep Is Your Love' was an R&B ballad but, when the film came out, it somehow became a disco ballad."

As well as making Stigwood, Travolta, and The Bee Gees filthy rich, *Saturday Night Fever* also transformed the lives of countless teenagers worldwide, among them London lad Georgios Panayiotou, now better known as George Michael. "Before *Saturday Night Fever* I was blind to that kind of music," he said. "You didn't hear a lot of dance on the radio, everybody was still into the 1960s and early-1970s idea of getting into your own thing at home. Saturday Night Fever got me out to the clubs."

Chanson D'Amour
Manhattan Transfer

Released January 1977
Atlantic *3374* (U.S.) / Atlantic *K 10886* (U.K. #1)

When Manhattan Transfer's first album wasn't much of a U.S. success, spending just four weeks on the album Top 40, Atlantic wheeled in super-producer Richard Perry – against the highly talented vocal ensemble's wishes – for album number two, *Coming Out*. 'Chanson D'Amour' was recorded as an afterthought at the end of a session in which little else had been accomplished and nailed in one take. The song had originally been a Number 6 *Billboard* hit for husband-and-wife team Art & Dotty Todd in 1958. While not particularly representative of Mantran's usual material, it was their biggest hit, and is particularly notable for its slight lyrics (there are in fact just four lines), questionable Anglo-French rhyming (encore, more, je t'adore), and those catchy 'rah-tah-tah-tah-tah' interjections.

Oxygène Part IV
Jean-Michel Jarre

Released July 1977
Polydor *PD 14425* (U.S.) / Polydor *2001 721* (U.K. #4)

Electronically-generated musical sounds had been incorporated into hit singles since the early 1960s, usually for their novelty value, and some massive international hits such as 'Telstar' by The Tornados and 'Reflections' by The Supremes had prominently featured electronics.

Robert Moog's new generation of controllable synthesizers inspired artists as diverse as The Beatles, The Byrds, and Stevie Wonder to increase the electronic content of their songs, and by the early 1970s German bands including Tangerine Dream and U.S. innovators such as Tonto's Expanding Head Band used nothing but synths to create their music. What much of this electronic music lacked, though, was worldwide popular appeal. Alongside Kraftwerk and Donna Summer, Jean-Michel Jarre took the final step of making music that was as danceable as it was cerebral.

His first album, an eight-part suite entitled *Oxygène*, was recorded during August 1976 in the 28-year-old French composer's studio, converted from his dining room, near the Champs-Elysées in Paris, with not a guitar in sight, and using state-of-the-art ARP, AKS, and RMI synthesizers plus a Mellotron and a 'rhythmic computer.'

'Oxygène Part IV' was released as a single in the late summer of 1977, in the midst of the punk boom, and became one of the first internationally successful 45rpm fusions of the undeniably futuristic sounds of synth technology with some infectiously memorable tunes and disco beats. It would prove to be the way that much music was made from now on, with Jarre ushering in the age of popular synthesized music that provided, at last, a viable alternative to the electric guitar.

Float On
The Floaters

Released July 1977
ABC *12284* (U.S. #2) / ABC *4187* (U.K. #1)

Disco and R&B act The Detroit Emeralds deservedly scored well with their spin-off group The Floaters as the languid ballad 'Float On' became an enormous hit on both sides of the pond. While the song, all icy guitar flicks and organ washes, insinuated itself into everyone's minds, the image of the band – Afro hairdos, polite suits, and all – was just right for the times. Unfortunately  they couldn't sustain any momentum and 'Float On' remained a one-off. But if you're going to join the ranks of one-hit wonders, you might as well have a smash hit.

Cold As Ice
Foreigner

Released July 1977
Atlantic *3410* (U.S. #6) / Atlantic *K 10986* (U.K. #24)

Heavy metal with touches of synth might be de rigueur today, but back in the late 1970s only a few bands were dabbling with such blasphemy. However, New York outfit Foreigner achieved the right blend of silky electronics and polite riffs and scored massive sales as a result. This little ditty was memorable solely for its "You're as cold as ice" line (which goes up a tone and back again, memorably) and made a good impression in Middle America – the Brits were less keen –ensuring a few years of touring success for Lou Gramm and his chums. Foreigner's eponymous debut LP from this year remains an AOR classic.

Uptown Top Ranking
Althia & Donna

Released December 1977
Warner Bros. *17098* (U.S.) / Lightning *LIG 506* (U.K. #1)

Althia Forrest and Donna Reid were a pair of Jamaican teenagers who topped the U.K. chart through a combination of pure luck and naive charm. While 'Uptown Top Ranking' was a semi-credible slice of warmed-up reggae, with their harmonies taken from the Bananarama school (in other words not really in harmony at all), it was the song's lyrics about a night out on the town that fuelled the imagination. "Shoulda see me and the ranking dread / Check how we jamming and ting!" intoned the twosome, and while only those familiar with Jamaican patois understood it, the feel-good vibe came through clear and strong.

Wuthering Heights
Kate Bush

Released January 1978
EMI America *8003* (U.S.) / EMI *2719* (U.K. #1)

This stunning debut single announced the arrival of the 19-year-old Kate Bush, perhaps the most naturally gifted British female musician of the modern era. At 15, Bush caught the attention of Pink Floyd's Dave Gilmour, who helped record the demo tape that earned her a deal with EMI. The label allowed Bush to spend the next two years studying music, dancing, and mime before she started work on her debut album, The Kick Inside. EMI at first chose 'James And The Cold Gun' to be her first single, but the precocious singer insisted that it should be this dazzling adaptation of Emily Bronte's classic mid-19th century novel of the same name.

'Wuthering Heights' opens with Bush's twinkly piano playing, quickly joined by her siren-like vocal, which weaves in and out of a complex melody and chord progression. Voice and piano are joined by warm synths, soaring strings, and, eventually, a lyrical guitar solo, as the song rises to a glass-shattering crescendo. Bush's choice of debut single was vindicated when it brought her unexpectedly immediate success, giving her a British Number 1 at the first attempt. The follow-up, 'The Man With The Child In His Eyes,' wasn't quite so popular in the U.K. but did provide the singer with a minor U.S. hit.

Bush continued an almost unbroken run of critical and commercial successes throughout the 1980s and early 1990s. Along the way she re-recorded 'Wuthering Heights' – for her 1986 anthology The Whole Story – but there is little doubt that the original remains the definitive version and one of the most striking debuts in the history of pop.

Mr. Blue Sky
Electric Light Orchestra

Released January 1978
Jet *5050* (U.S. #35) / Jet *UP 36342* (U.K. #6)

The definitive Electric Light Orchestra single, 'Mr. Blue Sky' demonstrates all of the group's strengths but also shows off the comical excesses that have regularly seen them dismissed as a bloated Beatles tribute act. Frontman Jeff Lynne – formerly of The Move – might just have got the last laugh, however, when he worked as producer with Paul McCartney, George Harrison, Ringo Starr, and, in effect, John Lennon on the two Beatles 1990s 'comeback' singles, 'Free As A Bird' and 'Real Love.'

Formed in 1971, ELO went through various changes of line-up in the early 1970s before eventually reaching a relatively settled membership that included Lynne, drummer Bev Bevan, bassist Kelly Groucutt, keyboardist Richard Tandy, violinist Mik Kaminski, and cellists Hugh McDowell and Melvyn Gale. The latter trio of string players was crucial to the group's sound, which drew most explicitly on Beatles songs like 'A Day In The Life' and 'I Am The Walrus.'

Prior to selection as a single, 'Mr. Blue Sky' made up the final part of 'Concerto For A Rainy Day,' a four-song suite that filled the third side of the double-disc set Out Of The Blue (1977). The most conventionally structured of the four songs, 'Mr. Blue Sky' does nonetheless stretch beyond five minutes, taking in the obligatory big string arrangement, a choir, vocoder'd vocals, and an extended false ending. An international chart hit, it has also become the unofficial theme tune of Lynne's hometown soccer club, Birmingham City.

Baker Street
Gerry Rafferty

Released February 1978
United Artists *1192* (U.S. #2) / United Artists *UP 36346* (U.K. #3)

The other song for which Gerry Rafferty is well known is Stealer's Wheel's 'Stuck In The Middle With You,' and while that was a good song, it was chiefly notable as an absolutely uncanny imitation of Bob Dylan. With 'Baker Street' Rafferty revealed a more original vision. It is an exquisite song about self-delusion and loneliness in the big city with a cleverly realistic lyric ("One more year and then you'll be happy…"). Rafferty devised instrumental parts for the song and Raphael Ravenscroft was brought in to transpose them to saxophone. The result was the cherry on the cake, perfectly complementing the air of aching melancholy.

Sultans Of Swing
Dire Straits

Released May 1978
Warners Bros. *8736* (U.S. #4) / Vertigo *6059 206* (U.K. #8)

The Out were a late-1970s power-pop band who once opened for the up-and-coming Dire Straits. Mark Knopfler, frontman and guitarist of Dire Straits, admired the great sound that Out guitarist George Borowski obtained from his ridiculously battered instrument. Knopfler wondered why Borowski didn't play solos. "I can't really play solos," came the guileless response, "I just play chords."

Not long afterwards, Knopfler was working on 'Sultans Of Swing,' a song about a "crap little band" he had seen playing when drinking in a pub, and he decided to put in a verse about the incident: "Check out Guitar George / He knows all the chords / Mind, he's strictly rhythm, he doesn't want to make it cry or sing / And an old guitar is all he can afford / When he gets up under the lights to play his thing."

It was this song that secured Dire Straits a record deal after a demo played on DJ Charlie Gillett's London radio show Honky Tonk in summer 1977 provoked record-company interest. However, it was not plain sailing after the band released 'Sultans Of Swing' as their debut single. The American record company barely promoted it or the group's first album, on which could be found a different, slightly smoother version of the track. Radio stations loved the band, however, and eventually the single climbed into the Top 10 in February 1979. This Stateside success prompted U.K. stations to play the record, even though BBC Radio 1 had declined previously on the grounds that the song had too many words, and the single went Top 10 at home too.

Le Freak
Chic

Released October 1978
Atlantic *3519* (U.S. #1) / Atlantic *K 11209* (U.K. #7)

While the punk wars raged and the roots of electro and hip-hop spread, Chic knocked out an effortless sequence of timeless disco singles, each of which evoked images of a night-time club existence that unified races and nations under one ineffable groove. This was an illusion, of course, but it says much for the super-clean, super-euphoric music of Nile Rodgers and Bernard Edwards that to this day the songs sound as if they come from another planet.

Guitarist Rodgers and bassist Edwards formed Chic in 1976 and soon recruited fellow New Yorker Tony Thompson, a drummer who had previously worked with LaBelle. The trio's earliest work, including the international debut hit 'Dance Dance Dance,' featured vocalist Norma Jean Wright, but she was forced to quit in 1978 due to complications with her recording contract. 'Le Freak' was the first Chic single to feature new vocalist Luci Martin, but it was inspired, in a sense, by another, more famous singer.

On new year's eve, 1977, Rodgers and Edwards were invited to meet Grace Jones at the world famous New York City disco club Studio 54 to discuss the possibility of the duo producing her next album. On arriving at the club's entrance, however, Rodgers and Edwards were stopped from entering by the venue's bouncers. Understandably irritated, they went back to Rodgers's nearby apartment and decided to vent their anger by composing a new song together. In its initial incarnation, the funky, chicken-scratch guitar riff was overlaid by a repeated cry of "Aaaaah, fuck off!" Sensibly, Rodgers later changed the lyric to "Freak out," and a disco classic was born.

'Le Freak' is more than just a fun song: as with so many of Chic's works, the world-class bass playing of Edwards inspired a swathe of rappers, samplers, and producers to improve their game. It formed the basis of The Sugarhill Gang's 'Rapper's Delight,' generally considered to be the first charting hip-hop single. 'Le Freak' quickly rose to the top of the *Billboard* Hot 100. It was followed midway through 1979 by another seminal Chic Number 1, 'Good Times,' which had the distinction of being the source material for Grandmaster Flash's landmark single 'Adventures On The Wheels Of Steel.' Together, these two songs represent a funkier, more colorful era in pop music, which was the most enduring legacy of disco (John Travolta's white suit notwithstanding).

NILE RODGERS: A CHIC PRODUCTION STYLE

Nile Rodgers formed Chic with Bernard Edwards in 1976, but the group's popularity began to dwindle at the start of the 1980s, and it was at that point that Rodgers's second career as one of the decade's biggest and most important record producers began to take off. He had already worked with Sister Sledge and Diana Ross, for whom he produced the smash hit 'I'm Coming Out,' and was invited to update the sound of 1970s pop chameleon David Bowie for his *Let's Dance* album (1983). Rodgers looms large over the record, painting its eight concise songs with a palette of shiny synthesizers, funky bass, and disco guitar licks. Let's Dance remains the biggest commercial success of Bowie's career and spawned three international hits: the title track, 'Modern Love,' and 'China Girl.'

Rodgers then turned his attentions to Madonna, for whom he produced the hits 'Material Girl' and 'Like A Virgin.' After that it was Mick Jagger and Duran Duran. In 1986 he finally got the chance to work with Grace Jones, on her *Inside Story* album; he also worked on movie soundtracks, including *Alphabet City* (1984) and *Coming To America* (1988).

Most of the albums Rodgers worked on during the 1980s were made at The Power Station in New York City (now known as Avatar Studios), with his one-time Chic bandmates Bernard Edwards and Tony Thompson regularly providing bass and drums. In 1992, Rodgers and Edwards reformed Chic (without Thompson) to make the *CHIC-ism* album and for a world tour. Rodgers was named Top Producer In The World by *Billboard* magazine in 1996, but a series of celebratory gigs in Japan was marred when Edwards contracted pneumonia and died suddenly.

During the 1990s and beyond Rodgers's work-rate slowed, but he continues to produce hit records, both for artists he has worked with previously in the early part of his career, including David Bowie and Duran Duran, and the likes of Samantha Cole and All-4-One.

After the U.S. terrorist attacks of September 11, 2001, he organized an all-star re-recording of the Sister Sledge classic 'We Are Family' and shortly thereafter founded the We Are Family Foundation to promote cultural and religious tolerance.

Rivers Of Babylon
Boney M

Released April 1978
Sire *1027* (U.S. #30) / Atlantic-Hansa *K 11120* (U.K. #1)

Rasputin
Boney M
Released September 1978
Sire *1049* (U.S.) / Atlantic-Hansa *K 11192* (U.K. #2)

Mary's Boy Child – Oh My Lord
Boney M
Released November 1978
Sire *1036* (U.S.) / Atlantic-Hansa *K 11221* (U.K. #1)

One of the most successful European pop acts of the 1970s, Boney M recorded two of the ten biggest-selling singles of all time in the U.K., a feat unmatched by any other group. Despite finding little success in the U.S., Boney M is one of a select few groups that could claim to have a truly global fan-base, with a following that stretches across Africa, India, and South-East Asia. Boney M was the brainchild of the German music producer Frank Farian, who recruited four West Indian session vocalists to front the group. They began to hit their stride with three U.K. Top 10 hits in 1977 before topping the charts early the following year with 'Rivers Of Babylon.' Originally a hit for the Jamaican rock-steady band The Melodians in 1969, the song set biblical lyrics – taken from Psalm 137 – against a gentle disco backbeat. In Britain, Boney M's version has been outsold only by Elton John's 'Candle In The Wind,' 'Do They Know It's Christmas?' by Band Aid (both of which were charity singles), Queen's 'Bohemian Rhapsody,' and 'Mull Of Kintyre' by Wings. It was also the group's only American hit.

Boney M followed 'Rivers Of Babylon' with the equally memorable 'Rasputin' – essentially a Russian history lesson set to four-to-the-floor drums and swooping strings. But that was soon eclipsed by the festive hit 'Mary's Boy Child – Oh My Lord,' Boney M's second U.K. chart-topper and the tenth best-selling single of all time in Britain. Despite their remarkable successes in 1978, the group had fallen into a steady decline by the end of the decade and split in 1981.

You're The One That I Want
John Travolta & Olivia Newton-John

Released March 1978
RSO *891* (U.S. #1) / RSO *006* (U.K. #1)

'You're The One That I Want' was the biggest of several international smash hits to be drawn from the *Grease* soundtrack album, which has sold in excess of 30 million copies worldwide.

The original stage version of *Grease*, written by Jim Jacobs and Warren Casey, first appeared in 1971. Six years later, when Robert Stigwood obtained the movie rights, it had notched up more than 2,000 Broadway performances. Newton-John was already an established singer with a string of hits and awards to her name, while John Travolta had found fame and fortune for his part in Stigwood's previous production, *Saturday Night Fever*, and had also toured in a stage production of *Grease*.

For the purposes of the movie version, Stigwood commissioned some new songs. Not surprisingly, given the success of *Fever*, he called on Barry Gibb of The Bee Gees to write the title song, while Gibb in turn invited former Four Seasons vocalist Frankie Valli to sing it. In addition, John Farrar, Olivia Newton-John's musical director, wrote her solo hit, 'Hopelessly Devoted To You' and the duet, 'You're The One That I Want,' which spent an impressive nine weeks at Number 1 in Britain. The follow-up, another Travolta/Newton-John duet, 'Summer Nights' (from the original *Grease* score), was Number 1 in Britain for seven weeks, making the couple one of the most successful double-acts of all time.

Miss You
The Rolling Stones

Released May 1978
Rolling Stones *19307* (U.S. #1) / Rolling Stones *EMI 2802* (U.K. #3)

The Rolling Stones didn't look like a good bet for a classic single in 1978. The band were viewed by most punks as bloated, indulgent parodies, and with guitarist Keith Richards facing long-term imprisonment for drug offences in Canada, the end of the one-time World's Greatest Rock'n'Roll Band looked a real possibility. But Richards paid his debt to society by playing a concert for the blind, thereby escaping prison, and the band regrouped for 'Miss You' and its parent album, *Some Girls* – their best work since 1972's *Exile On Main Street*.

With Bill Wyman's walking octave bass part and Mick Jagger's mincing, falsetto vocal, 'Miss You' took some tricks not from the new wave but from the other musical phenomenon of the time, disco. In many ways this was a re-run of how the band had started out – taking black music styles and regurgitating them with a sleazy panache and a carefully offhand pop sensibility. The single came not only in a standard 7-inch picture sleeve but also as a limited-edition pink vinyl 12-inch, a ploy that no doubt helped to secure its high chart placing.

Three Times A Lady
The Commodores

Released June 1978
Motown *1443* (U.S. #1) / Tamla Motown *TMG 1113* (U.K. #1)

The Commodores were formed by students attending the Tuskegee Institute in Alabama in 1967, including Lionel Richie, and chose their name at random from a dictionary. Chart success began with the instrumental 'Machine Gun' in 1974. Since all the other members of the group were writing up-tempo material, Richie made a conscious decision to write ballads since this would guarantee his material a place on their albums. Of course, he never expected them to be so successful, but following major chart hits with 'Sweet Love,' 'Just To Be Close To You,' and 'Easy,' Richie realized he had established a winning formula.

'Three Times A Lady' was the result of a conversation Richie had with his father at a party to celebrate his parents' 37th wedding anniversary. He recalled: "My father told me that in 37 years of marriage he'd never told my mother how much she meant to him. I decided I wasn't going to wait 37 years to tell my wife, Brenda." Richie sat down with the express intention of writing a declaration of love to his wife, and 'Three Times A Lady' was the result. He recalled how the song was written at the height of the 1970s disco phenomenon and that one radio programmer told him: "You are either the craziest man who ever lived, or the bravest, for releasing this song now." History proves that Richie was certainly not crazy, and the song swiftly rose to Number 1 on both sides of the Atlantic.

An Everlasting Love
Andy Gibb

Released July 1978
RSO *904* (U.S. #5) / RSO *015* (U.K. #10)

Andy Gibb, the younger brother of The Bee Gees, could hardly have picked a better time to launch his solo career. During 1977 and '78 the group were at the top of their game, their compositions dominating the charts and helping manager Robert Stigwood's RSO Records enjoy a remarkable 30 weeks at Number 1 on the *Billboard* singles charts in '78.

Andy's first three singles, 'I Just Want To Be Your Everything,' '(Love Is) Thicker Than Water,' and 'Shadow Dancing,' were all U.S. Number 1s. The first two were composed by Barry Gibb within two hours on the same evening, while 'Shadow Dancing' was a Barry-Robin-Maurice-Andy composition. 'Thicker Than Water' also carried an Andy Gibb composition credit, although apparently his sole contribution was the title. Barry co-produced the majority of Andy's biggest hits, to which he also often added his distinctive falsetto backing-vocals.

In the pre-*Saturday Night Fever* U.K. punk landscape, Andy's singles had not fared so well, and it was his fourth American hit, 'An Everlasting Love' (a Barry solo composition, and the first not to top the U.S. charts), that was his most successful single in Britain, reaching Number 10. Andy's instant success ultimately led to numerous personal and drug-related problems that in turn led to his untimely death in 1988 at the age of 30.

I Will Survive
Gloria Gaynor

Released December 1978
Polydor *14508* (U.S. #1) / Polydor *2095 017* (U.K. #1)

This marks one of many instances where a throwaway B-side has turned into an international hit. The A-side, recorded at a session overseen by veteran producer Freddie Perren, was a cover of a recent British Number 2, 'Substitute' by Clout. However, Perren had agreed to produce the record on condition that he and partner Dino Fekaris would supply the B-side, a move that would guarantee them 50 per cent of the royalties should 'Substitute' become a hit.

With this in mind, 'I Will Survive' was especially tailored for Gaynor, and Fekaris consulted her about subject matter that might appeal. However, when he arrived at the session he'd forgotten to bring the lyrics and had to quickly jot them down on a brown paper bag. As soon as she read them, Gaynor was immediately attracted to the defiant words. She was also stunned. How could this be a B-side? Surely it was a major hit. Her record company disagreed, and 'Substitute' was duly released with 'I Will Survive' hidden away on the back.

Gaynor decided to take matters into her own hands, persuading club DJs to flip the record. The breakthrough followed when 'Survive' became a favorite at New York's influential Studio 54 discotheque. Finally, after months of persuasion (and when it became apparent that 'Substitute' wasn't going to repeat its U.K. success), 'Survive' was re-released as the A-side and promptly shot to the top of the charts worldwide, selling several million copies and winning a Grammy for Best Disco Record. Gaynor has never been able to better this career blockbuster, a song that has since become a gay and feminist anthem and is recognized as something of a modern classic. 'I Will Survive' returned to the U.K. Top 5 in a 1993 remix, and anyone who has been near a karaoke bar will certainly have heard some awful versions as the song is one of the most-performed karaoke tunes.

Pump It Up
Elvis Costello & The Attractions

Released May 1978
Not issued U.S. / Radar *ADA 10* (U.K. #24)

Emerging in 1977, Elvis Costello found himself included as part of the British punk scene but soon revealed himself to be a far more enduring and diverse talent. 'Pump It Up' is the best-loved of his early new-wave hits. Born Declan McManus in 1955, Costello grew up with The Beatles and Motown, and worked as a computer operator before signing to the influential independent Stiff Records late in 1976. He made the acclaimed *My Aim Is True* album the following year before recruiting a backing band, The Attractions, with whom he would work, on and off, for the next two decades. The Attractions gave a harder-edged backing to Costello's songs, which tended to overflow with artful, acerbic wordplay.

The first fruit of Costello's work with The Attractions was the sneering, ska-influenced '(I Don't Want To Go To) Chelsea,' which preceded the release of his second full-length, *This Year's Model*. 'Pump It Up' was next out of the blocks, a raucous crystallization of Costello's new sound that's driven by Steve Nieve's monotonous organ and Pete Thomas's snare-heavy backbeat. In true Costello style, the punchy, catchy tune is topped by a barbed lyric about the perils of rock'n'roll decadence, written in late 1977 while he was on tour with Stiff label-mates Ian Dury and The Damned.

Most of Costello's singles, 'Pump It Up' included, were not issued in the U.S., but their parent albums invariably reached the *Billboard* Top 30 – no mean feat for such an idiosyncratically British artist.

No One Is Innocent (A Punk Prayer By Ronald Biggs) / My Way
The Sex Pistols

Released June 1978
Not issued U.S. / Virgin *VS 220* (U.K. #7)

Public Image
Public Image Ltd

Released October 1978
Not issued U.S. / Virgin *VS 228* (U.K. #9)

Less than a year after releasing their landmark debut album, *Never Mind The Bollocks*, The Sex Pistols were in disarray. The group's last proper single was the double A-side release, 'No One Is Innocent' / 'My Way,' recorded after frontman John Lydon (a.k.a. Johnny Rotten) had quit to form Public Image Ltd (PiL).

'No One Is Innocent' is a throwaway 'punk prayer' featuring a guest vocal by Ronnie Biggs, the notorious Great Train Robber who spent many years exiled in Brazil. Of more interest is the flipside, a rendition of 'My Way,' earlier popularized by Frank Sinatra. Here it is sung, lugubriously, by Sex Pistols bassist Sid Vicious. The single would be seen as Sid's swan song after the events of the next few months: he was charged with the murder of his girlfriend, Nancy Spudgeon, in October 1978, and died of a drug overdose the following April before the matter could be taken any further. By this stage the somewhat less volatile PiL had made its recorded debut with 'Public Image.' Like a lot of the group's best material, the single is driven by Jah Wobble's throbbing bass and the propulsive, Krautrock-derived drums, provided by Jim Walker, the first in a long line of apparently expendable kit men. Fighting for space atop the rhythm section are Keith Levene's sandblasted guitar and a ranting, raging vocal that could only have come from the larynx of a certain Mr. Lydon. It was the first in a line of great records from a group that, while lacking the sheer cultural impact of The Sex Pistols, created an equally impressive musical legacy.

Killing An Arab
The Cure

Released December 1978
Not issued U.S. / Small Wonder *SMALL 11* (U.K.)

Stark, minimalist, and hugely energetic, 'Killing An Arab' marked the start of The Cure's extraordinary career. Recorded on September 28, 1978, at Morgan Studios in London, England, it became their first single and, although it failed to chart, it plunged them into a worldwide debate about whether or not its lyric was racist. "It was a short poetic attempt at condensing my impression of the key moments in *L'Étranger* by Albert Camus," explained Cure mainman Robert Smith, clearly horrified by the interpretations of racism. The debate, fuelled by escalating Arab-Western tensions, still rumbles on – as does the one about whether The Cure are now, or ever were, Goths.

Ever Fallen In Love
(With Someone You Shouldn't've)
The Buzzcocks

Released September 1978
Not issued U.S. / United Artists *UP 36455* (U.K. #12)

This is the best-loved single by one of the enduring groups of the British punk era, marrying a melodic-minor chord progression with a frenetic performance and a lyric anyone could relate to. The group was formed in 1976 by singer-guitarists Pete Shelley and Howard Devoto, but Devoto appeared only on the Spiral Scratch EP before founding the more cerebral band Magazine. The first Buzzcocks single, 'Orgasm Addict,' was far too shocking for radio and didn't chart, but by the end of 1977 the group had built a wide and devoted following. 'Ever Fallen In Love' was one of five U.K. Top 30 hits they scored in 1978. It was not issued as a single in the U.S., but a cover version by Fine Young Cannibals reached Number 11 on the Billboard Hot Dance Music/Club Play chart in 1986.

Teenage Kicks
The Undertones

Released September 1978
Sire *49195* (U.S.) / Good Vibrations *GOT 4* (U.K. #30)

This seminal punk-influenced hit is perhaps best known for having been among the all-time favorites of the influential British DJ John Peel. The Undertones were formed in 1975 by vocalist Feargal Sharkey, guitar-playing brothers John and Damian O'Neill, bassist Mike Bradley, and drummer Billy Doherty. In the summer of 1978 they recorded 'Teenage Kicks,' their debut single, in a one-off deal for the small independent label Good Vibrations, based in their native Northern Ireland. Driven by a dirgey two-chord guitar riff, the song is peppered with handclaps and Sharkey's yearning cry: "I wanna hold her, wanna hold her tight / Get teenage kicks right through the night."

The single was immediately championed by Peel – who later named it as his favorite song of all time – and climbed into the U.K. charts, earning The Undertones a deal with the Sire label. The group had several other hits before splitting in 1983, while Sharkey topped the British charts two

years later with the solo single 'A Good Heart,' but nothing else that he or the group produced had the same visceral thrill as 'Teenage Kicks.'

Peel was, without exaggeration, the most important DJ in the history of British radio. He began his career in the U.S., where he worked using his real surname, Ravenscroft, for stations in Dallas, Oklahoma City, and San Bernardino. He returned to the U.K. in early 1967 and for several months had a show on the pirate station, Radio London, before landing a job with the newly created pop channel Radio One that summer.

For the next 34 years, until his sudden death in 2004, Peel regularly introduced listeners to new and exciting sounds. He was the first British DJ to play punk, reggae, and hip-hop, and an early champion of countless musical acts, from Captain Beefheart to T. Rex, The Sex Pistols to The Smiths, Pulp to The White Stripes. Notorious for playing records at the wrong speed, he was also the first British DJ to air the same record twice in a row. That record was, of course, 'Teenage Kicks.'

Hit Me With Your Rhythm Stick
Ian Dury & The Blockheads

Released November 1978
Epic *850726* (U.S.) / Stiff *BUY 38* (U.K. #1)

Milk And Alcohol
Dr. Feelgood

Released January 1979
Not issued U.S. / United Artists *UP 36468* (U.K. #9)

These two singles mark the commercial peak of pub-rock, the British music scene that laid the foundations for punk and then continued alongside it.

One of the most unlikely frontmen of the 1970s, Ian Dury taught painting at Canterbury College before turning to music. 'Hit Me With Your Rhythm Stick' followed the cult favorite 'Sex And Drugs And Rock And Roll' (1977) and displays all the hallmarks of Dury's best work, with its infectious combination of ramshackle rock'n'roll, the occasional hint of jazzy funk, and bawdy lyrical witticisms. Few people – including Dury himself – would have expected the single to top the U.K. charts, but it did so, for two weeks in early 1979, selling close to a million copies on the way.

Dury never matched that feat, but 'Reasons To Be Cheerful (Pt. 3)' did provide him with a successful British follow-up in 1979. He had high hopes for the caustic 'Spasticus Autisticus,' written in 1981 to commemorate the International Year of The Disabled, but it was banned by the BBC and, with little airplay, failed to chart.

In the same month that 'Hit Me With Your Rhythm Stick' topped the U.K. chart, Dr. Feelgood – who, like Dury, hailed from Essex, England – readied the irresistible 'Milk And Alcohol.' While the group never quite recovered from the departure of founding guitarist Wilko Johnson in 1977, this was their most successful single. It was co-written by Nick Lowe, the producer of a number of defining British albums of the era, including The Damned's *Damned Damned Damned* and several by Elvis Costello. 'Milk And Alcohol' features a suitably leering, cigarette-ravaged vocal delivery from frontman Lee Brilleaux over choppy, stop-start guitar and drums. It was issued as two different-colored 7-inch singles, one 'beery,' the other 'milky.'

Video Killed The Radio Star
Buggles

Released September 1979
Island *49114* (U.S. #40) / Island *WIP 6524* (U.K. #1)

'Video Killed The Radio Star' is the quintessential earworm: an irritatingly catchy novelty hit that gets stuck in the listener's head for days. It is also a perfectly crafted pop single and the first demonstration of the ingenious production talents of Trevor Horn, who went on to create some of the defining records of the 1980s.

British-born Horn formed Buggles in 1978 with keyboardist Geoff Downes, essentially as a vehicle for these two former session musicians to have a chart-topping hit. (Both had been members of the unsuccessful group Camera Club, which also included future pop star Thomas Dolby.)

'Video Killed The Radio Star' gave the duo exactly what they wanted at the first attempt, topping the U.K. singles chart and spending a total of 11 weeks in the listings. As well as Horn and Downes, the single featured keyboardist Hans Zimmer, who went on to become an Oscar-winning soundtrack composer, scoring movies including *Crimson Tide*, *Gladiator*, and *The Lion King*.

One of the great ironic pop hits, 'Video Killed The Radio Star' overflows with hook after hook, from the "ooh ooh" backing vocals to the many layers of overflowing keyboards. On close inspection, what at first sounds light and throwaway is revealed to be a cleverly constructed and rigorously detailed masterpiece of early synthesizer-pop. Similarly, the lyrics, far from being a string of half-baked phrases, are in fact a knowing deconstruction of the failings of the popular music industry.

Buggles followed 'Radio Star' with a handful of minor British hits over the next year, including 'The Plastic Age' and 'Clean Clean.' Neither Horn nor Downes had much interest in the further pursuit of pop stardom, however, and they split the group in 1980. The duo then joined the progressive rock group Yes, replacing departing members Rick Wakeman and Jon Anderson and producing the album *Drama*. After Yes disbanded in 1982, Downes formed Asia with Yes guitarist Steve Howe, Carl Palmer (the P in ELP), and John Wetton (once of King Crimson).

Horn meanwhile stepped away from the spotlight to embark on a highly successful career as a record producer. Among the countless acts whose rough diamonds he polished were ABC, Frankie Goes To Hollywood, Tina Turner, Pet Shop Boys, and tATu. He produced the charity hit 'Do They Know It's Christmas' for Band Aid and was a founding member of Art Of Noise, whose most notable releases include 'Close To The Edit' and 'Kiss,' a high-tech cover of the Prince original, recorded with Tom Jones.

Horn's style of production is difficult to categorize, not least because it has mutated over the years alongside the development of recording technology, but it is characterized by a sound that is rich and detailed but never cluttered. He will still be best remembered, however, for 'Video Killed The Radio Star,' which had the distinction – with fitting irony – of being the first song aired on MTV.

We Are Family
Sister Sledge

Released April 1979
Cotillion *44251* (U.S. #2) / Atlantic-Cotillion *K 11293* (U.K. #8)

Writer-producers Bernard Edwards and Nile Rodgers were at the top of their game following their success with Chic and, offered the pick of the Atlantic roster, decided to add their golden touch to Sister Sledge. Debbie, Kim, Joni, and Kathy Sledge had formed their group in Philadelphia in 1971 when the sisters were aged between 12 and 16, and they enjoyed some minor success, including a British Number 20 hit with 'Mama Never Told Me' in 1975. Edwards and Rodgers's subtly sparse production over catchy choruses gave the girls a trio of classic disco hits: 'He's The Greatest Dancer,' 'We Are Family,' and 'Lost In Music.' Both 'We Are Family' and 'Lost In Music' have returned to the U.K. charts on two separate occasions and 'He's The Greatest Dancer' formed the basis of Will Smith's 1998 U.S. chart-topper 'Gettin' Jiggy Wit It.' Unlike most disco hits of the era, the songs and production of Edwards and Rodgers had lasting quality that stands the test of time. Sister Sledge went on to more popularity in Britain, where they topped the charts in 1985 with 'Frankie,' which was not a hit in America.

Pop Muzik
M

Released April 1979
Sire *49033* (U.S. #1) / MCA *413* (U.K. #2)

In 1979 the synthesizer-sequencer explosion was yet to have a big impact in the U.K., although Gary Numan and Kraftwerk had made early inroads, and more than a few proto-New Romantic and hip-hop acts would be tweaking Wasp keyboards in the next year or two. This made M's splendid, utterly futuristic 'Pop Muzik' seem like a song from another galaxy, with its reverb-free percussion, relentless bassline, and those staccato lyrics, themselves something of a philosophical statement. 'Pop Muzik' was the brainwave of Robin Scott – educated at a London art school, even if the record sounded like it came from a bunker in Munich. The single made a huge splash and then dragged its maker down into obscurity.

Are 'Friends' Electric?
Tubeway Army

Released May 1979
Atco *7206* (U.S.) / Beggars Banquet *BEG 18* (U.K. #1)

Cars
Gary Numan

Released August 1979
Atco *7211* (U.S. #9) / Beggars Banquet *BEG 23* (U.K. #1)

Gary Numan was one of the first internationally successful exponents of synthesizer-pop, initially as the leader of Tubeway Army and then as a solo artist. Tubeway Army started out in a fairly perfunctory punk vein before Numan (born Gary Webb in London, England, in 1958) fell for the charms of the MiniMoog synthesizer, the pioneering mid-1970s work of Kraftwerk, and David Bowie's collaborations with Brian Eno. 'Are 'Friends' Electric?' was the group's fourth single. While the first three had failed to chart, this one went all the way to Number 1 in Britain, a

surprise given that it runs to more than five minutes, has no discernible chorus, and features several barely intelligible spoken-word sections. Its bleak, murky synth parts were later reworked to great effect by the 21st century girl group The Sugababes for their 2003 hit 'Freak Like Me.'

Within months of 'Friends' topping the U.K. chart, Numan had disbanded Tubeway Army and set out on his own. His first solo release, 'Cars,' gave him a second British Number 1 and his only U.S. Top 10 hit. Like its predecessor, 'Cars' has a bleak, post-modern lyric – in this instance inspired by a road-rage incident – but is set to a somewhat lighter musical backdrop. In the U.K. it has charted in three successive decades: first in its original form in '79; then with an 'E Reg' remix in 1987; and again in 1996, after its use on TV ads for beer.

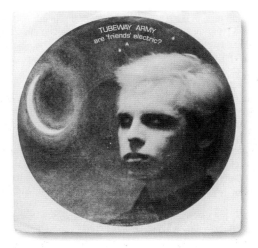

Don't Stop 'Til You Get Enough
Michael Jackson

Released August 1979
Epic *50742* (U.S. #1) / Epic *EPC 7763* (U.K. #3)

This was Michael Jackson's first solo Number 1 as an adult and introduced the chic, Quincy Jones-produced sound that would soon see him dubbed the King Of Pop. A year earlier, however, the idea of Jackson producing a huge international smash hit seemed unlikely. He had left Motown, the label for which he had recorded since the late 1960s, and was last seen playing the Scarecrow in *The Wiz*, the big-screen adaptation of *The Wizard Of Oz* that failed miserably at the box office. Nonetheless *The Wiz* was crucial to Jackson's career because it introduced Jackson to Quincy Jones, who served as the movie's musical director before becoming the perfect foil for the singer's growing talents in songwriting and arranging.

Jackson wrote 'Don't Stop' in 1978, and his original home demo – included on the recent expanded reissue of the *Off The Wall* album – shows that he knew exactly what he wanted from the song. The jangling, cowbell-laden rhythm, distinctive bass and guitar licks, and Jackson's newly developed falsetto are all there; the only extra ingredient the song needed was Jones's polished, spacious production sheen.

Issued at the height of summer 1979, the resulting single took three months to climb slowly but surely to the Number 1 spot on the *Billboard* chart, initiating Jackson's domination of the pop world for the next decade. It was quickly followed by two further U.S. Top 5 hits, *Off The Wall*'s title track and 'Rock With You,' both written by Rod Temperton, formerly of the disco group Heatwave.

Bat Out Of Hell
Meat Loaf

Released January 1979
Not issued U.S. / Epic *EPC 7018* (U.K. #15)

When Jim Steinman and Meat Loaf began work on the songs that became *Bat Out Of Hell*, they were intended for a futuristic musical based on Peter Pan entitled *Neverland*. The ten-minute epic was one of three videos specially commissioned by Columbia after witnessing Mr. Loaf's stunning performance at a U.S. convention. The album, released in America in October 1977, took about six months to take off and was a success in Britain first. In early 1978, the video of the title track was screened on the BBC's influential TV music show *The Old Grey Whistle Test* to such acclaim that it had to be shown again the following week. The album then hit the U.K. charts in March, some two months before its American Top 40 debut.

The juggernaut title track, the centerpiece of the album, was described by its writer as the result of his wish to create "the ultimate motorcycle crash song." Which makes the highlight of the track, and indeed the entire album, the motorcycle guitar effect played by producer Todd Rundgren. Steinman had wanted this all along, but Rundgren hated the idea, and it wasn't until the mixing stage that he plugged in his guitar and played the effect live in the studio. He continued into the following solo, to the utter amazement of all present – and all in one take.

Just about every adjective imaginable has been thrown at this track over the years. 'Bombastic' seems to top the list. This doesn't bother Mr. Steinman in the least. "Bombastic? Of course it's bombastic. I take that as a compliment. Rock'n'roll is the most bombastic form ever – heightened, oversized, gigantic, thrilling, and silly." 'Bat Out Of Hell' was not a single in the U.S., but in Britain it became the biggest of three hits from the LP, which went on to sell 37 million copies worldwide and spend a remarkable nine years on the British album charts.

My Sharona
The Knack

Released June 1979
Capitol *CL 16087* (U.S. #6) / Capitol *4731* (U.K. #1)

Back in '79, The Knack were hated by the critics for their cynicism, their refusal to speak to the serious music press, and the antediluvian (and anti-punk) nature of their British Invasion fashions and power pop sounds. A quarter of a century on, such passions seem barely comprehensible about a band whose only real prevailing impact on popular culture is this huge international hit. Written by their songwriting axis of Fieger & Averre, it boasts everything that made people both love and loathe them: it was naggingly catchy … at the same time as its heartless professionalism and stop-start rhythms made it somehow unlovely.

Goodbye Stranger
Supertramp

Released July 1979
A&M *2162* (U.S. #15) / A&M *AMS 7481* (U.K.)

"Just the thought of those sweet ladies / Sends a shiver through my veins" confided U.K.-born Rick Davies in this paean to the women of the world. Although the song sounded as if it had been written in a Chevy on Route 66 as the singer worked his way through a parade of females, in fact 'Goodbye Stranger' was stuffed with a very English reticence, perhaps the very quality that made it so memorable. Although the song didn't make much impact on the charts, Supertramp – whose line-up fluctuated endlessly – did go on to enjoy vast sales. The legacy of their work has endured, despite the fact that they themselves were among the most faceless of stars.

I Don't Like Mondays
The Boomtown Rats

Released July 1979
Columbia *11117* (U.S.) / Ensign *ENY 30* (U.K. #1)

Lest we forget, before becoming 'the man who organized Live Aid,' Bob Geldof was a pop star. 'I Don't Like Mondays' was his only Hot 100 hit with The Boomtown Rats in the U.S. (it scraped in at Number 73) but in Britain it was the second of two consecutive chart-toppers, following late-1978's 'Rat Trap.'

Geldof formed the six-piece group in Ireland in 1975 before dragging the whole lot of 'em across to London the following year, just in time for the punk trend. But the sound of The Boomtown Rats was closer to 1960s-style R&B than The Sex Pistols. The group was an immediate chart success in the U.K. and had notched up four hit singles and a pair of Top 20 albums before 'Rat Trap' reached Number 1.

'I Don't Like Mondays' is driven by sturdy piano chords pitched somewhere between David Bowie's early-1970s output and something from a stage musical. The lyrics were inspired by the murders committed by 16-year-old Brenda Ann Spencer at Cleveland Elementary School in San Diego, California, in January 1979. Spencer killed two adults and

wounded eight children and a police officer with a rifle she had been given for Christmas. When asked to explain her actions, she replied simply: "I don't like Mondays." Perhaps surprisingly, it didn't appear to bother anybody too much that Geldof had turned the words of a killer into a pop song. In fact, the meaning seemed to escape most radio DJs altogether – it was played regularly on Monday mornings during the 1980s to ease the masses back to work.

Message In A Bottle
The Police

Released September 1979
A&M *2190* (U.S.) / A&M *AMS 7474* (U.K. #1)

'Message In A Bottle' was the first of five British Number 1s for the group consisting of Sting (sole writer of all their hits), Stewart Copeland, and Andy Summers. The lead single from their second album *Reggatta De Blanc*, it was also A&M's first official British chart-topping single. The group's breakthrough had been a 1979 Number 32 hit in America with 'Roxanne,' which preceded major U.K. success, but their second album (a British Number 1) received a disappointing response Stateside. While 'Message In A Bottle' was a U.K. Number 1 it only reached Number 74 in America.

Of the group's trademark white-reggae sound – *Reggatta De Blanc* is a nonsense translation of the term – Sting said: "They're not straight reggae songs. What I do is weld elements of reggae into a rock setting." 'Roxanne' had originally been a ballad, and it was drummer Stewart Copeland who suggested adding a reggae beat.

Sting said he usually begins a song by finding a title. "It's common sense, really, because the title of the tune coincides with your hook-line, your chorus. So I write titles and work backwards from there." He added: "I never begin a song unless I have a metaphor," and the modest songwriter said he's particularly proud of 'Message In A Bottle.' "It's quite a cleverly put together metaphor: it develops and has an artistic shape to it."

While the *Reggatta* album received mixed reviews in Britain, it became the first of five chart-topping collections and gave the group another U.K. Number 1 single with 'Walking On The Moon.' And just in case you're curious, towards the end of that song Sting does indeed sing "Sending out an Esso Blue." He has a habit of playing with lyrics on the fade-outs of his songs: Esso Blue was a popular brand of British paraffin (kerosene) in the 1960s.

Hey Hey, My My (Out Of The Blue) / My My, Hey Hey (Into The Black)
Neil Young With Crazy Horse

Released August 1979
Reprise *49031* (U.S.) / Reprise *K 14498* (U.K.)

Young wrote this song, which name-checks Johnny Rotten, after his generation was derided as irrelevant by punks in the late 1970s. Two versions exist: a hard-rock take and an acoustic version, released as A- and B-side of this single with slightly different titles. The acoustic version contains the line "It's better to burn out than to fade away," and this unusual lack of complacency endeared Neil to younger musicians, not least of whom was Nirvana's Kurt Cobain, king of grunge. Cobain quoted the line in his suicide note, much to Young's distress.

Another Brick In The Wall (Part 2)
Pink Floyd

Released November 1979
Columbia *11187* (U.S. #1) / Harvest *HAR 5194* (U.K. #1)

Arguably the oddest Christmas Number 1 ever, 'Another Brick In The Wall' was Pink Floyd's first single in 11 years and, horror of horrors for their prog-rock album-orientated fans, it was set to a thumping disco beat. Written by Floyd's bassist, Roger Waters, the powerfully anti-establishment song was extracted from their double concept album (this is more like it) *The Wall*.

The track was recorded in France and Los Angeles, but the atmospheric children's choir section was added without any Floyd member present. "I sent the tape to England and got an engineer to summon some kids," recalled guitarist David Gilmour. "I gave him a whole set of instructions – 10 to 15-year-olds from north London, mostly boys – and I said, 'Get them to sing in as many ways as you like.'" The original intention was that the choir should be in the background, but the results were so strong that it was decided to feature them on their own.

Another distinctive element is the weird sound emanating from Gilmour's guitar at the end. How many effects pedals did it take to achieve that sound? "That's just Dave direct, with a little compression," explained producer Bob Ezrin, adding that it was also the first take. The song spent five weeks at Number 1 in the U.K., four weeks in America, and, as if to prove Waters's point about repressive educational systems, it was banned by South Africa's apartheid regime when black children began to adopt it as their anthem.

Heart Of Glass
Blondie

Released January 1979
Chrysalis *2295* (U.S. #1, U.K. #1)

Atomic
Blondie

Released February 1980
Chrysalis *2410* (U.S. #39, U.K. #1)

Blondie's first chart-topping hit in the U.S. and the U.K., 'Heart Of Glass' cemented the group's position as the most commercially successful act of the punk/new wave era. Blondie was formed in 1974 by vocalist Debbie Harry – a former Playboy bunny – and her boyfriend, guitarist Chris Stein. The group burst out of the blocks in 1976 with the organ-led punk-Motown hybrid 'X Offender' and in 1978 scored a pair of U.K. Top 10 hits, 'Denis' and '(I'm Always Touched By Your) Presence Dear.' By this stage they had expanded to a sextet, with drummer Clem Burke, bassist Nigel Harrison, keyboardist Jimmy Destri, and guitarist Frank Infante.

'Heart Of Glass,' the second single from the group's third and best album, *Parallel Lines*, was driven by a sparse, disco-inspired arrangement and Harry's angelic vocal. Both single and album were produced by Mike Chapman who, alongside regular collaborator Nicky Chinn, had sat at the helm of numerous British hits of the early-to-mid 1970s by The Sweet, Suzi Quatro, and others. Chapman was able to strip away some of the rough edges of Blondie's sound without dulling the group's impact, in the process turning them into an unassailable chart force. The following year's 'Atomic' also pitched itself somewhere between new wave and disco, and was given a similarly striking production job by Chapman. Although not as successful in the U.S. as some of Blondie's other hits – 'Call Me,' 'The Tide Is High,' and 'Rapture' completed a quartet of *Billboard* chart-toppers – it remains one of the group's best-loved songs.

Rapper's Delight
The Sugarhill Gang

Released September 1979
Sugar Hill *542* (U.S. #36) / Sugar Hill *SHL 101* (U.K. #3)

Although 'King Tim III' by The Fatback Band has the strongest claim to the title of first rap single, 'Rapper's Delight' was the genre's first Top 40 hit and without doubt one of the most important hip-hop recordings of all time.

Sylvia Robinson was a singer-songwriter-producer based in Englewood, New Jersey. She began to take note of the growing popularity of hip-hop in New York City during the late 1970s, promptly founding Sugar Hill Records to give this new music a commercial outlet. With the help of her son Joey, Robinson recruited three rappers, Big Bank Hank, Wonder Mike, and Master Gee – better known to their mothers as Henry Jackson, Michael Wright, and Guy O'Brien. She dubbed them The Sugarhill Gang. (According to hip-hop legend, Joey auditioned Jackson outside a pizza place, and Jackson's two comrades heard the performance and asked if they could have a go, too.)

Robinson was the brains behind the trio's debut single, 'Rapper's Delight,' which, like many early hip-hop records, used as its instrumental backing the hook from a recent disco hit – in this case, Chic's masterful 'Good Times.' What she couldn't do, though, was rap. Fortunately, Mike, Hank, and Gee knew all about that. The three of them trade effortless, joyous rhymes, which today sound a world away from the harsh, profanity-laden bile of much modern hip-hop.

'Rapper's Delight' only caught on locally at first, but then spread across the seas, even reaching the Top 10s in South Africa and Israel. Some estimates suggest total worldwide sales of over eight million copies. More massive hip-hop hits arrived in the subsequent months and years, but this is where rap's dominance of the airwaves and pop charts started.

London Calling
The Clash

Released December 1979
Not issued U.S. / CBS *8087* (U.K. #11)

Released in the final weeks of 1979, the apocalyptic 'London Calling' brought a fitting close to an erratic decade. The title track and opener from the group's third album, it was The Clash's highest charting single in the U.K. until a reissued 'Should I Stay Or Should I Go' was propelled to Number 1 in 1991 after featuring in a television advertisement for jeans. The song was not released as an A-side in the U.S. but featured as the B-side to the more upbeat 'Train In Vain (Stand By Me),' which gave The Clash their debut American hit in the early months of 1980.

Having burst onto the British punk scene in 1977 with the incendiary 'White Riot,' The Clash soon began to demonstrate a musical awareness that far outshone the majority of their peers. The group's third and finest collection, the double-disc album *London Calling* (1979), shows off a range of non-punk influences from ska and reggae to rockabilly. But there is nothing more powerful on that album than the anthemic title track.

'London Calling' kicks off with staccato guitar chords and a steady backbeat, but those features are almost blown out of the water by a monstrous rolling bassline. Joe Strummer revels in a call-and-response vocal with the other members of the group, variously putting down "phony Beatlemania" and announcing that "the ice age is coming." After two minutes he almost allows the song to self-destruct in a barrage of yelps, feedback, and – yes, it's true – Mick Jones's brief guitar solo, but pulls it back from the brink for a defiant final verse.

Brass In Pocket
The Pretenders

Released November 1979
Sire *49181* (U.S. #14) / Real *ARE 11* (U.K. #1)

Springing into life just as the U.K. punk scene began to fizzle out, The Pretenders had a much more enduring, classic pop-rock sound than most of their contemporaries, and in Chrissie Hynde were possessed of one of the greatest frontwomen of the time. Hynde was born in Akron, Ohio, but moved to Britain during the mid 1970s and worked for several years as a journalist on the NME music paper there.

In 1977 a demo tape of Hynde's self-penned songs caught the attention of the fledgling Real label, which requested that she put together a band. The Pretenders have been through countless line-up changes over the years, but were initially settled on the quartet of Hynde plus three British men: James Honeyman-Scott (guitar), Pete Farndon (bass), and Martin Chambers (drums).

The group's debut was a strident cover of The Kinks' 'Stop Your Sobbing' produced by Nick Lowe, best known at the time for his work with Elvis Costello. This and 'Kid' were minor U.K. hits during the first half of 1979 but paled in comparison to the group's third effort. 'Brass In Pocket' is driven by clean, stop-start Telecaster chords and Hynde's cool, cocksure vocal, a declaration that "I'm special, so special / I got to have some of your attention." Her bandmates join in, cooing the word "special" back in response, in the process eliminating any doubt there might be that Hynde's confidence could be misplaced.

Love Will Tear Us Apart
Joy Division

Released April 1980
Not issued U.S. / Factory *FAC 23* (U.K. #13)

The suicide of Joy Division's singer Ian Curtis in 1980 has cast a perpetual ghostly hue over the band's slim volume of recorded work. Yet even before his death there was something authentically other-worldly about Joy Division. A band inspired by punk but never a punk band, Joy Division initially favored a sort of monolithic rock, dominated by two-note guitar riffs, rigid drum patterns, and Curtis's forbiddingly gloomy baritone, with bassist Peter Hook providing most of the melody. The later addition of rudimentary synthesizer parts seemed to bring out a hitherto buried musicality in Curtis's voice, and on 'Love Will Tear Us Apart' the band crafted what is most definitely a pop single, albeit a rather dark, forlorn form of pop.

'Love Will Tear Us Apart' appeared in April 1980, just as the Joy Division story reached crisis point. Curtis was an epileptic and sometimes had seizures on stage. He cultivated a jerking, manically spasmodic dance routine that seemed to mimic the seizures, and audiences grew morbidly fascinated by his on-stage movements. Was he having a fit or just dancing?

The band was working a punishing schedule in early 1980, despite rumors of Curtis's declining health, exacerbated when some dates were cancelled on a European tour in January. Nonetheless, on their return the band started work immediately on the second album and released 'Love Will Tear Us Apart.' It was heaped with critical adulation but failed to reach beyond the independent charts. Then, on the eve of an American tour in early May, Curtis hanged himself. That summer a re-release of 'Love Will Tear Us Apart' gave the band their first British hit. It has since been covered by artists as unlikely as blue-eyed-soul boy Paul Young and the 1960s trouser-splitter, P.J. Proby.

Turning Japanese
The Vapors

Released January 1980
United Artists *1364* (U.S. #36) / United Artists *BP 334* (U.K. #3)

This A-side, an up-tempo live anthem chock-full of vocal and guitar hooks with a funky tempo change in the middle, borrowed as much from rock as it did from new wave. All of this made it an obvious chart candidate, boosted by the rumor that the title referred to masturbation, and specifically the facial expression at the climax of that activity. This was never confirmed by the band, who were discovered by Bruce Foxton of The Jam, and who went on to join the long line of new wave one-hit wonders, leaving this excellent ditty behind them.

Going Underground
The Jam

Released March 1980
Not issued U.S. / Polydor *POSP 113* (U.K. #1)

These days, a single entering the British chart at Number 1 is commonplace. When 'Going Underground' achieved that feat in March 1980 it was the first time it had happened since 'Merry Xmas Everybody' by Slade in 1973. There was a whiff of manipulation about the accomplishment: it was a double-pack single featuring bonus live tracks, and there was a convenient delay of a week from its originally announced release date due to a supposed pressing problem.

The Jam had undeniably built up a commercial strength through superb singles like 'The Eton Rifles,' and the ascent of 'Underground' to the top marked the start of The Jam in their pomp – which lasted until their dissolution in 1982. During that time they fulfilled the promise of the punk movement, to which they had come rather late in the day.

Technically this single was a double A-side, but few remember 'Dreams Of Children' today. It was 'Going Underground' that captured the imagination of DJs and the public, with a fearsome guitar riff, songwriter-guitarist Paul Weller's spat-out vocal, the thunderous rhythm work of drummer Rick Buckler and bassist Bruce Foxton, and a nuclear-nightmare lyric (now dated, then very resonant). Weller's lyrics could often be cringe-worthy but the cherry on the icing here was the superb couplet: "You choose your leaders and place your trust / As their lies wash you down and their promises rust."

Whip It
Devo

Released August 1980
Warner Bros. *49550* (U.S. #14) / Virgin *VS 383* (U.K.)

Ludicrous it may have sounded, but 'Whip It' contained all the hallmarks of the burgeoning new-wave sound – and more comedy than anybody else around at the time. The American punk-industrial-electronic quintet made sure everyone knew about their slightly unnerving connections – the Church Of The SubGenius among them – and kept the joke going on their songs, many of which, like this one, were packed full of vaguely homo-erotic innuendo. And all with a catchy chorus and a slinky synth bassline that sounded, at the time, like all our futures: "No one gets away, until you … whip it" they promised, and how we agreed. 'Whip It' was Devo's only Top 40 hit on either side of the Atlantic. Vocalist Mark Mothersbaugh has since found success with his soundtrack work, which includes writing the theme to the animated TV series *Rugrats*.

a native of Indiana, but while in the air force in the 1960s he found himself stationed in East Anglia, England. There he took and slightly modified the name of Gino Washington, a minor American rhythm & blues star. He fooled U.K. promoters and record labels into believing he was the real Washington. Before long, Geno's gravelly delivery and stage charisma had made him a star in his own right, and he secured four moderate chart hits. He also secured the wide-eyed admiration of young Kevin Rowland who, we are told by this song's lyric, saw him "back in '68 in a sweaty club." Rowland continues: "You fed me, you bred me, I'll remember your name." Rowland, who co-wrote the song with Kevin Archer, couldn't resist informing his erstwhile hero that he thought their roles were now reversed: "And now just look at me as I'm looking down on you / No, I'm not being flash, it's what I'm built to do." Rowland's rather whining voice never quite lived up to the bombast of his lyrics and certainly did not live up to the breathtaking majesty of the Midnight Runners' horn charts, but the record was still stirring enough to storm its way up the charts, a genuine word-of-mouth smash.

Antmusic
Adam & The Ants

Released November 1980
Columbia *0204* (U.S.) / CBS *9352* (U.K. #2)

'Antmusic' was a clarion call of pure post-punk groove, complete with drumming patterned after the Burundi tribes of Africa, some guttural chanting, and the sweetly rebellious vocals of a charismatic frontman. MTV launched in 1981 and played the single on heavy rotation, making an early video star out of the nattily coiffed and painted Adam Ant (who masqueraded as a pirate). 'Antmusic' helped the group earn a Grammy Award nomination for Best New Artist in 1982, the same year that Ant had his first American Top 20 hit as a solo artist, 'Goody Two Shoes.'

Geno
Dexys Midnight Runners

Released March 1980
Not issued U.S. / Late Night Feelings *R 6033* (U.K. #1)

Dexys frontman Kevin Rowland infamously took his music and his image very seriously indeed. 'Geno' was an extension of this passion. The song's subject, Geno Washington – real name George Washington – was

SINGLE FUTURE: VINYL, CASSETTE, OR CD ?

The cassette single burst on to the scene in 1980, with help from the irrepressible Malcolm McLaren, former manager of The Sex Pistols. In 1980, he persuaded EMI to issue the first cassette single to launch his new act, Bow Wow Wow. Not only did 'C30, C60, C90, Go!' champion the cause of home taping, then considered by record labels to be a form of piracy that was "killing music," it only included one song. He left the other side blank for buyers to use for their own piratical activities, a calculated attempt to bite the hand that was feeding him.

Bow Wow Wow were manufactured by McLaren to promote the Burundi-meets-Captain-Hook concept he had originally designed for Adam & The Ants; prized away from Adam, the original Ants now backed Annabella Lwin, a 14-year-old Burmese schoolgirl whom McLaren had found working in a London dry-cleaners. The cassette single reached only Number 34 in the British charts, despite its novelty value. McLaren followed it up with Your Cassette Pet, an eight-song cassette-only release, then gave up the campaign and turned to vinyl for the band's first album. Bow Wow Wow's heady mix of adolescent sexuality and art-school camp carried them along for a few scandalous years and even gave them a couple of British hits.

McLaren's was not an entirely original idea. 'Cassette culture' had been something of a post-punk cult in Britain for several years, allowing artists

to release music directly to their followers without using record companies. Bands would often mail out their music in exchange for a blank cassette and an addressed envelope. In America, however, the cassette single (sometimes known as the cassingle) had more prosaic origins. With cassette albums now dominating sales, record companies reasoned that there were now teenagers without turntables to play vinyl records.

The first major cassette single was Bryan Adams's 'In the Heat Of The Night,' issued on A&M in 1987. Later releases would have more than two songs, and for a time the cassette single did well. A poll by Arista that year showed that more than 40 per cent of cassette-single buyers had long given up buying 45s, but that 90 per cent said they would now start buying singles again. In 1989, De La Soul's 'Me Myself And I' became the first cassette-only single to enter the U.S. Top 40.

The cassette single's heyday was short. The introduction of the little 3-inch CD single, overpriced and initially unplayable on most machines, was a flop, but once CD singles began appearing on normal-sized discs, the commercial cassette single was doomed. By 2001 it had effectively died, along with its album-length predecessor. Blank CDs and file-sharing would replace it as an anti-commercial underground medium. The cassette has, however, achieved a kind of afterlife among enthusiasts and experimentalists.

Magic
Olivia Newton-John

Released May 1980
MCA *41247* (U.S. #1) / Jet *196* (U.K. #32)

Xanadu
Olivia Newton-John & Electric Light Orchestra

Released June 1980
MCA *41285* (U.S. #8) / Jet *185* (U.K #1)

Two years after her resounding success with both the movie and the soundtrack for *Grease*, Olivia Newton-John took on the silver screens of Hollywood once again with *Xanadu*. The feature film, directed by Robert Greenwald, co-stars Newton-John with leading man Michael Beck (fresh from his own success in *The Warriors*) and dancing legend Gene Kelly. The trailer promised that it would be "the most dazzling, romantic musical fantasy in years" with vibrant, disco-inspired dancing and roller-skating, a far-fetched plot line borrowing from Greek mythology, and a plethora of original songs done by Newton-John and Electric Light Orchestra (ELO) to fuel the performance sequences. *Xanadu*'s Greek muse Kira was a far-cry from *Grease*'s teenage Sandy, but each character that she played proved more than capable of belting out some lovely tunes.

Unfortunately, audiences didn't agree with the trailer's proclamation of excitement, and Universal Pictures had to swallow a well-publicized box office failure with *Xanadu*. Instead, the buying public confirmed its preference for Newton-John as a singer rather than a singer-actress, rewarding her efforts with platinum sales for the soundtrack and pop-chart placements for its two key songs, the smoldering ballad 'Magic' and the cosmic 'Xanadu,' both written by longtime Newton-John songwriter John Farrar plus ELO's Jeff Lynne. With sales of more than a million copies, 'Magic' topped the *Billboard* chart and gave Newton-John her first Gold single in America (and third Number 1) while U.K. fans made 'Xanadu' their Number 1 song from the movie.

(Just Like) Starting Over
John Lennon

Released October 1980
Geffen *49604* (U.S. #1) / Geffen *K 79186* (U.K. #1)

On December 8, 1980, the 20th century lost one of its most popular figures when John Lennon was shot dead outside his New York City apartment. Lennon was indeed starting over, having hardly touched a guitar during his five years as a house-husband bringing up Sean, his son with Yoko. Retiring to Bermuda in the summer of 1980 for a family holiday, Lennon began to write again. He said that all the songs on the *Double Fantasy* album came within a period of three weeks. He was without a record contract, and there was no lack of interest from bidding record companies, although John and Yoko signed with David Geffen because he offered to take on the record without hearing a note.

The album received mixed reviews, while '(Just Like) Starting Over,' a 1950s-sounding piece released shortly after his 40th birthday, was shaping up to be a moderate hit – it had already peaked at Number 8 in Britain before sliding to Number 21 – when tragedy struck. Ironically, Lennon had not had a British Number 1 since the demise of The Beatles,

but in the weeks following his death four of his songs would top the charts while another reached Number 2. First came '(Just Like) Starting Over,' which swiftly vaulted to Number 1, while a reissued 'Happy Xmas' rose to Number 2. In the new year, with accumulated back-orders of 300,000, 'Imagine' rose to the top, followed shortly afterwards by 'Woman,' the second single from *Double Fantasy*. Finally, in February 1981, Bryan Ferry and Roxy Music took 'Jealous Guy' to the top in a fitting tribute to one of the greatest icons in popular-music history.

There's No One Quite Like Grandma
St. Winifred's School Choir

Released November 1980
Not issued U.S. / Music For Pleasure *FP 900* (U.K. #1)

Among the longstanding U.K. yuletide traditions is the coveted Christmas Number 1. British bookmakers take millions in bets on the Christmas Day chart-topper. This phenomenon is peculiar to the U.K. charts, where national radio and television coverage enables a single released in early December to shoot to the top of the charts in a very short space of time. With records traditionally making great Christmas presents, there is also a history of offbeat middle-of-the-road singles topping  the U.K. charts at Christmas, records that youngsters can buy as gifts for older relatives, of which 'There's No One Quite Like Grandma' by St Winifred's School Choir is perhaps the best-known example.

Remarkably, the choir had already appeared on another U.K. Number 1, Brian & Michael's 'Matchstalk Men And Matchstalk Cats And Dogs,' which topped the charts there in April 1978. 'Grandma' was the first single ever released on EMI's budget label Music For Pleasure, usually strictly albums only, and featured seven-year-old soloist Dawn Ralph. While they only had one hit single, St Winifred's had a lengthy career – albeit with numerous personnel changes – and recorded nine albums over a period of ten years.

9 To 5
Dolly Parton

Released December 1980
RCA *12133* (U.S. #1) / RCA *25* (U.K.)

Country legend Dolly Parton had one of the largest crossover hits of her career with this title song to the soundtrack of *9 To 5*, an irreverent comedy movie starring Jane Fonda, Lily Tomlin, and Parton herself as resourceful working women wreaking revenge on an oppressive boss. From bleary-eyed coffee making in the morning to the chaotic juggling of duties once at the job, the record is a sassy and remarkably detailed tribute to the blue-collar nation, and was embraced dearly to the heart of America, particularly by women. The elusive Oscar agreed: '9 To 5' earned an Academy Award for Best Song.

Vienna
Ultravox

Released January 1981
Chrysalis *6597* (U.S.) / Chrysalis *CHS 2481* (U.K. #2)

In 1981 Midge Ure and his band of less-than-merry men sucked in their cheeks, applied a dab of panstick, and slipped into long trenchcoats for 'Vienna,' still one of the finest moments of early-1980s electro and by far Ultravox's best-known song to this day – even if the group was more experimental and just as ambitious on other recordings.

The song stood out from the rest of the synthesizer-rock pack for several reasons, firstly because of its stripped-down, less-is-more atmosphere. If you bought into the gothic imagery that adorned the jacket of 'Vienna' – and thousands of spotty, angst-ridden teenagers did – you could well believe that Midge and his men spent their time lurking around the Austrian capital's celeb-laden cemetery pouting over the tombstones of Mozart, Brahms, and a flock of Strausses, drinking absinthe. Secondly, the song took its time to build up to an epic climax, held down by an unforgiving rhythm section, a vocal melody that insinuated itself into your brain and wouldn't leave, and the big snare sounds of the era.

But aside from all the film noir pretension, 'Vienna' is simply a highly hummable pop tune, with its ethereal synth wash anchoring *that* bass and kick-drum riff with nihilistic precision. There's a tempo change towards the end, too, underpinning some gorgeous, reverb'd piano tinkles and Midge's wail of "It means nothing to meeeee!" – the best singalong party line of all Ure's considerable oeuvre.

(We Don't Need This) Fascist Groove Thang
Heaven 17

Released March 1981
Not issued U.S. / Virgin *VS 400* (U.K.)

When singer Glen Gregory joined ex-Human League computer boffins Martyn Ware and Ian Marsh to form the British group Heaven 17 (named after a bar in Anthony Burgess's novel *A Clockwork Orange*) they initially produced tinny, lightweight electronica of the weakest order. Gregory's medium-range vocals leavened the mixture somewhat, and in the process improved this A-side – which, remarkably, was initially banned by the BBC for its title. It wasn't until their excellent 1983 single 'Temptation' that Heaven 17 really found their feet, but as an example of early-1980s anti-capitalist pop propaganda, 'Fascist Groove Thang' does the trick perfectly: naive, tuneful, and faintly trashy music to be used once and thrown away.

Tainted Love
Soft Cell

Released July 1981
Sire *49855* (U.S. #8) / Some Bizzare *BZS 2* (U.K. #1)

Soft Cell's debut hit is an example of both the role of technology in creating new sound and the way that a good song can endure. As synthesizers became readily available and affordable in the early 1980s, many seized the chance to try to emulate Kraftwerk and David Bowie's 'Berlin' trilogy of albums. Among them were Marc Almond and Dave Ball, who formed Soft Cell, the archetypal synth-pop duo. The band released an EP and two singles in 1980 and '81 that caused some interest but didn't sell. Then they came across 'Tainted Love.'

The song had been written by one Ed Cobb, a 1960s songwriter-producer-manager who had once been a member of the hit vocal harmony group The Four Preps. In his stable of artists was the garage-rock band The Standells. Cobb wrote what became their biggest hit, 'Dirty Water,' with which 'Tainted Love' shares a powerful four-to-the-floor beat. 'Dirty Water' was covered by British band The Inmates, while 'Tainted Love,' which had been recorded by soul singer Gloria Jones in 1964, became a favorite in Britain's Northern Soul clubs in the late 1970s. Soft Cell kept the best of the original version of 'Tainted Love' – the solid, stomping beat – thus ensuring that their version would work as a dance number. But the instrumentation was entirely electronic, over which Almond performed theatrical vocal histrionics. The duo went on to have many more hits, but it is with this song that they will be forever associated.

Don't You Want Me
Human League

Released November 1981
A&M/Virgin *2397* (U.S. #1) / Virgin *VS 466* (U.K. #1)

With its fine melody, duologue lyric, and soap opera storyline, 'Don't You Want Me' was destined to become a karaoke favorite. Its monster synthesizer riff etched itself into the listener's memory as much as any guitar lick, completing the radio-friendly picture. The League had come a long way since their Kraftwerk-like gloom of two years ago when the line-up had included future Heaven 17 members Martyn Ware and Ian Craig Marsh.

The song was based on a photo-strip in a girl's magazine. The depiction of a starmaker scooping a nobody into celebrity seemed to allude to the real-life romance between frontman and writer Phil Oakey and vocalist Susanne Sulley, although perversely it was the group's other singer, Joanna Catterall, who sang the female lines. Another perverse touch came in Oakey's narrative where the girl bites that hand that feeds her.

While 'Don't You Want Me' wasn't a first of any kind – the U.K. charts were already awash with synth-pop – it was certainly the record that confirmed to any remaining doubters that synth-pop did not have to be merely a watery, weedy version of rock. The path was being set for the unthinkable: the demise of rock, which in the space of the next 15 years would be reduced to a mere sub-genre of popular music.

Meanwhile, as Ware and Craig Marsh happily received one per cent of the royalties for 'Don't You Want Me' in part return for giving up the rights to the Human League name, the League itself slowly went broke in a vain attempt to make another record with the impact of this one.

Rapture
Blondie

Released January 1981
Chrysalis *CHS 2485* (U.S. #1, U.K. #5)

It seems somewhat perverse to declare a record by a bunch of nerdy (white) New Yorkers and a former Playboy bunny to be one of the key moments in the development and popularization of rap music. But 'Rapture' is exactly that. Blondie had spent the previous half-decade becoming and then cementing their position as the biggest group of the punk/new wave era. By this stage they had chalked up a number of memorable transatlantic hit singles, among them 'Heart Of Glass,' 'Atomic,' and 'Call Me,' a collaboration with the disco producer Giorgio Moroder.

'Rapture' was taken from Blondie's fifth full-length effort, *Autoamerican*, which saw release in late 1980. Although the album itself is considered to be the point at which Blondie began to decline, its singles showed no signs of ill health – 'Rapture' followed 'The Tide Is High' to the top of the *Billboard* Hot 100.

The first (overlooked) half of 'Rapture' features one of Debbie Harry's finest vocal melodies, which soars seductively amid chiming bells and funky bass. Midway through, she ups the ante further, launching into a cool, collected rap that – while dismissed by some hip-hop purists – has the measure of many of the genre's early MCs. While it might not have the musical pedigree of Afrika Bambaataa or The Sugarhill Gang, 'Rapture' brought rap to suburban America for the first time, and it even had a heavy metal style guitar solo, preempting later rap-rock.

Once In A Lifetime
Talking Heads

Released February 1981
Sire *40649* (U.S.) / Sire *SIR 4048* (U.K. #14)

Talking Heads' best-loved song, 'Once In A Lifetime' represents the high-water mark of the group's association with über-producer Brian Eno. In the three years since recording their debut LP, *Talking Heads 77*, the quartet's output had evolved from taut post-punk to a funky melting pot of sound that drew as much on African polyrhythms as it did on more traditional, rock-based forms. Much of this can be put down to the influence of Eno, and also to the band's acceptance of their own limitations as musicians and subsequent hiring of talented guest players like the guitar virtuoso Adrian Belew.

'Once In A Lifetime' is the most immediate of the eight songs on the group's fourth full-length album, *Remain In Light*. Its verses are dominated by leader David Byrne's questioning spoken-word vocal, in which he ruminates on a wealthy, materialistic – but ultimately empty – world, over a backdrop of stop-start bass and watery keyboards. There is no real hook to speak of until the chorus, which is surprisingly euphoric, given that Byrne sings of letting "the days go by" and "the water hold me down."

Part of the song's lasting appeal was the accompanying promo video, which features Byrne's crazy-man dancing in front of some endearingly simple special effects. It remains a staple of music-television programming, while the song itself is one of the most distinctive singles of the early 1980s. No subsequent Talking Heads release so successfully melded their pop sensibilities and artistic invention, although they had a bigger hit four years later with 'Road To Nowhere.'

Ghost Town
The Specials

Released June 1981
2-Tone *2525* (U.S.) / 2-Tone *CHSTT 17* (U.K. #1)

Among the finest U.K. chart-toppers of the 1980s, 'Ghost Town' was The Specials' defining moment: an intoxicating mix of eerie fairground organ, dub bass, and timely lyrics about inner city violence. Released in the midst of rioting in London and Liverpool, it proved in effect to be the group's swan song, as three of its founding members left soon afterwards.

The Specials formed in 1978 and were soon at the forefront of a ska revival in the U.K., releasing their records on keyboardist Jerry Dammers's own 2-Tone label. The group's eponymous debut LP, released at the tail end of 1979, was produced by Elvis Costello and mixed reggae, punk, ska, and pop with impassioned socio-political lyrics. Three U.K. Top 10 hits and a second album, *More Specials*, followed in 1980 before the group unleashed its crowning achievement in the summer of 1981.

'Ghost Town' leaps from wistful to foreboding and back again across its six minutes, as vocalists Terry Hall and Neville Staples wonder "why must the youth fight among themselves?" Integral to the group's sound, as ever, is trombonist Rico Rodriquez, plus the super-tight rhythm section of bassist Horace Gentleman and drummer John Bradbury. Despite the group reaching their artistic and commercial high point, they were already on their last legs: by the end of 1981, Hall, Staples, and guitarist Lynval Goulding had left to form Fun Boy Three. The remaining members and various replacements carried on to increasingly diminishing returns as The Special A.K.A. before splitting in 1984.

O Superman
Laurie Anderson

Released October 1981
Warner Bros. *49876* (U.S.) / Warner Bros. *K 17870* (U.K. #2)

'O Superman,' an eight-minute spoken-word piece backed by minimal synthesizer passages, is one of the most unusual one-hit wonders of all time. Underpinned by a monotonous vocal sample, it was extracted from a lengthy stage work, *United States*, which performance artist Laurie Anderson eventually issued as a five-disc live set in 1985. The single was originally issued a month earlier on the independent One-Ten label, but a rush of orders – mostly from the U.K. – led to a recording deal with Warners and the company's subsequent re-release of the record. But nothing else Anderson recorded ever had the same commercial impact.

Radio Free Europe
R.E.M.

Released July 1981
Hib-Tone *HT 0001* (U.S.) / IRS *IR 9916* (U.K.)

'Radio Free Europe' marks the moment when post-punk turned into alternative rock. But at the time, R.E.M. didn't much care for it. They'd first attempted to record the song in February 1981, tried again in April, agonized over remixes, and finally released a version that none of them really liked. Lyrically incomprehensible (because writer-singer Michael Stipe wanted it that way), 'Radio Free Europe' nevertheless boasted a sound that cleverly combined traditional and avant-garde elements into something mysterious and yet radio-friendly. It was, however, a third version – recorded for the album *Murmur* – that rocketed all the way to Number 78 in America in August 1983, starting R.E.M. on the road to fame and fortune.

In The Air Tonight
Phil Collins

Released January 1981
Atlantic *3824* (U.S. #19) / Virgin *VS 102* (U.K. #2)

With this single, Phil Collins stepped out from the behind the drum-kit of the progressive group Genesis to become one most unlikely solo stars of the 1980s. The vast international success of 'In The Air Tonight' was all the more surprising given that the song is a bitter message to Collins's ex-wife set to a sparse drum-machine pattern and funereal electric-organ chords.

In 1979, Collins returned home from the latest in a run of lengthy world tours with Genesis to find his personal life in tatters: his wife had left him and taken their children with her. Not knowing what else to do with himself, he set up a small home studio – which consisted of a Rhodes electric piano, a Prophecy synthesizer, a Roland drum machine, and an 8-track recorder – and started pouring his heart out onto tape.

Collins recorded very quickly what he thought would be just a demo of 'In The Air Tonight,' writing the words as he sang them. Unable to replicate the original recording in a 'proper' studio the following year, he instead reworked the existing version. The main addition is the closing, tension-releasing drum fill, which was recorded, somewhat serendipitously, through the studio's 'reverse talkback' feed by accident, giving it a distinctive, highly compressed sound.

The success of the single sent Collins's full-length solo debut album, *Face Value*, into the upper reaches of the charts on both sides of the Atlantic and established a lucrative second career for the drummer. He had further solo hits throughout the 1980s, including seven U.S. chart-toppers, among them 'Against All Odds' and 'Groovy Kind Of Love.'

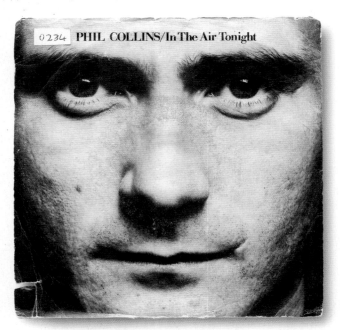

Rock This Town
The Stray Cats

Released January 1981
EMI America *8132* (U.S. #9) / Arista *SCAT 2* (U.K. #9)

This smart 1980s update of the '50s rockabilly sound came from three larger-than-life personalities who stood out amongst the synth-driven groups of the time. The refreshing trio hit first with this 45 in Britain, opening the gateway to hit-making back home in America. Singer-guitarist Brian Setzer, drummer Slim Jim Phantom, and upright-bass man Lee Rocker took The Stray Cats from their Long Island roots to London to work with veteran producer-guitarist Dave Edmunds. MTV ate up the visual presentation of the Cats and turned them into some of the first video stars.

Endless Love
Diana Ross & Lionel Richie

Released July 1981
Motown *1519* (U.S. #1) / Motown *TMG 1240* (U.K. #7)

Motown was always looking for that extra dollar, and teaming together two of their top artists, one of whom was the supreme ballad writer of the period, seemed bound to produce a winner. And indeed it did: 'Endless Love' became the company's biggest selling single of all time, shifting three million copies in America alone and spending nine weeks as the country's Number 1. It was written for the Brooke Shields movie of the same name, which also marked Tom Cruise's screen debut, but the film was a fiasco. Richie had already enjoyed three U.S. Number 1s, with 'Three Times A Lady' and 'Still' for The Commodores and 'Lady' for country star Kenny Rogers. 'Endless Love' was first commissioned as an instrumental, but Richie was asked for lyrics, and finally a female vocalist was suggested. Conflicting schedules called for the recording to be made at 3:30am in a Nevada studio, and while Ms. Ross hadn't heard the song before, the finished recording was in the can an hour and a half later.

Under Pressure
Queen & David Bowie

Released October 1981
Elektra *47235* (U.S. #29) / EMI *5250* (U.K. #1)

This sparse, under-produced collaboration is best known for its bassline, perhaps one of the most memorable and infectious in popular music history. It was the product of a spontaneous jam session between Queen and David Bowie at Mountain Studios in Montreux, Switzerland, in July 1981. The origins of the famous bassline are somewhat confused. Both Queen bassist John Deacon and Bowie have, surprisingly, denied writing it, each claiming it to be the work of the other. In 1990 Vanilla Ice recycled both the bass riff and the main piano part for his landmark hit 'Ice Ice Baby,' but has since claimed that he did actually sample the original. While 'Under Pressure' was not a major U.S. hit on its release in 1981, it has become one of the best known songs in both Queen and Bowie's catalogs, and remains a staple of the latter's live performances.

Start Me Up
The Rolling Stones

Released August 1981
Rolling Stones 21003 (U.S. #2) / Rolling Stones *RSR 108* (U.K. #7)

The last truly great Rolling Stones single, 'Start Me Up' is a gargantuan rocker cut from the same cloth as 1960s classics like 'Honky Tonk Women' and 'Satisfaction.' It demonstrated that Mick Jagger and Keith Richards still had a knack for a great tune, and also the extent to which they needed each other. The pair spent much of the rest of the 1980s somewhere between bickering and feuding, and the quality of the group's work suffered as a result.

'Start Me Up' was the first single drawn from *Tattoo You*, the 19th studio album from the self-proclaimed World's Greatest Rock'n'Roll Band. Like much of the group's work, it was produced by Jagger and Richards under the name The Glimmer Twins. Stripped back to its constituent parts, the song is amazingly simple: there is little more here than a pair of guitar riffs and a couple of repeated lyrics, but anything else would feel like padding. Richards's muscular guitar-playing dominates without ever becoming showy, while Charlie Watts provides a typically steady backbeat.

'Start Me Up' stormed into the upper reaches of the British and American charts, as did its parent album, but it marked the end of the Stones' run as a creative force. Amid Jagger and Richards's bickering about the direction the group should take and the unhelpful distractions of solo work, they slowly evolved into a spectacular live group that occasionally makes so-so records. But this single remains a live favorite, on a par with pretty much anything in the Stones' canon.

beast altogether, a harsh, confrontational look inside urban poverty and desperation, given voice by Melle Mel's urgent delivery. It's an unforgiving telegram sent from the heart of the crumbling and deadly Bronx in New York City where the twin effects of Reaganomics and a proliferating crack trade were colliding in a display of mass destruction.

Before 'The Message,' hip-hop was largely a happy-go-lucky, partying style, where you'd expect to find escapism rather than reportage. After its release, however, the genre would never be the same. In fact, hip-hop has subsequently been praised and prized for its ability to shine a mainstream light on the underexposed conditions of oppression. Without this song, the entire course of the genre could have been very different indeed, and some of its most prominent voices might never have surfaced.

'The Message' did not have the muscle to reach the higher American pop charts, peaking at Number 62, but it did receive attention overseas, hitting Number 8 in the U.K. and enjoying platinum sales within a month of its official release. Notable Los Angeles rapper (and later actor) Ice Cube would sample the backing track of 'The Message' to form the basis of his own rap song, 1992's 'Check Yo Self,' which transferred the original song's lament for a suffering city into a tune about accountability in the wake of self-destruction. And five years later another famous rapper, Puff Daddy, used a similar sample for his song 'Can't Nobody Hold Me Down,' pairing instrumental elements from 'The Message' with a vocal interpolation of lyrics from Matthew Wilder's 1984 song 'Break My Stride.'

Both are tributes to the iconic status and continuing relevance of 'The Message,' which remains a pivotal and influential song in hip-hop, one that has permanently pulled back the curtain on urban blight in America. Solutions to severe crime and poverty haven't been easy, nor have they been forthcoming, but 'The Message' shows that it's necessary to try.

The Message
Grandmaster Flash & The Furious Five

Released May 1982
Sugar Hill *584* (U.S.) / Sugar Hill *SHL 117* (U.K. #8)

Popular New York DJ Joseph Saddler (a.k.a. Grandmaster Flash) is one of hip-hop's most respected architects, an innovator of many of the techniques still used by professional DJs and a catalyst who brought the culture above ground. Most importantly, the legendary Flash has taught DJs how to create a lasting groove out of spare elements by manipulating records with the use of a mixer – so it followed that he'd make a great producer.

Saddler landed a recording contract with the burgeoning Sugar Hill Records, which had introduced itself to audiences with The Sugarhill Gang's 'Rapper's Delight' in 1979. He joined with several MCs to form Grandmaster Flash & The Furious Five, with a line-up that included brothers Melvin Glover (Melle Mel) and Nathaniel Glover (Kid Creole) along with Keith Wiggins (Cowboy), Eddie Morris (Scorpio), and Guy Williams (Rahiem).

Flash had already begun to make a name for himself in the recording world with his cut-up disco mega-mixes of songs from record labels like Salsoul and Casablanca, but 'The Message' was an entirely different

Planet Rock
Afrika Bambaataa & The Soul Sonic Force

Released June 1982
Tommy Boy *823* (U.S.) / Polydor *POSP 497* (U.K.)

Afrika Bambaataa is often called the godfather of hip-hop, and while he has some notable company – such as Kool Herc and Grandmaster Flash – the man born Kevin Donovan in Bronx, New York City, proudly carries a lot of the weight for what would eventually become global youth culture. 'Planet Rock,' produced by Arthur Baker and performed with Bambaataa's group Soul Sonic Force, is an urban tribute to the song that inspired it: 1977's 'Trans-Europe Express' by the German group Kraftwerk. It is also Bambaataa's enduring signature song.

Not only is the electro funk style of 'Planet Rock' prevalent today in a large palette of dance music styles, from house and drum'n'bass to techno and breakbeat, but the central instrument used in its creation, Roland's TR-808 drum machine, known simply as the 808, still beats in the heart of hip-hop around America, particularly in the South. It's traceable through the booty shake of provocative Miami bass records to the brilliantly rowdy crunk music that soundtracks an energetic youth in Atlanta. Without 'Planet Rock' many different artists would be searching for a production blueprint half as influential.

The song's impact is not only technical but also spiritual. 'Planet Rock' has a lesson to share that is still important, an ideal of multicultural harmony, on and off the dancefloor. Bambaataa walked the talk he talked: before making music he was a gang member, but later he renounced that life and formed the peaceful Zulu Nation, a collective that has celebrated more than 20 birthdays.

Mickey
Toni Basil

Released February 1982
Chrysalis *2638* (U.S. #1) / Radialchoice *TIC 4* (U.K. #2)

At a time when Toni Basil was an aspiring triple threat to the worlds of acting, dancing, and singing, she blended her various talents in this memorable, cheer-like tune based on a 1979 song, 'Kitty,' by the British band Racey. The video for 'Mickey,' featuring Basil fronting a sassy team of cheerleaders, became a popular mainstay of MTV. She spoke of the excitement of fitting into her old Las Vegas High School cheerleading outfit for the performance. Often called a one-hit wonder, Basil enjoyed a successful career as a choreographer after 'Mickey,' creating memorable dance moves for David Bowie and David Byrne.

I Love Rock'n'Roll
Joan Jett & The Blackhearts

Released February 1982
Boardwalk *135* (U.S. #1) / Epic *EPC A 2152* (U.K. #4)

The Arrows originally wrote this song in 1975, and pop tartlet Britney Spears would cover it in a lackluster way almost 30 years later, but it was Joan Jett and her Blackhearts who shot 'I Love Rock'n'Roll' to the top of the charts for eight weeks. The fiery Jett, who first debuted in the all-woman band The Runaways, took two attempts to make the song into a hit: her first version with former Sex Pistols Paul Cook and Steve Jones didn't catch on in anything like the same way as the Blackhearts take.

Ebony And Ivory
Paul McCartney with Stevie Wonder

Released April 1982
Columbia *02860* (U.S. #1) / Parlophone *6054* (U.K. #1)

The Girl Is Mine
Michael Jackson / Paul McCartney

Released November 1982
Epic *03288* (U.S. #2) / Epic *EPC A 2729* (U.K. #8)

While it may be a contrived song, 'Ebony And Ivory' gave Paul McCartney his lengthiest stay at the top of the U.S. singles charts – he was there for seven weeks – and it gave Stevie Wonder his first visit to Number 1 in Britain. Recorded for McCartney's *Tug Of War* album, the song marked his reunion with former Beatles producer George Martin and was recorded at Martin's Air studios on the picturesque island of Montserrat.

Later that year, McCartney was invited to contribute vocals to a Michael Jackson composition that put him on the biggest selling album of all time. Released as the first single from *Thriller*, 'The Girl Is Mine' was a sugary duet that gave little indication of how much of a blockbuster the album would become (it has sales of 54 million at the time of writing). McCartney recorded another duet with Jackson, 'Say Say Say,' for his 1983 album *Pipes Of Peace* before the pair fell out – Jackson used his *Thriller* millions to outbid McCartney for the Beatles copyrights owned by

ATV Music Publishing. Jackson paid $47.5 million (about £27 million) for the pleasure. Jackson had been calling McCartney and asking for financial advice; according to McCartney it was something of a running joke. "He'd say, 'I'm gonna buy your publishing, ya know!' I'd go, 'Ha! Good one, kid!' Then one day I get phoned up and they say, 'He's just bought your stuff!'" McCartney concluded: "All's fair in love, war, and business, I suppose. But it's a little galling now to find that I own less of 'Yesterday' than Michael Jackson. It's a thorn in my side."

Da Da Da
Trio

Released April 1982
Mercury *4019* (U.S.) / Mobile Suit Corporation *CORP 5* (U.K. #2)

In an era when synthesizers revved overtime and haircuts quickly fluffed and angled out of control, the German band known as Trio opted for more of a deconstructionist approach to their machine-driven ditties. The charm of the guiltily infectious 'Da Da Da' comes in its spare use of Casio beats and the vocal textures supporting a simple tune. The result has had a completely unexpected longevity for a Teutonic band that isn't Kraftwerk. Later, the song would enjoy a substantial new wind in America that blew it into the popular consciousness when it was picked up as a jingle for a car ad in 1997.

Eye Of The Tiger
Survivor

Released June 1982
Scotti Bros. *02912* (U.S. #1) / Scotti Bros. *SCT A 2411* (U.K. #1)

Survivor fan Sylvester Stallone asked the band to write a song for his certain-blockbuster movie *Rocky III*. But not even Stallone could have predicted the heavyweight knock down and drag out success of this monster song. The kudos included an Oscar nomination, a Grammy, a People's Choice Award, international chart placements, and Survivor's sole Number 1 hit. The sports world embraced 'Eye Of The Tiger,' which leaped from *Rocky* screens to real-life arenas, where it remained a motivational anthem. Strangely, in 1995 U.K. boxing champion Frank Bruno covered the song, which hit the Top 40 in Britain.

Do You Really Want To Hurt Me
Culture Club

Released September 1982
Epic *03368* (U.S. #2) / Virgin *VS 518* (U.K. #1)

The U.K.-based quartet that dubbed itself Culture Club was Boy George, Roy Hay, Mikey Craig, and Jon Moss. They began one of the most vibrant and successful careers in 1980s pop music with this sweet tune influenced by the easygoing rhythmic vibes of reggae toasters from the island of Jamaica. Boy George's honeyed soul voice went down the pop palate rather easily, and he managed to confound audiences on both sides of the Atlantic with his truly different androgynous look – braided long hair, lots of makeup, flashy outfits – and his ambiguously coy reactions to the constant questions about his sexuality.

Hungry Like The Wolf
Duran Duran

Released May 1982
Harvest *5134* (U.S. #3) / EMI *5295* (U.K. #5)

'Hungry Like The Wolf' was the fourth Top 20 hit in the group's native U.K. and the song that introduced Duran Duran to an eager America, ushering in a string of hits and hordes of female admirers. This potent,

extended sexual metaphor was a timely and unique combination of tough rock-guitar licks and frenetic beats, worthy of post-disco dancefloors – but was reportedly inspired by the innocent childhood fairy tale of *Little Red Riding Hood*. It also turned out to have an extended shelf life once the world embraced Duran Duran as a pop sensation.

Director Russell Mulcahy took Duran Duran to picturesque Sri Lanka to shoot the adventurous video, which most memorably features the thrilling tension of lead singer Simon LeBon pursued through a jungle by a painted she-wolf in heat. The quintet (originally Nick Rhodes, John Taylor, Andy Taylor, and Roger Taylor in addition to LeBon) fast became teen idols around the world, especially as the MTV audience devoured the video, which was considerably more filmic and action-packed than much of the competing material of the time. In 1984, 'Hungry Like The Wolf' won the Grammy for Best Video Shortform and made a notable contribution towards Duran Duran's second honor that year, for Best Video Album. Mulcahy would go on to shoot many of Duran Duran's most famous videos during the group's peak era of MTV superstardom.

Come On Eileen
Dexys Midnight Runners

Released June 1982
Mercury *76189* (U.S. #1) / Mercury *DEXYS 9* (U.K. #1)

Despite wearing clothes that were obsolete about ten minutes after they appeared and shooting a video that included the worst haircut crime ever committed – namely, the female mullet – Dexys Midnight Runners managed not to mess up their biggest hit. Depending on your point of view, 'Come On Eileen' was an elegantly catchy bit of pop folklore or a teeth-grindingly tinny gypsy lament: either way, it sank its teeth into everyone's cerebral cortex in 1982 and refused to let go for decades.

To this day, high school disco-themed dancefloors erupt as its first bars ring out – a stamping bass and drum intro followed by a whimsical violin melody – and people then either run for cover or celebrate its apparently eternal charm. Listen out for the many strokes of genius that punctuate the record, such as the chorus line, which drops down beguilingly from the verse, and the slow-shout-out break that builds to a fast ending.

Dexys, and specifically their maverick leader Kevin Rowland, couldn't have foreseen the song's enormous success – and failed to deal with it when it materialized, spiraling downward into eccentric inconsistency

after some decent singles ('Geno' was a triumph, as was 'Jackie Wilson Says') and a critically acclaimed album, *Don't Stand Me Down*. By that point the cowbilly wear had been ditched in favor of a preppy suit look that amused no one. But for a brief moment back there, Dexy and his Runners looked as if they might take over the world.

It Started With A Kiss
Hot Chocolate

Released July 1982
EMI America *8157* (U.S.) / RAK *344* (U.K. #5)

Formed in London in 1969, this multi-racial group's first recording was a reggae version of John Lennon's 'Give Peace A Chance' that they sent to The Beatles' Apple Records, who released it without success. They signed a new deal with Mickie Most in 1970 at the birth of his newly formed RAK label. Hot Chocolate went on to become the label's most consistently successful act, placing at least one hit on the U.K. charts every year between 1970 and 1984. They recorded a mixture of originals and custom-written material by contemporary writers. 'It Started With A Kiss' was composed by frontman and vocalist Errol Brown and was a U.K. hit on three separate occasions in 1982, 1993, and 1998, demonstrating the band's enduring popularity in Britain where their biggest international hit, 'You Sexy Thing,' also charted three times.

Sexual Healing
Marvin Gaye

Released October 1982
Columbia *03302* (U.S. #3) / CBS *A 2855* (U.K. #4)

'Sexual Healing' was a testimony to Marvin Gaye's continued talent after the glory years with the Motown label, earning two Grammys and an American Music Award and selling over a million copies. It introduced the legendary crooner to a fickle 1980s audience, who decided that this undeniably grooving ode to getting down was a goodie from an oldie. David Ritz wrote 'Sexual Healing' after witnessing the singer's pornographic magazine collection and went on to write *Divided Soul*, the revelatory biography about Gaye's life and his untimely death at the hands of his father in 1984.

Buffalo Gals
Malcolm McLaren & The World's Famous Supreme Team

Released November 1982
Island *99941* (U.S.) / Charisma *MALC 1* (U.K. #9)

The notoriously unctuous former manager of punk's defunct Sex Pistols re-emerged in an unusual way, as the impetus behind this hip-hop collaboration with two relatively unknown New York radio jocks called the World Famous Supreme Team. McLaren sniffed potential in the burgeoning rap scene and played a large role in transporting it to Britain. 'Buffalo Gals' has been sampled endlessly by hip-hop and electronica producers on both sides of the Atlantic. Certain snippets – including McLaren's introductory greeting, a Wild West-inspired "Helloooooooo!" – are iconic sounds in these genres, even though many listeners remain unaware of their origins.

1999
Prince

Released October 1982
Warner Bros. *29896* (U.S. #12) / Warner Bros. *W 9896* (U.K. #25)

In 1948 the great novelist George Orwell zeroed in on the year 1984 as the point of no return, but another visionary named Prince looked further ahead for his perpetually funky send-off to the end of time. Prince's first international hit expertly channels the pervasive panic about nuclear bombs, world wars, and other possibilities for Armageddon that gripped America in the 1980s under the presidential reign of Ronald Reagan (and the U.K.'s simultaneous rule by Margaret Thatcher). It is fitting that this lyrically and sonically innovative record served as a formal introduction to one of America's most singular soul talents since James Brown.

While his Minneapolis-bred backing band, The Revolution, were never meant to take center stage with the flamboyant Prince himself, '1999' is their biggest showcase – and particularly the duo known simply by their first names, Wendy & Lisa – as they sing and provide rhythmic counterpoints to his verses. The song was re-released in 1999 and managed the difficult feat of landing in the U.K. Top 10 and beating its original placement. Key lyrics such as "Two-thousand, zero zero / Party over / Oops, out of time" fit in perfectly with the end-of-the-world hysteria that surfaced just before the advent of Y2K, when there seemed to be some question marks over the world's future. Even in the 21st century club DJs continue to play '1999,' saving it for those moments when they want a large crowd reaction on the dancefloor.

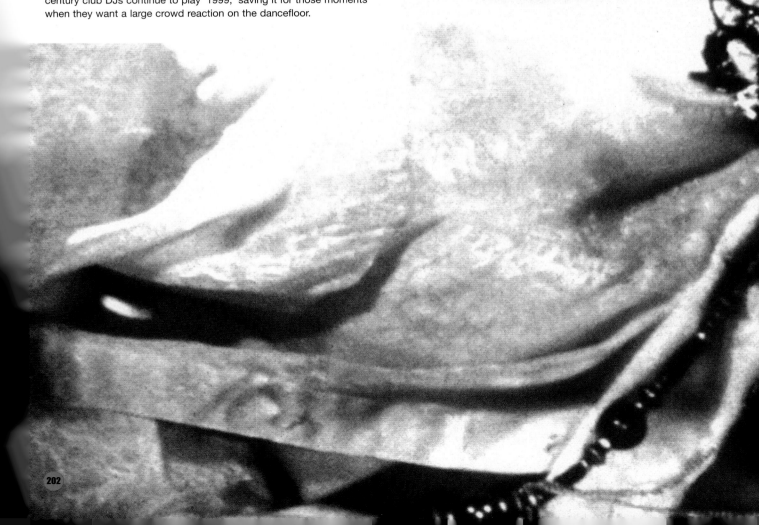

Golden Brown
The Stranglers

Released January 1982
Not issued U.S. / Liberty *BP 407* (U.K. #2)

Is it about a brunette? Is it about heroin? No one knows, possibly not even head Strangler Hugh Cornwell, whose laconic vocals sung over a fiendishly complex harpsichord-driven backing are one of this single's many high points. 'Golden Brown' was an unlikely hit given its unusual instrumentation and time signature, but the fact that it remains the group's best-known song (with 'Peaches') speaks volumes about The Stranglers' status as punk icons. After all, would a 'real' punk band have added a dreamy, reverb'd vocal melody as the outro of the song, a clean jazz drone instead of a proper guitar solo, and a military snare pattern? Probably not.

More than this, 'Golden Brown' says a lot about the tastes of the music-buying British public back in 1982 as punk's second wave took off and the twin demons of New Romanticism and synth-pop found a foothold. In retrospect, it doesn't seem to have been an era in which fans would have shelled out for what was practically a piece of classical music masquerading as a pop single. But they did anyway – in droves – which makes The Stranglers' achievement all the more notable. Perhaps this underlines that good music will find its way to market no matter what the prevailing trends indicate. Certainly the group themselves never equaled it again, despite semi-pop love songs such as 'Skin Deep' that tried and failed to replicate the classy, almost 1960s West Coast vibe of this most unusual recording.

House Of Fun
Madness

Released May 1982
Not issued U.S. / Stiff *BUY 146* (U.K. #1)

Following hot on the heels of The Specials, Madness were the most successful of the British ska-revivalists of the late 1970s and early 1980s. 'House Of Fun' was the highest charting of the group's many memorable U.K. hits. They formed in early 1979 in London, England, and by the end of the year had appeared twice on the British singles chart, with 'The Prince' – a giddy tribute to ska legend Prince Buster – and 'One Step Beyond.' Led by cheeky-chappy vocalist Graham 'Suggs' McPherson, the seven-piece line-up included a permanent two-man horn section, and the group maintained a fine line in snappy suits and crazy dancing.

The group had already reached the U.K. Top 10 on nine occasions – notably with 'Baggy Trousers' in 1980 – before 'House Of Fun' became their only Number 1. A typically fun-filled tale of adolescence, the song is driven by syncopated drums, nagging piano, and rapturous bursts of sax and trumpet. Its fairground feel is vaguely reminiscent of The Specials' landmark 'Ghost Town' but without the doomy overtones.

Two further huge hits followed, 'Driving In My Car' and 'Our House,' which became the group's only U.S. Top 10 hit early the following year. Their fortunes began to fade soon after, however, when their material took on a more melancholic edge. Although they continue to record and tour sporadically, Madness have never since been able to reach the heights of their 1980s heyday.

Rock The Casbah
The Clash

Released June 1982
Epic *03245* (U.S. #8) / CBS *A 2479* (U.K. #30)

British punk royalty The Clash will forever be remembered in the pop world for this, their biggest hit in America. Its rebellious mock protestation of an Arabian government unsympathetic to the power of a good rock jam moved audiences across the globe. The original cover art for 'Rock The Casbah' finds an Arab and a Hasidic Jew dancing with each other to the same groove, a peaceful thought that some still wish for, almost a quarter-century later. The song was a classic-rock radio mainstay for years until officially banned by radio giant Clear Channel in the wake of the U.S. terrorist attacks of September 11, 2001.

White Wedding
Billy Idoll

Released October 1982
Chrysalis *42697* (U.S. #36) / Chrysalis *CHS 2656* (U.K.)

For a great many artists, re-invention is the name of the game. David Bowie is the master of this particular skill, but failed British 1960s teen idol Shane Fenton's re-birth as mysterious glam-rocker Alvin Stardust is perhaps a better reference point for the transformation of Billy Idol. Born William Broad in London, England, he renamed himself Billy Idol while a member of The Bromley Contingent, cult followers of The Sex Pistols, played for a while with punk band Chelsea, and then made a splash as frontman of Generation X.

Unable to hit the big time in Britain, Idol relocated to New York City in 1981 where he teamed up with Kiss manager Bill Aucoin and guitarist-songsmith Stevie Stevens. As a solo act he contrived a new image that was part-metal, part-punk, and 100 per cent MTV-friendly. Conveying a rebellious persona with slick bondage-chic videos playing heavily on his grotesquely over-the-top variation on the petulant Elvis-James Dean sneer, Idol was ideal heavy-rotation fodder, securing his first American Top 30 entry with 'Hot In The City.'

His blisteringly powerful but hardly innovative follow-up was 'White Wedding.' Cleverly juxtaposing rebellious sentiments with traditional values, this was the one that eventually exported Idol's success back home, delivering his first British Top 10 entry when reissued in 1985.

New Year's Day
U2

Released January 1983
Island *99915* (U.S.) / Island *WIP 6848* (U.K. #10)

This school band made it all the way to the top, so keep up the group practice – you never know. They formed as Feedback and later The Hype before becoming U2 and winning a CBS contract in Ireland following a talent contest sponsored by Guinness. Two Ireland-only CBS singles topped the home charts before they secured an international deal with Island in 1980. 'New Year's Day,' from their third album, *War*, was U2's first British Top 10 single and their first proper U.S. single to make the charts, although only to Number 53. The album did better, making Number 12. ('Gloria' from their second album, *October*, had charted at Number 81 in the U.S. on the basis of import sales alone.)

It would be 1987's *The Joshua Tree* that turned U2 into a world-class act, but it was around this time that they transformed themselves into major-league players. That came from continual U.S. touring, as well as *War*, their first focused collection, including politically charged songs such as 'New Year's Day' and 'Sunday Bloody Sunday,' complete with Bono's flag-waving routine. 'New Year's Day' nearly didn't make the album at all. Bass player Adam Clayton came up with the bass riff at a soundcheck, Edge polished it on piano, but Bono had considerable problems coming up with a finished lyric. It's essentially a love song that moves further into politics, and the group were happy to let listeners draw associations with Lech Walesa's Solidarity movement. The song's line "Under a blood red sky…" was later appropriated as the title of their live mini-album that also included 'New Year's Day.'

Every Breath You Take
The Police

Released May 1983
A&M *2542* (U.S. #1) / A&M *AM 117* (U.K. #1)

Sting wrote 'Every Breath You Take' on a piano once owned by Noel Coward, while holidaying on the island of Jamaica at Golden Eye, the former home of James Bond author Ian Fleming. According to Sting himself, his most popular song appeared to him in the middle of the night and virtually wrote itself. He rose, went to the piano, wrote the song within ten minutes, and returned to bed.

'Every Breath You Take' was inspired by the break-up of Sting's first marriage, to actress Frances Tomelty, and is a prime example of the old music-business adage that simple songs are often the best. As the writer himself has freely admitted, the lyrics are taken virtually "straight out of a rhyming dictionary" while the melody is about as basic as it gets.

At first listen it appears to be a love song, but Sting has emphasized its ominous side. He said: "I consider it a fairly nasty song. It's about surveillance and ownership and jealousy." Summing up his most popular work, he concluded: "It's very simple, laughably simple, and at the same time it does have some kind of emotional relevancy. It's kind of mysterious that way."

'Every Breath You Take' was named Song Of The Year at the 1984 Grammy Awards before being reworked, 13 years later, by Puff Daddy and Faith Evans as 'I'll Be Missing You,' a tribute to Notorious B.I.G., the murdered rap star.

Mr. Roboto
Styx

Released February 1983
A&M *2525* (U.S. #3) / A&M *AMS 8303* (U.K.)

Arena rockers Styx took an unpredictable turn of sound and ideas with 'Mr. Roboto,' the group's infectious version of machine funk that also proved to be their odd little swan song. The strangely dramatic ditty is the centerpiece of Styx's perplexing *Kilroy Was Here* album, a rock opera of sorts that finds the hero (Kilroy) attempting an escape from a prison populated by robotic correctional officers. American audiences did not take to the overall concept as put forth by lead singer Dennis DeYoung, but still they wholeheartedly embraced 'Mr. Roboto' as the quirky piece of pop wonderment that it is.

Total Eclipse Of The Heart
Bonnie Tyler

Released February 1983
Columbia *03906* (U.S. #1) / CBS *TYLER 1* (U.K. #1)

Another dose of pomp and circumstance from *Bat Out Of Hell* composer Jim Steinman provided a transatlantic Number 1 for Bonnie Tyler (born Gaynor Hopkins, in Wales). A throat operation in 1976 to remove nodules on her vocal cords resulted in Tyler's trademark husky voice, and she arrived in the U.K. charts soon afterwards with 'Lost In France' and 'It's A Heartache' (which also made the U.S. country charts). Ms. Tyler recalled: "I didn't have any control over what I was doing at all. I was signed to a production company and the guys who managed me were also songwriters. So they'd only let me record their material. They wanted me to sing country songs because they were aiming at the Nashville market. Some of the material was quite good, I suppose, but after I'd had seven flops in a row in a two-year period my heart went out of it. When my contract expired, I just walked out."

A new deal with CBS-Columbia opened up some new possibilities, and among producers considered were Jeff Lynne, Phil Collins, and Jim Steinman. Tyler said she pestered Steinman with phone calls and demos until he finally agreed to take her on. Featuring Steinman's trademark overblown production, 'Total Eclipse' was, like most of his work, a song you either loved or loathed. The track featured contributions from Max Weinberg and Roy Bittan of Bruce Springsteen's E-Street Band and guitar by Rick Derringer. The mother album *Faster Than The Speed Of Night* was a U.K. Number 1, and Tyler teamed up with Steinman again in 1984 for the *Footloose* track 'Holding Out For A Hero.' In 1994 'Total Eclipse' would climb to Number 5 on the U.K. charts in a re-make by Nicki French.

True
Spandau Ballet

Released March 1983
Chrysalis *42720* (U.S. #4) / Reformation *SPAN 1* (U.K. #1)

Spandau Ballet had enjoyed eight previous appearances on the British Top 40, but Tony Hadley's sensitive vocals helped propel 'True' beyond the group's homeland and into the international pop pantheon. This love song proved to have a prolonged shelf-life that couldn't possibly have

been premeditated by the quintet, consisting of Hadley plus brothers Gary and Martin Kemp, John Keeble, and Steve Norman. In 1991, New Jersey-based hip-hop group P.M. Dawn cleverly sampled vocal tones and melodies from 'True' to build the backbone of the breakout song 'Set Adrift On Memory Bliss,' which topped the American charts and landed at Number 3 in Britain.

Rockit
Herbie Hancock

Released July 1983
Columbia *04054* (U.S.) / CBS *A 3577* (U.K. #8)

The noted jazz artist Herbie Hancock was briefly yet significantly at the center of the nascent recorded hip-hop world with 'Rockit,' the song that in a long and varied career is still his best known single and the one that crossed most boundaries.

While audiences loved the robotic voices and fresh synthesizer groove unique to 'Rockit,' but center-stage really belonged to the scratching sounds of New York hip-hop DJ Grand Mixer D.ST. He is recognized as a main architect of the technique of manipulating a record back and forth on a turntable while using a mixer to cut the sound in and out and make short, choppy musical phrases. It made an ideal counterpoint to Hancock's keyboards and helped push 'Rockit' to Number 71 in *Billboard's* Hot 100.

Hancock had always embraced technology and experimentation in his compositions, as had bassist Bill Laswell, who co-produced the song with Michael Beinhorn. But 'Rockit' gave Hancock a street relevance and impact while simultaneously grabbing mainstream honors, such as the 1983 Grammy for Best R&B Instrumental Performance. It's a rather tricky feat that he was never able to repeat with any other song.

The humorous video for 'Rockit' features Hancock jamming along with a band of robots and strange, self-playing instruments; it quickly became an MTV mainstay. Hancock cleaned up at the 1984 MTV Video Music Awards with 'Rockit,' taking home five moon-men statuettes for Best Concept Video, Best Special Effects, Best Art Direction, Best Editing, and, most interestingly, the fleeting honor of Most Experimental Video.

Flashdance . . . What a Feeling
Irene Cara

Released April 1983
Casablanca *811440* (U.S. #1) / Casablanca *CAN 1016* (U.K. #2)

This is the title cut from the soundtrack for the runaway smash movie *Flashdance*, the inspirational story of a Pittsburgh factory worker who beats incredible odds to live out her dreams to dance. It brought some top honors to Irene Cara, a singer who was seeing her own dreams unfolding. To paraphrase the song, Cara was taking her passion and making it happen. The enviable accolades for 'Flashdance … What A Feeling' included the Grammy for Best Female Pop Vocal and the Oscar for Best Song (awarded to *Flashdance* composer Giorgio Moroder). Cara had sung on another Academy Award-winning tune, 1980's 'Fame,' but 'Flashdance' swept the world.

Holiday
Madonna

Released October 1983
Sire *29478* (U.S. #16) / Sire *W 9405* (U.K. #2)

A buoyant, carefree ditty that seems tailor-made for Madonna, 'Holiday' was actually written by Lisa Hudson and Curtis Stevens with ex-Supremes singer Mary Wilson in mind. After Wilson declined the song, it was then recorded by the songwriters' friend, producer John 'Jellybean' Benitez, and the young Ms. Ciccone. 'Holiday' became the lead single from Madonna's debut self-titled album after it received tremendous response from the club DJs who had been sent promotional copies of the record (backed with another subsequent hit, 'Lucky Star'). To this day, DJs are an important part of the singer's career, often breaking each new song to the public. Her third single (following 'Everybody,' and 'Burning Up' / 'Physical Attraction'), 'Holiday' guaranteed Madonna's spot on the global dancefloor, a position she still occupies.

Just a few years after the song's release, 'Holiday' was being sampled and re-used by others. In 1986, Dutch duo MC Miker G and DJ Sven used the instrumental of 'Holiday' for their own 'Holiday Rap,' a novelty track that improved on Madonna's original for pop-chart domination when it reached Number 1 in 34 countries.

'Holiday' has since been sampled by Australian dance act The Avalanches and provided the concept for the bassline to Stardust's international club hit 'Music Sounds Better With You,' a catchy song from 2000 that Madonna later referenced by sampling it on 'Get Together' from her 2006 album *Confessions On A Dancefloor*. Madonna's third single was still an influential dance hit more than two decades after its release – and even an influence on her own career.

Uptown Girl
Billy Joel

Released September 1983
Columbia *04149* (U.S. #3) / CBS *A 3775* (U.K. #1)

This snappy tune is one of many of the diverse gems in the multi-platinum-selling Piano Man's vast catalog of hits. For the benefit of befuddled listeners who didn't know exactly who Billy Joel's 'Uptown Girl' was in real life, the question was answered definitively in the iconic video made to promote the song, which was an MTV favorite. It finds Joel playing a grease monkey ogling a beautiful lady in a colorful dress. She turns out to be none other than supermodel Christie Brinkley, who would soon be Joel's wife (and later, sadly, his ex).

White Lines (Don't Don't Do It)
Grandmaster & Melle Mel

Released October 1983
Sugar Hill *465* (U.S.) / Sugar Hill *SH 130* (U.K. #7)

After the international attention generated by Grandmaster Flash & The Furious Five's 'The Message,' the pioneering New York DJ known as Flash teamed up with Furious Five MC Melle Mel to bring another type of message record from the heart of the nascent hip-hop world. While 'The Message' encapsulated the volatility of urban oppression in the Bronx onto a record that the mainstream could instinctively feel and embrace, 'White Lines' decried cocaine. Abuse of the drug was one of the most insidious problems ravaging the city. While the song was clear in its avocation, it had an undeniable funk and groove that helped the hard lessons go down with a spoonful of sugar.

Much of the instrumental inspiration for 'White Lines' came from another song: 'Cavern' by Liquid Liquid, the underground New York post-punk group fronted by singer Sal Principato. 'Cavern' features the bassline that is now principally associated with Flash, and Principato's vocal inflections seem to dictate the melodic direction employed by Melle Mel on 'White Lines.'

As with 'The Message,' 'White Lines' was not a hit on the American pop charts but was a success in the U.K. Top 10. It remains a staple of club DJs worldwide, from hip-hop to house music aficionados. As a notorious party anthem, its central theme has surely been misinterpreted thousands of times on non-sober dancefloors. Even with the song's success in Britain, it was still a shocker when U.K. pop act Duran Duran covered 'White Lines' for their 1995 album *Thank You* and brought it back to the British pop charts.

Billie Jean
Michael Jackson

Released January 1983
Epic *03509* (U.S. #1) / Epic *EPC A 3084* (U.K. #1)

The second, biggest, and best of seven singles from *Thriller*, 'Billie Jean' set a crown upon the head of the King Of Pop and made him the first superstar of the MTV generation. Of course, Michael Jackson was already a star long before 'Billie Jean.' From 1969 and 'I Want You Back' onwards, rarely did a few months pass without a new Jackson hit making a large dent on the charts. For the most part, however, the first dozen or so years of his career were dominated by his work with his brothers as The Jackson 5. Solo hits such as 'Rockin' Robin' and 'Ben' in the early 1970s and 'Don't Stop 'Til You Get Enough' at the end of the decade were exceptions, not the rule.

In late 1982, Jackson released his duet with Paul McCartney, 'The Girl Is Mine,' as the first single from *Thriller*. While it reached the Top 10 in Britain and the U.S., not all of his critics were convinced. But his next release raised the bar significantly higher. 'Billie Jean' opens with a stark two-beat drum loop and what Jackson considered to be "the perfect bassline," which is eventually augmented by swift stabs of synthesized strings. The main focus is, naturally, Jackson's vocal. Legend states that Jackson nailed the lead part first take, before painstakingly building up the multi-tracked backing vocals.

Like the rest of its parent album, 'Billie Jean' was produced by Quincy Jones, but the song and arrangement are very much Jackson's own, as demonstrated by his 1981 home demo version – included on the 20th anniversary reissue of *Thriller* – on which all of the key components are already in place. Jones's main contribution was to make each of the instrumental and vocal parts sound as good as they possibly could. He did, however, have two major objections to Jackson's vision for 'Billie Jean.' He felt that the 30-second intro was much too long for a pop single, and wanted the title to be changed, fearing that listeners would associate the song with the tennis player Billie Jean King – but lost out on both counts.

Jackson's determination to retain the song's original title was largely due to its real-life roots. This cautionary tale of predatory female fans is based on a woman who had begun to call herself 'Billie Jean Jackson' and claim that the singer was the father of one – but not both – of her twin sons. This particular 'Billie Jean' was eventually institutionalized, but Jackson has since intimated in interviews that she wasn't the only crazed fan that he has had to inform, in no uncertain terms, that "the kid is not my son."

Released at the end of January, 1983 – less than two months after the perfectionist Jackson completed the final mix – 'Billie Jean' quickly rose to the top of the *Billboard* singles chart and soon also reached Number 1 in the U.K. and across Europe. Just as important as its chart position was the accompanying promo video, directed by Steve Barron. MTV at the time was dominated by white artists and initially refused to air 'Billie Jean' until a timely ultimatum came from Jackson's record boss, CBS President Walter Yetnikoff: start showing the video or there will be no more white CBS acts on MTV. (CBS owned the Columbia and Epic labels.)

By March the station had relented, and Jackson was the first black star of MTV. Others soon followed, among them Prince and Lionel Richie. But the 'Billie Jean' promo did more than just break down racial barriers. It paved the way for a brand new kind of music video. Before, videos tended to be little more than a performance piece; this, on the other hand, was more like a short film, with high production values and something approaching a narrative storyline. Before the year was out, Jackson had taken the form even further with the epic, horror-movie-styled *Thriller* video.

'Billie Jean' introduced the world to another of Jackson's innovations: his moonwalk dance, which he debuted on the U.S. TV special *Motown 25: Yesterday, Today, And Forever* in front of an audience of over 47 million viewers. The performance was integral to *Thriller* becoming the biggest selling album of all time, while 'Billie Jean' – still the only song to which Jackson moonwalks – remains his best-selling single. He followed it with another *Billboard* chart-topper, 'Beat It,' the third of an unprecedented seven hit singles to be drawn from *Thriller* and the fifth of 12 career U.S. Number 1s at the time of writing.

QUINCY JONES: POPULAR MUSIC'S RENAISSANCE MAN

A true everyman of the entertainment industry, Chicago-born Quincy Jones would earn himself the reputation of living legend by the time he hit 60 in 1993 and continues to operate effectively within the music and film businesses.

Like many music-biz moguls, Jones paid his dues on stage, honing a mastery of the jazz trumpet through a scholarship at the nascent Berklee School of Music in Boston and playing in the orchestra of jazz bandleader Lionel Hampton at the age of only 20. After moving into arranging – he worked with luminaries such as Count Basie, Cannonball Adderley, Tommy Dorsey, and Dinah Washington – Jones led a band assembled by jazzman Dizzy Gillespie and recorded his own debut album, *This Is How I Feel About Jazz*. He studied in Paris, which led to production work for the French Barclay label, where he worked with Jacques Brel, Charles Aznavour, Billy Eckstine, and Sarah Vaughan.

This might have been a career's-worth for many men, but Jones had much more to offer and went behind the scenes, becoming the first black senior exec. for a major U.S. record company when he was hired as Mercury's vice-president in 1961. Two years later he moved into film work, composing the score for Sidney Lumet's controversial *The Pawnbroker* and going on to soundtrack no fewer than 33 movies. A fruitful alliance with Frank Sinatra saw him arrange and conduct sessions for Sinatra's *It Might As Well Be Swing* LP, arrange the legendary *Sinatra At The Sands* album (recorded with the Count Basie Orchestra), and did the same for the singer's 1984 set *L.A. Is My Lady*.

Meanwhile, jazz wasn't enough to contain Jones. Alongside his own successful solo career he stepped into the pop and soul fields, working with Aretha Franklin, Paul Simon, and others. He was responsible for a major jazz coup, however, when he persuaded the ailing Miles Davis to perform a gig at the Montreux Jazz Festival, just months before the star's death in 1991.

By this time, Jones had become a staple of the modern black music mainstream, working with stars such as Rufus & Chaka Khan and – most famously – Michael Jackson, whose epoch-shaping *Off The Wall*, *Thriller*, and *Bad* albums he produced. Jones also worked on the 'We Are The World' single by U.S.A. For Africa in 1985, a sickly composition that was notable despite its musical shortcomings for the commercial boost it gave many of the black artists who contributed to it.

In the last two decades Jones has moved into film production, bringing movies such as the Steven Spielberg-directed *The Color Purple* to the screen and co-creating the renowned Will Smith TV comedy series *The Fresh Prince Of Bel Air*. In the course of his career Jones has scooped no fewer than 26 Grammy awards, and at the time of writing he is still active at the age of 73.

Sweet Dreams (Are Made Of This)
Eurythmics

Released January 1983
RCA *13533* (U.S. #1) / RCA *DA 2* (U.K. #2)

Vocalist Annie Lennox and multi-instrumentalist Dave Stewart, as Eurythmics, brought an emotional resonance to the often soulless sound of 1980s synth-pop. 'Sweet Dreams' was the duo's breakthrough hit and remains their most famous single. Lennox and Stewart formed the group in 1980; previously they were lovers as well as members of the modestly successful late-1970s pop act The Tourists. The duo's first album as Eurythmics featured contributions from Can's Holger Czukay and Jackie Liebezeit, and Blondie drummer Clem Burke, but was a critical and commercial failure. Stung by the reaction to their debut, the pair retreated to their London home studio and began experimenting with various analog synthesizers (even then seen as retro), alongside co-producer Andy Williams.

Stewart hit upon 'Sweet Dreams' almost by accident: the main riff came from the notes chimed out by a music box, replayed in reverse order on a rasping bass synth. Coupled with piston-like electronic drums, the instrumental track is strikingly minimalist and evocative of Kraftwerk's mid-1970s explorations, as such offering an effective contrast to Lennox's soulful vocal. It was her richly emotive voice that won over listeners from beyond the typical synth-pop market and made 'Sweet Dreams' a worldwide hit. Although the duo have had many more hits in the ensuing years, none has been as popular – or perhaps as good – as this song. 'Sweet Dreams' has since been recorded by a number of other artists, notably the shock-rocker Marilyn Manson (on his 1996 *Smells Like Children* EP).

Blue Monday
New Order

Released March 1983
Factory-Rough Trade *FACTUS 10* (U.S.) / Factory *FAC 73* (U.K. #9)

The biggest selling 12-inch single of all time, 'Blue Monday' is a near-perfect marriage of rock and dance music. After Joy Division frontman Ian Curtis committed suicide in 1980, few expected much from the group's three remaining members. Undeterred, guitarist (and now vocalist) Bernard Sumner, bassist Peter Hook, and drummer Stephen Morris regrouped the following year as New Order, recruiting keyboardist Gillian Gilbert and recording their debut album. *Movement* sounded too much like Joy Division Lite in places, but on the ensuing singles 'Everything's Gone Green' and 'Temptation' New Order started to experiment with electronic rhythms that bore the hallmarks of Kraftwerk and Afrika Bambaataa.

In late 1982 New Order started to work with Arthur Baker, the producer of Bambaataa's landmark single 'Planet Rock.' Baker helped crystallize the group's ambition, moving them towards a sound that fused 'real' and sequenced instrumentation. 'Blue Monday' was packaged in a stark, eye-catching jacket that resembled an oversized computer disk. It proved immediately that Sumner, Hook, and Morris could move out of the shadow of their former group.

Running to seven-and-a-half minutes and released only as a 12-inch, the single opens with a series of pulsating electronic rhythms, which are soon joined by sequenced bass and a synthesizer part evocative of Kraftwerk's 'Trans Europe Express.' Sumner's detached vocal arrives two minutes in, leading the song to its doomy epicenter with a lyric inspired by the recent Anglo-Argentinian Falklands War. The only live playing is Hook's melodic bassline, played high up the neck of the bass in what is now thought of as his trademark style. (Hook arrived at the style during the early days of Joy Division because he couldn't hear himself playing the lower notes, so weak was his amplifier.)

'Blue Monday' shot straight into the U.K. Top 10 on its release and became a huge club hit on both sides of the Atlantic. Part of its sales success was down to the fact that the group's concurrent album, *Power, Corruption And Lies*, contained an inferior demo version, making the 12-inch single an essential purchase. It was not a hit in the U.S. until the release five years later of 'Blue Monday 1988,' one of several subsequent remixes and reissues.

Let's Dance
David Bowie

Released March 1983
EMI America *8158* (U.S. #1) / EMI America *EA 152* (U.K. #1)

A switch of record labels from RCA to EMI America saw Bowie revitalizing his career and delivering his most commercial piece since the early 1970s. Simplicity itself, 'Let's Dance' presented the bare bones of rock'n'roll and was remarkably positive and uplifting in comparison with much of Bowie's earlier material. It has the most straightforward lyric in his catalog, and while he certainly could do much better, one has to admire the calculated in-your-face commerciality of this track, one that was obviously going to Number 1. And it was precisely the right move for the times. Dumping all his previous personas, here the former chameleon of rock became David Bowie, slick, modern Rock Star.

His interest in soul and disco music goes back to his 'thin white duke' mid-1970s period, so it's no surprise that when he decided to make a cutting-edge dance album in 1983 he chose one of the genre's masters, ex-Chic guru Nile Rodgers, to oversee production. Glossy hi-tech studio work by Rodgers coupled with a cameo guitar appearance by Stevie Ray Vaughan and radio-friendly mixing by Bob Clearmountain resulted in a chart-topping single on both sides of the Atlantic – Bowie's second Number 1 in America and third in Britain (fourth if you count 'Under Pressure,' his 1981 collaboration with Queen).

'Let's Dance' is a much-used title in the annals of pop, with four major hits bearing that name in Britain: first came Chris Montez in 1962; Bowie's hit was in 1983; that was succeeded by Chris Rea in 1987; and finally came boy-band Five, whose version reached Number 1 in August 2001. They are all different songs.

Relax
Frankie Goes To Hollywood

Released October 1983
Island *99805* (U.S. #10) / ZTT *ZTAS 1* (U.K. #1)

For a few brief months during 1984 it looked as if Liverpool's Frankie Goes To Hollywood, fronted by Holly Johnson, could be the biggest band of the 1980s. The group had spent two years going nowhere before they were spotted by Trevor Horn, the British production guru behind hits by Yes, Spandau Ballet, and ABC. "What I liked about the song was its structure," explained Horn. "It was like a radio jingle or a chant, except that Holly sang it like a wild animal."

Horn re-recorded the group's demo with The Blockheads (Ian Dury's backing band), transforming their promising, erotically-charged rave into a monstrously huge production that integrated their classically Liverpudlian four-on-the-floor beat into a soundscape where Giorgio Moroder met Phil Spector, complete with orgasmic sound effects.

With a new Holly Johnson vocal in place, the single was released and, to everyone's dismay, went nowhere. 'Relax' was rescued from oblivion on January 11, 1984, when BBC Radio One DJ Mike Read, having just realized that the lyric offered step-by-step advice on how to delay an orgasm, pulled it off his turntable and declared it obscene.

The resulting ban rocketed the song to Number 1, and the Frankies brilliantly milked the controversy to chalk up two more British chart-toppers, 'Two Tribes' and 'The Power Of Love,' becoming only the second band ever to score three consecutive Number 1s with their first three releases. (The first to achieve that was Gerry & The Pacemakers.) However, 'Relax' did not chart in America until a year later, reaching only Number 10, and both follow-ups floundered dismally there. Then, as suddenly as they'd arrived, the Frankies disappeared.

This Charming Man
The Smiths

Released October 1983
Not issued U.S. / Rough Trade *RT 136* (U.K. #25)

Following their debut single, 'Hand in Glove,' The Smiths released 'This Charming Man,' the second 45 from one of Manchester, England's most famous international exports. The influential rock quartet consisted of singer Morrissey, guitarist Johnny Marr, bassist Mike Joyce, and drummer Andy Rourke, and the single is a classic example of the special chemistry between the band's songwriters, Morrissey and Marr, and their innovative techniques. Morrissey's masterful, maundlin voice, prone to great emotion and hyperbole, had no peers, while Marr's guitar work showed a generation of self-taught bedroom musicians how to push the boundaries of their instrument.

Morrissey's lyrics to 'This Charming Man,' full of sexual ambiguity, obscure literary and filmic references, and with a clever semantic flow, would probably have made his hero Oscar Wilde proud. Diametrically opposed on the surface to the flamboyance of, say, Culture Club, Morrissey's words were in fact not too far from those of Boy George in that they encouraged fans to speculate – even though the singer has never quite publicly declared a sexual orientation.

The song's opening question – "Punctured bicycle / On a hillside, desolate / Will nature make a man of me yet?" – perfectly reflects the song's duality, its multivalent outlook on life. Benign and innocent, or titillating and devious; the audience is left questioning Morrissey's intentions, and the witty frontman would surely want it no other way. The single's sleeve did precisely nothing to distract potential fans from this overall confusion: it's a still of dreamy actor Jean Marais lying in reflection, taken from Jean Cocteau's 1950 fantasy romance epic *Orphée*.

Wake Me Up Before You Go Go
Wham!

Released May 1984
Columbia *04552* (U.S. #1) / Epic *A 4440* (U.K. #1)

Careless Whisper
George Michael

Released July 1984
Columbia *04691* (U.S. #1) / Epic *A 4603* (U.K. #1)

Teen duo Wham! got off to a shaky start. Their debut single, 'Wham Rap!,' flunked on first release and only became a U.K. hit after the success of their second single, 'Young Guns (Go For It).' In America, none of their first four singles even tickled the Top 40. Hardened industry cynics were writing them off as lightweights. Macho mainstream rock acts such as Prince and Bruce Springsteen dominated the era and Wham!'s carefully contrived image – James Dean but squeaky clean – looked laughable by comparison.

'Wake Me Up Before You Go Go' turned everything around. With a title based on a sign hung on Wham! member Andrew Ridgeley's bedroom door, it was a vibrantly energetic 1960s-Motown pastiche, which the dynamic duo made larger than life by prancing around in shorts and summer shirts on Britain's influential TV show *Top Of The Pops*. Instead of backing off from their lightweight image, they'd turned it up to 11 and confounded the critics. Suddenly it was cool to be young again. The song took them to Number 1 on both sides of the Atlantic, starting a run of hits that lasted until the duo split up – but cracks in the partnership were evident within weeks.

'Careless Whisper,' a tear-jerking ballad from the very first demo that had secured their deal with Innervision Records, came out in the U.K. as a solo release under George Michael's name but in America was credited to Wham! Featuring George Michael. Two years later, Ridgeley would be history and Michael a megastar.

Radio Ga Ga
Queen

Released January 1984
Capitol *5317* (U.S. #16) / EMI *QUEEN 1* (U.K. #2)

This was Queen's 22nd British Top 40 hit and their 11th in America. The group are especially notable in that all the individual members were bona fide songwriters with major hits to their credit. Among these, 'Bohemian Rhapsody' was by Freddie Mercury, guitarist Brian May wrote 'We Will Rock You,' bass guitarist John Deacon was responsible for 'Another One Bites The Dust,' while 'Radio Ga Ga' was by drummer Roger Taylor.

Originally the song was under consideration for Taylor's second solo album, and the title was inspired by some baby talk from his young son. Taylor says he wrote it after locking himself in the studio with a synthesizer and a drum machine, but after playing it to the band, Deacon came up with a bassline and Mercury, who was convinced it had hit potential, did some work on the lyrics.

The video for this anthemic piece – described in a *Melody Maker* review as "arrogant nonsense" – contained sequences from Fritz Lang's futuristic 1927 silent movie *Metropolis* intercut with staged scenes of synchronised handclapping, later impressively copied by tens of thousands of fans at stadium concerts.

The lyrics about the power that MTV had over former radio listeners seemed ironic since it was Queen's own 'Bohemian Rhapsody' clip that had helped usher in the video age. Composer Taylor explained: "It deals with how important radio used to be, historically speaking, before television, and how important it was to me as a kid. Today it seems that video, the visual side of rock'n'roll, has become more important than the music itself." Held at Number 2 in Britain by Frankie Goes To Hollwood's 'Relax,' the song nevertheless reached Number 1 in 19 countries.

Pride (In The Name Of Love)
U2

Released September 1984
Island *99704* (U.S. #33) / Island *IS 202* (U.K. #3)

This was U2's first single from their fourth studio album, *The Unforgettable Fire*, the first to be produced by Brian Eno and Daniel Lanois. The production duo functioned as surrogate band members, using the studio

as an instrument and turning U2 into a world-class act. Like many of the band's best songs, 'Pride' was the result of soundcheck jamming. Bono's original focus for the lyrics had been the kind of pride that comes before a fall. To be more precise, he was thinking of what he called the "Reaganesque pride that might cause nuclear war." That idea didn't work, but he found inspiration during a visit to a Chicago peace museum and an exhibit on assassinated civil-rights leader Martin Luther King Jr.

There were problems in the studio. A 'finished' version of the track wasn't working and was scrapped at the last moment, with the band starting again from scratch the next day as Pretenders leader Chrissie Hynde sang backing vocals. There was some concern over Bono's choice of subject. Guitarist Edge recalled: "Because of the situation in our country, non-violent struggle was such an inspiring concept. Even so, when Bono told me he wanted to write about King, at first I said: 'Woah, that's not what we're about.' Then he came in and sang the song and it felt right; it was great. When that happens there's no argument. It just *was*."

This was the group's biggest U.K. hit to date, reaching Number 3, and in fact remained their best British chart placing until 1988, when 'Desire' reached Number 1. They would go on to enjoy two U.S. chart-toppers from their next album, *The Joshua Tree*, and conquer the world with their performance at Live Aid.

You Spin Me Round (Like A Record)
Dead Or Alive

Released November 1984
Epic *04894* (U.S. #11) / Epic *A 4861* (U.K. #1)

'You Spin Me Round' was the biggest of ten U.K. hits for the British quartet fronted by the sexually ambiguous Pete Burns. They'd already hit the Top 30 with a cover of KC & The Sunshine Band's 'That's The Way I Like It' before engaging the services of up-and-coming writer-producers Mike Stock, Matt Aitken, and Pete Waterman.

It was Burns, impressed by the trio's production on hi-energy disco hits by Divine and Hazell Dean, who made the call. Waterman recalled: "There have been maybe a dozen extraordinarily important moments that have made me what I am today. That phone call was one of them."

Stock Aitken & Waterman were contracted to produce three tracks for Dead Or Alive's upcoming album, although 'You Spin Me Round' wasn't one of them. However, Waterman was so convinced it would be a huge hit that he spent most of the budget on the track – and it paid off when the record company agreed to let them produce the entire *Youthquake* album. Originally released in November 1984, 'You Spin Me' took over three months to climb to the summit: a remix gave it the extra push, and it reached Number 1 in Britain, later Number 11 in America.

The track is especially notable as the first Stock Aitken & Waterman production to hit Number 1. Probably the most successful writer-producers that Britain has ever seen, the trio would over the following years deliver dozens of hits for the likes of Bananarama, Mel & Kim, Kylie Minogue, Jason Donovan, and Rick Astley, achieving a total of 13 U.K. Number 1s between 1985 and 1990.

Twenty years after his only Number 1, Pete Burns, who has allegedly undergone extensive cosmetic surgery, is still a well-known figure in Britain and recently appeared on the U.K. cult television show *Celebrity Big Brother*.

Jump
Van Halen

Released January 1984
Warner Bros. *29384* (U.S. #1) / Warner Bros. *W 9384* (U.K. #7)

Still a quintessential rock anthem, 'Jump' finds the multi-platinum selling Van Halen – brothers Eddie and Alex Van Halen, Michael Anthony, and scene-stealer David Lee Roth – at their most vibrant. Lead singer Roth's flowing blond locks and gravity-defying acrobatics in the video were not in vain: they undoubtedly helped the band earn a 1984 MTV Video Music Award for Best Stage Performance In A Video. 'Jump' spent five weeks at Number 1 and marked the only time that Van Halen scored a chart-topper. It has been covered many times since, with veteran lounge lizard Paul Anka providing a memorable take on the song in 2005.

Drive
The Cars

Released July 1984
Elektra *69706* (U.S. #3) / Elektra *E 9706* (U.K. #4)

A group named The Cars and a song called 'Drive' – it sounds like a marketing ploy from the Ford Motor Company, although of course the group had actually been around for some years and had enjoyed their first of a dozen U.S. hits back in 1978. 'Drive' became a worldwide hit in 1984 but enjoyed a considerable revival and another trip into the U.K. Top 5 the following year after it featured in a moving video sequence of famine suffering at Live Aid. Writer Ric Ocasek then donated all subsequent royalties from the song to the Band Aid Trust.

Born In The U.S.A.
Bruce Springsteen

Released November 1984
Columbia *04680* (U.S. #9) / CBS *A 6342* (U.K. B-side; A #5)

It's surprising, considering how successful the *Born In The U.S.A.* album was, that none of the singles drawn from it – seven in the U.S. – reached Number 1 on either side of the Atlantic. The title track was inspired by a screenplay of the same name Springsteen had been sent. He originally recorded it at home on a 4-track machine in January 1982, together with the songs that would appear on his *Nebraska* album. Springsteen re-recorded it with The E-Street Band for the sessions that produced his bestselling album, nailing it live in the studio on the third take. It was released as the third single from an album that at the time of writing has sold over 15 million copies in America alone. In Britain it was the B-side of 'I'm On Fire,' a song more likely to attract U.K. airplay than this apparent celebration of American citizenship.

Springsteen has always been troubled by the continued misinterpretation of what is one of his favorite songs. Seen by many (including Ronald Reagan) as a gung-ho patriotic anthem, 'Born In The U.S.A.' was in fact about the bad treatment of homecoming Vietnam veterans, a theme to which Springsteen has often returned. With patriotism in mind, Chrysler offered $12 million to front an ad campaign; Springsteen rejected the idea. He did, however, allow 2 Live Crew to sample it for their 1990 Top 20 single 'Banned In The U.S.A.'

Girls Just Want To Have Fun
Cyndi Lauper

Released January 1984
Portrait *04120* (U.S. #2) / Portrait *A 3943* (U.K. #2)

Before the Spice Girls brought along their manufactured version of Girl Power, Cyndi Lauper had already provided it, the decade before, with 'Girls Just Want To Have Fun' – only she had musicianship and natural charisma. Her wild look in the video (orange hair, a myriad of baubles, and funky, gypsy-like clothes) made Lauper an MTV star; the network gave her the Video Music Award for Best Female Video in 1984. Her debut LP *She's So Unusual* featured three more hit songs after 'Girls' – 'Time After Time,' 'She Bop,' and 'All Through the Night' – and helped her take home the Grammy for Best New Artist.

Hello
Lionel Richie

Released March 1984
Motown *1722* (U.S. #1) / Motown *TMG 1330* (U.K. #1)

The success of this plaintive and romantic ballad provided a fourth Number 1 hit for Lionel Richie as a solo artist, apart from his considerable work with The Commodores. It was buoyed by the video, still one of Richie's strangest efforts and often viewed as somewhat camp (although that wasn't the intention). A mini-movie of sorts, it depicts a love story between Richie and a blind leading-lady who sculpts an uncanny likeness of Richie out of clay, despite her inability to see. With or without visuals, this song is demonstrative of a man at the peak of his powers.

Close (To The Edit)
Art Of Noise

Released June 1984
Island *99754* (U.S.) / ZTT *ZTPS 01* (U.K. #8)

'Close To The Edit' might not have aged particularly well, but in 1984 many considered its digital hums and orchestral stabs to be the sound of the future. It was the work of an unusual collective led by the record producer Trevor Horn, who had hit Number 1 in the U.K., as half of Buggles, five years earlier with 'Video Killed The Radio Star.' The group also included music journalist Paul Morley and arranger Anne Dudley, who later won an Academy Award for her work on the soundtrack to *The Full Monty*. 'Close To The Edit' was one of the first hit records to make use of the pioneering Fairlight CMI digital sampler. Horn and Morley left the group shortly after its release, leaving Dudley to carry on with two of Horn's former studio assistants, Gary Langan and J.J. Jeczalic.

Caribbean Queen
Billy Ocean

Released August 1984
Jive *9199* (U.S. #1) / Jive *77* (U.K. #6)

Born in Trinidad and Tobago, R&B singer-songwriter Billy Ocean (born Leslie Sebastian Charles) found pop stardom in the U.K., where he and his parents moved when he was eight. Ocean's Caribbean heritage gave his voice a sweet distinction truly his own, with a tone capable of leaping from high and light to low and sexy. After debuting in 1976 with a few minor hits, Ocean saw his propulsive 'Caribbean Queen' catapult him into an MTV star. He had tried a few different versions of the song but, alas, neither 'African Queen' nor 'European Queen' had the same ring.

I Just Called To Say I Love You
Stevie Wonder

Released August 1984
Motown *1745* (U.S. #1) / Motown *TMG 1349* (U.K. #1)

'I Just Called To Say I Love You' provides a convenient dividing line in the career of Stevie Wonder. During the 1970s he produced a string of classic albums – including *Talking Book*, *Innervisions*, and *Songs In The Key Of Life* – that demonstrate the perfect blend of technological experimentation and pop nous. In later years, though, he has seemed content to focus his work more exclusively on melody and song, and to pass on the sonic innovation baton to a younger generation of musicians. On this, the most commercially successful single of Wonder's career, the hook is so strong and memorable that it doesn't need to be backed by anything particularly revolutionary. A killer chorus and beautiful vocal delivery are more than enough.

far right > Ultravox frontman Midge Ure (second left), who co-wrote 'Do They Know It's Christmas?,' at work on the charity single with musicians including Genesis's Mike Rutherford (left) and Phil Collins (second right).

Smooth Operator
Sade

Released September 1984
Portrait *04807* (U.S. #5) / Epic *A 4655* (U.K. #19)

Jazz purists may spit at the immaculately pedicured feet of crooner Sade Adu, but the rest of the world doesn't care: her best songs, such as the huge hit 'Smooth Operator,' go down a treat with the after-dinner coffee and mints, and always will. The Sade brand was built on her voice, her looks, and her production, all things of great beauty and the perfect package for the suave yuppie 1980s. But beneath the superslick exterior there was real talent, as evidenced by the long and fruitful career the singer nurtured on the back of hits such as this. It's a safe bet that the likes of Katie Melua and Norah Jones wouldn't be around today if it hadn't been for Sade.

Do They Know It's Christmas?
Band Aid

Released December 1984
Columbia *04749* (U.S. #13) / Mercury *FEED 1* (U.K. #1)

We Are The World
U.S.A. For Africa

Released March 1985
Columbia *04839* (U.S. #1) / CBS *USAID 1* (U.K. #1)

Like millions of other British television viewers, Bob Geldof was shocked when he saw a BBC documentary film about famine in Ethiopia in fall 1984. At first he set himself a target of raising £70,000 (about $90,000) but then decided to record a charity Christmas record. According to Geldof, he knocked off the lyric in the back seat of a taxi between

meetings. Co-writer Midge Ure produced the entire backing track in his home studio, with the exception of Phil Collins's drums, which were added at the last minute, following the recording of the individual and massed vocals.

Geldof's methods of persuasion ensured one of the largest gatherings of stars ever seen in a recording studio, on November 25, 1984, including Sting, Bono, George Michael, Boy George, and David Bowie. Free studio time, manufacturing, and distribution were also arranged. The only body that failed to succumb to Geldof's tenacity was the British government, who refused to forgo their income from the V.A.T. (value-added tax) on sales of the record. Released on December 7, the disc immediately shot to Number 1 in Britain and sold over 3 million copies, while in America it reached Number 13 and sold a further million.

Following in the wake of Band Aid, Harry Belafonte began laying plans for a similar fund-raising project in America, named U.S.A. For Africa. Lionel Richie and Michael Jackson wrote 'We Are The World' in two-and-a-half hours, and it was recorded in Los Angeles on January 28, 1985, following the American Music Awards, which ensured that most of the top artists would be in town. Jones had sent a copy of the tape to all the participating musicians advising them in an accompanying letter to "check their egos at the door."

Contributors included Bob Dylan, Willie Nelson, Paul Simon, Ray Charles, Bruce Springsteen, and Diana Ross, in addition to Richie, Jackson, Stevie Wonder, and instigator Belafonte. Even Bob Geldof made the trip to appear on this American Band Aid offspring. Released on March 7, the single soon sold 7.5 million copies in America alone. In a remarkable demonstration of worldwide solidarity, on Easter Friday, April 5, 1985, at 15:50 GMT, 'We Are The World' was simultaneously broadcast by 5,000 radio stations around the globe.

Having got the ball rolling, Geldof then decided to go further by organizing a live-by-satellite worldwide concert. Staged on Saturday July 13, 1985, Live Aid, also known as The Global Juke Box, took place at London's Wembley Stadium and Philadelphia's JFK Stadium. Within a year, income from the various related projects had accumulated over $70 million in famine relief. Geldof was later rewarded for his efforts by a knighthood from the Queen, although he probably would have been more satisfied with a V.A.T. refund from the British government.

How Soon Is Now?
The Smiths

Released January 1985
Sire *S7155* (U.S.) / Rough Trade *RT 176* (U.K. #24)

'How Soon' was originally a B-Side to the 1984 single 'William It Was Really Nothing' but eventually became an A-side itself, as well as the most enduring song from the Manchester quartet (Morrissey, Johnny Marr, Andy Rourke, and Mike Joyce). It is a hallmark of the brief yet significant songwriting partnership of Morrissey and Marr, loved by guitar enthusiasts for Marr's adventurous, vibrato-laden technique (here including intricate multiple layers) and prized by lonely hearts across the globe for Morrissey's tender delivery. As with previous singles, the cover art depicted a young film actor – here Sean Barrett in 1958's *Dunkirk* – and Morrissey's ever-ambiguous lyrics continued to fuel speculation about the singer's sexuality.

'How Soon Is Now?' has enjoyed a strange afterlife among covers and songs that sample from it. In 1990, Marr's iconic opening chords were looped and sampled for Soho's 'Hippychick,' a female-led dance anthem that hit the U.K. Top 10 – higher than The Smiths ever got with the original. It was a strange choice given the isolationist nature of Morrissey's song, and a lot of Smiths fans despised it, but the considerably more upbeat 'Hippychick' solidified the versatility of Marr's singular talent.

A little over a decade later, 'How Soon Is Now?' received another unexpected revival when it was covered by Love Spit Love (an offshoot of British 1980s hit-makers The Psychedelic Furs) and used as the theme song to *Charmed*, an adventure show from TV mogul Aaron Spelling about young female witches.

Summer Of '69
Bryan Adams

Released June 1985
A&M *2739* (U.S. #5) / A&M *AM 267* (U.K.)

Born in 1959 in Kingston, Ontario, Bryan Adams signed to A&M Records in Canada in 1979 after they offered him $1 to record four songs. It was the best offer he could get at the time, and his first record for the company was the disco hit 'Let Me Take You Dancing,' which sold around 240,000 copies, mostly in the U.S. and Canada. The record was considerably speeded up to attain the required beats-per-minute for dancing purposes, and Adams ended up sounding like one of The Chipmunks. This is probably why 'Let Me Take You Dancing' is notable for its absence from Adams's many subsequent career collections. However, this initial success did enable him to splash out on his first car and, more importantly, won him a long-term contract with A&M.

It was his fourth album, *Reckless*, released in 1984, that gave Adams his big breakthrough, with a string of hits including 'Run To You' (originally submitted to Blue Oyster Cult), 'Heaven,' and 'Summer Of '69,' all composed with his first writing partner Jim Vallance. According to Adams, 'Summer Of '69' was mostly the work of Vallance and was "the hardest song on the album to write. The year is immaterial, although it was a great year – I was only ten, of course, but I remember the moon landing, the Beatles breaking up, Woodstock. … That song took more rewrites than any of the others, and I only let it go on [the record] because I didn't know what else I could do with it."

Money For Nothing
Dire Straits

Released July 1985
Warner Bros. *28950* (U.S. #1) / Vertigo *DSTR 10* (U.K. #4)

Many of Mark Knopfler's songwriting ideas come from real life experiences, the passing comments of friends, remarks on television, from movies, or a phrase read in a book. 'Money For Nothing,' described in a *Rolling Stone* review as "Led-Zep for yuppies," was just such a song. "I was in New York," Knopfler recalled, "it was one of those big appliance shops – at the back there were big walls of TVs all tuned to MTV. There was this Joe 'six-pack' figure there with his big checked shirt on and he was holding forth to an audience of one or two about the performances on MTV. The kind of stuff he was saying was so classic. I managed to eavesdrop for a couple of minutes, then I went and got a piece of paper and started writing down the lines." The situation aroused Knopfler's writing talents, and he instinctively felt that this was the basis for a song. Much of the lyrical content of the resulting song consisted of direct quotes from the guy in the shop.

Later, while recording was taking place at Air studios on the island of Montserrat, Knopfler happened to bump into Sting, who was spending some leisure time with his family while also working on demos for his debut solo album *The Dream Of The Blue Turtles*. Inviting him to the session, Knopfler suggested adding the hook "I want my MTV," the music station's contemporary advertising slogan, to the melody of Sting's own Police hit 'Don't Stand So Close To Me.' Thus, Sting got a share of the writing credit and royalties, and an international hit was born.

CD SINGLES: THE CHANGE FROM BLACK TO SILVER

After CD albums hit the Japanese and European markets in late 1982 and U.S. stores early the following year, it was only a matter of time before singles started to appear on the same format.

The Compact Disc was first conceived in the late 1960s, but it took over a decade of development and squabbling between electronics and recording companies – in particular Sony and Philips – before the technology became available to the public. Finally, in 1979, a series of standard specifications were set for the new format: the 120mm (four-and-three-quarter inch) diameter discs, made from polycarbonate, would hold a maximum of 74 minutes of 16-bit audio with a sampling rate of 44.1 kHz.

CD album sales were initially slow, and particularly in the U.S. didn't really pick up until 1986, but some labels had already begun to experiment with the format for singles. The first widely available CD single was 'Brothers In Arms' by Dire Straits, the title track from the group's 25-million-selling album of 1985. It was vastly outperformed, however, by the U.S. Number 1 hit 'Money For Nothing,' and in any case the CD version – issued to coincide with a European stadium tour – accounted for only a small percentage of sales. Like its big brother the CD album, the CD single took some time to establish itself as a viable alternative to vinyl and cassette, but by the early 1990s had become the most prevalent format in the singles market.

For a brief period, record companies experimented with issuing CD singles as smaller, three-inch discs, sometimes known as the CD3. The format never really took off, in part because the discs were somewhat awkward to use. They often had to be fitted into a plastic adapter – which increased their diameter to the regular CD diameter – before they would cooperate with some CD players. Storage was also a problem. No unified packaging format was agreed, and even if one had been devised, the discs would still not sit neatly among a collection of regular CDs. The CD3 was popular in Japan, but even there it was soon seen as something of a novelty item. While CD3s are still occasionally produced – such as U2's 2005 hit 'Sometimes You Can't Make It On Your Own' – they tend to be limited-edition oddities, almost always sold as well as, rather than instead of, a conventional CD single edition.

The CD arrived with the promise of crystal clear sound that would last forever but, as it turned out, both of these bold claims were wildly exaggerated. It did, however, offer room for much more music than the traditional seven-inch vinyl. Thus the process that had begun with the introduction of the 12-inch 'maxi' single continued, and the number – and length – of songs included on the average single increased. Where singles were once no more than an A- and a B-side, it soon became common for them to feature three, four, or more songs, bringing them up to the length of what was once referred to as an EP. In some instances during the 1990s, singles contained more music than most albums of the 1950s and '60s.

During the 1990s, the singles market expanded further, particularly in the U.K., when record labels hatched the idea of issuing two CD versions of a single – "CD1" and "CD2" – containing the same A-side but different B-sides. While it was often intimated that this was a helpful and considerate way of offering the die-hard fan even more songs by his or her favorite band, it was little more than a marketing ploy. Not only did two different editions of a single increase the label's potential earnings from the release in question, it also facilitated a higher chart placing, since many listeners would feel compelled to buy both.

left > Dire Straits performing 'Money For Nothing' with Sting (center) during the Live Aid concert at Wembley Stadium, London, England, on July 13, 1985.

Everybody Wants To Rule The World
Tears For Fears

Released March 1985
Mercury *880659* (U.S. #1) / Mercury *IDEA 9* (U.K. #2)

'Everybody Wants To Rule The World,' a superbly produced pop single with a highly effective guitar motif, was the seventh hit in Britain for the west country synth-pop duo who took their name (and a good deal of lyrical inspiration) from a book on primal-scream therapy by Arthur Janov. Their first U.S hit, it went straight to Number 1, as did the follow-up, 'Shout,' more mainstream pop than their gloomy earlier material and therefore somewhat more America-friendly.

In 1985 U.K. acts would hold the Number 1 spot on the *Billboard* singles chart for an impressive 25 weeks, and for 24 on the albums chart, all part of a mid-1980s British invasion of the U.S. charts. Conversely, in 1986 there were only eight weeks of singles chart-topping glory, and two on the albums charts.

Tears For Fears had spent many months perfecting the grandiose 'Shout,' an anthemic piece with endless overdubs, but 'Rule The World' was apparently a last-minute addition to the *Songs From The Big Chair* album, a half-completed song they didn't rate highly and that they finished in just three days. The *Songs* album topped the *Billboard* album charts for five weeks, shifting eight million copies, enough to keep the band in keyboard polish for the five years it took them to make the follow-up. A slightly modified version of the song hit the U.K. Top 5 the following year as 'Everybody Wants To Run The World' in support of Band Aid offshoot Sport Aid, during which 20 million people ran for Africa and raised $100 million.

Angel
Madonna

Released April 1985
Sire *29008* (U.S. #5) / Sire *W 8881* (U.K. #5)

Into The Groove
Madonna

Released June 1985
Sire *20335* (U.S. B-side) / Sire *W 8934* (U.K. #1)

Written by Madonna and Steve Bray, the breezy love song 'Angel' was produced by Nile Rodgers, legendary guitarist and hit-maker for disco superstars Chic (although 'Angel' itself is not heavy with guitar work). But it was 'Into the Groove,' the B-side of the 'Angel' 12-inch, taken from the 1985 film *Desperately Seeking Susan* (starring Madonna, Rosanna Arquette, and Aidan Quinn), that remains a more frequently visited Madonna classic. It's a pumping party jam styled after her earlier dance hits such as 'Burning Up' and beloved by her core home listening audience as well as professional DJs, who initially broke the song in nightclubs. 'Into the Groove' helped solidify Madonna's commitment to the dancefloor, something she has never abandoned.

Although 'Into the Groove' was in the film – the video was created from a montage of scenes – it's surprising to note that it wasn't on the released soundtrack for *Desperately Seeking Susan*. This seems to be

part of a pattern where Madonna's label does not always zero in on her key songs, only later catching up to the public's demand. But the song is forever associated with the deliciously mischievous personality of Madonna's Susan, one of the few well-liked characters she ever played. Susan danced and hustled her way through the Big Apple with a uniquely eclectic style and flair – much in the way the singer herself did in those early days of what has turned into a lengthy and iconic career.

The Power Of Love
Jennifer Rush

Released June 1985
Epic *05754* (U.S.) / CBS *A 5003* (U.K. #1)

The Power Of Love
Huey Lewis & The News

Released July 1985
Chrysalis *42876* (U.S. #1) / Chrysalis *HUEY 1* (U.K. #11)

Jennifer Rush (born Heidi Stern) grew up in Queens, New York City, but launched the successful phase of her professional career in Germany with a series of minor European hits. She was the daughter of an opera singer, Maurice Stern, and earned international attention for her startling vocal cords with the remarkable octaves and dizzyingly long notes she reaches on 'The Power of Love.'

The song topped charts all over the world, yet did not advance past number 57 in America. The ballad, which became the U.K.'s best-selling single of 1985 and landed a place in *The Guinness Book Of Records*, has been a

popular cover. It was re-made most notably by artists as varied as Air Supply, Laura Branigan, and Celine Dion. Branigan (1987) and Dion (1993) each took the song into the Top 40 with their respective versions and more or less kept to the ballad's original template.

Huey Lewis & The News, a pop-rock band from the San Francisco Bay Area, made their own song called 'The Power of Love' the same year as Rush's. Perhaps the title was lucky, or maybe the band was just talented, but it was also a remarkably successful song. A highlight and lead of the soundtrack for the Michael J. Fox time-travel comedy *Back To The Future* (in which Lewis made a cameo appearance), the group's 'Power of Love' was nominated for an Academy Award for Best Song.

Running Up That Hill
Kate Bush

Released August 1985
EMI America *8285* (U.S. #30) / EMI *KB 1* (U.K. #3)

Kate Bush's biggest international hit was one of the finest recordings of her career. 'Running Up That Hill' broke a three-year silence: as the first single from her landmark *Hounds Of Love* album, it was also her first offering since retreating to the English countryside to build a 48-track studio at the end of her garden. Bush spent much of her time off learning to work with new recording technology, particularly the cutting-edge Fairlight CMI, the first synthesizer to offer sampling and sequencing capabilities.

Opening as if it's emerging from thick fog, 'Running Up That Hill' makes good use of Bush's new toys, with unrelenting processed rhythms and disembodied, multi-layered synthesizer parts. Just as important, however, is the keen human element: a not-quite-persuasive-enough plea to God to fix a failing romantic relationship. The song was, in fact, originally called 'A Deal With God,' until Bush's label requested she change it, noting that songs that take the Lord's name in vain tended not to succeed on the American charts.

EMI had wanted to issue the more restrained 'Cloudbursting' as the first single from *Hounds Of Love*, but a change of name was as far as Bush was willing to compromise, arguing that 'Running Up That Hill' was a much truer reflection of the album as a whole. The relative performances of the two songs on the *Billboard* Hot 100 suggested she chose well: 'Running Up That Hill' became her biggest ever U.S. hit while 'Cloudbursting' failed to chart at all.

Dancing In The Street
David Bowie & Mick Jagger

Released September 1985
EMI America *8288* (U.S. #5) / EMI America *EA 204* (U.K. #1)

Bowie and Jagger's update of the classic Martha & The Vandellas 1964 hit 'Dancing In The Street' was that rare thing, a pop reworking of a soul classic that wasn't completely overshadowed by the original. It sold in vast quantities thanks to the emotional tie-in with Live Aid (which benefited from the record's sales revenue) and an iconic video in which the twosome, still in their prime, twirled the night away. The shouted, tension-building intro added value, and the song was not overproduced, a common mid-1980s studio blunder. Here then was firm evidence that spontaneous charitable ideas don't have to result in poor quality records, although the singers might now regret their choice of shirts in the video.

West End Girls
Pet Shop Boys

Released November 1985
EMI America *8307* (U.S. #1) / Parlophone *R 6115* (U.K. #1)

Pet Shop Boys frontman Neil Tennant worked for U.K. pop-music magazine Smash Hits (and, previously, for Marvel Comics) when he met future musical partner Chris Lowe in an equipment shop. The training in superheroes and teen idols was good for the duo, as their first single, 'West End Girls' (originally recorded by New York producer Bobby Orlando), eventually connected its charisma with a worldwide audience.

The song has disparate influences: Tennant's rap-like delivery and relative grittiness was inspired by 'The Message,' the raw hip-hop song about oppressive conditions in the Bronx by Grandmaster Flash & The Furious Five, and The Waste Land, a poem by T.S. Eliot. American gangster films also contributed to the vibe, but the lyrics dealt with the seediness of London's East End and the interaction of its ruffians with ladies from the posh West End.

After good club reaction but poor chart action, the song was reworked a year later by producer Stephen Hague, who lightened the Communist references, fattened up the sounds, and gave it an overall polish. The second time proved to be the charm: Hague's version shot to the top of the charts in America and in Britain, where 'West End Girls' was the first of four Number 1 hits from the album *Please*. The song's title has since inspired the names of at least two bands and a television show, and a steady stream of remixes has helped keep this dance classic alive in the clubs. It was crowned best song of the decade 1985-94 at the Ivor Novello awards, ahead of shortlisted singles by U2, Robert Palmer, Radiohead, and Massive Attack.

Kiss
Prince & The Revolution

Released February 1986
Paisley Park *28751* (U.S. #1) / Paisley Park *W 8751* (U.K. #6)

Manic Monday
The Bangles
Released January 1986
Columbia *05757* (U.S. #2) / CBS *A 6796* (U.K. #2)

Sign 'O' The Times
Prince
Released March 1987
Paisley Park *28399* (U.S. #3) / Paisley Park *W 8399* (U.K. #10)

Others might lay claim to having sold more records, but nobody wrote and recorded as many classic singles of the 1980s as Prince. 'Kiss' was the last of his great hits with his original backing group, The Revolution, while 'Sign 'O' The Times' marked the start of a new self-reliant and socially conscious phase of his career. He also provided the launching pad for another of the most successful acts of the late 1980s, The Bangles, when he wrote 'Manic Monday' for the all-girl quartet.

By 1986, Prince had reached the top of his game, both artistically and commercially, following a string of hit singles and albums that included '1999,' 'Little Red Corvette,' *Purple Rain*, and 'Raspberry Beret.' This remarkable run of success seemed to do nothing to dull his creativity or his perfectionism: he was never completely happy with 'Kiss,' and first gave it to the group Mazarati to record. On hearing their minimalist rendition, Prince realized the true worth of the song, claimed it back, and to the Mazarati recording added his own lead vocal and a stark acoustic guitar part.

The result is one of the finest songs in Prince's oeuvre and, like the earlier landmark single 'When Doves Cry,' another of his bass-less wonders: somehow, by removing the low-end, he managed to make it even funkier. Although 'Kiss' is credited to Prince & The Revolution, his backing band are missing in action, replaced by a simple drum-machine pattern and a subtle keyboard part. 'Kiss' quickly rose to Number 1 in the U.S., where it remained for three weeks, holding another Prince composition, 'Manic Monday' by The Bangles, off the top spot.

The Bangles had formed in 1982 as a garage-rock trio consisting of vocalist Susanna Hoffs and sisters Vicki and Debbi Peterson on guitar and drums. Despite adding a bassist, Micki Steele, and smoothing out the rough edges of their sound, the group struggled to crack the pop market with their full-length debut album, *All Over The Place* (1985). That soon changed when Prince – masquerading as 'Christopher' – donated this sure-fire hit, a knowing update of the classic Mamas & The Papas hit 'Monday Monday.' (Rumors that he gave up this instant classic – rather than record it himself – because of his interest in Hoffs have never been substantiated.)

'Manic Monday' soon climbed to Number 2 in Britain and America and propelled The Bangles' sophomore album, *Different Light*, into the upper reaches of the album charts on both sides of the Atlantic. After the lesser 'If She Knew What She Wants' came the group's first U.S. Number 1, 'Walk Like An Egyptian' – an irresistible novelty hit written by Liam Sternberg, who also wrote the theme to *21 Jump Street*. Several further memorable Bangles singles followed, including a cover of Simon

& Garfunkel's 'Hazy Shade Of Winter' and the transatlantic chart-topper 'Eternal Flame,' but nothing ever quite matched 'Manic Monday.'

Meanwhile, Prince spent most of the rest of 1986 touring with a stripped-down band in support of *Parade*, the album that included 'Kiss.' At the end of the year he started work on his epic, state-of-the-nation double album, *Sign 'O' The Times*. It was the first of his LPs since 1981's *Controversy* to be recorded without The Revolution and introduced a more refined, serious Prince sound.

The album's first single and title track is as stark musically as 'Kiss' – the bass is back, but there is little more alongside it than a drum-machine pulse and occasional snatches of guitar and keyboard. Prince constructed most of the music using the revolutionary Fairlight CMI synthesizer, which had become something of a holy grail for forward-thinking musicians in the 1980s, among them Kate Bush and Peter Gabriel.

'Sledgehammer,' which he described as "an attempt to re-create some of the spirit and style of the music that most excited me as a teenager – 1960s soul," was the first public unveiling of the new policy. Collins, of course, wasn't averse to remodeling 1960s soul styles for fun and profit, but where Collins favored Motown, Gabriel's inspiration was clearly the funkier, horn-driven grit of Stax. "Obviously there was a lot of sexual metaphor there," he explained. "I was trying to write in the old blues tradition, much of which is preoccupied with mating activities."

The song would have fared well on its own merits, but Gabriel's insurance policy came in the form of an innovative video helmed by young director Stephen R. Johnson, using a revolutionary new stop-motion technique that made real people appear to have been animated. Filmed over eight days at the famed Aardman studios in Bristol, England, the video immediately went into heavy rotation on MTV, propelling 'Sledgehammer' irresistibly to Number 1 on the *Billboard* chart. The accompanying album, *So*, quickly turned platinum, and on September 17, 1987, Johnson's video swept the board at the MTV Awards, winning in half of the 20 award categories.

Where 'Kiss' was a joyous, sexually charged affair, 'Sign 'O' The Times' is a doomy tirade against the dangers of drugs and the spread of AIDS – and is perhaps Prince's finest ever lyric. Despite its uncomfortable subject matter, the single soon climbed into the British and American Top 10s. It remains one of its creator's most important statements. Prince's purple period continued through to the end of the 1980s with further notable singles such as 'If I Was Your Girlfriend,' 'Alphabet St.,' and 'Batdance.'

Addicted To Love
Robert Palmer

Released March 1986
Island *99570* (U.S. #1) / Island *IS 270* (U.K. #5)

"We wanted to form the ultimate rock band," Duran Duran's John Taylor said with massive arrogance about his liaison in The Power Station with Robert Palmer. Yes, there was a time when Palmer's trebly, unthreatening pop was regarded as rock – in a kind of ageing-Lothario, upbeat-Bryan Ferry way. Surprisingly, 'Addicted To Love' is a credible supporting argument for these rock credentials, with the stop-start riff behind "You're gonna have to face it…" a triumphant live moment. The synth-brass sounds tinny today, and the video – featuring a bevy of guitar-playing ladies – is ludicrous rather than iconic, but the song's attractive, infectious qualities are still strong.

Sledgehammer
Peter Gabriel

Released April 1986
Geffen *28718* (U.S. #1) / Virgin *PGS 1* (U.K. #4)

For over two decades, as the frontman of Genesis and as a solo performer, Peter Gabriel's brilliance attracted massive critical acclaim without riches to match. In 1986, perhaps spurred by the solo success of Phil Collins, his replacement in Genesis, Gabriel made a conscious decision to become as successful as he was admired.

Take My Breath Away
Berlin

Released July 1986
Columbia *05903* (U.S. #1) / CBS *A 7320* (U.K. #1)

Veteran producers Giorgio Moroder and Tom Whitlock crafted this smoldering tune for Berlin, a Southern California band with a Teutonic name. Many will remember it as the theme to *Top Gun*, which starred Tom Cruise and Kelly McGillis in a romance taking flight. 'Take My Breath Away' helped propel sales in excess of one million copies for the *Top Gun* soundtrack, became an international hit, and earned both the Oscar and the Golden Globe Award for Best Song. Pop singer Jessica Simpson took the song back to the top of the charts in America when she covered it in 2004.

The Final Countdown
Europe

Released October 1986
Epic *06416* (U.S. #8) / Epic *A 7127* (U.K. #1)

With 'The Final Countdown' causing endless confusion in non-music media for years after its release – was it rock? was it metal? was it pop? – you'd be forgiven for thinking that the Swedish quintet responsible might wish to escape their best-known song. Not at all: Europe – now a laughing-stock in the U.K. but huge in their home country and Germany – released a whole album of songs featuring the parping synth horns of 'The Final Countdown' and even went so far as releasing a pre-millennium remix of the tune in late 1999. It's rock, Jim, but not as we know it.

RICK RUBIN: REVERED FOR RIFF AND RHYME

Jewish New Yorker Rick Rubin (born in 1963) reshaped the hip-hop and metal scenes several times over before settling into comfortable all-round maverick status in his middle age, and is the most influential producer on the American rock scene. Hiding behind a massive beard and shades, Rubin cultivates the appearance of an impassive guru – which makes it all the more remarkable that he started out as a classic rock nerd, citing Led Zeppelin as a big early influence.

Rubin made his first inroads into the record industry when he set up the Def Jam hip-hop label in 1984 with his college friend Russell Simmons. Their first big act was Run-DMC, led by Simmons's brother Joseph, but even this band was eclipsed by the enormous success of The Beastie Boys, a white Jewish act who performed rocked-up hip-hop. The combination of riff and rhyme was key to much 1980s rock, with Rubin crossing another boundary when he produced Slayer's colossal *Reign In Blood* album in 1986, acknowledged by many as the finest thrash-metal record ever made.

Rubin continued to work with Slayer, Danzig, and other moshers into the 1990s, but took a further step into godhood when he hooked up with The Red Hot Chili Peppers for their epoch-defining *Blood Sugar Sex Magik* LP in 1991. Landmark recordings with a revitalized Neil Diamond and with Johnny Cash, just before the legendary singer's death, as well as enormous success with the alt.metal band System Of A Down, ensured that Rubin's legacy is now set in stone. He remains one of the industry's most revered figures.

Walk This Way
Run-DMC

Released July 1986
Profile *5112* (U.S. #4) / London *LON 104* (U.K. #8)

The original version of 'Walk This Way' appeared on Aerosmith's 1975 album *Toys In The Attic*, reaching the American Top 10 as a single upon its re-release the following year. But the song's true potential was realized nearly a decade after its initial showing when it became the inspiration for a rap song from an upstart trio from Queens, New York City.

Run-DMC's DJ, Jam Master Jay, often created an instrumental version of 'Walk This Way' by cutting back and forth between two vinyl copies so that MCs Run and DMC could rhyme over the top. Def Jam's Rick Rubin, business partner of Run's brother Russell Simmons, suggested that Run-DMC release a single based on Aerosmith's original cut. It turned into a winner for Aerosmith as well as Run-DMC. Aerosmith's career was revitalized in the process, creating a second wind that helped sail the band towards at least another 20 years of multi-platinum success.

The song, from Run-DMC's seminal album *Raising Hell*, is remembered fondly for its music video, which was wildly popular on MTV. Mimicking the song's obvious sound-clash between rock and hip-hop, the video finds Run-DMC jamming in their own, enclosed room until the wall comes tumbling down at the behest of Aerosmith's Steven Tyler and Joe Perry.

Even 20 years later, artists and record company executives were still trying to recapture the magic of this merged-genres idea, but few have come close to the synergy of 'Walk This Way.'

Rock Me Amadeus
Falco

Released February 1986
A&M *2821* (U.S. #1) / A&M *AM 278* (U.K. #1)

Recorded by a quirky Austrian singer-songwriter resolutely determined to make his original mark on the international pop landscape, 'Rock Me Amadeus' stands as the only song in history sung in German that topped the charts in both the U.S. and Britain. For the lighthearted and colorful video, which was an MTV staple, Falco donned a powdered wig in tribute to his favorite original classical composer. It's true that Wolfgang Amadeus Mozart was never a rock star, but this rousing ditty did its part to immortalize him in a very 1980s way.

Venus
Banarama

Released May 1986
London *886056* (U.S. #1) / London *NANA 10* (U.K. #8)

Already a regular fixture on the Top 10 in their native U.K., Banarama were transformed into international superstars by the production trio Stock Aitken & Waterman, who worked their magic on over 200 British hits between the mid 1980s and the early 1990s. 'Venus' was originally a U.S. chart-topper in 1970 for the Dutch rock band Shocking Blue, but in the hands of S/A/W became a brash, glossy pop hit. The single's key element is the suspended chord with which it opens (and to which it periodically breaks down), which provided an effortless hands-in-the-air moment for clubgoers. The bass may now sound a little tacky, and the super-busy drum pattern is somewhat distracting, but perfect pop doesn't come much more perfect than this.

Nasty
Janet Jackson

Released May 1986
A&M *2830* (U.S. #3) / A&M *AM 316* (U.K. #19)

The youngest Jackson grew up in a show-business family and had been around the cameras since she was a small child, but her 1986 album *Control*, buoyed by this shockingly rebellious hit, marked Janet's coming-out party and launched her into the world of superstardom. 'Nasty' earned the American Music Award for Favorite Soul/R&B Single in 1987. That same year, Paula Abdul grabbed the MTV Video Music Award for Best Choreography for her work on the popular 'Nasty' video. Abdul would go on to enjoy her own relatively fruitful pop career, and later hosted the smash TV show *American Idol*.

The Lady In Red
Chris de Burgh

Released July 1986
A&M *2848* (U.S. #3) / A&M *AM 331* (U.K. #1)

Take a soupy bassline by Pino Palladino, a wash of smooth synth chords, and a rimshot-based drum pattern, add the happily-married musings of a blandly contented rocker on a day off, and you have the makings of a hugely successful suppertime love classic. Universally vilified by critics

who really should know better, 'Lady In Red' is a success because it links a popular activity – looking at a pretty female – with a spine-chilling vocal melody. All in all, it's hard to argue with a song that topped the charts in 25 countries and remains, to this day, one of the most instantly recognizable love songs of all time.

Don't Get Me Wrong
The Pretenders

Released October 1986
Sire *28630* (U.S. #10) / Real *YZ 85* (U.K. #10)

A breeze through some of Chrissie Hynde's most optimistic sentiments, the unforgettable 'Don't Get Me Wrong' – with its gorgeous ascending title melody – seems at first to be a long way from The Pretenders' punk roots. But then you recall that the group began their recording career with a cover of The Kinks' 'Stop Your Sobbing' – swiftly followed by the catchy pop hooks of Hynde's own 'Kid' and 'Brass In Pocket' – and you're left with the distinct impression that behind all the mid-1970s punk snarl was a songwriter whose sympathies lay more with Joe Jackson than Joe Strummer.

You Give Love A Bad Name
Bon Jovi

Released August 1986
Mercury *884953* (U.S. #1) / Vertigo *VER 26* (U.K. #14)

'You Give Love A Bad Name' is the ultimate fist-pumping rock anthem, and the first of Bon Jovi's four U.S. Number 1 hits. It also marked the start of the New Jersey quintet's collaborations with songwriter Desmond Childs, who helped bring the group's pop sensibilities to the fore, and in the process turning a reasonably successful rock act into international superstars. (He has also given the same treatment to Aerosmith, Alice Cooper, and Ricky Martin.) While it's easy now to mock the big hair and spandex outfits, it's hard to find fault with Bon Jovi's mix of hard-rock guitars and singalong choruses – a winning combination that made them one of the most successful bands of the 1980s.

Bad
Michael Jackson

Released September 1987
Epic *07418* (U.S. #1) / Epic *651155* (U.K. #3)

When it was time for Michael Jackson's first release since *Thriller*, the pressure was on for it to be equal to or better than that blockbuster hit. 'Bad' was conceived as a collaboration with Prince, but that didn't happen, and fans embraced the new record even as they were perplexed by Jackson's continually changing appearance. His skin appeared lighter and his nose more sculpted. What had been a rather cuddly persona on the *Thriller* album had also changed: 'Bad' is Jackson in unabashedly confrontational mode.

The public already knew from epics such as 'Thriller' that Jackson simply does not do small video productions. So it wasn't a great shock when he enlisted top director Martin Scorcese (*Taxi Driver*, *Raging Bull*) to create the video for 'Bad,' a choreographed fight dance in a New York subway station that features future movie star Wesley Snipes. The clip runs to 17 minutes (more than four times longer than the average music video) and was filmed in black-and-white as well as color. The video featured in a highly anticipated network television premiere, broadcast to millions of viewers.

Weird Al Yankovic, no stranger to lampooning Jackson, then presented 'Fat,' his parody of 'Bad' that grabbed the Grammy in 1988 for Best Concept Video. Miami rapper Trina later made a tribute to Jackson with 'Da Baddest Bitch,' a song (with an album of the same name) that used 'Bad' as part of its backing track, veering into the brazenly sexual territory to which Jackson could only hint coyly in his original.

Nothing's Gonna Stop Us Now
Starship

Released February 1987
Grunt *5109* (U.S. #1) / Grunt *FB 49757* (U.K. #1)

Starship was a descendent of the legendary San Francisco rock band named first Jefferson Airplane, then Jefferson Starship, and, following a legal dispute with founding (and parting) member Paul Kantner, simply Starship. After waning popularity over the course of 20 or more years, the group had two surprise Number 1 hits in 1985 ('We Built This City' and 'Sara') and two years later followed up with 'Nothing's Gonna Stop Us Now.' It was the last chart-topper in the fruitful and influential musical career of singer Grace Slick, who harmonizes beautifully with co-lead singer Mickey Thomas on this memorable power ballad.

I Wanna Dance With Somebody (Who Loves Me)
Whitney Houston

Released May 1987
Arista *9598* (U.S. #1) / Arista *RIS 1* (U.K. #1)

The boppy 'I Wanna Dance With Somebody' was the first single from Houston's sophomore album, *Whitney*, coming at the heels of an astounding debut that has since sold in excess of 24 million units and earned the elusive Diamond certification (for sales over ten million). The vibrant song was prepared to weather such pressure and break some new ground of its own for the singer. It went to Number 1 in five countries and remains a snapshot of the singer in the happiest and seemingly most innocent presentation of her public persona.

When Smokey Sings
ABC

Released May 1987
Mercury *888604* (U.S. #5) / Neutron *NT 111* (U.K. #11)

ABC executed a mid-career change of direction with this deft homage to Smokey Robinson, refining the sub-James Bond, sub-New Romantic pop with which they had peaked so perfectly on 'The Look Of Love' and 'Poison Arrow.' Aside from vocalist Martin Fry's Motown-style harmonies and the title, there was very little that was consciously retro about the song. Slickly emitted by a band who had mastered the art of late-1980s pop, 'When Smokey Sings' was the perfect disco anthem – piano flourishes and all. It's no surprise, then, to learn that this instant-classic single was co-produced by Chic's Bernard Edwards.

Pump Up The Volume
M/A/R/R/S

Released August 1987
4th & Broadway *7452* (U.S. #13) / 4AD *AD 70* (U.K. #1)

When AR Kane and Colourbox renamed themselves M/A/R/R/S for a one-off recording project in 1987, the result was the unexpectedly successful 'Pump Up The Volume,' a piano, beatbox, and bassline composition of indeterminate structure that appeared in a multitude of remixes for various geographic regions. The song became famous on two counts: first, because it was reportedly the first U.K. chart-topper to contain samples; second, because one of those samples was an audio snippet from 'Roadblock' by Stock Aitken Waterman.

In fact, the song is less important than the impact it made on the record-buying public and the music industry. It demonstrated that sampling technology had evolved to the point where stealing other people's sounds could be a chart-topping stratagem – and that doing so could lead to a whole swathe of musicians, producers, lawyers, and accountants simultaneously frothing at the mouth about the possibility of their property being swiped. This proved significant when S.A.W. successfully sued M/A/R/S for infringement of copyright, forcing the band to remove the offending sample from later pressings of the single.

Within a couple of months, the sampling trend began to expand dramatically as musicians discovered the possibilities that the idea offered. Add this to the arrival of hip-hop and house music, which was almost entirely digital (or at least machine-based) in its production, and the potential represented by 'Pump Up The Volume' becomes clear. Music was becoming virtual, and songs such as this one told us all about that new fact.

Push It
Salt-n-Pepa

Released December 1987
Next Plateau *315* (U.S. #19) / ffrr *FFR 2* (U.K. #2)

The misleadingly named Salt-n-Pepa – there were actually three of them – was the first female hip-hop act of note. Cheryl 'Salt' James and Sandy 'Pepa' Denton worked together in a Sears department store in Queens, New York City, before scoring an underground hit with their 1985 debut single 'The Show Stopper' (a response to Doug E. Fresh and Slick Rick's 'The Show'). By the time they cut their first full-length album, *Hot, Cool & Vicious*, the group also included DJ Pamela Green, while the bulk of the trio's songs were written by James's boyfriend, Hurby 'Luv Bug' Azor, a fledgling record producer.

Hot, Cool & Vicious spawned three minor chart hits: 'My Mike Sounds Nice,' 'Chick On The Side,' and a cover of Otis & Carla's 1960s-soul classic 'Tramp.' 'Push It' originally existed as the B-side of 'Tramp,' but the version that became Salt-n-Pepa's mainstream breakthrough was in fact a remix by the San Francisco-based radio DJ Cameron Paul.

Driven more by its instrumental hook than by Salt-n-Pepa's raps, 'Push It' at first sounded suspiciously like a novelty hit, but was the first of eight of the duo's singles to reach the *Billboard* Top 40. Half a decade later, after Green had been replaced by Deidre 'Spindarella' Roper, Salt-n-Pepa improved on the success of 'Push It' with 'Shoop' and 'Whatta Man' (a collaboration with another female trio, En Vogue). In doing so, they became one of only a small handful of hip-hop acts to have significant hits in both the 1980s and the '90s.

With Or Without You
U2

Released March 1987
Island *99469* (U.S. #1) / Island *IS 319* (U.K. #4)

The Joshua Tree was U2's finest moment of the 1980s, an album chock-full of big-hearted anthems that drew in fans from all districts of the rock metropolis. None came bigger or more overblown than the third track, 'With Or Without You,' the point at which for the first time producers Brian Eno and Daniel Lanois excelled themselves on behalf of the Irish quartet.

What makes this song sing with relevance is its indication – visible nowadays with the acuity of 20/20 hindsight – that the world's most earnest Christian rock band were about to undergo not one but two big changes. The fragile, surprisingly intimate two-note drone that opens the track and continues all the way to its heart-wrenching close is guitarist Edge at his understated best: remember his maxim that if you play only the root and octave of a chord, its 'sex' – major or minor – remains hidden, allowing all kinds of expansion.

Bono's lyrics are powerful and his vocals are by turns keening and emotional, allowing the song to build and build until – at last – the old lantern-jawed U2 we know from the days of *War* and *Boy* reveals itself. With this kind of disguised rocking-out hidden for so long before exposing itself, we can foresee that Bono and his chums were paying serious attention to the question of their own identity.

Of course, we know now that they took the issue a long way, morphing into a faux blues-soul act for the utterly pretentious *Rattle And Hum* before spreading their wings to achieve full potential as a self-aware act of great sophistication, post-*Achtung Baby*. 'With Or Without You' is the sound of the first steps in that process.

La Bamba
Los Lobos

Released July 1987
Slash *28336* (U.S. #1) / Slash *LASH 13* (U.K. #1)

Throwing R&B, soul, Tex-Mex, and traditional Latin music into their songs with infectious enthusiasm, Los Angeles quintet Los Lobos (it means The Wolves) had been gigging for a decade before their smash hit. 'La Bamba' was an old Ritchie Valens song covered for the new *La Bamba* movie.

The film could have been cheesy, but it covered serious topics, namely the short life and tragic death of Valens, who was only 17 when he died in a plane crash along with Buddy Holly and the Big Bopper. It caught the attention of cinema fans, and the associated soundtrack was a hit, led off by this song.

The flavor of the tune, in line with Valens's status as the first Mexican-American rock star, is entirely Latin, with squealing horns, Spanish-sounding guitar riff, frantic percussion, and of course the stop-start call of the title phrase that makes it so memorable. Nowadays, the song evokes the atmosphere of a Mexican restaurant in a dull city suburb, but back in 1987 it provided a distinctly exotic vibe when it landed in the charts and became deservedly popular on radio.

(You Gotta) Fight For Your Right (To Party!)
Beastie Boys

Released January 1987
Def Jam *06595* (U.S. #7) / Def Jam *650418* (U.K. #11)

With a name using an acronym that only the most die-hard fans know means "Boys Entering Anarchistic States Towards Inner Excellence," the Big Apple trio known as Beastie Boys hold the most excellent distinction of having the first Number 1 rap album in America (although at the time their white skin made them targets of criticism for participating in a largely black genre).

Producer Rick Rubin, who had released their AC/DC-sampling 'She's On It' for the *Krush Groove* movie soundtrack, had signed The Beastie Boys – resident New Yorkers Michael 'Mike D' Diamond, Adam 'MCA' Yauch, and Adam 'Ad-Rock' Horovitz – to his young record label Def Jam. The runaway success of *Licensed To Ill*, which spent five weeks in the top slot, was unquestionably buoyed by the anthemic '(You Gotta) Fight For Your Right (To Party!).'

'Fight For Your Right' is a more than convincing parody of the type of beer-soaked, panty-raiding rock jam that rules fraternity houses and dingy bars alike, all power guitar chords and messily shouted chorus. The three Beasties had prior experience with hardcore punk bands (including Ad-Rock's stint in the memorably named The Young & The Useless), so they drew upon their roots in thrashing rock for this novelty hit. An appropriately hedonistic video for the song, depicting the party that is every suburban parent's worst nightmare, made new MTV stars out of the Boys, and the band would evolve its image over the next several years through the lens of the music network.

98

Los Lobos saw their career plateau after 'La Bamba,' and they would never equal it commercially. However they remain a respected club-level draw, with a Spanish-speaking audience that seems certain to provide the group with a fanbase as long as they choose to continue.

I Think We're Alone Now
Tiffany

Released September 1987
MCA *53167* (U.S. #1) / MCA *1211* (U.K. #1)

Foolish Beat
Debbie Gibson

Released April 1988
Atlantic *89109* (U.S. #1) / Atlantic *A 9059* (U.K. #9)

Formulas for pop success are many and varied. Among the most consistently lucrative is the Svengali-like manipulation of the limited vocal talents of pretty teenage girls. From Marianne Faithfull to Kylie Minogue and beyond, there always seem to be older, wiser music-biz professionals lurking in the background – almost invariably men.

Producer George Tobin, a graduate of the Brill Building, heard big-voiced 12-year-old Tiffany sing while she was recording demos in his San Fernando Valley studio. Two years later, he advised her to record 'I Think We're Alone Now,' a 1960s smash for Tommy James & The Shondells. Tiffany didn't like the song but, persuaded by Tobin, she let him record the musical tracks over which she laid her vocal. The magic worked and the song, despite Tiffany's wobbly vocals, became an international success.

Sometimes, however, what you see isn't what it seems. Just as Tiffany hit Number 1, another pretty and precocious teen, Debbie Gibson, was notching up her second U.S. Top 5 hit, 'Shake Your Love.' Inevitably, the pair became locked in a media-inspired battle for the title of America's teen pop queen. In reality they were worlds apart. Gibson wrote her first song at the age of four, won a $1,000 prize in a songwriting contest at 12, and composed, recorded, and produced her own material, including 'Foolish Beat,' which became her first U.S. Number 1.

Both girls notched up sizeable strings of hits, leading Carole King, whose career straddled both the Brill Building and the singer-songwriter eras, to single them out as "artists of the MTV generation who have also accumulated years as they accumulate success."

left > Teen idol Debbie Gibson strikes a pose in a New York diner at the height of her fame.
above right > Los Lobos.
opposite > Left to right: Mike D, Ad Rock, and MCA of the Beastie Boys on stage in New York in 1987.

Dude (Looks Like A Lady)
Aerosmith

Released October 1987
Geffen *28240* (U.S. #14) / Geffen *GEF 29* (U.K.)

Given the apparently homophobic tendencies that Middle America has been known to exhibit, a song called 'Dude (Looks Like A Lady)' might be a startling title for a hit. But it's helmed by the veteran rockers Aerosmith, who with this song proved that folks listen to lyrics just a little bit less than they do a massively rockin' guitar riff. The song, from the group's *Permanent Vacation* album, also resurfaced on the soundtrack for the 1993 movie *Wayne's World 2*. Aerosmith appeared in this sequel to the blockbuster comedy starring Mike Myers and Dana Carvey, a spin-off from the popular *Saturday Night Live* sketch.

Heaven Is A Place On Earth
Belinda Carlisle

Released October 1987
MCA *53181* (U.S. #1) / Virgin *VS 1036* (U.K. #1)

After multi-platinum success fronting the fierce female rock group The Go-Gos, the charismatic Belinda Carlisle ventured out and continued on her own. She surprised and delighted an international audience with this first single, a singalong tune decidedly more pop-orientated than the group's heavy beats and strumming guitars. While the meteoric rise of 'Heaven' promised a skyscraping career for Carlisle, it would later prove to be the zenith of her solo years. It is possible to look at this positively: otherwise, Carlisle may never have reunited later with The Go-Gos.

Don't Dream It's Over
Crowded House

Released February 1987
Capitol *5614* (U.S. #2) / Capitol *CL 438* (U.K. #27)

Crowded House, born after the 1984 dissolution of Split Enz, a cult favorite Australian rock act that featured New Zealand-born brothers Neil and Tim Finn, became one of the most successful international bands that either of those countries have produced. Guitarist Neil Finn enlisted Split Enz drummer Paul Hester, bassist Nick Seymour, and guitarist Craig Hooper to form a new band called The Mullanes. They secured a record deal, moved way out to Los Angeles (without Hooper), and soon changed their name to Crowded House, reflecting the cozy new conditions they encountered in California.

'Don't Dream It's Over' keenly captures the tough exterior and tender interior of a great rock ballad, with a wonderfully rousing chorus and substantive lyrics. With a lack of gimmickry and no dramatic stories of rock-star type hedonism with which to promote the band, Crowded House took this simply sweet song to the upper reaches of the American pop charts in a surprise maneuver.

In 1987, 'Don't Dream It's Over' won the MTV Video Music Award for Video of the Year; Crowded House also took home a moon-man statuette for Best New Artist. The band followed up with another hit in 'Something So Strong' and would record for a further ten years (later, significantly, with brother Tim Finn). But nothing reached the same heights of 'Don't Dream It's Over,' the song that holds firm in its place as an all-time Crowded House favorite.

The One I Love
R.E.M.

Released September 1987
IRS *53171* (U.S. #9) / IRS *IRM 46* (U.K.)

Despite its apparently good natured title, R.E.M.'s breakthrough single is a moody dismissal of an ex-lover. Previously, the Athens, Georgia, quartet had barely scraped into the *Billboard* Hot 100, their highest chart success being 'Radio Free Europe,' which had peaked at a lowly 78. Perhaps most listeners didn't notice the sardonic mockery in Michael Stipe's voice, or perhaps they didn't care and were swayed instead by the jangling guitars and Mike Mills's harmonic backing vocals. Whatever the reason, 'The One I Love' set R.E.M. on the way to becoming one of the biggest groups of the subsequent decade.

Fairytale Of New York
The Pogues featuring Kirsty MacColl

Released November 1987
Not issued U.S. / Pogue Mahone *NY 7* (U.K. #2)

'Fairytale Of New York' is one of the most unusual, not to mention one of the best, festive hits in the history of the British singles chart. It arrived in the middle of an unexpected period of commercial success for The Pogues, an unruly bunch of Irishmen who mixed punk and traditional Celtic folk to great effect.

Much of The Pogues' finest work features a female counterpoint to gin-soaked frontman Shane McGowan, and this single is no exception. In the group's first few years, McGowan's foil was bassist and backing vocalist Cate O'Riordan, but she departed in 1986 after marrying Elvis Costello (they met when he produced The Pogues' seminal *Rum, Sodomy, And The Lash* album). Here that role is played by Kirsty MacColl, who had previously charted twice as a solo artist in the U.K. with the endearingly idiosyncratic 'There's A Guy Works Down The Chipshop Swears He's Elvis' (1981) and 'A New England' (1985).

'Fairytale Of New York' begins as a wistful, piano-led ballad before launching into a celebratory jig, which peaks when McGowan and MacColl begin to trade playful insults. Most memorable is the couplet: "Happy Christmas your arse / I pray God it's our last." Unlike most other holiday hits, which tend towards phony, cloying sentimentality, the feelings behind this single are genuine and easy to relate to. But it was still a surprise to most – perhaps even The Pogues themselves – when it climbed to Number 2 on the U.K. chart. The only thing more surprising was the appearance of Brat Pack actor Matt Dillon in the accompanying promo video, playing a policeman who pushes McGowan – in a shopping cart! – around New York City.

left > Kirsty MacColl joins The Pogues for a performance of 'Fairytale Of New York' on the group's December 1988 tour of the U.K.

I Should Be So Lucky
Kylie Minogue

Released January 1988
Geffen *27922* (U.S. #28) / PWL *8* (U.K. #1)

Especially For You
Kylie Minogue & Jason Donovan

Released December 1988
Not issued U.S. / PWL *24* (U.K. #1)

These two records illustrate how far Kylie Minogue's star rose in the space of 12 months. When the actress from the Australian soap *Neighbours* first materialized in the studio of Matt Aitken and Mike Stock in 1987, she found that the duo had never heard of her and had not even been told of her appointment. The pair proceeded to knock together a song for her in the space of 20 minutes. Aitken wanted to give her a Bananarama reject; Stock said that she should be so lucky to receive one of their seconds. With the phrase amended, a song about a girl lamenting her mediocre love-life was born. Its breathless peppiness and Minogue's celebrity kept it at Number 1 in Britain for five weeks.

Come 1988, not only had the pair given Minogue three more U.K. Top 5s, but also they had created a chart career for her *Neighbours* co-star Jason Donovan. There were no plans to record a duet with the two until a zealous Woolworths buyer, erroneously informed that they planned a joint single, ordered 400,000 copies.

STOCK AITKEN & WATERMAN SHOULD BE SO LUCKY

There was a dichotomy about Mike Stock, Matt Aitken, and Pete Waterman. Many critics seemed to despise their music – but the millions upon millions of people who bought the records clearly loved them. The statistics speak for themselves: the trio wrote and/or produced around 70 Top 20 U.K. hits in the space of eight years.

So how do we explain these extremes of love and hate? A big factor is that the three men – billed on their records as Stock/Aitken/Waterman and often referred to in print as S/A/W – were part of a new breed of songwriter. Modern technology enabled them to spurn the use of session musicians. Playing all the instruments they could manage, and using sequencers and synthesizers for the rest, they made their singles remarkably quickly. This also engendered a certain sameness, as well as a high-pitched, glaring sonic quality that for many summed up the emptiness and trashiness of the 1980s.

Pete Waterman was not a member of the writing team. Composers Mike Stock and Matt Aitken were musicians who once played in covers bands and were happy to give Waterman a third credit and (eventually) royalty on their songs, because his abilities to spot talent and make deals meant they could concentrate on writing. Early collaborations included novelty records and a Eurovision Song Contest entry for Cyprus. Hazell Dean's 'Whatever I Do (Wherever I Go)' – a British Number 4 in 1984 – was the first proper S/A/W hit, although they were happy to secure a Number 1 with Dead Or Alive's 'You Spin Me Round (Like A Record)' a few months later as mere producers. The team's further success with chanteuse Princess led the well-established girl trio Bananarama to request the services of S/A/W, who gave them a new lease on chart life that included the Top 10 U.K. hits 'Love In The First Degree' and 'I Want You Back.'

Black cockney sisters Mel & Kim were newcomers, however, and S/A/W made them famous with the sassy anthems 'Showing Out' and 'Respectable,' the latter becoming in 1987 S/A/W's first self-written chart-topper. Rick Astley – a fresh faced boy with an old man's voice – was another unknown to become a star under their aegis. He was one of the rare S/A/W American successes, scoring two Number 1s Stateside. Soon afterwards, S/A/W's Midas touch made actress Kylie Minogue the biggest selling singer in Britain.

The pivotal year was 1989. S/A/W started it with a Number 1 and closed it with the Christmas Number 1 (as producers) and Number 2, in between which had come two dozen U.K. Top 10s and half a dozen U.K. Number 1s. From that high point followed a gradual disintegration, starting with Aitken's departure from the team in 1991 and culminating in a bitter legal battle between Stock and Waterman over the latter's decision to sell the S/A/W recordings. At the time of writing it was announced that the three will be working together again. It remains to be seen whether they can pick up the thread of pure chart gold from the decade that they helped to define in Britain.

Doctorin' The Tardis
The Timelords

Released May 1988
TVT *4025* (U.S.) / KLF *003* (U.K. #1)

3:A.M. Eternal
The KLF

Released September 1989
Arista *2230* (U.S. #5) / KLF *005* (U.K. #1)

The Kopyright Liberation Front, to give it its full name, was the brainchild of Bill Drummond (who had earlier founded the Zoo record label in Liverpool, England) and Jim Cauty, a former member of Brilliant. The duo's first musical work together was an album, *1987 (What The Fuck Is Going On?)*, credited to The Justified Ancients Of Mu Mu. They chopped up – and mocked – records by artists including The Beatles, Led Zeppelin, and Abba, and the album's release was later blocked after the instigation of legal action by Abba.

Drummond and Cauty's next move was to aim a novelty hit at the top of the U.K. chart. 'Doctorin' The Tardis' was put together in a similar cut-and-paste fashion, and makes liberal use of two Gary Glitter songs – 'Rock And Roll (Part Two)' and 'Leader Of The Gang' – and the main theme to the British TV series *Dr. Who*. (Both the single's title and the alias Drummond and Cauty assumed for its release – The Timelords – refer to the long-running sci-fi show.) In a press release, Drummond described 'Doctorin' The Tardis' as "probably the most nauseating record in the world," noting that he and Cauty enjoyed "celebrating the trashier side of pop." The duo swiftly followed it with the mock how-to guidebook, *The Manual (How To Have A Number One The Easy Way)*.

Drummond and Cauty's biggest hits, however, came as The KLF around the turn of the decade. '3:A.M. Eternal' was initially issued in 1989 but didn't hit the charts until 1991. While the single hasn't aged particularly well, it does represent the cream of the contemporary U.K. house scene. It was followed by an improbable duet, 'Justified And Ancient,' recorded with "The First Lady Of Country: Tammy Wynette." All the while, Drummond and Cauty were still involved in various non-musical activities, which included sponsoring a prize for the worst British artist of the year, and – most controversially – setting fire to £1 million in banknotes, all in the name of art.

Roll With It
Steve Winwood

Released May 1988
Virgin *99326* (U.S. #1) / Virgin *VS 1085* (U.K.)

Steve Winwood is mainly remembered as the leader of the psychedelic rock group Traffic, with whom he recorded a number of hit singles and albums in the late 1960s and early 1970s. During the 1980s, however, the British singer and keyboardist carved out a new niche for himself as a solo star with a polished, soulful sound. 'Roll With It' was Winwood's second U.S. Number 1 (following 1986's 'Higher Love') and the biggest hit of his career. It was also his first single release since being tempted away from Island Records, for whom he had recorded since 1967, by a big-money deal from Virgin. Winwood's solo success started to dwindle soon afterwards, prompting him first to shrink from the media glare and then, in the mid 1990s, to return his attention to Traffic.

Never Tear Us Apart
INXS

Released June 1988
Atlantic *89038* (U.S. #7) / Mercury *INXS 11* (U.K. #24)

INXS had bigger hits, but 'Never Tear Us Apart' is arguably their finest moment, the fourth U.S. Top 10 entry from the Aussie world-beaters' multi-platinum album *Kick*. Keyboardist Andrew Farriss wrote the music in New Zealand while the rest of the band were playing tennis, but what he envisioned as an up-tempo Gene Vincent-style retro-rocker was dramatically slowed down by singer-lyricist Michael Hutchence. As a result, it presented them at their most poignantly tender, with Hutchence in fine voice, enhanced by Kirk Pengilly's haunting sax solo. At the funeral service following Hutchence's tragic death in 1997, his coffin was carried out to the sound of 'Never Tear Us Apart.'

Kokomo
The Beach Boys

Released July 1988
Capitol *69385* (U.S. #1) / Elektra *EKR 85* (U.K. #25)

When 'Kokomo' topped the charts, it was a landmark for The Beach Boys. As a group that had peaked over 20 years earlier, the song provided a fresh introduction to a generation gripped by new wave and heavy metal. The legendary group had last reached the Number 1 spot in 1966 with the Brian Wilson masterpiece 'Good Vibrations,' and indeed 'Kokomo' shared the mellifluous harmonies that are The Beach Boys' hallmark, but now spiced with some island flavor. The song, inspired by a resort in Montego Bay, Jamaica, made a filmic cameo with Tom Cruise in *Cocktail*.

Gigantic
The Pixies

Released August 1988
Not issued U.S. / 4AD *BAD 805* (U.K.)

Although it failed to chart, 'Gigantic' is a record of no small importance. While they never achieved widespread popularity at the time, Boston band The Pixies were a defining influence on many of those who followed in the late 1980s and early 1990s and have been acknowledged since as one of the most important rock groups of their time.

'Gigantic' is something of an oddity in their catalog in that it is sung by bassist Kim Deal (who tended then to go by the name Mrs. John Murphy). Most Pixies songs are front-ended by bandleader Black Francis's impassioned yelp, but here Deal offers up a smoother, softer vocal that wraps neatly around the song's four-chord riff. The other key element of 'Gigantic' is the change in dynamics from soft verse to loud chorus: less striking, perhaps, than in other Pixies songs of a similar vintage – 'Caribou,' for instance – but it was nonetheless this simple structure that provided the impetus for so many singles that followed, chief among them Nirvana's smash hit 'Smells Like Teen Spirit.'

The closest The Pixies came to a hit was when 'Planet Of Sound' scraped in at Number 27 on the U.K. chart in 1991. By that stage grunge, as it became known, was on its way to dominating the airwaves on both sides of the Atlantic, but the group that led the way was on the verge of splitting. The Pixies didn't achieve a level of commercial success to match the critical plaudits bestowed upon them until 2004, when they reformed for a world tour.

Kiss
Art Of Noise Featuring Tom Jones

Released October 1988
China *871038* (U.S. #31) / China *11* (U.K. #5)

In 1988 Tom Jones's commercial stock was low. The sometime Welsh love titan was more or less confined to Las Vegas residencies and country albums. However, during the long dark fog of near-obscurity that shrouded him post-Elvis, pre-*Reload* and indie credibility, Jones popped up on this corker of a Prince cover that made him cool again, albeit for about 20 minutes in 1988. The original clipped-funk stroke of genius was revamped and given new life courtesy of the Art Of Noise's studio technology, while Big Tom himself added some vaudeville macho-isms to the brew that made for a deserved international hit.

Sweet Child O' Mine
Guns N' Roses

Released June 1988
Geffen *27963* (U.S. #1) / Geffen *GEF 43* (U.K. #24)

Guns N' Roses were edgier and dirtier than all the tarted-up heavy metal groups that had preceded the band in Los Angeles, and they go down in history as one of the most distinctive rock bands ever to have walked the earth. GNR ferociously upped the ante for Sunset Strip debauchery with a decidedly more macho take on rock stardom than the spandex'd competition could muster. After making few waves with early singles 'It's So Easy' and 'Welcome To The Jungle' (which was later a massive hit), the mellow, almost gentle 'Sweet Child O' Mine' was the first Guns N' Roses Number 1 single and one of the best loved songs from the debut album, *Appetite For Destruction* – which, with more than 25 million copies sold (and the elusive Diamond certification in America), is one of the biggest sellers of all time.

The *Appetite* album was released in the summer of 1987 but 'Sweet Child O' Mine' wasn't a hit until 1988, demonstrating just a small piece of the longevity this album enjoyed in the popular landscape. The public loved the savage guitar grooves of Slash, the alluring, snarly warbles of wild frontman Axl Rose, and the social and pharmacological exploits of all of the band members (which, at this time, also included Duff McKagan, Izzy Stradlin, and Stephen Adler). An MTV favorite, the song earned the network's Video Music Award for Best Heavy Metal/Hard Rock Video as well as the American Music Award for Best Single Heavy Metal/Hard Rock.

Fast Car
Tracy Chapman

Released May 1988
Elektra *69412* (U.S. #6) / Elektra *EKR 73* (U.K. #5)

Tracy Chapman was born in Cleveland, Ohio, and went to university in Massachusetts, honing her performing and songwriting skills on the Boston folk circuit. She had begun writing poems and songs at the age of eight, and wrote the material on her debut album over a period of nine years. It was released in 1988 and earned excellent reviews, but the singer-songwriter was probably unprepared for the instant success she achieved with the record.

Chapman recalled that when she appeared at Nelson Mandela's 70th Birthday Concert at London's Wembley Stadium in 1988 "they didn't have a slot for me and I was kept waiting. It was just me and my acoustic guitar and I think they called me three times, hoping to put me on while the next act was getting ready." Sent back to her dressing room again, she was called out when Stevie Wonder was unable to appear after losing some computer software. It was all so sudden she had no time to feel the pressure of performing alone in front of the vast Wembley crowd and an enormous global television audience. Chapman delivered a show-stopping performance that sent her album soaring to the top of both the British and American charts.

'Fast Car' is about a couple trying to escape poverty for a better life, and would have sat well on any Bruce Springsteen album. It became the first of three hits from the album and won a Grammy award for Best Pop Vocal Performance. Chapman also won the Grammy for Best New Artist. Another of the album's highlights, 'Baby Can I Hold You,' written when she was just 18, became a huge international hit for Boyzone in early 1998.

Wild Thing
Tone Loc

Released December 1988
Delicious Vinyl *102* (U.S. #2) / Fourth & Broadway *BRW 121* (U.K. #21)

One of the most distinctive hip-hop hits of the late 1980s, 'Wild Thing' brought the deep-throated Tone Loc from underground obscurity to mainstream pop stardom in one giant leap. The record was written by Marvin Young, a.k.a. Young M.C., who went on to become a highly regarded producer and rapper in his own right, notably with his Grammy-winning single 'Bust A Move.'

'Wild Thing' was issued at the end of 1988 but didn't make it into the upper reaches of the *Billboard* chart until several months into the following year. It makes blatant – and unauthorized – use of a drum fill from Van Halen's 'Jamie's Cryin','' but the heavy-rock band didn't pursue the matter. Another hip-hop group of the time wasn't so lucky, however: the ever-controversial 2 Live Krew found themselves in a big bowl of legal hot water after taking guitar licks from Van Halen's 'Ain't Talkin' 'Bout Love' in 1989.

Tone Loc followed 'Wild Thing' with another *Billboard* Top 5 hit, 'Funky Cold Medina,' in the spring of 1989, but that was his last single of any real significance. In the 1990s he turned his attention to acting, appearing in a number of blockbuster hits, including *Heat* and *Ace Ventura: Pet Detective*.

Buffalo Stance
Neneh Cherry

Released November 1988
Virgin *99231* (U.S. #3) / Circa *YR 21* (U.K. #3)

The stepdaughter of jazz trumpeter Don Cherry, Neneh Cherry brought a tough and streetwise yet sassy and feminine vibe to 'Buffalo Stance,' an R&B song with a hip-hop swagger, back when such a thing did not exist. She performed the New York-flavored song on British TV chart show *Top Of The Pops* while pregnant, igniting a firestorm of judgment in the media. But the headstrong Cherry didn't seem to care one bit; her cut was a favorite of nightclub DJs everywhere, and even reached the top of the American dance-music chart.

Girl You Know It's True
Milli Vanilli

Released September 1988
Arista *9781* (U.S. #2) / Cooltempo *COOL 170* (U.K. #3)

High from the tremendous success of the guilty-pleasure R&B-dance hit 'Girl You Know It's True,' the duo known as Milli Vanilli won two American Music Awards, including Favorite Single Pop/Rock and Favorite New Artist. But the statuettes were returned in disgrace in a widely-broadcast press conference after it had been revealed that uncredited studio singers hired by producer Frank Farian were behind Milli Vanilli, rather than Fabrice Morvan and Rob Pilatus, the visual representation of the group. There has never been a bigger embarrassment in pop music. The scandal became comedic fodder for late-night TV and must surely have contributed to the events preceding Pilatus's suicide in 1998 at age 33.

1989

Like A Prayer
Madonna

Released March 1989
Sire *27539* (U.S. #1) / Sire *W 7539* (U.K. #1)

After five years in the charts, Madonna Louise Vernon Ciccione saw her career at a plateau. The 'shocking' sex themes she had explored in 'Like A Virgin' and the ditzy dancefloor stuff she did so well along the lines of 'Get Into The Groove' were becoming outmoded. Her enormous fanbase would require something a little more intellectually satisfying to retain their attention, and so in due course Madonna explored her troubled Catholic background with 'Like A Prayer,' a gospel workout that would have been about a tenth as controversial without its accompanying video.

Over the excellent, bouncing rhythm – bass was supplied by sessioneer extraordinaire Guy Pratt – and the soaring, uplifting gospel-choir vocals, Madonna sings out: "Just like a prayer / I'll take you there," while walking through a candlelit church. In due course she approaches the altar and kneels to pray to the figure of Jesus, eyes closed on a crucifix. And lo! After a couple of seconds, Jesus opens his eyes and, stepping down from his rather uncomfortable position, embraces Madonna passionately – which sent middle America into a froth of self-righteous horror. The fact that Jesus was played by a black actor served only to strengthen the resulting Bible Belt protests.

All these years later it seems rather harmless, especially as Madonna has now settled into an inoffensive role as lady of the manor in ye olde England. But back in 1989 it seemed as if a good deal of America expected Madonna to be struck down by a thunderbolt from above.

People Hold On
Coldcut Featuring Lisa Stansfield

Released March 1989
Tommy Boy/Warner *922848* (U.S.) / Ahead Of Our Time *CCUT 5* (U.K. #11)

Lisa Stansfield had been a presenter on a U.K. TV show that was a weekly dance party, but her career jumped when she paired up with Coldcut's Matt Black and Jonathan More to record 'People Hold On.' This jubilant party anthem, evocative of the developing house music genre of the time, landed on the group's debut album *What's That Noise?* as its highlight. Stansfield would later chart with more hits and eventually won a Brit Award (the U.K. equivalent of a Grammy) while Coldcut launched their independent record label Ninja Tune and nurtured the careers of several hip-hop and electronica artists.

Me Myself And I
De La Soul

Released April 1989
Tommy Boy *7926* (U.S. #34) / Big Life *BLR 7* (U.K. #22)

In 1989 American hip-hop was the province of scary, sweaty hood-dwellers such as Ice-T and NWA – who sold gazillions of records while threatening to beat up on you and insult your lady friend – or ridiculous party-rappers like Will Smith and M.C. Hammer, who did little other than dance inventively in large trousers. Someone clearly had to fill the gap, and while the U.K. scene soon supplied non-violent, non-trivial bands like Massive Attack and Soul II Soul, the U.S. provided the excellent De La Soul, who pioneered the 'Daisy Age' style of laidback beats and peaceful, intelligent rhymes.

Although Daisy Age was – like romo and cowbilly – an idiotic term dreamed up by some rookie journalist, it actually described the mellow, organic vibe of De La Soul's tunes rather well. Laying out their wares

with their debut single 'Me Myself And I' were the New York trio of Kelvin 'Posdnuos' Mercer, David 'Trugoy The Dove' Jolicoeur, and Vincent 'Maseo' Mason. They smothered the tasty samples and relaxed, unhurried beats with a conversational rapping style that drew its inspiration from nursery-rhyme surrealism and everyday observations rather than the bloody confrontations that illustrated the gangsta-rappers' work so vividly. They spoke too of black power and traditional relaxants such as marijuana, but without the penetrating, aggressive overtones that would populate albums by Dr Dre and Ice Cube.

Life for De La Soul was, you inferred from their music, about taking it easy rather than getting annoyed, and perhaps that is the reason why the public on both sides of the Atlantic took to them so readily.

Back To Life
Soul II Soul

Released June 1989
Virgin *99171* (U.S. #4) / 10-Virgin *TEN 265* (U.K. #1)

Londoner Jazzie B's collective of singers, musicians, and dancers made an international splash with this Caron Wheeler-fronted groove where Wheeler's tuneful vocals provide the perfect foil to the propulsive dance beats and soaring strings. Along with 'Keep On Movin',' the song is a highlight of Soul II Soul's debut album *Club Classics Vol. One*. The album title turned out to be an apt prediction for these Soul II Soul songs, particularly 'Back To Life,' which was later covered most notably by American R&B star Mary J. Blige and sampled by British electronica producer Wookie.

Soul II Soul continued to release albums and singles until 1995, but were never able to match the success of 'Back To Life.' The group's Nellee Hooper, though, has since carved out a niche as one the most acclaimed producers of recent times. His CV includes such high-profile acts as U2, Björk, Madonna, and Gwen Stefani, as well as a BAFTA Award – the British equivalent of an Oscar – for his work on the soundtrack to Baz Luhrmann's cinematic adaptation of *Romeo And Juliet*.

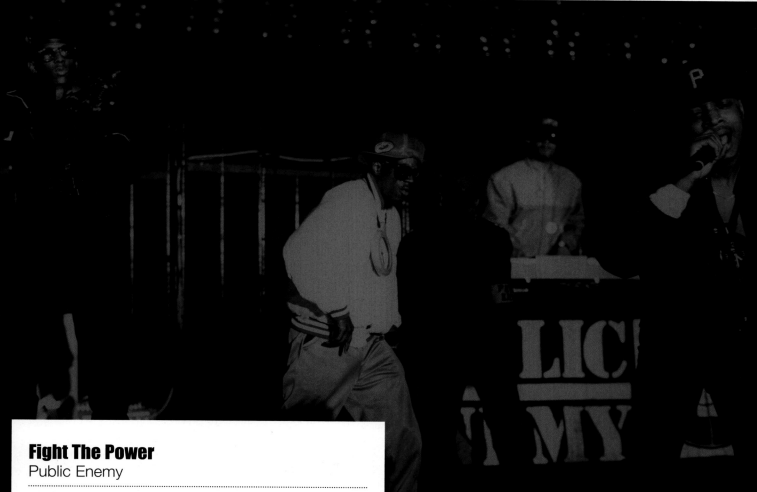

Fight The Power
Public Enemy

Released June 1989
Motown *MOT 4647* (U.S.) / Motown *ZB 42877* (U.K. #29)

The most important rap group of all time reached their apex with this era-defining single, which featured on the soundtrack to Spike Lee's similarly pivotal *Do The Right Thing*. The seeds of Public Enemy were sown in the early 1980s when rapper Chuck D and Hank Shocklee, leader of a local DJ crew, started performing regularly on a New York radio show hosted by Bill Stephney. Stephney became the group's publicist, while Shocklee formed a production team, The Bomb Squad, with his brother Keith and Eric 'Vietnam' Sadler. From the start, the membership of Public Enemy was closer to that of a political organization than a regular group. Next to join was a second rapper, Flavor Flav, DJ Terminator X, and 'Minister Of Information' Professor Griff.

The group launched in full force in 1987 with a debut album, *Yo! Bumrush The Show* on the influential Def Jam label, home to Run DMC. A year later Public Enemy unleashed *It Takes A Nation Of Millions To Hold Us Back* – regularly cited as the greatest hip-hop album ever – and its resplendent singles 'Bring The Noise' and 'Don't Believe The Hype.'

Borrowing its title from a 1975 Isley Brothers hit, 'Fight The Power' is a crystallization of the sound and ideas of *Nation Of Millions*. It was issued on the Motown label in a one-off deal, as was the *Do The Right Thing* soundtrack album. Like all of Public Enemy's singles it was only released as a DJ-friendly 12-inch, hence its failure to reach the *Billboard* pop chart. (It did, however, top the *Hot Rap* listings.)

The single is underpinned by a typically frantic Bomb Squad production, dominated by relentless drums, pulsating two-note bass, snatches of funk guitar, and intermittent wailing sirens. The state-of-the-nation lyrics are among Chuck D's finest. The first two verses are a call to his fellow black Americans to fight oppression and institutional racism; in the third, his tone becomes more incendiary as he rails against a list of what in his view were racist celebrity figures. Most striking is his put-down of Elvis Presley: "A hero to most, but he never meant shit to me." John Wayne and Bobby McFerrin are among his other targets.

Chuck D saw rap music as "the black CNN" – a voice for a section of the community generally ignored by the mainstream media. Both 'Fight The Power' and *Do The Right Thing* – which was set against a backdrop of inner-city racial conflict – demonstrated an open distaste for cozy, white America, and stirred up waves of controversy and debate. But Public Enemy's defining single was soon overshadowed by an interview that Professor Griff gave to the *Washington Times* later the same summer, in which he claimed Jews were to blame for "the majority of wickedness that goes on in the world." The ensuing storm drew attention away from one of the most powerful moments in rap history, and – even though Griff was eventually fired – cast an unfortunate shadow over the rest of Public Enemy's career. None of the group's subsequent releases – which include the Buffalo Springfield-sampling 'He Got Game' (1998) – have come close to matching the visceral thrill of 'Fight The Power.'

She Drives Me Crazy
Fine Young Cannibals

Released January 1989
IRS/MCA *53483* (U.S. #1) / London *LON 199* (U.K. #5)

The U.K. trio of singer Roland Gift and musicians David Steele and Andy Cox took their name from *All The Fine Young Cannibals*, a 1960 movie starring Robert Wagner and Natalie Wood. As part of the rhythm section of successful pop-ska act The (English) Beat, Steele and Cox brought hit-making know-how to Fine Young Cannibals, but it was the suave Gift who made the group stand out. Gift was capable of reaching into the falsetto range, and his inimitable vocal tone helped catapult the jangly guitars and boogie-inducing groove of 'She Drives Me Crazy' into the upper reaches of the pop charts.

Hangin' Tough
New Kids On The Block

Released July 1989
Columbia *68960* (U.S. #1) / CBS *BLOCK 3* (U.K. #1)

New Kids On The Block was the brainchild of Maurice Starr, the eccentric manager who first put himself on the industry map with the multi-platinum success of New Edition. Starr manufactured the white NKOTB in the same way as he had the black New Edition, even trawling the same city limits of Boston to find the right talented and adorable candidates in brothers Jordan and Jonathan Knight, Donnie Wahlberg, Joey McIntyre, and Danny Wood. After failing to hit pop gold with the self-titled debut album, a new hope emerged when MTV picked up 'You Got It (The Right Stuff),' the first single from NKOTB's second album *Hangin' Tough*. Greeted with a warm reception from its female audience, the network soon moved on to the title track. The *Hangin' Tough* album eventually sold more than 12 million copies, a staggering figure that set the standard for subsequent boy-bands to try to emulate.

Ride On Time
Black Box

Released August 1989
RCA *62003* (U.S.) / Deconstruction *PB 43055* (U.K. #1)

Italian dance producers Black Box reached into the annals of disco, beefing up earlier grooves for modern listeners in a winning formula that enjoyed exposure in nightclubs around the world and helped usher in the house music genre. While slinky, dark-skinned model Catherine Quinol provided the visual representation for the group on record jackets and videos, the vocals on Black Box's hits were made by sampling black vocalists Loleatta Holloway and Martha Wash. Snippets from Holloway's 1980 tune 'Love Sensation' formed the basis of 'Ride On Time,' a huge U.S. club hit and the U.K.'s best-selling single of 1989.

Love Shack
The B-52's

Released September 1989
Reprise *22817* (U.S. #3) / Reprise *W 9917* (U.K. #2)

Swing The Mood
Jive Bunny & The Mastermixers

Released July 1989
Music Factory/Atco *99140* (U.S. #11) / Music Factory Dance *MFD 001* (U.K. #1)

It seemed as if pop music was in safe hands early in 1990 as the gorgeously infectious 'Love Shack' from the perennially eccentric B-52's landed on the charts. Part 1950s hop anthem, part '60s surf jingle, and a looney tune of the most traditional stripe, 'Love Shack' was ostensibly the tale of "a little known place where we can get together" but in truth was an excuse for everyone to get highly silly, with more impressionable teens even adopting a beehive hairdo in the video's honor. The B-52's attempted more hits in the same vein but soon fell from grace as the joke wore off. They did retain some critical credibility thanks to the occasional kudos-enhancing move, such as singer Kate Pearson adding guest vocals to R.E.M.'s ultra-irksome but popular 'Shiny Happy People' a year later.

As we know, pop music is an evil mistress, and late in '89 came the devilish noise of Jive Bunny, a remix duo who sampled Bill Haley's 'Rock Around The Clock', added a cheap backbeat, and created a 'song.' The Bunny's 'Swing The Mood' caused grown men to weep after the third playback and reduced the work rate, the sperm count, and probably the will to live during its long, agonizing chart run. Air-headed radio DJs indulged the monster with far too much airplay, and for a while it seemed as if the future might not after all be an Orwellian boot stamping on a human face but the sound of the late, disembodied Haley stuttering "Ah one-one-one-one-one…" et cetera and repeat forever.

left > New Kids On The Block on tour in Holland in 1990. Clockwise from top right: Jordan Knight, Jonathan Knight, Joey McIntyre, Donnie Wahlberg, and Danny Wood.

It all came to a head one Friday evening in November 1989 when the British chart TV program *Top Of The Pops* staged an all-time coup by featuring Happy Mondays and The Stone Roses – two brand-new bands out of Manchester – on the same show. The Mondays, usually credited with pipping the Roses to the post and kick-starting the 'Madchester' scene, peaked a year later with 'Kinky Afro,' an insanely funky paean to not much in particular. The band's attraction centered on frontman Shaun Ryder – soon to emerge as drugs hoover for a generation – who mouthed his meaningless verse with high insouciance, while tambourine-player and all-round fifth wheel Bez did his strange funky-chicken dance.

The Stone Roses, meanwhile, were heavier and grumpier, lacking the Technicolor cartoon flash of Ryder and his chums but boasting supreme musicianship. Frontman Ian Brown kept his trancey, low-in-the-mix vocals understated (the birth of 'shoegazing'), while guitarist John Squire wah-wah'd up a storm and the expert rhythm section of Gary 'Mani' Mounfield and Alan 'Reni' Wren brought Motown to a new generation. The non-LP track 'Fool's Gold' may have been the better song, but the Mondays had the gift of the gab and, as it turned out, more staying power – despite the sea of drugs that nearly sank them on several occasions.

Like The Stone Roses without the attitude or Happy Mondays with an IQ, James rode the coat-tails of the Madchester movement with 'Sit Down,' a fantastic three-chord trick that in Britain became a student-disco staple for years. Anchored by a lolloping snare-drum pattern and an octave-laden bassline, it appeared at first glance to be no more than a request to, well, to take a seat. But frontman Tim Booth was always a clever fellow (he worked with cerebral soundtrack writer Angelo Badalamenti in later times) and had more up his sleeve, working in an almost political message, with lines such as: "Those who feel the breath of silence / Sit down next to me."

Standing somewhat to one side of all this was Primal Scream, the brainchild of sometime Jesus & Mary Chain drummer Bobby Gillespie. 'Loaded' was the perfect fusion of rock and dance beats, entering the indie-dance canon as an all-time classic tune of the era. Aided by the often surly Gillespie and his knack for a soundbite – he too enjoyed recreational substances, and saw no reason to hide the fact – the Scream founded a long and profitable career that continues to this day.

Fool's Gold
The Stone Roses

....

Released November 1989
Jive *1315* (U.S.) / Silvertone *ORE 13* (U.K. B-side; A #8)

Sit Down
James
Released June 1989
Not issued U.S. / Rought Trade *RT 225* (U.K.)

Loaded
Primal Scream
Released February 1990
Not issued U.S. / Creation *CRE 070* (U.K. #16)

Kinky Afro
Happy Mondays
Released July 1990
Not issued U.S. / Factory *FAC 302* (U.K. #5)

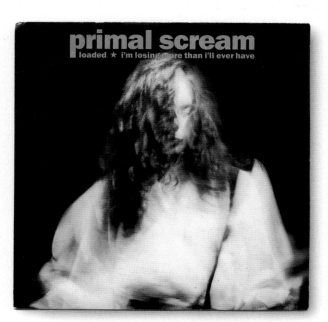

As the 1980s faded from view in Britain, permanently taking with it the post-punks and the New Romantics, a new sound was emerging from the Midlands. House music and hip-hop had begun to make their presence felt in clubland worldwide, but the 1960s pop of The Beatles and The Byrds was also experiencing a renaissance – particularly in Manchester and Liverpool. A small cadre of bands was emerging who liked house and pop, and didn't see why they should be mutually exclusive. Thus was the concept born of 'rock music you can dance to.'

1990

Nothing Compares 2 U
Sinéad O'Connor

Released January 1990
Ensign/Chrysalis *23488* (U.S. #1) / Ensign *ENY 630* (U.K. #1)

This intensely heartfelt performance was too much for some: one reviewer called it "a pointless and embarrassing over-sentimental paw … a waste of talent." Millions of others clearly thought otherwise, making this single and the album *I Do Not Want What I Haven't Got* reach Number 1 on both sides of the Atlantic, an accomplishment Ms. O'Connor has found hard to follow. 'Nothing Compares' remains her only major hit single, and its huge success was undoubtedly assisted by a stark video shot in one take after a more lavish production didn't work. The tears are genuine.

O'Connor would become better known for her non-musical activities, such as tearing up a picture of the Pope John Paul II on live television, and has since claimed that she hated the fame that 'Nothing Compares' brought her. It was her manager who suggested she record what was until that point a little-known gem written by Prince in 1985. The man who seems to write ten songs before breakfast had given this song to The Family, a group signed to his Paisley Park label that included former members of The Revolution and future members of The New Power Generation. It was only an album track at the time, and the Purple One didn't perform or record it himself until after O'Connor had made it internationally popular. A live-in-the-studio duet with Rosie Gains recorded in 1992 appears on Prince's *The Hits/The B-Sides* three-CD collection.

U Can't Touch This
M.C. Hammer

Released February 1990
Capitol *15571* (U.S. #8) / Capitol *CL 578* (U.K. #3)

Ice Ice Baby
Vanilla Ice

Released September 1990
SBK *07335* (U.S. #1) / SBK *18* (U.K. #1)

These songs established recycling as an easy formula for hit-making – and a formula that would be revisited a decade later by Sean 'Diddy' Combs and others in pursuit of pop success. Two of the biggest blockbuster rap singles to date, these infectious tunes are known for their big, obvious samples lifted from other popular songs. 'U Can't Touch This' was made with the help of Rick James's saucy 'Super Freak,' while 'Ice Ice Baby' is built on the instrumental bed of 'Under Pressure' by Queen & David Bowie.

Vanilla Ice followed M.C. Hammer into the pop charts and would often be compared with him. They shared some surface similarities, such as the gift of dancing feet and a propensity for wearing parachute pants. But behind the scenes, Hammer's upbringing and outlook were very different from Ice's. M.C. Hammer had a reputation for benevolence and helping his community while Vanilla Ice quickly became known for a selfish, snobbish attitude.

M.C. Hammer was born Stanley Kirk Burrell and grew up on the rough streets of Oakland, California, but opted towards bubblegum when it came to his music. He simply had no interest in perpetuating the violent lifestyle he saw on the streets. Meanwhile, Vanilla Ice began life as Robert Van Winkle, a kid from suburban Texas who pretended to come from the inner city of Miami and professed to be hard on boastful songs like 'Ice Ice Baby.' Both 'U Can't Touch This' and 'Ice Ice Baby' helped their respective albums each sell over ten million copies.

Dub Be Good To Me
Beats International

Released February 1990
Elektra *64970* (U.S.) / Go! Beat *GOD 39* (U.K. #1)

Norman Cook was a former guitarist with The Housemartins now turned DJ-producer, and would later be known as multi-platinum artist Fatboy Slim. He scored an early Number 1 single in his native U.K. with this lively version of an American R&B hit. 'Dub Be Good To Me' is a cover of 1982's 'Just Be Good To Me' by Atlanta's S.O.S. Band. The original was crafted by Jimmy Jam and Terry Lewis, the super-producers credited for catapulting Janet Jackson into maverick pop stardom. Cook preserved much of the melodic integrity of their song, revving it up a little with a bassline borrowed from punk band The Clash.

The Power
Snap!

Released March 1990
Arista *2013* (U.S. #2) / Arista *113133* (U.K. #1)

Less than one year after the music world was outraged by the unmasking of Milli Vanilli as the secret studio project of German producers and not two spunky young black men, Germany would again concoct a hugely successful pop sham in Snap!, whose high-energy dance hit 'The Power' is unabashedly constructed from vocal samples. The samples were swiped (and uncredited) from the relatively unknown house music diva Jocelyn Brown ('I'm Gonna Get You') and rapper Chill Rob G ('Let The Words Flow'), although in 'live' performances and on the video, the singing and rapping is represented by stand-ins Jackie Harris and Turbo B, respectively.

Killer
Adamski

Released March 1990
MCA *24049* (U.S.) / MCA *1400* (U.K. #1)

Seal (Sealhenry Samuel) later became internationally famous, sold over 10 million albums, and married a supermodel. But on this record, he was a newcomer vocalist guesting on a haunting U.K. chart-topper, grabbing the spotlight through the sheer power of his raw, emotive voice. Adamski had been buoyed by the U.K. Top 20 success of his rave anthem 'N.R.G.,' but now the more subtle yet grooving 'Killer' became the producer's career highlight. While Adamski never stopped making music (latterly as Adam Sky), he never did repeat these chart feats and the success of his album *Doctor Adamski's Musical Pharmacy*. But from 'Killer' and Seal's later solo hit 'Crazy' a unique, enduring star was born.

World In Motion
ENGLANDneworder

Released May 1990
Not issued U.S. / Factory/MCA *FAC 293* (U.K. #1)

Oh, how the British public laughed when New Order – the warmer, clubbier reincarnation of the much darker and more depressing Joy Division – released this excellent song for England's World Cup team, one of only two decent soccer tunes in recorded history. (The other was Skinner & Baddiel's ludicrously singable 'Three Lions' in 1996.) Somehow, art activist Keith Allen was involved. Somehow, England player John Barnes was persuaded to perform a surprisingly on-point rap – and somehow agreed to do a lame (and mildly racist) visual gag in the video in which his cropped head was mistaken for a microphone. Somehow, it was all rather good – perhaps because of the song's unique selling point, the pronunciation of 'England' as 'En-ger-land.'

Groove Is In The Heart
Deee-Lite

Released August 1990
Elektra *64934* (U.S. #4) / Elektra *EKR 114* (U.K. #2)

Deee-Lite was a trio comprised of the vivacious American singer Lady Miss Kier Kirby and the turntable-studio wizards known as Supa DJ Dmitry Brill (from the former Soviet Union) and Jungle DJ Towa 'Towa' Tei (of Japan). They captured the

lovely utopian bubble of glamorous and internationally savvy New York City club life and brought it to the mainstream for everyone's enjoyment. 'Groove Is In The Heart' features guest vocals from Parliament-Funkadelic's inimitable Bootsy Collins and rapper Q-Tip from A Tribe Called Quest. The whimsical, bouncy beat hugs Lady Kier's pop-culture-packed lyrics tight and just right. The single was unlucky not to top the U.K. chart – it sold exactly the same number of copies as Steve Miller Band's 'The Joker,' but stalled at Number 2

because of an obscure (and never-before enforced) chart ruling, which states that, in the event of a tie, the single with the highest sales increase on the previous week should be awarded the Number 1 spot.

Unbelievable
EMF

Released October 1990
EMI *50350* (U.S. #1) / Parlophone *R 6273* (U.K. #3)

This first song from an unknown U.K. dance-rock group called EMF was a surprise hit on both sides of the Atlantic. 'Unbelievable' is a guitar-driven groover featuring odd vocal samples from the controversial American comedian Andrew 'Dice' Clay, attempting to convey just how shocking the song's main character is. EMF is said to stand for Epsom Mad Funkers, but many say it is really Ecstasy Mother Fuckers, the name of a secret song on EMF's debut album *Schubert Dip*. Given the band's place on the cusp of Britain's then-burgeoning acid-house rave scene, it's not hard to believe.

Sadeness Part 1
Enigma

Released November 1990
Charisma *98864* (U.S. #5) / Virgin International *DINS 101* (U.K. #1)

Gregorian chant set to a gentle dance beat: 'Sadeness' must surely rank as one of the strangest international hits in the history of popular music. It was the debut single by Enigma, the brainchild of the Romanian-born German-based composer Michael Cretu, who later re-christened himself Curly MC. Gregorian chant had been a regular component of new age music for some time, but the simple addition of an electronic backbeat brought these ancient sounds into the upper reaches of the charts across Europe and America. Alongside typically drippy synths and a panpipe melody, the single also features a breathless vocal from Cretu's wife, Sandra (calling herself F. Gregorian). Enigma have had several other big hits since, but none has had the surprise impact of 'Sadeness.'

There She Goes
The La's

Released October 1990
London *869370* (U.S.) / Go! Discs *GOLAS 5* (U.K. #13)

The La's (so named after the Merseyside slang for 'lads') crashed and burned in spectacular style after peaking with a near-perfect single, 'There She Goes.' Frontman Lee Mavers was dubbed "the Syd Barrett of the 1990s" by an over-excited press, although there are parallels between The La's man and the dotty old Pink Floyd bod, as Mavers too vanished from view, attaining an almost mythical status as a flawed genius who lost his way.

Rumors circulated for years that Mavers was on the point of returning with more perfect pop in the mold of 'There She Goes,' but we had to wait until 2005, when the band re-formed … a decade too late. However, their finest three minutes remains Mavers's legacy: 'There She Goes' boasts an unforgettable arpeggiated intro, the singer's gorgeous falsetto, and a surprisingly elegant bass part from John Power, who went on to form the briefly popular Britpop band Cast.

Enjoy The Silence
Depeche Mode

Released February 1990
Sire/Reprise *19885* (U.S. #8) / Mute *BONG 18* (U.K. #6)

Depeche Mode were one of the defining British groups of the 1980s, but their biggest and best-remembered hit didn't arrive until the start of the subsequent decade. Hailing from unfashionable Basildon, south-east England, the synth-pop quartet were a regular fixture on the charts in their homeland from 1981 onwards but didn't begin to make it into the American market until several years later. 'People Are People' (1984) looked like being the group's lone U.S. hit until (somewhat fittingly) the 1987 *Music For The Masses* album brought them into the mainstream. Depeche Mode ended the 1980s on a high note with the strident robotic blues vamp 'Personal Jesus,' a Top 30 hit on both sides of the Atlantic.

The follow-up was even better and even more successful. Produced by Flood – whose resumé includes U2, Smashing Pumpkins, and P.J. Harvey – 'Enjoy The Silence' is propelled along by neat, sequenced bass and drums and foreboding mock-choral synthesizer chords. Dave Gahan turns in one of the finest vocal performances of his career, his baritone delivery perfectly suited to multi-instrumentalist Martin Gore's despairing lyric. His message seems to be that the more you talk, the more you erode the magical mystery of a new romance – not the most positive of sentiments, but hard to dispute.

Epic
Faith No More

Released February 1990
Slash *19813* (U.S. #9) / Slash *LASH 21* (U.K. #37)

From San Francisco's Faith No More, 'Epic' was one of the most bizarre hybrid songs to hit the pop charts in the 1990s, a rock-rap-funk mixture similar to the hits of L.A.'s Red Hot Chili Peppers. The minor-key wails of frontman Mike Patton are effective at the same time as they seem a highly unusual choice for popular melodies. There was a ruckus among activists when the explosive performance video for 'Epic' was seen, including goldfish that have fallen out of their tank and gasp desperately for air, but the band helpfully tried to reassure everyone that no fish were harmed during the filming.

Tom's Diner
DNA Featuring Suzanne Vega

Released March 1990
A&M *1529* (U.S. #5) / A&M *AM 592* (U.K. #2)

The endearingly melancholic Suzanne Vega, a poet-turned-folk-singer raised in New York City, could never have predicted that she'd have one of her biggest hits with this club jam that originated as a bootleg release by a pair of creative British DJs. Vega wrote 'Tom's Diner' in the early 1980s and held onto it until '87, when she released the album *Solitude Standing*. The original is performed a cappella – simply Vega's voice, with no instrumentation to back her up, not even her trusty guitar. Three years later, DNA grafted the original onto a chugging beat by Soul II Soul and pressed up illegal white labels, vinyl records devoid of images or information. The recording's popularity among DJs spread quickly, and with Vega's permission an official release eventually emerged on her record label, A&M.

While DNA later released another mix of a Vega song ('Rusted Pipe'), the group never became known pop stars, instead fading back into the faceless dancefloor world from whence they came. In 1991, 'Tom's Diner' was celebrated with its own tributary compilation, *Tom's Album*, featuring versions from little-known bands like Bingo Hand Job, a special collaboration between R.E.M. and Billy Bragg. Tom's Restaurant, the real-life New York coffee shop where 'Tom's Diner' was written, would later return to the spotlight on television, starring as the local coffee shop for the gang on smash situation comedy *Seinfeld*. While the exterior of the real restaurant was shown, the interior was shot on a sound stage in Los Angeles.

Freedom
George Michael

Released October 1990
Columbia *73559* (U.S. #8) / Epic *GEO 3* (U.K. #28)

'Freedom' marked the point of George Michael's transformation from camp 1980s pop idol to serious musical artiste. That earlier role had served Michael well: after Wham!, his highly successful duo with Andrew Ridgeley, came to the end of its natural life, he embarked on a run of eight U.S. Top 5 hits – five of them chart-toppers – between 1987 and 1990, a feat not achieved by a British act since The Beatles. Those hits included the mildly controversial 'I Want Your Sex,' 'Faith,' 'Father Figure,' and 'Praying For Time.'

'Praying For Time' was the first single to be drawn from Michael's *Listen Without Prejudice: Vol. 1*, which introduced the pop world to a newly mature and sensitive version of the star – not to mention one capable, for the first time, of producing a solid, musically diverse album. An effortlessly funky, house-inflected affirmation of life, love, and liberty, 'Freedom' was the second single to be drawn from the album, and the second Michael single to bear that title (the first was a 1984 Wham! hit). It was obviously a matter of great importance to the singer to maintain his independence, and two years later he took his label, Sony, to court, citing restraint of trade. (He was dismayed at Sony's apparent reticence to back his newly serious material and image, which was borne out in lower chart placings from 'Freedom' onwards.) He lost the case but was eventually freed by Sony, and was able to resume his career almost as if nothing had happened after a four-year hiatus.

Wicked Game
Chris Isaak

Released November 1990
Reprise *19704* (U.S. #6) / London *LON 279* (U.K. #10)

Falling
Julee Cruise
Released November 1990
Warner Bros. *4346* (U.S.) / Warner Bros. *W 9544* (U.K. #7)

Go
Moby
Released March 1991
Instinct *EX 229* (U.S.) / Outer Rhythm *FOOT 15* (U.K. #10)

The common thread here is the cinematic auteur David Lynch: Isaak and Cruise were given a leg up by their prominence in his work, while Moby's first U.K. hit sampled the *Twin Peaks* theme.

Chris Isaak was already a cult favorite, having made three albums of gentle 1950s-style rock, but none had reached the charts. 'Wicked Game' is built around a slow, sensual slide-guitar line and Isaak's delicate, cracked croon, and was originally featured on the singer's 1989 set *Heart Shaped World*. It was given a new lease on life the following year when Lynch used it in the nightmarish road movie *Wild At Heart*, and he also directed the song's promo video.

Julee Cruise, by contrast, was something of a pet project for Lynch and his regular musical collaborator, Angelo Badalamenti. 'Falling' is a vocal version of the orchestral theme to Lynch's landmark television series *Twin Peaks* (in which Cruise also had a small, recurring role). It was a surprise

U.K. hit as *Peaks* became the most talked-about TV series in years.

Moby first issued an embryonic version of his *Twin Peaks*-sampling 'Go' while 'Falling' was still on the U.K. chart. A refined version of the ambient techno song reached the British Top 10 a year later. It was the first hit in a long and eclectic career for the New York-based electronic musician, who reached his commercial peak a decade later with his ten-million-selling *Play* album, which spawned the singles 'Porcelain,' 'Why Does My Heart Feel So Bad,' and 'South Side.'

Smells Like Teen Spirit
Nirvana

Released October 1991
DGC *19050* (U.S. #6) / DGC *DGCS 5* (U.K. #7)

'Smells Like Teen Spirit' confirmed the rumblings that had been emanating from Seattle since the spring of 1989. Something called grunge was happening up in that Northwestern backwater. Those in the know, having sniffed the air, now realized that grunge might have the same power as punk had a decade and a half earlier: the power to turn the music business upside down.

At first, the front-runner in the race to make grunge go global was Mudhoney, a raw but melodic quartet signed to the tiny Sub-Pop label. Before long, however, another Sub-Pop act, Nirvana, led by the enigmatic Kurt Cobain, was turning heads. The group's early singles and live shows confirmed them as a force to be reckoned with, and the British rock press in particular began hailing them as potential saviors of a corporate music scene that had grown bloated and out of touch with younger listeners.

In the year prior to the release of 'Teen Spirit,' the charts were dominated by slickly processed pop, rock, and dance from the likes of Mariah Carey, Bryan Adams, Madonna, Michael Bolton, Janet Jackson, Extreme, Whitney Houston, and Paula Abdul. Talented as these artists were, their music was calculated, sophisticated, and rooted in their ability to turn on a sanitized semblance of sincere emotion whenever they opened their mouths. Nirvana was the antithesis of almost everything these artists stood for. Nirvana's music was about chaos, confusion, and spontaneity.

So it was appropriate that 'Smells Like Teen Spirit' was sparked to life by a misunderstanding. Cobain and his friend Kathleen Hanna of punk-feminist band Bikini Kill had spent an evening together at his apartment on North Pear Street, Olympia, 60 miles south of Seattle. During the evening, Hanna spray-painted the graffiti "Kurt smells like Teen Spirit" on one of the walls. "I took that as a compliment," Cobain explained in a subsequent interview. "I thought she was saying that I was a person who could inspire. I just thought that was a nice little title." What Hanna meant, however, was much more literal: that Cobain smelled like the female under-arm deodorant Teen Spirit. "I didn't even know that deodorant existed," claimed Cobain, "until after the song was written."

Having found a title, Cobain next had to put some music together. "I was trying to write the ultimate pop song," he revealed in 1994. "I was basically trying to rip off The Pixies. ... We used their sense of dynamics, being soft and quiet, then loud and hard." What he came up with gave a good indication of Cobain's eclectic musical tastes. To The Pixies' dynamics he added the primitive drive of The Kingsmen's 'Louie Louie,' a long-time favorite of Seattle rockers, combined with more than a hint of the chord changes of 'More Than A Feeling' by prog-rock giants Boston.

Lyrically, the song is – to be generous – impervious to logical examination. Cobain snarls out a long string of loosely rhyming non sequiturs, clearest of which is the phrase "Here we are now, entertain us," derived from a line Cobain used to break the ice at social gatherings. Elsewhere, he growls a terse and inscrutable list that runs: "A mulatto, an albino, a mosquito, my libido." Despite the lack of traditional meaning, the almost stream-of-consciousness words are delivered with a numbed conviction that spoke volumes about Cobain's state of mind – despairing, angry, vulnerable – and were a perfect match for the millions of disaffected teenagers who found it impossible to relate to the phony glamour that surrounded Whitney, Madonna, and their ilk.

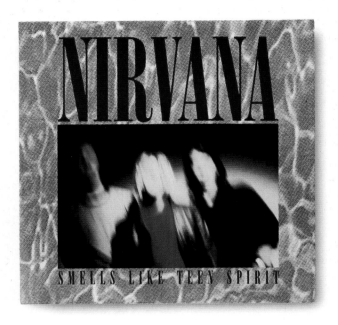

Jonathan Poneman of Sub-Pop was there in Seattle's OK Hotel on April 17, 1991, when Nirvana played 'Smells Like Teen Spirit' live for the very first time. Poneman recalled: "I remember going, 'Wow, God, this is a really good song.' Then it comes to the chorus and everyone went, 'Oh my God, this is one of the greatest choruses of any songs I've ever heard!'" But Poneman didn't get the opportunity to release the song, because Nirvana moved to DGC Records, a subsidiary of Geffen, at the end of the month.

'Smells Like Teen Spirit' was recorded at the start of May 1991 in Sound City Studios, Van Nuys, California, during sessions with producer Butch Vig for the group's second album, *Nevermind*. Their indie debut, *Bleach*, had cost slightly over $600. This major-label follow-up ran to $120,000.

Like Sub Pop's Poneman, Vig was immediately blown away by the song. "I kept having them play it over and over again, because it was so fucking good," he revealed later, adding that the song was more or less complete by the time he heard it. He did admit, however, to having done "some minor tweaking of the arrangement" that included having Cobain repeat during each chorus a brief guitar ad-lib, which originally appeared only at the end of the song.

In advance of release, the single was sent out to American radio DJs on August 27, 1991, while the band was touring in Europe. Geffen's marketing team and Nirvana's management company, Gold Mountain, were completely taken aback by the response. "We thought it was gonna be the college/alternative-rock track," remembered Danny Goldberg of Gold Mountain, "and the feeling was that 'Come As You Are' was a more melodic song so it would be more of a pop song." Instead, 'Teen Spirit' took off immediately at all levels of rock and pop radio.

Director Sam Bayer's memorable video for 'Teen Spirit' had its first MTV play on September 29, but the song took off first in Britain, entering the U.K. singles chart at the end of November, swiftly followed by its U.S. chart debut on December 7. In both territories, the single stopped just outside the Top 5, but there was no mistaking its impact. A whole new generation of record buyers had been galvanized, and grunge was set to be rock's dominant force for the rest of the decade already underway.

Unfinished Sympathy
Massive Attack

Released February 1991
Virgin *DMD 1662* (U.S.) / Wild Bunch *WBRS 2* (U.K. #13)

Regularly cited among the greatest singles of the 1990s if not all time, 'Unfinished Sympathy' introduced the world to Massive Attack and the 'trip-hop' sound that the group pioneered. Robert Del Naja (a.k.a. '3D'), Adrian Vowles ('Mushroom'), and Grant Marshall ('Daddy G') were part of a music collective based in Bristol, England, known as The Wild Bunch, before forming Massive Attack in 1987.

This was the group's third single, and the second to be drawn from their milestone debut album, *Blue Lines*. Both album and single laid out the ground rules for what became known as trip-hop, the first legitimate British response to rap music, and inspired a host of similar artists, notably occasional Massive Attack member Tricky, and Portishead, both from the Bristol area.

'Unfinished Sympathy' is built around a jangly, slowed-down hip-hop beat and a moving, cinematic string arrangement. The remarkably soulful vocal is by Shara Nelson, who also stars in the memorable promo video for the song. In it she is filmed walking the backstreets of Los Angeles, apparently unaware of everything going on around her. It was one of the first music videos to be shot in one continuous take.

The single is something of an oddity in the group's catalog in that it was credited simply to Massive. They were persuaded to drop the "unpatriotic" Attack during the first Gulf War, a step that Del Naja continues to regret. He was a vocal critic of the second war in Iraq a decade later. In the intervening years Massive Attack had continued to make records of the highest quality, including the U.K. hit singles 'Protection,' 'Karmacoma,' and 'Teardrop,' which featured a gorgeously ethereal vocal by former Cocteau Twins mouthpiece Elizabeth Fraser.

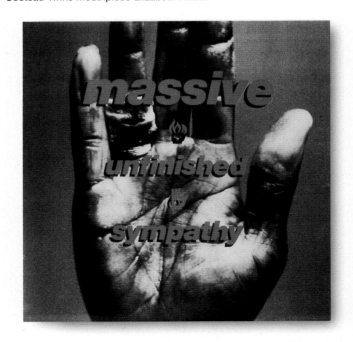

Losing My Religion
R.E.M.

Released February 1991
Warner Bros. *19392* (U.S. #4) / Warner Bros. *W 0015* (U.K. #19)

After a decade building a slow success, R.E.M. was ready for the big time at the start of the 1990s. Surprisingly, however, the song that confirmed the group's status among rock music's elite was a morose ballad dominated by a mandolin, an instrument not usually considered as a leading voice in rock music. The only other notable hit to feature it prominently is 'Maggie May' by Rod Stewart, released two decades earlier. But in the hands of R.E.M.'s Peter Buck, the mandolin offers a fine counterpoint to sad strings and a maudlin Michael Stipe vocal – written, according to its author, as a follow-up to 'Every Breath You Take' by The Police.

'Losing My Religion' was helped along by a memorable video starring Stipe and Saint Sebastian, and it became the best-known song of the group's career, winning a Grammy for Best Pop Performance (By A Duo Or Group With Vocals). It went down well everywhere, in fact, except Ireland, where the single was banned because of its religious content – somewhat ironic, given that the offending word is used purely metaphorically.

R.E.M. scored another U.S. Top 10 hit several months later with 'Shiny Happy People,' a bouncy duet with Kate Pierson of The B-52's. The group quickly grew to hate that song, however, and has never performed it live, unless you count a rendition given on TV's *Sesame Street* more than a decade later, when it was re-christened 'Furry Happy Monsters.'

(Everything I Do) I Do It For You
Bryan Adams

Released June 1991
A&M *1567* (U.S. #1) / A&M *AM 789* (U.K. #1)

This epic ballad was written for and featured in the movie *Robin Hood: Prince Of Thieves*, and spent a record 16 weeks at Number 1 in the U.K. during the summer of 1991.

Adams was originally commissioned simply to add words to a theme written by Michael Kamen, whose work encompasses numerous film scores, 11 ballets, and guest appearances with musicians ranging from Kate Bush to Metallica. In the end, though, Adams and his producer, Mutt Lange, came up with a song that bore little relation to Kamen's music for the movie (but for which Kamen nonetheless retained a co-writing credit).

Neither Kamen nor the producers of *Robin Hood: Prince Of Thieves* were keen on Adams's song, and relegated it to the movie's end credits. The public disagreed, however, and sent 'Everything I Do' to the top of the charts on both sides of the Atlantic and 28 other countries around the world. In the U.S. – where it spent seven weeks at Number 1 – it ranks second only to the charity hit 'We Are The World' by U.S.A. for Africa among the biggest-selling singles of all time.

Despite its huge international success, 'Everything I Do' is loathed as much as it is admired, in part because of its apparent disinclination towards leaving the charts – not to mention the airwaves – and also, perhaps, because of Adams's clean cut looks and squeaky-clean persona. What is undeniable, though, is that the song contains a strong vocal melody, an expertly assembled build-up, and a weighty, lighters-aloft ending that gets people cheering around the jukebox every time. Love it or hate it, 'Everything I Do' is one of the biggest and most easily recognizable records of the 1990s.

Enter Sandman
Metallica

Released August 1991
Elektra *64857* (U.S. #16) / Vertigo *METAL 7* (U.K. #5)

'Enter Sandman' finds Metallica at their most approachable, but without losing any of the band's famous metal edge they had carefully cultivated in their first ten years of ear-blistering life. The lead single off the album *Metallica*, the infamous multi-platinum selling effort colloquially known as *The Black Album*, it helped propel that record into the band's most popular effort ever. The song gained new life once adopted into the sports world as a steely anthem of intimidation, and a popular professional wrestler named Jim Fullington even adopted the moniker of The Sandman.

Do The Bartman
The Simpsons

Released January 1991
Not issued U.S. / Geffen *GEF 87* (U.K. #1)

'Do The Bartman' was a spin-off from the long running animated TV series *The Simpsons* and is the work of the pseudonymous John Jay Smith, better known to the world as Michael Jackson. Series creator Matt Groening finally admitted at the 1998 Second Annual World Animation Celebration that Jackson had written the song, expressing his surprise that nobody had discovered the truth earlier.

'Do The Bartman' bears many of the hallmarks of Jackson's work of the time, and the backing vocals sound suspiciously like him . . . mainly because they are by him (and the song's producer, Bryan Loren). If those weren't big enough clues, our Mr. Smith is also name-checked in the lyrics: "If you can do the Bart you're bad like Michael Jackson."

'Do The Bartman' was the opening track on *The Simpsons Sing The Blues*, an album of songs sung by different characters from the series. The lead vocal here is rapped by Nancy Cartwright, the regular voice of bratty pre-teen Bart. The single was not granted a physical release in the U.S., although the album cut made Number 11 on *Billboard*'s Airplay chart, and the video was still Number 1 on MTV for the first three months of 1991. A single was released in the U.K., where it topped the chart, despite the fact that *The Simpsons* was shown only on satellite television in Britain until 1996. Its enduring legacy – aside from the story of its mysterious author – is that anybody aged six to 16 at the time of the song's release can most likely still recite Bart's rap.

The Shoop Shoop Song (It's In His Kiss)
Cher

Released January 1991
Geffen *19659* (U.S. #33) / Epic *6566737* (U.K. #1)

Covering a 1963 hit by Merry Clayton was a masterstroke by sliced-and-diced cyborg pop lady Cher, once of Sonny & Cher fame, especially as it also appeared on the soundtrack for the *Mermaids* movie, in which she starred as mum of wayward goth brat Winona Ryder. Cher had previously tried her hand at watered-down hair-rock – remember the hideous 'If I Could Turn Back Time,' in whose video she appeared in almost nothing but greenish tattoos? – and would eventually strike it big with house-trance in the late 1990s. But this classic bit of soul was a triumph, not to be repeated.

Mama Said Knock You Out
LL Cool J

Released January 1991
Def Jam *73706* (U.S. #17) / Def Jam *6564470* (U.K. B-side)

"Don't call it a comeback!" shouts a rugged LL Cool J on this American Top 20 hit. "I've been here for years!" He was born James Todd Smith but his new name stood for Ladies Love Cool James, and he was one of the first world-famous rappers as well as one of the first artists on New York City's legendary Def Jam label.

After debuting as a hard-edged teenager with obvious sex-symbol potential, he had become known for entertaining the ladies just a bit more than the men as he started to grow up and come across with near-ballads like 'I Need Love.' The fickle streets had started to turn away from him until the reaffirmation of 'Mama Said Knock You Out,' a pounting, unrelenting song and the title track of his fourth album. In the rap world, one's inner-city credibility is paramount, and this song was the sound of LL vehemently taking back that credibility and never letting it go.

With the help of legendary hip-hop DJ-producer Marley Marl at the controls, 'Mama Said' is anything but soft and is indelibly complimented by its gorgeous black-and-white video featuring LL in a boxing ring. The *Mama Said* album featured a further hit in 'Around The Way Girl' while songs like 'The Boomin' System' and 'Jingling Baby' earned heavy club rotation. The album went double-platinum and cemented LL Cool J's place in the hip-hop pantheon for years to come.

Summertime
DJ Jazzy Jeff & The Fresh Prince

Released June 1991
Jive *1465* (U.S. #4) / Jive *JIVECD 279* (U.K. #8)

This Philadelphia hip-hop duo, which debuted in 1987 and enjoyed the fruits of multi-platinum sales, had its last major hit in 1991 with the enduring jam 'Summertime.' The song, perfect for outdoor barbecues, pool parties, and slow cruising in a caravan of cars, is decidedly more laidback than their earlier successes with cheeky songs like 'Parents Just Don't Understand.' Alongside these achievements, the charismatic Will Smith (a.k.a. The Fresh Prince) had started an acting career with his lead role in the popular situation comedy *The Fresh Prince Of Bel-Air*. The transition was so successful that by the end of the 1990s Smith would no longer be known principally as a rapper: he became a full-fledged blockbuster movie star demanding millions of dollars.

99

The group's relative silence off the small screen (*Bel-Air* enjoyed frequent cameos from Jazzy Jeff) had built up anticipation for the 1991 release of the *Homebase* album, which was nicely buoyed by the reception for 'Summertime.' To paraphrase the rap star LL Cool J, people called it a comeback, although DJ Jazzy Jeff and the Fresh Prince had been there for years. In one of the ultimate honors for any song,

'Summertime' grabbed a Grammy for Best Rap Performance By A Group. Not a bad way to put a cap on a successful career, for while Jazzy Jeff and Will Smith have remained the tightest of friends and talked about future collaborations, they've never released another proper album together since *Homebase*.

I'm Too Sexy
Right Said Fred

Released July 1991
Charisma *98671* (U.S. #1) / Tug *SNOG 1* (U.K. #2)

When we first heard 'I'm Too Sexy' we all said no, this can't be a real song, it's a nursery rhyme, or a parody of a gay disco anthem. In fact, Right Said Fred's debut single was both, becoming iconic for its proud-to-be-out associations and its none-more-simple bass and drums motif with a bit of brass tacked on top. The shaven-headed, muscular British band – baritone singer Richard Fairbrass, his songwriter-instrumentalist brother Fred, and guitarist Rob Manzoli – added to the song's impact with their unique look and defied all criticism by sustaining their career a lot longer than they should have done. Remarkable.

Set Adrift On Memory Bliss
PM Dawn

Released August 1991
Gee Street *866094* (U.S. #1) / Gee Street *GEE 33* (U.K. #3)

It's certainly a long way from Jersey City to London, but brothers Prince Be (Attrell Cordes) and DJ Minute Mix (Jarrett Cordes) bridged many international gaps of sound and style with their hippified take on hip-hop as PM Dawn. They scored a massive crossover hit with the creative 'Set Adrift on Memory Bliss,' which lifts the familiar melodic stabs from 'True,' the 1983 hit ballad from U.K. pop group Spandau Ballet. 'Set Adrift' was included on PM Dawn's loftily named and sampladelic 1991 album *Of The Heart, Of The Soul And Of The Cross: The Utopian Experience*.

O.P.P.
Naughty By Nature

Released September 1991
Tommy Boy *988* (U.S. #6) / Big Life *BLR 74* (U.K. #35)

The New Jersey trio had an international hit with this hilarious ode to fooling around. Rappers Treach (Anthony Criss) and Vinnie (Vincent Brown) plus DJ Kay Gee (Keir Gist) hail from the ghetto of East Orange and shared tough childhood experiences, heavily reflected in the group's songs. But 'O.P.P.' is different, almost bubblegum, largely because of the song it samples heavily: 'ABC' by The Jackson 5. While the polite explanation for the acronym 'O.P.P.' is that it stands for Other People's Property, the more crass definition replaces the last word with names for male and female genitalia. Committing adultery never sounded so funky.

Finally
Ce Ce Peniston

Released October 1991
A&M *1586* (U.S. #5) / A&M *AM 858* (U.K. #2)

The gorgeous and poised Cecelia Peniston was simply not satisfied to rest on the laurels earned from her title as Miss Black Arizona of 1989. Instead, just a few short years later she'd be known as the queen of the dancefloor with one of the most infectious and bestselling club hits of the 1990s. 'Finally' is a love song with oomph, a sassy anthem with universal appeal. The album of the same name generated two more pop hits ('We Got a Love Thang' and 'Keep On Walkin'') and earned Peniston two *Billboard* Music Awards.

Don't Let The Sun Go Down On Me
George Michael & Elton John

Released November 1991
Columbia *74086* (U.S. #1) / Epic *657646* (U.K. #1)

There was no reason why a live version of Elton John's 1974 hit 'Don't Let The Sun Go Down On Me' should become a hit now, but this didn't deter his chum George Michael, who pulled out a spiffing version of the old chestnut and watched it race up the charts like a rat up a drainpipe. The song is unremarkable if you're familiar with the original melodic piano-ballad, other than the money-shot moment when Big George says to the fawning audience: "Ladies and gentlemen … mister Elton John!" The venue goes berserk, Reg comes on and does his stuff, hugs are exchanged, and another trillion dollars go into the accounts of Messrs. Panayiotou and Dwight.

Black Or White
Michael Jackson

Released November 1991
Epic *74100* (U.S. #1) / Epic *657598* (U.K. #1)

After Michael Jackson was *Bad*, the emboldened artist took a step further and became *Dangerous*, speaking out more loudly against his self-inflicted oppression and alienation from the rest of the world. While he continued to have hits, Jackson's public persona only grew stranger.

Regular television network Fox and the three major American music cable networks (MTV, VH1, and BET) premiered the memorable video, which features a morphing of the faces of a diverse group of people (much like the famous video for Godley and Creme's 'Cry'). Protestors subsequently forced the excising of one violent scene of Jackson smashing a car window, but it's less clear why the scene featuring Fox cartoon characters Homer and Bart Simpson hit the cutting room floor. Perhaps it was just to get Fox on board in the early stages?

In a way that has been repeated countless times in his obstacle-laden career, Jackson's intentions for this song ended up hideously twisted against him in what could be considered a major backfire. "It don't matter if you're black or white," he sings, clearly troubled. But no sooner had the song hit the airwaves than late-night talk-show hosts and aspiring stand-up comedians alike had concocted dozens and dozens of jokes, questioning Jackson's strangely morphing skin color. He claimed it was due to the melanin-depleting skin disorder vitiligo, but folks weren't so sure.

Baby Got Back
Sir Mix-A-Lot

Released April 1992
Def American *18947* (U.S. #1) / Def American *DEFA 20* (U.K.)

The urban music world, which stars the complementary genres of R&B and hip-hop, has a fondness – even an unabashed joy – for a woman's backside. While it is a frequent subject of songs and in videos, it was Seattle's most famous rapper Sir Mix-A-Lot (born Anthony Ray) who broke the ice with 'Baby Got Back,' his chart-topping paean to the beauty of the big ol' booty.

In his raucously funny lyrics, Mix-A-Lot takes pains to detail the type of posterior he finds most appealing. He wants a lady with an "LA face and an Oakland booty." No skinny girls with flat rumps are desired over here; that type of woman is only for the pages of *Cosmo*, not black men with real needs. "36-24-36?" he asks, somewhat sarcastically. "Only if she's five three!"

The accompanying video for 'Baby Got Back' couldn't possibly be more descriptive of the song itself, with its giant ass mountains, suggestively moving fruit and vegetables, and, perhaps most importantly, a voluptuous, gyrating dance troupe to drive home the point. 'Baby Got Back' stayed in the Number 1 slot for four weeks and shocked critics when it won an elusive Grammy for Best Rap Solo Performance. Sir Mix-A-Lot later attempted to be a breast man with the racy 'Put 'Em On The Glass,' which featured a soapy car-wash video, but neither that song nor any other overshadowed his butt of a joke.

Jump
Kris Kross

Released April 1992
Ruffhouse *74197* (U.S. #1) / Ruffhouse *657847* (U.K. #2)

In their early teens, Atlanta's Chris Kelly and Chris Smith were respectively dubbed Mack Daddy and Daddy Mack, and they shot to fame with the catchy hip-pop song 'Jump.' But it wasn't the rapid-fire lyrical delivery that got Kris Kross noticed, it was the truly odd way they would wear their clothes: all completely backwards. The young artists were an early success story for Jermaine Dupri, the producer and music executive who launched his own hit-making record label, So So Def, and later created multi-platinum work with artists such as Mariah Carey and his girlfriend Janet Jackson.

Jump Around
House Of Pain

Released July 1992
Tommy Boy *7526* (U.S. #3) / Ruffness *XLS 43* (U.K. #8)

The rap community is not typically characterized as having Irish pride, yet House Of Pain briefly changed that with this enduring anthem from MCs Everlast (Erik Schrody) and Danny Boy (Dan O'Conner) plus DJ Lethal (Leor Dimant). They came from the same underground Los Angeles scene that gave us compatriots Cypress Hill, but 'Jump Around' is a raucous party jam that still, years after its release, can ramp up the energy on any dancefloor. After House Of Pain disbanded, Everlast enjoyed a moderately successful solo career, while DJ Lethal joined multi-platinum rock group Limp Bizkit.

End Of The Road
Boyz II Men

Released July 1992
Motown *2178* (U.S. #1) / Motown *TMG 1411* (U.K. #1)

I Will Always Love You
Whitney Houston

Released November 1992
Arista *12490* (U.S. #1) / Arista *120657* (U.K. #1)

For 36 years, nobody was able to match Elvis Presley's 11-week stint at Number 1 on the *Billboard* singles chart with his 1956 hit 'Hound Dog' / 'Don't Be Cruel.' Then his record was broken twice in the space of four months by two of the biggest R&B acts of the 1990s.

Boyz II Men (Nathan Morris, Wayna Morris, Shawn Stockman, and Michael McCary) formed in 1989 at the High School Of The Creative And Performing Arts in Philadelphia, Pennsylvania. After auditioning backstage at a New Edition gig, the group signed to Motown, and hit Number 2 in the U.S. with their debut single, 'It's So Hard To Say Goodbye To Yesterday,' in 1991. By the following fall, the group had perfected their smooth, soulful sound, and had found the perfect collaborator in the form of songwriter Kenneth 'Babyface' Williams. He provided them with 'End Of The Road,' which spent 13 weeks at Number 1 on the *Billboard* Hot 100 and is Motown's most successful single of all time.

A few months later, Houston's cover of Dolly Parton's enduring country hit 'I Will Always Love You' was the soaring crescendo to *The Bodyguard*, which starred Houston and Kevin Costner in a musically-driven romance. With 14 weeks at Number 1 in the U.S., the song shattered the record set by 'End Of The Road.' Houston later won Grammys for Record Of The Year and Best Pop Vocalist, Female. But her record would be surpassed a few years later by another Boyz II Men single, this time a collaboration with Mariah Carey, 'One Sweet Day,' which topped the charts for an incredible 16 weeks.

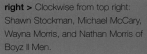
right > Clockwise from top right: Shawn Stockman, Michael McCary, Wayna Morris, and Nathan Morris of Boyz II Men.

THE BABYFACE SOUND: FROM WHITNEY TO OUTKAST

Kenneth 'Babyface' Edmonds, a youthful looking man well deserving of his nickname, is one of the most celebrated songwriters and producers in the history of R&B music. Honored a remarkable three times with the Grammy Award for Producer Of The Year, he is also a groundbreaking record-label executive, a rare combination indeed.

Since co-founding the Atlanta-based LaFace Records with Antonio 'LA' Reid in 1989, Babyface has released multi-platinum albums from such distinctive megastars as TLC, Toni Braxton, and OutKast. LaFace has inspired the creation of many other labels and enjoys near-universal credit for kick-starting the city of Atlanta as a new Mecca for black music.

From his early days as part of the sweet-soul-harmony band known as The Deele (with Reid), and then a string of hit R&B singles and albums on his own, he went on to work with icons such as Madonna and Whitney Houston, and crafted a record-breaking hit for Boyz II Men. Given all this, Babyface would have had a fulfilling career had he stopped in the early 1990s and rested on his laurels. Yet his passion and determination have kept him relevant to the current business of making music, with no end in sight. His winning smile, his tender lyrics, and his gift for soliciting the best from everyone he works with continue to keep Babyface at the heart of popular music production.

Mr. Loverman
Shabba Ranks

Released July 1992
Epic *74257* (U.S. #40) / Epic *659 0782* (U.K. #3)

Oh Carolina
Shaggy

Released November 1992
Virgin *12672* (U.S.) / Greensleeves *GRE 361* (U.K. #1

With his cover of the 1960 Folkes Brothers song 'Oh Carolina,' Shaggy (born Oroville Richard Burrell) might be the only artist ever to have hit the pop charts who served as a soldier in the Gulf War. And along with Shabba Ranks, then a label-mate of Michael Jackson, Shaggy was one of the few 1990s reggae artists originally from Jamaica to have enjoyed success away from the island. Not since the days of Bob Marley, that is. Both artists played up their accents, their deep voices, and their all-around masculine sex appeal to generate hordes of adoring female fans. Men liked them too, even if they didn't want to admit it too loudly, mainly because these sizzling songs from exotic sex symbols probably helped them get women.

Not long after the success of 'Mr. Loverman,' Shabba Ranks (known to his loving mother as Rexton Rawlson Fernando Gordon) fell out of favor with the general public on both sides of the Atlantic, coming under fire for his unabashedly homophobic lyrics in some other songs. Apparently it wasn't enough to cultivate an image as a ladies' man; it was also imperative to declare a stubborn intolerance for difference. This was all quite badly timed, what with the rise of political correctness. The combination proved damaging to Shabba, and we did not hear much more from him.

Would I Lie To You
Charles & Eddie

Released September 1992
Capitol *44809* (U.S. #13) / Capitol *CL 673* (U.K. #1)

It seems not to matter how weak a song's production is or how insipid its sentiments, as long as the top-line melody is catchy enough to stay in the listener's head until old age sets in. This was certainly the case for 'Would I Lie To You,' the career high of Edward Chacon and the late Charles Pettigrew, a soul duo whose knack for a super-bland R&B lick made them stars. The song is notable for the singers' keening falsettos – always a reliable banker in these diluted days – and the interchange of improvised lines that the men throw in from time to time. It's that simple.

Connected
Stereo MC's

Released September 1992
Gee Street *864744* (U.S. #20) / Fourth & Broadway *BRW 262* (U.K. #18)

British pop music has been popular in America since The Beatles, but it has been markedly difficult for the isle's urban sounds to make an impact beyond its shores. Stereo MC's shook up American dance floors and hit the Top 20 in their native U.K. with 'Connected,' which has a catchy shuffle beat provided by Nick Hallam and the mellifluous tones of singer-rapper Rob Birch. While not the big breakthrough that the band and the genre itself might have banked on, its simultaneous presence on radio, clubs, and MTV is exactly the strategy for success that more recent urban artists from Britain have adopted abroad.

Tears In Heaven
Eric Clapton

Released January 1992
Duck-Reprise *19038* (U.S. #2) / Reprise *W 0081* (U.K. #5)

Songs about real-life tragedies are usually mawkish and embarrassing, but Eric Clapton pulled off a coup with 'Tears In Heaven,' which he wrote in the aftermath of the death of his five-year-old son Conor. The song was both catchy enough to pull in public attention and sober enough to serve the subject, with Clapton never making it sound routine or forced, although he admitted that it was sometimes difficult to perform.

The wider impact of 'Tears In Heaven' was twofold. First, it demonstrated that Clapton, who had been in career doldrums for at least two decades after the scintillating work he put in with John Mayall, Cream, and others in the 1960s, could still be a chart-topper. As a piece of songwriting, 'Tears' is perfect. Second, it showed that Clapton could deliver the goods as an acoustic musician as well as in electric mode. His preferred method over the years had always been with the help of a battered electric guitar, but his command of the acoustic instrument here was flawless.

It should also be noted that 'Tears In Heaven,' released as a single alongside Clapton's bestselling MTV *Unplugged* album, ushered in a new awareness of the acoustic medium to the grunge generation of 1992. The album showed that Clapton could rearrange his classic hits for a largely acoustic set and still sound cool (try the revised version of 'Layla'), and was among the first in an unplugged fad that lasted a few years but never produced an album as good as Clapton's, with the possible exceptions of those by Nirvana and Neil Young.

The Drowners
Suede

Released May 1992
Not issued U.S. / Nude *NUD 1S* (U.K.)

Suede never matched the commercial success or the lasting appeal of contemporaries such as Blur, Pulp, and Oasis, but they were first out of the blocks when it came to reinvigorating British guitar-based music in

the early 1990s. The group's androgynous, post-glam sound and image – a mixture of The Smiths and David Bowie – stirred up an instant media storm, and put them on the cover of key U.K. music paper *NME* before they'd even released a single. Dominated by Bernard Butler's bruising guitar chords and Brett Anderson's arch vocal, 'The Drowners' more than matched the hype, scraped in at Number 49 on the chart, and opened the floodgates for the ensuing Britpop tide.

Friday I'm In Love
The Cure

Released May 1992
Elektra *64742* (U.S. #18) / Fiction *FIC 42* (U.K. #6)

The entire blame for the drunken crab dance that is The Cure's rise from post-punk upstarts to international goth megastars can be laid at the feet of Robert Smith. His near-schizophrenic musical eclecticism has enabled the band to thrash out a cacophonous maelstrom on albums like *Pornography* and *Faith*, then craft chart hits spanning everything from electro-pop ('Let's Go To Bed') to jaunty swing ('The Love Cats') and nightmarish goth ('Lullaby').

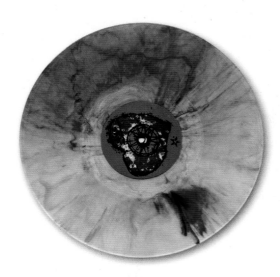

'Friday I'm In Love' was the second single from the Number 1 album *Wish* and, once again, it rang the changes. "It's a dumb pop song," Smith admitted cheerfully, "but it's quite excellent, actually, because it's so absurd. It's so out of character – very optimistic and really out there in happy land."

Examined clinically, it's just one of hundreds of songs that use the days of the week as a starting point – others include 'Friday On My Mind' by The Easybeats and 'Thursday's Child' by David Bowie. But Porl Thompson's jangly guitar lines and the song's irrepressibly happy mood made 'Friday' The Cure's second biggest British hit single, peaking at Number 6. "People think we're leaders of some sort of gloom movement," Smith complained. "I could sit and write gloomy songs all day long, but I just don't see the point."

Creep
Radiohead

Released September 1992
Capitol *44932* (U.S. #34) / Parlophone *6078* (U.K. #7)

Radiohead's breakthrough hit 'Creep' became something of an albatross from which the group struggled to escape for the next few years. Like a lot of the group's early material it is heavily indebted to the loud-soft dynamics and bleak lyrical sentiments of The Pixies and Nirvana. This meant that the quintet from Oxford, England, had a ready-made fanbase in the U.S., where the single gave them a debut hit. But back home 'Creep' was deemed too miserable for radio in 1992 and didn't chart until it was reissued a year later. Even then, Radiohead were sneered at as a faux-grunge band that had lucked out in America.

Radiohead referred to 'Creep' as "our Scott Walker song," but "our Hollies song" might have been more appropriate. Distinct similarities to 'The Air That I Breathe' meant that its credits were retroactively altered to include Albert Hammond and Mike Hazelwood, composers of the 1960s hit.

Supposed unintentional plagiarism aside, the most memorable moment in 'Creep' is the atonal crunch of Jonny Greenwood's guitar before each chorus. According to legend he arrived at the sound by accident as a way of expressing his irritation at a slow song he didn't much care for. He wasn't alone: frontman Thom Yorke used the band's next single, 'My Iron Lung,' to express his disdain for live audiences who turned up wanting to hear this song but no others. He needn't have worried too much: by 1997 Radiohead were the most important band on the planet.

Jeremy
Pearl Jam

Released September 1992
Epic *77935* (U.S.) / Epic *658 2582* (U.K. #15)

On January 8, 1991, Jeremy Wade Delle, a distraught 16-year-old student at Richardson High School in Dallas, Texas, shot himself dead in front of his classmates during an English lesson. After reading about it in a newspaper, Eddie Vedder of recently formed Seattle-based grunge hopefuls Pearl Jam found himself moved to write a song about it that very night.

Drawing on his own recollections of a fellow student in junior high school in San Diego, California, who had gone on a shooting spree, Vedder came up with a lyric that Pearl Jam guitarist Jeff Ament realized would fit with "two pieces of music that I wrote on acoustic guitar with the idea I would play them on a Hamer 12-string bass I had just ordered." The song evolved further during the recording process at Seattle's London Bridge studio. "I had an idea for the outro," said Ament. "I overdubbed a 12-string bass part and we added a cello part – big-time production for us."

Released as the third single from their multi-platinum debut album *Ten*, 'Jeremy' failed to chart significantly in America, but the award-winning video by director Chris Cafaro became a long-running staple on MTV. "The message of the video was a warning of the exact thing that happened at Columbine," explained Ament, referring to the 1999 U.S. school massacre. "Parents and teachers don't always pay attention to what's going on." It's a testament to the increasing power of MTV that, despite its humble chart record, 'Jeremy' remains the song most closely identified with Pearl Jam.

1992

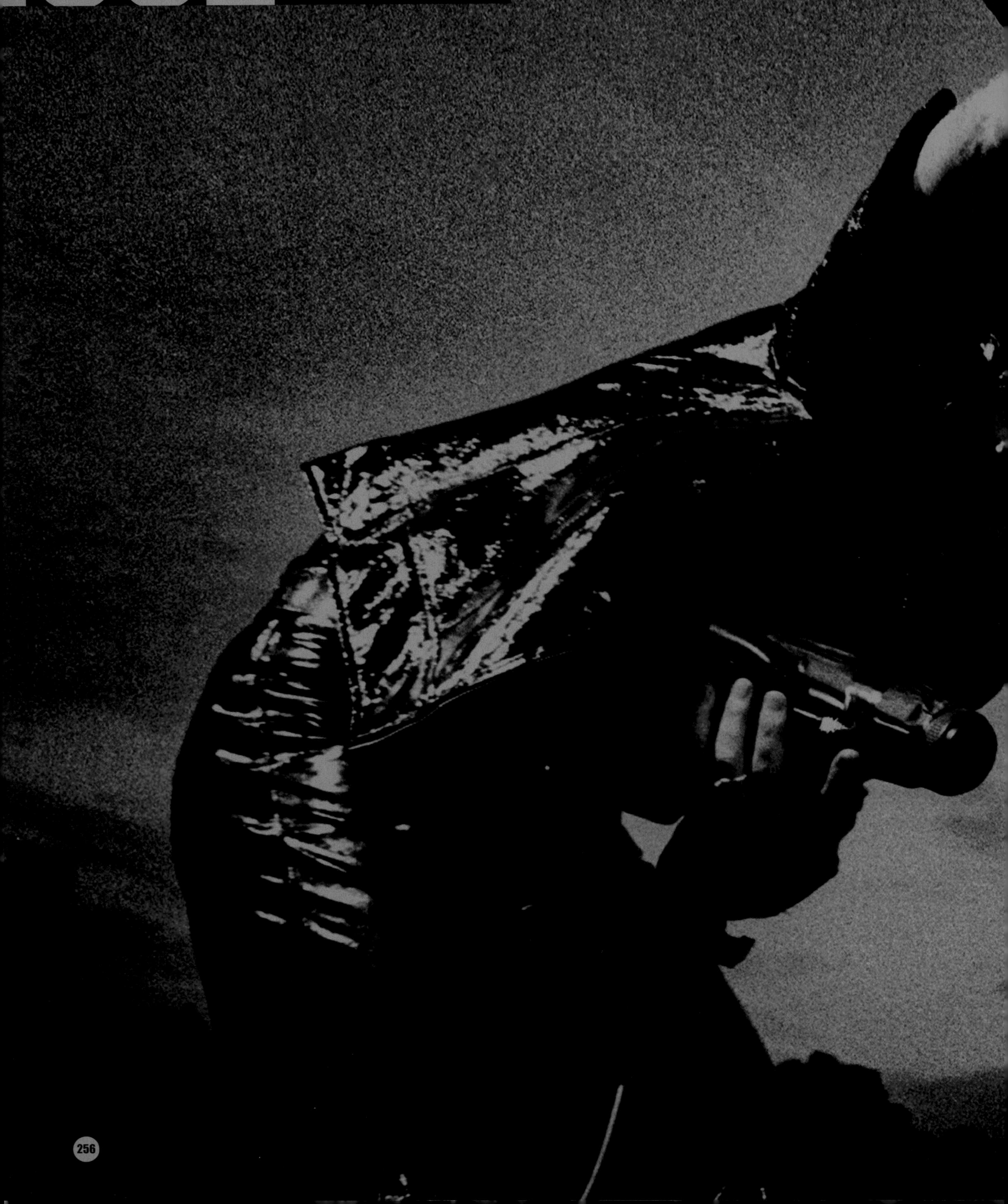

One
U2

Released March 1992
Island *866533* (U.S. #10) / Island *IS 515* (U.K. #7)

Driven by Edge's subtle, soulful guitar chords and Bono's plaintive vocal delivery, 'One' remains among U2's finest singles. It was the third of three classic singles drawn from the group's sixth studio album, *Achtung Baby*, all released in the space of four months (the other two were 'The Fly' and 'Mysterious Ways').

Achtung Baby is famous as the album where U2 cast off their trad-rock shoes and restyled themselves as post-modern, electro-tinged experimentalists. This is clear enough on songs such as 'Fly,' which bears the hallmarks of producer Brian Eno's work in the late 1970s with David Bowie. The album as a whole is rather impressively layered with multi-tracked, effects-laden guitars, towering synthesizers, and forceful rhythms inspired by (then) cutting-edge dance beats. 'One,' however, is a much more simple, stately affair, anchored not by tinkering with the latest studio gadgetry but by an elegant four-chord riff, everyman lyrics, and a magisterial singalong chorus.

The song's words are ambiguous enough to apply to any situation (which represents a large part of its appeal), but the fact that profits from sales of the single were given to AIDS charities suggests that it might have been written with those suffering from the disease in mind. In later years, Bono has often found himself castigated for sanctimoniously pontificating about global issues, but it's hard to find fault with his genuinely affecting tone here. The lasting popularity of 'One' was demonstrated in 2006 when the lyrics were chosen as the greatest of all time by viewers of the music-TV channel VH1 in Britain.

Are You Gonna Go My Way
Lenny Kravitz

Released February 1993
Not issued U.S. / Virgin America *VUS 65* (U.K. #4)

From the album of the same name, 'Are You Gonna Go My Way' finds superstar Lenny Kravitz in the purest and most rockin' moment of his career. Four years since his startling debut album *Let Love Rule* shocked the world, here he was revved up to full throttle. And once he had everyone's attention, Kravitz wasn't about to let go for anything. From the signature guitar riffs and the way the song's structure builds up and releases tension to Kravitz's inimitably sexy and soulful snarls, the track is solid from top to bottom – with maximum tenacious funk.

Linger
The Cranberries

Released February 1993
Island *862800* (U.S. #8) / Island *IS 559* (U.K. #14)

Proof that suspended drone chords will always elevate a song from the mundane to the magical, 'Linger' is a mournful ballad that bears many listens before becoming too mawkish to bear. The Cranberries, later known for their political angst and singer Dolores O'Riordan's tabloid antics, hit an early creative peak with their debut single, which dealt expertly with the ruins of a relationship without ever employing maudlin imagery or petty rent-a-ballad tricks. In fact, the song arrives with a beautiful guitar figure, hits you with a clutch of heart-stopping choruses, and goes away without outstaying its welcome. Shame they never equaled it again.

Everybody Hurts
R.E.M.

Released April 1993
Warner Bros. *18638* (U.S. #29) / Warner Bros. *W 0169* (U.K. #7)

Having climbed to the top of the pop ladder two years earlier with 'Losing My Religion,' R.E.M. consolidated their position among the key rock bands of the 1990s with another moving ballad. The unusually direct lyrics of 'Everybody Hurts' were later used by the British charity Samaritans in advertising aimed to discourage young men from committing suicide.

In the liner notes to *The Best Of R.E.M.*, bandleader Michael Stipe reflected on the song, concluding that "the reason the lyrics are so atypically straightforward is because it was aimed at teenagers. … I've never watched *Buffy The Vampire Slayer*, but the idea that high school is a portal to hell seems pretty realistic to me. It's hard for everyone."

The song features one of the finest vocal performances of Stipe's career; the music was written by drummer Bill Berry, although he was supplanted for the recording by a Univox drum machine. The strings were arranged by former Led Zeppelin bassist John Paul Jones. Aside from the almost-raucous bridge, the rest of the arrangement is as spartan as the lyric, with only gentle electric guitar arpeggios, a simple electric organ figure, and on-beat bass. Like 'Losing My Religion,' the single's success was aided by an affecting promo video.

Cats In The Cradle
Ugly Kid Joe

Released March 1993
Stardog *864888* (U.S. #6) / Mercury *MER 385* (U.K. #7)

And so it was decreed in the Book Of Rock that any band worth its salt shall release a ballad as their third single. Lo! This proved to be the case with Ugly Kid Joe, whose big hit – 'Everything About You' – had been mildly diverting in 1992, and who now wanted to show off their sensitive side with a cover of Harry Chapin's 'Cats In The Cradle.' In fact their version wasn't half bad, with singer Whitfield Crane showcasing a sensitive, sub-Cobain bark that perfectly suited the song's father-and-son theme. Acoustic motifs lent the record sophistication and the future looked temporarily bright for UKJ, although they folded in due course.

What's Up
4 Non Blondes

Released May 1993
Interscope *98430* (U.S. #14) / Interscope *A 8412* (U.K. #2)

Iron-lunged Linda Perry and her band, 4 Non Blondes, did well to nick the chord sequence for this song from a million old hits (including Bobby McFerrin's 'Don't Worry, Be Happy'). Adding a vocal hook consisting of variations on the word "yeah" ensured that Generation X didn't have to work too hard to get the message and, behold, 'What's Up' was a huge hit. It helped, too, that Perry's repeated question of "What's going on?" wasn't aimed at anything in particular. Unfortunately, grunge was on its way out in 1994 and nu-metal was on its way in, which made the neither-here-nor-there 4 Non Blondes instantly unfashionable.

I'd Do Anything For Love (But I Won't Do That)
Meat Loaf

Released September 1993
MCA *54626* (U.S. #1) / Virgin *VSCDT 1443* (U.K. #1)

Meat Loaf's massive success with this song, which topped the charts in no fewer than 28 countries across the globe, is an ideal case study for a comeback that was utterly against the odds and yet surpassed all previous efforts. In his nearly 20-year career, Meat was never as big as he was after 'I Will Do Anything For Love (But I Won't Do That).'

Most critics and armchair pundits had already declared the singer's career long over, gone with the heyday of the *Bat Out Of Hell* album and his rendition of 'Hot Patootie' as the Eddie character in cult classic flick *The Rocky Horror Picture Show*. But his dedication to staying on the road and performing live helped keep his name out there, and people became increasingly interested.

'I Will Do Anything' was certainly a leftfield selection for the hell-raising Mr. Loaf, whose mother named him Marvin Lee Aday when he was born in Dallas, Texas, in 1947. The song's almost operatic arrangement and its regal vocal feel were accurately captured by the dark environs of the video. It helped the *Bat Out Of Hell II* album go on to sell over ten million copies – and, to top it all off, Meat Loaf took home a Grammy for Best Rock Solo Performance in 1994.

No Limit
2 Unlimited

Released January 1993
Radikal-Critique *15499* (U.S.) / PWL Continental *PW 256* (U.K. #1)

Dutch techno had its oh-so-brief moment in the global spotlight when 2 Unlimited took a simple, bleepy tune called 'No Limit' and spun it into world pop success. 'No Limit' did not land in the *Billboard* Hot 100 in America – which wasn't such a surprise, since few techno songs did. However, this oversight might have seemed rather strange to the rest of the world, given that 35 countries embraced the song as a Number 1 hit. Despite that success, 2 Unlimited never became pop stars with any sustainable appeal or longevity.

Nuthin' But A "G" Thang
Dr. Dre

Released February 1993
Death Row *53819* (U.S. #2) / Death Row *A 8328* (U.K. #31)

Dr. Dre was easily the most important hip-hop producer of the 1990s, and he brought his innovative G-Funk sound to the mainstream with 'Nuthin,' which also introduced the wider world to a certain Snoop Doggy Dogg. Before striking out on his own, both as producer and solo artist, Dre was a founding member of the late-1980s West Coast hip-hop group N.W.A., with whom he made the seminal *Straight Outta Compton* LP.

Built around a sample from 'I Want'a Do Something Freaky To You' by smooth 1970s funk artist Leon Haywood, 'Nuthin But A "G" Thang' was the finest example yet of the production style Dre had begun to develop around the turn of the decade. All the hallmarks of his best work are here: the Funkadelic-inspired beats, the stop-start liquid bass, the subtle funk guitar, and the heavy-breathing backing vocals. Dre's talents were many and varied, and he was one of the most clued-up talent spotters around, for 'G Thang' also marks the first time that Snoop Doggy Dogg made it into the *Billboard* Hot 100. Within a year Snoop would reach the Top 10 with two singles of his own, 'What's My Name' and 'Gin & Juice,' in the process becoming the first widely recognized gangsta rapper.

'Nuthin' But A "G" Thang' remains the biggest of Dr. Dre's solo hits, although he did guest on BLACKstreet's 1996 chart-topper 'No Diggity' (which he also produced). Since then, Dre has spent most of his career behind the mixing desk, fashioning hits for such hip-hop heavyweights as 2Pac and Eminem, as well as doling out more pop-orientated fare to the likes of Mary J. Blige and Gwen Stefani.

Whoomp! (There It Is)
Tag Team

Released June 1993
Life *79500* (U.S. #2) / Club Tools *SHXCD 1* (U.K. #34)

The Atlanta-bred duo of DC The Brain Supreme and Steve Roll'n are not exactly household names, but their one hit 'Whoomp! (There It Is)' did win the curiously widespread fame enjoyed by other big 1990s novelties such as 'Macarena' and even 'Achy Breaky Heart.' Tag Team's hit was part of the club-driven, hip-hop-wise style of bass that was springing out

of both Atlanta and Miami, and manages perfectly to encapsulate the frenetic energy of the genre. DC The Brain Supreme can still be found holding it down as the DJ at various Atlanta-area strip clubs, the very spots where many urban hits are discovered.

Human Behaviour
Björk

....

Released June 1993
Elektra *66299* (U.S.) / One Little Indian *112* (U.K. #36)

Venus As A Boy
Björk

....

Released August 1993
Elektra *66273* (U.S.) / One Little Indian *122* (U.K. #29)

'Human Behaviour' and 'Venus As A Boy' launched the solo career of one of the most idiosyncratic talents of the late 20th century. Born and raised in Iceland, Björk had sung in various bands since her teens, most notably The Sugarcubes, who had a U.K. Top 20 hit with the aptly titled 'Hit' in late 1991. Within a year, however, the group's vocalist, nearing the end of her 20s, decided to relocate to London, England, and strike out on her own. There she began working with the cream of the U.K.'s dance music musicians and producers, including keyboardist and programmer Marius De Vries and Soul II Soul founder Nellee Hooper.

The first fruits of their work together was 'Human Behaviour,' a vibrant, up-tempo tune driven by striking, multi-timbral percussion and Björk's cooing vocal and faux-naive lyrics, which according to the singer detail "an animal's point of view on humans." The accompanying promo video was the first of a number of memorable collaborations between Björk and the French director Michel Gondry, and was named Best Breakthrough Promo at the 1994 MTV Awards.

Björk followed 'Human Behaviour' with the similarly exuberant 'Venus As A Boy,' which was the only one of her early singles to feature on the *Greatest Hits* disc of her career-spanning *Family Tree* box set. It's easy to see why – with its sensuous blend of bottle-like percussion sounds, lilting strings, and simple but effective lyrics, 'Venus' has aged much more gracefully than the rest of Björk's early 1990s material and, indeed, the majority of the pop music of the time.

Dreamlover
Mariah Carey

....

Released August 1993
Columbia *77080* (U.S. #1) / Columbia *6594445* (U.K. #9)

Mariah Carey's summertime ditty borrows familiar melodic elements from 'Genius of Love' by Tom Tom Club. Of the dozens of songs that have sampled that 1982 hit, Carey's 'Dreamlover' remains the Club's favorite. "She must have been quite a little girl when [our] song came out, like eight or ten years old," said Tom Tom Club's Tina Weymouth. "I think it reminds her of a happy time in her life, and what she's done with it is very sweet." Weymouth and fellow Tom Tom Club member/husband Chris Frantz are fond too of Carey's remix, which features a guest rap from the late Ol' Dirty Bastard.

Loser
Beck

Released March 1994
DGC-Bong Load *21930* (U.S. #10) / Geffen *GFS 67* (U.K. #15)

'Loser' was the defining moment in the popularization of lo-fi music and introduced the world to one of the most eclectic, multi-talented performers of the 1990s. Lo-fi is an umbrella term for music recorded using somewhat primitive means but that nonetheless succeeds despite the relatively low production values. Its emergence coincided with the arrival of cheap 4-track tape recorders in the 1980s, which allowed musicians to make recordings at home on a low budget. But it did not filter into the mainstream until the likes of Beck, Pavement, and Elliott Smith began to make waves in the first half of the '90s.

Born in 1970 in Los Angeles, Beck Hansen spent some time within the New York avant-folk East Village coffee-house scene in the late 1980s before returning to the West Coast and making a clutch of one-off singles for various independent labels in the early '90s. One of these was 'Loser,' first recorded for the tiny Bong Load imprint. It was among the earliest of the genre-bending experiments for which he became famous, mixing his love for Delta Blues with a keen admiration for hip-hop, particularly Public Enemy. (Beck went on to make his finest album, *Odelay*, with that legendary group's production team, The Bomb Squad.)

Musically, 'Loser' is remarkably simple, consisting of little more than a looped drumbeat and a couple of dirty, bluesy guitar lines. It was recorded, fittingly, on a 4-track machine by Beck and co-author Carl Stephenson, another musician clearly schooled in the lo-fi aesthetic. The vocal is an ironic half-spoken, half-sung semi-rap about being a social outcast. The mocking tag-line – "I'm a loser baby / So why don't you kill me?" – was a jokey response to the singer's inability to rap like Public Enemy's Chuck D. He can't, of course, but that doesn't limit the appeal of a song that eventually became known as the anthem of a supposed 'slacker generation' – ironic given that the pre-fame Beck worked long, low-paid hours to support his musical endeavors.

The initial 1993 release of 'Loser' by Bong Load had been a small-scale affair and had resulted in little airplay and no chart success. But it did spark a bidding war between major labels. Beck ultimately signed to Geffen, who offered him the freedom to carry on making occasional lower-profile albums for smaller labels. (In fact this only happened once, in 1995, when *One Foot In The Grave* was released by K Records. Beck had intended his 1998 set, *Mutations*, to be given a similarly low-key release, but Geffen intervened, and the label has since taken charge of all the singer's subsequent work.)

The first thing Geffen did after signing Beck in 1994 was to reissue 'Loser,' and with major label money behind it, the single was a memorable, inspirational international hit. Beck has since recorded a number of other highly acclaimed albums and singles, but none will be as fondly remembered as this.

She Don't Use Jelly
The Flaming Lips

Released August 1994
Warner Bros. *218131* (U.S.) / Warner Bros. *W 0246* (U.K.)

'She Don't Use Jelly' was a surprise one-off hit (Number 55 in the U.S.) for one of the few truly original bands of modern times. The Flaming Lips started out from Oklahoma in the mid 1980s as an outré psychedelic act but had mellowed sufficiently to sign a deal with Warners in 1992. Even so, few would have expected this alt-bubblegum curio to reach the charts. An even more surreal touch came as the band rode the crest of their 15-minute fame-wave by performing the song on *Beverly Hills 90210* and receiving the backing of the teen soap's Steve Sanders (played by Ian Ziering), who announced: "I've never been a big fan of alternative music, but these guys rocked!"

Girls And Boys
Blur

Released March 1994
SBK *58115* (U.S.) / Food *47* (U.K. #5)

Parklife
Blur

Released August 1994
Not issued U.S. / Food *53* (U.K. #10)

With these two singles, Blur announced themselves as the leading lights of Britpop, the dominant trend in British music and culture during the mid 1990s. The London-based group's second album, *Modern Life Is Rubbish* (1993), was essentially a template for the bands that followed. Often thought of as a response to grunge, Britpop grouped together a loose affiliation of bands inspired by British guitar-led pop of the 1960s and 1970s.

Blur, however, were always a step ahead of their contemporaries, whose records were often mere carbon copies of The Small Faces, The Beatles, and others. 'Girls And Boys,' the first single from the group's third full-length effort, *Parklife,* has a disco backbeat and funky bassline reminiscent of Blondie and provided by the under-appreciated rhythm section of Dave Rowntree and Alex James. Guitarist Graham Coxon adds spiky, staccato chords, while vocalist Damon Albarn offers the main hook, an infectious, tongue-twisting chorus about "Girls who are boys / Who like boys to be girls …"

'Girls And Boys' was Blur's highest-charting single in the U.K. so far, and gave the group a rare U.S. hit (Number 59), but it was 'Parklife' that confirmed the quartet as the darlings of British music. A joyous faux-cockney romp, it features a guest spoken-word vocal by Phil Daniels, star of the movie version of The Who's *Quadrophenia*. His dulcet tones perfectly compliment Albarn's arch lyric, which includes such gems as: "John's got brewer's droop / He gets intimidated by the dirty pigeons."

Black Hole Sun
Soundgarden

Released August 1994
Not issued U.S. / A&M *5807532* (U.K. #12)

With its spacious, dreamy verses and bruising chorus, 'Black Hole Sun' was one of the finest alternative rock singles of the decade. Because they were from Seattle and making heavy, guitar-based music, Soundgarden were lumped in with grunge, but had actually been in existence for several years before Nirvana, Pearl Jam, and the others

came along. Like the majority of the group's singles, 'Black Hole Sun' – which features on their fourth album, *Superunknown* – was not issued as a physical single in America, but the album cut made Number 24 on *Billboard*'s Airplay chart and was a huge MTV hit.

All I Wanna Do
Sheryl Crow

Released June 1994
A&M *0702* (U.S. #2) / A&M *580842* (U.K. #4)

This breezy, carefree hit, tailor-made for summer afternoons on the open highway, provided the launch-pad for one of the most popular adult-orientated rock acts of the 1990s. Before achieving her chart breakthrough with 'All I Wanna Do,' Sheryl Crow worked as a session singer, most notably touring with Michael Jackson. She sought a record deal of her own but found that the imagination of most major labels extended little further than wanting to turn her into a grown-up Debbie Gibson.

Crow signed to A&M in 1991 and made an aborted first attempt at recording her debut with Police producer Hugh Padgham, whose polished pop sheen was not to her taste. Instead she started working informally with a group of seasoned session musicians, including her boyfriend, Kevin Gilbert, and producer-guitarist Bill Bottrell. These clever creative types named their Tuesday-night musical evenings the *Tuesday Night Music Club*, and gave the same name to the record they recorded together, which became Crow's debut. The album did little business until 'All I Wanna Do' was sent out to radio stations. Carefully driven by lilting slide-guitar and handclaps, the single was – somewhat ironically, given Crow's dismay at the earlier attempts to make her album – much more slick and polished than the rest of *Tuesday Night*. Crow found the lyrics in a book of poetry by Wyn Cooper, who earned an unexpected fortune from the song when it became one of the biggest hits of 1994.

Sabotage
Beastie Boys

Released July 1994
Capitol *58171* (U.S.) / Capitol *CL 716* (U.K. B-side; A #19)

From the fourth album *Ill Communication*, 'Sabotage' wasn't exactly what one would call a runaway chart-topping sensation for the Beastie Boys, that wacky rapping trio of Ad-Rock, MCA, and Mike D who first stormed the world in the late 1980s with drunken antics and clever rhymes. But it has a fond place in the hearts of so many fans because it was a tune that proclaimed in no uncertain terms that the group was not only here to stay, it planned on causing some serious damage as well. The song's power guitar chords and squelchy scratches are perfectly matched by the urgency of the vocal delivery.

The downright silly music video for 'Sabotage' made it an instant favorite on MTV, which aired it as if the Beastie Boys were one of the only bands on the planet. Directed by longtime cohort Spike Jonze (who has worked with artists such as Björk and Fatboy Slim), it parodies 1970s cop dramas like *Chips* and *Starsky & Hutch* with hilarious pomp and circumstance. Handlebar mustaches, loud suits, and spirited chases – it's all there, and then some. Other songs such as 'Sureshot' and 'Get It Together' were consistent enough to keep Beastie Boys fans excited about the album, but 'Sabotage' ultimately provided the rocket-fuel blast to take *Ill Communication* through sales of more than three million copies in the United States alone.

Gin & Juice
Snoop Doggy Dogg

Released February 1994
Death Row *98318* (U.S. #8) / Death Row *A 8316* (U.K. #39)

Regulate
Warren G & Nate Dogg

Released May 1994
Death Row *98280* (U.S. #2) / Death Row *A 8290* (U.K. #5)

These two hip-hop mega-hits are bound together by family ties. Snoop Doggy Dogg was discovered by and worked closely with hip-hop super-producer Dr. Dre, the half brother of Warren G – who launched his own musical career with a collaboration with Snoop's cousin, Nate Dogg. Both singles are rooted in the G-funk sound Dre developed to such striking effect on his own U.S. Number 2 hit 'Nuthin' But A "G" Thang' and the accompanying album, *The Chronic*.

'Gin & Juice' is the second and most memorable of Snoop Doggy Dogg's early hits, which wisely stick closely to the sound of the two Dr. Dre singles on which he had previously appeared, 'Deep Cover' and the 'G Thang.' With 'Gin & Juice,' Dogg was confirmed as one of the most distinctively talented rappers of his generation. His laidback and apparently effortless style seemed somewhat at odds with his image, defined by his complicity in a gang-related shooting the previous year. (Dogg was acquitted, on grounds of self-defense, but related charges hung around him for the next few years.)

Like his half-brother, Warren G is a skilled rapper and producer (although both are more adept at the latter than the former). 'Regulate' is smoother and slicker than the bulk of Dre's work. Similarly, at a time when angry, confrontational gangsta rap was becoming increasingly widespread, the lyrics and delivery here hark back to the gentler themes of early-1980s hip-hop and are complemented neatly by Nate Dogg's soulful vocal delivery.

Bump N' Grind
R. Kelly

Released February 1994
Jive *42207* (U.S. #1) / Jive *368* (U.K. #8)

From the freakily titled album *12 Play* came this breakthrough single from Chicago singer Robert Kelly. He had already made waves as part of the R&B group Public Announcement before striking out with this overtly sexual opus. "I don't see nothing wrong with a little bump'n'grind," he sings suggestively, and neither did the legions of loyal female fans that the song and video netted for Kelly. Given his later troubles with the law relating to charges of child pornography, 'Bump N' Grind' and related songs like 'Downlow' seem all the more ironic with the benefit of hindsight.

The Most Beautiful Girl In The World
The Artist Formerly Known As Prince

Released March 1994
NPG-Bellmark *72514* (U.S. #3) / NPG *60155* (U.K. #1)

With its video evoking the sheer goodness of Mother's Day celebrations, 'Most Beautiful Girl' is a sweet ballad in praise of women that stands in stark innocence when compared to the remarkably unbridled and risqué songs that are liberally sprinkled through Prince's catalog. The song was inspired by Prince's lust for Vanessa Marcil, a gorgeous American actress known primarily for her roles in *General Hospital*, *Melrose Place*, and most recently *Las Vegas*.

Although the song earned Prince his first Number 1 hit in Britain, it is more significant to note 'Beautiful Girl' as a useful marker for his change of name to The Artist Formerly Known As Prince – or simply The Artist, represented by his own proprietary logo, which fused the male and female signs together with a flourish. This infamous shift was a result of Prince's dissatisfaction with his prohibitively long-term recording and publishing contracts at Warner Brothers. It was an upset so profound that he took to writing the word 'slave' on his face in public and comparing his plight to segregationist times. He began to speak of "emancipation from the chains that bind" and ceased promoting earlier work issued under the Prince name. Ironically, his publishing contract with Warner-Chappell expired on December 31, 1999, giving the Artist his name back and, no doubt, the urge to party like it's 1999.

7 Seconds
Youssou N'Dour Featuring Neneh Cherry

Released June 1994
Sony *77482* (U.S.) / Columbia *660508* (U.K. #3)

The combination of washed-up female rapper and Afrobeat star doesn't sound promising on paper, but when Senegalese singer Youssou N'Dour teamed with Neneh Cherry for this ambient trip-hop composition, the

world stopped to listen. For '7 Seconds' they took a Bach-originated descending bassline, smothered it in a nice warm synth-wash, and added alternating vocals for the verse before a dramatic drop to the chorus line – so simple it had to be a hit.

'7 Seconds' equalled Cherry's highest ever chart placing in the U.K., although she bettered it early the following year when she appeared on the British Number 1 charity single 'Love Can Build A Bridge' alongside Eric Clapton and The Pretenders' Chrissie Hynde. She had a further U.K. Top 10 hit in 1996 with 'Woman,' which evoked '7 Seconds' in its use of a similar descending chord progression. N'Dour, meanwhile, never troubled the charts again, but continues to make records, and maintains a devoted following across Europe and Africa.

Love Is All Around
Wet Wet Wet

Released May 1994
London *856194* (U.S.) / Precious *JWL 23* (U.K. #1)

Rock observers had been waiting for years for some canny pop chancers to update the excellent 1967 Troggs hit 'Love Is All Around' and knew that when it came it would hit big. But no one could have predicted the impact in Britain of Wet Wet Wet's sickly-sweet version of Reg Presley's cheery tune, assisted by the *Four Weddings And A Funeral* soundtrack on which it appeared. The song went on to become the longest-reigning Number 1 single in the U.K., notching up no fewer than 15 weeks at the top (although it made only Number 41 in America). Pellow and his pals deserved the success: they added a cunning orchestration and an upgraded vocal melody on the last chorus, adding up to a big improvement on the original.

Kiss From A Rose
Seal

Released July 1994
ZTT-Sire *17896* (U.S. #1) / ZTT *ZANG 52* (U.K. #4)

After the runaway success of Seal's first self-titled album in 1991, expectations were high for the follow-up. When it arrived – another eponymous set – 'Kiss From A Rose' was an immediate high point, even if the rest of the album struggled to match up.

It's clever stuff. Although 'Kiss From A Rose' masquerades quite efficiently as a mere lover's ballad from start to finish, Seal throws in every sub-Bacharach & David trick he can think of to make it fly. For starters, there's that lovely clarinet theme; then he opens each chorus with a highly hummable wail of "Bay-bee!" that covers close to an octave in a word; then for good measure he throws in a vocal round composed of multiple croons of "I've been kissed by a rose". The man has obviously studied the fine art of songwriting, and is a master musician too.

Surprisingly, 'Kiss From A Rose' was only a minor hit in the U.K. on its initial release in 1994, and was not issued at all in the U.S. at the time. Then, the following summer, it was used on the soundtrack to *Batman Forever*, its glittering production well matched by the movie's glossy look, and gained a new lease of life on both sides of the Atlantic. Seal's slick music fell out of vogue shortly afterwards, but songs such as this remain among the finest singer-songwriter records of the decade.

Here Comes The Hotstepper
Ini Kamoze

Released October 1994
Columbia *77614* (U.S. #1) / Columbia *6610472* (U.K. #4)

Ini Kamoze (born Cecil Campbell) remains one of the few Jamaican dancehall acts to make an impact on the charts in America and Britain. Disco aficionados recognized the instrumental in 'Hotstepper' as that of 'Heartbeat' by Taana Gardner, a song released in 1981 through New York's West End Records. Unfortunately, Kamoze was about a decade too early to fully capitalize on the dancehall craze that later hit America hard, thanks to artists such as Sean Paul and Elephant Man. Instead, he brought a brief flash of island fire to transatlantic airwaves with this international smash – and was never heard from again.

Back For Good
Take That

Released April 1995
Arista *12848* (U.S. #7) / RCA *1271462* (U.K. #1)

"I wrote 'Back For Good' in 10 minutes," grinned Take That songwriter Gary Barlow after the song became a gigantic success. He might well grin: the tune used the same ascending chord sequence as a stack of other hits. Cleverly, he used the same chords in the verse and the chorus but separated the two with a simple bridge, adding a standard middle-eight. The only other touch of sophistication was the alternating lead and backing vocals, which flipped around for the outro. So that's how to write a hit.

Barlow and his crew (Jason Orange, Howard Donald, Mark Owen, and some show-off kid called Robbie Williams) are still the supreme boy-band in Britain, following their 2005 comeback, even as the genre passes its first decade in business. Among the first of the newer breed of deliberately manufactured pop acts, Take That manage to retain some credibility by writing many of their own hits and possessing genuine vocal talent. And they launched Williams's phenomenally successful solo career.

Only the Irish quintets Boyzone and Westlife came close to unseating Take That from their British throne, although innumerable acts such as East 17 have tried and failed to do so. This is because Take That have the songs, no matter how anodyne the delivery or ludicrous the dance routines – a lesson that wannabe boy-bands should note. 'Back For Good,' although it's cheesier than a bowl of Parmesan, and is the group's only U.S. hit, is the gold standard that the kids and their managers should aim for.

Buddy Holly
Weezer

Released April 1995
Not issued U.S. / Geffen *GFS 88* (U.K. #12)

"Oo-wee-oo, I look just like Buddy Holly / Oh-oh, and you're Mary Tyler Moore," warbled Weezer singer Rivers Cuomo in the L.A. quartet's breakthrough single, 'Buddy Holly,' an entertaining mish-mash of influences that would inspire a whole raft of nerdy oh-so-ironic alternative-rock bands (There was no physical single in the U.S., but the album cut made Number 18 on *Billboard*'s Airplay chart.)

It was probably the extremely popular video that was responsible for the band's subsequent rise to a respectable B-league status in alt.rock. Thanks to the magic of movie technology, Weezer were superimposed onto the stage of Arnolds, the diner in the old *Happy Days* sitcom. Cuomo and band walked through the song dressed in the 1950s preppie wear that characters such as the young Ron Howard had worn in the original series – in other words, they looked like geeks of the highest order.

The song was inspired by the band's incessant comments about Cuomo's then-girlfriend, a highly eccentric Korean, hence the line "Your tongue is twisted, your eyes are slit." It became something of a teen anthem, helped by the resolution to a payoff line: "I don't care what they say about us anyway." The evolving emo generation bought into the song with enthusiasm, responding in droves to the 'geeks rule' ethos and Weezer's tongue-in-cheek approach. Thousands even bought a pair of horn-rimmed glasses – as it happened, the one essential nerd accessory that Cuomo didn't use in the 'Buddy Holly' video. Is that ironic irony, or irony squared? Either way, Weezer are responsible for a lot, even if their career never again rose to these same heights.

Free As A Bird
The Beatles

Released December 1995
Apple *58497* (U.S. #6) / Apple *R 6422* (U.K. #2)

'Free As A Bird' was built around an opaque demo vocal from the 15-years-late John Lennon and was The Threetles' sort-of-comeback single, issued to tie in with the start of the remarkable *Anthology* compilation albums and TV series. Lennon's vocal sounded disappointingly weak and thin – an inevitable result of the passage of time and the condition of the pre-digital tapes – and doubly so in comparison with that of Paul McCartney, who chipped in on the middle section and elsewhere. But the production was fat, warm, and organic, with Ringo's drum sound right on the money, Macca's bass as huggable as always (and he didn't overdo the fills), and George's guitar as ever a thing of beauty, especially the masterful slide intro.

What of the song itself? The structure was based on a descending chord sequence straight out of Beatles cliché, but worked well enough and could have come from any of a dozen 1960s bands with a knack for a semi-classical progression. The sentiments that 'Free As A Bird' expressed were more or less contained in the title. But this was that unique thing – at least until the follow-up single 'Real Love' came along – *a new song by The Beatles*. Very few people were going to argue with that. And in case anyone wasn't sure, they stuck a fade-out on the end that could have come straight off *Revolver*. You half expected McCartney to mutter "cranberry sauce" two octaves too low.

Alright
Supergrass

Released July 1995
Capitol *82277* (U.S.) / Parlophone *R 6413* (U.K. #2)

As Britpop flourished and grunge waned, the cheekiest of the cheeky new British bands was Supergrass, who seemed to leap straight out of the radio, simultaneously warm and dated like the 1970s and new and glistening like the '90s. Kicking off with a wonky piano break and adding a melodic bass lick, the song bounded along like an overenthusiastic puppy, weaseling its way into everyone's psyche and making Supergrass, three scamps from Oxford, into willing stars. In due course all this cheeky-chappy foolishness began to wear thin and the band adopted a more grown-up approach, but 'Alright' remains a prime early candidate for 'grass greatness.

Common People
Pulp

Released May 1995
Island *7138* (U.S.) / Island *CID 613* (U.K. #2)

The Britpop years may have been dominated by Blur and Oasis, but the era's finest single came from Pulp. A nerdy anti-hero in the Buddy Holly mold, Jarvis Cocker formed Pulp in 1981 but didn't achieve anything approaching success for over a decade. That finally changed with 'Common People,' his amusing almost-true story of a snooty Greek art student who couldn't quite bring herself to rough it. Pitched somewhere between krautrock and glam-pop, the single became an instant classic in the U.K. but did little business elsewhere. It was given a bizarre new reading in 2004 when it was covered by *Star Trek*'s William Shatner.

Wonderwall
Oasis

Released October 1995
Epic *78216* (U.S. #8) / Creation *CRE 215* (U.K. #2)

Love 'em or hate 'em, Oasis were the biggest British group of the 1990s, and their 'Wonderwall' one of the decade's defining singles. Led by the irrepressible Gallagher brothers – vocalist Liam and songwriter-guitarist Noel – Oasis came bursting out of Manchester in 1994 with the U.K.'s fastest-selling debut album ever, *Definitely Maybe*, which drew on the best bits of the past three decades of British music: The Beatles, T. Rex, The Sex Pistols, etc.

The following year the group became embroiled in a high-profile, press-orchestrated feud that pitched the five working class lads from the industrial north of England against Blur, four former art students from down south. The rivalry reached its peak in August when both issued new singles on the same day: and Blur's chirpy 'Country House' beat Oasis's tepid 'Roll With It' to Number 1.

Had Oasis chosen to release this instead, Blur might not have been so lucky. Taking its name from the 1968 film of the same name, which featured a soundtrack by George Harrison, 'Wonderwall' is one of the finest and most elegant songs in the Noel Gallagher songbook, and features one of his younger brother's strongest and most affecting vocal performances. Eight other Oasis singles have gone one better on the U.K. chart – including 'Don't Look Back In Anger' (1996) and 'All Around The World' (1998) – but this remains the group's defining moment. It has become a regular fixture on British polls to find the greatest singles of all time and is the band's only significant U.S. hit to date.

Don't Stop (Wiggle Wiggle)
The Outhere Brothers

Released February 1995
Aureus *AU1200-1* (U.S.) / Eternal *YZ 917* (U.K. #1)

This year, concern about obscene lyrics on rap and heavy-rock records resulted in potentially offensive releases being stickered with parental advisory warnings. Unexpectedly, sales went up, because we now knew which records were cool without having to listen to them first.

Perhaps worried that their single might not get stickered, foul-mouthed Chicago rap duo The Outhere Brothers made the parental warning an integral part of their single's cover design. 'Don't Stop' zoomed to Number 1 in the U.K., but it wasn't until the equally naughty follow-up, 'Boom Boom Boom,' had spent four weeks at Number 1 that the authorities finally noticed and banned it, which of course enhanced sales still further.

Scatman (Ski-Ba-Bop-Ba-Dop-Bop)
Scatman John

Released May 1995
RCA *64379* (U.S.) / RCA *281712* (U.K. #3)

Surely the combination of jazz scatting and house-trance could never work? That's what many thought in horror as 'Scatman (Ski-Bap-Bop-Ba-Dop-Bop)' ascended the British charts in 1995. But it did work, with Scatman John – an American, John Paul Larkin, who had learned to scat to overcome a stutter – doing his rapid-fire thing over a euphoric house groove that in fact worked rather well on the dancefloor. The rapped verses were nothing special and the song grated after a couple of listens, but if you were 13 years old it probably sounded like the best thing ever recorded. Larkin didn't have long to enjoy his newfound fame, succumbing to lung cancer in 1999.

Waterfalls
TLC

Released June 1995
LaFace *24107* (U.S. #1) / LaFace *298812* (U.K. #4)

From the blockbuster album *CrazySexyCool*, which spawned multiple hits and has sold over ten million copies in America, this is considered by many fans to be the signature song from Tionne 'T-Boz' Watkins, Lisa 'Left Eye' Lopes, and Rozonda 'Chilli' Thomas, the R&B supernova known as TLC. Although the life of the Atlanta-bred outfit was cut short with Left Eye's tragic death in a car accident in Honduras in 2002, TLC are one of the most successful female groups of all time.

Most of their songs tended towards the lighter and funkier side, but 'Waterfalls' is a cautionary tale ("Don't go chasing waterfalls / Please stick to the rivers and the lakes that you're used to"), ushering in new respect as the group proved they could bring substance to their songs. The memorable video features computer-generated sequences of the ladies dancing on water as various characters are shown traveling the wrong paths, leading to destruction and untimely ends.

'Waterfalls' was nominated for two Grammys and helped TLC take home the award for Best R&B Album for *CrazySexyCool*. The song was produced by Organized Noize (Patrick 'Sleepy' Brown, Ray Murray, and Rico Wade), the studio wizards credited for nurturing and developing the career of another wildly successful group, Atlanta hip-hop duo OutKast. In fact, it was TLC who gave OutKast their first visible guest appearance in the early 1990s thanks to the remix of the TLC single 'What About Your Friends.'

I Got 5 On It
Luniz

Released June 1995
Noo Trybe *38474* (U.S. #8) / Virgin America *VUSCD 101* (U.K. #3)

The San Francisco Bay Area has been a fertile ground for hip-hop music of all flavors, but this ode to smoking marijuana has transcended local fame while remaining a homegrown staple. Oakland's Luniz (Yukmouth and Numskull) twisted up their original version, which features a hook from R&B singer Michael Marshall, and made a remix, legendary for its inclusion of top Bay Area rap stars Shock G, E-40, Spice 1, Dru Down, and Richie Rich, all together on one track. There was U.S. Top 40 success for the original (Number 8) as well as the remix (Number 28).

I Wish
Skee-Lo

Released July 1995
Sunshine *78032* (U.S. #13) / Wild Card *5777752* (U.K. #15)

Rappers by nature are usually much more boastful than shy, but not Skee-Lo (a.k.a. Antoine Roundtree). His sole U.S. hit 'I Wish' is quite possibly the most unegotistical tune ever to have been set to a hip-hop beat. Over a multi-layered pastiche of clever samples and a patented West Coast bounce, he rhymes: "I wish I was a little bit taller / I wish I was a baller / I wish I had a girl who looked good / I would call her." The song was pervasive enough to earn the album of the same name a Grammy nomination for Best Rap Album.

One Of Us
Joan Osborne

Released December 1995
Mercury *852368* (U.S. #4) / Blue Gorilla *JOACD 1* (U.K. #6)

Once in a blue moon, pop music's perennial concerns about love, intoxication, and dancing in the moonlight are briefly joined by a one-off hit single that seems to swim in deeper waters. 'One Of Us,' written by Eric Bazilian of The Hooters, was that record for this year.

Osborne, very much in the prevailing mode of Alanis Morissette and Sheryl Crow, invited us to ponder how it might be "if God was one of us … just a stranger on a bus." The single went gold, the accompanying album, *Relish*, went triple platinum, and Prince described it as "a great melody and an important statement." What more can you ask?

Gangsta's Paradise
Coolio Featuring L.V.

Released August 1995
MCA Soundtracks *55104* (U.S. #1) / Tommy Boy *MCSTD 2104* (U.K. #1)

What could actress Jodie Foster and music legend Stevie Wonder possibly have to do with a West Coast gangsta rap song? Plenty, for hip-hop artist Coolio (a.k.a. Artis Ivey) and L.V. (a wheelchair-using R&B singer) recorded this song for the soundtrack of *Dangerous Minds* (a movie starring Foster as a teacher at a troubled school), basing it on Wonder's 'Pastime Paradise.' Coolio had worked the same trick a year earlier on 'Fantastic Voyage,' which drew on The Ohio Players' song of the same name and hit Number 3 on *Billboard*.

'Gangsta's Paradise' earned Coolio a Grammy for Best Rap Solo Performance and topped the charts on both sides of the Atlantic, making it the U.K.'s first gangsta rap chart-topper and the first hip-hop single to sell over a million copies there. Like many big hits before – among them 'Beat It' by Michael Jackson and Nirvana's 'Smells Like Teen Spirit' – the most successful single of Coolio's career received the dubious honor of being parodied by Weird Al Yankovich, who re-titled the song 'Amish Paradise.'

You Are Not Alone
Michael Jackson

Released August 1995
Epic *78002* (U.S. #1) / Epic *662 3102* (U.K. #1)

Scream
Michael Jackson & Janet Jackson

Released June 1995
Epic *78000* (U.S. #5) / Epic *662 0222* (U.K. #3)

Constant controversy was still a staple of Michael Jackson's diet by 1995, even if he felt he hadn't done much to heat up the oven. Written by R&B crooner R. Kelly, 'You Are Not Alone' is mainly remembered for its accompanying visuals. At the time Jackson was married to Lisa Marie Presley, daughter of Elvis, and the video is an awkward physical display – semi-nude – of a relationship that continues to puzzle the general public. Many commented on how Jackson's skin tone appears almost as milky white as his wife's.

The 1989 single 'Leave Me Alone' had been Jackson's first overt attack on the paparazzi and media that feasted on all the truths and half-truths of his life, which at that time included stories like buying the bones of the Elephant Man and sleeping in a hyperbaric chamber. With the help of sister Janet, 'Scream' revisits the same topic in much more confrontational form ("Just stop pressuring me / Makes me want to scream").

'Scream' was produced by Jimmy 'Jam' Harris and Terry Lewis, the Minneapolis duo who had groomed Janet for international superstardom with her 1986 album *Control*. Where the animated video for 'Leave Me Alone' softened the message of the song with its cuteness, the black-and-white flick for 'Scream' featured the Jackson siblings scowling and executing aggressive choreography. It reportedly cost $7 million to film – a price which, more than a decade on, still seems staggering and extravagant. To put it into perspective, Michael Jackson's breakthrough video for 'Thriller' cost a mere $800,000.

Missing (remix)
Everything But The Girl

Released October 1995
Atlantic *87124* (U.S. #2) / Blanco y Negro *NEG 84CD* (U.K. #3)

DJs and remixers have been responsible for giving previously unseen success to some unlikely artists through dancefloor hits. Such is the case with the U.K.'s Everything But The Girl (partners Tracey Thorn and Ben Watt). No one would have expected the mellow twosome to craft songs for dance parties, but the band's only American hit was a club-friendly take on EBTG's original acoustic song 'Missing,' souped up with a lively beat by New York house music legend Todd Terry. Watt later turned much of his attention to DJing, starting a British club night called Lazy Dog and touring all over the world.

One Sweet Day
Mariah Carey & Boyz II Men

Released November 1995
Columbia *78074* (U.S. #1) / Columbia *6626035* (U.K. #6)

Judged on musical content alone, 'One Sweet Day' doesn't sound like a particularly remarkable single, but this duet by two of the hottest R&B acts of the decade holds the record for the longest stint at the top of the *Billboard* Hot 100.

The song itself was borne out of tragedy. In January 1995, David Cole, one half of C&C Music Factory and a close friend and frequent collaborator of Carey's, died following an unspecified illness. At the same time as Carey's grief began to blossom into a song, Boyz II Men were working on a musical tribute to their murdered road manager, Khalil Roundtree. On hearing that they were both working on similar efforts, the two acts decided to pool their resources, resulting in this collaborative effort.

'One Sweet Day' shot straight in at Number 1 on the U.S. charts and remained there for a total of 16 weeks. Neither act was a stranger to long stays at the top: Boyz II Men had twice held the same record, with 'End Of The Road' (13 weeks) and 'I'll Make Love To You' (14 weeks); two of Carey's previous singles, 'Dreamlover' and 'Fantasy,' had sat at the top of the pile for eight weeks each. 'One Sweet Day' was up for Record Of The Year and Best Pop Collaboration (With Vocals) at the 1996 Grammy Awards, bringing Carey's total nominations for the year to six. She left empty-handed, however, but not before she had made her humiliation very clear, and declined to attend another Grammy event until 2006.

Spaceman
Babylon Zoo

Released January 1996
EMI *10485* (U.S.) / EMI *CDEM 416* (U.K. #1)

Boosted by its use in a TV ad for Levi's jeans, 'Spaceman' was the kind of one-hit-wonder single that polarizes opinion. Babylon Zoo singer Jas Mann, a sort of proto-Marilyn Manson, had the right look, a killer PR campaign, and a fairly decent song in 'Spaceman.' But the decision to switch the song mid-way through from sub-Depeche Mode miserabilia to shrieking, warp-speed fast-forward gimmickry provoked delight and disdain in equal measure. The double-speed section of the song was in fact not part of the original, but was taken from a remix by the legendary American DJ and record producer Arthur Baker.

Firestarter
The Prodigy

Released March 1996
Maverick *17387* (U.S. #30) / XL *70CD* (U.K. #1)

Born Slippy
Underworld
Released July 1996
TVT *8731* (U.S.) / Junior Boy's Own *JBO 44CDS* (U.K. #2)

Setting Sun
Chemical Brothers
Released October 1996
Astralwerks *6176* (U.S.) / Freestyle Dust-Virgin *CHEMSD 4* (U.K. #1)

For a brief period, as the Britpop scene began to implode in a cocaine fog, British music was dominated by electronic acts, who at one point even threatened to break into the U.S. mainstream. The biggest of these was The Prodigy, whose harsh but hook-laden techno hits had made regular appearances on the U.K. chart since the early 1990s.

On 'Firestarter,' the group's former concert dancer Keith Flint takes center stage, delivering a John Lydon-style rant about his not-so-latent pyromania, over a barrage of ferocious beats and distorted guitar samples. The accompanying promo video, set on a disused London Underground line, drew countless complaints, but that did nothing to halt the single's unstoppable rise to the top of the U.K. chart. The similarly menacing 'Breathe' repeated the feat, while the subsequent Prodigy album, *The Fat Of The Land*, was a transatlantic Number 1.

Several months after 'Firestarter' came the definitive hit by the more cerebral techno trio Underworld. The group had existed in various forms since 1983 but was thrust into the mainstream when 'Born Slippy' – an infectious blend of freeform vocals, delayed piano chords, and frenetic programmed rhythms – was featured on the soundtrack to the cult hit movie *Trainspotting*. The Chemical Brothers, meanwhile, were the kings of big beat, an upbeat strand of electronica. 'Setting Sun' featured a guest vocal by Oasis's Noel Gallagher, giving him a second U.K. Number 1 hit of 1996 (and U.S. Number 80) following his own group's 'Don't Look Back In Anger.'

Ironic
Alanis Morissette

Released March 1996
Maverick-Sire *17698* (U.S. #4) / Maverick *W 0343CD* (U.K. #11)

While Alanis Morissette doesn't appear to understand the titular concept of her biggest hit – "rain on your wedding day" might be irritating, but there's nothing explicitly ironic about it – she certainly knows her way around a radio-friendly pop chorus. The success of this single – and its follow-up, 'You Learn' – helped make her *Jagged Little Pill* the biggest-selling debut album of all time. (She had made an earlier dance-pop record as a teenager but that sold only in her native Canada.)

Morissette first caught the attention of rock audiences in summer 1995 with the release of the furious, vengeful 'You Oughta Know.' The song's lyric became the cause of much speculation when it was revealed to be about the lecherous, manipulative behavior of an unnamed music-industry figure. The singer has never revealed his identity, aside from whispering it to Larry David in an episode of *Curb Your Enthusiasm*.

Impressive as 'You Oughta Know' was, Morissette needed something gentler and more melodic to facilitate her mainstream breakthrough. 'Ironic' was just the ticket, and its jangly guitars and angsty – but not too angsty – vocals became a regular fixture on rock and pop radio stations throughout the spring and summer of 1996. With this proper smash hit in the bag, Morissette cemented her position on the crest of the wave of female alternative rock performers – Tori Amos, Jewel, Joan Osborne, and the rest – who flooded the market during the mid 1990s.

Macarena
Los Del Rio

Released May 1996
RCA *64407* (U.S. #1) / RCA *1345372* (U.K. #2)

'Macarena' sees an obscure Spanish song gets reworked into an international dance smash. One of the biggest novelty hits of all time, the Latin song introduces the world's easiest and most inane dance. Its

sheer simplicity helped catapult the song into worldwide domination, with a shelf life far longer than it deserved (it charted for well over a year in some countries). The unlikely hit stayed in the Number 1 spot in America for 14 weeks, a feat achieved by very few artists, among them the mighty Elvis Presley.

Wannabe
The Spice Girls

Released July 1996
Virgin *38579* (U.S. #1) / Virgin *VSCDX 1588* (U.K. #1)

The Spice Girls' remarkable debut and instant signature song 'Wannabe' was put together by Richard Stannard and Matt Rowe, a successful songwriting team. The duo had written three hits for East 17, the British boy-band of the moment, and agreed to work with the five-woman vocal group after seeing a showcase performance they gave late in 1994.

The Girls' claims of self-determination went too far when publicists insisted that the group – none of whom played musical instruments – wrote all of the lyrics and most of the music for their records, which is clearly untrue. Certainly it's unlikely that, despite the formal credits, they co-wrote 'Wannabe,' but their personalities and outlook can surely be discerned in the lyric and sentiment of this, the second song that Stannard and Rowe devised for the Girls. (The first, 'Feed Your Love,' was ultimately rejected as too raunchy for their intended audience.)

Rowe set up a drum loop, and its strutting nature reminded him of 'You're The One That I Want' from the movie *Grease,* which in turn led to a song with a certain feistiness. It's hard not to imagine the composers bombarded with ideas by their eager charges among the song's tidal wave of catchphrases and sarcastic remarks. A few hard-rock guitar riffs and the most inane euphemism ever devised for sexual congress, "Zig-a-zig-ahh," completed the ridiculously catchy and quotable anthem.

The song's key phrase is "If you wanna be my lover / You gotta get with my friends," a declaration that no man will come between the girls and their female mates. It's easy to mock The Spice Girls' toytown feminism manifested in that line and in their slogan Girl Power (appropriated from now-forgotten girl duo Shampoo). British journalist Julie Burchill pointed out that a predilection for wearing skimpy outfits is a freedom that men have never tried to deny women.

But the group struck a chord with (largely pre-pubescent) women around the world – and apparently with many others. For a while, everyone seemed to go Spice Girls mad. They had five U.S. Top 10 hits. In Britain, the only one of their ten singles that didn't make Number 1 ('Stop') got to the second spot.

Many people were troubled by the group because they pretended to be something they were not. They were not the significant talents they claimed or any sort of liberationists, but a classic bubblegum pop band, ciphers who by hard work, physical attractiveness, and engaging personalities sold the art of their highly-skilled backroom boys with massive success. Just like proto bubblegum band The Monkees, it may take the space of a generation for those who resent the fraudulence of The Spice Girls to forget that baggage and recognize their records as pop of the highest quality.

Lovefool
The Cardigans

Released September 1996
Not issued U.S. / Stockholm *5710502* (U.K. #2)

Abba proved that Swedish pop could capture the fickle hearts of an international audience and put them in a trance, and this was reinforced by the success of The Cardigans' single 'Lovefool.' It is filled with the irresistible coos of lead singer Nina Persson, then a delicate blonde with limitless sex-symbol appeal singing "Love me, love me." The song made a memorable addition to the soundtrack of Baz Luhrmann's *Romeo + Juliet*, with Clare Danes and Leonardo DiCaprio as the star-crossed lovers. ('Lovefool' made Number 2 as an album cut on the U.S. airplay chart but wasn't a single.)

California Love
2Pac Featuring Dr. Dre And Roger Troutman

Released April 1996
Death Row *854652* (U.S. #6) / Death Row *DRWCD 3* (U.K. #6)

No Diggity
BlackSTREET Featuring Dr. Dre

Released October 1996
Interscope *97007* (U.S. #1) / Interscope *IND 95003* (U.K. #9)

By 1996 it looked possible that the promising career trajectories of producers Teddy Riley and Dr. Dre had already reached their peaks. Riley (of Virginia Beach, VA) had been known as the father of new jack swing, a streetwise brand of R&B. It was best represented by his protégé Bobby Brown, a former singer from New Edition who hit the multi-platinum jackpot with the Riley-produced album *Don't Be Cruel* (1990). And Dr. Dre (Andre Young) had been known as the hip-hop producer with the Midas touch, first in bringing his group NWA to the forefront and then doing the same with rapper Snoop Doggy Dogg. But now their hits failed to flow so freely as they had in the past.

'No Diggity' and 'California Love' changed all that, putting both back into the pop spotlight. Riley's R&B group BlackSTREET performed 'No Diggity' with all the swagger of street rappers, which proved successful when combined with guest hip-hop verses from Dre and female MC Queen Pen. The song went on to win a Grammy for Best R&B Performance By A Duo Or Group.

Meanwhile, Dre had a special song cooked up to celebrate the release from prison of controversial rapper Tupac Shakur (a.k.a. 2Pac), in collaboration with Dre himself and Roger Troutman, the funkily vocoder'd frontman of Zapp. 'California Love' remains one of the best-loved songs from 2Pac and was unfortunately one of his last hits. The rapper died tragically in September 1996 after being shot in Las Vegas.

DON'T FORGET ABOUT DRE

Simply put, Dr. Dre is the platinum standard in hip-hop, the pinnacle of success that millions dream of yet never achieve. His songwriting virtuosity, which samples and draws from soul, rock, and funk in equal measures, parallels the skills of some of the greatest writers in music, and has won him accolades from just about every corner of the music industry, including the Grammys, which named him Producer Of The Year in 2000. Those unfamiliar with this titan of urban sounds may draw an easy analogy: Dr. Dre is the Quincy Jones of hip-hop, setting trends and staying ahead of the curve at all times.

After forming the controversial gangster-rap supergroup NWA (it stands for the incendiary Niggaz With Attitude) with Ice Cube, Eazy E, MC Ren, and Yella, he left to become an accomplished solo star in his own right with one of the most celebrated hip-hop albums, *The Chronic* (1992). He is also known for nurturing and developing the careers of some of pop music's brightest modern stars, including Snoop Dogg, Tupac Shakur, Eminem, and 50 Cent, whose work is indelibly associated with Dre's magic. Dre's ever-evolving sound, rooted in George Clinton's messy funk and given a spicy twist all his own, is easily the most emulated and the most ripped-off in the history of the genre.

The man born Andre Young began his musical career when he DJ'd in his hometown of Compton, in the rough South Central portion of Los Angeles, peddling mixtapes at flea markets and swap meets. He went on to regional success with his first two groups, the World Class Wrecking Cru and, later, NWA. The P-Funk flavored hits of *The Chronic* such as 'Nuthin' But a "G" Thang' and 'Let Me Ride' were anthems that put Dre in the public eye through constant video, radio, and club rotation. But Dre seemed only too happy to retreat from the solo spotlight to focus all his energies into the studio as he crafted the careers of others.

His first major artist was Snoop Dogg (born Cordozar 'Calvin' Broadus), a young rapper introduced to Dre by his own stepbrother Warren G (Warren Griffin III), who was in a group called 213 with Snoop. Their perfect chemistry began right from the start, when Snoop and Dre recorded Dre's debut solo single 'Deep Cover' on the first day they worked together. Dre's perfectionist approach and ear for talent would allow him to repeat this feat again with both Eminem and 50 Cent.

Some of Dre's most promising studio assistants and protégés have gone on to lucrative careers of their own – including Scott Storch, the man behind hits for artists such as Beyoncé, Lil Kim, and Fat Joe. Meanwhile, Dre's Aftermath label, which he established after famously leaving Suge Knight's Death Row Records, continues to dictate industry standards in hip-hop with such popular artists as Busta Rhymes and The Game.

Virtual Insanity
Jamiroquai

Released August 1996
Sony *OSK 0857* (U.S.) / Sony *S2 663613* (U.K. #3)

British group Jamiroquai were long reviled as lukewarm poster-boys for those members of the Gap generation who found acid jazz too funky. But the group at last found their commercial and critical groove with 'Virtual Insanity,' a nifty bit of coffee-table fatback with a nod to Stevie Wonder that everyone could enjoy. Sucked in by that stop-start line, "Future … feels like … virtual insanity," plus a dose of strings and, of course, Stuart Zender's unparalleled bass playing, millions endorsed mouthy little Jay Kay's band and elevated them to the super-league. The award-winning video and Kay's enviably cool dancing helped, of course, and a career in modern funk was assured.

Un-Break My Heart
Toni Braxton

Released October 1996
LaFace *24200* (U.S. #1) / LaFace *1410632* (U.K. #2)

Gorgeous singer Toni Braxton commanded the American pop charts for 11 weeks with this Number 1 hit ballad. Penned by Diane Warren, whose songs have been recorded by everyone from Natalie Cole to Kiss, 'Un-Break My Heart' is both poignant and hopeful. The song helped to bring multi-platinum honors to Braxton's second album, *Secrets*. Unfortunately, less secret was the fact that within two years of this triumph, Braxton would file for bankruptcy. But ten years later she became a star on Broadway who maintained a reasonably successful position in R&B.

I Believe I Can Fly
R. Kelly

Released December 1996
Jive *42422* (U.S. #2) / Jive *JIVECD 415* (U.K. #1)

Most would agree that rabbits can't take flight, but please don't tell that to the veteran cartoon character Bugs Bunny, who believes not only that he could fly, but that he could touch the sky. One of the dear hare's favorite songs must be 'I Believe I Can Fly,' the theme song to *Space Jam*, a movie starring Bugs and basketball megastar Michael Jordan (among other *Looney Tunes* and NBA icons). While Jordan battles to regain his prodigious talent – which has been taken by Bugs and friends – there's an epic song of empowerment guiding him along to victory over his awfully cute alien abductors.

This inspirational ode to positive achievement from Chicago-born singer-songwriter Robert Kelly stands apart from the bulk of his musical catalog, which is laden with an abundance of sexual innuendo. Despite his certain specialty, the prolific Kelly does have a proven talent for writing sports-oriented songs. He would later provide 'The World's Greatest,' a theme to go along with the movie *Ali*, about boxer Muhammad Ali.

The song netted three Grammy Awards (Best R&B Song, Best Original Song From A Soundtrack, and Best R&B Male Vocal Performance). The impeccably rowdy cover band Me First & The Gimme Gimmes (best known for their 'Somewhere Over the Rainbow' theme song for HBO's *Taxicab Confessions*) later tackled 'I Believe I Can Fly' in their own inimitable style, transforming a ballad to something far more visceral.

Killing Me Softly
Fugees

Released June 1996
Not issued U.S. / Columbia-Ruffhouse *663343* (U.K. #1)

The Fugees offered a welcome alternative to the trend among 1990s hip-hop acts for tales of drug runnin', gun totin' gangstas. This, their most memorable single release, was a heartfelt modernization of Roberta Flack's soulful 1973 chart-topper 'Killing Me Softly With His Song.' The Fugees' version is dominated by Lauryn Hill's powerful, emotive vocal delivery, underpinned by subtle instrumentation and augmented by the occasional encouragement – "One time!" – from her fellow Fugees, Pras Michel, and Wyclef Jean.

Michel and Jean, both Haitian immigrants, formed the group with Hill in her native East Orange, New Jersey, in the early 1990s. The trio made its recorded debut in 1994 with *Blunted On Reality*, an album that set socially conscious lyrics against jazz and reggae-inflected music. It didn't sell well, but was followed two years later by the *Billboard* chart-topper, *The Score*. 'Killing Me Softly' was one of four international hits drawn from the album (although some, like 'Killing Me,' were U.S. airplay hits and not physical singles); the others were the upbeat calling card 'Fu-Gee-La,' the darker 'Ready Or Not,' and a cover of Bob Marley's 'No Woman, No Cry.'

Back in 1996, just as 'Killing Me Softly' started to take over the airwaves, Lauryn Hill's voice was the key ingredient of another notable hip-hop R&B hit, 'If I Ruled The World' by Nas. Since the release of his 1994 debut, *Illmatic*, Nas has been one of the prominent figures in the rap world, chalking up a number of hit singles and albums. He is perhaps most famous for a heated public feud with Jay-Z, although the pair had reconciled their differences by 2005, and at the time of writing were rumored to be working on a collaborative album.

Meanwhile, with the world seemingly at their feet, the Fugees had in fact drifted apart within a year of the release of 'Killing Me Softly.' The trio spent the best part of a decade working on solo projects to varying levels of critical and commercial success before reuniting in 2005 for the so-so 'Take It Easy.'

I'll Be Missing You
Puff Daddy & Faith Evans Featuring 112

Released June 1997
Bad Boy 79097 (U.S. #1) / Puff Daddy 1499102 (U.K. #1)

Mo Money Mo Problems
The Notorious B.I.G. Featuring
Puff Daddy & Ma$e

Released July 1997
Bad Boy 79100 (U.S. #1) / Puff Daddy 1492492 (U.K. #6)

'I'll Be Missing You' is, quite simply, one of the biggest hip-hop records of all time. Released in tribute to the recently murdered Notorious B.I.G. – and featuring a guest vocal by his widow, Faith Evans – it made a global star of Sean 'Puffy Daddy' Combes, his close friend and Bad Boy Records label boss. It also inaugurated a new kind of hit-making. Going above and beyond mere sampling, the single is based almost entirely on The Police's 1983 hit 'Every Breath You Take.'

Rap in the mid 1990s was dominated by a feud between a pair of record labels from either side of the U.S. – Puff Daddy's New York-based Bad Boy imprint and Marion 'Suge' Knight's L.A.-centric Death Row. The bad blood stemmed from Death Row artist 2Pac Shakur's claims that he had slept with Faith Evans; by the time the hostilities had ended, both 2Pac and B.I.G. had been shot dead, six months apart, by assailants still unidentified to this day.

Puff Daddy had already topped the U.S. singles chart several months before B.I.G.'s death with his debut release, 'Can't Nobody Hold Me Down.' But 'I'll Be Missing You' took him into a completely new league. It spent 11 weeks atop the *Billboard* Hot 100 and was a Number 1 hit in the U.K. and countless other territories. Nominally composed by another rapper, Sauce Money, the single's main chord progression and chorus vocal-melody are lifted straight out of 'Every Breath You Take.'

Puff Daddy made no bones about this brazen act of musical recycling, and the original song's composer, Sting, didn't mind much either as he

received the lion's share of the ensuing royalties on ten-million-plus sales. It did, however, provoke heated debate within the music industry, with many critics questioning the artistic value of a record that added little to The Police's original, aside from Puff Daddy's rap. That didn't stop many other artists using the same trick to huge commercial success. Puff Daddy himself repeated the feat in 1998 with 'Been Around The World' – essentially 'Let's Dance' by David Bowie – and 'Come With Me,' which modeled itself on Led Zeppelin's 'Kashmir' and guest-starred that group's guitarist, Jimmy Page.

With a sad inevitability, The Notorious B.I.G.'s career reached its high-water mark in the months after his death. His second album – titled, with grim foresight, *Life After Death* – topped the U.S. chart in the week of his death, while its first two singles were also American Number 1 hits.

'Mo Money Mo Problems' was his biggest and most memorable single, and like 'I'll Be Missing You' it made liberal – although not quite so liberal – use of a sample, this time 'I'm Coming Out' by Diana Ross. To that it added a fat, dirty bassline, funky guitar, guest raps by Puff Daddy and Bad Boy stable-mate Ma$e, and a prescient chorus vocal line: "The more money we come across / The more problems we see." In the self-destructive gangsta-rap wars of the time, little could be mo' true.

Candle In The Wind 1997
Elton John

Released September 1997
Rocket 568108 (U.S. #1) / Rocket PTCD 1 (U.K. #1)

As unlikely as it might seem now, so long after the event, in 1997 the world was briefly united in grief following the death of Diana, Princess Of Wales. It drove many of the normally stoic and reserved populace of her native Britain into an unprecedented state of public mourning, which in turn led Elton John to rewrite and reissue his 'Candle In The Wind' and, in the process, notch up the biggest-selling single of all time.

The original version of the song, written in tribute to the actress Marilyn Monroe, was a U.K. Number 11 hit for Elton early in 1974. He later became a close friend and confidante of the princess and, in the days immediately following her death (on August 31, 1997) asked his regular collaborator Bernie Taupin to rework the lyric to reflect her life and the impact of her death.

The new version was ready in time for Elton to perform it at Diana's funeral on September 6 at Westminster Abbey, London, and to record it with former Beatles producer George Martin that same day. 'Candle In The Wind 1997' went on sale exactly one week later, hitting Number 1 in pretty much every country with a singles chart, paving the way to eventual worldwide sales of over 33 million copies. Incredibly, the single spent three years in the Canadian singles chart, where it clung to the top spot for 45 weeks. And it was important in the rejuvenation of Elton's career, pushing his well-timed solo album *The Big Picture* into the U.S. and U.K. Top 10s.

left > Notorious B.I.G. (left) with friend and label boss Puff Daddy.
right > Elton John performing at the funeral of Princess Diana.

99

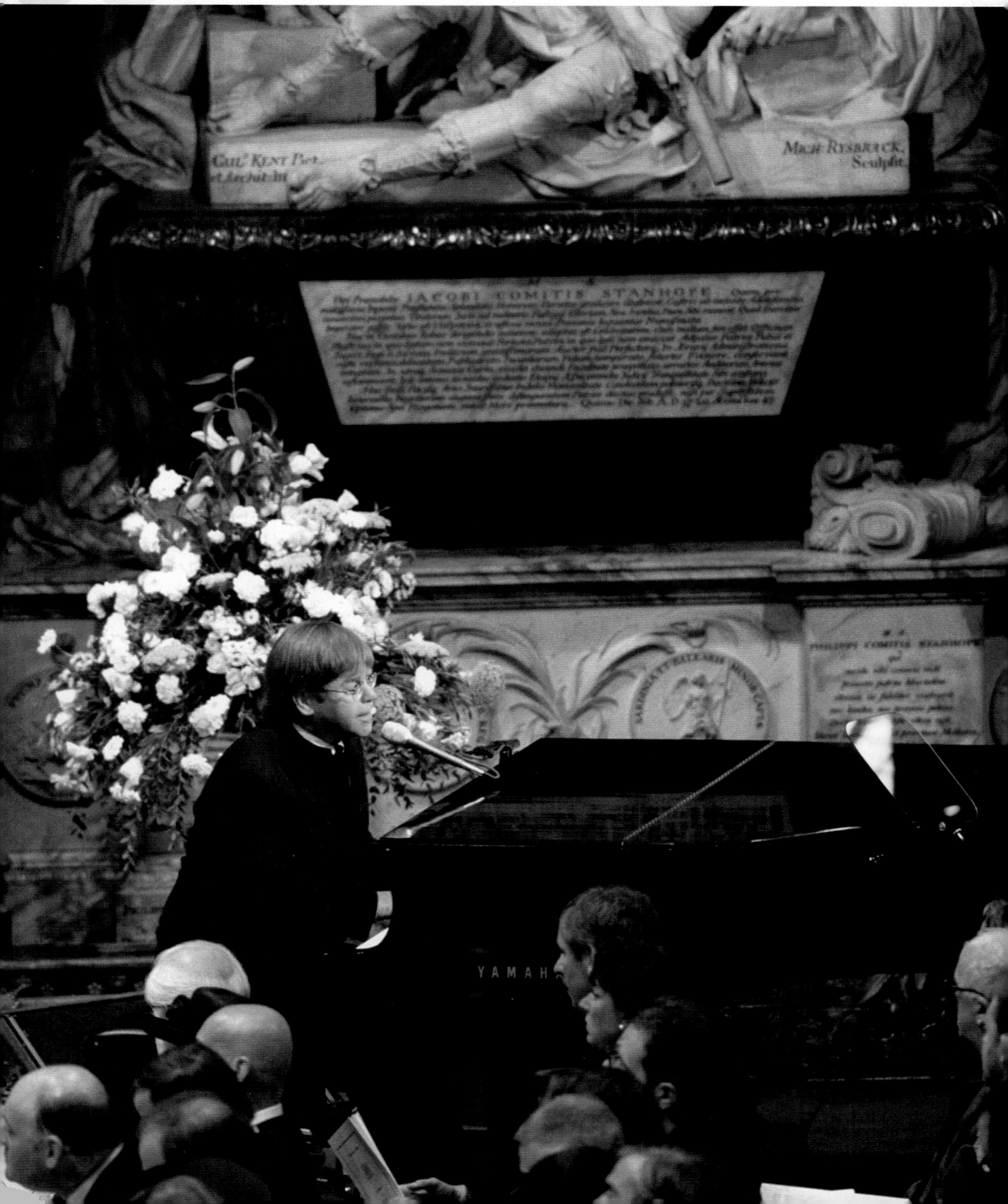

Your Woman
White Town

Released January 1997
Chrysalis-EMI *58638* (U.S. #23) / Chrysalis *CDCHS 5052* (U.K. #1)

'Your Woman' was one of the most unlikely U.K. chart-toppers ever. It was a kitsch pop bedroom recording by a British Asian student, Jyoti Mishra, built around a trumpet part sampled from a 1930s recording. The single was given a limited release in 1996 on an EP entitled *Abort, Retry, Fail?*. Mishra sent out only five promotional copies. One landed on the desk of a late-night radio DJ, Mark Radcliffe, who played it while filling in as presenter of the BBC Radio 1 breakfast show. The resulting major-label reissue gave Mishra a one-off Number 1 hit and a very fleeting – and ultimately unwanted – taste of fame.

Da Funk
Daft Punk

Released February 1997
Virgin *38587* (U.S.) / Virgin *VSCDT 1625* (U.K. #7)

Sexy Boy
Air

Released February 1998
Caroline *06645* (U.S.) / Virgin *VSCDT 1672* (U.K. #13)

In the late 1990s, a strange thing happened: all of a sudden, French music was cool outside France. The seeds were sown with the 1996 compilation album *Super Discount*, put together by the house DJ Etienne de Crecy, and mainstream success came early the following year with Daft Punk's major-label debut.

'Da Funk' is, essentially, low-tech techno. A prime example of the less-is-more philosophy, it is made up of little other than a squelching synth melody, one-note bass, and a beat that sounds as if it were recorded out of a passing car window. Parisians Thomas Bangalter – the son of a disco producer – and Guy-Manuel De Homem Christo first issued the single on the dance label Soma in 1995, but the Virgin reissue was a U.K. Top 10 hit, thanks it part to a memorable promo video, directed by Spike Jonze and starring a walking, talking dog. The follow-up, 'Around The World,' was a minor U.S. hit, and in 1998 Bangalter recorded one of the European club hits of the summer, 'Music Sounds Better With You,' under the alias Stardust.

By the time that single had hit the charts, Daft Punk had a rival as kings of French pop in the shape of another Parisian duo, Air. Nicholas Godin and Jean-Benoit Dunckel released three singles between 1995 and 1996, later reissued collectively as *Premiers Symptomes*. 'Sexy Boy' was their first for Virgin, following hot on the heels of their acclaimed full-length debut, *Moon Safari*. Like the rest of the album, the single is built around warm, retro synths, gentle beats, and charming Franglais vocals.

right > The French electronica duo Daft Punk, who insist on wearing masks for all publicity photos.

Bitch
Meredith Brooks

Released May 1997
Capitol *58634* (U.S. #2) / Capitol *CDCL 790* (U.K. #6)

In 1995, Alanis Morrissette's notorious single 'You Oughta Know' made it the rage for women to show rage in pop. Meredith Brooks was a singer from Oregon known for making much milder music, but when she hit the pop charts with 'Bitch' two years later the song was instantly charged as derivative of Morrissette's amped-up paean to failed love. However, 'Bitch' doesn't have the bitter ring – it's a feminist-positive anthem. Brooks reclaims the word as a term of empowerment, not degradation. The Grammy Awards didn't think Ms. Brooks was such a bitch, giving her a nomination for Best Vocal Peformance.

Tubthumping
Chumbawamba

Released August 1997
Republic *56146* (U.S. #6) / EMI *CDEM 486* (U.K. #2)

English group Chumbawamba, an ultra-left-wing collective that had slogged through the morass of activist-pop for years with little commercial impact, surprised absolutely everybody when they hit the Top 10 with 'Tubthumping,' a highly catchy shoutalong that temporarily mesmerized everyone. Unfortunately, Britpop Britain only heard the line "He drinks a vodka drink … he drinks a cider drink" and assumed it was a simple drinking song, missing out entirely on the subtext of escapist futility. Other than singer Danbert Nobacon chucking a bucket of water over U.K. deputy prime minister John Prescott at the 1998 Brit Awards, 'Tubthumping' was Chumbawamba's only moment in the sun.

Paranoid Android
Radiohead

Released May 1997
Not issued U.S. / Parlophone *CDODATAS 01* (U.K. #3)

Issued to great fanfare as "the 'Bohemian Rhapsody' of the 1990s," this six-minute epic was one of the most ambitious British rock singles of the decade. According to vocalist and songwriter Thom Yorke, however, it was inspired by the cut-and-paste feel of The Beatles' 'Happiness Is A Warm Gun' and not Queen's rock operatics. Bassist Colin Greenwood corroborated the story in a contemporary interview, claiming that 'Paranoid Android' was about "taking things apart and sticking them back together again to see if they made any sense."

It started life as three separate songs: the tricksy, time-shifting opening; a maudlin, choral centerpiece; and, sandwiched either side of that, a jerky, Pixies-style freak-out dominated by Jonny Greenwood's ferocious lead guitar. Yorke's lyric was, by all accounts, inspired by a nightmarish night-out in the media glitz of Los Angeles. Despite being – in the words of its critics – pompous, overblown, and much too long, 'Paranoid Android' debuted at Number 3 on the U.K. singles chart. It served as the perfect introduction to Radiohead's third album, *OK Computer*, which reset the parameters within which a modern rock band could or was supposed to operate. Also, it finally gave the group a more fitting legacy than "that band who did 'Creep.'"

Bitter Sweet Symphony
The Verve

Released June 1997
Hut-Virgin *38634* (U.S. #12) / Hut *HUTDG 82* (U.K. #2)

This swirling, string-driven epic, topped off by a chest-beating vocal, was one of the decade's greatest singles. True to its title, it was also something of a bitter-sweet success for The Verve, who didn't earn a penny in publishing royalties from the record. The problem stemmed from a four-bar sample of an orchestral rendition of The Rolling Stones's 'The Last Time,' discovered by Verve frontman Richard Ashcroft on an album by The Andrew Loog Oldham Orchestra.

Ashcroft then wrote the rest of the music himself – including the main orchestral hook – but despite clearing the Oldham sample, he was then sued by Allen Klein, whose ABKCO Records holds the rights to all of the Stones's material from the 1960s. Following an out-of-court settlement, all copyright on 'Bitter Sweet Symphony' reverted to ABKCO – despite Mick Jagger and Keith Richards giving The Verve's song their blessing, and the fact that it bore no resemblance to 'The Last Time.'

Regardless of the legal wrangling, however, few could deny that The Verve had created a modern classic. The song climbed into the upper reaches of the charts on both sides of the Atlantic; in Britain its rise to the top was halted only by another landmark 1990s single, 'I'll Be Missing You' by Puff Daddy. The Verve followed up with a stirring ballad, 'The Drugs Don't Work,' which gave them their only British Number 1 hit, and then their third and final studio album, *Urban Hymns*.

Torn
Natalie Imbruglia

Released November 1997
Not issued U.S. / RCA *1527982* (U.K. #2)

It seems rather unlikely that a former Australian soap actress would hit international pop-music paydirt by covering an obscure song by a band from Los Angeles, but such is the tale of Natalie Imbruglia's first and most popular single 'Torn.' After appearing on the popular Aussie television serial *Neighbours* – a veritable feeding ground of homegrown talent that has gone on to worldwide success – Imbruglia tried her hand at a music career and released a cover version of a song from Ednaswap, the now defunct band fronted by Anne Preven, whose lyrics immaculately captured the contradictory dilemmas of everyday life.

TO CHART OR NOT TO CHART?

During the 1990s, a number of hugely popular records failed to make it onto the *Billboard* Hot 100 because they were not given a commercial release in a physical format. Sales of singles had been in decline since the 1970s, prompting many record labels not to bother manufacturing them at all, and instead to release tracks to radio stations only. The labels also hoped that, by not making a single available to the public, they would encourage greater sales for their artists' albums (which, of course, made more money). A direct result of this, however, was that many of the decade's most memorable songs, including Alanis Morissette's 'You Oughta Know,' The Cardigans' 'Love Fool,' and 'Torn' by Natalie Imbruglia, were not in fact Hot 100 hits in the U.S. (the latter song did, however, top the *Billboard* Airplay chart). Eventually, in December 1998, the regulations by which the Hot 100 chart is compiled were altered to reflect the declining importance of the physical single so that, for the first time, records could enter the chart without a single copy being sold.

On & On
Erykah Badu

Released January 1997
Kedar-Universal *56002* (U.S. #12) / Universal *UND 561117* (U.K. #12)

Erykah Badu – born Erica Wright in Dallas, Texas – remains one of the most startling talents the world of soul music has ever seen, a virtuoso in a sea of conformity. Her breakthrough single 'On & On' has a fresh, bluesy feel and an immediacy of emotion lacking in much contemporary R&B, as well as a low-end groove to appeal to modern ears. The song helped propel her debut album *Baduizm* to Number 2 in America, and its video gave a visual introduction to the eccentric singer with the throwback voice and the otherworldly look.

Return Of The Mack
Mark Morrison

Released March 1997
Atlantic *84868* (U.S. #2) / WEA *040CD* (U.K. #1)

Alas, the Mack known as Mark Morrison never revisited the chart glory of this catchy chart-topper. But it wasn't his lack of talent or a dearth of well-crafted tunes that prevented Morrison – born in Germany and brought up in England – from reaching similar heights. Rather, his cluttered arrest record reveals a range of charges from assault to weapons violations. Morrison's run-ins with the law made him a notorious 'bad boy' in the eyes of the British press, but that and his constant assertions of innocence failed to help him continue to sell records.

MMMBop
Hanson

Released May 1997
Mercury *574261* (U.S. #1) / Mercury *5745012* (U.K. #1)

'MMMBop' was a peppy, infectious tune that catapulted young brothers Isaac, Taylor, and Zachary Hanson from making kid-friendly cover songs of oldies into massive international fame. But it might not have reached its heights of glory if some experienced underground producers hadn't made a savvy remix. The song was originally conceived as a ballad, but in the hands of The Dust Brothers – Los Angeles production duo John King and Mike Simpson – it turned into an infectious pop hit with the briefest touch of hip-hop breakbeat momentum.

King and Simpson were responsible for giving the critically acclaimed Beastie Boys album *Paul's Boutique* its sampladelic flair, and later helped bring new success to singer Beck. Their production for 'MMMBop' is comparatively spare, accented by scratchy noises and the brothers' punchy, high-note harmonies and their prodigious work on keys, guitar, and drums. Not since the Jacksons has America seen such a talented family, although the Hansons have more unity.

'MMMBop' helped them earn three Grammy nominations, for Record Of The Year, Best Pop Performance By A Duo Or Group, and Best New Artist. The memorable video features a bevy of performance sequences and was directed by the famous youth-culture film director Tamra Davis (*CB4*, *Half Baked*, *Crossroads*). Almost a decade after their first hit,

Hanson continue to enjoy a successful career, releasing albums together through their own independent record label, 3CG (it stands for 3 Car Garage).

How Do I Live
LeAnn Rimes

Released July 1997
Curb *73022* (U.S. #2) / Curb *CUBCX 30* (U.K. #7)

A simple, moderately affecting ballad from identikit blonde country singer LeAnn Rimes, 'How Do I Live' was the postman's whistling choice for much of 1997 thanks to its killer title melody and the chance – fully exploited by Rimes – to launch a lung-busting epic climax at its end. As with so much modern country-pop (think Shania Twain, The Dixie Chicks), it's the precision-engineered production that makes the song so shiny, with all the melodies waterfall-perfect and the vocals a thing of great beauty. Yes, it's covered in a layer of pure cheese, but as modern country goes, you could do much worse.

You Make Me Wanna ...
Usher

Released August 1997
LaFace *24265* (U.S. #2) / LaFace *1560652* (U.K. #1)

Usher was an entertainer more or less since birth, made his recorded debut at age 14, and went on to establish himself as a nationally-known teen heartthrob by the time he was 19 with 'You Make Me Wanna.' As an R&B singer with extraordinary pipes – and dance moves that seem as if handed down by Michael Jackson himself – Usher still relishes the heartthrob role a decade or so later. Even before he was legal he was a ladykiller, crooning slick lines like this song's infectious chorus: "You make me wanna leave the one I'm with / And start a new relationship / With you ... ."

Barbie Girl
Aqua

Released September 1997
MCA *55392* (U.S. #7) / Univeral *UMD 80413* (U.K. #1)

By 1997 techno had been hijacked by the Nickelodeon kids' channel and other cultural media aimed at the under-12s, and children's music has been based on Eurobeats ever since. But all this plinky-plinky rubbish never seemed destined to break through into the adult world until the advent of Danish-Norwegian quartet Aqua, who made you listen to it whether you wanted to or not.

The quartet – singer Lene Nyström Rasted, rapper-comic stooge René Dif, and keyboard players Søren Nyström Rasted and Claus Norreen – nailed a moderately clubby beat to a sickly Barbie-and-Ken love story, delivered in helium vocals, and made a bazillion euros out of it.

How could this happen, and how was it permitted? The secret lay in the fine looks of singer Lene, the daft interplay between her and rapper Dif,

It's worth considering the fate of a host of girl bands in the late 1990s. Remember B*Witched from Ireland, a kind of Corrs for kids? Once thought to be The Next Big Thing, they in fact became The Next Forgotten Thing, despite a signature tune ('C'est La Vie') and a selling point (Irishness). All Saints avoided this fate, narrowly, because they had 'Never Ever' – a real song.

Angels
Robbie Williams

Released December 1997
Capitol *7788192* (U.S.) / Chrysalis *CHSLH 5072* (U.K. #4)

As the world moved toward the 21st century, it seemed as if rock music was an art form that would be left in the 20th, a relic of a bygone age and superseded by house, techno, rap, and other musical styles. Then in Britain along came an artist who seemed to embody both in spirit and output all the attributes of that once all-powerful, now marginalized genre.

Robbie Williams affected rock'n'roll irreverence and cheeky likeability while releasing records infused with the great melodies, memorable licks, knowing lyrics, and potential for communal live singalongs that always characterized the greatest rock music. Remarkably, he was a former member of a boy-band, and hitherto had seemed a talentless twerp.

'Angels' was the song that weakened the resistance of those who could not take seriously as a legitimate rock artist someone who had been in Take That. Although Guy Chambers provided the melodic foil to Williams's lyrics, the song started life as a collaboration between the artist and budding songwriter Ray Heffernan, who provided the verse and its melody. But it was the combination of Chambers's grand, sweeping chorus melody and Williams's affectingly vulnerable words that gave 'Angels' the air of a modern classic. No Williams concert would now be complete without a mass singalong of the chorus with its climactic phrase that nobody quite understands: "I'm loving angels instead."

and the none-more-unforgettable line "I'm a Barbie girl / In the Barbie world" that you had to sing, like it or not. The bat-like vocal frequencies remained stuck in the listener's head – and inspired much conjecture as to whether Lene's natural range was really that high.

When two more singles appeared, the broadly similar 'Doctor Jones' and the much more acceptable ballad 'Turn Back Time,' they revealed just how much studio treatment had been required to give 'Barbie Girl' its day-glo, amphetamine feel. Unfortunately, that same near-psychotic look and sound made the band rapidly obsolete, and they split in 2001, although the song is probably still played to this day at Copenhagen infant-school discos.

Never Ever
All Saints

Released November 1997
London *570178* (U.S. #4) / London *LONCD 407* (U.K. #1)

After endless accusations of being "the new Spice Girls" (which, rightly, they laughed away), London quartet All Saints delivered this classy chunk of gospel and saw their detractors fall silent and their stock go stratospheric. Most people didn't realize why it sounded so familiar, but then it didn't occur to them that the girls had adapted a hymn, 'Amazing Grace.' Luckily, their perfect harmonies disguised the lift.

As with Take That's 'Back For Good' – the gold standard in boy-band pop – 'Never Ever' has gone down as the manufactured-girl-band song to beat, alongside '2 Become 1' by the aforementioned Spice ladies. It's a simple, affecting ballad, which bandleader Shaznay Lewis had written in the aftermath of a failed relationship, and boasts the chorus line: "Never ever have I ever felt so low," which itself is a catchy tongue-twister.

The song was the boost that the band needed, although their progress faltered with the next two singles, a weak remake of the Chili Peppers' 'Under The Bridge' and the R&B-by-numbers 'Bootie Call.' But then in 2000 All Saints triumphed with two excellent singles produced by William Orbit before quitting in the following year.

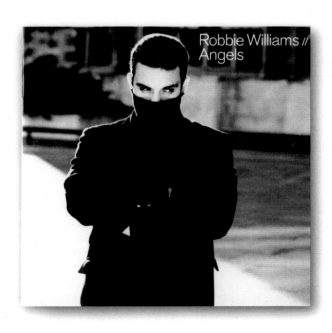

Robbie Williams // Angels

... Baby One More Time
Britney Spears

Released November 1998
Jive *42545* (U.S. #1) / Jive *0522752* (U.K. #1)

This arresting, instantly memorable mega-hit provided the perfect introduction to the most iconic popular music star of the turn of the century. While the global resurgence of teen-orientated pop had begun several years earlier with the rise of The Spice Girls and The Backstreet Boys, no one else could match the near-global ubiquity of young Britney Spears.

Like all great pop prodigies, Britney – born in Kentwood, Los Angeles – started singing and dancing locally almost as soon as she could string a sentence together. In 1990, at the age of eight, she appeared on a nationally televised *Star Search*. As with future pop starlets Christina Aguilera and Justin Timberlake – with whom she had a very public and allegedly chaste relationship for several years – she then worked as a mouseketeer on the Disney Channel's *New Mickey Mouse Club*.

In between times, Spears had studied at the Professional Performing Arts School in New York City. At 15 she signed a deal with Jive Records – nominally an independent label, but home to such big sellers as R. Kelly and The Backstreet Boys – and began work on a debut album with a number of hot songwriters and producers, including Eric Foster White and Max Martin. It was Martin who wrote and produced 'Baby One More Time,' the song that gave Spears an international Number 1 hit at the

first attempt and provided the perfect springboard to her ensuing superstardom. Like The Spice Girls and their 'Wannabe,' Britney's debut is somewhat unconventional in structure. It doesn't rely on a big, hook-laden chorus, but instead is made up of several interlocking parts that, while not particularly remarkable on their own, add up to one of the most striking, catchy pop hits of recent times.

The key elements are the vocal melodies and Britney's coy, suggestive delivery; the instrumental parts – rock-ballad drums, vaguely funky bass, washes of synth strings – are rarely more than perfunctory, aside perhaps from the juddering piano chords that open each verse. The lyrics, too, are unusual: "I must confess / That my loneliness is killing me" seems on paper as if it belongs to an angst-ridden rock song, not a bright, bouncy pop single.

Just as important to the success of 'One More Time' was the accompanying music video, which cast the 17-year-old Spears as a modern-day Lolita in skimpy school uniform. Integral to the Britney Spears phenomenon was the intriguing juxtaposition of the singer's regular espousal of her good, pure values – particularly sexual abstinence – and her raunchy, provocative music and image.

The furious debate about what was and wasn't decent peaked the following summer when Britney made a scantily-clad appearance on the cover of *Rolling Stone*. By then, 'Sometimes' and '(You Drive Me) Crazy' had followed 'Baby One More Time' into the upper reaches of the charts across the Western world, and Britney had cemented her position as the biggest solo female artist of her time.

MAX MARTIN: POP'S SWEDISH CHEF

When the Britney Spears hit '. . . Baby One More Time' took over the airwaves in late 1998 and into '99, many were surprised to discover that the song was the handiwork of a songwriter-producer based in Sweden. Max Martin (born Martin Sandberg in Stockholm in 1971) started working for the Swedish pop label Cheiron at the age of 21. Alongside the label's founder, Denniz PoP, he co-wrote and produced a string of European hit singles and albums in the mid 1990s for artists including Ace Of Base and Rednex.

The duo's big break came in 1996 with an invitation from the American record company Jive to contribute to the eponymous debut album by the label's boy-band, The Backstreet Boys. Both Backstreet Boys and the singles 'Quit Playing Games (With My Heart)' and 'As Long As You Love Me' were remarkably successful across mainland Europe and, eventually, in the U.S. too.

Over the next few years Martin and PoP consolidated a highly successful relationship with Jive. In 1997 they provided The Backstreet Boys with several more international hits, notably the self-mythologizing 'Everybody (Backstreet's Back),' which paired their trademark dance-pop with a theatrical Phantom Of The Opera feel. After launching the Swedish

singer Robyn out into the pop world with 'Show Me Love,' Martin and PoP worked on the debut by another American Jive act, *Nsync.

In 1998, PoP succumbed to cancer, leaving Martin to assume the reigns of Cheiron. Now he wrote and produced the majority of his hits alongside another fellow Swede, by the name of Rami. One of this new pairing's first collaborations was '. . . Baby One More Time,' Britney Spears's debut single, which gave Martin his first U.S. Number 1 hit.

Over the course of the following year, Max Martin became the world's most in-demand songwriter-producer for hire, helming further hits for Britney and The Backstreet Boys as well as new clients, among them Celine Dion, Bryan Adams, and former Take That star Gary Barlow. In 1999 and 2000 Martin was named Songwriter Of The Year by the American Society Of Composers, Authors, & Publishers.

At the start of the 21st century Martin closed down Cheiron and formed a new hit factory, Maratome. Despite the change of name and support personnel, the hits kept coming. Chief among them was 'Since U Been Gone,' which transformed 2002 *American Idol* winner Kelly Clarkson from pop puppet to almost-serious artiste in 2004.

While Hill's solo success was phenomenal, and certainly the loudest of the three at the time, it is Wyclef Jean who has emerged as the soloist with longevity, both in his own work and in producing others (such as the Columbian megastar Shakira). Jean's catchy, jangly hip-pop tune 'Gone Till November' asserted that his own career was definitely on the up.

Gettin' Jiggy Wit It
Will Smith

Released February 1998
Columbia *78804* (U.S. #1) / Columbia *6655605* (U.K. #3)

The indefatigable Will Smith based 'Gettin' Jiggy Wit It' on a fantastic three-chord sample from 'He's The Greatest Dancer' by Sister Sledge. Smith peaked as a hip-hop artist in 1998, just before acting became his main career, and never did do better than this cheerful, up-tempo piece of nonsense. Although the title was in hip-hop lingo and Smith has always made much of his Philly-ghetto roots, the production and promotion of this single screamed 'major-label act!' His credibility among the genuine hip-hop elite has always been tarnished by his populist vibe and cheesy grin. But do we need another too-serious, too-violent rapper? No. Which is why we love Big Will.

Gone Till November
Wyclef Jean

Released February 1998
Ruffhouse *78752* (U.S. #7) / Columbia *6658712* (U.K. #3)

Doo Wop (That Thing)
Lauryn Hill
Released September 1998
Ruffhouse *78868* (U.S. #1) / Ruffhouse *6665152* (U.K. #3)

Ghetto Supastar (That Is What You Are)
Pras Michel Featuring Ol' Dirty Bastard & Introducing Mya
Released June 1998
Interscope *95021* (U.S. #15) / Interscope *INC 95593* (U.K. #2)

After the phenomenal success of the Fugees, whose sophomore album *The Score* remains one of the most successful hip-hop albums of all time, the group slowly began to show cracks in its foundation and decided to part ways. In 1998, all three members (Lauryn Hill, Wyclef Jean, and Pras Michel) set out to recapture that achievement – only they did it individually, as solo artists.

Led by the rap-R&B hybrid hit 'Doo Wop (That Thing),' Hill's multi-platinum *The Miseducation Of Lauryn Hill* was nominated for a staggering 11 Grammys and grabbed five, including Best New Artist, Best R&B Song, and Best R&B Vocal Performance. Michel, meanwhile, came out with his debut album *Ghetto Supastar*, lending its title cut to the soundtrack for the Warren Beatty movie *Bulworth*. R&B ingenue Mya sang the hook – an odd lift from 'Islands In The Stream,' the 1983 chart-topping duet between Dolly Parton and Kenny Rogers – while the Wu-Tang Clan's madcap Ol' Dirty Bastard traded rap verses. It gave Michel another taste of mainstream success, but this would prove fleeting.

It's Like That
Run-D.M.C. Vs. Jason Nevins

Released March 1998
Columbia *665293* (U.S.) / Sm:)e *SM 90652* (U.K. #1)

This updated version of Run-D.M.C.'s 'It's Like That' didn't dent the American pop charts but soared to the top in the U.K. and almost 30 other countries. It was also a smash on dancefloors around the world, employed by DJs of many genres who were looking to inject a little hip-hop flavor into the mix. Detractors griped that Jason Nevins, the New York-based DJ-remixer responsible for the song's second-time-around, did little more than add a peppier, metronomic beat while leaving the 1983 original largely untouched. But Nevins's skill was to unearth a classic at precisely the right time and reap the benefit.

Feel It
The Tamperer Featuring Maya

Released April 1998
Jive *46506* (U.S.) / Pepper *0530032* (U.K. #1)

With its unforgettable chorus line – "what's she gonna look like with a chimney on her?" – 'Feel It' was one of the finest European dance-pop hits of the late 1990s. The musical backdrop of jangling bells and up-tempo house rhythms was the work of a pair of Italian DJs, Alex Farfoli and Mario Fargetta. Their female compatriot, Maya, provided the empowering vocal, which is centered on an oddly playful threat of revenge against somebody foolish enough to have slept with her man. The single was hugely successful across Europe, as was the follow-up, 'If You Buy This Record Your Life Will Be Better,' although it seems doubtful they could have proved such a bold sales pitch.

Dance The Night Away
The Mavericks

Released April 1998
MCA *72056* (U.S.) / MCA Nashville *MCSTD 48081* (U.K. #4)

Led by the jovial, goateed Raoul Malo, The Mavericks are a U.S. country band with Tex-Mex influences. Their music is melodic, radio-friendly, and highly inoffensive – the three golden qualities for modern commercial success, some might say. The very catchy 'Dance The Night Away' was a worldwide hit, even if its blandness was almost breathtaking. But nobody complained because the band had worked to earn their recognition – 'Dance' was taken from their fifth album. Two further singles scraped the British Top 50 but The Mavericks never had such success in their home country.

The Boy Is Mine
Brandy & Monica

Released May 1998
Atlantic *84089* (U.S. #1) / Atlantic *AT 0036CD* (U.K. #2)

This sassy and technically superior pop anthem finds vocalists Brandy Norwood and Monica Arnold in a fictional clash of fierce lyrics and trilling diva ad-libs. Both had been popular R&B stars since their early teenage years, and 'The Boy is Mine' (released on both of their albums of the time) brought the singers to new heights of mainstream recognition. Amid rumors that they were not getting along too well, at the time of writing this record unfortunately marked the last collaboration from these two young talents. But the tale has a happy ending: they've both since blossomed into mothers and maintained successful solo careers.

What Can I Do
The Corrs

Released August 1998
Atlantic *84444* (U.S.) / Atlantic *AT 0044CD* (U.K. #3)

A relative flop on its first release but a big old smash hit after a brush-up and a remix from Tin Tin Out, 'What Can I Do' is a highly attractive three minutes of pop fluff from the perennially attractive Corrs, the prettiest band (excluding their brother) ever to have come out of Ireland. Andrea Corr fronts the quartet and supplies tin whistle, her two sisters Sharon and Caroline are on violin and drums, and brother Jim is on guitar. They struck gold by providing the Celtic-friendly music-buying public with a resolutely Irish sound – a clever move in America and the UK.

'What Can I Do' was in fact the fifth single from The Corrs – the world had been slow to catch on, at least initially – and the band gave the impression in interviews that the way to stardom had been no easy ride. However, once this single hit in Britain it became obvious that the time was ripe for 'Irish pop,' and The Corrs capitalized with a series of similarly chirpy tunes that boasted the latest in crisp production and a media-friendly home-country image that neither overdid the Irish angle nor neglected it entirely. There was always a violin or tin whistle solo lurking in the background.

'What Can I Do' had such a commercial whack in Britain that a leading bank used it to soundtrack a TV ad, with Andrea and the family changing the lyrics to "What can we do to make you happy?"

I Don't Want To Miss A Thing
Aerosmith

Released August 1998
Columbia *78952* (U.S. #1) / Columbia *6664082* (U.K. #4)

Like the proverbial bolt from the blue, this power-ballad gave Aerosmith a third peak in a sporadic four-decade career of extreme ups and downs. After an initial period of success in the mid 1970s, several members of the group had battled hard-drugs addiction prior to a Run-D.M.C.-inspired comeback in the mid-to-late 1980s. But it appeared that their popularity – and creativity – had begun to wane by the time they issued a career retrospective, *Big Ones*, in 1994.

Then came 'I Don't Want To Miss A Thing,' written for the band by the phenomenally successful songwriter Diane Warren. A huge international hit, the song was given a further boost by its inclusion on the soundtrack to the movie *Armageddon*, which, coincidentally, starred Aerosmith vocalist Steven Tyler's daughter, Liv.

Rosa Parks
OutKast

Released November 1998
LaFace *4367* (U.S.) / Not issued U.K.

One of the most successful hip-hop groups of all time, Atlanta's OutKast (Andre 'Andre 3000' Benjamin and Antwan 'Big Boi' Patton) have also touched on many controversial moments in their career, whether by accident or design. OutKast's third album Aquemini, a masterpiece of soul and hip-hop otherworldliness, is now best remembered for featuring the single 'Rosa Parks.'

The lively and funky song is named after Rosa Parks, the civil rights activist. In 1955 in Montgomery, Alabama, Parks famously refused to move to the back of the segregated bus she was on, which sparked a nationwide uproar. The song makes reference to this event in part of the chorus ("Ah ha / Hush that fuss / Everybody move to the back of the bus . . ."), but otherwise the song is not about her. 'Rosa Parks' was nominated for a Grammy for Best Rap Performance By A Duo Or Group, and the song would later surface as part of an emotional battle.

OutKast's huge success during the coming years was not enough to shield its members from the certain pain of an unlikely lawsuit. Representatives for Parks launched a suit against the group and its record companies in 1999, claiming that the song was both a copyright infringement and defamed her character. After a battle with many dramatic twists and turns that managed to reach all the way up to the U.S. Supreme Court, the case was settled out of court in April 2005, just six months before Parks's death at age 92.

My Heart Will Go On
(Love Theme From 'Titanic')
Celine Dion

Released February 1998
550 Music-Epic *78825* (U.S. #1) / Epic *6655472* (U.K. #1)

When director James Cameron unleashed his mega-movie *Titanic* in 1997 – then the most expensive film ever made – he required a suitably epic song to soundtrack its key subplot (the relationship between the two leads) with plenty of hooks to deploy at key moments throughout the film.

Thus, Swiss-American chanteuse Celine Dion – one of the world's biggest singing stars following the success of her albums *Falling Into You* (1996) and *Let's Talk About Love* (1997), which between them sold over 60 million copies worldwide – performed 'My Heart Will Go On.' The single sold in enormous quantities thanks to its winsome Hollywood-Celtic flute melody, slick orchestration, and money-shot line of "Near ... far ... where*eeeeeeeeeever* you are." This last songwriting conceit, an operatic moment of almost Wagnerian pomp, had the delivery boys whistling for months.

Even the song's creators must have been startled by its success – Dion herself didn't think much of the song to begin with, and took some convincing to record it. While some might have found 'My Heart Will Go On' to be rather too overwrought and overblown, the record did nonetheless deserve its fame. Composer James Horner came up with a melody to die for, and while the title meant very little, moviegoers certainly got the message as Leonardo DiCaprio sank into the icy depths. The single won an Academy Award for Best Original Song – just one of a record-equalling 11 Oscars picked up by *Titanic*.

Ray Of Light
Madonna

Released April 1998
Maverick *17206* (U.S. #5) / Maverick *W 0444CD* (U.K. #2)

By the mid 1990s it looked as if Madonna's career was on its last legs after just over a decade at the top of the pop ladder. She was pushing 40 – about 120 in pop years – and with singles such as 'Human Nature' ('95) and 'One More Chance' ('96) she seemed unable to match the luster of earlier mega-hits.

Then came perhaps the most surprising change of direction in her chameleon-like career. Madonna decided to star in the cinematic adaptation of Andrew Lloyd Webber's *Evita*. The movie was a big box-office hit, but more importantly seemed to reignite her passion for music.

The singing lessons she took prior to accepting the role didn't hurt, either: her 1998 'comeback' single, the icy ballad 'Frozen,' showed off one of the best vocal performances of her career.

The follow-up, the pulsating future-disco cut 'Ray Of Light,' was even better. For the first time in years it seemed that Madonna had broken free from the shackles of controversy – the church-baiting 'Like A Prayer' or the over-sexed 'Justify My Love' – and made the music itself her focus once again. Not that 'Ray of Light' was entirely free of controversy. Soon after it rose into the British and American Top 5, the song was found to be based quite substantially on 'Sepheryn,' a 1970s song written by Curtis Muldoon and Dave Curtiss. Both were more than a little miffed at the way Madonna's producer William Orbit had co-opted their song but cheered up somewhat when they were awarded a large chunk of the royalties.

Believe
Cher

Released October 1998
Warner *17119* (U.S. #1) / WEA *175CD* (U.K. #1)

Cherilyn Sarkisian, a sprightly 53 but looking 20 years younger when her career was saved by 'Believe,' had struggled for credibility since the 1980s. The one-time Mrs. Sonny Bono had scored a few minor hits with a soft-rock approach that made much of her surgically-enhanced youthfulness, but by 1998, Top 5 hits had become thin on the ground since 'If I Could Turn Back Time,' a grisly rock ballad from 1989.

Cher then stunned her detractors with the massive-selling 'Believe,' a song that fell somewhere between kitchen-sink techno, cheesy house-trance, and plain old sugary pop. Its success came from two key elements: the chorus line of "Do you believe in life after love?" specifically the yodel in the middle of the word "believe," and the masterful decision by the producers to employ a vocoder-like effect on her voice towards the end of the song. Although this turned her voice into a digitized soup and was slightly nauseating for some listeners, many loved it and the song shot up the charts. The whole thing shifts upwards in key at one point, a classic maneuver that nearly always makes a struggling song sound suddenly fresher. So, Cher was on a career high again, and capitalized on the success with – yes! – another house tune, 'Strong Enough,' that also featured a pitch-shifted vocal.

If You Had My Love
Jennifer Lopez

Released May 1999
Epic-Work *79163* (U.S. #1) / Columbia *6675772* (U.K. #4)

There are countless examples of movie stars making lame attempts to record a pop song, usually resulting in the actor in question quickly retreating to his or her primary occupation in the midst of negative reviews and poor sales. There are also musicians who make dire big-screen appearances. Jennifer Lopez, however, appears equally adept in both roles. Having established herself as the world's highest-paid Latin American actress with *Out Of Sight*, in which she starred with George Clooney in 1998, she decided the following year to launch a pop career. 'If You Had My Love' was the first of many smash hit singles that, as well as establishing Lopez as one of the most famous women in the world, helped to bring Latin-flavored pop into the mainstream.

Genie In A Bottle
Christina Aguilera

Released June 1999
RCA *65692* (U.S. #1) / RCA *1705482* (U.K. #1)

Following the pattern of all great pop idols, once Christina Aguilera hit the popular consciousness, she seemed as if she was there to stay and had always been a big household name. It happened for Aguilera in the summer of 1999, when America became blanketed by the ubiquity of 'Genie In A Bottle.' The young woman from near Pittsburgh served time as a pre-teen in TV's *Mickey Mouse Club* with future stars Justin Timberlake and Britney Spears and went on to sing the key song 'Run To You' in the Disney movie *Mulan*. All that and her extraordinary pipes helped net a recording contract with RCA.

One of the more overt songs on her debut album *Christina Aguilera*, 'Genie' features the chorus: "If you want to be with me / Baby there's a price to pay / I'm a genie in a bottle / You gotta rub me the right way." While Aguilera seemed to spend much time in her early interviews disputing the meaning of the song, it seemed to be contradicted by her

sexy dance moves and bottle-blonde looks displayed in the video and her performances. All of a sudden, Britney Spears had a significant threat to the throne of teen queen, and the two former mouseketeers continued to skyrocket to worldwide fame. Aguilera took home the coveted Grammy Award for Best New Artist in 2000.

I Try
Macy Gray

Released October 1999
Epic album cut (U.S. #5) / Epic *6681832* (U.K. #6)

From the time when Erykah Badu's first album broke in 1997 until about 2003, neo-soul looked like a force to be reckoned with. Badu, Jill Scott, and Macy Gray boosted the trend, mixing up vintage Motown influences with hip-hop sounds and urban production. Gravelly voiced Gray scored one of the genre's biggest hits with 'I Try,' a gospel-infused hymn to a broken heart anchored by a simple piano and bass rhythm that, in combination, made a pure torch anthem. The single was nominated for three Grammys at the 2001 awards ceremony, at which it won in the category of Best Female Pop Vocal Performance.

Caught Out There
Kelis

Released November 1999
Virgin *38677* (U.S.) / Virgin *VUSCD 158* (U.K. #4)

Got Your Money
Ol' Dirty Bastard Featuring Kelis

Released November 1999
Elektra *67022* (U.S. #33) / Elektra *E 7077CD* (U.K. #11)

Harlem's own Kelis Rogers may not be the most successful R&B singer in America but she is one of the true modern innovators in the genre – and one of the musicians others turn to when they're ready to rip off someone. She has only partially been recognized for her ability to set the pace. Kelis's debut single 'Caught Out There' brought some Alanis Morrissette-style rage to the urban pop world with the snarled chorus of "I hate you so much right now!" The video helped contextualize the aggression, fronted by a cute and diminutive female with a giant, colorful Afro, and got people talking about this different new artist.

Ol' Dirty Bastard (or ODB; born Russell Jones) was a key part of the acclaimed New York rap group Wu-Tang Clan until his death in late 2004. He was an incomparable figure of unabashed craziness known for fathering many children, ingesting many confusicants, and releasing groundbreaking records. For his biggest solo hit he recruited Kelis to sing the hilarious R&B hook ("Hey, Dirty / Baby, I got your money / Don't you worry") that helped portray ODB as a comically ruthless pimp.

The popularity of the song, and its blaxploitation-styled video, kick-started a great demand for Kelis to guest on other songs, starting a side career of sorts for the singer. She would later grace tunes by hip-hop stars such as Busta Rhymes, Clipse, and P. Diddy, and married the Big Apple rap star Nas.

My Name Is
Eminem

Released February 1999
Aftermath 95040 (U.S. #36) / Interscope *INC 95638* (U.K. #2)

A few short months after Britney Spears and her 'Baby One More Time' gave the imminent millennium a new queen of pop, this landmark single announced the king. A calling card for the most successful white rapper of all time, Eminem's debut single had all the hallmarks of his best work. Its creator is one of a very small handful of performers who can honestly claim to have irreversibly altered the landscape of popular music in the past two decades.

According to hip-hop legend, Dr. Dre – a founding member of NWA and producer of countless other rap acts of the 1990s – found Eminem's demo tape on the floor of the garage of Interscope Records head Jimmy Iovine. The young rapper, born Marshall Mathers in 1973 in Kansas City, had been struggling to find a record deal; he assumed this was largely because of the color of his skin. His main antecedent, Vanilla Ice, had come to be seen as something of a laughing stock, and few other white rappers had managed any notable success. But Dr. Dre saw something special in Eminem and, after watching him perform at the 1997 Rap Olympics, brought the rapper to Interscope and started production work on what eventually would become *The Slim Shady LP*.

In 1998 Eminem made his first, tentative steps to fame, first appearing on Kid Rock's *Devil Without A Cause* and then issuing a low-profile taster for his debut album proper, 'Just Don't Give A Fuck.' As soon as 'My Name Is' reached radio at the tail end of the year, however, any plans that Interscope had to slowly ease Eminem into the mainstream quickly disappeared.

In just three rapid-fire verses, the rapper – in his Slim Shady guise – sets out his bitter, angry stall, railing against his mother (who, famously, "smokes more dope than I do"), teachers ("I smacked him in the face with an eraser, chased him with a stapler"), record company executives, and a host of celebrities, from The Spice Girls to Pamela Anderson. By the time of the subsequent release of *The Slim Shady LP*, Eminem had added a catalog of songs about rape, murder, child molestation, drug abuse, and more. This naturally provoked widespread controversy and moral condemnation, as well as furious debate about whether there could be any artistic value in music that focused on such repellent subject matter.

The rapper soon found himself labeled a misogynist, a homophobe, and, generally speaking, a vile, immoral, bad influence on youth. In his defense, he always maintained that the lyrics are from the perspective of his Slim Shady character and that he doesn't advocate rape, murder, and the rest – duh! – but that his freedom of speech should allow him to rap about whatever he chooses. Race seems to be the only contentious area he generally avoids, perhaps because, as his 2002 single 'Without Me' suggests, he feels a modicum of guilt for "being the worst thing since Elvis Presley" for using "black music so selfishly."

Inevitably with Eminem records, the focus tends to fall on the lyrical content – as jaw-dropping as ever here both for clever wordplay and unspeakable nastiness – while Dr. Dre's stellar production work is all but ignored. On 'My Name Is' Dre underpins the vocal tracks with an uncluttered backdrop of stark, stop-start bass and drums and occasional bursts of keyboard. The song embodies elements of the 1975 recording 'I Got The . . .' by the British-African poet and musician Labi Siffre (who insisted Eminem remove certain homophobic lyrics from 'My Name Is' before clearing the sample).

As well as having a remarkably catchy single on his hands, Eminem also began to reap the benefits, for the first time, of being white. Where before the color of his skin had proved a stumbling block to acceptance in the hip-hop world, now that he'd got there he found it opened up an unparalleled market for rap music across white America.

Within weeks of its release, 'My Name Is' found its way into the U.S. Top 40 and peaked at Number 2 in Britain. It was followed by a single that many critics felt was even better. 'Guilty Conscience' casts Dr. Dre as the rapper's good side, as bad Marshall rants about problems with his wife, Kim, and the various unpleasant ways he would respond to finding her in bed with another man. (These two childhood sweethearts went through a very messy, very public divorce in the early 2000s, only to remarry in 2006.)

As with Britney Spears, Eminem's musical worth began to falter the more he became a 'media star,' but few – if any – other rappers of the time could match the artistic and commercial success of his early work. Even when the controversial lyrics and odious Slim Shady persona are stripped from 'My Name Is,' what remains is, indisputably, a great record.

Cowboy
Kid Rock

Released October 1999
Lava-Atlantic *84520* (U.S.) / Atlantic *AT 0076CD* (U.K. #36)

Detroit-bred Kid Rock, born Robert Ritchie, began his music career as a DJ and rapper under the tutelage of veteran artist Too $hort, but remained an underground artist until he incorporated a wider palette of rock and country-inspired sounds into his strangely original mix – just as he does on 'Cowboy.' Thankfully this combination, true to his roots, was what people wanted to hear, otherwise he might have suffered the indignant fate of Vanilla Ice and other neglected white rappers. Strangely, while 'Cowboy' wasn't a runaway pop smash, the album on which it appeared, *Devil Without A Cause*, sold more than 11 million copies.

All The Small Things
Blink-182

Released November 1999
MCA *155606* (U.S. #6) / MCA *MCSTD 40223* (U.K. #2)

Never mind the bollocks, this is the new punk, circa 1999. Courtesy of accomplished producer Jerry Finn, this song from Southern California's Blink-182 (from the cheekily titled album *Enema Of The State*) was the perfect companion to Blink's rough but cuddly image. Even the British, purveyors of fine punk bands like The Clash and The Sex Pistols, were quick to accept Blink-182's 'All The Small Things' as the new pop incarnation of a formerly rebellious musical genre. The video, which lampoons the vids of antiseptic boy bands such as Backstreet Boys and *NSYNC, made it a certified MTV hit.

Praise You
Fatboy Slim

Released January 1999
Astralwerks *66254* (U.S. #36) / Skint *42CD* (U.K. #1)

Fatboy Slim is one of several aliases used over the years by Norman Cook (Quentin to his mum), one of very few British electronic musicians to achieve widespread success in America. He began his musical career in the mid 1980s as bassist in The Housemartins, then formed Beats International, whose 'Dub Be Good To Me' was a U.K. Number 1 hit in 1990, and had further success later in the decade as Freak Power and Pizzaman.

In 1996 Cook signed to the cult Brighton-based label Skint and became Fatboy Slim, issuing a debut album of brash, infectious techno, *Better Living Through Chemistry*, that spawned an entire genre of its own, dubbed big beat. In 1998 his remix of 'Brimful Of Asha' by the British Asian indie group Cornershop was an unexpected U.K. Number 1, setting the stage for two huge Fatboy Slim hits later in the year, 'The Rockafeller Skank' and 'Gangster Trippin'.'

Both were soon eclipsed by 'Praise You,' which added infectious piano chords and a powerful, stop-start breakbeat to a gospel vocal sample. It remains the most successful and most memorable single of Cook's career, in part because of the accompanying promo video. In it, director Spike Jonze leads a pretend dance troupe through a series of ironic moves outside a California theatre. Despite its minimal production values, the promo was a multiple award-winner, and proved instrumental in establishing Fatboy Slim as a mainstream pop success in America.

Kiss Me
Sixpence None The Richer

Released February 1999
Squint *79101* (U.S. #2) / Elektra *E 3750CD* (U.K. #4)

Texas quintet Sixpence None The Richer took their name from a phrase used in a C.S. Lewis book and are one of the ultimate one-hit-wonder bands. They enjoyed a huge hit with the excellent 'Kiss Me' and then vanished from public view faster than you can say "universally ignored La's cover version." The single was a breath of fresh air in the nu-metal-plagued music scene of 1999, all winsome vocals and super-fragile guitars. Perhaps on paper this doesn't sound like the combination for a potential hit, but the song is proof that a winning melody will always comes through. SNTR's version of the aforementioned 'There She Goes' was dull, however, so it was bye-bye from them forever, with or without a kiss.

Windowlicker
Aphex Twin

Released March 1999
Sire *35007* (U.S.) / Warp *WAP 105* (U.K. #16)

'Windowlicker' remains the finest individual statement by one of the late 20th century's greatest musical innovators. The English eccentric Richard D. James began working as Aphex Twin in the early 1990s, producing a run of highly acclaimed albums and singles that run from soothing ambient tones to mind-melting drum'n'bass. 'Windowlicker' mixes hyperactive programmed drum rhythms and bass pulses with ironically moaning and cooing vocal samples. The latter element was intended to parody the overt sexualization of modern pop music, as was the promo video, which stars a group of half-naked dancers with faces manipulated to resemble a grotesque variation of James's own.

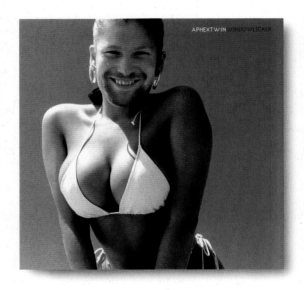

You Get What You Give
New Radicals

Released March 1999
MCA album cut (U.S. #36) / MCA *MCSTD 48111* (U.K. #5)

'You Get What You Give' was one of the biggest international hits of the summer of 1999, a bright, shiny, unashamedly *pop* single clearly inspired by 1970s rock and soul. In 2004 it was praised by Joni Mitchell, who included it on an *Artist's Choice* compilation of favorite songs, for "rising from the swamp of 'McMusic' like a flower of hope."

A rallying cry to disaffected youth, it was the work of Gregg Alexander (born Grosse Pointe, Michigan), who formed New Radicals with the express purpose of scoring a big worldwide hit single. Having achieved that at the first attempt, he split the 'band' – he was the sole member – and turned his attention to writing for and producing other artists. He has since worked with Rod Stewart, Hanson, and Ronan Keating, among others, and won a Grammy for his song 'The Game Of Love,' performed by Santana and Michelle Branch.

'You Get What You Give' is driven by emphatic piano chords, melodic guitar licks, and an instantly memorable vocal line. While most of the lyric is inoffensive feel-good fare, the closing lines were designed by Alexander to test the priorities of the music media.

As he expected, little attention was given to the couplets about what he deemed important political issues – "health insurance, rip-off lying / FDA, big bankers buying" – but his petty faux-sniping at fellow celebrities Courtney Love, Marilyn Manson, and Beck drew countless unwarranted column inches of muck-raking.

Flat Beat
Mr. Oizo

Released March 1999
Not issued U.S. / F Communications-Pias *F 104CD* (U.K. #1)

This deliciously frantic techno song by an inventive French electronica artist will forever be identified with a creature named Flat Eric. The cute and cuddly yellow puppet served as the mascot for a memorable commercial for jeans in Europe where Flat Eric happily jerks and shimmies to Mr. Oizo's thumping beat. Later, Oizo's Paris-based record label F Communication privately questioned its decision to license this song to the Levi's corporation after receiving dozens of phone calls per week inquiring not about Oizo but where they could get their very own Flat Eric to take home.

Everybody's Free (To Wear Sunscreen)
Baz Luhrmann

Released June 1999
EMI *887176* (U.S.) / EMI *CDBAZ 001* (U.K. #1)

Perhaps the only well-known film director to release a chart-topping single – and definitely the only such person from Australia – Baz Luhrmann, 37 years old in 1999, recorded 'Everybody's Free (To Wear Sunscreen)' partly as an elaborate joke and partly as a serious health message. The song takes its lyrics from a *Chicago Tribune* article that provided a list of practical advice, including the use of sun protection, although the lyrics were erroneously attributed to the novelist Kurt Vonnegut. Pop pickers watched in confusion as the song became a summer hit in '99 while Luhrmann prepared to hit the headlines with his extravagant *Moulin Rouge* movie. It seems highly improbable that he will attempt to invade the charts again.

Smooth
Santana Featuring Rob Thomas

Released July 1999
Arista *13718* (U.S. #1) / Arista *1748762* (U.K. #3)

This song was Number 1 in the U.S. for an astonishing 12 weeks – something that the legendary Bay Area guitarist Carlos Santana might never have conceived possible in his long and storied career. For his album *Supernatural*, Santana sought the contributions of a youthful mix of guest artists, including R&B singer-rappers Lauryn Hill (formerly of Fugees) and Cee-Lo (of Goodie Mob). But it was 'Smooth' and its smolderingly sexy vocals courtesy of Matchbox 20 lead singer Rob Thomas that provided the fuel *Supernatural* needed to win the Grammy for Album Of The Year.

Sing It Back
Moloko

Released August 1999
Warner Bros. *44687* (U.S.) / Echo *ECSCD 82* (U.K. #4)

This U.K. dance act, fronted by the gorgeous and talented Irish lead singer Roisin Murphy, became pop stars as this song from their second album went from club hit to mainstream hit, all thanks to a funky remix from German DJ-producer Boris Dlugosch. While not a chart-buster in America, where the video received almost no airplay, 'Sing It Back' won loyal fans for Moloko amongst U.S. dance-music aficionados. The song received many additional remix treatments, all extending its shelf-life in the clubs well beyond the woefully short span of a typical house-music tune.

Steal My Sunshine
Len

Released November 1999
Under The Covers *9906* (U.S. #9) / Columbia *6685062* (U.K. #8)

Whaddya know, a Canadian alt.rock band. When siblings Marc and Sharon Costanzo released a blend of hip-hop beats, attitude, and simple pop humability in 1999 and named it after its persistent chorus line, they had no idea that it would be a global hit and that they would dematerialize from the limelight shortly afterwards. Bizarrely, Marc delivered his raps in a hoarse, almost death-metal grunt while Sharon sang her chorus line in a flat tone that seemed to indicate a complete lack of interest. But the public didn't care and watched keenly for a follow-up. Sadly, nothing of note was forthcoming, and Len were history.

Re-Rewind The Crowd Say Bo Selecta
Artful Dodger Featuring Craig David

Released December 1999
Republic *156916* (U.S.) / Public Demand-Relentless *RELENT 1CDS* (U.K. #2)

Fill Me In
Craig David

Released April 2000
Wildstar-Atlantic *88101* (U.S. #15) / Wildstar *CDWILD 28* (U.K. #1)

Although U.K. garage was viable by the end of the 1990s, the genre lacked personalities, in stark contrast to the superstar DJs and MCs in drum'n'bass, hip-hop, and R&B. Many urban-music fans wondered if garage might languish behind the scenes as a result, but those fears were dispelled by the production duo known as Artful Dodger. With effortless aplomb, their snappy beats and bass underpinned the nonsensical line from prodigy Craig David: "When the crowd say bo – selecta."

The Artful Dodger vanished shortly afterwards, but David became a megastar, albeit with an entirely different musical approach. Stripping his solo recordings of the hard, urban production of 'Re-Rewind,' David took a more soulful tack, and one aimed more directly at mainstream ears. His move to a softer sound paid immediate dividends as he topped the British singles chart twice in 2000, with 'Fill Me In' and '7 Days.' Both reached the American Top 20 in early 2001 – no mean feat for a previously unknown British singer.

Independent Women Part 1
Destiny's Child

Released September 2000
Columbia *79493* (U.S. #1) / Columbia *6705932* (U.K. #1)

It was ironic that Destiny's Child – a Supremes for the 21st century – reached their artistic and commercial peak during the most tumultuous phase of their career. 'Independent Women Part 1' climbed to Number 1 on the *Billboard* Hot 100 – and stayed there for 11 weeks – just months after two former members of the group, LaTavia Roberson and LeToya Luckett, took legal action against their ex-colleagues and their manager, Matthew Knowles, citing breach of partnership.

Houston, Texas-based Knowles had started the group in 1990 when his daughter, Beyoncé, and Roberson were both only nine years old. By 1993 he had added Luckett and his niece, Kelly Rowland, to the group. After several years of performing in the Houston area, the teenage group signed to Columbia in 1997. The quartet scored a number of international hits, including 'No, No, No' and 'Bills, Bills, Bills,' but by the time 'Say My Name' topped the U.S. singles chart in March 2000, Roberson and Luckett were on their way out. Both disliked the way Knowles handled the group's affairs and his apparent favoritism towards his daughter and niece. They didn't intend to quit – but found themselves suddenly replaced by Michelle Williams and, briefly, Farrah Franklin (who only lasted five months before leaving for unspecified reasons).

In the meantime, with lawsuits pending from Roberson and Luckett, Destiny's Child released the lesser 'Jumpin' Jumpin'' before the trio of Knowles, Rowland, and Williams hit their stride on 'Independent Women Part 1.' A glorious slab of R&B-pop reminiscent of Michael Jackson at his peak in the late-1970s and early-'80s, the single was included in the remake of *Charlie's Angels*, guaranteeing it worldwide exposure. A transatlantic Number 1 hit, it was also included on the group's third full-length effort, *Survivor* (2001) – as was 'Part 2,' a slightly slower reading of 'Independent Women' with different lyrics and space-age sound-effects. By the time of the album's release, Roberson and Luckett had settled out of court with their former bandmates but continued to pursue their former manager.

Part of the settlement between the four original members of Destiny's Child was an agreement that neither side would criticize the other publicly, but this didn't stop the new-look trio issuing *Survivor*'s title track as their next single. Most listeners realized that the not-so-subtle call-and-response lyrics were aimed squarely at Roberson and Luckett ("You thought that I'd be weak without you / But I'm stronger … You thought I wouldn't sell without you / Sold nine million"). That's what the axed duo themselves thought, too, prompting a further lawsuit.

Nevertheless, 'Survivor' gave Destiny's Child another massive international hit, which they followed with the similarly successful 'Bootylicious,' a storming ode to the power of the rump. In 2002, each member of the trio started work on individual projects. Inevitably, it was Beyoncé who achieved the greatest solo success, first as an actress – in *Austin Powers In Goldmember* – and then with her ubiquitous 2003 hit 'Crazy In Love.'

The Bad Touch
The Bloodhound Gang

Released March 2000
Polygram International *497267* (U.S.) / Geffen *4972672* (U.K. #4)

A comedy band with comedy songs, The Bloodhound Gang have somehow managed to sustain a reasonably successful career since 1992, when alternative rock and nu-metal were still in their infancy. At the end of the 1990s the rock-buying public seemed to go mad for lightweight, irreverent pop acts – such as Weezer – and pop-punk bands – like Green Day. In the midst of all that, this Pennsylvanian quintet's amusing frat-boy blend of smutty humor and synth-rock provided them with a batch of hits. The biggest, 'The Bad Touch,' was an ode to sex ("You and me baby, we ain't nothing but mammals / Let's do it like they do on the Discovery Channel") accompanied by a 'funny' video.

Porcelain
Moby

Released June 2000
V2 *27650* (U.S.) / Mute *CDMUTE 252* (U.K. #5)

South Side
Moby Featuring Gwen Stefani

Released January 2001
V2 *27665* (U.S. #11) / Not issued U.K.

The New York-based producer Moby (born Richard Melville Hall, a descendent of the author of *Moby Dick*) is one of America's most notable and outspoken artists in the field of electronic music. He is known as much for trying a vast array of sounds and styles as he is for talking about social and political issues, showing that an artist can be both entertaining and intelligent. With his propulsive techno anthems, Moby has been a fixture on the international scene since the 1990s heyday of rave culture.

He took a distinct left-turn with his 2000 album *Play*, where he took recordings of blues musicians by sound anthropologist Alan Lomax into his sample palette. *Play* pleasantly surprised critics and fans, opening up his audience base with a thoughtful balance of classic and modern elements.

A British Top 10 hit, 'Porcelain' did not fare nearly as well on the American pop charts for Moby (which seemed to suit him well). But it was an undeniable hit with executives on Madison Avenue: 'Porcelain,' like most of *Play*, was licensed throughout the world for use in film and television and was used to sell a number of brands and products – a car, a department store, a liqueur – which seemed like a

testimonial to its versatility and broad appeal. With several hundred licenses for a multitude of applications, *Play* has since been cited and studied by the music industry and the advertising industry as a test-case of potential salesmanship.

Early in 2001 Moby redressed the failure of *Play*'s singles on the U.S. *Billboard* chart with the release of a re-recorded version of the album's 'South Side.' A key element in its mainstream success was the guest vocal by Gwen Stefani of the ska-pop group No Doubt, whose past hits included 'Just A Girl' and 'Don't Speak.' It was the first of two smash-hit collaborations for Stefani in early 2001: she also sang on Eve's U.S. Number 2 hit 'Let Me Blow Ya Mind.'

I'm Outta Love
Anastacia

Released September 2000
Epic *79354* (U.S.) / Epic *6695782* (U.K. #6)

Although Anastacia is a strikingly beautiful woman with a powerful stage show and an equally impressive set of lungs, her brash, slightly aggressive demeanor has caused more than a few fans to back away in fear over the years. Nonetheless, there's no denying the power of her voice and songwriting, and this single was a remarkable introduction to both. Labeled by many critics as "the new Tina Turner" for her bulging-neck-veins fortissimo, Anastacia gave it maximum power in 'I'm Outta Love,' a very hum-able tune with a stamping beat and wall-of-sound backing that resembled a hybrid of The Supremes and Cher. Surprisingly, despite achieving smash-hit status across Europe, the single stuttered in at a lowly 92 in her native America.

Since I Left You
The Avalanches

Released September 2000
Modular *010* (U.S.) / XL Recordings *XLS 134CD* (U.K. #16)

Australian electronica quartet The Avalanches (Robbie Chater, Tony Diblasi, Gordon McQuilten, and Darren Seitmann) gained international attention with this creative and lively slice of sampladelia that is reminiscent of U.K. pop band St. Etienne.

A hit in the land down under, the song missed the American pop charts but still managed to make an impression among underground tastemakers in both regions as a significant club hit. It's a versatile tune that won favor among DJs of varying styles. In Britain, the single was successfully reissued on XL Recordings, home of techno terrorists Prodigy, while in America they signed with the major label Sire.

The Avalanches were cheekily vocal about the fact that the *Since I Left You* album was made possible with the liberal use of over 900 samples from records of just about every style imaginable, and they promoted the record with a special DJ mix that dipped into everyone from Hall & Oates to some obscure German electronica. It was impossible to legally clear all of the album's samples for use, so listeners were left guessing about the correct origins of many of the eclectic sounds. As far as we can tell, the song seems inspired by bright 1960s pop, but it could just as easily have been made by pillaging modern country songs.

B.O.B. (Bombs Over Baghdad)
OutKast

Released September 2000
LaFace *24500* (U.S.) / LaFace-Arista *1822942* (U.K.)

Ms. Jackson
OutKast

Released November 2000
LaFace *24516* (U.S. #1) / LaFace-Arista *1836822* (U.K. #2)

OutKast's fourth album *Stankonia* showed the group in transition into popular consciousness, and the lead single 'B.O.B. (Bombs Over Baghdad)' burst onto the scene with a techno-like pace, moving with the ferocity of a roaring train. A metaphor for the group's bombastic potency, the song was a hit on radio as well as MTV, although it was later banned by the corporate radio giant Clear Channel in the aftermath of the attacks on the U.S. in September 2001.

'Ms. Jackson,' on the other hand, strips the group of a considerable amount of its machismo, something few rappers like to have taken away. An ode to their "babymama's mamas," the song is written as an apology to the mothers of their former girlfriends (and mothers of their children), because they broke up with the girl even after they had a child together. Many still believe the main inspiration for the character of 'Ms. Jackson' to be the mother of soul singer Erykah Badu, with whom OutKast's André Benjamin had a son named Seven.

'Ms. Jackson' later received the Grammy for Best Rap Performance By A Duo Or Group, the award that had earlier eluded the pair for 'Rosa Parks.' OutKast also achieved Grammy nominations for 'Ms. Jackson' for Best Shortform Video and for Record Of The Year, the latter a rare feat for any hip-hop artist. *Stankonia*, meanwhile, won the Grammy for Best Rap Album and was nominated for Album Of The Year – an honor the group would grab in 2004 for the follow-up double album *Speakerboxxx / The Love Below*.

Stan
Eminem

Released November 2000
Interscope album cut (U.S.) / Interscope *97470* (U.K. #1)

Thank You
Dido

Released January 2001
Arista *13922* (U.S. #3) / Cheeky-Arista *1853042* (U.K. #3)

A haunting tale of obsessive fandom, 'Stan' captures Eminem at the height of his fame and the peak of his creative powers. It also helped the British singer-songwriter Dido, whose 'Thank You' is sampled in the chorus.

Eminem's proper debut single, 'My Name Is,' was issued less than two years earlier, but in the intervening period he had achieved more than most performers do in their entire careers – and generated more controversy. 'Stan' was the third single to be drawn from *The Marshall Mathers LP*, which sold over two million copies in its first week on sale and was the first rap album ever to be nominated for Album Of The Year at the Grammys.

But it took 'Stan' to cement Eminem's role as one of the biggest stars of the popular-music mainstream. The single is more considered and melodic than his previous releases, mostly through its liberal use of the chorus vocals and instrumental backing from 'Thank You.' Over shuffling acoustic guitars and subtle programmed drums, Eminem performs the first three verses in the character of Stan, a devoted fan who becomes so enraged by the rapper's failure to respond to a series of letters that he kills himself and his pregnant wife by driving off a bridge. The final verse contains the rapper's belated response as he realizes all-too-late that the Stan to whom he is replying is the same fan whose suicide he has just heard about.

Despite its bleak, unsettling lyrical content, 'Stan' was a huge international hit and in the week before Christmas 2000 gave Eminem his second British chart-topping single ('The Way I Am' had been a U.K. Number 1 six months earlier). As was the case with the majority of the rapper's singles, 'Stan' was not released commercially in the U.S. but quickly became a staple of music television and radio programming, and made Number 51 on the *Billboard* Hot 100.

At the 2001 Grammy Awards ceremony, Eminem performed the song with Elton John singing Dido's parts, in response to widespread criticism of the rapper's lyrics by the Gay And Lesbian Alliance Against Defamation (who still picketed the event). The duet with Elton raised a few eyebrows, but in many ways the combination of Eminem – America's most controversial rapper – and Dido – a hippy-dippy English songbird – was just as surprising.

Dido made her first appearances on record in the mid to late 1990s with the dance-pop group Faithless, fronted by her brother, Rollo. Born Florian Cloud de Bounevialle Armstrong, Dido studied at the Guildhall School Of Music in London from the age of six before completing a law degree.

Her full-length solo debut, *No Angel* (1999), was helped first when 'Here With Me' was used as the main theme to the sci-fi TV series *Roswell* and then by Eminem's adoption of 'Thank You.' By the middle of 2001, 'Thank You' had become a British and American hit in its own right, while the gentle, ethereal songs of *No Angel* found their way into over 13 million record collections across the world.

Yellow
Coldplay

Released July 2000
EMI *889077* (U.S.) / Parlophone *CDR 6538* (U.K. #4)

Can it really be this long since Chris Martin and his band released their second proper single, the fragile 'Yellow'? Nowadays the quartet are a globally successful chart act, walking into America with a shy smile and a keyboard flourish and hobnobbing with the great and the good of Hollywood thanks to Martin's marriage to A-league actress Gwyneth Paltrow. Yet it all started so quietly. This single crept into the U.S. charts at Number 48.

'Yellow' is a simple song, elevated to the realms of the extraordinary by three key attributes. First, there is Martin's killer falsetto in the bridge. Everyone likes a romantic, spiralling boy-wail (in this case on the line "Your *skin*, oh yeah your skin and bones") and Coldplay's version was no exception. Second, the clever decision at the end of the song to play the same chords that have made up the whole song so far – but switching them from major to minor: not a common move, but here a stroke of genius. Finally, the band filmed an excellent less-is-more video featuring Martin ambling along a beach as dawn breaks, mouthing the words in slow motion (in fact he had to sing it at double speed for the shoot). Although he resembled the science geek you used to pick on at school, the song's sheer quality ensured classic status for the video. More hit singles and three hit albums followed, and the rest is history.

Beautiful Day
U2

Released September 2000
Island *562972* (U.S. #21) / Island *CID 766* (U.K. #1)

Although the 1990s had started well for U2 – when, as now, they were the biggest band in the world – they had lost their way by the *Pop* album of 1997 and needed to reclaim some relevance as the new decade began. Fortunately, 'Beautiful Day' and its parent album *All That You Can't Leave Behind* were just what was needed, ushering in a whole new sound, steeped in vintage vibes, exuding middle-aged cheerfulness, and attracting a new generation of listeners.

Astoundingly, 'Beautiful Day' marked the first time that Bono, Edge, Adam Clayton, and Larry Mullen Jr. displayed a tendency towards plagiarism, inadvertently or otherwise. As Bono's vocal broke into "Touch me ... take me to that place" and then "Teach me … I know I'm not a hopeless case" it was obvious that the melody was similar to the 1985 hit 'The Sun Always Shines On TV' by Norwegian trio A-Ha. But it's safe to assume that everyone's favorite Irish rockers wouldn't have deliberately pinched the idea. Indeed, Bono had once sarcastically dedicated a live rendition of their hit 'One' to British garage man Craig David, whose song 'Walking Away' had borrowed the chord sequence of the U2 tune with cheeky nonchalance.

'Beautiful Day' marked the resumption of U2's keen performance in the singles charts, and it isn't too much to say that without it they might have gone down a steady route into obscurity – one to which their arch experiments with electronica on *Pop* could only lead. As it is, they seem now to be well set for the rest of their lives.

Rollin'
Limp Bizkit

Released October 2000
Flip/Interscope *06406* (U.S.) / Interscope *IND 97474* (U.K. #1)

Taken from the Number 1 multi-platinum-selling album *Chocolate Starfish And The Hotdog Flavored Water*, 'Rollin'' is one of Limp Bizkit's most memorable anthems. The Florida band, fronted by angsty lead singer Fred Durst (a tabloid favorite for his escapades), had burst into the pop world three years earlier with a bombastic cover of George Michael's ditty 'Faith.'

Limp Bizkit followed up two years later with the crass 'Nookie' and the hip-hop savvy 'N Together Now,' a song produced by legendary DJ Premier and featuring rapper Method Man of Wu-Tang Clan. But 'Rollin'' – a perfect anthem for SUV road rage – rocks the hardest.

Feel Good Hit Of The Summer
Queens Of The Stone Age

Released November 2000
Interscope *497443* (U.S.) / Interscope *497455* (U.K.)

Stoner-rock had been something of a niche interest before Queens Of The Stone Age came along. Genre pioneers Kyuss and Monster Magnet were reliable festival draws but hardly troubled the charts. That changed when the notoriously hard-partying QOTSA landed in the lower U.K. charts with the very cheeky 'Feel Good Hit Of The Summer,' a one-note grind featuring as its sole lyric the line "Nicotine, valium, vicodan, marijuana, ecstasy, and alcohol" and the one-word chorus of "C-c-c-c-c-cocaine!" Rob Halford of Judas Priest lent his robust vocals to the song, which became much-loved for its simplicity and catchiness and its controversial subject – a killer combination.

Modern Age
The Strokes

Released January 2001
Beggars Banquet *85024* (U.S.) / Rough Trade *RTRADCD 010* (U.K.)

Hotel Yorba
The White Stripes

Released November 2001
XL Recordings *XLS 139* (U.S., U.K. #26)

New York quartet The Strokes and Detroit duo The White Stripes had been performing and recording since the late 1990s, but their first widely successful releases came in 2001 – and boy, did they make an impact. The two bands are rather different in style but were lumped together initially thanks to their stripped-down music, ineffably cool pouts, and the fact that their names began with 'The' (hysteria began to build when The Hives joined in the fuss).

The Strokes' signature song remains the fantastic 'Last Nite,' which leads off the *Modern Age* EP. It's a combination of simple, trancey blues-rock riffing, a look that was pure marketing heaven, and a lean, economical sound akin to Blondie and the other tight, funky post-punk acts. With their gorgeous curls and skin-tight black jeans, they looked as if they'd been pulled straight from 1981 and the oh so fashionable bars of New York's Lower East Side, where they had made their name. Frontman Julian Casablancas personified their appeal with his Italian-American sneer and a penchant for flinging the mic-stand about between puffs on his Marlboro. Fortunately, all this was backed up by some solid songwriting.

The more enigmatic Jack and Meg White (vocals-guitar and drums respectively – there is no bassist in The White Stripes) were less immediately digestible but appear to be the more durable act. With their raw, powerful sound derived from vintage American blues, the duo struck gold with 'Hotel Yorba,' their first proper single. Massive success came in 2003 with the Stripes' biggest song to date, 'Seven Nation Army,' and their future seemed assured.

Clint Eastwood
Gorillaz

Released March 2001
EMI *879050* / Parlophone *CDR 6552* (U.K. #4)

The idea of a cartoon rock band wasn't exactly original – remember The Archies? – but with his animated Gorillaz project, sometime Blur frontman Damon Albarn offered up some of the most innovative pop music of the new millennium. 'Clint Eastwood' mixes the haunting, minor-key melodicism of The Specials with producer Dan 'The Automator' Nakamura's slick rhythms and an icy cool rap by Del Tha Funkee Homosapien.

Albarn and Jamie Hewlett, creator of the cult comic-book series *Tank Girl*, first conceived of the idea of a "virtual hip-hop group" in the late 1990s. While Hewlett came up with the visuals, Albarn started putting the music together with a host of collaborators from the worlds of rock and rap, including Nakamura, DJ Kid Koala, and the former Talking Heads rhythm section of Chris Frantz and Tina Weymouth.

The resulting *Gorillaz* album was filled to the brim with genre-blending, thoroughly modern pop, and the most joyous music Albarn had made since the early days of Blur. 'Clint Eastwood' was the second single to be drawn from the album, following the low-key release of 'Tomorrow Comes Today' in late 2000 (for which the musicians behind Gorillaz tried but failed to keep their identities secret). 'Clint Eastwood' continued Albarn's run of chart success in the U.K. but more crucially provided the first step towards the kind of U.S. success that had always eluded him with Blur, with a Number 57 entry on the *Billboard* Hot 100.

Where's Your Head At
Basement Jaxx

Released November 2001
Astralwerks *38803* (U.S.) / XL Recordings *XLS140CD* (U.K. #9)

Based on a big distorted keyboard riff sampled from Gary Numan, Basement Jaxx's most memorable single to date was a blast right from its first bars. The song was loaded with sirens from the DAT tape marked 'Chemical Brothers' and had an infectious four-to-the-floor beat in a clubland groove nailed to some amusing vocals – and that was it. Crowds loved the single, especially when it was coupled with the rather outrageous rock act that the band put on. However, 'Head' wouldn't have done half as well without its accompanying video, a genuinely unnerving clip in which an unsuspecting laboratory visitor is threatened by half-human half-monkey mutants.

Get Ur Freak On
Missy Elliott

Released March 2001
Elektra *67190* (U.S. #7) / East West-Elektra *E 7206CD* (U.K. #4)

In four breathtaking minutes, 'Get Ur Freak On' demonstrates exactly why Missy Elliott was one of the hottest musical talents of the late 1990s and early 2000s. It was also one of the first major hits to blend cutting-edge hip-hop with Middle Eastern instrumentation.

After working with Jodeci and New Edition, Elliott got her break half a decade earlier when she and long-standing collaborator Timbaland contributed seven songs to teen R&B star Aaliyah's big-selling *One In A Million* (1996). Missy's own debut, *Supa Dupa Fly*, arrived a year later and was soon propelled up the charts on the strengths of the sterling single 'The Rain,' which made clever use of an Ann Peebles sample. The multi-talented, larger-than-life star soon became something of a style icon, too, appearing in ad campaigns for Gap and Sprite as singles like 'She's A Bitch' and 'Hot Boyz' became hits.

Over the years Elliott has racked up a host of hits as a solo performer, among them 'Work It' (2002), and produced chart smashes for numerous other artists. It's unlikely, however, that anything else she does will be able to eclipse the scattershot rhythms, tricksy tabla patterns, and cocksure vocals of 'Get Ur Freak On.' The only drawback for Elliott is that, since the release of this single and the accompanying *Miss E . . . So Addictive* album, expectations for her subsequent releases have been impossibly high – although she almost topped 'Get Ur Freak On' with 'Work It.'

Family Affair
Mary J. Blige

Released July 2001
MCA *155859* (U.S. #1) / Uptown-MCA *MCSTD 40267* (U.K. #8)

The sensational soul singer Mary Jane Blige (originally from Yonkers, New York) has been consistently praised for her heartfelt lyrics and phenomenal vocal tone, but 'Family Affair' made longtime fans want to know who produced the equally strong instrumentation behind her. The answer is Dr. Dre, the legendary hip-hop producer who's largely responsible for the careers of blockbuster artists such as Snoop Dogg and Eminem. This pairing of two supernovas in the urban music world shot straight to the top of the American pop charts thanks to Dre's funk-infused strings and Mary's uplifting and celebratory singing.

Fallin'
Alicia Keys

Released June 2001
J Records *21041* (U.S. #1) / J Records *1903692* (U.K. #3)

Alicia Keys (born Alicia Cook) has traveled a long and hard road in the music business, from years spent playing a small piano in a cramped apartment she shared with her mother Terri in the rough Hell's Kitchen section of Manhattan, to the pinnacle of international pop success and humanitarian activism. After the heartbreak of a failed record deal that collapsed on itself before she was even old enough to drive, Keys caught the attention of wizened Arista Records music executive Clive Davis, who had launched the careers of serious legends like Whitney Houston and Santana. After leaving Arista, Davis kicked off his new venture J Records with the startling talent of this extraordinary singer-songwriter wise beyond her tender years.

With simple yet deep lyrics that resonate with anyone who has wrestled with the rollercoaster emotions of love, the aching piano ballad 'Fallin'' made Alicia Keys an instant heartthrob and a household name in record time. The song cleaned up at the 2002 Grammy Awards, where she brought home statuettes for Song Of The Year, Best R&B Song, and Best R&B Vocal Performance. The song was also a catalyst for the rest of Keys's multi-platinum-selling debut album *Songs In A Minor*, which gathered a host of gongs from the NAACP Image Awards, the *Billboard* Awards, the Soul Train Awards, and the Teen Choice Awards.

Rock The Boat
Aaliyah

Released September 2001
Priority *46109* (U.S. #14) / Blackground-Virgin *VUSCD 243* (U.K. #12)

'Rock The Boat' was not Aaliyah Haughton's biggest hit. That may have been 'One In A Million' in 1996, or 2000's 'Try Again,' both Number 1 singles in America – and both produced by Virginia studio wizard Timbaland for the young star, who got her start as a protégé (and secret love interest) of R. Kelly. But 'Rock The Boat' accidentally became more than just a sultry song with a barely veiled nautical metaphor for sexual intercourse. The Detroit-born R&B star died tragically in a plane crash – along with some of her employees and personnel from her label, Virgin Records – after video director Hype Williams shot the song's beautiful performance video on Abaco Island in the Bahamas. Aaliyah's star power had been soaring high in music and in film alike, with starring roles in *Romeo Must Die* and *Queen Of The Damned*, and she was just 22 years old.

At the time of the accident, Aaliyah had been quietly dating New Yorker Damon Dash, an outspoken man who was then the business partner of rapper Jay-Z in the Roc-A-Fella empire, a massive, multi-tiered company that earned millions in the clothing and music industries. The typically vocal Dash remained respectful and relatively quiet about the shock of her death, although he admitted frankly that he couldn't listen to the radio or watch television because of the heavy airplay that 'Rock The Boat' was enjoying.

Can't Get You Out Of My Head
Kylie Minogue

Released September 2001
Capitol *77685* (U.S. #7) / Parlophone *CDRS 6562* (U.K. #1)

'Can't Get You Out of My Head' was a comeback single for the former soap-opera actress who most people thought had run the full course of her European pop success. But it proved that Australian beauty Kylie Minogue could be remembered for more than covering 1960s hit 'The Locomotion' and having the most prized posterior this side of bootylicious American actress-singer-dancer Jennifer Lopez. A household name in Europe, Kylie turned this song into her introduction to most American audiences, who had barely made a note of 'The Locomotion' when she trotted it out in the 1990s.

'Can't Get You Out of My Head' received dozens of unofficial, underground remixes from aspiring bedroom producers all over the world. These versions, sometimes called mash-ups, helped extend the shelf-life of the original song, which was played well beyond its original point of expiration. (One version memorably paired Minogue's solo voice with the instrumental backing to New Order's 'Blue Monday.') The song was penned by the British duo of Rob Davis, formerly the bassist in 1970s glam-rock band Mud, and Cathy Dennis, who had international chart success in the '90s as part of dance act D Mob. This global hit for Minogue gave Dennis a second wind, and she later wrote more pop hits, including 'Toxic,' the biggest song so far for another modern pop sensation, Britney Spears.

Get The Party Started
Pink

Released October 2001
Arista *15074* (U.S. #4) / LaFace-Arista *1913372* (U.K. #2)

Beautiful
Christina Aguilera

Released December 2002
RCA *98364* (U.S. #2) / RCA *6502462* (U.K. #1)

The colorfully-dressed all-female rock band from the San Francisco Bay Area known as 4 Non Blondes are remembered, sometimes derisively, as a one-hit wonder for their unusual 1992 hit 'What's Up.' But a decade later, former 4NB guitarist Linda Perry went on to craft memorable hits for young pop stars Pink and Christina Aguilera, and earned a distinction as one of America's most promising and in-demand 'new' producers.

Perry's 'Get The Party Started' was one of two songs she wrote for Pink's sophomore album *M!ssundaztood*. It helped Pink transform her image from lightweight R&B crooner to gutsy rock singer with a slice of sassy and jangly guitar pop. Pink has since been viewed as an artist capable of a much more versatile range than many had thought possible, something the artist herself had been telling her record-label executives from day one.

After shocking the public with the raunchy single 'Dirrty,' Christina Aguilera followed it up with Perry's 'Beautiful,' a plaintive ballad for self-esteem with its stirring chorus: "You are beautiful / No matter what they say / Words can't bring you down." The song brought back what people loved best about Aguilera: her remarkable voice, but not her somewhat childish attempt to be a sex kitten. 'Beautiful' was nominated for a Grammy for Song Of The Year.

Pop
*NSYNC

Released June 2001
Jive *42933* (U.S. #19) / Jive *9252422* (U.K. #9)

I'm a Slave 4 U
Britney Spears
Released October 2001
Jive *42967* (U.S. #27) / Jive *9252892* (U.K. #4)

Lapdance
N*E*R*D Featuring Lee Harvey & Vita
Released May 2001
Virgin *38786* (U.S.) / Virgin *VUSCD 196* (U.K. #33)

Mouseketeers have to grow up eventually, and 2001 was a key year in the development of the lives of former Mickey Mouse Club members Britney Spears and Justin Timberlake, then the lead singer of boy-band *NSYNC. The former couple in puppy love were morphing into young adults under the extreme heat of the world's spotlight. Instead of remaining in creative stasis, they tried to make records in a more mature style that broke away a little from the earlier work. *NSYNC's 'Pop' was a breakbeat-heavy tune directed by American electronica producer BT (Brian Transeau) and it gave the band a new edge with DJs on the club scene – just as its members were becoming old enough to get into clubs and drink legally.

By 2001, The Neptunes (Pharrell Williams and Chad Hugo) had built their name as producers with the gold and platinum touch, largely in the hip-hop world with artists such as N.O.R.E. and Jay-Z. Working with pop princess Britney Spears on the successful single 'I'm A Slave 4 U' forced a broader definition of their capabilities across musical boundaries. Spears was intrigued by the growing reputation of The Neptunes as hitmakers, but few could have predicted how utterly combustible their collaboration would be. Where Spears's earlier recorded efforts hinted at sex in the hands of an innocent sweetheart, the video for 'I'm A Slave 4 U' found her in hot pink leather and chaps, writhing around a sweaty room with an erotic arrangement of equally drenched dancers. Her contrived goody-two-shoes image was gone for good, but thankfully the song's lyrics were not entirely explicit and still left a little something to the imagination.

'I'm A Slave 4 U' was not Spears's biggest hit by a long shot, stalling at Number 27 on the *Billboard* Hot 100. But its water-cooler potential – the ability to generate office talk and other forms of mainstream buzz – exceeded that of every song she had put out so far, and it remains one of her most controversial cuts. The second single from the *Britney* album was 'I'm Not a Girl, Not Yet a Woman,' but the imagery and lyrics Spears portrayed with 'I'm A Slave 4 U' had many fans unsure if that was a true statement.

So shocking was Britney Spears's song upon its release that another steamy Neptunes production was almost lost in the shuffle. The soaring chords and urgently plucky rhythms of 'Lapdance,' recorded under Williams and Hugo's relatively shortlived guise as N.E.R.D. (standing for No one Ever Really Dies), features the little-known female rapper Vida singing the spicy hook: "Baby, you want me? / Well, you can get this lapdance here for free." But compared to Spears, who had the sweat literally licked off of her in her video, the more urban-focused 'Lapdance' failed to raise quite as many eyebrows in America.

IN SEARCH OF THE NEPTUNES

Poseidon, who also answers to the catchy little name of Neptune, is the eternal god of the sea, the overlord of all things aquatic and fluid. He's an unlikely mascot for a town, yet Neptune is the centerpiece of a myriad of activities in Virginia Beach, VA. His gargantuan statue likeness watches over the Virginia Beach boardwalk with commanding grace, while turtles, fish, and other sea creatures cling on for dear life.

He was no doubt a powerful icon to the young Virginia Beach natives Pharrell Williams and Chad Hugo, for when they officially formed a studio production team they called themselves The Neptunes, later the recipients of a Grammy Award for Producer Of The Year (2004). They learned throughout the 1990s under the wing of R&B producer Teddy Riley (known as the inventor of new jack swing for artists such as Bobby Brown), but by the turn of the century Williams and Hugo would come to eclipse Riley's significant achievements in the recording industry and set off into the deep end of superstardom, crafting hits for a diverse array of artists.

The Neptunes' electronic bleeps, punchy rhythms, and sweet soul hooks became signature stamps that many wanted to collect. This meant not only a heavy demand for Williams and Hugo but also resulted in a slew of inferior copycat productions by amateurish producers who wanted to cash-in on an apparent formula for victory.

Williams and Hugo first started creating a buzz with rap songs like N.O.R.E.'s 'Superthug' (1998), Mystikal's 'Shake Ya Ass' (2000), and Jay-Z's 'I Just Wanna Love U (Give It 2 Me)' (2000), but by 2001 they were crafting songs for pop tartlet Britney Spears, the best example being her controversially mature 'I'm A Slave 4 U.' They've since gone on to record with Usher, Beyoncé, Toni Braxton, Gwen Stefani, Mariah Carey, and others in the pop world, but have maintained a close tie with their beloved hip-hop and R&B flavors, fostering groups such as the street-edged Clipse and the singer Kelis, for whom they've produced several memorable songs including her hits 'Caught Out There' (1996) and 'Milkshake' (2004). They've worked with hip-hop stars like Nelly, Busta Rhymes, Fabolous, and LL Cool J, although they explored the fringes of rock with their N.E.R.D. group, a project that spawned one album, *In Search Of*. They've also given rap icon Snoop Dogg the biggest hits of his career with 'Beautiful' (2003) and 'Drop It Like It's Hot' (2004).

Despite having a population of less than half a million, Virginia Beach has come to be known as a breeding ground for distinctively different musical talent. Besides The Neptunes and their mentor Teddy Riley, the town is also the place where rap-R&B superstars Jodeci, Missy Elliot, and Timbaland all grew up. Maybe there really is something in those waters of Neptune.

It Wasn't Me
Shaggy

Released January 2001
MCA *155782* (U.S. #1) / MCA *1558022* (U.K. #1)

Because I Got High
Afroman

Released August 2001
Universal *015310* (U.S. #13) / Universal *MCSTD 40266* (U.K. #1)

Two of the most hilarious odes to non-accountability in music emerged in 2001 – and became not just cult hits but international hits. 'It Wasn't Me' was the bestselling song in the U.K. that year and the largest in Jamaican singer Shaggy's career, while 'Because I Got High' was a surprise triumph from a relatively unknown rap artist. Shaggy's anthem is about not being a cheater, even in the face of obvious and damning evidence such as being caught red-handed in the sexual act, and is as gut-bustingly funny as Afroman blaming everything in his life on smoking too much marijuana.

Izzo (H.O.V.A.)
Jay-Z

Released July 2001
Roc-A-Fella *588701* (U.S. #8) / Roc-A-Fella *5888152* (U.K. #21)

From the critically acclaimed and multi-platinum-selling album *The Blueprint*, 'Izzo (H.O.V.A.)' was produced by Chicago's Kanye West, who later became an internationally acclaimed solo artist on the level of a blockbuster rapper like Jay-Z (the alias of Brooklyn-born Sean Carter). Loyal to the man who gave him his greatest fame as a producer, West signed to Jay-Z's label Roc-A-Fella. 'Izzo' samples and loops the briefest snippet of Michael Jackson in his Jackson 5 days and speeds it up even faster than the young chipmunk could do on his own, exemplifying the creative production style that became West's signature. Several years later, it was still being 'borrowed' by countless hip-hop producers worldwide in their fruitless quest to capture his winning formula. West's first solo breakout hit, 2003's 'Through The Wire,' applied the technique to Chaka Khan's hit 'Through The Fire.'

But 'Izzo' is not just simply a showcase for the prodigious Kanye West; musical titan Jay-Z is spotlighted rather well here, too. Lyrically, the song demonstrates Jay-Z's considerable talent for wordplay: 'H.O.V.A.' is an abbreviation for "Jay-Hova," a play on Jehovah to indicate his rap-god status; 'Izzo' appropriates a type of West Coast hip-hop slang that throws the 'izz' sound in the middle of words, a style popularized by L.A. rapper Snoop Dogg. 'Izzo (H.O.V.A.)' earned Jay-Z a Grammy nomination for Best Rap Solo Performance.

Gotta Get Thru This
Daniel Bedingfield

Released December 2001
Island *570976* (U.S. #10) / Relentless *RELENT 27CD* (U.K. #1)

The New Zealand-born and British-bred singer-producer Daniel Bedingfield scored an international hit with this catchy take on the rollicking, funky dance music that's been referred to variously as U.K.

garage and 2-step. Listeners who first heard 'Gotta Get Thru This' were not immediately aware that vocalist Bedingfield was male, since the singing was considerably speeded up. It was a surprise hit in America, a country that didn't take to the genre the way it took to this song.

Hero
Enrique Iglesias

Released October 2001
Interscope *497613* (U.S. #3) / Interscope *IND 97671* (U.K. #1)

Whenever, Wherever
Shakira

Released November 2001
Sony International *672196* (U.S. #6) / Epic *6724262* (U.K. #2)

The turn of the century brought a new appreciation for Latin American pop stars in Britain and America, a phenomenon that brought new success for Spain's Enrique Iglesias and Columbia's Shakira, singers who had already enjoyed success in the Spanish-speaking world.

After scoring his first American chart-topper in 1999 with 'Bailamos,' Enrique, son of legendary singer Julio Iglesias, returned to the Top 10 in 2001 with 'Hero' from his album *Escape*. That same year, Shakira – a star in her native Columbia since she was a pre-teen – debuted her first U.K. album *Laundry Service* and the breakout hit 'Whenever, Wherever.' Both artists have had hits by mixing Spanish and English in the same songs, but of course their mainly English versions have done best in the English-speaking territories.

It hurts neither Iglesias nor Shakira that each has become a sex symbol, which they both exploited fully in their videos for these songs as well as in their careers generally. The video for 'Hero' features an adventure plot with the damsel in distress played by Iglesias's then-girlfriend Jennifer Love Hewitt, an attractive American movie actress who got her start as a star of the Fox television drama *Party Of Five*. Meanwhile, Shakira's visual take for 'Whenever, Wherever' has her rolling around in mud and shaking her body suggestively while wearing a tight leather bikini top.

Ain't It Funny
Jennifer Lopez Featuring Ja Rule & Caddillac Tah

Released January 2002
Epic *672390* (U.S. #1) / Epic *6724922* (U.K. #4)

Foolish
Ashanti

Released March 2002
Murder Inc. *588986* (U.S. #1) / Murder Inc. / Mercury *0639942* (U.K. #4)

During the first half of 2002, the hip-hop label Murder Inc. and it's biggest star, Ja Rule, held an 18-week stranglehold on the *Billboard* Hot 100's Number 1 spot.

Born Jeffrey Atkins in Queens, New York City, Ja Rule wrote and produced several hits with R&B hooks – and lent his lyrical talents to a few R&B songs and helped make them hits as well. The first time he had success with the formula was with New Jersey singer Christina Milian on the sexy 'Between Me & You' and then with Baltimore's Lil' Mo on 'Put It On Me,' but his next single, 'Always On Time,' brought it straight to the top. A burgeoning chanteuse from Long Island, New York, named Ashanti Douglas sang the 'Always On Time' hook, and by the time the two performers appeared together in the video, yet another star was born, and Ja Rule had his first Number 1 single.

After two weeks at the top, 'Always On Time' was replaced by an even bigger hit, 'Ain't It Funny,' the first of two hip-hop-savvy collaborations between Ja Rule and the Bronx-born actress-dancer-singer Jennifer Lopez. Both 'Ain't It Funny' and 'I'm Real' appeared on a remix album called *J To Tha L-O! The Remixes*. The songs, which sampled classic hip-hop joints like Craig Mack's 'Flava In Your Ear,' lent the critically panned Lopez some credibility in the hip-hop world, which she had long tried to join. (She continued to espouse her "street" credentials with 'Jenny From The Block,' a Number 3 hit on the *Billboard* Hot 100 later in 2002.)

In the meatime, Ashanti had signed to Murder Inc. and been busying herself working on a record of her own, with help from label boss Irv Gotti and, naturally, the omnipresent Mr. Rule. Follwing 'Ain't It Funny'"s six-week stint at Number 1, Ashanti's solo debut, 'Foolish,' hit the top spot, and hung on in there for a total of ten weeks. Ja Rule didn't feel the need to put in an appearance on this particular record, but did pop up in the video, which was fashioned after the much-loved gangster movie *Goodfellas*.

Hot In Herre
Nelly

Released May 2002
Fo' Real *279* (U.S. #1) / Universal *MCSTD 40289* (U.K. #4)

Dirrty
Christina Aguilera Featuring Redman

Released October 2002
RCA *97635* (U.S. #48) / RCA *1962722* (U.K. #1)

St. Louis-based rapper Nelly had a runaway hit with 'Hot In Herre,' a catchy and flirty tune produced by Pharrell Williams of The Neptunes that spent seven weeks atop the American charts and snagged a Grammy for Best Male Rap Solo Performance. In addition to ruling clubs, radio, MTV, and BET for months, the song unintentionally inspired a hit from another pop artist (Christina Aguilera) and a film from an internationally famous fashion photographer (David LaChappelle).

After Nelly's anthem started to wane just a little, Canadian electro DJ Tiga followed it up with his own version of 'Hot in Herre.' Tiga ended up with an international club hit and released a memorable video featuring marionette puppets singing the lyrics. 'Hot' also inspired songbird Christina Aguilera in the slangified spelling of her own 'Dirrty' later that year. Musically, Aguilera's surprisingly raunchy tune derives from 'Let's Get Dirty,' a song by East Coast rapper Redman, produced by Rockwilder.

Aguilera's camp secured production by Rockwilder and a guest appearance by Redman to make 'Dirrty.' Her song is indelibly associated with its David LaChappelle-directed video in which Aguilera, clad in skimpy underwear and chaps, writhes with female dancers in a muddy underworld replete with illicit fighting and strange fetishes. Among the cast of performers are dancers from South Central Los Angeles who practice a style called krumping. LaChappelle's experience shooting 'Dirrty' inspired him to create his award-winning documentary Rize in 2005, a chronicle of krumping (and its predecessor, clowning).

Gimme The Light
Sean Paul

Released October 2002
VP *6400* (U.S. #7) / VP-Atlantic *AT 0146CD* (U.K. #5)

The sounds of Jamaica were pivotal in creating the foundation for American hip-hop, but styles such as reggae and its lively sub-strain of dancehall have traditionally only been popular in U.S. cities with sizeable Caribbean populations, such as New York and Miami. Sean Paul Henriques kicked the door down with 'Gimme The Light,' a smash with club DJs that broke through to radio and video outlets.

The chart-topping follow-up single 'Get Busy' and album *Dutty Rock* (which got the Grammy for Best Reggae Album) helped cement dancehall as a viable sound within the American urban-music scene in 2003. That year he also added his vocals to two of the biggest international hits of the summer – Beyoncé's 'Baby Boy' and 'Breathe' by Blu Cantrell.

A Moment Like This
Kelly Clarkson

Released October 2002
RCA 6022 (U.S. #1) / RCA 60622 (U.K. B-side)

Kelly Clarkson was catapulted to fame as the winner of the first season of *American Idol*, the U.S. version of the British TV talent show *Pop Idol*. There is nothing particularly remarkable about the Texan singer's debut single, but there didn't need to be. Given the platform of such a successful television series, there was no question that 'A Moment Like This' would become a smash-hit on the *Billboard* charts, establishing a pattern that has since been followed by each of the subsequent *American Idol* winners.

To her credit, Clarkson seems like one of the few winners of *Idol* with the talent to last more than a couple of polished, throwaway pop ditties. By 2004 she had re-cast herself as rock chick par excellence with the international hit 'Since U Been Gone,' which was written for her by Max Martin, the Swedish composer of Britney Spears's breakthrough hit '. . . Baby One More Time.'

Cry Me A River
Justin Timberlake

Released December 2002
Jive 40073 (U.S. #3) / Jive 9254612 (U.K. #2)

As the most sought-after member of the blockbuster boy-band *NSYNC, Memphis-born Justin Timberlake was always touted as the one from the group who was most likely to have a successful solo career. But the extent of the multi-platinum success of Timberlake's debut effort *Justified,* an album that generated several hits, was still largely a surprise.

Most of *Justified* was breezy and fun, but the most talked about and easily the most scathing song on the record is 'Cry Me A River.' Produced by and featuring Timbaland (a.k.a. Tim Mosley, the Virginia-based producer of R&B hits for Aaliyah and Missy Elliot), the song is a tale of a cheating, dumped girlfriend and the ways of dealing with the consequences of her misguided actions.

It was widely rumored that 'Cry Me A River' was based on Timberlake's own tumultuous breakup with fellow pop-star Britney Spears (who allegedly cheated on him with her choreographer, Wade Robson). Their relationship had been dissected in the media for years, down to every last little detail, and Timberlake did nothing to discourage the widely held interpretation of the song. The video only added fuel to the already raging flames of the scandal by featuring a blonde Britney look-alike model as the target of Timberlake's hurtful revenge. It should come as no surprise that it was a favorite of the MTV video countdown program *Total Request Live* and a regular subject visited in gossip magazines such as *U.S. Weekly* and *Star*.

TV IDOLS: A NEW OLD WAY TO FABRICATE POP STARS

The idea of the manufactured pop act is nothing new – it dates back almost as far as pop music itself – but *Pop Idol*, *American Idol*, and the various spin-off TV shows that air around the globe have made the ploy even more transparent, not to mention even more successful.

The basic premise of the show – which in the U.K. was superseded by *The X-Factor* – is that a series of open auditions are held from which a "final 12" performers are selected to compete to become that year's idol. Every week, each of them sings a song before a panel of judges, who offer instant criticism. Viewers vote for their favorite, and the least popular act is voted off, until only one remains. Over the course of the series the performers are taught singing techniques and dance steps,

often by visiting guest musicians eager to put in an appearance – and plug their latest product – on what has become the top-rated show on American television.

Each year's winner is guaranteed a hit or two straight away, but few seem destined for enduring success – after all, it's never too long before the next *Idol* comes along. The true, lasting star is Simon Cowell, the main judge on both the British and American versions of the show, who is loved and hated in equal measure for his blunt put-downs of most of the performers. On the strength of this he has become one of the highest-paid stars in the history of American television, not to mention one of the most influential figures in the popular music industry.

Hate To Say I Told You So
The Hives

Released February 2002
Burning Heart *60157* (U.S.) / Burning Heart *BHR 1059* (U.K. #23)

Garage-rock had already been re-re-established in the U.K. thanks to The Strokes and The White Stripes by the time that Swedish quintet The Hives arrived with this addictive single, which scraped in at Number 86 in America. But it was this song that made many listeners aware of the power of punked-up rock'n'roll, especially when pumped out by Scandinavians in suits. Led off by an overdriven guitar (and breaking down at one point to a similarly distorted bass part), 'Hate To Say I Told You So' is powered by a simple four-note riff and fueled by the deranged wails of Howlin' Pelle Almqvist. Impeccably good; unforgettably raw.

Freak Like Me
Sugababes

Released April 2002
Universal International *582898* (U.S.) / Island *CID 798* (U.K. #1)

'Freak Like Me' is the most commercially successful example of the mash-up, a club remix that combines the musical elements of one song with the vocal parts of another – and one of the most memorable U.K. hits of recent times. In this case, the three Sugababes sing the lyrics to Adina Howard's 1995 single of the same name against the powerful synthesizer frame of Gary Numan's 1979 British Number 1 'Are Friends Electric,' as reworked by the DJ-producer Richard X. The single helped to establish Sugababes, who despite their ever-changing line-up were among the most successful British girl-bands of the new millennium. Numerous hits followed, including 'Round Round,' 'Hole In The Head,' and 'Push The Button,' all U.K. Number 1s.

Toxicity
System Of A Down

Released March 2002
American album cut (U.S.) / Columbia *6725022* (U.K. #25)

Having prepared the way with the stunning 'Chop Suey!,' America's finest Armenian metal quartet shed the last remaining vestiges of the nu-metal tag with this epic song, which was also the title of their second and most accessible album. Singer Serj Tankian laid his heavily vibrato'd vocals over a dense but funky guitar soup, with the listener's ears drawn inexorably to the stop-start riff in the bridge and the chorus line: "The toxicity / Of our cities." The tune ends rather insanely with a snatch of Eastern melody and Tankian's mad yelp. The future would be even madder for this ambitious, unique band. While their singles were not major chart hits in the U.S. – this one peaked at Number 70 – *Toxicity* was the first of the group's three Number 1s on the *Billboard* album chart.

Let's Push Things Forward
The Streets

Released April 2002
Not issued U.S. / Locked On-679 *679L 005CD* (U.K. #30)

Aside perhaps from the likes of Massive Attack, there was little in the way of a viable U.K. alternative to hip-hop during the 1980s and 1990s. At the dawn of the 21st century, however, British urban music found a new lease on life with the sounds of 2-step and U.K. garage – essentially vocal versions of earlier, less mainstream strands of jungle and drum'n'bass. This new music made its first impact on the charts with hits by The Artful Dodger, Oxide & Neutrino, and the shortlived So Solid Crew (essentially a poor man's Wu Tang Clan). But the genre's first true star was Mike Skinner, a.k.a. The Streets.

Born in 1978, Skinner grew up on the outskirts of the typically British city of Birmingham and started experimenting with music at a young age. The title of his second single, 'Let's Push Things Forward,' is representative of his music-making philosophy: the instrumental parts are clean, sleek, ultra-modern, and the words describe British urban life in a way never before heard on record. Steering clear of the sensationalism of a lot of U.S. hip-hop, Skinner instead reports on the mundane matters of life – cans of beer, Indian take-outs, darts – in a striking mock-cockney voice. Making explicit the comparison between his lyrics and those of his American counterparts, he said: "Around here, we say birds, not bitches." Skinner continued from strength to strength over the next few years, confirming his mainstream pop-star status with his first U.K. Number 1, 'Dry Your Eyes,' in late 2004.

House Of Jealous Lovers
The Rapture

Released April 2002
DFA *2121* (U.S.) / Output *OPRDFA 001* (U.K.)

Losing My Edge
LCD Soundsystem

Released July 2002
DFA *2123* (U.S.) / Output *OPRDFA 002* (U.K.)

It was only a matter of time, following the arrival of The Strokes, The Hives, and the rest, for a new bunch of bands to mine the dancier, funkier end of late-1970s and early-'80s punk and new wave. Two of the first and best of these were The Rapture and LCD Soundsystem. Both issued their defining singles in 2002, but it took a little longer for them to achieve noteworthy commercial success.

The Rapture had been in existence since the late 1990s but didn't begin to hit their stride until they made the *Out Of The Races And Onto The Tracks* EP, which echoed the work of Public Image Ltd and Talking Heads two decades earlier. 'House Of Jealous Lovers' took things a step further, adding an irresistibly funky backbeat and singalong chorus to the usual angular guitars and throbbing bass.

A 2003 reissue of 'Jealous Lovers' on Mercury Records reached Number 23 on the U.K. singles chart. The original version had been put out by the fledgling DFA Records, founded in 2001 by the New York-based producer James Murphy and his regular English collaborator Tim Goldsworthy (formerly of U.N.K.L.E.). Part of the reason for forming the label was to create a platform for Murphy's own recordings as LCD Soundsystem. His debut, 'Losing My Edge,' is a sarcastic send-up of too-cool-for-school music fans – most of the lyrics are simply the names of hip bands – set to a gritty, electro-punk backing.

A Little Less Conversation
Elvis Vs. JXL

Released June 2002
RCA *060575* (U.S. #50) / RCA *1943572* (U.K. #1)

It wasn't entirely surprising that a classic such as Elvis Presley's 1968 ditty 'A Little Less Conversation' would be remixed for current ears by someone like Junkie XL, a.k.a. Tom Holkenborg, a Dutch-born DJ-producer known for bombastic techno and breakbeat cuts. Hip-hop and electronica artists often look to the past for present inspiration. What was more shocking was that a remix such as this was picked up to be a part of an official Elvis release (the *30 #1 Hits* album) after the single became a Number 1 hit in several countries as, essentially, a bootleg. It then became the theme to TV's *Las Vegas*.

Ignition–Remix
R. Kelly

Released December 2002
Jive *40065* (U.S. #2) / Jive *9254972* (U.K. #1)

Even as controversial R&B singer R. Kelly (Chicago-born Robert Kelly) faced international scandal stemming from numerous counts of child pornography against him in Illinois and Florida, his pop music mettle and his status as an urban legend grew ever stronger. Nowhere was this more in evidence than with the radio and video release of 'Ignition–Remix' from Kelly's two-million-plus-selling album *Chocolate City*.

Following the dramatically repentant 'Heaven, I Need a Hug,' a radio-circulated song apparently in direct response to the charges, and never formally released, 'Ignition–Remix' found the singer returning to his more salacious roots with a unapologetically infectious song that bored into pop psyches like a worm on a mission, just as his best melodies always have. Once again pondering his all-time favorite topic – sex, of course – Kelly sets up this mid-tempo bouncer with a simple (and totally inane) metaphor about male and female anatomy and car keys and ignitions.

Kelly's instincts for putting out 'Ignition–Remix' at this time were frighteningly on target. Stoked by the real-life headlines, the titillating motor of this song ran strong, stopping just shy of the top spot in America but netting Kelly his second-ever U.K. Number 1 (the first was 1996's 'I Believe I Can Fly'). More than that, however, it symbolized Kelly's continued foothold in pop music, no matter how the details of his personal life unfurled.

Hey Ya!
OutKast

Released November 2003
LaFace *54962* (U.S. #1) / Arista *6579532* (U.K. #3)

An inescapable slice of experimental pop infectiousness, 'Hey Ya!' may well be one of the biggest crossover records in history. It was released only as a DVD single in the U.S., but the deceptively simple tune has introduced countless ears around the world to the mercurial sound of OutKast, where hip-hop is really only a starting point for musical fun.

'Hey Ya!' peaked at the top of the *Billboard* Hot 100 and at Number 3 in the U.K., and was a fixture on global dance floors and radio airwaves for at least a year following its release. The song was instrumental in the meteoric and sparkling performance of the unique long-player *Speakerboxxx / The Love Below*, a double-album showcasing the individual and collective talents of OutKast members Andre '3000' Benjamin and Antwan 'Big Boi' Patterson.

'Hey Ya!' is nonsensical at times but offers a somewhat twisted take on the clichés of the love song, questioning what makes love real and true. But the song's lyrics and overall message were quickly relegated to the background amid the public fervor for the catchy keys and booming bass of the backing track, although Benjamin's requests to "shake it like a Polaroid picture" became an oft-repeated phrase from the song, much to the delight of the camera corporation.

Directed by Bryan Barber, the video for 'Hey Ya!' casts the song in a new, imaginative light. Both amusing and technologically tricky, it is a

cheeky parody of The Beatles' iconic 1964 TV appearance on *The Ed Sullivan Show*. But instead of the fab four, the band performing is The Love Below – all its members are played by Benjamin himself, including the sassy backup singers, The Love Haters, who are all clad in jockey garb. Since Benjamin wrote, produced, sang, and played most of the instruments on the song, the depiction is not really such a stretch. Barber also directed 'The Way You Move' – released as a joint DVD single with 'Hey Ya!' – and *My Life In Idlewild*, OutKast's HBO-funded movie musical inspired by The Love Below. Almost a mini-movie in itself, the 'Hey Ya!' video is a whimsical introduction to Benjamin's genuine love for acting, which he has gone on to explore more formally, notably in John Singleton's movie *Four Brothers* (2005).

'Hey Ya!' was well celebrated, grabbing Video Music Awards from MTV and MTV Europe. It also copped the 2004 Grammy for Best Urban/Alternative Performance, although the band's live performance of the song at the ceremony was criticized by several Native American organizations, who opposed the Indian-styled costuming and choreography. Undeterred by what might have been a momentary lapse of judgment, the song went on to top critics' polls at *Village Voice* and *Rolling Stone*, the latter saving it a place in its 500 Greatest Songs Of All-Time list.

In Da Club
50 Cent

Released January 2003
Interscope *497856* (U.S. #1) / Interscope *4978742* (U.K. #3)

By the time 'In Da Club' journeyed from the streets of New York City to top the *Billboard* Hot 100, where it stayed for nine weeks and became the bestselling single of 2003, 50 Cent had already gained and lost a record deal and been at death's door. Born Curtis Jackson in Queens, the former drug dealer was contracted to Columbia and startled the hip-hop industry with the sizable hit 'How To Rob,' an antagonistic song about stealing respect – and possessions – from rap stars. After recording *Power Of The Dollar* (2000), and following an incident in which he was shot nine times, 50 Cent was dropped before he could release the album, and he returned to his old life in the rap underground.

The attack added to the rapper's growing legend in New York, which he capitalized on over the next two years through his own independent mix-tape releases. These caught the attention of hip-hop luminaries Eminem and Dr. Dre, who signed him and produced his debut album *Get Rich Or Die Tryin'*. The upbeat first single 'In Da Club' became an inescapable presence on radio and MTV as well as in the clubs. But the most enduring legacy of 50 Cent's first hit may be its infectious chant, which has now become standard drunken-birthday-party fare: "Go shorty, it's your birthday / We go'n' party like it's your birthday."

Milkshake
Kelis

Released August 2003
Star Trax-Arista *54243* (U.S. #3) / Virgin *VSCDX 1863* (U.K. #2)

With this playfully suggestive single, the American R&B singer Kelis finally found success in her homeland, having already established a strong following in Europe. After graduating in 1998 from New York City's Fiorello H. LaGuardia High School of Music & Art and Performing Arts, Kelis Rodgers met and started working with The Neptunes, who had just started on their way to becoming the most sought-after production duo of modern times.

The Neptunes produced Kelis's first two albums, *Kaleidoscope* (1999) and *Wanderland* (2001), but both floundered in America. She scored minor British hits with the singles 'Caught Out There' (with its memorable chorus line of "I hate / You so much right now"), 'Good Stuff' (both 1999), and 'Young, Fresh, N' New' (2001), but her only taste of chart success in the U.S. was with her guest appearance on Ol' Dirty Bastard's 'Got Your Money.'

Three things contributed to the reversal of Kelis's fortunes in America. The first was her relationship with and subsequent marriage to the high-profile rapper Nas; the second was a move to The Neptunes' Star Trax label, who put more effort into promoting her; and the third was the release of her finest single to date. 'Milkshake' bounces along on warm synths, stop-start drums, and a vocal that sounds like a warped playground chant. The lyrics – a not-very-veiled declaration of just how great are the singer's breasts – stirred up a heap of conjecture and controversy, but in the end that served only to help Kelis to her biggest international success so far. (Two further European smash hits followed: 'Trick Me' and 'Millionaire,' a duet with OutKast's Andre 3000.)

Crazy In Love
Beyoncé

Released June 2003
Columbia *79949* (U.S. #1) / Columbia *6740672* (U.K. #1)

'Crazy In Love' launched the solo career of erstwhile Destiny's Child singer Beyoncé, and immediately made her one of the biggest popular-music stars of the early 21st century.

Columbia Records executives were initially unsure about Beyoncé's choice of the song as her first proper solo single, fearing its harder-edged sound might alienate sections of her existing fan base. They were eventually convinced, however, by the addition of a rap from the singer's beau, hip-hop renaissance man Jay-Z, which gave the song indisputable star power. Earlier in the year Beyoncé had appeared on his U.S. Number 2 hit ''03 Bonnie And Clyde.' Here he returns the favor, first announcing that the duet is "history in the making," and then taking the opportunity to declare himself to be "cut from a different cloth / My texture is the best fur / Of chinchilla."

The main musical hook of 'Crazy In Love' is a thrusting horn sample, taken from the Chi-Lites' 1971 hit 'Are You My Woman.' The backing track – which flits, rhythmically, between a jangling, hi-hat-heavy breakbeat in the verses to four-to-the-floor disco in the chorus – was the work of a then struggling producer, Rich Harrison.

After working on Mary J. Blige's 1999 full-length *Mary*, Harrison found himself in something of a slump until Beyoncé chanced upon an embryonic version of what became 'Crazy In Love.' The singer enlisted him to finish off the music, adding the bulk of the lyrics and melody herself. The main vocal highlight arrives in the bridge, the "uh oh uh oh uh oh no no" neatly encapsulating the rest of the lyric's theme of romantic insanity.

'Crazy In Love' was an instant smash hit, climbing high up the charts in Britain, North America, Japan, Australia, and across Europe. Within a month of its release, Beyoncé had become the first female artist to simultaneously top the album and singles charts in the U.S.A. and the U.K. when her full-length debut, *Dangerously In Love*, joined it at Number 1. The single was also one of the first true successes of legal downloading, chalking up 100,000 sales in the U.S.A. alone. It won Grammy Awards for Best R&B Song and Best Rap/Sung Collaboration; a club mix by Maurice Joshua, 'Krazy In Luv,' was named Best Remixed Recording. Its success was further boosted by an extravagant promo clip, directed by Jake Nava, which features an exploding car and numerous costume changes.

All in all, the single and its star became so ubiquitous that it afforded Beyoncé that ultimate signifier of fame: she was able to drop her surname – Knowles, by the way.

opposite > OutKast's Andre 3000 performing 'Hey Ya!' on February 17th, 2004 at the Brit Awards in London, England. Beyoncé then joined the stage for a rendition of her 'Crazy In Love.'

Mundian To Bach Ke
Panjabi MC

Released January 2003
Sequence *8012* (U.S. #32) / Showbiz-Instant Karma *KARMA 28CD* (U.K. #5)

'Mundian To Bach Ke' was the first major U.K. hit to fuse modern hip-hop and electronica with bhangra, a form of Indian and Pakistani dance music. A remix by Jay-Z then helped the song into the U.S. Top 40. Western ears had begun to warm to Middle Eastern and Indian sounds, most notably with the success of Missy Elliott's tabla-laden smash-hit 'Get Ur Freak On.' The British-Asian electronic musician Talvin Singh had a brief period of fame in Britain when his solo debut album *OK* (1998), which fused Hindi classical music with drum'n'bass, won the U.K.'s Mercury Music Prize.

Panjabi MC (born Rajinder Rai) made the Indian influence more explicit in his music, rapping and singing in both English and Punjabi and using traditional bhangra instruments such as dhol drums and a one-string instrumental called the tumbi. Rai had started his musical career in the early 1990s and found widespread success within Asian communities across Europe. 'Mundian To Bach Ke' – which translates as 'Beware Of The Boys' – was originally issued in 1998 on the Big Star label but was re-released and first charted five years later, at a time when other British-Asian musicians, including the producer Rishi Rich, were finding fame. Key to the song's success is its use of the distinctive bassline and other musical figures from the theme to the TV series *Knight Rider*. After topping the singles chart in Germany and reaching the Top 5 in Britain, 'Mundian' caught the attention of Jay-Z, who liked the song so much that he remixed it, adding his own rap to the new version.

All The Things She Said
t.A.T.u.

Released January 2003
Interscope *019354* (U.S. #20) / Interscope *0196972* (U.K. #1)

"Sex sells" is a well-known axiom in just about every industry there is, but with t.A.T.u., the music business hadn't seen such an overstated attempt to embody the phrase since Brooklyn rapper Lil Kim's oversexed antics made headlines in the 1990s. Until t.A.T.u., Russian pop artists had very little success on the international charts. 'All The Things She Said' brought water to that desert-like drought, and it was not too surprising when the public thirstily drank it up.

But the success of 'All The Things' was not simply because the song resonated with the public. Full of high notes but little in the way of a catchy hook or melody, it is not the sort of tune that normally dominates pop charts. Instead, record-buyers picked up on the implied lesbian relationship between members Elena Sergeevna Katina and Yulia Olegovna Volkova, which was precisely what t.A.T.u.'s calculating manager Ivan Shapovalov intended them to notice.

Photographs showing the pair kissing, cuddling, and holding hands, their antics in live performances, and the video for 'All The Things She Said' all played up this pretend imagery, with two very young-looking performers clad in even younger-looking clothing meant to evoke the classic Catholic schoolgirl. It was not a lasting formula for success – especially when they 'came out' to say that they are both heterosexual women who date men.

Hurt
Johnny Cash

Released April 2003
Universal *779982* (U.S.) / American-Lost Highway *0779982* (U.K. #39)

In the last years of his life Johnny Cash achieved an entirely unpredicted last dose of fame thanks to the motivating force of the equally great Rick Rubin. Beginning with *American Recordings* in 1994, the pair recorded several albums mixing Cash originals with often surprising covers.

Among the most incongruous of these, seemingly, was Cash's reading of 'Hurt' by the industrial rock group Nine Inch Nails. Nails mainstay Trent Reznor has been something of an unsung hero in modern metal, discovering and nurturing Marilyn Manson, for example, before watching his protégé eclipse him totally. Reznor had struck a gloomy strain of gold with 'Hurt,' which dealt with the keen misery of life through a miasma of drug withdrawal and gothic darkness. Cash sang Reznor's lines in his gruff, beautiful voice and gave the song renewed meaning, ironically introducing Cash to a new generation of listeners just months before his wife died. He followed her four months later. Of course, in this modern age, the song's starkest impact came in the accompanying video clip, which had Cash in a darkened room at home. In one unforgettable shot he sits before a piano with closed lid – a sign, or even an admission, that his life was drawing to a close. The video won several awards as the industry tried to pay Cash due recognition before it was too late.

I Luv U
Dizzee Rascal

Released May 2003
Not issued U.S. / XL Recordings *XLS 165CD* (U.K. #29)

Hot on the heels of The Streets came the prodigiously talented rapper and producer Dizzee Rascal, still only 17 when 'I Luv U' made its way into the British Top 30. Born Dylan Mills in 1985 to Ghanaian immigrants, Dizzee learned to make music on school computers and at 15 started MC-ing at raves and on London pirate-radio stations. 'I Luv U' is typical of the grime style, of which Dizzee Rascal is the chief exponent: the beats are harsh and unvarnished and sound more like malfunctioning underground trains than drums; the lyrics, which detail an accidental teenage pregnancy, are fittingly spat out rather than rapped.

Where Is The Love
Black Eyed Peas

Released June 2003
A&M *000714* (U.S. #8) / A&M *9810996* (U.K. #1)

A guest appearance here by former *NSYNC lead Justin Timberlake helped establish Black Eyed Peas as one of the most popular hip-pop groups of the early 21st century. The Los Angeles based trio of will.i.am, aple.de.ap, and taboo – who all sign their names in kd lang-style lowercase – went on to recruit the sassy, sexy vocalist Fergie as a permanent fourth member of the band, and she seemed to be the key ingredient in the sustained popular success that the group has enjoyed since. Fergie made her debut on the naggingly insistent follow-up 'Shut Up,' a British Number 2 hit.

Bring Me To Life
Evanescence

Released June 2003
Wind-Up *673573* (U.S. #5) / Epic *6739762* (U.K. #1)

Although gothic metal had previously been a strictly niche interest with little or no commercial effect, Evanescence – a kind of slightly darker Linkin Park with the amazing vocals of the 22-year-old Amy Lee – took the recipe straight to the charts with this melodic, anthemic slice of gloom. 'Bring Me To Life' was accompanied by a video in which Lee jumped off a building and sang the song on her way down, scoring with its combination of Lee's soaring larynx and some rapped interludes, plus the requisite big guitars and some wicky-wack scratching. The gates duly opened for a flood of Evanescence-style female-fronted bands such as Lacuna Coil and Nightwish.

Mad World
Michael Andrews Featuring Gary Jules

Released December 2003
Universal *9816488* (U.S.) / Sanctuary *SANXD 250* (U.K. #1)

The movie *Donnie Darko*, a kind of teen *American Beauty* loaded with gothic miserablism and an exciting new face in Jake Gyllenhaal, was briefly the toast of the critics in 2003, spurring this soundtrack song into the charts. Gary Jules and Michael Andrews's piano-and-vocal cover of Tears For Fears' excellent 1981 hit 'Mad World' was bleak, disturbing, and very catchy, although Jules's voice – like Michael Stipe with added vibrato – became somewhat irksome after a few hearings. In due course *Donnie* fever subsided, the song slipped away, and the twosome dematerialized, leaving us all free to enjoy *American Pie 2* and *Terminator 3* instead.

I Believe In A Thing Called Love
The Darkness

Released September 2003
Atlantic *301349* (U.S.) / Must Destroy *DARK 01CD* (U.K. #2)

We still don't know whether England's hair-metal heroes The Darkness are supposed to be a joke or not, but it's an irrelevant point when their songs sound this charismatic. 'I Believe In A Thing Called Love' was delivered with an ironic wink by singer Justin Hawkins in bat-alarming falsetto tones, but avoided misinterpretation as mere comic vaudeville by the strength of the riffs that he and his brother Dan delivered. 'Older' rock fans were delighted by the band's espousal of AOR/chart-metal sounds from the 1980s – think Whitesnake, Foreigner, Boston – while younger listeners were kept amused by Hawkins's catsuit.

Maps
The Yeah Yeah Yeahs

Released September 2003
Interscope *207322* (U.S.) / Dress Up-Polydor *9811413* (U.K. #26)

At first, The Yeah Yeah Yeahs appeared to be heading for success purely by virtue of coming from New York City and peddling a punky, garage-rock-derived sound. With the thoughtful, expansive 'Maps,' however, they proved themselves to be a fine band in their own right. Like The White Stripes the group lacks a bassist, but they more than make up for this with the effects-laden guitar work of Nick Zinner and Brian Chase's sturdy backbeat. The real star of the show is vocalist Karen O, a mutant cross-breed of P.J. Harvey and Chrissie Hynde. Her fearful vocal plea on 'Maps' – "they don't love you like I love you" – was aimed at her then-boyfriend, Angus Andrew of the avant-rock group Liars.

Take Me Out
Franz Ferdinand

Released February 2004
Sony *76774* (U.S.) / Domino *RUG 172CD* (U.K. #3)

Scottish quartet Franz Ferdinand are not at all apologetic for co-opting the styles of Talking Heads and Gang Of Four for their trademark brittle, arty sound. The band were immediately popular on their arrival on the indie scene in 2004 and caused a whole generation to consult the 20th-century history books. 'Take Me Out' was a glorious blast through a simple chord progression heard a trillion times before, but it still worked perfectly – perhaps because it was so jerky and awkward.

The Ferdinands plunged into the song with unrestrained abandon – listen to the laughing tone of the "I say, you don't know…" lines – and deliver a committed performance on stage, while the slightly garage-style production values of the record make it sound as if it should have been delivered in a middle-American college campus in 1981 – or perhaps a club in Manchester, England, in 1990. Listen too for the all-band tempo change in the intro, which lends some hands-in-the-air excitement, and the sudden stop-and-shout moments that come straight from vintage post-punk.

The song was a huge hit in Britain (but only made Number 66 in the U.S.), revitalizing the U.K. art-rock circuit (or what was left of it in our corporate era) and arousing a brief revival of the pencil moustache. With their skinny frames, sensible haircuts, decidedly intellectual tastes, and oh-so-crisp post-mod fashion sense, Franz Ferdinand seemed for a while to be the future of British pop. Indeed they continue to ascend the chart of cool – unlikely progress for a band who started so explosively.

Take Your Mama
Scissor Sisters

Released April 2004
Universal *21236* (U.S.) / Polydor *9866277* (U.K. #17)

Scissor Sisters highlighted a softening attitude during the mid 2000s towards music that drew unashamedly and pretty much entirely on the past. There's nothing particularly innovative about 'Take Your Mama' – it sounds like two parts Elton John, one part Bee Gees, and George Michael stirred-in to taste – but innovation is not what's required. The brash, glam New York quintet – they started out playing at burlesques – realized early in their career that the most important ingredient in the recipe for pop success is a cool, catchy chorus. And 'Take Your Mama,' which could well have fallen off the back of Elton's 1972 opus *Goodbye Yellow Brick Road,* certainly has that component firmly in place.

Scissor Sisters are also in possession of two fine focal points in the form of extravagant co-vocalists Jake Shears and Ana Matronic. 'Take Your Mama' was the biggest of five U.K. hits from the group's eponymous debut, which ended up as Britain's best-selling album of 2004. Scissor Sisters didn't achieve the same level of success in the U.S., although one of several follow-ups to 'Take Your Mama,' 'Filthy / Gorgeous,' topped the Hot Dance Club Play chart.

Irish Blood, English Heart
Morrissey

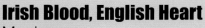

Released May 2004
Attack-Sanctuary *86000* (U.S.) / Attack *ATKXS 002* (U.K. #3)

'Irish Blood, English Heart' began a highly successful comeback for the former Smiths frontman, following almost a decade in the musical wilderness. After the band split in 1987, Morrissey stepped effortlessly into a solo career with the singles 'Suedehead' and 'Every Day Is Like

THE FUTURE OF THE DIGITAL SINGLE

Commentators often speak in long, hyperbolic sentences about revolutions in the music industry, many of which never survive to make the long-term history books. But there can be little doubt of the huge impact that download technology is having on how music is discovered, purchased, and listened to.

Many people think of online downloads as synonymous with MP3, the most prevalent of a number of audio file formats. The term MP3 is derived from the long-winded MPEG-1 Audio Layer 3, the third iteration of an audio-visual file compression format that dates back to the late 1970s. It wasn't until 1994, however, that a series of standardized specifications for MP3 were devised by a group of European audio engineers headed by a German, Karlheinz Brandenberg.

Put simply, MP3 technology allows sound to be stored digitally in a fraction of the space required by CD audio files. (The smaller file sizes do have an effect on the resulting sound quality, but not as noticeably as some of the format's detractors would suggest.) MP3 was important because, firstly, it allowed users to store a greater number of song files on their computers' hard drives, which back then were a fraction of the gargantuan sizes of today. Secondly and even more importantly, the technology made it possible for music to be 'shared' over the internet.

MP3 files – 'MP3s' – first came into use in 1995 but did not begin to enter the public consciousness until the turn of the century. Partly this was because of the controversy surrounding the Napster software program, which allowed its growing army of users to share their newly digitized record collections. Most record companies were very slow to respond to the capabilities of digital audio, but they woke up when fans began freely and illegally to download their product. After much outcry and declarations about the end of the music industry as we know it, Napster and other similar file-sharing systems were forced to close in their then current form.

What the slothful music industry lacked was a way of making their music available for sale over the internet. In 2003, that gap in the market was filled by Apple Computer's iTunes Music Store, which allowed users to buy individual tracks by a growing number of artists for 99¢ each (79p in the U.K.). Other similar download music retailers followed, but Apple continues to dominate both the market for this and for portable digital audio players, with its acclaimed iPod (a Walkman-sized personal jukebox, capable of holding thousands of songs).

So what effect has this had on the single? Certainly not as much as it has on the album, which remains in a state of flux as web-savvy consumers opt to download one or two favorite tracks rather than forking out for a full set of 13-or-so songs and finding many of them to be mediocre. Since singles by their very nature are almost always focused on one song alone, how you listen to it (or purchase it), whether on your gramophone or your iPod, is not a matter of huge consequence. Naturally, B-sides are now of less importance, both to consumers and record labels – but they have been for many years, at least since there became no need to turn over a slab of vinyl to hear them.

Since 2003, singles charts in the U.S. and the U.K. have been modified to reflect the growing number of download sales. The effect of this is harder to judge in the U.S. since chart placings on the *Billboard* Hot 100 are generally more a reflection of airplay than record sales. *Billboard* added a Hot Digital Tracks listing to its vast roster of charts in 2003 but did not begin to incorporate download sales into its main charts until February 2005. The first digital download single to sell over a million copies in the U.S. was Gwen Stefani's 'Hollaback Girl' (2004). At the time of writing, the biggest-selling download has been 2005's 'Since U Been Gone' by 2002 *American Idol* winner Kelly Clarkson.

In the U.K., a specific download chart was introduced in September 2004. Those who expected this to become a platform for less commercial music were somewhat disappointed to find that the first act to top this particular chart was the bland Irish boy-band Westlife, with an unremarkable live rendition of 'Flying Without Wings.'

Until recently, chart regulations in Britain were more stringent than in the U.S., requiring a physical product to be on sale before a record is allowed entry into the main Top 40. The rules were finally relaxed in 2006, just in time for hip-hop duo Gnarls Barkley to fly in at Number 1 with what became the year's biggest hit in Britain, 'Crazy.'

Sunday' and the accompanying album *Viva Hate* (all 1988). The 1990s were less kind to him, however: his recorded output was spotty, he was labeled a racist by the media after several vague – and perhaps misunderstood – statements and an onstage appearance draped in the Union Jack flag, and he was sued, successfully, by former bandmate Mike Joyce over a royalty dispute. By the end of the decade he had lost his recording contract with Island Records and relocated to Los Angeles, where he led a solitary, almost reclusive existence.

Morrissey started his road back to success in 2003 with a world tour – which he embarked upon, unusually, without a record to promote – and a new deal with Sanctuary (or, more precisely, the label's former reggae imprint, Attack, which the singer now controls). To the surprise of many, he then started work with Jerry Finn, the producer best known for his work with pop-punk act Blink-182. Finn, however, lends 'Irish Blood, English Heart' a powerful, polished sheen: the perfect backdrop for a typically defiant lyric, in which the poet-laureate of pop declares: "There is no one on earth I'm afraid of / And no regime can buy or sell me."

Vertigo
U2

Released November 2004
Island *9868183* (U.S. #31) / Island *CIDX 878* (U.K. #1)

The Irish rock behemoth's finest single for a decade, 'Vertigo' returned some much-needed raw power to U2's sound after too long a deviation with dance beats and group-up balladry. Arriving with the odd cry of "uno, dos, tres, catorce!" ("one, two, three, fourteen!"), this is an uptempo rocker power-driven by sheet-metal guitars and fuzzy bass. Bono turns in a fine vocal, complete with one or two more apparently off-the-cuff lines of Spanglish thrown in for good measure, and there is a typically strident performance from unsung hero Larry Mullen Jr. on drums. 'Vertigo' won three awards at the 2005 Grammys, and was notable as part of a widespread cross-promotional ad campaign with Apple's iTunes Music Store, which sold a download of the single before it was available anywhere else.

Yeah!
Usher Featuring Lil' Jon & Ludacris

Released January 2004
Arista *59149* (U.S. #1) / Arista *6606002* (U.K. #1)

This high-energy R&B-rap song blared out of radios, dominated dance floors, and enjoyed heavy video rotation on MTV, VH1, and BET (a rare feat). Singer Usher was well used to accolades, but this record gave him his longest-running American chart-topper. He also acquired some needed street credibility from the collaboration with producer and pop culture star Lil Jon and rapper-actor Ludacris. All three made their careers in the urban music mecca of Atlanta, and this song pays tribute to that city through lyrical references to other songs amid calls to perform some lively dance steps invented in Atlanta.

'Yeah!' was just one of four huge U.S. Number 1 hits for Usher in 2004. It spent 12 weeks atop the *Billboard* Hot 100 during the spring; the only record able to take away the top spot was his own follow-up, 'Burn,' which clung on for a further seven weeks. With the release of his third chart-topper of the year, 'Confessions Part II,' Usher became the first solo artist to have three singles in the *Billboard* Top 10 at once. The similarly successful 'My Boo,' a duet with Alicia Keys, followed, meaning that in 2004 Usher spent a record-breaking total of 28 weeks at Number 1.

Toxic
Britney Spears

Released February 2004
Jive *59214* (U.S. #9) / Jive *6602092* (U.K. #1)

This was a year of scandal and regular tabloid appearances for Britney Spears. The young pop tartlet married twice, first in January to a childhood pal in a 55-hour Las Vegas gag, and later in the year to backup dancer Kevin Federline, whom she had dated for about three months. 'Toxic' fell right between the nuptials.

Britney owed much of her earlier success to songs penned and produced by a Swede, Max Martin, and now she again looked to Sweden for hits. Bloodshy and Avant (Christian Karlsson and Pontus Winnberg) had

enjoyed European success with American pop singer Christina Milian and hit the spot again with this track, which has club-inspired breakbeats, and violin lines reminiscent of James Bond films. British songwriter Cathy Dennis, who co-wrote Kylie Minogue's 'Can't Get You Out Of My Head,' signed on to pen the catchy lyrics.

Fans who reckoned she would never top her racy video for 'I'm A Slave 4 U' had to think again: this one has her donning many disguises as a female assassin, and plays on her supposed promiscuity by placing the singer in multiple situations with different men. 'Toxic' has proved to be Spears's greatest musical triumph, netting her a Grammy for Best Dance Recording.

This Love
Maroon5

Released March 2004
J Records *63388* (U.S. #5) / J Records *6608452* (U.K. #3)

Los Angeles-based band Maroon5 took home the coveted Grammy Award for Best New Artist in 2005, owing largely to this remarkably infectious pop single from an album released almost three years earlier. 'This Love' is a simple yet clever power-guitar tune with near universal appeal, and it proved inescapable throughout 2004 on American radio and on MTV. The band has, to its possible regret, become noted for its extracurricular activities: singer Adam Levine has the rugged good looks and the fickle attitude of a famous Hollywood bachelor, and has since been a fixture in tabloid magazines, linked to young celebrities such as Jessica Simpson and Lindsay Lohan.

Drop It Like It's Hot
Snoop Dogg

Released September 2004
Geffen *357411* (U.S. #1) / Geffen *2103461* (U.K. #10)

Rapper-actor Snoop Dogg is about as American as apple pie. He's been an iconic figure of popular culture since his recorded debut early in the 1990s, but the top spot on the American pop charts eluded him until the release of the sizzling, snappy, and Snoopendous 'Drop It Like It's Hot' in 2004, made with the help of the hit-making producer Pharrell Williams (of Neptunes/N.E.R.D. fame). The song received numerous awards in America (including two Grammy nominations) while in Britain it took home the 2005 MOBO for Best Video thanks to its clever black-and-white treatment.

You Had Me
Joss Stone

Released November 2004
EMI *867482* (U.S.) / Relentless-Virgin *RELDX 13* (U.K. #9)

Dusty Springfield aside, Britain has produced few female soul vocalists of particular note, and even fewer with the talent and popular appeal to achieve longstanding international success. A rare potential exception to that rule arrived in 2003, from rural Devon, England, at just 16 years old. Joss Stone had traveled a year earlier to New York City where she caught the eye – and ears – of S-Curve Records founder Steve Greenberg. During the spring of 2003 he took charge of Stone's debut album, *The Soul Sessions*, alongside singer-producer Betty Wright. That album spawned a minor U.K. hit early the following year with a re-reading of a White Stripes song, 'Fell In Love With A Boy,' which showed off the remarkably mature voice that Stone had developed while listening to soul legends such as Aretha Franklin. An even better single followed later in the year. 'You Had Me,' the first track drawn from her second album, *Mind, Body & Soul*, is a strident, mid-tempo funk number reminiscent of 1970s Stevie Wonder that contains the kind of chorus that buries itself deep in the listener's head after even a single listen. Stone's first U.K. Top 10 hit, it did not chart in the U.S. but was nonetheless instrumental in helping Mind, Body & Soul climb to Number 11 on the Billboard albums chart there, making the singer's future look decidedly rosy.

Goodies
Ciara

Released May 2004
LaFace *57550* (U.S. #1) / BMG *6665881* (U.K. #1)

The teenage R&B singer and dancer Ciara Harris was discovered in Atlanta by Jazze Pha (Phalon Alexander), a DJ and producer whose father, James Alexander, had been a founding member of soul greats The Bar-Kays. Jazze Pha produced most of Ciara's debut album *Goodies*, but the title track was crafted by Lil Jon (Jonathan Smith). Lil Jon was another producer known for a local style of hyped-up dancefloor records termed 'crunk' after an energetic Atlanta youth culture that had been bubbling for some time. The song features a guest performance from platinum-selling North Carolina rapper Petey Pablo, who tried valiantly to contain his passion for the sexy Ciara in his verse, mainly because she wasn't quite 18 when they recorded it.

The combination of Ciara's R&B vocals and Lil Jon's crunk beats were initially described as 'crunk & B,' but use of the term faded after Ciara's subsequent singles showed her ability to move beyond that sound. Video director Benny Boom gave the public their visual introduction to Ciara. He set 'Goodies' in an Atlanta car wash for a dance performance showcasing her formidable moves, including a back bend reminiscent of the slow motion action dodging executed by Keanu Reeves in *The Matrix*. 'Goodies' brought Ciara to the top of the American charts for seven weeks, a goal she had envisioned while still in high school. She might not necessarily have predicted that she'd repeat the feat in the U.K. and Canada as well, but this proved a harbinger of international sucess.

What You Waiting For
Gwen Stefani

Released September 2004
Interscope *00350711* (U.S.) / Interscope *9864986* (U.K. #4)

"Take a chance, you stupid ho'," shouts Gwen Stefani on her first single, 'What You Waiting For.' Strangely, she's chastising herself – for a lack of confidence that's manifesting itself as writers' block. It must've been frightening for the lead singer of the award-winning Southern California-reared No Doubt to go solo at the height of her band's success; that inner turmoil is reflected in the frenetic tick-tock pace of the song. The video introduces her memorable Harajuku Girls, brightly dressed and sassy Japanese dancers whom she would use on subsequent singles and the tour for her *Love Angel Music Baby* album.

Unwritten
Natasha Bedingfield

Released December 2004
BMG download only (U.S. #1) / Phonogenic-BMG *6663522* (U.K. #6)

Prior to achieving success of her own, Natasha Bedingfield looked on as her older brother, Daniel, scored a run of international hits in the early 2000s, notably the U.K. Number 1 'Gotta Get Thru This.' She studied psychology – in part, apparently, because "I knew it'd make me a better songwriter" – before making *Unwritten*, an album of breezy up-tempo pop-dance songs. It spawned three British hits in 2004, including the chart-topping 'These Words,' which put Natasha and Daniel in the *Guinness Book Of Records* as the only brother and sister to both achieve solo Number 1s in the U.K.

It took over a year, though, for 'Unwritten' to receive any significant attention in America. As with several other slow-burning hits of recent times, it was given a boost when performed by a contestant on *American Idol*. It was also used as the theme to the MTV reality show *The Hills*. By the spring of 2006, the single had been certified five times platinum in the U.S. as one of only a handful of records so far to sell over a million copies as a download-only single. Even more impressively, Bedingfield was the first British woman to top the Hot 100 since *Billboard* magazine began compiling its various musical hit parades in 1940.

Jailhouse Rock
Elvis Presley

Released January 2005
Not issued U.S. / RCA *6667152* (U.K. #1)

In The Kitchen / Trapped In The Closet
R. Kelly

Released April 2005
Jive *69126* (U.S.) / Not issued U.K.

In 2005, RCA hit upon an inventive way of celebrating 50 years of Elvis hits in Britain. Over the course of 18 weeks, the label reissued each of the king's Number 1 singles, one per week, in chronological order. The first of these was 'All Shook Up,' but it was ineligible for the chart because it was packaged within a collectors-edition box big enough to house all 18 singles. (Had it been allowed to chart, it would have hit Number 2.) The following week's 'Jailhouse Rock' then provided the first U.K. chart-topper of 2005; it was followed a week later by a reissue of the double A-side 'One Night' / 'I Got Stung,' which now has the distinction of being the 1,000th record to top the British singles chart.

Not all of the subsequent 15 Elvis singles released made it to the pole position, but each of them made it into the Top 5, demonstrating – as if there were any need – that Elvis remains among the most enduringly popular performers in the history of music. RCA's clever reissue strategy was asking to be copied, and it was perhaps inevitable that the first artist to attempt to match Elvis's feat came from the king of pop, Michael Jackson, during the spring and early summer of 2006.

Jackson did not fare nearly as well, however: none of his repackaged hits made it into the Top 10 (and most lingered around the Number 15 spot before dropping off the chart after a week). Perhaps this was partly bad timing: RCA had commenced the Elvis singles series in January, traditionally the easiest time to score a British Number 1 hit, given the lack of major releases in the post-Christmas lull. Also, Jackson's sequence of past hits made the stores less than a year after his trial on several counts of child molestation and abduction. Although he was acquitted on all counts, the case did little for his reputation.

Meanwhile, on the other side of the Atlantic, R. Kelly – a man who could at times rival Michael Jackson both for unsavory media stories and sheer madness – issued the first in a different kind of multi-part series. The B-side to his rather mundane single 'In The Kitchen' offered up the first 'Chapter' of 'Trapped In The Closet,' a series of 12 narrative songs all set to the same musical backing. None of the 'Closet' series made a serious indentation on the *Billboard* charts, but they became a fixture on urban radio as fans waited to hear the next installment of Kelly's soap-opera-style relationship drama.

Kelly's summer 2005 *TP.3 Reloaded* album collected the first five parts of the series and offered up a promo video for each of them, in which he and some friends act out the story. Both the audio and video Closets are frequently hilarious, but it's not always clear if this is intentional, such is the apparent determination in both his wordplay and acting. At the end of the year the prolific singer released a DVD of all 12 chapters, complete with bonus material and an enlightening director's commentary.

Ghetto Gospel
2Pac Featuring Elton John

Released June 2005
Not issued U.S. / Interscope *9882168* (U.K. #1)

Nasty Girl
The Notorious B.I.G. Featuring Diddy, Nelly, Avery Storm, & Jagged Edge

Released December 2005
Bad Boy *94143* (U.S.) / Bad Boy *ATO229CDX* (U.K. #1)

Dozens of musicians can say that they worked with the late Tupac Shakur (a.k.a. 2Pac), either on collaborations when he was alive or songs constructed after his violent death in 1996 at age 25. But there was surely no collaboration more unusual than the unlikely ballad 'Ghetto Gospel,' constructed using a sample from Elton John's 1971 composition 'Indian Sunset' for the documentary *2Pac: Resurrection*. Like Elvis Presley, 2Pac has had a thriving career in the afterlife, with millions of posthumous record sales. Unlike Elvis, however, 2Pac had a sense of impending doom and worked tirelessly to amass a catalog of material that could see the light after his demise.

On the day that 2Pac was shot and killed, his great rival The Notorious B.I.G. denied any involvement, stating that he had been busy in the studio, working on a song called 'Nasty Girl.' A few months later, B.I.G. was murdered too. 'Nasty Girl' remained unfinished for almost a decade. It was eventually completed in 2005 for inclusion on the posthumous collection *Duets: The Final Chapter*, and on the finished version B.I.G. vies for time on the mic with Diddy (a.k.a. Puff Daddy, his former friend and label boss), Nelly, the hotly tipped Avery Storm, and the R&B vocal group Jagged Edge. (The accompanying all-star promo video also features Usher, Pharrell Williams, and the supermodel Naomi Campbell.) Ironically, neither 2Pac nor Notorious B.I.G. had topped the British singles chart during their lifetimes, but both managed to achieve the feat posthumously with these singles, less than a year apart.

Candy Shop
50 Cent Featuring Olivia

Released July 2005
Universal *9880609* (U.S. #1) / Interscope *9881293* (U.K. #2)

Superstar rapper 50 Cent's trip to the 'Candy Shop' earned him his third U.S. Number 1 and added to the growing list of controversies in his fast-moving career. He'd been incarcerated for drug-related offenses, he'd been shot at, and he'd engaged in countless feuds with other hip-hop performers. Now he was criticized for the thinly veiled sexual connotations of this hit that paraphrased commercials for M&Ms, the candy that "melts in your mouth, not in your hand." Widespread parental disapproval did little to halt the success of 'Candy Shop,' which, like his 2003 breakthrough hit 'In Da Club,' spent nine weeks at the top of the *Billboard* Hot 100. (In between, he'd spent five weeks at Number 1 with '21 Questions,' a collaboration with Nate Dogg.)

Perhaps more surprising than any of his gritty, foul-mouthed songs was 50 Cent's political stance. He backed George W. Bush in the 2004 U.S. election and defended the president's widely criticized response to the

well and truly over. Then, seemingly out of nowhere, came her smash comeback album *The Emancipation Of Mimi* and 'We Belong Together,' which provided Carey with the 16th Number 1 hit of her career. The record spent nearly a quarter of 2005 in that top pop spot. Crafted by Atlanta-based music mogul and longtime friend Jermaine Dupri (along with his secret weapon, young songwriter Johnta Austin), it has a savvy hip-hop feel in the way that Carey makes her lyrics flow, but it is still a sweet love song. It's a combination that proved irresistible and opened up a world of possibilities for a talented artist still finding her considerable voice.

Gold Digger
Kanye West

Released August 2005
Roc-A-Fella *000511811* (U.S. #1) / Universal International *5885699* (U.K. #2)

Kanye West was at first known as the highly skilled producer behind artists such as Jay-Z but has since stepped out from behind the mixing board to establish himself as one of the finest and most successful hip-hop performers of the early 21st century. One of several excellent singles to be drawn from his acclaimed second album *Late Registration*, 'Gold Digger' spent ten weeks at Number 1 in America. It also stands at the time of writing as the fastest-selling download ever.

Somewhat strangely, 'Gold Digger' features both a repeated vocal sample from Ray Charles's 'I've Got A Woman' and, in its intro, an imitation of the jazz-soul legend's voice by the actor-singer Jamie Foxx. (Foxx had recently won the Academy Award for Best Actor for his portrayal of Charles in the biopic *Ray*.) The rest of the song is dominated by a sparse, irresistibly funky backing track and West's somewhat tongue-in-cheek lyrics about gold-diggin' women who "ain't messin' with no broke niggas." It is often remarked that West's skills as a rapper fall far short of his abilities as a producer, but it's difficult to fault his vocal performance on 'Gold Digger,' which ended up as big a crossover smash as OutKast's 'Hey Ya' had been two years previously.

West followed up with two more sterling singles – 'Heard 'Em Say' and 'Touch The Sky' – that showed off the gifts of *Late Registration*'s unexpected co-producer, Jon Brion, previously best known for his work with Fiona Apple and on the soundtracks to such movies as *Magnolia* and *Eternal Sunshine Of The Spotless Mind*.

destruction caused by 2005's Hurricane Catrina. While Kanye West, his rival at the top of the rap game, declared on live television that George Bush "doesn't care about black people," 50 Cent proclaimed him to be "incredible … a gangsta. I wanna meet George Bush, just shake his hand and tell him how much of me I see in him." The president would surely agree.

We Belong Together
Mariah Carey

Released July 2005
Def Jam-Island *000516211* (U.S. #1) / Def Jam-Island *9883483* (U.K. #2)

During the 1990s it became customary for Mariah Carey to spend weeks at the top of the *Billboard* Hot 100. At the start of the new decade, however, her career looked all but over. The singer started 2001 well, signing a deal with Virgin Records worth a reported $80 million. But by the end of that year her semi-autobiographical movie and album project,

Glitter, was a huge critical and commercial failure, and the singer was reported to have suffered a physical and emotional breakdown. This followed several promotional appearances that could only be described as unusual. In one instance she turned up on MTV's *Total Request Live* handing out popsicles before performing something akin to a striptease; in others she just rambled on about nothing in particular.

In 2002 Carey suffered the indignity of being bought out of her contract by Virgin. She subsequently signed to Def Jam, but it seemed that her days of dominating the singles chart were

Speed Of Sound
Coldplay

Released May 2005
EMI *8729862* (U.S. #8) / Parlophone *CDR 6664* (U.K. #2)

Axel F
Crazy Frog

Released May 2005
Gusto *21495* (U.S.) / Gusto *CDGUS 17* (U.K. #1)

In May 2005 an unusual battle raged for the top spot on the U.K. singles chart. In the left corner, representing good, honest – if a little dull – rock music, was the London-based quartet Coldplay; in the right corner, a spin-off from one of the most irritating TV ad campaigns in history, and the most potent example of the power of the ringtone. It had become apparent shortly into the new millennium that consumers didn't just want their music available on CD and as a download, but wanted to consume music through their cell phone, translated into a polyphonic series of bleeps or as a 'realtone,' in which actual music blared from your mobile.

Coldplay had by this stage become one of the biggest bands in the world. Their importance was such that shares in their parent label, EMI, dropped significantly when it was announced that the forthcoming album *X&Y* – from which 'Speed Of Sound' was taken – would be delayed.

Driven by stately guitar and piano amid big, roomy drums, the single is one of the group's finer efforts, but not exactly the kind of grandstanding musical rebirth hinted at before its release. It does have the notable distinction of being the first single for 37 years by a British group to go straight into the U.S. Top 10. The last one to achieve such a feat was The Beatles' 'Hey Jude.'

As successful as it was in America, in the U.K. 'Speed Of Sound' couldn't match the commercial clout of 'Axel F,' which was issued on the same day and sold four times as many copies in its first week as Coldplay's single (mostly to kids who didn't know any better). Almost certainly the most diabolical release to top the British chart – to call it a song is stretching the point – 'Axel F' had a strange and convoluted genesis. The main musical element is a souped-up version of the theme to the 1984 Eddie Murphy movie *Beverly Hills Cop*. Layered over the top are a series of migraine-inducing vocal parts, chief among them a feat of strained vocal gymnastics originally performed in 1997 by a Swedish teen, Daniel Malmedahl.

Despite its dubious musical merit, 'Axel F' and the accompanying Crazy Frog video had become ubiquitous in the U.K., largely because of the blanket advertising bought up on its behalf by the new media company Jamba! According to *The Guardian* newspaper, Crazy Frog-related ads were shown over 2,000 times a day on British television in May 2005. Their main aim was to sell Crazy Frog ringtones. The success of the single was secondary; it was recorded on Jamster!'s behalf by the German duo Bass Bumpers, who wisely chose to release it under a pseudonym. The ringtone itself remains, to date, the most lucrative of all time; it has earned Jamster! over £14 million in Britain alone (about $26 million) and untold additional riches across the U.S. and Europe.

Jamster! found itself censured soon after 'Axel F' topped the charts (it made only Number 50 in America). The U.K. Advertising Standards Authority upheld countless complaints that it wasn't entirely clear that the ringtone sale led to a subscription service and not simply a one-off payment. Also, the animated Crazy Frog's genitalia was visible. The result was that the vile creature was banned from the airwaves until after 9:00pm.

You're Beautiful
James Blunt

Released June 2005
Custard download only (U.S. #1) / Atlantic *AT 0207CD* (U.K. #1)

A lovelorn ballad about glimpsing an ex-girlfriend on the subway, 'You're Beautiful' unexpectedly became one of the biggest hits across Europe during the summer of 2005. Early the following year it rose to the top of the *Billboard* Hot 100, making Blunt the first British artist to have an American Number 1 since Elton John topped the charts with 'Candle In The Wind' in 1997. Given the fey, lightweight feel of this breakthrough hit for Blunt, it came as a surprise to some to discover that he had served in the British Army prior to embarking on a musical career. Although repeated exposure to 'You're Beautiful' seemed to invoke feelings of despair and irritation in many listeners, the single remained a radio staple on both sides of the Atlantic for the best part of a year. The great Weird Al Yankovic was sufficiently moved by Blunt's song to record his own special kind of tribute: 'You're Pitiful.'

Bad Day
Daniel Powter

Released July 2005
Warner Bros. download only (U.S. #1) / WEA *W 682CD* (U.K. #2)

Like James Blunt's similarly themed 'You're Beautiful,' 'Bad Day' was a British hit in the summer of 2005 but took a further year to top the U.S. chart. Its slow climb to Number 1 harked back to an earlier age, when records would slowly pick up momentum as they spread into different radio markets. It has become more common today for singles to perform well for a few weeks but then quickly slide down the charts. Surprisingly, Powter's breakthrough hit stalled at Number 3 in his native Canada, where it was a hit in early 2005. It then found widespread success across Europe, but was largely ignored in the U.S. until it was chosen as the song to be played whenever a contestant was voted off the 2006 season of *American Idol*. It was also heard often during the 2006 NBA playoffs following the elimination of several teams on their home courts. Despite these intrinsic links with failure, 'Bad Day' provided Powter with one of the biggest-selling downloads of all time in the U.S., where over a million internet-savvy music fans have paid for the privilege of saving the song onto their hard drives.

I Bet You Look Good On The Dance Floor
Arctic Monkeys

Released October 2005
Domino *3533392* (U.S.) / Domino *RUG 212* (U.K. #1)

'I Bet You Look Good On The Dance Floor' was one of the biggest British grassroots successes of recent times. Before even releasing a record, the band had built up a wide fanbase through word-of-virtual-mouth on the internet and on the strength of live performances in the north of England. The teenage quartet's first widespread release, 'Dance Floor' entered the U.K. singles chart at Number 1 and made Arctic Monkeys the most talked about British band in years.

It's a measure of the group's innocence that, just a couple of years earlier, school friends Alex Turner and Jamie Cook had asked for guitars for Christmas, and then started learning their trade by picking out the chords to songs by The White Stripes and The Vines with the help of bassist Andy Nicholson and drummer Matt Helders. In the blink of an eye, the four lads from Sheffield were well on the way to joining their idols in the big league, thanks largely to the promise shown in a set of demos the band made available for free on the internet.

'Dance Floor' is pitched midway between the early-21st-century vogue for scratchy new wave and the confident swagger of 1990s favorites Oasis. The record is dominated by jagged guitar chords and Turner's stream-of-consciousness-style vocal about "dancing to electro-pop like a robot from 1984" along with typically teenage feelings of romantic insecurity. It was followed to the top of the British chart by 'When The Sun Goes Down' in January 2006. A week later, Arctic Monkeys' first full-length became the fastest-selling debut album of all time in the U.K. It reached Number 24 in America, where the group is beginning to make a considerable mark.

King Of The Mountain
Kate Bush

Released November 2005
EMI *45087* (U.S.) / EMI *EM 674* (U.K. #4)

After all but disappearing for more than a decade, Kate Bush returned with this elegiac homage to Elvis Presley, the most successful solo artist in chart history. Bush's last single release had been 'And So Is Love,' from her underwhelming seventh album *The Red Shoes* (1993), which amounted to her only 1990s output. In the intervening years, her stock continued to rise. She was regularly named among the most innovative and influential women in pop and name-checked by other artists, from John Lydon to OutKast. Earlier in 2005, the British new-wave group The Futureheads hit the U.K. Top 10 with a well-received cover of Bush's 'Hounds Of Love,' the title track from her much-loved 1985 opus.

One of the year's most hotly anticipated releases, 'King Of The Mountain' is built around mournful synths, reggae bass, and lightly flicked guitar chords. It develops slowly over its four-and-a-half minutes, never quite reaching the expected climax. The lyrics reference *Citizen Kane* as well as Elvis, to whom Bush remarks that "another Hollywood waitress / Is telling us she's having your baby." A taster for the double-disc set *Aerial*, the single was issued on CD, as a digital download, and – harking back to an earlier time – a seven-inch picture disc, with artwork by Bush's son, Bertie.

So Sick
Ne-Yo

Released January 2006
Def Jam *000619011* (U.S. #1) / Def Jam *9854185* (U.K. #1)

Ne-Yo was still in his early 20s when 'So Sick' became a transatlantic chart-topper, but he had already carved out a career as a notable R&B songwriter, generating hits for artists such as Mary J. Blige, Jamie Foxx, and Rihanna. Born Shaffer Chimere Smith of African-American, Puerto Rican, and Chinese descent, he was given the nickname Ne-Yo by a friend who compared his ability to 'see' music to the visionary skills of

Keanu Reeves's character Neo in the *Matrix* movie trilogy. It was therefore surprising when he called upon the Norwegian production team Stargate to craft 'So Sick,' restricting his own contribution to the lyrics, which declare him to be "so sick of your love songs / So sad and slow / But I just can't turn off the radio." Perhaps in response to this, Ne-Yo unleashed countless remixes of 'So Sick' to radio stations across the U.S., featuring duets with the likes of LL Cool J and 2Pac (the latter surely one of the most prolific dead men ever).

Beep
Pussycat Dolls Featuring will.i.am

Released February 2006
Universal *9852859* (U.S. #13) / Universal *9852861* (U.K. #2)

For the last two decades, the flow of countless hip-hop records has been interrupted by the beeping-out or muting of profanity. Often, this ends up making the radio edit of a single sound like a cell phone call from Outer Mongolia in which every other word is just about intelligible. 'Beep' takes a rather more amusing, self-referential tack, building the interruptions into the framework of the song.

Each line of the vocal ends with a beep – "you got a real big heart, but I'm lookin' at your [beep]," for instance – leaving it to the listener to

decide which choice expletive should fill in the gap. The combination of this smutty gimmickry, a guest appearance by Black Eyed Peas vocalist will.i.am, and an infectious, stop-start backing track ensured that 'Beep' was an international hit. (Perhaps surprisingly, the single was most successful in New Zealand, where it spent eight weeks at Number 1.)

'Beep' was the third U.S. hit for Pussycat Dolls, who started life in the mid 1990s as a burlesque dance troupe. With an ever-changing line-up, they performed a Thursday night residency at The Viper Room in Los Angeles from 1995 to 2001 before the group's creator, choreographer Robin Antin, decided to try his hand at pop music. Prior to focusing on music, the Dolls were regularly

joined onstage at the Viper by high-profile female celebrities, from Britney Spears to Paris Hilton, all keen to unleash their wild side and become a pussycat for the night.

S.O.S.
Rihanna

Released February 2006
Def Jam *00631511* (U.S. #1) / Universal *9877821* (U.K. #2)

The latest in a line of teen-pop superstarlets, Rihanna was one of the biggest hits on the American and British singles charts in the first half of 2006. The Barbadian singer earned a deal with Def Jam at just 16 years old after auditioning for the label's CEO, the sometime rapper Jay-Z, who snapped her up on the spot. She hit Number 2 in the U.S. and the U.K. in 2005 with her debut single, 'Pon De Replay,' which merged R&B-pop with elements of Jamaican dancehall and West Indian calypso rhythms.

Its success was soon eclipsed by 'S.O.S.,' which is derived from a sample of Soft Cell's 1981 electro-pop classic 'Tainted Love,' itself a cover of a 1960s song by northern-soul singer Gloria Jones. The enduring chart success of 'S.O.S.' was such that, a few months later,

Rihanna achieved the rare feat of having two songs in the *Billboard* Top 10 at once, when the smooth ballad 'Unfaithful' was released in June.

Crazy
Gnarls Barkley

Released March 2006
Downtown *70002* (U.S. #2) / WEA *401CD* (U.K. #1)

'Crazy' became one of the most talked-about records of 2006 because it was the first song to top the British singles chart on the strength of downloads alone. It was also one of the most memorable hits of recent times, with Danger Mouse's widescreen-technicolor production style providing the perfect foil for singer-rapper-songwriter Cee-Lo Green's infectious, gospel-inspired vocal melody.

The success of 'Crazy' was a career high for both parties. Green had found sporadic success since the mid 1990s as a member of the hip-hop group Goodie Mob, as a solo artist, and as a writer and producer of hits for other artists, including Busta Rhymes and Pussycat Dolls.

Danger Mouse, meanwhile, first drew attention for the illicit *Grey Album*, which mixed a cappella versions of Jay-Z's *Black Album* with instrumental tracks from *The Beatles* (a.k.a. *The White Album*). He then co-produced the acclaimed *Demon Days* by Gorillaz, which spawned the British hits 'Feel Good Inc.,' 'Dare,' and 'Dirty Harry.'

'Crazy' took advantage of a slackening in U.K. chart regulations that, for the first time allowed singles to enter the Top 40 without being available in a physical format. It subsequently spent nine weeks at Number 1 – making it the longest-reigning British chart-topper since Wet Wet Wet's 'Love Is All Around' hung on to pole position for 15 weeks in 1994.

Smile
Lily Allen

Released July 2006
Capitol *digital download* (U.S.) / EMI/Regal *REG135* (U.K. #1)

Rehab
Amy Winehouse

Released November 2006
Universal *digital download* (U.S.) / Island/Universal *953* (U.K. #7)

In 2006, a pair of London-born twentysomethings became the U.K.'s new queens of pop, and looked set the following year to buck the trend and match that success in the U.S.

Lily Allen is a very modern phenomenon, her fame initially deriving, almost entirely, from the popularity of her Myspace.com profile. Within a few months of her joining the website, the songs she posted there – notably 'LDN,' a joyous paean to her home city – made her a star in the virtual world even before she'd signed a record contract. After inking a quick deal with EMI, by way of the indie subsidiary Regal, Allen topped the British chart with her first single proper, the sunny, ska-tinged 'Smile.' An album, *Alright, Still*, quickly followed, drawing rave reviews and spawning an equally good follow-up, 'Littlest Things.'

Where Allen's look and vocal style are as light and breezy as her songs, Amy Winehouse – despite being similarly small of frame – has the voice and manner of a hardened soul singer. 'Rehab' was the first single to be taken from her second album, *Back To Black*, a winning modernization of

the girl-group sound of the 1950s and 1960s recorded in collaboration with producer-du-jour Mark Ronson. (British born but based in New York City, Ronson was also responsible for Allen's 'Littlest Things,' and in 2007 made a covers album, *Version*, that features guest vocals by both Allen and Winehouse.) Like 'Smile,' 'Rehab' is a three-minute burst of pop at its finest. Over hip-hop-style bass and drums and Motown-inspired brass, strings, and bells, Winehouse sings unapologetically, not to mention autobiographically, about her refusal to enter a drying-out clinic in 2005 at the behest of her record label.

While neither 'Smile' nor 'Rehab' was a significant American hit, both singles' parent albums subsequently performed strongly on the *Billboard* chart. *Back To Black* entered the *Billboard* albums chart at Number 7 in March 2007 – a record for a British female artist.

Promiscuous
Nelly Furtado Featuring Timbaland

Released June 2006
Geffen *000756611* (U.S. #1) / Geffen *1706030* (U.K. #3)

My Love
Justin Timberlake Featuring T.I.

Released November 2006
Jive *702049* (U.S. #1) / RCA *88697020502* (U.K. #1)

In the summer and fall of 2006, Nelly Furtado and Justin Timberlake both returned to the top of the pop ladder after a break of several years with their strongest and most commercially successful material to date. Both had a pair of international mega-hit singles, all four of which were the work of one man: the hip-hop super-producer Timbaland best known, prior to this, for his work with Missy Elliott and Aaliyah.

First out of the blocks was the Canadian singer-songwriter Furtado, who had first risen to international prominence in 2000 with the bright, breezy 'I'm Like A Bird.' Under Timbaland's stewardship, her songs and image became harder, meatier, and sexier. Many of the songs on Furtado's 2006 album *Loose* bear the influence of 1980s-style pop, notably 'Promiscuous' and 'Maneater,' which topped the British singles chart. Furtado's first and (to date) only U.S. Number 1, 'Promiscuous' was also named Best Pop Song at the 2006 *Billboard Music Awards*.

Arriving a full four years after his solo debut, *Justified*, Timberlake's *FutureSex/LoveSounds* was by far and away the most eagerly anticipated release of 2006. It didn't disappoint, particularly in terms of its singles. First came the aggressive, robotic, and downright fantastic 'SexyBack,' which was notable, given Timberlake's past life as a boy-band pin-up, for its profanity-laced lyrics. Even better, however, was the slow-burning 'My Love,' a duet with the rapper T.I., which somehow manages to sound both irresistibly seductive and like something from another planet at the same time.

Grace Kelly
Mika

Released January 2007
Island/Universal *1721083* (U.S. / U.K. #1)

If ever there was such a thing as a dead cert in popular music, it was Mika. This doe-eyed, androgynous singer-songwriter of decidedly cosmopolitan heritage and upbringing is for all intents and purposes a 21st century Freddie Mercury (with a hint of Elton John and the Scissor Sisters thrown in for good measure). Prior to launching what looks like it could well be a lengthy international pop career, Mika (born Michael Holbrook Penniman in Beirut in 1983 to Lebanese and American parents) studied at the Royal College Of Music in London, performed in the same city's Royal Opera House, and wrote jingles for British Airways and the Orbit brand of chewing gum.

After signing to Universal Music Mika was given time to hone his songs in London and Los Angeles before releasing the low-key single 'Relax, Take It Easy' in the fall of 2006. Then, amid considerable expectation and relentless marketing, came 'Grace Kelly,' a nonchalant 1970s-style piano ballad aimed in mocking satire, apparently, at musicians who change their sound in pursuit of commercial success. The single hit Number 1 in the U.K. on the strength of downloads alone and broke into the upper reaches of charts across Europe, selling close to two million copies in the process. American success is sure to follow.

This Ain't A Scene, It's An Arms Race
Fall Out Boy

Released January 2007
Universal *1718545* (U.S. #2) / Universal *171838* (U.K. #2)

Alongside My Chemical Romance, Fall Out Boy are the most successful of the wave of 'emo' groups that emerged in the U.S. during the early 2000s. The term emo was originally used to describe one of the more extreme subgenres of hardcore punk during the 1980s, but has since come to define all manner of American rock groups tied together by little more than the fact that their often-bleak lyrics are in some way or other 'emotional.' Taking their name from a comic-book character featured sporadically in *The Simpsons*, Fall Out By are nominally led by guitarist and singer Patrick Stump, but are for all intents and purposes the vehicle of bassist and lyricist Pete Wentz.

Wentz's confessional writing style, characterized by such rambling song titles as 'I've Got A Dark Alley And A Bad Idea That Says You Should Shut Your Mouth (Summer Song),' has won him and his group millions of (mostly teenage) admirers across the U.S. and beyond; his appeal seemed only to grow when he attempted suicide in 2005 at the age of 25, seemingly inspired by the death, a year earlier, of the singer-songwriter Elliott Smith. Since then, however, a fitter, happier Wentz has provided his group with an arsenal of material that has helped Fall Out Boy cross over toward genuine pop stardom, cemented by the success of the pulsating pop-punk of 'This Ain't A Scene … ,' which narrowly missed the top spot on the singles charts on both sides of the Atlantic.

Ruby
Kaiser Chiefs

Released February 2007
B-Unique *digital download* (U.S.) / B-Unique *BUN119* (U.K. #1)

With 'Ruby,' Kaiser Chiefs confirmed their status among the leading lights of British guitar-based music. The group, named after a South African soccer team, formed almost a decade earlier when Leeds school friends Nick Hodgson, Simon Rix, Nick Baines, and Andrew White spotted singer Ricky Wilson fronting a Rolling Stones tribute band. The band's early singles – 'Oh My God,' 'I Predict A Riot' (both 2004), and 'Everyday I Love You Less And Less' (2005) – demonstrate their widespread appeal, invoking the soccer-stadium sing-along style of Oasis one minute and the doomy romanticism of The Smiths the next.

'Ruby,' the lead single from Kaiser Chief's second full-length album, *Yours Truly, Angry Mob*, is pitched in much the same vein. The verses are reminiscent at times Morrissey, which comes as no surprise when you learn that 'Ruby' was produced by Stephen Street, whose past credits include a number of albums by both The Smiths and their erstwhile frontman. The chorus, meanwhile, evokes another of Street's former charges, Blur, with its feel-good vocal melody and naggingly insistent synthesizer lines. 'Ruby' gave Kaiser Chiefs a first chart-topper in the U.K., and provided a timely boost to the group's profile in America, hitting Number 18 on *Billboard*'s Modern Rock listings.

Give It To Me
Timbaland Featuring Nelly Furtado & Justin Timberlake

Released February 2007
Interscope *008759* (U.S. #1) / Interscope *???* (U.K. #1)

On 'Give It To Me,' the man behind some of the greatest singles of the past decade, from 'Get Ur Freak On' to 'Maneater,' steps out from behind the mixing desk – with a little help from his superstar friends.

When successful producers attempt solo careers, the results are often disappointing. Timbaland's closest rivals among the great R&B/hip-hop producers of the early 21st century, Pharrell Williams and Chad Hugo (better known as The Neptunes), have consistently churned out big, memorable hits for others, but their solo output has been rather more spotty. Timbaland too had made several other records under his own name prior to 2007, but none had come close the artistic or commercial success of his work with Aaliyah, Missy Elliott, and company. This time around, however, success seemed inevitable.

In 2006, Timbaland raised his profile significantly by not only producing four of the year's biggest hits – 'Promiscuous' and 'Maneater' by Nelly Furtado, and 'SexyBack' and 'My Love' by Justin Timberlake – but by appearing as a guest vocalist on three of the four as well. Leaving nothing to chance, he invited Furtado and Timberlake back to sing on the first single to be drawn from his new solo venture, *Timbaland Presents Shock Value*, and then upped the publicity ante further by laying into his former collaborator Scott Storch (who co-wrote the Timberlake hit 'Cry Me A River' with Timbaland) in the lyrics. Timbaland's verses also seem to take a swing at some of the other stars who have crossed his path over the years, including Prince and Janet Jackson.

In truth this could just as easily have been another Timbaland-produced hit for Furtado or Timberlake, but only the truly hard-hearted would begrudge this hit-maker extraordinaire enjoying his own three-and-a-half minutes at the top.

Makes Me Wonder
Maroon 5

Released March 2007
A&M/Octane *12098* (U.S. #1 / U.K. #2)

'Makes Me Wonder' announced the welcome return of one of the hottest pop-rock properties of the mid 2000s. The Californian quintet had first found international success in 2004 with the transatlantic smash-hit 'This Love,' but took their time over recording a follow-up to their 2002 debut album *Songs About Jane*. In the intervening years singer Adam Levine guested on Kanye West's 'Heard 'Em Say,' a Top 30 hit in Britain and America, while drummer Ryan Dusick was forced to quit the group because of persistent wrist and shoulder problems.

Levine has claimed in interviews that 'Makes Me Wonder''s somewhat oblique lyrics concern his dissatisfaction with the course of the Iraq war and US foreign policy in general, although it's hard to tell from the music, which sticks mostly to the breezy template of Maroon 5's earlier tunes. As with a number of other hits of 2006–7, there is also a distinct whiff of 1980s pop in the production. But the single's place in pop history was sealed not by its lyrical or musical content but by its rise in the US from Number 64 one week to Number 1 the next – the biggest jump to the top spot in the history of the *Billboard* Hot 100.

CLASSIC
TRACKS
BACK TO
BACK
SINGLES

CLASSIC TRACKS BACK TO BACK ALBUMS

Thunder Bay Press

An imprint of the Advantage Publishers Group

10350 Barnes Canyon Road, San Diego, CA 92121

www.thunderbaybooks.com

Volume copyright © 2008 by Outline Press Ltd.

Text © 2008 by Outline Press Ltd.

ISBN-13: 978-1-59223-872-9

ISBN-10: 1-59223-872-6

The Library of Congress has cataloged the original Thunder Bay edition as follows:

Albums : the stories behind 50 years of great recordings / editors, Simon Smith &
Tony Bacon.
   p. cm.
  ISBN-13: 978-1-59223-295-6
  ISBN-10: 1-59223-295-7
 1. Popular music--Discography. 2. Popular music--Biography. 3. Sound
recording industry. I. Smith, Simon, 1966 Apr. 1- II. Bacon, Tony, 1954-

  ML156.4.P6A47 2008
  781.64'0266--dc22

            2007048467

WITH CONTRIBUTIONS FROM

JOHNNY BLACK

MARK BREND

MICHAEL HEATLEY

JOHN MORRISH

RIKKY ROOKSBY

THOMAS JEROME SEABROOK

DAVID SIMONS

COMMISSIONING EDITOR: MARK BREND

MANAGING EDITOR: THOMAS JEROME SEABROOK

EDITORS: SIMON SMITH & TONY BACON

DESIGN: MAIN ARTERY

Origination by Global Graphics (Czech Republic) & DL Repro Ltd. (England)
Printed by Colorprint Offset Ltd. (Hong Kong)

1 2 3 4 5 12 11 10 09 08

THUNDER BAY
P·R·E·S·S

CLASSIC TRACKS
BACK TO BACK ALBUMS

The Stories Behind 50 Years of Great Recordings

Introduction

Classic Tracks Back To Back: Albums profiles 400 of the most important albums of the past six decades.

The age of the 12-inch vinyl album began in the mid 1950s with *In The Wee Small Hours* by Frank Sinatra **8**. Other early landmarks include the soundtrack to *Rock Around The Clock*, featuring the famous title song by Bill Haley **14**, and the first greatest-hits album of note, *Elvis' Golden Records* **35**.

In the 1960s, bands such as The Beatles and The Beach Boys began to exploit the full potential of the long-playing record on such 'concept' albums as *Revolver* **68** and *Pet Sounds* **76**. Some albums, such as *The Doors* **84**, provided their creators with widespread international success at the first attempt; others – *The Velvet Underground & Nico* **90**, for example – sold poorly at first, but have since come to be acknowledged as all-time classics.

As the 1960s gave way to the '70s, the popular-musical album seemed to grow more extravagant with each passing year. The Who unveiled the first 'rock opera' in the shape of *Tommy* **118**, before Pink Floyd took progressive rock out into the stratosphere with *The Dark Side Of The Moon* **156**. The latter part of the decade saw the arrival of disco and punk, but both were overshadowed by the huge commercial success of *Hotel California* by The Eagles **184**.

The 1980s are not generally renowned for having produced the greatest music, but did give birth to some of the biggest-selling albums of all time, including Michael Jackson's *Thriller* **211** and *Born In The U.S.A.* by Bruce Springsteen **225**. Elsewhere, Prince combined funk, rock, soul, and pop to great effect on *Sign 'O' The Times* **237**, while the advent of the compact disc gave a new lease of life to reissues of music from the past.

The 1990s were dominated by alternative rock, best exemplified by Nirvana's *Nevermind* **254**, and hip-hop, which confirmed its standing in the musical mainstream with the success of albums by The Fugees **280**, The Notorious B.I.G. **283**, and Jay-Z **289**.

The early 21st century found the album in a state of flux as internet downloads of individual songs began to take precedence, but albums such as *Kid A* by Radiohead **296** and Wilco's *Yankee Hotel Foxtrot* **303** showed that there was still life in the old format yet.

A-Z listing of featured artists

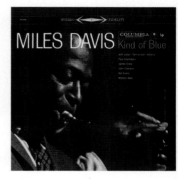

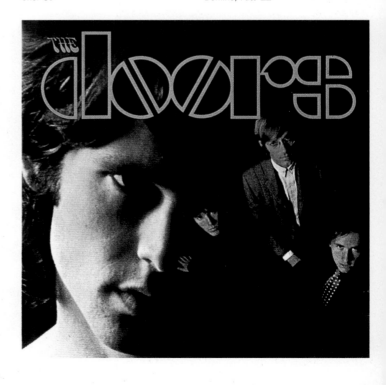

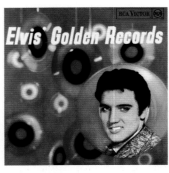

The stories behind 50 years of great recordings

■ *Gene Vincent & His Blue Caps at Capitol Studios, Hollywood, in 1956.*
Left to right: Cliff Gallup, Gene Vincent, Willie Williams, Dickie Harrell,
and Jack Neal.

1955

In The Wee Small Hours
Frank Sinatra

Capitol W581 (U.S.A.) / CAPS1008 (U.K.)
Released April 1955

The year 1955 was remarkable both in the career of Francis Albert Sinatra and in the development of the album.

Not only did Sinatra successfully take on the role of tormented heroin-addicted card dealer Frankie Machine in *The Man With The Golden Arm* but he released an album, *In The Wee Small Hours*, which showed the world the enormous potential of the 12-inch format.

It was his first to be conceived from the off as a full-length, 12-inch album, and, unlike previous collections, was designed to be listened to in the order laid down. Just reading through the titles tells a story, and, with eight songs on each side now available to him thanks to the new long-player (LP) format, he had double the space in which to tell that story.

Sinatra had been making the painful transition from teen idol – with a following consisting almost exclusively of bobby-soxers – to an entertainer of much greater stature. As a solo performer between 1943 and 1952 he had clocked up an amazing 86 hits during his time on the Columbia label, and alongside his recording success there were appearances in popular movies such as *Anchors Aweigh* and *On The Town*. But by the mid 1950s, as his personal life ran into difficulties, so his musical fortunes were beginning to fade. *In The Wee Small Hours*, however, was to prove to be the album that turned his career around and was the first of many hit albums and singles to come.

In so many ways the album bears the imprint of the second Mrs Sinatra, high-flying actress Ava Gardner, from whom he'd split in late 1953 amid much rancor. The pair's affair had, for a couple of years, run parallel to his first marriage to Nancy, but when that ended things got worse rather than better. Sinatra had wanted a child, but Gardner had twice ended pregnancies, telling him: "We don't have the ability to live together like any normal married couple." This was hard coming on top of the bad publicity that leaving his family had attracted, and his attempts to rekindle the relationship, including a journey to Africa where she was filming, proved fruitless.

The combination of two strong, successful characters hadn't been the recipe for long-term success – according to legend, Gardner dumped him via an MGM press release – and in its aftermath Sinatra had embraced the high-rolling Las Vegas lifestyle with a vengeance. Breakfasting at five in the afternoon, he now lived a nocturnal life, making the newly written title song by David Mann and Bob Hilliard a particularly appropriate one. The cover, too, depicts late-night desolation particularly effectively, showing a solitary Sinatra smoking a cigarette under a streetlight's baleful glow.

He entered KHJ Studios in Hollywood in the company of arranger-conductor Nelson Riddle and pianist Bill Miller on February 8th 1955 for the first of five sessions – the others were on February 16th and 17th and March 1st and 4th. With a musical recipe of less-is-more, he had a firm vision of what he wanted to achieve, using a basic rhythm section of guitar and celesta that built on Miller's piano and was augmented by Riddle's strings at appropriate moments.

Riddle had followed in Sinatra's footsteps by joining Tommy Dorsey's band as trombonist in 1944, albeit three years after Sinatra had gone solo,

Continued on next page

1955

before settling in California after national service and moving into arranging. Riddle and Sinatra brought out the best in each other, and it was no surprise that Riddle served as musical director on most of the singer's popular television specials. The relationship with Riddle – otherwise best known for his work with Nat King Cole on songs such as 'Unforgettable,' 'Somewhere Along The Way,' and 'Ballerina' – had only begun in 1953 but was to be a mutually beneficial teaming for the individuals concerned, and Riddle succeeded Axel Stordahl as Sinatra's arranger of choice.

The material on this album, as with all Sinatra's Capitol releases, was selected by the singer and his A&R man, Voyle Gilmore, who also gets a production credit. Then Sinatra and Riddle would work out how to give it the kind of treatment they wanted. "My father was paramount when it came to that," son Christopher Riddle told Spencer Leigh in 2003, "and Frank became more and more comfortable with my father's decisions because he understood that my father was making things that slotted in with him perfectly. He was creating wonderful orchestrations, which would enhance him and make him sound better than anything he could come up with. Frank would say to my dad, 'Make it sound like this' or 'Make it sound like that' or whatever. Sometimes Nelson would be saying in the arrangement, 'Hello, Frank, I remembered what you said and here is my little musical rejoinder.'"

The sessions would begin at eight in the evening and extend until well past midnight. Part of this was down to Sinatra's notorious perfectionism, cutting his vocal short 27 times in a single song to correct either himself or the orchestra. Yet he seemed able to re-establish the mood the instant he began to sing again.

In 1963 Sinatra would explain to *Playboy* magazine that he was ideally suited to singing sad songs: "Being an 18-karat manic depressive and having lived a life of violent emotional contradictions I have an over-acute capacity for sadness as well as elation." He also stated that: "When I sing, I believe, I'm honest," and the honesty shines through, especially here in Hoagy Carmichael's 'I Get Along Without You Very Well,' a song that epitomizes the mood of the entire album and highlights Sinatra's vocal prowess.

Track three on Side One, 'Glad to Be Unhappy,' the first of three Rodgers & Hart tunes, showcased a voice now deeper and more ravaged than the light tenor of early days, and it would be this, plus Sinatra's mastery of phrasing, that gave standards, such as Duke Ellington's 'Mood Indigo' and Arlen & Harburg's 'Last Night When We Were Young,' an added dimension. 'Can't We Be Friends?' by the husband and wife team of Paul James (James Paul Warburg) and Kay Swift tells an all too familiar tale: "She didn't mean it, / I should have seen it, / But now it's too late."

The first side ends with 'When Your Lover Has Gone,' penned by Edgar Swan, a number Sinatra had originally recorded back in 1944 with Axel Stordahl handling the orchestration. With a decade of life lived since then, Sinatra's vocal performance effortlessly surpasses the earlier version – and

Continued on next page

1955

legend has it that he broke down in the studio and cried after concluding the master take. It is certainly a fitting point to remove the stylus and pause for thought.

Side two kicks off with Cole Porter's 'What Is This Thing Called Love?' – a question Sinatra must have spent much time considering. Riddle's clarinet theme here is arguably as persuasively haunting as Porter's original melody.

With track 11, Alec Wilder's 'I'll Be Around,' the possibility of a brighter future is at least hinted at. Two Broadway show tunes by the masters, Rodgers & Hart, help bring the album to its conclusion: 'It Never Entered My Mind' (from the 1940 show *Higher And Higher*) has been described by one critic as "perhaps the definitive musical evocation of loneliness," while 'Dancing On The Ceiling,' from 1930's *Evergreen*, again sees Sinatra daring to hope.

The final track of any album is, inevitably, the one the listener is left with, and for track 16 Sinatra returned to a song he'd written with Sol Parker and Hank Sanicola back in 1941, 'This Love Of Mine.' It is the only Sinatra writing credit on the label, and it gave him and his fans a message of hope in the belief that "This love of mine goes on and on." If Ava Gardner was listening, and there was little doubt she was, the message was that he intended to put her in the past. He'd sung out his blues and was ready to move on.

> "BOB [HILLIARD] AND I HAD WRITTEN THE SONG AND HAPPENED TO BE IN NEW YORK EN ROUTE TO VISIT A PUBLISHER. AS WE WERE WALKING ALONG THE STREET, BOB SAID, 'HEY, THERE'S SINATRA AND NELSON RIDDLE.' SURE ENOUGH, THEY WERE WALKING AHEAD OF US, SO WE CALLED OUT TO THEM AND SHOWED THEM THE SONG. FRANK LIKED IT, AND ASKED, 'IS IT PUBLISHED YET? WE'LL USE IT ON THE ALBUM WE'RE WORKING ON RIGHT NOW.'"
>
> DAVE MANN, CO-WRITER (WITH HILLIARD) OF 'IN THE WEE SMALL HOURS.'

In The Wee Small Hours reached Number Two in the *Billboard* charts, proving that, while the album was sophisticated enough to appeal to jazz fans, Sinatra still commanded as big a popular audience as ever. Most importantly, it achieved its objective in winning Sinatra the attention and affection of the male half of the species, who, prior to this release, would have considered him an irredeemable teen idol. As it stands, bar-room crooners all the way through to Tom Waits have listened and learned, while in a bizarre gender reversal Carly Simon covered the title track in 1993 for the movie *Sleepless In Seattle*.

Time is a healer, they say, and Frank Sinatra's recording career bears out the saying. A year after these sessions he was busy waxing another very different masterpiece in *Songs For Swinging Lovers*. He'd spent 1955 making no fewer than five movies and, as he ended the year back in harness at The Sands, the Las Vegas hotel he co-owned, he started the new year of 1956 on an upbeat note.

It's hard to believe the man who steamed into 'You Make Me Feel So Young' was the same who'd ripped the heart out of his audience with 'I Get Along Without You Very Well,' but the evidence was there for all to hear.

Sinatra would cannily continue the pattern of alternating slow, sad albums and up-tempo swingers to the end of the decade, augmenting them where appropriate with Christmas albums, compilations, and soundtracks. Interestingly, however, it would be his 1958 release, *Frank Sinatra Sings For Only The Lonely* – which reunited him with Nelson Riddle – that bore comparison with *In The Wee Small Hours*, in the eyes of the critics and the

singer himself. When aficionados laud Sinatra's output in the 1950s, it is usually these two albums plus *Songs For Swinging Lovers* on which they base their argument. The fact that artists such as Linda Ronstadt brought Riddle out of retirement three decades later to try to achieve the same effect that he had with Sinatra – and as he had with Peggy Lee, Dean Martin, Dinah Shore, and others – says it all.

Sinatra recordings were the yardstick by which all other vocalists would be judged when it came to dealing with the American Popular Songbook. Sarah Vaughan, Ella Fitzgerald, and Tony Bennett have all put up worthy challenges, but it is easy to state a case for Sinatra offering the definitive performance of each and every song *In The Wee Small Hours* contains. One critic summed it up, accurately, as "an album so desolate you feel like you're in a basement bar in Manhattan on a rainy, miserable night and you can smell the bourbon and Lucky Strikes."

Rita Kirwan of *Music* magazine was one of the favored few to witness the sessions back in 1955, and her account of the end of one night's proceedings – appropriately in the wee small hours of the morning – gives an evocative flavor: "Sinatra takes a gulp of the lukewarm coffee remaining in the cup most recently handed to him, and then he lifts the inevitable hat from his head a little, and plops it right back, almost as if he'd wanted to relieve pressure from the hat band. The studio empties fast; just music stands and chairs remain. Sinatra flops on to one of the chairs, crosses his legs and hums a fragment of one of the songs he's been recording. He waves to the night janitor now straightening up the studio and says, 'Jeez. What crazy working hours we got. We both should've been plumbers, huh?'" If you want your waterworks testing, then this is the album.

Liberace At The Hollywood Bowl Liberace

Columbia CL 600 (U.S.A) / Philips BBL 7159 (U.K.)
Released March 1955 (U.S.A.) / January 1958 (U.K.)

An American of Polish-Italian descent, pianist Liberace was a self-made legend, and his performance at the Hollywood Bowl was pure wish fulfillment.

Four years earlier, to the very night, he'd performed to an empty auditorium, having saved enough money to rent the Bowl on an off night. This time around he fully lived out his dream, with his brother George conducting the orchestra, before a wildly enthusiastic, standing-room-only crowd of some 20,000.

Liberace At The Hollywood Bowl, as released in 1955, is an edited version of the first half of the concert; *Hollywood Bowl Encore*, an edited version of the second half, was released three months later. (A four-record boxed set of 78s from the Hollywood Bowl Concerts is particularly collectable.) A double CD set issued in 2002, 15 years after Liberace's death, includes all of the music performed that night in original sequence. He had yet to incorporate 'I'll Be Seeing You' into the act as his finale, but the music – as glitzy and exotic as the wardrobe he preferred – displays all the musical frills and trills for which he became famous throughout the world.

The material ranges from classics to popular tunes and includes standards such as 'Stardust' and 'As Time Goes By' as well as a humorous version of 'Chopsticks.' His style, epitomized by the candelabra on the grand piano and aped by the likes of Elton John, would last longer than the music, but *Liberace At The Hollywood Bowl* is probably the album to have. It's just a pity they didn't film it.

Tamboo
Les Baxter, His Orchestra And Chorus

Capitol T-655 (U.S.A.) / LC6807 (U.K.)
Released June 1955

The long career of pianist, saxophonist, conductor, composer, and arranger Les Baxter encompassed swing, jazz, and movie soundtracks, but it is as the founding father of the 1950s genre exotica that he is best remembered.

Like all genres, exotica resists easy definition. In its portrayal of various imagined traditional forms of music from 'exotic' parts of the world – predominantly Polynesian, Afro-Caribbean, and Hawaiian – it betrayed a debt to Hollywood stereotypes of the time, all rustling grass skirts and whooping Tarzan cries. Crucially, it has no roots in any real non-Western musical tradition, but it is an imagining of what such music might sound like. Its chord progressions and grooves owe something to jazz, but it lacks that genre's sense of artistic gravity. Sometimes it was meant to serve as light background music, at other times it was overtly showy and attention grabbing. Perhaps it is best to think of exotica as a fantastic country, part Hawaii, part Africa, part West Coast technological paradise, populated by seasoned musicians who had already worked extensively in jazz, light classical, soundtrack music, and pop, being served endless cocktails by many dusky maidens. And in their midst was Les Baxter.

It all started in 1951, when Baxter released *Le Sacre Du Sauvage*, later reissued in expanded form as *Ritual Of The Savage*, both on Capitol. As *Variety* magazine put it: "Les Baxter . . . has started a whole new trend on wax with his quasi-exotic sounds." It included what would become exotica's theme song, 'Quiet Village,' later a hit for Martin Denny. *Le Sacre Du Sauvage* was the first of a long run of albums for Capitol that lasted until 1962, including such evocative period pieces as *Skins! Bongo Party With Les Baxter*, *The Primitive And The Passionate*, and *Jungle Jazz*. *Tamboo* was one of these, appearing in 1955. Like all Baxter's work it conjured up a fantasy world, an alternative to the harsher urban sounds of the newly emerging rock'n'roll.

Exotica petered out in the early 1960s, and Baxter spent the rest of his career composing soundtracks for b-movies. He died in 1996, living just long enough to see his music rediscovered by a new generation of musicians and enthusiasts, and many of his albums reissued.

1956

Rock Around The Clock (Original Soundtrack)

Decca DL 8225 (U.S.A.) / Brunswick LAT 8117 (U.K.)
Released March 1956

The Girl Can't Help It (Original Soundtrack)

Key Cat # (U.S.A.) / Capitol EAP 1-823 (U.K.)
Released December 1956

When it became clear that rock'n'roll was no passing fad, Hollywood moved quickly to cash in.

Producer Sam Katzman, a veteran of many years' service on second features for Columbia, signed Bill Haley and named the singer's first movie *Rock Around The Clock* after his trademark hit. Its unexciting storyline – failed manager discovers rock'n'roll, "like hillbilly with a beat," and steers

band, The Comets, to stardom – and bargain-basement production values were masked by the excitement of the music. (Perhaps the movie's greatest legacy is the portrayal of black act The Platters as the equals of their white counterparts in a society still inclined to buy 'vanilla' cover versions.)

The movie's success swiftly inspired a follow-up, *Don't Knock The Rock*. Little Richard co-starred in the latter, and it was one of his hits that titled *The Girl Can't Help It*. Directed by Frank Tashlin, this appeared in late 1956 and boasted appearances by Gene Vincent, Eddie Cochran, and Fats Domino alongside the 'Georgia Peach.' Julie London's 'Cry Me A River' is probably the standout track of a movie that, with a budget permitting the casting of blonde bombshell Jayne Mansfield as the heroine, Edmond O'Brien as her gangster boyfriend, and Tom Ewell as the agent charged with making Mansfield a star. It proved rock'n'roll could inspire a major movie and not just cheap

exploitation features, and it was also one of the first rock movies to be shot in color, a luxury afforded to few bar Elvis Presley until well into the following decade. Indeed, the footage of Gene Vincent playing 'Be Bop A Lula' is the only known color footage of the man and his – largely – original Blue Caps in existence (the guitarist featured here is not Cliff Gallup).

The soundtrack veers from the sublime Eddie Cochran – bizarrely portraying an example of how you don't need talent to succeed in rock'n'roll – to Ray Anthony, the man who dubbed Edmond O'Brien singing 'Rock Around The Rock Pile.'

Having opened the rock-movie era, Sam Katzman more or less brought down the curtain with 1961's *Twist Around The Clock*, leaving a gap in the market to be to be to be filled by more imaginative movie-makers later in that decade.

The Platters **The Platters**

King/Federal 549 (U.S.A.) / Parlophone PMD 1058 (U.K.)
Released May 1956

With sales of over 50 million records, The Platters are the bestselling black doo-wop band of all time, and this album contains their first singles.

Coached by Buck Ram, a white lawyer in his 40s, they proved right his assertion that mixing orchestral arrangements with an R&B beat was a recipe for success. They'd been releasing singles since 1953, but the first two million-sellers were 'Only You,' released in 1955, and the chart-topping 'The Great Pretender,' released in early 1956. Pioneering DJ Alan Freed, a champion of black music, arranged for The Platters to appear in the movie *Rock Around The Clock*, and across-the-board success was the result. This album consists of material cut for King/Federal prior to that breakthrough and clearly shows their gospel roots, and it became the first by a rock'n'roll group to make the U.S. Top Ten.

Tony Williams' high lead voice was the band's secret weapon. The line-up was completed by Zola Taylor, Paul Robi, Herb Reed – who continues to lead

a line-up today – and David Lynch. The album opens with an earlier version of 'Only You (And You Alone),' but also contains a number of less successful singles, 'Give Thanks,' 'Tell The World,' 'Shake It Up Mambo,' and 'I'll Cry When You're Gone.' Other selections range from the onomatopoeic 'Voo-Vee-Ah-Bee' to a doo-wop take on movie theme 'Roses Of Picardy.' The Platters' inclusion on the soundtrack of *American Graffiti* and induction into the Rock'n'Roll Hall Of Fame in 1990 was well-deserved recognition. This is where that long-running story started.

Calypso **Harry Belafonte**

RCA Victor 1248 (U.S.A.) / RD 27107 (U.K.)
Released June 1956

Harold George Belafonte made 1957 the year of the 'Calypso Boom,' and this, his third album, was the catalyst. It was also the first LP ever to be certified a million-seller.

Belafonte, an actor of West Indian parentage, had trained alongside such classmates as Marlon Brando, Walter Matthau, and Tony Curtis, but broadened his options to include music when he figured he'd not be able to emulate their successes. His musical journey gathered momentum when he signed a recording contract with RCA in the early 1950s, and his first two albums, eclectic reflections of global folk music, were both successes, with the second, *Belafonte*, a chart topper.

But it was a meeting with Irving Burgie – an American with a Barbadian mother who performed West Indian songs as Lord Burgess and His Serenaders – that turned Belafonte on to calypso in particular. The album *Calypso* was the result, though the project initially found "significant resistance" among the RCA hierarchy. So he took his plan directly to company president, George Merek, who gave him the green light to proceed. He was rewarded with an unprecedented 31 weeks at the top of the U.S. charts. (It would not be until 1962 and *West Side Story* that *Calypso*'s run at Number One would be bettered.)

Burgie was credited with the majority of the songs, which had been well rehearsed before Belafonte entered the studio with The Tony Scott Orchestra, conductor Norman Luboff, and guitarist Millard Thomas. Ironically, then, it was the one piece of improvisation, 'Day O,' that would give the album its opening signature track and inspire a plethora of imitators. This number is accompanied by a 'version,' entitled 'Star O,' on Side Two, but the album, described as "a cross section of folk music from Jamaica, Trinidad, and other islands," is by no means full of soundalike filler. 'I Do Adore Her' and 'Come Back Liza' are evocative ballads, while 'Man Smart (Woman Smarter),' later covered by artists as diverse as The Carpenters and Robert Palmer, could be termed the first feminist folk song. 'Jamaica Farewell' was the hit single selected by RCA, but when future actor Alan Arkin's folk group, The Tarriers, reached Number Four with a cover of 'Day O' – retitled 'The Banana Boat Song' – Belafonte's version was issued and peaked just one place below its competitor despite being second off the blocks.

Boosted by this, *Calypso* stayed on the *Billboard* chart for 99 weeks, and inspired many folk singers and groups to pick up their acoustic guitars – most notable among which were The Kingston Trio, named after the capital city of Jamaica. Indeed, the following decade found at least one song of West Indian origin in every self-respecting folk act's repertoire. Little wonder the album gets a five-star rating at the *All Music Guide* website, which believes it remains "a record of inestimable influence" today.

Resisting the impulse to record a follow-up album immediately, Belafonte instead spaced out his calypso albums, releasing them at five-year intervals in 1961, 1966, and 1971.

As well as singing stardom, Belafonte's later career embraced movies and television, though his more recent activities, since an appearance on 1985's U.S.A. For Africa all-star single, have been in the political world.

From Studio To Turntable

From the crude wax disks of the 1940s to the virtually limitless sound-manipulation properties of modern-day digital audio, recording technology has made enormous strides over the last half-century. Many of today's listeners will have been born too late to recognize the sound of a needle descending on to vinyl, and have no other point of reference than affordable, near-perfect sound.

The various studio enhancements have had a profound impact on the record business as a whole, altering the manner in which musicians perform in the studio and the way composers craft new songs. But what effect did all this have on the music world? There are those who claim that the evolution in music-making machinery has enhanced the creative process, while digital detractors blame sampling, sequencing, and other button-pushing activities for the general decline in studio ingenuity.

Perhaps the most heated debate concerns the impact of technology on the long-playing, vinyl album, introduced during the late 1940s and all but replaced by the Compact Disk some 40 years later. Supporters cite the durability and high-fidelity of the digital medium, not to mention the longer running times of the average CD release. Analog romantics, on the other hand, often prefer a warm piece of old vinyl to a shrill digitally mastered reissue, and mourn the loss of the double-sided track line-up of the turntable era.

In order to understand our place in music history in the early 21st century, it's helpful to start by returning to a time when recording methods were very different.

State-of-the-art record making in 1945 – which involved cutting a groove along a wax disk using a magnetically driven needle – was light-years ahead of the earliest days of sound reproduction, when musicians would gather around a large funnel-shaped horn and create acoustic vibrations that formed grooves on a turning cylinder.

In the mid 1920s the condenser microphone, manufactured by the Neumann company, ushered in the era of electrical recording. For the first time vocalists could sing at normal volume, rather than bellowing over a wailing orchestra. Even so, making records during the 1930s and 1940s was a far from leisurely process. The sound produced by studio performers was simultaneously printed on to a rotating wax disk – known as the master – from which copies could later be cut. Once the recording was under way, there was no turning back. Any mistake would ruin the disk and force the group to start again with a fresh master.

The medium would soon change, and in dramatic fashion. While stationed in Britain during World War II, Lieutenant Jack Mullin, a trained electronics engineer, became intrigued by the lifelike quality of the classical-music radio being broadcast from Germany. After the war ended he made a remarkable discovery: the broadcasts were not live, they just sounded that way. Some years earlier the Germans had devised an ingenious method for recording and reproducing sound using a roll of magnetic tape that was spooled between two reels on a machine called a magnetophon. Mullin immediately requested a demonstration. "I really flipped – I couldn't tell from the sound whether it was live or a playback."

A year later Mullin and business partner Bill Palmer played a sample recording to executives of NBC, who were immediately struck by the high quality of the sound. By 1948 the Ampex Corporation had introduced its Model 200, the first in a long line of industry-standard tape-recording units. It was Bing Crosby who saw the enormous potential of the new apparatus. Crosby had earlier almost single-handedly changed the practice of vocal recording from operatic to intimate by moving closer to the mike. He now became the first popular artist to utilize the new Ampex recorder.

Continued on page 17

1956

Sings The Rodgers & Hart Songbook Vol. 1
Ella Fitzgerald

Verve MGV 4002-2 (U.S.A.) / HMV CLP 1116 & 1117 (U.K.)
Released August 1956 (U.S.A.) / May 1957 (U.K.)

Part of her 'Songbook' series of recordings of the late 1950s – others include George and Ira Gershwin and Cole Porter – Ella Fitzgerald here turns her attention to the songs of Rodgers & Hart.

She entered the newly opened Capitol Records Studio A in Hollywood with producer Norman Granz on August 27th 1956 and emerged four days later with a classic. Lorenz Hart's sophisticated and witty lyrics were natural partners for Richard Rodgers' music throughout a 24-year partnership that produced 40-plus shows and movie scores. Yet, just as with Fitzgerald's versions of Cole Porter songs, it is as if these were written just for her. As Deena Rosenberg commented in the liner notes: "When songs from the musical theater are taken outside the theater, each performer can choose whether to imitate the original version or to evolve a more personal one. Ella's interpretation . . . leaves the listener with the feeling that there is little more to say."

Perfect pitch and diction, not to mention a vocal range of more than two octaves, were the Fitzgerald hallmarks, as may be heard here on 'The Lady Is A Tramp,' 'Where Or When,' and over a dozen more. Buddy Bergman's orchestral arrangements are noticeably sweeter than those employed on the two-volume *Cole Porter Songbook* project or, indeed, Nelson Riddle's Gershwin treatments, but somehow this adds to the charm.

Ira Gershwin once commented in awe: "I never knew how good our songs were until I heard Ella Fitzgerald sing them." Rodgers & Hart would doubtless agree.

Memorial Album **Hank Williams**

MGM E-202 (U.S.A.) / D137 (U.K.)
Released September 1956 (U.K.)

***Memorial Album* is one of several releases that cashed in on the passing of country giant Hank Williams, who died in the back of a Cadillac driving him to a gig on New Year's Day 1953, nine months short of his 30th birthday.**

Newspapers of the time quaintly described him as a "star hillbilly singer," but the songs he wrote and sang in his brief life proved instrumental in bringing hillbilly music into the mainstream. And, while the scant 8-track selection on *Memorial Album* is hardly representative of his work, no one could deny the quality of the material here.

The rough and ready 'Cold Cold Heart' and 'Hey Good Lookin'' were 1951 country chart toppers, while 'Half As Much' made Number Two the following year. Most telling, though, is the number of cover versions of his songs recorded during his lifetime and which attest to Williams' immediate influence. Tony Bennett, then in the spring of his career, cut 'Cold Cold Heart,' Joni James recorded 'Your Cheatin' Heart,' and Frankie Laine tried 'Kaw-Liga' for size. All feature on *Memorial Album* in their original form. Half a century later, and with Williams as influential as ever, now on a new alt.country generation personified by the likes of Ryan Adams, the covers keep on coming.

A colorful personal life, alcohol, and prescription drugs proved a fatal combination, but Hank Williams shook up the world of country music and the reverberations continue, thanks to the raw emotion of tracks like these.

Ellington At Newport **Duke Ellington**

Columbia (U.S.A.) / Philips BBL 7152 (U.K.)
Released November? 1956

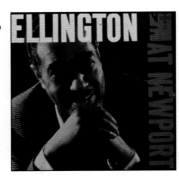

Pre-war jazz giant, Duke Ellington, took the opportunity to prove that class is permanent when he and his band were invited to play the third *Newport Jazz Festival* in 1956.

Having suffered the onslaught of rock'n'roll and the post-war financial pressures that made touring with big bands an impossibility, Ellington and band were at a low ebb when they opened the Saturday evening entertainment on July 7th.

With the program running late, they took the stage again at midnight with the prospect of losing most of the audience – but, after playing a specially commissioned 'Newport Jazz Festival Suite,' Ellington threw caution to the wind and gave tenor saxophone player Paul Gonsalves his head on 'Diminuendo and Crescendo in Blue,' a number from some 20 years previously. "Just get out there and blow your tail off," he advised, and, as the crowd applauded wildly, the set and the band's fortunes were transformed by a 27-chorus improvisation. Four encores and a cover story from *Time* magazine later, Duke Ellington and his band faced a far rosier future.

"The event marked not only the turning point in one concert," reported the magazine, "it confirmed a turning point in a career." Historian Mark Tucker depicted it as "a high point in his performing career comparable in some ways to the opening at London's Palladium in 1933 and the Carnegie Hall debut in 1943." In 1999 Columbia released *The Complete Ellington At Newport*, a double-CD set including the renowned concert in its entirety – and in stereo – as well as the studio recreations issued on the original *Ellington At Newport* album. The release was supervised by original producer George Avakian.

Continued from page 15

The arrival of the tape machine coincided with yet another astonishing studio breakthrough. In 1947 the Neumann company once again made history with the introduction of its famous U47 condenser microphone (the first mike capable of both direct and omni-directional recording), which was distributed by the Telefunken Company (hence its nickname of Telly). It was followed in 1949 by the slightly modified M49. Both offered stunning range and clarity, and helped usher in the golden age of vocal sound. (As a measure of their quality, they remain among the most respected – and expensive – vocal microphones on the vintage market.)

These technological advances represented a major turning point for the industry at the close of the 1940s. To recording engineers, magnetic tape was a blessing. Reel-to-reel tape machines could be stopped and restarted quickly and easily in the event of a mistake. Engineers could also edit together several different takes of the same song by cutting out the best sections of the tape using a razor blade, then sticking them back together to form a final master. The continuity that tape provided helped keep the momentum going during a session.

The Echo Revolution

In the early days of record-making, engineers would mike up a large room or concert hall to give a recording its proper ambience. However, with the introduction of the vocal microphone (and, later, separate recording tracks), singers were often isolated in an enclosed space known as a vocal booth in order to provide some degree of sound separation. For many vocalists, the results were simply too 'dry,' hence the need to replenish some of the ambience removed during the isolation process.

In 1947 the Chicago-based engineer Bill Putnam achieved an echo-laden sound on 'Peg-O-My-Heart' by Jerry Murad and his group, The Harmonicats, by recording part of the song in the marbled restroom at the nearby Civic Opera House. 'Peg-O-My-Heart' went on to become the first ever million-selling hit. Putnam later refined the concept by building a series of echo chambers – isolated reverberant rooms – made of reflective plaster. He then fed individual recording signals directly from the console to the room through a basic loudspeaker, which would be returned with a lone microphone.

By the early 1950s echo chambers had become the leading source of studio-sound enhancement. Over the years engineers refined the art of chamber construction, adding rounded corners (made from plaster-coated chicken wire), making the rooms asymmetrical, or pointing the speakers against the wall instead of facing the microphone for a rolling-reverb effect. No two echo chambers sounded alike, simply because each one was individually built, and many engineers still maintain that the best echo chambers were unparalleled as a reverb source, even by today's standards.

It was the guitarist and inventor Les Paul who, during the early 1950s, helped define the sound of the echo chamber. While experimenting in his home studio in 1949, Paul discovered tape echo, whereby a signal from one tape head was fed to a second machine running at a slower speed then returned to the original. Tape echo neatly replicated the actual reflections found in reverberant rooms, but Paul took the invention one step further. Using his own echo chamber, constructed underground adjacent to his New Jersey home, Paul tried sending a recorded signal to the echo chamber by way of the tape-delay unit. By inserting a multisecond delay between the original dry signal and the returned chamber signal, Paul created an entirely unique reverb effect that would become the toast of the studio industry.

The tape delay was just one of many groundbreaking devices that emerged from Paul's garage during this time. His most notable brainwave made it possible to record individual parts one after the other, using an Ampex 300 tape machine outfitted with a second playback head. Paul's invention – which he called "sound on sound" – gave birth to the era of multitrack recording, and, in time, would change the course of popular music.

Meanwhile, recording researchers continued to break new ground. The first mechanical rival to the echo chambers came from Germany's EMT corporation, which introduced the first plate reverb systems. The EMT 140 model in particular, introduced in 1957, immediately became a viable form of studio sound enhancement. A plate reverb consisted of a long thin sheath of sheet metal that was housed in a protective wooden enclosure. Sound would be fed into a driver at one end of the plate, and the resulting reverberation would be picked up at the other and sent back to the recording console. The plate could also be dampened

Continued on page 19

1956

Elvis Presley Elvis Presley

RCA LPM1254 (US) / HMV CLP1093 (UK)
Released March 1956

Elvis Elvis Presley

RCA LPM1382 (U.S.A.) / HMV CLP1105 (U.K.)
Released October 1956

While the impact of Elvis Presley is nearly always measured in singles, it was a landmark day when, on January 10th 1956, he walked into the RCA Victor recording studios in Nashville to begin his first album-recording session for his new employers.

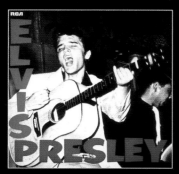

While success at Sun had come out of the blue, a $40,000 transfer fee now sat on his shoulders. Would the young man who'd only turned 21 a couple of days earlier still be able to deliver?

His first two days in the studio provided the answer in the shape of five tracks, three of which – 'Money Honey,' 'I'm Counting On You,' and 'I Got A Woman' – would grace his first album *Elvis Presley*, released just two months later. One of the others recorded at these sessions was the Number One single 'Heartbreak Hotel,' which, as was the custom in those days, was not included on the album. Five of the 12 tracks had been recorded at Sun Studios, so they only needed to be topped up by seven more to complete a historic LP.

Presley was backed not only by his familiar rhythm section of Scotty Moore, Bill Black, and D.J. Fontana but also by vocal group The Jordanaires. Those seasoned sessioneers were unimpressed by the raw newcomer, but his pledge that, "If one of these songs goes big, I want you to record with me all the time," proved their passport to fame and fortune. The relatively untutored Presley also caused the studio staff problems, his hard-strummed guitar tending to bleed into the vocal microphone because

he played the guitar high on his chest. The solution was to use a felt pick that muted the sound somewhat.

The cover of the album has itself become iconic and much-imitated, most notably by The Clash with *London Calling* (1979). Earliest pressings had the name Elvis in light pink (it darkened on later examples). Presley was in green across the bottom, the name framing a monochrome photograph by William S. 'Popsie' Randolph of the guitar-strumming singer in full cry.

Several of the songs on the album would have been familiar through original versions by Ray Charles ('I Got A Woman'), Little Richard ('Tutti Frutti'), The Drifters ('Money Honey'), and Rodgers & Hart ('Blue Moon'). Interestingly, 'Blue Moon,' 'I Love You Because,' and 'I'll Never Let You Go,' ballads all, were songs well-established in the Presley repertoire that had been recorded at Sun but were considered unsuitable for release by Sam Phillips, the Sun Records supremo who discovered Presley. However, their inclusion here results in a more varied LP, emphasizing the broad base of his musical roots.

The album opens with 'Blue Suede Shoes,' a song Presley's former Sun stablemate Carl Perkins, who

composed it, had taken into the U.S. Top Five. Unfortunately for Perkins, his involvement in a near-fatal car crash slowed his progress, and he had to watch the rival version become a hit – but was doubtless consoled by the royalties.

Presley's own musical career would soon be slowed up, too, for while movies would prove amazing vehicles in which to promote the star, his output would lose the edge that had made it such vital listening for millions of teenagers the world over. Needless to say, his screen test with Paramount Studios, undertaken shortly after the album sessions, led to an immediate three-picture deal. Shooting of the first, *Love Me Tender*, would begin in late August, just before the sessions for second album *Elvis*.

This was committed to tape during the first three days of September at Radio Recorders in Hollywood, though one track, 'So Glad You're Mine,' which opens Side Two, was held over from the RCA Studio sessions earlier in the year. The sleeve is known to exist in at least 11 different versions, because of the advertisements for different RCA albums alongside an essay on the star.

Again, no room was found for the Number One single 'Don't Be Cruel' b/w 'Hound Dog,' while there had been a session in between albums one and two to produce music for *Love Me Tender*. This had, however, seen Presley recording with session men, much to his annoyance, so when he reconvened with Moore, Black, Fontana, and The Jordanaires – whose Gordon Stoker also contributed piano – the assembled cast had a point to prove. Thirteen tracks were waxed in the three-day session, which not unnaturally resulted in a more cohesive whole than its two-stage

Continued on page 20

Continued from page 17

through a movable pad, which allowed the engineer to control the length of the decay. Plate reverbs also had company in the form of spring reverb units, which mimicked natural reverb by attaching feeds to either end of a generous expanse of wrapped spring coil.

■ *(Left to right) Elvis Presley, Bill Black, Scotty Moore, and Sam Phillips.*

Sam Phillips And Sun Records

Before the 1950s audio limitations were such that it would have been nearly impossible to distinguish the sound of one studio from the next. Tape recording, however, opened doors unimaginable just a few years earlier. By the start of the decade studio owners had begun to take advantage of the improved technology, using emerging sound-sculpting tools such as echo and delay to create exciting new records. Such haphazard creativity helped bolster the reputation of a select few studios during this time and, in turn, helped fortify the careers of some soon-to-be legendary recording artists.

It would be wrong to assume that Elvis Presley knew exactly what he was doing when he began his long career in 1954 with 'You're a Heartbreaker,' 'I'm Left, You're Right, She's Gone,' and the various other cinder blocks of rock'n'roll. In fact, it was how little he knew that ushered in the most explosive period in pop history.

Not that it was all left to chance: Presley had the look and the style, an intuitive sense of timing, and, when it came to selecting songs, impeccably good taste. All that was needed was to get the goods down on tape. That was easier said than done, however. In order to complete the equation, it would be necessary for Elvis and his regular collaborators, Scotty Moore and Bill Black – whom Elvis had met at Sun Studios in Memphis – to hook up with a forward-thinking studio technician who'd be willing to break a few rules. That person turned out to be Sun's own Sam Phillips.

A former audio engineer at a Memphis radio station, Phillips opened his one-man studio operation, Sun Records, at 706 Union Avenue in the winter of 1950. Originally outfitted with a 16-inch acetate disk cutter, the studio later upgraded with a pair of Ampex tape units.

"The sound of Sun was determined by its limitations," notes Ernst Jorgensen, longtime Presley archivist. "Sam had a very small space, and as a result there were no drums – just room enough for acoustic guitar, electric, and bass. So in order to make it sound fuller, he created this embellishment – and that became

Continued on page 21

predecessor. Engineer Thorne Nagar was influential in guiding the still-inexperienced band through the recording process, and, though no producer was credited for either album, the powers behind the throne were undoubtedly RCA executives Steve Sholes and Chet Atkins.

The Little Richard songbook was on this occasion raided no fewer than three times – for the opener 'Rip It Up' as well as 'Long Tall Sally' and 'Ready Teddy' – while Otis Blackwell contributed 'Paralyzed.' Jerry Leiber and Mike Stoller, the white songwriting and production team that had penned tracks for several classic black vocal groups, followed up 'Hound Dog,' their Number One for Presley, with 'Love Me,' which reached Number Two as a single in its own right.

But perhaps the track for which the album will most often be associated in many people's minds is the one that has been most lampooned over the years: 'Old Shep.' Presley first performed the song at the Mississippi-Alabama Fair at ten years of age, and he clearly enjoyed the memory. Furthermore, his piano playing on the track was his first recorded performance on that instrument.

Released in mid October, *Elvis* entered the U.S. pop chart at Number Seven, an impressive debut that would only be beaten four years later by *GI Blues* and remains his second highest *Billboard* LP-chart entry. One month later it hit the top, staying there for five weeks – as against its predecessor's ten – and making many a Christmas-present list. Once deposed by Nat King Cole it hung around at Number Two for another 11 weeks, ten of them consecutive, so it's no surprise that *Elvis* was certified three million copies sold in 1960.

These two chart-topping albums in the space of seven months – not to mention a rush of singles and EPs – confirmed that Elvis Presley and rock'n'roll were no mere flashes in the pan.

'S Wonderful **Ray Conniff**

Columbia 925 (U.S.A.) / CBS 24 (U.K.)
Released December 1956

Massachusetts-born Conniff, a seasoned back-room boy who came good as a performer thanks to Columbia A&R svengali Mitch Miller, found a hit formula with this album.

It was a formula he reproduced more than 30 times in the dozen years that followed, to the undying delight of fans of easy listening.

He began arranging as a youngster in 1933, and went on to work with the likes of Artie Shaw before the war and Harry James after. In fact, he had first arranged this album's Gershwin-penned title track while working with Shaw, and he had also arranged the hit version of 'September Song' reprised here, for James.

Having joined Columbia in 1954 and worked on hits by stars such as Guy Mitchell, Rosemary Clooney, Johnny Mathis, and Marty Robbins, Conniff was eventually given his own album by Miller. Orchestral versions of such popular standards as 'Begin The Beguine,' 'Stardust,' and 'I Get A Kick Out Of You' effectively updated the pre-war big band sound for the 1950s, a distinctive innovation being the use of wordless vocals delivered by a male-female chorus. This blend was often imitated, but never eclipsed.

After this album's spring 1957 chart success, peaking just outside the U.S. Top Ten, better-performing follow-ups *'S Marvelous* and *'S Awful Nice*

led eventually to 'proper' singing on 1960's *It's The Talk Of The Town*, while Conniff's version of 'Lara's Theme,' from the hit movie *Dr Zhivago*, made the U.S. Top Ten singles in 1965. His music also found favor in the U.S.S.R., where he recorded in 1974 with a local choir supplying vocals. This, however, is the album that started it all – wordlessly.

Finger-Style Guitar **Chet Atkins**

RCA Victor LPM1383 (U.S.A.) / Not issued in U.K.
Released September 1956

Inspired by the thumb-and-finger-picking style of Merle Travis, Chet Atkins developed his own variation while trying to copy the records, and in doing so made history.

One of the major architects of country music's Nashville Sound, Atkins has been said to be the most recorded solo instrumentalist in history. Signed to RCA Victor in 1947 as a singer and guitarist, Atkins also helped to promote the careers of Hank Williams and Elvis Presley, but his own albums of instrumental music were highly influential in their own right on aspiring guitarists. Albums cut with the likes of Mark Knopfler attest to this.

This 1956 offering is an album of two very different sides: a rhythm section supports Atkins on the first side, cutting such well-known numbers such as 'In The Mood;' while the second side has the likes of 'Gavotte in D' and 'Waltz in A-Flat' performed solo in a more classical style. (Not to say that he was averse to using the studio here, as Side Two's 'Unchained Melody' features a delayed, overdubbed chorus.)

Each year, until his death in 2001, Atkins was proud to see fans, guitar enthusiasts, and students from across the nation and overseas meet in Nashville for a four-day convention. "I was kind of an innovator and I could pull it off very well," he admitted. "I can see that now. At the time I thought I was terrible, but that kept me improving and trying to learn to play better." This album remains a primer for Mark Knopfler and his fellow Atkins-ites.

1957

Around The World In 80 Days
(Original Soundtrack)

Decca 79046 (U.S.A.) / Brunswick LAT 8185 (U.K.)
Released April 1957

Just as Hollywood enlivened the post-war cultural landscape, so movie soundtracks dominated the popular music charts, despite the mounting challenge of rock'n'roll.

The U.S. Top Five had featured hits from *My Fair Lady*, *The Eddy Duchin Story*, *The King And I*, and *High Society* the previous year, and in July 1957 it was time for Victor Young's score for *Around The World In 80 Days* to take its place there. Sadly, Young himself was not around to witness this feat, having unexpectedly passed away in November 1956 at the age of 56.

While such numbers as 'Invitation To A Bull Fight' and 'India Country Side' really only work in the context of the film, there is a real song – and a classic at that – in the title track, which inspired covers from artists as celebrated as Frank Sinatra, Bing Crosby, The Maguire Sisters, and, most successfully in chart terms, orchestral maestro Mantovani. Interestingly, a single pairing Victor Young's instrumental version with Crosby's vocal reached a peak of Number 13 in the same week this album topped the chart.

A tug of war between Decca and RCA-Victor that delayed release for some six weeks (producer Mike Todd favoring RCA) failed to dent the soundtrack's commercial potential, and though it was knocked off the top by yet another soundtrack – that of Elvis Presley's second movie, *Loving You* – it would regain the summit for another nine weeks before once again deferring to The King, this time with *Elvis' Christmas Album*.

Only three soundtracks would achieve pole position in the U.S.A. in 1958, an indication that the balance of pop power was changing. But, just as the movie starring Shirley MacLaine and David Niven remains a classic, so the soundtrack retains its charm.

■ *Beale Street, Memphis, in the 1950s, home of Sam Phillips's legendary Sun Studios*

Continued from page 19

the *sound*." That sound was the product of tape echo. "It wasn't necessarily that Sam had this vision of how everything should work," says Jorgensen, "it was just what he had and how he made it work. If you listen to some of the early Sun ballads, you can hear him changing that echo effect – trying to find the right balance."

On vocals, tape echo nicely replicated the actual reflections found in small rooms or echo chambers. When applied to Moore's strident guitar lines, Black's bass, and Presley's briskly strummed acoustic, the combined 'slapback' effect was something else altogether. "Elvis's acoustic – which was always miked up on its own right up to the beginning of the 1960s – had this breezy and melodic sound," says Jorgensen, "but at the same time, you've got this incredibly percussive thing going all the way through on account of Bill's slap-bass playing. I've had to argue with people who insist that there's real percussion going on in there! When, in fact, it's just the combination of the playing and the echo."

By 1955 Phillips had fully mastered the sounds that would soon reverberate around the world. "Sam was a very different type of producer – mainly because he didn't work with big 'professional' artists," continues Jorgensen. "Time wasn't really a factor. As a result, Elvis had the luxury of being able to let things happen – to create the songs spontaneously."

Moving to Multitrack

Studio technology continued its rapid development through the 1950s. Working in conjunction with Les Paul and David Sarser early in the decade, Ampex brought multitrack recording into the marketplace with the introduction of its revolutionary 3-track tape machine. By 1955 Ampex had patented Sel-Sync, a mechanism that made it possible for an overdubbed part to be easily synchronized with a previous track.

Though most of the major studios bucked the multitrack trend, the more adventurous independent labels were intrigued. One such company was New York-based Atlantic Records, whose visionary young engineer, Tom Dowd, saw multitrack as a powerful tool and a most worthy investment. In the early 1950s Dowd began recording jazz sessions using both a mono machine and a 2-track recorder for back-up. This allowed Atlantic to compile a backlog of stereo material well before stereo had even hit the mass market. "When stereo came in," said Dowd years later, "while everyone else was making fake stereo, we already had the real thing."

Atlantic didn't stop there. In 1957 the label acquired (at considerable expense) an Ampex 8-track machine, making it the first in the business to have such recording capability.

Recording artists still went about the business of making records as they had for years, arriving well-rehearsed and cutting upward of ten songs or more in a matter of hours. The real difference was in the dramatically improved fidelity of the new equipment. Recording engineers quickly came of age, learning how to place the microphones around the room in order to capture the best dynamics of a studio performance.

The results of their efforts were stunning. Scratchy 78s from the 1940s were replaced by such albums as Sinatra's *Songs For Swingin' Lovers*, with a sound that was almost like being inside Capitol's Studio A during the actual performance. The life-like quality of the vinyl LP lit a fire under the careers of crooners like Ella Fitzgerald, Nat 'King' Cole, Johnny Mathis, and many others, creating a pop-vocal explosion that would last well into the 1960s.

The advanced sound quality of the LP set the stage for an unprecedented hi-fi boom. Acoustic Research developed its famed AR-1 speaker, which, in tandem with the Dynakit power amplifier, became one of the top sellers in home audio. Variable-groove recording made its debut, increasing the music capacity of the LP. The mastering process evolved: multiple 'mother' positive disks, cut from the original negative master, were used to make 'stampers,' each one capable of producing copies of an LP, further streamlining the production process.

The record industry was more than happy to cash in on the audiophile market. Since recording artists were typically capable of recording an entire album's worth of material in a single day, labels could expect multiple products by a hit performer during the course of a year. By the mid 1950s, album sales were brisk.

The Tommy Steele Story Tommy Steele

Not issued in U.S.A. / Decca LF 1288 (U.K.)
Released June 1957

It didn't take long for Britain's first home-grown rock'n'roll star to steer into the middle of the road. Tommy Steele, a former seaman, had encountered American music on his travels, and, just as he entered his 20s, manager John Kennedy aimed him at the teen rock'n'roll market.

His first single, 'Rock With The Caveman,' saw him backed –

uncredited – by top British jazzman Ronnie Scott. However, it was when he reached Number One in the U.K. with 'Singing The Blues' in early 1957 that he became a household name. Immediately following this plans were announced for a movie – the low-budget, semi-factual *The Tommy Steele Story* (aka *Rock Around The World*) – based on the life story of the former Tommy Hicks. The album of the same name hit the top in July.

The movie, shot in black and white and running to a scant 82 minutes, also featured jazzman Humphrey Lyttleton, The Chas McDevitt Skiffle Group, The Tommy Steele Calypso Band, and Chris O'Brien's Caribbeans, and took the story from Steele's supposed discovery in a coffee bar to the (then) present. Two tracks, 'Butterfingers' and 'Water Water,' became Top Ten singles, while this album and a book were perfectly timed tie-ins. But by the end of the year he was courting future wife Anne Donati and appearing in Christmas pantomime, leaving the British rock'n'roll stage to the likes of Cliff Richard and his fellow Larry Parnes protégé Marty Wilde.

Steele did score another Number One with the soundtrack to *The Duke Wore Jeans*, but by 1959 and *Tommy The Toreador* – with its novelty hit 'Little White Bull' – the world of musicals that has sustained his career ever since was already beckoning. Yet, despite the brevity of his rock'n'roll career, Steele did serve as a prototyoe for early British rockers.

Here's Little Richard Little Richard

Specialty 2100 (U.S.A.) / London HA-O 2055 (U.K.)
Released July 1957

Jerry Lee Lewis Jerry Lee Lewis

Sun 1230 (U.S.A.) / London HAS 2138 (U.K.)
Released December 1957

Rock And Rollin' With Fats Domino Fats Domino

Imperial 9004 (U.S.A.) / London HA-P 2041 (U.K.)
Released November 1955 / March 1957

While the electric guitar rather than the piano has generally been considered rock'n'roll's primary instrument, in their own very different ways, Little Richard, Jerry Lee Lewis, and Fats Domino all sought to overturn the stereotype.

Richard Wayne Penniman, otherwise known as Little Richard, grew up one of 13 children and emerged as an unashamed attention-seeker. Bursting on to the charts in 1956 with 'Tutti Frutti,' he appeared in such rock exploitation movies as *Don't Knock The Rock*, *The Girl Can't Help It*, and *Mister Rock'n'Roll* before quitting music to enroll in a Seventh Day Adventist college. This divide between rock and religion has continued to dog the God-fearing piano-thumper, as he has retired and returned many times during his career. His first album, *Here's Little Richard*, remains, however, a classic of its kind, produced by Bumps Blackwell in New Orleans and containing two bona fide U.S. Top Ten hits in 'Long Tall Sally' and 'Jenny, Jenny.'

made his name and inspired the 1989 movie, *Great Balls Of Fire*, was essentially the 18 months from early 1957 to mid 1958, of which this album is a snapshot.

If Lewis blazed brightly but briefly, New Orleans native Antoine 'Fats' Domino's first LP, *Rock And Rollin' With Fats Domino* – originally released as *Carry On Rockin'* – took its time to chart, being the third of his albums to grace the Billboard listings in 1957 once retitled and reissued. The catalyst was a string of his singles, and 'Ain't That A Shame' from this album not only made the Top Ten back home but gave him his third U.K. hit. He received sterling support from drummer Cornelius Coleman and guitarist Walter Nelson, but it was Domino's bejeweled fingers caressing those trademark piano triplets, combined with his rich, slightly melancholy vocal, that provided the hooks.

Purists say Domino cut his crucial material prior to his commercial breakthrough, which, by that reckoning, makes this album the last of the best. And even when the hits dried up – and with at least 22 million-selling singles there were many – Domino continued to tour into the 1990s to a loyal worldwide audience.

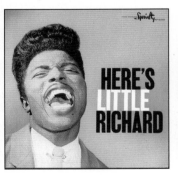

Jerry Lee Lewis, The Killer, was another artist from the Sun Records' stable from which Elvis had prematurely bolted. But, within a year of his eponymous debut album, Lewis's career was already on the slide thanks to publicity surrounding his bigamous marriage to a 13 year-old second cousin. Prior to that, his impact, thanks to television appearances on the *Steve Allen Show*, had been of Presley-esque proportions, surmounting the piano – often literally – to push debut single 'Whole Lotta Shakin' Goin' On' to the U.S. Number Three spot in the summer of 1957.

His second album, *Volume 2*, made the U.K. Top 20, but the impact was already waning. He would rise again later in the 1960s as a country singer, with a more world-weary, less physical stance than the wildman heard in the decade that gave birth to rock'n'roll. The amazingly short period that

1958

Things Are Swingin' Peggy Lee

Capitol 1049 (U.S.A.) / T1049 (U.K.)
Released October 1958 (U.S.A.) / January 1959 (U.K.)

This was the fourth U.S. Top 20 album for Peggy Lee and it ranks alongside similarly themed albums released by Capitol label mates Frank Sinatra (*Songs For Swingin' Lovers*) and Dean Martin (*This Time I'm Swingin'*).

Lee – born Norma Delores Egstrom in Jamestown, North Dakota, in 1920 – had enjoyed two decades in the business before her definitive version of 'Fever,' previously a hit for Little Willie John, brought worldwide renown in 1958. Lee added her own lyrics to the first couple of verses and supplied the arrangement. The album exhibits the classic, warm 1950s-era Capitol stereo sound with the exception of 'You Don't Know' and 'Fever,' both recorded in mono because of technical problems.

As well as 'It's a Wonderful World,' 'It's Been A Long, Long Time,' 'Life Is For Livin',' and 'Fever,' the album includes two self-penned numbers: the title track and 'It's A Good, Good Night,' both of which compare well with the aforementioned tunes.

Peggy Lee's last hit record came in 1969, when 'Is That All There Is?' made it to the U.S. Top 40, but her albums still sell in healthy numbers. The following year saw her star in the show *Side By Side By Sondheim*, which she clearly enjoyed – and, being a musical institution, she was able to pick and choose her projects. By the time of her death in 2002, her continued popularity had long been assured, and her passing was mourned by millions throughout the world.

1958

South Pacific (Original Soundtrack)

RCA Victor 1032 (U.S.A.) / RB16065 (U.K.)
Released March 1958

West Side Story (Original Soundtrack)

Columbia 2070 (U.S.A.) / CBS 4676061 (U.K.)
Released October 1961

These two movie soundtracks topped the U.S. charts nearly four years apart, confirming the enduring appeal of the American musical.

Interestingly, the original Broadway cast album of *West Side Story* had been released simultaneously with the *South Pacific* soundtrack, but only when the show became a movie itself did the cash registers start ringing. *South Pacific* was the work of Richard Rodgers and Oscar Hammerstein II, the most successful partnership in the history of Broadway musicals. Composer Rodgers and librettist Hammerstein had both worked successfully with others, but the impact of this and their other hit shows – *Carousel*, *The King And I*, and *The Sound Of Music*, for example – was such that few now think of one without the other.

The pair of New Yorkers had scored their first hit with *Oklahoma!* in 1943, and *South Pacific* – based on a novel, *Tales Of The South Pacific*, by James A. Michener – opened on Broadway six years later with the largest advance ticket sales ever registered. The tale of a U.S. Navy nurse and a suave French planter thrown together in wartime made such an impact that it won the Pulitzer Prize for Drama – the first musical ever to achieve the honor. The main protagonists' slow-starting romance is paralleled by a tragic inter-racial liaison between a young American lieutenant and an island girl, which ends in the former's death, so adding an extra dimension to the story.

The role of Frenchman Emile de Becque had been written by Rodgers specifically for opera star Ezio Pinza, who starred opposite Mary Martin in the Broadway production, but in the movie it is played by Rossano Brazzi. Mitzi Gaynor beat Doris Day, Elizabeth Taylor, and Audrey Hepburn to the role of Nellie Forbush, the woman who falls for him on 'Some Enchanted Evening.' On the soundtrack only Gaynor did her own singing, the remainder of the cast being voiced by others, with opera singer Giorgio Tozzi singing the male lead. The orchestra was conducted by longtime Rodgers & Hammerstein associate Alfred Newman. Movie-goers enjoyed the bonus of 'My Girl Back Home,' a number cut from the stage production for time reasons but restored to the score here. Extensive location shooting led to the decision to record the soundtrack at the 20th Century-Fox sound stage in Hollywood before shooting began. This meant that, while performers could lip-synch to the recording, it did lead to some rather wooden performances.

South Pacific had followed the successful *Oklahoma!* on to the big screen, and its setting on the Hawaiian island of Kauai, combined with the new Todd-AO 65mm process, which offered previously unseen clarity, made it an immediate winner. Director Joshua Logan's casting was panned by critics, however, who also slated the movie for its length (170 minutes) and the over-use of colored filters. But songs such as 'Bali Ha'i,' 'I'm Gonna Wash That Man Right Out Of My Hair,' and 'Happy Talk' – which became an unlikely U.K. Number One in 1982 in the hands of Captain Sensible from punk band The Damned – certainly stand the test of time. Besides, the public voted with their wallets and made it Number One. And when it did so, the original cast recording, having already notched up an incredible 208 chart weeks, followed it up to Number Two to make an amazing double. In Britain, the soundtrack topped the charts in May 1958, clocking up 313 weeks on the listings.

The appeal of *West Side Story* lies in the way it integrates song, dance, and narrative, showing how the movie musical could still be relevant in a new decade. The combination of young, thrusting lyricist Stephen Sondheim and seasoned composer Leonard Bernstein was perfect. The music was almost entirely a joint venture, with only the themes of 'Maria' and 'Cool' pre-dating their collaboration. Work began in autumn 1955 and was completed in the summer of 1957, Bernstein having taken a six-month sabbatical in the middle to work on *Candide*.

By updating Shakespeare's *Romeo And Juliet* and transplanting it to a big-city New York setting, Sondheim and Bernstein were eventually rewarded, despite the relatively moderate success of the original stage show, with a movie soundtrack album that broke all records with a 54-week residency at Number One in the U.S. and 175 chart weeks in Britain, where it also made the top spot. The movie itself received 11 Academy Award nominations and won ten Oscars – only two other movies, *Ben-Hur* (1959) and *Titanic* (1997), have earned more – including Best Picture, Best Supporting Actor (George Chakaris), Best Supporting Actress (Rita Moreno), and Best Direction (Robert Wise and Jerome Robbins). Robbins had also choreographed the work for the stage show, and co-director Wise would go on to mastermind another big-budget musical, *The Sound Of Music*, in 1965.

All the voices bar that of Russ Tamblyn (Riff) were dubbed by other singers, notably Marni Nixon (Maria), Jim Bryan (Tony), and Betty Ward (Anita). Individual songs, such as 'Maria' and 'Tonight,' picked up pop covers from artists as diverse as P.J. Proby, Johnny Mathis, and Shirley Bassey, while some six years later, at the height of the Vietnam War, British rock group The Nice used 'America' as the soundtrack to torching the Stars and Stripes on stage, much to Bernstein's displeasure.

It was the fact that the gangs represented racial groupings – The Jets white teenagers and The Sharks Puerto Ricans – that gave *West Side Story* an added contemporary dimension. Natalie Wood didn't convince everybody as Latina heroine Maria who falls for Tony, but it emerged as a powerful modern parable that would show the way for the likes of Bob Fosse's *Sweet Charity* and *Cabaret*.

The belated success of *West Side Story* certainly proved the power of the big screen to change people's perceptions. "Suddenly everyone could hum everything," said a bemused Sondheim of a show many critics had initially decried for not possessing memorable melodies. The *joie de vivre* seen here would inspire the likes of *Fame* in the following decade.

■ *Main picture: Russ Tamblyn (Riff) in* West Side Story. *Left: Mitzi Gaynor washes that man right out of her hair in* South Pacific.

1958

Johnny's Greatest Hits Johnny Mathis

Columbia 8634 (U.S.A.) / Fontana 1STP (U.K.)
Released March 1958

Fans of Johnny Mathis clearly couldn't get enough of the suave San Franciscan, and this, the first greatest-hits album of the pop era, proved it.

The brainchild of Columbia Records A&R director, Mitch Miller, it gave new life to such hit singles as 'It's Not For Me To Say,' 'Chances Are,' and 'The Twelfth Of Never,' and, crucially, bought Mathis time to record a new album. The music owes much to the work of arranger Ray Conniff, a big-selling orchestra leader in his own right, whose work on the likes of 'Wonderful! Wonderful!' and 'When Sunny Gets Blue' had been accomplished with a maximum of ten musicians in a de-consecrated church in New York.

The result was a Number One album that stayed on the *Billboard* listings for just two and a half months short of 500 weeks – a record for longevity it would take something of the magnitude of Pink Floyd's 1973 release, *Dark Side Of The Moon*, to eclipse. By the time Mathis topped the U.S. albums chart again in 1959 with a collection of standards and show tunes, Columbia had already released *More Johnny's Greatest Hits*, which attained a highly respectable Number Two. He'd go on to register 26 Top 40 albums by the end of the 1970s – at which point his chart career began to slow up, though he continues to record new material and release albums to this day – including three more greatest-hits-style compilations. A profitable format was born.

One Dozen Berrys Chuck Berry

Chess LP-1432 (U.S.A.) / London HAM 2132 (U.K.)
Released March 1958

While primarily considered a singles artist, Chuck Berry also turned out albums on a regular basis.

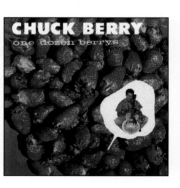

His sole U.S. Top Ten LP came as late as 1973 with the all-star *London Sessions*. His other two Top 40 albums were a live set and a hits collection, underlining the fact that his self-contained three-minute story-songs, powered by trademark Gibson guitar riffing, were ideal for being spread over two sides of seven-inch plastic.

Indeed, this, his second full-length Chess album – and the first to be released in the U.K. – contains a number of tracks previously issued as singles, both a- and b-sides. These were 'Oh Baby Doll' b/w 'La Juanda' (June 1957), 'Rock And Roll Music' b/w 'Blue Feeling' (September 1957), and the million-selling 'Sweet Little Sixteen' b/w 'Reelin' And Rockin'' (January 1958). 'La Juanda' appears in a different mix from the single release, while, in a labor-saving tactic, 'Blue Feeling' is on the album twice, in its original form and at half speed, entitled 'Low Feeling.'

Berry would record at Chess Studios in Chicago in batches between concert dates, having taken the decision to discard his touring band in favor of picking up local backing musicians from town to town. The resulting transportation and wage savings meant he could afford to fly, but a valuable by-product was that, by giving Berry the opportunity to rehearse with new musicians, he was given the musical inspiration for new compositions. Other songs, he later admitted in his autobiography, were attempts to clone his successes, as with 'Oh Baby Doll,' which was a self-confessed rewrite of early hit 'School Day.'

The visual content of his writing was striking. 'Reelin' And Rockin'' was inspired by seeing bluesman Big Joe Turner through the window of a Chicago club to which Berry, then 16, was too young to be admitted. 'Sweet Little Sixteen,' on the other hand, was his retelling of an occasion, backstage at a gig at the Ottawa Coliseum, when he observed a young female fan intent on getting the autograph of Paul Anka. Berry's observational qualities and ability to sum up the spirit of youth in a few well-turned words or phrases are his much-imitated calling cards.

One Dozen Berrys contained the new songs 'Guitar Boogie,' 'In-Go,' 'Rock At The Philharmonic,' 'It Don't Take But A Few Minutes,' and 'How You've Changed.' Life would change for him a couple of years later, after a conviction for transporting a minor across a state line for immoral purposes led to him spending 1962 and 1963 in prison.

But even if Leonard Chess hadn't stockpiled material to release in order to keep Berry's name fresh in record buyers' minds, his influence would still have been undiminished. As proof, tracks on this album alone attracted covers by, among others, The Beach Boys, The Beatles, and The Rolling Stones – not a bad fan club.

Sam Cooke **Sam Cooke**

Keen A-2001 (U.S.A.) / HMV CLP1261 (U.K.)
Released March 1958

Sam Cooke was one of the most important early figures in the creation and development of what we now know as soul music, and Otis Redding and Marvin Gaye were among his earliest disciples.

Sam Cooke, the singer's first totally secular album, was cut for Bob Keene's Keen label and not for Specialty, with whom Cooke had been signed as a gospel artist. His aim was to flee his musical roots and cross over into the popular market, but this was blocked by Specialty, as it would lose him the following he had won while singer with The Soul Stirrers. The minister's son had created waves since replacing R.H. Harris as their lead singer, but label boss Art Rupe was opposed to his first ventures away from gospel under the name of Dale Cook.

Orchestra leader Bumps Blackwell, who gets a credit on the sleeve, was instrumental in the switch. He struck a deal with Rupe to forego any future royalties for his work with Little Richard – Blackwell had production credits on many of Richard's biggest early hits – in order to take Cooke away and sign to Keen. He'd been impressed by a Soul Stirrers' gospel show at the Shrine Auditorium in Los Angeles and had seen the potential immediately. "My initial impression was 'This cat should be pop,'" he told Cooke's biographer Daniel Wolff. "That was just too much voice to be in such a limited market."

After initial attempts to cut pop material at J&M Studio in New Orleans proved unsuccessful, the scene shifted to Los Angeles in 1957. Blackwell wisely attempted to meld blues chord structures with teen-centered lyrics "because white girls are buying records these days." White vocal trio The Pied Pipers were recruited to add background sweetening, and an early result, 'You Send Me,' sold 1.7 million copies when backed with

'Summertime' on a January 1957 single. It topped the U.S. chart and made the U.K. Top 30.

Cooke's eponymous album, released that March, was arguably overloaded with familiar ballads, such as 'Ol' Man River,' 'Moonlight In Vermont,' and 'Danny Boy,' not to mention interpretations of such jazz standards as 'Ain't Misbehavin'' and 'That Lucky Old Sun,' but, nevertheless, it reached Number 16 in March 1958.

In the light of his being forced to record material he felt inappropriate, as well as an ill-starred Copacabana concert in which he was obliged to dress in a suit with tails, Cooke decided to rebel against Blackwell's aim to capture a white audience. They split after a second Keen album, *Encore*, and, by early 1960, Cooke was recording for RCA – who paid a $100,000 transfer fee – with producers Hugo and Luigi.

But Cooke's complicated private life, which included losing his first wife in an auto accident in 1959, led to his fatal shooting in 1964 after an unsavory motel incident with sexual overtones. Some 200,000 fans paid their respects at two memorial services, but the true legacy of Sam Cooke was in those he inspired. Otis Redding, another soul legend to meet an untimely end, covered 'Shake' and used it to make the breakthrough to a white audience on his own terms that Cooke would surely have achieved had he lived. 'You Send Me' alone has been covered by artists as diverse as Steve Miller, Rod Stewart, and Aretha Franklin, while The Rolling Stones, Bryan Ferry, and Cat Stevens are others to dip into his songbook.

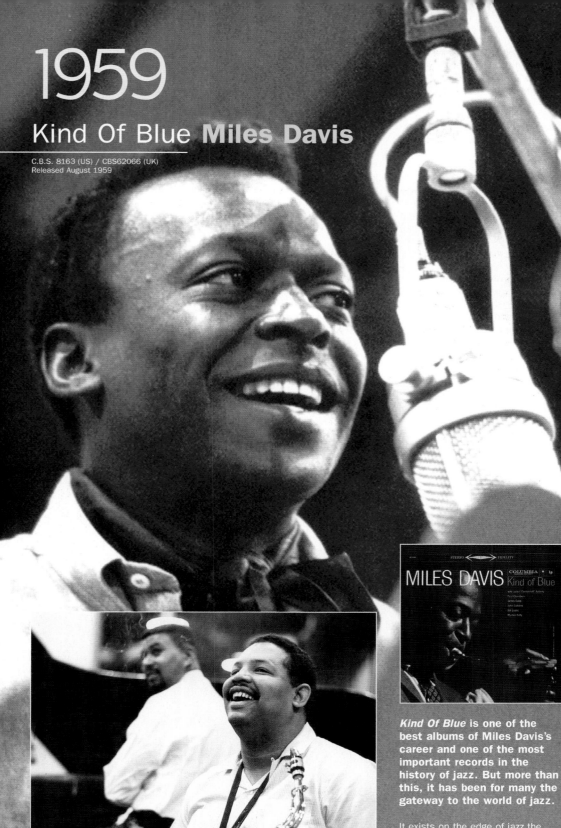

1959

Kind Of Blue **Miles Davis**

C.B.S. 8163 (US) / CBS62066 (UK)
Released August 1959

■ *Main Picture: A rare smile from Miles Davis. Left: Alto-sax player 'Cannonball' Adderley. Right: Davis takes a breather as John Coltrane (left), Adderley, and pianist Bill Evans play on.*

Kind Of Blue is one of the best albums of Miles Davis's career and one of the most important records in the history of jazz. But more than this, it has been for many the gateway to the world of jazz.

It exists on the edge of jazz the way the Statue of Liberty stands before the promise of New York City and the U.S.A. itself, holding a beacon up to the musically hungry, offering solace to fatigued ears, hearts, and minds. For 40 years it has sold largely by word-of-mouth, finding a home even in record collections that are otherwise jazz-free. Its appeal is international, and in the last decade it has actually increased its sales rate, now past five million.

Like many famous albums, *Kind Of Blue* has a legend attached: that its five tracks were cut in two days and improvised on the spot. This is not quite true, but not far off. Recording began on March 2nd 1959 at Columbia's 30th Street Studio in New York. Now demolished, the studio was a big space, a hundred feet square with high ceilings; it could hold a symphony orchestra and classical recordings were often made there. Engineers and musicians valued its reverberant sound, resulting from the natural wooden surfaces. The five musicians who assembled

there were a jazz supergroup: Miles Davis on trumpet, Julian 'Cannonball' Adderley on alto sax, John Coltrane on tenor sax, Bill Evans on piano – replaced on one track by Wynton Kelly – Paul Chambers on upright bass, and Jimmy Cobb on drums. The producer was Irving Townsend.

The first session ran from 2.30pm to 5.30pm, followed by a second from 7.00pm until 11.00pm. *Kind Of Blue* is marked by restraint and a brooding thoughtfulness. Davis was exploring a new style, 'modal jazz,' which used scales other than the common major and minor. The emphasis was to be on the improvisation of lines of single notes. Solos became more important and could be longer. Tempos got slower to accommodate this melodic soloing. The complex chords and rapid changes of earlier jazz were to be simplified. Davis told the *Jazz Review* in 1958: "Guys give me tunes and they're full of chords. I can't play them . . . I think a movement in jazz is beginning away from the conventional string of chords, and a return to emphasis on melodic rather than harmonic variation. There will be fewer chords but infinite possibilities as to what to do with them."

Bill Evans's sleevenotes made a fashionable connection with a type of Japanese art in which the artist must paint spontaneously. This fixed the notion that the whole album had been created from nothing and chimed with the Beat Generation's interest in Zen. In fact, 'All Blues' and 'So What' had been played live a couple of times. Though all the music is credited to Miles Davis this has been disputed: it has been argued that Bill Evans sketched out 'Blue In Green' and co-wrote 'Flamenco Sketches.' But composition in this sense only means basic ideas and structure. Where the players did have written directions they amounted to no more than a few notes and scales on paper. Davis wanted spontaneity in the playing. He didn't want to rehearse the tunes. On occasion, instructions as to who was to solo next were given during the recording itself. So, in this sense, the legend of *Kind Of Blue*'s spontaneous creation has a kind of truth.

The March 2nd session started with 'Freddie Freeloader,' a 12-bar blues-based structure to ease the musicians in, and the only track with Wynton Kelly playing piano instead of Evans. They did three aborted takes before the fourth and final run through nailed it. The recording was done on a state-of-the-art 3-track tape. A small amount of echo was added to the mix in addition to the studio's natural reverb, which can be heard in the middle of the stereo image if you listen on headphones.

The second track to be recorded is the album's most famous, 'So What,' named after a favorite dismissive term of Davis's. 'So What' gives the album its beguiling introduction, with an atmospheric passage for piano and bass in a free rhythm. Unexpectedly, this colorful section gives way to a two-chord riff, one that musically sounds like the 'So What' of the title. There is a neat call-and-answer idea between the bass and the other instruments. Miles Davis said the inspiration for the music came from two sources. One was the African folk rhythms and timings he had recently heard when watching the Ballet Africaine perform. The second was American church music, recalled from childhood when he lived on his grandfather's farm: "I added some other kind of sound I remembered from being back in Arkansas, when we were walking home from church and they were playing these bad gospels. That feeling is what I was trying to get close to . . . six years old, walking with my cousin along that dark Arkansas road." A complete fourth take did the business. The first day's recording was completed with the delicate ten-bar sequence of 'Blue In Green.' The solos are provided by trumpet, piano, and tenor saxophone, with Adderley sitting out.

Kind Of Blue's second session took place on the afternoon of Wednesday April 22nd. The first track recorded that afternoon was 'Flamenco Sketches.' The bass pattern had been played by Evans in a song called 'Peace Piece' on the album *Everybody Digs Bill Evans* earlier that year. The five scales that form the basis of 'Flamenco Sketches' had been worked out

Continued on next page

■ *Main Picture: Davis and pianist Bill Evans step back to discuss the recordings. Below: Davis advises Evans while bassist Paul Chambers looks on. Right: John Coltrane in contemplative mood.*

on the morning of the first session in March, when Evans went to Davis's apartment. It got its name because one of the scales – the Phrygian – has a Spanish flavor and is often heard in flamenco music. The first take was complete and became the only one that wasn't used from the entire sessions. (It has been added to the most recent CD edition of the album.) The finished second take took another five more tries, culminating in a complete take six. The Spanish feel of 'Flamenco Sketches' later bore fruit in Davis's 1964 album, *Sketches Of Spain*. After the concentrated effort of 'Flamenco Sketches,' the ensemble recorded the bouncy 'All Blues.'

The album was released on August 17th 1959, with a cover shot of Davis taken at the Apollo Theater that further cemented the importance of the trumpeter as an African-American hero. The album sold steadily, and within about a year student jazz bands were doing covers of its tunes. It found a crossover audience and influenced many musicians throughout the 1960s.

During the 1990s it was discovered that a motor problem on the recording machine had caused the tape to run a fraction slower than it should have during the March session. Consequently, the playback was slightly faster than actual time, and for over 30 years the world had heard three of *Kind Of Blue*'s tracks not as they were played. The current CD version has the tracks at the right speed and pitch. If you don't know *Kind Of Blue*, take the advice of San Francisco columnist C. H. Garrigues: "Buy it and play it, quietly, around midnight . . ."

1959

Elvis' Golden Records Elvis Presley

RCA LPM 1707 (U.S.A.) / RB 16069 (U.K.)
Released April 1958

50,000,000 Elvis Fans Can't Be Wrong: Elvis' Golden Records Vol.2
Elvis Presley

RCA LPM 2075 (U.S.A.) / RD 27159 (U.K.)
Released December 1959

Fourteen million-selling singles, seven of which were chart toppers, made *Elvis' Golden Records* a greatest-hits compilation by anyone's definition.

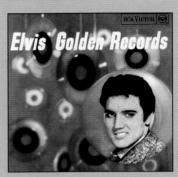 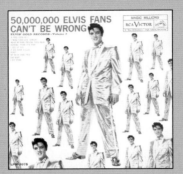

Eschewing the early Sun releases, the album kicks off with the seminal 'Heartbreak Hotel' and ends with 'Jailhouse Rock,' which had topped the U.S. charts earlier in 1958. Other Number Ones include 'I Want You I Need You I Love You,' 'Don't Be Cruel,' 'Hound Dog,' 'Too Much,' and 'All Shook Up.'

Maybe the Christmas album that had preceded it had made fans feel they were buying less essential material, as *Elvis' Golden Records* entered *Billboard*'s album listings at a modest Number Nine. It rose only six places further, though it enjoyed a further 23 chart weeks after the singer's death in 1977 to add to an initial 40, and has five times gone platinum. (Curiously, British release was on RCA's classical imprint, Red Seal.)

'Wear My Ring Around Your Neck' was a result of Elvis's last studio session before being drafted into the U.S. Army, but he managed to sneak into the studio again in Nashville in June to provide more product to be released as singles. It was clear, however, that the goose was laying fewer golden eggs, and an album of b-sides and EP tracks, *For LP Fans Only*, was cobbled together as a spring 1959 stopgap.

The second volume of *Golden Records*, *50,000,000 Elvis Fans Can't Be Wrong*, emerged just in time for Christmas 1959, and boasted an eye-catching image of Presley in a gold lamé suit. It is, inevitably, a slighter collection than its predecessor, with just five singles released since early 1958 with their b-sides padding out the tracklist. The movie theme 'King Creole' (unreleased as a single in the U.S. but a big British hit) is a surprise omission, but the singles, including two Number One hits – 'Don't' and 'A Big Hunk O'Love' – were all genuine million-sellers. 'Hunk' and its b-side, 'My Wish Come True,' would be the last of the June 1958 Nashville recordings to make it to single, manager Colonel Tom Parker putting the brakes on and hoping thereby to create a demand for new product to coincide with Elvis's March 1960 demobilization.

Reflecting the fact, perhaps, that Presleymania had subsided somewhat during his years in the Army, this second hits collection peaked at a modest Number 31 and would take until 1966 to exceed a million dollars' sales; *Golden Records*, on the other hand, was so certified in 1961. In Britain, however, it reached Number Four in mid 1960, thus setting the pattern of greater European chart success than in Presley's native country that would continue until his death. Subsequent compilation albums have proved even more of a moneymaking phenomenon, and still rarely a year passes without a 'new' title charting in Britain and/or the U.S.A., while 2002's *Elv1s 30 #1 Hits* topped the U.K. charts on the 25th anniversary of his passing.

The Birth Of Stereo

Record companies seemed to have learned from the 'war of the speeds' debacle, at least in the short term. So when stereo came along, a standard was agreed before marketing began.

Attempts to provide a spacial dimension to sound were, of course, nothing new. In 1881, in Paris, Clément Ader, an eccentric inventor and pioneer of aviation, demonstrated a system called the Théâtrophone, which transmitted the sound from a series of microphones in front of the stage at the Paris Opéra to listeners at the International Electrical Exhibition. Because listeners used two earpieces and because the microphones were spaced, a kind of stereophony was the result. Ader went on to market the system commercially as a wired predecessor of wireless.

In the 1920s new understanding of the mechanisms of hearing brought the first two-eared hearing aids and, as a spin-off, further experimentation with multichannel sound. But what we know today as stereo was really invented, and patented, by the EMI engineer Alan Blumlein in 1931. Frustrated by the way sound failed to follow the characters on the movie screen, he began thinking of practical ways of adding a directional element to recorded sound. He also tried to persuade his EMI bosses that stereo – or 'binaural,' as he called it – would breathe life into the good but flat recordings then being made.

> ### "EVERYONE SAT DOWN, SCRATCHED THEIR COLLECTIVE HEADS, AND ASKED, 'WHAT SHALL WE CALL THIS NEW SOUND?' FINALLY OUR PR PEOPLE TOOK THE HINT WHEN WE SAID IT REPRESENTED A LIFE-LIKE EXPERIENCE, AND SETTLED ON 'LIVING STEREO.'"
> ### *PRODUCER JACK PFEIFFER ON RCA'S 1950S TECHNOLOGY*

In his patent he created a theoretical stereo recording chain, from microphone placement to disk cutting, but was not able to carry it all out in practice before being moved by EMI first to television and then to war work. Nonetheless, right through 1932 and 1933, EMI allowed him to build microphones, circuitry, and a stereo disk-cutting lathe and experiment with them.

In 1934 his whole kit was moved to EMI's new studios at Abbey Road, in London. In the room later made famous by The Beatles, Blumlein made his first stereo music recording, two tracks by Ray Noble's Dance Band. Finally, on January 19th 1934, Blumlein recorded a rehearsal of Mozart's 'Symphony No. 41,' conducted by Sir Thomas Beecham. Then he moved on to his real interest, stereo movie soundtracks, which he pursued until ordered to move on to EMI's electronic television system, then still locked in battle with John Logie Baird's mechanical system.

Blumlein's original stereo patent expired in 1947, five years after his death in an airplane crash while testing an airborne radar system. It was extended for five years, and then expired altogether. EMI never used his work commercially, not taking an interest in stereo again until its arch-rival Decca came up with a system in 1955.

In the meantime, Bell Laboratories in the U.S.A. had in 1931 begun working with the great conductor Leopold Stokowski, who was unhappy with the recorded sound he was getting with his Philadelphia Orchestra. A new cutting lathe was developed and then, in March 1932, two years before Blumlein's experiments, a stereo recording of Scriabin's 'Poem Of Fire' was produced, using two separate grooves on the same wax disk. Two styli and cartridges were required to play it back.

This was obviously not the way forward, however, though public demonstrations of stereo continued throughout the 1930s and work on multichannel sound didn't stop. Disney, with *Fantasia*, and the new Cinerama and Cinemascope

Continued on page 38

1959

Exotica Vol. 1 **Martin Denny**

Liberty 3034 (U.S.A.) / London SAHW 6062 (U.K.)
Released April 1959

Exotica Vol. 2 **Martin Denny**

Liberty LST 7034 (U.S.A.) / London SAHW 6076 (U.K.)
Released July 1959

While the name Martin Denny means little in Britain, the classically trained pianist's musical recipe, an "exotic fruit salad," titillated America's taste-buds to such an extent that 1959 saw him score a Number One album in *Exotica* and a Number Two single in lead track 'Quiet Village.'

A job as a bar pianist in Hawaii in 1954 led to Denny forming a quartet, and the response to his music, which contained Polynesian and Asian influences – as *Mojo* magazine put it in 1995: "Hawaiian melodies, Latin rhythms and all-American sentiments" – was immediate and positive.

Les Baxter – another pianist, arranger, and composer, who had been working in a similar field for most of the decade, and who is the true founding father of the genre that became known as exotica – contributed three tracks, 'Quiet Village,' 'Stone God,' and 'The Love Dance.'

The record, cut at Honolulu's Webley Edwards studio, cost well under a thousand dollars to make. Since spoof bird calls, improvised by musicians Arthur Lyman (vibes), Augie Colon (percussion), and John Kramer (double bass), had proved a surprise hit in concert, they reprised these in the studio, while frog noises were generated by Denny using a grooved percussion instrument. The album was recorded twice: the 1956 mono version featuring Arthur Lyman, and the stereo his replacement, Julius Wechter.

Denny's early releases were lavished with near-unanimous critical acclaim. The *Seatle Times* proclaimed Denny, somewhat ironically, to be "just what the doctor ordered to banish the Presleys and [Rick] Nelsons from teenagers affections." The *San Francisco Examiner*, meanwhile, heaped praise on "the most exciting group of musicians I have ever heard."

In the wake of this initial success Denny recorded no fewer than 36 further albums of "exotic mood music" for Liberty, rejoicing in such titles as *Primitiva*, *Hypnotique*, and *Romantica*. Many featured model Sandy Warner on the cover, underlining the genre's label as "bachelor-pad music," while the mid 1960s saw Denny's work percolate into ballet as well as being used as background music in locations as disparate as restaurants and massage parlors.

In the 1990s Creation Records' Rev-Ola subsidiary put Denny's music back on the market in digital form, bolstering his cult status, while the Scamp label combined the first two volumes of *Exotica* on a 1997 CD.

In just a few years Buddy Holly inspired the formation of countless groups and provided them with songs to cover – and in the case of The Hollies a name. The Beatles' earliest recordings included a demo of 'That'll Be The Day,' and The Rolling Stones' first Top Ten hit was a version of 'Not Fade Away.' 'It's So Easy' certainly sounds like an anticipation of Merseybeat. Later movies and stage musicals have put Holly's music before the public again and supported a stream of compilations.

Have 'Twangy' Guitar Will Travel
Duane Eddy

Jamie LP 3000 (U.S.A.) / London HAW2160 (U.K.)
Released June 1959

In the late 1950s Duane Eddy's instrumental hits helped put the electric guitar at the very heart of popular music.

Eddy's trademark was 'twangy' guitar motifs and melodies played on the lower strings. The combination of metal strings, low pitched notes, and undistorted amplification created his signature sound, along with studio reverb and echo. The idea of making the electric guitar the focus of a recording was itself revolutionary.

Eddy once said: "My background was more country than pop. There are two types of guitar players, the players who have developed their skills to a point where they can play anything in any style, and me. I can't do that . . . I found a sound, the so-called twangy guitar sound, and I stayed with it."

Between 1958 and 1963 his releases were often in the Top 40. Among the most famous are 'Rebel Rouser' and 'Peter Gunn,' the latter a television series theme on which his guitar is joined by growling sax. 'Peter Gunn' was covered in 1986 by U.K. group Art Of Noise, an update that earned them a Grammy. One way or another, the Eddy sound was emulated by Eddie Cochran, The Ventures, The Shadows, and other instrumental groups. It fell from favor when The Beatles put the emphasis back on vocals, and amplifier distortion replaced twang as the definitive rock sound. One of the greatest homages to his work is the playing of Vic Flick on the James Bond soundtracks from 1962 onward.

The Buddy Holly Story **Buddy Holly**

Coral 57279 (U.S.A.) / 9105 (U.K.)
Released May 1959

Released three months after Holly's death in a plane crash on February 3rd 1959, T*he Buddy Holly Story* was an early example of the posthumous album achieving huge sales on the wave of public sympathy that follows a performer's untimely death. (Hank Williams's *Memorial Album*, 1955, was another.)

This was the first album of Holly material released after his death, and it stayed on the charts for three years. The crash at Clear Lake, Iowa, was later put into song by Don McLean as 'the day the music died' in his tribute song, 'American Pie.'

Buddy Holly's professional career lasted little more than two years. Born in Lubbock, Texas, in 1936, Holly recorded his first demos in 1954 and 1955, followed by others in Nashville in a rockabilly style as a solo artist for Decca. His first single was issued in July 1956. After his Decca contract was terminated because of a lack of commercial success, he went to Clovis, New Mexico, and met producer Norman Petty. With his new group, The Crickets, Holly re-recorded 'That'll Be The Day,' which became a Top Three single on both sides of the Atlantic in 1957, the first of a sequence of million-sellers. By late 1958 Holly was second only to Elvis in popularity.

Of the 12 tracks, 11 are mono, and the album lasts a mere 26 minutes. It opens appropriately with 'Raining In My Heart,' with its evocative pizzicato strings. 'Early In The Morning' is a gruffer, more forceful vocal than you expect from Holly. 'Peggy Sue' is memorable for its fast, distant drumming and Holly's trademark 'hiccup' vocal. The guitar solo required someone other than Holly – who, in order to maintain the rhythm, was unable to stop strumming to flick the pick-up switch – to kneel down in front of him to change the setting on his Stratocaster at the start and end of the solo, thus creating a striking change in tone and volume. Other hits from 1957 and 1958 were 'Maybe Baby,' 'Everyday,' with its slapped thigh rhythm and musical chimes, the rocking 'Rave On' and 'Think It Over,' the sarcastic 'That'll Be The Day,' with its famous blues guitar intro, the Latin-influenced 'Heartbeat,' and the high energy of 'Oh Boy!'

The album ends with Holly's first single of 1959, a cover of Paul Anka's 'It Really Doesn't Matter Anymore.' Its bittersweet resignation at the end of a relationship was inevitably heard after Holly's death as a deeper world-weariness, as though he were singing about parting from life. (Otis Redding's 'Dock Of The Bay' and Jimi Hendrix's 'Voodoo Chile' are two later singles whose lyrics were similarly recontextualized by their performers' deaths.) This track is in stereo and shows an expansion of Holly's original sound with smooth strings and harp glissandos.

Continued from page 36

systems explored multichannel systems in movies, for example, and in the early 1950s record companies began recording in stereo, but without a feasible stereo disk-playing system the commercial possibilities remained limited.

Research continued, and, in 1952, experimenter and audio engineer Amory Cook released binaural disks in which two entirely separate grooves were cut for left and right channels. Enthusiasts needed a record deck with two pickup cartridges alongside each other. It was extremely difficult to place the needles in the grooves accurately enough to get both channels to start together.

In 1957 three more refined systems were placed before the U.S. record industry: Decca's 'vertical-lateral' system, a system offered by Columbia, and a third devised by Westrex, manufacturers of record-cutting lathes.

Both Blumlein's and Keller's stereo experiments in the 1930s had used the side-to-side and up-and-down movements of the stylus in the groove to provide two channels. However, both had also – independently of one another – devised a much better system, in which the two channels were recorded on opposite sides of the V-shaped groove, though neither seems to have been able to make this '45/45 system' – so called because each channel is at that angle to the disk surface – work at the time, not least because of having to use shellac. The Westrex system – apparently devised in ignorance of Blumlein's patents (which had languished in EMI's vaults before expiring) as well as Keller's work – was another such 45/45 system. It had the great advantage of nominal compatibility with mono: two channels playing the same sound in phase produce a sideways movement that is reproduced on mono equipment as the two channels added together to make one sound.

For once the industry agreed on a common system – and the best system – and started planning a controlled transition to stereo, though not without the odd hiccup. A small company called Audio Fidelity sent some tapes to Westrex to have a master cut "for test purposes." One side contained various sound effects, with test tones, and the other was taken from a stereo tape recording of The Dukes Of Dixieland. To the annoyance of the entire industry, Audio Fidelity immediately put the disk on sale, purely so that it could claim to be the first. At that stage there was not even a commercially available stereo cartridge to play the record – but nonetheless it sold well.

Within a year of Westrex's first demonstration of the system, every significant company was offering stereo records. But the buyers were less enthusiastic. They needed something to convince them to make the expensive transition to stereo. For classical listeners, that came in the shape of Decca's record of Wagner's *Das Rheingold*, the beginning of the first complete recording of The Ring Cycle, and a tour de force of stereo sound and effects, produced by John Culshaw in London.

Meanwhile, the sensation for pop listeners was bandleader Enoch Light's *Persuasive Percussion*, which made great use of ping-pong directional effects. However, it would be a while before stereo settled down as a great boon for classical listeners and a new wave of hi-fi enthusiasts. By 1968 all classical records were being released in stereo.

For pop listeners, playing singles on small record-players, it was largely irrelevant, at least until the late 1960s and the rise of the album market. In 1969 EMI took the controversial decision to release The Beatles' *Abbey Road* LP in stereo only. This forced people at the very least to change their record-player cartridges, since, despite their theoretical compatibility, mono cartridges and styli very quickly destroyed stereo records.

1959

Film Encores **Mantovani**

London 1700 (U.S.A.) / SKL 4002 (U.K.)
Released April 1959

The dapper, Venice-born Annunzio Paolo Mantovani was one of the most successful orchestra leaders in history, with a career spanning six decades.

The son of a violinist who played at Milan's La Scala opera house under Toscanini, he followed his father's instrumental example, came to London at the age of 16, and, four years later, was conducting the Hotel Metropole's orchestra. Al Bowlly was just one of the famous singers with whom he worked. He scored U.S. hits in 1935 and 1936 with 'Red Sails In The Sunset' and 'Serenade In The Night.' After a spell as a musical director in London's West End, Mantovani turned his attention to the U.S.A. again in the 1950s.

His trademark 'cascading' strings sound, concocted with the assistance of arranger Ronnie Binge, was unveiled in 1950, when he revived the pre-World War I song 'Charmaine' to million-selling effect. This proved the key to further success, and, though he'd reprised his theatrical past with success for 1955's *Song Hits From Theatreland*, which took him into the *Billboard* Top Ten for the first time, the release that took him to the very top in July 1959 was this specially recorded movie-theme collection.

Decca Records, pioneers in the new technique of stereo recording, allowed Mantovani to choose the repertoire, and his selections clearly struck a chord with the public. *High Noon*, *My Foolish Heart*, *Intermezzo*, and *Three Coins In The Fountain* were all represented by their title themes, while 'Over The Rainbow' from *The Wizard Of Oz* and 1955 chart topper 'Unchained Melody' from *Unchained* were numbers everyone could sing.

Surprisingly, given his past singles success, none of the tracks were spun off as hits in their own right. But follow-up albums in very much the same vein, such as *Songs To Remember* (1960), kept the pot boiling, even if critics claimed any one album was indistinguishable from any other. The new medium of television helped Mantovani maintain his popularity, and his flamboyance at the podium was matched by a tendency to hold notes longer than his competitors. The former violinist is also said to have been the first million-selling stereo recording artist but, said his son Kenneth, he never regarded himself as a pop star. "He went off to work and played records – he had his job to do – but then came home just like any other father."

Mantovani's 40-piece orchestra continued to sell records worldwide despite ever-changing fads and fashions, fighting off competition from many similarly configured orchestras, notably that of Percy Faith. Though he was never to repeat the Number One success of *Film Encores*, the similarly titled *Continental Encores* gave Mantovani a U.K. chart album – the first of 11 – in the same year, 1959. Fifty-one albums charted in the U.S.A., mostly in the Top 50, and all – bar the score to 1964 Broadway hit *Kismet* – were instrumental. He died in Tunbridge Wells, Kent, in 1980, but his music and his orchestra play on.

1960

String Along **The Kingston Trio**

Capitol 1407 (U.S.A. & U.K.)
Released July 1960

Joan Baez *Joan Baez*

Vanguard VSD2077 (U.S.A.) / Fontana STFL6002 (U.K.)
Released October 1960

Folk was the youthful sound of the pre-beat early 1960s, and the Kingston Trio and Joan Baez were leading exponents.

String Along was The Trio's fifth studio album, and all had reached Number One. The three San Franciscan students – Dave Guard, Nick Reynolds, and Bob Shane – had moved on somewhat from their first album, which had been released just over two years earlier, by introducing 12-string guitar and exotic percussion to the mix, which led to comparisons with The Everly Brothers.

One song on the album, 'Bad Man's Blunder,' was recorded as an act of charity for one for the song's writers, Cisco Houston, who was hospitalized and facing large medical bills. Released as a single, it only made Number 37 and is even today classed by *Billboard* as a novelty number. The second single, 'Everglade,' fared even worse, peaking at Number 60, a far cry from their chart-topping days of 1958 when 'Tom Dooley' ruled the roost. Though they'd enjoy four more Top 40 entries in 1962 and 1963, The Trio's days as a chart act were numbered, something Guard's replacement by John Stewart could not reverse.

Joan Baez had hitched a lift on the Kingston Trio's coat-tails, along with Peter, Paul, and Mary, Judy Collins, and others. She enjoyed her first break in 1958 when performing as guest of Bob Gibson at the first *Newport Folk Festival*.

Signed by Vanguard Records, apparently because co-founder and producer Maynard Soloman was an idealist like herself, she released her first, eponymous album in November 1960, but would later gain in notoriety thanks to a personal association with Bob Dylan and a link with the protest movement, particularly her work in mobilizing public opinion against U.S. involvement in the Vietnam War. Her breakthrough in Britain came in 1965 when she played the Royal Albert Hall, and her fifth album, issued hard on the heels of single 'We Shall Overcome,' breached the Top Three, while *Joan Baez* finally made it into the UK chart at Number Nine.

This first album, which Baez recorded at the age of 19, was cut in a New York hotel bedroom and relied upon traditional folk standards – many, like 'Silver Dagger' and 'Mary Hamilton,' from Scotland – and included such staples as 'House Of The Rising Sun,' the spiritual 'All My Trials,' and the Spanish political song, 'El Preso Numero Nuevo.' Simplicity and sincerity were the keywords, both musically and lyrically, and Solomon had to work hard to convince Baez to employ another musician, guitarist Fred Hellerman, to fill out her sound.

Baez would record 16 more albums for Vanguard before signing with A&M in the 1970s. If she'd made the move to a major label earlier or become Dylan's labelmate on CBS she might have done even better even quicker, but by giving folk the kind of sex appeal the likes of The Kingston Trio lacked she did the genre a great service.

1960

Unforgettable **Dinah Washington**

Mercury 20572 (U.S.A.) / MMC14048 (U.K.)
Released February 1960

The trade papers called her 'Queen Of The Jukeboxes,' while she herself preferred 'Queen of the Blues.' What's certain is that Dinah Washington brought her bluesy delivery to the jazz world until her untimely death at the age of just 39, three years after this release.

Born Ruth Lee Jones in Tuscaloosa, Alabama, in 1924, Washington lived life to the full, marrying no fewer than seven times and showing a partiality to drink, but this became part of the appeal of a performer who demanded fans accept her just as she was. It certainly gave her the emotional armory to invest every song on this ballad-heavy album with the necessary gravitas. As one critic put it: "Nearly all the tunes are ballads, and they're all about loneliness, about women wronged, and yet always hoping for that good man to come to whom they can offer their great gift: complete devotion." 'Unforgettable' itself is, of course, the Nat King Cole classic, and it's a measure of Washington's self-belief that she thought she could put her own stamp on such a song.

Washington had first crossed to the pop chart in 1950 with a sensual reading of 'I Wanna Be Loved,' and her audience grew from the black record-buying public to a much wider market. 'What A Difference A Day Makes' and duets with fellow Mercury artist Brook Benton opened up new vistas, but it was the likes of *Unforgettable*'s 'This Bitter Earth' – her fifth R&B singles chart topper – that exemplified a bleaker setting for her talents.

In 1964 the 21-year-old Aretha Franklin was moved to record a tribute to Washington. Also titled 'Unforgettable,' it was a timely reminder of a sadly missed singer.

It's Everly Time **The Everly Brothers**

WB WS 1381 (U.S.A.) / Warner Bros WS8012 (U.K.)
Released April 1960

One of the great male duos in popular music, the Everly Brothers' voices match as though a singer is harmonizing with himself. Their presence loomed large in popular music between the death of Buddy Holly and 'Love Me Do.'

Signed in 1956 to Cadence, their first success came with 'Bye Bye Love' (1957), which started a run of hits: 'Wake Up Little Susie,' 'All I Have To Do Is Dream,' 'Claudette,' 'Bird Song,' 'Till I Kissed You,' and 'Walk Right Back.' Their harmony vocals and acoustic guitars were country in origin, but guitarist Chet Atkins helped with arrangements to give The Everlys a stronger beat.

In 1960 The Everlys signed the first million-dollar music industry contract, with Warner Brothers. Shortly after, 'Cathy's Clown' went to Number One in the U.S.A. (five weeks) and the U.K. (nine weeks). *It's Everly Time* was recorded in March 1960 at RCA's Nashville Sound Studio B. The follow-up to 'Cathy's Clown,' 'So Sad,' is a strong meditative opener. The husband-and-wife team of Felice and Boudleaux Bryant, who wrote hits for Roy Orbison, provided five of the tracks, of which 'Sleepless Nights' shows off their skills to great effect, with its impressively unpredictable chord sequence sinking through various keys.

The Everlys were a huge influence on many 1960s' acts, such as The Beatles, The Hollies, The Searchers, and Simon and Garfunkel. Graham Nash recalled: "I remember going to a school dance and listening to The Everly Brothers do 'Bye Bye Love.' It paralyzed me. I had to stop what I was doing, which was walking across the dance floor. And I stopped because I was so shocked musically . . . something inside of me said, 'I want to make people feel what I feel at this moment.'"

The Sound Of Fury **Billy Fury**

Not issued in U.S.A. / Decca LF1329 (U.K.)
Released May 1960

This ten-inch debut album by the Liverpudlian Fury was cut in just two sessions at Decca's West Hampstead studio in London in January and April 1960.

The album mimicked the legendary Sun Sound better than any other British rock'n'roller, and would subsequently be hailed as the first great U.K. rockabilly album. Boasting material penned under Fury's pseudonym, Wilbur Wilberforce, it was an album that its producer Jack Good regarded as 'remarkable.' Good got two bass players in to achieve an authentic slap bass sound: Alan Weighell played the note on electric bass and Bill Stark just slapped his upright. Piano player Reg Guest was the band leader; a group of singers called The Four Jays – later to become a Brian Epstein beat group, The Fourmost – played The Jordanaires; and Joe Brown provided lead guitar. Brown recalled: "I got 26 shillings for the whole session, and it was done in virtually one take, most of it – two takes at the most. We went in with chord sheets and down it went in a couple of hours. Whole album."

On this album Fury's reference point was Eddie Cochran, whom Brown had backed on his U.K. appearances, with touches of Presley ('Since You've Been Gone'), but he achieved some kind of originality with the ballad 'You Don't Know.' Lead track, 'That's Love,' was put out as a single in the U.K. in the month of the album's release, peaking one rung lower than *The Sound Of Fury*, which reached Number 18.

While superficially derivative, *The Sound Of Fury* was influential because the likes of Johnny Kidd And The Pirates, Joe Brown's band The Bruvvers, and Sounds Incorporated all used it as a blueprint to create British rock'n'roll.

Time Out **The Dave Brubeck Quartet**

Columbia CL1397 (U.S.A.) / Fontana TFL5085 (U.K.)
Released June 1960

Time Out is rightly regarded as an all-time great jazz album. Recorded in the same studio as Miles Davis's *Kind Of Blue*, it achieved a similar crossover success.

With a delightful balance of the cerebral and the expressive, *Time Out* is an album for people who think they don't like jazz.

IIn 1954, the year he joined Columbia, Brubeck was already famous enough to make the cover of *Time*. The concept behind *Time Out* was to experiment with unusual time signatures such as 9/8 and 5/4. The Quartet comprised Brubeck on piano, Paul Desmond on alto saxophone, Eugene Wright on bass, and Joe Morello on drums. The seven tracks were recorded on June 25th, July 1st, and August 18th 1959. Among them was 'Take Five,' where the group manage to give the most extraordinarily relaxed lilt to a 5/4 beat. The melody was written by Desmond, whose lazy, purring lines are beautifully articulated, while Brubeck keeps things simple with the accompaniment so the others won't get lost.

Amazingly, 'Take Five' became a pop hit in 1961, reaching Number 25 in the U.S.A. and spending almost ten weeks in the U.K. Top 20. The LP had unprecedented sales for a jazz record. Brubeck had managed to promote jazz to a middle-class white audience that had previously missed it. It was also a big hit with a college audience who saw themselves as too hip for rock'n'roll or Bobby Vee. *Time Out* was the natural soundtrack to 'heavy' conversations about French poetry, existentialism, Marx, Kerouac, and the Bomb. Its successor, *Time Further Out*, is also worth a listen.

1960

The Eddie Cochran Memorial Album
Eddie Cochran

Not issued in U.S.A. / London HAG 2267 (U.K.)
Released September 1960

Singer-guitarist Eddie Cochran was one of the early rock'n'roll greats, and one of the first U.S. artists to tour extensively in Britain.

Tragically he met his end, aged just 21, in a car crash near Chippenham, in south-west England, in April 1960. This resulted in a wave of public sympathy that propelled the poignantly titled 'Three Steps To Heaven' to Number One in Britain, though it failed to chart in his country of origin.

The shamelessly titled *Eddie Cochran Memorial Album* was issued later that year by his British label, Decca/London, and reached Number Nine in the U.K. (It would re-chart in 1963, peaking at Number 11.) As well as the posthumous chart topper it contained Eddie's previous four British hits – 'Summertime Blues,' 'C'Mon Everybody,' 'Somethin' Else,' and a cover of Ray Charles' 'Hallelujah I Love her So,' with which he opened his shows. DJ John Peel later rated seeing Cochran perform this as one of the earliest highlights of his own personal musical journey, while the Joe Meek-produced Heinz hit, 'Just Like Eddie,' celebrated Cochran's life in song.

It was Cochran's guitar work that proved most influential at the time on the likes of George Harrison, notably the latter's adoption of the semi-acoustic Gretsch and employing such tricks as using an unwound third string to assist note bending. Since then Cochran's songs have attracted covers from The Who, Blue Cheer, The Sex Pistols, and The Faces among many others. The Rolling Stones used his '20 Flight Rock' as their stage intro music in the early 1980s. In the same decade 'C'Mon Everybody' received advertising's ultimate accolade, the Levi's television commercial. So Eddie Cochran's music truly is his memorial.

1961

Hey, Lets Twist! (Original Soundtrack)

Roulette 25168 (U.S.A.) / Columbia DB4803 (U.K.)
Released November 1961

Among the last of the pre-Beatles rock-exploitation movies, *Hey, Lets Twist!* was named for the latest dance craze.

Shot in black and white, it was set in the Peppermint Lounge, the New York venue on West 45th Street where middle-aged trendsetters let their hair down. Fueled by press and television interest, the Twist – which had enjoyed a first flourishing in August 1960 in the hands of Chubby Checker – was temporarily back in the news, and a movie resulted.

Joey Dee And The Starliters were the house band at the Peppermint Lounge, and they scored a U.S. chart-topping single with the movie-featured 'Peppermint Twist,' written by Dee and his producer, Henry Glover. Singers Jo-Ann Campbell ('Let's Do My Twist') and Teddy Randazzo ('It's A Pity To Say Goodnight') also participated in the movie, the soundtrack of which reached Number 18 in the U.S.A. in March 1962. Yet, such was the rapid fall off of public interest that the title track, released as a single in January, could barely scrape into the Top 20. (Britain remained relatively immune, Dee's dance disk stalling three places short of the Top 30.)

Dee, born Joseph DiNicola, chose to continue in the movie world, and the CD reissue of *Hey, Lets Twist!* teamed this with the soundtrack of *Two Tickets To Paris*, his other movie of note, from October 1962. Henceforth, the only interest in his Starliters was the membership of three Young Rascals-to-be and, briefly, one James Marshall Hendrix.

The Shadows The Shadows

Columbia 1374 (U.S.A.) / 33SX 1374 (U.K.)
Released September 1961

The Shadows were the U.K.'s most successful instrumental group of all time, with numerous hits between 1960 and the beginning of the 21st century. This debut album was heavily influenced by Duane Eddy, and helped popularize the electric guitar.

The instrumental single had a higher profile in the early 1960s than at any period since, with records such as 'Stranger On The Shore' (by jazz clarinettist Acker Bilk) and 'Telstar' (by The Tornados) reaching Number One. Popular music was making use of new technology, and The Shadows' success was partly down to their exploration of the novel sounds that could be created. The electric guitar was newly established in the rock quartet line-up of two guitars, bass, and drums, and was the hippest instrument in the world – as evidenced by its role in the James Bond movies and many television themes of the day.

The Shadows originated with Hank Marvin and Bruce Welch playing skiffle in a London coffee bar. Marvin had taken up the guitar in 1957 at 16. As The Drifters they became Cliff Richard's backing group. One of the enduring figures of the British popular-music scene, Richard has topped the U.K. singles chart more often than any other artist bar Elvis and The Beatles – though, despite a couple of U.S. chart hits, he has never achieved sustained success in the U.S.A.

The group started recording as The Shadows in 1960. Jerry Lordan's tune, 'Apache' (July 1960), became their first U.K. Number One, and it topped the *New Musical Express* (U.K.) poll for best British instrumental of the year. Marvin's tone was cool and mostly clean. He played one of the first Fender Stratocasters imported into the U.K., using melodies on the lower strings as Eddy did but also higher lead breaks. His sound was shaped by echo, early examples of string-bending, and vibrato from the Strat's tremolo arm. For a generation of players inspired by Marvin's lead playing on tracks like 'Shadoogie' and 'Nivram,' he was the first British guitar hero. The 1999 EMI CD remaster of this album includes mono and stereo mixes of the 14 tracks.

The Soul Of Ike And Tina Turner
Ike And Tina Turner

Sue P-2001 (U.S.A.) / Kent K519 (U.K.)
Released October 1961

While the stormy relationship between Ike and Tina Turner has been chronicled and dissected in book and movie form, there's little doubt that Ike coaxed some amazing vocal performances out of his sometime wife. This album, which was not released in Britain until 1984, contains many early examples.

Tina's act combined sex and religion, inspiring worship and lust from a mainly male audience. "I styled her that way," Ike said. "I made it happen. The lights came down on her, there was no spotlight on me."

With the recording of 'A Fool In Love,' which, as *Billboard*'s review accurately reported, had "a touch of gospel style in the screaming passages," the Turners hit a groove they would retread relentlessly until Phil Spector got involved with production in the mid 1960s. The exuberant 'I Idolize You' from this album also scored, and was teamed on a single with the teen-slanted 'Letter From Tina,' while 'It's Gonna Work Out Fine,' 'Poor Fool,' and 'Tra-La-La-La-La' were further examples of Ike's successful formula. Legend has it Tina was only offered a shot at 'A Fool In Love' when a session singer failed to show. If so, it was a happy accident indeed.

Spector's input opened up a whole new world for Tina, and would inevitably weaken Ike's hold on her. The 1980s and 1990s saw her reap the rewards that decades of hard work had prepared her for, but *The Soul Of Ike And Tina Turner*, an early entry on a formidable resume, remains something she can be proud of.

1962

Jazz Samba **Stan Getz, Charlie Byrd**

Verve 8432 (U.S.A.) / Verve SULP 9013 (U.K.)
Released September 1962

The combination of jazz guitarist Charlie Byrd, tenor saxophonist Stan Getz, and a new type of Brazilian rhythmic music, brought back by Byrd from a tour of South America, catapulted artists and genre on to the charts in 1963.

The bossa nova craze helped Getz become one of the most successful jazzmen ever to cross over to the mainstream, thanks to four Top 40 LPs within a couple of years. This album of instrumentals, produced by Creed Taylor, was the first. While Getz's existing fans may have been dismayed at the saxophonist 'selling out' to commercialism, no one dared argue that he had not paid his fair share of dues, having served in the bands of such respected leaders as Jack Teagarden, Stan Kenton, Benny Goodman, Tommy Dorsey, and Woody Herman.

Getz first became interested in bossa nova in December 1961, when Byrd played him an LP by João Gilberto. Getz saw in the music an excitement and immediacy that was missing from contemporary jazz. He asked Byrd to put together and rehearse a rhythm section for a prospective jazz-samba album, and to call him in when the band was ready.

On February 13th 1962 Getz flew to Washington, D.C., to cut the album. The recording studio was, in fact, a church hall. Two drummers, Bill Reichenbach and Buddy Deppenschmidt, were employed at the sessions in imitation of Brazilian polyrhythmic jazz groups. The other musicians were bassist Keter Betts and Byrd's brother Gene, on bass and guitar respectively. The sextet cut the seven songs on *Jazz Samba* in three hours, after which Getz flew straight back to New York for dinner.

"I JUST THOUGHT IT WAS PRETTY MUSIC. I NEVER THOUGHT IT WOULD BE A HIT."

STAN GETZ

Having chosen not to rehearse with Byrd and his band before the sessions, Getz relied on his finely honed improvisational ability, and nowhere is this more in evidence than on the opening track, 'Desafinado,' co-written by Brazilian father of the bossa nova, Antonio Carlos Jobim. This reached the U.S. Top 20 when released as a single, while Getz would make the Top Five in 1964 with 'The Girl From Ipanema,' for which he teamed up with singer Astrud Gilberto. (Their 1964 LP *Getz/Gilberto* won a Grammy Award.) But this U.S. Number One album, which reached Number 15 in the U.K., was the start of it all.

Green Onions **Booker T. And The MGs**

Stax 701 (U.S.A.) / London HAK 8182 (U.K.)
Released October 1962 (U.S.A.) / July 1964 (U.K.)

Here, one of the 1960s' greatest studio session groups grabs the spotlight for once, instead of backing more famous acts, such as Otis Redding and Wilson Pickett.

Renowned for their disciplined but gritty style, The MGs were the house band of the Stax label, based in Memphis – hence MGs: Memphis Group – with an equivalent role to The Funk Brothers over at Motown in Detroit. The quartet's line-up was Booker T. Jones (organ), Steve Cropper (guitar), Al Jackson (drums), and Lewis Steinberg (bass).

The album originated when the group recorded 'Behave Yourself' and 'Green Onions' after a studio session with rockabilly star Billy Lee Riley in June 1962. The remaining ten tracks were cut that August and included Ray Charles's 'I Got A Woman,' 'Twist And Shout,' 'Stranger On The Shore,' Smokey Robinson's 'One Who Really Loves You,' and 'Mo' Onions,' an attempt to re-write the title track. 'Green Onions' wasn't first choice as a single but when it got airplay it was released and became a Top Three U.S. million-seller, with Booker only 16 at the time. The album, produced by Jim Stewart, followed three months later. In the U.K., where the group had a cult following, it came out in mono on the London label in 1964 and nearly reached the Top Ten.

Reissued by Atlantic in 1966 – again in mono – it finally came out in stereo in late 1969. Despite the album's success, Booker T. carried on music studies at Indiana University until 1966.

Main picture: Booker T. And The MGs' Steve Cropper at Stax Studios. Below: a set of publicity shots of the group from the mid 1960s.

Al Jackson, JR

Booker T

Donald "Duck" Dunn

Steve Cropper

1962

Modern Sounds In Country And Western Music
Ray Charles

ABC-Paramount 410 (US) / HMV CLP 1580 (UK)
Released April 1962

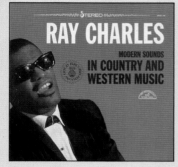

**Having dominated black music in
the late 1950s, pianist-vocalist
Ray Charles delighted in
breaking musical boundaries,
and never more so than with this
hugely popular excursion into
country.**

Charles had already passed through
several distinct musical incarnations,
starting with the night-club style of
the late 1940s, through to the
classic R&B Atlantic material of the
1950s, before he signed for ABC-
Paramount in 1959. He was one of the few artists of the period who
demanded – and got – total control over his recorded material, as well as
retaining ownership of the masters. The freedom this gave him was
reflected in the eclectic nature of his output, which has influenced several
succeeding generations of artists.

Each phase of his work has its own special appeal, but it was during the
1960s that Charles was at his boldest and most prolific, and enjoyed his
greatest commercial success. He'd already explored the jazz sphere, with
1961's *Genius + Soul = Jazz*, on which he'd been assisted by members of
Count Basie's band. That album reached U.S. Number Four and emboldened
him to try a daring incursion into country music. This, however, did not meet
with the approval of ABC president Sam Clark. "He felt I was making a
mistake," said Charles later, "but I felt if I lost any fans he would gain as
many as I would lose." The result was the bestselling album of his career. It
was *Billboard*'s Number One for 14 straight weeks and remained on the pop
chart for three weeks short of two years.

Charles had long enjoyed country music, having listened to the *Grand Ole
Opry* on the radio during his youth in Greenville, South Carolina, and gigged
with a country band, The Florida Playboys, in Tampa in 1947 as a sideline
alongside his main job with Charlie Brantley's Honeydrippers.

Producer Sid Feller took the helm in the studio – though, like Sam Clark, he
had taken some convincing. "I hadn't known what the hell he was talking
about, but hell, it worked – he loved the simple, plaintive lyrics, and thought
giving the music a lush treatment would make it different."

Having mixed the sacred and the profane in gospel and R&B in the 1950s,
Charles was now playing country with what was effectively a big band.
(Ironically, in the 1980s he would to all intents and purposes become a
country singer by recruiting steel guitars and the like to his arrangements.)
Repertoire sources ranged widely: the Webb Pierce-Everly Brothers classic
'Bye Bye Love,' Big Bill Broonzy's arrangement of 'Careless Love,' and Hank
Williams's 'You Win Again' and 'Hey Good Lookin'' were highlights. Other
writers included Eddy Arnold, Floyd Tillman, and Jimmie Davis, a prolific
singer-songwriter – he co-wrote 'You Are My Sunshine' – and sometime
Louisiana governor.

Perhaps the greatest performance was on Don Gibson's 'I Can't Stop Loving
You,' an unusual choice in that Gibson's own version had sold a million just
four years earlier, albeit as a b-side. It was hidden away as second-to-last
track, reflecting Sid Feller's low opinion of it. But when Tab Hunter recorded
a soundalike version for single release, Charles's hand was forced, and it
became first of an unusually large number of singles to be taken from the
album, boosting sales to unexpected heights. The song reached Number
One, and the follow-up, the Cindy Walker–Eddy Arnold-penned 'You Don't
Know Me,' stalled just one place short.

Two sessions – in New York and Los Angeles – was all it took to complete
the album in February 1962. Big-band arrangements on the half-dozen New
York tracks were essayed by Gerald Wilson and Gil Fuller, while strings on
the Los Angeles cuts were by Marty Paich – whose son David would emerge
two and a half decades later as leader of AOR supergroup Toto. The songs
were recorded live in the studio, six or seven a day at a total cost of
$22,000.

This was all the more remarkable given Charles's turbulent private life, which included a heroin habit that was making him distinctly unreliable as a performer. Indeed, he'd escaped a drug bust in Indianapolis on a technicality just before the sessions for this album started. He had money to indulge such foolishness, Ray Charles Enterprises having grossed a staggering $1.5 million in 1961.

A follow-up was expected, and, having been recorded on east and west coasts exactly like its predecessor, *Modern Sounds In Country And Western Music Volume Two* was duly released in late 1962. It visited near-identical song sources, reached Number Two during a 67-week chart stay and yielded Top Ten hit singles in 'You Are My Sunshine' and 'Take These Chains From My Heart.' In Britain the album hit Number Six, a position he would never again surpass.

Other related albums include *Crying Time* and *Country And Western Meets Rhythm and Blues*, both recorded in 1965. Ray Charles was nothing if not prolific, and *Modern Sounds* – ABC's first million-seller – was just one of six of his albums to make the U.S. Top 40 in 1962. (That said, three were compilations of his Atlantic material designed to cash in on his success.)

While *Modern Sounds* turned a whole lot of newcomers on to the Ray Charles phenomenon, Charles's loyal fans stayed with him no matter which musical route he took. Jazz magazine *Downbeat* voted him best male singer five years in a row from 1961, even though he was straying into other fields, while *Billboard*'s chart records show he was the ninth bestselling artist in the U.S.A. in the 1960s – a decade where musical fads and fashions came and went with breathtaking rapidity.

In a sense, it didn't matter what style he chose: Ray Charles's innate character shone through. "Some people say my style comes from the church-singing in gospel choirs," he said, "some people say it's jazz, but really I just sing about life." With earnings at $1.6 million in 1962, life was rich indeed.

Spinning Gold

When partners Stan Ross and Dave Gold signed the $175-a-month lease agreement on a property located at the corner of Santa Monica and Vine in the fall of 1950, they had no idea that their start-up enterprise would one day become a major piece of pop-music lore.

"It was an old building that had been previously used by a dentist," says Gold. "Given the equipment we were using at the time, making records was like pulling teeth."

It didn't happen overnight, but by the turn of 1960s the disparate elements combined to make Gold Star Recording Studios the most sought-after independent facility in Hollywood. Over the next decade Gold Star's 23-feet by 35-feet recording-room would play host to a diverse crowd of characters, from Sonny & Cher ('I Got You Babe') and The Beach Boys ('Good Vibrations'), to rockers The Who ('I Can See For Miles') and Iron Butterfly ('Inna Gada Da Vida').

In Dave Gold the studio had a master technician who built from scratch many of the studio's best pieces of machinery. Gold's twin echo chambers – perfected near the end of the 1950s – produced some of the finest recording effects in all of pop music. Ross and his cousin Larry Levine, who signed on in 1952, were pioneers in the engineering trade, and their miking and mixing techniques became the backbone for scores of hit records over a 30-year period. Rounding out the essential ingredients was Gold Star's inimitable house band, dubbed The Wrecking Crew,

Continued on page 49

1963

The Freewheelin' Bob Dylan Bob Dylan

Columbia CL 1986 (U.S.A.) / CBS62193 (U.K.)
Released May 1963

Dylan's second album, *The Freewheelin' Bob Dylan*, introduced protest lyrics into the consciousness of the pop audience. Blues and folk artists had always used songs to comment on the injustices of politics, war, and society but, for mainstream record buyers, Dylan's angry invective was a revelation.

In 1958, against a background of bobby-soxers and rock'n'rollers, a huge folk boom had swept the U.S.A. after The Kingston Trio's ground-breaking Number One single 'Tom Dooley.' Many of the hits generated in its wake, however, were sanitized and bowdlerized before they reached the mass market. Dylan's vision of folk music had little truck with this comfortably commercial niche.

On September 29th 1961 the *New York Times* music critic Robert Shelton raved over a Dylan gig at Gerdes Folk City, describing him as "a cross between a choirboy and a beatnik" who was "bursting at the seams with talent." Shortly afterward, Dylan was signed to Columbia by revered A&R man John Hammond, who had previously discovered Billie Holiday and would subsequently nurture Bruce Springsteen. Dylan was quickly tagged 'Hammond's folly' because few Columbia executives could see much commercial potential in this raspy-voiced troubadour, whose eponymous 1962 debut album consisted largely of folk-blues covers, giving little indication of what was to come.

Recording for *Freewheelin'* started in April 1962 at Columbia's Studio A in New York City, and carried on sporadically for a year, during which dozens of tracks were recorded and discarded while Dylan was finding his own voice as a writer. Musically, *Freewheelin'* remained firmly in the same style as the debut – one man and his finger-pickin' guitar – but the youth of America had never heard anything resembling the lyrics of tracks like 'A Hard Rain's A-Gonna Fall,' a vision of impending apocalypse conjured through metaphorical images of trees dripping blood, dead oceans, and empty diamond-studded highways.

It's indicative of just how far Dylan's lyrics stood apart from mainstream pop that, on the same day as the final *Freewheelin'* session, Jan & Dean recorded 'Surf City' in Los Angeles, a vibrant teen anthem celebrating the joys of the Californian lifestyle with "two girls for every boy." Significantly, at the start of 'Bob Dylan's Blues' Dylan referred sarcastically to this yawning gulf, observing: "Tin Pan Alley – that's where most of the folk songs come from nowadays." *Freewheelin'* also included the achingly beautiful lament for love gone wrong that is 'Don't Think Twice, It's All Right,' but it was the uncompromising protests – 'Masters Of War' and 'Blowin' In The Wind' – that spoke loudest to Americans terrified by the Cold War and disgusted by the treatment of racial minorities in their land of the free.

Freewheelin' stalled at Number 22 in the *Billboard* albums chart because, for the moment, Dylan's audience consisted largely of young radical intellectuals. This was a relatively small but disproportionately influential cohort, some of whom – Phil Ochs, Tim Rose, and Barry McGuire to name a few – would themselves become protest songwriters and spread the word. By 1965, however, when The Byrds turned his 'Mr Tambourine Man' into an international pop hit, Dylan began to be regarded as a spokesman for his generation.

In The Wind Peter, Paul & Mary

Warner Bros 1507 (U.S.A.) / Warner Bros WM8142 (U.K.)
Released October 1963

Having helped introduce American youth to folk music, Peter Yarrow, Paul Stuckey, and Mary Travers did another service with their third album by including three songs by the then cult folkie Bob Dylan.

Granted, there was a certain amount of nepotism involved, as the trio and Dylan shared a manager, Albert Grossman, but titling their album after a song of his nailed their colors firmly to the Zimmerman mast and undoubtedly gave their stablemate – whose first album had signally failed to chart – much-needed exposure.

Both 'Blowin' In The Wind' and 'Don't Think Twice, It's Alright,' which reached Numbers Two and Nine as U.S. singles before the realease of *In The Wind*, also appear on Dylan's 1963 LP *The Freewheelin' Bob Dylan*, though the Peter, Paul & Mary album track, 'Quit Your Low Down Ways,' would wait until 1991 to be anthologized by its author on a retrospective box set.

In Britain, where they toured before Dylan, *In The Wind* would prove the trio's most successful album, peaking at Number 11 in 1964 in the wake of the title track's Number 13 success. Back home, it took only two weeks to hit the top, displacing their debut album, which had just reassumed the Number One slot. Dylan found such lofty heights harder to reach, and only when *Planet Waves* reached pole position in 1974 could he look down on all comers. By that time the winsome Peter, Paul & Mary were three years into their solo careers – though they have subsequently re-formed.

Continued from page 47

a rotating cast of session players that included drummer Hal Blaine, bassist Carole Kaye, guitarists Glen Campbell and Billy Strange, and many others.

It was a combination of ingenuity and technical know-how that kept Gold Star in the black during the early years. When a deal on a recording console fell through, Gold simply got out the toolbox and went to work. "As a last resort, I got some old chassis together, a bunch of tubes, and turned it into a four-input unit," says Gold. "It was pretty crude, but it worked. And that's what we used for several years."

"All the Columbia records made in New York during that time had the most wonderful echo sound," says Ross. "It was because they had these beautiful echo chambers there. I used to love to hear that on a recording – so right away, that was something we wanted to have on our own productions."

It would take some doing before the Gold Star crew hit on a winning formula. "We started by using this long hallway that we had off the original Studio A," says Gold. "We opened the door on one end and put a microphone at the other end. Then we'd just put the singer down there. It wasn't very much, but it did the job for the time being."

Gold then embarked on a string of echo experiments, most of them less than extraordinary. "I tried using springs, which were OK for instruments but never really sounded good with vocals. We then constructed this long 4-by-4 crawlspace that ran above the hallway. We painted the walls in order to make it more reflective – it's a wonder we didn't die in the process. But that didn't work either. During this one session, we tried putting this female singer in the bathroom – which wasn't half bad, except the song was called 'Well of Loneliness,' and we couldn't stop cracking up!"

By 1956 it was decided that a proper echo chamber was the only way to go. "I did a bunch of research, and finally came up with something that looked like it might work," says Gold, who formulated a cement-plaster concoction especially for the walls of the chamber (its ingredients remain a secret). "We built these two trapezoid-shaped rooms right behind Studio A," says Gold, "with isolation walls and a cement slab that separated them from everything else in the building. And then we put up that concrete mixture, about 2 inches thick. The thing is, when you were building echo chambers, it was always hit or miss – there were certain things you had to do in there but there were never any guarantees it would sound good once you were finished." To Gold's amazement, his new chambers sounded good – really good. "At that point all we had to do was figure out the right kind of mike and speaker to use – which turned out to be an RCA ribbon mike and a 12-inch speaker powered by a ten-watt amp. But really, just about anything would've worked in there."

In 1958 – the year The Champs cut the chart-topping 'Tequila' at Gold Star – a ramshackle group of teens known as The Teddy Bears pulled into Gold's place for the purpose of recording some sides for the fledgling Dore Records label. Leading the pack was 18-year-old Bronx native Harvey Phillip Spector, a recent graduate of local Fairfax High School. "Phil came to Gold Star because he'd heard I was a Fairfax alumnus," says Ross. "He may have gone to a few other places as well at the time, but I don't think too many people really wanted to deal with him – he was a pretty unusual character."

Intended as a b-side, the Spector-penned 'To Know Him is To Love Him' became an out-of-the-blue Number One hit. Unable to repeat that success, Spector returned to New York, ostensibly to become a court stenographer. Within two years he was back in the business, determined to parlay his lone credit as a hit-maker into a successful career in record production. It worked, and by 1961 Spector had compiled an enviable string of hits, most notably Curtis Lee's 'Pretty Little Angel Eyes' and The Paris Sisters' ethereal 'I Love How You Love Me.' Just 21, Spector had fame, money, and the respect of the entire industry.

Near the end of 1962 Spector flew to Los Angeles to cut 'He's a Rebel' for The Crystals. "And it was from that session that he realized he could capture this one particular sound he'd been hearing in his head at Gold Star," says Levine. "Who knows why that was – it's just something that happened while he was there."

In order to achieve his sound, Spector loaded up Gold Star's recording-room with multiple bassists, guitarists, and percussionists, then pumped everything through the studio's echo chambers, with the echo return on full. Spector called his peculiar brand of musical cacophony the 'Wall Of Sound.'

Continued on page 51

1963

Live At The Apollo **James Brown**

King 826 (U.S.A.) / London HA8184 (U.K.)
Released June 1963

This frenzied, sweat-drenched aural-sex workout catapulted James Brown to the forefront of the rapidly evolving 1960s' soul scene, paving the way for the birth of funk.

Ray Charles, whose 1955 smash 'I Got A Woman' is often cited as the first song to be labeled 'soul,' has described the genre as "the fusion of gospel and blues." Certainly, the word 'soul' was common currency among black American musicians from the early 1950s, cropping up in the titles of jazz instrumentals, in gospel band names – such as Sam Cooke's early combo The Soul Stirrers – or as rock'n'roll song titles – Little Richard's 'Ooh! My Soul,' for example.

By the time James Brown, a regular fixture in the 1950s' R&B charts, started scoring Top 40 pop chart success in the early 1960s, the term was being widely applied to more pop-oriented R&B acts, such as Little Anthony & The Imperials, The Clovers, and The Coasters. However, despite his chart hits, Brown felt he was still not reaching the widest possible audience. Inspired by a Top 20 placing in 1960 for Ray Charles's live album, *In Person*, Brown decided that an in-concert release could reveal the power of his super-charged stage shows to an audience that only knew him through his studio recordings.

Unfortunately, Brown was contracted to King Records of Cincinnati, run by Syd Nathan, a formerly shrewd entrepreneur who was losing his touch. With soul album sales generally low, Nathan figured that if an act was performing regularly, there would be no demand for a recorded version, and refused to fund it.

Furious, Brown put $5,700 of his own money up to finance the recording at the end of a week's residency in the legendary Harlem Apollo. The day was bitterly cold, so Brown's crew perked the audience up with free coffee, and, from start to finish the gig was dynamite. Brown's musical director, Bobby Byrd, has recalled: "There was tension, you know, we were nervous about recording and all. But the minute we hit the stage – magic!" Brown and his tightly drilled band pounded out the hits – 'I'll Go Crazy,' 'Please Please Please,' 'Night Train,' and the rest – while the engineers caught their manic live urgency on tape.

Even so, on release, Nathan's continuing reluctance was evidenced by an initial pressing of a mere 5,000 copies. There was like-for-like competition in the market place with Little Stevie Wonder's live album, *12 Year Old Genius*, but within days R&B radio DJs were playing the entire Apollo album end to end, and King Records was obliged to order the first of many re-pressings.

In a staggering 66 weeks on the pop LP chart, it peaked at Number Two, held off the Number One slot by an album that was its polar opposite, Andy Williams's *Days Of Wine And Roses*.

Live At The Apollo not only earned James Brown the title of the 'Hardest-Working Man In Showbusiness' but proved that in-concert albums could be very good for business indeed, attracting a vast new audience to an already established artist.

A Christmas Gift For You From Phil Spector
Phil Spector

Philles PHLP 4005 (U.S.A.) / London HAU8141 (U.K.)
Released November 1963

Before Phil Spector became a producer, the key factors for hit records were melody, words, arrangement, and performance; after Spector, the unique sonic landscape of a record was often equally important.

One of many contenders for the title of 'First Rock Concept Album,' *A Christmas Gift For You* is also considered the first bona fide rock'n'roll Christmas album.

Spector learned his craft as an apprentice to Jerry Leiber and Mike Stoller, one of the greatest songwriting and production teams of the 1950s. His first solo production, 'To Know Him Is To Love Him,' for his own band The

Teddy Bears, went to Number One in the U.S.A. in 1958, after which there was no stopping him. By the age of 20 he was head of A&R for Atlantic Records in Los Angeles, and two years later he started his own label, Philles, almost immediately scoring another Number One with The Crystals' 'He's A Rebel.'

A ruthless manipulator, Spector didn't let The Crystals sing on the tracks issued under their name. That job went to Darlene Love, lead vocalist of another band of Spector protégées, The Blossoms. "When Phil told me he was planning a rock'n'roll Christmas album," Love recalls, "I thought he was crazy. Nobody had done anything like that before." Rock'n'rollers had, of course, made Christmas albums, but their raw style was invariably toned down to fit what was perceived as the Spirit of Christmas. Spector's innovation was that this would unmistakably be rock'n'roll music.

By the time recording started in mid 1963, Spector had become known for his Wall Of Sound production technique, which he had developed at the Gold Star Studios in Los Angeles. Indeed, the specific qualities of that studio were essential to the effect he created. First of all, Gold Star boasted superb echo chambers, which, when fully open, produced a vast cavernous wash of reverb and sympathetic harmonic vibrations. Secondly, the walls of the recording-room were painted with a lead-based paint, which caused any noise to ring around in the air. Finally, the facilities were relatively primitive, with no means of equalization or compression.

All of this suited Spector ideally. His technique was the opposite of everything that sophisticated studios strove to achieve. While they recorded every instrument clearly and separately, Spector would cram Gold Star's little 22-by-32-foot room with upward of 30 musicians, none of whom were isolated from each other by sound baffles. He would then let the resulting sounds intermingle freely into a huge sonic soup. Individual instruments might be swamped to the point of inaudibility, but the overall sound is massive.

That Wall Of Sound when paired with appropriately seasonal sound effects and applied to such numbers as 'Frosty The Snowman' and 'White Christmas' – sung by Spector's stable of hitmakers, including Darlene Love, Bob B. Soxx And The Blue Jeans, The Crystals, and The Ronettes – resulted in a timelessly exciting Christmas album.

Shortly after its release, however, President John F. Kennedy was assassinated and the U.S.A. was plunged into mourning. Out of respect Spector re-called the album from the shops, so it didn't even have a chance to chart, despite which its reputation has grown over the years.

Continued from page 49

The song that would become the prototype for all Wall projects was 'Zip-A-Dee-Doo-Dah,' a hit for Bob B. Soxx & The Blue Jeans (featuring Spector mainstay Darlene Love). "We'd been working on it for around three hours, and he kept boosting the levels, till it finally reached the point where everything was pinning," says Levine. "It was my first session with Phil, I really didn't have the nerve to say anything to him at first. Finally I couldn't take it any more, so I just shut down all the mikes at once! Phil accepted that graciously – he started screaming at me! I told him I had no option but to do that. So slowly I started bringing the mikes back up one at a time, balancing them as I was going along. I got to the last microphone, which was Billy Strange's guitar, and Phil jumps up and says, 'That's it – that's the sound – let's record!' I told him I didn't have the guitar mike up yet, but that was what he wanted. So we went with it. And it was the most incredible recording experience I'd ever had." Incredibly, Levine and Spector mixed the entire spectacle to a single track of an Ampeg 3-track machine.

There's no doubt that Spector knew exactly what he was doing when he created the Wall – but in all likelihood it wouldn't have been quite the same without the elements that existed at Gold Star. Though many tried to replicate the sound, few even came close.

Homemade Mixers

Most of the best professional studios in existence today utilize the same type of equipment made by a handful of famous-name audio manufacturers – the way it's been for many years. This was not the case at the start of the 1960s, when record labels typically had their own research and development staff construct customized mixing consoles from scratch, each one specifically designed to match the particular nuances of the recording-rooms as well as the needs of the engineers who operated them. Such gadgetry helped give a studio its 'signature' sound.

"Every place had a hand-made console," recalls studio session guitarist Al Gorgoni. "That was a big part of it. The sound was homemade! And the resident engineer really knew the board, all of its little functions, and you could really hear that on the finished product as well. Unfortunately, house engineers have become a thing of the past."

"What differs from how things are manufactured today," remarks producer Jim Reeves, a former engineer with CBS Records, "is that, in the designing stage of these consoles, the recording engineers actually sat with the design staff and communicated what those demands in the modern recording process were. As a result, the consoles were specifically designed to make sense for us 'users.'"

In 1960 most studio mixing consoles utilized the same basic design (largely attributed to Universal Audio's Bill Putnam), which included anywhere from six to ten microphone inputs, a handful of channel faders, 'send' and 'return' functions for adding echo, and so forth. Many engineers, however, frequently saw fit to augment the console's functions based on their own particular needs.

When Atlantic Records moved into roomier facilities on New York's West 60th Street in 1959, house engineer Tom Dowd took the opportunity to toss out his old mixing console and began building his own revamped unit that would include a revolutionary new concept: sliding faders. "The equipment most places were using in those days consisted of hand-me-down stuff from broadcast facilities, including consoles that had these big fat 3-inch knobs," says Dowd. "The problem was that you couldn't get two or three under your hands. It wasn't just inaccurate, it was plain stupid. Eventually I found a manufacturer who was making slide wires – faders were linear instead of cylindrical and traveled five inches up and down. Because of the narrow width of these things, I could fit them into a board half as wide. Which enabled me to put a whole group of faders in two hands, which is what I'd wanted to do all along. Finally, I could play the faders like you could play a piano."

Above all, mixing consoles that were built in-house as opposed to on an assembly line were made to last. "All the consoles I used at Columbia were completely dependable," says Roy Halee, ex-Columbia engineer for Simon & Garfunkel and many others. "With the idea being that with 50 or more musicians, you can't afford breakdowns. And they never did – not once."

1963

Please Please Me **The Beatles**

Not issued in U.S.A. / Parlophone 46435 (U.K.)
Released March 1963

With their second Parlophone single, 'Please Please Me,' closing in on the top of what was then known as 'The Hit Parade' in the U.K., producer George Martin hastily scheduled recording time for The Beatles' first LP.

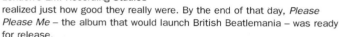

Years of constant gigging had made The Beatles a solid live act, but it wasn't until February 11th 1963 that Martin and the rest of the staff at London's EMI Recording Studios realized just how good they really were. By the end of that day, *Please Please Me* – the album that would launch British Beatlemania – was ready for release.

Beginning at 10am with the tricky two-part vocal harmony of 'There's a Place,' the group proceeded to knock out 11 more songs in under 12 hours, among them 'Baby It's You,' 'Misery,' 'Chains,' and 'Anna,' leading up to the grand finale, John Lennon's historic rendering of Bert Berns's 'Twist and Shout,' completed in a single take just after 10pm. It mattered little that Lennon was nursing a bad cold and spent the day downing throat lozenges in order to keep up the pace. "I don't know how they do it," remarked producer Martin near the end of the marathon session. "We've been recording all day, but the longer we go on, the better they get."

Though EMI already had in its possession a 4-track recorder, Martin and crew – engineers Norman Smith and Richard Langham – cut the entirety of *Please Please Me* live to 2-track (a McCartney double-track vocal on 'A Taste of Honey' and a harmonica add-on to 'There's a Place' would be patched in later). The band set up in a configuration that would change little over the following years. Harrison's and Lennon's Vox AC30 guitar amplifiers were placed gingerly atop folding chairs, and situated perilously close to Ringo Starr's kit. Neumann vocal and instrument microphones, fastened atop a set of rolling stands, stood nearby, with cables strewn across the parquet floor, and little or no baffling dividing the individual players.

"The first album was basically just an effort to capture the feeling of their stage act, which they'd really mastered by then," says Langham. "There were just two mikes on Ringo's drums, with very little baffling, maybe just a low drum screen, and that was about it, really. It was very typical of the method used for artist's tests or commercial tests."

If anything, the wide-open arrangement gives *Please Please Me* a sense of urgency that's still palpable over 40 years on. Lennon and McCartney's locked harmonies verge on distortion; Starr's snare drum, aided by the ample leakage, resonates loudly throughout EMI's massive Studio 2. In short, The Beatles sound like a band on a mission.

"You listen to 'I Saw Her Standing There,' or anything on that first album," remarks EMI engineer Richard Lush, "and you hear the drums going all over the vocal mike, there are things like limiters going on and off, as soon as the music stop the drums comes up. It's so unlike anything you'd hear today. But it just adds to the overall excitement of the recording. Face it – when something like 'Twist and Shout' comes on that's live or has a bit of vibe to it, your ears always prick up."

The 12 Year Old Genius **Little Stevie Wonder**

Tamla 240 (U.S.A.) / Oriole PS40050 (U.K.)
Released July 1963

Having failed to make a mark with first album, *Tribute To Ray Charles*, Stevie Wonder was recorded live, and like James Brown at the Apollo, Wonder's in-concert charisma put him on the musical map.

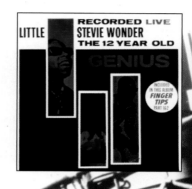

It wasn't such a gamble, given his show-stopping performances on the Motortown Revue tours, at which Wonder – born Steveland Morris – performed out front with vocals and

harmonica rather than, as later, ensconced behind keyboards. Suffice to say that 'Little' Stevie – he dropped the diminutive in 1964 – did not seem out of place beside the more mature talents of Marvin Gaye, The Supremes, The Miracles, and Mary Wells.

The album's blues-based opening song, 'Fingertips,' recorded at the Regal in Chicago, was label boss Berry Gordy's choice as a single, and repaid his faith by selling a million. Split over two sides, it topped the U.S. charts six weeks after release. *The 12 Year Old Genius* followed suit a fortnight later, deposing Andy Williams in August 1963 and becoming not only the first live chart topper but the first of Stevie's three U.S. Number One albums – though he'd have to wait 11 years for the next.

> # "I LISTENED TO EVERYTHING I COULD HEAR. MUSIC WAS MY COMMUNICATION TO THE WORLD. DIFFERENT LANGUAGES, VOICES, SINGERS – I HEARD EVERYTHING."
> ### STEVIE WONDER

Material ranges from more chantalong material, such as 'La La La La La,' through the self-penned 'Drown In My Own Tears' and Ray Charles's 'Hallelujah I Love her So,' to the more sophisticated 'Masquerade Is Over,' one of several tracks first heard earlier that year on *The Jazz Soul Of Little Stevie*. And, while the result was impressive, Wonder found the title 'genius' hard to live with. Happily, he overcame the child-prodigy tag – he is still the youngest singer to top the U.S. albums chart – to sustain a 40-year-plus recording and performing career.

Call Me/That's The Way Love Is **Bobby Bland**

Duke 77 (U.S.A.) / Vocalion 8034 (U.K.)
Released September 1963

Hedging its bets by being named after both sides of what was then his biggest pop hit, this album was a long-awaited pop album-chart breakthrough for Robert Calvin Bland, whose journey to *Billboard*'s listing included a stint as driver and valet to B.B. King.

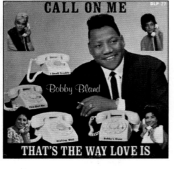

Bobby 'Blue' Bland hedged his bets, straddling blues, gospel, and soul, but perhaps not moving with the times in the same way as the likes of Marvin Gaye. Hence his core audience, right through to the 1990s, was a black one.

As was usual for black-music albums of the time, this was a collection based on successful singles. 'Call Me,' with its staccato trumpets, is, against type, Latin in flavor, and it reached Number 22 in the pop chart, while 'That's The Way Love Is,' a R&B chart topper in its own right, hit Number 33 as the b-side.

The songs were written by a combination of trumpeter-arranger Joe Scott – the man who helped shape Bland's musical style after he signed for Duke Records in 1955 – his manager Don Robey, and one Deadric Malone, creator of the majority of tracks here. *Black Music* magazine suggested Malone was in fact a *nom de plume* of Robey. Certainly, the duo/triumvirate steered Bland's career until the parting of the ways in the late 1960s brought a dip in fortunes.

Over in Belfast, Northern Ireland, one man who was clearly listening to Bobby Bland was Van Morrison, whose hero-worship is such that he has invited Bland to open for him on a number of occasions.

The Ventures In Space **The Ventures**

Dolton 8027 (U.S.A.) / Liberty LBY1189 (U.K.)
Released December 1963

The Ventures were the most successful instrumental group of the 1960s. When they weren't covering others' hits, they wrote tunes such as 'Fear,' that now seem like the soundtracks of long-lost b-movies.

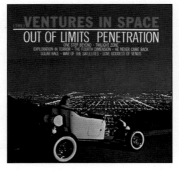

The group formed in Seattle in 1959 by Bob Bogle and Don Wilson. They were joined by Nokie Edwards – who at first played bass then switched to lead guitar when Bogle took up bass himself – and drummer Howie Johnson. Their 1960 debut single, as The Versatones, was on their own Blue Horizon label. They quickly learned how to arrange music to fit their style, and became very prolific. The first hit was 'Walk Don't Run,' and they had four hit albums in 1961. During the 1960s they released 33 albums that charted, more than half of them reaching the Top 40, and selling a million LPs in 1963 alone, the year that *In Space* was first released (1970s reissue pictured).

The main characteristic of The Ventures' music is the guitar instrumental, often powered by a galloping shuffle from the rhythm section. Guitar techniques taken from Duane Eddy and other rock'n'rollers are spiced with primitive string-bending, effects such as echo, reverb, and tremolo, and many tracks feature unconventional chord changes and juxtapositions. Some tracks – 'Moon Child,' for example – are reminiscent of The Tornados' 'Telstar' and British instrumental outfit The Shadows, though in comparison with the latter The Ventures have a more garage sound and a liking for unusual instrumentation. (This tendency had been evident on their 1962 hit, 'The 2,000 Pound Bee,' where the guitar is put through a fuzzbox, an effect virtually unknown at the time.)

The Ventures survived the British Invasion of the mid 1960s by finding a new market in Japan, where they went on to sell over 30 million albums. Their influence can be heard in the playing of guitarists such as Jerry Garcia (Grateful Dead) and Jorma Kaukonen (Jefferson Airplane), and elements of their music can be heard from Quicksilver Messenger Service's *Happy Trails* to more recent albums by the likes of Liverpool band The Coral.

The Beatles At Abbey Road

The former EMI engineer Richard Langham still remembers the first few hints of early Beatlemania invading the all-business environment at EMI's Studio 2 at 3 Abbey Road, London SW8.

"It was a freezing cold day," says Langham. "We were outside getting all The Beatles' gear out of the van to bring into the studio. I noticed these bits of paper falling out of the backs of the amplifiers – they were all these little folded notes that the girls had thrown on to the stage that they'd read and then tossed into their amps! I knew right then that this was going to be a very interesting time."

Up to the late 1950s EMI's Abbey Road premises – a nine-bedroom Victorian residence transformed into a three-room record-making facility in 1931 – had been the exclusive domain of classical and jazz artists, such as pianist Fats Waller and violinist Yehudi Menuhin. Though a few teen pop hits by British heart-throb Cliff Richard helped boost EMI's profit margin as the 1960s approached, few could have predicted the long-term impact on corporate earnings that began with the June 1962 audition by four working-class youths from Liverpool.

Much of the credit for the kinetic feel of the early Beatles albums goes to first engineer Norman Smith, who decided right from the start that the band would fare much better by working as they did on stage, without the constraints of imposing baffling screens. Against the advice of EMI heads, Smith turned Studio 2 into one large, open recording space. His hunch was correct, and any leakage merely added to the overall energy of the recordings.

"The whole thing about The Beatles' records is that they've got excitement," says former EMI engineer Richard Lush. "You put on a record like 'Twist and Shout' – I mean, the vocal performance on that song is just staggering, especially when you bear in mind that John had already been there for 12 hours, singing his guts out live to 2-track. It's absolutely amazing."

Amazing, yes – but in 1963 The Beatles, like many other professional outfits of the time, had spent their formative years playing several shows a day, five, six, seven days a week. By the time they made their debut inside a professional studio, they had the stamina, the energy, and, most of all, the expertise to make a great-sounding recording – often without the aid of overdubs or edits.

"Both John and Paul could step up to that vocal mike and nail those takes again and again," says Lush. "You put on *Anthology* and hear all the various takes and false starts – each time they come back, they're always right there, they just never hit a bum note. That kind of precision comes from working together constantly – to be able to instinctually pull it off without fail."

Within two years of the band's initial audition, four Beatles albums had topped the *Billboard* chart – each one conceived at 3 Abbey Road. The former gneral manager of Abbey Road, Ken Townsend, has observed: "Let's face it, there's a certain kind of spontaneity that occurs when you aren't multitracking everything. The Beatles' first few years proved that."

■ *John Lennon and Paul McCartney at work in Abbey Road Studios with producer George Martin. Between May 1963 and 1965 The Beatles – and, to a lesser extent, The Rolling Stones – held a strangehold over the U.K. albums chart. During that period The Beatles spent a total of 83 weeks at Number One with albums including* Please, Please Me, With The Beatles, *and* A Hard Day's Night.

1964

All Summer Long **The Beach Boys**

Capitol S+/T 2110 (U.S.A. & U.K.)
Released July 1964

Beach Boys Concert **The Beach Boys**

Capitol S+/T 2198 (U.S.A. & U.K.)
Released November 1964

The Beach Boys' albums of the early 1960s demonstrate the group's swift progression from idealistic, surf-obsessed rock'n'roll to music of the depth and magnitude of *Pet Sounds*.

As with all the group's work, the unifying thread here is the combination of the three Wilson brothers' voices with those of their cousin, Mike Love, and neighbor, Al Jardine, to create one of the finest vocal harmony groups of all time. The Beach Boys worked at a prodigious rate throughout the

1960s, producing two or three albums per year while touring solidly. Their debut, *Surfin' Safari* (1962), and *Surfin' U.S.A.* (1963), are fairly one-dimensional, feelgood tributes to sand, sea, and beautiful girls; *Surfer Girl* and *Little Deuce Coupe* (both 1963) show the first signs of Brian Wilson's capacity for delicate, melancholic songs, notably *Surfer Girl*'s 'In My Room.'

All Summer Long was recorded in April and May 1961 at Western Recorders in Hollywood. The album is the first on which Brian Wilson took complete control of The Beach Boys' sound; he fired his overbearing father, Murray, the group's manager, during the opening session.

All Summer Long contains some of the strongest and most memorable songs of The Beach Boys' early career, among them 'Little Honda,' 'Wendy,' and 'I Get Around,' which became the group's first U.S. Number One hit single and reached Number Seven in the U.K. Of the less well-known tracks, 'Girls On The Beach' is one of Wilson's finest pre-*Pet Sound*s ballads, while the wistful title track now reads like a farewell to the sun and surf that dominated the group's first phase. The album itself peaked at Number Four in the U.S.A. It was not issued in the U.K. until the following summer, where it failed to chart.

"PEOPLE BEGAN TO REALIZE THE POTENTIAL IMPACT OF THE GROUP AND GIVE CONSIDERATION TO THE BEACH BOYS AS A MAJOR ATTRACTION."

CONCERT PROMOTER FRED VAILS

Shortly after the release of *All Summer Long*, and with the album still riding high in the U.S. *Billboard* chart, The Beach Boys played two shows at the Civic Auditorium in Sacramento, California, on August 1st, both of which were recorded. Assisted by the engineer Chuck Britz, Brian pieced together the best of both performances the following month for the live set *Beach Boys Concert*. Ever the perfectionist, he also re-recorded some of the group's vocals. The album features renditions of a number of earlier Beach Boys hits, alongside covers of 'Johnny B. Goode' and 'Monster Mash.'

Beach Boys Concert reached Number One in the U.S.A. in December, a feat unmatched by any of the group's albums apart from the 1974 compilation *Endless Summer*. The album also marked the end of Brian Wilson's role as a touring member of the group. In late 1964, after suffering the first of several mental breakdowns, Wilson would retire from live performance and concentrate his efforts exclusively on studio work.

Muddy Waters: Folk Singer Muddy Waters

Chess 1483 (U.S.A.) / Pye International NPL 28040 (U.K.)
Released April 1964

The legendary blues singer and guitarist Muddy Waters began his recording career in the early 1940s, when Alan Lomax tracked him down in Mississippi for the Library Of Congress Archive Of Folk Song.

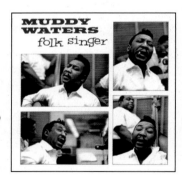

Waters's international profile began to rise in the mid 1960s, as the Chicago-blues style he had pioneered in the 1940s and 1950s became the primary influence on a wave of British R&B groups. However, on *Folk Singer* Waters capitalized on the growing popularity of folk by reverting to a stripped-down, live acoustic setup, predating the idea of the 'MTV Unplugged' album by two decades.

Muddy Waters: Folk Singer was recorded in September 1963 at Tel Mar Studios in Chicago. Alongside Waters on the album are Buddy Guy on second acoustic guitar, Clifton James on drums, and Willy Dixon, who also produced the sessions, on bass. Most of the songs are Waters's own compositions, performed in a style reminiscent of his very first Chess recordings in the late 1940s. The album also includes a version of Dixon's chain-gang song, 'My Captain,' and a reading of John Lee 'Sonny Boy' Williamson's 'Good Morning Little School Girl.'

A 1999 reissue of the album adds two 1964 sessions featuring a larger ensemble of backing musicians, among them James Cotton on harmonica and J.T. Brown on tenor saxophone and clarinet. These more electrified recordings illustrate the two sides of Waters's music in the mid 1960s.

1965

A Love Supreme
John Coltrane

Impulse! A77 (U.S.A.) / MCA DMCL 1648 (U.K.)
Released February 1965

One of the most important jazz recordings of all time, the influence of *A Love Supreme* extends way beyond the world of jazz to rock and fusion musicians, including Carlos Santana.

Saxophonist John Coltrane made his name as a sideman with, among others, Miles Davis, on whose epochal *Kind Of Blue* he had played in 1959. Coltrane didn't begin to concentrate fully on his own career until 1960, when he made the relatively conventional albums *My Favorite Things* and *Coltrane Plays The Blues*. By the mid 1960s, however, Coltrane had found a freer, more experimental sound, which reached its apex on *A Love Supreme*. The album was envisioned by its creator as a "humble offering" to God – whom he had found in the midst of his

lengthy battle with heroin addiction – and is divided into four distinct parts: 'Acknowledgement,' 'Resolution,' 'Pursuance,' and 'Psalm.' Expanding deliriously on these four central themes, Coltrane's passionate tenor saxophone work is, of course, the focal point, but the music is held together by the exemplary rhythm playing of drummer Elvin Jones, bassist Jimmy Garrison, and pianist McCoy Tyner. As was typical of jazz albums of the time, *A Love Supreme* was recorded live in one session, on December 9th 1964, with producer Bob Thiele at Van Gelder Studio, New Jersey. The LP's sleevenotes contain a lengthy piece written in thanks to The Lord by Coltrane.

His most fully realized artistic statement, *A Love Supreme* is also the bestselling album in Coltrane's catalog, eventually selling over a million copies worldwide. Coltrane's life and music would become more turbulent in the years that followed, and his album releases grew more and more chaotic before his death in 1967 from liver cancer. In the last year of his life Coltrane's band featured his wife, Alice, who would go on to make a number of acclaimed albums of her own, including 1970's richly orchestrated *Universal Consciousness*.

A Love Supreme has been reissued in several slightly different forms since Coltrane's passing. Most notable is the 2002 Deluxe Edition, a two-CD set combining previously unheard recordings with a newly remastered version of the album itself, sourced from tapes discovered in the late 1990s in the vaults of EMI in London.

1965

The Sound Of Music (Original Soundtrack)

RCA Victor 2005 (US) / 90368 (UK)
Released March 1965

When it opened in March 1965, the movie version of *The Sound Of Music* became the highest-grossing movie to date in the U.S.A., and would, a year later, be named Best Picture at the Academy Awards.

The movie was adapted from the 1959 Broadway musical of the same name, the last of many collaborative efforts by Rodgers & Hammerstein. The musical, in its turn, was based on a book by Howard Lindsay and Russel Crouse, which drew heavily on the autobiography of Maria Von Trapp.

Columbia had already issued an original-cast recording from the Broadway production five years earlier, when RCA Victor decided to issue an album of songs from the movie version. Though this recording of the stage show had been highly successful, and could be found in many record collections across the U.S.A., it didn't stop the new version selling well. *The Sound Of Music* reached Number One in the U.S.A. and the U.K., and remained on the albums charts on both sides of the Atlantic for several years. Between 1965 and 1969 the soundtrack album spent a total of 70 weeks at the top of the U.K. charts, and has sold over 11 million copies since its original release.

The original 1959 stage cast had featured the then 45-year-old singer Mary Martin – at whose request Richard Rodgers and Glendenning Hammerstein had written the show – in the role of the 21-year-old Maria. By the time the movie version went into production Martin was 50 and deemed too old to be considered for the lead. Instead, Maria would be played by Julie Andrews, who had recently won an Oscar for her performance in the title role of another piece of sentimental musical cinema, *Mary Poppins* (1964). Andrews's performances, both on screen and on the soundtrack, are exemplary throughout. However, some of the other actors' voices are dubbed over by stronger singers – though both Christopher Plummer (Captain Von Trapp) and Peggy Wood (Mother Abbess) are credited on the sleeve, neither's voice is actually heard on record.

As well as the change of lead actress, the movie version of *The Sound Of Music* cut some of the less upbeat songs from the stage production, such as 'How Can Love Survive?' and 'No Way To Stop It.' Of the songs that remain, however, many have become popular standards, including the title track as well as 'Do-Re-Mi,'

'Climb Every Mountain,' 'My Favorite Things,' and 'Edelweiss.' The movie version also adds a new song, 'I Have Confidence,' with both words and music having been written by Rodgers after Hammerstein's death in 1960.

The Sound Of Music remains one of the most successful soundtrack albums of all time, surpassed only by the likes of *Saturday Night Fever* (1977) and *The Bodyguard* (1992).

What Now My Love?
Herb Alpert And The Tijuana Brass

A&M 3265 (U.S.A. & U.K.)
Released April 1965

Herb Alpert was one of popular music's first renaissance men. As well as being one of the biggest-selling instrumental pop performers of all time, he is the founder, and 'A,' of A&M – 'M' is business partner Jerry Moss – the record label that has over time been home to many successful artists.

Alpert began his musical career as a songwriter, collaborating with Lou Adler on the Sam Cooke hit 'Wonderful World.' After setting up A&M in 1962 he had an immediate U.S. Top Ten hit with his single 'The Lonely Bull.' During the 1960s Alpert had a run of 11 Top 20 albums in the U.S.A., of which *What Now My Love?* was the most successful, spending nine weeks at Number One. *What Now My Love?* captures the trumpet-playing Alpert and his band – which included pianist Lou Pagani and guitarist John Pisano – at their peak, mixing original pieces with interpretations of contemporary pop and Broadway hits, all set in a style dubbed 'Ameriachi' by music critics.

It was through the success of Alpert's own recordings that A&M was able to develop a roster of impressive, emerging stars. Among the label's signings in the late 1960s were The Carpenters, Humble Pie, Cat Stevens, and Burt Bacharach. A&M grew vastly in stature over the next two decades, until 1990, when Alpert and Moss sold the label to Polygram for $500 million. The duo have since founded a new label, Almo Sounds, which continues to issue Alpert's work as well as material by other artists, including Garbage.

The Paul Butterfield Blues Band
The Paul Butterfield Blues Band

Elektra EKL/EKS 7294 (U.S.A. & U.K.)
Released October 1965

One of the most gifted harmonica players of his generation, Paul Butterfield led the U.S.A.'s first great white blues band.

Born in Chicago in 1942, Butterfield started performing in local blues clubs in the late 1950s. In 1963 he recruited Howlin' Wolf's rhythm section – drummer Sam Lay and bassist Jerome Arnold – and guitarist Elvin Bishop, and completed the classic line-up of his unusually racially integrated Blues Band the following year with the addition of slide guitarist Mike Bloomfield.

After signing to Elektra, the group entered the studio with producer Paul Rothschild during the summer of 1965 to cut the 11 songs on their debut album . The material is mostly made up of ragged reinterpretations of classic Chicago blues, from Willie Dixon's 'Mellow Down Easy' to Muddy Waters's 'I Got My Mojo Working.' Butterfield's harmonica dominates, but the twin-guitar interplay of Bloomfield and Bishop proved equally influential. Having witnessed a blistering performance by the group at the 1965 *Newport Folk Festival*, Bob Dylan was so impressed that he recruited Bloomfield for his own set later the same evening.

The Paul Butterfield Blues Band was not a huge commercial success on its release in 1965, but it paved the way for numerous other white blues groups of the mid to late 1960s.

Look At Us **Sonny & Cher**

ToAtco LP 33-177 (U.S.A.) / Atlantic ATL 5036 (U.K.)
Released August 1965

To all intents and purposes, the album that put Salvatore 'Sonny' Bono and his teenage bride Cherilyn 'Cher' Lapierre on the map in the summer of 1965 was little more than a vehicle for the duo's massively successful first hit single, 'I Got You Babe' – but what a single it was.

Written by Bono – a proven composer who had co-written The Searchers' 'Needles and Pins' – the Number One smash showed just how much Bono had learned during his long apprenticeship with Phil Spector. Like most of Spector's works, the Bono-produced *Look at Us* – which peaked at Number Two on the *Billboard* chart and also sported the Bono-penned follow-up 'Just You' – was recorded at the famed Gold Star Recording Studios, which in 1965 still only used three tracks, with an array of Spector regulars, including guitarist Barney Kessel, drummer Hal Blaine, and bassist Lyle Ritz.

A unique sound-balancing method devised by engineer and Gold Star co-owner Stan Ross ensured that Harold Batiste's majestic arrangement of 'I Got You Babe' got the attention it deserved. "We had this deal with KHJ, the local station, to play the acetates of the new songs just after they'd been cut," says Ross. "I'd sit there in the studio and listen to the broadcast over the speakers we had in there. When I'd cut the master, my EQ adjustments would be based on what I'd heard coming back over the airwaves! That way I knew exactly how it would sound over every other station in the country from that point forward. It was that simple."

1965

Bringing It All Back Home **Bob Dylan**

Columbia CL 2328 (U.S.A.) / CBS 62515 (U.K.)
Released March 1965

Highway 61 Revisited **Bob Dylan**

Columbia CL 2389 (U.S.A.) / CBS 62572 (U.K.)
Released August 1965

A brand new and enduring musical genre, folk rock, sprang into being partly as a result of Bob Dylan's fifth album, *Bringing It All Back Home*. As with most such revolutionary moments there was no master plan. It happened because it had to.

With his early acoustic albums Dylan had revolutionized the early-1960s folk scene simply by writing his own songs. Chart-topping albums and singles by The Kingston Trio, The Highwaymen, and The Rooftop Singers testify to the massive popularity of folk music at the time, but all of these acts covered traditional songs. The scene generated very little in the way of original material until Dylan came along, at which point the floodgates opened and every sensitive teenager who could pick three chords on a battered acoustic guitar suddenly became a folksy singer-songwriter. Dylan was also seen as the inventor of protest music, so the eyes of the music community were firmly fixed on him, watching his every move.

However, when he went into Columbia's New York studios on January 13th 1965 to begin recording sessions for *Bringing It All Back Home*, he was not planning to invent a new electric-folk style. One entire side of the album, in fact, remained firmly in his acoustic, solo-troubadour mode.

There were, however, certain songs that he felt were not going to work without additional instrumentation. "I had this thing called 'Subterranean Homesick Blues,'" he explained later. "It just didn't sound right by myself." Maybe that's because its rapid-fire, semi-rapped lyric bears more than a passing resemblance to Chuck Berry's 'Too Much Monkey Business,' a rock'n'roll classic that Dylan would have known well.

The popular notion that Dylan was a Greenwich Village folkie who made a shocking volte-face into rock'n'roll is one that has long muddied the waters around his next move. Dylan grew up in the 1950s listening to rock'n'roll, particularly enjoying Buddy Holly, The Everly Brothers, and Elvis Presley, of whom he has said: "When I first heard Elvis' voice I just knew that I wasn't going to work for anybody; and nobody was going to be my boss . . ." On June 5th 1959 when he left Hibbing High School, Minnesota, the school yearbook noted that he intended "to follow Little Richard," and one of his first paid jobs was a brief stint as pianist in teen idol Bobby Vee's band. So his decision to bring in rock players for 'Subterranean Homesick Blues' was more a return to his roots than a radical restructuring of folk idioms.

Continued on next page

As a guitarist, Dylan chose Bruce Langhorne, whom he'd worked with in 1962, during rarely mentioned unreleased electric sessions for the album *The Freewheelin' Bob Dylan*. Dylan's producer, Tom Wilson, chose the rest of the band, including John Sebastian, later to form The Lovin' Spoonful, and John Hammond Jr, who has subsequently become a highly regarded bluesman.

> ## "I'VE WRITTEN SOME SONGS THAT I LOOK AT, AND THEY JUST GIVE ME A SENSE OF AWE. STUFF LIKE 'IT'S ALRIGHT MA,' JUST THE ALLITERATION IN THAT BLOWS ME AWAY."
>
> *BOB DYLAN*

Photographer Daniel Kramer, who attended the sessions, vividly recalls the excitement and elation when 'Maggie's Farm' was first played back: "There was no question about it – it swung, it was happy, it was good music, and, most of all, it was Dylan." The rock instrumentation also worked a treat for another up-tempo Chuck Berry-style workout, 'Outlaw Blues,' and for the hilariously surreal 'On The Road Again.' The guitars are also plugged in, but appropriately more mellow, for two of Dylan's most memorable love songs, 'She Belongs To Me' and 'Love Minus Zero/No Limit.'

The album gave him his first Top Ten entry, and 'Subterranean Homesick Blues' sneaked into the Top 40 singles chart, but, even more significantly, one of the album's acoustic tracks, 'Mr Tambourine Man,' went to Number One in June in an electrified version by The Byrds. Folk rock had arrived, and the overwhelming mass of white American teens embraced it immediately, soaking up similarly styled hits from Simon & Garfunkel, The Turtles, and Barry McGuire.

Unfortunately, to the folk fraternity who had previously adored him, amplified folk was a crime against nature. When Dylan debuted his new electric band at the *Newport Folk Festival* on July 25th he was booed off the stage, and similar demonstrations of dismay and anger greeted him wherever he toured for the rest of the year.

He was, nevertheless, not about to turn back. *Highway 61 Revisited* followed just six months after *Bringing It All Back Home*, and this time the electricity crackled and fizzed from every groove.

Guitarist Mike Bloomfield once claimed that the sessions were chaotic because "no one had any idea what the music was supposed to sound like." Neither Dylan nor producer Tom Wilson, according to Bloomfield, directed the musicians: "It was a matter of pure chance." More likely it was a matter of choosing the right musicians to start with, then giving them their creative head.

The opening swagger and swirl of Al Kooper's organ and Paul Griffin's piano on 'Like A Rolling Stone' left no doubt that in a few short months Dylan had made a quantum leap and was now the king of a hill built by his own hand. Snarling and sneering his way through the vitriolic lyric, Dylan had never before sounded so sure of himself. He was certainly confident enough to release it as a six minute single against the advice of Columbia Records, who insisted that radio wouldn't play anything over three minutes in length. It went Top Five on both sides of the Atlantic.

Bloomfield's stinging lead guitar kicks 'Tombstone Blues' into a higher rock'n'roll gear than Dylan had

ever previously managed, but the album's real strength is not its style but its content. Such songs as 'It Takes A Lot To Laugh, It Takes A Train To Cry,' and 'Ballad Of A Thin Man' are beautifully understated, with every instrument perfectly complementing Dylan's straggling melodies. The lyrics, too, had leaped ahead, with virtually every line of 'Desolation Row' elegantly conjuring word pictures that combine into a dark and surreal movie playing in the back of the listener's head.

Arguably, *Highway 61 Revisited* also marks the dividing line between rock'n'roll and rock. Here was a music too cerebral to be pop, too bluesy and ballsy to be folk rock, and, most significantly, it was also too sophisticated to be rock'n'roll.

Even 40 years after its release this is a hard album to fault. The worst that can be said is that it stands responsible for countless crimes against songwriting committed by legions of inferior artists who misguidedly imagined themselves to be the next Bob Dylan.

1966

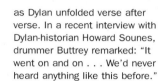

Blonde On Blonde **Bob Dylan**

Columbia 841 (US) / CBS S+/66012 (UK)
Released May 1966

The first double album in rock,
Blonde On Blonde **stands as the culmination of a period of intense activity for Dylan, having been released within a year of his equally highly regarded** ***Bringing It All Back Home*** **and** ***Highway 61 Revisited.***

After a hectic period that had seen the inauguration of his new electric sound, Dylan decamped to Columbia Music Row Studios in Nashville, Tennessee, to begin work on his seventh studio album. This was one of the first instances of a rock musician recording in the home of country music with Nashville musicians, though Dylan

did bring with him organist Al Kooper and guitarist Robbie Robertson of The Band. The other musicians at the *Blonde On Blonde* sessions were guitarist and bandleader Charlie McCoy, drummer Kenny Buttrey, bassist Henry Strzelecki, Wayne Moss on guitar, and Hargus 'Pig' Robbins on piano, all veterans of the Nashville scene. The sessions were produced by Bob Johnston and were completed in eight days in February and March 1966.

Dylan himself turned up four hours late for the first day of recording – St Valentine's Day 1966 – with the lyrics to the song with which he wished to begin still not finished. The Nashville players had to wait several more hours as he continued to write. They were eventually called down to the studio in the middle of the night, at which point Dylan presented them with a brief fragment of 'Sad-Eyed Lady Of The Lowlands.' Without the luxury of a rehearsal, the band went straight into the recording of what would end up as an 11-minute epic. More used to playing on two-minute country tracks, the band looked at one another in disbelief

as Dylan unfolded verse after verse. In a recent interview with Dylan-historian Howard Sounes, drummer Buttrey remarked: "It went on and on . . . We'd never heard anything like this before."

Many at the time assumed that this epic song, which closed the album, was about Joan Baez, but the sad-eyed lady in question was, in fact, Dylan's new wife Sara. Notoriously guarded about his private life, Dylan went to great lengths to keep the marriage a secret, even going so far as to hide Sara in a walk-in closet when a pair of DJs came to interview him backstage at a gig in Vancouver, BC. Sara would later inspire a less cheerful song cycle on *Blood On The Tracks* (1975), often referred to as Dylan's 'divorce album.'

Dylan worked through the rest of the *Blonde On Blonde* material in much the same way over the next few days. Each song was recorded live, mostly in one or two takes. Dylan rarely played the band more than a verse or two before the red light came on. Despite this, the Nashville musicians' playing on *Blonde On Blonde* is exemplary, lending the album a more fluid, expansive quality than the harsh folk rock of the previous year's *Highway 61*. In return, Dylan credited the players by name on the record's sleeve, which at the time was highly unusual. Their appearance on the album also raised the profile of country music considerably within the rock audience and helped pave the way for future country-rock crossovers.

As with 'Sad-Eyed Lady,' Dylan would often finish writing the songs on the day of recording. He arrived at the studio one morning with the freshly written, cinematic lyrics to 'Stuck Inside Of Mobile With The Memphis Blues Again' on headed hotel notepaper. Among the other key tracks on the album are 'Just Like A Woman' and 'Leopard-Skin Pill-Box Hat,' both believed to be about the model Edie Sedgwick, and the delicate 'I Want You.'

Perhaps the most infamous song on *Blonde On Blonde* is 'Rainy Day Women # 12 & 35.' Deciding that he couldn't do it justice with "a bunch of straight people," Dylan insisted that, in the words of the song, "everybody must get stoned" before the recording began. Somewhat reticent to begin with, the inebriated musicians swapped instruments and, with the addition of trombonist Wayne 'Doc' Butler, cut the song in the sloppy marching-band style that Bob wanted. The end result is the most off-kilter piece in the Dylan canon.

Blonde On Blonde was mixed in Los Angeles in mid March 1966 by Dylan and Bob Johnston. By this stage it had become clear that there was much more material than would fit on a traditional LP, thus giving birth to the first double-album set in rock music. Numerous other artists have since followed Dylan's lead, often with mixed results; most lack the consistency and focus of *Blonde On Blonde*. Among the other late-1960s' double-vinyl releases that succeeded Dylan's magnum opus are Frank Zappa's *Freak Out* (1966), Donovan's *A Gift From A Flower To A Garden*, Captain Beefheart's Trout Mask Replica (both 1967), and *Electric Ladyland* by Jimi Hendrix (1968). Two more achievements: Blonde On Blonde's 'Sad-Eyed Lady Of The Lowlands' was the first song to fill an entire side of vinyl and was then the longest popular song on record.

Blonde On Blonde was released in May 1966 while Dylan was in the midst of his controversial first electric tour of the U.K., and the album reached the Top Ten in both the U.S.A. and Britain. Two months later Dylan was injured in a mysterious motorcycle accident, after which he became somewhat reclusive, bringing to an end the most frenetic period of his career. His next release, the country-tinged *John Wesley Harding*, would not emerge for another 18 months.

Blonde On Blonde appeared in a strange disparity of mixes on its

release around the world. As was the case at the time, the mono mix took precedence, but, strangely, the stereo version of the album featured shortened versions of several of the songs. One song, '4th Time Around,' added a harmonium part missing on the mono version. The original U.K. release of the album was mistakenly cut from an early master and included odd fragments of music at the end of several of the songs. In 1968 the mono versions of the album were dropped, eventually to be replaced in 1970 by yet another new stereo mix, which altered the lengths of eight of the 14 tracks.

About The Sleeve

Not only was *Blonde On Blonde* the first rock double album, it was also the first to be issued in a gatefold sleeve. The artwork was designed by Josephine DiDonato, who has also produced album sleeves for Wynton Marsalis, Tony Bennett, and Harry Connick Jr.

The front and back covers of the LP are made up of an iconic portrait of Dylan in a double-breasted brown suede jacket and black-and-white checked scarf, photographed by Jerry Schatzberg. The sleeve opens to reveal a collage of smaller, monochrome images, again taken by Schatzberg. The layout of these images has changed since *Blonde On Blonde* was first released in 1966. There were originally nine images spread across the two sides of the inner sleeve; most were of Dylan himself but there were also shots of the actress Claudia Cardinale, an unidentified woman – seen whispering in Dylan's ear – and a self-portrait by the photographer. After objections from Cardinale over the inclusion of her photograph, a replacement sleeve was issued in the U.S.A., removing the images of both Cardinale and the unknown woman. The U.K. edition retains the original artwork.

After *Blonde On Blonde*, the gatefold-sleeve album became more commonplace for both single and double albums, most notably The Beatles' *Sgt Pepper's Lonely Hearts Club Band*.

Tale Of The Tape

The success of stereo records destroyed the nascent home-tape market, except for those who needed a recording capability. But tape didn't die.

The vinyl LP record achieved remarkable levels of fidelity – plenty of people still prefer its sound to that of CD – but it was not a portable medium for music. The single was better, but it was still no fun to lug a portable record-player and a box of records with you to the beach or a picnic. And then there was the problem of in-car entertainment. In 1955 Dr Peter Goldmark, head of CBS's research laboratories and overseer of the LP project, had created the Highway Hi-Fi system, but it used special 16rpm records. Then, in 1960, several U.S. car manufacturers adopted the RCA Auto Victrola, an in-car autochanger stacked with 14 singles. It lasted only a couple of years.

The time was right for another look at tape. There had been some developments over the years. In 1959, the 4-track format doubled playing time, but that didn't solve the fundamental problem with tape, which was consumer resistance to its awkwardness. RCA, perhaps fulfilling the promise it had made at the time of the LP rpm debacle, came up with an idea to tackle that. Called simply the Sound Tape Cartridge, it was uncannily like a larger version of the later Philips Compact Cassette. It placed two spools of ¼-inch tape in a seven-inch by five-inch plastic box normally running at 3¾ inches per second to provide 30 minutes of playing time. Like Compact Cassette, the tape format was 4-track, allowing stereo on each side. RCA duly produced a portable machine and a library of pre-recorded titles for it.

Unfortunately, the system was chronically unreliable and disappeared within a couple of years. A system by 3M, in which tape was reeled out of a cartridge into the player and then wound back at the end, proved another dead end. But then the background music industry had the brilliant idea of creating a cartridge in which the tape was pulled out of a central spool and then fed back in a continuous loop. The Fidelipac system of 1962 was a 2-track development of that concept, initially used for broadcast, and then adapted for in-car use. A 4-track version followed, doubling the playback time. It was marketed by a former used-car salesman, Earl 'Madman' Muntz. This was a Californian success in the early 1960s, particularly among the Hollywood crowd – Frank Sinatra, James Garner, and Peter Lawford were among those who had Muntz Fidelipac players. In 1964 pre-recorded tapes began to appear, as well as the first home players.

But then Bill Lear, creator of the Learjet business aircraft, announced his own Stereo-8 system. He had previously installed Muntz's machines on his airplanes, now he changed the design of the cartridge (apparently to circumvent any patents on the Muntz system). He also fitted a new playback head to the player, with eight tracks of sound across the ¼-inch tape providing four selections of stereo music. When each selection finished, the loop tape was in position to play it again, but the playback head now moved across to the next pair of tracks and played those. In that way it would instead automatically switch to the next pair of playback heads and so play different music.

What made the Stereo-8 system succeed was not so much down to its inherent qualities as Lear's business abilities. The system wasn't perfect, and Lear's great mistake was to place the pinch wheel, the essential moving part in any tape system, inside the cartridge rather than leaving it in the player; this meant it had to be cheap, which made it unreliable. Despite this, he persuaded RCA to provide music and Ford to fit the machines as options on its 1966 models. It was an immediate and lasting success, spawning home models and rising to take a quarter of the U.S. home-music market by the mid 1970s. Elsewhere, however, it was much less successful. Player manufacturers began to lose interest after 1975, and large-scale production of tapes ended in 1983.

The system also had some bizarre musical side-effects. Ideally the format required four musical selections of identical lengths: the maximum was 20 minutes. In order to achieve this equality, albums were given different running orders. In some cases, songs were faded out and in again to cross the join. (Notoriously, the 8-track version of *Sgt Pepper* not only had the tracks in the wrong order it had a crudely edited special version of 'Sgt Pepper's Lonely Hearts Club Band (Reprise)' with the last ten seconds repeated to make that selection the right length.)

1966

Sounds Of Silence **Simon & Garfunkel**

Columbia CS9269 (U.S.A.) / CBS 62690 (U.K.)
Released January 1966

Unknown to the record-buying public, Simon & Garfunkel's first hit album came into being solely because of studio trickery and the vision of a producer.

In June 1965, when Bob Dylan ran late for a *Highway 61 Revisited* recording date, producer Tom Wilson found himself with a studio full of musicians twiddling their thumbs. "We had no idea what we were going to work on," remembers guitarist Vinnie Bell. "There were no artists . . . and we had no music. They just played a demo of these two guys singing." The two guys were Paul Simon and Art Garfunkel, a folksy acoustic New York duo, who had broken up when their debut album stiffed. The track, 'The Sound Of Silence,' wasn't actually a demo, it came from that failed album, *Wednesday Morning, 3am*. Wilson got the studio crew to add electric instruments to the track, and the result was so successful that it was released as a single that, with folk rock emerging as a new genre, promptly shot to Number One.

Simon & Garfunkel quickly reunited and were given a month in which to cobble together a cash-in album. As Garfunkel recalls: "We were under the influence of big business. We had this Number One single, and it was a case of business trying to make the music conform to the situation."

Astonishingly, the pressure-cooked duo came up with a genuinely memorable album that includes not just the classic title track, but another Simon-composed cornerstone of the genre, 'I Am A Rock.'

The Monkees **The Monkees**

Colgems COS-101 (U.S.A.) / RCA SF-7844 (U.K.)
Released October 1966

The Monkees were the first manufactured pop group, but it's worth remembering that the system used to record music under The Monkees moniker had long been standard practice in the music industry.

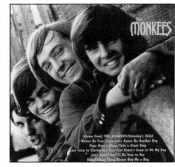

Such teen idols as Frankie Avalon, Bobby Vee, and Bobby Vinton, were routinely fitted up with songs by Brill Building tunesmiths and then presented with a backing track recorded by session men to which they would add their vocals. There was never any pretence that such Motown groups as The Four Tops or The Supremes played on or wrote the songs they sang, but The Monkees' svengali, Don Kirshner, realized that in order to launch The Monkees as a viable American alternative to The Beatles, they had to appear to be a credible rock band. And that's where the lies had to start.

Inspired by the success of The Beatles' movie, *A Hard Day's Night*, Kirshner, of the successful Aldon Music publishing company in New York, conceived a scheme to manufacture an equally lovable pop band, and felt that a weekly television show in the wacky Beatles'-movie style was the ideal means of delivery.

Having recruited four handsome boys via trade-magazine adverts, Kirshner hired professional writers, including Neil Diamond, and teams such as Tommy Boyce and Bobby Hart, Carole King and Gerry Goffin, to knock out enough songs for a debut album. The crack Los Angeles session-player mafia, known as The Wrecking Crew, was employed to create backing tracks to which The Monkees added vocals, and then mimed to on television.

The formula worked, the album sold four million copies, and The Monkees were trapped into living Kirshner's lie for some while to come. Tempting as it is to dismiss The Monkees as pop trash, such songs as 'Last Train To Clarkesville' and 'Take A Giant Step' are hard to resist, and the two songs on the album with composer credits for Monkee Mike Nesmith – 'Papa Gene's Blues' and 'Sweet Young Thing' – revealed that here was a *bona fide* talent in waiting.

Eventually, of course, The Monkees turned on Kirshner, demanded the right to compose their own songs and play on their records, and promptly saw their career flush itself down the drain. Kirshner, having learned his lesson, next transformed the popular *Archie* comic-book characters into a television cartoon band called The Archies and had another huge international smash with 'Sugar Sugar' – and, being cartoons, they never insisted on writing their own songs.

Collecting 8-track tapes and equipment has become a contemporary obsession in the U.S.A., and enthusiasts have come up with various reasons for the format's death: the most likely culprit, though, was a European invader, the Philips Compact Cassette.

When it was introduced in 1963 the Compact Cassette was intended to be a simple, sturdy, reliable, and low-fidelity home-and-office recording medium. No one seems to have foreseen its success as a carrier for music. It used narrow ⅛-inch ferric tape moving at a slow 1⅞ inches per second. But it did permit 30 minutes of recording (later 45 then 60 minutes) on each side of the tape, it was portable, and its efficient design meant it had sufficiently low power requirements to permit battery use. As so often, convenience was about to win out over sound quality.

In 1965 Philips freely licensed its new technology to rival manufacturers of tapes and machines, who agreed to abide by its technical specifications. By 1966 pre-recorded cassettes had begun to appear on the market, but the real breakthrough for cassette's acceptance as a serious music medium was the arrival of Dolby B, a noise reduction system, available on new machines from 1970 onward. The Dolby system and Dolby-processed tapes soon became near-universal. Together with improved tape formulations and more precisely player mechanics, they ensured a long life for cassette. The arrival, in 1979, of the portable playback-only cassette machine, better known as the Sony Walkman, took its fortunes to new heights. (It also accustomed the population at large for the first time to the appealing new sensation of listening on headphones, a pleasure previously little known outside hi-fi circles.)

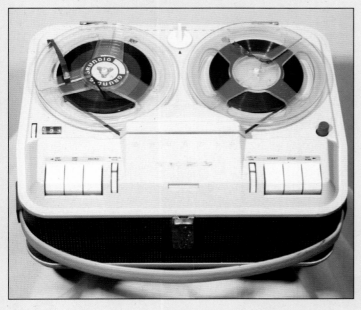

Cassette reached its peak in the late 1980s, when it dominated the market for recorded music, though in due course it was to be crushed by CD almost everywhere. Philips itself stopped making pre-recorded cassettes in 2000. Since then recordable CD has effectively finished it off in the West, though it remains important in some parts of the world, notably the Indian sub-continent.

Not everyone was satisfied with trying to extract high-quality sound from a medium so inherently limited as the cassette, however. In 1976, Sony introduced Elcaset, a new system using standard ¼-inch tape, running at 3¾ inches per second in a larger and more precisely engineered cassette. Several Japanese manufacturers took up the standard, but no pre-recorded tapes were available and the system rapidly foundered. The machines were capable of excellent results but standard cassette was much improved by the time of their introduction. In any case, by 1977 Sony was already working on a digital-disk system, and audio enthusiasts were inclined to wait for that. In 1980 the remains of the Elcaset production run were unceremoniously auctioned off to a company in Finland, where the system lived on for a few years.

1966

Revolver **The Beatles**

Capitol 2576 (U.S.A.) / Parlophone PMC/PCS 7009 (U.K.)
Released August 1966

With *Revolver* The Beatles moved toward using the studio as an instrument in itself, rather than merely a room in which recording takes place.

Because of this, as well as a new sophistication in the band's songwriting, these 14 tracks advanced the boundaries of what was considered possible in popular music. Only three years earlier The Beatles were playing Merseybeat; now they were mixing up Indian and blues influences. *Revolver*, and in particular the track 'Tomorrow Never Knows,' helped create and popularize the taste for psychedelic music that would soon become a defining trait of the hippie movement.

With George Martin once more at the producer's helm, the recording sessions started early in April and lasted until June. *Revolver* featured an intriguing mix of up-tempo numbers, melodious ballads, and songs that defied categorization. *Revolver* gave Harrison his best opportunity thus far to shine in his own right – his seminal slashed chords on 'Taxman' sounded harsher and more angular in 1966 than they do now. Instead of stealing from Chuck Berry, the lead-guitar break has an Indian influence in its phrasing. The lyric theme of 'Taxman' had a wide appeal. The British Labour Party was re-elected in March 1966, and the government introduced a new, high, top rate of tax. 'Doctor Robert' has a similar blues-rock feel. Many of *Revolver*'s songs have unexpected twists in them: 'I Want To Tell You' is a Harrison song that fades in with its dissonant piano playing a deliberate wrong note for several bars.

'Good Day Sunshine' offered two rollicking pianos and two drum kits, and a second verse that unpredictably terminates early in a piano solo. 'And Your Bird Can Sing,' where Lennon takes the lead vocal, is the best rocker on the album, with carefully plotted harmonized guitar breaks and a steadier beat. (For the comical chaos of some Beatles sessions, seek out the version on *Anthology 2*.) Less predictable because of its asymmetrical phrasing is 'She Said She Said,' with its static background and a lyric that mixes metaphysics ('I know what it's like to be dead') with recollections of childhood, which was a central theme of British psychedelia. 'Got To Get You Into My Life' is a fine soul tune, complete with brass section and an adventurous melody, and this was probably influenced by the many mid-1960s' chart hits written for the Motown label by Holland-Dozier-Holland.

Of the ballads, 'Eleanor Rigby' is the standout, creating in just over two minutes an unforgettable glimpse of old age and loneliness, a world normally avoided in the lyrics of popular song. McCartney sings over an octet of four violins, two violas, and two cellos. 'Here, There and Everywhere' is a more traditional love song. Apparently inspired by an early listen to The Beach Boys' *Pet Sounds*, it doesn't quite emulate the less-predictable movement of Brian Wilson's chord patterns, and consequently its tenderness comes over as sentimental in a way that *Pet Sounds* avoids. The piano figure on the somewhat bitter 'For No One' sounds as if influenced by The Beach Boys, whose work at the time often featured eighth-note piano chords.

Revolver also has one of the most popular children's pop songs of all time, 'Yellow Submarine,' sung by Ringo Starr to a battery of sound effects, such as breaking surf, clinking glasses, a brass band, engine-room clatters, and mock-nautical orders. Dylan's 'Rainy Day Women # 12 and 35' has been cited as an influence, but so is the 1950s' BBC radio comedy series

The Goon Show. 'Yellow Submarine' has an appropriately jaunty verse tune and an effective lower vocal harmony line to buttress the chorus. Lennon's adult counterpart is 'I'm Only Sleeping,' a narcoleptic acoustic strum with one of his typical narrow-range melodies, some fluid shifts in song structure, tape-speeded vocals, and serpentine flickers of two 'backward' guitars.

For millions of young people *Revolver* also opened a door on Indian music and the 'mystic' East. It was musically courageous for a band in The Beatles' position to put 'Love You To' on a rock album in 1966, dominated as it is by Indian instruments and open imitation of Indian music. But exotic as it was, Harrison's homage to the culture he was coming to revere couldn't compete with the impact of the album's closing track, 'Tomorrow Never Knows,' one of the most revolutionary statements ever made in popular music. The first song to be worked on, 'Tomorrow Never Knows' was

inspired by Lennon's considerable LSD intake and his reading of *The Psychedelic Experience* by Tomothy Leary, Ralph Metzner, and Richard Alpert, which itself alluded to the *Tibetan Book Of The Dead*. The lyric of the song summarized what was to become the core tenet of the counter-culture, that belief in the power of reason, which had dominated Western science and philosophy for two centuries, was inadequate to explain or penetrate the mystery of existence.

As rockets put U.S. and Soviet astronauts into outer space, 'Tomorrow Never Knows' pointed to a new frontier: inner space. The mind had to be turned off, transcended, in order for reality and the self to be fathomed. This would be a revolution in human consciousness, from which would evolve a utopia of enlightened beings.

Work on the song – originally entitled 'The Void' – started on April 6th with the basic rhythm tracks.

Musically, 'Tomorrow' ambitiously attempts to approximate this new vision of reality. Starting with sitar, it opens out a soundscape that breaks with Western musical tradition in abandoning musical progression. The drum pattern and virtually a single chord sustain the track, along with five tape loops – a 'seagull' effect (McCartney laughing); an orchestral chord of B-flat major; a Mellotron flute; another Mellotron oscillating a string tone from B-flat to C; and an ascending sitar phrase – all subjected to tape-speeding and other effects. Lennon's lead vocal was put through a Leslie cabinet. The Beatles had managed to get a piece of essentially avant-garde music across to millions, but, being who they were, couldn't resist the facetious bit of piano at the end. Here was the start of the psychedelic 1960s, which in many ways is what people have come to think of as the 1960s.

'She Said She Said' was the last song to be recorded, on June 21st 1966. The sessions also produced

'Paperback Writer,' their 12th British single, recorded on April 13th and 14th along with its b-side, 'Rain.'

Two days after finishing *Revolver* The Beatles were back on the road playing in Germany on the 24th. The U.S. version omits 'And Your Bird Can Sing,' 'I'm Only Sleeping,' and 'Doctor Robert,' all of which had been included on *Yesterday And Today*, a U.S.-only Beatles LP released two months before *Revolver*.

It was common practice in the 1960s for the tracklistings of albums to differ on either side of the Atlantic. The Beatles are the best example of this; the original U.K. versions of each of the group's albums up to and including *Revolver* were altered for their U.S. issue, often to take in non-album singles (which tended not to feature on the U.K. editions). Much of The Rolling Stones' output of the time was given the same treatment, notably *Out Of Our Heads* (1965) and *Aftermath* (1966).

1966

Otis Blue **Otis Redding**

Atlantic SD33284 (U.S.A.) / 587036 (U.K.)
Released February 1966

**In the mid 1960s Otis Redding's
popularity rivaled that of James
Brown. Nicknamed 'Mr Pitiful' for
his plaintive phrasing, and
drawing on blues, pop, and
gospel, Redding's soul appeal
crossed racial boundaries, as
was evident during his seminal
set at the 1967** *Monterey Pop*
festival.

The bulk of *Otis Blue* was recorded
on July 27th 1965 at the Stax
studios in Memphis, backed by
Booker T. And The MGs and The Memphis Horns. Ten of the 11 tracks were
laid down between 10am on the 27th and 8am the following morning, with
an eight-hour intermission for the musicians to play a club gig! One other
song had been recorded the previous April. Wayne Jackson of The Memphis
Horns: "Otis would come into a session, get his guitar out and start singing
his song – he'd walk round the studio and sing it to Duck [Dunn, bass] until
Duck was in the groove, sing it to the drummer, come round to me and
Andrew [Love, the saxophonist] and sing us the horn parts. Once everybody
was in the groove then Otis would go to the microphone . . . and we'd start
recording. He was the most charismatic of all the people we worked with,
the most exciting to be around."

Otis Blue is a warm, confident record, with three Sam Cooke tunes,
including 'Wonderful World,' and The Temptations' 'My Girl,' showing the
grittier R&B feel of Stax. Two Redding originals – 'Respect' and 'I've Been
Loving You Too Long' – were subsequently covered by Aretha Franklin and
Tina Turner.

In December 1967, three days after cutting what was to be his biggest hit,
'Dock Of The Bay,' Redding died in a plane crash, aged just 26.

Blues Breakers With Eric Clapton John Mayall

London LL3492 (mono) LL492 (stereo) (U.S.A.) / Deram LK 4804 (U.K.)
Released July 1966

Nicknamed 'The *Beano* **Album,'
after the comic that Eric Clapton
is reading on the sleeve, this
record advanced rock guitar from
the twangy sound that had
dominated the early 1960s,
establishing Eric Clapton as the
new guitar supremo and
accelerating the British blues
boom.**

Clapton joined Mayall after having left
The Yardbirds in March 1965. He'd
wanted to continue playing straight
blues, and was not happy with The Yardbirds' new more chart-friendly
direction. Mayall said: "I'd known about Eric, of course, before he joined . . .
but when I heard the b-side to 'For Your Love' ['Got To Hurry'], I knew he
was the guitarist for the band. And he didn't take much persuading."

Clapton joined a line-up that included Mayall on vocals, keyboards, and
harmonica, John McVie on bass – later the 'Mac' of Fleetwood Mac – and
Hughie Flint on drums. Flint commented: "It was frustrating in the Blues
Breakers before Eric came in because we couldn't really get the Chicago sound
that John wanted. As soon as Eric came in, the band completely transformed . . .
We were able to play all the blues standards by people like Buddy Guy and
Freddie King – just the music that John loved . . . When Eric came in, all of us
were a bit overawed by the way he played guitar. I'd never heard a blues guitarist
like this outside of the Americans." The press thought the same. *Melody Maker*
(U.K.) said: "No British musicians have sounded like this on record."

The album included Clapton's first vocal (Robert Johnson's 'Ramblin' on My
Mind'), and covers of famous blues numbers, such as Freddie King's

'Hideaway' and Otis Rush's 'All Your Love.' On Ray Charles's 'What I'd Say' the band throw in The Beatles' 'Day Tripper' riff for good measure.

Clapton plugged a Gibson Les Paul – then, incredibly, out of production – into a Marshall JTM 45 amplifier, and horrified the engineers by recording at high volume. Clapton went after a Les Paul after seeing one on the cover of the album *Freddie King Sings The Blues*. He first used this set-up for the Mayall single 'I'm Your Witchdoctor' b/w 'Telephone Blues,' produced by Jimmy Page, who acknowledged that Clapton was the first to combine the Les Paul with Marshall amplification, a guitar tone that would come to define heavy rock. By the end of the 1960s the Les Paul would be widely regarded as the premier rock guitar.

Clapton said: "I suppose my aim was to get some kind of thickness that would be a combination of the way all of the musicians I heard played, plus the sustain of a slide guitar . . . When they tried to set up the recording, I wouldn't let them put the microphone anywhere near my amplifier." The lead breaks are typified by stinging distortion on the edge of feedback and vibrato, effortless sustain, wild and subtle string-bending, and a precocious command of the Chicago electric blues idiom. Some of the playing contains the blueprint for Cream's approach to the blues. The effect of the record is summed up by Queen's Brian May: "He was what turned me away from The Shadows style and sent me back to listening to B.B. King, Bo Diddley, and all those people. I didn't realize the depth or emotion there was in the music until I saw Eric Clapton. That somehow made it accessible for me." May was only one of thousands who started investigating the blues originals.

1966

Aftermath
The Rolling Stones

London PS476 (U.S.A.) / Decca SKL 4786 (U.K.)
Released April 1966

The Rolling Stones' fourth album, *Aftermath*, **was the first on which singer Mick Jagger and guitarist Keith Richards wrote every song.**

Well into the mid 1950s, the roles of songwriter and performer had been almost entirely separate in popular music. Songs were composed by so-called 'Tin Pan Alley' tunesmiths – such as Irving Berlin, Harold Arlen, and Cole Porter – and sung by specialist singers like Frank Sinatra, Ella Fitzgerald, and Bing Crosby. The distinction between the two jobs was, however, much less pronounced in folk and blues circles, where a Woody Guthrie or a Leadbelly would habitually write and perform his own songs. As rock'n'roll evolved, emerging young artists – notably Chuck Berry, Buddy Holly, and Bob Dylan – drew their inspiration from blues, folk, and country music, and so considered it perfectly normal to write their own material. Thus, the boundaries between folk, blues, and popular music became increasingly blurred.

With the arrival of The Beatles and their in-house writing team of Lennon & McCartney, the floodgates burst wide open, and The Stones were in the vanguard of innumerable British bands that decided to follow The Fab Four's lead. Mick Jagger has admitted that their first attempt at composition was "a horrible song," adding: "It was pop, and we didn't record it, because it was crap." To their surprise, Jagger & Richards found that their earliest songs – 'As Tears Go By,' written for Marianne Faithfull, is an obvious example – didn't match their personalities. "We were these two rebellious band members and we would write nice little tunes, but sentimental stuff."

By the end of 1965, however, they'd got the hang of it, and set to work on their first entirely self-composed album. Recording started at the end of a grueling U.S. tour with a five day session, between December 6th and 10th, at the RCA Studios, Los Angeles. From the outset it was obvious that this would be the first real Rolling Stones album. With the solitary exception of a sprawling semi-jam, 'Goin' Home,' The Stones' original incarnation as R&B wannabes was swept aside. Gone were the regurgitated hymns to American cars, bars, and boardwalks, replaced by songs about suburban housewives on tranquillizers, brain-dead dolly birds, and the corrupted values of modern life. And if these songs, shot through with misogynistic, narcissistic, and sneering lyrics, revealed The Stones as being far from lovable 'mop-tops,' at least they now had their own identity.

Though Jagger & Richards were writing the songs, Brian Jones gave the album much of its musical appeal. The baroque dulcimer in 'Lady Jane,' the sitar in 'Mother's Little Helper,' the marimbas on 'Under My Thumb,' these are all Jones's contributions, and they lift the tracks out of the riff-rock ruts they might otherwise have sunk into.

The release of *Aftermath* affected the band in three important ways: first, it brought them a new level of respect, placing them on a par with The Beatles, The Who, and The Kinks; second, generating their own material gave Jagger & Richards full creative control of the band's musical direction; and, finally, it earned them songwriting royalties that, before very long, would prove very lucrative.

Andrew Loog Oldham

For much of the 1960s The Rolling Stones' career was nurtured by Andrew Loog Oldham, who acted as the group's manager and producer. He quickly established the group as the bad boys of the mid-1960s' British music scene, providing a direct contrast to The Beatles' clean-cut image.

A former publicist, Oldham produced all of The Rolling Stones' albums from the group's 1964 debut, *The Rolling Stones* (called *England's Newest Hit Makers* in the U.S.A.), up to *Between The Buttons* (1967). He also formed The Andrew Loog Oldham Orchestra, issuing a series of albums of symphonic renditions of contemporary groups' songs. His reinterpretation of The Stones' 'The Last Time' was later sampled by The Verve, and formed the backbone of the group's 1997 British hit single 'Bittersweet Symphony.'

In 1965 Oldham founded Immediate, one of the best known British independent record labels of the 1960s. The company was initially highly successful, issuing albums by artists including The Small Faces and The Nice, but was bankrupt by the end of the decade. By this stage Oldham had also been relieved of his duties with The Rolling Stones.

Oldham continued to work sporadically as both producer and manager of other acts through the 1970s, but never again reached the level of success he had achieved with The Rolling Stones.

1966

Pet Sounds
The Beach Boys

Capitol ST2458 (U.S.A.) / MS2197 (U.K.)
Released May 1966

Pet Sounds, a new high in studio creativity in the mid 1960s, became possible after December 23rd 1964, when Brian Wilson suffered a severe mental breakdown on a flight to Houston, leading him to retire from touring and become a studio-based artist.

With their latest single, 'Dance, Dance, Dance,' easily making the U.S. Top Ten, December had been an intensely busy month for The Beach Boys. They had been shuttling across the U.S.A. between recording sessions, live gigs, and television appearances, most of the pressure falling squarely on the shoulders of the band's presiding genius Brian Wilson. Not only was he a performing band member but also their songwriter, arranger, and producer. As Brian's brother Carl noted: "He never did like touring, ever. He didn't like flying, or being away from home, or anything."

Adding to his mental anguish was the fact that earlier that month he had married Marilyn Rovell of Californian girl group The Honeys, but the relationship was already fraught with tension because Wilson was convinced that his new bride was having an affair with his band's lead vocalist, Mike Love. Brian, a 22-year-old survivor of parental abuse, found such burdens intolerable, and he had lately turned to marijuana in search of an escape from his torments.

So, two days before Christmas The Beach Boys boarded a plane in Los Angeles, heading for a gig in Houston, but, before it landed, Brian had snapped. He charged up and down the aisle, screaming abuse at staff, passengers, and the other Beach Boys until his brothers wrestled him to the floor and, reluctantly, had him sedated.

Brian began seeing a psychiatrist and concluded that the best way to deal with his unbearable workload was to stop playing in the band. "It was bound to happen," reckoned Carl philosophically. "He just said, 'I don't want to tour. I want to stay home. I want to make good music.'" From that moment on the studio was Brian Wilson's home. He became increasingly aware that a recording studio could be as much of a creative tool as any musical instrument, and *Pet Sounds* became the embodiment of that philosophy.

Hand in hand with this realization came another change in Wilson's world view. In the spring of 1965 he took LSD for the first time, and told Marilyn that the experience had been a spiritual confrontation with God. Now the stage was set. Though it would ultimately wreak havoc with his already parlous mental state, the perceptual changes triggered in Wilson by the drug would directly contribute to his creativity over the coming months.

Despite the fact that no firm plan – or even title – for the new album had yet entered Wilson's head, the earliest recording to appear on what was to become *Pet Sounds* took place on July 12th 1965 at Wilson's favorite studio, Western Recorders in Hollywood. Beach Boy Al Jardine had brought Wilson a somewhat gloomy Caribbean folk song, 'The Wreck Of The John B.' In the space of one day Wilson refashioned it as 'Sloop John B,' using the finest West Coast session players available – including The Wrecking Crew, who played on Phil Spector's biggest hits. Wilson pushed the tempo up and introduced an optimistic glockenspiel backing. "All we had to do was show up and sing," recalled Jardine.

As instrumentalists, the other Beach Boys were beginning to find themselves effectively – and infuriatingly – redundant, but Wilson applied the same rigorous standards to himself. He was a perfectly capable bass guitarist, but, for recording sessions, he used legendary session bassist Carol Kaye. "Sure, I could play bass," Wilson has explained, "but I could see the bigger picture if I left that to someone else so I could stay in the control booth and produce the session." However, even with Kaye on board, virtually every bass note was written by Wilson, and he had the final say on every aspect of the production. He was in total control and this would be the blueprint for every track on *Pet Sounds*.

Wilson's right-hand man at the console was Chuck Britz, who helped make the most of Wilson's increasingly complex compositions. "Chuck Britz," Wilson later observed, "taught me how to concentrate on what I was listening to . . . how to get my soul right into the music." It was Britz who masterminded the magnificent reverberation heard on 'Good Vibrations' and other Beach Boys classics. Western Recorders' live echo chamber had been haphazardly constructed from cinder block, but produced one of the finest reverb effects of the time. "Something about those cement blocks seemed to be able to expand the sound even more than usual," recalled Britz. "It was so warm – Brian's voice, in particular, sounded great in that chamber."

It was around this time that advertising copywriter Tony Asher dropped by the studio and was introduced to Wilson. The pair threw some ideas around, and Wilson – never a sophisticated lyricist – was sufficiently impressed by the young wordsmith to file his name mentally for future reference.

The instrumental parts for another *Pet Sounds* track, 'You Still Believe In Me,' were recorded on November 1st, under the title 'In My Childhood.' Neither this nor 'Sloop John B' were, however, recorded as part of any album. They were simply tracks.

Everything changed on December 6th, the date of the U.S. release of The Beatles' new album, *Rubber Soul*. In Wilson's own words: "When

Continued on next page

1966

I heard *Rubber Soul*, I said, 'I have to top that.' Then I did *Pet Sounds* and McCartney said, 'I'll top that with *Sgt Pepper*.'"

Wilson had noticed that every track on *Rubber Soul* seemed to have been recorded with the same care and attention normally lavished on a single. Until this time pop albums were regarded by the music industry as a way to cash in on hit singles. Rock'n'roll was regarded as a passing phase, so an album tended to consist of nine formulaic tracks quickly recorded to fill up the space between two or three carefully created singles. Wilson now decided that his next album would meet and even exceed the quality levels set by *Rubber Soul*, so that the entire album would stand as a coherent and creative whole.

Within days Wilson was back in Western Recorders finishing off 'Sloop John B.' After trying out every member of the band on lead vocals, he decided to do it himself, much to Jardine's dismay, and paid guitarist Billy Strange $500 to add a distinctive 12-string guitar backing.

For most of January 1966 The Beach Boys were touring the Far East, leaving Brian in Los Angeles, where he took full advantage of their absence to push ahead. On January 18th he entered Western to work on the instrumental track 'Let's Go Away For A While.' *Pet Sounds* was officially under way.

Wilson had also now begun working with Tony Asher as a lyricist, sometimes presenting him with complete instrumental tracks, sometimes just with melodies or even fragments of melodies. "The general tenor of the lyrics was always his," says Asher, "and the actual choice of words was usually mine. I was really just his interpreter."

"THE MUSIC OF *PET SOUNDS* WAS CREATED SOLELY FOR THE PURPOSE OF MAKING PEOPLE FEEL GOOD. I WANTED TO CREATE MUSIC THAT PEOPLE WOULD FEEL WOULD GET TO THEIR FEELINGS MORE."

BRIAN WILSON

By the 22nd Wilson had shifted to Gold Star Studios and moved on to another new song, 'Wouldn't It Be Nice.' Mark Linett, who later produced the stereo and 5.1 Surround Sound versions of *Pet Sounds*, points out that the richness of sound on tracks made at Gold Star came, to some extent, from the relatively small size of the studio. "You hear these huge records that Brian and Phil Spector made and you think it must be an enormous space," he explains. "Well, no, it's a very small space, because that allowed the coincident information to be useful. If you were in a huge room like Studio 1 at Western, the bounceback from instruments to the other mikes would have been objectionable, whereas in a small room, it added another dimension." The depth of sound on the album is all the more remarkable given that Wilson mixed it in mono. (His reluctance towards working in stereo was due in no small part to the fact that he was deaf in one ear.)

Returning to Western on the 24th Wilson laid down tracks for the haunting ballad 'You Still Believe In Me.' In his ongoing efforts to find new sounds he devised a piano introduction that required sessioneer Larry Knechtel to play the keyboard while another musician clambered inside the piano and plucked the strings to make them ring out.

The Beach Boys' Far Eastern tour ended with a gig in Hawaii on the 29th, after which they took a well-earned rest while Wilson ploughed on with the new album. The collaboration with Asher was proving fruitful. Listening to Wilson speak about his high-school crush on a girl called Carol Mountain, Asher had written a lyric titled 'Carol, I Know,' but Wilson mis-heard the phrase and sang it as the much more poignant 'Caroline, No.' One of the pair's loveliest songs, recording of 'Caroline, No' was started on January 31st.

Suitably refreshed after their break, the other Beach Boys joined Wilson in Western Studios on February 9th. As Asher has pointed out, they were "hoping for and expecting more of what had been hits for them all along." Instead they were confronted by a radically more sophisticated style and

Continued on next page

sound, which didn't seem to require any input from them other than their voices. "We were a surfing group when we left the country," observed Al Jardine, "and now basically we came back to this new music."

Asher has confirmed that the band were unenthusiastic about the new songs and couldn't understand why their proven hit-making formula needed changing. "There was resistance," Wilson revealed. "There was a little bit of inter-group struggle. It was resolved in that they figured it was a showcase for Brian Wilson, but it was The Beach Boys. In other words, they gave in."

Wilson was back in Western on the 11th without the other Beach Boys, working on what he has described as "one of the sweetest, most loving songs that I ever sang," 'Don't Talk (Put Your Head On My Shoulder).'

During a session on the 14th, Wilson made his first use of an electro-theremin in the backing for 'I Just Wasn't Made For These Times.' Played by another session musician, Paul Tanner, the instrument was a variation on an earlier device invented in the 1920s by Russian scientist Leon Theremin. Both instruments emit the same eerie sound, half-way between a violin and a soprano voice, but the original theremin was apallingly difficult to master, because pitch and volume were varied by the performer's hands moving around in a magnetic field generated by the instrument. Accurate production of notes was much simpler on the electro-theremin which used a slider control for pitch and an amplifier for volume.

The following day saw the entire band rendezvous at the petting paddock in San Diego Zoo to shoot the album's cover. The best that can be said of the result is that it has a certain naive charm, and it ties in with the title, which Wilson says was chosen "because we specialized in certain sounds. It was our best – the songs were our 'Pet Sounds.'"

Later the same day they reassembled at Western and recorded 'That's Not Me,' a song whose lyric deals with Wilson's rationale for giving up touring. The track is remarkable for being the only one on *Pet Sounds* to feature the band playing its own instruments, though even here they were augmented by session players.

With the album sessions in full swing, Wilson now set to work on 'Good Vibrations,' but this classic single would not be completed in time to be included on the album.

Much of the next month and a half was occupied by the band adding its vocals under Brian's supervision. Recalling this long and painstaking process, Mike Love has stated: "If there was a hint of a sharp or flat, we would have to do it again until it was right." Frequently, Wilson would stop the group to pick up on some tiny error which no one else had even noticed. Even at this point, however, there were three new songs still to be recorded, 'Here Today,' 'I'm Waiting For The Day,' and, taking pride of place, 'God Only Knows.'

After a couple of days of Brian working on backing tracks without the band, they joined him in Columbia Studio A on March 10th. "When I walked in on 'God Only Knows,'" remembers Beach Boy Bruce Johnston, "I realized that something wonderful was happening." The song wasn't completed until a month later, when Carl Wilson recorded his transcendently beautiful lead vocal, widely regarded as his finest moment with the band. With 'God Only Knows' in the can, *Pet Sounds* was effectively complete.

Pet Sounds was released on May 16th, but, though now recognized as a landmark album, it stalled at Number Ten in the US chart because Capitol Records simply didn't get behind it. "They didn't promote *Pet Sounds*," reasons Johnston, "because they said it wasn't commercial and people wouldn't understand it."

The British audience liked it better, sending it to Number Two, and unswerving British devotion to *Pet Sounds* has seen it re-evaluated over the years, often topping critics' polls as the best album of all time. In Paul McCartney's own words: "It blew me out of the water," and there's no question that it set a new benchmark that The Beatles now felt they would have to top. Speaking of *Pet Sounds* some years later, The Beatles' producer George Martin observed that: "It gives you an elation that is beyond logic." And that, surely, is the point at which music intersects with magic.

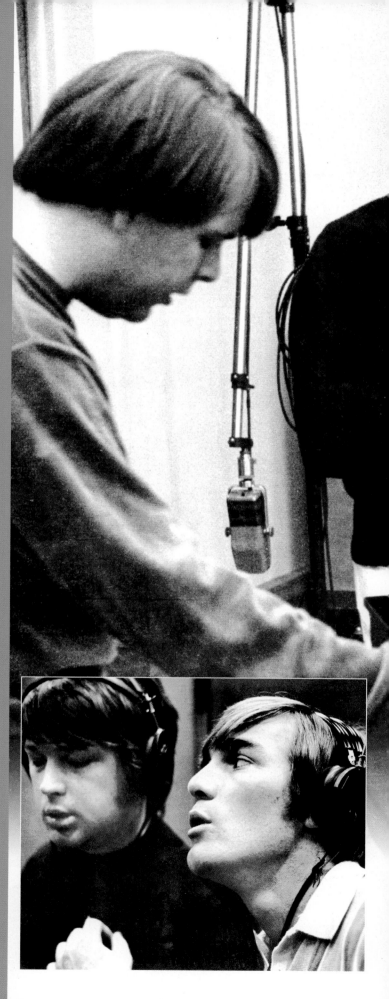

1967

I Never Loved A Man (The Way I Loved You)
Aretha Franklin

Atlantic 8139 (U.S.A.) / 587/588 085 (U.K.)
Released March 1967

Recorded in a handful of sessions between Muscle Shoals, Alabama, and Manhattan during the winter of 1967, Aretha Franklin's premier Atlantic album – which eventually settled at Number Two in the U.S.A. on its way to selling over a million copies – helped bring soul music to a worldwide audience.

A showcase for top songwriters – including King Curtis ('Save Me') and Chips Moman ('Do Right Woman, Do Right Man') – *I Never Loved A Man* also included a pair of fine originals in 'Baby, Baby, Baby' and 'Don't Let Me Lose This Dream.' But it was the cover of Otis Redding's 'Respect' that gave Franklin her first Number One single and brought her the richly deserved title of 'Queen of Soul.'

Few people had ever heard of the 25-year-old pianist-vocalist before her March 1967 soul breakout. Signed by Columbia in 1960, Franklin spent six frustrating years as a Dinah Washington-style pop balladeer until Atlantic's Jerry Wexler saw in her the makings of a world-class artist who'd simply been playing for the wrong team. Shortly after he recruited Franklin in late 1966 the pair headed for Alabama, where a revelatory one-off session at FAME Studios produced the stunning title track, written by Franklin's friend Ronnie Shannon. Rush-released as a single in late February, 'I Never Loved a Man' immediately shot up the charts, leaving Wexler and Franklin just weeks to polish off the remainder of the album at Atlantic's New York studios.

Over the next eight years Wexler would go on to cut an additional 14 albums with Franklin, his most valued client of all. "In this business, it's so important to be able to work on the music only when it's needed – because if it ain't broke, don't fix it," says Wexler. "With Aretha, there was never any second-guessing. In the studio, she was nothing short of miraculous."

Surrealistic Pillow **Jefferson Airplane**

RCA Victor LSP-3766 (U.S.A.) RD/SF 7889 (U.K.)
Released March 1967

On November 15th 1965, with an unprecedented $25,000 advance, Jefferson Airplane became the first West Coast hippy band to be signed up by a major record label, RCA, the home of Elvis Presley.

They were launched as a "San Francisco sextet singing in the folk-rock vein," but their debut album, *Jefferson Airplane Takes Off*, didn't trouble the charts.

Surrealistic Pillow – so named by Jerry Garcia of The Grateful Dead, who produced it – was their second effort, recorded over 13 days during November 1966. This one amped up The Airplane's quirky 'folksydelia' with rockier riffs, but the principal change was the arrival of the band's new vocalist Grace Slick. And with her came two songs, 'White Rabbit" and 'Somebody To Love,' written for her previous band, The Great Society. 'White Rabbit,' perhaps the quintessential Haight-Ashbury hit, was inspired by Slick's observation that virtually every great children's story – from *Peter Pan* though *The Wonderful Wizard Of Oz* to *Alice's Adventures In Wonderland* – involved children ingesting strange substances then having fantastical dream-like adventures.

> ### "I TOOK ACID AND LISTENED TO MILES DAVIS'S *SKETCHES OF SPAIN* FOR ABOUT 24 HOURS STRAIGHT."
> *GRACE SLICK ON THE INSPIRATION BEHIND 'WHITE RABBIT'*

The band's other major songwriter, Marty Balin, also contributed several powerful tracks, while guitarist Jorma Kaukonen provided the shimmering acoustic solo piece, 'Embryonic Journey,' but it was Slick's songs that would provide the two hits that would establish The Airplane as a major chart force. The album peaked at Number Three that spring, and was declared gold on July 24th, opening the floodgates for Frisco's hippy bands.

The Elektra Records Story

In the mid 1960s, Elektra Records radically expanded the horizons of rock by insisting on excellence and innovation in every aspect of its operations.

While a college student at St John's, Annapolis, Maryland, company founder Jac Holzman had more interest in electronics, radio, and tape recorders than in his scheduled classes. Inspired by a classical concert he had attended, Holzman decided to start his own record company, and, on October 10th 1950, he named it Elektra Records.

Elektra's first release, *New Songs*, by contemporary classical composer John Gruen, was a commercial disaster. Holzman relocated to Greenwich Village, opened a record store to generate cash, and recorded a second album, the memorably titled *Jean Ritchie Singing The Traditional Songs Of Her Kentucky Mountain Family*. This garnered critical acclaim and sold enough copies to put Elektra on a firmer footing.

Adding blues to its folk-based catalog in 1954, Elektra moved to bigger offices. Always politically active, Holzman boldly signed singer-guitarist Josh White to Elektra when White's former label, Decca, dumped him because he had been blacklisted during Senator Joe McCarthy's Communist witch-hunt. The early-1960s' folk boom boosted Elektra's fortunes, and Holzman's earlier reservations about rock music were swept away when, on July 25th 1965, he watched Bob Dylan go electric at *Newport Folk Festival*. "Dylan and folk music and Elektra were never the same again," he has said.

Determined to get behind the new, politically aware, intellectually challenging form of rock that was emerging, Holzman first signed Los Angeles-based Love – "Five guys of all colors, black, white, and psychedelic – that was a real first. My heart skipped a beat. I had found my band!" – and then The Doors.

Suddenly, without compromising its principles, little Elektra was scoring hit singles and competing in the same arena as giants Columbia, Capitol, and RCA. Entering its golden age, Elektra signed a string of ground-breaking acts, each of which explored the outer fringes of rock. To name just three: The Holy Modal Rounders, who invented psychedelic folk; Ars Nova, who took the combination of baroque and rock to its logical conclusion; and The Stooges, who were hammering out punk years before its time.

The label's big, blocky 'E' logo became a hallmark of quality, not just for Elektra's choice of artists but for exquisite sound reproduction and imaginative sleeve designs. Holzman's unswerving commitment to quality also meant that when album sales began to overtake singles in the late 1960s, his label was perfectly placed to reap the benefits, because knocking off quick hits had never been a feature of Elektra's recording policy.

Throughout this period Elektra also continued to record cutting-edge singer-songwriters, including Tim Buckley and Phil Ochs, while its classically oriented sister label, Nonesuch, scored a totally unexpected international smash with Joshua Rifkin's recordings of piano rags by Scott Joplin.

By the start of the 1970s, however, Holzman was wearying of the business and had moved to Hawaii. Elektra was merged, first with David Geffen's Asylum Records, then with Warner Brothers, thus forming WEA (Warner/Elektra/Asylum). Under new management the label continued to sign quality artists and achieved higher sales figures than ever, but the Holzman fingerprint was gone and Elektra's unique identity was lost for ever.

The Doors **The Doors**

EKS-74007 (U.S.A. / U.K.)
Released January 1967

The Doors' debut album broke new ground by fusing elements of theatre, poetry, and psychology into a hard rock format.

The Doors was recorded over six days in August 1966 at Sunset Sound, Los Angeles. Much of the album's impact comes from the exotic blending of Ray Manzarek's keyboards (splicing New Orleans stride and classical discipline) with Robbie Krieger's swooping fretwork (sometimes bluesy, sometimes evoking Indian ragas), while drummer John Densmore employed every percussion trick in the book to illustrate Jim Morrison's story-songs without ever skipping a beat. The real jolt, however, was Morrison's intimidating and surreal lyrics, exploring areas formerly taboo, even in rock.

'Light My Fire,' the Krieger-composed hit single, gave the band superstar status. But the key track is 'The End,' which had been recorded by the light of a single candle. This brooding, hallucinatory, gothic nightmare set to music was wholly new in its musical structure and oedipal lyrics.

In a world where the most outrageous of mainstream rock bands could achieve notoriety simply by turning their amplifiers up or introducing sexual or socio-political themes into their lyrics, The Doors' music was remarkably sophisticated, and Morrison's lyrics, probing the murkier depths of the human psyche, were downright shocking.

1967

Forever Changes **Love**

EKS 74013 (U.S.A. / U.K.)
Released November 1967

Frequently hailed as a classic of psychedelia, Love's third album, *Forever Changes*, is actually that much rarer artifact: an album that exists in its own category.

As the first rock band signed to the previously folk-dominated Elektra Records, the Los Angeles-based Love had a lot to prove. Initially touted as the 'new Byrds,' their eponymous 1966 debut album certainly ploughed a similar folk-rock furrow, but by the time of its successor, *Da Capo*, they were clearly heading in another, more idiosyncratic direction.

At the heart of the band was Arthur Lee, whom Elektra Records' president, Jac Holzman, has called "one of the few geniuses I have met." Born in Memphis, Lee had grown up with eclectic musical tastes that embraced soul, R&B, folk rock, and MOR. He seemed equally at home rocking out with his friend Jimi Hendrix or chilling out to the smooth sounds of Nat 'King' Cole, and elements of both are clearly audible in *Forever Changes*.

Recording began at Sunset Sound, Los Angeles, in June 1967, but, by that point, the band was falling apart. There had been personnel changes, much internal bickering, and escalating hard-drug problems. Things were so bad that Elektra Records' producer Bruce Botnick, who was to co-produce the album with Neil Young, decided to dispense with the services of all the band members except Lee, and brought in the Los Angeles crack team of session players, The Wrecking Crew, to create the instrumental backings.

The first two tracks to be recorded – 'The Daily Planet' and 'Andmoreagain' – were completed with Lee arranging, playing, and singing, while the other band members merely watched from the sidelines. Horrified by the ease with which they had been replaced, they demanded their old jobs back. "The band was so shocked," remembers Botnick, "that it caused them to forget about their problems and become a band again."

When the sessions resumed on August 11th, Lee had usurped Young, and the rest of the band had replaced The Wrecking Crew. Precisely what happened next remains a matter of whose version you'd most like to believe – virtually all of the participants have offered dramatically different scenarios, and, given how stoned they apparently were during the sessions, their recollections can hardly be relied upon.

What is irrefutable is that Lee wrote most of the songs, though the band's other guitarist-vocalist, Bryan MacLean, composed the best-remembered track, 'Alone Again Or,' as well as the haunting 'Old Man.' The other major contributor to the album's unique sonic palette was David Angel, an orchestral arranger who had previously worked with Andy Williams and Herb Alpert's Tijuana Brass.

Angel's input is evident from the opening track, the lovely 'Alone Again Or,' where shimmering strings and mariachi horns, courtesy of members of The Los Angeles Philharmonic Orchestra, brilliantly intensify the drama of the band's delicately finger-picked acoustic-guitar patterns. In a way, the track represents the whole album in microcosm. The musical elements – acoustic guitars, strings, horns, understated bass and drums – are all here. Having

been blown away by the guitar pyrotechnics of his now internationally acclaimed old associate Hendrix, Lee had astutely decided there was no point in trying to compete. Instead, *Forever Changes* would be largely acoustic and focused on well-constructed songs rather than on instrumental virtuosity. Lyrically, too, the mood of other-worldly strangeness in MacLean's song sets listeners up for Lee's similar – if noticeably weirder – approach throughout the subsequent tracks. However, Lee's obsessive need to control every aspect of the album is demonstrated in the mixing of 'Alone Again Or,' because, lacking confidence in MacLean's singing, Lee turned down the composer's lead vocal, burying it under his own harmony part.

Lee was the principal element that ensured *Forever Changes* would stand apart from the general run of West Coast psychedelia at the time. Unlike the rainbow-eyed battalions of hippie bands promoting love, peace, and brotherhood, Lee saw the world as a dark, dangerous place on the brink of self-destruction. "When I did that album," he has said, "I thought I was going to die."

At just 22 years old he was convinced that he would not live beyond 26, and the album brims over with dire portents of the apocalypse he believed was imminent. 'The Daily Planet,' for example, is a damning indictment of the tedium of modern life generally and, very specifically, of the part played by toy guns in conditioning children for war. The title of the song 'The Red Telephone' refers to the hotline linking The White House to The Kremlin, to be used only on the brink of nuclear attack. And, in 'A House Is Not A Motel,' he asserts: "By the time that I'm through singing / The bells from the schools of wars will be ringing." Given all of this, it should be an intensely depressing album, but the sheer beauty of the music conspires – at least at first – to sugar the bitter pill of Lee's lyrics. As a result, when the lyrics do finally seep through after repeated listens, their impact is significantly greater.

The innovations on *Forever Changes* are too many to document here, but a few examples will serve to give a flavor: 'The Good Humor Man He Sees Everything Like This' employs cut-up tapes of horn parts to simulate the sound of a needle jumping in a vinyl groove; 'Maybe The People Would Be The Times Or Between Clark And Hilldale' features an ingenious lyrical device of holding back the final word of the verse and then using it as the first word of the next; the otherwise tightly constructed 'Live And Let Live' ends with a guitar solo that deliberately falls apart.

When recording finished in September Love had fashioned an album as innovative as *Sgt Pepper* or *Are You Experienced?*, but with an entirely different mood and musical landscape. So different, indeed, that the world wasn't quite ready for it. On release, *Forever Changes* staggered to Number 154 on the *Billboard* album chart before disappearing back below the horizon. Only the passage of time and the persistence of critical acclaim has elevated it to the status of an all-time classic – but it still hasn't gone gold.

Resurgent interest in Love – and *Forever Changes* in particular – peaked in 2003 when, several months after the 25th anniversary of its original release, Lee began performing the album in its entirety with his new band and an eight-piece Scandinavian string and horn section. *Forever Changes Concert* captures one such performance, taped at the Royal Festival Hall in London on January 13th 2003. Lee was one of several artists to revisit a past masterwork in a live setting: Beach Boys founder Brian Wilson performed *Pet Sounds* in full on his 2000–1 tour, while David Bowie reworked his landmark *Low* (1977) on stage in 2002.

1967

Disraeli Gears **Cream**

Atco SD33232 (U.S.A.) / Reaction 594003 (U.K.)
Released November 1967

Eric Clapton, Jack Bruce, and Ginger Baker were dubbed rock's first 'supergroup,' choosing the name Cream in ironic acknowledgment of the fact. Their second album, *Disraeli Gears*, with its classic psychedelic sleeve, mixes heavy blues with rock riffery.

Disraeli Gears was recorded on 8-track in ten days at Atlantic Studios in New York with Tom Dowd producing. 'Sunshine Of Your Love' has a classic and memorable riff, and songs such as 'World Of Pain,' 'Dance The Night Away,' and 'We're Going Wrong' have pretty chord sequences and a delicate touch. The heavy riffing and Baker's distinctive drumming – Keith Moon

meets the whirling dervishes – are juxtaposed with poetic lyrics sung in a relaxed if moody style, a contrast heightened by the mix itself. Singeribassist Jack Bruce said: "I had this idea that you could have very heavy, wild instrumental stuff but a gentle, lyrical vocal . . . very rhythmic backing, very smooth voices on top. It would've been easy to scream something, but then it's one-dimensional."

Clapton's fuzzy front pickup on 'Swlabr' is one of the definitive tones in rock guitar, and 'Tales Of Brave Ulysses' a fine early deployment of the wah-wah pedal. The album influenced legions of guitarists. Eddie Van Halen said: "I

started out playing blues; I learned from the *Blues Breakers* album. Then I learnt [some of the Cream solos] note-for-note." And Buddy Guy: "My favorite is 'Strange Brew.' I was really impressed by the tone [Clapton] was getting, plus the way he was playing." *Disraeli Gears* gives ample evidence of a creative partnership, the potential of which was perhaps never fully realized at the time. An expanded remastered version of the album was released in 2004.

■ *Above: Ginger Baker (left), Jack Bruce (center), and Eric Clapton pose with local children in Battersea Park, London, during the summer of 1967. Pictures from this photo session were used on the psychedelic collaged sleeve of* Disraeli Gears, *which was designed by Martin Sharp. The design was subtly different on the U.S. (left) and U.K. (right) editions of the album (back covers pictured). Sharp's design was adapted again for the 1997 retrospective collection,* Those Were The Days.

The Velvet Underground & Nico
The Velvet Underground

Verve V6 5008 (U.S.A.) / S+/VLP9184 (U.K.)
Released March 1967

White Light/White Heat
The Velvet Underground

Verve V6-5046 (U.S.A.) / S+/VLP9201 (U.K.)
Released December 1967

On release, *The Velvet Underground And Nico* barely limped into the *Billboard* chart at Number 197 before promptly disappearing without trace, but it is now acknowledged as one of the most influential albums of all time.

The Velvets, whose music can now be seen as New York's brutally realist street-wise riposte to San Francisco's hippy dreams, was launched largely from a platform provided by their association with the 1960s' most celebrated pop artist, Andy Warhol. As an outrageous quartet they had become New York's hottest rock ticket during 1966, but, by the time they started recording their debut album, they had been joined by Warhol's protégée, the striking blonde German actress, model, and chanteuse, Nico.

■ *Above: The Velvet Underground with Nico (left). Right: the line-up for the band's second album, by which time the German singer had departed.*

Keen to establish Nico as next in his line of 'superstars,' Warhol financed the album, securing three days at a studio on Broadway, at a cost of $2,500. In return, the band would feature Nico as a vocalist and credit Warhol as producer, though he rarely showed his face at the studio. Lou Reed, the band's principal songwriter, found Nico's presence hard to take – and there were, undeniably, solid musical reasons for not wanting her in the band. A perforated ear-drum made her deaf in one ear and, as a result, she would often lose control of her vocals. Multi-instrumentalist John Cale recalls: "We'd hear her go off-key or hit the wrong pitch. We would sit there and snigger."

According to drummer Mo Tucker time was so limited that most of the tracks were recorded live with virtually no overdubs. "We went in the studio for just eight hours to do it, and all the gigs we'd done just paid off. It wasn't a case of 'Let's do it again; let's overdub here.' What you hear is exactly what we played, mistakes and all."

It could be said that this was exactly what the music required. Held together by Tucker's rudimentary pounding drum patterns, The Velvets incorporated lashings of feedback, distortion, and screeching electrified viola into songs whose chord progressions were primitive in the extreme. To invest more time and effort into capturing their crazed cacophonies in perfect hi-fi would have been to miss the point.

The recording of Reed's epic 'Heroin' is a good example of how poor recording facilities served to enhance the visceral intent of the material. "The guys couldn't have their amps up loud in the studio," recalls Tucker, "so I couldn't hear anything. When we got to the part where you speed up, it became this mountain of drum noise. I couldn't hear shit. So I just stopped and, being a little wacky, they just kept going." And that's the version that ended up on the album.

As well as the minimalist, and often discordant, sonic assault of the music, what set Velvet Underground songs apart from the mainstream was Lou Reed's unblinkingly nihilistic lyrics. Then as now, variations on teen romantic themes provided the words for most chart hits. Though folk rock had broadened the scope to cover socio-political issues, and the San Francisco bands were exploring free love and dope-related ideas, nothing prepared the public for Reed's tales of sado-masochism, alienated junkies, and teenage girls turning blue.

The completed album was first rejected by Atlantic Records (who didn't want drug songs), then by Elektra (who hated the violas), before producer Tom Wilson secured them a deal with MGM's jazz subsidiary, Verve, which was trying to revamp

itself for the psychedelic era. According to Cale, however, Wilson insisted on re-recording some tracks in California, resulting in marked disparities in sound quality across the album.

When the album hit the streets it was embraced by the more adventurous record critics of the day but, despite being dressed up in its famed Warhol banana cover, rejected by the public, who were not yet ready to move on from pop, protest, and psychedelia. Verve's commitment to the band wavered, and the label now put its promotional efforts into its other major signing, The Mothers Of Invention. Ironically, as Reed has pointed out, "that was one of the reasons why we could do what we wanted."

With Nico now out of the band, what they wanted for their second album, *White Light/White Heat*, was to go beyond the limits of the first one. "It was a very rabid record," explains Cale. "The first one had some gentility, some beauty. The second one was consciously anti-beauty." Cale also notes that the chaotic nature of their lives on the road is reflected in the album. "We decided to go in and turn all the instruments up and fuck the engineer."

The album's centerpiece is, unquestionably, the relentlessly churning 17-minute 'Sister Ray.' There already existed a vogue for lengthy album tracks, which tended to be excuses for bands to show off their ensemble improvisational skills, but in The Velvets' hands that notion went out the window. Instead, Reed sets up a simple, dirty guitar riff that gets increasingly basic as the track evolves, while the rest of the band fights for attention. "When Cale came surging through the wall of sound on his first solo," explained Sterling Morrison, "all of a sudden, the organ is way louder than me or Lou. I couldn't turn up; I was already maxed out. At one point, I was down at the bridge pickup on my Stratocaster, so I decided to get a little more oomph on the neck pickup. So I switched to that, which was good." On purely musical merits, 'Sister Ray' is hard to justify, but as an organically evolving, living, gasping sonic monster, it remains unsurpassed in the annals of rock.

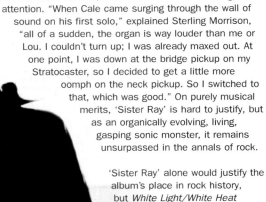

'Sister Ray' alone would justify the album's place in rock history, but *White Light/White Heat* also includes Cale's horrific spoken-word tale, 'The Gift,' and the indescribably nightmarish 'Lady Godiva's Operation,' plus a trio of more conventionally excellent rock workouts.

Despite the poor performance of both albums on release, their influence has been enormous, with bands as diverse as R.E.M., Nirvana, and The Strokes having cited them as inspiration.

Songs Of Leonard Cohen **Leonard Cohen**

Columbia 9533 (U.S.A.) / CBS 63241 (U.K.)
Released December 1967

Already in his 30s, Cohen was a successful poet and novelist and well known in his native Canada before the release of this debut album thrust him into the international spotlight.

Where Dylan's greatest lyrics achieve much of their dazzling effect by being inscrutable, surreal, stream of consciousness, Cohen's most enduring songs are usually easy to understand. The only smoke and mirrors element with Cohen was how he pulled off the clever trick of writing almost exclusively about love and sex, while making it feel like the stuff of arcane metaphysics.

The religious allusions of 'Sisters Of Mercy,' for example, make it seem much more than a song about a night in the company of two mini-skirted girls, which is what it actually is. "I suppose I always wanted to be a pop singer," he said many years later while talking about this album, going on to explain that he'd rather be the kind of writer whose songs "were sung by the women washing their clothes" than be considered an intellectual.

None of this, however, detracts from Cohen's achievements on this album, evoking powerful emotions with a limited vocal range, a finger-picking guitar accompaniment, and the ability to spin an engaging yarn. In 'Suzanne,' for instance, her "place by the river" is brought vividly to the mind's eye with judicious details about "tea and oranges that come all the way from China." Cohen felt that producer John Simon's over-dubbed strings, choirs, and percussion marred his songs, but their timeless ability to stir the heart isn't undermined.

Exploring The Possibilities Of The Studio

1967

The summer of 1967 – the 'Summer Of Love' – officially got under way at midnight on June 1st, when radio stations across the U.S.A. were given the go-ahead to begin broadcasting *Sgt Pepper's Lonely Hearts Club Band*, The Beatles' long-awaited psychedelic masterpiece and the band's first full-length release since *Revolver* nine months earlier.

An album packed with swirling guitars, panning vocals, crossfades, odd sound effects, and a fade-out finale nearly as long as the band's first single, *Sgt Pepper* represented a major departure from conventional rock recording. Though its hallucinogenic imagery and trippy sitars haven't aged all that gracefully, nearly 40 years on it remains one of only a handful of undisputed landmark rock recordings.

Above all, the arrival of *Sgt Pepper* signaled a complete transformation for The Beatles, a band that had long exhibited remarkable studio economy, writing and recording almost non-stop while issuing upward of three albums per year. By 1967, however, the rules of in-studio etiquette were being rewritten as the era of multitrack recording fully took hold. While bands still cut their rhythm tracks as a live unit, more often than not vocals, percussion, lead guitar, and other instrumentation were added as carefully conceived overdubs. After spending an unprecedented four months inside EMI's Studio 2 at work on *Revolver*, The Beatles allowed themselves a half-year assembling the bits and pieces that would become *Sgt Pepper*, along with the February 1967 double a-side single 'Penny Lane' / 'Strawberry Fields.'

In 1967 The Beatles were still working exclusively with 4-track machines, so EMI's staff had grown accustomed to taping such complex pieces as 'Strawberry Fields' and 'All You Need Is Love' using virtually the same machinery as in the early days – though this did, on occasion, cause a few headaches, as former EMI engineer Richard Lush recalls: "I remember the night we did 'All You Need Is Love,' which was being recorded and broadcast live to hundreds of millions of people. We had two tape machines there, one playing the backing track for the song, the other recording the live vocals, orchestra, and the rest. I remember George Martin saying, 'Just make sure you record on the right machine, otherwise it's going to be very quiet in here!' You've never seen two guys run to a pub as fast as [engineer] Geoff Emerick and I did the second that show ended."

It wasn't until mid 1968, in fact, that the group finally doubled its capacity with the 8-track taping of 'Hey Jude,' albeit at neighboring Trident Studios. Not that the problems came to an end once EMI finally secured its first 8-track unit during the making of *The Beatles* (better known as *The White Album*) in mid 1968. "The machine we got from 3M was a bit of a disaster, because it didn't have a bloody clock on it," recalls Lush. "They'd be out there recording five takes of a song and ask to hear it back – except you didn't know where to look! We ended up having to make all these little marks on the tape, but the problem was you never knew which chorus you were on, and of course there were a couple of things that got [accidentally] wiped along the way."

Coincidentally or not, the beginning of the 8-track era at Abbey Road marked the beginning of the end for The Beatles, whose disintegration can be traced to *The White Album* sessions when, ironically, improved technology made it possible for the four members to work individually for the first time.

"Great things were still happening, obviously," says Lush. "You listen to John's demos from the time – things like 'Happiness Is A Warm Gun' and 'Glass Onion' – and you hear the work that the band did to the songs in the final product. But there was less

Continued on page 94

Sgt Pepper's Lonely Hearts Club Band **The Beatles**

Capitol 2653 (U.S.A.) / Parlophone PCS 7027 (U.K.)
Released June 1967

Whatever else *Sgt Pepper* may or may not be, it unquestionably established in the minds of the record-buying public a blueprint for what a truly great album should be.

It was not the first concept album, it was not the first psychedelic album, it may not even be the best album The Beatles ever made, but it did set the benchmark by which all subsequent albums were judged for decades after.

It was Paul McCartney's ongoing love-hate relationship with The Beatles' mega-success that provided the background to his invention of an imaginary band. Already, in 1965, in an effort to establish whether or not Beatles songs were hits just because of the band's fame McCartney had written the single 'Woman' for pop duo Peter & Gordon under the pseudonym Bernard Webb, and only revealed that he was the composer after it became a hit. And by 1967 The Beatles were even more successful, so when he dreamed up Sgt Pepper's band it should have

Since its first release in 1967, Sgt Pepper has been reissued in a variety of alternative jacket designs. Below, a picture-disk edition from the late 1970s.

been no surprise to anyone because, as he said: "it would be nice to lose our identities, to submerge ourselves in the persona of a fake group."

As their producer George Martin remembers it: "Paul came in with this song, 'Sgt Pepper,' and he was kind of identifying it with The Beatles themselves. We recorded the song, and then the idea came to make it into the concept for the whole album."

Concept albums had been around for some years, beginning with LPs unified by having a single theme – dreams, weather, travel – running through all of the songs, and continuing with the likes of 1965's *Beach Boys' Party!* album, which pretended to be a party at which The Beach Boys just happened to be in attendance with their instruments. The arrival of psychedelia, however, gave such albums a shot in the arm, and The Beatles were among the first to recognize the potential of setting an entire album inside its own parallel vision of reality.

The first Beatles album that could be called psychedelic was *Revolver*, but *Sgt Pepper* would take several giant steps further. To achieve McCartney's vision, they effectively took over Abbey Road's main studio for an unprecedented 129 days, during which, as staff engineer Peter Vince recalls: "We actually sat around a lot of the time doing nothing, waiting for them to come up with ideas. But you had to be there because suddenly they'd get the idea and want to go straight for it. They were the innovators of working through the night and very long hours. Prior to them, everyone went home at 10pm."

Viewed with a critical eye, the album might be said to offer only three songs that can be regarded as truly imaginative leaps forward, those being 'Lucy In The Sky With Diamonds,' 'She's Leaving Home,' and 'A Day In The Life.'

This trio is the creative core on which the album's gigantic reputation rests. There's also a brace of universally popular singalongs, 'With A Little Help From My Friends' and 'When I'm Sixty-Four.' Both are very much in McCartney's irresistibly tuneful but irrefutably lightweight tradition, though much enhanced by Martin's clever arrangements and production wizardry.

Crucially for justifying the album's now legendary status, even the less groundbreaking songs – 'Fixing A Hole,' 'Good Morning Good Morning,' 'Getting Better,' 'Being For The Benefit Of Mr Kite,' and 'Lovely Rita' – are rendered magical and fascinating by careful attention to detail, intelligent use of sound effects, and convincingly dynamic performances. This leaves the conceptual bookends – two versions of the title song – and one of Harrison's by now obligatory Indian-flavored tracks, 'Within You Without You.'

So, that's *Sgt Pepper's Lonely Hearts Club Band* neatly summarized, but the whole has become so much more than the sum of those parts. Over the years, every track has been subjected to relentless analysis, scrutiny, deconstruction, and dismemberment, to such an extent that we now know, for example, that 'When I'm Sixty-Four' had actually been written by McCartney back in the days when The Beatles played The Cavern Club in Liverpool. Lyrically and musically it's his tribute to his 64-year-old father, Jim, who had played in dance bands during the war. "It was a pastiche," notes George Martin, "a kind of send-up of the old stuff. Paul always had that sneaking regard for the old rooty-tooty music."

We know, too, that 'A Day In The Life,' Lennon's principal contribution to *Sgt Pepper*, came about through the accidental proximity of a copy of a newspaper. "I was reading the *Daily Mail* one day and noticed two stories,"

Continued on page 96

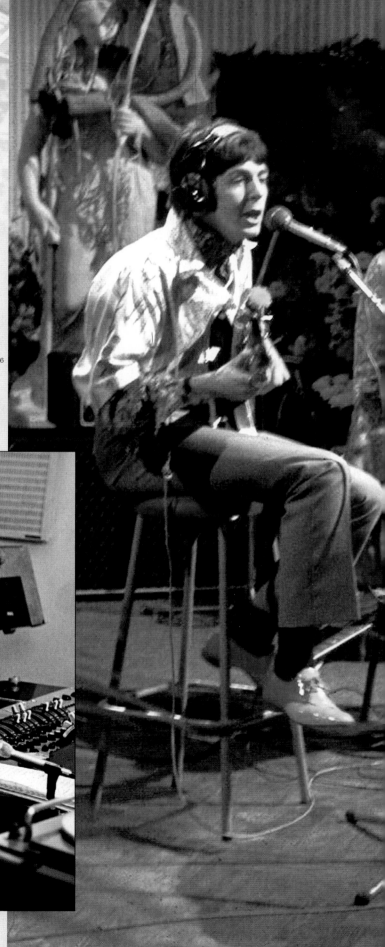

group effort – and it's through interaction that real ideas develop. Because nine times out of ten, it's one bloke sitting in a room, and it's his view on it all. There's something that occurs when you introduce an idea to different people . . . and that was such an important element for The Beatles."

The trend toward a more leisurely use of recording time went hand in hand with the increasingly sophisticated perception of rock music that arrived in 1967. The year of *Sgt Pepper* also saw the world's first successful rock-concert extravaganza – the *Monterey International Pop Festival* – as well as the birth of Jann Wenner's *Rolling Stone* magazine, which ushered in the era of serious rock criticism. With such acts as Jimi Hendrix and Frank Zappa's Mothers of Invention pushing the creative envelope, rock'n'roll was no longer considered the exclusive domain of the teeny bopper but a mature, complex genre. And, as record executives were beginning to find out, it was one with tremendous financial potential.

All of these factors gave rise to the methodical approach to record-making that would define the waning years of the 1960s and beyond. (Not surprisingly, it also had a profound impact on the number of albums produced each year: after releasing a total of 14 U.S. albums during the period from 1964 to 1967, the industry's leading maker of product, The Beatles, offered just one collection, *The White Album*, in 1968.)

In the wake of *Sgt Pepper*, pop artists around the world unleashed albums that used conventional instrumentation and studio gadgetry in unconventional ways. On their November 1967 second effort, *Again*, Los Angeles rockers The Buffalo Springfield – the first major group to sport a three-guitar line-up – unveiled a staggering array of acoustic and electric-guitar tracks, leads, and colorations that would help shape an entire nation of studio accompaniment in the years that followed. Up the coast in San Francisco, Moby Grape, yet another three-guitar

Continued on page 96

■ *Main picture: The Beatles perform 'All You Need Is Love' as part of* Our World, *the first ever satellite-linked television broadcast, at Abbey Road Studios on June 25th 1967, three weeks after the release of* Sgt Pepper. *Below: (left to right) manager Brian Epstein, producer George Martin, and engineer Richard Lush look on from the control room.*

Continued from page 92

Continued from page 94

outfit, delivered their self-titled Columbia debut, a brilliant collection of expertly crafted songs and choice guitar work. In sharp contrast to the silly self-consciousness of the era, The Who's late-December release, *The Who Sell Out*, celebrated the charmingly crass commercialism that was and still is pop radio, featuring original radio jingles and capped by 'I Can See For Miles,' the band's first foray into the U.S. Top Ten.

Not to be outdone were The Grateful Dead, the most notorious band among 1967's psychedelic crowd. Signing with Warner Brothers in 1967, the band insisted on a clause that allowed them as much studio time as they felt necessary to complete a recording project. The unfettered access gave The Dead the opportunity to learn first hand the machinations of a modern studio, but it was an expensive lesson.

In 1968 the band issued *Anthem Of The Sun*, an ambitious mix of live and studio tracks – most averaging around ten minutes in length – that featured experimental sound montages and quirky instrumentation. The Grateful Dead continued their overdubbing exploits on their next effort, *Aoxomoxoa*, this time with the help of a 16-track machine. With neither album selling well outside of the group's San Franciscan fan base, The Dead's total tab for *Anthem Of The Sun* and *Aoxomoxoa* reached nearly $200,000. By that time psychedelia, The Grateful Dead's natural musical home, was already a waning force. New arrivals like The Beatles' *White Album* and The Rolling Stones' *Beggars Banquet* signaled the coming of a more acoustic, song-based pop format. By the end of 1969 the message from Warner Brothers' top brass was unequivocal: the band's next album had better be cheap – and good.

Standing on the sidelines during this period of technological upheaval was Bob Dylan, who'd spent the greater part of 1967 holed up in Woodstock, New York, following a motorcycle accident a year earlier. For Dylan, the overly meticulous trend in record-making was anathema. A noted technophobe, Dylan frequently recorded entire albums in a week or less, and had little use for conventional studio methods. "A Dylan session was completely different," remarks Columbia engineer Frank Laico. "For one thing, Dylan wanted everyone close together – in fact, he wanted to be on top of the drums, which was unique! That was OK – in fact, I never liked it in later years when the bands would be spread apart, to the point that the different players were situated in separate rooms. What's the point?"

"I didn't know how to record the way other people were recording and I didn't want to," Dylan later observed. "The Beatles had just released *Sgt Pepper*, which I didn't like at all. I thought it was a very indulgent album, though the songs on it were real good. I didn't think all that production was necessary because The Beatles had never done that before."

When he eventually returned to the studio to schedule a series of recording sessions in the waning days of 1967, Dylan knew exactly what he wanted: an album that was the diametric opposite of the industry's accepted standard of the time. "Every artist in the world was in the studio trying to make the biggest-sounding record they possibly could," recalled Dylan's producer, Bob Johnston. "So what does Dylan do? He comes to Nashville and tells me he wants to record with a bass, drum, and guitar."

It took Dylan and his Nashville cats all of three days to nail down *John Wesley Harding* (1968), a collection of sparse, acoustic songs that was as majestic for its simplicity as any multitrack manifesto. "We went in and knocked 'em out like demos," remembers session drummer Kenny Buttrey. "It seemed to be the rougher the better. Dylan would hear a mistake and laugh a little bit to himself as if to say, 'Great man, that's just great. Just what I'm looking for.' . . . He knew everything and knew exactly what he wanted."

Coming just months after *Sgt Pepper*, *John Wesley Harding* signaled an entirely new direction in pop music – and, for many, a complete repudiation of obsessive multitracking. Following Dylan's lead, over the next several years groups such as The Grateful Dead, The Band, and Crosby, Stills, Nash & Young helped launch a spirited back-to-basics trend, and, by the start of the 1970s, an unprecedented revolution in acoustic-based music.

Continued from page 93

he explained. "One was about the Guinness heir who killed himself in a car. On the next page was a story about 4,000 holes in the streets of Blackburn. Paul contributed the beautiful little lick 'I'd love to turn you on.'" It's common knowledge, too, that a Victorian circus poster provided the lyrics for 'Being For The Benefit Of Mr Kite;' that 'Lovely Rita' was inspired by a real encounter with a female traffic warden; and that Lennon regarded 'Good Morning Good Morning' as "a throwaway, a piece of garbage."

What isn't always appreciated, however, is the context in which *Sgt Pepper* was being made. While The Beatles were undeniably in the vanguard of psychedelia, they were certainly not blazing that path alone. To name just a couple of others, there were The Byrds in Los Angeles, Jefferson Airplane in San Francisco, both of whom were pushing back the frontiers musically, and there's no doubt that McCartney in particular kept himself well abreast of what those transatlantic innovators were up to.

However, back in London, Pink Floyd were actually in Abbey Road Studios working on their debut album, *Piper At The Gates Of Dawn*, at precisely the same time as The Beatles were making *Sgt Pepper*.

On learning that they were next door, Paul, George, and Ringo dropped in to say hello, and Floyd's co-manager, Andrew King, remembers the visit. "The Beatles came through to have a look at us. McCartney, dressed in a loud, yellow-checked overcoat, was very friendly and encouraging, but we also went through and saw them mixing 'Lovely Rita.' We didn't stay long, though, because the atmosphere was, well, it was a very bad vibe in there." King's partner, Peter Jenner, has noted: "I'm sure The Beatles were copying what we were doing, just as we were copying what we were hearing down the corridor."

Elsewhere in Abbey Road, The Pretty Things were in the early stages of recording tracks for their rock-opera, *S.F. Sorrow*. "There really was no sense of competition," states Pretties' guitarist Dick Taylor. "Lennon was always very supportive, and I seem to remember we borrowed Ringo's snare drum at one point. We all shared an interest in experimenting with sound and it wasn't about rivalry."

One major advantage that The Beatles had over bands such as Pink Floyd or The Pretty Things was the size of their budget. Depending on whose figures you choose to accept, recording *Sgt Pepper* cost between $60,000 and $240,000 (between £25,000 and £100,000 at 1967 rates of exchange), either of which were staggering amounts in those days. And, naturally, the most extravagant album in rock history to date would have to be clad in the most extravagant cover.

On March 30th The Beatles came together in artist Peter Blake's Chelsea studio to have their picture taken for the cover. Work on the revolutionary design, an ambitious life-sized collage of The Beatles' heroes, had been going on for some time before their presence in the studio was required. Brian Epstein's personal assistant, Wendy Hanson, had spent an entire week doing nothing but obtaining clearances from celebrities who were to be included. "I spent many hours and pounds on calls to the States. Fred Astaire was very sweet; Shirley Temple wanted to hear the record first; I got on famously with Marlon Brando, but Mae West wanted to know what she would be doing in a Lonely Hearts' Club."

Even though Blake only charged a surprisingly reasonable £200 for his work – cheap for an artist of his stature – he has commented: "The Beatles were at their absolute peak. If we decided to do something, they could go to EMI and say, 'This is what we want to do.' If they said 'No,' then EMI wouldn't get the record. They were very powerful, so it meant that we could break through lots of barriers."

Part of the cover's impact derives from the fact that it is a gatefold sleeve, but Blake claims that this was a pragmatic rather than an artistic decision. "It was going to be a double album," he says. "It ended up as only one record, but it was a double-sleeve. They thought that there would be more material but there wasn't enough for two records, so then we compiled this sheet of things you could cut out, the Sergeant's stripes and the like, for inclusion in one of the pockets."

Released on June 1st 1967, *Sgt Pepper* soared to Number One in the albums chart two days later, a slot it held for 22 weeks, selling so well that it even turned up in the singles chart at Number 21.

band's mentally ill leader, Syd Barrett. "Working with Syd was sheer hell," says EMI engineer Norman Smith. "I don't think I left a single Floyd session without a splitting headache. Syd never seemed to have any enthusiasm for anything. He would be singing a song and I'd call him into the control room to give a few instructions, then he'd go back out and not even sing the first part the same, let alone the bit I'd been talking about."

Andrew King seemed to see a different side to Barrett. "It was the most intensely creative time of Syd's life. He was not like a dominant band leader so much as he was Hale-Bopp [comet] and they were dragged along in the tail. I remember watching him mixing on a 4-track desk and he played it like it was an instrument."

Whichever version is true, *Piper At The Gates Of Dawn* – its name drawn from a chapter title in Kenneth Grahame's book *The Wind In The Willows* – was destined to prove a one-off, a completely unique listening experience. Barrett's songs are peopled by dwarves, scarecrows, fairies, and weird felines, drifting through fantastical landscapes conjured up by a veritable sonic kaleidoscope of strange electronic noises, stuttering guitar rhythms and curiously looping drum patterns.

Piper At The Gates Of Dawn Pink Floyd

Not issued in the U.S.A. / Columbia SCX 6157 (U.K.)
Released August 1967

At the same time as The Beatles were recording *Sgt Pepper*, their Abbey Road neighbors, Pink Floyd, were in the process of recording their first album, *Piper At The Gates Of Dawn*.

Riding on the success of their first major hit single, 'See Emily Play,' the band had moved into Studio 3 at Abbey Road to work on the album, which would prove to be the first and last flowering of the genius of the

Peter Jenner has, however, pointed out that the carefully constructed songs on the album bear very little resemblance to what Pink Floyd did on stage, because: "If we'd put out what we were playing live, it wouldn't have sold at all." Jenner states that only the extended spacey instrumental, 'Interstellar Overdrive,' resembled a live Floyd track. "They played it twice," he says, "one version recorded straight on top of the other. They double-tracked the whole track. Why? Well it sounds pretty weird doesn't it? That big sound and all those hammering drums."

Their Satanic Majesties Request
The Rolling Stones

London 2 (U.S.A.) / Decca TXS103 (U.K.)
Released December 1967

Nudged along by *Sgt Pepper* and *Piper At The Gates Of Dawn*, even The Rolling Stones decided to go trippy on their next album, *Their Satanic Majesties Request*, but the results were, to say the least, patchy.

The best tracks were lavishly produced, convincingly weird-sounding songs about cosmic journeys, alienation, and the future, with more than a hint of Pink Floyd in their ever-shifting electronic landscapes, but guitarist Keith Richards has since admitted: "I liked a few songs, like '2,000 Light Years,' 'Citadel,' and 'She's A Rainbow' but, basically, I thought the album was a load of crap."

A harsh judgment, perhaps, but it certainly didn't feel like a real Stones album. Not even its $25,000 (£10,000) state-of-the-art three-dimensional cover image – clearly intended to out-weird *Sgt Pepper* – could dispel the uncomfortable feeling that The Stones had merely seen a bandwagon passing and were struggling to clamber aboard.

1968

Greatest Hits Diana Ross And The Supremes

Motown 663 (U.S.A.) / STML 11063 (U.K.)
Released January 1968

The Four Tops Greatest Hits The Four Tops

Motown 662 (U.S.A.) / STML 11061 (U.K.)
Released January 1968

The Hollies Greatest Hits The Hollies

Epic 32061 (U.S.A.) / Parlophone PCS 7057 (U.K.)
Released August 1968

Record-players in the 1960s had mechanical devices for stacking 45s above the turntable. After the first had played, the arm would swing back out from the run-off groove, the next 45 dropped on to the previous disk, and the needle lowered on to the run-in edge to play it.

Mostly it worked, though by the fourth or fifth single the needle often looked like it was on a roller-coaster, as 45s were not perfectly flat; sometimes the needle fell off and hit the edge of the turntable with a ghastly noise.

But there was another way to hear a run of favorite singles: the greatest-hits album.

Here was a winning concept that pleased everyone. The listener got all the hits on a single LP if they didn't buy them first time out on singles, and those who already had copies got a new pressing to replace crackling 45s – and the record companies had no qualms about persuading the public to purchase the same song twice. These albums also brought these songs to an audience too young to buy the singles on their first release. And, as some acts in that chart-focused decade never made memorable albums, it is the greatest-hits compilation that best represents their music. Nowhere is this truer than with Motown.

As much as any white rock or pop acts, the team of writers, sessioneers, and performers in Detroit helped Motown typify the sounds of the 1960s. In its golden era the label permanently occupied large areas of the Top 20. Berry Gordy's shrewd business sense meant it wasn't long before Motown capitalized on the greatest-hits concept, with U.S.-released collections by Marvin Gaye (1964 and 1967), Mary Wells (1964), The Miracles (1965), The Marvelettes (1966), and The Temptations (1966). Those by The Four Tops and The Supremes were issued in the U.K. on the Tamla Motown label in 1968 and both went to Number One.

sell out big venues several nights consecutively, notably the Royal Albert Hall in London. Like The Supremes, it was Holland-Dozier-Holland who were the driving force behind their success, and when the songwriting trio left Motown in 1968 The Tops suffered.

The greatest-hits format was used by many labels. The Rolling Stones put out *Big Hits: High Tide And Green Grass* in 1966, and The Hollies had a career-boost with their U.K.-only collection in 1968. All bar one of the tracks on The Hollies' album – among them 'Just One Look,' 'Bus Stop,' and 'Carrie Anne' – had been U.K. Top Ten hits over a five-year period, and featured the vocal harmonies of Allan Clarke and Graham Nash, the latter of whom later formed a supergroup trio with David Crosby and Stephen Stills. The U.S. edition of *The Hollies Greatest Hits*, issued in 1973, adds the 1969 hit 'He Ain't Heavy, He's My Brother.'

There were also greatest-hits miscellanies that drew on a range of artists on a single label. Motown issued no fewer than 11 volumes of *16 Big Hits* between 1963 and 1969 before replacing it with the 'Motown Chartbusters' series. Numbers One to Five (1970–1) make a brilliant introduction to the label, while numbers Three and Four, with their metallic colors, are among the most effective sleeve-art designs of their era.

For much of the 1960s The Supremes were Motown's flagship act, rivaling The Beatles, The Beach Boys, and Elvis in popularity. Initially overshadowed by The Marvelettes, everything changed when they hooked up with songwriting team Holland-Dozier-Holland for their first Number One, the foot-stamping 'Where Did Our Love Go.' Ten of the 12 tracks on Diana Ross And The Supremes' *Greatest Hits* were U.S. Number Ones, and the entire record was written by Holland-Dozier-Holland. By 1967 The Supremes were charting with the lyrically daring 'Love Child' and 'Reflections,' a track musically sophisticated enough to rival Brian Wilson.

The Supremes now tend to be assessed in the light of Diana Ross's subsequent solo career, but that shouldn't detract from their impact at the time. The popularity of Motown with white audiences may be said to have helped to shift racial attitudes in the U.S.A. and the U.K. However, in November 1968 The Supremes found themselves on a British Royal Command Performance bill with The Black And White Minstrels, a popular British television cabaret act of the time that featured blacked-up white men and white women. Ross protested and added a brief eulogy for Martin Luther King – who had been assassinated in April that year – that was edited out of the television broadcast. The next day she found herself answering press criticism of her 'controversial' behavior.

When 'Baby I Need Your Loving' hit the charts in 1964 The Four Tops had been together for ten years. It was 'I Can't Help Myself' (1965) where they really started to sound like a 'Hitsville' act, and by the mid 1960s they were able to

1968

At Folsom Prison
Johnny Cash

Columbia CS-9639 (U.S.A.) / CBS 63308 (U.K.)
Released March 1968

By January 1968 the U.S.A. was experiencing a major wave of social and political upheaval. The war in Vietnam had boiled over, hastening the demise of President Lyndon Johnson's administration and creating a firestorm of political tension throughout the country.

As rock music increasingly became the voice of dissent, Nashville, the acknowledged seat of social conservatism in music, stood in sharp contrast with its tales of drinking, divorce, and redneck mayhem.

Few knew about the raucous side of life better than Johnny Cash, who'd had his share of booze, pills, and bruises during his first dozen years in the business. Not surprisingly, some of Cash's most ardent fans were the U.S.A.'s most dangerous criminals, and for years Cash had performed free concerts at high-security prisons throughout California. Cash was still on the jail trail in 1967 when he approached his label, Columbia, with the idea of cutting a live date from inside one such correctional facility. After convincing label heads that a concert before convicts was worth a shot, on January 13th 1968 producer Bob Johnston procured a pair of 4-track recorders and headed out to Folsom Prison, the hardball correctional facility located 100 miles east of San Francisco. There he was joined by Cash along with backing band The Tennessee Three – guitarist Luther Perkins, bassist Marshall Grant, and drummer W.S. Holland – plus vocalists The Statler Brothers, as well as Cash's wife-to-be, June Carter.

It would be a gig like no other. Performing before a crowd of 2,000 potentially violent inmates inside a thunderously reverberant prison cafeteria with armed guards taking aim from the catwalks overhead, Cash, clad in characteristic black, never lets up, delivering classic renditions of 'Jackson' (a duet with Carter), '25 Minutes To Go' (a darkly humorous tale of a convict's final moments before his execution), as well as the ballad 'Green, Green Grass Of Home' with unparalleled conviction. But the clincher was 'Folsom Prison Blues,' originally a hit for Cash on the C&W chart in 1956, early in his career. To this day, the knowing cheer that follows the line "I shot a man in Reno, just to watch him die" remains one of the most eerie moments in live recording.

Issued on March 1st – the same day Cash and Carter were wed – *At Folsom Prison* became an instant success, going gold by year's end and achieving multiplatinum status in 2003. On the heels of the crossover smash hit of the re-released 'Folsom Prison Blues' single – a C&W chart Number One and Number 32

in the pop chart – record companies by the score began hauling tape machines in and out of correctional facilities in order to capitalize on the trend. Among the many artists who went from working the bar crowd to the behind-bars crowd were Big Mama Thornton, B.B. King, and, of course, The Man In Black himself, who repeated his feat a year later with the million-selling 'A Boy Named Sue,' recorded live at San Quentin Prison, California.

Sweetheart Of The Rodeo **The Byrds**

Columbia CS 9670 (U.S.A.) / CBS 63353 (U.K.)
Released August 1968

Having pioneered the psychedelic movement in music in 1966 with their album *Fifth Dimension*, The Byrds – along with Bob Dylan and The Band – were among the first to react against it.

Sweetheart Of The Rodeo marked a return to the folksy roots of American music, to simple melodies, sweet close-harmony vocals, and comprehensible lyrics – much like Dylan's *John Wesley Harding* and The Band's *Music From Big Pink* (both also 1968).

When The Byrds assembled to begin recording in Nashville during March 1968 they were in a state of disarray, having lately replaced two founder members – drummer Michael Clarke and singer-songwriter David Crosby – with Kevin Kelley and Gram Parsons. It was Parsons, with his roots in country and soul, who was most responsible for The Byrds' whole-hearted plunge into music formerly associated with rednecks and truck drivers.

As well as guitarist Clarence White, who would later join The Byrds full-time, the band was augmented in Nashville by a squad of the finest session players money could buy, including John Hartford on banjo, Earl Ball on piano, Roy Huskey on bass, and, most significantly, Lloyd Green and Jaydee Maness on pedal-steel guitars. It was the prominence of the slippery quicksilver swooping and soaring of those guitars that made *Sweetheart* sound unlike any album previously marketed at rock fans. With hindsight, of course, it's easy to see country rock as a logical development for a band whose bass player, Chris Hillman, had earned his chops in bluegrass bands, and whose leader, Roger McGuinn, had served his time as a Greenwich Village folkie. At the time, however, it didn't seem that way. Country was seen as a reactionary right-wing music, whereas rock tended to be left wing and radical, so a switch from one to the other was not just a bold move, it was potentially career-busting.

What saved the project was the sincerity The Byrds brought to the album, playing it absolutely straight – except perhaps for McGuinn's exaggerated dopey-hick vocal on 'The Christian Life' – and picking a selection of great songs that straddled folk, soul, and country, alongside a couple of fine Parsons originals and two recent Dylan songs.

A certain amount of mystery still shrouds McGuinn's decision to remove Parsons's lead vocals from several cuts, replacing them with his own. Parsons's former producer, Lee Hazlewood, started the problems by threatening to sue because he still had him under contract, but there's also little doubt that McGuinn was unhappy to have Parsons's voice dominating the album. For one thing, though Parsons's singing was always deeply emotional, it wasn't always strictly in tune; for another, The Byrds had been McGuinn's band from the start, and he wasn't about to accept being relegated to the role of back-up singer.

Though critics received the album warmly, the public's confusion about the new direction meant that *Sweetheart* was not a big seller. Nevertheless, a year later The Beatles would be singing 'Get Back,' and country rock would emerge as a powerful new force in the early 1970s when The Eagles took The Byrds' new direction to its logical conclusion.

The Circle Game **Tom Rush**

Elektra EKL 4018 (mono) / EKS 74018 (stereo) (U.S.A. & U.K.)
Released May 1968

Tom Rush started his career as one of many acoustic singer-songwriters thrown up by the folk boom of the early 1960s.

And, like many of those performers, he, too, later went 'electric,' with a 1966 album, *Take a Little Walk With Me*, which had one electric side (mainly cover versions of old 1950s' rock'n'roll songs) and one acoustic side.

Rush's next album, *The Circle Game*, didn't appear for another two years, by the standards of the time an unusually long gap between releases. With its subtle orchestrations, impeccable musicianship, and consistently strong material, *The Circle Game* marked a step forward, not only for Rush but the singer-songwriter movement in general. Rush's unaffected, almost casual vocal delivery and the pervading atmosphere of confessional intimacy was a forerunner of later, more popular albums by the likes of Jackson Browne, James Taylor, and Joni Mitchell. Indeed, Rush did much to bring these three artists to public attention by covering songs of theirs on *The Circle Game*

before any of them had released albums of their own. Rush modestly disavows any special foresight on his part, saying in *Rolling Stone* magazine in 1975: "If I hadn't done it, those people would have gotten recorded anyway. They were just too good to go unnoticed."

Rush himself contributed just two songs to *The Circle Game*: the first, a neat guitar instrumental called 'Rockport Sunday,' segues into the album's closing song, 'No Regrets.' The most enduring of Rush's compositions, it was later a hit single for both The Walker Brothers and Midge Ure.

1968

Days Of Future Passed **Moody Blues**

London 18012 (U.S.A.) / Deram SML 707 (U.K.)
Released January 1968

The Who Sell Out **The Who**

Decca DL4950 (U.S.A.) / Track 613002 (U.K.)
Released January 1968

Ogden's Nut Gone Flake **The Small Faces**

Immediate Z1252008 (U.S.A.) / IMSP 012 (U.K.)
Released June 1968

The Kinks Are The Village Green Preservation Society **The Kinks**

Reprise 6327 (U.S.A.) / Pye NSPL 18233 (U.K.)
Released November 1968

S.F. Sorrow **The Pretty Things**

Rare Earth 506 (U.S.A.) / Columbia SCX6306 (U.K.)
Released December 1968

The Beatles' *Sgt Pepper* raised the stakes for rock groups who wanted to be seen as important in the grander scheme of things.

As the counter-culture got into its stride, a number of bands began to realize that LPs could be more than a miscellany of ten songs. One answer to this was the so-called concept album. The concept album could satisfy creative ambition, garner publicity, and sell records, all at once. A number of such albums appeared in 1968, as bands tried to catch up with The Beatles, though how substantial or convincing the concept was varied from record to record.

The Moody Blues were best known for their hit 'Go Now,' but with the departure of vocalist Denny Laine they needed a new musical direction.

Their record company, Decca, asked them to record Dvořak's *New World Symphony* with an orchestra for a demonstration record to show off the label's new 'Deramic' sound. Instead, the band ended up writing *Days Of Future Passed*, a song-sequence that went from dawn to midnight. Kitted out in a boldly colored pop-art sleeve, it launched The Moodies' career as an albums band and managed several hits, notably the wildly romantic 'Nights In White Satin.' *Days* was well-recorded for its time, though much of the orchestration is MOR, with the 'morning music' resembling the busy-busy scores once featured on travel documentaries. 'Dawn Is A Feeling' is the highlight of the first side. Side Two is more engaging, having 'Nights' and 'Tuesday Afternoon,' the latter a U.S. hit and glorious Mellotron-driven pop for the 'Summer Of Love.'

Between 1964 and 1968 The Who released singles that were among the hardest rock of the time, musically powerful and lyrically adventurous, as Pete Townshend showed himself to be a courageous chronicler of the teenage experience. *The Who Sell Out* is a sequence of songs linked by Radio London jingles and pastiche commercials, as heard on 1960s' British pirate radio. It had one hit single, 'I Can See For Miles' – the band's first U.S. Top Ten hit – and several songs that anticipated the themes and procedures of The Who's 1969 rock-opera, *Tommy*.

A few months later in the year The Small Faces released *Ogden's Nut Gone Flake*, its famous circular sleeve based on an Edwardian tobacco tin. Side One was a miscellany of songs that included the hit 'Lazy Sunday' and the powerful 'Afterglow.' The second side was comprised of six songs that told the story of Happiness Stan, the boy who searched for the missing half of the moon. Between tracks there were short spoken links by British comedian Stanley Unwin, renowned for his ability to re-order the English language into hilarious but strangely comprehensible gobbledygook.

Like The Who, by 1968 The Kinks were looking for a new direction after enjoying a run of hits that included such classic songs as 'You Really Got Me' and 'Waterloo Sunset.' The Kinks were sidelined musically in 1967–8 when beat-pop gave way to heavy blues and psychedelia, so they adjusted by becoming an albums band. *The Kinks Are The Village Green Preservation Society* looked back on and celebrated the culture of a pre-1960s England that was already receding fast. Failing to chart in either the U.S.A. or the U.K., the LP was described by singer-songwriter

■ *Main picture: The Pretty Things. Far left: The Moody Blues. Above left: The Small Faces. Below left: The Kinks.*

Ray Davies as "the most acclaimed flop of all time," but it has since established itself as an enduringly eccentric evocation of British life.

Another important concept album of the same period is The Pretty Things' *S.F. Sorrow*. It is now recognized as the first rock-opera, but, as guitarist Dick Taylor remembers, when recording began, that wasn't the plan.

"We'd recorded two tracks, 'Bracelets Of Fingers' and 'I See You' before the concept came up." From the start, though, it had been about experimentation: "I'd bought a bagpipe chanter in a junkshop, which turned out to be in the right key for the tooty bits in 'Bracelets Of Fingers.'"

Once the rock-opera concept emerged, vocalist Phil May supplied a plot based on a short story he'd written about World War II, featuring a central character who was an amalgam of May himself and his foster father, Charlie.

The songs follow this composite, S.F. Sorrow, from birth to death, with love, work, war, and burning airship disasters in between, and the story-telling element lent itself naturally to the inclusion of unusual sounds to represent events in Sorrow's life. "Our basic principle," says Taylor, "was that if it made a noise we would bring it to the studio, and find a way to incorporate it into a track." The pegs and strings from an old upright piano, for example, were scavenged to create a home-made zither which provided eerie twanging sounds on 'Death.'

The rock-opera idea was so new that EMI found it difficult to market the album, but the press recognized it as a milestone. A few months later, however, The Who stole much of The Pretties' thunder when they unveiled *Tommy*.

NBC Special
Elvis Presley

RCA LSP4088 (U.S.A.) / RCA RD8011 (U.K.)
Released December 1968

The erstwhile King Of Rock'n'Roll rode out the British Invasion, psychedelia, and all of the other movements in 1960s pop by starring in a series of lame movies.

In the process he came to bear an increasing resemblance to the bland performers he had swept away in 1956, becoming more safe MOR entertainer than focus of teenage rebellion. But in 1968 he slimmed down, poured himself into a black leather suit, and re-launched himself as a rock star, stepping out in front of an audience for the first time in years on a live televised concert, and he rarely looked or sounded better.

The combination of nerves and excitement re-created in Presley the fizzing kinetic energy of his youth. He delivered a masterful performance throughout, particularly during the section with guitarist Scotty Moore and drummer DJ Fontana, who had worked with him on his seminal material in the 1950s. The three old friends sat close to the studio audience in a television producer's contrivance of an improvised jam session, Elvis strumming electric guitar, irrepressible and in great voice.

Recorded at NBC Studios and Western Recorders, Burbank, California, in June 1968 but not broadcast or released until December of that year, the *NBC Special* album – later reissued as *TV Special* – rejuvenated Presley, propelling him into the second great phase of his career. The following year he recorded his best studio album since the 1950s, *From Elvis in Memphis*, and scored with the classic hit singles 'Suspicious Minds' and 'In The Ghetto.'

Presley would never hit these heights again. Soon he was drawn into a money-spinning routine of Las Vegas cabaret seasons, precipitating a slow decline and that tragic early death.

1968

Astral Weeks
Van Morrison

Warner Bros WS1768 (U.S.A.) / K46024 (U.K.)
Released November 1968

Astral Weeks is frequently cited as one of the great albums of popular music, as well as a highpoint of Van Morrison's career. Like Miles Davis's *Kind Of Blue*, the spontaneity and speed of its recording is part of its legend.

Van Morrison came to fame as the singer with Northern Irish band Them on hits such as 'Baby Please Don't Go' and 'Here Comes The Night.' After going solo Morrison had a hit with 'Brown-Eyed Girl.' Warner Brothers signed him in early 1968, and *Astral Weeks* was his first release on the label. Morrison was provided with a select group of jazz musicians, including guitarist Jay Berliner, Richard Davis on double bass – who had worked with Miles Davis – and Modern Jazz Quartet drummer Connie Kay, plus horn player John Payne, and percussionist Warren Smith Jr. Lewis Merenstein produced, and Louis Fallon took care of some aspects of the arrangements.

The first session was held at Century Sound Studios on West 52nd Street in New York on September 25th 1968. Work began at 7pm, and the musicians made rapid progress – for the jazz musicians the chord sequences were straightforward and repetitive. Arriving around 9pm meant Berliner missed being on 'Cyprus Avenue' and 'Madame George.' The first session also saw 'Beside You' and 'Astral Weeks' completed; 'Beside You' had previously been recorded for the Bang label.

The following morning there was an aborted session, so the remaining songs were recorded on October 15th. 'Slim Slow Slider' ran to over 13 minutes as an improvisation but was trimmed back to 3 minutes 20 seconds for the record. The first four songs were grouped by producer Lewis Merenstein under the phrase 'In The Beginning,' and the second side was titled 'Afterwards,' thus hinting at some sort of hidden narrative to the songs.

It is unfortunate that the words were not printed on the sleeve, since they are more like extended poems than lyrics, full of images and phrases that tease and

provoke the imagination. The tunes are love songs dominated by nostalgia for youth, love, and the desire for rebirth. Such numbers as 'Cyprus Avenue' are located in personal memories of childhood, but most people will have similar memories attached to wherever they grew up, giving this song, as with many others on the album, a universal appeal. Much of the lyrical content was written by instinct: Morrison described 'Madame George' as "just a stream-of-consciousness thing, as is 'Cyprus Avenue.' Both those songs came right out. I didn't even think about what I was writing. There are some things that you write that just come out all at once, and there's other things that you think about and consider where you'll put each bit."

Morrison described *Astral Weeks* as "probably the most spiritually lyrical album I've ever done." 'Madame George' includes a significant reference to "child-like vision," and the album's very title suggests the spiritual dimension, 'astral' being a term that came from the counter-culture's metaphysical lexicon, most commonly associated with the phrases 'astral projection,' an out-of-body experience, and 'astral plane,' a Theosophical concept of a dimension beyond the material world ruled by emotion and imagination. The duration of an 'astral week' could not be measured by earthly clocks, and its quality would transcend the mundane.

The music is introspective, relatively free-form, and atmospheric, with diluted elements of folk, blues, gospel, and rock. The songs themselves depart from the obvious demarcations of

verses, choruses, and bridges, to stretch out past the five-minute mark in five of the eight tracks. The music uses an instrumentation that would have struck its audience as unusual and sophisticated. There is light percussion instead of the expected big beat and the double bass lends a jazzy feel. Other sounds include vibraphone, strings, flute, acoustic guitars, soprano saxophone, and, on 'Cyprus Avenue,' a harpsichord.

It seems that much of the time the players were allowed to come up with their own parts. This gives the performances a certain spontaneity at the same time as it makes the tracks ramble. Guitarist Jay Berliner said: "I played a lot of classical guitar on those sessions and it was very unusual to play classical guitar in that context. What stood out in my mind was the fact that he allowed us to stretch out. We were used to playing to charts, but Van just played us the songs on his guitar and then told us to go ahead and play exactly what we felt." This means that though the album was recorded very quickly, the songs were not literally improvised.

If the album has a weakness it is the vocal melodies. After only a couple of tracks it is evident that Morrison's tunes are largely taken from a small number of vocal tricks and phrases. Essentially, he sings much the same melody throughout: it is certainly distinctive, but could tend to monotony once this is noticed. (The exception is 'The Way Young Lovers Do,' which does achieve greater melodic distinction.) Morrison's lack of vibrato can also seem rather out of place and somewhat harsh at times for the material, particularly at the end of 'Beside You.'

Astral Weeks didn't sell well on first release – a figure of 20,000 has been mentioned – and Morrison understood he needed to record something thereafter that would have more immediacy and a wider appeal, which resulted in the R&B of *Moondance* (1970). Nevertheless, *Astral Weeks* continues to find new listeners and remains a record that, in its own way, suggested new expressive possibilities for the album.

Electric Ladyland
Jimi Hendrix

Reprise 2R6307 (U.S.A.) / Track 2657001 (U.K.)
Released October 1968

**Jimi Hendrix's third studio
album was a double vinyl, and
the last he recorded with The
Experience. One of the all-time
great rock albums, *Electric
Ladyland* mixes blues, rock,
psychedelia, soul, jazz, and
proto-funk in highly imaginative
ways. It topped the U.S. chart
and provided four hit singles.**

As a double, with the extended
nature of some of the individual
songs, *Electric Ladyland*
demonstrated Hendrix's desire to
expand his music beyond the
restrictive verse-chorus limits of the
single. Some early tracks were cut
in London, others at the Record
Plant in New York in spring of
1968. His restless ambition led to
protracted sessions and many re-
recordings in pursuit of his vision.
Manager Chas Chandler perceived
this as self-indulgence and lack of
focus, and he quit.

Hangers-on in the studio – 'electric
lady' was a Hendrix term for
groupie – didn't help. Relationships
between the band members –
especially between Hendrix and
bassist Noel Redding – were at an
all-time low, to the extent that
some of the bass parts were not
played by Redding at all, and his
one song on the album, 'Little Miss
Strange,' is almost as dwarfed by
its surroundings as is 'Sloop John
B' on *Pet Sounds*. Engineer Eddie
Kramer helped Hendrix by supplying
effects such as phasing and
varispeeding of the tape. Guest
musicians included Buddy Miles
and Al Kooper, as well as Chris
Wood, Dave Mason, and Stevie
Winwood of Traffic.

Here was a rock record where there
seemed to be no boundaries: on
'Burning Of The Midnight Lamp'
Hendrix pitted harpsichord against
wah-wah Fender Stratocaster;
'Rainy Day' was a one-chord jazz-
inspired vamp where Hendrix
dueled with saxophone player
Freddie Smith as though modal jazz
was back in fashion. While the
cover of Earl King's 'Come On'
nodded to the traditional
excitement of blues rock, '1983 (A
Merman I Should Turn To Be)' and
'Moon, Turn The Tides . . . Gently
Gently Away' were impressionistic
science-fiction epics that
demanded headphones so you
could get lost in their watery world.
(It is astonishing to think that
Hendrix drew such sounds from a
Fender Stratocaster, the same
model of guitar Buddy Holly was
strumming on 'Peggy Sue' only ten
years earlier.) 'Have You Ever Been

Trout Mask Replica
Captain Beefheart And His Magic Band

Straight Records/ Reprise RS 2027 (U.S.A.) / STS1053 (U.K.)
Released November 1969

Uncle Meat
Frank Zappa And The Mothers Of Invention

Bizarre 2024 (U.S.A.) / Transatlantic TRA 197 (U.K.)
Released April 1969 (U.S.A.) / September 1969 (U.K.)

One of the most idiosyncratic albums ever released, *Trout Mask Replica* has been cited as a defining influence on innumerable avant-garde rock acts, but in fact sounds like nothing else ever recorded.

 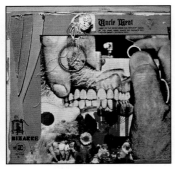

Having made the comparatively straightforward, blues-based *Safe As Milk* and the somewhat more challenging *Strictly Personal*, Captain Beefheart [...] Frank Zappa's Straight

Earlier that same year, Zappa himself had issued a complex double album with his own band, The Mothers Of Invention. *Uncle Meat* blends the experimental rock of his earlier releases – notably *We're Only In It For The Money* – with the more kinetic side of contemporary composer Steve Reich. The album's focal point is the six-part epic 'King Kong,' a template for much of the jazz rock of the future. Several months later, Zappa released the more concise *Hot Rats*, which featured the unmistakable vocal talents of Captain Beefheart on the track 'Willie The Pimp.'

The Velvet Underground
The Velvet Underground

MGM 4617 (U.S.A.) / CS 8108 (U.K.)
Released March 1969

Having horrified the ruling hippy cadre with their decadent and hedonistic debut album and reduced rock to a minimalist onslaught with their second, The Velvets did a complete volte-face on their third offering.

The naked aggression that had been one of their distinguishing features was now replaced by resignation and despair. The stories in Lou Reed's songs still originated in the gutters of the Big Apple, but the music was delicate, pretty, and restrained. This was largely because John Cale, who had been tussling with Reed for control of the band, had been maneuvered out in late 1968. With Cale's experimental, avant-garde tendencies excised, [...] came the core of The Velvets, whose other members

To Electric Ladyland?' has the light soul feel of Curtis Mayfield, while by contrast 'Crosstown Traffic' is blistering full-on rock. Like Muhammad Ali, Hendrix could float like a butterfly and sting like a bee. 'House Burning Down' makes extraordinary use of foxtrot rhythm and has an outro with one of Hendrix's most far-out pieces of guitar. It is followed by an audacious and authoritative re-imagining of a Dylan song, 'All Along The Watchtower,' a song that, like 'House Burning Down,' reflected the incendiary atmosphere of the U.S.A. in 1968. The apocalyptic imagery in 'Watchtower' matched the spirit of the year.

There are two arrangements of 'Voodoo Chile,' which had developed from the band playing Muddy Waters's 'Catfish Blues.' One is a slow blues jam, the other an up-tempo rock arrangement that evolved over eight takes and closed the record. This 'Slight Return' version gave Hendrix a posthumous U.K. Number One in 1970.

1968

About The U.K. Sleeve

The gatefold sleeve of the U.K. release of *Electric Ladyland* featured 19 naked women against a dark background. Apparently, the group photos used on the U.S. cover didn't make it to the U.K. in time, leaving the record company's art department to come up with something.

It was every male teenage rock fan's fantasy, but Hendrix himself commented: "I wouldn't have put this picture on the sleeve myself but it wasn't my decision. It's mostly all bullshit." Though Hendrix may not have liked it, it was publicity and it fed the sexual aura about him – it even had to be displayed in record stores in a brown-paper wrapper, as if it was a pornographic magazine. However, as the women were from a variety of racial groups, a cosmopolitan, multiracial world – albeit one of sex – was evoked. Maybe that message could be said to have redeemed, at least in part, its sexism at a time when racial barriers were still strong.

success between 1969 and 1975.

'Prog,' as it later became known, was a kind of displacement-activity response to the apparent failure of the 1960s counter-culture: by 1969 the revolution may have been lost, but it could be carried on by artistic means through a music that challenged The Establishment. Philosophical lyrics, complex music, and performer virtuosity all suggested an assault on the citadels of high culture – in the case of *In The Court Of The Crimson King* the sleeve itself featured a 'high art' reference in adapting a picture by the visionary poet and artist William Blake.

The Rolling Stones' historic July concert. By the time *In The Court of The Crimson King* was released, there was a stir about the band, and the album made the U.S. Top 30 and the U.K. Top Five.

In Fripp they had an experimental and cerebral guitarist, and they set themselves against the prevailing back-to-roots and heavy-blues/hard-rock trends, combining folk, classical, jazz, and rock influences into a unique fusion. The songs were multisectioned and often grandiose. The album's highpoint was the scampering guitar-sax riffing on the apocalyptic '21st-Century Schizoid Man,' while such Mellotron ballads as 'I Talk With The Wind' could have featured on a Moody Blues album. The pioneering music here led to the likes of ELP, Genesis, and Yes finding an audience.

Crosby, Stills & Nash Crosby, Stills & Nash

Atlantic SD8229 (U.S.A.) / 588189 (U.K.)
Released May 1969

Déjà Vu Crosby, Stills, Nash & Young

Atlantic SD7200 (U.S.A.) / 2401001 (U.K.)
Released March 1970

Through the 1960s, power in the music industry gradually moved from managers, promoters, producers, and songwriters, to the performers themselves.

Many followed The Beatles' example and wrote their own material, and by 1968 a small number of musicians were venerated as rock equivalents of the virtuosos of classical music. If one rock superstar made a band great, the logic ran, surely four superstars would make a group four times greater. Thus was born that triumph of faith over human nature, the supergroup.

In fact, the majority of supergroups comprised of members of other successful bands usually turned out less than the sum of their joint reputations, often staying together – as with Eric Clapton's Blind Faith – for only one album of middling achievement. In Humble Pie's case, the combination was Steve Marriott (ex-Small Faces) and Peter Frampton (ex-Herd) along with Jerry Shirley and Greg Ridley (ex-Spooky Tooth). Their first two albums were strongly influenced by The Band, but the fourth, *Rock On* (1970), was a bestseller. Playing more aggressive rock, for a while, at least, they almost lived up to expectations.

Stephen Stills had an early taste of the supergroup when he played on *Super Session*, a project arranged by keyboard player Al Kooper, where Stills shared guitar duties with Mike Bloomfield of The Paul Butterfield Blues Band. Previously Stills had been a member of Buffalo Springfield along with Neil Young. In 1969, David Crosby (ex-Byrds), Graham Nash (ex-Hollies) sang together with Stills at a party in Los Angeles. Genuinely surprised by how well their voices blended, they got together and recorded *Crosby Stills & Nash*, which made the U.S. Top 30 and U.K. Top Ten. As well as the hit single 'Marrakesh Express,' the album includes the multisectioned 'Suite:

Judy Blue Eyes,' written for Judy Collins, and Crosby's 'Long Time Gone,' inspired by the assassination of Robert F. Kennedy; 'Lady of The Islands' was about Joni Mitchell, and 'Guinevere' was written for Crosby's girlfriend Christine. *Crosby, Stills & Nash* is a classic album of acoustic guitars and vocal harmonizing, with 'Wooden Ships' evoking the Woodstock Nation-era perfectly.

The following year the trio became a quartet with the addition of Neil Young, and they cut *Déjà Vu*, which yielded several hit singles in the U.S.A. An intoxicating mixture of folk rock, open-tuned balladry, and spiky electric work-outs, it made CSN&Y the quintessential hippie spokesmen, and it was thought they might become that elusive thing, an 'American Beatles.' However, internal band relationships were soon strained, and with four such accomplished songwriters there was bound to be tension as each contested space for their songs.

Graham Nash looked back on the achievement: "In our first year together, we spent probably eleven months together, 24 hours a day . . . with just a couple of guitars [we] would sit people down and say, 'Listen to this,' and . . . rip off these ten songs, do them brilliantly, and floor people . . . Musically, we ate, drank, and slept together every night. I was with Joni, and that was flowering. Stephen was with Judy Collins, and that was flowering. David was with Christine, and that was flowering. Within a year, it had all changed. My relationship with Joni had turned sour, Stephen had stopped going with Judy, and David's girlfriend Christine had been killed. We were knocked for a loop. We were all romantic people, and our love-lives were in shambles. Then bring in Neil and plug into his insanity, and it's amazing *Déjà Vu* ever got recorded."

Cloud Nine The Temptations

Gordy 939 (U.S.A.) / Motown STML 11109 (U.K.)
Released September 1969

By 1968 Motown was fighting to keep its finger on the pulse.

The U.S.A. was experiencing civil unrest to a soundtrack of acid rock, socially aware pop, and Sly Stone's bad-ass funk. If the label was to remain "the sound of young America" it had to get hip to what was happening. Enter the psychedelic funk and hard rhythms of The Temptations' *Cloud Nine*.

Signed in 1961, The Temptations didn't break into the charts until 'The Way You Do The Things You Do' in 1964, notching up 14 Top Ten singles and 32 Top Ten R&B hits in the U.S.A. over the next eight years. Melvin Franklin provided the bass vocal, the middle range was handled by Paul and Otis Williams, and melodies were usually sung by David Ruffin or Eddie Kendricks. By the time of *Cloud Nine*, however, Ruffin had been replaced by Dennis Edwards.

Producer Norman Whitfield was attuned to rhythm. He said: "When we first did [*Cloud Nine*] with The Temptations, I started studying African rhythms on my own, and I wanted to know how to make a song have as much impact without using a regular 2/4 or 4/4 backbeat. And it turned out to be very successful." He updated the Motown sound with adventurous productions and songs built with a few basic chords and riffs.

One day in 1968 Whitfield came into the studio declaring he wanted to do something fresh and set the musicians jamming. The result was 'Cloud Nine,' with its prominent groove and wah-wah guitar. Lyrically, too, this drugs song was a change from the band's usual themes. *Cloud Nine* led to further recordings by The Temptations in a similar vein, such as 'Psychedelic Shack,' 'Papa Was A Rolling Stone,' and 'Ball Of Confusion.' In the 1970s the album proved a major influence on the development of disco.

■ *Main Picture: (Left to Right) David Crosby, Graham Nash, and Stephen Stills. Left: (Left to Right) Nash, Crosby, Neil Young, and Stills.*

1969

Dusty In Memphis
Dusty Springfield

Atlantic SD8214 (U.S.A.) / Philips SBL7889 (U.K.)
Released March 1969

The highpoint of Dusty Springfield's career,
***Dusty In Memphis* is an album of**
sophisticated and sexy 'blue-eyed' soul and pop
that matched one of the best singers the U.K. has
ever produced with a classic U.S. session team.

The 14 hits she had scored thus far, starting in 1963 with 'I Only Want To Be With You,' were often big Phil Spector-style orchestrations that were perfect settings for her husky voice. But she had a passion for Motown and R&B, so it seemed entirely appropriate that she should go to Memphis in September 1968 to record. The experience was not a happy one, however, as there were disagreements about the songs and working methods in the studio, so she ended up adding the vocals later at Atlantic Studios in New York.

She later said: "I hated it at first . . . because I couldn't be Aretha Franklin. If only people like [co-producer] Jerry Wexler could realize what a deflating thing it is to say 'Otis Redding stood there' or 'that's where Aretha sang.' Whatever you do, it's not going to be good enough. Added to the natural critic in me, it was a paralyzing experience. I was someone who had come from thundering drums and Phil Spector, and I wanted to fill every space. I didn't understand that the sparseness gave it an atmosphere. When I got free of that I finally liked it, but it took me a long time. I wouldn't play it for a year."

She might have thought it wasn't good enough, but 'Son Of A Preacher Man' is a standout track by any standards, one of her finest vocals, and a deserved hit. Recent CD issues of the album include extra tracks from the sessions. Unfortunately it wasn't a chart success on its release, and signaled the beginning of Springfield's commercial decline.

The Gilded Palace Of Sin
The Flying Burrito Brothers

A&M SP 4175 (U.S.A.) / AMLS 931 (U.K.)
Released April 1969

When Gram Parsons quit The Byrds after their country-rock classic, *Sweetheart Of The Rodeo*, he set about founding The Flying Burrito Brothers, and was soon joined by another disillusioned Byrd, bassist Chris Hillman.

The Gilded Palace Of Sin, however, proved to be much more than just a successor to *Sweetheart*. Whereas The Byrds had retained much of the traditional elegance of country music, The Burritos dragged it kicking and screaming into the rock age, letting rip with distorted steel guitars and studio effects right there alongside the mandolins and honky-tonk pianos.

> "IN THE BURRITOS, WHEN GRAM WAS A COHERENT GUY, WE HAD THIS WONDERFUL VISION. WE WERE SHARING THE HOUSE TOGETHER, HAD BOTH COME OFF A COUPLE OF UNPLEASANT RELATIONSHIPS, AND TOOK SOLACE IN EACH OTHER AS FRIENDS. BUT WE ALSO WROTE SOME GREAT SONGS."
>
> *CHRIS HILLMAN ON HIS RELATIONSHIP WITH GRAM PARSONS*

Parsons and Hillman hit their songwriting peaks with this album, and it is Parsons's impassioned, soulful performances on the tracks 'Hot Burrito No. 1' and 'Hot Burrito No. 2' that are the bedrock of his huge reputation. But the album's real and lasting achievement lies in its fusing of country performance techniques with rock attitude and amplification, thus kicking open the doors of the Nashville establishment for every inspired young cowboy who felt that the people's music had stagnated. Its impact was not felt so much in sales as in the slew of young acts who followed in its wake, from The Eagles to The Nitty Gritty Dirt Band, Commander Cody, and The Ozark Mountain Daredevils.

Back To Basics

At the start of 1969 Paul McCartney had undertaken his 'back-to-the-egg' campaign in a desperate attempt to keep The Beatles from falling apart.

Coming on the heels of the raw-but-revelatory double disk *The Beatles* (aka *The White Album*), McCartney's 'Get Back' project called for a series of completely live tracking sessions reminiscent of the band's earliest studio dates. By that point, however, McCartney's bandmates had little use for anything of the kind, as was later revealed on the dysfunctional *Let It Be* movie and album, released post-breakup in the spring of 1970. Instead, *Abbey Road*, the album that resulted from these sessions and the group's final recorded work, would be unlike anything previously attempted by the band, an entire collection of songs built around an intricate framework of guitar colorations and carefully constructed vocal harmonies, all rampantly overdubbed. Perhaps more than any other Beatles album, *Abbey Road* celebrated studio technology.

Despite their striking differences, the sessions for *Let It Be* and *Abbey Road* were very close in time, with the group setting down a rhythm track for John Lennon's 'She's So Heavy' at Trident Studios in London only weeks after the legendary January 30th 1969 rooftop concert. By then The Beatles were a group teetering on the brink of collapse; that they summoned the strength to return to the sanctity of Abbey Road that summer certainly surprised producer George Martin, who thought he'd seen the last of them.

Utilizing both Studio 2 and Studio 3 the group gradually put together its most polished and intricate work over eight consecutive weeks in July and August. As always, there were new sounds. For Ringo Starr, it was the deadened tom-tom tones (the result of a new set of calf-head skins acquired just prior to the *Abbey Road* sessions) that gave 'Come Together' its distinctive thud. Meanwhile, George Harrison, an early proponent of electronic music, turned his bandmates on to the sounds of the original Moog synthesizer, a prominent component of 'Here Comes The Sun' and 'Maxwell's Silver Hammer.'

Though it wasn't John Lennon's cup of tea – "We put out something slick to preserve the myth," he later claimed – *Abbey Road*'s ornate Side Two neatly predicted the gussied-up production values that would come to define 1970s guitar rock. It mattered little that the outgoing band could only muster a handful of completed songs; to this day, the side-long medley that is the album's crowning achievement sounds like a carefully constructed set of overtures rather than what it really was: a hodgepodge of discarded Lennon & McCartney bits and pieces.

On August 20th 1969 – almost seven years to the day that the band's lead-off single 'Love Me Do' was recorded – The Beatles convened inside Studio 2's control-room to preview a final mix of 'She's So Heavy,' then went their separate ways. "It felt comfortable being back there with George Martin," Ringo remembered years later. "We knew the place; we felt at home. It was like, 'Here we are again, lads.'"

Without a doubt, the most compelling statistic in Fab Four folklore is the sheer speed with which Lennon, McCartney, Harrison, and Starr arrived, conquered, compiled, and then fled, shedding their stylistic skin with each and every album, often many times in a single year. Though they both benefited from and helped inspire the enormous technological advances in the world of recording, The Beatles made their mark largely on the strength of studio ingenuity rather than studio machinery. The day the group called it quits, studios around the globe were already busy installing machines capable of recording upward of 32 individual tracks. The Beatles never made it beyond eight.

"It seems that whenever you get that kind of economy, things do tend to happen in a more creative manner," remarks Beatles historian Mark Lewisohn. "Even in later years, when The Beatles were in the vanguard of a more relaxed and stretched form of recording, there was still an undercurrent of economy in the their work. And I truly believe that they benefited from it."

1969

Led Zeppelin
Led Zeppelin

Atlantic SD8216 (U.S.A.) / 588171 (U.K.)
Released April 1969

Led Zeppelin II
Led Zeppelin

Atlantic SD8236 (U.S.A.) / 588198 (U.K.)
Released October 1969

These two albums simultaneously took heavy blues to its ultimate expression and wrote much of the rule book for heavy rock in the 1970s.

Led Zeppelin's debut is a record where many aspects of 1960s music cross-pollinated and bloomed. The immediate sources are late Yardbirds (courtesy of Page), blues (from Cream, Hendrix, British blues), a little touch of art rock, and a real understanding of the greater possibilities the album format offered over the 45rpm single.

'Good Times Bad Times' blasted off Zeppelin's recorded career with a double-punch E-chord, a chorus of pure power-pop, and a Jimmy Page guitar solo played on a Telecaster through a Leslie speaker, a one-man blizzard of notes, all in a mere 3 minutes 43 seconds. Likewise, nothing could be further from the turgid clichés of Zeppelin-inspired heavy metal than 'Communication Breakdown,' a taut two-minute blast of power that evoked the energy of The Who's 'I Can't Explain' and The Kinks' 'All Day And All Of The Night.' It is impeccably played garage rock, a sonic onslaught punctuated by another mad Page solo careering off the splash of Bonham's cymbal white-noise. By contrast, the English folk-guitar of Bert Jansch, Davey Graham, and John Renbourn led to 'Black Mountainside,' a DADGAD-tuned instrumental based on Jansch's 'Black Waterside,' itself a traditional tune.

Unlike many of their later imitators, Zeppelin benefited from the wide-ranging musical tastes of its members. Bonham and Plant had played blues and R&B; Plant had recorded pop material for CBS on a couple of singles that sounded not unlike Long John Baldry; and both liked the West Coast rock scene of Moby Grape, Love, and Buffalo Springfield. Jones enjoyed jazz and classical, and shared Bonham's fondness for Motown and Stax, which would have a significant effect on the Zeppelin groove. The fact that Page and Jones were experienced sessioneers-arrangers gave them an ear for detail that made *Led Zeppelin* remarkably polished for a debut. Zeppelin were a band of virtuosos who knew how to be a team.

Scrutiny of Led Zeppelin's body of work led to the discovery of all manner of specific 'steals' and alleged similarities between their songs and those of

others. Leaving aside obvious blues debts – now settled legally – many such claims stem from a basic misunderstanding about the inevitability with which ideas in popular music will be recycled. When *Led Zeppelin* was released, eyebrows were raised by the fact that the earlier Jeff Beck album *Truth* – which featured Rod Stewart on vocals – also had a version of Willie Dixon's 'You Shook Me.' It was said Page and Plant had stolen their thunder – but, evidently their thunder wasn't loud enough. (And, as Plant has pointed out, there were hundreds of bands in the U.K. at the time covering the song.) In the Zeppelin version everyone except Bonham gets a solo – Plant on harmonica, Jones on the organ, and finally Page on backward-reverb guitar that allows him to pile up chiming lead over Bonham's drum barrage. Other bands may have played this song but not with Zeppelin's dramatic sense – which made them immediately successful live. Similarly, 'I Can't Quit You Baby,' another Dixon song, had been covered by John Mayall, whose version is at once more authentic but anemic by comparison. (Zeppelin's studio cut is bettered by a live version taped at the Royal Albert Hall, London, on January 9th 1970, where the band play with amazing ferocity.)

Sources and influences are one thing, but the true measure of Led Zeppelin is how far they transcended those influences. Zeppelin had more imagination than most bands, more structure than Hendrix or Cream, better songs and a wider range of styles than Free, and more punch than anyone – with the possible exception of The Who. Even the acoustic track 'Babe I'm Gonna Leave You' – a traditional song also recorded by Joan Baez – is played powerfully. The descending finger-picking could be the intro to something by Simon & Garfunkel, but there's no mistaking the band on the crashing choruses.

The band's ambition was signaled by the epics that close each side of the vinyl. Side One ends with 'Dazed and Confused,' developed from The Yardbirds' 'I'm Confused.' In the middle section Jones and Bonham play call-and-answer, while Page conjures eerie sounds from the guitar with a violin bow and a wah-wah. The whole track is an artful orchestration of dynamics and ensemble playing. Side Two closes with 'How Many More Times.' A fusion of Albert King's 'How Many More Years' and 'The Hunter' – the latter written by members of Booker T. And The MGs – it boasts the hardest riff on the album.

For *Led Zeppelin II* the band found themselves in the unenviable position of having to write and record a follow-up while criss-crossing the U.S.A. on an exhausting tour. Playing to increasingly large audiences, within six months they were a headline act. Riffs and ideas began to emerge from their on-stage improvisations. Their power and dynamics drew an increasingly frenzied response. Stoned audiences got up and danced. This probably focused the musical direction of *Led Zeppelin II*, as the blues element of the first album was evened out with hard rock riffs.

'Whole Lotta Love' was their first undisputed classic and a strong contender for the track that 'invented' heavy metal. It is a musical jackhammer that melded lyrics from Willie Dixon's 'You Need Love' with a gargantuan three-note riff, and the result is undeniably raw and exciting. In the middle section Page and engineer Eddie Kramer pushed technology to the limits, creating a soundscape of simulated sex best appreciated on headphones. Page used a Theremin for some high-pitched wails. A thunderous snare roll from Bonham leads the band into Page's guitar solo, its phrases crunchingly punctuated by the rhythm section.

There are more electrifying riffs to be found on 'Heartbreaker,' with its frenetic guitar break, 'Living Loving Maid,' the start and finish of 'Moby Dick' (a drum solo), and the bulk of 'Bring It On Home.' On 'Ramble On' and 'What Is And What Should Never Be' explosive choruses detonate more delicate verses that evoked Tolkein and West Coast rock respectively. Zeppelin understood the power of dynamic contrast. There is even a beautiful ballad in 'Thank You,' with tumbling cascades of 12-string guitar and a slow Hammond fade. *Led Zeppelin II* is an album to which you can go berserk or – and this is rare for a hard rock album – you could just sit down and listen. Either way it is rewarding.

Building on the success of the first album (which made Number Ten in the U.S.A. and Number Six in the U.K.) *Led Zeppelin II* topped the charts on both sides of the Atlantic.

1969

Tommy **The Who**

Decca DL7205 (U.S.A.) / Track 613013/4 (U.K.)
Released May 1969

Quadrophenia **The Who**

MCA 210004 (U.S.A.) / Track 2657013 (U.K.)
Released November 1973

Tommy and **Quadrophenia** stretched the notion of what the rock album could be and are among the best attempts to use the LP for a group of inter-related songs. **Tommy** not only to saved The Who's career but gave them commercial success and critical standing.

By 1968 the band were creatively and financially in a fix, their troubles exacerbated by the costly habit of smashing equipment. Between 1964 and 1967 The Who had charted with a sequence of superb, bold singles, such as 'My Generation' and 'The Kids Are Alright,' but the failure of the barnstorming 'I Can See For Miles' to fulfill Townshend's expectations in the U.K. charts shocked him – though it did become their first U.S. Top Ten hit. With the onset of heavy blues rock and psychedelia, a gulf between chart pop and album rock opened up. To maintain credibility The Who needed to make a play for the latter audience. The likes of The Beatles' *Sgt Pepper*, The Pretty Things' *S.F. Sorrow*, and The Small Faces' *Ogden's Nut Gone Flake* seemed to point one way forward, and The Who's manager, Kit Lambert, repeatedly pushed the idea of a rock-opera at Townshend until it took hold.

Townshend was primed to write something like *Tommy* because he had a group of themes in his head that needed expression: childhood memories, psychedelic trips, how a rock band relates to its audience, reflections on the counter-culture, and the spiritual teachings of Meher Baba. He had already written multisectioned songs, but he wanted *Tommy* to be a multilayered entity: it would rock and it would roll, and appeal to a young audience; it would be something The Who could reproduce in concert; it was to be a spiritual parable. He later said: "I wanted it to have a rock-singles

level and a bigger concept level. I wanted it to appeal as a fairy-story to young people and to be intellectually entertaining. But I also wanted it to have a spiritual message, too." *Tommy* ranged from popular culture and the hippy world – pinball, LSD, inner space, guru figures – to references to Britain during World War II and to 1950s holiday camps. Townshend told the *New Musical Express* (U.K.) that *Tommy* "can be taken as one of three things – a spiritual symbol, the life of a pop star, or a rock'n'roll album."

By May 1968 Townshend had imagined the character of a "deaf, dumb, and blind kid," the antithetical figure for a society in thrall to sensory overload. The writing and recording process was held up by tours, so the songs assembled themselves like a jigsaw puzzle. Some – 'We're Not Gonna Take It' and 'Sensation,' for example – were composed before *Tommy* was conceived. One of its strongest songs, 'Pinball Wizard,' arose almost by accident because Townshend knew that Nik Cohn, an influential rock critic and author, was a pinball enthusiast. There was never a clear narrative. Townshend's versions of the story, as told to journalists, were often contradictory as he changed his mind and groped toward artistic coherence. The band got on with recording their parts with no idea what the story was about, but trusting that Townshend knew what he was doing. Entwistle came up with two important contributions to the drama in 'Fiddle About' and 'Cousin Kevin,' and Keith Moon had the basic idea for 'Tommy's Holiday Camp.'

Tommy was billed as the first rock-opera – though it would be more accurate to say rock cantata. This claim was symptomatic of how rock was defining itself as a more serious form of creativity than disposable pop. One way to do this was to imitate classical forms within a rock context – which is what, to a degree, *Tommy* does – so there is some attempt to repeat themes, hence the inclusion of an 'Overture,' and the way 'Christmas' anticipates 'See Me, Feel Me.'

The recording went on through the autumn and winter of 1968 at IBC in London. Multitrack machines now made it easier for groups with only four members to build up a layered sound. Townshend resisted the idea, briefly entertained, of orchestrating parts of *Tommy*, and the band confined themselves to instruments they could play or sounds they could make in the studio. Entwistle added French horn, there are backward tapes on 'Amazing Journey,' buried sitar on 'Cousin Kevin,' and fairground barrel-organ for 'Tommy's Holiday Camp.' Throughout, Townshend's acoustic-guitar playing is as important as his electric. Many songs went through repeated re-recordings until he was happy with them. Kit Lambert pushed the band through the inevitable moments of despair to complete the 24 tracks, and the fact that *Tommy* did eventually hit the record shops was a minor triumph in itself. The album was a U.K. Number Two and U.S. Number Four, staying on the U.S. charts for 47 weeks. Its triple gatefold sleeve was impressive, the lattice-work sky depicting the theme of inner space. As the first album of its kind it had considerable novelty value.

Unfortunately, the album's mix didn't do justice to the band's power. This has been partly remedied by the 1996 CD reissue which went back to the original 8-track tapes – an unusual step, as CD remastering of classic albums is normally from quarter-inch stereo masters which do not permit any remixing at all.

For a time *Tommy* rejuvenated and dominated The Who's live act – especially for Daltrey, who, with his fringed jacket and long curly hair, was able to project the character of Tommy – though eventually it was trimmed back to a few key tracks, such as 'Pinball Wizard,' with its prime power-chording and mike-swinging abandon, 'See Me, Feel Me,' 'I'm Free,' and 'Listening To You.' They used its material to great effect at *Woodstock* in the summer of 1969, and live versions of many of the album's songs can be heard on *The Who Live At The Isle Of Wight* and the extended reissue of *Live At Leeds*.

Thereafter, *Tommy* became something of a parasite, sucking some of The Who's vitality, as a variety of re-workings drained the band's time and energy. The first was Lou Reizner's 1972 orchestral version, with guest

■ *The Who at IBC Studios, London. Main Picture: Bassist John Entwistle (left), Roger Daltrey, and producer Kit Lambert look on as Pete Townshend plays the Hammond organ. Above left: Daltrey. Right: Entwistle pauses for thought while Townshend (right, and inset) re-strings his guitar.*

singers and The London Symphony Orchestra and Chamber Choir. This often gains in richness over the original *Tommy* what it loses in punch. Here, Ritchie Havens's version of 'Eyesight To The Blind' is a career highpoint; Steve Winwood, Sandy Denny, Maggie Bell, and Ringo Starr all perform their tracks superbly; and there is an exhilarating combination of voices on '1921.' Rod Stewart's 'Pinball Wizard' is surely preferable to Elton John's, which came only a few years later when, in August 1975, Ken Russell's movie version of *Tommy* was released, complete with new soundtrack. London's West End saw a stage version in 1979; in 1989 another star-studded version was filmed in Los Angeles and released as a video, *Live Tommy*; while in the 1990s surviving members of The Who did a new concert version, and there was also a Broadway stage musical.

The drawback of Tommy's success was that it obliged Townshend and The Who to better it. The first project intended to follow it up was called *Lifehouse*, but this collapsed for many reasons, leaving a bunch of superb songs to be released as *Who's Next* and its satellite singles. The real successor was *Quadrophenia* (1973), as under-rated as *Tommy* is over-rated, a more consistent and powerful set of songs.

Quadrophenia was a play on the concept of schizophrenia. The central character, a mod called Jimmy, manifested four characters, equivalent to the four members of The Who. On the cover their faces are placed in the mirrors on his scooter. The story loosely takes Jimmy through a process of progressive disillusionment. He argues with his parents, loses his job, ruins his best suit, smashes up his scooter, watches the band he loves get too successful, quarrels with his girlfriend, and sees the 'ace face' he had looked up to working as a menial bell-boy at a seaside hotel in Brighton. He takes pills on a train to the coast from London's Waterloo Station and has a spiritual experience of sorts on a rock in the sea, stripped psychologically to "the bare bones of what I am." The lavish packaging sketched all this with several thousand words of monologue and a number of black-and-white photographs.

Revealingly, *Quadrophenia* is dedicated "to the kids of Goldhawk Road, Carpenders Park, Forest Hill, Stevenage New Town and to all the people we

Continued on page 121

1969

Continued from page 119

played to at the Marquee and Brighton Aquarium in the summer of '65." It's full of nostalgia for the days when The Who were a mod band, and views that period through the lens of the later-1960s desire for transcendence. The problem is that, conceptually at least, the album is unable to reconcile its bleak vision of Jimmy's life and times with its apparent desire to go back and re-live it. The Who's history as a band and the individual members are mixed up with the story in such a way as to make its nostalgia also narcissistic. In one of the cover photographs this narcissism is allowed to violate time: Jimmy (supposedly in 1965) is outside the Hammersmith Odeon watching The Who (1970s vintage) making their way to a limo. In this respect, the snatch of 'The Kids Are Alright' faintly echoing at the end of 'Helpless Dancer' is poignant and symptomatic.

Whatever these problems, the music was consistently good. Townshend brought the band only rough demos, allowing more input during the recording. Some of the 8-track demos carried over on to the 16-track master. Entwistle wrote and overdubbed 50 horn parts. Each band member had a theme, gathered in the opening track 'I Am The Sea:' 'Helpless Dancer' (Daltrey's theme), 'Is It Me?' (Entwistle's theme), 'Bell Boy' (Moon's theme), and 'Love Reign O'er Me' (Townshend's theme). Lyrically, there is plenty about a rock band growing older and away from its audience, making *Quadrophenia* itself a meditation on the line "Hope I die before I get old" from 'My Generation.' The sea and the beach provided a unifying imagery. Townshend said: "It's more a series of impressions. Of memories. You see a kid on a rock in the middle of the sea, and this whole thing explains how he got there." The music evokes this superbly.

There are 17 tracks, including several instrumentals. Synthesizers were again used here, as they had been on The Who's earlier album, 1971's musically innovative *Who's Next*. The Who managed to sustain the intensity throughout. Side Three's sequence of '5.15,' 'Sea and Sand,' 'Drowned,' and 'Bell Boy' is among the finest material they ever recorded. There were impressive sound effects and links, such as the sound of rain and storm, a radio broadcast, or Townshend walking along shingle. It was initially thought the album would be released in quadraphonic sound but that never materialized. Many people complained that the album is not mixed as well as it could be. Daltrey was allegedly unhappy with how his vocals sat in the music, and this opened up conflict between him and Townshend. (Two days of rehearsals before a tour due to start on October 28th 1973 in Stoke ended in a punch-up between the two that left Townshend unconscious.)

Where the album faltered in The Who's intentions was that it failed to find much space in their live set. They started off with the noble intention of replicating the whole thing live with backing tapes, a huge undertaking. But the tapes didn't work properly, throwing the band off, and they felt constrained at having to play to fixed structures and tempos. Consequently, much of the album was soon dropped from concerts, leaving only such gems as '5.15,' 'Bell Boy,' and 'Drowned' remaining in their sets into the mid 1970s.

In the U.S.A. the album went gold in one day, becoming the highest-charting Who album at Number Two, and *Quadrophenia* later became a movie. Despite this, the mod imagery of the story had a limited understanding beyond the U.K. As rock critic and biographer of the band Dave Marsh has pointed out, mod defied translation, being "the only important aspect of 1960s British pop culture not adopted by Americans." It also became a milestone that indicated The Who would not be able to escape from or improve on their 1960s heritage.

■ *A still from the 1979 movie version of* Quadrophenia, *which starred The Police frontman and future solo performer Sting (center). The GS on the fairing of his motorbike stands for his real name, Gordon Sumner.*

1970

On Her Majesty's Secret Service (Original Soundtrack)
John Barry

EMI 90618 (U.S.A) / United Artists UAS29020 (U.K.)
Released January 1970

In their quest for new markets record companies discovered that people would buy the music soundtrack to movies they had enjoyed. No franchise has been more successful in this respect than the James Bond movies.

These appeared as albums in their own right with impressive movie-poster sleeves, and have been trawled for many Bond greatest-hits compilations. In the Bond movies the music was a crucial part of the glamour, doing much to establish the erotic, action-packed world of Ian Fleming's secret agent. The magic of the movies may wane with maturity but the music doesn't, and the man responsible for formulating the Bond-music style in the 1960s was John Barry.

Barry knew from the age of nine that he wanted to be a composer. Helping his father run a cinema had exposed Barry to countless movie soundtracks, though he was initially drawn to classical music. However, his discovery of swing jazz broadened his horizons, and he took up the trumpet. This combined knowledge of brass instrumentation and the syncopation of jazz became crucial for his work as a composer.

By the late 1950s Barry was working on British television series, such as *Six-Five Special* and *Oh Boy!*, playing in his band, The John Barry Seven. By the early 1960s he was scoring movies – *From Russia With Love* (1963) and *Zulu* (1964) are early examples – and he has since gone on to compose for over 60 movies, becoming the most successful British movie composer ever. Rarely has any soundtrack music achieved the level of identification with its subject as Barry's has with the Bond movies – not to mention the hit single theme songs. In the 1990s his popularity once again soared, and the influence of Barryesque harmony, themes, and instrumentation could be heard in mainstream pop. He gave concerts of his music and released solo albums, such as *The Beyondness Of Things* (1998).

The soundtracks of *From Russia With Love*, *Goldfinger*, and *Thunderball* are saturated with the Cold War atmosphere of the pre-psychedelic 1960s. Barry always found the right singer for the title songs: Shirley Bassey's strident 'Goldfinger' and breathy 'Diamonds Are Forever,' Tom Jones's hormonal 'Thunderball,' and Louis Armstrong's touching 'We Have All The Time In The World' from *On Her Majesty's Secret Service*. Many of the songs – the latter, for example – were penned with Burt Bacharach's lyricist Hal David.

On Her Majesty's Secret Service, like every John Barry Bond soundtrack, repays close attention to detail. Trumpets blare, timpani boom, snare drums crack and rattle, strings soar and counterpoint the brass – usually on angular intervals – and such exotic instruments as the cimbalom evoke far-flung corners of the world. The chord sequences are often unusual, outside the norms of popular music, and each tends to be a mini-essay on the use of dissonance to achieve a sexy, violent atmosphere. Even 'Do You Know How Christmas Trees Are Grown?' – which features a children's choir – has some unexpected chord changes in it. Just as Bond had all the latest gadgets, so did Barry: he gave the electric guitar and electric bass prominent roles in his orchestra, and the title track of *On Her Majesty's Secret Service* is a lovely slice of 1960s pop with pioneering use of synthesizer.

Bridge Over Troubled Water
Simon & Garfunkel

Columbia CK-9914 (U.S.A.) / CBS 63699 (U.K.)
Released January 1970

The first major album release of the 1970s was also one of the decade's most important – *Bridge Over Troubled Water* **was a mammoth achievement on nearly every level.**

The album owed as much to the production wizardry of longtime Simon & Garfunkel associate Roy Halee as the song contributions of Paul Simon, who outdid himself with, in addition to the towering title track, such pop masterworks as 'The Boxer' and 'The Only Living Boy in New York.' The technical explorations that had begun with 1968's *Bookends* – natural echoes, delays, and volume swells – were evident right from the start of the *Bridge* sessions, which got under way on November 16th 1968 with the taping of 'The Boxer,' the album's designated first single, at Columbia's Music Row Studios in Nashville.

Session man Fred Carter Jr, who was detailed to handle guitar duties, spontaneously devised the song's beautifully cascading intro – which, ironically, was almost assigned to another instrument altogether. "I came up with this thing and played it to Paul," says Carter, "and he said, 'I love it . . . but I think it needs to be played on a concertina.' So there was some dude from Italy doing his first tour of the U.S.A., who just happened to be Italy's greatest classical concertina player. So Paul brings him in with an interpreter, and we sat there all day and went over the lick, and they wrote it out for the guy, who then played it. And afterward Paul says, 'Naw, that's not it.' And he dismissed the guy and he walks out in bewilderment, and we went right back to where we were, and got it in about the third take."

When Garfunkel accepted an offer to appear in the Mike Nichols movie *Catch-22*, work on *Bridge* effectively ground to a halt for the better part of a year. But, after reconvening at Columbia's Studio B in New York in the late fall of 1969, Halee, Simon, and Garfunkel took little more than three weeks to complete the bulk of the album, during which time Garfunkel cut his now-famous title-track vocal and numerous other sonic journeys were attempted – for example, drums were overdubbed using an open elevator shaft for reverb; vocals were taped in a nearby chapel; random instruments and entire orchestral sections were 'flown in' at will. All of these imaginative leaps would ultimately test the limits of Columbia's 1969 recording capability, forcing Halee to wire up multiple machines in order to handle the multitude of tracks, as well as the patience of boss Clive Davis, who at one point wondered aloud if all of these "extras" were really necessary.

> **"WHEN THE TWO OF THEM WERE SINGING LIVE, SOMETHING WOULD HAPPEN IN THE SOUND FIELD BETWEEN THEIR VOICES THAT WAS MAGICAL. THE MINUTE YOU'D PUT [SOMETHING] BETWEEN THEM, IT WENT AWAY. SO I'D ALWAYS INSIST, 'YOU GOTTA DO IT LIVE.'"**
> *PRODUCER ROY HALEE ON WORKING WITH SIMON & GARFUNKEL*

By the time *Bridge Over Troubled Water* was finished so too, to all intents and purposes, was the career of Simon & Garfunkel. Regardless, *Bridge* would become their crowning achievement, scoring a multitude of Grammys and topping albums charts the world over. In the U.K. the album charted for more than 300 weeks, 41 of them at Number One.

Tea For The Tillerman **Cat Stevens**

Columbia CK-9914 (U.S.A.) / CBS 63699 (U.K.)
Released January 1970

Cat Stevens was one of the most popular and prolific British singer-songwriters of the 1970s. *Tea For The Tillerman* **was his breakthrough album.**

Born in London in 1947 to a Greek father and a Swedish mother, Stevens was a teen-pop idol in the late 1960s, but was forced to take a sabbatical from the music business after contracting tuberculosis in 1968. When he returned two years later it was with a more mature sound in the James Taylor mold. *Mona Bone Jakon* (1970) was a minor U.K. hit, but it was *Tea For The Tillerman*, released just five months later, that first brought Stevens widespread international success.

Produced by former Yardbird Paul Samwell-Smith, *Tea For The Tillerman* doesn't deviate much from the gentle folk-pop sound of its predecessor, but it does have a more confident and optimistic feel, which undoubtedly gave it a wider popular appeal. The album peaked at Number 20 in the U.K. and Number Eight on the U.S. *Billboard* chart in early 1971, and includes several of Steven's most famous songs, notably 'Father And Son' and 'Wild World.'

Stevens recorded seven further international hit albums during the 1970s, among them *Teaser And The Firecat* (1971) and *Buddah And The Chocolate Box* (1974). He retired from music in 1979, however, after becoming a Muslim and changing his name to Yusuf Islam.

1970

Curtis **Curtis Mayfield**

Curtom 8005 (U.S.A.) / Buddah 2318 015 (U.K.)
Released September 1970 (U.S.A.) / February 1971 (U.K.)

Curtis Mayfield had enjoyed considerable success in the early and mid 1960s as lead vocalist and songwriter in The Impressions, whose hits included 'Gypsy Woman' (1962) and 'People Get Ready' (1965).

Mayfield was a rare commodity in the 1960s, a soul singer also capable of writing his own material. He was also among the first performers to speak about African-American pride in song. By the dawn of the 1970s, alongside Marvin Gaye and Stevie Wonder, he was one of a peerless triumvirate of soul-music auteurs, innovating not just with the social consciousness of their lyrics but also by integrating funk and psychedelia into their music.

Still only 28, Mayfield had left The Impressions in 1970 to pursue a solo career. *Curtis*, his solo debut, was issued on his own Curtom label, also home to, among others, the remaining members of The Impressions as well as The Staple Singers.

Curtis remains Mayfield's defining statement, though it would be surpassed commercially by his soundtrack to the 'blaxploitation' movie *Superfly* (1972). *Curtis* has latterly become known as the '*Sgt Pepper* Of Soul,' though it confounded some critics on its original release, with *Rolling Stone* magazine hoping that Mayfield was "just in a slump" and would "soon be writing tunes with real life in them again." Both statements are somewhat puzzling, given the power of songs like 'Miss Black America' and 'Give It Up' and Mayfield's mastery of such a wide sonic palette. *Curtis* reached Number 19 in the U.S.A. on release, while the single '(Don't Worry) If There's A Hell Below We're All Going To Go' peaked at Number Three, though neither album nor single charted in the U.K.

Loaded **The Velvet Underground**

Cotillion SD9034 (U.S.A.) / Atlantic 2400111 (U.K.)
Released September 1970

Loaded saw the ever-changing Velvet Underground mutate yet again, but it also brought their golden era to an end.

Recorded under difficult circumstances during the summer of 1970, the album was a triumph of creativity over adversity. The band was simultaneously holding down an exhausting ten-week residency at Max's Kansas City, drummer Mo Tucker was taking time out to look after her newborn daughter, and guitarist Sterling Morrison was studying part-time at college.

Yet, from the breezy harmony vocals and chiming guitars of the opener, 'Who Loves The Sun?' *Loaded* overturned all expectations. Their first three albums, though stylistically different, all shared a disturbing emotional intensity that was assumed to be the band's defining characteristic, but now they sounded like they were having fun. If the lyric of the album's first acknowledged classic, 'Sweet Jane,' wallows in sordid details of New

York's decadent sub-culture, the track's simple, churning guitar riff is positively celebratory, as is 'Rock & Roll,' Reed's hymn to the delights of pop radio.

In late August, on the last night of their Max's Kansas City residency, Reed quit. He'd simply had enough. For the next two years he lived with his parents in Freeport, Long Island, working as a $40-a-week typist in his father's accountancy firm. Bassist Doug Yule, assisted by producer Geoffrey Haslam, brought the album to completion and, as with every Velvet Underground album, it was largely ignored by the record buying public at the time. Fortunately, given the glorious '20/20 vision' of hindsight, *Loaded* now stands revealed as a classic.

John Barleycom Must Die **Traffic**

United Artists 5500 (U.S.A.) / Island Records 9116 (U.K.)
Released July 1970

While most of the psychedelic and progressive rock of the late 1960s and early 1970s was dominated by the sound of the electric guitar, Traffic ploughed a more individualistic furrow, one built around the expressive playing of organist-guitarist Steve Winwood and flautist-saxophonist Chris Wood.

Winwood had begun his musical career in 1964 at the age of 15 as keyboard player and vocalist in The Spencer Davis Group, before forming Traffic with Wood, guitarist Dave Mason, and drummer Jim Capaldi. Traffic's early work betrayed a deep love for The Beatles' *Revolver*, but over time the group began to develop a sound all of their own, drawing on folk, jazz, and R&B. Mason quit the group in 1969, leading to the temporary dissolution of Traffic, and Winwood, now 22, originally intended *John Barleycorn Must Die* to be his solo debut, planning to play all the instruments on it himself. He began recording the album with producer Guy Stevens in February 1970, but soon realized he needed to replace Stevens with Island Records head Chris Blackwell and bring his erstwhile Traffic collaborators back into the fold – though, in truth, Capaldi's and Wood's contributions often seem like mere backdrops to Winwood's multitracked keyboard parts and impressive, soulful vocals.

John Barleycorn Must Die contains six expansive songs that sit apart from Traffic's late-1960s material, sounding closer in mood to the jazz rock of Santana or Tim Buckley. Nonetheless, the album was Traffic's most successful commercially, reaching the Top 20 both in the U.S.A. – where it went gold – and the U.K.

Fire and Water **Free**

A&M 4268 (U.S.A.) / Island ILPS 9120 (U.K.)
Released July 1970

Fire and Water is a definitive slice of blues-based hard rock. Formed in the shadow of Cream and the British blues boom, Free cut seven albums in their short, turbulent career (1968–73).

Simon Kirke was a solid drummer, Andy Fraser's bass work was adventurous in the best tradition of Jack Bruce, and the late Paul Kossoff remains unequalled as a master of 'one-note-says-it-all' lead guitar. In Paul Rodgers Free had a voice of striking assurance for someone so young. His delivery seemed effortless, rasping one moment and purring the next.

Partly as a result of Rodgers's blues-inflected tunes, much of Free's music is imbued with an obscure sorrow for woman lost or woman found and then lost. Lyrically, at least, their most famous song, 'All Right Now,' is atypical, and its enduring popularity obscures other fine songs in their canon. The brooding 'Fire And Water' and the loping menace of 'Mr Big' show how Free thrust the space in their music to the fore. They didn't go for Wall Of Sound-type onslaught or mass overdubs, preferring to walk the space like a tightrope.

There's tension, too, between the macho thump of the rockers and the vulnerability of the ballads. It's deceptive music because it sinks in slowly, and when hooked you can't say exactly why. Hard rock gets harder, heavier, and happier than Free, but it doesn't get any more bruised than 'Don't Say You Love Me.'

1970

Bitches Brew Miles Davies

Columbia 26 (U.S.A.) / CBS 66236 (U.K.)
Released May 1970

The late 1960s was a period of great transition for Miles Davis. With *Miles In The Sky* and *Filles De Kilimanjaro* he had begun to turn to electric instrumentation, while the line-up of his touring band, no longer a traditional quintet, seemed in a constant state of flux.

Just as importantly, though, Davis and his producer Teo Macero were in the midst of devising a whole new way of making albums, essentially a precursor to the sampling and sequencing methods used so prominently from the 1980s onward. Macero would record the band live in the studio and then, under Davis's direction, piece together whole new compositions by cutting up and splicing together pieces of tape. This method was used to great effect on the album *In A Silent Way*, recorded in early 1969, which also marked the first time Davis used three electric-piano players and guitarist John McLaughlin on record.

Bitches Brew took both processes a step further. While *In A Silent Way* had made use of rock instrumentation, Davis's next recordings drew more explicitly on the sound and feel of hard rock and funk. Following sessions for *A Tribute To Jack Johnson* – which would not be released until 1971 – Davis and his band recorded the six expansive pieces that would make up *Bitches Brew* over three days in August 1969. The caliber of the band was high, and many of the players Davis assembled had already enjoyed or would go on to achieve success in their own right. The musicians included McLaughlin, saxophonist Wayne Shorter, bass clarinet player Bernie Maupin, the aforementioned trio of keyboardists (Joe Zawinul, Chick Corea, and Larry Young), two bassists (Dave Holland and Harvey Brooks), two drummers (Jack DeJohnette and Lenny White), and Jumma Santos and Don Alias on percussion.

Much of the lengthy material on *Bitches Brew* was recorded in short sections to be pieced together later. The epic title track, built around staccato bass, over-lapping, discordant electric pianos, and hypnotic funk drumming, was originally conceived as a five-part suite, though only three parts made the final cut. A fourth section was retitled 'John McLaughlin' and also included on the album. Davis's trumpet is often drowned in extreme echo, adding to the dark, foreboding feel of the track. The equally moody and chaotic opener, 'Pharaoh's Dance,' required 19 edits when Davis and Macero began post-production; several two-bar fragments are looped to disorientating effect, while further use was made of echo and reverb. With its melodic Fender Rhodes electric piano and obvious Latin feel, 'Spanish Key' is as close as *Bitches Brew* gets to light relief, though the choppy guitar lines and frantic horn solos never truly allow the listener to settle. 'Miles Runs The Voodoo Down' betrays more than a hint of the influence of Jimi Hendrix before the album closes with a version of Shorter's 'Sanctuary,' almost unrecognizable from the version Davis had recorded in the 1950s, as included on the compilation *Circle In The Round*.

Though there was some resistance from jazz purists at the time, *Bitches Brew* was an instant critical and commercial success, becoming Davis's only album to reach the *Billboard* Top 40 and the first to achieve gold. As well as casting a huge shadow on much of the jazz that followed – in a way comparable, perhaps, only to The Beatles' impact on popular music – *Bitches Brew* also had a profound impact on rock and funk musicians, from Carlos Santana to the influential Krautrock group Can.

Abraxas **Santana**

Columbia 30130 (U.S.A.) / CBS 64087 (U.K.)
Released September 1970

Emerging in the late 1960s from the Bay Area scene that also gave birth to Jefferson Airplane and The Grateful Dead, Santana reached their creative peak with *Abraxas*, a successful fusion of Latin rhythms and psychedelic guitar playing.

Named for their guitarist, The Santana Blues Band, as it was originally known, developed a strong live reputation before cutting its eponymous Columbia debut in 1969. Santana entered the studio to record their sophomore album in April of the following year, just as Columbia was gearing up for the release of Miles Davis's epochal *Bitches Brew*. The band shared Davis's pioneering spirit in its desire to fuse what were then considered disparate musical styles to create a wholly new sound, and there would also be a striking similarity between the sleeves of *Abraxas* and *Bitches Brew*.

As with its predecessor, *Abraxas* featured Mexican-born Carlos Santana alongside keyboardist Gregg Rolie, bassist David Brown, drummer Bob Livingstone, and percussionists Marcus Malone and Jose 'Chepito' Areas, whose conga and timbales work give it a distinct Latin flavor. Drawing on rock, blues, jazz, and salsa, the album features probably the best known recording of Santana's career, a cover of Fleetwood Mac's 'Black Magic Woman,' which peaked at Number Four on the U.S. singles chart. *Abraxas* topped the *Billboard* chart immediately on its release, and soon provided a second hit single, a frenetic rendition of Tito Puente's 'Oye Como Va.' Santana consolidated its success the following year with *Santana III*, after which the original line-up split, leaving Santana to follow a more jazz-based aesthetic for subsequent, less commercially successful releases.

1970

Woodstock **Various Artists**

Cotillion CT3-500 (U.S.A.) / Atlantic 2663001 (U.K.)
Released August 1970

The *Woodstock* triple album stands as a glorious audio celebration of the crowning moment of 1960s hippiedom, when half a million young people came together on Yasgur's Farm in upstate New York for a weekend of peace, love, and music. Maybe.

Viewed from another perspective, this lavishly produced, sprawling three-album set might be seen as the beginning of the cynical and ruthless exploitation of stoned-out traditional hippies by stoned-out capitalist hippies. It's often conveniently forgotten that *Woodstock* was set up to be a massive money-making enterprise, and only became a free festival after the fences were trampled down. Part of that enterprise was the movie and this companion live album, the combined effect of which was to turn *Woodstock* into the most mythologized rock concert of all time.

The original vinyl is, undeniably, nicely packaged in a full-color, triple-fold-out sleeve, but is it a great album? In truth, probably not. The recording quality is entirely acceptable, but many of the performances are sloppy or lackluster. With its stage announcements, mini-interviews, and crowd chants it works well as a documentary of the event but, for the most part, the studio versions of most of the songs featured here are superior. Nevertheless, buoyed up by the burgeoning *Woodstock* myth, the album went gold two weeks after release and dollar signs began appearing in the eyes of record executives around the globe as it dawned on them that a triple album recorded live over a period of three days was sitting at Number One on the albums chart.

Compared with the costs of putting a superstar band into a studio for six months – which was beginning to become the norm – recording a live album was astonishingly cheap and the profits could be enormous. There had been successful live albums in the past – *James Brown Live At The Apollo* and

the double *Live Dead* by The Grateful Dead being notable examples – but there were no successful triple live albums until *Woodstock*. What *Woodstock* said to the marketing departments was that if a live concert could be adequately 'eventized' – built up in the public's imagination – then there were huge profits to be made from recording it.

Woodstock Two, naturally, was released soon after, and 1971 brought a three-LP set entitled *The First Great Rock Festivals Of The Seventies*, featuring live recordings from the *Atlanta Pop Festival* and *The Isle Of Wight*. Before long, no self-respecting festival could consider itself complete without an attendant album of 'classic' live performances. A nicely boxed set, *The Last Days Of The Fillmore*, appeared in 1972, but most of what appeared was shoddily produced until 1978, when The Band's superb guest-star-studded movie-album tie-in *The Last Waltz* was released.

The respective merits of such albums is, however, not the central issue. The real point is that the *Woodstock* triple spawned an entirely new and lucrative marketing phenomenon that, in essence, was built around the realization that concert souvenirs could be sold to people who hadn't actually been there.

■ *Main picture: to save time between performances, there were two circular stages at Woodstock, one of which could be set up while the other was in use and then pulled into place when needed. Right: Janis Joplin on stage at the festival, on August 16th 1969.*

Workingman's Dead The Grateful Dead

Warner Bros. WS-1869 (U.S.A. & U.K.)
Released June 1970

American Beauty The Grateful Dead

Warner Bros. WS-1869 (U.S.A. & U.K.)
Released December 1970

They recorded just three studio albums in their final 15 years, but back in 1970 The Grateful Dead somehow managed to assemble their two best works all within the space of five months.

Workingman's Dead, the group's first studio release since 1969's *Aoxomoxoa*, marked the beginning of a new, more efficient era for The Grateful Dead, and with good reason. In trouble with the law following a marijuana bust in New Orleans and in debt to Warner Brothers to the tune of nearly $200,000 for studio excesses incurred during the band's previous two albums – *Anthem Of The Sun* and *Aoxomoxoa* – The Dead had no choice but to make their next album on the cheap.

This led chief songsmith Jerry Garcia and lyricist Robert Hunter to reach back to their folk roots and come up with a collection of tight, melodic songs with a simple, acoustic framework. By the end of 1969 the set included the slow blues 'Black Peter,' the countrified 'High Time,' and the epic 'Uncle John's Band,' the latter a nod to the three-part harmonizing of colleagues Crosby, Stills & Nash. To make the imminent recording process as smooth as possible, the band diligently began rehearsing the new tunes. "Jerry and I worked out the two acoustic-guitar parts well beforehand, in hotel rooms, in the practise studio, whenever we got the chance," Bob Weir recalls. "Each of us came up with some part that contrasted with what the other was playing. One of us would play the root chords, and the other would invert the chords up the neck. We really had it down by the time we went in to cut the album." In February 1970 the band entered San Francisco's Pacific High

Recording, the studio operated by Alembic, the Dead-associated musical-instrument manufacturer. Unlike the group's previous efforts, *Workingman's Dead* was the product of a band that knew exactly what needed to be done right from the start – and the simplicity of the arrangements made the going that much easier. "We were set up in what looked like a little crescent around the drums," Weir recalls, "almost elbow to elbow. It was pretty tight. There's a lot of live leakage because of that, but that was fine."

On the strength of FM-friendly cuts 'Uncle John's Band' and 'Casey Jones,' *Workingman's Dead*, issued in early June 1970, made it all the way into the *Billboard* Top 25, becoming the group's first bona fide hit album. But there was more to come. Even before the release of *Workingman's Dead* a whole new crop of Hunter-Garcia songs began popping up on the group's set lists. 'Attics of My Life,' 'Till The Morning Comes,' and 'Candyman' sported captivating Garcia melodies and tight, meticulously arranged three-part harmonies, while 'Friend of The Devil' and 'Ripple' continued the bluegrass spirit of *Workingman's Dead*.

By midsummer the band was back in the studio, ready to crank out its second album in the space of a year. For the making of *American Beauty* they chose a new location, Wally Heider's in San Francisco, and a new producer, 20-year-old Steve Barncard, who'd recorded Garcia's famous pedal-steel

overdub for the Crosby, Stills, Nash & Young hit 'Teach Your Children' some months earlier.

At Barncard's suggestion the band set up in Heider's upper-level Studio C, birthplace of classic recordings by the likes of Creedence Clearwater Revival, Jefferson Airplane, and CSN&Y. Even with drummer Bill Kreutzmann perched just a few feet away, Barncard insisted on cutting the band's acoustic guitars live. "That was so important – especially when there would be any interplay between the two acoustic guitars," Barncard recalls. "The reason those rhythm tracks are so tight is because they were set up really close together, just sitting in these plastic chairs facing each other, with very little obstruction. I may have had a few small baffles around the drums, but that was it. When they were recording, they liked to be able to look at each other's fingers, pick up on accents, and so forth. The interplay was a very big part of those sessions. One of the reasons it was such a fun record to make was that the band got the basic arrangements together well ahead of time. They were just completely prepared and professional in their approach. I'll never forget hearing the sound of Phil, Jerry, and Bob's second vocal pass on 'Attics of My Life' coming through the monitors. It was as pure a recording process as you could get."

David Grisman overdubbed mandolin parts on 'Ripple' and 'Friend of The Devil,' and guitarist Dave Nelson supplied some quick string work on the Phil Lesh album opener 'Box of Rain.' "Phil had given me the chord chart the previous night," Nelson recalls. "It was just a ton of what seemed like totally random chords thrown together. Every line was similar to the last, but not quite [the same]. I took that piece of paper to the session the next day. I ran my Telecaster straight into the board, they put on the track, and I just read it straight off the chart – solo break and all. I had no idea what I was doing or what it was sounding like, but there it was."

Workingman's Dead was still selling well by the time *American Beauty* entered the charts that fall, and, by Christmas, The Grateful Dead had their second Top 30 album of the year. Both would eventually become million-sellers.

1970

1970

Paranoid Black Sabbath

Warners 1887 (U.S.A.) / Vertigo 6360011 (U.K.)
Released September 1970

Who first conjured heavy metal out of the pit? The metal bands with huge libidos borrow from Led Zeppelin and the flashy neo-progressives look up to Deep Purple, but the prophets of doom are the spawn of Black Sabbath.

The sound of Sabbath was defined by Tony Iommi's guitar – an ultra-fuzzy proto-grunge that sounded like it had just crawled out of the primeval soup and was trying with its one brain cell to go back. Iommi doubled up his riffs but kept the parts simple, while Ozzy Osbourne seemed to sing as if chained up somewhere down the corridor. The Birmingham, UK, outfit wrote the odd tearjerker ballad – 'Changes,' for example – but their real calling was to express downer sentiments evoked by pentatonic riffs fit to make a television evangelist's head revolve.

Sabbath took the Book Of Rock and handed it on with 90 percent of its pages missing: blues, psychedelia, hippie mysticism, soul basslines, folk, rock'n'roll – you name it, Sabbath dumped it. And they were asexual, immune to the erotic pulse that dated back to Elvis's gyrations. Sabbath was for boys "worried about girls," "not interested in girls," or whose idea of a sex-guru was author Dennis Wheatley. Sabbath's hit 'Paranoid,' with its distinctive riff, has Ozzy finishing with his woman because she couldn't help him with his "mind." 'Iron Man' is the ultimate detuned riff, and 'War Pigs' compares generals with witches – thus cementing the military-occult axis that would become the mainstay of heavy metal. Sabbath were 'No Futurist's' before British punk bands like The Pistols ever shook a safety pin, and their continued influence is evident in the likes of Metallica.

■ *Black Sabbath recording* Paranoid *at Parr Street Studios, Liverpool, England. Main picture (left to right): Bill Ward, Ozzy Osbourne, 'Geezer' Butler, and Tony Iommi. Below: Ward at the drums, and Osborune at the piano.*

After The Gold Rush **Neil Young**

Reprise RSLP 6383 (U.S.A. & U.K.)
Released September 1970

Harvest **Neil Young**

Reprise MS 2032 (U.S.A.) / Reprise K/K4 54005 (U.K.)
Released March 1972

After successful spells in Buffalo Springfield and alongside Crosby, Stills & Nash, Neil Young established himself as one of the most influential songwriters of his generation with *After The Gold Rush*.

Having spent much of the previous year on tour or in the studio with CSN&Y, in early summer 1970 Young regrouped with his regular backing band, Crazy Horse, which was comprised of guitarist Danny Whitten, bassist Billy Talbot, and drummer Ralph Molina. He also recruited the then-unknown 17-year-old guitarist-pianist Nils Lofgren in an effort to move away from the hard-rock sound of his previous solo release, *Everybody Knows This Is Nowhere*.

Young's early solo work tended toward the lavish. The multilayered arrangement of his 'Expecting To Fly' – from the Buffalo Springfield album *Again* – was a three-and-a-half minute sound fantasy punctuated by abrupt stereo pans, subtle edits, and keyboard parts that were felt rather than heard. By the time he came to make *After The Gold Rush*, though, Young had settled on a simpler, sparser sound. He had also set up a basic studio in the basement of his new home in the Topanga Canyon hills of Los Angeles, which he soundproofed with lead and pine milled from the trees in his backyard. A modest collection of gear included a Scully 8-track, a small mixer, and a handful of mikes.

"There was a shitload of room on those recordings," Young told writer Jimmy McDonough, "because there wasn't anything else goin' on. The song was it . . . and everything else was supporting it."

The songs in question, inspired largely by the Dean Stockwell-Herb Berman screenplay that gave the album its title, stick in the main to the country-folk that had served him so well on CSNY's *Déjà Vu*, with even the rockier tracks underpinned by Lofgren's stately piano playing. Perhaps the most important of the album's ten originals is 'Only Love Can Break Your Heart,' the single that first brought Young mainstream attention, while another key track is the cautiously optimistic 'Don't Let It Bring You Down.' More infamous, however, is 'Southern Man,' the scathing attack on racism and bigotry in the Deep South of the U.S.A. that prompted Lynyrd Skynyrd to reply in 1974 with 'Sweet Home Alabama.'

Though not entirely successful with the critics – *Rolling Stone* magazine's Langdon Winner concluded that "most of this music was simply not ready to be recorded" – *After The Gold Rush* struck an immediate chord with the disillusion felt by many after the death of the 1960s dream. By Christmas, it had become Young's first Top 10 hit album, and remained on the U.S. chart for over a year on its way to selling two million copies.

Young built on the success of *After The Gold Rush* two years later with the lighter *Harvest*, which became the biggest-selling album of his career. Perhaps surprisingly, given its commercial success, *Harvest* contains a strange disparity of styles, from the country-edged 'Out On The Weekend' and 'Heart Of Gold' – the only U.S. Number One hit single of his career – to the ragged rock of 'Old Man' and 'Words (Between The Lines Of Age).' It also includes two songs recorded with The London Symphony Orchestra, and the stark anti-heroin ballad 'The Needle And The Damage Done.'

1970

Apple STCH 639 (U.S.A. & U.K.)
Released June 1970

**All Things Must Pass introduced
the rock world to the mixed
pleasures of the studio triple
album. Box sets had previously
been the reserve of classical
labels releasing operas, choral
works, and symphony cycles,
works whose length necessitated
three or more 12-inch LPs.**

By contrast, in the 1950s and early
1960s single-oriented pop struggled
to get to grips with even a single
album. Record companies often
threw LPs together by combining a couple of hits with eight tracks of
indifferent 'filler' until the artistic ambition of rock led groups to make
albums where all the tracks counted, and eventually to stretch themselves
across four sides of vinyl. But six?

For Harrison, a triple album was a personal statement in the context of The
Beatles' post-split politics. As a musician his input had not always been fully
appreciated, and it had always been a bone of contention that he lacked an
outlet for his songs in the band, owing to the songwriting dominance of
those other two guys. Consequently he had a large backlog of songs – 'Wah-
Wah,' for example, a track on this album, actually dated back to early 1969,
and was written at the time of Harrison's temporary walk-out (captured on
film during the making of *Let It Be*) after yet another studio row between
Lennon and McCartney – and now was the time to release them.

At its best, *All Things Must Pass* balances the emotional uplift of 1960s
pop with spiritual concerns, keeping its feet on the floor even when its head
is in the clouds. This is exemplified in the swooning rush and barbed lyric of

■ A year after the release of **All Things Must Pass,** *George Harrison
organized* **The Concert For Bangladesh,** *the first major charity rock-music
event. Responding to the plight of refugees during the 1971 Bangladeshi
struggle for independence from West Pakistan, Harrison arranged two
nights of all-star performances at Madison Square Garden, New York.
Among the guests were Bob Dylan (center) and Leon Russell (right),
pictured below with Harrison, as well as Ringo Starr, Badfinger, and Eric
Clapton.*

Awaiting On You All,' as well as the famous 'My Sweet Lord,' surely one of the greatest religious songs of the past 50 years. The infamous legal action, in which Harrison was judged to have plagiarized The Chiffons' 'He's So Fine,' may or may not have been a victory for copyright law but was a moral and artistic injustice. For, whatever the similarities of melodic phrase and harmony, 'He's So Fine' is mere candyfloss compared with the thumping majesty, the fabulous key-change, and slide-guitar breaks of Harrison's enlightened fusion of Christianity and Hinduism.

Harrison's muse can be melancholic, as on a song like 'Let It Roll,' but the album also has 'If Not For You,' the beautiful 'I'd Have You Anytime' – co-written with Bob Dylan – and the sunny 'What Is Life,' with its huge sound and driving beat. In the sleevenotes to the remaster of 2001, Harrison wrote that he would have liked "to liberate some of the songs from the big production," which he now thought "a bit over the top." (Some will be thankful he didn't, for *All Things Must Pass* is perhaps the last great example of Phil Spector's Wall Of Sound production.) Harrison explained: "Some of the sessions were very long in the preparation of the sound and the arrangements had at times various percussion players, sometimes two or three; two drummers, four or five acoustic guitars, two pianos, and even two basses on one of the tracks. The songs were played over and over again until the arrangements were sorted out so that the engineer in the control-room could get the sound with Phil Spector. Many of the tracks were virtually live." A number of guests were featured, including Ringo Starr, Eric Clapton, Peter Frampton, members of Delaney and Bonnie, Badfinger, and Procol Harum.

In 1971–2 Harrison enjoyed the greatest commercial success of any of the ex-Beatles. This was all the more remarkable given the cost of production of the triple album. Perhaps it could have been better shorter, perhaps the all-star jams were expendable, but *All Things Must Pass* stands as Harrison's monument.

Taproot Manuscript Neil Diamond

Universal 73092 (U.S.A.) / Universal UNLS 117 (U.K.)
Released October 1970

This extraordinary album, which Diamond described as "an attempt to convey my passion for the folk music of that black continent," pre-dated Paul Simon's African-inspired *Graceland* project by over 15 years.

'African Trilogy,' which makes up one half of *Taproot Manuscript*, was acknowledged on release as "a stunning example of pop crossbreeding" by *Time* magazine, but because its creator had written hits for The Monkees and spent most of his subsequent career in sequined shirts crooning to moist housewives, it has been ignored by the rock cognoscenti.

"The 'Trilogy' took 18 months to write," Diamond has said, "but it gave me far more satisfaction than anything I'd done before." It was also a nightmare for everyone else involved in it at Western Sound in Los Angeles. Engineer Armin Steiner described Diamond as the "most incredible mass of self-torture I have ever seen," and tales of his endless bickering over Marty Paich's lovely orchestral arrangements are legendary. The end result, however, was an impressive six-song suite based on African themes, featuring ambitious use of sound effects, exotic instruments, and vocal textures unheard of in popular music at the time. Undeniably much more pop-oriented than Simon's *Graceland*, it nevertheless explored similar issues, with lyrics touching on poverty, natural disasters, and the effects of Christianity on indigenous African cultures.

The album, which went gold two months after release, includes not just a classic Number One hit in 'Cracklin' Rosie' but also 'Done Too Soon,' which sounds uncannily like the inspiration for Billy Joel's 1989 smash hit 'We Didn't Start The Fire.'

Vanity Lables

During the 1960s and 1970s there was a fashion for successful pop and rock groups to form their own 'vanity' record labels, often in association with a major-label parent company, through which they would issue their own music as well as records by other artists.

This trend was started by Frank Sinatra, who in 1961 set up the highly successful Reprise label, initially to issue his own *Sinatra Swings* – the title of which had to be changed from *Swing Along With Me* after his paymasters at Capitol claimed it was too similar to the earlier *Come Swing With Me*. Much of Sinatra's subsequent recorded output, which began to head in a more jazz-based direction, was issued on Reprise. In its infancy, the label also issued albums by Sammy Davis Jr, Dean Martin, and Bing Crosby. Warner Brothers bought a majority shareholding in 1963, but the label has continued as a separate entity since.

In 1967, in the week that 'Good Vibrations' went gold, The Beach Boys launched Brother Records. The label issued all of the group's albums and singles from *Smiley Smile* onward, though their records also bore the imprint of the group's parent label at the time, Capitol. When The Beach Boys signed with Reprise in 1970 the group's albums were credited to Brother/Reprise. Brother Records also issued an album by The Flame, a group produced by Dennis Wilson.

Many bands started their own labels for financial reasons, so that they could invest their earnings in a company and limit the amount of tax they would have to pay. This was particularly true of The Beatles, who formed Apple Records in 1968. Two years earlier George Harrison had sung "It's one for you, 19 for me" in the song 'Taxman,' drawing attention to the fact that the Labour government had introduced stiff taxation for big earners, taxing them at 95 per cent on their higher-level income.

The first release on Apple was John Lennon and Yoko Ono's controversial *Two Virgins* album, which Apple's parent companies – Capitol in the U.S.A. and EMI in the U.K. – refused to distribute because of its 'obscene' cover, on which Lennon and Ono appeared naked. Apple issued all of the group's albums from *The Beatles* (aka *The White Album*) onward, many of the four Beatles' early solo projects, and albums and singles by other artists, including the popular singer Mary Hopkin. Apple began to dwindle in the mid 1970s, but re-emerged in the 1990s with the launch of The Beatles' *Anthology* series.

In 1969, shortly after issuing the symphonic rock concept album *On The Threshold Of A Dream*, The Moody Blues founded Threshold Recordings. The label's first release was the group's own *To Our Children's Children's Children* later the same year. They also opened a chain of record-stores under the name Threshold.

In 1974, after recording five globally successful albums, Led Zeppelin created their Swan Song label. As well as issuing the group's albums after *Physical Graffiti* in 1975, the label was also home to a number of other groups, including Bad Company and The Pretty Things, and helped fund the cult comedy movie *Monty Python And The Holy Grail* (1975).

1970

Sweet Baby James **James Taylor**

Warner Brothers 1843 (U.S.A.) / K46043 (U.K.)
Released February 1970

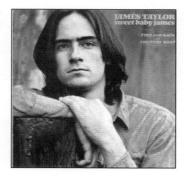

James Taylor was one of the first of a new breed of West Coast singer-songwriters to achieve widespread commercial success.

Sweet Baby James is thought by many to be Taylor's first album, but he had in fact recorded a lesser-known, eponymous debut for The Beatles' Apple label in 1968, which featured Paul McCartney on bass. While *James Taylor* limped to Number 62 on the U.S. *Billboard* albums chart, its follow-up faired much better, reaching the Top Ten on both sides of the Atlantic. Two of its gentle, folk-rock songs were U.S. hit singles, 'Fire And Rain' and 'Country Road,' which featured backing vocals from Joni Mitchell. Taylor repaid the favor by appearing on Mitchell's landmark *Blue*, issued the following year. He also contributed to Carole King's *Tapestry*.

Taylor's own career continued to go from strength to strength throughout the 1970s and beyond. All but one of his 12 subsequent album releases of the next 30 years achieved gold or platinum status in the U.S.A.

1971

Blue **Joni Mitchell**

Reprise 2038 (U.S.A.) / K44128 (U.K.)
Released August 1971

In May and June 1971 they locked the doors to the A&M Studios in Los Angeles as Joni Mitchell bared her soul to record her fourth LP, an album she has described as "probably the purest emotional record I will ever make in my life."

Stephen Stills and James Taylor made contributions, and Mitchell brought a new sophistication to the singer-songwriter idiom, both musically and lyrically, as she mulled over adult relationships. For young women struggling with moody boyfriends the world over she became a wise older sister who knew how they felt. Her vocals were instantly recognizable: a slow, wide vibrato, with unpredictable swoops in the phrasing. So was her guitar work, owing to unusual tunings that gave unique chords, as evident on the likes of 'This Flight Tonight.' She once observed: "For some reason, once I got the open tunings I began to get the harmonic sophistication that my musical fountain inside was excited by. Once I got some interesting chords to play with, my writing began to come."

She had already written hits in 'Big Yellow Taxi' and 'Woodstock,' but she was moving away from her folk beginnings into a more crossover style. For the upbeat 'Carey' she employed light percussion and bass, two guitars, and her own multitracked backing vocals, but generally the record has a sparse sound. 'My Old Man,' 'Blue,' and 'Little Green' have not much more than voice with piano or guitar. The lyrics are haunted by journeys and lovers, none more so than 'The Last Time I Saw Richard,' which closes the record with a narrative that juxtaposes different outlooks on life and where they lead.

Tapestry **Carole King**

ODE 77009 (U.S.A.) / A&M AMLH2025 (U.K.)
Released February 1971

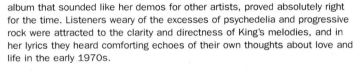

Tapestry established Carole King as the first superstar female singer-songwriter. Joni Mitchell, Janis Ian, Laura Nyro, and others had preceded her and blazed a trail, but none had achieved the kind of sales figures and chart accomplishments that King would with this album.

Since starting in the music business in 1959 King had, together with her Brill Building lyric-writing husband Gerry Goffin, composed over 100 Top 40 hits, including eight Number One singles, for the likes of Little Eva, The Drifters, and The Monkees, but she was not regarded as a singer-songwriter because those songs had been written for other artists.

Encouraged by her friend James Taylor, King had taken her first step as a solo songwriter in 1970 with the album *Writer*, but only because the success of The Beatles and Bob Dylan had encouraged so many artists to write their own songs that she was finding it hard to make a living. *Writer* had sold a miserable 6,000 copies, but with *Tapestry*, recorded at A&M Studios in Hollywood, the decision to make a stripped-back, piano-based

album that sounded like her demos for other artists, proved absolutely right for the time. Listeners weary of the excesses of psychedelia and progressive rock were attracted to the clarity and directness of King's melodies, and in her lyrics they heard comforting echoes of their own thoughts about love and life in the early 1970s.

'Will You Love Me Tomorrow,' written for The Shirelles a full decade earlier, was miraculously transformed by King's new treatment. The girl-group version had seemed fraught with all the insecurities and double standards of the traditional boy-girl relationships of that earlier era, whereas King's own version comes across as a mature, clear-headed appraisal of the uncertainties of any relationship in any era. Her determination to survive and move on from a failed relationship in 'It's Too Late' and her promise of life-long loyalty in 'You've Got A Friend' were philosophical touchstones for a newly liberated sisterhood of women.

Even so, King never sought to ingratiate herself with the hardline feminists. She was a model of the new woman – hard working, financially independent, the equal of any man she encountered in the music business – but she took her role as a mother as seriously as her career. She frequently stated that she had never encountered sexual discrimination in her working life, and she was happy to acknowledge that she had called the album after a piece of tapestry she had been working on as relaxation between takes.

On June 19th 1971 Tapestry hit Number One on the *Billboard* albums chart for the first of a staggering 15 weeks on its way to notching up 10 million sales in two years. At the Grammys, King collected Best Album, Best Song, Best Record, and Best Female Vocalist, and the album went on to spend 302 weeks on the charts, securing it the distinction of being the longest-charting album ever by a female solo artist.

In short, King's achievements with *Tapestry* paved the way for every Tori Amos, Alanis Morrisette, and Avril Lavigne to follow in its wake.

■ *Sessions for Carole King's Tapestry. Above: King at the mixing desk in A&M Studios, Hollywood, with producer Lou Adler. Opposite: James Taylor and Joni Mitchell add their backing vocals.*

1971

Stoney End **Barbra Streisand**

Columbia PCQ-30378 (U.S.A.) / CBS 64269 (U.K.)
Released February 1971

Already an emerging Broadway star, Barbra Streisand became one of the most commercially successful singers of the early 1960s with *The Barbra Streisand Album* (1962), an album of torch songs and standards that stood apart from the prevailing trend for rock'n'roll.

The singer spent much of the rest of the decade working on stage and screen, winning an Academy Award for her role in the movie adaptation of the musical *Funny Girl*, in which she had also starred on Broadway.

With her movie career on the wane, Streisand made her first attempt at a return to the pop market in 1969 with *What About Today?*, which drowned great songs by Lennon & McCartney, Bacharach, and others in insipid, Las Vegas-style arrangements. Needless to say, the album sold poorly. On *Stoney End*, however, Streisand made a more successful attempt at lending her powerful voice to the popular music of the time.

The title track, perhaps surprisingly, is a straight version of a song by the eclectic late-1960s singer-songwriter Laura Nyro, which provided Streisand with a U.S. Top Ten hit in early 1971. The rest of the album sits closer to Joni Mitchell – whose 'I Don't Know Where I Stand' Streisand covers – than the show tunes for which she was best known. It also includes songwriting contributions from Gordon Lightfoot and Randy Newman, who plays piano on several tracks. *Stoney End* reached Number Ten in the U.S.A. and laid the foundations for a career resurgence that culminated with starring roles in the movie musicals *The Way We Were* (1973) and *A Star Is Born* (1976).

Sticky Fingers **The Rolling Stones**

Rolling Stones COC59100 (U.S.A. / U.K.)
Released April 1971

The first album on The Stones' own label, Rolling Stones Records, *Sticky Fingers* found the band digging ever deeper into rootsy veins of Americana, with bohemian, good-vibes producer Jimmy Miller at the helm.

The hit single 'Brown Sugar' defines the sloppy-rock groove of the entire proceedings, but guitarist Keith Richards's increasing use of the open-G tuning he had learned from Ry Cooder adds much swampy ambience and a country feel.

In some ways, it's a grab-bag of tracks recorded over the preceding two years, some using the band's newly acquired mobile recording studio parked outside Mick Jagger's country home, Stargroves, others at their favorite London studio, Olympic, and still more in Muscle Shoals, Alabama, in search of authentic Southern accents. Despite this, the album sounds remarkably coherent, with tracks seeming almost to merge into each other.

The album's extraordinary sleeve, however, probably attracted more attention than its music. Shot by Andy Warhol, who had previously devised the peelable banana cover for The Velvet Underground, this one featured a grainy black-and-white close-up of a jeans-clad groin into which a fully functioning metal zipper was inserted. The Stones were presumably sniggering up their sleeves at the thought of countless female fans enjoying the vicarious little thrill of unzipping what they assumed to be Jagger's jeans, unaware that the groin in the photograph belonged to gay icon Joe Dallesandro. As a sales-boosting gimmick it was a stroke of genius but, in practice, the zipper played havoc with the cover of whichever album it was shelved beside.

■ *The Rolling Stones maintain their modesty with the help of a copy each of their* Sticky Fingers *LP, the sleeve artwork for which was designed by Andy Warhol.*

Who's Next **The Who**

Decca DL79182 (U.S.A.) / Track 2408102 (U.K.)
Released September 1971

**The Who's finest single album,
Who's Next was a landmark in its
innovative use of synthesizers
and sequencers in rock. It is also
one of the finest examples in
rock history of artistic victory
snatched from the jaws of defeat.**

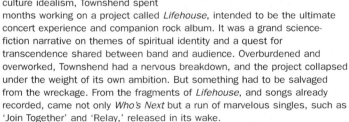

The success of *Tommy* had left The
Who, and Pete Townshend in
particular, with the challenge of where
to go next. Immersed in spiritual
ideas and the afterglow of counter-
culture idealism, Townshend spent
months working on a project called *Lifehouse*, intended to be the ultimate
concert experience and companion rock album. It was a grand science-
fiction narrative on themes of spiritual identity and a quest for
transcendence shared between band and audience. Overburdened and
overworked, Townshend had a nervous breakdown, and the project collapsed
under the weight of its own ambition. But something had to be salvaged
from the wreckage. From the fragments of *Lifehouse*, and songs already
recorded, came not only *Who's Next* but a run of marvelous singles, such as
'Join Together' and 'Relay,' released in its wake.

Who's Next caught The Who at their peak, doing full justice to their power.
'Baba O'Reilly' and 'Won't Get Fooled Again' became anthems to rival
anything from their chart heyday in the 1960s. Both feature explosive power-
chording from Townshend, Moon's whirlwind drumming, Entwistle's melodic
bass, and Daltrey's commanding vocals, as well as an underlay of
sequencer – and in the case of 'Baba O'Reilly' a violin break. Every one of
the nine tracks is a gem, from the muscular spirituality of 'Bargain,' the
moving 'The Song Is Over,' and the black humor of 'My Wife,' to the
romantic resolve of 'Getting In Tune,' the agit rock of 'Going Mobile,' and
the majestic vocal harmonies and dynamic climax of 'Behind Blue Eyes.'

■ *Above: The Who on the British TV show* Top Of The Pops *in 1971.*

Pictures At An Exhibition
Emerson, Lake & Palmer

Manticore 66666 (U.S.A.) / Island HELP 1 (U.K.)
Released December 1971

**As its political and social
influence waned with the end of
the 1960s, rock compensated by
taking itself more seriously. It
wanted to be seen to be Art, and
this led to a skirmish with the
frock-coated world of classical
music.**

The Who had already messed about
with Edvard Grieg's 'Hall Of The
Mountain King' and parodied 'Land Of
Hope And Glory.' When Deep Purple
recorded their *Concerto For Group
And Orchestra* in 1970 at the Royal Albert Hall with The London
Philharmonic, the rebels were not just at the gates, it seemed they were in
the palace. ELP went one better. In the immortal words of Peter Sellers,
they started "muckin' abaht with the classics." The result was *Pictures At
An Exhibition*, recorded live at Newcastle City Hall in March 1971.

In ELP Keith Emerson's keyboards took the place of guitar in the standard
power trio, with Greg Lake on bass and vocals, and Carl Palmer on drums.
Emerson performed with the flamboyance and theatrics of Hendrix, while
the band pursued elaborate and hard-hitting pieces. Composed by Modest
Mussorgsky as a set of piano pieces, *Pictures At An Exhibition* had
received many orchestral treatments, most successfully by Ravel. The
point about 'prog' going 'classical' was that the bands couldn't lose:
impressed by technique, half the audience considered the band a cut
above the average for tackling it (and themselves a cut above the average
rock fan for listening to it); the other half thought it was a rebel wheeze,
like taking a spray-can to a Constable painting. ELP gave *Pictures* a
thorough rock mugging and threw in B. Bumble & The Stinger's 1960s hit
'Nut Rocker' for good measure. In a continuation of this theme, later in
the 1970s they had a singles hit with a version of Aaron Copland's
'Fanfare For The Common Man.'

Electric Warrior
T. Rex

Reprise 6466 (U.S.A.) / Fly HiFly6 (U.K.)
Released September 1971

The first LP Marc Bolan made with the four-piece band T. Rex, *Electric Warrior* is the album that opened the door for glam rock, pre-dating Bowie's *Ziggy Stardust* by a year.

Periodically, rock renews itself by returning to its 12-bar roots. Despite his four mostly acoustic albums cut as the two-man Tyrannosaurus Rex, Bolan had always been a fan of rock'n'roll. By 1970 he had returned to electric guitar, reaching a new audience with the album *T. Rex* and his first big hit 'Ride A White Swan.' His songwriting began to filter the raw excitement of rock'n'roll through an eclectic post-Hendrix, post-Dylan sensibility, which took T. Rex beyond the 1950s pastiche of Sha Na Na or the *Grease* soundtrack. Bolan's lyrics mixed up his earlier Tolkeinesque wizards-and-elves imagery with such elements of Americana as DJ Alan Freed, Fender guitars, the *Dr Strange* comics, and Cadillacs. His distinctive woodland warble floated over Chuck Berry-derived riffs, with funky congas, and dappled English strings courtesy of producer Tony Visconti.

Electric Warrior contains two hit singles – the classic boogie 'Get It On' (aka 'Bang A Gong' in the U.S.A.) and 'Jeepster' – alongside gentle ballads 'Girl' and the reincarnation song, 'Cosmic Dancer,' with its spooky backward lead guitars, the chugging 'Mambo Sun,' and the doo-wop-derived 'Monolith,' which was 'Duke Of Earl' meets Arthur C. Clarke. (Bolan can be heard on the tapes joking with Visconti that the take should be titled 'Duke Of Monolith.') Against prevailing denim trends, Bolan dressed up in satin and Lurex, and, in the wake of *Warrior*, toured to scenes of 'T. Rexstasy' reminiscent of Beatlemania.

What's Going On
Marvin Gaye

Tamla Motown TS 310 (U.S.A.) / STML11190 (U.K.)
Released May 1971 (U.S.A.) / September 1971 (U.K.)

A star in the sunset of Motown's golden Detroit era, *What's Going On* is the most significant album that the label released.

What's Going On strikes a creative balance between Gaye's personal and public concerns, and is where the label almost exclusively associated with hit singles belatedly discovered the album as an artistic entity in its own right. It gave Marvin Gaye a road back from the wilderness in which he'd found himself following the death of singing partner Tammi Terrell. *What's Going On* revitalized Gaye's music, satisfying on the one hand his long-held ambition as a singer to perform more sophisticated material, and on the other his generous impulse to respond to the plight of his brother Frankie and the thousands like him serving in Vietnam, and to the social upheaval in the U.S.A. at the close of the 1960s.

It might have been Gaye's vision and voice, but both in the writing and the playing *What's Going On* is a team effort. By 1970 Gaye had the reputation at Motown of being difficult to work with. David Van DePitte was assigned as producer and arranged the orchestral parts, but found that Gaye hadn't finished the songs and kept taking time off. Recording sessions for the title track

were on June 1st, with vocals overdubbed on July 6th, 7th, and 10th, and strings on September 21st 1970. The basic tracks for the remaining songs were recorded on March 17th, 19th, and 20th, with overdubs on March 24th, 26th–30th 1971. Obie Benson of The Four Tops was called in to help finish songs, and the LP became the last hurrah for Motown's session players, with Funk Brothers veterans James Jamerson and Bob Babbitt (bass), Joe Messina and Robert White (guitars), Earl Van Dyke (piano), and Jack Ashford (percussion) actually getting credits on the sleeve for once, instead of being unnamed session players. Jamerson's bass lines are frequently astonishing in both their rhythm and jazz inflections. Jamerson hardly ever talked about a day's recording when he got home, but after cutting 'What's Going On' he reputedly told his wife the track was a masterpiece.

In contrast to the anguished vocals that were *de rigueur* for most male singers at Motown, and which Gaye had used on such hits as 'I Heard It Through The Grapevine,' here he tried singing in a more relaxed way. He said: "I felt like I'd finally learned how to sing. I'd been studying the microphone for a dozen years, and suddenly I saw what I'd been doing wrong. I'd been singing too loud, especially on those Whitfield songs. It was all so easy. One night I was listening to a record by Lester Young, the horn player, and it came to me. Relax, just relax." He also multitracked his voice, blurring the distinction between lead and backing vocal, so that many of the songs have multiple vocal lines weaving in and out of each other. (The idea for this came from the happy accident of a playback when he heard two of his vocal tracks at once instead of one.)

Unfortunately, when Motown's boardroom first heard the final tapes they rejected the album, and Gaye had to deliver them an ultimatum to get it released. He commented: "[Motown] didn't like it, didn't understand it, and didn't trust it. Management said the songs were too long, too formless, and would get lost on a public looking for easy three-minute stories. For months they wouldn't release it. My attitude had to be firm. Basically I said, 'Put it out or I'll never record for you again.' Berry Gordy eventually said, 'Marvin, we learn from everything. That's what life's all about. I don't think you're right, but if you really want to do it, do it. And if it doesn't work you'll learn something; and if it does I'll learn something.' The album was called *What's Going On.* I learned something." Gaye's confidence was vindicated, for *What's Going On* became Motown's biggest selling album to date, yielding three hit singles – the title track, 'Mercy Mercy Me,' and 'Inner City Blues.'

In strictly musical terms it is a cohesive album. This is partly because of the linking of one track to another so that the music unfolds continuously, with the occasional jolt of a sudden tempo and key change as one groove runs straight into the next. Other factors are the recycling of vocal phrases and the re-using of chord progressions on more than one song. The bridge of 'What's Going On' becomes the intro of 'What's Happening Brother,' and the main progression of the former crops up again in 'Mercy Mercy Me.' The

music has far more of a jazz feel than was usual with Motown, the overall sound an ambient groove. There were innovative production touches, the heavily reverbed congas, for example – used most effectively on the droning melancholy of 'Inner City Blues' – with strings, brass, and celeste adding lushness and sparkle to the album.

Written and conceived in a generous and humane spirit, the lyrics touch on many issues of the day, making the record a State Of The Union address from a President Of Soul: the Vietnam War, poverty and crime in the inner cities, drugs, unemployment, ecology, all were handled with a poignant grace, along with Gaye's ever-faithfuls, love and religion. Gaye told Smokey Robinson: "God is writing this album. God is working through me." Sensual and spiritual, only occasionally does the record slip into sentimentality, on 'Save The Children,' for instance.

In 2001 Motown issued an exemplary 'deluxe' edition with two separate mixes, one from Detroit in April 1971 which is 'drier,' the other prepared in May in Los Angeles and used for the LP release. It also contains a live performance of much of the album from a concert at the Kennedy Center in Washington on May 1st 1972. Three decades later, *What's Going On* still retains its freshness and humanity.

1971

There's A Riot Goin' On Sly & The Family Stone

Epic 30986 (U.S.A.) / EPC/40 64613 (U.K.)
Released November 1971

"One of the most drugged-sounding albums yet to be released," according to a *New Musical Express* **(U.K.) review at the time, Sly Stone's dark, political masterpiece would prove inspirational to countless musicians of disparate genres, from 1970s disco to hip-hop in the 1990s.**

Having studied music and composition at university and worked as a DJ in the early 1960s, Sylvester Stewart formed The Family Stone in 1966, rechristening himself Sly Stone in the process. The band had early hits with the kinetic, funky 'Dance To The Music,' 'Everyday People' – which topped the pop and R&B charts – and its parent album, *Stand*, before bridging the gap between black and white audiences with a triumphant performance at *Woodstock*. Subsequent single releases, 'Thank You (Falettin Me Be Mice Elf Again)' and 'Family Affair,' also reached Number One in the U.S.A.

'Family Affair' was also the first single to be drawn from Stone's epic masterwork, *There's A Riot Goin' On*. Where the bulk of the band's previous offerings had been in tune with the optimism of the late 1960s, *There's A Riot Goin' On* took *Stand*'s 'Don't Call Me Nigger, Whitey' as a starting point. Stone's songs became overtly political in nature, a cynical commentary on the decline of U.S. values and civilization. Given its lyrical content, the album's iconic sleeve – a stark image of the Stars and Stripes – could not be more fitting.

Musically, while retaining the commercial edge that had served his band so well in recent years, Stone began to delve further into his melting pot of taut funk, psychedelic soul, rock, and blues. Perhaps the biggest influence on the record's sound was Stone's prodigious intake of cocaine, which is surely responsible for its bleak, hazy overtones. His propensity for repeatedly overdubbing his band's performances with his own often sloppy playing also led to the master tapes becoming warped in places. Where it is left untouched, the playing of The Family Stone – arguably the first fully racially integrated band – is exceptional, in particular Greg Errico's staccato drum breaks and Larry Graham's peerless bass work. Stone also makes early use of a drum machine on some tracks, including 'Family Affair.'

Despite its somewhat claustrophobic tone and uncompromising lyrical agenda, *There's A Riot Goin' On* kept Sly And The Family Stone's run of success going, topping the U.S. albums chart and also making the U.K. Top 40. As well as 'Family Affair,' the album also spawned 'Runnin' Away,' perhaps the most perfect pop moment in Stone's career. The rest of *Riot* is built around two lengthy, thematically similar, jazzy funk songs, 'Africa Talks To You (The Asphalt Jungle)' and 'Thank You For Talkin' To Me Africa,' a slowed-down remake of the earlier single 'Thank You (Falettin Me Be Mice Elf Again).'

Stone would never again hit the commercial and artistic peaks of *There's A Riot Goin' On*, falling into a desperate period of drug dependency and eventual bankruptcy by the late 1970s.

Maggot Brain **Funkadelic**

Westbound 2007 (U.S.A.) / 6310 200 (U.K.)
Released August 1971

Throughout the 1970s, funk pioneer George Clinton led two of the genre's most important groups, Parliament and Funkadelic.

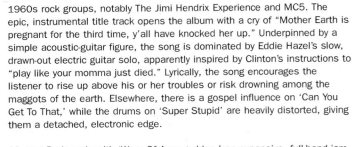

Though the membership of both overlapped, Clinton used Parliament as an outlet for his more groove-orientated, upbeat material, while Funkadelic's recordings had more of a social and political conscience.

After working as a songwriter for Motown in the 1960s, Clinton formed Funkadelic in 1969 and recorded the group's eponymous debut the following year. Funkadelic issued *Free Your Mind And Your Ass Will Follow* in early 1971 before starting work on *Maggot Brain*. Like *There's A Riot Goin' On* by Sly And The Family Stone, which was released in November 1971, *Maggot Brain* betrays the influence of late-

1960s rock groups, notably The Jimi Hendrix Experience and MC5. The epic, instrumental title track opens the album with a cry of "Mother Earth is pregnant for the third time, y'all have knocked her up." Underpinned by a simple acoustic-guitar figure, the song is dominated by Eddie Hazel's slow, drawn-out electric guitar solo, apparently inspired by Clinton's instructions to "play like your momma just died." Lyrically, the song encourages the listener to rise up above his or her troubles or risk drowning among the maggots of the earth. Elsewhere, there is a gospel influence on 'Can You Get To That,' while the drums on 'Super Stupid' are heavily distorted, giving them a detached, electronic edge.

Maggot Brain ends with 'Wars Of Armageddon,' an expansive, full-band jam, on which Clinton, keyboardist Bernie Worrell, and Funkadelic's three guitarists battle for control. *Maggot Brain* failed to chart on release in either the U.S.A. or the U.K., but is now regarded as one of the finest funk records of the era.

Clinton continued to record at a prodigious rate throughout the 1970s, and retained the socio-political edge to his work with Funkadelic even as his contemporaries moved towards more throwaway, hedonistic material in the latter part of the decade. In 1978 Funkadelic issued one of their best-loved and most commercially successful albums, *One Nation Under A Groove*, which features an updated version of 'Maggot Brain.' The title track was a hit when issued as a single on both sides of the Atlantic.

1971

[Untitled] IV
Led Zeppelin

Atlantic SD7208 (U.S.A.) / 2401012 (U.K.)
Released November 1971

After the bafflement in the music press over the acoustic leanings of their third album, Led Zeppelin came back to remind the world that no one could rock their audience like they could.

The biggest-selling hard-rock album ever, Zeppelin's fourth brought the band's acoustic and electric, mystical and erotic aspects into perfect balance. These eight tracks have the strength of rain-washed granite.

IV, as it has become known, was recorded using The Rolling Stones' mobile facility at Headley Grange, a large Victorian house in Hampshire, U.K., and in London, during the winter of 1970–1. The band's genius for dynamics and strange 'look-Ma-no-time-signature' riffs drives 'Black Dog,' and 'Rock and Roll' blasts like a supercharged V8 running on jet fuel. 'Misty Mountain Hop' matches a concrete-demolishing riff with tales of hippy days in the park, and 'Four Sticks' pits stratospheric singing and churning drums with innovative synthesizers. 'Going To California' set romantic disillusionment to delicate acoustic guitar and mandolin. 'When The Levee Breaks' took Memphis Minnie's 1929 blues and rewrote it to enormous proportions, lifting off from Bonham's much-sampled battering intro. (This classic drum sound was achieved with ambient miking in Headley Grange's hall and an echo unit.)

At the album's heart are 'The Battle Of Evermore' and 'Stairway To Heaven.' Page had picked up a mandolin one night during a holiday he and Plant were enjoying in a cottage in Wales, and wrote 'Evermore' with the first shapes his fingers found. Despite the absence of electric instruments, the song still has an extraordinary intensity and haunting atmosphere, as it pictures the eternal battle between good and evil with images drawn from J.R.R. Tolkein's *The Lord Of The Rings*, at the time a cult book among the hippies. It is also one of the few Zeppelin songs to feature a guest musician, the late Sandy Denny, then ex-singer with British folk outfit Fairport Convention. The balance between Plant's voice and hers is superb.

To feel the full effect of 'Stairway To Heaven' always listen to 'The Battle of Evermore' first. One of rock radio's most played tracks, 'Stairway To Heaven' is neither the pompous anthem ridiculed by fashionable prejudice nor the backward-message-infested Satanism of twisted imaginations. 'Stairway' sustains the mystic pastoralism of 'The Battle of Evermore,' with its idealized English country landscape – reminiscent of the paintings of Samuel Palmer – inhabited by the mysterious figures of the May Queen, the piper, and a Celtic goddess promising spiritual wisdom and redemption. The inspiration came partly from Plant's reading of Lewis Spence's *The Magical Arts In Celtic Britain*. 'Stairway' is a tautly constructed eight-minute masterpiece of arrangement, carefully building from acoustic guitar and recorders to multiple electric guitars and Zeppelin at full throttle, and the lone-voice ending. Every individual's performance is exemplary, with Bonham's drum entry giving the song a spine-tingling lift-off, and Page supplying one of the rock's most expressive solos over Jones's Motown-inspired bass line.

Fittingly, the use of 'runic' symbols to name the album, the absence of words from the sleeve, the juxtaposition of urban destruction with the hermit's mountain-top light of wisdom, gave the vinyl album a mystique no CD could match – a perfect package for music that remains timelessly potent.

Hunky Dory **David Bowie**

RCA AFL-1 4623 (U.S.A.) / SF/PK 8244 (U.K.)
Released December 1971

The Rise And Fall Of Ziggy Stardust And The Spiders From Mars
David Bowie

RCA AFL-1 4702 (U.S.A.) / SF/PK 8267 (U.K.)
Released June 1972

The first classic Bowie release, *Hunky Dory* marked the start of an impressive run of high-quality albums throughout the 1970s; the following year's *Ziggy Stardust*, meanwhile, is the first of his character-based concept albums and the best-loved release of his career.

Having begun his career in the mid 1960s as Davy Jones, the rechristened David Bowie first hit his stride, artistically and commercially, with the single 'Space Oddity,' which was given a wider exposure when used to accompany television pictures of the first moon landing in 1969. In spite of this, its parent album, *Man Of Words, Man Of Music* – later retitled *Space Oddity* – and the follow-up, *The Man Who Sold The World*, both failed to chart. The latter had a surprisingly hard, almost heavy-metal sound, but when it came to recording *Hunky Dory* Bowie had returned, for the most part, to the acoustic guitar-based, singer-songwriter sound of his earlier work. What elevated the album above his late-1960s material, 'Space Oddity' aside, was Bowie's newly developed and highly ambitious capacity for bridging the gap between highbrow and lowbrow art forms, taking classic pop and peppering it with cabaret stylings and sexually ambiguous lyrics.

Hunky Dory includes several songs that have since become touchstones in the Bowie canon, notably the euphoric 'Changes' and 'Life On Mars' – originally composed with Sinatra in mind – a pair of peerless piano-led pop singles. The other key ingredient of the success of the album was the first appearance of Bowie's mythical backing group, The Spiders From Mars, who add an early glam feel to the likes of 'Andy

Warhol' and 'Queen Bitch.' The album also features Rick Wakeman, who would soon join Yes, on piano.

Though *Hunky Dory* failed to make a big impact on the charts on its release, its success was buoyed by the first issue of 'Changes' as a single – it would reach Number One in the U.K. when reissued alongside 'Space Oddity' in 1975 – and the controversy sparked by Bowie's proclamation in *Melody Maker* (U.K.) that he was bisexual. Bowie had already started work on his next album by the time *Hunky Dory* saw release in December 1971. In fact, he had issued embryonic versions of two songs – 'Moonage Daydream' and 'Hang On To Yourself' – from *Ziggy Stardust* under the pseudonym Arnold Corns six months previously. He had begun to conceive the idea of a concept album for which he would 'become' the title character, an amalgam of Bowie's good friend (Z)Iggy Pop, cult 1960s performer The Legendary Stardust Cowboy, Vince Taylor (the 'French Elvis'), and various aspects of Japanese culture, which gave Ziggy his distinctive shock of red hair.

While the Ziggy character was integral to Bowie's mainstream breakthrough, it is the quality of the music found on *Ziggy Stardust* that cemented its status as one of the most important British records of the time. Like *Hunky Dory* the

album was produced by Ken Scott, who had previously worked as an engineer on The Beatles' *Magical Mystery Tour* and *The Beatles* (aka *The White Album*). With Wakeman now devoting his time to Yes, The Spiders also have a larger role to play on this album; virtually all of the material is built on the four-piece rock-band dynamic, with occasional flourishes of strings and piano. The album begins with one of Bowie's strongest songs, the apocalyptic 'Five Years,' which is followed by the more upbeat 'Soul Love' and 'Moonage Daydream.' However, the key musical ingredient of the album's success, is 'Starman,' which reached the U.K. Top Ten on its release as a single. As the album progresses, guitarist Mick Ronson – who was also responsible for the impressive string arrangements – is given more of a chance to shine, on the heavier 'Suffragette City,' the proto-punk 'Hang On To Yourself,' and the title track. *Ziggy Stardust* closes with perhaps its finest moment, the slow-burning 'Rock'n'Roll Suicide.'

Bowie spent much of 1972 and the first half of the following year performing – in character – the songs from *Ziggy Stardust* to a devoted fan base, many of whom had begun to attend his concerts in Ziggy-inspired costume. On July 3rd 1973 he shocked a packed audience at London's Hammersmith Odeon with the words: "Not only is this the last show of the tour, it's the last show that we'll ever do." The performance was filmed by noted documentary-maker D.A. Pennebaker and released as a home video in 1982. What Bowie in fact meant with his stark on-stage declaration was that it would be the last appearance by Ziggy Stardust And The Spiders From Mars. His career was only just beginning, with *Ziggy Stardust*'s impressive follow-up, *Aladdin Sane*, already in stores, and true international success soon to come.

1972

Pink Moon Nick Drake

Island SMAS-9318 (U.K.) / ILPS 9184 (U.K.)
Released February 1972

Though ignored in his lifetime, Nick Drake has since become one of the best loved singer-songwriters of the 1970s.

Drake's work has a somber majesty quite apart from his contemporaries. His first two albums, *Five Leaves Left* (1969) and *Bryter Layter* (1970), both have a distinct melancholy, but are brightened by Robert Kirby's baroque string arrangements and a number of impressive guest musicians, including John Cale, formerly of The Velvet Underground. Island Records and Drake himself had high hopes for both LPs, but neither registered with the listening public – total sales of all Drake's albums during his lifetime, in fact, reached less than 5,000 copies.

Thoroughly dejected after pouring his heart and soul into those first two albums, Drake retreated to Island head Chris Blackwell's Spanish villa to write the songs that would become *Pink Moon*. He recorded the album in two late-night sessions in October 1971 with his friend John Wood, a veteran of the late-1960s English folk scene. On both occasions Drake arrived at the studio after midnight, sang a handful of songs, and left. With the exception of the title track, which includes a brief piano motif, all of the recordings feature just Drake's fragile vocal and nimble, close-miked guitar playing, performed mostly in one take. The resulting album is less than half an hour of haunting, delicate music comparable to nothing except, perhaps, Robert Johnson's sparse delta blues. Like its predecessors, *Pink Moon* sold poorly on release, and would prove to be Drake's last album proper.

On November 25th 1974 he died after an overdose of sleeping pills. However, Drake's profile began to rise after his death, and numerous performers started to acknowledge a debt to his work. Interest had grown sufficiently by 1986 for Hannibal Records to issue a collection of unreleased recordings, *Time Of No Reply*, and a boxed set of that and his three full albums, *Fruit Tree*. In 2002 he was given further exposure when the title track from *Pink Moon* was used as the soundtrack to a car commercial.

Sail Away Randy Newman

Reprise 2064 (U.S.A.) / K44185 (U.K.)
Released June 1972

Born into a musical family – two of his uncles wrote movie scores – Newman made his recording debut with the flop single 'Golden Gridiron Boy' in 1962.

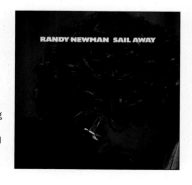

He didn't make another record of his own for several years, instead finding work as a staff songwriter and arranger, first for Liberty Records and then Warners. In the mid-to-late 1960s the likes of Dusty Springfield, Peggy Lee, Alan Price, and Gene Pitney had hits with Newman's songs, but his own albums *Randy Newman*

Creates Something Under The Sun (1968) and *12 Songs* (1970) sold poorly despite strong reviews.

Sail Away was the first of Newman's albums to achieve any commercial success of note, though he remained a cult figure for most of the 1970s. Part of the reason for this was his subtle, acerbic wit, which confounded most listeners; his limited vocal abilities also put pop audiences off his songs unless somebody else was singing them. The majority of Newman's songs were written in character, including *Sail Away*'s title track, on which he adopted the persona of a slave-trader in Africa.

Musically, the album finds a common ground between the rich orchestrations of *Something Under The Sun* and the stripped-back blues rock of *12 Songs*. Among the strongest tracks on the album are the sardonic 'Political Science' and 'You Can Leave Your Hat On,' later a hit for both Joe Cocker and Tom Jones. *Sail Away* ends with the bitter anti-religious rant 'God's Song (That's Why I Love Mankind).' The album failed to chart on release, but is now regarded as a cult classic.

'Hot Hits' And 'Top Of The Pops' Compilations

In the late 1960s through to the mid 1970s some of the biggest-selling compilation albums in the U.K. did not feature any original artists at all.

Two competing budget-priced series, 'Top of The Pops' – named after the long-running BBC television chart show – and 'Hot Hits' spawned dozens of releases, each full of the hits of the day performed in the style of the original versions by faceless session men. Or at least, that was the idea. All too often the results were a bland and unintentionally comic mixture of awkwardly mimicked vocal inflections and tired instrumental impersonations. Nonetheless, the albums sold in their millions, and even scored high chart positions until it was decided that they didn't qualify on account of their low price.

There were no credits on the albums, so you never knew who had heroically attempted singing first in the style of Engelbert Humperdinck and then Donny Osmond. But in later years, long after the albums had been rendered obsolete by cheap compilations of original hits by the real artists, pop historians discovered that artists of the caliber of David Bowie and Elton John had served time on pop's cover-version production line before they, too, had hits of their own that would be perfunctorily rendered down by their former colleagues.

Nuggets Various Artists

Elektra 7E-2006 (U.S.A. & U.K.)
Released September 1972

Released at a time when rock music was taking itself increasingly seriously, the *Nuggets* compilation was a reminder of more innocent times.

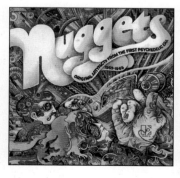

Compiled by Lenny Kaye, later of The Patti Smith Group, *Nuggets* collected 27 classic U.S. garage-rock tracks from the mid 1960s, when countless U.S. teenagers had enthusiastically bashed out imitations of then current British-invasion bands such as The Beatles, The Rolling Stones, and The Yardbirds. The recording careers of most of these teenagers went no further than a locally released single – all of the ambition, frustration, and energy of youth condensed into three minutes. A few, including The Electric Prunes, The Standells, and The 13th Floor Elevators, all of whom feature on

Nuggets, sustained careers for several years, releasing albums, having hits, and even, in the case of The Electric Prunes, touring internationally.

It is a telling comment on how fast music was developing that, by the time *Nuggets* appeared in 1972, a mere four to six years since the singles featured had originally been released, it seemed like a monument to a bygone age. *Nuggets* has been reissued several times since, culminating with a greatly expanded four-CD boxed set in 1998. Several of the songs featured on the original vinyl-double are now acknowledged classics of their time, including 'I Had Too Much To Dream Last Night' by The Electric Prunes and 'You're Gonna Miss Me' by The 13th Floor Elevators. The *Nuggets* concept itself has proved influential, with several similar series of other psychedelic garage-rock compilations following in its wake, including *Pebbles* and *Rubble*.

■ *The Electric Prunes, one of the higher-profile acts featured on* Nuggets.

Machine Head **Deep Purple**

Warners 2607 (U.S.A.) / Purple TPSA 7504 (U.K.)
Released April 1972

Machine Head captured the British heavy-rock group Deep Purple at their creative peak, and includes the group's best-loved song, 'Smoke On The Water.'

The first of many incarnations of Deep Purple was formed in 1967 by guitarist Richie Blackmore, drummer Ian Paice, and keyboardist Jon Lord; vocalist Ian Gillian and bassist Roger Glover joined in 1969, and first featured on the band's fourth album, the ambitious rock-classical hybrid *Concerto For Group And Orchestra* (1970). After making the U.K. hit albums *Deep Purple In Rock* and *Fireball*, the group decided to record its seventh album using the Rolling Stones' mobile studio. On December 7th 1971 the group arrived in Montreux, Switzerland, and intended to set up camp in the casino. Before they could do that, however, a fire broke out at a Frank Zappa concert in the theater connected to the casino, destroying the entire complex. Deep Purple moved to the Grand Hotel across town, and quickly set to work on a song, 'Smoke On The Water,' inspired by the fire. Other songs recorded at the Grand Hotel for *Machine Head* include 'Highway Star,' 'Lazy,' and 'Pictures Of Home.'

Issued on the band's own Purple label in the U.K., *Machine Head* was their first bona fide international hit album. It topped the U.K. chart and reached Number Seven in the U.S.A., and helped to establish Deep Purple – alongside Led Zeppelin and Black Sabbath – as one of the most important British heavy-rock acts of the 1970s.

The Quadraphonic Debacle

Stereo records and compact cassette were two examples where the music and electronic industries rationally adopted a single standard to everyone's benefit, especially that of the consumer. That was not always the case. The worst example must be the quadraphonic fiasco of the early 1970s.

Quadraphonic – or surround – sound came about because of a sense among mainly classical listeners that standard two-channel stereo was flat and could not recreate the ambience that you hear in a concert hall. But, even at that time, such listeners did not constitute a huge market. In due course it would become clear that a more impressive effect could be provided by mixing records so that instruments could be heard right around the listener. Sometimes they even moved.

With eight, 16, or 24 individual audio tracks to play with, it was a relatively simple matter to mix pop material down to four channels. Creating a system for getting those channels into the home, however, was a different matter. First, in 1969, came a four-channel open-reel tape deck that simply took all four tracks of a standard quarter-inch tape and played them simultaneously rather than using them for two lots of stereo material. Pre-recorded tapes were soon available. Then, in 1970, the Quad-8 8-track format was introduced, along with players and a selection of recordings. To compensate for the halved playing time, thinner tape was used, which did not help their already doubtful reliability. Initial offerings were enhanced versions of old recordings, including the 1965 soundtrack of *The Sound of Music*. Later, albums would be specially mixed for quad, including directional effects. But Quad-8 was dead before the end of the decade, with the final release apparently being Tomita's *Kosmos* in 1978.

Neither reel-to-reel nor 8-track presented any serious technical problems. Putting four channels of information on to the two sides of a vinyl groove, however, was a different matter. There were two main approaches. The first of these, matrixing, which was adopted by CBS for its SQ system and Sansui for its rival QS, meant mathematically combining four channels of recorded sound into two channels to be cut into a normal stereo groove on the disk. They were then decoded at the playback end and turned back into four channels to be amplified and reproduced over four loudspeakers. Stereo listeners would hear a combination of all four channels.

The CD-4 system, however, was much more ambitious as well as being fiendishly complicated. Devised in Japan by JVC, then a subsidiary of RCA, it required different groove dimensions and, eventually, a different stylus and reformulated vinyl. Each side of the groove now carried the sum of front and back channels on that side, but also an extra signal at an inaudibly high frequency. This was used to carry an encoded version of the difference between front and rear channels. At playback, the difference signal was used to separate out front and back sounds. Because the main audible groove carried combined front and back signals, stereo compatibility was achieved.

All this was a considerable engineering challenge, which made the equipment expensive and JVC late into the market. The first disks, marketed in Japan, were simply not durable enough. The improved disks did not appear in the U.S.A. until 1973, some time after the matrix systems. But it did work, producing a high degree of channel separation, which is more than can be said for the early matrix systems, which were inclined to leave the public wondering what the fuss was about. Few members of the public were as interested in quadraphony as the manufacturers and record companies, and by 1977 it was effectively dead, though matrixing did re-emerge later in the Dolby Surround system for home video.

1972

Talking Book **Stevie Wonder**

Motown TS319 (U.S.A.) / STMA 8007 (U.K.)
Released October 1972 (U.S.A.) / January 1973 (U.K.)

Talking Book belongs to the third flowering of Wonder's career. His breakthrough had been as 'Little' Stevie Wonder, the '12-year-old genius' of 1963's 'Fingertips'.

After his voice broke in 1966 he had given Motown hits such as 'My Cherie Amour' and 'Signed, Sealed, Delivered.' In 1971 the 21-year-old signed a new contract that gave him more creative freedom. He hooked up with Bob Margouleff and Malcolm Cecil of Tonto's Expanding Headband, pioneers of early synthesizers and programming. Vast sums were spent as the three labored in Electric Lady Studios in New York, finishing about 75 songs and leaving several hundred others in sketched forms. The first release from this material was *Music Of My Mind* (1972), which features the minor U.S. hit 'Keep On Running' and 'Superwoman (Where Were You When I Needed You).' Partly recorded during the same sessions, *Talking Book* followed, the critical and commercial success of which made Wonder one of the most influential black musicians of the early 1970s.

A multi-instrumentalist himself, Wonder was less reliant on having a team of session players around him, and the development of multitrack recording was making it easier for a musician of his ilk to make albums on a DIY basis, and instruments such as the clavinet and electric piano came to the fore. Perhaps surprisingly, however, the first voice heard on *Talking Book* belongs to Jim Gilstrap, who trades a couple of lines with fellow Wonderlove backing singer Gloria Barley on the opening 'You Are The Sunshine Of My Life' before Wonder himself joins in.

The album includes 'You Are The Sunshine Of My Life' and 'Superstition' – the latter written for Jeff Beck, who also played on 'Looking For Another Pure Love.' However, when Wonder heard Beck's version he withdrew permission, deciding the song was too good to give to someone else. Motown agreed, and the rush-released single was a big hit. It was his first U.S. Number One hit since 'Fingertips (Part 2),' which had topped the U.S. singles chart nine years earlier. There was also a timely black-consciousness significance to *Talking Book*'s cover, which depicts Wonder sitting on the ground looking distinctly African.

Wonder's run of classic 1970s recordings continued the following year with the release of *Innervisions*, which features the international hit singles 'Higher Ground' and 'Living For The City.'

■ *Right: Stevie Wonder working on* **Talking Book** *at Electric Lady Studios, New York, on February 22 1972. Electric Lady had been founded in the late 1960s by Jimi Hendrix.*

School's Out **Alice Cooper**

Warner Brothers 2623 (U.S.A.) / K56007 (U.K.)
Released July 1972

Along with The New York Dolls, it was Alice Cooper and *School's Out* that epitomized the U.S. version of glam rock.

The title track was a huge hit single on both sides of the Atlantic and the LP had a run of 32 weeks on the U.S. albums chart. The early versions of the semi-gatefold sleeve featured a pair of paper knickers wrapped around a school desk.

The Alice Cooper Band was originally on Frank Zappa's Straight label, and played the clubs of Los Angeles. Heavily in debt, they moved to Detroit, eventually signing with Warner Brothers. Their music was part Stones, part trashy adaptation of the garage rock of the likes of The MC5, and, like The Stones, they were a five-piece, with Glen Buxton and Michael Bruce on guitars. Their third album, *Love It To Death*, yielded a hit in 'I'm Eighteen,' and their fourth, *Killer*, opens with the live favorite 'Under My Wheels.' Cooper developed a highly theatrical act, with props that included a live snake, chopped up dolls, electric chair, and guillotine, and the singer plastered in mascara. This soon made them a top live draw.

School's Out is a concept album only insofar as it evokes a *West Side Story* world of teen delinquency. Many of the songs have above-average arrangements, but the title track was the standout moment, a classic school-day blues song that belonged to a tradition that went back to Chuck Berry's 'Ring Ring Goes The Bell.' It has a great riff and a memorable word play on the word "principles." Cooper's influence can be felt in later acts such as Guns N'Roses, Mötley Crüe, and Marilyn Manson.

I'm Still In Love With You **Al Green**

Hi Records 32074 (US) / London SHU 8443 (UK)
Released October 1972

I'm Still In Love With You is the centerpiece of a trio of classic Al Green albums that also includes *Let's Stay Together* (1972) and *Call Me* (1973).

Considered by many to be the greatest soul singer of the 1970s, Green was the primary beneficiary of the Hi Records house band, which included the exemplary five-piece Memphis Horns.

From the age of nine, in the late 1950s, Al Green had toured with his siblings as the gospel quartet The Green Brothers before scoring a Number Five hit on the U.S. R&B charts with 'Back Up Train' (1968), recorded with The Soul Mates. Green signed with bandleader and Hi Records executive Willie Mitchell in 1969, and recorded the albums *Green Is Blues* and *Al Green Gets Next To You* (1971). Neither was a commercial success, but Green's fortunes changed when the classic title track to *Let's Stay Together* (1972) topped the U.S. singles chart.

Green followed that album six months later with his masterpiece, *I'm Still In Love With You*. His fourth album to be recorded with the Hi Records band, it was co-produced by Green and Mitchell, and features the singer's first explorations into country and rock material. Most of the songs are Green originals, but he finds room for impressive renditions of Roy Orbison's 'Pretty Woman' and 'For All The Good Times' by Kris Kristofferson. The album failed to chart in the U.K. but reached Number Four in the U.S.A., where the title track was also a hit when issued as a single.

Exile On Main Street
The Rolling Stones

Rolling Stones 2900 (U.S.A.) / 69100 (U.K.)
Released June 1972

Here is an example of a rock band really taking advantage of the space offered by the double-vinyl format.

Exile On Main Street occupies a special position in The Rolling Stones' catalog, often acclaimed as the definitive expression of their 1970s-era music. It was the follow-up to *Sticky Fingers* (1971) and made Number One on both sides of the Atlantic. It is also an example of a band recording in unusual circumstances, breaking the rule that records are supposed to be made in recording studios.

Part of the album's legend is the situation in which it was recorded. Using The Rolling Stones' 16-track mobile unit, the band wrote and recorded the 18 songs in the greatest amount of disarray and informality that could be imagined, living in Richards's house, Château Nellcote, at Villefranche-sur-Mer in the South of France, between May and September 1971. The building had allegedly been used as the local Gestapo headquarters in World War II, which gained The Stones another brownie point in the decadence stakes. The decision was partly a result of tax exile, partly the desire to avoid the sterilities of being in a studio, and have the chance to blur the work-party boundary. Keith Richards said: "Suddenly for *Exile* we all left England and went to France and recorded in my house – and after that slowly everybody dispersed to different parts of the globe, so the lull in that period was more to do with just the geographical difficulties of getting it together."

The house was cold and damp, and overdubs were done in the kitchen while people were eating or talking. Band members came and went unpredictably with lovers and wives. Mick Jagger was often absent, leaving Richards as the prime architect of the material. The air of dishevelment runs right through to the sleeve's hand-written notes and raggedly assembled assortment of black and white photos by Robert Frank. The romanticizing of this *mise-en-scène* is evident when one critic invites us to listen to 'Loving Cup' and "imagine condensation streaming down the cellar walls, rattling chandeliers, and the ever-present mood-music of the mistral, the French summer wind that reportedly takes on a deeply ghostly aspect."

It did mean The Stones could record whenever inspiration struck. Of 'Happy,' on which Richards sang lead, he said: "The basic track was Bobby Keys on baritone sax, myself on guitar, and Jimmy Miller on drums. 'Happy' was cut one afternoon because the whole record was cut in the basement of my villa with The Stones' mobile truck parked in the driveway. So sometimes I would be ready to play and some of the guys would come over early. It was really like a warm-up, but had this idea for a song."

Exile drew on a blend of country blues, Chuck Berry, and Stax/Volt R&B, and is characterized by a murky production in which the lead vocals are pulled back – though the mix sounds clearer on the 66-minute CD reissue. The core of the music is the guitar interplay between Richards and Mick Taylor. There are up-tempo rockers ('Rip This Joint,' 'Happy,' and 'All Down The Line'), country rock songs ('Sweet Virginia'), as well as blues material such as the cover of Slim Harpo's 'Hip Shake' and 'Stop Breaking Down' (the latter recently revived by The White Stripes). Guest musicians included Bobby Keys (saxophone), Jim Price (trumpet and trombone), Nicky Hopkins (piano), and Al Perkins (slide guitar). The extra time allowed by having four sides to play with was exploited by arranging the 18 songs into four sections: Side One was full of rockers, Side Two was acoustic in emphasis, Side Three had some gospel touches, and Side Four had four upbeat soul-influenced songs.

band's best music; the less committed may find that the LP's material is remarkably uninspiring for an album about which such big claims are made, and that *Sticky Fingers* is far more focused. The standout track is 'Tumbling Dice,' the epitome of The Stones' distinctive groove and a hit single. Richards himself conceded that double albums are problematic: "Double albums have a lot going against them. You know there's gonna be a certain amount of confusion, with so much material . . . in the beginning we didn't want to make a double album, but it all just poured out." Contrary to the legend, not all the songs came out in the South of France. 'Shake Your Hips,' 'Shine A Light,' and the basic track of 'Stop Breaking Down' were first recorded in October 1970 in London, 'All Down The Line' was put down in October 1969 in Los Angeles, and 'Loving Cup' went all the way back to the spring of 1969.

Producer Jimmy Miller commented: "Basically, *Exile on Main Street* was an idea to try and get back to good old rock'n'roll. Looking back over the recent albums, we felt there was a need to re-establish the rock thing." Not positively received at the time, *Exile* over the years has come to be influential as an example of how a rock album might be made as much as for its music.

1972

Foxtrot Genesis

Charisma CAS1058 (U.S.A. & U.K.)
Released October 1972

One of the most enduring rock bands from the 1970s to the 1990s, Genesis had an impressive run of success across three decades on both sides of the Atlantic. *Foxtrot* finds the group at the start of its creative peak, and was the first Genesis album to chart in the U.K.

Vocalist and songwriter Peter Gabriel formed Genesis in 1967 with fellow pupils at the private school he attended, Tony Banks (keyboards) and Mike Rutherford (bass). The group released the albums *From Genesis To Revelation* (1968) and *Trespass* (1970), but didn't begin to reach its full potential until guitarist Anthony Phillips and drummer Chris Stewart were replaced by Steve Hackett and Phil Collins. This new-look Genesis, now signed to manager Tony Stratton-Smith's Charisma label, recorded *Nursery Cryme* in 1971, which began to show signs of the expansive, theatrical progressive rock the group would soon make its own. The follow-up, *Foxtrot*, is where the five members of Genesis finally reach their potential.

Working much faster than many of their prog rock contemporaries – who would take months to finish each album – Genesis recorded *Foxtrot* at Island Studios in Basing Street, London, between August 6th and 11th 1972. The album sessions were produced by David Hitchcock and engineered by John Burns. The band performed at the *Reading Festival* and then completed a short tour of Italy before mixing *Foxtrot* on the 25th, 26th, and 27th of the same month. The album's sleeve credits give an indication of how far the group had grown as musicians: Gabriel plays flute and oboe on some songs, while Rutherford provides flourishes of cello on others.

> ## "WE WORKED ON A PIECE THAT WAS 30 MINUTES LONG. I FELT WE'D OUTSTAYED OUR WELCOME BY THE TIME WE WERE FIVE MINUTES INTO IT."
> ### GENESIS GUITARIST STEVE HACKETT

Foxtrot opens with one of the band's best-loved songs, 'Watcher Of The Skies,' a powerful distillation of the group's sound, drenched in Mellotron strings. 'Time Table' evokes the more theatrical moments of David Bowie's recent *Hunky Dory* (1971) and *Ziggy Stardust* (1972), while 'Get 'Em Out By Friday' is a more sustained psychedelic piece. The 23-minute, seven-part epic 'Supper's Ready' dominates *Foxtrot*'s second side, leaping backward and forward from acoustic guitar-led whimsy to all-out rock. Peter Gabriel's lyrics and vocal performances are complex and extravagant throughout, giving some indication of the multilayered concept albums he would conceive shortly after *Foxtrot*.

Foxtrot peaked at Number 12 in the U.K., but Genesis didn't reach the U.S. albums chart until the release of the following year's *Selling England By The Pound*. That album was succeeded in late 1974 by the two-disk set *The Lamb Lies Down On Broadway*, after which Peter Gabriel left the group to pursue a solo career. Phil Collins then took over as the chief creative figure in Genesis, leading the band in a more pop direction.

■ *Genesis frontman Peter Gabriel on tour in support of* Foxtrot *at the City Hall in Newcastle, England.*

Something/Anything? Todd Rundgren

Bearsville 2BX 2066 (U.S.A.) / K65501 (U.K.)
Released February 1972

With its numerous false starts, breakdowns, and other charming imperfections, Todd Rundgren's one-man, double-disk *Something/Anything?* proved to an entire generation of do-it-yourselfers that the hits really could come from the home.

By the start of the 1970s portable multitrack technology had enabled multitalented types – Paul McCartney with *McCartney* and Pete Townshend with *Who Came First?*, for instance – to create an entire album's worth of material unassisted. Rundgren, a budding producer whose credits included The Band's *Stage Fright* (1970) and Badfinger's *Straight Up* (1971), was not to be outdone. Late in 1971 Rundgren set up shop inside ID Sound, a small Los Angeles studio, and began work on his first full-fledged solo effort. Manning the controls was James Lowe, a Los Angeles-based engineer and frontman for 1960s rockers The Electric Prunes. "ID was one of the first independents in Los Angeles," recalls Lowe, "the kind of place where you could go and really get hands-on and no one would bother you. Plus, it had the full compliment of Sennheiser and Neumann mikes, and really nice homemade effects as well."

Rundgren arrived at the studio with a large parcel of ideas – "a bouquet of ear-grabbing melodies," as he'd later call them – few of them fully formed. "The album was the demo – it all went down right there," says Lowe. "A lot of times Todd only had a rough sketch of a song, and it would just develop through the recording. It's a great way to work – things are happening spontaneously and that's when the real magic can happen."

Rundgren began each song by situating himself inside ID's closet of a drum-room. "I was never sure exactly where the song was going until we'd laid down about four or five tracks," says Lowe. "He'd leave these blank spaces all over the place – there would be like eight or 12 bars of nothing – and then he'd just go back afterward and pop in a piano or guitar in that spot." One thing was certain, Rundgren wanted the new work to have a muscular, uncompromising veneer. When it came time to track the pop rave-up 'Couldn't I Just Tell You,' Rundgren's acoustic guitar was sent through a compressor set to high gain. "That sucking limiter thing just worked great on that song," says Lowe. "Most of the tracks were right on the edge like that – we were really trying for something with a little more bite."

Guitar and vocal parts were later added up at Rundgren's place in Nichols Canyon, using a borrowed Scully 8-track machine. During one such living-room session, Lowe snapped a photograph of the artist striking a mock-Nixon pose from atop a makeshift platform, with wires and crumpled paper strewn across the floor and a vocal microphone taped unceremoniously to the handle of a floor mop. "I had a wide-angle lens," recalls Lowe, whose shot was later used for the album's gatefold, "in order to take in the full scope of the mess!"

With finishing touches applied at New York's Record Plant and Bearsville Studios, *Something/Anything?*, released in early 1972, spawned a pair of smash singles in 'I Saw The Light' and, more than a year later, 'Hello It's Me,' a remake of Rundgren's Nazz-era cut – and Rundgren's first and last trip to the Top Ten, though he had other lower-placed chart singles under his own name as well as many hits produced by him. The album consolidated Rundgren's reputation as a hit-making wunderkind – a label he promptly refuted with the formation of the left-of-center Utopia a short time later.

1973

Dark Side Of The Moon
Pink Floyd

Harvest 11163 (U.S.A.) / SHVL 804 (U.K.)
Released March 1973

"No," says Roger Waters, **"it's not our best album.** *The Wall* **is deeper and more musically powerful."**

Having composed the bulk of both albums, the estimable Mr Waters is more than entitled to his opinion, but the international record-buying public begs to differ. Over the past three decades we've shelled out for a mere 23 million copies of *The Wall*, while lapping up 34 million copies of *Dark Side Of The Moon*, which isn't bad for an album with somewhat humble beginnings.

"It began in a little rehearsal room in London," remembers Floyd guitar supremo Dave Gilmour. "We had quite a few pieces of music, some of which were left over from previous things." During the closing weeks of 1971, that room in Broadhurst Gardens, West Hampstead, saw the gestation of an epochal album, rich in sonic experimentation, powerful melodies, and startling lyrical concepts, which would elevate Pink Floyd from major-league cult status into the world's biggest rock band.

"At some point during the proceedings," Gilmour has said, "Roger came up with the idea of making it a piece about madness." Mental illness was something about which Pink Floyd knew a great deal, having watched their first leader, Syd Barrett, reduced from brilliantly inventive songwriter to incoherent babbler through the onset of schizophrenia exacerbated by the frequent ingestion of LSD. Understanding that the 'madman' in *Dark Side Of The Moon* is Syd Barrett is essential to grasping why Waters's concept galvanized the band, sparking them to new creative heights.

Having spent the previous five years in a wilderness of pleasantly inconsequential electronic noodling, Pink Floyd now surged forward to create a genuinely ground-breaking album that charted one man's retreat into paranoid insanity via the medium of impeccably languid rock songs linked by beautifully realized electronic sound collages.

Dave Gilmour has asserted that another major reason why *Dark Side* differed from previous Pink Floyd albums was that "we'd played it live before we recorded it." He's absolutely right, and not only did the Floyd play it live, they developed it from gig to gig.

They emerged from West Hampstead on January 20th 1972 to give their first live performance of a musical suite entitled *Eclipse: A Piece For Assorted Lunatics*, at The Dome, Brighton, U.K., but it was very much a work in progress. Waters confirms, for example, that: "The actual song, 'Eclipse,' wasn't performed live until Bristol, Colston Hall, on February 5th. I can remember one afternoon rolling up and saying, 'Hey chaps, listen, I've written an ending.' So when we started performing the piece called 'Eclipse,' it probably did have 'Brain Damage,' but it didn't have, 'All that you touch, all that you see, all that you taste.'"

Critic Derek Jewell of the London *Sunday Times* saw the piece, now entitled *The Dark Side Of The Moon*, at London's Rainbow Theatre on the 17th, by which time it had been hammered into a shape that more closely resembled how the finished album would turn out. "In their own terms," wrote Jewell, "Floyd strikingly succeed. They are dramatists supreme."

Tours of the Far East, North America, and Europe enabled the band to fashion the material still further so that, according to Gilmour, when recording finally began at EMI's legendary Abbey Road Studios on June 1st 1972, "we all knew the material. The playing was very good. It had a natural feel."

Intriguingly, the first track they worked on was 'Us And Them,' which keyboardist Rick Wright had originally composed for the film *Zabriskie Point* in 1969. It failed to make the film's final cut so now, with additional input from Waters, it was pressed into service for the new album. A week later

1973

recalls as having been composed very quickly, in a mere 24 hours. "I knew there had to be a song about money in the piece," explains Waters, "and I thought that the tune could be a song about money, and having decided that, it was extremely easy to make up a seven-beat intro that went well with it. I often think that the best ideas are the most obvious ones."

The following day they laid down the basic track for 'Time,' the music of which is credited to the whole band but with lyrics by Waters. "For me it was the first time we'd had great lyrics," reckons Gilmour. "The others were satisfactory, or perfunctory, or just plain bad. On *Dark Side*, Roger decided he didn't want anyone else writing lyrics."

Before the month was out they'd also set to work on the basic track for 'The Great Gig In The Sky,' a wordless Rick Wright composition evoking Waters's fear of dying in a plane crash, and notable for session singer Clare Torry's astonishing gospel-blues wailing, intended to represent the pain and ecstasy of life and death.

Work on *Dark Side* was inconveniently derailed by further tours of the U.S.A. and Europe, not to mention the recording of a soundtrack, *Obscured By Clouds*, for the film *La Vallée*, plus work on a ballet score for French choreographer Roland Petit.

During October 1972 they returned to Abbey Road and, among other things, decided to bring in an outside musician to add sax solos to 'Money' and 'Us And Them.' "There were several big names we could have gone to," points out Gilmour, "but it can be tedious bringing in these brisk, professional session men. A bit intimidating." Instead, they called up their old Cambridge mate Dick Parry, who did them proud.

The final burst of studio sessions did not begin until January 18th 1973. During the last two weeks of the month they completed the spooky instrumental 'On The Run,' which had been recorded earlier as a guitar and keyboard piece. Now they added synthesizer sequences courtesy of a newly arrived EMS VCS Synthi-AK, then overlaid them with synthesized airplane sounds and running footsteps recorded in an echoey tunnel near London's Science Museum.

One of the most distinctive and, at the time, avant-garde aspects of the album was its ingenious use of spoken-voice samples, another innovation that Gilmour attributes to Waters. "He wanted to use things in the songs to get responses from people. We wrote a series of questions on cards and put them on a music stand, one question on each card, and got people into the studio and told them to read the first question and answer it. Then they could remove that card and see the next question and answer that, but they couldn't look through the cards so they didn't really know what the thread of the questions was going to be until they got into it."

Interviewees included roadies and their girlfriends, Jerry the Irish doorman at Abbey Road, and Paul and Linda McCartney, who turned out to be "much too good at being evasive for their answers to be usable."

The unseen questions included: When did you last hit someone? Were you in the right? Would you do it again? And, most crucially, What does the dark side of the moon mean to you? It was Jerry the doorman who responded with the astonishingly appropriate: "There is no dark side of the moon, really. It's all dark." Placed in the context of the closing track, 'Eclipse,' this spontaneous response resonates with as much power as if it had been written by a playwright.

It's worth noting that, though Waters was undoubtedly the primary architect of *Dark Side*, the album was made at a time when he and Dave Gilmour were working in harmony, with each contributing a unique set of attributes to the project. "I think I tend to bring musicality and melodies," is how Gilmour explains it. "Roger was certainly a very good motivator and obviously a great lyricist. He was much more ruthless about musical ideas, where he'd be

happy to lose something if it was for the greater good of making the whole album work. So, you know, Roger'd be happy to make a lovely sounding piece of music disappear into radio sound if it was benefiting the whole piece. Whereas I would tend to want to retain the beauty of that music."

The final studio session was held on February 1st 1973. "We'd finished mixing all the tracks," remembers Gilmour, "but until the very last day we'd never heard them as the continuous piece we'd been imagining for more than a year. We had to literally snip bits of tape, cut in the linking passages and stick the ends back together. Finally, you sit back and listen all the way through at enormous volume. I can remember it. It was really exciting."

The tone of the album is set from the opening seconds, when an ominous overture employs a heartbeat to underscore ticking clocks, cash registers, manic laughter, and screams, before giving way to the liquid slide guitar intro of 'Breathe.' Waters's stark lyrics tie the tracks together as much as the music, dealing in turn with the big issues of birth, time, death, and money before introducing the theme of madness with 'Us And Them,' and developing that idea to its logical but shattering conclusion on 'Brain Damage.' Looking back at that particular song, Roger Waters has said that the title line was: "Me, speaking to the listener, saying, 'I know you have these bad feelings and impulses, because I do, too, and one of the ways I can make contact with you is to share the fact that I feel bad sometimes.'"

Though many of the ideas – tape-loops, voice samples, sound effects, etc. – were not new, even in a pop context, the use of them on *Dark Side* to sustain a mood that permeates the entire work was startlingly innovative. And that's where Nick Mason deserves a hearty pat on the back. While the contributions of Waters, Gilmour, and Wright are self-evident, it's all too easy to see Mason as Floyd's Ringo, contributing not much more than a solid thump as and when required. *Dark Side* engineer Alan Parsons has pointed out that this view could hardly be more misguided: "He was always the guiding light in matters to do with the overall atmosphere," says Parsons, "and he was very good on sound effects and psychedelia and mind-expanding experiences."

It would be heartening to conclude that the album went on to massive success simply on its sublime musical merit, but no one in Pink Floyd is sufficiently self-delusional to believe that's the case. "It wasn't only the music that made it such a success," says Mason. "EMI/Capitol had cleaned up their act in America. They put money behind promoting us for the first time. And that changed everything."

Gilmour, too, has stated that, rather than the cerebral complexities of 'Brain Damage' or 'Eclipse,' it was the rootsy funk of 'Money' that reached out and grabbed the band a new audience. "It started from the first show in America. People at the front shouting at us to play 'Money!' and to give them something they could shake their asses to!"

Whatever the reasons, after its release on March 24th 1973 *Dark Side* went on to achieve astronomical worldwide sales. though, astonishingly, it has never topped the U.K. chart, and spent only one week at Number One in the U.S.A.

Perhaps unsurprisingly, Roger Waters never had any problem seeing the sow's ear behind the silk purse of Pink Floyd's greatest moment. "We'd cracked it. We'd won the pools. What are you supposed to do after that? *Dark Side Of The Moon* was the last willing collaboration. After that, everything with the band was like drawing teeth; ten years of hanging on to the married name and not having the courage to get divorced, to let go; ten years of bloody hell. It was all just terrible. Awful. Terrible." Certainly Pink Floyd's internal wrangles seem to have intensified after *Dark Side*, even though it finally put paid to the notion that the band could never creatively equal the work they had done on their first album when Syd Barrett was in the driving seat.

When all's said and done, *Dark Side Of The Moon* is a prime example of the progressive-rock concept album at its very best, one that survived the Year Zero of punk and subsequent movements to be rediscovered by new generations – as well as by those who liked it first time round but, having assigned it once to the trashcan of 'dinosaur rock,' now find that they probably always rather liked it after all.

1973

The Faust Tapes **Faust**

Not issued in the U.S.A. / Virgin VC501 (U.K.)
Released 1973

A hyperactive patchwork of song fragments, *The Faust Tapes* afforded the cult German band a brief window of commercial success when the recently formed Virgin Records decided to sell it for the price of a single.

Faust was the brainchild of Uwe Nettelback, a journalist-turned-producer who, despite not playing on any of their records, is the band's key figure. The group began rehearsing and then recording in his converted schoolhouse studio; their chaotic, sound-collage debut, *Faust*, was issued in 1971 by Virgin on clear vinyl housed in an eye-catching transparent sleeve. The follow-up, *Faust So Far*, is more song based but retains the first album's fiercely individual, experimental streak. Neither sold more than a couple of thousand copies.

The material that became *The Faust Tapes* was not originally intended for commercial release, but Virgin hit upon the idea of issuing it at a cost of just 49 pence – less than a dollar at the time. Taken from recordings made between 1971 and 1973, the album was a disorienting collection of 26 mostly untitled pieces of music, ranging from full songs to 30-second snapshots of ideas, several of which would turn up in more coherent form on *Faust IV*. The songs ranged from free jazz to psychedelic pop, but Virgin's marketing gimmick worked: all 60,000 copies of the original pressing sold within a couple of months, making *The Faust Tapes* the most mythical of the various Krautrock albums released around the same time – including Can's *Tago Mago* and Neu!'s *75*, both of which, along with *The Faust Tapes*, are often cited as seminal influences by such musical luminaries as David Bowie and Radiohead.

Paris 1919 **John Cale**

Reprise MS 2131 / K44239 (U.K.)
Released March 1973

Clasically trained and inclined toward the avant-garde, Cale's first three solo albums after leaving The Velvet Underground explored the territory of angry rock and minimalism.

But this fourth offering, with its heavily orchestrated introspective musings on religion, ghosts, and the British class system, came as a bolt from the blue.

Recorded in Los Angeles, largely at Sunset Sound, with the members of

---

Of Fortune,' for example, though pinned down by solid drums, seem to drift on currents of sound.

Cale's voice is, as always, an uncertain instrument, but reservations about his singing are swept away in the face of such inscrutable lines as: "If the sacheting of gentlemen gives you grievance now and then, what's needed is the memory of planning lakes." Listeners may never work out exactly what that means but, unlike most willfully contrived and obscure lyrics, there's a feeling that they definitely do mean something.

■ *Roxy Music on stage in Los Angeles in December 1972, in the midst of the group's only tour of the U.S.A. with keyboardist Brian Eno (left). Eno left Roxy Music shortly after the release of* For Your Pleasure. *He went on to record a number of acclaimed solo albums and to become one of the most important producers of recent times, helming albums by artists including David Bowie, Talking Heads, and U2.*

For Your Pleasure **Roxy Music**

Warner Brothers 2696 (U.S.A.) / Island ILPS 9232 (U.K.)
Released July 1973

Along with David Bowie, Roxy Music were the intelligent art-rock end of glam, drawing on cultural references hitherto regarded in rock circles as hopelessly Establishment and unhip.

Bryan Ferry's donning of a tuxedo was almost as rebellious a gesture in 1973 as safety-pins were in 1976, except it was a revolt into style. Rock convention stated that 'proper' music – that is, music that annoyed your parents – had its Year Zero in 1956. This meant crooners such as Sinatra *et al.* and the songs they sang were out, as was anyone who dressed up in anything other than denim. But, in Roxy's case, the male rock fan forgave them Eno all tarted up because they had drummer Paul Thompson, who looked like a regular guy and laid down a muscular beat, the bug-eyed Phil Manzanera on guitar, and a *femme fatale* on the record sleeve.

And Roxy Music didn't just look different, they sounded different from the average rock band. Eno supplied on-tap synthesizer weirdness and Andy Mackay's saxophone conjured visions of space-age rock'n'roll on songs such as the stomping 'Editions Of You' and the witty 'dance' single 'Do The Strand.' Manzanera played expressive lead in 'Strictly Confidential,' and a brilliant freak-out solo through a blizzard of phasing in the dramatic 'In Every Dream Home A Heartache,' a song that showcased the band's imagination. As for Ferry, his robot crooner vibrato and echo-laden electric piano brought an unforgettable brooding power and regret to such art deco nocturnes as 'Beauty Queen' and 'For Your Pleasure.'

1973

Goodbye Yellow Brick Road Elton John

MCA 10003 (U.S.A.) / DJM DJLP 1001 (U.K.)
Released November 1973

This 17-song double album cemented Elton John's international standing.

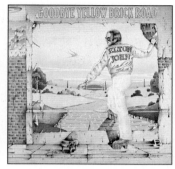

The former Reginald Dwight embarked on his career under the name of Elton John as a piano-playing singer-songwriter, composing music for Bernie Taupin's Wild West-infatuated lyrics. Once glam rock took off in Britain, Elton had license to dress up, wear outrageous spectacles and platform boots, and come on like a 1970s Little Richard.

Goodbye Yellow Brick Road was cut at the popular Château d'Hérouville studios in France in not much over two weeks. The original intention had been to record in Jamaica, but sessions were quickly aborted because of problems with the studio and a heavy atmosphere.

The album opens in somber mood with 'Funeral For A Friend' and the Marilyn Monroe-elegy 'Candle In The Wind,' one of the album's four single hits. 'Bennie And The Jets' was a nod in the direction of Bowie's Ziggy, complete with dubbed audience noise and the evocative couplet "You're gonna hear electric music / Solid walls of sound." It gave Elton his first R&B hit and a U.S. Number One. The album had up-tempo rockers – the fairground jive of 'Your Sister Can't Twist' and the Stonesy rocker 'Saturday Night's Alright For Fighting,' for example – which Taupin gave an English flavor, and the stately 'Goodbye Yellow Brick Road.' The likes of 'This Song Has No Title' and 'Grey Seal' had gospel-tinged melodies and progressions that could have come from the earlier Elton John of Tumbleweed Connection. Goodbye Yellow Brick Road reached Number One across the world and spent two years on the U.S. and U.K. albums charts.

The Singles 1969–1973 The Carpenters

A&M 3601 (U.S.A.) / AMLH/CAM 63601 (U.K.)
Released November 1973

The biggest-selling musical act of the 1970s, brother-and-sister duo Richard and Karen Carpenter had their greatest success with *The Singles 1969–1973*. Issued at the height of their fame, it spent 115 weeks on the *Billboard* albums chart.

Keyboardist-arranger Richard and drummer-singer Karen recorded an unreleased album for the RCA label in 1966 before signing to A&M Records in 1969. The Carpenters scored an impressive run of light and breezy Top 20 hit singles in the early 1970s, including the chart toppers 'Close To You' and 'Top Of The World.' They were the most successful of a number of wholesome, MOR performers to dominate the charts in the 1970s, the ranks of which also included Barbra Streisand and Bread. *The Singles 1969–1973* contains all of their hits, from their first release, a cover of The Beatles' 'Ticket To Ride,' to 'Yesterday Once More,' which reached Number Two in the U.K. and the U.S.A. in June 1973.

The Carpenters' career began to decline within a year of the release of *The Singles* album, as their light, harmonic pop had fallen from fashion by the latter half of the decade, while both siblings were beset by ill-health. Karen died tragically in 1983 as a direct result of the anorexia from which she had suffered throughout most of her adult life, bringing worldwide recognition to the condition for the first time. The Carpenters' music has continued to sell strongly since her death, in particular this collection, which has sold seven million copies in the U.S.A. alone.

Tales From Topographic Oceans **Yes**

Atlantic 18122 (U.S.A.) / K/K4 80001 (U.K.)
Released December 1973

The pinnacle of prog ambition in the 1970s, *Tales From Topographic Oceans* is an album that continues to divide not just critics and fans but also the group itself: keyboardist Rick Wakeman left shortly after the album's completion, unhappy with the direction Yes was taking.

After scoring four consecutive U.K. Top Ten albums – including *Close To The Edge* (1972) and the triple-vinyl live set *Yessongs* (1973) – Yes spent the latter half of 1973 attempting to fashion a record that would top all of the group's previous releases. Public anticipation for *Tales* was so high that the album, a double, achieved gold status in the U.K. on the strength of pre-sale orders alone. The LP's subject matter is rooted in the spiritual text *Autobiography Of A Yogi* by Paramhansa Yogananda, and is divided into four distinct sections, sporting names like 'The Revealing Science Of God,' each of which fills one side of vinyl.

Tales From Topographic Oceans is a sprawling, richly orchestrated work, awash with sudden changes in tempo and time signature, searing guitar solos, synthesizer flourishes, and impenetrable lyrics about Eastern mysticism – the kind of album that would today be derided as being hopelessly overblown and pretentious. Many critics at the time shared this view, but there was clearly a market for the band's prog excesses in its day: *Tales From Topographic Oceans* was the group's biggest commercial success to date, topping the U.K. albums chart and peaking at Number Six in the U.S.A.

Blackboard Jungle Dub
Lee Perry And The Upsetters

No Catalog Number
Released 1973

One of the key figures in the development and popularization of reggae, the eccentric Lee 'Scratch' Perry has produced hundreds of records in a career spanning five decades.

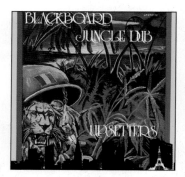

In the late 1960s and early 1970s he worked closely with The Wailers (featuring Bob Marley), whose backing band contained several members of Perry's own band, The Upsetters. Perry was also one of the earliest innovators of dub, a bass-and-drum-heavy, effects-laden variant of traditional reggae. Perry and other producers, including King Tubby – who is also credited for work on this album – had begun issuing alternative, 'dub' mixes of songs they worked on as single b-sides, effectively creating the concept of the remix. However, The Upsetters' *Blackboard Jungle Dub* is considered to be the first full dub album.

Perry's rich, spacious productions are all the more impressive given his primitive working methods. Perry's recording set-up in the 1970s consisted of a basic Teac 4-track recorder, a small mixing desk, and a few early effects units, including an Echoplex delay unit, which he would use to achieve his distinctive, echoing snare drum sound. In 1973 Perry built his Black Ark Studio in his own back yard, which allowed him to work full time on developing his sound. Perry continued to release dub albums and singles at a prodigious rate, his recordings proving inspirational to other reggae producers as well as the likes of The Clash.

In 1977 Perry brought an end to the Black Ark phase of his career, burning down his studio after claiming it had been beset by evil spirits. Black Ark

was just one of a number of famous studios to be destroyed by fire. The Caribou Ranch studio in Nederland, Colorado, burned down in 1985 after previously playing host to artists including Steely Dan, Neil Young, and Chicago. Easley McCain Studios in Memphis suffered a similar fate in 2005. Wilco, Jeff Buckley, and The White Stripes had all recorded there.

Countdown To Ecstacy **Steely Dan**

ABC 779 (U.S.A.) / PROBE SPB 1079 (U.K.)
Released July 1973

A flawless marriage of Brill Building pop suss, jazz elegance, and rock attitude makes this the most consistently satisfying Steely Dan artifact.

Founders Walter Becker and Donald Fagen had honed their skills working as staff songwriters at ABC Records, but forming their own band gave them a free hand to let their musical imaginations run riot. Their debut, *Can't Buy A Thrill*, included two major hit singles, 'Do It Again' and 'Reelin' In The Years,' but what *Countdown* lacks in hits is more than compensated for in sophistication. On *Thrill* the band was relatively inexperienced, but by *Countdown* they'd toured together, so, as Becker explains: "The musicians got to hear the songs and participate in developing the arrangements at an earlier stage. Because we knew what the band sounded like, we had a more developed conception of it, and it became a more integrated framework."

By this time the band had lost its original vocalist, David Palmer, so Fagen's intellectual sneer moved front and center, proving to be a better vehicle for the band's scathingly acerbic critiques of the U.S.A.'s foibles. The Stax

saxophone and stuttering guitar battle in the middle of 'My Old School,' the swing-meets-heavy-metal groove of 'Bodhisattva,' and the strutting cynicism of 'Showbiz Kids' make this perhaps the high-water mark of studio-perfect rock because the passion remains intact throughout.

Unfortunately, however, the album proved too cerebral for the MCA executives charged with marketing it. Promotion was minimal and sales were poor, but the passage of time has accorded *Countdown To Ecstacy* the status it always merited.

1973

Tubular Bells
Mike Oldfield

Virgin 13135 (U.S.A.) / V2001 (U.K.)
Released May 1973

Tubular Bells was a music-industry ground-breaker of epic proportions, cobbled together, as it was, by a teenage guitar geek.

Mike Oldfield would be the first to admit that he was something of a social misfit, a prodigiously talented young musician whose guitar was his life. He didn't set out to create an album that would expand the horizons of electric guitar as none had done since Hendrix, or an album that would break every rule about how to make hit records, or even an album that would make it possible for rock composers to be spoken of with the same respect as classical composers, but he achieved all three just by doing what came naturally to him.

The seed of *Tubular Bells* was sown on July 10th 1971, when Kevin Ayers And The Whole World played their final gig together in London, leaving Mike Oldfield, their 16-year-old guitarist, out of a job. Ayers, however, had also given the lad his key to fame and fortune, an old Bang & Olufsen tape recorder. "By soldering a few wires together and blocking off the tape with cigarette packets and things," recalls Oldfield, "I was able to multitrack on it. I took the insides out and did all kinds of strange things with tape loops and decided that I'd better have one of these Terry Riley things in there to start my very first demo. And that was the opening theme for *Tubular Bells*, which I played on a Farfisa organ."

Oldfield lugged his lo-fi, warts'n'all demo round to the smart offices of several top record company A&R men, only to find that "they all looked at me as if I was mad. They all said, because there was no vocals, no words, no drums or anything, that it was not marketable" – and, in a year when the British charts were dominated by the likes of Donny Osmond, David Cassidy, and Gilbert O'Sullivan, who could blame them?

Indeed, it might all have ended right there if Oldfield's next group, The Arthur Lewis Band, hadn't been chosen by chance to make some test recordings at Virgin's soon-to-be-opened Manor Studios in Oxfordshire. During some downtime at The Manor, Oldfield played his demo for studio boss Tom Newman. "He was just a funny little hippie," recalls Newman, but he was sufficiently impressed to allocate some recording time.

So, in late 1972 Oldfield squirreled himself away in the bowels of The Manor and set to work in earnest, piecing *Tubular Bells* together from what Newman had first heard as "half a dozen little unconnected pieces," and playing virtually all the instruments himself. As Oldfield remembers it: "I made up a list for Virgin of all the instruments I would need, and they ordered everything up for me. I had seen a set of tubular bells when I did some recording in Abbey Road, so I thought I may as well have some tubular bells, they might come in handy."

Though The Manor was being built from scratch as a state-of-the-art recording facility, it was still a time when editing of tracks was done by cutting up the tapes with a razor blade. From the start Oldfield pushed the existing technology to its limits. "I remember, on the second day of actual recording, explaining to Tom that I had this organ chord which I wanted to slowly slide into another chord," he says. "It would be simplicity itself with modern synths, but the only way we could do it then was to get the maintenance engineer to come in and record the first organ chord on a tape

loop, which he then put on to this great big machine with a huge dial on it and, as he turned the dial, the machine sped up which caused the chord to go up in pitch."

Tom Newman has vivid memories of some of the Heath Robinson/Rube Goldberg-like contraptions Oldfield used to achieve his guitar effects. "He had this awful home-made electronics box full of horrid transistors, covered in faders and knobs, which he called his Glorfindel. It was a piece of plywood filled with junk that he could plug his guitar into and sometimes a sound would come out. Most of the time it was terrible. It would go 'Eeeeoww, Arrrk!' It was like tuning a radio set. Then he would kick it and all of a sudden this glorious, amazing guitar sound would come out."

Much of the actual recording was carried out late at night, after the imbibing of far too much Guinness at a local hostelry. As a result, entire days of recording were sometimes wiped by accident and, as Oldfield readily admits, the tubular bells themselves were somewhat the worse for wear by the time they were put on tape. "Instead of using the little mallet provided, I hit the bell using a proper metal hammer," he explains, "because I wanted it to sound much bigger. I really wanted a huge cathedral bell, but all we had was these little bells. Anyway, I hit it so hard that I cracked it and there was so much gain wound up on the microphone channel that there's noticeable distortion."

On hearing the completed masterwork, Virgin supremo Richard Branson was far from convinced. According to Newman, getting his boss to release the record "was like dragging stuff uphill through treacle." In due course, however, Newman won Branson over and *Tubular Bells* entered the U.K. album chart on July 14th 1973. It wasn't exactly an overnight smash, but persistent marketing kept it moving up, peaking at Number Three in the U.S.A. in March 1974 and finally reaching the top of the

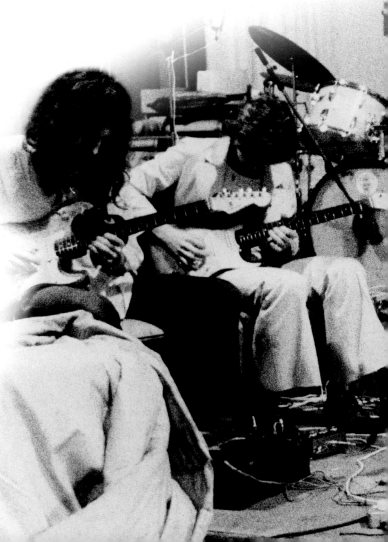

U.K. chart on October 5th 1974, one week after its follow-up, *Hergest Ridge*, had hit the top spot.

Ultimately, it became the second bestselling album in the U.K of the 1970s, outsold only by Simon & Garfunkel's *Bridge Over Troubled Water*. And, as if to prove all those doubting A&R men wrong, after *Tubular Bells* appeared on the soundtrack of the movie *The Exorcist* an edited excerpt became a U.S. Top Ten single.

■ *Main picture: Mike Oldfield (center) in rehearsals for a live performance of* Tubular Bells *at the Queen Elizabeth Hall, London, in June 1973. Among the guest musicians were Gong's Steve Hillage (left) and Mick Taylor of The Rolling Stones (second left).*

The Origins Of Virgin Records

Quite apart from the innovative characteristics of the music, *Tubular Bells* has a second claim to rock'n'roll greatness. Being the first record released by Virgin Records, it was also the start of the Richard Branson empire, which has since blossomed into a global conglomerate built on megastores, airlines, railways, telecommunications, and much, much more.

Branson, having left his private school with minimal formal qualifications, founded Virgin as a cut-price mail-order record store, but it was unquestionably the massive sales generated by *Tubular Bells* that transformed the toothy-grinned charmer into a business mogul, who went on to sell Virgin Records to EMI in March 1992 for £560 million (about $1,033 million at the time).

Branson's canny business instincts remain his empire's greatest asset, though his clever manipulation of his own image runs it a close second. He knows that to be seen abseiling down the side of a skyscraper or ballooning across the world's oceans brings the kind of advertising money can't buy. Pegged early on as "the hip capitalist," he is famous for apparently knowing nothing about music. "It was a bit beyond him," says Mike Oldfield, who points out that Branson's real gift was for employing people who did know what they doing. Those people signed Phil Collins, Culture Club, The Sex Pistols, and countless other acts that probably made Branson richer than any of them.

1973

Raw Power **Iggy Pop**

Columbia KC 3211 (U.S.A.) / CBS 65586 (U.K.)
Released May 1973

Among the most aptly named albums ever recorded, *Raw Power* captures the violent, proto-punk energy of Iggy And The Stooges right before the group imploded.

Born James Jewel Osterberg, Iggy Pop began his musical career as drummer in The Iguanas before forming The Stooges with bassist Dave Alexander and siblings Ron and Scott Asheton on guitar and drums respectively. The Stooges' eponymous debut, produced by John Cale, sounded like a more visceral Velvet Underground – and at the time Iggy was dating that group's sometime chanteuse Nico. Neither *The Stooges* (1968) nor *Fun House* (1970) sold more than a couple of thousand copies at the time, leading to the end of The Stooges' relationship with their label, Elektra. In 1972 the group split temporarily. Later that year, by chance, Iggy ran into David Bowie – a big fan of The Stooges – and Tony DeFries of Bowie's MainMan management team. Bowie would, over the course of the next year, become a crucial figure in resuscitating the careers of not just Iggy but also The Velvet Underground's Lou Reed, whose album *Transformer* (1972) he produced.

Bowie and MainMan brought Iggy to Britain with a slightly reconfigured line-up of The Stooges: Alexander was no longer in the group, while Ron Asheton had switched to bass to make way for new guitarist James Williamson. Somewhat surprisingly, given The Stooges' chaotic recent past and penchant for drink and drugs, MainMan allowed Iggy to produce himself what would become *Raw Power* at CBS Studios in London. Iggy's main aim was to capture the raw energy of what he still considers, 30 years after the fact, to be the finest and most powerful rock group of the time. To that end, everything on the record is bursting with distortion; the songs sound as though they could explode at any moment.

There are some touches, though, that distinguish The Stooges from other pre-punk garage-rock groups of the time: 'Penetration' makes use of a celeste – a keyboard instrument containing tuned bells, used in Tchaikovsky's 'Dance Of The Sugar Plum Fairy,' from *The Nutcracker Suite* – while 'Search And Destroy' contains the sound of sword fighting. According to Iggy, the latter sound is authentic: "We got some old sabers from an antique store. That was maybe a little unnecessary production touch which we took out of these new mixes." The "new mixes" to which Iggy is referring feature on a 25th anniversary edition of *Raw Power* issued in 1997 on the Legacy division of Columbia Records. When Iggy had handed in what he thought was the finished version of *Raw Power* to MainMan in early 1973 Tony DeFries hated the sound of the album and enlisted Bowie to remix the songs at Western Sound in Hollywood. While Iggy was reasonably happy with Bowie's mix, it didn't exactly stick to his original aim for the album, which was to show off the "rip-snortin' super-heavy, nitro-burnin', fuel-injected rock band that nobody in this world could touch at that time." Some of Bowie's changes and additions to the album were in too much of an eccentric, quintessentially English vein for Iggy's liking, hence his decision to return to the album two and a half decades later.

Like its predecessors, *Raw Power* was not a commercial success, though the Bowie connection helped boost its sales slightly. The album was, however, highly influential on most of the punk groups that followed, on either side of the Atlantic, from The Ramones to The Sex Pistols.

The Stooges backstage at the Whiskey A-Go-Go, Los Angeles, on October 30th 1973: Iggy Pop (seated, left), Scott Asheton (seated, right), Scott Thurston (standing, left), Ron Asheton (center), and James Williamson (right).

1974

Autobahn Kraftwerk

Vertigo 2003 (U.S.A.) / 6360 (U.K.)
Released November 1974

Though Kraftwerk perfected their sinisterly synthetic pop on later albums, it was *Autobahn* that woke the world up to the potential of electronic sounds.

Kraftwerk's earlier albums consisted largely of ambient instrumental noodlings, similar to their German contemporaries Tangerine Dream and Ash Ra Tempel, but with *Autobahn* they created a template for much of the cutting-edge pop and rock that was to follow. Florian Schneider recalls that *Autobahn* emerged when they returned to their whimsically named Düsseldorf studio, Kling Klang, after a long motorway drive. "When we came in to play, we had this speed in our music. Our hearts were still beating fast, so the whole rhythm became very fast."

Taking a revolutionary departure from their usual entirely instrumental approach, they decided to add some lyrics about driving on the Autobahn. Then, as lyric collaborator Emil Schult explains: "Ralf [Hutter, of Kraftwerk] specifically asked me to write some lyrics, and it took me one day. Ralf went over them and corrected them a little bit, and it was singable, so it became a song."

To capture sounds of passing traffic, several *Autobahn* journeys were undertaken in Hutter's Volkswagen – what else? – with the microphone of a portable tape recorder dangled out of the window. Despite its engine noises, evocative Doppler shifts, and rhythmic precision provided by their newly acquired custom-built 16-step analog sequencer, *Autobahn* wasn't intended as a map of the future: Kraftwerk themselves saw it as being similar in many ways to The Beach Boys' 'Fun, Fun, Fun.' Hutter and Schneider were fascinated by how Beach Boys songs, crammed with references to woodies, perfect waves, and beach bunnies, conjured instant mental pictures of West Coast teen society.

"A hundred years from now," explained Hutter, "when people want to know what California was like in the 60s, they only have to listen to a single by The Beach Boys." *Autobahn* was Kraftwerk's first attempt to do the same thing for their homeland, but 1970s Germany was radically different from 1960s California. "Walk in the street and you have a concert – cars playing symphonies," pointed out Hutter. "Even engines are tuned, they play free harmonics. Music is always there – you just have to learn to recognize it."

The 22-minute long 'Autobahn' is the album's centerpiece, and though other tracks are clearly descended from their earlier ambient output, Hutter's unlikely Beach Boys analogy is borne out by the unmistakable surf-rock drum patterns and chugging rhythms in 'Kometenmelodie 2.'

An edited version of 'Autobahn' reached Number 25 on the U.S. singles chart, but, just as the crooners of the mid 1950s couldn't grasp the significance of Elvis Presley, the music critics of the 1970s were so steeped in the traditional verities of the 12-bar and the blustering machismo of rock that many saw it as little more than a bizarre electronic novelty, a lifeless Teutonic descendant of 'Route 66.' It was, however, just a matter of time before nothing would ever be the same again, and Kraftwerk's influence was soon celebrated in the work of artists as diverse as Afrika Bambaataa, David Bowie, Depeche Mode, New Order, Orbital, The Chemical Brothers, and Michael Jackson.

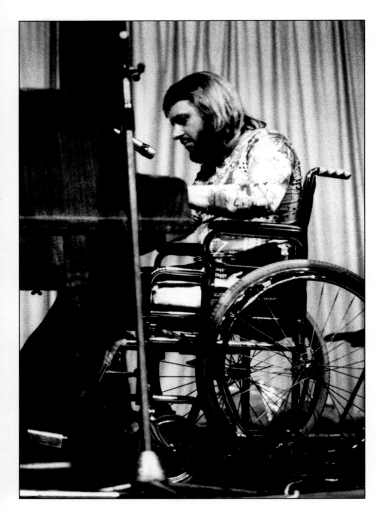

Head Hunters **Herbie Hancock**

Columbia 32731 (U.S.A.) / CBS CBS/40 65582 (U.K.)
Released January 1974

One of the most influential figures in jazz of the later 20th century, Hancock made perhaps the definitive jazz-funk album, *Head Hunters*, an early example of the potential of the synthesizer.

A prodigiously talented pianist, Herbie Hancock had a huge influence on the changing direction of The Miles Davis Quintet of the mid 1960s before forming his own sextet in 1968. Hancock's band made four albums in the early 1970s, experimenting with funk and cutting-edge synthesizers, but split because of financial difficulties. His next act was to form a stripped down funk group to record *Head Hunters*. Clearly inspired by James Brown and Sly Stone, Hancock's rich synthesizer playing on the album is more rhythmic in feel than the piano flourishes that made his name in the previous decade. Hancock also makes use of an early sequencer, which allowed him to program synthetic bass parts over which his band could perform.

Perhaps surprisingly, for a record so groundbreaking, *Head Hunters* was an instant commercial hit, becoming the first jazz album to achieve platinum status. Hancock remained popular throughout the 1970s, playing to stadium-sized audiences across the U.S.A. and releasing a series of albums that developed on themes introduced on *Head Hunters*. Hancock later had a pop hit with the robotic funk single 'Rockit' in 1983, while also making frequent returns to the acoustic jazz of his roots.

Court And Spark **Joni Mitchell**

Asylum 7E1001 (U.S.A.) / SYLA 8756 (U.K.)
Released March 1974

***Court And Spark* is a high point both in Joni Mitchell's career and for the 'sophisticated' end of the singer-songwriter genre.**

In contrast to the stark *Blue*, *Court And Spark* had a band sound, courtesy of Tom Scott's jazz-rock LA Express. Guitarists Larry Carlton, José Feliciano, and Robbie Robertson also assisted, while David Crosby and Graham Nash did some backing vocals. Elements of light rock and jazz dovetailed in a fine batch of songs about life and love. It went gold and had three hit singles: the ecstatic 'Help Me,' the playful 'Raised On Robbery,' and the breezy 'Free Man In Paris.'

Mitchell tells a salutary tale about sharing a house with David Geffen, head of Asylum Records, who at this time was hoping to release Dylan's new album, *Planet Waves*. When Mitchell had finished *Court And Spark* she took it home to play to Geffen. "I was so excited the night I finished it I brought it back to the house to play it. There were a bunch of people there, including Dylan [who] . . . fell asleep and snored all the way through it. When the record came to the end, the people went, 'Huh?' Then they played *Planet Waves* and everybody jumped up and down. There was so much enthusiasm . . . for the first time in my career I felt this sibling rivalry. It was an ordinary record for Bobby, a transitional piece, and yet everybody was cheering. Finally, one of the women took me aside and said, 'Don't pay them any attention. Those boys have no ears.'"

Rock Bottom **Robert Wyatt**

Virgin13112 (U.S.A.) / V/TCV 2017 (U.K.)
Released July 1974

During the late 1960s Robert Wyatt was the drummer in the art-rock collective Soft Machine. After playing on their first four albums he began to tire of the role, so in 1971 he left to form Matching Mole, in which he sang as well as drummed.

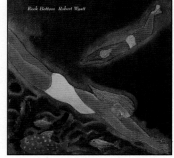

Two albums later, Wyatt fell from a third-storey window at a party, suffering a spinal fracture that has left him wheelchair bound ever since. During a lengthy period of convalescence, realizing he would not be able to resume his duties in Matching Mole either as a drummer or as a touring musician, Wyatt began to re-imagine his career a solo performer, and *Rock Bottom* was the result.

Though Wyatt had written most of the material for *Rock Bottom* before his accident, the album clearly reflects his difficultly in dealing with his paralysis. Recorded by Pink Floyd's Nick Mason, the six stately songs are given time and space to develop by an impressive array of guest musicians, chief among them Mike Oldfield. Most deal with the insular life that Wyatt and his soon-to-be wife Alfie had adopted, notably the heartbreaking opener 'Sea Song,' on which he declares, in his trademark wistful falsetto, "When you're drunk, you're terrific." Though not a particular commercial success, *Rock Bottom* is rightly regarded as one of the real high points in progressive rock. Two months later, in a typical example of his idiosyncratic career, Wyatt had a U.K. hit with a cover of The Monkees' 'I'm A Believer,' and he continues to make the occasional, often highly political, album into the 21st century.

1975

Horses **Patti Smith**

Arista 4066 (U.S.A.) / ARTY 122 (U.K.)
Released December 1975

Patti Smith was one of the foremost poets of the punk era, while *Horses*, her debut album, remains one of the best-loved records to come out of New York in the 1970s, ranking alongside albums by The Ramones, Talking Heads, and Television.

Horses was produced by John Cale, formerly of The Velvet Underground, whose influence is clear on a number of its songs. Another key contributor was guitarist Lenny Kaye, who had regularly backed Smith on the New York performance-poetry circuit in the early 1970s and who had, in 1973, compiled the influential *Nuggets* album of 1960s garage rock. The album also features pianist Richard Sohl, bassist Ivan Kral, and drummer Jay Dee Daugherty.

Horses opens with a brief spoken-word passage that segues neatly into an energetic rendition of Van Morrison's 'Gloria.' There are also suggestions of reggae (on 'Redondo Beach') and several reflective, piano-led epics. 'Break It Up' was co-written by Television frontman Tom Verlaine, who also plays guitar on the track.

Smith recorded three more albums in the late 1970s before retiring to concentrate on married life with her husband, ex-MC5 guitarist Fred 'Sonic' Smith, and only returned to her musical career after his death in 1995. She marked the 30th anniversary of *Horses* with a live recreation of the album at the 2005 *Meltdown* festival in London.

■ *Patti Smith on stage in early 1976 with bassist Ivan Kral.*

Natty Dread **Bob Marley**

Island ILPS 9281 (U.S.A. & U.K.)
Released May 1975

Live! **Bob Marley**

Island ILPS 9376 (U.S.A. & U.K)
Released December 1975

The most iconic reggae performer of all time, Bob Marley made his international commercial breakthrough in 1975 with these two albums.

Both contain versions of his classic 'No Woman No Cry,' and the live set also features a rendition of his 'I Shot The Sheriff,' a major hit for Eric Clapton the previous year. With these songs, Marley brought reggae to a truly global audience for the first time.

Before Marley's arrival on the international music scene as a solo star, The Wailers – Marley, Peter Tosh, and Bunny Livingston (aka Bunny Wailer) – had established themselves as huge stars in their native Jamaica. During the 1960s and early 1970s the group worked with two of the most influential and pioneering figures in Jamaican music, 'Sir' Coxsone Dodd and Lee 'Scratch' Perry, producing numerous domestic hits. Among them, 'Trench Town Rock,' issued on The Wailers' own Tuff Gong label, topped the Jamaican singles chart for five months in 1971.

The Wailers signed with Chris Blackwell's Island Records in 1972, shortly after the release of a one-off single on CBS, 'Reggae On Broadway,' the group's first international release. Blackwell was at the helm of much of Marley's material from this point on, including *Catch A Fire* (1973), one of the first full reggae albums and the first to reach a wider, more rock audience. By the time *Natty Dread* was recorded, Bob Marley And The Wailers – as they were now called, Tosh and Wailer having left – had built up a strong live following, but had yet to achieve any hit records outside Jamaica.

Natty Dread was colored by the presence of a number [...] including American guitarist Al Anderson – who, along w[...] introduced a more pronounced rock edge to Marley's m[...] drummer Remi Kabaka. The album is also the first of M[...] I-Threes, three female backing singers – one of whom w[...] who had replaced his former partners on vocal duties. N[...] some of Marley's strongest songs, including 'Rebel Musi[...] The album's key moment is the soulful ballad 'No Woma[...] version of which provided Marley with his first U.K. hit sir[...] album's release. *Natty Dread* itself peaked at Number 43[...] edged into the lower reaches of the Top 100 in the U.S.A[...]

Shortly after the release of *Natty Dread*, Marley embarke[...] of the U.K. that culminated in an appearance at the Lyce[...] London. *Live!* captures that performance, from July 18th [...] recorded with the same band that features on *Natty Drea*[...] peak of his powers here, successfully recasting his tradit[...] music for a rock audience. The material is split equally be[...] from *Natty Dread* and older songs, including 'Burnin' And [...] The Sheriff.' The musicians are barely audible on 'No Wor[...] they are overtaken by an ecstatic crowd singing every wor[...] Later reissued with the more informative title *Live At The* [...] improved slightly on *Natty Dread*'s chart placing, reaching [...] U.K. and Number 90 in the U.S.A. Marley achieved further [...] success the following year with *Rastaman Vibration*, which [...] Top Ten.

Born To Run
Bruce Springsteen

Columbia 33795 (U.S.A.) / CBS CBS69170 (U.K.)
Released November 1975

Born To Run, **Bruce Springsteen's breakthrough album, is one of the definitive rock albums inspired by life in the city.**

It dramatizes the romantic longings of urban life, offering snapshots of tenements, streets, and highways, where radios blare through summer windows, bikers pose with their machines, and lovers make out on the beach. At the album's heart are the car and the open road, and the idea of driving away together and escaping. This is most clearly caught in the famous title track, but it informs each of the record's eight songs, right from the opener 'Thunder Road,' a tale of broken-hearted boys crying over graduation gowns. No matter how desperate the characters, in Springsteen's mini-*West Side Story* there is always a better place at the freeway's end. Much of his career since has questioned that, but *Born To Run* is a city to visit when you need the strength to dream.

Springsteen made a long journey to find the music of his third album. In the late 1960s he was a long-haired guitarist playing heavy blues rock on a Les Paul in bands such as Earth, Child, Clearwater Swim Club, and Steel Mill. Then he appeared in a series of short-lived outfits, including Dr Zoom And The Sonic Boom and The Bruce Springsteen Band, all the while gaining vital experience as a live performer. Springsteen collaborator 'Miami' Steve Van Zandt commented: "He was into songwriting very early on and was always quite good at it. There weren't that many people writing back then; it was still the era of the old Brill Building thing."

By 1971 Springsteen knew it was time for a musical change: "I moved from hard rock to rhythm-and-blues-influenced music and I began to write differently." He played solo for noted A&R man John Hammond at CBS in May 1972. Hammond saw Springsteen as a new folk singer in the Dylan mold and signed him on that basis, but when recording for the first album started in June 1972 Springsteen insisted on using a band. By this point he had seven years of songwriting behind him, in a number of different styles. His lyrics were wordy and the impressionistic songs had cinematic qualities, and he was also experimenting with longer forms that would work well live. He later called the resulting album – *Greetings From Asbury Park, NJ* – "an acoustic record with a rhythm section."

In 1973 many critics dismissed Springsteen as a mix of Dylan and Van Morrison. His own personality and musical strengths were obscured. The first version of The E Street Band toured with Chicago to promote *Greetings*. For the second album, *The Wild, The Innocent And The E Street Shuffle* (1974), Springsteen wanted to inject a dose of bar-band sparkle'n'clatter into the new songs to up the energy of the band's live show, and 'Rosalita' quickly established itself as one of the highlights of the set. In May 1974 journalist – and later Springsteen producer as well as manager – Jon Landau wrote the famous review that featured the quote: "I saw rock'n'roll future and its name is Bruce Springsteen."

His first two albums had sold moderately, and Springsteen was building a reputation as a live act, but even as his profile grew, the band was almost broke and nearly dropped by CBS. His third album had to be a killer. Roy Bittan replaced David Sancious on piano and Max Weinberg came in on drums.

After protracted and psychologically bruising sessions at 914 Sound Studio, Blauvelt, New York, and the Record Plant, New York City – with Springsteen, Jon Landau, and Mike Appel on production duties – *Born To Run* was released in August 1975, and it was the album that put him on the road to stardom. Springsteen said in 1978: "When I did *Born To Run*, I thought, 'I'm going to make the greatest rock'n'roll record ever made.' The only concept that was around *Born To Run* was that I wanted to make a big record, you know, that sounds like these words. Just like a car, zoom, straight ahead, that when the sucker comes on it's like wide open. No holds barred!"

Not for nothing did Springsteen name-check Roy Orbison in 'Thunder Road.' Roy Bittan confirmed: "He said he wanted a record where the singing sounded like Roy Orbison." Reaching past hard rock, Springsteen's musical landmarks were to be found in the late 1950s and early 1960s: Orbison, Presley, The Righteous Brothers, The Ronettes, The Beach Boys, Bo Diddley, Duane Eddy, Phil Spector. Critic Greil Marcus once described 'Born To Run' as a "'57 Chevy running on melted-down Crystals records." Springsteen himself said in 1987: "I wanted to make a record that would sound like Phil Spector. I wanted to write words like Dylan. I wanted my guitar to sound like Duane Eddy." The album, according to Springsteen, spoke "the traditional language of rock'n'roll." He never had forgotten the magical immediacy of mid-1960s pop and rock. One Springsteen biographer, Chris Humphries, describes him in concert as "a one-man history of rock'n'roll, a human jukebox," while another, Dave Marsh, calls him "the living culmination of 20 years of rock'n'roll tradition."

In 1980 Springsteen commented: "I've been influenced by a lot of people. Elvis was one of the first. Otis Redding, Sam Cooke, Wilson Pickett, The Beatles, Fats Domino, Benny Goodman, a lot of jazz guys. You can hear them all in there if you want to." Bo Diddley is the main rhythm reference for 'She's The One,' a cool jazz influence breathes through the wistful 'Meeting Across The River,' 'Tenth Avenue Freeze-Out' is updated Stax soul, while 'Jungleland' and 'Backstreets' closed each side of the vinyl record with an epic long-form song. The instrumentation is suitably impressive. Piano and glockenspiel glitter on the tracks like tarmac strewn with diamonds, and electric guitars and saxophone blend together in droning power-chords.

Born To Run simplified Springsteen's musical vision. He lost some of the funk and the street-dandy poetry but gained power and a bigger audience. The title track, with its Duane Eddy riff and unpredictable twisting and turning bridge, duly took its place in the pantheon of 'greatest-ever rock songs.' Live, it never failed to reduce artist and audience to one quivering mass of defiance and longing, growing more poignant as the years have passed. In October 1975 both *Time* and *Newsweek* put him on their covers – he was Rock's New Sensation.

■ *Below: Springseen with guitarist 'Miami' Steve Van Zandt (right).*

1975

Discreet Music **Brian Eno**

Antilles 7030 (U.S.A.) / Obscure OBS 3 (U.K.)
Released December 1975

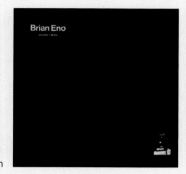

This extraordinary album took a slew of avant-garde ideas and seeded them into the heart of popular music culture where, amazingly, they took root and flourished.

In the early 1970s Eno was the flamboyant keyboard player of Roxy Music, an eccentric muso clad in peacock feathers and makeup, who coaxed weird electronic bleeps out of primitive synthesizers. He quit Roxy in 1973 to pursue a solo career, which took a radical turn on January 18th 1975 when Eno walked in front of a London taxi. Confined to a hospital bed for weeks, virtually immobile, he found himself listening one day to an album of harp music with the volume turned down too low to hear properly. Unable to move to turn it up, he found himself hearing the music as an aspect of the ambience of the room – like the changing qualities of the light or the sounds of the weather outside – and, to his surprise, he found that he enjoyed it that way.

On his release from hospital he decided to create a piece of music designed to be listened to at a low volume. He also decided that, rather than being composed, it should be generated. To achieve this he played a couple of simple melody lines on a synthesizer, which were harmonically compatible but of different lengths. He then fed both pieces through an echo unit and a delay system that looped them so that they would play simultaneously and repeatedly. Being of unequal length they would inevitably drift out of sync, creating a potentially endless pattern of variations.

Unusual as this was in a pop–rock context, *Discreet Music* was not a revolutionary work per se. Indeed, most of Eno's innovations had clear precedents in the avant-garde fields of minimalism and electronic composition. There had even been earlier electronic albums that found some acceptance with the rock audience, notably Terry Riley's *Rainbow In Curved Air* (1969), and two German works, Kluster's *Klopfzeichen* (1970) and Tangerine Dream's *Electronic Meditation* (1970). Eno himself, in collaboration with King Crimson guitarist Robert Fripp, had helped pioneer the use of ambient music loops on their 1973 album *No Pussyfooting*, and the original intention for *Discreet Music* was that it would become a musical background on top of which Fripp would improvise.

Many experimental composers set out to shock the musical establishment, but Eno took pains in the album's sleeve note to point out that his concepts owed more to the spirit of the early 20th century composer Erik Satie, "who wanted to make music that could 'mingle with the sound of the knives and forks at dinner.'" For some, this reduced Eno's composition to the same level as the despised Muzak systems, but others perceived it as a refreshing contrast to the self-aggrandizing high-volume bluster of rock music. Yet, without Eno's standing in the rock world, *Discreet Music* would have been confined to a much smaller audience, and it was his work with rock giants such as U2 and Talking Heads that would ultimately introduce many of Eno's ideas to vast mainstream audiences.

Blow By Blow **Jeff Beck**

Epic PE33409 (U.S.A.) / EPC69117 (U.K.)
Released March 1975

Blow By Blow **was the nearest the mercurial Jeff Beck ever came to making an album consistently worthy of his undoubted guitar talents, and it stands as a good example of the jazz rock fusion style that was a minor thread in music during the first half of the 1970s.**

Beck came to fame in The Yardbirds in the mid 1960s, contributing idiosyncratic lead to some of their best material – and for a short time having as guitar partner Jimmy Page before Beck left to form his own band and Page went on to form Led Zeppelin out of the ashes of The Yardbirds. In 1968–9 Beck released *Truth* and *Beck-Ola* with a line-up that included Rod Stewart and Ronnie Wood before they re-emerged as The Faces. After further recordings with The Jeff Beck Group and the heavy-rock Beck, Bogert & Appice, Beck, with producer George Martin at the helm, made the all-instrumental *Blow By Blow*. The music put aside heavy riffs and three-chord blues for more complex progressions while still retaining some commercial appeal. Beck multiplied the lead parts by overdubbing and Jan Hammer played keyboards. Martin gave Beck's playing the backdrop of attractive strings and rhythm arrangements, and their partnership was kept for a second album, *Wired* (1976).

''Cause We've Ended As Lovers' is possibly the standout track here. However, Beck seemed fated never to find the right context or compromise by which his guitar skills could reach a wider public. He was also a stern critic of himself, once saying: "Emotion rules everything I do . . . I can switch on automatic and play, but it sounds terrible. I've got to be wound-up, in the right mood."

■ *Below: Brian Eno in his home studio during the mid 1970s.*

Gratitude **Earth, Wind & Fire**

Columbia 33694 (U.S.A.) CBS S80995 (U.K.)
Released December 1975

The year 1975 was a turning point for Chicago-based Earth, Wind & Fire. With the smash 'Shining Star' propelling parent album *That's The Way Of The World* **to the top of the albums chart, EWF suddenly found themselves playing arenas to capacity crowds.**

At Christmas they returned with *Gratitude*, a double-disk set of mainly live material, culled from the group's summer 1975 North American tour. It also included four new studio tracks: the single 'Sing A Song,' 'Can't Hide Love,' 'Celebrate,' and 'Gratitude,' all recorded the previous June at Colorado's Caribou Ranch. "We didn't have time to do a whole new studio album," explained Maurice White, "so we just started taping all our shows."

In concert, the phenomenal vocalizing of Philip Bailey breathed new life into the ballad 'Reasons,' while EW&F's impossibly funky horn section took 'Shining Star' up yet another notch – listening to Don Myrick's lyrical sax work during 'Reasons,' an awe-struck Bailey gushes to the audience: "He plays so beautiful. Don't you agree?"

Like its predecessor, *Gratitude* also climbed to the Number One spot, selling over a million copies in the process. Sadly, the joy surrounding EWF's newfound success was tempered by the loss of Charles Stepney – co-writer of 'Reasons' and 'That's The Way Of The World – who died suddenly from a heart attack while the hit 'Sing A Song" was still in rotation.

As the first platinum-selling black R&B group, EWF became a major source of inspiration for scores of next-generation artists, among them multi-instrumentalist Lenny Kravitz, whose 1991 hit 'It Ain't Over 'Til It's Over' sounded strikingly similar to EW&F's 'That's The Way Of The World.'

1975

Blood On The Tracks **Bob Dylan**

CBS 33235 (U.S.A.) / CBS 69097 (U.K.)
Released January 1975

The Basement Tapes **Bob Dylan**

Columbia 32235 (U.S.A.) / CBS CBS/40 88147 (U.K.)
Released July 1975

Creatively, the early 1970s were a quiet time for Bob Dylan. The release of the much-maligned double album of covers and half-finished scraps, *Self Portrait* (1970), was followed by the pleasant but modest *New Morning*, after which there was no new material at all until 1973, when the soundtrack to *Pat Garrett And Billy The Kid* – a Sam Peckinpah movie in which Dylan appears – was released.

Early the following year saw the release of Dylan's and The Band's last studio collaboration, *Planet Waves*. Both albums had flashes of the old genius, but hard-line disciples of the one-time spokesman for a generation feared that their guru's creative fire had been all but extinguished by years of family life with wife Sara, the subject of *Blonde On Blonde*'s 'Sad-Eyed Lady Of The Lowlands.'

But by 1974 Dylan's life of apparent domestic bliss was crumbling. His marriage was in ruins, destroyed by the stress of enduring constant harassment from adoring fans and Dylan's alleged infidelities during a 1974 tour. It was from this sorry situation that Dylan drew inspiration for an artistic revival, writing a set of songs that detailed his pain, anger, frustration, and longing with an artistry that eclipsed even his greatest work from a decade earlier.

Sessions for *Blood On The Tracks* were unusually protracted, at least by Dylan's usually spontaneous – and somewhat slapdash – standards. Recording started in New York during September 1974 when he booked studio time without even deciding who was going to accompany him. Producer Phil Ramone roped in ace session players Deliverance at the last moment, and a few songs were recorded. Dylan quickly dispatched Deliverance, however, and regrouped with a trio comprised of pedal-steel guitarist Buddy Cage, bassist Tony Braun, and organist Paul Griffin. With this stripped-down line-up Dylan recorded more songs, and a ten-song version of the album was completed, slated for release on Christmas Day 1974.

Promotional copies were pressed and sent out to radio stations, while Dylan took a copy back to the Minnesota farmhouse he was sharing with his brother David. There, listening through the songs, he persuaded himself that the mood was too mellow and, perhaps that the lyrics were just a little too obviously autobiographical. On Christmas Eve, the day before the album was due to be released, Dylan gave the order to stop production, stating that he wanted to re-record some songs.

A few days later he was in a studio in Minnesota with the cream of the local scene's musicians, where he re-cut the songs. Lyrics were edited and rewritten, tempos changed, and

additional arrangement touches added. The album's two pivotal songs, 'Idiot Wind' and 'Tangled Up In Blue,' were among those reworked, becoming tougher, more energized, more caustic, and closer in spirit to classic Dylan from the mid 1960s in the process.

The revised version of the album was finally released in January 1975, to immediate critical acclaim and huge sales, eventually peaking at Number One in the U.S.A. and Number Four in the U.K. Bootleg versions of the earlier, scrapped version of the album – a much slower, more maudlin affair than the official release – have been circulating widely ever since.

Released later the same year, the songs on *The Basement Tapes* had been recorded by Dylan with The Band in 1966 and 1967 while the singer was apparently recuperating after a mysterious motorcycle accident. When the material was eventually released, it was during one of the busiest, most artistically rewarding periods of Dylan's career. The album appeared six months after *Blood On The Tracks* and six months before *Desire* (1976), at a time when he was touring with a revolving cast of singers and poets – including Joan Baez and Allen Ginsberg – on the 'Rolling Thunder Revue.'

The music Dylan and The Band had recorded was sent out as publishers' demo tapes in the late 1960s, resulting in hits for other artists, including 'Mighty Quinn,' a U.K. Number One for Manfred Mann. These recordings were among the first by any artist to be widely bootlegged, appearing from 1968 onward under various titles.

According to Dylan's recent autobiographical tome, *Chronicles: Volume One* (2004), the motorcycle incident was not quite as serious as he had claimed at the time: "I'd been hurt, but I recovered. Truth was that I wanted to get out of the rat race." Dylan spent several months with his wife Sara and newborn son Jesse at his home in Woodstock, New York, before inviting The Band to join him to work over some of his new songs. The musicians worked in near seclusion in the relaxed atmosphere of The Band's Big Pink recording base. In contrast to Dylan's output of the time, the frantic *Highway 61 Revisited* and *Blonde On Blonde*, much of the material on *The Basement Tapes* has an exuberant, playful feel, closer in spirit to the material recorded not long afterward for *John Wesley Harding* (1968).

Among the many highlights of the eventual 24-track, double-album issue of *The Basement Tapes* is his own version of 'This Wheel's On Fire,' already a U.K. hit for Julie Driscoll with Brian Auger And The Trinity, and the humorous 'Tears Of Rage,' on which Dylan sings: "I can drink like a fish / I can crawl like a snake / I can bite like a turkey / I can slam like a drake." The songs reveal Dylan and The Band at their most carefree, leading *Village Voice* critic Robert Christgau to remark: "What is most lovable about the album is simply the way it unites public and private, revealing a Dylan armed in the mystery of his songs but divested of the mystique of celebrity with which he has surrounded his recording career for almost a decade."

On its official release in July 1975 *The Basement Tapes* peaked at Number Seven in the U.S.A. and Number Eight in the U.K. For the previous seven years, however, most of the songs had been available in bootleg form, housed inside a plain white cover, decorated only with the title *The Great White Wonder*. While the practice of bootlegging music was not new, the success of *The Great White Wonder* was unprecedented: the album is claimed to have sold over 350,000 copies, though more conservative estimates place the figure closer to half of that. Whatever the actual sales, the popularity of *The Great White Wonder* gave a clear indication that music fans were willing to buy often poor-quality recordings of private tapes and live performances by the artists they admired.

The practice of bootlegging soon developed into a whole underground industry of its own. Among the notable pirate versions to follow *The Great White Wonder* into record shops were *Stampede* by The Who (a recording – in rather bad taste – of a performance at which twelve audience members were crushed to death), numerous live recordings of The Grateful Dead (which the group, unusually, encouraged), and the multipart series of Beatles rarities, *Unsurpassed Masters*.

1976

Desire **Bob Dylan**

Columbia 33893 (U.S.A.) / CBS CBS/40 86003 (U.K.)
Released January 1976

Desire and its predecessor, Blood On The Tracks, represent Dylan at the top of his second peak, his mid-1970s renaissance. They also confirmed the suspicion, long held by the cognoscenti, that no matter how far down he might go, Dylan could never be counted out.

Anyone who had labored through *Self Portrait* in 1970 or *Planet Waves* in 1974 had every reason to believe that Dylan was a spent force. *Blood On The Tracks* was an assured return to form, but if anyone had any lingering doubts, just a few bars of *Desire*'s opening track, 'Hurricane,' was enough to sweep away the memories of half a decade of sub-standard material.

Sessions for the album had begun on July 28th 1975 at Columbia Studios in New York City. Emmylou Harris was on harmony vocals, Scarlett Rivera, a busker plucked from the streets of Greenwich Village, was on violin, and Eric Clapton was playing guitar. "It ended up with something like 24 musicians in the studio, all playing these incredibly incongruous instruments – accordion, violin . . ." recalled Clapton later. "It really didn't work. He was after a large sound, but the songs were so personal that he wasn't comfortable with all the people around. It was very hard to keep up with him. He wasn't sure what he wanted. He was really looking, racing from song to song. The songs were amazing." In consequence, from that first session, only 'Romance In Durango' made it to the finished album.

A few days later Dylan returned to the studio with no producer and an almost entirely different band, though Scarlett Rivera was still aboard. "The sessions were outrageous," she revealed subsequently. "There was just a rundown of the songs and, once the structure was understood, the red light went on." In this mood of unrehearsed spontaneity, they knocked off 'One More Cup Of Coffee,' 'Mozambique,' 'Hurricane,' and several others.

Clapton's assessment proved accurate, because the songs, mostly co-written with off-Broadway songwriter Jacques Levy, were extraordinary, particularly 'Sara,' an uncharacteristically transparent proclamation of undying love for his wife, from whom he was soon to part. 'Hurricane,' a powerful plea for the release of convicted murderer Ruben 'Hurricane' Carter, reasserted Dylan's role as a fighter for justice, a man of the people standing up against the system. And 'One More Cup Of Coffee' pulls off the classic Dylan trick of creating a startling contrast by interspersing seemingly mystical verses with a prosaic but evocative chorus.

If the band was somewhat loose, Rivera's soaring violin lines were more than enough to maintain the musical interest and, for his part, Dylan's vocals sounded more passionate than they had for years. "He wanted very unpolished and unaffected performances," explained Rivera. "He was really looking for lots of heart and genuine expression, as opposed to precision playing and a flawless performance."

The critics were divided on the merits of *Desire*, some clearly unable to hear the quality of the songs because of the slackness of the music, but the public had no such qualms, and the album reached Number One on the U.S. albums chart on February 7th 1976, staying there for five solid weeks.

Stupidity Dr Feelgood

Not issued in the U.S.A. / United Artists UAS 29990 (U.K.)
Released September 1976

**The quintessential English
pub-rock band, Dr Feelgood hit
the top of the U.K. chart with
Stupidity, recorded at two 1975
live performances.**

Dr Feelgood emerged from Essex,
England, in the early 1970s, their
frantic rock'n'roll soon earning a
devoted local following. The band at
the time was focused around twin
frontmen Lee Brilleaux (vocals and
harmonica) and hyperactive guitarist
Wilko Johnson. On the strength of
their impressive live performances Dr Feelgood signed a multialbum deal
with United Artists. Their first, *Down By The Jetty*, was recorded,
unfashionably, in mono; the follow-up, *Malpractice*, was a minor U.K. hit, as
was the single 'Back In The Night.'

Given that Dr Feelgood spent so much time on the road, leaving few
opportunities for studio recording, the decision was made by United Artists
to capture the band in their favorite environment, live on stage. The two
sides of *Stupidity* were recorded at separate live shows, the first at
Sheffield's City Hall, the second right in the band's backyard, at the Kursaal
in Southend, Essex. The album includes definitive versions of many of the
band's best-loved songs, including Johnson originals 'She Does It Right' and
'Roxette.' Its success briefly put Dr Feelgood's corner of Essex on the
musical map, as other local acts including Eddie And The Hot Rods and The
Kursaal Flyers had U.K. chart hits.

The band never really recovered, and was never able to repeat its early
commercial success, after the departure of maniacal guitarist Johnson in
1977, though they continue to tour to the present day, albeit with a
completely changed line-up. Brilleaux had remained in the band, but by the
time of his untimely death from cancer in 1994 he was the only remaining
original member.

■ *Above: Wilko Johnson (left) and Lee Brilleaux of Dr Feelgood, on stage
in 1976. Dr Feelgood was one of the leading lights of pub rock, a pre-
punk style that emerged from North London and Essex, England, during
the mid 1970s as a reaction to the excesses of progressive rock.*

This was a band whose first gig, in early 1974, was so bad that many of their friends stopped speaking to them afterward. Vocalist Joey Ramone, however, was undaunted, believing firmly that by that time "rock'n'roll had got so bloated and lost its spirit. We stripped it down and re-assembled it under the influence of The MC5, The Beatles and The Stones, Alice Cooper and T. Rex."

So The Ramones persevered, tightened up, and won a sizeable live following. Even so, Hilly Kristal, owner of legendary New York venue CBGB's, vividly remembers the night when MOR queen Linda Ronstadt and her entourage pitched up at the club to see what the fuss was about. "They lasted less than five minutes. She literally flew out the door holding her ears."

The buzz was enough, however, to get them a low-budget deal with Sire Records, who put them into Plaza Sound Studios at Radio City Music Hall, New York City, to start recording the album on February 2nd 1976. Production on the album was in the hands of Sire's in-house A&R man Craig Leon with some assistance from Tom Erdelyi, aka Tommy Ramone, the band's drummer. Leon recalls: "A lot of people didn't even think they could make a record. There were weeks of pre-production on a very basic level, like when the songs started and when they ended."

Once the band was fully rehearsed it became a matter of deciding on a sound. Leon's point of reference for the guitars was the rasping din on 'Silver Machine,' the only hit single by British acid-rock warriors Hawkwind – bassist Lemmy, who sang lead on 'Silver Machine,' went on to form Motörhead. To achieve the huge yet dry overall ambience of the album he put each musician's amps into separate rehearsal halls so that "you could crank it up and still get isolation."

To the uninitiated, every Ramones song sounds identical to every other Ramones song, but, as with dub reggae or blues, the subtle differences emerge with repeated listens. Each compact capsule is crammed with minimalist hooks, hints of Phil Spector, almost buried Byrds-like guitars, and much more.

When it was finished, on February 19th, it had cost a mere $6,400 at a time when superstars could easily eat up – or snort up – half a million dollars in the studio, and all 14 tracks take up a mere 29 minutes. Punk rock, as we know it today, was born.

The Ramones The Ramones

Sire 7520 (U.S.A.) / 9103 253 (U.K.)
Released May 1976

The Ramones is the album that invented the 1970s incarnation of punk rock.

The term 'punk' had been used in the 1960s, usually applied to what were more commonly called garage bands, such as The Standells, ? And The Mysterians, and The Sonics. There's no denying that The Ramones shared with these bands not just a certain brazen attitude but a slavish devotion to the notion that a great song never lasted more than three minutes and never employed more than three chords. The slogan on The Sonics' first album – "Four great guys, three great chords" – would have been equally valid for The Ramones a decade later.

1976

Arrival **Abba**

Atlantic 18207 (U.S.A.) / Epic EPC/40 86018 (U.K.)
Released January 1977 (U.S.A.) / November 1976 (U.K.)

One of the most successful pop acts of all time, Abba achieved so much commercial success during the mid 1970s that the group was listed on the Swedish stock exchange as one of the nation's biggest exports.

They had seven Number One albums and nine chart-topping singles in the U.K., and achieved the kind of pan-European success that others could only dream of. While Abba was not quite so universally popular in the U.S.A., the group did top the *Billboard* singles chart with the disco classic 'Dancing Queen,' included on *Arrival*.

Songwriting duo Benny Andersson and Björn Ulvaeus formed Abba in 1971 with their partners, vocalists Anni-Frid Lyngstad-Fredriksson and Agnetha Fältskog-Ulvaeus. All four had achieved fame independently in Sweden, but Abba's wider breakthrough came when the group won the 1974 Eurovision Song Contest with 'Waterloo,' which subsequently topped the U.K. chart and reached Number Six in the U.S.A. Abba consolidated this success with the albums *Waterloo* (1974) and *Abba* (1975), a first *Greatest Hits* compilation (1976), and a string of international hit singles, among them 'SOS,' 'Mamma Mia,' and 'Fernando.'

As with previous Abba albums all songwriting and production duties on *Arrival* were handled by Andersson and Ulvaeus. The duo wrote in a very methodical way, reminiscent of the conveyor-belt-like practices of Tin Pan Alley. They would turn up at their shared office in the morning, pull out their acoustic guitars, and churn out hits day after day. *Arrival* was recorded at various points between the summers of 1975 and 1976 at Metronome, Glen, and KMH studios in Stockholm, Sweden, the sessions broken up by the group's hectic promotional schedule in support of *Abba* and *Greatest Hits*. Abba started work on the basic backing track to 'Dancing Queen' in August 1975, adding string parts and vocals the following month. 'Knowing Me, Knowing You,' and 'That's Me' were cut in March 1976, with the rest of the album completed in the summer of the same year.

Musically, *Arrival* has a much more synthesized sheen than previous Abba recordings, which tended to be based around the traditional pop instrumentation of piano and guitar. The songs stick mostly to the template of *Waterloo* and *Abba*, but add elements of the disco sounds that were beginning to dominate the singles charts in Europe and the U.S.A., and occasionally feature more adult lyrical themes than on earlier hits. 'Money Money Money' has a cabaret feel, while the power ballad 'Knowing Me, Knowing You' describes the decline of a marriage, presaging the split between Björn and Agnetha Ulvaeus, who had married shortly after the group's formation in 1971. Both songs were huge international hits. 'Knowing Me, Knowing You' topped the U.K. singles chart, as did 'Dancing Queen,' which was also the group's sole U.S. chart topper.

The first Abba record sleeve to feature the group's distinctive mirror-image logo, with the first 'B' reversed, *Arrival* topped albums charts across Europe on its release in late 1976 and reached Number 20 in the U.S.A. when it was issued there early the following year. *Arrival* has sold over ten million copies worldwide, just edging past *The Album* (1978) and *Voulez-Vous* (1980) as the band's biggest-selling studio album. Its sales have since been eclipsed by the definitive hits collection *Abba Gold*, which prompted revival in the band's fortunes during the 1990s and has sold in excess of 25 million copies.

■ *Main picture: Abba on stage at the 1974 Eurovision Song Contest, an annual televised event in which various European nations each performs a song, with the winner decided by a public phone vote. The event was inaugurated in 1956 in a spirit of European unity, and over the years has enlarged to include former Eastern-bloc countries, as well as Israel and Turkey. Left to right: Benny Anderson, Anni-Frid Lyngstad-Fredriksson, Björn Ulvaeus, and Agnetha Fältskog-Ulvaeus. Above: Anderson and Ulvaeus contemplate the mix of another pop hit later in the 1970s.*

The Rock Radio Revolution

In an effort to provide a refuge from the commerciality of AM pop radio, during the late 1960s a group of upstart U.S. broadcasters launched a succession of 'alternative' rock radio stations on the FM band, a frequency normally reserved for classical music and public-affairs programming.

Instead of the usual parade of Top 40 hits, stations such as Boston's WBCN, New York's WNEW, and San Francisco's KSAN aired obscure album cuts and works by lesser-known artists and gave equal time to lyrical content deemed unsuitable for mainstream radio. WBCN's Charles Laquidara, WNEW's Pete Fornatale, and KSAN's Tom Donahue weren't just DJs but bona fide heroes of the underground, who frequently aired their views on subjects ranging from the war in Vietnam to the presidency of Richard Nixon. Playlists were non-existent, and the improvisatory nature of the broadcasts was infectious. By the start of the 1970s the massive popularity of FM began to have a direct impact on the recording arts. One of the first bands to capitalize on the format was Led Zeppelin, whose music was specifically tailored to the burgeoning FM movement, defying the conventional wisdom that hit singles sold albums.

But, as the popularity of FM rock radio grew, stations found themselves in direct competition with one another and, eventually, began awarding air space to big-money advertisers such as McDonald's and Coca-Cola. By the mid 1970s the subversive nature of early FM had all but disappeared, replaced by the increasingly structured AOR format, as FM jocks became largely indistinguishable from the AM broadcasters they'd once rebelled against. By then rock'n'roll, for years the voice of the young and disenfranchized, was rapidly becoming the domain of the corporate consultant, who studied the demographics and installed rigid playlists that favored laidback acts along the lines of Fleetwood Mac and The Eagles. As the business of making rock became bigger, recording artists demanded and received fatter contracts and increasingly indulgent terms and conditions.

1970s Studio Excess

With cash – and cocaine – flowing freely during the early 1970s, major recording studios were given a plush facelift. Expensive lighting, fancy decor, fully equipped kitchens, and top-notch recreational facilities replaced the humble interiors of yesteryear. At the same time, studio owners began to rethink the layout of the recording space, the result of the latest innovation in tape technology: with 16-track – and soon to be 24-track – engineers could have a dedicated track for each band member for the first time. At the time, however, some of the industry's best studios still utilized large, open tracking-rooms that in many instances pre-dated the era of the multitrack. With all the instruments blending together as a result of the live environment, it didn't matter if there were 16 tracks or 160 tracks. Studio heads quickly realized that without addressing the issue their investment would be wasted.

"So, in a further attempt to really isolate the instruments, in order to take full advantage of the 16-track technology, they started to deaden the studios," recalls Chris Huston, studio designer and noted producer-engineer for Van Morrison, James Brown, The Who, and many others. "The idea was that, with that many tracks, you could really control things, you could create something by having the ability to isolate and replace entire sections of a song. That immediately became apparent to those in the recording industry. And in order to pull it off, you had to also re-think the way the studio was constructed, because up until that point you didn't have the wherewithal to really hone those parts individually. So, in turn, they began this new studio prototype: one where leakage could be maintained, if not completely eliminated. It was a tremendous change in the method of modern recording up to that point. And it turned everything on its tail."

Unfortunately, the redesign had the unintended affect of stripping away any innate room sound – an element that had played such a large part of the recording process for so many years. "When we were doing 4- and 8-track, I could listen to a record that was made in New York and tell you which studio it came from," says engineer Shelly Yakus.

Continued on page 183

1976

Frampton Comes Alive! **Peter Frampton**

A&M 3703 (U.S.A.) / A&M AMLM 63703 (U.K.)
Released January 1976

As 1975 unfolded, Peter Frampton, a British export based in the U.S.A., was a moderately successful 24-year-old solo artist in need of a commercial breakthrough.

A skilled songwriter whose winsome good looks belied an extraordinary lead-guitar talent, the ex-Humble Pie member arrived at San Francisco's Winterland Ballroom on the night of June 14th backed by a tight new band and sporting an assortment of road-tested songs from his back catalog. At showtime, engineer Chris Kimsey – who had worked with The Rolling Stones and Ten Years After – snapped on a multitrack tape machine backstage and hoped for a few good takes.

The resulting work, issued the following January as *Frampton Comes Alive!*, made the industry reassess the power of live recordings and made Frampton an icon overnight. Sporting superior versions of studio tracks 'Show Me The Way,' 'Somethin's Happening,' and 'Lines on My Face' – and showcasing Frampton's acoustic side as well – the double-disk *Frampton Comes Alive!* spent ten weeks at the top of *Billboard*'s album chart, spawned three hit singles, and sold eight million copies in its first year alone. The album's trump card was, and still is, the stadium-sized 'Do You Feel Like We Do?' an extract from 1973's *Frampton's Camel* that somehow blossomed into a rocker of epic proportions, aided in no small part by Frampton's powerful solo breaks and expert timing.

In hindsight it's not too difficult to understand why *Frampton Comes Alive!* became the single-biggest live album in history – or, in the estimation of Wayne Campbell from *Wayne's World*, an album so popular "it was delivered

in the mail along with samples of Tide." To his credit, Frampton understood the potential impact that a house full of unabashed – and uncoached – fans might have on the world at large if properly recorded. Of course, one can't create pandemonium in a vacuum – and to that end Frampton did his part by delivering some of the most melodic guitar work ever cut live. Eventually, the sound of 4,500 ecstatic Winterland fans was enough to convince 16 million record buyers that they were missing out on something huge.

It was a formula much too good to be ignored, and in the years that followed artists ranging from Bob Seger to Cheap Trick would follow the *Frampton Comes Alive!* blueprint all the way to the bank, even as Frampton himself was quickly unraveling from the experience. He eventually regained his composure in the 1980s and 1990s. Today, it's hard to get past Frampton's cheesecake cover photo, gimmicky talkbox work, and bizarre lyrics – "I have itchy fingers / And butterflies are strange" – yet, 30 years later *Frampton Comes Alive!*, which was repackaged in 2001 as a 'deluxe' CD set featuring four bonus tracks and an informative John McDermott essay, still sounds better than almost anything else that came out of that schizoid summer of 1976 and serves as a reminder of the magical possibilities that will always exist within the context of live performance.

Boston **Boston**

Epic BL34118 (U.S.A.) / EPC 81611 (U.K.)
Released February 1976

This is the story of how one man's musical obsession, a multitrack tape machine, and a home studio resulted in a multiplatinum record.

When the rock establishment in the U.K. was overthrown by punk in the mid-to-late 1970s, no such sweeping change took place in the U.S.A. There, the counter-culture rock of the late 1960s slowly mutated into AOR as its audience left their youth behind. A generation of musicians who'd grown up listening to blues-influenced hard rock, all riffs and solos, turned from revolution to rock's megawatt onslaught. One such was Tom Scholz, who had gained a Masters Degree in engineering at Massachusetts

and in his spare time put together a 12-track home studio. This background in electronics would eventually lead him into the field of inventing guitar effects-units such as the highly successful Rockman headphone amplifier.

A perfectionist and multi-instrumentalist, Scholz labored away, overdubbing parts until he reached a layered sound that was to influence profoundly the U.S. rock mainstream. In this process he was assisted by Barry Goudreau (guitar), Fran Sheehan (bass), Sib Hashian (drums), and Brad Delp (guitar and vocals). Scholz shaped heavy guitar riffs, amped-up old-time rock'n'roll, and short lead breaks with a pop sensibility, focusing on four-minute, verse-chorus songs that would appeal to a wide listenership with their straightforward lyrics. Scholz enthusiastically stacked vocal harmonies like The Eagles and created guitar choirs reminiscent of Queen. Legend has it that some of the home recordings ended up as the finished album.

The elegant punch of 'More Than A Feeling' is where everything cohered perfectly. A track best appreciated in its edited single form, it dusts off a few familiar chord progressions, adding for spice the lovely E-flat to E minor chord change heard between the chorus and guitar break. The melodic lead-guitar solo sounds as if it had escaped the mind of The Shadows' Hank Marvin in the early 1960s, lingering in the ether until Scholz made it the jewel in a more hi-tech musical crown. The rest of the album has a breezy, down-the-freeway vibe, though nothing matches the melodic strength of 'More Than A Feeling.'

For many years *Boston* was the biggest-selling debut album by a rock band in the U.S.A. Boston had created a radio-friendly, well-crafted sound that established certain rules for U.S. commercial rock. It persisted, in ever-more stifling form, for a decade until indie bands such as R.E.M. and the grunge explosion challenged and overthrew it – and, despite the persistence of a certain rumor, 'Smells Like Teen Spirit' does not have the same chords as 'More Than A Feeling,' though there is a rhythmic similarity which might be intentional irony on Kurt Cobain's part.

Scholz's perfectionism and periods of litigation combined to stretch out Boston's lifespan. *Don't Look Back* came out in 1978, *Third Stage* in 1986, and *Walk On* in 1994.

■ *Left: Peter Frampton on stage in 1976, using a talkbox to achieve the unusual vocal sound heard on* Frampton Comes Alive!

Continued from page 181

"When we went to 16-track, it was tougher, and when we went to 24 I couldn't tell anymore. The studios in New York all had distinctive sounds, a combination of the rooms, the equipment, and the main engineers. . . . I learned the sound of Bell, of A&R, of Mediasound, of Mira Sound. You could hear it on the radio. But it all went out the window with 24-track; 16 tracks on two-inch tape was as far as you could go and still maintain the personality of a room. The 24-track machines started to eat up the clarity of the instruments."

Once again, the ramp-up in recording technology helped shape the method of music making. Taking full advantage of the sophisticated multitrack machinery, in the U.K. art-rock groups such as Emerson, Lake & Palmer, Yes, and King Crimson issued lengthy, complex works built around layers of guitar, synthesizer, and carefully overdubbed vocals. The extended nature of albums such as Yes's double-disk opus *Tales From Topographic Oceans* (1974) was a far cry from the two-hits-eight-covers format of 1960s pop.

Funky Drumming And The Disco Explosion

During the 1960s the likes of Stevie Wonder and Marvin Gaye achieved stardom by creating pop music that easily crossed racial barriers. With the start of the 1970s, however, the sound of black America began to change rapidly. In early 1970 James Brown – the 'Godfather Of Soul' – released back-to-back singles, 'Funky Drummer' and 'Brother Rapp,' both built around long, repeating drum grooves that became the basis for funk, a highly rhythmic brand of soul music that would dominate the charts through the early part of the decade. Because most funk hits used the same tempo, dance-club DJs could segue from one song to the next without interruption, keeping the dance floor filled in the process. The phenomenon was not lost on record producers of the time, who began substituting an electronic-drum program in place of a real drummer. The machine-made drum track had an unpredictable – and explosive – side-affect. Unlike a real drummer – whose tempo may vary ever so slightly – a programmed drum track could keep the beat and hold it indefinitely, making it possible to assign an exact number of beats per minute for any given song. Before long, DJs were provided with special extended remixes of hit songs on 12-inch vinyl, each one bearing a 'BPM' designation. By matching songs according to their BPM, DJs could guarantee a virtually endless stream of dance music.

As it turns out, the dominant BPM of the decade – 120 – belonged to disco, a big, brassy synthesis of white pop and black rhythm popularized by mega-artists such as The Bee Gees and Donna Summer. Through to the end of the decade nearly every aspect of popular culture, from fashion trends to dance steps, were dictated by disco's unrelenting beat. Meanwhile, programmed drums and synthesizers were forming the basis for techno pop, spearheaded by Germany's Kraftwerk – whose hit 'Autobahn' became the first Top 40 record comprised entirely of electronic rhythms and instrumentation. Within a few years, the likes of The Human League, Soft Cell, and Yazoo (known as Yaz in the U.S.A.) were reaching the charts without the aid of a human drummer.

The Birth Of The Breakbeat

Not everyone was as enamored of the mechanized rhythms dominating the airwaves of the late 1970s, however. Just across the East River from Manhattan, a whole new sub-genre was brewing. Many Jamaicans had relocated to the Bronx during the early 1970s, and the neighborhoods were filled with the sounds of dub reggae, with improvised 'raps' over Jamaican recordings that poured forth from large, mobile sound systems. One such immigrant was a 22-year-old Bronx DJ named Kool Herc, who worked clubs and local parties using a pair of turntables, one microphone, a monstrous sound system, and a revolutionary new approach to spinning records. Herc discovered that dancers loved the long drum breaks on James Brown records. Using two copies of 'Funky Drummer,' Herc figured out a way to extend the drum passage indefinitely by 'cutting' back and forth between each disk. Herc's invention – which he called the 'breakbeat' – set in motion the events which would form the basis for rap.

Like Herc, young Joseph Saddler began his own career in the mid 1970s spinning records at block parties and dance clubs around the Bronx. But Saddler – aka Grandmaster Flash – wasn't your average kid with two turntables and a microphone. Manipulating the disks with a free hand, the teenage DJ devised a method for 'performing' the mixes, using cutting and other techniques that added a rhythmic flair to the non-stop stream of dance grooves. Additionally, Flash's stage show included a team of poetic 'MCs' – whom he later dubbed the 'Furious Five' – including soon-to-be rap stars Melle Mel and Kid Creole. The MCs introduced a completely new approach

Continued on page 185

1976

Hotel California **The Eagles**

Asylum 1084 (U.S.A.) / K/K4 53051 (U.K.)
Released December 1976

The Eagles were one of the most popular U.S. groups of the 1970s. *Their Greatest Hits*, released in early 1976, is one of the biggest-selling albums of all time in the U.S.A., having sold over 25 million copies, and set the stage perfectly for *Hotel California*.

The Eagles came together in 1971, having previously served as part of Linda Ronstadt's backing group. Indeed, all of the founding members of The Eagles were experienced country-rock session musicians before achieving fame in their own right. Vocalist and guitarist Bernie Leadon had been a member of former Byrd Gene Clark's group Dillard And Clark and one of Gram Parson's Flying Burrito Brothers, while bassist Randy Meisner had served in Rick Nelson's band; drummer-backing vocalist Don Henley had issued one album with his group Shiloh, and guitarists Glenn Frey and Don Felder had performed with Bob Seger and Stephen Stills respectively.

The musicians were encouraged to form The Eagles by Ronstadt's manager, John Boylan, who then found the group a deal with David Geffen's recently formed Asylum label. An eponymous debut established The Eagles' sound in 1972, a highly polished update of the country-and-folk-tinged rock that had begun to emerge from the West Coast of the U.S.A. in the late 1960s.

After making the concept album *Desperado* in 1973 The Eagles topped the U.S. pop singles chart with 'The Best Of My Love,' taken from the group's third full-length release, *On The Border* (1974). That single's success set the stage for their mainstream breakthrough, which they achieved with the following year's *One Of These Nights*, the group's first U.S. chart-topping album.

> ## "['HOTEL CALIFORNIA'] SORT OF CAPTURED THE ZEITGEIST OF THE TIME, WHICH WAS A TIME OF GREAT EXCESS IN THIS COUNTRY, AND IN THE MUSIC BUSINESS IN PARTICULAR."
> ### *DON HENLEY, LOOKING BACK ON THE SONG IN 1995*

By the time The Eagles released the phenomenally successful retrospective set *Their Greatest Hits*, Bernie Leadon, the chief country influence in the group, had quit. He was replaced by Joe Walsh, a heavy rock guitarist, known at the time both as a solo artist and member of The James Gang. While Walsh brought a more commercial rock edge to the group, it was drummer Don Henley who took over as the chief creative figure and lead vocalist from 1975 onward.

Henley wrote six of the nine songs that feature on *Hotel California*, including the famous title track. As on that song, most of his compositions paint California – and the U.S.A. in general – as a troubled, nihilistic land, on the verge of collapse under the weight of its own decadence. The album details, but also makes pains to disapprove of, the various excesses to which a popular rock group in the 1970s might succumb.

The Eagles spent the bulk of the time between the releases of *Their Greatest Hits* and *Hotel California* in the studio, perfecting the songs that would be included on the latter album. This lengthy gestation can be attributed both to the fact that they were conscious of how great a

launching pad the success of *Their Greatest Hits* was – and so wanted to ensure they made the most of that opportunity – and the knowledge that they had to formulate new working methods in the wake of Leadon's departure.

The Eagles maintained their trademark vocal-harmony style, but where some of the group's earlier work tended toward a pastoral, folksy feel, they now, with the addition of Walsh, had a solid, powerful sound more in tune with the commercial rock of the era.

Hotel California was recorded between March and October 1976 at Criteria Studios in Miami, Florida, and The Record Plant in Los Angeles. The album was produced by Bill Szymczyk, who had previously worked with artists including B.B. King and The J. Geils Band as well as recording all of The Eagles' albums since *Desperado*.

Sessions for *Hotel California* were strained and drawn out at times, particularly when it came to recording the title song. They had spent several months working in vain on 'Hotel California' until Felder, who came up with the song's distinctive 12-string guitar intro, decided that the group should try to recapture the spirit of an earlier demo recording. Remembering that the demo in question was at his home, Felder telephoned his cleaner, asking her to play the recording down the line to the group so that they could reacquaint themselves with their earlier performance.

Hotel California achieved gold status in the U.S.A. after its first week on sale in December 1976, selling over 500,000 copies. It rose to Number One on the U.S. *Billboard* albums chart the following month and peaked at Number Two in the U.K. The album has since sold over 20 million copies worldwide, 16 million in the U.S.A. alone. At the 1977 Grammy Awards it was named Album Of The Year, with Szymczyk winning the producers' award.

The first single to be drawn from the album was 'New Kid In Town,' which topped the U.S. chart and reached Number 20 in the U.K. This was followed by *Hotel California*'s six-and-a-half minute title track, now regarded as an all-time classic rock single. 'Hotel California' is built around a slightly reggae-tinged drum rhythm – likely

Continued from page 183

inspired by Bob Marley's *Rastaman Vibration*, which had in 1976 become the first hit reggae album in the U.S.A. – and the dueling lead-guitar parts, played by Walsh and Felder.

For such a commercially successful song Henley's lyrics are strangely opaque, describing a hotel that "could be heaven or . . . hell," and from which guests can never escape. Like 'New Kid In Town,' 'Hotel California' topped the U.S. singles chart, giving The Eagles the fourth of five career Number One hits – the others being 'Best Of My Love,' 'One Of These Nights,' 'New Kid In Town,' and 'Heartache Tonight.'

In the wake of the vast success of *Their Greatest Hits* and *Hotel California*, bassist Randy Meisner left to embark on a solo career, but The Eagles maintained their popularity with *The Long Run* (1979) and *Eagles Live* (1980) before deciding to disband in 1981.

All five members of the group continued to make records throughout the 1980s and 1990s before reuniting in 1994 for the live album *Hell Freezes Over*. The group's high standing in popular music was confirmed in 1998 when The Eagles were inducted into the Rock'n'Roll Hall Of Fame.

■ *The Eagles perform in London, England, in April 1977, in support of their bestselling album* Hotel California. *Left to right: Rick Meisner, Don Felder, Glenn Frey, and Joe Walsh.*

to rapping by trading verses at will and working out meticulously coordinated routines. They were an immediate sensation in the dance clubs of New York. At a time when both rock- and disco-album production had become bloated and unimaginative, rap was unique, a homemade art form comprised almost entirely of 'borrowed' ingredients. More important, rap became a forum for urban musicians who were unable to afford major-label studio time or expensive instruments. Kurtis Blow's 1980 hit 'The Breaks' underscored rap's street appeal: though it barely cracked the pop charts, the legendary track still sold a million copies in New York City alone. Within a few years, rap had become a mainstream phenomenon, thanks in large part to the worldwide acceptance of hip-hop artists such as Run-DMC and Public Enemy.

The automated rhythms and instruments that were the lifeblood of rap, techno, and other genres of the late 1970s, however, further reduced the element of live studio performance. Combined with the industry's insatiable demand for track space, over the next several years the recording business continued its rapid transformation. Albums such as Steely Dan's *Aja* (1977) typified the changed environment. As Brian Wilson had done with The Beach Boys recordings a decade earlier, Steely Dan leaders Donald Fagen and Walter Becker cut tracks using a small army of virtuoso session players, among them guitarist Larry Carlton and drummer Bernard Purdie. Unlike Wilson, however, tunes such as 'Deacon Blues' and 'Josie' were assembled block by block, with an obsessive attention to detail – the finished work was apparently remixed at least a dozen times before the duo authorized its release. Though smartly packaged and brimming with top-flight jazz rock, to many listeners – and more than a few critics – the perfectionism that was at the core of *Aja* was somewhat off-putting.

1977

David Bowie Low

RCA 2030 (U.S.A.) / PL/PK 12030 (U.K.)
Released January 1977

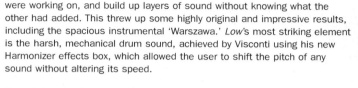

At the height of punk in the U.K., David Bowie was one of the few acceptable faces of the old guard, and the first two albums in his so-called 'Berlin trilogy,' _Low_ and _"Heroes,"_ had a huge impact on much of the synthesizer pop that would follow them.

Though David Bowie had reached his mid-1970s peak with the international hit albums _Young Americans_ and _Station To Station_, his personal life was in turmoil, brought on by the collapse of his marriage and a growing drug dependency. With that in mind Bowie moved to Berlin with his friend Iggy Pop in 1976, purportedly to clean up. There he immersed himself in Germany's burgeoning music scene, taking a particular liking to Neu! and Kraftwerk, who had already started to impact on the Bowie sound on _Station To Station_'s epic title track.

Having worked during the summer on Iggy's _The Idiot_, Bowie decamped, on September 1st, to Château d'Hérouville Studios just outside Paris to begin work on _Low_ with producer Tony Visconti. Also present at the sessions was art rock pioneer Brian Eno, formerly of Roxy Music, whose 1975 solo album _Another Green World_ was another big influence on _Low_. Making use of numerous new synthesizers, including the Mini-Moog, Bowie and Eno soon instituted some curious recording methods. For example, they would enter the studio separately, turn down all but the rhythm tracks of the song they were working on, and build up layers of sound without knowing what the other had added. This threw up some highly original and impressive results, including the spacious instrumental 'Warszawa.' _Low_'s most striking element is the harsh, mechanical drum sound, achieved by Visconti using his new Harmonizer effects box, which allowed the user to shift the pitch of any sound without altering its speed.

Bowie's label RCA was, by all accounts, horrified when presented with _Low_; the label's head is said to have offered Bowie a house in Philadelphia if only he would, please, record another album in the vein of _Young Americans_. While _Low_ was clearly the most experimental release of his career thus far, the first side of the album is made up of fairly conventional songs, and provided Bowie with another international hit single, 'Sound And Vision.' More problematic to the record company was the almost entirely instrumental second side, then highly unusual on a pop record by an established star. Perhaps symbolically, this farewell to the first commercial phase of his career was issued the week after Bowie's 30th birthday, its striking cover image – the artist in profile, taken from the movie _The Man Who Fell To Earth_, in which he had starred – a marked contrast to the extravagant sleeves of his earlier albums. _Low_ has become the most admired recording in the Bowie catalog, and has influenced numerous musicians since, from the electro-pop stars of the early 1980s to Trent Reznor of Nine Inch Nails. The success of _Low_ has also inspired other acts to take similar stylistic sidesteps at the height of their commercial appeal, including Talk Talk and Radiohead.

Several months after the release of _Low_, which peaked at Number Two in the U.K. and reached the U.S. Top Ten, Bowie was back in the studio, this time at Hansa Studios, situated right next to the Berlin Wall, to record _"Heroes."_ Again working alongside Eno and Visconti, Bowie also recruited King Crimson's Robert Fripp, who provides the searing lead-guitar part on the title track, one of the most memorable of all Bowie's recordings. _"Heroes"_ is both a refinement and a more extreme version of _Low_: the first, song-based side is snappier, while the second-half's instrumental material is more obtuse than anything on its predecessor. Bowie completed his Berlin trilogy with the less successful _Lodger_ in 1979.

■ **Below: rather than promote Low, David Bowie chose to go out on tour, incognito, as the keyboardist in Iggy Pop's band.**

My Aim Is True **Elvis Costello**

Columbia JC 35037 (U.S.A.) / Stiff SEEZ/ZSEEZ 3 (U.K.)
Released August 1977

Issued at the height of punk, *My Aim Is True* established Costello as one of the enduring talents of the era.

Born Declan McManus, Elvis Costello signed to the independent label Stiff Records in 1977 and promptly started work on his debut album, ditching his country-rock backing group in the process. Stiff paired him with producer Nick Lowe and the U.S. rock quintet Clover – here called Shamrock – two of whom would go on to found Huey Lewis And The News. Lowe was, at the time, the in-house producer at Stiff, having helmed numerous albums since the label's inception – of particular note is The Damned's *Damned Damned Damned*, the first British punk album.

However, *My Aim Is True* is not a punk album. While Costello's vitriolic lyrics and sneering vocal drew comparisons with punk acts, his music demonstrated an awareness and acceptance of rock history. There is a hint of the folksy singer-songwriter in the album's ballads, including the single 'Alison,' while 'Watching The Detectives' has a reggae beat. *My Aim Is True* was released in an eye-catching sleeve, designed by Barney Bubbles, with a photograph of a pigeon-toed, bespectacled Costello, looking more like the computer programmer McManus had once been than the rock star Costello was to become.

Aja **Steely Dan**

A.B.C. 1006 (U.S.A.) / ABCL/+C 5225 (U.K.)
Released September 1977

Steely Dan is not your typical rock band. For a start, there are only two permanent members of the group, the songwriting duo of Donald Fagen and Walter Becker, who formed Steely Dan as a reaction against the huge-selling soft-rock groups of the era.

Aesthetically, Becker and Fagen's albums stood apart from most of their contemporaries, particularly in 1977, in that they were always immaculately produced and full of musical complexity. *Aja* captures the group at its critical and commercial peak. Becker and Fagen did initially operate within the confines of the traditional rock band, recording and touring the albums *Can't Buy A Thrill* (1972) and *Countdown To Ecstasy* (1973) with a permanent drummer, guitarist, and vocalist. However, the duo became disillusioned with that line-up and with life on the road, which led to the break up of the original five-piece, leaving Becker and Fagen to concentrate exclusively on studio work.

Somewhat surprisingly, given that they refused to tour it, *Pretzel Logic* (1974) was the duo's greatest success to date, thanks in no small part to

the inclusion of the biggest hit single of their career, 'Rikki Don't Lose Than Number,' which peaked at Number Four in the U.S.A. *Pretzel Logic* introduced a more pronounced jazz edge to Steely Dan's music, which became more apparent on *Katy Lied* (1975) and *The Royal Scam* (1976). On these albums Becker and Fagen had begun to draw on a pool of impressive session musicians in their attempts to produce the slickest, most densely layered recordings possible.

Work started on *Aja* in the latter part of 1976 at Village Recorders in Los Angeles and a number of other studios in and around Hollywood. Writing about the album retrospectively, *Rolling Stone* magazine called *Aja* "music so technically demanding its creators had to call in a-list session players to realize the sounds they heard in their heads but could not play." Where Steely Dan's earlier works had been mostly guitar based, on *Aja* the songs are led by swathes of keyboards and saxophone. The sessioneers in question included Wayne Shorter, best known as the saxophonist in the second great Miles Davis quintet during the mid-to-late 1960s.

Aja is a rich, textured album, and one that was often used in electrical stores to demonstrate the capabilities of new hi-fi systems. Though the performances are full of complex musical flourishes, the songs on *Aja* are simpler and more immediate than on previous Steely Dan albums. The net result of this was that *Aja* is the most successful album of the group's career, reaching Number Three in the U.S.A. – where it was among the first albums to be awarded the newly founded platinum status – and Number Five in the U.K. It spawned a trio of U.S. hit singles, 'Peg,' 'Deacon Blues,' and 'Josie,' and even earned the respect of the jazz world, resulting in an album of covers of Becker and Fagen songs by Woody Herman. Legal wrangling between the label ABC and its new parent company MCA stalled the release of a follow-up. Becker and Fagen took a 20-year break from recording together after *Gaucho* (1980), but made a successful return in 2000 with the multiple Grammy Award-winning *Two Against Nature*.

Heavy Weather **Weather Report**

Columbia 34418 (U.S.A.) / CBS 81775 (U.K.)
Released March 1977

The definitive jazz supergroup of the 1970s, Weather Report played a concise, melodic form of the jazz-rock fusion that had emerged in the late 1960s.

The group was formed in 1971 by the composer and keyboardist Joe Zawinul and saxophonist Wayne Shorter, fresh from their work on Miles Davis's epochal albums *In A Silent Way* (1969) and *Bitches Brew* (1970). At the time of *Heavy Weather*, the group's seventh album, Weather Report also featured bassist Jaco Pastorius, drummer Alex Acuna, and percussionist Manolo Badrena.

By this stage, Zawinul had begun to experiment with cutting-edge synthesizer technologies. Moving away from the more traditional Fender Rhodes electric piano, Zawinul worked with an ARP 2600 – originally conceived as an entry-level keyboard for synthesizer novices – and a more complex Oberheim Polyphonic synthesizer, which also has the capacity for creating and storing eight-note sequences that could be repeated at the user's will.

Buoyed by Zawinul's synthesizer playing, the eight short songs – short at least by the standards of jazz fusion – have a warm, smooth feel that helped propel *Heavy Weather* up the U.S. pop charts, where the album peaked at Number 30. Recorded at Devonshire Sound Studios in North Hollywood, California, *Heavy Weather* opens with Zawinul's 'Birdland,' which has since become a jazz standard, and has been covered by numerous other artists, including the vocal quartet Manhattan Transfer. Another highlight is Shorter's frantic 'Palladium.' Demonstrating that Weather Report was not just about Shorter and Zawinul, *Heavy Weather* also includes compositions by the group's other members, among them Pastorius's 'Teen Town,' with its infectious disco beat.

1977

Never Mind The Bollocks Sex Pistols

Warner Brothers 3142 (U.S.A.) / Virgin V2086 (U.K.)
Released November 1977

This is *the* seminal punk album, where British rock rediscovered its energy. On its much-anticipated release it seemed a blast of untrammeled anarchy, setting fire to a music scene that, by 1976, was a dank mixture of chart bubblegum, the dregs of glam rock, and the lofty dinosaur bands of prog.

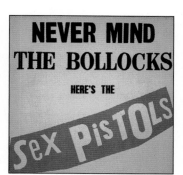

The Pistols, with help from manager Malcolm McLaren, were the most dramatic expression of punk's do-it-yourself ethic, and represented a genuine youth rebellion in contrast to the plastic version offered by supposed teen acts such as The Bay City Rollers. The first paradox is that musically The Sex Pistols were not new but grounded in 1950s rock'n'roll and 1960s garage rock; the second is that, for all its snarling nihilism, *Never Mind The Bollocks* is riotous fun.

It came suitably attired in a lurid pink and yellow sleeve unlike anything else in the racks. The prominent use of 'bollocks' led to shops refusing to display it, nor could it be advertised on television. It contains four Pistols hits: 'Anarchy In The U.K.' (the first significant punk single, at least as far as the wider public was concerned, though The Damned's 'New Rose' got there first), 'Pretty Vacant,' 'Holidays In The Sun' (with its goose-stepping intro), and 'God Save The Queen.' An incendiary rock single, 'God Save The Queen' was released to coincide with Queen Elizabeth II's silver jubilee – an occasion of great pomp and circumstance – and it made a big noise on

a small island, cementing The Pistols' reputation as Public Enemies Numbers One To Four. The single was originally to be put out on A&M but withdrawn, then issued by Virgin after the band had been signed by Richard Branson. The problems with A&M and an earlier bust-up with EMI were immortalized on the album's closing track, 'EMI.' Other cuts include the incoherent abortion horror-show 'Bodies,' the sinister 'Submission,' the sarcastic 'Liar,' and the hilariously knuckle-headed 'Seventeen,' with its refrain, "I'm a lazy sod."

The Pistols' sound had two main ingredients. The first was Johnny Rotten's vocal style, one of the most recognizable in rock history. Like Dylan, his refusal to pitch conventionally expressed rebellion, and the off-key sneering comes across powerfully, displaying a knack for forcing a note that doesn't fit against the underlying chord, as with the era-defining phrase "we mean it, maann" from 'God Save The Queen.' The lyrics are given further force by sarcastic touches such as the rolled 'r' in 'moron' and the pseudo-exultant exclamation of 'money,' touches that fitted Rotten's spiky-haired Artful Dodger persona. The second ingredient was Steve Jones's multitracked guitar onslaught. The semitone shifts for many of the riffs stem from such rock'n'roll influences as Eddie Cochran, and Jones recycled Chuck Berry lead breaks on a Les Paul played through an overdriven Vox AC30 amplifier with only one speaker working. By way of example, the lead solo on 'God Save The Queen' is not far removed from Brian May's Berry homage on Queen's 'Now I'm Here' (1974) – but the intent is entirely different.

It was a long time since a band had played with such ferocity, The Pistols' attitude giving what was left of the legacy of the 1960s a good kicking. This band wasn't interested in peace and love; it wasn't even interested in longevity or taking their rebellion any farther, and *Never Mind The Bollocks* is the only proper studio album The Sex Pistols completed, the band's fate sealed after Rotten left in January 1978 at the end of their one and only U.S. tour.

After Rotten's departure Sid Vicious – who, despite being perhaps the best-remembered and most iconic bandmember today, even though he played on almost no recordings – became the focus of what was left of the group until they finally fell apart.

■ *Below (left to right): Glen Matlock, Johnny Rotten, and Steve Jones.*

Talking Heads 77 **Talking Heads**

Sire 9103 328 (U.S.A.) / 9103 328 (U.K.)
Released October 1977

Marquee Moon **Television**

Elektra 7E-1098 (U.S.A.) / K52046 (U.K.)
Released February 1977

The New York new wave was a markedly different beast from its British offspring, punk rock. Punk focused heavily on just two elements of the New York scene, specifically the simplistic energy of The Ramones and the fashion sense of Richard Hell, using the former as a musical manifesto and the latter as a style template.

Meanwhile, back in the Big Apple, bands falling under the new-wave umbrella were about as musically diverse as it was possible to be, sharing little other than their emergence in the same time and place. The romantic Hispanic rock of Mink De Ville bore little resemblance to, for example, the trashy pop ethic of Blondie, and the two bands who formed the vanguard, Television and Talking Heads, were both different again.

The Lower East Side art rock of Talking Heads, with its staggered rhythms and sudden tempo changes, seemed a deliberate rejection of earlier rock

structures. The guitars were tuned oddly, David Byrne's singing was self-consciously strained, the lyrics didn't always rhyme and often sounded like the incoherent babble of asylum inmates. Byrne has explained his oblique approach to the lyric of *Talking Heads 77*'s signature song, 'Psycho Killer,' by saying that he intended it "to be like Randy Newman doing Alice Cooper. One way of telling the story would be to describe everything that happens – 'He walks across the room, he takes so many steps, he's wearing such-and-such.' That tells you everything that's going on, on one level, but it really doesn't involve you emotionally. The other extreme is to describe everything as a series of sensations. I think that sometimes has more power, and affects people a little stronger."

Television wrote punchy, concise lyrics that sounded as if they might have come from a Mike Hammer pulp detective novel, and conjured up dark, sinister atmospheres through the interplay of the guitars of Richard Lloyd and Tom Verlaine. By all accounts their early gigs were appallingly bad, but they persevered. "Television rehearsed for six to seven days a week for four to six hours a day," says Lloyd. "We were both really roughshod musicians on one hand, and desperadoes on the other, with the will to become good." By the time of Marquee Moon, their rhythms were tight and choppy and their coruscating, mercurial lead lines frequently recalled the heyday of San Francisco acid rock, as did the extended lengths of their improvisations.

Producer Andy Johns, who'd previously worked on *Goat's Head Soup* for The Rolling Stones, remembers Television as a hard band to fathom. "My first impression was that they couldn't play and couldn't sing and the music was very bizarre. But after we finished mixing, we went to some rehearsal place and played it on these large speakers, and I was bowled over." The centerpiece of *Marquee Moon* is the epic title track, a U.K. hit single despite its ten-minute running time. It was Talking Heads, however, who proved themselves able to change and adapt with the times, becoming one of the most successful bands of the 1980s, while Television, who initially looked a much safer bet for long-term stardom, rapidly crashed and burned amid serious ego clashes.

■ *Above: Talking Heads on stage in London, England in late 1976, just prior to the release of their debut album.*

1977

Bat Out Of Hell
Meat Loaf

Epic 34974 (U.S.A.) / EPC/40 82419 (U.K.)
Released October 1977 (U.S.A.) / January 1978 (U.K.)

One of the biggest selling albums of the 1970s, *Bat Out Of Hell*, contains some of the most extravagant, operatic rock music ever recorded.

Born Marvin Lee Aday in Dallas, Texas, in 1947, the powerful singer Meat Loaf acquired his nickname at a young age on account of his sizeable figure. In the late 1960s he moved to Los Angeles and fronted the psychedelic rock group Popcorn

Blizzard, who opened for the likes of The Who and Ted Nugent in 1967 and 1968. Meat Loaf quit the group in 1969, and for much of the next decade concentrated his energies on appearing in a number of high-profile musical roles in Los Angeles and on Broadway, though he did find time to record the album *Stoney & Meat Loaf* (1971) with the female soul singer Stoney, for Motown Records' Rare Earth subsidiary. This period of Meat Loaf's career is best known for his performance as Eddy – on stage and screen – in the *Rocky Horror Picture Show* (1975).

While working in musicals Meat Loaf began an association with the songwriter and producer Jim Steinman. A classically trained pianist, Steinman wrote the musical *More Than You Deserve*, in which Meat Loaf starred, before the pair began touring the U.S.A. as part of the *National Lampoon Show* in 1976. That year Meat Loaf made his first serious foray into the rock'n'roll world, lending his immense vocal presence to half of the songs on his old friend Ted Nugent's *Free For All*.

In 1977 Meat Loaf and Steinman started work on an ambitious musical album project, *Neverland*, based on the story of *Peter Pan*, for which the duo signed a development deal with the label RCA. When they objected to Steinman's choice of Todd Rundgren as producer, he and Meat Loaf left the label and signed instead with Epic. By this stage the *Neverland* songs had mutated into a new project, *Bat Out Of Hell*.

Meat Loaf, Steinman, and Rundgren recorded *Bat Out Of Hell* in the summer of 1977 with a group of accomplished session players, most notably

drummer Max Weinberg, a member of Bruce Springsteen's E Street Band. There is a suggestion of Springsteen's music in both the piano playing and the narrative songwriting style of *Bat Out Of Hell*, particularly in titles such as 'All Revved Up With No Place To Go.' The album also draws on the pomp and circumstance of Richard Wagner, and includes lavish arrangements conducted by The New York Philharmonic Orchestra's Gene Orloff.

Befitting an album of such ostentatious ambition, *Bat Out Of Hell* was recorded at a number of studios on the East Coast. Most of the songs were cut at Bearsville Sound and The Hit Factory, both in New York, with some additional tracking at Rundgren's own Utopia Sound, also in New York, and House Of Music in West Orange, New Jersey. No stranger to epic, overblown productions on his own solo works, the multi-instrumentalist Rundgren colors Steinman's already vast compositions with a widescreen sonic backdrop that jumps effortlessly from ferocious, apocalyptic hard rock to extravagant show tunes.

There are only seven songs on *Bat Out Of Hell*, but any fears that the listener is being short-changed are allayed by the fact that three of them are close to ten minutes long. *Bat Out Of Hell* threatens to collapse under the weight of its own bombast at times, particularly on the album's most infamous moment, midway through the three-part 'Paradise By The Dashboard Light,' when baseball announcer Phil Rizzuto is called in to provide a brief interlude of commentary that serves as a hilarious extended sexual metaphor.

The most striking elements of *Bat Out Of Hell*, however, are the vocals. Meat Loaf possesses a voice that could match Steinman's grandiose, theatrical compositions. Drawing on his stage experience, Meat Loaf is simply as close as rock music gets to opera. His voice isn't to everybody's taste, however: the *Rolling Stone* review of *Bat Out Of Hell* concluded that "his phrasing is way too stage-struck to make the album's pretensions to comic-book street life real. He needs a little less *West Side Story* and a little more Bruce Springsteen." This was a commonly held view among many critics, who thought *Bat Out Of Hell* was simply too overblown.

Given the album's enormous sales to date, initial chart placings were relatively modest – it entered the U.S. albums chart at Number 14 on its release and reached Number 9 in the U.K. early the following year – but began seriously to pick up momentum over the course of 1978. (In the U.K., the defining moment in Meat Loaf's rise to stardom was a show-stopping performance of the nine-minute title track on the influential television music program *The Old Grey Whistle Test*, which proved so popular that it was shown again the following week, despite its length.) The album's popularity grew on the strength of a series of epic singles, including the title track and 'Paradise By The Dashboard Light.' By 2004 *Bat Out Of Hell* had sold over 34 million copies worldwide, with sales of 16 million in the U.S.A. alone, placing it among the five bestselling albums of all time. It also spent 474 weeks on the U.K. charts, just 3 weeks short of the record of 477, held by Fleetwood Mac's *Rumours*. Until the release of Alanis Morissette's *Jagged Little Pill* in 1995, it was the bestselling U.S. debut of all time.

Bat Out Of Hell continues to shift an average of 200,000 copies per year, and as such is perennially one of the strongest-selling back-catalog albums by any artist. This can partly be attributed to the various different editions that have been released over time. The album sold strongly when it was first issued on CD in 1983, and was given a new lease on life when the singer recorded *Bat Out Of Hell II: Back Into Hell* in 1993. While this second volume of collaborations between Steinman and Meat Loaf – who had not worked together since falling out while making *Dead Ringer* (1981) – sat at Number One around the world, the original *Bat Out Of Hell* re-entered the U.K. chart at Number 19. In 2002 Epic issued a remastered edition in the high quality SACD format, while two years later Meat Loaf recorded *Bat Out Of Hell Live: With The Melbourne Symphony Orchestra*, which is exactly what its title suggests, the original album performed in its entirety, live on stage with a full orchestra.

Saturday Night Fever **(Original Soundtrack)**

R.S.O. 4001 (U.S.A.) / 2658 123 (U.K.)
Released November 1977

One of the biggest movies of the 1970s, *Saturday Night Fever* introduced disco to the mainstream and made John Travolta a superstar. The accompanying soundtrack album was even more successful, spending 24 weeks at Number One in the U.S.A.

The movie was based on a 1975 *New York* magazine article about the New York disco scene, 'Tribal Rites Of The New Saturday Night,' by the British rock writer Nik Cohn. (Two decades later it emerged that Cohn had invented most of the details in his article – including the character of Vincent, who was the inspiration for Tony Manero, the Travolta character in the movie – after spending a dull, uneventful weekend hanging around in New York clubs.)

The album was dominated by The Bee Gees, and marked the peak of the second and most memorable phase of the group's career across four decades. British-born brothers Barry, Maurice, and Robin Gibb began their musical journey as The Bee Gees in their adopted homeland of Australia in the early 1960s, but returned to the U.K. by the time their 'Spicks And Specks' topped the Australian singles chart in 1967. The Bee Gees had ten more Beatles-inspired hits in Britain and the U.S.A. over the next two years, but the brothers' careers began to slip in the 1970s. The group's fortunes began to improve when they issued the disco-inspired *Children Of The World* (1976), which led to them being asked to contribute to the *Saturday Night Fever* soundtrack. While it does contain songs by other artists, notably Kool And The Gang and KC And The Sunshine Band, *Saturday Night Fever* is generally considered to be a Bee Gees album. The group performs half of the album's songs, while several others – 'If I Can't Have You,' recorded by Yvonne Elliman, and the classic 'More Than A Woman,' sung by Tavares – were written by the Gibbs. In that respect, *Saturday Night Fever* demonstrates that, as well as being a phenomenally successful act in their own right, The Bee Gees were also among the dominant pop songwriters of the era.

Both album and movie open with a Bee Gees' song that has come to encapsulate the entire disco era, 'Stayin' Alive,' which already sat atop the U.S. singles chart when *Saturday Night Fever* opened at movie houses across the U.S.A. (The track showcases the falsetto vocals that have subsequently become the group's trademark style and which were used on this album for the first time.) The soundtrack album spawned two further Number One hits for them, 'Night Fever' and 'How Deep Is Your Love?'

Most of The Bee Gees' songs included on *Saturday Night Fever* had been written before the brothers had been approached to contribute to the movie soundtrack, and they had been intended for the follow-up to *Children Of The World*. They were recorded with the Turkish producer Arif Mardin, who had played a key role in establishing Atlantic Records, producing many of the label's biggest acts in the 1960s and 1970s. Mardin had previously worked on The Bee Gees' *Mr Natural* (1974), and had been largely responsible for shifting the group's sound away from 1960s pop toward soul and disco.

Saturday Night Fever topped the charts on its release in both the U.S.A. and the U.K., and has since shifted over 25 million copies worldwide, making it the most successful movie-soundtrack album of all time and re-establishing The Bee Gees among the pre-eminent stars of the pop scene. In 1999 *Saturday Night Fever* was recast as a stage musical in London to great success.

1977

Fleetwood Mac
Rumours

Warner Bros 3010 (U.S.A.) / K56344 (U.K.)
Released February 1977

Rumours went platinum within a month of release and is now approaching 20-times platinum – but these staggering sales figures reveal only a small part of the album's significance in rock history.

Technically, this classic album pushed production standards up to new levels, and, musically, it raised the stakes in terms of song quality, performance, and meticulous attention to detail. It was also the album where the artists' real lives became virtually indistinguishable from the songs they were singing. This had happened before, with The Mamas & The Papas, and it would happen again with Abba, but *Rumours* was the moment when the phenomenon of confessional pop-song writing really captured the imagination of the record-buying public.

Fleetwood Mac had started life in the mid-1960s as a British blues quartet, later becoming a quintet, and had the competition beaten hollow until their brilliant songwriter-guitarist, Peter Green, went off the rails. After other personnel hiccups – including the religious conversion of guitarist Jeremy Spencer and the declining mental health of another guitarist, Danny Kirwan – they relocated to California, where they noodled around for several years until drummer Mick Fleetwood heard the album *Buckingham-Nicks* by

aspiring songwriters Lindsay Buckingham and Stevie Nicks. Fleetwood invited them to join the band, and the first album with this new line-up, *Fleetwood Mac*, took off like a rocket. On February 15th 1976 they began recording the follow-up, *Rumours*, at the Record Plant, Sausalito, California.

"The Record Plant was this amazing hippy place," recalls Stevie Nicks. "We like to say we were all hippies but, in the beginning, we really weren't. But we went up to this incredible studio, which was all decorated with Indian saris and beautiful colors, there were little hippy girls everywhere making cookies. It was such a beautiful thing. You walked in and you were like, 'Aaaaah! I love this place.'"

Regrettably, however, the band had brought their own snakes into this hippy garden of paradise, because the two romantic relationships in the band, Buckingham and Nicks and John and Christine McVie, were rapidly disintegrating. The first thing they had to do was work out how to continue functioning as professionals when their personal lives had become seething cauldrons of disappointment, mistrust, and anger. "There was pain, there was confusion," says Buckingham, "and it all added up to make *Rumours* a soap opera on vinyl."

The bandage they used to cover their open sores was work. "We had two alternatives," explains Christine McVie. "Go our own ways and see the band collapse, or grit our teeth and carry on playing with each other. Normally, when couples split they don't have to see each other again. We were forced to get over those differences." This need to maintain the band trapped them in an environment where they were precluded from expressing publicly, or even privately, their true feelings. Almost inevitably, their emotional turmoil found its way into the songs.

Bassist John McVie was not a songwriter, so Christine's eloquently regretful reflections on their crumbling marriage, 'Don't Stop,' 'Songbird,' and 'Oh Daddy,' have no response from him. "I'd be sitting there in the studio while they were mixing 'Don't Stop,'" he reflects, "and I'd listen to

■ *Main picture: Christine McVie. Above right: Mick Fleetwood. Below right: Stevie Nicks.*

the words, which were mostly about me, and I'd get a lump in my throat. I'd turn around and the writer's sitting right there."

Buckingham and Nicks, however, were both songwriters, and their compositions effectively became substitutes for conversations they should have been having. "When we were writing and recording these songs," says Nicks, "I don't think we really thought about what the lyrics were saying. It was only later down the line that Lindsey did come to question the lyric of my song 'Dreams,' and my answer was that it was my counterpart to 'Go Your Own Way.'"

"The spark for that song," admits Buckingham, "was that Stevie and I were crumbling. It was totally autobiographical."

Mick Fleetwood remembers Stevie being particularly upset by the words "crackin' up, shackin' up" being directed at her by Lindsey through his song. For her part, Nicks felt that 'Dreams' was much more empathetic than 'Go Your Own Way.' "In my heart," she told him, "'Dreams' was open and hopeful, but in 'Go Your Own Way,' your heart was closed."

As well as their personal problems, they soon found that the Record Plant was a strange place in which to work. There was a sunken pit in one of the studios, known as Sly Stone's Pit, which Fleetwood remembers as being, "usually occupied by people we didn't know, tapping razors on mirrors." Cris Morris, the engineer who had helped build the studio, points out that "a lot of other musicians dropped by. Van Morrison hung out a lot. Rufus and Chaka Khan, Rick James."

It wasn't long, though, before Fleetwood Mac, who were now reaping the huge financial benefits of the success of their previous album, found themselves indulging in narcotic recreational pursuits. "It was the craziest period of our lives," says Fleetwood. "We went four or five weeks without sleep, doing a lot of drugs. I'm talking about cocaine in such quantities that, at one point, I thought I was really going insane."

Somehow, however, ground-breaking work continued to get done. In the powerfully driving 'Don't Stop,' for example, the voices of Buckingham and McVie were deliberately equalized and compressed to such an extent that they sounded almost identical. "We were trying to get unique sounds on every instrument," remembers Morris. "We spent ten solid hours on a kick-drum sound in Studio B. Eventually we moved into Studio A and built a special platform for the drums, which got them sounding the way we wanted."

Though the basic tracks were completed in Sausalito, there was a period of several months in Los Angeles, largely given over to the mixing process as well as vocal, guitar, and percussion overdubs.

"Looking back at it from 56 years old," said Nicks in 2004, "all I can think is, 'Thank God it wasn't worse.' Thank God we didn't get into heroin. We were lucky that we were always able to get ourselves together to make the music. Maybe it was the music that saved all of us."

1978

Blue Valentine **Tom Waits**

Elektra 6E 162 (U.S.A.) / Asylum K 53088 (U.K.)
Released October 1978

Blue Valentine was Waits's penultimate album for Elektra, before he signed to Island and moved into more experimental territory, and is the culmination of the first phase of the singer's career.

Waits signed to Elektra in 1973 after being spotted performing at the Troubadour in Los Angeles by Frank Zappa's manager Herb Cohen. His early albums – including *Closing Time* (1973) and *Nighthawks At The Diner* (1975) – showed Waits to be a talented writer who could, apparently effortlessly, get into the mindset of the low-life, Bourbon-soaked characters that populated his songs.

By the late 1970s, however, Waits's hobo act had begun to grow stale. Realizing this, he expanded his repertoire beyond his usual first-person tales of life in the gutter, balancing them with aching romantic balladry. Waits also widens his musical pallet here, shifting the emphasis away from his own piano playing on some tracks and instead making use of guitarists Roland Bautista and Ray Crawford, who give 'Twenty-Nine Dollars' and 'Whistlin' Past The Graveyard' more of an R&B feel. The influence of swinging 1950s jazz still looms large, though, particularly on 'Romeo Is Bleeding,' while 'Somewhere' and 'Kentucky Avenue' stand apart from the rest of the album with their rich, orchestral arrangements.

Blue Valentine didn't chart on its release in 1978, but is now considered among the strongest works in the career of one of the greatest songwriters to emerge in the 1970s.

Some Girls **The Rolling Stones**

Rolling Stones COC 39108 (U.S.A. & U.K.)
Released June 1978

Though still routinely described as 'The Greatest Rock'n'Roll Band In The World,' by 1978 The Rolling Stones were looking like they would be swept away by the new generation of faster, tougher punk bands.

The band's recent studio albums had sounded tired and pedestrian, with just one or two songs reminding everyone what they were capable of. Coming a year after 1977's routine live set, *Love You Live*, *Some Girls*, the first Stones studio album of the punk era, came at a crucial juncture in the band's career. British critics in particular were gleefully anticipating the dismissal of the record as yet more evidence that the old guard had finally been displaced.

Grudgingly, even the hardest-bitten of hacks had to admit that *Some Girls* was a good album. A disco-influenced hit single, 'Miss You,' was just one highlight among the best set of Stones songs since the classic double, *Exile On Main Street*, six years earlier. The fast three-chord rocker 'Respectable' matched the young punks for energy, while guitarist Keith Richards's one lead-vocal contribution, 'Before They Make Me Run,' was a simultaneously vulnerable and defiant riposte to the drug-related legal troubles he had recently been experiencing.

The Rolling Stones continue to tour and record to this day. Though there have been hit singles and chart albums aplenty since *Some Girls*, many hail it as the last great Stones album.

Outlandos D'Amour The Police

A&M 4753 (U.S.A.) / AMLH 68502 (U.K.)
Released November 1978

A strange *ménage à trois*, The Police set out on their path to becoming the biggest band of the 1980s with this unusually eclectic album.

Prior to forming the band in 1977, Sting was a free-improvising jazz bassist from Newcastle, Andy Summers was a journeyman London-based rock guitarist, whose career stretched back into the early 1960s, and American drummer Stewart Copeland was a refugee from early 1970s prog outfit Curved Air. They came together on a largely pragmatic basis, because the mid-1970s punk-rock explosion led to a huge demand for new live acts. Dying their hair blond and masquerading as punks, they hitched a ride on the bandwagon and attracted enough attention to enable them, on January 19th 1978, to start recording their debut album in Surrey Sound Studios, Leatherhead, U.K. The sessions, in the £10-an-hour studio – which Sting remembers as "a cruddy, funky place with egg cartons on the wall" – were financed by £1,500 (about $3,000 at the time) borrowed from Copeland's rock-entrepreneur brother, Miles.

The album was somewhat musically diverse for a band hoping to pass itself off as punks. 'Next To You,' 'Peanuts,' and 'Truth Hits Everybody' certainly had enough reckless energy to pull off the deception, but beautifully crafted and executed songs such as 'Can't Stand Losing You' and 'So Lonely' can now clearly be seen as the work of musicians infinitely more sophisticated than the average punk hopeful.

Among the songs they recorded was one that Sting had knocked out in October of 1977 after an eye-popping walk through the red-light district of Paris. The song, named after Roxanne, the beloved of Cyrano de Bergerac in the play *Cyrano*, tells of a man's love for a prostitute whom he hopes to rescue from her seedy existence. "I was about to sing the first line," remembers Sting, "when I noticed a stand-up piano. I was tired, I'd been up all night, so I just sat down. I thought the piano lid was closed, but it was open, so I wound up playing this incredible chord with my arse. It was this sort of atonal cluster that went nicely against the G minor we were playing. We thought it was funny, so we left it in." The most distinctive aspect of the track, however, is the way in which it artfully combines rock attitude with reggae rhythms. "Bob Marley was the link," admitted Sting later. "'Roxanne' has a real Bob Marley feel. He's half white, so he's sort of a cultural go-between."

Even so, no one in The Police thought much of 'Roxanne.' Only Miles Copeland spotted it as a potential hit, and scored the band a deal with A&M Records on the strength of that one song. British radio wouldn't play it, deeming the subject matter unsavory, but a year later it broke out from a small station in Austin, Texas.

Though it never went higher than Number 32 in America, 'Roxanne' made The Police seem glamorous back in Britain and, by continuing to blend rock with reggae, they went on to conquer the world.

1978

Van Halen **Van Halen**

Warner Brothers 3075 (U.S.A.) / K56470 (U.K.)
Released February 1978

The air-brushed album cover looked silly, an over-the-top rendering of 'You Really Got Me' appalled many a Kinks fan, and yet, on their massive-sounding, exuberant Warner Brothers debut, Van Halen brought a touch of punk attitude to mainstream U.S. rock.

Southern California's Van Halen offered proof positive that they were no run-of-the-mill heavy-rock band, because behind the macho swagger lay four supremely talented individuals, who could play and write – and, apparently, drink, snort, and screw – rings around the competition.

It was immediately apparent that the driving force behind the band was 22-year-old guitar virtuoso Eddie Van Halen. Today, many can still recall first hearing Eddie's album-opening 'Eruption,' a spellbinding amalgam of hammer-ons, whammy-bar dives, and scorching volume, performed from start to finish in a single take. Mercurial, witty, impatient, and devil-may-care, Van Halen was the first guitarist since Hendrix to shake up rock guitar by opening a door to new sonic possibilities, notably in his use of 'tapping.' While he didn't invent the technique – whereby notes are produced by banging fretting fingers on the neck – he certainly popularized it. (A host of less talented rockers abused the technique through the 1980s until grunge rose up out of Seattle and cried 'Enough!')

The guitar pyrotechnics found a perfect complement in David Lee Roth's vocals. A vocal gymnast of the highest order, Roth's feral howl has the pheromone content of a sweaty football dressing-room, and he sings most of the album with a confident, gum-chewing insouciance. As a rhythm section, bassist Michael Anthony and drummer Alex Van Halen supply bottom end to spare.

The road to *Van Halen* began in mid 1977, when producer Ted Templeman accepted an invitation to check out the band – whose Gene Simmons-financed demo had already been rejected by scores of major companies – at Starwood, the venue where Van Halen had built a local audience. A contract was offered and demo sessions arranged. "As it turns out, we didn't need the extra studio time," recalls Templeman's longstanding engineer Donn Landee. "They cut 28 songs in about two hours. That's when we knew we had a band that could play."

On the first week of January 1978 Van Halen convened inside Sunset Sound's Studio 1. In order to capture the raw energy of the group's club work, Landee and Templeman decided on a no-overdubs approach. "There are only a couple of spots where we added anything afterward – on 'Runnin' With The Devil' and 'Jamie's Cryin'" – and those were done in one take," says Landee. "And we didn't use very many tracks at all. Alex's drums were probably cut using only four mikes total. You just don't need a lot of tracks to get a great sound."

To compensate for the live, one-guitar approach Landee placed Eddie's track slightly off-center in the mix, with a splash of delayed echo from Sunset Sound's extraordinary live echo-chamber filling up the opposite channel. "It made sense, because we didn't want to overdub guitars," he recalls. "If you put the guitar right down the middle with everything else, you'd wind up with the whole band in mono! So it seemed like a reasonable idea." That is, until a month later, when Eddie, vacationing in Italy, happened to get into a rental car that was short one channel, "at which point I got a panicked phone call from the other side of the world wondering why he couldn't hear his playing!"

Completed in less than three weeks, *Van Halen* – which settled at Number 19 on the *Billboard* albums chart – took just seven months to be certified platinum. All told, more than 10 million copies have been sold in the 27 years since its release.

The Last Waltz **The Band**

Warner Brothers 3WS-3146 9 (U.S.A.) / K66076 (U.K.)
Released April 1978

The final live gig by the definitive line-up of The Band set new standards for how a much-loved rock group should say goodbye.

Not only did they have the good grace to bow out while they were still at the top, they invited their pals along for the party and had the home movie shot by Martin Scorsese. This marketing-man's dream took place on November 25th 1976 at Winterland, San Francisco, with guest appearances from Bob Dylan, Neil Young, Joni Mitchell, Emmylou Harris, Muddy Waters, Stephen Stills, Dr John, Eric Clapton, Ronnie Hawkins, Van Morrison, Neil Diamond, and Ringo Starr.

Everything about the event was over the top. There was a 38-piece orchestra, three teams of ballroom dancers, and a food bill that came to $42,000, not including the 400 pounds of fresh salmon specially flown in by Dylan. There was even an all-white room, decorated with sheepskin rugs, Groucho Marx noses, and a glass-topped table complete with razor blades. Despite much behind-the-scenes grief – drummer Levon Helm didn't want to do the concert, Dylan made everyone jump through hoops, music director John Simon claims he never got paid – *The Last Waltz* remains a landmark

not just for its consistently superb music but for Warners' brilliantly manipulative marketing. Sold on the back of one event, we got the triple album, the movie, the home video, the double-CD reissue, the DVD, and the boxed-set four-CD reissue. As their fellow Canadian Leonard Cohen almost said: "Hey, that's the way to say goodbye."

▪ *The Band and friends on stage at Winterland, San Francisco, on November 25th 1976. Above (left to right): Van Morrison, Bob Dylan, and Robbie Robertson. Below: Rick Danko with Robertson.*

1979

Rust Never Sleeps Neil Young And Crazy Horse

Reprise 2295 (U.S.A.) / K54105 (U.K.)
Released July 1979

The punk movement poured scorn on the reigning rock aristocracy as bloated, out of touch, and indulgent, so it was no surprise that most survivors of the 1960s viewed the new bands with something between suspicion and disdain.

Neil Young was one of the few members of the old guard to respond with enthusiasm to the likes of The Sex Pistols. Galvanized by the energy of the new wave, he recorded one of his great albums, *Rust Never Sleeps*. Throughout his career Young has bounced back and forth between country-folk acoustic ballads and raging, ragged rock. On *Rust Never Sleeps* he does both styles, performing Side One in acoustic-troubadour guise, then calling up long-serving backing band Crazy Horse for a second side of fierce electric rock. The result is a perfectly balanced set of consistently strong material. 'Thrasher' is one of Young's most affecting acoustic songs; while the electric 'Powderfinger' features one of the best recorded examples of his brink-of-collapse lead-guitar playing. The album's key song, 'My My, Hey Hey,' appears twice, in both acoustic and electric versions, the former subtitled 'Out Of The Blue,' the latter 'Into The Black.' In it Young name-checks The Sex Pistols' singer Johnny Rotten, having delivered one of rock music's most evocative slogans: "It's better to burn out than to fade away."

Off The Wall Michael Jackson

Epic 35745 (U.S.A.) / EPC/40 83458 (U.K.)
Released August 1979

After recording four albums as a teenager in the early 1970s and achieving countless hits as a member of The Jackson 5, Michael Jackson relaunched his solo career in 1979 with the more mature sounding *Off The Wall*.

The album marks the beginning of Jackson's association with studio wizard Quincy Jones, who would go on to produce Jackson's *Thriller* (1982), the biggest-selling album of all time.

Shortly after recording *Destiny* with fellow Jackson siblings Randy, LaToya, and Rebbie – as The Jacksons – Michael started work with Jones in Los Angeles on what would be his first solo release as an adult. Jones and Jackson had first worked together on *The Wiz*, a musical version of *The Wizard Of Oz* that also starred Diana Ross and Richard Pryor, for which Jones wrote the score. *Off The Wall* is best known for its lead track, one of Jackson's finest singles, 'Don't Stop 'Til You Get Enough,' which topped the U.S. chart in advance of the album's release. The album itself is a near-faultless collection of soulful funk and smooth balladry, which also spawned the hits 'Rock With You' and 'She's Out Of My Life.' *Off The Wall* peaked at Number Three in the U.S.A. and Number Five in the U.K., and has sold over eight million copies worldwide.

Off The Wall may stand a long way short of being Jackson's biggest commercial success but it remains his strongest artistic statement. Reviewing a reissued edition of the album in 2001, *Rolling Stone* magazine decided that it "remains a perfect album . . . the rhythm never lets up, and neither does the quality," while two years earlier, *Q* magazine declared that *Off The Wall* contained "some of the best melodies in the history of pop."

Bop Till You Drop Ry Cooder

Warner Brothers WB 7599-27398-2 (U.S.A. & U.K.)
Released August 1979

A prominent member of Hollywood's studio-session scene during the 1960s and 1970s, Ry Cooder added his trademark slide licks for everyone from Paul Revere And The Raiders to The Rolling Stones – who had appropriated the open-G tuning method, favored by Cooder, for 'Honky Tonk Women.'

It was Cooder's second solo effort for Reprise, *Bop Till You Drop*, that gave the guitarist the dubious distinction of having the first popular-music album recorded entirely in the digital domain, utilizing a 3M 32-track recorder at Amigo Studios in North Hollywood. With support from drummer Jim Keltner, bassist Tim Drummond, and slide-guitar ace David Lindley, *Bop Till You Drop* featured competent updates of such old staples as 'Little Sister,' 'The Very Thing That Makes You Rich (Makes Me Poor),' and 'Go Home, Girl.' "He sends shivers down my spine," remarked no less an observer than the great Pops Staples of The Staples Singers. "He comes out with these old tunes your parents taught you, and it's like going back in time." Despite having engineering ace Lee Herschberg on board – whose previous clients had included Frank Sinatra and Rickie Lee Jones – Cooder, who would continue to serve as a sideman for the likes of Eric Clapton, Randy Newman, and John Hiatt, would later dismiss the technologically advanced *Bop* as a thin-sounding experiment. (Historical footnote: in early 1979 Stephen Stills had actually prepared his own all-digital effort, but it was never released, giving Cooder the non-analog accolade.)

Unknown Pleasures Joy Division

Not issued in the U.S.A. / Factory FACT10 (U.K.)
Released August 1979

One of the most revered bands of the post-punk era in the U.K., Joy Division's debut was also the first release of note on the influential independent Manchester-based Factory Records.

A local television presenter, Tony Wilson, formed the label in 1978, several months after he had started a popular alternative-music club night in Manchester, also called Factory. Joy Division was one of the first bands to play at the club, alongside other notable post-punk acts Cabaret Voltaire and The Durutti Column. All three were included on the label's inaugural EP release, *A Factory Sampler*.

Joy Division had already built up a fiercely devoted live following by the time they began recording their debut in July 1979 with Martin Hannett, producer of many early Factory releases. *Unknown Pleasures* is built around Peter Hook's droning bass lines and the abrasive guitar playing of Bernard Albrecht, with Stephen Morris's distinctive drum sound – which Hannett achieved by recording him on the roof of the studio – pinning it all down. The final and most important element of the band's sound was frontman Ian Curtis's despairing lyrics, sung in a low monotone, which has often been affected by later alternative-rock acts.

The album's £8,000 ($14,000) production costs came out of Tony Wilson's life savings; fortunately for him, *Unknown Pleasures* was greeted with

overwhelming critical praise on its release in the U.K., and became a permanent fixture on the U.K. independent chart for several years. However, the album was not issued in the U.S.A. at the time – the group apparently having turned down a large distribution deal with Warner Brothers – and remained unreleased there until 1989.

On May 18th 1980, shortly before the release of the second Joy Division album, *Closer*, and on the eve of their first U.S. tour, Curtis hanged himself. The remaining trio, augmented by keyboardist Gillian Gilbert, went on to achieve considerable international success as New Order.

Metal Box [US title: Second Edition]
Public Image Ltd

Warner Brothers 3288 (U.S.A.) / Virgin METAL 1 (U.K.)
Released November 1979

The second release from former Sex Pistol John Lydon's second band of note, *Metal Box* was issued in the U.K. as three 45rpm 12-inch disks in a film canister embossed with their name.

Formed soon after Rotten – now reclaiming his family name of Lydon – left The Sex Pistols in 1978, Public Image Ltd were, from the outset, a much more musical outfit than his former band. The membership of PiL, as they are often known, was completed by guitarist Keith Levene, once of The Clash, and Lydon's old friend, bassist Jah Wobble, as well as a series of session drummers. Debut album *Public Image* had been recorded before the band had had much time to develop their sound; a year later, however, PiL had carved out a niche all of their own, as showcased on *Metal Box*.

Self-produced by the band at various studios in Oxford and London, *Metal Box* marks one of the first occasions of a rock band experimenting with elements of dub and world music as well as dance rhythms, over which Lydon rants about his dying mother and his general resentment toward the world. The album draws heavily on the trio's extensive record collections, notably Captain Beefheart, Lee 'Scratch' Perry, and German prog band Can. The eleven lengthy songs stick to an extreme tonal dynamic, all bass and treble with hardly any middle. In the U.S.A. *Metal Box* was issued in a more conventional sleeve in 1980 as *Second Edition*; the cost of the original packaging was so high that Virgin only produced 60,000 copies, and vetoed the band's plan to include a lyric sheet. The album includes the minor U.K. hit single 'Swan Lake' (aka 'Death Disco').

Journey Through The Secret Life Of Plants
Stevie Wonder

Tamla 371 (U.S.A.) / Tamla Motown TMSP 6009 (U.K.)
Released November 1979

In 1976 Stevie Wonder issued the sprawling, multiple Grammy Award-winning *Songs In The Key Of Life*, considered by many to be one of his strongest artistic statements.

It took Wonder over three years to release a follow-up, an incredibly long time by 1970s standards, when most acts were set into a pattern of producing a new studio album every year. When it eventually arrived, *Journey Through The Secret Life Of Plants* seemed like a rather odd choice of successor to its hugely popular predecessor. The mostly instrumental album is apparently the soundtrack to a documentary of the same name, which never actually saw a full release.

Most of the tracks are wordless, heavily synthesized pieces that tend to sit closer to classical music than the soulful R&B Wonder is known for. When he does sing, however, his vocal performances are often unusual – on 'Venus Fly Trap And The Bug,' for example, his voice resembles that of Tom Waits.

Despite its unconventional musical content, *Journey Through The Secret Life Of Plants* reached Number Four in the U.S.A. on release and Number Eight in the U.K., demonstrating Wonder's undeniable popularity at the time, when even a quirky, pseudo-symphonic soundtrack album could become a huge hit. Two of the album's more traditional songs, 'Send One Your Love' and 'Outside My Window,' were minor hit singles on both sides of the Atlantic. *Journey Through The Secret Life Of Plants* remains an intriguing oddity in the canon of an unquestionably great artist.

The Wall **Pink Floyd**

Harvest 36183 (U.S.A.) / SHDW 411 (U.K.)
Released December 1979

The Wall was Pink Floyd's most ambitious, sprawling concept album ever, a mammoth touring stage production, a full-length movie, and, some years later, a star-studded one-off concert in Berlin. It was also, as guitarist Dave Gilmour has pointed out, "the last embers of Roger's and my ability to work collaboratively together."

Roger Waters still rates *The Wall* as the best idea he ever had, and its songs of alienation, bitterness, and rage against the machines are generally viewed as the nearest he has come to an autobiography in music. The album's seed lies in an incident during a concert at Montreal's Olympic Stadium on July 6th 1977. It was the end of a lengthy tour, and Waters was increasingly disillusioned with his relationship with the audience. "There was a fan clawing his way up the storm netting to try and get to us," he remembers, "and I just snapped and spat at him. I was shocked, disgusted by myself as soon as I did it, but, after I'd thought about it, the idea of actually building a wall between us and the audience, it had wonderful theatrical possibilities."

The band was suffering tax problems, so the double album was recorded partly in France and partly in Los Angeles, but no expense was spared. "We got hand-built 16-track recorders from LA and carted them at great expense to France," remembers Gilmour. "They kept breaking down every two minutes. There was a whole range of new technology and all these new people we'd brought in to make this record a huge sonic advance."

In retrospect, Gilmour has reservations about the album. "I still think some of the music is incredibly naff," he says, "but *The Wall* is conceptually brilliant. At the time I thought it was Roger listing all the things that can turn a person into an isolated human being. I came to see it as one of the luckiest people in the world issuing a catalog of abuse and bile against people who'd never done anything to him."

The album included what would turn out to be Pink Floyd's first single for eleven years, the controversial 'Another Brick In The Wall.' The song, with its violently anti-education theme, was written by Waters, but the disco beat that helped propel it to Number One in the U.S.A. and the U.K. was suggested by producer Bob Ezrin, and the kids' choir was recorded in north London without any member of the band present. Other than 'Another Brick,' the album's most memorable track – and another source of friction between Waters and Gilmour – is probably 'Comfortably Numb.' "Roger was taking more and more of the credits," complains Gilmour. "In the songbook for this album against 'Comfortably Numb' it says 'Music by Gilmour and Waters.' It shouldn't. He did the lyrics. I did the music."

Though *The Wall* stalled at Number Three in the U.K., where the legacy of punk was still in full flow, the band must have taken some slight comfort when it topped the U.S. charts for 15 straight weeks.

1979

London Calling **The Clash**

CBS 36328 (U.S.A.) / CBS CLASH3 (U.K.)
Released December 1979

Though their early song '1977' had proclaimed "No Elvis, no Beatles or Stones," The Clash were always infatuated with classic rock images.

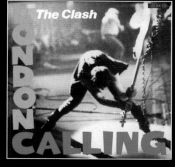

The sleeve of *London Calling* was a case in point, with an evocative photo of bassist Paul Simonon in a Who-like act of guitar destruction framed by graphics copied from Elvis Presley's 1956 debut album. It was a bold move, claiming for themselves some of rock's most potent myths, but it was easily matched by the quality of the music. Inside the sleeve was a double album of musical variety drawing on the full gamut of popular-music styles of the previous 25 years, a broad-minded approach that would have been unthinkable in the cultural revolution that had reached its peak little more than two years earlier.

From the start The Clash was the most musically adventurous of the first wave of British punk bands, grafting dub and reggae into their sound while still demonstrating only a rudimentary grasp of their instruments. By the time of *London Calling*, the band's third album, competence had caught up with ambition and The Clash had the guts to blend rockabilly, epic pop, jazz, and ska into the mix as well. That stylistic variety combined with a strong set of material, drawn mainly from the band's songwriting team of Joe Strummer and Mick Jones, made *London Calling* that rare rock phenomenon, a consistently good double album that maintains interest through all four sides of vinyl. Credit is due both to the band and producer Guy Stevens – who had previously worked with Jones's favorite band Mott The Hoople – that such a mixed bag ended up sounding like a unified statement rather than a collection of pastiches. It was good value, too, with the band insisting that it be sold for the price of a single disk.

London Calling marked a breakthrough in the U.S.A. The band's biggest American hit single, 'Train In Vain,' was an unlisted 'secret' track at the end of Side Four of the original vinyl release. The album was eventually voted by readers of *Rolling Stone* magazine as the best rock record of the 1980s – though it had first been released two weeks before the end of the previous decade. It did well at home, too, with the title track – featuring a backward guitar solo, the likes of which had not been heard on a rock record since the psychedelic age – becoming the band's biggest British hit single yet.

The Clash was a contradiction, both iconoclastic and traditionalist, and in Strummer and Jones there were two powerful musical voices that were often in conflict: Jones the melodic rock traditionalist, Strummer the sloganeering black-music evangelist. It was on *London Calling* that these opposing forces were most successfully balanced in creative tension. Though there was still great music to come, The Clash would never be this consistent or this good again.

1980

The Blues Brothers (Original Soundtrack)
The Blues Brothers

Atlantic 16017 (U.S.A.) / W50715 (U.K.)
Released June 1980

As The Blues Brothers, comedians John Belushi and Dan Aykroyd recorded several hit albums, wrote and starred in a hugely popular movie, and helped introduce soul and blues to a new audience in the early 1980s.

The duo's characters, Jake and Elwood Blues, started life as a sketch on *Saturday Night Live*, the U.S. variety show that also launched the careers of Eddie Murphy, Mike Myers, and countless others. By the time the big-screen version of *The Blues Brothers* was released, Belushi and Aykroyd had already topped the U.S. albums chart with *Briefcase Full Of Blues* (1978).

Though they sold strongly, The Blues Brothers' albums met with a mixed critical reception. While some were just happy to see the blues gain further exposure, others were angered by what they saw as the devaluing of a classic musical genre by a pair of greedy comics. While there may have been a hint of truth in these accusations, Aykroyd and Belushi did recruit a band of exemplary musicians to back them on screen and on record. Among them were two of Booker T.'s MGs – guitarist Steve Cropper and bassist Donald 'Duck' Dunn – and trumpet player Alan Rubin, who had previously worked with such musical luminaries as Frank Sinatra, Duke Ellington, and The Rolling Stones. As Jake and Elwood, Belushi's vocals and Aykroyd's harmonica playing are hardly flawless, but what does become clear throughout their recordings is that the duo have a genuine love for the music.

The Blues Brothers remains the most enduring of the duo's albums, mainly because, like the movie itself, it includes cameo appearances by a number of true stars of blues and soul: Ray Charles duets with Jake on 'Shake A Tail Feather,' while James Brown sings 'Old Landmark,' Cab Calloway powers through 'Minnie The Moocher,' and Aretha Franklin turns in a storming rendition of 'Think,' which she had first recorded at the peak of her powers in 1968. Any comparisons to this quartet of blues and soul legends would prove unfavorable to Belushi, but he handles the remaining six vocal tracks well, particularly the closing 'Jailhouse Rock.' The only unfortunate omission is John Lee Hooker, who has a guest role in the movie but didn't make the soundtrack album. *The Blues Brothers* was produced by Bob Tischler, with whom Aykroyd and Belushi had previously worked on a *Saturday Night Live* album, and who had recently produced another pair of comedy records for the *National Lampoon* team, *Gold Turkey* (1975) and *That's Not Funny, That's Sick* (1977).

Somewhat unwisely, MCA, the musical arm of Universal – who produced the movie – declined to release the accompanying album, leaving it instead to Atlantic Records to reap the financial rewards. *The Blues Brothers* reached Number 13 in the U.S.A. on its release and remains an international cult favorite. Aykroyd and Belushi capitalized on their success with a tour in the latter part of 1980 as well as a third album as Jake and Elwood, *Made In America*. After issuing a 'best-of' album in 1981, The Blues Brothers' career ended the following year when Belushi died of a drug overdose. In 1998 Aykroyd made a less successful follow-up movie, *Blues Brothers 2000*, in which James Belushi took on the role his brother had made famous.

Searching For The Young Soul Rebels
Dexy's Midnight Runners

Not issued in the U.S.A. / Parlophone 7213 (U.K.)
Released July 1980

Dexy's Midnight Runners had considerable success in the U.K. in the early 1980s, blending contemporary new-wave pop with 1960s-style brass arrangements.

The group was formed in 1978 by vocalist Kevin Rowland, whose backing musicians included a three-piece horn section. Dexy's were well on the way to becoming one of the iconic British pop acts of the era by the time the group issued its debut album, *Searching For The Young Soul Rebels*. 'Geno,' Rowland's enthusiastic tribute to the soul singer Geno Washington, had already topped the U.K. singles chart, while the group was just as well-known for its image – based at this point on the New York dockers' uniforms in Martin Scorsese's *Mean Streets* – as its music.

Searching For The Young Soul Rebels was produced by Pete Wingfield, who had in the 1970s worked as a session keyboardist for the likes of Van Morrison and Jimmy Witherspoon. The album's release was briefly held up when Rowland 'kidnapped' the master tapes, holding them hostage until Parlophone offered him a higher royalty rate. Despite the group's lack of cooperation with the music press – Rowland chose to communicate with fans via full-page magazine advertisements rather than speak to journalists – the album was hailed as a modern classic on its release. A relentless reimagining of Rowland's soul heroes, topped off by the singer's witty lyrics and theatrical vocal delivery, *Searching For The Young Soul Rebels* peaked at Number Six in the U.K. and spawned a further Top Ten hit single, 'There, There, My Dear.'

1980

Back In Black **AC/DC**

Atco CS-16018 (U.S.A. & U.K.)
Released July 1980

**A quarter-century after its arrival,
Back In Black remains, for many,
the essential hard-rock record of
the modern era.**

Like many milestone efforts, *Back In
Back* had little to do with pop trends
of the time – which, in 1980, were all
about skinny ties and Farfisa organs.
Instead, with *Back In Black*, AC/DC –
guitarists Angus and Malcolm Young,
bassist Cliff Williams, drummer Phil
Rudd, and singer Brian Johnson –

delivered a set of ironclad songs that are stripped to the bone, jacked up at
the bottom, and outfitted with some of the most tastefully lean guitar
accompaniment on record. Helping the band achieve its megaplatinum apex
were producer Robert John 'Mutt' Lange – an unlikely ally, whose ear for
slick pop nevertheless lent a subtle but essential mainstream sensibility to
the proceedings – and Tony Platt, an engineer of impeccable taste, whose
patience and mixing skills brought it all together on tape.

Back In Black marked a turning point in AC/DC's career. *Highway to Hell*,
issued a year earlier, had finally pushed the group into platinum territory.
But as the band was pulling together material for the all-important follow-up,
in February 1980 original vocalist Bon Scott died an alcohol-related death,
and the band's future seemed uncertain. Determined to push on in spite of
the circumstances, in March the group hired Newcastle-based vocalist Brian
Johnson to fill Scott's shoes, then immediately began rehearsing at
London's E'Zee Hire Studios. As a diversion, that May the group repaired to
the tropical surroundings of sunny Nassau and the newly constructed
Compass Point Studios, where they prepared to cut tracks for their
forthcoming Atco effort.

With AC/DC it had always been about the riff, and on *Back In Black* there
are plenty of them: 'Hell's Bells,' 'Shoot To Thrill,' 'Have A Drink On Me,'
and the unrelenting title track featured the dynamic interplay between
Angus's right-channel Gibson SG lead guitar and brother Malcolm's left-
channel Gretsch rhythm. From his control-room vantage point, Platt

realized the sound he was after was already coming through the monitors. Processing and other add-ons were purposely left off the rhythm tracks. "We all had a good idea of how we wanted it to sound right from the start," says Platt, "and so our goal was to get it on tape there, rather than leaving it for the final mix. Being restricted to 24 tracks meant that a lot of the decisions would be made early on, which also added to the feeling of immediacy. But most of all, they just played it like it is! There was hardly any patching required – we'd just cut takes until we had a nice balance of perfection and feel."

As so often happens, the makeup of the studio itself helped determine the recording dynamics. "The setup and approach was quite different from *Highway*," notes Platt, who'd come aboard during the mix phase of the previous album. "*Highway* had been recorded in a very dead studio, so much so that during mixing I'd fed various parts back through the speakers and into the studio, recording the result for extra ambience. So when it came time to do *Back In Black*, the idea was to get that ambience on tape right from the start. The room at Compass Point was fairly large but had a lowish ceiling, which concerned me a little as I didn't want the room to compress the sound. We spent some time choosing the right position for the drums by hitting a snare in various parts of the room. I discovered a 'sweet spot' where the snare suddenly sounded bigger, deeper, fuller, and – most important – snappier. I subsequently discovered that there was a void above this position that was obviously allowing the sound to rise without choking it!"

■ *Main picture (left to right): Cliff Williams, Malcolm Young, Simon Wright, Angus Young, and Brian Johnson, who joined AC/DC in 1980, a month after the death of original vocalist Bon Scott (pictured above).*

For Angus's solo tracks – which were overdubbed – Platt employed two amplifier stacks, one in the main room and another in a live chamber at the far end of the building. "We used Angus's radios to transmit to these amps," says Platt. "The radios actually proved to be quite an important part of the sound, as they added some mid bite. I used two Neumann U67s on each cabinet, so I could pan the result where I wanted. And absolutely no compression was used at all."

Despite the volume at hand, Platt encouraged leakage in order to maintain the ambient element. "We kept Cliff's bass in a separate booth so that Angus and Malcolm's guitars could really bleed into the room," says Platt. "There was some screening over the amps, but it was minimal. For Phil's drums, I kept several room mikes up at all times, which I would move around depending on the effect I wanted to achieve. But, really, it was mainly just tuning the drums carefully to get the sound as close to where we wanted it, with the overheads providing most of the texture."

For newcomer Johnson, cutting vocal parts worthy of his predecessor was only half the battle; crafting lyrics that fit the AC/DC sex/rock/mayhem mold turned out to be the most daunting task of the entire six-week affair. "Because the lyrics were written as we went along, all of Brian's vocals were overdubs," says Platt. "But that turned out to be for the best anyway, as one of Mutt's finest attributes as a producer is his ability to enable the singer to perform to the best of his abilities."

Mixing for the album took place at Electric Lady Studios in New York shortly after the sessions were completed. "The size of the sound is really a combination of things," says Platt. "The tuning is good, the arrangements are spacious, and the recording isn't heavily processed, aside from some subtle addition of delays and light reverb just for extra ambience. I remember we also monitored quietly so we could balance carefully."

Coming after years of synthesized disco and overproduced AOR, *Back In Black* proved once again the resilience of live, loud, and melodic rock, and listeners immediately responded. At 20 million and counting, today the AC/DC's seventh major-label release ranks as the sixth bestselling album of all time.

"Probably the biggest buzz I've ever had during my time in the business was walking into Madison Square Garden one evening and hearing *Back In Black* coming over the house PA," notes Platt. "The engineer told me he always used that album to run up a PA, because if it sounded good with *Back In Black* playing, then he knew he had it! I can't think of a better endorsement than that."

1980

The Game Queen

Elektra 513 (U.S.A.) / EMI EMA 795 (U.K.)
Released July 1980

Five years after the release of 'Bohemian Rhapsody' – and having survived the punk-rock boom that killed off many of their contemporaries in the late 1970s – Queen issued their most diverse studio album, *The Game*, which was also the only one of the group's 14 full-length efforts to top the U.S. albums chart.

After recording the modestly successful *Queen* (1973) and *Queen II* (1974), Queen issued a run of five studio albums throughout the remaining years of the 1970s that each entered the upper reaches of the charts on both sides of the Atlantic. The group ended the decade, and the first phase of its career, with the double-album set *Live Killers* (1979), recorded earlier that year on the huge arena tour in support of *Jazz* (1978). In the final months of the 1970s they issued the rockabilly-inflected single 'Crazy Little Thing Called Love.' The first of the group's singles to top the U.S. singles chart, the song peaked at Number Two in the U.K., and would also be included on *The Game*.

The Game was recorded in two stages at Musicland Studio in Munich, Germany, with producer-engineer Josh McRae. Initial sessions were booked for June and July 1979, but produced little more than 'Crazy Little Thing Called Love' and a clutch of rough versions of other songs. The bulk of the recording was completed between February and May of the following year. The opening 'Play The Game,' one of four hit singles drawn from the album, sets the tone. Beginning in the vein of a typical stomping Queen song from the 1970s, 'Play The Game' features an unexpected synthesizer solo midway through. During the 1970s Queen's album sleeves and promotional posters had been decorated with the phrase "no synthesizers were used on this record," a fairly transparent attempt by the group to align themselves with the serious hard rock of the likes of Led Zeppelin. By the time the group came to make *The Game*, however, Queen had succumbed to the power of the synthesizer. Guitarist Brian May provides most of the keyboard parts, and was largely responsible for the group's change in direction.

Issued in the summer of 1980, *The Game* quickly rose to the top of the albums charts in the U.S.A. and the U.K. as well as elsewhere in Europe. The album's success can partially be attributed to the trail of hit singles – 'Crazy Little Thing Called Love,' 'Save Me,' and 'Play The Game' – that preceded its release. *The Game* also spawned a fourth huge hit single, 'Another One Bites The Dust,' which has become one of Queen's best-known songs. The track is emblematic of the new musical direction Queen took in the 1980s: based around taut, funky bass and drums, and featuring occasional flourishes of warm synthesizer, the song is about as far as the group could get from their earlier, theatrical heavy rock.

After *The Game* Queen moved into ever more pop-orientated territory. The following year the group performed a duet with David Bowie on the single 'Under Pressure,' a song which features on both Queen's *Hot Space* (1982) and various hits compilations by both acts. While Queen's popularity began to dwindle in the later 1980s, particularly in the U.S.A., the group continued to record until Freddie Mercury's death in 1991.

Fresh Fruit For Rotting Vegetables
Dead Kennedys

Faulty-IRS SP 70014 (U.S.A.) / Cherry Red B-RED 10 (U.K.)
Released November 1980

Inspired by the British punk scene, The Dead Kennedys became one of the defining U.S. hardcore groups of the 1980s, mixing visceral rock with fiercely political lyrics.

Frontman Jello Biafra (born Eric Boucher) launched the famed underground rock label Alternative Tentacles in 1979, which issued the group's debut single, 'California Über Alles.' (In a busy year, the 21-year-old Biafra had also run, unsuccessfully, for mayor of San Francisco.) The band signed a distribution deal with another nascent independent label, Faulty, for the release of its full-length debut, *Fresh Fruit For Rotting Vegetables*. Faulty was a subsidiary of IRS, the label founded by Miles Copeland, a former record producer and manager of The Police, as well as being the brother of The Police's drummer Stewart.

Fresh Fruit For Rotting Vegetables was produced by the group's guitarist East Bay Ray and recorded at Moibus Music in San Francisco in the winter of 1980. The album is an unrelenting barrage of raw, guitar-led punk and left-wing, satirical lyrics, typified by song titles such as 'Let's Lynch The Landlord' and 'Chemical Warfare.' Though it failed to chart in the U.S.A., it reached Number 33 in the U.K. and spawned the memorable single 'Holiday In Cambodia.' The album is now considered to be one of the most important underground rock records of the early 1980s. The following year The Dead Kennedys issued the equally polemical *In God We Trust Inc.*, which included the single 'Nazi Punks Fuck Off.'

Peter Gabriel 3 Peter Gabriel

Mercury SRM13848 (U.S.A.) / Charisma CAS4019 (U.K.)
Released June 1980

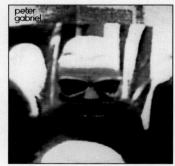

Who would have guessed that the eccentric art rock of early Genesis would lead to two very different but successful careers for singer Peter Gabriel and drummer Phil Collins? Or that the two would collaborate so effectively on Gabriel's third solo album, a record on which the approach to arrangement and production would be so influential throughout the 1980s?

Peter Gabriel 3 showed that in rock music there were other types of song to sing, other themes about which to write, other beats to pound, and instruments other than guitars to be played. All this was contained on the chilling opener, 'Intruder.' Cymbals and hi-hats were put aside: the beat came from Phil Collins's stark snare and bass drum recorded with distant mikes in a large room but then subjected to compression and 'gating,' an electronic process that cuts off a signal before its sound naturally fades. The result was a drum sound that crackled with focused energy, and was much imitated.

Here Gabriel wrote more from rhythms than chord sequences or melodies, experimenting with the then state-of-the-art computer-controlled CMI Fairlight synthesizer. Several tracks feature marimba and the fretless bass sound popularized by Jaco Pastorius. The Jam's Paul Weller steps up to play the fiery guitar riff on 'And Through The Wire' and Kate Bush sings on the sardonic parody of international politics, 'Games Without Frontiers,' which was a hit single. An album whose themes were alienation and psychosis closes with an elegy for murdered South African civil-rights activist Steve

Biko, a track that includes African singing fading in and out of the mix. In a time when world music was not a recognized genre 'Biko' was both exotic and highly political.

Remain In Light Talking Heads

Sire SRK/SRC 6095 (U.S.A. & U.K.)
Released October 1980

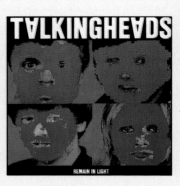

By adding African percussion, funk, and electronic production techniques to their art-rock repertoire, Talking Heads reached a creative peak, and the apex of their association with producer Brian Eno, with *Remain In Light*.

They had released an acclaimed debut, *Talking Heads 77*, on Sire before cutting the more experimental *More Songs About Buildings And Food* and *Fear Of Music* with Brian Eno, the producer fresh from making the critically lauded *Low* and *"Heroes"* with David Bowie. *Fear Of Music*'s opening track, 'I Zimbra,' was the first suggestion of the sound Talking Heads would arrive at on their next release, as the group began to draw on the polyrhythmic drumming of African music.

Eno and Talking Heads began recording *Remain In Light* at Compass Point Studios in the Bahamas in July 1980, with additional tracking and mixing taking place in New York and Los Angeles. As well as the original quartet of frontman David Byrne, guitarist Jerry Harrison, bassist Tina Weymouth, and drummer Chris Frantz, the recordings were augmented by Eno, two percussionists, backing vocalist Nona Hendryx, trumpeter Jon Hassell, and guitarist Adrian Belew, fresh from his work on Bowie's *Lodger*. Belew makes sublime use of wah-wah and delay effects on his guitar playing, while all four core members dabble with synthesizers. The album's eight tracks, all co-written by Eno, started life as lengthy, percussive, full-band jams; the tapes of these performances were manually sliced up and reconfigured as looped grooves and then padded out with additional instrumentation and Byrne's expansive vocal melodies.

> **"WE WANTED TO DEVELOP AN UNDERSTANDING OF THE AFRICAN MUSICAL CONCEPT OF INTERLOCKING, INTERDEPENDENT PARTS AND RHYTHMS THAT COMBINE TO MAKE A COHERENT WHOLE."**
> *TALKING HEADS FRONTMAN DAVID BYRNE*

Remain In Light begins with 'Born Under Punches,' a single looped funk groove that gradually grows as Byrne adds layers of vocals and the rest of the band make subtle changes to the rhythm. These hypnotic, multilayered beats are unrelenting throughout what is by far the most cohesive album in the Talking Heads catalog. The best known song here is 'Once In A Lifetime,' a flop on its original single release but now considered by many to be Talking Heads' greatest individual statement. *Remain In Light* became their biggest album hit to date, its commercial success only exceeded by the later, more pop-orientated *True Stories* (1986) and *Naked* (1988) at the end of the band's career. It remains one of the finest rock records of the decade.

A year after making *Remain In Light*, Byrne and Eno reconvened for the collaborative album *My Life In The Bush Of Ghosts*. The latter album develops many of the themes of the former, again merging world music with new studio technology. As on *Remain In Light* the pair built up their songs from tape loops and electronic percussion but also began to make innovative use of found-sound samples, including elements of Egyptian and Lebanese music as well as fragments of American talk radio stations and ambient static. The album – a minor hit in both the U.S.A. and Britain – has since become a signpost for the many musicians who have followed Byrne and Eno toward genre-bending, patchwork methods of working.

1981

Escape **Journey**

Columbia 37408 (U.S.A.) / CBS CBS/40 85138 (U.K.)
Released August 1981

Founded by Neal Schon, a former member of Santana, Journey started life as an instrumental trio before adding vocalist Steve Perry and becoming a huge-selling arena-rock act.

Formed in 1973, Journey was named by the winner of a San Francisco radio contest, and recorded three modestly successful jazz-rock albums before Perry joined the group in 1977. His smooth vocal delivery and the group's arrival at a more concise, hard-rock sound immediately reaped dividends, with *Infinity* (1978) selling a million copies in the U.S.A. alone. By the end of the 1970s Journey had also become a hugely popular live act, regularly filling large venues across North America and Europe.

The group's fourth album with Perry, *Escape*, was Journey's mainstream breakthrough. Produced by Kevin Elson and Mike 'Clay' Stone and recorded at Fantasy Studios in Berkeley, California, *Escape* has a more polished, commercial sound than its predecessors.

The album spawned a trio of Top Ten hits in the U.S.A. – the ballads 'Don't Stop Believin',' 'Who's Crying Now,' and 'Open Arms' – and sold over nine million copies worldwide. *Escape* topped the U.S. albums chart and reached Number 32 in the U.K., and was followed by two more big sellers, *Frontiers* (1983) and *Raised On The Radio* (1986), after which the group split and Perry became a recluse.

Though Perry returned for the reunion album *Trial By Fire* a decade later, subsequent Journey albums have been made without his involvement and with Schon as the only original group member.

No Sleep 'Til Hammersmith **Motörhead**

Not issued in the U.S.A. / Bronze BRON/+G/C 535 (U.K.)
Released July 1981

**Motörhead were fronted by one
of the enduring figures of British
heavy rock, bassist-vocalist
Lemmy (born Ian Kilminster), and
laid the foundations for thrash
metal with a series of visceral
albums in the late 1970s and
early 1980s.**

Originally a member of the progressive
acid-rock group Hawkwind, Lemmy
formed Motörhead in 1975 with
guitarist 'Fast' Eddie Clarke and
drummer Phil 'Philthy Animal' Taylor.

The group built up a devoted following in the U.K. with the albums *Motörhead*
(1977), *Overkill*, *Bomber* (both 1979), and *Ace Of Spades* (1980).

In March 1981 Motörhead scheduled a four-date U.K. tour specifically to
record *No Sleep 'Til Hammersmith*, as nobody had ever thought to tape the
group's live act before. The 'Short Sharp, Pain In The Neck Tour' took in
performances at the West Runton Pavilion, Leeds Queen's Hall, and two
dates at the Newcastle City Hall. The songs on *No Sleep 'Til Hammersmith*
were recorded at the final three gigs by Vic Maile, who had previously
recorded Dr Feelgood's live album *Stupidity* (1976). *No Sleep* takes in
material from all four of Motörhead's studio album releases to date,
including 'Iron Horse' and the classic 'Ace Of Spades.'

No Sleep 'Til Hammersmith reached Number One in the U.K. on its release,
the only Motörhead album to do so, and remains the group's defining
moment. Though Motörhead never rose beyond the level of cult act in the
U.S., the group proved inspirational to many of the huge-selling heavy-metal
acts that followed in the later 1980s.

■ *Above (left to right): Phil Taylor, Lemmy, and Eddie Clarke of Motörhead.*

Damaged **Black Flag**

S.S.T. SST 007 (U.S.A. & U.K.)
Released November 1981

**Alongside The Dead Kennedys,
Black Flag was one of the most
important U.S. hardcore punk
groups of the early 1980s.**

Black Flag were formed in 1977 by
guitarist Greg Ginn and bassist Chuck
Dukowski, but the group didn't reach
its full potential until vocalist Henry
Rollins joined in 1980. By this stage
the group also included rhythm
guitarist Dez Cadena and drummer
Robo.

The group recorded *Damaged* themselves in West Hollywood over three
weeks during the summer of 1981, keeping to a budget of $8,500. The
resulting album – 15 angry, disaffected songs crammed into a half-hour
record – was clearly too much for MCA-Unicorn, the label to which the
group had signed in 1980, who refused to issue it. Claiming that it was
too outrageous, they particularly objected to such songs as 'Padded Cell'
and 'Police Story,' which detailed the group's recent battles with the
LAPD, who had assumed, incorrectly, that Black Flag was a cover for a
drugs' ring.

Undeterred, Ginn released *Damaged* on his own SST label – later home to
such influential bands as Hüsker Dü and The Minutemen – prompting legal
action from MCA-Unicorn, who sued the group and succeeded in blocking
them from recording as Black Flag for two years. The band eventually paid
out a six-figure sum to free themselves from their contract and issued seven
further albums between 1984 and 1986 before splitting up.

The muscular, tattooed Rollins has since become one of rock's unlikely
renaissance men, recording several spoken-word albums and publishing
volumes of poetry, short stories, and autobiography via his 2.13.62 imprint.

1981

Dare! **The Human League**

A&M 4892 (U.S.A.) / Virgin T/TP/TCV 2192 (U.K.)
Released October 1981

Non-Stop Erotic Cabaret **Soft Cell**

Sire 3647 (U.S.A.) / Some Bizarre BZ LP/MC 2 (U.K.)
Released December 1981

Hailing from the industrial English city of Sheffield, also home to contemporaries ABC, The Human League was the first synthesizer pop group to achieve widespread international fame.

Drawing on David Bowie's pioneering work with Brian Eno in the late 1970s on the albums *Low* and *Heroes* as well as his knack for capturing the cultural zeitgeist, The Human League peaked with *Dare!*, which spawned the Number One hit single on both sides of the Atlantic, 'Don't You Want Me.' The first, more avant-garde incarnation of The Human League was founded by former computer operators Martyn Ware and Ian Craig-Marsh alongside vocalist Phil Oakey. The trio soon recruited Adrian Wright, who became the group's visual technician, creating projections in front of which the other members performed. The Human League's line-up marked something of a sea change in popular music, as it was no longer necessary for a group to have a guitarist, bassist, or drummer when all of those sounds and more could be synthesized using keyboards and drum machines.

After several unsuccessful singles and an album, *Reproduction* (1979), Ware and Craig-Marsh left to form Heaven 17. They were replaced by Ian Burden on bass and synthesizers and a pair of backing vocalists, Jo Catherall and Susanne Sulley. This new Human League issued a trio of U.K. hit singles, of which 'Love Action (I Believe In Love)' reached Number Three, before commencing work on *Dare!*. The album was produced by the group and Martin Rushent, an engineer-cum-producer who had previously worked with T. Rex, The Stranglers, and Buzzcocks.

In contrast to The Human League's earlier experimental offerings, *Dare!* is a bright, polished collection of well-crafted love songs, underpinned by Rushent's sequencer-heavy style of production. The group's sound was bolstered by the addition of guitarist Jo Callis, who added melodic hooks to a predominantly synthesizer-based sound. Once again turning to Bowie's work – notably 'Sound And Vision' and 'Fashion' – as a template, the album also drew on the flamboyance of Roxy Music and the robotic groove of Kraftwerk. *Dare!* topped the U.K. albums chart in late 1981 and reached Number Three on its release early the following year in the U.S.A. As well as 'Don't You Want Me' and the previously issued 'Love Action'

and 'The Sound Of The Crowd,' *Dare!* featured a further U.K. hit single, 'Open Your Heart.'

Another important synth-pop act to emerge in 1981 was Soft Cell, whose 'Tainted Love' had already topped the U.K. singles chart by the time The Human League came to release *Dare!*. Though Soft Cell was ultimately overshadowed commercially by The Human League, the group issued the similarly innovative *Non-Step Erotic Cabaret*, which peaked at Number Five in the U.K. The album also contains two further U.K. hits, 'Bedsitter' and 'Say Hello, Wave Goodbye,' but failed to make as much of an impression in the U.S.A., where it peaked at Number 22.

■ *Above: Adam And The Ants. Below: Soft Cell. Left: The Human League.*

Prince Charming Adam And The Ants

Columbia 37615 (U.S.A.) / CBS CBS/40 85268 (U.K.)
Released November 1981

Adam And The Ants started life in the late 1970s as a fairly perfunctory, gloomy, post-punk act, whose debut, *Dirk Wears White Sox* (1979), failed to chart.

Former Sex Pistols manager Malcolm McLaren then hijacked the group's three backing musicians – rechristening them Bow Wow Wow and teaming them up with teenage singer Annabella Lwin – but not before he had encouraged frontman Adam Ant (born Stuart Goddard) to adopt a more theatrical image. Ant recruited a new band to record the Technicolor, rock'n'roll-influenced *Kings Of The Wild Frontier* (1980), which gave him a pair of U.K. hit singles, 'Ant Music' and 'Dog Eat Dog.'

Adam And The Ants' third album, *Prince Charming*, is an even more exuberant conceptual piece. Ant adopted the character – and costume – of an 18th-century highwayman on the record's sleeve and on the single 'Stand And Deliver,' which topped the U.K. singles chart, as did the follow-up 'Prince Charming.' A third single, 'Ant Rap,' peaked at Number Three in early 1982. The album was produced by Chris Hughes – who in another incarnation was the drummer in Tears For Fears – a highly sought-after producer and session musician. (Having produced all of Adam And The Ants' albums, Hughes went on to work with, among others, Paul McCartney, Enya, and Tori Amos.)

Despite a lukewarm critical response and few strong songs beyond the three hit singles, *Price Charming* entered the U.K. albums chart at Number Two, though it fared less well in the U.S.A., where it stalled at Number 94. Ant split the group in early 1982 to pursue a solo career.

1981

Face Value Phil Collins

Atlantic 16029 (U.S.A.) / Virgin V2185 (U.K.)
Released February 1981

Having achieved considerable international success during the 1970s as a member of Genesis, Phil Collins launched his solo career in 1981 with *Face Value*.

Originally the group's drummer, Collins emerged as the key figure in Genesis after the departure of Peter Gabriel in 1975, taking on the roles of chief songwriter and vocalist and steering the group toward a more adult contemporary pop sound. Collins started work on *Face Value* alone on an 8-track recorder before enlisting the help of Hugh Padgham, who had recently engineered Peter Gabriel's third solo album – on which Collins had guested – and produced *Ghost In The Machine* by The Police. Collins played all of the drum and synthesizer parts himself, while the guest musicians include Eric Clapton and the Earth Wind & Fire horn section. *Face Value* features eleven Collins originals that draw on recent changes in his personal life, from 'In The Air Tonight,' which details the collapse of his marriage, to 'This Must Be Love,' about the optimism of a new relationship.

Despite its sparse, somber arrangement and bitter lyrics, 'In The Air Tonight' reached Number Two in the U.K. singles chart and made the U.S. Top 20. *Face Value* itself peaked at Number Seven in the U.S.A. and topped the U.K. chart, outselling all of Collins's previous albums with Genesis.

Street Songs Rick James

Motown 12153 (U.S.A.) / MOT-5405 (U.K.)
Released November 1981

A blend of funk, rock, soul, and contemporary pop, Rick James's sound predated that which would propel Prince to superstardom, and helped revive the then-floundering Motown Records label.

Before signing to Motown, James had been a member of 1960s Toronto band The Mynah Birds with a pre-fame Neil Young, though the group never released a record. James signed to Motown in 1977 and hit the U.S. albums chart with his demo tape, issued as *Come Get It!*. By the time he began recording *Street Songs*, his fifth solo album, James was Motown's hottest property, and the label gave him free reign to write, produce, and perform most of the album himself. James worked on the album between December 1980 and July 1981 at a number of studios in and around Hollywood, employing an array of impressive guest musicians. Chief among them was Stevie Wonder, who guests on harmonica, while The Temptations provide backing vocals. On 'Fire And Ice' James performs a duet with the disco singer Teena Marie, whose own debut, *Wild And Peaceful*, he had produced in 1979.

Street Songs reached Number Three on the U.S. albums chart on its release in late 1981 and sold over a million copies, making it the biggest-selling album of James's career. Its success was due in no small part to the inclusion of his best known single, 'Super Freak (Part 1),' which reached the *Billboard* Top 20.

1982

■ *A still from the promo video for Michael Jackson's 'Thriller,' the title track from his landmark album. 'Thriller' was, at the time, the most expensive promo video ever made.*

Thriller Michael Jackson

Epic 38112 (U.S.A.) / EPC/40/CD 85930 (U.K.)
Released December 1982

The biggest-selling album of all time, *Thriller* has become a watershed in the history of popular music, selling in excess of 50 million copies worldwide. Incredibly, seven of the nine tracks also became huge hit singles.

Being an international star was nothing new to Michael Jackson, but his 1979 album *Off The Wall* had established him as a solo performer of astonishing ability and limitless mainstream potential. Produced by Quincy Jones, the album had given Jackson his first two U.S. Number One

singles in 'Don't Stop 'til You Get Enough' and '...... ...' and would eventually sell over seven million copies worldwide. Jackson remained loyal to his musical family, however, recording *Triumph* with the other Jacksons the following year. That album's high point is his 'This Place Hotel,' an early example of the horror-movie imagery he would develop further on *Thriller*.

Jackson began work on *Thriller* in March 1982 at Westlake Audio in Los Angeles, California. He was reunited on the album with Quincy Jones, a producer, composer, and record-company executive who had previously worked with artists including Miles Davis and Frank Sinatra. *Thriller* took its predecessor as a blueprint, perfecting its disco pop while adding heavy-rock elements to the funk tracks and making the soulful ballads even sweeter, giving the album a near-universal appeal.

Jones's production is one of the keys to the album's success, providing Jackson with a sparse but powerful backdrop over which to demonstrate his improved vocal abilities: gone for the most part is the adolescent falsetto of his earlier hits, replaced instead by a deeper, more determined delivery. The lyrical themes of *Thriller* are also more adult, as Jackson rails against press intrusion into his life on 'Wanna Be Startin'

Somethin'" and sounds almost paranoid on 'Billie Jean,' with its repeated refrain of "The kid is not my son." While the words seem downcast at times, the music remains vital throughout and – crucially to its enduring appeal – free of the schmaltzy over-production of much of the pop music of its era.

As well as containing some of the strongest hooks of Jackson's career, *Thriller* also featured several notable guest stars. The singer performed a duet with Paul McCartney on the album's first single, 'The Girl Is Mine' – the two would reconvene the following year for 'Say Say Say.' Of more historical importance is the guitar solo on 'Beat It,' provided by Eddie Van Halen at a time when a collaboration between a black pop star and a white heavy-metal musician was unprecedented. Many other black performers would follow Jackson's lead in subsequent years and work with rock musicians to boost their crossover appeal: Run DMC, for example, scored a Number Four hit in the U.S.A. in 1986 with 'Walk This Way' featuring Aerosmith. Jackson himself would repeat the feat a decade later, working with Guns N' Roses guitarist Slash on *Dangerous*.

Another contributor to *Thriller* was Vincent Price. Price had begun his acting career in the 1930s, starring in numerous darkly comic horror movies before switching tack in the 1970s and becoming a television chef. He returned to his earlier role on *Thriller*, providing a suitably spooky voice-over on the title track. The rest of the performers were Los Angeles session musicians, though one of the album's backing vocalists

would go on to have a hugely successful solo career in her own right: Jackson's sister Janet, already a sitcom star, would later record one of the decade's biggest selling albums, the hip-hop flavored *Control* (1986).

Jackson was adamant while making *Thriller* that it would vastly outsell *Off The Wall*, telling Jones that he intended it to be the most successful album of all time. He demonstrated his dedication to the project when he scrapped the album after the first official playback for label executives. Jackson and Jones returned to Westlake Audio to undertake a radical remix, so pushing the album several months behind schedule. On its eventual release in December 1982, however, *Thriller* entered the U.S. *Billboard* chart at Number One, where it would remain for an unrivalled 37 weeks of a two-year residency. The album also topped the U.K. chart and numerous others across Europe. Just as Jackson had planned during its lengthy gestation, *Thriller* would go on to become the bestselling album of all time, achieving worldwide sales of over 51 million copies.

Jackson helped maintain *Thriller*'s momentum by drawing an unprecedented seven hit singles from it. The first of these was the Paul McCartney collaboration 'The Girl Is Mine,' which was followed in early 1983 by 'Billie Jean' and 'Beat It.' Both releases topped the U.S. singles chart; the former was almost titled 'Not My Lover' after Quincy Jones opined that listeners might too readily associate the song with the tennis player Billie Jean King. ('Beat It' was successful enough that it inspired a

Weird Al Yankovich parody, 'Eat It,' itself a U.S. chart hit.) In May 1983 Jackson performed 'Billie Jean' on a television special commemorating 25 years of Motown Records. It was at this moment that Jackson became pop music's first megastar, inaugurating his moonwalk dance in front of an audience of 47 million.

Jackson released four more singles from *Thriller* during the remainder of the year; 'Wanna Be Startin' Somethin',' 'Human Nature,' 'PYT (Pretty Young Thing),' and the album's title track. All four reached the U.S. Top Ten and were hits in Britain. 'The Lady In My Life' proved to be the only song on *Thriller* not to be issued separately: an eighth song from the album, 'Baby Be Mine,' was also issued as the b-side to 'Human Nature.'

During 1983 Jackson also entered into a mutually beneficial relationship with MTV, becoming the first real star of the fledgling television station. 'Billie Jean' was the first video by a black artist to be playlisted by MTV, and also marked the first time a music video told a story while promoting a song. Jackson and director John Landis took the process a step further with the 'Thriller' promo. The extravagant piece, in which a werewolf

Above: Paul McCartney – who featured on the first single to be drawn from Thriller, *'The Girl Is Mine' – and his wife Linda pose with Jackson at the 1983 Brit Awards ceremony. Left: Jackson with his pet monkey, Bubbles, and an unnamed llama.*

Jackson dances with a troupe of other creatures of the night, ended up costing twice its already huge $600,000 budget. These costs were recouped in March 1984 with the VHS release of *The Making Of Michael Jackson's 'Thriller,'* which became the bestselling music video ever. By the time of its release, Jackson had won in a record eight categories at both the American Music Awards and the Grammys, bringing a fitting conclusion to a period of unparalleled success.

> ## "ALL THE BRILLIANCE THAT HAD BEEN BUILDING INSIDE MICHAEL JACKSON FOR TWENTY-FIVE YEARS JUST ERUPTED."
> *QUINCY JONES, PRODUCER OF THRILLER*

Michael Jackson's star showed no sign of falling during the rest of the 1980s. After a final tour with The Jacksons in 1984, Michael co-wrote the global hit single 'We Are The World' with Lionel Richie and bought the music publishing company ATV, which held the rights to much of the Lennon & McCartney songbook. His next solo release, *Bad* (1987), inevitably failed to reach the artistic and commercial heights of its predecessor, but still sold over 25 million copies and spawned four U.S. Number One hit singles. Though Jackson's career began to decline in the 1990s amid much negative publicity, *Thriller* remains one of the most important albums of all time.

The Digital Revolution

After the quadraphonic debacle, both industry and consumers were wary of new technology. Nonetheless, in the studio world things were changing all the time. Tom Stockham of the Massachusetts Institute of Technology had devised a digital audio recorder, using a computer tape transport, as early as 1962.

In 1975 he started a company called Soundstream with loudspeaker-maker Malcolm Low and launched the first commercial digital recording service in the world. In 1976 he recorded The Santa Fe Opera and then, in 1978, recorded Frederick Fennell and The Cleveland Symphonic Winds for Telarc. This would be the first commercially released digital recording. The first digitally recorded pop or rock album to be released was Ry Cooder's *Bop Till You Drop*. Both those records were released on album and cassette, garnering considerable interest from audiophiles and enthusiasts, though Cooder was scathing about both the sound and the complexities involved in pioneering it. But while there was keen interest there was, as yet, no digital delivery system for the home.

That came with Compact Disc, introduced in 1982, but a playback-only medium for the first ten years of its life. The CD was first conceived in 1969 by Dutch physicist Klass Compaan, but ten years passed before the format was ready to be officially unveiled. The CD is an amalgam of several technologies introduced in the 1960s and 1970s, including the laser and digital recording systems. Philips and Sony were at the forefront of the new medium's development and were jointly responsible for setting a number of standards for the format in 1979. All CDs would be recorded in 16-bit audio, with a sampling rate of 44.1 kHz (44,100 samples per second). Produced from polycarbonate, the disks were intended to be four and a half inches (115mm) in diameter, but were expanded to nearly four and three-quarter inches (120mm) to allow for just over 74 minutes of audio. All involved were optimistic that CDs would revolutionize the way we listen to music.

The first commercial CD players went on sale in Japan in October 1982, alongside an initial catalog of 112 CD titles. Europe and the U.S.A. followed in February and June of 1983 respectively. Many of the first titles were classical and jazz recordings or, in Japan, karaoke collections; among the early rock and pop titles on offer were Billy Joel's *52nd Street* and Michael Jackson's *Off The Wall*. The general trend tended to be for major-label hits of the past few years. Aside from Japan, traditionally more receptive to new technology and where demand almost immediately outstretched supply, CD sales began slowly, with many consumers unsure whether the new format would take off, and neither willing nor able to meet the high cost of the first CD players. Early CD machines, such as the Sony CDP 101, sold for around $1,000, with the disks themselves priced between $15 and $20, limiting their mainstream appeal. Research commissioned by Sony Japan suggested that virtually all CDs were being sold to young men in their 20s and early 30s, whose primary interest was in the high sound-quality of the format. Some industry people began to worry that this might limit the CD market to audiophiles and never expand it to what Sony had predicted would be "a music revolution in the home." Regardless, major record labels continued to expand their catalogs. One of the first new albums to be issued on CD was Bruce Springsteen's *Born In The U.S.A.*, which went on to become one of the biggest-selling albums of all time.

Initially, all CDs were manufactured either by PolyGram in Germany or by Sony Japan; the first major U.S. pressing plant did not open until late 1984. Up to 1986, the majority of CDs sold in the U.S.A. were imported from abroad. CDs sold modestly for the first couple of years before a sudden upsurge around Christmas 1985 that left record shops completely out of stock and pushed yearly sales up to 22 million. The same year also saw the introduction of the DiscMan. While such portable CD players would not become commonplace for several years, they gave CDs a further advantage over 12-inch vinyl albums because music fans could now listen to them while on the move.

The size of the CD meant that a new packaging format had to be created. It was decided that CDs should be sold in 12-inch by six-inch cardboard 'long-boxes,' perhaps because they could be displayed in the same racks as vinyl records. It was also considered that these large rectangular packages would be more of a deterrent to retail theft than something of five inches in diameter. However, as complaints were made about the amount of cardboard wasted in the production of the long-boxes, they

Continued on page 215

1982

Rio **Duran Duran**

Capitol 12211 (U.S.A.) / E.M.I. 3411 (U.K.)
Released January 1983 (U.S.A.) / May 1982 (U.K.)

Duran Duran was the most enduring and successful of the new-romantic groups to emerge from the U.K. in the early 1980s.

The group's second full-length effort – and international breakthrough album – *Rio* typifies the decade's pop, not just musically but also visually, particularly in the title track's famous video, in which the group cavorts with beautiful models on a yacht.

Duran Duran was formed in 1980 by DJ-turned-keyboardist Nick Rhodes and bassist John Taylor, who named the group after a character in the kitsch sci-fi classic movie *Barbarella* (1967). The group was augmented by drummer Roger Taylor, guitarist Andy Taylor, and vocalist Simon Le Bon. In 1981 they signed to EMI – which hoped to capitalize on the success of fellow new romantics Culture Club and Spandau Ballet – and recorded an eponymous debut, which peaked at Number Three in the U.K., remaining on the chart for 118 weeks. The album was not initially successful in the U.S.A., but entered the *Billboard* Top Ten two years later, with 'Durandemonium' at its peak following the release of *Rio*.

Central to Duran Duran's success was the group's image, carefully cultivated in press shots and a series of videos directed by Russel Mulcahy. Having previously directed the video to Buggles' novelty hit 'Video Killed The Radio Star,' Mulcahy cast Duran Duran as hedonistic playboys in the promotional movie that accompanied the group's debut single, 'Planet Earth.' The image stuck, and Mulcahy continued to work with the group throughout the 1980s, directing memorable videos for 'Girls On Film,' 'Rio,' and 'Wild Boys,' among others. Also integral to Duran Duran's visual appeal were the high-fashion record sleeves, designed by Malcolm Garrett, in particular *Rio*'s iconic cover.

Having already conquered the U.K. and much of Western Europe with their eponymous debut album, the group began to set its sights on the U.S. market while making *Rio*. Like its predecessor, *Rio* was produced by Colin Thurston, who had earned his spurs engineering David Bowie's *"Heroes"* and Iggy Pop's *Lust For Life* in Berlin in 1977 before working on albums by The Human League and Magazine. Thurston lends *Rio* a lush, exuberant feel throughout, whether on the upbeat synth-pop of 'Hungry Like The Wolf' and the title track or on more subtle ballads, such as 'Lonely In Your Nightmare.' While the album is often dominated by dayglo synthesizer flourishes and electronic drum-machine rhythms, *Rio* also reveals Duran Duran as a group of talented musicians, particularly in the case of bassist John Taylor and drummer Roger Taylor.

Rio reached Number Two in the U.K. on its release in 1982, while three singles from the album – 'Hungry Like The Wolf,' 'Save A Prayer,' and the title track – entered the Top Ten. In the U.S.A. the album's release was held over until early 1983, at which point it reached Number Six, while 'Rio' peaked at Number Two several months later. In the remaining months of 1983 Duran Duran reached the top of the singles and albums charts in the U.K. for the first time, with 'Is There Something I Should Know' and *Seven And The Ragged Tiger* respectively.

The Lexicon Of Love **ABC**

Mercury SRM-1-4059 (U.S.A.), Neutron NTRS1 (U.K.)
Released September 1982 (U.S.A.) / July 1982 (U.K.)

With their dramatic, synthesized pop, ABC became an instant international success with their first single, 'Tears Are Not Enough,' and the album *The Lexicon Of Love*.

Based in Sheffield, England, ABC earned considerable critical acclaim from the outset for their classic pop songwriting as well as former fanzine editor Martin Fry's crooning vocal delivery, which was often likened to that of Bryan Ferry and David Bowie. Though signed to Phonogram in the U.K., the group was allowed to issue their debut through their own Neutron imprint.

What lifted *The Lexicon Of Love* above the often throwaway fare of ABC's early-1980s contemporaries was the innovative production style of Trevor Horn. His warm, dense arrangements, augmented by Anne Dudley's sweeping orchestrations, proved the perfect foil for Martin Fry's theatrical vocals. Horn, who had scored an international hit with 'Video Killed The Radio Star' as a member of Buggles two years previously, would become one of the most successful producers of the 1980s, working with Yes, Pet Shop Boys, Frankie Goes To Hollywood, and Tina Turner, among others. He also later formed techno-pop group Art Of Noise with Dudley and music journalist Paul Morley.

The Lexicon Of Love quickly rose to the top of the U.K. albums chart on its release and made the Top 30 in the U.S.A. The album spawned four hit singles, including 'The Look Of Love' and 'Poison Arrow,' both of which reached the *Billboard* Top 40. Though the band would never repeat the critical and commercial success of their debut – in part because of Martin Fry's ill health, which limited their activity in the mid 1980s – ABC did achieve an isolated international hit in 1987 with the nostalgic 'When Smokey Sings.' They continued to tour and record sporadically through the 1990s.

Nebraska **Bruce Springsteen**

Columbia 38358 (U.S.A.), CBS 40 25100 (U.K.)
Released September 1982

In stark contrast to the glossy production techniques employed on most early-1980s albums, *Nebraska* marks the first instance of an artist issuing a collection of songs recorded in demo form.

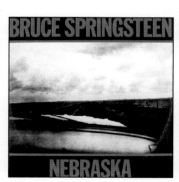

In late 1981, following a lengthy world tour in support of *The River* (1980), Springsteen enlisted his guitar technician, Mike Batlan, to find him "a little tape machine – nothing too sophisticated, just something I can do overdubs on." Batlan duly purchased a Teac 144 Portastudio – a basic 4-track tape recorder that had been on the market since 1979 – and set it up in Springsteen's home in Long Branch, New Jersey.

Springsteen originally intended to cut rough demos of his new songs before recording them properly with The E Street Band. To this end, he worked through the songs quickly, mostly in one or two takes, with just acoustic or electric guitar, harmonica, and vocals. It soon became clear that these demos fell into two distinct categories: half were typical Springsteen rockers – these would later form the basis of *Born In The U.S.A.* (1984) – while the rest had a sparse fragility at odds with his earlier work.

> **"I GOT THIS LITTLE CASSETTE RECORDER, PLUGGED IT IN, TURNED IT ON, AND THE FIRST SONG I DID WAS 'NEBRASKA.' I ONLY HAD FOUR TRACKS, SO I COULD PLAY THE GUITAR, SING, THEN DO TWO OTHER THINGS. THAT WAS IT."**
>
> *BRUCE SPRINGSTEEN*

Some attempts were made to rework this set of songs with subtle instrumentation from the full band, but recordings repeatedly stalled as Bruce felt unable to match the feel of his original tapes.

When it was eventually decided to issue the demos as the follow-up to *The River*, Columbia insisted attempts be made to clean up the original tapes, though little could be done about the sound of a record that had been mastered on an old Panasonic boom box. While the primitive nature of the recordings is often exaggerated – Springsteen still used high-quality Shure microphones and a Gibson Echoplex unit – *Nebraska* remains one of the most rough-sounding releases of a major-label star. The album includes some of the strongest songs in the Springsteen canon, from the title track, a first-person retelling of the Charlie Starkweather killings – also the subject of Terrence Mallick's 1973 movie *Badlands* – to the epic 'Highway Patrolman.'

The Nightfly **Donald Fagen**

Warners 23696 (U.S.A.) / 923696 1/-4 (U.K.)
Released October 1982

After making a series of albums as Steely Dan between 1972 and 1980 alongside Walter Becker, Donald Fagen launched his solo career with the acclaimed conceptual set *The Nightfly*.

While it doesn't deviate far from the Steely Dan sound, *The Nightfly* is a stronger, more cohesive collection of songs than anything Fagen had recorded with Becker since the duo's defining work, *Aja* (1977).

Fagen had made his first tentative steps toward working apart from Steely Dan shortly after the release of the group's *Gaucho* in 1980, when he contributed to the score of Martin Scorsese's *King Of Comedy*. Stepping away from the biting cynicism of Steely Dan, Fagen conceived *The Nightfly* as an evocation of his teenage years, and to that end the songs succeed as snapshots of the period of post-war optimism of the years before the assassination of John F. Kennedy. Produced, like all of Steely Dan's work, by Gary Katz, *The Nightfly* is faultlessly performed by a revolving cast of over 30 session players, who give the album a lavish, smoky, jazz feel. Alongside seven Fagen compositions – held together by the conceit of a hip DJ speaking across the airwaves to Fagen's disaffected youth – is a rendition of the Leiber & Stoller song 'Ruby Baby.' Of the originals, 'IGY (International Geophysical Year)' and the Cold War drama 'New Frontier' were both minor hit singles in the U.S.A. *The Nighfly* itself reached Number 11 in the U.S. albums chart on its release, peaking at Number 44 in the U.K.

Continued from page 213

were eventually replaced by the hastily conceived and now familiar jewel-box.

A major limitation of the vinyl LP had been its maximum playing time of a little over 40 minutes. Artists were quick to exploit the capacity of the CD, which effectively doubled the prospective length of the albums they made. Albums in the 1960s and 1970s typically ran to around 35 minutes, but in the CD era were more likely to hit 50 or 60 minutes. The dynamic of the album also changed; traditionally conceived as two – or more – sides of vinyl, on CD it became a single body of work. These technical advances were not without drawbacks: many artists were overeager to use up all the available space, often resulting in bloated, unfocused albums. The potential length of CDs also had an effect on reissues of older titles. Earlier double-albums, such as Bob Dylan's *Blonde On Blonde*, could be re-pressed on a single disk, while for the first time lengthy classical pieces could be heard in one sitting. Back-catalog sales rose significantly in the latter half of the 1980s as consumers were encouraged to replace their vinyl with remastered CD editions. Past favorites, such as Simon & Garfunkel's *Bridge Over Troubled Water* and Pink Floyd's *Dark Side Of The Moon*, were given a new lease on life by the prospect of hearing them in an enhanced digital format for the first time.

In 1986 three million CD players were sold across the U.S.A. as sales of the traditional LP began to decline. For a brief period in the mid 1980s the cassette led the soundcarrier market, but it would soon be usurped by the CD. Worldwide CD sales reached one billion in 1990, by which time vinyl was increasingly perceived as a niche market. By 1995, 70 percent of all soundcarriers sold worldwide were CDs.

Tape did not give up that easily, however. In the early 1980s the Japanese giants Sony and Matsushita separately developed digital recording systems intended for home use. In 1983 they and some 80 other manufacturers agreed a common system – known as R-DAT or DAT – using the revolving-head recording technology familiar from video recorders. Unfortunately, the new technology terrified the record companies because of its capacity for making perfect copies of CDs, which they were just beginning to sell in large volumes as replacements for people's vinyl record collections. Consequently, they sought a modification of the DAT standard so it would not record CDs, followed by a more general system to stop DAT making digital copies of digital copies – copies of copies tend to proliferate much faster than copies of originals. At the same time they lobbied to prevent the import of DAT recorders without these limitations. In the end, Sony and Phillips agreed not to introduce DAT until the incorporation of SCMS – serial copy management system, the copy-protection system required by the record companies.

In the U.S.A., DAT machines without anti-copying systems were banned in 1987, and lobbying against the machines continued even beyond their eventual introduction in 1990, eight years after their original launch. The issue was not resolved until the Audio Home Recording Act of 1992, which applied to all digital recording devices though not, fatefully, to home computers, which were at the time considered unlikely ever to have the storage capacity to record CDs. SCMS was now mandatory, and manufacturers of machines and tapes also had to pay a levy to copyright owners. Interestingly, in 1988 Sony had taken over CBS Records and now began to see the copyright question from the other side of the fence. Besides, without machines reaching homes, record companies had no interest in producing pre-recorded tapes, essential if DAT was to replace the cassette. In the end, it settled down as an expensive, high-quality medium for studio mastering use and, later, for computer backup.

While Sony was embroiled in copyright wars over DAT, Phillips in Holland had another idea. Its Digital Compact Cassette, introduced in 1992, was a stationary-head digital recording medium using a cassette sufficiently similar to the existing compact cassette to allow old analog cassettes to be played in the same machines. However, the system did not record as much data as DAT, so the audio had to be compressed to fit. It was launched with "a huge selection of prerecorded titles," taking in everyone from The Cure to Ella Fitzgerald. In-car and portable players were made available. It was a success – but only in The Netherlands, where it seized a good share of the market – and it lasted until 1996, when production was halted. Elsewhere, it fought a grim and eventually losing battle with Sony's next invention, the MiniDisc, introduced the same year.

MiniDisc (MD) was intended by Sony to be a replacement for cassette and had several advantages: it offered the instant accessibility that people were getting used to with CD, and it also looked new and exciting compared with the Phillips machine, which was still identifiably a cassette recorder. It also lent itself to portability and came accompanied with a initial flurry of prerecorded music. But MiniDisc initially used a slightly more aggressive version of audio compression than DCC, and some claimed it was audible. MD never captured the American market, and the dream of a mass market for prerecorded disks soon faded. It lives on in a kind of limbo, assailed on one side by recordable CD and on the other by portable MP3 players such as the iPod. Sony, however, has not given up. In 2004 it introduced HiMD, using a 1GB disk that will hold 45 hours of music and can also be used for computer storage.

1982

The Kids From Fame Kids From Fame

RCA 4249 (U.S.A.) / MGM KIDLP004 (U.K.)
Released October 1982

The Kids From Fame was a spin-off from the early 1980s NBC television series Fame.

The television show, which ran for six years between 1982 and 1987, was itself a by-product of the 1980 movie of the same name about a New York school for performing-arts students. Both the movie and television versions gave the 'students' regular opportunities to sing, and, given the popularity of both, an album of songs by them was inevitable.

The Kids From Fame features ten songs, some sung by the entire Fame ensemble, others performed by individual members of the cast,. All are in the standard pop vein of the time, taking in saccharine ballads and disco pop, all decorated by then cutting-edge synthesizer sounds. The album was only a minor hit in the U.S.A., particularly when compared with the success of the television series. Nonetheless, it was followed in 1983 by a second album, Songs, and the concert recording The Kids From Fame Live, which captured the group on stage at the Royal Albert Hall in London, performing 'Don't Stop 'Til You Get Enough,' 'We Got The Power,' and other pop hits. In the early 2000s Fame became an internationally successful musical, at a time when nostalgia for the music and styles of the 1980s was at its highest.

Hex Enduction Hour The Fall

Not issued in the U.S.A. / Kamera KAM 005 (U.K.)
Released March 1982

Hex Enduction Hour is arguably the best-loved of countless album releases by The Fall, the cult British group fronted by the eccentric Mark E. Smith.

Smith founded The Fall in Manchester, England, in 1977, and remains the only constant in an ever-changing membership. The group inaugurated its scratchy post-punk sound on two albums from 1979, Live At The Witch Trials (actually a studio album) and Dragnet. Then came Totale's Turns, Grotesque (both 1980), and the mini-LP Slates (1981).

The Fall started work on Hex Enduction Hour in late December 1981 at the disused Regal Cinema in Hitchin, England, before decamping – improbably enough – to a cave in Iceland to finish the album in early 1982. The eleven songs on Hex are dominated by Smith's freeform vocal rants, the scattershot attack of the group's two drummers, Paul Hanley and Karl Burns, and the spiky guitar interplay between Marc Riley and Craig Scanlon. The other musicians on the album are bassist Steve Hanley and percusssionist-vocalist Kay Carroll.

Hex opens with 'The Classical' – essentially The Fall's mission statement – and closes with 'And This Day,' an epic onslaught of relentless dissonance. In between, the songs' violence and cynicism is born out in titles like 'Hip Priest' and 'Who Makes The Nazis?' The album barely scraped into the U.K. chart, and was not issued in the U.S.A. until 1989, but remains a landmark of early 1980s art rock.

1983

Let's Dance David Bowie

EMI America 17093 (U.S.A.) / AML 3029 (U.K.)
Released April 1983

Having recorded a run of innovative albums between 1970 and 1980, from the glam rock Ziggy Stardust (1972) to the electronic explorations of Low (1977), on Let's Dance Bowie changed direction again, opting for a contemporary pop sound, which brought him the biggest commercial success of his career.

Having retreated from the limelight to make his 'Berlin trilogy' of albums – Low, "Heroes" (both 1977), and Lodger (1979) – Bowie began to make more decisive inroads into the mainstream market again with Scary Monsters And Super Creeps (1980). That album featured collaborations with Pete Townshend and Robert Fripp and gave Bowie four U.K. hit singles, 'Ashes To Ashes,' 'Fashion,' 'Up The Hill Backwards,' and the title track. Despite its chart success, Scary Monsters was still a fairly abrasive, experimental record in places. The following year Bowie issued his second volume of greatest hits, Changestwobowie. This release marks a turning point in his career. Throughout

the 1970s Bowie was renowned for setting trends and inspiring whole new musical genres. From *Let's Dance* onward his records tended to draw more explicitly on the sound of the times rather than leading them.

Let's Dance is notable for the fact that none of Bowie's regular musical collaborators from the 1970s appears on it. Dispensing with Tony Visconti, Bowie recruited the disco producer Nile Rodgers, who had achieved enormous success in the late 1970s as the key creative figure in Chic and had since made records with Diana Ross and Debbie Harry. Rodgers looms large over the sound of *Let's Dance*, which, though clearly still a David Bowie record, has a distinctly polished, dance-pop feel. The album has a bright synthesizer sheen throughout, and is laced with disco guitar hooks, played by Rodgers himself. In place of Carlos Alomar, who had featured on every Bowie album since *Young Americans* (1975), is Stevie Ray Vaughan, the guitarist who went on to lead the blues revival of the 1980s. (Vaughan's appearance on *Let's Dance* predates his own solo debut, *Texas Flood*, by three months, demonstrating that Bowie still had a knack for spotting fresh talent.)

Let's Dance was recorded at Mountain Studios in Switzerland, where Bowie was living as a tax exile. Side One of the vinyl opens with a trio of international single hits, each of them primed for the mainstream but retaining enough individuality to keep them apart from standard pop fare. The first track, 'Modern Love,' is followed by a cover of Iggy Pop's 'China Girl,' which Bowie had produced for Pop's 1977 album *The Idiot*. Bowie covered the song to help his friend – who was languishing in a period of diminishing success – by way of the huge royalty payments that started to go Pop's way as the song raced into the Top Ten of the U.S. and U.K. singles charts. The third song in

this opening salvo is the title track, one of Bowie's best-known songs and the only one of his singles to top the charts on both sides of the Atlantic. Though the rest of *Let's Dance* doesn't quite maintain the momentum of these three, there are few weak moments, resulting in the most aurally satisfying Bowie album of the 1980s. *Let's Dance* topped the U.K. albums chart on its release, and reached Number Four in the U.S.A.

Let's Dance was just one of a number of big-selling albums of the 1980s produced by Nile Rodgers. Rodgers had previously been best known as a member of Chic, the most influential disco group of the late 1970s. The band scored several huge international hits between 1977–9, most notably 'Le Freak' and 'Good Times,' but the group's popularity fell in the early 1980s.

Undeterred, Rodgers turned his hand to writing for and producing other artists, including Sister Sledge and Diana Ross. *Let's Dance* was the first of a run of hugely successful albums produced by him. He followed it with work on Madonna's *Like A Virgin* (1984), Duran Duran's *Arena* (1984), and Mick Jagger's solo debut, *She's The Boss* (1985). Most of Rodgers's 1980s productions were recorded at The Power Station in New York (now known as Avatar Studios), where he made regular use of his former Chic bandmates Bernard Edwards and Tony Thompson, on bass and drums respectively. The Power Station also lent its name to the pop supergroup formed in 1985 by the British soul singer Robert Palmer alongside Thompson and several members of Duran Duran, whose work Rodgers produced.

■ *Below: Nile Rodgers (left) and Bernard Edwards (center) pose with David Bowie at the 1983 Frankie Crocker Awards in New York.*

1983

Synchronicity **The Police**

A&M 3735 (U.S.A.) / AMLX63735 (U.K.)
Released June 1983

As well as being the multiplatinum tombstone on the grave of The Police's career, *Synchronicity* illustrates how, by the mid 1980s, recording technology had advanced to such a degree that it was possible for a feuding band to record an album in the same studio without actually having to see each other.

Sting, in the process of breaking up with his actress wife Frances Tomelty, had written several songs, including 'Every Breath You Take,' at Golden Eye, the house formerly owned by James Bond author Ian Fleming in Jamaica. Armed with this material, The Police started work on *Synchronicity* on December 5th 1982 at Air Studios on the Caribbean island of Montserrat. Producer Hugh Padgham recalls: "Though the island is a kind of tropical paradise, making the album turned into a nightmare." This was because, as well as Sting's split from Frances, guitarist Andy Summers's marriage was disintegrating. To compound their misery, the always edgy relationship between Sting and drummer Stewart Copeland had deteriorated

to the point where the pair could not bear to be together. "For acoustic reasons, all of the band members played in different rooms," says Padgham tactfully, "but I'd have to admit that it was also a very convenient way of keeping them all apart." One specific bone of contention at this time was Sting's insistence that Stewart should drum in a more conventional rock mode, rather than his trademark reggae style.

After two weeks nothing had been completed, Padgham wanted to go home, and manager Miles Copeland had to fly in to force them back to work. Even so, Summers recalls "six weeks" being spent trying to record the bass and snare drum for 'Every Breath You Take,' which Copeland still regards as a wonderful song blighted by "an utter lack of groove. It's a totally wasted opportunity." At the start of 1983 recording moved to Le Studio, located in a ski resort near Montreal. "Sting would go skiing in the mornings," says Padgham. "Stewart would come in and lay down some complex drum track, then Sting would come back while Stewart was skiing, and say, 'What the fuck's that? Take it off.'"

Caught in the middle, Summers assumed the role of peacemaker. "Whenever Sting and I had our fists around each others' throats," remembers Copeland, "Andy would hold a two-inch tape – the ring of good vibes – over our heads, chanting 'I am nothing' until we stopped." Eventually, however, *Synchronicity* was completed and, as Padgham observes: "Ultimately, out of all that tension, came a quite wonderful album." The record-buying public certainly agreed, because on July 23rd 1983 it topped the U.S. albums chart for the first of 17 weeks, and had gone four-times platinum before the end of 1984.

Sting has since described *Synchronicity* as virtually a solo album. "Songs like 'Every Breath You Take' and 'Wrapped Around Your Finger' were all about my life," he points out. "I couldn't involve this kind of personal work in a democratic process, at least not about the issues. So it was very clear to me during the making of this record that this was the end of The Police."

Murmur by his suitably mumbled delivery. The focal point is often Peter Buck's distinctive guitar playing, which drew equally on The Byrds and the more contemporary sound of post-punk, while drummer Bill Berry and bassist Mike Mills provide a steady backdrop. *Murmur* reached the U.S. Top 40 on its release, and includes several fan favorites, notably a re-recorded version of the band's debut single 'Radio Free Europe' and 'Perfect Circle,' the latter still a staple of R.E.M.'s live performances 20 years after its release.

Under A Blood Red Sky **U2**

Island 414-818008-1 (U.S.A.) / IMA 3 (U.K.)
Released December 1983

This 8-track mini-album recorded the spirit and fire of U2's shows around the time of the *War* tour.

Formed in Ireland in the late 1970s, U2 had by 1983 released three albums. *Boy* and *October* had been moody, fragmented experiments in guitar rock, dominated by The Edge's heavily echoed riffs and guitar phrases; their third album, *War*, showed a considerable focusing of the band's music, with producer Steve Lillywhite creating a viciously compressed, explosive drum sound. The Cold War tension and barely restrained anger of the songs had a theatrical directness that was bound to electrify audiences. It was as if U2 had arrived to be to the 1980s what The Who had been to the 1960s: a counter-cultural rock band and a fantastic live act.

It made perfect sense, therefore, to get this stage act down on vinyl. Very wisely, U2 side-stepped the temptation of the live double album, and instead *Under A Blood Red Sky* came out as a mini-album at a reduced price – possibly, in part, to tempt those who had bought the video of the same name (of a show at Red Rocks, Arizona) that had been released earlier that year, though of the songs here, only 'Gloria' and 'Party Girl' are actually from the Arizona show. Other tracks, including '11 O'Clock Tick Tock' and 'New Year's Day,' showed that The Edge had discovered an echo-drenched guitar style that was neither riff nor lead but somewhere in between. The album features a passionate rendition of 'Sunday Bloody Sunday' and touching renditions of 'Party Girl' and the Biblical '40.' Unfortunately, a snippet from Stephen Sondheim's 'Send In The Clowns' sung by Bono during one of the songs required a five-figure sum in copyright settlement.

■ *Below: U2 frontman Bono patrols the stage on the group's 1982 U.S. tour.*

Murmur **R.E.M.**

IRS 70604 (U.S.A. & U.K.)
Released May 1983

R.E.M.'s full-length debut, *Murmur*, introduced the sound that would dominate much of the alternative rock of the next decade.

Having already developed a cult following on the strength of the mini-album *Chronic Town*, R.E.M. started work on *Murmur* on January 6th 1983 at Reflection Sound Studios in Charlotte, North Carolina. The album sessions were produced by Don Dixon and Mitch Easter, who had recorded *Chronic Town* at his own Drive-In Studio, also in North Carolina. The band spent the best part of the next six weeks recording, adding multiple layers of arpeggiated guitar to a quiet, subtle backbeat. Still painfully shy at this point, Michael Stipe insisted on performing all his vocal parts alone in the dark.

The sound of *Murmur* is a darker, more obtuse version of the jangly, folk-tinged rock R.E.M. would perfect on the multiplatinum albums *Out Of Time* and *Automatic For The People* in the early 1990s. Stipe's trademark oblique lyrics are already in place, and are lent a further air of mystery on

1983

Eliminator ZZ Top

Warners 23774 (U.S.A.) / W3774/+4 (U.K.)
Released June 1983

occasional co-songwriter. In 1970 Gibbons and Ham recruited bassist Dusty Hill and drummer Frank Beard – curiously the only member of the trio without a full set of facial hair. ZZ Top produced five blues-based albums for London Records in the 1970s before signing to Warners in 1978. The group's Warners debut, *Deguello* (1979), demonstrated with a series of wry, surreal songs, that ZZ Top were not the simple, rustic trio most people had taken them for in the past, but musically the group was still mining 1960s-style blues rock. *El Loco* (1981) continued in a similar vein, adding a smutty sense of humor to songs such as 'Pearl Necklace' and 'Tube Snake Boogie,' before the group – or perhaps Ham – decided a change of sound was needed in order to achieve true international stardom.

Few would have expected ZZ Top to adopt the synth-pop stylings that dominated the singles charts in the early 1980s, but that is exactly the route the group took. *Eliminator* retains the driving blues guitars of previous ZZ Top albums, but adds a layer of synth hooks that immediately brought mainstream acceptance to the trio of two bearded and one mustachioed Texans. Produced, like all of ZZ Top's recorded output, by Ham, the album also sticks to the lyrical themes of its predecessors. Even if the group didn't quite look the part, ZZ Top's songs about fast cars and faster women were suddenly in vogue, dovetailing neatly with the international playboy image of the likes of Duran Duran. ZZ Top also adopted a similar promotional angle to Duran Duran, filling their music videos with scantily clad beauties as well as the obligatory red coupe. ZZ Top's videos – for 'Sharp-Dressed Man,' 'Gimme All Your Lovin,'' and 'Legs' – were rivaled only by Michael Jackson when it came to heavy MTV rotation in 1983.

Having achieved modest success in the U.S.A. during the 1970s with a traditional, guitar-based sound, bearded blues-rock trio ZZ Top began working with synthesizers on *Eliminator*, achieving widespread international fame in the process.

Eliminator also established a strong visual image for the band. The record's sleeve – an airbrushed image

of a red Ford coupe – stands among the most iconic album covers of the 1980s, while the videos for 'Gimme All Your Lovin' and 'Legs' were MTV staples during the cable music channel's formative years.

ZZ Top was first conceived in the late 1960s by guitarist Billy Gibbons and Bill Ham, who, throughout the group's career, has been an unofficial fourth member, serving as manager, producer, and

Eliminator reached Number Nine in the U.S.A., and was ZZ Top's first hit album in the U.K., where it peaked at Number Three. Of the three singles to be drawn from *Eliminator*, 'Legs' was the most successful, charting at Number Eight in the U.S.A. and Number 16 in the U.K. ZZ Top followed the album with the equally successful – but less artistically rewarding – *Afterburner* (1985), which was essentially 'Eliminator II'.

Swordfishtrombones Tom Waits

Island 90095 (U.S.A.) / ILPS/ICM 9762 (U.K.)
Released September 1983

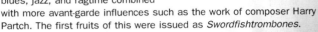

Tom Waits first emerged in the early 1970s under the guidance of Frank Zappa's manager Herb Cohen, recording seven albums of woebegone, after-hours balladry for Elektra in the U.S.A. and Asylum Records in the U.K. between 1973 and 1980.

After fulfilling his Elektra-Asylum contract with *Heart Attack And Vine*, Waits began to experiment with a wholly new sound, a melting pot of blues, jazz, and ragtime combined with more avant-garde influences such as the work of composer Harry Partch. The first fruits of this were issued as *Swordfishtrombones*.

Recorded at Sunset Sound in Los Angeles in August 1982 with producer Biff Dawes, *Swordfishtrombones* ditches the traditional arrangements and rich orchestral flourishes of Waits's earlier work in favor of a more idiosyncratic palette of weird instruments. Waits himself switches from piano to harmonium, while an impressive array of guest musicians, including Larry Taylor and Victor Feldman, conjures up a vaudeville opera with marimbas, African talking drums, and the sound of a chair being dragged across the studio floor. The songs are pitched somewhere between Kurt Weill and Howlin' Wolf, and Waits's lyrics, delivered in his trademark raw-throated voice, are as obscure as the musical settings behind them, as he sings of eggs that "chase the bacon from the fryin' pan" and "a hummingbird trapped in a closed-down shoe store."

Waits evidently had some trouble persuading a record label to take a chance on *Swordfishtrombones*, as it didn't see release until 13 months after its completion. Eventually issued by Island Records, with whom Waits would remain until the late 1990s, the album became an instant cult favorite, and is now regarded by many as one of the finest albums of the 1980s.

Can't Slow Down Lionel Richie

Motown 8051 (U.S.A.) / MOT-6059 (U.K.)
Released December 1983

A former member of The Commodores, Lionel Richie as a solo performer was one of the most successful male vocalists of the 1980s. As well as being a hugely popular ballad singer, he also wrote and produced hits for other artists, including 'Lady,' a U.S. Number One hit for Kenny Rodgers.

Formed in 1968, The Commodores' early output was dominated by hard funk, but Richie's lush ballads gradually came to the fore in the 1970s. Richie left the group to pursue a solo career in 1982, releasing a self-titled debut album that spawned three U.S. Top Ten hits; his second solo album, however, elevated him to the ranks of superstardom. Using Michael Jackson's recent *Thriller* (1982) as a blueprint, *Can't Slow Down* aimed to cover all bases of the mainstream pop market, adding funky dance pop and watered-down elements of hard rock to the expected ballads. Richie co-wrote and produced all eight songs on the album, and spent six months honing the sound of the album at a variety of studios across the U.S.A.

On its release in late 1983 *Can't Slow Down* quickly rose to the top of the U.S. albums chart, eventually selling ten million copies in the U.S.A. and over 15 million worldwide. The album also gave him five U.S. Top Ten singles and won the 1984 Grammy Award for Album Of The Year. Of the singles, 'Hello' and 'All Night Long (All Night)' both topped the U.S. chart, selling a million copies each.

1984

Diamond Life **Sade**

Portrait 39581 (U.S.A.) / Epic 26044 (U.K.)
Released February 1985 (U.S.A.) / July 1984 (U.K.)

Among the most striking female singers to emerge in the 1980s, Sade achieved widespread international fame with the jazz-inflected *Diamond Life*, one of the biggest-selling debuts of the decade.

Born Helen Folasade Adu to an English mother and African father in the Nigerian city of Lagos in 1959, Sade grew up in London. In the early 1980s, while studying fashion at St Martin's College and occasionally modeling, she began to draw record-company interest as vocalist in the funk-rock collective Pride. Initially reticent to leave the eight-piece group behind and sign a major label deal as a solo performer, Sade stalled for a year before inking a contract with Epic in 1983, but only after she had been assured that the label would also take on guitarist-keyboardist Stuart Mathewman and bassist Paul Denman.

Sade started work on her debut album shortly thereafter, adding keyboardist Andrew Hale and drummer Paul Cooke to the band. Also featuring on *Diamond Life* are Mathewman's trumpet-playing sibling Gordon and percussionist Martin Ditcham, who would later work extensively with Talk Talk. *Diamond Life* was produced by Robin Millar, who lends the album a slick, light-jazz feel despite a lack of prior experience as producer. (Following the worldwide success of *Diamond Life*, Millar produced albums for Everything But The Girl, Fine Young Cannibals, and Big Country, among others.) The songs have an elegant cool, their precise guitar and keyboard licks offset by Sade's effortless vocal delivery, reminiscent at times of her childhood idols Billie Holiday and Nina Simone. There are suggestions of Afrobeat rhythms beneath the songs' sophisticated jazz-club stylings, but they are rarely allowed to spill over to the surface. Very few of the nine songs edge beyond mid-tempo, but then they were not intended to – *Diamond Life* is the perfect coffee-table or dinner-party album.

Diamond Life gradually climbed up the U.K. albums chart during the latter part of 1984, peaking at Number Two on the strength of the singles 'Your Love Is King' and 'Smooth Operator,' a collaboration between Sade and former bandmate Ray St John. Sade signed to the CBS subsidiary label Portrait for the U.S. release of the album in early 1985, where it reached Number Five and earned platinum status soon after 'Hang On To Your Love' and 'Smooth Operator' entered the Top Ten.

Sade kept up the momentum with a cameo role in the movie *Absolute Beginners*, which also starred David Bowie, in which she sang 'Killer Blow.' In late 1985 she issued a quick follow-up album, *Promise*, which proved even more popular than *Diamond Life* and gave her the international hit 'The Sweetest Taboo.' After winning a Grammy Award for Best New Artist, Sade's popularity was such that even her album tracks were being heavily rotated on U.S. radio stations. She continues to record and tour in the 21st century, and has to date sold over 40 million albums worldwide.

Like A Virgin **Madonna**

Sire 9251571 (U.S.A. & U.K.)
Released November 1984

Signed to Leo Stein's Sire Records in 1983, Madonna Louise Veronica Ciccone quickly broke into the mainstream with a pair of 1984 singles, 'Lucky Star' and 'Borderline,' and by year's end, her self-titled debut had gone platinum.

Nothing, however, could have prepared listeners for the singer's next move. In November came a single, 'Like A Virgin,' written by pop tunesmith Billy Steinberg, the title track from Madonna's forthcoming second album that revealed a tougher, hard-pop Madonna, a sound so irresistible that even rock radio took notice.

Manning the controls inside New York's Power Station Studio C for the making of *Like A Virgin* was Chic producer Nile Rodgers, who surrounded the singer with an economical rhythm section consisting of Chic bassist Bernard Edwards and drummer Tony Thompson, with Rodgers himself handling guitar duties. "Tony's got such a great way with drums – he plays so hard and so loud he just fills up the room with sound," notes Rodgers's engineer Jason Corsaro. "I realized that it was something that had to be captured. I mean, if you've got a drummer who sounds so beautiful in the room, why would you want to take that away?" Initially, Corsaro's attempts at beefing up the backing were met with resistance. "The folks at Power Station were always telling me, 'You can't put R&B drums in the big room, they have to go in the dead room!' But that didn't make any sense to me – I knew there had to be a way to capture the power of the drums and keep the rhythm intact at the same time."

Corsaro eventually figured out a unique method that involved equal parts mike placement and just plain technical creativity. "By being too close, I knew I was going to miss a lot of those dynamics. By the same token, that music demanded a strong groove. So I started cutting the room tracks in time with the drums. Everyone thinks it was gated, but I actually wrote the parts into the computer as we were mixing! When I added Tony's drums on top of that, the sound was incredibly powerful. It was just what I wanted – a rock, room sound, but also very R&B." As a result of the minimalist mix, Thompson's drum kit became the featured instrument on 'Like a Virgin.' "That's one of the things that made the song so special," says Corsaro. "Because there was nothing but guitar and bass, the drums had so much space to fill. You could hear what Tony was doing so clearly."

Corsaro still had some selling to do during the initial playbacks. "To tell you the truth, Nile wasn't that into it in the beginning of the record," recalls Corsaro. "It really went against the grain of the early-'80s dance sound – I think he was looking for something a bit more 'normal.' But Madonna and her manager absolutely loved it. And that was all he needed to hear."

Corsaro's sound innovation was instrumental in helping to cross Madonna into the rock mainstream – an almost unheard-of feat at the time. "I was thrilled when they picked 'Like a Virgin' for the first single," says Corsaro. "It became the first dance-pop record to have a real rock drum sound. Of course, since then Madonna's proved herself quite capable of keeping up with new ideas – it's really one of her finer attributes."

Reaching Number One on December 22nd 1984, the title track to *Like A Virgin* remained at the top of the charts for the first five weeks of 1985, becoming Madonna's biggest career single. The album – which itself hit Number One in February – provided three additional smash hits in 'Material Girl,' 'Angel,' and 'Dress You Up.' Madonna never looked back, dominating the pop charts with ten straight Top Five singles and massive album sales through the remainder of the decade.

Welcome To The Pleasuredome
Frankie Goes To Hollywood

Island 90232 (U.S.A.) / ZTT-Island ZTT1Q (U.K.)
Released November 1984

Frankie Goes To Hollywood was one of the biggest British pop phenomena of the mid 1980s, thanks in no small part to the slickly orchestrated campaign of controlled controversy that propelled the group's records to the top of the U.K. charts.

Having formed in Liverpool in 1980, Frankie Goes To Hollywood teamed up with producer Trevor Horn, who signed the group to his ZTT label in 1983. (At this time Horn was best known as a performer on Buggles' novelty hit 'Video Killed The Radio Star,' though his production credits did by now include ABC's *Lexicon Of Love*.) The group's first single, the high-octane 'Relax,' sold a million copies in the U.K. after it was banned by the BBC because of its sexually suggestive lyrics. The accompanying homoerotic promo video was also banned, serving only to boost the group's popularity. In the meantime, Paul Morley, the music writer and promotional director of ZTT, began cleverly to insinuate the group into the national consciousness, largely by way of a series of hugely popular 'Frankie Says . . .' T-shirt slogans.

Welcome To The Pleasuredome, the group's double-album debut, arrived in late 1984, with Frankiemania continuing to rise in the U.K. following the release of 'Two Tribes,' which had spent nine weeks at Number One – 'Relax' taking the Number Two spot for some of that time – during the summer. Horn's disco-pop production is exemplary throughout, but few of the album tracks are as memorable as the singles, and covers of Gerry And The Pacemaker's 'Ferry 'Cross The Mersey' and Bruce Springsteen's 'Born To Run' are unnecessary filler. 'The Power Of Love' provided Frankie with a third consecutive U.K. Number One hit, while the album itself also topped the British charts.

Frankie was far less popular in the U.S.A., but did manage a Number Ten placing when 'Relax' was reissued in early 1985.

Make It Big **Wham!**

Columbia 39595 (U.S.A.) / Epic EPC/40 86311 (U.K.)
Released November 1984

Wham! was one of the most internationally successful British pop acts of the 1980s. The duo's popularity peaked with *Make It Big*, which topped the charts in the U.S.A. and the U.K., as did three of the singles drawn from it.

George Michael, who wrote all of the duo's hits and produced the album, was clearly the dominant member of the pair, and few were surprised when he disbanded the group to embark on a solo career in 1986.

Wham!'s debut album *Fantastic!* shows few signs of the songwriting talents Michael would harness on *Make It Big* and in his solo work, and failed to make much of an impact outside the U.K. He and partner Andrew Ridgeley started work on a more mature follow-up in July 1984 with engineer Chris Porter, who had recently worked with Elaine Paige and The Alarm. Like many pop albums of the time, *Make It Big* contains a lot of filler between the songs earmarked as singles, but the singles themselves are near faultless. 'Wake Me Up Before You Go-Go' and the ballad 'Careless Whisper' – written when Michael was just 17 – had already topped the singles charts on both sides of the Atlantic and across Europe by the time *Make It Big* was released in late 1984. 'Everything She Wants' provided Wham! with a third U.S. chart topper, while 'Freedom' reached Number One in the U.K. *Make It Big* has sold over five million copies in the U.S.A. alone, while in 1985 Michael became the youngest ever winner of Britain's Ivor Novello Songwriter Of The Year award.

1984

Born In The U.S.A.
Bruce Springsteen

CBS 38653 (U.S.A.) / CBS86304 (U.K.)
Released June 1984

The commercial peak of Springsteen's career, *Born In The U.S.A.* sold more than ten million copies in the U.S.A. alone and gave him several hits, including the passionate 'Cover Me' and the poppy 'Dancing In The Dark.'

That many see Springsteen as the acme of American 'blue-collar' rock, a guy who sings about cars, girls, and not much else, is largely down to this album's international success. For many it fixed him for ever in their minds as a crude, sweaty stadium rocker, a Rambo of the six-string, populist and simplisitic.

Recording the acoustic demos of *Nebraska* made Springsteen go for a leaner band sound and more straightforward song structures when he returned to electric rock. The band played together in the studio and recorded as directly as possible. Guitarist Steve Van Zandt noted: "That was literally live, at least the eight or nine things we did before I left. If Bruce wanted to sing it again, we'd play it again; that's how live it was."

The title track was crucial, seemingly inescapable in 1984. Festival crowds sang it with gusto when it boomed out through PA systems, whether they were American or not. Springsteen said: "I had written a catchy song . . . probably one of my best since 'Born To Run.' I knew it was going to catch people – but I didn't know it was going to catch them like *that*, or that it was going to be what it was." 'Born In The U.S.A.' started life as a two-chord acoustic song during the *Nebraska* sessions, but was amped-up by The E Street Band with unparalleled ferocity and single-mindedness. Drummer Max Weinberg recalled: "Bruce started playing this droning guitar sound. He threw that lick out to [keyboardists] Roy [Bittan] and Danny [Frederici], and the thing just fell together. It absolutely grabbed us. We played it again and got an even better groove on it. At the end as we were stopping, Bruce gave me the high sign to do all these wild fills, and we went back into the song and jammed for about ten minutes, which was edited out. I remember that night as the greatest single experience I've ever had recording, and it set the tone for the whole record."

From celebrating the mythical romance of the American Dream earlier in his career, Springsteen was now exposing the plight of those who crawl at its margins and under its shadow. But this focus was often blurred by the radio-friendly bounce of 'Glory Days,' the perceived nostalgia of 'My Home Town,' and the apparent flag-waving of the chorus of 'Born In The U.S.A.' Despite the fact that the verses of that song painted a bleak picture of life in the U.S.A., they could be overlooked in the light of the seemingly patriotic refrain, as happened when President Ronald Reagan and others ignored Springsteen's ambivalence and co-opted the song for simplistic jingoism.

Its composer has reservations about the album that made him a global star. In 1987 he said: "I wasn't satisfied with the *Born In The U.S.A.* record. I did not think I made all the connections I wanted to make on it." It was his last studio album with The E Street Band for over a decade.

1984

and sporting a pair of National Health Service glasses. His lyrics were allusive, anguished, and droll. He said: "It was always important to me to use lines that hadn't been said before, because it wasn't enough to use the usual pop terminology." His melodies were free of blues inflections, one reason why the music sounds so English. While 'What Difference Does It Make' and 'Hand In Glove' were hits, the album also features the sad dignity of 'Still Ill' and the creepy beauty of the controversial 'Suffer Little Children,' a song about the infamous 'Moors Murders' that took place in and around the band's home town of Manchester during the mid 1960s.

A Walk Across The Rooftops **The Blue Nile**

A&M 5087 (U.S.A.) / Linn Records LinnLP LKH 1 (U.K.)
Released April 1984

This most retiring of bands has made a career out of eschewing the promotional treadmill of record/video/tour/record, instead choosing to spend years fashioning infrequent albums that are adored by the cognoscenti.

The Blue Nile was formed in 1981 by three Glaswegian university graduates, Paul Buchanan, Robert Bell, and Paul Joseph Moore. That same year an early demo found its way to Robert Stigwood's RSO Records, resulting in a single, 'I Love This Life,' being released in 1981, just weeks before the company went out of business. After this false start the band came to the attention of Linn, a Scottish company known for its upmarket record turntables. Sensing a marketing opportunity for its hi-fi products, Linn formed a label, signed The Blue Nile, and released *A Walk Across The Rooftops*, the band's debut album.

Sales were initially slow, but the album's humane, meticulously crafted electronic white soul gradually drew in a coterie of fanatical admirers. Eventually it quietly slipped into the U.K. album charts and got a release in the U.S.A. on the A&M label. Most bands would have grabbed the moment and toured non-stop for a year on the back of this breakthrough, then quickly recorded a follow-up. Not The Blue Nile. They refused to play live, instead retreating from view to agonize over their next record for five years. *Hats*, as the follow-up was called when it finally appeared in 1989, was felt by many to be even better than *Rooftops*. This time, the band deigned to tour.

The Smiths **The Smiths**

Warner Brothers 25065 (U.S.A.) / Rough Trade RTD25 (U.K.)
Released February 1984

One of the most original of bands of the 1980s, The Smiths were reminiscent of early R.E.M.: they were arty, they appealed to students, had unusual lyrics, plenty of Rickenbacker jangle, an unconventional vocalist, and a healthy contempt for chart formulas.

Guitarist Johnny Marr – whose work with The Smiths made him one of the most important British guitarists of the decade – summed up the group's spirit when he said: "We were against synthesizers, the Conservative government, groups with names like Orchestral Maneouvres In The Dark, the English Monarchy, cock-rock guitar solos, and the American music scene at the time. We stood for the Englishness of The Kinks, T. Rex and Roxy Music . . . We were into The Rolling Stones, The MC5, The Patti Smith Group, Oscar Wilde, [playwright] Sheleagh Delaney, and certain actors."

Recording the debut LP was a trial. The Smiths junked a whole batch of songs and had to start over. When they performed on television their first hit single 'This Charming Man' – not included on the album – they looked like nothing else on the U.K. music scene. Singer Morrissey was the anti-rock star, with a bunch of gladioli hanging out of the back pocket of his jeans

1985

Songs From The Big Chair Tears For Fears

Mercury 824300 (U.S.A.) / MERH 58 (U.K.)
Released March 1985

Tears For Fears – duo Roland Orzabal (vocals, guitar, keyboards) and Curt Smith (vocals, bass) – emerged during the new-romantic, synth-pop period of the early 1980s, taking their name from psychotherapist Arthur Janov's book _Prisoners Of Pain_.

Their debut album, _The Hurting_, contained the hit 'Mad World,' and was followed by _Songs From The Big Chair_, the fifth-bestselling album of 1985. It had three big hits in 'Shout,' 'Head Over Heels,' and 'Everybody Wants To Rule The World.' 'Everybody' was a melody of Beatles-like catchiness, sung and played with such conviction it sounds like they were polishing the platinum disk even as the tape rolled.

The album had structural twists and turns, sculpted melodies, freaky guitar solos, bold singing, and imaginative textures. It was lyrically unified by the theme of psychological exploration and catharsis. Side Two of the vinyl best illustrates the record's dramatic ebb and flow. After the deep blue of the smoky night-club 'I Believe,' 'Broken' kicks in and takes rock somewhere you didn't know was on the map. Its anguish lightens into the walking-on-air 'Head Over Heels,' its Bowie-esque la-la-and-handclaps coda segueing into a cooking live reprise of 'Broken.' A measure of peace comes with the bewitching 'Listen,' with its haunting chords, fluid female vocal, and mysterious mantra-like chant. Time has not been kind to pop music from this period with its tinny, artificial beats and one-finger synth playing, but _Songs From The Big Chair_ is an exception, leaving an impression greater than the sum of its parts.

Rum, Sodomy And The Lash The Pogues

Not issued in the U.S.A. / Stiff SEEZ 58 (U.K.)
Released August 1985

Blending a punk-rock sensibility with traditional Irish folk music, The Pogues built up a devoted cult following in Europe and the U.S.A. in the 1980s.

Shane McGowan formed the group in 1982, adding several folk musicians to the more conventional punk core of his previous group, The Nipple Erectors. The group soon built a reputation on the strength of McGowan's shambolic, drunken stage act and the battered elegance of 1984's debut album _Red Roses For Me_. The following spring The Pogues recruited Elvis Costello – whose own work had begun to betray more rootsy influences by the mid 1980s – to produce what became _Rum, Sodomy And The Lash_.

'The Sick Bed Of Cúchulaínn' set the tone for the album, erupting midway through from whiskey-soaked ballad to rousing, accordion-led punk folk. _Rum, Sodomy And The Lash_ continues in this vein, mixing traditional Irish songs with McGowan originals. The album's centerpiece, 'A Pair Of Brown Eyes,' was a minor U.K. hit single. The Pogues would never again quite match the aching beauty of the songs on here. This was partly a result of the departure of bassist and backing vocalist Cate O'Riordan, who left the

group after marrying Costello in 1986, while McGowan began to descend into drug and alcohol abuse, his unpredictable behavior resulting in him being sacked in 1991. The Pogues did, however, manage an unlikely festive hit in 1987, when 'Fairytale Of New York' – a duet with Kirsty MacColl, featuring the line "Merry Christmas, my arse / I pray God it's our last" – reached Number Two in the U.K.

Hounds Of Love Kate Bush

EMI ST17171 (U.S.A.) / KAB 1 (U.K.)
Released September 1985

After the artistically successful but under-selling _The Dreaming_ (1982), _Hounds Of Love_ – recorded at Windmill Lane Studios and Abbey Road between spring 1984 and summer 1985 – brought Kate Bush back from the commercial wilderness and won her new fans in the U.S.A.

Album-opener 'Running Up That Hill,' a powerfully melancholic tale of communication failure between lovers, was the first of several singles. It was originally titled 'A Deal With God,' but Bush bowed to record-company advice that having the word God in the title would limit airplay in certain countries. The bold, galloping drum rhythm of 'Running Up That Hill' never lets up, with thunderous fills that punctuate the closing section. (Minus hi-hats and cymbals, Bush first encountered this stripped-back drum style when she sang on Peter Gabriel's third album.) 'Cloudbusting' features another innovative approach to percussion with its march-like rhythm track.

Side One of the vinyl offered five individual songs, whereas Side Two was a suite of inter-connected pieces, 'The Ninth Wave,' based on the memories and hallucinations of someone floating in the sea. Her most ambitious piece, it gave ample opportunity to make use of the exotic sounds of her brother Paddy's collection of unusual instruments, as well as Pink Floyd-inspired sound effects. Bush also made pioneering use of the Fairlight synthesizer system.

> **"I WANTED TO TRY AND GET ACROSS A SENSE OF POWER, AND THE WAY I RELATED TO THAT WAS VERY MUCH WHAT I CONSIDER VERY GOOD MALE MUSIC – THE KIND OF POWER I FOUND THERE WAS NOT WHAT I FOUND IN A LOT OF FEMALES' MUSIC."**
> **KATE BUSH, SPEAKING IN 1989**

In almost every way the distance between _Hounds Of Love_ and her 1978 breakthrough hit 'Wuthering Heights' is enormous. The degree of progression in her music is remarkable, and not driven by fashion or style-hopping. It is always in an integral relationship with her music's emotional core.

After _Hounds_, Bush recorded _The Sensual World_ (1989), which expressed a more feminine energy. Using The Trio Bulgarka to add plangent East European folk harmonies to several songs, as well as draw on the musical skills of violinist Nigel Kennedy, The Chieftains, and the Breton harp player Alan Stivell were inspired choices. Both albums show Bush's depth as a songwriter, whether in singing about love failing or lost, or reaching back to forgotten regions of childhood. She has a fine ear for melody and an ability to invent new arrangements for her songs, and she does all this without recourse to blues-inspired vocal clichés.

Bush is unquestionably one of the greatest female singer-songwriters to emerge from the U.K. Without her example things might have been very different for all the rebellious women who came through in the 1990s, such as Björk, Alanis Morissette, and Tori Amos.

1985

Biograph Bob Dylan

Columbia 38830 (U.S.A.) / CBS 66509 (U.K.)
Released November 1985

A career-spanning collection of hits, misses, and previously unissued recordings, the five-LP/three-CD set *Biograph* was the first widely successful boxed set by a rock artist.

While other acts had issued two- or three-volume packages of vinyl in the past, *Biograph* started a trend for lavishly packaged, multidisk sets of a single artist, intended as *the* definitive representation of a performer's work.

Compiled by Columbia to commemorate 24 years of Bob Dylan on record, *Biograph* was conceived as a comprehensive assessment of his career to date. The original ten sides of vinyl are arranged thematically rather than chronologically, making their way through the various aspects of Dylan's music. Side One of the first disk is, perhaps surprisingly, devoted to his love songs, while the rest of *Biograph* works its way through other areas, including Dylan's early protest songs, his first experiments with an electric band, and his most overtly Christian period. This arrangement allows key moments in the Dylan songbook – 'Like A Rolling Stone' or 'Blowin' In The Wind,' for example – to sit comfortably alongside lesser-known or never-before-heard recordings, which include 'Percy's Song' and 'Lay Down Your Weary Tune.' The downside of this scattershot approach is that the listener is left unaware at times of the many patterns, changes, and reinventions of Dylan's career. Perhaps heeding this, the compilers of the majority of the box sets that followed *Biograph* – including Dylan's later all-rarities set, *The Bootleg Series* (1991) – have tended to stick to a more rigid, year-on-year sequence.

Biograph also established another key ingredient of the box set: accompanying the music is an extensive booklet, which features notes by Dylan himself on each of the songs and several biographical pieces, aimed at reminding the listener just how important is the man and his music. As a further selling point these sleevenotes include a number of previously unpublished photographs.

Following the success of *Biograph*, other artists and their respective labels were quick to put together box sets of their own. The subjects of these sets tend almost without exception to be heavyweights of the worlds of rock and, to a lesser extent, jazz, weighted so as to appeal to fans old and new, with a selection of classic material for the uninitiated and an assortment of unreleased cuts for the devoted completist.

A year after *Biograph*'s release, Bruce Springsteen assembled a five-disk volume of concert recordings, *Live 1975–85*. By far the most commercially successful box set ever produced, *Live 1975–85* was one of the first albums to be given diamond status at the inauguration in 1999 of the award for sales of over ten million copies in the U.S.A. That a multivolume collection of live recordings could stand alongside *Sgt Pepper's Lonely Hearts Club Band* or *Dark Side Of The Moon* in sales terms is quite an astonishing achievement, considering the fact that most box sets are aimed at a small section of the record-buying public.

Of the countless other box sets issued over the course of the next two decades, several deserve a brief mention. A number of these contain their respective acts' entire discography, including The Velvet Underground's *Peel Slowly And See* and Led Zeppelin's *Complete Studio Recordings* (both 1993); all 13 U.K. Beatles albums were made available in 1988, housed inside an expensively priced mock bread bin. Sony has to date issued seven deluxe sets compiling the complete sessions from various periods in Miles

Davis's career, several of them with engraved metal spines. The Beach Boys' *Good Vibrations* collection neatly sums up 30 years of the band and includes half an hour of previously unheard material from the then incomplete *Smile* album. Beyond rock and jazz, box sets are less common. One notable exception, however, is *Tommy Boy's Greatest Hits* collection, five CDs of music from the pioneering rap label packaged within an eye-catching, scaled-down reproduction of a crate full of vinyl.

Riptide Robert Palmer

Island 90471 (U.S.A.) / ILPS 9801 (U.K.)
Released November 1985

In a career spanning five decades, Robert Palmer sang with The Alan Bown Set and Vinegar Joe before launching a solo career in the 1970s.

Establishing himself as a versatile white soul singer, Palmer had a number of minor hits in the U.S.A. and Britain in the late 1970s and early 1980s. In 1985 he found a wider mainstream audience as a member of the pop supergroup The Power Station, alongside members of Chic and Duran Duran. 'Some Like It Hot' and a cover of the T. Rex classic 'Get It On' both featured on *The Power Station* and both reached the U.S. Top 20.

The stage was therefore set for Palmer's solo career to move up a gear. *Riptide* was recorded in the Bahamas with several of the musicians Palmer had worked with earlier in the year with The Power Station, including Duran Duran's Andy Taylor. Producer Bernard Edwards lends *Riptide* a polished, 1980s pop sheen that stands some way apart from Palmer's previous blues- and soul-influenced work. It was his first to enter the Top Ten in the U.K. and the U.S.A., but is best remembered for the huge U.S. Number One hit it spawned, 'Addicted To Love.' The memorable promo video had Palmer performing with a 'band' of guitar-wielding models in mini-skirts and became an MTV staple. *Riptide* also featured 'I Didn't Mean To Turn You On,' which peaked at Number Two in the U.S.A. in the summer of 1986.

Brothers In Arms Dire Straits

Warner Brothers 2-25264 (U.S.A.) / Vertigo VERH 25 (U.K.)
Released May 1985

A classic record of the 1980s, *Brothers In Arms* is one of the biggest-selling albums of all time, reaching Number One in at least 25 countries, with worldwide sales in excess of 20 million, and many of the tracks becoming hit singles.

Dire Straits were fortunate enough to be the right band at the right time with the right product to benefit from a new music medium: *Brothers* was one of the first rock albums released on CD. Philips, who were making CD hardware, claimed later that this was "the key album in transforming CD from a new-fangled curiosity into a mass-market music carrier." Hi-fi stores liked its pristine production for demoing CD players and systems. (It was estimated that at one point, when CD players were still luxury items, everyone who had a player had a copy of the album.)

After their first two albums in 1978–9 and the wiry Fender-guitar licks of 'Sultans of Swing,' Dire Straits got more ambitious. By their fourth LP, *Love Over Gold*, they had left their pub-band origins far behind, stretching songs

such as 'Telegraph Road' to 14 minutes. But, after the double-live *Alchemy*, Knopfler decided to trim back to more focused, hooky songs.

Brothers captured the mood of the time. It rocks – but not too much – and it doesn't scream at you, so millions who would normally never buy a rock album bought it. Knopfler's subdued gravelly voice seems reassuringly grounded – worse things happen at sea, it implies. He comes across as an unpretentious Man Of The People, like a commercial version of J.J. Cale. The gleaming steel guitar on the cover promises the illusion of rootsy authenticity delivered in a high-gloss digital package. The lyrics are straightforward. It has radio-friendly breezy tunes like the gentle regret of 'So Far Away,' 'Why Worry,' 'Your Latest Trick,' and 'Walk Of Life.' There is even an anti-war song in 'Brothers in Arms.' The sound combines guitars with ear-candy synth-pads and post-Phil Collins drum rolls.

Knopfler changed his trademark Fender guitar tone for an overdriven Les Paul on 'Money For Nothing,' the album's liveliest track, a harmonic-popping distant relative of 'Jumping Jack Flash,' with a guest vocal by Sting. The story goes that Knopfler wanted to emulate ZZ Top's guitar sound but they wouldn't tell him how, so he approximated it by wedging a wah-wah pedal half-open. 'Money For Nothing' might have been intended as a satire on the consumerism of the decade, but was all-too-quickly assimilated as an anthem for it, especially with its innovative video all over MTV. *Rolling Stone* called it "Led Zep for yuppies."

Whatever the quality of the record as a whole, its title track was genuinely impressive. The real vocalist with Dire Straits is the lead guitar, and 'Brothers In Arms' is one of Knopfler's greatest moments. Refusing to show off, he wrests from the Les Paul something magisterial. Rarely has the electric guitar possessed such dignity.

Studios Out Of Cities

From the jazz age through the 1960s the majority of recording sessions took place in the heart of the world's great cities – New York, Los Angeles, Philadelphia, London, and other metropolitan areas. But, beginning in the 1970s, the forces that fueled the flight from the cities to the suburbs – traffic, neighbors, crime – led many studio owners to open shop in outlying areas.

Built by artist manager Albert B. Grossman in 1970, Bearsville Studios in upstate New York offered all the amenities of a big-city studio in a relaxing, rural environment, and quickly gained favor among artists looking for an escape from the congestion of midtown Manhattan. The following year producer James Guercio opened the full-service Caribou Ranch Studio in the foothills of the Rocky Mountains near Boulder, Colorado. The studio featured upmarket accommodation that included cabins with brass beds and fieldstone fireplaces, as well as a full-time kitchen staff who served up sumptuous meals around the clock. Similarly, Longview Farms, located midway between Boston and New York in rural western Massachusetts, provided a peaceful respite from the noisy distractions of the city. Those who wished to lie in the sand while laying down tracks could head to a 'destination' studio such as Compass Point in the Bahamas, or George Martin's AIR Studios on the tiny Caribbean island of Montserrat. Albums recorded at AIR include *Synchronicity* (1983) by The Police, *Brothers In Arms* (1985) by Dire Straits, and Sting's *Nothing Like The Sun* (1987). Compass Point, meanwhile, was the recording location of The Rolling Stones' *Emotional Rescue* (1980) and several of Robert Palmer's albums, including *Secrets* (1979) and *Riptide* (1985).

The rise of the destination studio proved to be the final nail in the coffin for the older, no-frills recording establishments. Though the rock era had all but displaced the large jazz orchestras of yesteryear, during the 1970s many of the mammoth studios originally constructed to hold such ensembles were still in place. For years the big, reverberant live rooms of such facilities as Abbey Road in London and 30th Street Studio in New York had helped define the sound of pop radio. "Those studios had what you'd call a 'fingerprint' sound," remarked Jimmy Johnson, producer for Wilson Pickett, Aretha Franklin, and many others. "The kind of places where you hear a record on the radio today and know immediately where it was cut. And *that's* what made them so special."

At the start of the 1980s a major economic recession in U.S. album sales helped trigger the music industry's first major revenue falloff in nearly three decades. After years of rampant excess, record-company bosses frantically sought to cut loose all the extra baggage. Accountants crunched the numbers and then called for the removal of some of the biggest studios. Their rationale: smaller bands – and even smaller digital recording equipment – required considerably less space than was needed from a studio designed before the multitrack era. A few larger rooms survived the changeover, such as Capitol Studios in Los Angeles and Abbey Road, but in the city of New York, where soaring real-estate values put a premium on midtown property, one by one stately old facilities – including RCA, Mediasound, the Pythian Temple, Webster Hall, and 30th Street Studio – were sold and transformed into offices, apartments, and nightclubs.

Audio experts bemoaned the passing of the big-studio era, claiming that records produced within a smaller, more controlled environment were not nearly as vital sounding. "It really represented the changing of the guard," remarked one producer. "When you had that kind of room, you're moving air – and it made such a difference in the sound of the recording."

1986

Graceland **Paul Simon**

Warner Bros 25447 (U.S.A.) / 925447 (U.K.)
Released October 1986

Paul Simon's second Grammy-winner focused international attention on apartheid and energized the emerging world music scene.

Graceland may not have contributed directly to the downfall of apartheid, but, in retrospect, it's hard to understand the barrage of criticism Simon attracted from anti-apartheid groups for working with the South African musicians on this genre-busting album. "*Graceland*'s instincts were right," he insists, "and it called into question a lot of thinking, which is good."

On March 29th 1985, largely because he had heard the track 'Gumboota' on the South African compilation *Gumboots Accordion Jive Hits Volume II*, Simon started two weeks of work with local musicians in Johannesburg. But the big change on *Graceland* was not that Simon was working with non-white musicians – his previous solo albums were peppered with exotic international sounds, and even in the days of Simon & Garfunkel he had championed world music long before it became a cause célèbre, introducing South American instrumentation on 'El Condor Pasa.' What made this album different was that, in the past, Simon had tended to write songs and then create music tracks for them in the studio. Simon explained: "I thought, I have enough songwriting technique that I can reverse this process and write this song after the tracks are made."

This set him off on a journey of discovery in which he learned a great deal simply from observing the – to Western eyes – unusual techniques of his South African collaborators. "African guitarists and the bass players were altering what they were playing from verse to verse," he explains. "Choruses didn't have to always be the same. They could repeat, they could use material from a verse, they could introduce some new lyric idea and retain elements from one chorus to the next, like in that song 'Graceland.' None of the choruses are exactly symmetrical."

Happily, the resulting fusion of Western folk rock with township jive, kwela, and mbaqanga styles on *Graceland* seems to have prompted the revitalizing of Simon as a songwriter. Tracks such as 'Diamonds On The Soles Of Her Shoes' or 'The Boy In The Bubble' demonstrated a vigor and imagination that had been lacking in his work for some while. The first flash of Ladysmith Black Mambazo's vocal harmonies in 'Homeless' is a heart-stopper, as are Baghiti Khumalo's mercurially slithering basslines in 'You Can Call Me Al,' but it was Simon's determination to make the best album he possibly could that elevated it into the highest reaches of the pantheon of classic rock albums.

"When I was working on *Graceland*," he has said, "I was thinking, 'If I don't make this interesting, I will never get my generation to pay attention.' They are not paying attention any more to records. They were, at a certain point, certainly around the time of *Bridge Over Troubled Water*, but they no longer look to records to have their lives illuminated. They look to movies or literature."

Graceland certainly made music relevant again, not just for Simon's old audience but for a whole new generation.

Elektra 9-60439-1 (U.S.A.) / Music For Nations MFN60 (U.K.)
Released March 1986

In the U.S.A. in the late 1970s and early 1980s a new movement in heavy metal was beginning to emerge.

MASTER OF PUPPETS

Drawing on the heritage of the original exponents of the genre – Led Zeppelin, Deep Purple, and, most importantly, Black Sabbath – as well as the so-called New Wave Of British Heavy Metal of the late 1970s, which included Iron Maiden, Saxon, and Tygers Of Pan Tang, this new incarnation was defined by detuned riffing played at lightning speed that owed little to the blues-based hard rock of the late 1960s and early 1970s. Anthrax, Slayer, and Megadeth were just three of the big names purveying this new sound. When the dust settled, however, Metallica emerged as kings of the pack.

Formed in Los Angeles in 1981, Metallica went through several personnel changes before settling on the four-piece line-up of James Hetfield (guitar and vocals), Kirk Hammett (lead guitar), Cliff Burton (bass), and Lars Ulrich on drums. After issuing *Kill 'Em All* (1983) on the independent label Megaforce, the group signed to Elektra for *Ride The Lightning* (1984), which

Neither album stands out particularly from the thrash metal of the time and both betray the usual hard-rock influences – Motörhead and Ted Nugent, for example – but there are suggestions of the force that Metallica would soon become. Another band might have been content, with their fan base rapidly growing and the rock press heaping praise upon their albums, to continue in the same vein and become bona fide rock stars in the Def Leppard mold. Metallica, however, had a different agenda, and decided it was time to reinvent the thrash-metal genre.

In September 1985 the group returned to Sweet Silence Studios in Copenhagen, Denmark, where they had recorded *Ride The Lightning*, to begin work on the third Metallica album. As with its predecessor, *Master Of Puppets* was produced by Flemming Rasmussen who, prior to working with Metallica, had engineered albums by the singer-songwriters Cat Stevens and Bert Jansch in the 1970s. Rasmussen's only previous heavy-metal production experience lay with Rainbow's *Difficult To Cure* (1981), but his uncluttered style is perfect for the visceral assault of Metallica. The group spent the last four months of 1985 in Copenhagen perfecting the eight songs on *Master Of Puppets*, but there is little evidence of over-elaboration. Though often musically complex, few songs sound as if they are comprised of any more than the four members of Metallica playing together.

'Battery' opens the album with ominous, intertwining flamenco guitar figures before the more familiar heavy guitar chords thunder in and out of conventional time signatures. The title track rides in on stop-start guitar and cymbal crashes, building to a frenetic crescendo then switching to an expansive mid-section closer to Queen than Aerosmith. The album has the feel of a horror-movie soundtrack throughout, particularly on 'Welcome Home (Sanitarium).' *Master Of Puppets* reached Number 29 in the U.S.A. and Number 42 in the U.K., making it Metallica's most successful album to date. Tragically, however, it was the last the group recorded with bassist Burton, who died in a road accident while the group was on tour in Scandinavia.

Slippery When Wet Bon Jovi

Mercury 830 264-2 (U.S.A.) / Vertigo VERH/+C 38 (U.K.)
Released September 1986

The biggest U.S. hard-rock group of the 1980s, Bon Jovi had a latent pop sensibility that helped elevate them above their peers in the world of heavy metal.

The group had a minor U.S. hit with debut single 'Runaway' (1984) shortly after settling on a line-up of vocalist Jon Bon Jovi (born John Bongiovi), guitarist Richie Sambora, keyboardist David Bryan, bassist Alec Such, and drummer Tico Torres. After releasing an eponymous debut and *7800 Degrees Fahrenheit* (1985) Bon Jovi enlisted the help of producer Bruce Fairbairn for what they hoped would be their breakthrough third album. (Fairbairn was best known at that point for his work with Blue Öyster Cult, but would later become one of the biggest rock producers of the late 1980s, producing albums by, among others, Aerosmith and AC/DC.) The group also turned to songwriter Desmond Child, who co-wrote *Slippery When Wet*'s two U.S. Number One hit singles, 'You Give Love A Bad Name' and 'Livin' On A Prayer.'

Bon Jovi recorded 30 songs for possible inclusion on the album and then played the rough mixes to several groups of New York and New Jersey youths, basing the tracklisting on their opinions. While Bon Jovi's earlier material drew most obviously on 1970s heavy metal, *Slippery When Wet* betrays the influence of Bruce Springsteen, who, like Jon Bon Jovi, hails from New Jersey. On its release in the fall of 1986, *Slippery When Wet* far exceeded the group's expectations, topping the U.S. albums chart and reaching Number Six in the U.K. It has since sold over 12 million copies in the U.S.A. alone.

■ *Clockwise from top: Cliff Burton, James Hetfield, Lars Ulrich, and Kirk*

1986

Guitars, Cadillacs, Etc., Etc. **Dwight Yoakam**

Reprise 2-25372 (U.S.A.) / Warner Brothers 925372 (U.K.)
Released March 1986

With his major-label debut, Kentucky-born, Ohio-bred Dwight Yoakam joined roots-based newcomers such as Randy Travis and Steve Earle in helping to establish the formidable new-country trend of the mid 1980s.

A singer-songwriter with a cowboy hat slung deviously over one eye and a throaty voice to match, Yoakam had spent his formative years with one ear on The Rolling Stones and the other on Buck Owens, and the convergence of styles would set the tone for Yoakam's solo career, which began at the age of 21 with an exploratory visit to Nashville in the fall of 1977.

Nashville at the time, however, had little use for a traditionalist with a rock sensibility. Frustrated, Yoakam charted a course for downtown Los Angeles, the polar opposite of Music City. Performing in the same clubs that housed regional punk acts – the likes of X and The Dead Kennedys – Yoakam began to establish himself as the hip alternative to contemporary country, even garnering a loyal fan base around Hollywood known as 'cowpunks.'

Enter guitarist-producer Pete Anderson, who, like Yoakam, had been weaned on a steady diet of C&W and rock'n'roll. In Yoakam, Anderson heard the direction Nashville needed to take and insisted that the singer immediately commit a handful of his originals to tape. Financial backing came in the form of a $5,000 credit-card advance from Tulsa drummer Richard Coffey, a friend of Yoakam's, who received a portion of the publishing for his trouble. In early 1984 Yoakam, Anderson, and a hastily assembled backing crew entered Excalibur Studio, an independent 24-track facility conveniently located behind a sewing-machine repair shop in nearby Studio City, and proceeded to hammer out six songs, including Yoakam originals 'It Won't Hurt' and 'South Of Cincinnati,' along with a cover of the Johnny Cash classic 'Ring Of Fire.'

"Excalibur was the kind of kind of place where you could just walk in, hand them $200 and go to work for eight hours or so and get as much done as possible," recalls Anderson. "That's how we recorded most of the EP – just get a bit of money, grab Brian Levi the engineer, run over there, and get tracking."

With funds running dry, Yoakam, Anderson, and Levi repaired to another low-budget facility, Hit City West, and proceeded to mix the songs in a series of overnight cram sessions. "We'd arrive at 11.30, have the tapes up by midnight, and start mixing non-stop," says Anderson. "There was no automation, so there we are, the three of us on our knees in front of the board at four in the morning, holding down mutes, going, 'OK, ready? Un-mute the mandolin! Didja get it?! Ride it up! Pull it down!' All night long. We even wild-tracked a few parts, just flying 'em in from tape. That was a *job*."

That November, Oak Records – a Los Angeles independent known for its hardcore punk roster – printed up 5,000 copies of Yoakam's debut EP, entitled *Guitars, Cadillacs, Etc., Etc.* Then Yoakam and Anderson sat back and waited for the big fish to bite, at one point even turning down alt-rock specialists IRS Records. "We were thinking, 'We're gonna be patient and get ourselves a nice major-label deal and then make them do things our way,'" recalls Anderson. "You would've thought we were nuts."

When Warner/Reprise came calling in May of 1985 Yoakam and Anderson were ready. Their list of demands included the stipulation that all six songs previously issued on the *Guitars, Cadillacs* EP be used untouched on Yoakam's full-length debut. "That was all part of it. We told them, 'You get what you get – we're not touching these tracks.' We just didn't feel like they needed to be done over again."

After recording four additional tracks, including Johnny Horton's 'Honky Tonk Man' and Yoakam's own 'Guitars, Cadillacs' at Capitol's Studio B – birthplace to innumerable Buck Owens classics – the album was complete. Released the following March, the 'extended' *Guitars, Cadillacs, Etc., Etc.* quickly tore up the country charts, made impressive inroads on the pop side as well, and spawned a handful of hit singles in 'Honky Tonk Man' (which went to Number Three) 'Guitars, Cadillacs' (Number Four), and 'It Won't Hurt' (Number 31). By 1999 *Guitars, Cadillacs, Etc., Etc.* had reached double-platinum status, making Richard Coffey's original credit-card loan one seriously profitable investment.

Control **Janet Jackson**

A&M 5106 (U.S.A. & U.K.)
Released March 1986

Being the kid sister of 'The King Of Pop' was no picnic for Janet Jackson during the early part of the 1980s. After appearing as backing vocalist on brother Michael's *Off The Wall* album in 1979, the younger Jackson went solo, but her first two offerings – 1983's *Janet Jackson* and 1984's *Dream Street* – failed to find significant audiences.

In 1985 the 19-year-old Jackson teamed up with Jimmy Jam and Terry Lewis, the renegade production team from Minneapolis, who had got their start in the business after being unceremoniously dumped by Prince. Setting up shop in their modest but comfortable Flyte Tyme Productions facilities, Jam and Lewis constructed a set of spare but supple grooves around a handful of Jackson's autobiographical lyrics. When the dust had settled the trio had compiled an entire album's worth of material that included 'What Have You Done For Me Lately,' 'Control,' and 'Nasty.' In Jam and Lewis, Jackson had finally found a winning formula. And the rest, as they say, is history.

According to Jam, the looseness that marked the *Control* recording sessions was key to the album's success. "When you come right down to it, it's the element of spontaneity that gives a record like *Control* its energy," says Jam. "The kind of thing that happens naturally during a live recording. You just have to be ready for it and know how to properly bottle it. With Janet, I just wanted to let it happen, I didn't want to have to tell her what I was after. Still, I think there are times when the singer needs to be coached, and Janet is no exception. Sometimes I would get her to use hand gestures, or have her put her hand on her hip, just to throw a little body language into the song. Prince used to say, 'Records should always be visual.' Meaning that when you're hearing a recording, you should also get a sense of what was going on in that room. The difference might be subtle, but believe me, it works."

Within months of its spring 1986 release, *Control* had gone multiplatinum – on its way to selling over five million copies – while spinning off five Top Five hit singles, including the Number One smash 'When I Think Of You,' a first-ever trip to the top for both artist and production team. Over the next 15 years Jam and Lewis would produced an additional 15 chart toppers, good enough to tie them for second place alongside Elvis Presley producer Steve Sholes on the all-time list of producers of Number Ones – only The Beatles' George Martin has more.

"If you look at the careers of Steve Sholes and George Martin, the one thing they both have in common is that each one had a single artist who defined what they did," says Jam. "With us, obviously, it's Janet. That's really what makes it happen. When you pick great artists to work with, they can't help but make you look good."

Raising Hell **Run-DMC**

Profile 1217 (U.S.A.) / London LP/C 21 (U.K.)
Released June 1986

The first hip-hop act to produce cohesive, fully-realized albums, Run-DMC brought its pioneering rap-rock hybrid into the mainstream with *Raising Hell*.

Though Run-DMC would soon be overtaken by more radical, politicized groups such as Public Enemy, *Raising Hell* remains one of rap's most important early statements.

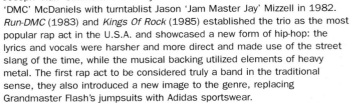

Run-DMC was formed by rappers Joseph 'Run' Simmons and Darryl 'DMC' McDaniels with turntablist Jason 'Jam Master Jay' Mizzell in 1982. *Run-DMC* (1983) and *Kings Of Rock* (1985) established the trio as the most popular rap act in the U.S.A. and showcased a new form of hip-hop: the lyrics and vocals were harsher and more direct and made use of the street slang of the time, while the musical backing utilized elements of heavy metal. The first rap act to be considered truly a band in the traditional sense, they also introduced a new image to the genre, replacing Grandmaster Flash's jumpsuits with Adidas sportswear.

Raising Hell expanded on the template of its predecessors, keeping the trio a step ahead of their contemporaries. The sound is much denser than on the first two full-length Run-DMC efforts, adding layer upon layer of sonic bells and whistles to their sparse backbeat of drum machine and record scratching. Where the guitar parts on both *Run-DMC* and *Kings Of Rock* sound as if added as afterthoughts, here they are fully integrated into the sound. On 'It's Tricky' Run-DMC even make use of the main riff from 'My Sharona' by new-wave band The Knack. The rhymes on *Raising Hell* are more forceful than before, and draw on a wider range of subjects – for instance, 'Peter Piper' takes its inspiration from a number of fairy tales, including the story of Mother Goose.

The most important element of *Raising Hell*, however, was the appearance of Steven Tyler and Joe Perry of Aerosmith on a cover of their 1977 hard-rock hit 'Walk This Way.' It was issued as a single shortly after the release of the album, and almost single-handedly brought about hip-hop's mainstream breakthrough. In the U.S.A. the single reached Number Four, while its parent album eventually climbed to Number Three and became the first hip-hop record to achieve platinum status, selling over a million copies. The memorable promo video for the single also established Run-DMC as the first rap act to be featured regularly on MTV. In it, Run-DMC and Aerosmith are seen rehearsing either side of a brick wall, before knocking it down and performing together. This simple but effective symbolism neatly summed up exactly what was beginning to happen to music in the late 1980s. Run-DMC further developed its appeal to a white audience when the trio toured with The Beastie Boys shortly after the release of *Raising Hell*.

The Queen Is Dead **The Smiths**

Sire 25426 (U.S.A.) / Rough Trade ROUGH96 (U.K.)
Released June 1986

The definitive British guitar band of the 1980s, The Smiths were at their commercial and creative peak when it came to the recording of *The Queen Is Dead*.

Their previous effort, *Meat Is Murder* (1985), had topped the U.K. albums chart and provided the anthemic single 'How Soon Is Now?' Consequently, the band was under intense pressure to match its success with their third album. Undeterred, frontman Morrissey conceived *The Queen Is Dead* as a lament for the declining standards of British society since the 1950s.

Recorded during the winter of 1985 at various studios around the U.K., *The Queen Is Dead* was produced, like its predecessor, by Morrissey and guitarist Johnny Marr with engineer Stephen Street. The album's songs range from such ironic snapshots of British life as 'Frankly, Mr Shankly,' whose title character is deemed "a flatulent pain in the arse," to the mournful 'I Know It's Over,' in which the narrator "can feel the soil falling over my head." The orchestrations on the latter and several other tracks on *The Queen Is Dead* are credited to The Hated Salford Ensemble.

The Queen Is Dead reached Number Two on its release in the U.K., and was a minor hit in the U.S.A. The Smiths' success brought about a resurgence of guitar-led pop in Britain after a period dominated by synthesizers. The Smiths split a year later, after recording *Strangeways Here We Come*, their biggest U.S. success. Two decades after its release *The Queen Is Dead* is regularly acclaimed as one of the finest British albums of all time.

■ *Run-DMC and Aerosmith recording 'Walk This Way' at Magic Venture Studio, New York, on March 9th 1986. Standing (left to right): Joseph 'Run' Simmons, Darryl 'DMC' McDaniels, Jason 'Jam Master Jay' Mizzell, Run-DMC publicist Bill Adler, and Aerosmith guitarist Joe Perry. Seated: Steven Tyler, and producers Russel Simmons and Rick Rubin.*

1987

Permanent Vacation **Aerosmith**

Geffen 24162 (U.S.A.) / 924 162-2 (U.K.)
Released August 1987

Aerosmith was hugely popular in the U.S.A. in the 1970s as part of the country's first wave of hard-rock groups. The band took on the mantle of The Rolling Stones, who had started to become a little too ancient for younger audiences, churning out numerous blues-based rock hits throughout the 1970s.

By the end of the decade, however, Aerosmith appeared to be washed up, particularly when guitarist Joe Perry – the Keith Richards equivalent to vocalist Steven Tyler's Mick Jagger – quit the group in 1979. Aerosmith had begun to halt a slow and steady decline into obscurity and drug addiction by reforming and signing to Geffen in 1984, but it took the success of Run-DMC's rap-rock cover of 'Walk This Way' (1986) to revive completely the group's fortunes.

Buoyed by the success of the single – which was billed as a collaboration between Run-DMC and Aerosmith and promoted by a video featuring the two acts performing together – the group started work on its proper comeback album. They recruited the team responsible for the recent huge success of Bon Jovi's *Slippery When Wet* (1986) to help them make *Permanent Vacation*. Producer Bruce Fairbairn gives the album a rich, modern sheen, while songwriter Desmond Child took rough drafts of Perry's and Tyler's songs and turned them into hook-laden, pop-rock gems. These efforts paid off handsomely, resulting in Aerosmith's strongest and best-selling album since the mid 1970s and a pair of U.S. hit singles, 'Angel' and 'Dude (Looks Like A Lady).'

Kick **INXS**

Atlantic 81796 (U.S.A.) / Mercury 832 721-2 (U.K.)
Released November 1987

After forming in Sydney, Australia, in 1977, INXS gradually built up an international following through the 1980s.

The band eventually scored a U.S. Top Five hit with 'Sweet As Sin' (1986), a single drawn from the group's fifth album, *Listen Like Thieves*, which peaked at Number 11. Its success paved for the way for a mainstream breakthrough on

both sides of the Atlantic, but few could have anticipated *Kick*'s popularity.

INXS entered Rhinoceros Studios in Sydney in March 1987 with Chris Thomas, whose various credits as musician, producer, and mixer take in such landmark albums as *The Beatles* (aka *The White Album*, 1968), *Dark Side Of The Moon* (1973), and *Never Mind The Bollocks, Here's The Sex Pistols* (1977). The resulting album, completed in the early summer at Studio de la Grande Armee in Paris, is the most potent of the group's career, taking in hard rock, string-drenched balladry, and soulful horn arrangements, each song equipped with a powerful pop hook to drive it up the singles charts if necessary. 'Need You Tonight' topped the U.S. singles chart prior to the release of *Kick*, while 'New Sensation,' 'Devil Inside,' and 'Never Tear Us Apart' all entered the Top Ten. All four singles reached the U.K. Top 30, as did 'Mystify.'

INXS helped maintain the album's momentum with a year-long worldwide tour, dubbed 'Calling All Nations.' *Kick* has sold over ten million copies, and was certified six-times platinum in the U.S.A. shortly before the death of frontman Michael Hutchence in 1997.

Appetite For Destruction Guns N' Roses

Geffen 24148 (U.S.A.) / WX 125+C (U.K.)
Released July 1987

Guns N' Roses was the quintessential American heavy-rock act of the 1980s, a potent blend of the best elements of Aerosmith, The Sex Pistols, The Rolling Stones, industrial quantities of hairspray, and rock star bad behavior.

Despite the group's image – something akin to a late-1980s version of The Stones at their most debauched – Guns N' Roses was also one of the few bands of the era to think beyond sex, drugs, and rock'n'roll. Songs such as 'Welcome To The Jungle' and 'Paradise City' focus on crime and poverty in inner-city U.S.A., while 'Mr Brownstone' is a first-person tale of heroin addiction.

The group was formed in 1985 by vocalist Axl Rose and guitarist Izzy Stradlin, with bassist Duff McKagen, drummer Steven Adler, and lead guitarist Slash joining in time for the release of the self-financed EP *Live ?!*@ Like A Suicide* and a residency at the famous Troubadour club in Los Angeles. The Guns N' Roses live experience caught the attention of David Geffen, who signed the group in March 1986.

The following month the group started work on its debut album at Rumbo Studios, Los Angeles, but nothing from those sessions was deemed good enough for release. The poor quality of these recordings was attributed to Slash's growing drug dependency, prompting an ultimatum by Rose: clean up or leave the group.

The band resumed work on what would become *Appetite For Destruction* at Take One Studio in Burbank, California, with Mike Clink on production duties. Clink had previously engineered albums by UFO, Jefferson Starship, and Joe Cocker, but had little experience as producer prior to working on Guns N' Roses' debut. (He would later work with Metallica, Whitesnake, and Megadeth.) Guns N' Roses spent five months perfecting the sleazy, blues-based metal of *Appetite For Destruction*, after which Geffen sat on the record for the best part of a year, waiting for the hype around the group to reach fever pitch before unleashing the album. The album's cover – a painting of a woman being raped by a robot – caused a huge media storm and the first of many accusations that Rose was a bigoted misogynist. The group eventually responded to calls to change the artwork, replacing it with a stark image of a cross on a black background, augmented by caricatures of the five group members as skulls.

Appetite For Destruction grew in popularity over the next year as Guns N'

Roses became America's most notorious band, eventually reaching Number One in August 1988. Four months later, following the release of *GNR Lies*, Guns N' Roses became the only act to have two albums in the U.S. Top Five simultaneously during the 1980s. *Appetite For Destruction* peaked at Number Five in the U.K. and has sold over 20 million copies worldwide, establishing it as one of the biggest-selling debut albums of all time. Its most famous song, the melodic 'Sweet Child O' Mine,' topped the U.S. singles chart in the summer of 1988, while 'Welcome To The Jungle' was a hit on both sides of the Atlantic.

■ *Left to right: Slash, Duff McKagan, and Axl Rose of Guns N' Roses.*

Hysteria Def Leppard

Mercury 830675 (U.S.A.) / Vertigo 830675 (U.K.)
Released August 1987

The biggest British heavy-rock act of the 1980s, Def Leppard battled against adversity to produce their definitive work, the 12-million selling *Hysteria*.

The group's previous album, *Pyromania* (1983), had introduced a new form of highly polished, melodic heavy rock, and was an international bestseller, shifting ten million copies globally. The group began work on what it hoped would be a quick follow-up in late 1984, but these plans were suddenly derailed when drummer Rick Allen lost an arm in a car wreck on New Year's Eve. Consequently, Def Leppard was effectively on hiatus for most of 1985, as Allen first recovered in hospital and then began to adapt to a new way of drumming, which made use of a Fairlight drum machine and a specially arranged kit.

The group started work afresh with regular producer Robert 'Mutt' Lange in early 1986, slowly piecing together the meticulous, glossy songs that would feature on *Hysteria*. The sessions were interrupted by Def Leppard's participation in the 'Monsters Of Rock' tour across Europe, which marked Allen's first live performances since his accident.

Def Leppard completed work on *Hysteria* in the early months of 1987, eventually releasing it that summer after a three-year absence. The album sold modestly to begin with, but gradually rose to the top of the U.S. charts and Number Two in the U.K., remaining a permanent fixture in the upper reaches of both charts well into 1989, buoyed by the release of six singles from the album, notably the U.S. Number One hit 'Love Bites.'

1987

Sign 'O' The Times Prince

Paisley Park/Warners 25577 (U.S.A,) / WX 88/+C (U.K.)
Released March 1987

With *Sign 'O' The Times* Prince struck the perfect balance between his catchy, pop-oriented hits and his most forward-thinking, adventurous work.

In 1985 Prince had founded his Paisley Park label and studio complex, a move that afforded him even more creative freedom than before. He had also announced a break from live performance for the foreseeable future, allowing him to devote his time exclusively to making records. He had recorded most of his 1980s output with his backing group The Revolution, but opted to produce and perform virtually every note of *Sign 'O' The Times* himself, with the exception of the occasional horn part or female backing vocal. Musically, *Sign 'O' The Times* serves as both a culmination of everything Prince had recorded previously and an indication of the directions he would take in the future. The album takes in sparse electronic funk, gospel-tinged rock, psychedelic pop-soul, and more across its 18 tracks, giving it the sort of sprawling, kaleidoscopic feel common among double albums. Prince originally conceived *Sign 'O' The Times* as a triple, with the working title of *Crystal Ball*, but eventually relented to pressure from Warners and trimmed it down to a double.

Many critics saw *Sign 'O' The Times* as a late-1980s update of Sly And The Family Stone's *There's A Riot Goin' On* in terms of its socially aware lyrics and all-encompassing musical themes. Prince's album, however, takes a much more moralistic viewpoint than the cocaine psychosis of Stone's early 1970s masterpiece. 'Sign 'O' The Times' sets the tone as Prince warns of America's problems with AIDS and drug abuse against a stark bass and drum-machine backing. 'Play In The Sunshine' and 'Housequake' are more upbeat, euphoric affairs, while Prince shows his more soulful side on 'The Ballad Of Dorothy Parker.' The remaining tracks continue in a similar vein, jumping from genre to genre, issue to issue at the drop of a hat. Among the many highlights of the remainder of the album, 'If I Was Your Girlfriend' is Prince at his pop-soul best, while the nine-minute 'It's Gonna Be A Beautiful Night' provides a fitting climax.

Sign 'O' The Times reached Number Six in the U.S.A. and Number Four in the U.K. on its release, eventually selling over ten million copies and reconfirming Prince's commercial potential after the more experimental, less popular albums *Around The World In A Day* (1985) and *Parade* (1986). The title track, 'U Got The Look,' and 'I Could Never Take The Place Of Your Man' all reached the Top Ten of the U.S. singles chart, while 'If I Was Your Girlfriend' was a U.K. hit.

For most of the 1980s Prince recorded at such a rate that for every song that saw the light of day on record numerous others remained unheard in the vaults of Paisley Park. Within six months of the release of *Sign 'O' The Times* he had readied a follow-up, the so-called *Black Album*. Shortly before it was due to go on sale, however, Prince withdrew the album, claiming it to be too immoral for public consumption. The *Black Album* was eventually issued in 1994 in the midst of Prince's long-running dispute with Warners, during which he declared himself to be the label's slave, changing his written name to a symbol and being referred to as The Artist Formerly Known As Prince.

■ **Prince leaps through the air in Rotterdam, The Netherlands, on his 1987 European tour in support of Sign 'O' The Times.**

Whitney **Whitney Houston**

Arista 208141 (U.S.A.) / AL-8405 (U.K.)
Released June 1987

Whitney was the first album by a female performer to debut at Number One in the U.S.A., while the four singles drawn from it completed a record-breaking run of seven consecutive chart-topping singles.

Born into a musical family – her mother is R&B singer Cissy Houston, while Dionne Warwick is a cousin – Houston started her pop career as a backing singer, performing with Lou Rawls and Chaka Khan among others. Her solo debut, *Whitney Houston*, sold 13 million copies, making it the biggest-selling female debut until it was eventually overtaken by Alanis Morissette's *Jagged Little Pill* in the late 1990s. *Whitney Houston* spawned a trio of U.S. Number One hit singles, including 'The Greatest Love Of All,' leading to impossibly high expectations for her sophomore offering.

The production on *Whitney* was shared between Michael Masser, who concentrated on the ballads, and John 'Jellybean' Benitez, who was largely responsible for the more upbeat, disco-pop tracks. *Whitney* was Houston's international breakthrough, and served as a template for much of the contemporary R&B that followed in the late 1980s and early 1990s. While sales of *Whitney* didn't quite match those of *Whitney Houston*, it did beat its predecessor in terms of the number of hit singles it contains. The Grammy-winning 'I Wanna Dance With Somebody Who Loves Me,' 'Didn't We Almost Have It All,' 'So Emotional,' and 'Where Do Broken Hearts Go' all reached Number One in the U.S.A., and were all hits across Europe.

Introducing The Hardline According To Terence Trent D'Arby **Terence Trent D'Arby**

Columbia 40964 (U.S.A.) / CBS 450911 (U.K.)
Released October 1987 (U.S.A.) / July 1987 (U.K.)

Terence Trent D'Arby is perhaps best remembered for announcing his emergence on the pop scene with the bold claim that his debut, *Introducing The Hardline According To Terence Trent D'Arby*, was the greatest and most important album since The Beatles' *Sgt Pepper*.

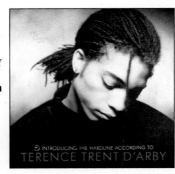

After serving in the U.S. Army, New York born D'Arby moved to London, England, where his demo tape caught the attention of CBS record executives. He was given an unusual amount of creative freedom when it came to recording his debut album, which he wrote and produced himself and on which he plays a variety of instruments, from piano and drums to clarinet and saxophone. This maverick spirit drew comparisons with Prince, whose genre-bending artistic leaps had clearly inspired D'Arby's attempts at assimilating elements of rock, pop, funk, and soul.

While not quite as good as D'Arby claimed it to be, *Introducing The Hardline* earned favorable reviews on its release across Europe in the summer of 1987. The album reached Number One in the U.K., where the singles 'If You Let Me Stay,' 'Wishing Well,' and 'Sign Your Name' all reached the Top Ten. The album took longer to catch on in the U.S.A., but eventually rose to Number Four and sold two million copies after 'Wishing Well' had topped the singles chart. D'Arby returned two years later with the conceptual *Neither Flesh Nor Fish*, but its self-consciously important themes put off many fans of his debut. After that D'Arby continued to achieve modest success in the U.K., but his career in the U.S.A. never recovered.

1987

The Joshua Tree **U2**

Island 422-842298-1 (U.S.A.) / U26 (U.K.)
Released March 1987

**The Joshua Tree was one of the
biggest albums of the mid
1980s, shifting over 12 million
copies, and the first platinum-
selling CD in the U.S.A. The
album took U2 on to the covers
of *Rolling Stone* and *Time* as the
world's premier rock band.**

Anton Corbijn's widescreen
photograph on the dramatic black-
and-gold cover has the band dressed
like characters from a spaghetti
Western, emphasizing the image of
U2 as a pure, austere force of nature, something that could resist the
materialism of the decade. The LP's title comes from a desert town in
California associated with the death of singer-songwriter Gram Parsons as
well as being home to a cactus capable of surviving terrible droughts. U2's

1987

international success came about partly because they were willing to take up the burden of being a rock band with seriousness of purpose. U2 were in a tiny minority of bands at the time who still played as though the music could change the world and whose lyrics expressed social, religious, and political themes. In this sense U2 are heirs to The Who, though without The Who's self-destructive streak of cynicism. For U2 the bitter wisdom of 'Won't Get Fooled Again' wasn't enough. You couldn't stop there. You had to hang on to an idealism that was ready to be fooled again, and again, for however long it took to get things done. There are other resemblances, too, notably that both are formidable live acts; Bono's voice has something of the power of Daltrey; and both bands have a guitarist with an immediately recognizable sound.

The Joshua Tree was released two years after their previous album, *The Unforgettable Fire*, had surprised many with its experimental approach. (This change in sound was due largely to the arrival of Brian Eno as the group's producer.) Realizing that they had gone as far as they could enthusing audiences with the naked aggression of the songs on *War* and *Under A Blood Red Sky*, U2 had decided to take a left turn and dismantle their rock machine. *The Unforgettable Fire* expanded their sound; *The Joshua Tree* is all the richer for that expansion, even though it was U2's most direct and disciplined set of songs to date.

Behind these songs was a widening of musical horizons as the band outgrew some of their teenage prejudices against older artists and Irish and American roots music. Touring the U.S.A. brought them into contact with genres of music that lay at the foundations of rock itself. Bono was inspired

by Coltrane's *A Love Supreme*, and The Edge looked back to Hendrix and blues rock to see what he could adapt. They were exposed to reactionary forms of Christianity, which led them to redefine their own faith. Bono in particular gained new insights into the relationship between social justice, poverty, and a radical Christianity that was far beyond that which the television evangelists were pushing. The group's political awareness grew with their involvements with Live Aid and Amnesty International. Bono's trip to Nicaragua led directly to the seething anger of 'Bullet The Blue Sky,' a song in which rock's sheer noise finds a commensurate theme. 'Mothers of The Disappeared' raised awareness of the plight of those kidnapped by the authorities in Argentina.

The writing of the music took a new direction. As they re-engaged with the notion of songs with verses and choruses, individual members started developing ideas in advance and presenting them to the others instead of getting material from jamming. They were now able to wear some of the styles of other bands while still sounding like U2. There is certainly no mistaking Bono's vocals and The Edge's echoed guitar patterns, heard to such brilliant effect on the opener 'Where The Streets Have No Name.'

U2's core sound arose the day The Edge got his hands on an echo device, which enabled him to side-step accepted notions of how rock guitar should sound – low overdriven riffs, barre chords, lead solos played on pentatonic scales. He once said: "Really I just started writing with the echo and it all happened . . . Parts that would have sounded at best bland without the echo suddenly sounded amazing." On 'Where The Streets Have No Name' the intro has The Edge playing a four-note figure on the higher strings. What makes this motif work is the echo; he plays it with a delay timed so that a rhythm is set up between the notes and their echoes, so it has rhythmic *and* melodic interest.

The new medium of CD really brought over the crisp high-end sparkle of

much of The Edge's guitar work. The opener, along with 'I Still Haven't Found What I'm Looking For,' 'With Or Without You,' and 'Bullet The Blue Sky' are immediately recognizable U2 classics. 'With Or Without You' demonstrates that even at the height of their stadium phase their sense of arrangement was far ahead of most rock bands. In 1987 The Edge said: "I now see that one of the great things is being able to do something original within a cliché." When it is not hovering on a D chord, 'With Or Without You' comprises a single four-bar, four-chord sequence that has been used on many hits, including Men At Work's 'Down Under,' The Police's 'So Lonely,' 'Since You've Been Gone' by Rainbow, and more recently by Busted.

U2's arrangement has two major differences. First, this progression is subjected to a dynamic in which the song starts quietly and slowly builds to a roaring climax, dies away, and then has a partial recovery. In other words it has an overarching form. In 'With Or Without You' everyone holds back until this dramatic climax is reached at around three minutes in. Second, at no time are the four chords fully articulated. Most bands would have had a couple of acoustic guitars merrily strumming their way through these changes, but U2 avoid this. Instead the chords are implied in the musical space between the bass root notes and The Edge's guitar parts – none of which are straightforward chords.

Aside from its most famous tracks, *The Joshua Tree* has the band venturing into unusual territory with the elegiac 'One Tree Hill,' the dark 'Exit,' and the anti-drug 'Running To Stand Still,' while 'In God's Country' is remarkable for its combination of power and wistfulness.

The Joshua Tree made U2 into international superstars, and marked a distinct turning point in the group's career. Four years later they returned with *Achtung Baby*, which showcased a harder-edged sound informed by dance music and a new image for the group, in particular Bono, who traded his cowboy shirt and hat for wraparound shades and leather trousers.

La Bamba (Original Soundtrack) Various Artists

Slash-Warners 25605 (U.S.A.) / Slash-London 828058 (U.K.)
Released August 1987

Gipsy Kings **The Gipsy Kings**

Elektra 60845 (U.S.A.) / Telstar 2355 (U.K.)
Released February 1988

With *La Bamba*, the soundtrack to a biopic of Mexican rock'n'roll singer Richie Valens, Los Lobos became the first act of Mexican extraction to enjoy widespread chart success in the U.S.A. since Valens himself in the 1950s.

Prior to recording *La Bamba*, Los Lobos had begun to enjoy modest success with a sound that mixed rock, country, and blues with traditional Spanish and Mexican music. After forming in Los Angeles in 1973, the group inked a deal with the Warners subsidiary Slash in 1983 and issued the acclaimed *How Will The Wolf Survive?* the following year. The album didn't make huge inroads into the charts, stalling at Number 47 in the U.S.A. and Number 77 in the U.K., but it did attract the attention of writer-director Luis Valdez, at the time in the early stages of making a movie about the life of Valens, who had died in the airplane crash in 1959 that also killed Buddy Holly and The Big Bopper. In 1986 Valdez invited Los Lobos to contribute to the soundtrack to the movie, a collection of re-recordings of Valens's hits. Eight out of the 12 songs on the album are by the band.

Valens's shimmering, upbeat rock'n'roll worked well in the context of the five-piece, acoustic-based Los Lobos. The band race through the first half-dozen songs, including the memorable title track – a Number One hit single in Britain and the U.S.A. – before a quartet of guest performers arrive for the more eclectic second half of the album. Former Klique vocalist Howard Huntsberry sings 'Lonely Teardrops,' while singer-songwriter Marshall Crenshaw offers a reading of Buddy Holly's 'Crying, Waiting, Hoping.' Bo Diddley's classic 'Who Do You Love' follows The Stray Cats' 'Summertime Blues' before Los Lobos finish with two more Valens songs.

The success of *La Bamba*, on screen and on record, catapulted Los Lobos into the mainstream in the summer of 1987, leaving the group in a difficult position. *La Bamba* – which sold two million copies in the U.S.A. on its route to the top of the albums chart, and was also a hit across Europe – was not particularly representative of the band's sound. Spurning the chance to consolidate its popular appeal, the group decided to return to the more idiosyncratic Tex-Mex sound of its earlier albums and never again came close to matching the success of *La Bamba*.

The following year The Gipsy Kings achieved international success with a similarly Spanish-edged sound. Hailing from Arles in the south of France, The Gipsy Kings brought flamenco-guitar-led pop to the mainstream for the first time. They group had already had a number of hits in France before *Gipsy Kings* entered the U.K. Top Ten in the summer of 1988. The single 'Bamboleo' was also a hit in the U.K., while the album reached Number 57 in the U.S.A. In 1989 The Gipsy Kings recorded *Mosaïque*, which added modern production techniques to the group's traditional sound, consolidating its popular appeal.

1988

Pontiac **Lyle Lovett**

MCA/Curb 42028 (U.S.A. & U.K.)
Released January 1988

**Lyle Lovett was associated with
the burgeoning alternative-
country scene when he emerged
in the mid 1980s, but in truth
his music had more in common
with the singer-songwriters of
the 1970s, from Randy Newman
to James Taylor.**

Released in 1986, Lovett's self-titled
debut album may have had a country
sheen but it also drew on elements of
rock, jazz, and soul. Five singles from
Lyle Lovett reached the U.S. Country
Top 40, but the singer was deemed a sell-out by Nashville traditionalists.
Regardless of this, Lovett had begun to develop a more mainstream following
after the release of his debut, setting the stage for the follow-up to be a bona
fide crossover hit.

Pontiac was recorded using a newly installed digital 32-track system at
Soundstage Studios in Nashville, with Tony Brown, previously the
keyboardist in Emmylou Harris's group, on production duties. Harris herself
provides backing vocals on *Pontiac*, as does Vince Gill, while the cutting-
edge nature of the album's gestation is illustrated by a logo on the front
cover that declares it to be a 'Digital Recording.' The album contains 11
Lovett originals that veer from the stark, surrealist opener 'If I Had A Boat'
("If I were Roy Rogers . . . we'd go riding through the movies") to the breezy
'LA County.' *Pontiac* was well received by rock critics, leading to strong
sales of over 500,000 in the U.S.A. Lovett continues to record ever-more
idiosyncratic albums into the 21st century and has also carved out a second
career as an actor, earning widespread acclaim for his role in Robert
Altman's *Short Cuts* (1993).

Surfer Rosa **The Pixies**

Electra 61295 (U.S.A.) / 4AD CAD803 (U.K.)
Released March 1988

**Among the most important
alternative-rock albums of the
1980s, The Pixies' debut played
a large part in giving birth to the
music that became known as
grunge.**

The Pixies' sound had already been
established on 1987's mini-album
Come On Pilgrim – which included a
clutch of fan favorites, 'Caribou,' 'The
Holiday Song,' and 'Nimrod's Son.'
The follow-up was the band's first full-
length effort, recorded in the fall of
the same year at Q-Division in their native Boston, Massachusetts,
alongside Steve Albini, who would become the most sought-after producer
around when grunge broke in the 1990s. They worked quickly, laying down
the instrumental tracks in two weeks and adding the vocals in another two
days. Albini's production style is sparse and economical, which is well suited
to the band's abrasive sound.

The album is driven by the twin-guitar assault of frontman Black Francis
(born Charles Thompson IV) and lead player Joey Santiago, showcasing the
quiet-verse-loud-chorus aesthetic that would so influence Nirvana and

others. Equally distinct is Francis's manic, Latin-inflected vocal delivery,
which was apparently inspired by a Thai rock-star friend who told him to
"scream it like you hate that bitch!" The album also has a powerful melodic
edge, particularly when Francis's voice is twinned with the less abrasive
tones of bassist Kim Deal.

Despite unanimous critical praise, *Surfer Rosa* failed to chart on its release.
The album's key moment is the epic 'Where Is My Mind?' The track was
given wider exposure a decade later when used memorably over the end
credits of the movie *Fight Club*, which brought about a long-deserved
commercial acceptance of The Pixies, and *Surfer Rosa* in particular. In 2005
the band reunited for a triumphant world tour.

Tracy Chapman **Tracy Chapman**

Elektra 60774-2 (U.S.A. & U.K.)
Released April 1988

**The spirit of the folk era
resurfaced in the late 1980s,
thanks in part to the appearance
of Boston-based newcomer Tracy
Chapman, whose self-titled
Elektra debut reintroduced
audiences to the simple
pleasures of unplugged music.**

The highlight of the set was the
lead-off single 'Fast Car,' the story
of a working-class couple struggling
to escape the ravages of urban
poverty. (Chapman's stunning solo
performance of the song at the 1989 Grammy presentation – where she
received the award for Best Female Pop Vocal – remains a memorable
moment in pop music.)

By 1984 Chapman, then a 20-year-old sophomore student at Tufts University, had begun performing her own tunes at clubs around the Boston area. Through a friend, Chapman was introduced to producer David Kershenbaum, who was immediately struck by Chapman's plaintive songs and vocal range, which bore a strong resemblance to Joan Armatrading with whom Chapman has often been compared. By the end of 1986 Chapman had inked a deal with Paul Rothschild's reputable label, Elektra Records, and prepared to cut a debut album at Kershenbaum's Los Angeles studio. Kershenbaum, who'd recorded Joe Jackson's *Look Sharp!* album using minimal overdubs for less than $10,000, employed a similar approach for Chapman, whose vocals and acoustic guitar were recorded live over a spare rhythm section consisting of drummer Denny Fongheiser and bassist Larry Klein.

"The difference between 'Fast Car' and some of the other songs on the album was when it hit the chorus, Denny really opened up with those big toms," Kershenbaum told writer Robyn Flans. "That was a wonderful exercise in dynamics, because it was so vulnerable in both the message and presentation. It was Tracy and her acoustic guitar, Larry and a little rhythm from Denny. And it took a while to get to the chorus, which worried some people. It broke rules of great song construction, and I wouldn't advise people to try it, but for some reason, it milked it so much that when it hit the release of the large chorus, it blew you over."

In the spring of 1988 *Tracy Chapman* made its debut on *Billboard*'s album chart and quickly pushed its way through a sea of hair bands and hip-hop acts on its way to the Number One position, while the single 'Fast Car' eventually topped out at Number Six. "What happened was something that none of us had dreamed – the album was gold before the single ever really got on the radio," remembers Kershenbaum. "It was one of those records where people still walk up to me and tell me exactly where they were and what they were doing when they first heard 'Fast Car.'"

Spirit Of Eden **Talk Talk**

EMI America 46977 (U.S.A.) / Parlophone 746977 (U.K.)
Released September 1988

TALK TALK

SPIRIT OF EDEN

At their commercial peak after *The Colour Of Spring* (1986), Talk Talk abruptly changed direction for the avant-garde, jazz-inflected ambience of *Spirit Of Eden*.

The group had initially ridden in on the back of the new romantics, in the wake of the likes of Duran Duran, and scored international hits with 'Talk Talk' and 'It's My Life.' After the critical and commercial success of *The Colour Of Spring*, the group's label, Parlophone, gave Talk Talk free rein to produce the follow-up themselves, anticipating more of the same thoughtful pop rock. Instead, guided by frontman Mark Hollis and multi-instrumentalist Tim Friese-Green, Talk Talk decamped to an old church in Suffolk, England, where the group spent a year perfecting the six otherworldly songs on *Spirit Of Eden*.

"THE MOST IMPORTANT THING WITH THIS ALBUM WAS JUST TO HAVE THE RIGHT FEEL – FOR IT TO HAVE AN ABSOLUTE CALM, BUT FOR IT TO HAVE AN ABSOLUTE INTENSITY INSIDE OF THAT."

TALK TALK FRONTMAN MARK HOLLIS

Unlike the three previous Talk Talk albums, which were recorded as a four-piece, *Spirit Of Eden* features a dozen guest players, including the classical-crossover violinist Nigel Kennedy and various brass instrumentalists. These 16 musicians, augmented in places by the choir of Chelmsford Cathedral, conspired to produce a work of hushed complexity. The album's delicate ambience was achieved using distant miking techniques.

Though Hollis and engineer Phill Brown used only pre-1967 analog equipment for the initial, semi-improvised recordings, they made pioneering use of digital technology in the second phase of creating *Spirit Of Eden*. The songs were pieced together and refined using a digital tape machine, in a manner that recalled the way Teo Macero shaped Miles Davis's late-1960s albums out of snippets of live and studio performances. The resulting music, unlike any rock album before or since, sits somewhere between Davis's *In A Silent Way* (1969), Brian Eno's early ambient work, and Erik Satie's sparest piano pieces. Needless to say, the album sold poorly. Dropped by Parlophone, Talk Talk made one more album, the majestic *Laughing Stock* (Polydor, 1991), before disbanding.

Nothing's Shocking **Jane's Addiction**

Warners 25727 (U.S.A.) / WX 216 (U.K.)
Released September 1988

Los Angeles-based Jane's Addiction stood apart from the often histrionic, over-egged heavy metal of the city's other rock groups of the time, typified by Guns N' Roses.

Instead, Jane's Addiction fused elements of folk, funk, and metal, creating a sound that, while nowhere near as commercially successful, stands up better to historical reassessment than the work of the group's peers.

Jane's Addiction formed in 1984, earning a deal with Warners three years later on the strength of a self-released, eponymous live album. The group recorded its debut album proper in early 1988 at Eldorado Studios in Los Angeles with producer Dave Jerden – who had previously worked with Talking Heads, The Rolling Stones, and Red Hot Chili Peppersduties.

Nothing's Shocking is an eclectic, challenging album, with songs ranging from visceral hard rock to instrumental jazz noodling. There is a lyrical intensity to most of the songs, be it the bleak 'Jane Says,' a tale of heroin addiction, to 'Ted, Just Admit It . . .' written about the serial killer Ted Bundy. The album's most striking element is Perry Farrell's unique vocal style, an eerie, siren-like wail that somehow stands out from but sits perfectly with the music beneath it.

Nothing's Shocking failed to chart on its release on either side of the Atlantic, but has since come to be recognized as an alternative-rock classic. The band achieved greater commercial success with the more streamlined *Ritual De Lo Habitual* (1990), which spawned a minor U.K. hit, 'Been Caught Stealing.'

1988

It Takes A Nation Of Millions To Hold Us Back
Public Enemy

Def Jam 4303 (U.S.A.) / 462415 (U.K.)
Released July 1988

Generally considered to be the greatest hip-hop album of all time, Public Enemy's second release was one of the landmark successes of the seminal hip-hop label Def Jam.

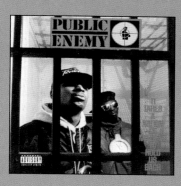

Def Jam Records was formed in 1984 by New York University students Rick Rubin and Russell Simmons, whose younger brother Joseph had already begun to have considerable success as one third of Run-DMC. Though Run-DMC was already signed to Profile Records, Rubin, and to a lesser extent Simmons, were responsible for producing much of the trio's early output, including the albums *Kings Of Rock* and *Raising Hell*. Rubin also produced LL Cool J's *Radio* (1985) and The Beastie Boys' debut, *Licensed To Ill* (1986), both of which were issued on Def Jam and helped establish the label as

the home of the bulk of the most important – and bestselling – hip-hop releases of the late 1980s.

In 1987 Def Jam signed the upcoming hip-hop group Public Enemy, whose first release, *Yo! Bum Rush The Show*, was released in the fall of that year. While Run-DMC had begun to move rap toward a more hardcore sound, Public Enemy took this process a step further, with rappers Chuck D and Flavor Flav advocating social revolution in their lyrics while production duo The Bomb Squad created a fierce collage of sound unlike anything heard previously. The group's setup was also highly unusual: while most hip-hop acts were in the Run-DMC mold of two or three rappers and a DJ, Public Enemy resembled something closer to a political organization. Alongside Chuck D, Flavor Flav, DJ Terminator X, and in-house production team The Bomb Squad, at the core of the group was publicist Bill Stephney and 'Minister of Information'/choreographer Professor Griff.

Yo! Bum Rush The Show was a minor success, failing to ignite the interest of many outside the hip-hop underground, but its follow-up, *It Takes A Nation Of Millions To Hold Us Back*, would prove impossible to ignore. Recorded

shortly after the first album at a number of studios around New York, *Nation Of Millions* is a refinement of the ideas and ideals of its predecessor. Chuck D had by this stage arrived at a more direct, focused lyrical style, and delivers his compelling rhetoric in a deep, authoritative voice while the more flamboyant Flavor Flav provides the lighter entertainment with a series of short, comical asides. D's raps covered a variety of subjects, from white supremacy and black nationalism to the manipulative nature of the record industry.

Equally radical here is the layered sonic backdrop provided by The Bomb Squad, led by producer Hank Shocklee. In the late 1970s and early 1980s most hip-hop records involved a rapper performing over the top of another record spun by a DJ, the most famous example being The Sugarhill Gang's 'Rapper's Delight,' which utilized a repeated break from Chic's 'Good Times.' By the mid 1980s, however, hip-hop producers had begun to make use of the new technology of the sampler, a digital recording device that allows the user to capture a short element of an existing recording and then repeat it to create something new.

Public Enemy's Shocklee took this process several steps further than his predecessors, who had tended to use samplers simply to loop a bar or two of an old funk or soul song. One of the major limitations of the earliest samplers was that they could only store a couple of seconds of music in their memory; Shocklee used this to his advantage, weaving together complex, claustrophobic rhythm tracks out of the tiniest fragments of other songs, utilizing literally hundreds of sonic fragments of other people's music to create something wholly original.

Where Run-DMC and others had taken samples from heavy-rock records, the sound sources on Public Enemy's album were more disparate: *Nation Of Millions* contains pieces of free jazz and avant-garde compositions, as well as the obligatory funk drum breaks. Occasionally The Bomb Squad throws in a recognizable sample – such as the guitar break from David Bowie's 'Fame' used in 'The Night Of The Living Baseheads' – but they have usually passed before the listener catches on. Most striking is the repeated use throughout the album of tiny snatches of squawking saxophones and sirens, which give the beats an unrelenting, uneasy feel. After The Bomb Squad had pieced together the basic rhythmic structure of each song, Chuck D and Flavor Flav would add their vocal parts. Shocklee would then finish the potent sonic brew by adding more sound effects and samples, including a number of well-chosen snatches of spoken social commentary.

At the time there were no laws in place to regulate the plundering of past recordings by Public Enemy and others. With the success of *Nation Of Millions* and other artists' albums – notably The Beastie Boys' *Paul's Boutique*, which used The Bomb Squad's production style as a template – the original performers started to become antagonized by hip-hop acts' unsanctioned recycling of their back catalogs. Record labels and industry lawyers moved quickly to put a system in place whereby the creators of the original music would be compensated financially for any samples used, and by the early 1990s artists would have to pay to clear each individual sample or risk being sued for a large chunk of their songs' royalties. Such an arrangement would be unmanageable for a outfit such as Public Enemy, who would sometimes use more than a dozen samples in a single song, and indeed the group had to change its sound in the 1990s to incorporate live instrumentation.

It Takes A Nation Of Millions To Hold Us Back was released in the summer of 1988 to high praise from rock and rap critics alike. It charted at Number 42 in the U.S.A. and reached the Top Ten in the U.K., where it also spawned two hit singles, 'Don't Believe The Hype' and 'Bring The Noise.' In 1995 the *New Musical Express* (U.K.) declared *Nation Of Millions* the greatest hip-hop album ever – an opinion later shared by numerous other publications – stating: "This wasn't merely a sonic triumph. This was also where Chuck D wrote a fistful of lyrics that promoted him to the position of foremost commentator/documenter of life in the underbelly of the U.S.A."

Public Enemy continued to rise in popularity after the album's release, scoring an international hit with the classic 1989 single 'Fight The Power,' which was given prominence on the soundtrack to Spike Lee's movie *Do The Right Thing*.

■ *Left to right: Professor Griff, Chuck D, Flavor Flav, and Terminator X.*

1988

Daydream Nation **Sonic Youth**

Torso 2602339 (U.S.A.) / Blast First BFFP 34 (U.K.)
Released October 1988

Daydream Nation was one of the more unusual successes of U.S. alternative rock of the 1980s.

While most of their contemporaries, including R.E.M. and The Pixies, were fairly reliant on conventional song structures, Sonic Youth took as their blueprint The Velvet Underground at their most freeform and eccentric. The group was founded in 1981 by guitarist-vocalist Thurston Moore and bassist Kim Gordon (the pair later married). Guitarist Lee Ranaldo joined in 1982, while drummer Steve Shelley arrived shortly after the release of *Bad Moon Rising* (1985), the first Sonic Youth album to gain international exposure.

Sonic Youth continued to hone their sound on the well-received *Evol* (1986) and *Sister* (1987) before recording an ironic tribute to Madonna and other pop stars of the time, *The Whitey Album* (1988), as Ciccone Youth. Returning to their day jobs, the group recorded what has come to be known as their defining work in July and August 1988 at Greene Street Recording, New York. *Daydream Nation* was produced by the group and Nick Sansano, who would later work with Public Enemy and The Manic Street Preachers among others. It veers – often without warning – from hypnotic psychedelia to balls-out art rock, and takes in such fan favorites as 'Teenage Riot' and 'Eric's Trip.' Although the album failed to chart, its word-of-mouth success earned Sonic Youth an unlikely major-label deal with David Geffen's DGC, for whom the group continues to record today.

■ *Left to right: Thurston Moore, Steve Shelley, Kim Gordon, and Lee Ranaldo of Sonic Youth.*

1989

The Lion **Youssou N'Dour**

Atlantic 91253 (U.S.A.) Virgin 91253 (U.K.)
Released August 1989

Following the success of Paul Simon's *Graceland* (1986) African music started to find a wider audience among Western listeners in the later 1980s. Youssou N'Dour was the biggest star of this burgeoning world-music market, and *The Lion* was his first internationally released album.

N'Dour started performing in his native Senegal as a teenager in the mid 1970s. By the age of 21 he had assumed control of the group Super Etoile De Dakar, which became hugely popular across Africa and developed a cult following in Europe and the U.S.A. In the mid 1980s N'Dour's expressive, five-octave voice featured prominently on both *Graceland* and Peter Gabriel's *So* (1985), which introduced him to a wider, more mainstream Western audience for the first time. Gabriel later invited N'Dour to record an album of his own at the former Genesis frontman's newly built Real World Studios. The resulting album, *The Lion*, consists mostly of re-recorded versions of older material, but did also include a handful of songs sung in English. Musically, the album is built on the

mbalax style N'Dour had helped pioneer with Super Etoile De Dakar, which blends elements of African, Cuban, and Western pop music. The single 'Shakin' The Tree,' a duet with Gabriel, was a minor U.K. hit single.

N'Dour had his biggest chart hit five years later when '7 Seconds,' recorded in collaboration with Neneh Cherry, reached Number Two in the U.K. Other African performers to find success in the post-*Graceland* music world include Baaba Maal and Orchestra Baobab.

▓ *Real World Studios (pictured above and below) was founded by Peter Gabriel in 1988 on the outskirts of the English village of Box, Wiltshire. The main recording-room is surrounded on three sides by a river that runs around the grounds of the studio. As well as Youssou N'Dour, the many bands and musicians to have recorded at Real World since the late 1980s include Kylie Minogue, James, and The Super Furry Animals. Left: N'Dour at the North Sea Jazz Festival in The Hague, Denmark, in July 1989.*

1989

The Stone Roses The Stone Roses

Silvertone 1184 (U.S.A.) / ORE 502 (U.K.)
Released April 1989

The Stone Roses is regularly touted as one of the greatest albums of all time in the U.K., where it cast a long shadow over much of the guitar-based music of the 1990s. In the U.S.A., however, The Stone Roses never rose beyond the level of a cult act.

The band was formed in Manchester, England, by vocalist Ian Brown, guitarist John Squire, and drummer Alan 'Reni' Wren in 1984, but they didn't really get going until bassist Gary 'Mani' Mounfield joined three years later. The singles 'Elephant Stone' (1988) and 'Made Of Stone' (1989) failed to chart, but generated high expectations among British tastemakers and trendsetters. *The Stone Roses* didn't disappoint; only The Smith's *The Queen Is Dead* comes close in terms of importance and influence among British guitar-based music. Produced by John Leckie, the album welded subtle dance rhythms to melodic, 1960s-style psychedelic guitar pop, each song topped by Brown's shamanic vocal delivery. The album's highlights include the slow-burning 'I Wanna Be Adored,' 'She Bangs The Drum,' and the eight-minute closing track 'I Am The Resurrection.'

> "WHEN I'VE HEARD ONE OF OUR SONGS ON THE RADIO, WHEN IT'S JUST BEEN BASS, DRUMS, AND ONE GUITAR LINE, I'D SAY THEY'RE AS DANCEABLE AS ANY HOUSE RECORD I'VE EVER DANCED TO. IT'S JUST ABOUT CREATING A GROOVE WITH SPACE AROUND IT."
>
> STONE ROSES FRONTMAN IAN BROWN

The Stone Roses was not a huge success initially, stalling at Number 19 on the U.K. chart, but seems to grow in stature with every passing year. In the wake of its success, countless other British groups – from The Charlatans and Happy Mondays through to Blur, Oasis, and The Verve – have scored U.K. hits owing a debt to The Stone Roses' sound. The Stone Roses themselves never really capitalized on this, however. After one more terrific single, 'Fools' Gold,' the group disappeared, eventually returning in 1994 with the disappointing *Second Coming* before splitting in acrimony.

■ *The Stone Roses make their U.K. television debut on* The Late Show *on November 21st 1989. Forty seconds into their rendition of 'Elephant Stone,' the group exceeded the BBC volume regulations, causing a power cut.*

Club Classics – Volume One Soul II Soul

Virgin 91267 (U.S.A.) / 10-Virgin DIX 82 (U.K.)
Released April 1989

Soul II Soul was the most influential U.K. dance act of the late 1980s and early 1990s, and launched the career of the producer Nellee Hooper, who later worked with U2, Madonna, and numerous others.

In 1988 Hooper, vocalist-keyboardist Jazzie B, and multi-instrumentalist Phil 'Daddae' Harvey issued a pair of singles, 'Fairplay' and 'Feel Free,' that made only minor dents in the U.K. charts but were big club hits. They gave little indication, however, of the artistic and commercial success that would follow with *Club Classics*, an album that actually lives up to its boastful title.

Preceded by the international hit single 'Keep On Movin',' *Club Classics* is a slick blend of R&B, soul, disco, and world-music influences. The album's smooth hip-hop beats, lush string arrangements, and dub reggae bass were a key influence on much of the British dance music of the 1990s. Alongside the group's core trio, an important presence on *Club Classics* is Caron Wheeler, who sang on and co-wrote 'Back To Life,' which topped the U.K. singles chart and reached Number Four in the U.S.A. The album itself also reached Number One in the U.K., peaking at Number 14 in the U.S.A., where it quickly sold two million copies. In the wake of the success of *Club Classics* Nellee Hooper became one of the hottest producers of the early 1990s, working with Sinead O'Connor ('Nothing Compares 2 U'), Massive Attack (*Blue Lines*), Björk (*Debut*), and Madonna (*Bedtime Stories*).

Disintegration The Cure

Elektra 60855 (U.S.A.) / Fiction FIXH14 (U.K.)
Released May 1989

One of the most enduring bands to emerge in the aftermath of punk in the U.K., The Cure were one of the principal acts responsible for laying the foundations of Gothic rock in the early 1980s.

The group looked to have peaked with the album *Pornography* in 1982, but gradually reestablished themselves later in the decade with a more pop-orientated sound. *Disintegration* was The Cure's biggest critical and commercial success. Already adored across Europe, the band had begun to make inroads into the U.S. market with the retrospective singles collection *Staring At The Sea* (1986) and the album *Kiss Me Kiss Me Kiss Me* (1987), which displayed a harder-rock sound than the group's earlier efforts.

Disintegration was recorded alongside David Allen, who had worked on synthesizer-pop group The Human League's breakthrough album *Dare!* before producing all of The Cure's albums between 1983 and 1996. *Disintegration* is essentially a refinement of everything that preceded it. Retaining the gloomy lyricism that had made The Cure one of the best-loved cult bands of the 1980s, the album adds a heightened pop sensibility to the arena-ready rock of *Kiss Me Kiss Me Kiss Me*. Key to *Disintegration*'s success was the upbeat single 'Lovesong,' which provided the group with a Number Two entry on the U.S. pop charts. The album itself reached Number 12 in the U.S.A. and Number Three in the U.K., and provided further chart hits on both sides of the Atlantic with 'Pictures Of You' and a remixed version of the song 'Lullaby.' Though frontman Robert Smith would claim in interviews around the release of the album that the group would soon

disband, The Cure have continued to tour and record into the 21st century, though never with the commercial success of *Disintegration* and its follow-up *Wish* (1992).

The Healer John Lee Hooker

Chameleon 74808 (U.S.A.) / Silvertone ORE 508 (U.K.)
Released October 1989

The Complete Recordings Robert Johnson

Columbia 46222 (U.S.A.) / 467246 (U.K.)
Released November 1990

One of the most important blues guitarists of all time, John Lee Hooker enjoyed a career that spanned over 50 years, from 1948 until his death in 2001. Hooker recorded little of note during the 1980s, however, until *The Healer*, which prompted a resurgence of interest in both his work and the blues generally.

In 1988 Hooker and slide guitarist-producer Roy Rogers set upon the idea of recording an album of collaborations with other musicians, in a similar vein to the series of LPs Hooker cut with Canned Heat, Van Morrison, and others in the early 1970s. Recorded at Russian Hill Recording Studios in San Francisco, The Plant in Sausalito, California, and Leon Haywood Studios in Los Angeles, *The Healer* features contributions from, among others, Keith Richards, Carlos Santana, Bonnie Raitt, Los Lobos, Charlie Musselwhite, and Canned Heat. None of them was able to outshine Hooker himself on the album, however, which contained his most vital performances in two decades, and the single 'I'm In The Mood' won a Grammy for Best Traditional Blues Recording.

The impressive guest list caught the attention of the mainstream press for the first time since Hooker's brief appearance in *The Blues Brothers* (1980), resulting in his strongest ever album sales. The album's popularity also prompted the release of countless CDs of material from Hooker's back catalog, as well as that of other Delta Bluesmen, notably *The Complete Robert Johnson* (1990).

Perhaps the best-loved of all the Delta blues singers, Johnson began writing and performing his own material as a teenager in the late 1920s. Legend states that he sold his soul to the devil in exchange for his peerless guitar skills. He made a number of recordings in the 1930s, which were issued in the U.S.A. on the Vocalian-Arc label. Johnson died in 1938, at the age of 27, having been poisoned by a jealous barman. His recorded output was first compiled in the midst of the mid-1960s blues revival as *King Of The Delta Blues Singers* (1966). *The Complete Recordings* builds on that set, and contains each of the 37 songs Johnson recorded in his lifetime.

Meanwhile, the John Lee Hooker revival continued into the early 1990s with *Mr Lucky* (1991), which peaked at Number Three in Britain, and the U.K. Top 20 hit, a re-recording of his 1962 hit 'Boom Boom' (1992), though neither had any serious impact in the U.S.A.

1989

Paul's Boutique **Beastie Boys**

Capitol 91743 (U.S.A.) / EST 2102 (U.K.)
Released July 1989

Somewhat under-appreciated on release in favor of the harder, gangsta rap typified by NWA, The Beastie Boys' second album has since been recognized as one of the high points of late-1980s hip-hop.

In 1986 The Beastie Boys issued what would become the biggest-selling rap record of the 1980s, *Licensed To III*. The album was sonically similar to the rap-rock hybrid of Run DMC's *Raising Hell* but has a jovial, frat-party feel quite apart from many of the band's hip-hop contemporaries. Most of the success of *Licensed To III* was down to the crossover appeal of the guitar-led single 'Fight For Your Right (To Party)' and the controversy that arose from the trio's apparently sexist lyrics.

Paul's Boutique is a completely different animal. Though some songs, such as 'Shake Your Rump,' wouldn't have been out of place on The Beastie Boys' debut, much of the album is a showcase for the deft production style of The Dust Brothers, Mike Simpson and John King. The duo was among the first to use a digital sampler, which allowed them to produce a much more precise, cohesive sonic backdrop than on the often primitive recordings of their peers. Following the lead of Public Enemy's production team The Bomb Squad, The Dust Brothers looked beyond the obvious guitar and drum samples used by most hip-hop record makers, instead taking elements from songs by the likes of Pink Floyd, Curtis Mayfield, Sly Stone, and The Ramones; one track, 'The Sounds Of Silence,' uses as its hook a couple of chords from 'The End' by The Beatles. The result is a psychedelic sound collage, often drowned in reverb that sounds nothing like anything that came before. In addition, the three Beastie Boys' vocal contributions take in a wider variety of subjects than on *Licensed To III*, and showcase a markedly improved delivery style.

Paul's Boutique reached Number 14 on its release in the U.S.A., but failed to match the success of its predecessor by some way. Many critics had already labeled The Beastie Boys as one-hit-wonder chancers who could never make another *Licensed To III*, and in many ways they were right: *Paul's Boutique* is a far more musically impressive statement than the group's debut, and one that would inspire a host of other artists and producers, in hip-hop and beyond. The Beastie Boys followed it with the more commercially successful albums *Check Your Head* (1992) and *III Communication* (1994), on which the group's members started to play their own instruments for the first time.

Straight Outta Compton NWA

Ruthless 57102 (U.S.A.) / 4th & Broadway 534 (U.K.)
Released August 1989

The first widely successful gangsta rap album, *Straight Outta Compton* established NWA as the first West Coast alternative to the New York-based hip-hop scene.

Niggaz With Attitude was formed in the mid 1980s by rappers Ice Cube, MC Ren, and Eazy-E, turntablist DJ Yella, and Dr Dre, who would go on to become perhaps the most important hip-hop producer of the next two decades. The group played a key role in the compilation album *NWA And The Posse* (1987), before Eazy-E formed his own Ruthless Records to issue *Straight Outta Compton*, the label allegedly funded by illegal activity.

Containing the infamous single 'Fuck The Police,' which drew a written warning from the FBI, *Straight Outta Compton* is a continuous stream of visceral, violent raps set against a backing of harsh drum-machine programming and occasional stabs of funk guitars and horns. Dr Dre had yet to arrive at the richer production style that would bring him so much commercial success in the 1990s, but the musical backing he provides here is the perfect accompaniment to the album's vocal focus.

Straight Outta Compton reached Number 37 in the U.S. albums chart on release, and immediately stirred up controversy as debate raged over whether the members of NWA were violent misogynists or simply seeking to document urban life. Such arguments have continued long since the band split in 1992, as a succession of artists from 2Pac to Eminem have kept up the gangsta-rap tradition.

As Nasty As They Wanna Be 2 Live Crew

Luke XR-107 (U.S.A.) / Atlantic 91651 (U.K.)
Released June 1989

Their third and most successful album, 2 Live Crew's *As Nasty As They Wanna Be* was one of the first albums to be labeled with a 'Parental Advisory' sticker to warn against its explicit content and also to be legally branded obscene.

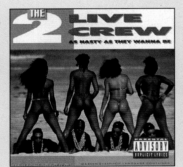

In 1985 two high-ranking U.S. politicians' wives, Tipper Gore and Susan Baker, formed the Parent's Music Resource Center, having been shocked at the lyrical content of some of the music their young daughters were listening to. There had been a long history of records being banned or censored, from Duke Ellington's so-called "devil's music" to the Frank Zappa single 'I Don't Wanna Get Drafted,' but never before had a system been set up to categorize "obscene" music. On the back of Gore's and Baker's campaigning, a growing number of albums – which tended to be by rap and hard-rock artists – were displayed with a warning in the late 1980s.

Not only was *As Nasty As They Wanna Be* one of the first to fall into this category, it was eventually banned outright in Florida. Taking the sexually charged, violent content of NWA's recently issued *Straight Outta Compton* several steps farther, the album's lyrical content borders on the pornographic. The majority of the album's 18 tracks, which include 'Me So Horny' and 'Bad Ass Bitch,' are frank, voyeuristic accounts of casual sex; equally offensive to many was the cover art, which depicted the group's

four members peering up from a beach at a quartet of scantily clad women.

The Parental Advisory sticker has since become an industry standard. In 1991 Wal-Mart, the largest music retailer in the U.S.A., announced it would no longer stock albums with "Explicit Content," prompting many artists to issue two versions of their albums, one of them cleaned up.

3 Feet High And Rising De La Soul

Tommy Boy TB1019 (U.S.A.) / DLS1 (U.K.)
Released March 1989

De La Soul's debut, *3 Feet High And Rising*, introduced an optimistic, 'daisy age' alternative to the gritty, political hip-hop of many of the group's peers.

De La Soul was formed in 1987 by a trio of rappers, David 'Trugoy The Dove' Jolicoeur, Kelvin 'Posdnuos' Mercer, and Vincent 'Pacemaster Mase' Mason, in Long Island, New York. In late 1988 the group started work on their first album with producer 'Prince Paul' Huston, a founder member of early-1980s rap crew Stetsasonic, at Calliope studio in New York.

Taking a similar approach to The Beastie Boys' *Paul's Boutique*, *3 Feet High And Rising* was built out of elements of a wide variety of music, from Johnny Cash to Steely Dan. The best-known song on the album, 'The Magic Number,' features elements of 'You Showed Me' by The Turtles, which prompted legal action from the cult 1960s group. The implications of The Turtles' eventual court victory affected not just De La Soul but hip-hop production methods in general. From the early 1990s onward all samples had to be cleared and paid for before an album could be released, leading many hip-hop acts to switch to using more live instrumentation.

Reaching Number 24 in the U.S.A. and number 13 in the U.K., *3 Feet High And Rising* opened the doors for a wave of other rap acts with a similarly positive outlook, including A Tribe Called Quest and The Jungle Brothers. De La Soul's debut is also notable for the spoof game-show segments interspersed between the album's songs; comic interludes between tracks would soon become a regular ingredient of hip-hop albums.

■ *Posdnuos (left) and Pacemaster Mase of De La Soul.*

1990

The Immaculate Collection **Madonna**

Sire 7599 26440 (U.S.A. & U.K.)
Released November 1990

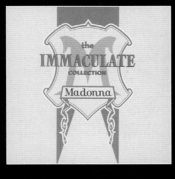

The pre-eminent female performer of the 1980s, Madonna ended the first phase of her career with an unusual retrospective set, the biggest-selling best-of album of all time by a female artist.

The Immaculate Collection contains most of Madonna's hits from 1983 to 1990, but presents many of them in remixed form, with some sped up or shortened from their original length. The album was also the first to make use of QSound, a newly developed mixing technique that purported to simulate quadraphonic, three-dimensional sound using only two speakers. The year 1990 proved to be one of the busiest and most controversial years of Madonna's career. Prior to the release of *The Immaculate Collection* she issued *I'm Breathless*, a selection of songs "inspired by the film *Dick Tracy*," in which she also starred.

She also embarked on the Blonde Ambition Tour, which tied in with the greatest-hits theme of *The Immaculate Collection*. The notorious tour introduced Madonna's conical, Jean Paul Gaultier-designed bra to the world and drew protests from religious and conservative groups, who objected to the lewd dance routines, which included simulated sex with hermaphrodites. The singer was captured during the tour in the documentary feature *Truth Or Dare* – originally titled *In Bed With Madonna*, under which name it was released in the U.K. and elsewhere, but the name was changed for U.S. release.

The Immaculate Collection features 16 of Madonna's biggest hits to date – arranged in chronological order, from 'Holiday' and 'Material Girl' to 'Like A Prayer' and 'Vogue' – and two previously unheard cuts, both of which also became international hit singles, which makes for a highly impressive tracklisting. Of the new songs, the hypnotic, hip-hop-influenced 'Justify My Love' stands as one of Madonna's most controversial releases, largely because of the media storm surrounding the raunchy video, which was banned in Britain and the U.S.A. Despite this – or perhaps because of it – 'Justify My Love' was Madonna's seventh U.S. Number One hit single and marked the start of the most overtly sexual period of her recording career. Subsequent years saw the release of her soft-porn book, *Sex*, and the albums *Erotica* (1992) and *Bedtime Stories* (1994). The other exclusive track on *The Immaculate Collection*, 'Rescue Me,' reached Number Nine in the U.S.A. and Number Three in the U.K. The album itself surprisingly failed to top the U.S. albums chart, but soon became Madonna's biggest-selling album to date, selling over 23 million copies worldwide.

Some of the songs suffer from the exaggerated panning and separation of the QSound mixes, resulting occasionally in a strange, displaced sound. Once heralded as a revolution in audio technology, QSound was briefly popular in the early 1990s but failed to achieve the sort of music-industry dominance its creators had hoped for. While Sting and Luther Vandross both recorded Grammy Award-winning albums in the format in 1991, QSound has since only really been used on video-game soundtracks.

I Do Not Want What I Haven't Got
Sinead O'Connor

Ensign 21759 (U.S.A.) / CHEN 14 (U.K.)
Released March 1990

Though often better known for her controversial statements and actions, Sinead O'Connor was one of the most striking pop vocalists and performers of the early 1990s.

After issuing a debut album, *The Lion And The Cobra*, in 1987, O'Connor's career stalled briefly as she and drummer John Reynolds had a son and then divorced, events which would inform the mood of her second full-length album. O'Connor recorded *I Do Not Want What I Haven't Got* at STS Studios in her native Dublin, Ireland, during the summer of 1989. Among her collaborators here were former Smiths bassist Andy Rourke, ex-Public Image Ltd bassist Jah Wobble, and Nellee Hooper of Soul II Soul. Hooper was responsible for the stark arrangement of the Prince composition, 'Nothing Compares 2 U,' which topped the singles charts on both sides of the Atlantic. The striking, confessional nature of 'Nothing Compares 2 U' was a good indication of what else lay on *I Do Not Want What I Haven't Got*. The album jumps from string-drenched balladry and traditional Celtic folk to slick pop and the arresting a cappella title track, the common link throughout being O'Connor's impassioned vocal delivery.

I Do Not Want What I Haven't Got reached Number One in the U.S.A. and the U.K., but O'Connor's musical career soon began to take a back seat to the various controversies she got caught up in – be it refusing to sing 'The Star-Spangled Banner,' turning down Grammy Awards, or ripping up a photograph of the Pope on *Saturday Night Live*.

Violator **Depeche Mode**

Sire 26081 (U.S.A.) / Mute STUMM 64 (U.K.)
Released March 1990

Depeche Mode was one of only a handful of British acts to achieve true stardom in the U.S.A. in the 1990s.

The group was originally part of the early-1980s new-romantic scene, but soon moved toward a darker, more claustrophobic sound. *Music For The Masses* (1987) cemented a strong international following for the group, but what Depeche Mode really lacked – particularly in the U.S.A. – was a bona fide hit that would take them to the next stage. Issued in late 1989, 'Personal Jesus' was the group's most striking single yet. Built on a robotic blues stomp, with an insistent, echoing vocal, it reached the Top 30 in Britain and the U.S.A. The follow-up, an apocalyptic disco ballad by the name of 'Enjoy The Silence,' was even better, and became the group's biggest ever U.S. hit, peaking at Number Eight. That set the stage perfectly for *Violator*, recorded throughout the latter half of 1989 with Flood, producer and engineer of albums by U2, Nick Cave & The Bad Seeds, and Erasure. While nothing else on the album quite matches the power of the two singles that preceded its release, *Violator* is remarkably consistent both in the sound and the quality of the songs. Among the other highlights are the staccato funk of the opening 'World In My Eyes' and the bleak 'Waiting For The Night.'

Violator was a trans-Atlantic Top Ten hit, and has sold six million copies worldwide. The follow-up, *Songs Of Faith And Devotion* (1993), fared even better, topping the U.S. and U.K. charts, but *Violator* remains the group's defining work.

Soundtrack From Twin Peaks **Angelo Badalamenti**

Warner Brothers 26316 (U.S.A. & U.K.)
Released September 1990

Opening with one of the most memorable and evocative pieces of music ever written for television, *Soundtrack From Twin Peaks* was as much of a surprise hit as the much-heralded series, which first aired in 1990.

Twin Peaks was the brainchild of Mark Frost and the cinematic auteur David Lynch, best known for the cult-classic movies *Eraserhead* (1977) and *Blue Velvet* (1986). *Twin Peaks* marked Lynch's first foray into television.

Angelo Badalamenti, who had previously scored *Blue Velvet* and worked as an arranger for Pet Shop Boys and Liza Minnelli, was employed to write the main theme and incidental music for the series. 'Twin Peaks Theme' opens the album, riding in on delicate electric piano and strings, softly brushed drums and a distinctive, dreamy lead line, played on a six-string bass. Elsewhere, Badalamenti's smoky jazz on 'Freshly Squeezed' and 'Dance Of The Dream Man' is perfectly suited to the otherworldly atmospheres of *Twin Peaks*, and the stark, piano-led 'Laura Palmer's Theme' neatly encapsulates the double life of the title character, whose death provides the story around which the series is based. The three vocal tracks on *Soundtrack From Twin Peaks* are sung by Julee Cruise, and had all previously featured on her Lynch- and Badalamenti-produced album *Floating Into The Night* (1989). Cruise became something of a pet project for Lynch, and was given further exposure when she appeared in *Twin Peaks* as a nightclub singer. *Soundtrack From Twin Peaks* unexpectedly reached Number 16 on the U.S. albums chart, while 'Twin Peaks Theme' won a Grammy Award for Best Instrumental Pop Performance.

1991

Nevermind Nirvana

DGC 24425 (U.S.A. & U.K.)
Released September 1991

Ten Pearl Jam

Epic 47857 (U.S.A.) / 468884-2 (U.K.)
Released August 1991

**Without question the most influential rock album of the 1990s,
Nevermind signaled the arrival of the decade's most enduring white
youth-culture movement: grunge.**

Like many revolutionary albums before it, *Nevermind* came out of left field
and was roundly dismissed by many U.S. critics who heard it only as a
dirtier, simpler form of heavy metal. It took interest from the U.K. to launch
the album on its way to achieving ten-times platinum status before the start
of the new millennium.

Nirvana's debut album, *Bleach*, had much of the same raw-yet-melodic
sound as *Nevermind*, and a couple of great Kurt Cobain compositions,
'About A Girl' and 'Negative Creep,' that should have alerted critics to the
fact that something fresh was happening. What *Bleach* lacked, however, was
Dave Grohl's drumming. When Grohl replaced Chad Channing, producer
Butch Vig immediately noticed how "Dave was incredibly powerful and dead
on the groove. I could tell from the way Kurt and Chris were playing with him
that they had definitely kicked their music up another notch in terms of
intensity." Now they had the sound that Cobain once described as "The Bay
City Rollers getting molested by Black Flag," and all they had to do was get
it on tape.

Cobain described the process of creating songs for *Nevermind* by saying:
"We downed a lot of cough syrup and Jack Daniels and just lounged on the
couch in the recreation area of the studio for days on end, just writing down
a few lyrics here and there." In stark contrast, Vig recalls that Cobain was in
good spirits during the making of *Nevermind*, and worked long days,
beginning around noon and ending after midnight. "I think it took five or six
days in all," says Vig. "Dave was set up in the middle of the room. We built
a big drum tunnel on the front of his bass drum, so we could mike it from a
distance and still isolate it from all the bleed in the rest of the room. Chris
had his SVT bass rig off to the side, but he could play in the room. His
headphones were set up next to the drums. Kurt's amps were in a little
isolation area, but he was also in the room and he could sing into a mike."
Most tracks, he reckons, required only two or three takes.

'Smells Like Teen Spirit,' the song that would rocket them into the U.S. Top
Ten singles chart, came about as the result of a misunderstanding between
Cobain and a girlfriend. "We were kinda drunk, and we were writing graffiti
all over the walls of my house," he explained. "She wrote 'Kurt smells like

1991

teen spirit.' And earlier on, we were having this discussion on teen revolution and stuff like that, and I took that as a compliment. I thought she was saying I was a person who could inspire. I just thought that was a nice little title. And it turns out she just meant that I smelled like the deodorant, I didn't even know that deodorant existed until after the song was written."

Surprisingly, given the elemental passion on 'Teen Spirit,' Cobain's musical inspiration for the track is said to have been Boston's bombastic pomp-rock classic, 'More Than A Feeling.' Vig was immediately impressed by 'Teen Spirit,' and insisted that they play it over and over again. "There wasn't much that needed to be done with the song," he points out. "I think we did a little arranging. At the end of each chorus, there's a little ad-lib thing Kurt did with the guitar. Originally that only happened at the end of the song; he did it a whole bunch of times. I suggested moving that up into each chorus and cutting the choruses down a little bit."

The album's other really well-known cut, the chilly but compelling 'Come As You Are,' is much harder to get a handle on. Is it, as some Nirvana-watchers have suggested, an open invitation to the band's fans to join in their fun, or is it something much more sinister? "The lines in the song are really contradictory," said Cobain. "Y'know, one after another, they're kind of a rebuttal, to each line, and they're just kinda confusing I guess. It's just about people, and uh, what they're expected to act like." He has also claimed that: "At the time I was writing those songs, I really didn't know what I was trying to say. There's no point in my even trying to analyze or explain it." Given that the songs, though oblique, seem to be the work of an intelligent lyricist, it's hard to know how serious Cobain was being when he made these kinds of comments. There's so much variety on the album – from the punky thrash of 'Territorial Pissings' to the richly melodic 'Lithium,' or the acoustic strum of the nightmarish 'Polly,' detailing a horrific rape he'd

■ *Above and below: Nirvana record a live session for the Dutch radio stations VARA and VRPO on November 25th 1991, two months after the release of the group's groundbreaking* Nevermind *album. Opposite: Stone Gossard and Eddie Vedder of Pearl Jam on stage on the New York leg of the* Lollapallooza *festival in 1992.*

read about in a newspaper – that it's hard to accept *Nevermind* as anything other than the work of a rational, self-aware songwriter.

Like Bob Dylan, Cobain saw no merit creating a perfect take, preferring instead to leave each song fresh and vital, mistakes and all. "He really wanted to do everything on the first or second take," says Vig. "He'd do a couple of takes and say, 'That's it. I'm not gonna do it any more.' The tricky part was trying to figure out how to motivate him to give really good performances." The resourceful Vig, however, would record every word Cobain sang, including warm-ups, and would then piece a final take together from the best-sung lines from three or four versions.

Recording In The 1990s

After a decade of arena rock, hip-hop, and hair bands, the change that swept over the recording industry at the start of the 1990s was swift and dramatic.

It began with the re-emergence of 45-year-old Neil Young – whose full-tilt performance of 'Rockin' In The Free World' on *Saturday Night Live* served as a prelude to his landmark *Ragged Glory* – and continued with the arrival of a new crop of young bands, many of whom hailed from the rain-soaked metropolis of Seattle, Washington. Joining the likes of Nirvana, Pearl Jam, and Mudhoney were a contingent of upstart producers and engineers, whose use of old-school techniques and technology helped put some of the dynamics back into the recording environment.

One of the best of the behind-the-board bunch was Butch Vig, producer of Nirvana's *Nevermind*, Smashing Pumpkins' *Gish* and *Siamese Dream*, and many others. During the 1990s Vig worked much of his magic from his own hand-built recording facility, Smart Studios, located in downtown Madison, Wisconsin. It was there that, in 1995, Vig teamed with guitar buddies Duke Erikson and Steve Marker, plus Scottish vocalist Shirley Manson, to form Garbage. With Garbage, Vig found the perfect outlet for his old-school-rules-new-school-tools production style, which involved recording spontaneous song fragments live then cobbling together the disparate elements in a manner reminiscent of Vig's hero Brian Wilson. "Most of our songs come from simply improvising while we're running our 48-track Pro Tools," says Vig. "We compile bits and pieces, cut them up, and edit them together, and keep working on them until eventually it sounds like a song that was written on an acoustic guitar!"

Recording *Dookie*, the major-label debut from Bay Area's Green Day, in 1994 was UK-born, San Francisco-based engineer Neill King, who'd cut his teeth with the likes of Elvis Costello, Madness, and The Smiths and knew a little something about harnessing studio energy. Rather than try to contain Tre Cool's voluminous drum sound, King had the band set up in the expansive, wood-laden Fantasy Studio A, then proceeded to make the most of the enormous ambience. "There are huge ceilings in there, so I just put up a bunch of room mikes and tried to capture the sound of Tre's kit that way," says King. "If you can get it sounding really good in the room, it's going to come across so much better on record than just close-miking everything."

Meanwhile, up at Boston's Q Division Studios, singer–songwriter Aimee Mann was capping a masterful year in music with her second effort, *I'm With Stupid*, an album recorded during 1994 but not issued until early 1996, owing to record-company shenanigans. Its distinctive edge was the product of co-writer, producer, and multi-instrumentalist Jon Brion, who learned the art of creative dabbling from old heroes such as The Beatles and The Zombies. Brion's quest for unique guitar tones often led him down some fairly unusual paths. "On 'Long Shot' I had Aimee record consecutive rhythm-guitar tracks, each one played the same but with different colorations each time," says Brion. "For the first track, I'd say, 'OK, let's go with all red things – this guitar is red, that fuzz box is red, that amp's got a little red on it, fine, go . . .' For the second part, I had her play a Tele through a Matchless amp with a Vox Tonebender; on the next track, she's playing the worst guitar in the building through the cheapest fuzz pedal we could find into a Kustom head. I know it sounds crazy, but eventually you get that cool juxtaposition. It always seems to pan out in the end."

The leaner, meaner production style of the 1990s was just the ticket for veteran songwriter–guitarist Tom Petty. After a fruitful four-year stint with producer Jeff Lynne, Petty handed the control-room keys to Def Jam's Rick Rubin and Rubin's trusted engineer Jeff Scott. In late summer 1993, Petty and Rubin checked into Sound City in Van Nuys, a mammoth structure with several decades-worth of California pop lore behind it (and birthplace to Petty's 1979 commercial breakout *Damn The Torpedoes*).

Released in the fall of 1994, the resulting album, *Wildflowers*, left the impression of a middle-aged tug-of-war, an effect made all the more pronounced by the immediacy of Rubin's production work. Says Joe Baresi, assistant engineer on the album: "*Wildflowers* is a great example of the kind of sound you can get out of a great studio with the right people running it."

Sweetened with some remixing by Andy Wallace, Vig's production was undeniably a major factor in the success of the album. Though he would no doubt have preferred Cobain's vocals to be higher in the mix, he was able to create a sound that was balanced beautifully between grunge distortion and pop clarity. It was a combination that worked equally well for hi-fi quality FM stereo radio and for lo-fi student or underground stations, and it appealed to pop fans and metalheads alike. Just about the only person in the U.S.A. who didn't like it was Kurt Cobain: "Our music, especially on this album, is so slick-sounding," he grumbled. "A few years ago, I would have hated our band, to tell you the truth."

> "A LOT OF THE TIME I WRITE A SONG AND WHEN SOMEONE ASKS ME ABOUT IT I'LL MAKE UP AN EXPLANATION ON THE SPOT, BECAUSE I WRITE LYRICS IN THE STUDIO, AND I HAVE NO IDEA WHAT I'M TALKING ABOUT HALF THE TIME."
> *KURT COBAIN*

From the outside, however, everything looked fine, and when the little band from Aberdeen, Washington, reached Number One in the U.S. albums chart on January 11th 1992 it sparked an explosion of interest in the so-called 'Seattle Sound' that would change the lives of dozens of local musicians, not least among them being the five members of Pearl Jam.

The core of Pearl Jam lay in 1980s Seattle favorites Mother Love Bone, whose promising career ended with the heroin-related death of singer Andrew Wood. While guitarist Stone Gossard and bassist Jeff Ament were struggling to regroup, Jack Irons, former drummer of The Red Hot Chili Peppers, suggested they should consider recruiting a young San Diego surfer, Eddie Vedder, who also wrote songs. As Vedder recalls it: "Jeff sent me a tape of three songs, and I sent him back a mini-opera." The tape he received consisted of instrumental backing tracks, which he transformed into complete songs with the addition of lyrics and vocal melodies. Among them were 'Once' and 'Alive,' both of which wound up on *Ten*. It was clear that Vedder worked well with Gossard and Ament, so they played a few gigs and recorded a bunch of demos as Mookie Blaylock, a name borrowed from a favorite basketball player, which they soon realized was too much of a joke to be taken seriously.

So, on May 11th 1991, when the now renamed Pearl Jam began recording their Epic Records debut album at London Bridge Studios, Seattle, Washington, with producer Rick Parashar. The old Mookie demos were rerecorded without too much alteration, because the band had been playing them live for months and knew exactly how they should be done.

Musically, Pearl Jam and Nirvana had very little in common, beyond a raw, raging power that had been missing from rock for too long. Where Nirvana kept things deliberately simple and grungy, Pearl Jam sounded more like a souped-up, socially-aware, essence of Led Zeppelin with a hint of Southern rock thrown in for good measure, all topped off with Vedder's heart-stoppingly powerful vocals. The first track they completed was 'Alive,' the

stirring twin-guitar-powered rocker that would become their first single. The cut that would put them on the map, however, was 'Jeremy,' based on the true story of Jeremy Wade Delle, a seriously disturbed 16-year-old student at Richardson High School in Dallas, Texas, who had shot himself dead in front of his class on January 8th 1991. Vedder combined Delle's story with his own recollection of a fellow-student in junior high school, in San Diego, California, who had taken a gun to his class and gone on a shooting spree, though with less disastrous results. He and Pearl Jam guitarist Jeff Ament then put music to the words and, though it was never a huge hit, the accompanying video walked off with no less than four MTV Video Music Awards, including Video Of The Year, Best Group Video, Best Metal/Hard Rock Video, and Best Direction.

Parashar's contribution to the album extended beyond faithfully recording the band's music into helping them actually make it. "Rick's a super talented engineer-musician," notes Jeff Ament, and he adds that, on a day when guitarist Stone Gossard was sick: "Ed, Rick, and I conjured up the art piece that opens and closes the record. That was so fun, I wanted to make a whole record of that kind of stuff."

When the album was released on August 27th 1991, insiders realized that Mookie Blaylock might be gone but it wasn't forgotten, because *Ten* had been the number on his New Jersey Mets shirt. "I think we all felt pretty good about the record," remembers Gossard, "but we didn't feel like it was the end-all recording, by any means. And I think we kind of felt like, wow, we set the deal up the way we wanted, people seem to be into hearing us play, and at that point Mother Love Bone was helping us get some attention. So we were feeling positive."

Epic Records secured an attention-grabbing promotion for 'Alive,' by having it pre-released via a Coca-Cola promotion. But Vedder soon found himself dismayed by the machinations of the industry, hating the endless round of hand-shaking, back-slapping company functions the band had to attend. It must have stung him badly when Kurt Cobain dismissed Pearl Jam as "corporate" rockers.

A slow-burner, *Ten* didn't peak until almost a year later, when it hit Number Two on the *Billboard* chart in the week of August 22nd 1992 and went on to eclipse *Nevermind* with its rapid progression to five-times platinum status, making Pearl Jam, briefly, more popular than Nirvana.

Tragically, one curious side-effect of the popularity of Seattle's grunge-era bands was the, presumably unintended, glamorization of self-loathing. Cobain seemed to feel he had betrayed his own integrity by finding fame and fortune, and Vedder clearly felt tainted by the embracing tentacles of the business without which he would never have become a superstar. Other Seattle bands, notably Alice In Chains, expressed similarly negative feelings about themselves, and when significant numbers of high-profile icons all seem to share the same philosophy, some of it will inevitably rub off on their fans.

The horrific circumstances of Kurt Cobain's death sent shock waves around the world, but the media glamorization of that waste of an enormous talent simply shored up the impression that such behavior was, somehow, the epitome of cool.

Metallica **Metallica**

Elektra 61113 (U.S.A.) / Vertigo 5100221 (U.K.)
Released August 1991

Metallica are to heavy metal what the stealth bomber is to aviation: darker and meaner than anything else.

With their seminal 1986 album *Master Of Puppets* they had jettisoned the more cartoonish aspects of earlier versions of heavy metal and played up the existential despair. They had popularized a new harmonic vocabulary for the genre, using unusual scales for their riffs and solos. In came the 'scalloped' power-chord with its thumping top and bottom-boosted EQ. Along with the extreme riffing they also had a maniacal sense of arrangement.

In 1991 the eponymous fifth album, in its blacker-than-black sleeve, took head-banging to new levels of precision and went to Number One on both sides of the Atlantic. It was composed with a desire to match riffs to more commercial songs and reduce the length of instrumental passages. 'Enter Sandman' is the standout track and an obvious hit single, and quickly established itself as one of those licks that every aspiring heavy-metal guitarist had to learn to play. Drummer Lars Ulrich commented: "I always find that the first song that you write for an album has a certain magic to it, and that was 'Enter Sandman.' This song just has such a feel to it that we felt it should be the first new thing people heard." They made dramatic use of strings on 'Nothing Else Matters,' with vocalist James Hetfield singing a love song that manages to sound like a curse at the same time.

The whole pantomime of heavy metal has little to do with any recognizable world of ordinary human experience. But it's a vicarious thrill to ride the back of this particular beast. Earlier Metallica albums are more thrashy and frenetic, with epic convoluted songs. With this album they cut the waffle and perfected their style. Ever since, they've been trying to escape the black-hole event horizon of their own darkness.

Blood Sugar Sex Magik **Red Hot Chili Peppers**

Warners 26681 (U.S.A.) / WX 441 (U.K.)
Released September 1991

Blood Sugar Sex Magik, **The Red Hot Chili Peppers' fifth album, arrived just as Nirvana had begun to open the doors for alternative rock in the mainstream, and was the group's commercial breakthrough.**

RHCP had made four albums of funky punk in the 1980s before inking a deal with Warners in 1990. The group recruited Rick Rubin, co-founder of Def Jam Records, to produce *Blood Sugar Sex Magik*. Though best known for his pioneering work with Run-DMC and Public Enemy, Rubin had plenty of experience with rock bands, too, having produced albums by The Cult and Slayer among others. Rubin helped refine the RHCP sound, which had previously tended at times to drift into jam-band territory. *Blood Sugar Sex Magik* is dominated by the bruising, sexual funk of 'Give It Away' and 'Suck My Kiss,' while the mournful 'Under The Bridge' narrowly missed out on the top spot of the U.S. singles chart.

Blood Sugar Sex Magik was a big hit in the U.S.A. and across Europe, eventually selling more than seven million copies worldwide. The group took four years to follow it with the half-baked *One Hot Minute* (1995), before returning to form with *Californication* (1999).

1991

Screamadelica Primal Scream

Sire 26714 (U.S.A.) / Creation CRE076 (U.K.)
Released September 1991

Loveless My Bloody Valentine

Sire 26759 (U.S.A.) / Creation CRE060 (U.K.)
Released November 1991

In the fall of 1991 independent label Creation Records released two of the most innovative British albums of the 1990s: Primal Scream's dance-rock hybrid *Screamadelica* and the pioneering noise-pop of *Loveless* by My Bloody Valentine.

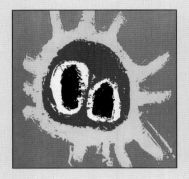 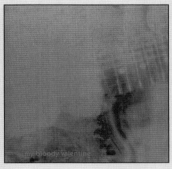

Having recorded a pair of albums of guitar-led rock in the late 1980s, Primal Scream was drawn to the growing acid-house scene and its upbeat, euphoric dance music. Inspired by these new, cutting-edge sounds, frontman Bobby Gillespie asked DJ Andrew Weatherall to remix 'I'm Losing More Than

I'll Ever Have' from the group's eponymous second album. Weatherall removed the drums, bass, guitars, and vocals from the original, a mid-tempo rocker reminiscent of The Rolling Stones, keeping only the piano and horn parts from the song's outro. Adding a new drum beat, dub bass, a soulful vocal sample, and some fresh guitar lines, Weatherall created 'Loaded' (1990), a single that would not only earn Primal Scream its first U.K. hit, but also bridge the gap between rock and dance audiences.

Inspired by the success of 'Loaded,' Primal Scream set about recording an album with the same crossover appeal. The group again worked with Weatherall on eight of the album's 11 tracks – though this time the producer worked with the band from the outset rather than remixing finished tracks – including the epic single 'Come Together' and a version of The 13th Floor Elevators' 'Slip Inside This House.' *Screamadelica* also features a contribution from Jimmy Miller – famous for his work with The Rolling Stones – on soulful opener 'Movin' On Up,' and techno act The Orb assist on the electronic psychedelia of 'Higher Than The Sun.' The resulting album still stands as a unique, genre-bending statement, and was Creation Records' most successful release to date, reaching Number Eight in the U.K. albums chart.

After making a series of fairly lightweight EPs in the mid 1980s, My Bloody Valentine recorded the acclaimed *Isn't Anything* in 1988. The album's droning, layered guitars and dreamy vocals inspired a host of imitators and raised expectations for My Bloody Valentine's second full-length album, particularly after the group issued the *Glider* EP, a richly textured work that made *Isn't Anything* sound like a rough sonic template.

My Bloody Valentine started work on the follow-up to *Isn't Anything* in mid 1989, but it soon became apparent that, given guitarist-songwriter Kevin Shields's growing perfectionism, the group would not be issuing any new material soon. The recording of *Loveless* eventually spanned more than two years, 16 engineers, and countless studios across the U.K., almost bankrupting Creation, who are rumored to have invested over $500,000 in its gestation, a huge sum for a small independent label.

The resulting album was undoubtedly worth the wait in terms of artistic merit, but failed to recoup its production costs, leaving Creation in a fragile

state until its huge worldwide success with Oasis later in the 1990s. *Loveless* is a near-perfect work, founded on an impenetrable wall of dense, searing guitars and deftly programmed rhythms, which mark My Bloody Valentine as one of the first rock bands to utilize digital sampling. Despite the album's moderate commercial success it casts a long shadow over much of the experimental rock that followed it. My Bloody Valentine disbanded in the mid 1990s after Shields decided there was no way the group could top *Loveless*. In 2000 he joined Primal Scream as additional guitarist and occasional producer.

Spiderland **Slint**

Touch & Go T&Glp*64 (U.S.A. & U.K.)
Released March 1991

Though never commercially successful, *Spiderland* was a defining, pioneering influence on post-rock, one of the dominant forms of experimental music in the 1990s and early 2000s.

While it has since become an umbrella term for any group that dares reach beyond the boundaries of conventional rock music, post-rock was originally typified by droning, hypnotic soundscapes with abrupt dynamic shifts and long, complex song structures.

Spiderland was Slint's second and final album. The group was formed in 1988 by Louisville, Kentucky, schoolfriends Brian McMahan on guitar and vocals and Britt Walford on drums, with guitarist David Pajo and bassist Ethan Buckler (replaced by the time *Spiderland* was cut by Todd Brasher). The album was recorded in the fall of 1990 by Steve Albini – one of the key record producers of the 1990s – and Brian Paulson, an engineer who would later work with Beck and Wilco. Its central track, 'Good Morning, Captain,' is emblematic of the whole album in its shifts from quiet, foreboding verses to loud, distorted choruses. The long list of bands inspired by Slint – and this album in particular – includes Mogwai, Tortoise, and Godspeed You Black Emperor!

After Slint disbanded, Pajo joined the equally influential Tortoise, appearing on their highly regarded *Millions Now Living Will Never Die* (1996) before forming his own groups Aerial M and Papa M. McMahan founded The For Carnation, and both he and Pajo have featured on albums by the otherworldly singer-songwriter Will Oldham – aka Palace Music and Bonnie 'Prince' Billy, among other pseudonyms – who took *Spiderland*'s enigmatic cover photograph.

Seal **Seal**

Sire 26627 (U.S.A.) / ZTT ZTT9 (U.K.)
Released May 1991

The London-born soul singer Seal topped the U.K. singles chart in 1990 with his first release, 'Killer,' a collaboration with the techno producer Adamski. Shortly thereafter he started work on his full-length debut with producer Trevor Horn, who also signed Seal to his ZTT label.

Seal was preceded by a huge international hit single, 'Crazy,' which reached Number Two in the U.K. in late 1990 and Number Seven in the U.S.A. the following spring. The light, funky house production of 'Crazy' gave a good indication of the sound of half of the songs on the album; the rest of the tracks on *Seal* are guitar- and piano-led ballads, typified by 'Whirlpool,' which serve mainly to show off Seal's striking vocal ability. The sweeping string parts on the album were arranged by Anne Dudley, a member of Trevor Horn's Art Of Noise group, who would later go on to compose movie soundtracks.

Seal sold three million copies worldwide and spawned two further U.K. hit singles, 'Future Love Paradise' and a remixed version of 'Killer.' The album also earned the artist a prestigious Ivor Novello Award for songwriting in 1992.

Seal issued a second eponymous album three years after the release of his debut. Again produced by Horn, *Seal* (1994) featured contributions from Joni Mitchell and Jeff Beck and included the U.S. Number One hit single 'Kiss From A Rose,' which was featured on the soundtrack to *Batman Forever* (1995) and cemented his reputation as the pre-eminent British soul singer of the 1990s.

1991

Ropin' The Wind **Garth Brooks**

Capitol 96330 (U.S.A.) / ESTU 2162 (U.K.)
Released September 1991

Garth Brooks was the first country artist to achieve multiplatinum sales figures in the U.S.A. *Ropin' The Wind* was the first country album to debut at Number One on the *Billboard* Top 200, where it remained for 18 weeks.

After issuing an eponymous debut in 1989, Brooks began to gain attention outside the country-music world with the following year's *No Fences*, which reached Number Three on the pop albums chart. *Ropin' The Wind* was Brooks's third album in 22 months. Like its predecessors, the album was produced by Allen Reynolds, who had previously worked with Don Williams, Patsy Cline, and Emmylou Harris. It is built on a solid country foundation but also draws on the arena rock of The Eagles and Journey. It was also the first of his albums to blend traditional country elements with 1970s-style rock – most notably on a version of Billy Joel's 'Shameless' – which angered some C&W purists. Despite this, Brooks did more than anybody else to bring country music into the mainstream in the 1990s, while retaining a country audience – 'What She's Doing Now,' 'Shameless,' and 'The River' all reached the Number One spot on the country singles chart.

No Fences and *Ropin' The Wind* both sold over ten million copies, and Brooks issued eight more hit albums in the 1990s, while his run of multiplatinum successes was broken only by *The Life Of Chris Gaines* (1999). That album – for which the singer took off his stetson, grew a goatee, and dabbled in pop rock – remains something of an oddity in the Brooks catalog. He returned to what he does best – and the top of the U.S. albums chart – on *Scarecrow* (2001).

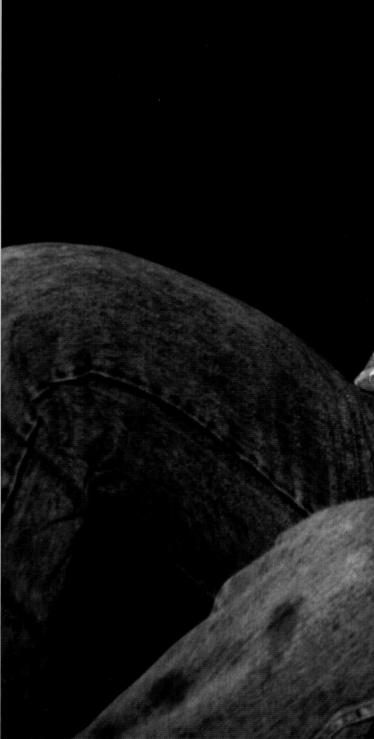

1992

Unplugged **Eric Clapton**

Reprise 45024 (U.S.A.) / Duck-Warners 480 (U.K.)
Released August 1992

Unplugged EP **Mariah Carey**

Columbia 52758 (U.S.A. & U.K.)
Released March 1992

Uptown MTV Unplugged **Various Artists**

MCA 10858 (U.S.A. & U.K)
Released June 1993

Unplugged **Neil Young**

Reprise 45310 (U.S.A.) / 9362 45310 (U.K.)
Released June 1993

MTV Unplugged In New York **Nirvana**

DGC 24727 (U.S.A.) / GED24727 (U.K.)
Released November 1994

In the early 1990s there was no greater signifier of the importance or musical worth of a group or singer than being invited to tape a set for MTV's *Unplugged* series. After airing on MTV, many of these performances were also issued on record. Some – the sets by Eric Clapton and Nirvana, for example – have become significant albums in their own right.

MTV hit upon the idea of *Unplugged* after watching the overwhelming response to an acoustic rendition of 'Wanted Dead Or Alive' at the cable television station's 1989 Music Awards by Jon Bon Jovi and Richie Sambora. At first *Unplugged* tended to group together two or three complementary acts, but by mid 1990 had settled into putting the spotlight on one established performer per show. The Eagles' Don Henley was the first artist to be given a whole *Unplugged* of his own, while other early successes were Elton John and Aerosmith.

Not many of the earliest *Unplugged* performances were issued on record, and those that did become available in album format – including Paul McCartney's set – tended to be seen as novelty items and were not particularly successful. That began to change with the release of two big-selling sets in 1992. The first of these was the three-million-plus selling *Unplugged* EP by Mariah Carey, which compiled the seven songs from her March 16th performance at the Kaufman Astoria Studios in Queens, New York. Carey was backed by harpsichord, celeste, a string quartet, an eight-member vocal workshop, and the horn section from *Saturday Night Live*.

Released later in 1992, Eric Clapton's performance remains the biggest-selling *Unplugged* album of all. It has sold more than seven million copies in the U.S.A. alone, where it reached Number One, and achieved the Number Two slot in the U.K. Clapton's set was taped at Bray Film Studios in Windsor, England. It was Clapton's first performance since the tragic death of his young son Conor, and marked the first public airing of his heartfelt tribute to his son, 'Tears In Heaven.' Clapton also worked through a number of his best-known songs, and a series of blues classics, including Muddy Waters's 'Rollin' And Tumblin'' and Robert Johnson's 'Malted Milk.'

The idea behind the series had originally been to show popular groups and their music in a different light. Too often, though, it became simply an uninspiring

acoustic set of the artist in question's greatest hits performed in a way that barely deviated from the recorded versions. To that end, *Unplugged* was often at its most interesting when it showcased artists from outside the guitar-based rock world. One of the more unusual sets was a showcase for Uptown Records taped on February 6th 1993 at Universal Studios, Los Angeles. It featured performances by Mary J. Blige, Father MC – later better known as Puff Daddy – and others, backed by The Swing Mob. Blige was surprisingly outshone by Jodeci, particularly on a version of Stevie Wonder's 'Lately,' which reached Number Four on the U.S. singles chart.

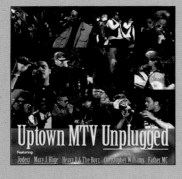

However, some rock artists did go to greater lengths to give their fans – and MTV – something different. One such performer was Neil Young. Though a short acoustic set had been a staple of his live performances for years, Young made an effort to present some of his songs in new and unusual settings at the taping, recorded the day after the Uptown Records set at the same venue. Most striking was his version of 'Like A Hurricane,' previously a harsh guitar-rock track, here reset for pump organ and harmonica. While other songs – particularly 'Needle And The Damage Done' and selections from his recent 'comeback' album *Harvest Moon* (1992) – hardly differed from the studio versions, Young had at least offered a bit of variety and the sense that this was a one-off performance. Both Young's *Unplugged* and the Uptown Records stable's set were issued in album form in June 1993. Young's was the more successful, reaching Number 23 in the U.S.A. and Number Four in the U.K.

For many, the most memorable *Unplugged* was recorded at Sony Music Studios in New York City on November 18th 1993. Right up until the taping there was some concern as to whether Nirvana, and frontman Kurt Cobain in particular, would be fit to perform. In the event, Cobain and his group gave one of the most striking live television performances ever witnessed. Ignoring 'Smells Like Teen Spirit,' the group concentrated on subtle renditions of lesser-known songs, including 'About A Girl' and 'On A Plain,' and made use of non-rock instrumentation such as accordion and cello. The performance also revealed Cobain as a superb interpreter of other people's songs, breathing new life into David Bowie's 'The Man Who Sold The World' – embellished by a hint of cheekily distorted guitar – and the stark blues of a version of Leadbelly's 'Where Did You Sleep Last Night.'

Nirvana's *Unplugged* took on greater significance by virtue of being the final live taping of the group before Cobain's suicide in April of the following year. Issued six months after his death, *MTV Unplugged In New York* serves as a fitting epitaph for the career of perhaps the most important rock singer and songwriter of his generation. It topped the charts on both sides of the Atlantic and has since sold nearly four and a half million copies in the U.S.A. alone. Inevitably, no subsequent *Unplugged* set could come close to the emotional resonance and iconic status of Nirvana's performance or the record sales of Eric Clapton's set. With the exception of the occasional, isolated highlight, such as Bob Dylan's 1994 performance, the series began to dwindle in the later 1990s, when it was dominated by middling alternative-rock acts. MTV tried to relaunch the show as *Unplugged 2.0* in 2001, at which point R.E.M. became the first group to feature on the program twice. *Unplugged 2.0* never reached the heights of the early-1990s tapings, however, and was canceled in 2002.

Warner Bros 45505 (U.S.A.) / 9362450552 (U.K.)
Released October 1992

After five albums with the IRS label, R.E.M. signed to Warner Brothers, and in the process moved away from being a college-radio rock outfit toward a more mature, commercial sound.

Their 'second' career commenced with *Green*, but it was their seventh album, *Out Of Time*, that made them a huge international act on the back of the popularity of 'Losing My Religion.' These circumstances turned *Automatic For The People* – the title is the motto of a restaurant called Weaver D's Delicious Fine Foods, in Clarke County, Georgia, where the staff acknowledge any order with the word 'automatic' – into something of a challenge as a follow-up record.

Sessions took place in studios right across the U.S.A. As the band jammed ideas, it seemed to Buck that "a lot of the songs are kind of like old folk or blues songs." 'Drive' makes an unusual album opener and was the first single. 'Try Not To Breathe,' 'The Sidewinder Sleeps Tonite,' and 'Man On The Moon' are infectious, upbeat R.E.M. songs. (The maddeningly indecipherable hook-line on 'Sidewinder' is apparently "Call me when you try to wake her.") Several tracks – notably 'Sidewinder' – benefit from the production and arrangement skills of Led Zeppelin's John Paul Jones. Buck praised Jones for being able to write string parts that were "nonsweet." These, along with the bold 'Ignoreland,' are counter-balanced by quieter material, such as the piano-led 'Nightswimming' and the plangent, hymn-like 'Find Me A River.'

Knowing their rock music recording history also helped some of the tracks. 'Star Me Kitten' has the band using a similar vocal texture to 10cc's 'I'm Not In Love.'

The subject-matter is often dark. Themes of mortality, suicide, AIDS, and memory make the songs somber but not so bleak as to make the record a depressing listen. The lyric of 'Find Me A River,' for example, is genuinely poetic and beautiful in its regret, while 'Everybody Hurts' features one of Stipe's most clearly focused lyrics. He explained: "That was written for teenagers, basically, saying don't kill yourself . . . My sister is a teacher and someone she knows, who is 15, tried to kill himself, and it led to this song. The idea was to write something that would appeal to someone who is having trouble."

Automatic For The People was both a commercial high-point for R.E.M. – around the time of this album's release they were bigger than U2 – as well as a critical one. The album has been praised for its cohesiveness, for its ability to be positive while dealing with some dark themes, even as it gave R.E.M. a brace of hit singles. Fulfilling such different criteria is no mean feat.

Ingénue kd lang

Sire 7599 26840 (U.S.A. & U.K.)
Released March 1992

kd lang – she insists on the lower-case letters – became one of the most controversial figures in country music when she emerged in the late 1980s.

Like Garth Brooks, she mixed traditional C&W elements with other rock-based styles. What caused more of a stir, however – at least among Nashville's elder statesmen – was the fact that lang is an out lesbian, though by the time of *Ingénue* she was more of a pop star than a country singer.

A real-life Canadian cowgirl, lang released four albums of rockabilly-tinged country in the 1980s. *Absolute Torch And Twang* (1989) was the first to make a dent on the U.S. pop chart. As its title suggests, the album marked the beginnings of lang's move away from country toward adult contemporary ballads. Issued in the immediate aftermath of her first public admission of her homosexuality, *Ingénue* has a pronounced pop edge, though it does betray slightly the influence of Patsy Cline. Produced by lang and the multi-instrumentalist Ben Mink, the album was lang's first since her debut to be recorded without her backing group The Reclines. They are replaced by Mink's programmed rhythms and an assortment of session musicians playing everything from marimbas to tamboura. Mink also co-wrote the lion's share of the songs with lang, including the U.K. Top 20 hit single 'Constant Craving,' which won a Grammy for Best Female Pop Vocal Performance. The album itself reached Number Three in the U.K. and Number 18 in the U.S.A., and sold 1.6 million copies worldwide.

Connected Stereo MC's

Gee Street 514061 (U.S.A.) / 4th & Broadway BR 589 (U.K.)
Released October 1992

Stereo MC's was the first widely successful British hip-hop group. The group was formed by rapper Rob Birch and producer-DJ Nick 'The Head' Hallam in 1985.

The duo set up their own Gee Street label using the £7,000 (about $14,000) they were paid to vacate their flat by property developers before recruiting vocalist Cath Coffey and drummer Owen If. Their first offering *33-45-78* (1989) and follow-up *Supernatural* (1990) failed to chart, but the group scored an unexpected U.S. hit in the summer of 1991 with 'Elevate My Mind.'

Connected was Stereo MC's breakthrough album. The album was a huge success in the U.K., where it peaked at Number Two, buoyed by the popularity of its title track, a Top 20 hit on both sides of the Atlantic. With its shuffling drums, funky horn sample, and Birch's laconic vocal delivery, 'Connected' was typical of the Stereo MC's sound.

The album is more laidback and melodic than a lot of U.S. hip-hop of the time, but retains the kind of cool, urban sound required for success in the rap market. Despite the high chart placing for 'Connected,' the album stalled at Number 92 in the U.S.A. Back in the group's homeland, *Connected* spawned three further Top 20 hit singles, 'Step It Up,' 'Ground Level,' and 'Creation.'

Poised for further mainstream success, Stereo MC's effectively retired for the remainder of the 1990s. When the group returned nine years later, it was with the lukewarm *Deep Down & Dirty* (2001), which quickly fell off the radar.

Rage Against The Machine
Rage Against The Machine

Epic 52959 (U.S.A.) / 472224 (U.K.)
Released November 1992

Rage Against The Machine was one of the first groups to find a viable common ground between rock and hip-hop in the 1990s.

The group's sound prefigured that of Korn, Limp Bizkit, and other so-called rap-metal acts. RATM was also highly politicized, and regularly lent its support to various left-wing causes. Unsurprisingly, then, the songs on *Rage Against The Machine* are doggedly polemical, a sequence of revolutionary tracts about the state of the U.S.A. in the late 20th century.

RATM started work on its debut in early 1992 with producer Garth Richardson, who had previously worked with Red Hot Chili Peppers. While that group's punk-funk influence can be detected on the album, RATM has a much harder, angrier sound. 'Bombtrack' opens the album with a supercharged Led Zeppelin riff, while vocalist Zack de la Rocha seems to delight in yelling the mantra "Fuck you, I won't do what they tell me" over 'Killing In The Name.' Song titles 'Take The Power Back' and 'Bullet In The Head' speak for themselves; the aggression never lets up. While much has been made of de la Rocha's impassioned raps over the alternative-metal backing and the influence this had on subsequent groups, what is most striking about *Rage Against The Machine* is Tom Morello's guitar playing. Only Radiohead's Jonny Greenwood could claim to have coaxed so many otherworldly sounds out of a guitar in the 1990s. *Rage Against The Machine* has sold three million copies worldwide, while 'Bullet In The Head' was a U.K. Top 20 hit.

The Bodyguard (Original Soundtrack)
Whitney Houston / Various Artists

Arista 18699 (U.S.A.) / 7822-18699 (U.K.)
Released November 1992

One of the most successful female vocalists of the 1980s and 1990s, Whitney Houston made her big-screen debut in the romantic thriller *The Bodyguard* (1992).

The movie was a box-office success, but was outshone by its soundtrack, which is dominated by Houston. Its success was due in no small part to the inclusion of her rendition of Dolly Parton's 'I Will Always Love You,' which spent a then-record 14 weeks at Number One in the U.S.A.

For such a successful album *The Bodyguard* is an uneven affair. It opens with 'I Will Always Love You' and five more Houston songs that wouldn't have seemed out place on 1990's *I'm Your Baby Tonight*. The rest of the material is in the typical big-budget soundtrack vein: Lisa Stansfied, Joe Cocker, and Curtis Stigers each provide a song, and Kenny G offers up a couple of slices of his mellow jazz. The album is rounded off by an extract from the movie's orchestral score and lengthy versions of 'I'm Every Woman' and 'Queen Of The Night' by Houston. Nothing unpleasant, then, but not what you would expect to find at the top end of a list of all-time big-selling albums. Needless to say, *The Bodyguard* did sell by the truckload – it is one of the biggest-selling albums of all time, having sold 17 million copies in the U.S.A. alone – topping albums charts across the globe and winning Houston a pair of Grammy Awards.

1993

Siamese Dream **Smashing Pumpkins**

Caroline 88267 (U.S.A.) / Hut HUT011 (U.K.)
Released July 1993

While most of their grunge contemporaries were inspired by 1970s punk and 1980s metal, Smashing Pumpkins drew more heavily on earlier psychedelic and progressive-rock groups as well as the recent dreamy, wall-of-sound productions of My Bloody Valentine.

The group's sophomore effort, *Siamese Dream*, is one of the best alternative-rock albums of its time. Debut album *Gish* (1991) had marked Smashing Pumpkins as a band of immense potential, but the group was in a state of crisis as the tour in support of the album ended the following summer. Frontman Billy Corgan was battling depression and writer's block, guitarist James Iha and bassist D'Arcy Wretsky were in the midst of a turbulent romantic break-up, and drummer Jimmy Chamberlain was struggling with heroin and alcohol addiction. Chamberlain spent a month in rehab before the group decamped to Atlanta, Georgia, hoping the drummer would find it less easy to maintain his drug habit away from The Pumpkins' home city of Chicago.

Smashing Pumpkins started work on *Siamese Dream* in December 1992 at Triclops Sound alongside Butch Vig, who had produced *Gish* as well as Nirvana's recent breakthrough album *Nevermind*. The group opted to record the album's basic tracks in a live setting, despite Chamberlain's erratic appearances at the sessions as his drug problems continued. Already something of a perfectionist when it came to recording, Corgan then built up numerous layers of guitar and keyboards, giving the songs an impressive, widescreen feel. Corgan brought in a violinist and cellist to embellish the album's quieter moments, while R.E.M.'s Mike Mills plays piano on closing track 'Luna.'

Siamese Dream is an accomplished, diverse work, both heavier and more melodic than much of the alternative rock of the early 1990s. Despite Corgan's apparent writer's block, it includes some of the strongest songs of his career, either as chief Smashing Pumpkin or later as the key figure in alternative-rock supergroup Zwan. The album's rich production stands apart from the rawness of other grunge bands, evoking early Pink Floyd, Queen, and The Cure in places. Opening track 'Cherub Rock' is a powerful statement of intent, riding in on insistent, multitracked guitar and drums, with the rest of the album divided between spacious atmospherics and unrelenting heavy rock.

Siamese Dream reached the Top Ten in both the U.S.A. and the U.K., where it spawned two hit singles, 'Disarm' and the ironic 'Today,' which was promoted by a music video in which Corgan drove an ice cream van. 'Disarm' is among the album's high points, an arresting blend of fiercely strummed acoustic guitar, bells, strings, and Corgan's pleading vocal. Though the group would make three more albums – including the commercially and critically successful *Mellon Collie And The Infinite Sadness* – *Siamese Dream* remains the most complete statement of Smashing Pumpkins' career.

■ *Left to right: D'Arcy Wretsky, Jimmy Chamberlain, Billy Corgan, and James Iha.*

Tuesday Night Music Club **Sheryl Crow**

A&M 0126 (U.S.A.) / 540 126 (U.K.)
Released October 1993

**Sheryl Crow scored a huge
international hit with the rootsy,
countrified rock of
her debut. A highly collaborative
affair, the album was conceived
and recorded, as the title
implies, at a regular Tuesday-
night jam session attended by
Crow and her musical friends.**

Prior to launching her solo career,
Crow worked as a teacher in her
native Missouri before moving to Los
Angeles in search of work as a

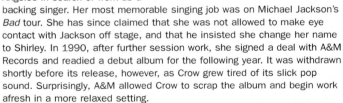

backing singer. Her most memorable singing job was on Michael Jackson's
Bad tour. She has since claimed that she was not allowed to make eye
contact with Jackson off stage, and that he insisted she change her name
to Shirley. In 1990, after further session work, she signed a deal with A&M
Records and readied a debut album for the following year. It was withdrawn
shortly before its release, however, as Crow grew tired of its slick pop
sound. Surprisingly, A&M allowed Crow to scrap the album and begin work
afresh in a more relaxed setting.

In 1992 Crow was introduced to a group of Los Angeles-based session
players by her then-boyfriend Kevin Gilbert, who had made an ill-fated

attempt at remixing the tapes of her scrapped work from the previous year.
This loose collective of musicians had been meeting once a week at
producer Bill Bottrell's Toad Hall studio for the 'Tuesday Night Music Club.'
Crow was invited to join them and, as the only member of the club with a
record deal, became the focus of the weekly songwriting and jam sessions.
Over the course of the year the musicians assembled the laidback, bluesy
songs that feature on her second attempt.

Tuesday Night Music Club was not particularly successful on its initial release
in 1993, but eventually climbed into the U.S. Top Five on the strength of the
international hit single 'All I Wanna Do.' Ironically the only song on *Tuesday
Night Music Club* that Crow didn't have a hand in writing, its sound was
emblematic of the album as a whole. While 'All I Wanna Do' initially seems
quite loose, with its rambling pedal steel and Crow's laidback vocal delivery,
the song is in fact underpinned by a slick, lightly funky backing.

Producer Bottrell laid similarly polished foundations beneath the other
songs, from the opening 'Run, Baby, Run' – which borrows a riff from The
Beatles' 'I Want You' – to the smoky jazz of 'We Do What We Can.' Lyrically,
the album is split between typical post-breakup fare – 'Can't Cry Anymore,'
'Nobody Said It Would Be Easy' – and the more upbeat self-encouragement
of 'Strong Enough' and 'Solidify.'

On subsequent albums Crow's songs became more political, addressing
such issues as abortion and nuclear war. For *Tuesday Night Music Club*,
however, she keeps to the tried and tested themes of classic romantic rock.
The album eventually shifted ten million copies worldwide, while the singer
consolidated her success through the 1990s with the Grammy-winning
albums *Sheryl Crow* (1996) and *The Globe Sessions* (1998).

1993

The Chronic **Dr Dre**

Death Row 57128 (U.S.A.) / Interscope 7567 92233 (U.K.)
Released February 1993

Behold, the birth of G-funk: *The Chronic* introduced the sound that would dominate hip-hop for the rest of the 1990s.

After leaving NWA, the group with whom he had revolutionized West Coast rap, Dre formed Death Row Records with Marion 'Suge' Knight in 1992. His first release was a single, 'Deep Cover,' a collaboration with the then-unknown rapper Snoop Doggy Dogg. As well as being one of the finest hip-hop producers of all time, Dre also had a knack for finding and launching new talent. Dogg became Dre's protégé in the same way Eminem did in the late 1990s.

'Deep Cover' and *The Chronic*, issued nine months later, marked an important change in the way hip-hop records were made. Before, they had tended to be built around a frenetic, James Brown-style drum loop. As suggested by its marijuana-referencing title, *The Chronic* pioneered a more laidback sound that drew on George Clinton's work with Funkadelic and Parliament. Dre had also begun to make more use of live instrumentation than had previously been heard on rap records. His liquid basslines and synthesizer squeals would soon become ubiquitous. Dogg featured on half of the songs on *The Chronic*, including the Number Two U.S. chart entry 'Nuthin' But A "G" Thang.' It was no surprise, therefore, that by the end of 1993 Dre had produced Snoop's own debut, *Doggystyle*. *The Chronic* peaked at Number Two in the U.S.A., while *Doggystyle* went one better, topping the charts in December 1993.

Republic **New Order**

Qwest 45250 (U.S.A.) / Centredate 828413 (U.K.)
Released May 1993

Republic was New Order's sixth and bestselling album, but found the group in a state of flux.

New Order had emerged from the ashes of the cult post-punk quartet Joy Division after the suicide of vocalist Ian Curtis in 1980. New Order adopted a more synthesized, beat-driven sound, and had numerous U.K. hits throughout the 1980s. True U.S. success proved elusive until the release of *Republic* – which, coincidentally, followed *Violator*, by another British electronic group of the 1980s, Depeche Mode, into the upper reaches of the U.S. albums chart.

By this stage, however, New Order had begun to fragment. Rumors of internal conflict were rife and matters were not helped by the fact that all four members of the group had started working on side projects by 1989: Bernard Sumner collaborated with former Smiths guitarist Johnny Marr as Electronic, bassist Peter Hook fronted Revenge, and drummer Stephen Morris and keyboardist Gillian Gilbert formed The Other Two. To exacerbate matters, Morris and Gilbert were upset that the *Republic* sleeve design had originally been intended for their *The Other Two And You* (1993) album, until it was co-opted by the other members of New Order.

Given the tension within the group *Republic* sounds subdued and disjointed in places, but still contains flashes of New Order's best work, particularly on the aptly titled 'Regret.'.

Music Box **Mariah Carey**

Columbia 53205 (U.S.A.) / 474270 (U.K.)
Released September 1993

Mariah Carey was the most successful female performer of the 1990s, during which time she released nine huge albums and had 13 U.S. Number One hit singles, more than any other woman in history.

Unlike many of her contemporaries, Carey also writes or co-writes most of her material. She also had the advantage – until their 1997 divorce – of being married to Columbia Records boss Tommy Mottola. Her eponymous debut (1989) and second release *Emotions* (1991) were both multimillion sellers, but drew accusations that she over-used her much vaunted five-octave voice. Stung by these criticisms, she aimed to make her third album more subtle musically and less reliant on vocal gymnastics. Her two dozen collaborators on *Music Box* include the Brazilian pop maestro Walter Afanisieff, who co-authored half of the album, David Cole and Robert Clivilles of C&C Music Factory, and Babyface, who duets with Carey on the slick ballad 'Never Forget You.' *Music Box* spent a total of eight weeks atop the U.S. albums chart and was the first of Carey's albums to reach Number One in the U.K. The biggest-selling album of Carey's career, it has sold more than 27 million copies worldwide, and spawned her eighth and ninth U.S. chart-topping singles, 'Hero' and 'Dream Lover.' Subsequent albums could not quite match the sales of *Music Box*, but none of her albums during the 1990s shifted less than nine million copies, bringing her total sales for the decade to an incredible 140 million albums.

Enter The Wu-Tang (36 Chambers) **Wu-Tang Clan**

Loud-RCA 66336 (U.S.A.) / 74321 20367 (U.K.)
Released November 1993 (U.S.A.) / May 1994 (U.K.)

Wu-Tang Clan introduced a new modus operandi for hip-hop groups, using *Enter The Wu-Tang* to establish the Wu brand, before launching various solo projects, a clothing line, and even a Wu-Tang comic.

From the start, Wu-Tang Clan was not your typical rap group. Led by the production wizard RZA, the collective was influenced as much by chess and kung-fu movies as it was by other hip-hop acts. Unlike other more intellectual hip-hop groups, however, Wu-Tang Clan retained a hardcore edge to its music. The group signed an unusual deal with RCA in 1992, which allowed all of its members to pursue parallel solo careers. Work began shortly thereafter on *Enter The Wu-Tang* at Firehouse Studio in the group's native New York. The songs are raw and sparse and held together by samples from martial-arts movies. Lyrically, the album is intense and often violent, but more literate than any other hip-hop group: who else has rhymed "elephant tusk" with "Egyptian musk," or made reference to the Emancipation Proclamation in song?

Enter The Wu-Tang was a critical and commercial hit on its release in late 1993. Within the next couple of years it was followed by hit albums by group members including Method Man, Raekwon, and Ol' Dirty Bastard, confirming The Clan as one of the 1990s most important hip-hop empires.

1994

American Recordings **Johnny Cash**

American 45520 (U.S.A.) / 74321 23685 (U.K.)
Released May 1994 (U.S.A.) / October 1994 (U.K.)

**American Recordings was the
first in what became a series of
four albums of rock covers and
Cash originals recorded by the
legendary country singer during
the latter part of his life. The
albums were not a huge
commercial success, but were
unanimously adored by critics
and introduced Cash's music to a
younger generation.**

In 1992 Cash's recording contract
with Mercury Records expired. With
his country audience dwindling, some assumed this would mean the end of
his 40-year career, but Cash had other ideas. The following year he
unexpectedly signed a new deal with Rick Rubin's American label. Rubin had
been one of the most important producers of the previous decade, having
worked with both rock and hip-hop artists, most notably on the Run-DMC
album *Raising Hell* (1986), which brought those two disparate genres
together for the first time. As producer of 'The American Series,' Rubin
guided Cash toward a similar stylistic crossover – essentially, *American
Recordings* is a set of rock songs performed by a country artist in a folk
style.

The album was recorded in late 1993 at Rubin's Los Angeles home and at
the Cash residence in Hendersonville, Tennessee. There were no other
musicians present at the sessions: Rubin simply plugged in a microphone

and recorded Cash alone, backed only by his own acoustic-guitar playing.
They taped over 70 songs in all, of which eleven feature on *American
Recordings*. Two more songs were taken from a solo live performance at the
Viper Room in Los Angeles.

American Recordings does contain a clutch of Cash originals, old and new,
but – like the three albums that follow it – is dominated by his
interpretations of other people's songs, and the way he manages, without
fail, to make each one his own. The highlights include his rendition of Nick
Lowe's 'The Beast In Me,' and readings of Leonard Cohen's 'Bird On A Wire'
and 'Down There By The Train' by Tom Waits. The most important song,
however, in terms of finding Cash a new audience, is the murder ballad
'Delia's Gone.' The accompanying video, in which Cash kills and buries the
model Kate Moss, brought the singer to the attention of the MTV generation
for the first time.

Shortly after the release of *American Recordings*, Cash enthused: "I'm more
proud of it than anything I've ever done in my life. This is me. Whatever I've
got to offer as an artist, it's here." Music critics lapped up the album, with
Rolling Stone magazine declaring it to be "unquestionably one of his best
albums" and remarking that "his voice is the best it has sounded in 30
years." Though it failed to chart in either the U.S.A. or the U.K., *American
Recordings* sold solidly through the 1990s and early 2000s and won a
Grammy Award for Best Contemporary Folk Album.

The three subsequent albums in the series are more collaborative affairs,
while the more surprising song choices tended to be Rubin's suggestions.
Unchained (1996) featured contributions from Tom Petty And The
Heartbreakers, and a version of 'Rusty Cage' by the heavy-rock group
Soundgarden. Cash's output slowed after he was diagnosed with Parkinson's
Disease in 1997, but his ill-health did nothing to detract from the subtle
beauty of his final pair of albums. *American III: Solitary Man* (2000) includes
covers of songs by U2 and Nick Cave, while *American IV: The Man Comes
Around* (2002) is best remembered for Cash's stark reading of Nine Inch
Nails' claustrophobic 'Hurt.'

Interest in these albums inevitably peaked after Cash's death on September
13th 2003. The five-disk set *Unearthed* (2003) is made up mostly of previously
unissued recordings from the previous ten years of American sessions.

Grace **Jeff Buckley**

Columbia 57528 (U.S.A.) / 475928 (U.K.)
Released August 1994

The only full-length album Jeff Buckley completed during his lifetime, *Grace* has become one of the best-loved albums of the 1990s.

Buckley struggled throughout his short career against the expectations of being the son of a father he barely knew, cult singer-songwriter Tim Buckley. The lives and careers of Jeff and Tim shared a number of parallels: both were among the outstanding vocalists of their respective generations, both made highly individual and expressive music, and both died too young.

Brought up by his mother, Buckley met his father only briefly, shortly before Tim's death from a drug overdose in 1975. His haunting performance of his father's 'Once I Was' sparked a major-label bidding war, eventually won by Columbia, who issued the *Live At Sin-E* EP the following year. He started work on his first full-length album in the fall of 1993 with his newly formed band, which comprised bassist Mick Grondahl, drummer Matt Johnson, and guitarist Michael Tighe. The album's sessions were produced and engineered by Andy Wallace, who had worked on Run-DMC's 'Walk This Way' before mixing Nirvana's *Nevermind*. An audacious debut, *Grace* draws on the sound and emotional power of Led Zeppelin and Van Morrison. The key ingredient is Buckley's voice, which resembles a somewhat more subtle Robert Plant in its five-octave range. He steps effortlessly from delicate crooning to a soaring falsetto on the album's ten songs, which include well-chosen covers of Leonard Cohen's 'Hallelujah,' Jim Shelton's 'Lilac Wine,' and Benjamin Britten's 'Corpus Christi Carol.'

Buckley's own songwriting contributions are equally as impressive as his vocal

performances. The first two songs on *Grace* were co-written alongside Gary Lucas, guitarist in the final incarnation of Captain Beefheart's Magic Band. Of these, opening track 'Mojo Pin' had previously been issued in more skeletal form on the *Sin-E* EP, while the title track is classic epic rock. 'Last Goodbye,' meanwhile, grows into a deft Middle Eastern string arrangement, while 'Lover, You Should've Come Over' is underpinned by stately acoustic guitar and organ. The album closes with two of its most powerful songs: 'Eternal Life' is as close as Buckley gets to the sound of early-1990s alternative rock, while 'Dream Brother' evokes his father's 'Dream Letter,' gradually building to a cathartic crescendo after a tabla-laden intro.

The final line of 'Dream Brother' – "Asleep in the sand, with the ocean washing over" – would prove eerily prophetic. On May 29th 1997, during the recording of what would have been his second album, provisionally titled *My Sweetheart, The Drunk*, Buckley took a swim in a treacherous part of the Mississippi, and was sucked under the water as a steamboat passed. He was 30 years old.

While *Grace* had only sold modestly on its initial release, reaching Number 50 on the U.K. albums chart, it has grown in stature and influence substantially since Buckley's passing. Numerous bands and artists, including Radiohead and Coldplay, have cited *Grace* as a key influence on their work. Since Buckley's death, his mother, Mary Guibert, has coordinated the release of a number of posthumous albums, most notably *Sketches For: My Sweetheart The Drunk*, a collection of demos and unfinished recordings from 1997.

Jeff Buckley was just one of a number of performers following in the footsteps of a famous musical parent to emerge in the 1980s and 1990s. John Lennon's first son, Julian, the subject of Paul McCartney's 'Hey Jude,' released his debut album *Valotte* in 1984, which also provided him with four hit singles. His later releases were less successful, however. Lennon's son with second wife Yoko Ono, Sean, recorded two albums in the late 1990s for The Beastie Boys' Grand Royal label. Carnie and Wendy Wilson, daughters of Beach Boy Brian, and Chynna Phillips, daughter of John and Michelle of The Mamas And The Papas, formed Wilson Phillips, selling four million copies worldwide of their eponymous debut in 1990. Dweezil Zappa, son of Frank, has made four albums of experimental metal; while Loudon Wainwright III's son Rufus has carved out a career of his own, making extravagant, orchestral pop since the late 1990s.

Definitely Maybe **Oasis**

Epic 66431 (U.S.A.) / Creation CRECD 169 (U.K.)
Released February 1995 (U.S.A.) / September 1994 (U.K.)

Park Life Blur

SBK-Food 29194 (U.S.A.) / EMI-Food FOOD10 (U.K.)
Released April 1994

Different Class **Pulp**

Polygram 524165 (U.S.A.) / Island 8041 (U.K.)
Released October 1995

Suede Suede

Columbia 53792 (U.S.A.) / Nude NUDE1 (U.K.)
Released April 1993

Brit-pop emerged in the mid 1990s in Britain. It started as an anti-grunge movement around 1992 and developed into a collective desire to relive the 1960s and make Britain swing again.

The rehabilitation of The Beatles' reputation with the release of the *Anthology* and *Live At The BBC* CDs fueled an interest in the 1960s. Suddenly the Union Flag was hip again and on the cover of magazines, and the key bands included Oasis, Blur, Pulp, Suede, Supergrass, Elastica, and Sleeper. The Beatles connection was worked most strongly by Mancunian band Oasis. Their debut, *Definitely Maybe* (1994), brims with no-nonsense, WYSIWYG swagger. It has 'Rock'n'Roll Star,' the powerful 'Live Forever,' and the T. Rex-Chuck Berry-inspired 'Cigarettes And Alcohol.' Oasis offer juggernauts of layered guitars turned up to 11, and Liam Gallagher sings in a voice part-Johnny Rotten and part-John Lennon – taking as his cue Lennon's vocalization of the word 'shine' on 'Rain.'

The Beatles influence also shaped the 1995 follow-up *What's The Story (Morning Glory)?*, with the Lennonesque ballad 'Don't Look Back In Anger,' while 'Roll With It' sounds like a 1990s 'Hard Day's Night.' 'Cast No Shadow' has slide guitar and strings eerily evocative of *All Things Must Pass*. After that, arrogance, drugs, and fame sent Oasis into a creative tailspin, despite sell-out megagigs.

In contrast to Oasis, Blur were based in London, and their influences were at the time more along The Kinks-Small Faces axis of 1960s pop than The Beatles so beloved of their rivals. *Park Life* offers more eccentricity and more focused evocations of everyday life than Oasis's work. The press attempted to fan inter-band antagonism between the two groups, emphasizing the polar opposites of northern working-class Oasis versus southern art-school Blur. Eventually Blur withdrew from the Brit-pop scene and had deconstructed their sound by the time they recorded the grungy 'Song 2' with its memorable "woo-hoo" catchphrase.

In some ways Pulp resembled a Human League reborn for the 1990s, with a Morrisseyesque figure penning the words. The admirably unpretentious Jarvis Cocker wrote sensitively and wittily about a whole range of subjects on *Different Class* (1995), which included a clutch of timely U.K. hit singles, among them 'Common People' and 'Sorted For Es and Whizz.' And who else but Cocker could have put a song like 'Help The Aged' on an album like *This Is Hardcore* (1997), with its magnificently sleazy title track, in which the spirit of lounge MOR gets hijacked by a John Barry orchestration and a Led Zeppelin drumbeat?

Brit-pop wasn't just about evoking the 1960s, however – at times Oasis could sound as though they wanted to be Slade. While no one stepped up to be the 1990s T. Rex or Roxy Music, Suede emerged in 1993 to play at being Bowie – their third single, 'Animal Nitrate,' sounds like an outtake from *Ziggy Stardust*. Their debut album went to Number One in the U.K. and won the 1993 Mercury Music Prize. Suede – and in particular singer Brett Anderson – made the right glam moves in terms of the bisexual, are they/aren't they game – witness the two people kissing on the cover of their debut album and the naked figure on the cover of the second, *Dog Man Star* (1994). Resident guitar star Bernard Butler, who did a mean line in Mick Ronson-style riffs, left in 1994 and has since pursued a solo career – though in 2005 Butler and Anderson returned as The Tears.

The high point of Brit-pop coincided with the election of a Labour government in May 1997 after 18 years of Conservative rule. The new administration actively and publicly courted the aristocracy of British culture, both popular and more rarified, in an attempt to ride a wave of credibility in the new world order of 'Cool Britannia.' The 'movement,' however, didn't last.

1994

The Downward Spiral Nine Inch Nails

Nothing/TVT 92346 (U.S.A.) / Island ILPSD 8012 (U.K.)
Released March 1994

The most successful industrial-rock act of the 1990s, Nine Inch Nails is the recording pseudonym of Trent Reznor, also the producer of much of Marilyn Manson's early material.

A classically trained pianist, Reznor wrote and played the entirety of the first two Nine Inch Nails releases, *Pretty Hate Machine* (1989) and *Broken* (1992), the latter a Top 20 hit in the U.S.A. and U.K. For *The Downward Spiral* Reznor recruited a number of session musicians, including drummers Chris Vrenna and guitarist Adrian Belew, most famous for his work with David Bowie and Talking Heads in the late 1970s and early 1980s. Belew's appearance offers a clue to the sound of *The Downward Spiral*, which in places feels like an updated, heavier take on Bowie's *Low* (1977) and *Scary Monsters* (1980), as well as earlier industrial-rock acts such as Ministry and Skinny Puppy. The album's session drummers also make a big impact, particularly on the oppressive, multilayered rhythms of 'Piggy.'

The Downward Spiral was met with much public disapproval on release for

its recording location. In 1993 Reznor had begun renting the Los Angeles house where The Manson Family had murdered actress Sharon Tate in 1969. Deciding his new home would provide a suitable recording environment, Reznor built a studio in the basement. Despite this controversy the album remains Reznor's greatest artistic success and also the biggest-selling Nine Inch Nails album. The single 'Closer' was a hit on both sides of the Atlantic, and was followed a year later by the remix collection *Further Down The Spiral*.

Dummy Portishead

Polygram 828552 (U.S.A.) / Go Beat 828552 (U.K.)
Released August 1994

A number of trip-hop acts – so called because they merged slowed-down hip-hop beats with jazzy, psychedelic instrumentation – emerged in the early 1990s from the English city of Bristol. Portishead's debut, *Dummy*, was the short-lived genre's most successful album.

In 1991 Massive Attack issued what is generally considered to be the first trip-hop album, *Blue Lines*, a mix of soulful vocals, stoned raps, and edgy dub and hip-hop samples. One of the engineers on the album was Geoff Barrow, from the nearby sleepy coastal town of Portishead. Two years after the release of *Blue Lines* Barrow formed a group of his own with vocalist Beth Gibbons and guitarist Adrian Utley. Taking the name of Barrow's hometown, the trio recorded *Dummy* at State Of The Art and Coach House Studios in Bristol with engineer Dave McDonald during the latter part of 1993 and the early months of 1994.

Building on the rather more sparse sound of Massive Attack's debut, Barrow and Utley created a claustrophobic, cinematic backdrop for Gibbons's haunting, melancholic vocals. Half-speed drum-fills and eerie, droning organs vie for space with a few well-chosen samples from recordings by artists including Weather Report, Isaac Hayes, and Johnny Ray. Preceded by the singles 'Numb' and 'Glory Box,' a minor hit in the U.S.A., *Dummy* was released to widespread critical praise on both sides of the Atlantic. The album reached Number Two in the U.K., where it was awarded the Mercury Music Prize for Album Of The Year.

A month after the release of *Dummy* came Massive Attack's excellent sophomore album *Protection*. The latter group's former rapper, Tricky, released his similarly acclaimed debut, *Maxinequaye* (1995), a gritty, harder-edged take on the Portishead sound. All three acts distanced themselves from the trip-hop tag, however, particularly as a number of watered-down imitators began to hit the U.K. charts in 1996 and 1997.

Weezer **Weezer**

Geffen 24629 (U.S.A. & U.K.)
Released August 1994 (U.S.A.) / February 1995 (U.K.)

When grunge began to implode following the death of Kurt Cobain, Weezer was one of the first groups to fill the void. The group's awkward, nerdy, hook-laden rock also helped lay the foundations for 'emo' (emotional hardcore), as typified by Jimmy Eat World and The Get Up Kids, in the late 1990s.

Weezer was formed in 1993 in Los Angeles by guitarist-vocalist Rivers Cuomo, bassist Matt Sharp, and drummer Patrick Wilson, and within a year had earned a deal with Geffen. The group quickly started work on a debut album with producer Ric Ocasek, former frontman of the late-1970s new-wave group The Cars.

On the album's release, most reviewers recognized that Weezer sounded like a cross between The Pixies and The Beach Boys. Brian Bell, who joined Weezer just three days before the recording sessions began, provides most of the angular lead-guitar parts reminiscent of the former group. He is also responsible, alongside Sharp, for the breezy Californian harmonies that neatly offset Cuomo's melodies. This blend of wiry alternative rock and pop hooks was crucial to making *Weezer* one of the biggest albums of 1994. Just as important, however, was the Spike Jonze-directed video to the single 'Buddy Holly,' still regarded as one of the finest of all time. In it, through clever editing, Jonze slotted the group into an episode of *Happy Days*. 'Buddy Holly' was an international hit, as was *Weezer*, which peaked at Number 16 in the U.S.A. and Number 23 in the U.K.

CrazySexyCool **TLC**

LaFace 26009 (U.S.A.) / Arista 26009 (U.K.)
Released November 1994

TLC had a huge international hit with their second album, *CrazySexyCool*, just as the personal lives of the trio started to resemble some kind of warped soap opera.

The group had made their recording debut in 1992 with *Oooooooohhh . . . On The TLC Tip*, an album of youthful exuberance rooted in the softer side of early-1990s hip-hop and urban pop. TLC opted to aim for a more

mature, soulful sound with the follow-up, which was recorded in the summer of 1994 with producers Dallas Austin and L.A. Reid, head of the group's label LaFace. *CrazySexyCool* resembles Prince in places, most obviously when the group cover his 'If I Was Your Girlfriend,' while there are also suggestions of *Very Necessary*, the album on which TLC's predecessors Salt 'N' Pepa attempted a similar transition from raucous rap to a more mature R&B sound.

CrazySexyCool was preceded by a single, 'Creep,' a U.S. Number One hit. The album's worldwide exposure was further enhanced by the release of 'Waterfalls,' one of the defining R&B pop hits of the mid 1990s, which spent seven weeks at the top of the U.S. chart and was also hugely successful across Europe. Shortly before the release of *CrazySexyCool*, the group's Lisa 'Left Eye' Lopes burned down the mansion of her NFL wide-receiver boyfriend Andre Rison in a fit of rage. She was eventually sentenced to five years probation after admitting an alcohol problem. In early 1995, as *CrazySexyCool* sat in the upper reaches of albums charts across the globe, TLC filed for bankruptcy, claiming to be $3.5 million in debt. The situation was not helped by the huge insurance payments Lopes faced after the arson incident or by the group's claims that they were not being paid adequate royalties for their hugely successful second album. In 1996 Tionne 'T-Boz' Watkins announced she was suffering from sickle cell anemia, while Rozonda 'Chilli' Thomas was going through a messy public breakup with producer Austin, with whom she had recently had a son. Despite these personal setbacks, TLC remain one of the biggest-selling female R&B groups of all time, while *CrazySexyCool* contains some of the finest urban pop of the decade. Tragically, Lopes was killed in a car crash in 2002.

1995

The Bends **Radiohead**

Capitol 29626 (U.S.A.) / Parlaphone PCS 7372 (U.K.)
Released March 1995

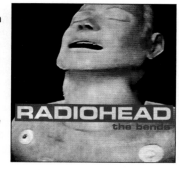

Radiohead shook off the one-hit-wonder tag with *The Bends*, which built on the epic rock of early U2 and R.E.M. to often startling effect. The album in turn inspired a wave of new British bands, notably Travis and Coldplay.

Radiohead scored an unexpected international hit in 1993 with the single 'Creep,' but many critics considered its parent album, *Pablo Honey*, to be a lightweight attempt at jumping on the grunge bandwagon. Stung by these criticisms, the group felt under intense pressure to record a worthy follow-up, resulting in several months of strained recording sessions in mid 1994, during which numerous songs were scrapped or repeatedly reworked.

The band eventually completed the album early the following year, re-recording its twelve songs in two weeks after a confidence-boosting U.S. tour. *The Bends* was produced by John Leckie, a former Abbey Road engineer, who had worked on Pink Floyd's *Dark Side Of The Moon* and John Lennon's *Plastic Ono Band*. Radiohead's three guitarists dominate *The Bends*, though the most striking element is Thom Yorke's vocal delivery. Apparently, Yorke found the confidence to let loose his emotive falsetto after witnessing a live performance by Jeff Buckley. The album also contains a much wider range of material than *Pablo Honey*, particularly on the opening 'Planet Telex,' with its delayed piano-chords and staccato drum loop.

The Bends reached Number Six in the U.K. albums chart, where its profile grew with the success of the singles 'High And Dry,' 'Fake Plastic Trees,' and 'Street Spirit,' a Number Five U.K. chart entry. The album peaked at Number 88 in the U.S.A., where Radiohead toured in support of R.E.M. and Alanis Morissette in an attempt to broaden their appeal.

A Live One **Phish**

Absolute A-Go-Go 61772 (U.S.A.) / Not issued in the U.K.
Released July 1995

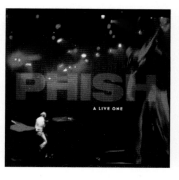

Taken from a series of performances recorded in late 1994, the two-disk set *A Live One* was intended as the definitive representation of the Phish concert experience.

Phish was formed in 1983 by Vermont University friends Trey Anastasio (guitar and vocals), Jon Fishman (drums), and Jeff Holdsworth (guitar); bassist Mike Gordon joined the following year. The group self-released their debut album, *Junita*, in 1988, before signing to Absolute A-Go-Go and starting to develop a strong live following across the U.S.A., particularly on the college circuit.

Like The Grateful Dead before them, Phish are well known for vastly expanding their recorded works on stage; studio versions of their songs are often seen as templates to be developed further in a live setting. In its original form on *A Picture Of Nectar* (1992), 'Tweezer' runs to just under nine minutes – here the song is stretched out to more than half an hour. Some of the songs on *A Live One* are also given a new musical lick of paint and taken off into the uncharted waters of jazz, funk, and psychedelia. The album also includes seven songs previously unheard on record, some of which would later see release in studio form on subsequent Phish albums.

Fittingly, *A Live One* was the first of the group's albums to reach the U.S. Top 20, and it was the first of numerous live releases from the group. A six-CD set, *Hampton Comes Alive*, followed in 1996, and in 2001 the group started the 'Live Phish' series, which within a couple of years numbered 20 double-disk concert recordings. Even that isn't enough for many Phish fans, who continue to trade bootlegs of Phish gigs on tape and over the internet with the band's blessing. Phish fandom is apparently a uniquely North American experience, however; outside the U.S.A., the group – and similar acts such as The Spin Doctors – is virtually unheard of.

■ *Below: Radiohead perform on the U.K. TV music show* Later With Jools Holland *in 1995. Left to right: Ed O'Brien, Phil Selway, Thom Yorke, and brothers Colin and Jonny Greenwood. Opposite: Alanis Morissette.*

Jagged Little Pill **Alanis Morissette**

Maverick 9362-45901 (U.S.A. & U.K.)
Released August 1995

Jagged Little Pill is the 12th biggest-selling album of all time and has shifted 16 million copies in the U.S.A. alone.

Morissette's success helped sell alternative rock to a more adult audience for the first time and also opened the doors for a number of other rock-orientated female performers in the mid-to-late 1990s, notably Joan Osborne, Jewel, and Fiona Apple.

Though *Jagged Little Pill* is generally considered to be Morissette's debut, her musical career began a decade earlier. She first came to prominence in her native Canada after joining the cast of children's variety show *You Can't Do That On Television* at the age of ten. Using the money made from her television career, the precocious starlet pressed 2,000 copies of her self-penned debut single, 'Fate Stay With Me,' on her own Lamor Records label. Her next move was to sign to MCA Records, which issued the pop-dance *Alanis* in 1991. Both the album and its single 'Too Hot' made the Top Ten in Canada but failed to make an impact elsewhere, despite a tour in support of Vanilla Ice. Her second album, *Now Is The Time* (1992), failed to match the success of the debut and resulted in the end of her association with MCA, which opted not to renew her contract.

In 1993 Morissette moved to Los Angeles where she met producer and songwriter Glen Ballard. He had made his name as a member of Quincy Jones's studio team and previously worked on Barbra Streisand's *Till I Loved You* and Paula Abdul's *Forever Your Girl* (both 1988) as well as the Wilson Philips self-titled debut, which had earned him several Grammy Awards. He had also played keyboards on Michael Jackson's *Bad* (1987).

Though Morissette and Ballard were both best known for their work in the pop sphere, they made a conscious effort to move toward an edgier, alternative-rock sound in their work together. Ballard provided the perfect musical backdrop for the vituperative lyrics that Morissette had begun writing, which dealt with failing relationships and her attitude toward the Catholic Church, as well as her quest for self-improvement and personal reinvention. By this stage, Morissette's image had mutated as far as her music: no longer the teen-pop princess, she now looked the part of a rock star, complete with the obligatory leather pants.

The duo's demo tape sparked a bidding war among the major labels, eventually won by Madonna's fledgling Maverick Recordings, a Warner

Brothers subsidiary. After inking the deal, Morissette headed straight for Westlake Studios in Hollywood, where she and Ballard began the task of fleshing out the material on her demo into a full album. Flea and Dave Navarro of Red Hot Chili Peppers added bass and guitar to several tracks, which were largely built around Ballard's thick power chords and driving rhythms. While a few of the songs sound too polished, given the angst-ridden nature of the vocals, most of the album successfully combines an alternative-rock edge with a pop sensibility, which is what its two creators set out to achieve.

Back in Canada *Jagged Little Pill* was met with a degree of skepticism, with many considering Morissette's change of sound and image to be a transparent attempt to jump on the alternative-rock bandwagon. This was less of a problem in the rest of the world, however, where hardly anybody had been aware of her previous career – and Alanis herself is even prone to referring to it in interviews as "my debut."

Jagged Little Pill soon climbed to the top of the U.S. *Billboard* charts, which it would dominate for much of the next 18 months. Key to the album's success was the single 'You Oughta Know,' a bitter tirade aimed at a record company executive who took advantage of a young Alanis. The song caused a stir on its release for the explicit sexual content of the lyrics – the result being that Morissette soon had an army of devoted, neo-feminist fans. The album spawned several other international hit singles, including the more jangly, acoustic-guitar-led 'Hand In My Pocket' and 'Ironic,' both of which were hugely successful across Europe.

As well as its flurry of single releases, *Jagged Little Pill*'s momentum was maintained by Morissette's incessant touring around the globe. Shortly before the album's release she had put together an impressive live band that included guitarist Jesse Tobias, formerly of the band Mother Tongue, and drummer Taylor Hawkins, who would later join Foo Fighters. At the 1996 Grammys Morissette was nominated in six categories, of which she won three, including Album Of The Year. *Jagged Little Pill* soon surpassed Whitney Houston's *Whitney* as the biggest-selling U.S. debut album of all time, and worldwide sales have passed the 33 million mark.

The French Album [U.K. title: D'Eux] **Celine Dion**

550 Music / Epic 67101 (U.S.A.) / Sony International 80219 (U.K.)
Released October 1995 (U.S.A.) / September 1998 (U.K.)

At her peak in the mid 1990s, Celine Dion worked at a prodigious rate, issuing new albums regularly in both French and English, which helped make her one of the decade's dominant pop figures.

Dion had achieved considerable success since the early 1980s, particularly in France and her native Canada. Toward the end of the decade she was advised by manager – and future husband – Rene Angelil to remake her image in order to match that success in the U.S.A. This soon achieved the desired result, and Dion sang the title track to the 1992 Disney movie *Beauty And The Beast*, following it with her biggest-selling solo album to date, *The Color Of My Love* (1993). In the meantime, albums such as *Dion Chante Plamondon* (1994) and *Des Mots Qui Sonnent* (1995) helped maintain her profile in French-speaking territories.

The French Album was Dion's first attempt to bridge her two separate fan bases. Written in the main by Jean-Jacques Goldman – a singer and songwriter who had achieved fame in his own right in France – the album kept to the sugary, adult-contemporary-pop formula of her recent U.S. hits but with French lyrics. The ploy worked, and the album sold well across the globe. In 1998 it was reissued as *D'Eux* and reached the U.K. Top Ten. By then Dion had sold 25 million copies each of *Falling Into You* (1996) and *Let's Talk About Love* (1997), making her one of the best-selling female pop artists of all time.

1995

Post 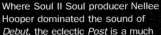 Björk

Elektra 612740 (U.S.A.) / One Little Indian TPLP51 (U.K.)
Released June 1995

A child star in her native Iceland, Björk fronted post-punk groups Kukl and The Sugarcubes before moving to London in the early 1990s and recording the euphoric dance-pop album *Debut* (1993), which sold three million copies worldwide and provided her with the U.K. hits 'Venus As A Boy' and 'Big Time Sensuality.'

Where Soul II Soul producer Nellee Hooper dominated the sound of *Debut*, the eclectic *Post* is a much clearer representation of Björk herself. The album is built on collaborations with some of the most highly regarded electronic musicians of the time, including 808 State's Graham Massey, Howie B, and Tricky, who duets with Björk on the edgy closing track 'Headphones.' *Post* opens with one of the most striking of Björk's songs, the punishing programmed bass-and-drum assault of 'Army Of Me.' The remainder of the album takes in melodic drum & bass and richly orchestrated electronic torch song, while a quirky cover of the jazz standard 'It's Oh So Quiet' provided Björk with an unlikely pan-European hit single. Though the song is musically unrepresentative of the overall sound of *Post*, it does hint at the many idiosyncratic moves of Björk's career.

Post is also the album where Björk comes into her own as a singer, though hers is a voice that continues to divide opinion. To some Björk is one of the finest and most individualistic vocalists of recent times; to others she sounds like a malfunctioning firework. *Post* reached Number 32 in the U.S.A. and Number Four in the U.K., where it provided her with five hit singles.

To Bring You My Love **PJ Harvey**

Island 524085 (U.S.A.) / 8053 (U.K.)
Released February 1995

After two albums of angst-ridden alternative rock, PJ Harvey developed a richer, blues-based sound on *To Bring You My Love*.

Harvey split up her original power trio shortly after touring in support of her second album, *Rid Of Me* (1993), a ferociously sexual record produced by grunge stalwart Steve Albini. She then started work on *To Bring You My Love* in September 1994 at Townhouse Three in London, gathering together an impressive avant-rock supporting cast, including multi-instrumentalists John Parish and Mick Harvey – no relation, but a member of Nick Cave's Bad Seeds – Tom Waits's guitarist Joe Gore, and Eric Drew Feldman, once of Pere Ubu.

To Bring You My Love remains the most consistent body of work of Harvey's career, and was hailed as a masterpiece by many critics on its release. The title track, which opens the album, quotes a line from Captain Beefheart's 'Sure 'Nuff 'N Yes I Do' from *Safe As Milk*, a key influence on some of *To Bring You My Love*'s guitar-led material. Other songs are driven by trippy, downbeat drum loops and mournful organ, reminiscent at times of Portishead's recent *Dummy*, while the vituperative relationship dramas of Harvey's earlier songs are replaced by dark, uneasy meditations on lost children and the slow inevitability of death. *To Bring You My Love* is Harvey's most successful album to date in the U.S.A., where it entered the charts at Number 40 and won a Grammy for Best Alternative Rock Album. In the U.K. the album spawned three minor hit singles, 'Down By The Water,' 'C'Mon Billy,' and 'Send His Love To Me.'

Garbage **Garbage**

Almo Sounds 80004 (U.S.A.) / Mushroom 31450 (U.K.)
Released August 1995 (U.S.A.) / October 1995 (U.K.)

Garbage's eponymous first album added a pop sensibility to the dreamy soundscapes of My Bloody Valentine's *Loveless*.

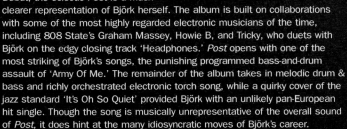

Unusually, the group was founded by a trio of record producers: Butch Vig, Steve Marker, and Duke Erikson. Of the three, Vig had been the most successful by far, having produced such landmark albums as Nirvana's *Nevermind* (1991) and Smashing Pumpkins' *Siamese Dream* (1993). Rather than continue in his role as the most sought-after producer of the decade, however, Vig started playing with Erikson and Marker in the latter's basement studio in Madison, Wisconsin. In 1994 the trio recruited the Scottish-born singer Shirley Manson after seeing her singing with her group Angelfish on MTV. Manson gave Garbage a powerful, sexy focus, and in the early days of the group she was often likened to The Pretenders' Chrissie Hynde.

As might have been expected, given the pedigree of its creators, *Garbage* is immaculately produced. The album is built on a bedrock of stuttering drum loops, heavily processed guitars, and shimmering keyboards, over which Manson weaves a web of smooth, sultry vocals. *Garbage* was a Top 20 hit on both sides of the Atlantic, and in the U.K. the album also provided four hit singles, including 'Only Happy When It Rains,' 'Queer,' and 'Stupid Girl.' As well as the usual CD issue, the album was released as a double LP – which ran at 45rpm – and as a boxed set of six seven-inch records.

Tragic Kingdom **No Doubt**

Trauma/Interscope 92580 (U.S.A.) / 90003 (U.K.)
Released October 1995 (U.S.A.) / June 1996 (.U.K)

No Doubt provided a welcome antidote to the relentless misery of most 1990s alternative rock. Drawing on new wave and ska, the group's upbeat guitar-pop brought them widespread international success late in the decade. *Tragic Kingdom* was the group's breakthrough, eventually selling 15 million copies worldwide.

The band formed in Orange County, California, in 1987, but their early momentum was halted by the suicide of original vocalist John Spence in 1990. Now with Gwen Stefani on vocal duties, the albums *No Doubt* (1992) and *The Beacon Street Collection* (1995) sold poorly, but did just enough to resume an interrupted relationship with Interscope, who gave 1980s singer Matthew Wilder – best known for his 1983 smash 'Break My Stride' – the job of producing the group's major-label debut.

While *Tragic Kingdom* evokes the sound of Madness and The Specials in places, as big an influence during the album's gestation was the end of the seven-year relationship between No Doubt vocalist Gwen Stefani and the band's bassist Tony Kanal. Fortunately, though, the album isn't all doom and gloom, as the singles 'Just A Girl' and 'Spiderwebs' testify. Both were big hits on U.S. radio in 1996 as *Tragic Kingdom* made its slow climb to the top of the *Billboard* chart. In the U.K. the album wasn't a particular success until the release, in early 1997, of the ballad 'Don't Speak,' a Number One hit.

The key element of No Doubt's appeal was Stefani's über-cool, Madonna-light image, the antithesis of her intense, angsty mid-1990s peers. After two more No Doubt albums she launched the inevitable solo career with *Love Angel Music Baby* in 2004.

1996

Odelay **Beck**

DGC 24823 (U.S.A.) / Geffen 24908 (U.K.)
Released June 1996

**An eclectic, multitalented
singer-songwriter, Beck drew
on everything from hip-hop to folk
rock to create *Odelay*, a landmark
of 1990s genre-bending.**

Beck first came to prominence in 1994
with the single release of 'Loser,' which
became the alternative-rock anthem of
the summer. 'Loser' announced the
arrival of not just a major new talent
but also a whole new genre, christened
lo-fi by the music press. Lo-fi had its
roots in U.S. underground rock of the
1980s, from R.E.M. to Beat Happening, and describes music recorded cheaply,
often on a 4-track at home. Beck was one of several important artists to
emerge in the mid 1990s who stuck to this lo-fi aesthetic; others include
Pavement and Liz Phair.

Though most of his key albums were released by DGC, Beck had an unusual
clause in his contract that allowed him to issue some of his more
experimental offerings through smaller independent labels. In 1994, as well
as his DGC debut *Mellow Gold*, which sold well on the strength of 'Loser,'
Beck put out the albums *Stereopathic Soul Manure* (on Flipside) and *One
Foot In The Grave* (on K Records, generally considered to be the original lo-fi
label). Beck spent much of 1995 on tour before starting work on the
'official' follow-up to *Mellow Gold* with highly regarded production duo The
Dust Brothers.

The Dust Brothers' role in the making of *Odelay* is significant because
Beck's album has a number of ideological similarities to its producers'
earlier work with The Beastie Boys on their groundbreaking *Paul's Boutique*
(1989). Like The Beastie Boys, Beck drew on any number of disparate
artists and genres; *Odelay* is an eclectic melting pot of ideas, on which Beck
and The Dust Brothers take elements of folk, rock, hip-hop, psychedelia,
jazz, blues, movie soundtracks, and the avant-garde to create a dense,
original collage of sound. Beck's music has the playfulness of The
Beastie Boys but is closer thematically to the sardonic, slacker-
generation attitude of movies like *Reality Bites* (1992) than the latter
group's frat-party humor.

Odelay was issued to unanimous critical plaudits in the summer of 1996.
The album's release was followed by the single 'Where It's At,' a sparse
blend of hip-hop beats, a single distorted guitar, and off-hand vocals

that became a minor hit in the U.S.A. and U.K. *Odelay* itself reached the Top
20 in both countries as well as numerous others across Europe. The album
spawned three further singles, including the wiry blues of 'Devil's Haircut'
and a more upbeat, psychedelic piece, 'The New Pollution.' Each of the
single releases from *Odelay* arrived backed with various remixes by eye-
catching artists, including Aphex Twin and Oasis guitarist Noel Gallagher,
demonstrating the respect Beck already commanded among his peers.

Since *Odelay* Beck has continued to jump from genre to genre in the manner
of David Bowie in the 1970s. The low-key, Brazilian-tinged *Mutations* (1998)
was originally intended to be released on the tiny independent label Bong
Load before DGC realized the record's potential and snatched up the rights
to it. *Midnite Vultures* (1999) was clearly inspired by Prince's erotic funk,
while on *Sea Change* (2002) Beck veered toward richly orchestrated folk
rock before touring with The Flaming Lips as his backing band.

The Score **The Fugees**

Ruffhouse/Columbia 67147 (U.S.A.) / 483549 (U.K.)
Released February 1996

**The Fugees' second album and
mainstream breakthrough, *The
Score*, provided a much-needed
alternative to the trend for
aggressive gangsta rap in the
mid 1990s.**

The Fugees formed in 1992 in New
York City when rapper Lauryn Hill
began to work with MCs Prakazrel
'Pras' Michel and Wyclef Jean, first
cousins of Haitian decent who had
grown up in New Jersey. The group's
name was a reference to the cousins'
refugee status.

The Fugees' debut, *Blunted On Reality* (1994), did little on its release to
distinguish the group from their rap contemporaries, but a closer inspection
reveals a love of reggae and jazz beneath the album's hard hip-hop exterior.
These influences became more apparent on *The Score*. Much of the album
was recorded at the group's Booga Basement Studio in East Orange, New
Jersey, and The Crib in New York. A number of other songs were cut at

Anchor Studios in Kingston, Jamaica. Pras and Hill were responsible for creating most of the album's beats, as well as providing vocals, while Wyclef and another cousin, Jerry Duplessis, assisted with general production.

Shortly after the album's release Hill described it as an "audio film . . . it's almost like a hip-hop version of *Tommy*, like what The Who did for rock'n'roll." While her claims may be slightly exaggerated, *The Score* has a distinctly cinematic feel, and there is a definite thread running through it. Hill's vocals shine throughout, and she sounds equally at home rapping or singing in a sweet, soulful voice reminiscent at times of Nina Simone.

The Score's key track is 'Killing Me Softly.' Based on Roberta Flack's 'Killing Me Softly With His Song,' it provided The Fugees with a huge worldwide hit single, proving to mainstream audiences that hip-hop didn't always have to be about the dark side of life. 'Ready Or Not,' built around an uncleared sample of Enya's 'Song For Boadecia,' was another big international success. Enya's label, Island Records, threatened legal action against The Fugees before the Irish new-age singer intervened, deciding she was happy for the group to use her song after all – for a hefty fee – particularly after discovering that they were not "pro-crime" gangstas. The core trio's love of reggae is represented most directly with a version of Bob Marley's 'No Woman No Cry,' which featured a guest vocal by his son Ziggy and would eventually be the fourth international hit single to be taken from the album, after 'Fu-gee-la.'

Though the group never officially disbanded, there have to date been no further Fugees albums. All three members have since gone on to successful solo careers. Wyclef Jean recorded the Afro-Caribbean-styled *The Carnival* in 1997 and had a hit on both sides of the Atlantic with the single 'Gone Till November,' while Pras released the more hip-hop orientated *Ghetto Supastar*. After several years out of the public eye, Hill eclipsed both her former bandmates with *The Miseducation Of Lauryn Hill* (1998), for which she earned five Grammy Awards. The album topped the U.S. charts, as did her debut solo single, 'Doo Wop (That Thing).'

Spice Spice Girls

Virgin 42174 (U.S.A.) / 2812 (U.K.)
Released February 1997 (U.S.A.) / October 1996 (U.K.)

One of the biggest-selling girl groups of all time, Spice Girls exploded on to the pop scene in the summer of 1996 with debut single 'Wannabe' and the album *Spice*.

Spice Girls had been assembled by father-and-son management team Chris and Bob Herbert in 1994, but the monster outgrew its creator after a year and signed with Simon Fuller's more powerful 19 Management, who also handled Annie Lennox. After honing their talents for a further year, the five girls unleashed 'Wannabe,' which topped the charts in 23 countries. As important as Spice Girls' music, however, was their quasi-feminist 'Girl Power' philosophy, which helped the group become a cultural phenomenon, just as likely to be discussed in broadsheet newspapers as teen magazines. Each girl cultivated a distinct personality, be it 'Scary Spice' Melanie Brown or 'Baby Spice' Emma Bunton.

Spice was put together by a host of highly regarded figures in British pop, including production team Absolute, with string arrangements by Craig Armstrong and mixing by Mark 'Spike' Stent. While there was nothing particularly original about the music on *Spice*, its tight, catchy dance-pop sold in extraordinary numbers across the globe, providing three more huge hit singles, 'Say You'll Be There,' '2 Become 1,' and the double a-side 'Mama' / 'Who Do You Think You Are?' The group followed *Spice* with the album and movie *Spiceworld* (both 1997) before becoming a four-piece – after Geri 'Ginger Spice' Halliwell left – and then drifting into solo careers of varying success.

Antichrist Superstar Marilyn Manson

Nothing-Interscope 90006 (U.S.A. & U.K.)
Released October 1996

Marilyn Manson was the latest in a long line of shock rockers, from Alice Cooper to G.G. Allin, and quickly became the most controversial rock performer of the 1990s.

Former music journalist Brian Warner renamed himself Marilyn Manson in 1989, when he began to recruit like-minded musicians in the Florida area. (Like Manson, each of the group members was given the first name of a doomed actress and the surname of a serial killer.) Manson soon became associated with Trent Reznor of Nine Inch Nails, to whose Nothing label he signed. *Portrait Of An American Family* (1994) and *Smells Like Children* (1995) had more shock value than musical worth, but a cover of The Eurythmics' 'Sweet Dreams (Are Made Of This)' started to generate interest outside the industrial-rock underground.

Antichrist Superstar was Manson's first serious attempt at commercial success. Produced by Reznor and Skinny Puppy's Dave Ogilvie, the album was still intended, first and foremost, to stir up controversy, particularly among right-wing and Christian groups. Unlike its predecessors, however, it has a solid musical backing, driven by doomy guitar, synthesizer lines, and harsh, programmed percussion. The album reached Number Three in the U.S.A. in late 1996, shifting two million copies. In the U.K. it grew in popularity after 'The Beautiful People' and 'Tourniquet' both made the Top 30 when issued as singles in the summer of 1997. Manson's follow-up, *Mechanical Animals*, was a bigger commercial success, but by that stage the singer's work had begun to slip into self-parody.

Richard D. James Album Aphex Twin

Elektra 62010 (U.S.A.) / Warp WARP 43 (U.K.)
Released November 1996

Aphex Twin is one of the most important and innovative electronic musicians of all time, and the best-known act on the roster of the pioneering Warp Records label. Though he is perhaps better known for his Brian Eno-style ambient experiments, his defining work is the *Richard D. James Album*.

Aphex Twin started making music as an escape from the boredom of life in rural Cornwall, England. His early work alternated between the hard techno of 'Digeridoo' (1991) and the subtle soundscapes of *Selected Ambient Works Volume II* (1994). The *Richard D. James Album* takes elements of both strands of his previous work. *New Musical Express* (U.K.) called the album "drill'n'bass," but that only tells half the story: the stark, compressed beats are overlaid with melodic synthesizer flourishes and lush string arrangements. In the fast-moving world of electronic music, many records once deemed cutting edge soon sound tired and dated. A decade after its release, *Richard D. James Album* still holds up and still sounds like a blast from the future.

Ever the eccentric – he claims to live in a bank vault and drive a tank – Aphex Twin chose not to release another album for five years, limiting his output to two groundbreaking singles, the industrial nightmare 'Come To Daddy' (1997) and the mutant breakbeats of 'Windowlicker.' Shortly thereafter various rock groups, including Radiohead and Linkin Park, began to cite Aphex Twin as a key influence on their work.

1996

All Eyez On Me 2Pac

Death Row Records 52404 (U.S.A.) / 524249 (U.K.)
Released March 1996

Life After Death The Notorious B.I.G.

Bad Boy / Arista 78612 73011 (U.S.A. & U.K.)
Released March 1997

No Way Out Puff Daddy And The Family

Bad Boy / Arista 8612 73012 (U.S.A. & U.K.)
Released July 1997

In the mid 1990s gangsta rap was the dominant force across the charts and airwaves of the U.S.A. At the time, two of the genre's biggest stars, 2Pac and The Notorious B.I.G., were involved in a high-profile feud. In the space of six months, between September 1996 and March 1997, both were shot dead; neither's killer has, to date, been apprehended.

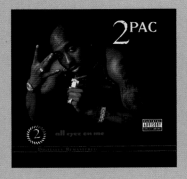

The most notorious of all rap labels, Death Row Records was formed in 1991 by Marion 'Suge' Knight, whose aim was to create the Motown Records of the 1990s. The Los Angeles-based label dealt exclusively in the gangsta rap that had been introduced to the mainstream by the likes of NWA several years previously. Death Row became an immediate success with the release of *The Chronic*, the debut solo album by Dr Dre, formerly of NWA, which would eventually sell over ten million copies. Its next big success was Snoop Doggy Dogg's debut, *Doggystyle* (1993), also a U.S. Number One. The biggest star to emerge from the Death Row stable, however, was Tupac '2Pac' Shakur. 2Pac's earliest solo recordings, which include *Strictly 4 My NIGGAZ* (1993) and *Thug Life Volume 1* (1994), were issued on Interscope Records and failed to sell beyond the hip-hop underground, but he made his mainstream breakthrough in 1995 with *Me Against The World* and the U.S. hit single 'Dear Mama,' which demonstrated an affinity for sentimental balladry as well as hard-hitting raps.

Unlike many of his contemporaries, 2Pac really did come from the background of bleak, inner-city violence he rapped about. He had already faced charges, which were subsequently dropped, of shooting two off-duty police officers and attacking Allen Hughes, the director of the movie *Menace II Society* (in which he was to have appeared). 2Pac was then jailed in 1995 for sexual assault, just as *Me Against The World* was climbing to the top spot on the U.S. albums chart. By this stage, 2Pac and Knight had begun a bitter feud with various associates of the New York-based label Bad Boy, in particular its founder Sean 'Puff Daddy' Combs and his biggest star, Christopher 'The Notorious B.I.G.' Wallace.

While the exact origins of the hostilities between these two rap labels from opposite sides of the U.S.A. are unclear, the tension was raised significantly with 2Pac's claims, in interviews and on record, that he had slept with B.I.G.'s wife Faith Evans, an up-and-coming R&B singer; 2Pac also suspected B.I.G. of being behind a 1994 incident in which he was shot

several times in the lobby of a New York recording studio. The conflict between these two stars then became entangled with a separate disagreement between Combs and Knight, which again centered on one's infidelities with the other's wife. Knight publicly insulted Combs at the 1995 Soul Train Music Awards before posting a $1.4 million bail bond that saw the release of 2Pac from prison after the rapper had served only eight months of a four-and-a-half year sentence.

In return 2Pac started work on his debut album for Death Row, released the following year as *All Eyez On Me*. This two-disk set gave 2Pac his second U.S. Number One album and spawned his first chart-topping single, 'California Love,' a smooth piece of Dre-produced rap-funk and one of the biggest hits of the summer of 1996. The single's b-side, 'Hit 'Em Up,' summed up 2Pac's feelings toward the Bad Boy family, when he asks: "Who shot me? You punks didn't finish. Now you're about to feel the wrath of a menace, nigga."

The song was, to all intents and purposes, a declaration of war between the presiding rap labels of the East and West coasts, and this war would have its first casualty on September 13th 1996, when 2pac Shakur died in a Nevada hospital. Six days earlier, he had been shot repeatedly while riding away in Suge Knight's limo from a Mike Tyson-Bruce Seldon boxing match. Shortly before the shooting, 2Pac and Knight had been involved in the assault of a member of the powerful Crips gang; Knight is claimed to have deep affiliations with their arch-rivals, The Mob Piru Bloods. Numerous allegations have since been made – against B.I.G., Combs, Knight himself, and The Bloods organization – but no arrests have ever been made. Knight was subsequently arrested for parole violation after the assault incident, and would spend five years in prison, during which time Death Row's influence and popularity fell.

Bad Boy Records, which had recently become part of Arista, enjoyed better fortunes in the wake of 2Pac's death. The label's biggest release to date, The Notorious B.I.G.'s sophomore album *Life After Death* was issued in March 1997. It was the follow-up to his multiplatinum debut *Ready To Die* (1994), which had made him the U.S.A.'s biggest-selling male artist of 1995 and reinvigorated East Coast hip-hop. Several days before *Life After Death* hit the stores, its title became strangely prescient as, like his great rival 2Pac, The Notorious B.I.G. was shot dead in a drive-by shooting in Los Angeles. As with 2Pac's murder, the killer is still at large. *Life After Death* was hugely successful in the wake of The Notorious B.I.G.'s death, topping the U.S. albums chart and spawning a pair of Number One singles, 'Hypnotize' and 'Mo Money, Mo Problems.'

Three months after B.I.G.'s death, his former employer Puff Daddy and his widow Faith Evans released a single in tribute to him. 'I'll Be Missing You,' which utilized the chords and chorus melody of 'Every Breath You Take' by The Police, topped the singles charts in the U.S.A. and the U.K. Stepping away from his roles as producer and label executive, Puff Daddy issued his full-length solo debut, *No Way Out*, shortly after. Puff Daddy – later rechristened P Diddy – has since gone on to become the acceptable face of rap, scoring numerous hits on both sides of the Atlantic, introducing his own clothing line, and dating the actress and singer Jennifer Lopez.

Two of rap's biggest and most talented stars, however, were long gone as the genre they helped popularize grew into a period of mainstream respectability. Both 2Pac and The Notorious B.I.G. have become increasingly popular since their deaths, due in no small part to the regular posthumous releases of half-finished and reworked material. In 2002 noted British documentary-maker Nick Broomfield made *Biggie And Tupac*, an ultimately inconclusive investigation into the rappers' lives and deaths, which serves as a stark warning of what can happen when life too closely imitates art.

■ *Main picture: Notorious B.I.G. on stage in 1996. Inset: Tupac Shakur*

1997

Buena Vista Social Club **Buena Vista Social Club**

Nonesuch 79478 (U.S.A.) / World Circuit WCD050 (U.K.)
Released June 1997

The Buena Vista Social Club is a group of musicians who have been meeting to sing and play together in Cuba since before Fidel Castro's rise to power in 1959.

In March 1996 the U.S. guitarist Ry Cooder traveled to Cuba to jam with them and record some songs, even though most of them were then in their late 70s or early 80s.

One of the constants of Cooder's varied career as solo performer, session musician, and movie-soundtrack composer has been his desire to explore new styles, from Tex-Mex to Dixieland jazz. Having all but exhausted the musical heritage of North America, Cooder chose Cuba as the destination for his next project. Cuban music had been popular in the U.S.A. in the early part of the 20th century but had fallen

into obscurity after the 1959 Revolution and subsequent U.S. blockade. Cooder sought to rekindle interest in Cuban song by working with veteran musicians from the island, including the vocalist Ibrahim Ferrer, the pianist Ruben Gonzalez, and the guitarist Compay Segundo. Most of these men were by now in semi-retirement, living in dilapidated apartments in Havana – Ferrer had even turned to shining shoes to earn some much-needed cash.

The performances on *Buena Vista Social Club* have a relaxed atmosphere, evoking a time long before Cuba became, at least in the eyes of the U.S. Government, an ideological pariah state just off the coast of Florida. The songs themselves often date back to the 1950s and beyond and take in a variety of styles. There are piano instrumentals and acoustic folk ballads, joyous traditional dance tunes, and a bolero sung by Segundo and his former lover Omara Portuondo. They were captured with warmth and intimacy by Cooder using analog recording techniques; any digital embellishments would have sounded incongruous alongside such evocative music. The two-week sessions at EGREM Studios in Havana also resulted in the albums *Introducing Ruben Gonzales* and The Afro-Cuban All Stars' *A Toda Cuba Le Gusta*.

Buena Vista Social Club was met with unanimous critical praise on its release the following summer. The album was a minor chart hit in the U.S.A. and across Europe, but gradually sold over a million copies, so making it the biggest success of Cooder's career and bringing unparalleled mainstream exposure to Cuban music.

Not everybody was happy to see the album's release, however. Cooder was fined $100,000 by the U.S. State Department for breaching the embargo with Castro's "evil" communist empire. That didn't stop Cooder from returning to Cuba the following year to make another album with Ibrahim Ferrer. This time he took with him the movie director Wim Wenders, who

caught the recording sessions and a pair of live performances in a heart-warming documentary, also called *Buena Vista Social Club*. (Cooder had previously provided the seminal, evocative solo-guitar soundtrack to Wenders's 1984 movie *Paris, Texas*.) Issued in 1999, the film was also very well received, topping numerous critics' polls and gaining an Academy Award nomination for Best Documentary.

Time Out Of Mind Bob Dylan

Columbia 68556 (U.S.A.) / 486936 (U.K.)
Released October 1997

Bob Dylan's 31st studio album was recorded with Daniel Lanois, producer of Dylan's *Oh Mercy* (1989) and U2's *Joshua Tree* (1987).

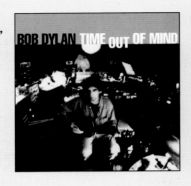

Lanois had given Dylan's sound a subtle modern update on *Oh Mercy*, an album hailed as a major comeback – it had come at the end of a decade Dylan himself admits "left me pretty whitewashed and wasted out professionally." The albums he made in the intervening period – the sub-standard *Under The Red Sky* (1990) and the traditional-folk sets *Good As I Been To You* (1992) and *World Gone Wrong* (1993) – suggested that Dylan wasn't quite out of his slump yet. At the very least, they implied a lack of solid new material.

Time Out Of Mind redressed that balance in some style with Dylan's strongest set of songs since the mid 1970s. The production is gentle, allowing the songs to shine, though sometimes the ethereal background textures that Lanois creates are at odds with the stark bitterness of Dylan's lyrics. Dylan is unrelentingly downcast throughout, from the opening lines of 'Love Sick' – "I'm walking through streets that are dead . . . my feet are so tired . . . the clouds are weeping" – to the 17-minute closer 'Highlands.' The latter song is reminiscent of 'Desolation Row,' the lengthy final track on *Highway 61 Revisited* (1965), in the way the narrative unfolds, never rambling, despite its length and monotonous structure.

Time Out Of Mind reached Number Ten in the U.S.A. and the U.K. and won Dylan three (more) Grammys, including Album Of The Year.

Come On Over Shania Twain

Mercury 536003 (U.S.A.) / 558000 (U.K.)
Released November 1997 (U.S.A.) / March 1998 (U.K.)

The biggest-selling album of the 1990s, *Come On Over* by the country-pop crossover singer Shania Twain has sold over 35 million copies worldwide.

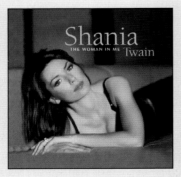

Taking a leaf out of Michael Jackson's book, Twain drew eight singles from the album, of which three reached the U.S. Top Ten. She was also the first country-based performer truly to engage with MTV audiences.

Canadian-born Twain had recorded an eponymous debut in 1993, but her career didn't take off until she met – and eventually married – the rock producer Robert 'Mutt' Lange. He guided her second album, *The Woman In Me* (1995), toward a more rock-orientated sound, propelling Twain to mainstream pop stardom.

Come On Over was essentially more of the same, but with even more hooks and a more polished, commercial sound. There are still country

elements, such as the fiddles on 'Man! I Feel Like A Woman,' but even they have been processed to fit with the record's modern pop sheen. Twain updated her image accordingly, and now looked less like a country singer and more like she'd just walked out of the pages of *Vogue*. This immediately boosted her appeal internationally. Twain had previously never charted in the U.K., but *Come On Over* climbed to Number One and gave her six Top Ten hit singles, including 'That Don't Impress Me Much,' 'From This Moment On,' and 'Don't Be Stupid.' The latter song charted three full years after the album's release, highlighting the incredible longevity of – and colossal marketing push behind – *Come On Over*.

1997

OK Computer **Radiohead**

Capitol 55229 (U.S.A.) / Parlophone NODATA02 (U.K.)
Released June 1997

With *The Bends*, released in 1997, Radiohead had demonstrated that there was still an audience for intelligent, serious rock at a time when the often throwaway conviviality of Brit-pop dominated guitar-based music in the U.K.

Another group might have been happy with having produced one of the most acclaimed albums of the decade, but Radiohead clearly had plans for a more ambitious follow-up even as *The Bends* was climbing up the U.K. albums chart. The group recorded one of the songs that would feature on *OK Computer*, 'Lucky,' for the *Help* compilation album in September 1995. A number of the biggest British groups of the time were asked to contribute a song to the album – which aimed to raise money for and focus attention on the children caught up in the war in the former Yugoslavia – with all of them having to be recorded during a 24-hour period. Most bands donated a cover or a reworking of an older song; Radiohead's offering was not only a brand new composition but also one of the group's most striking recordings to date.

Around the same time Radiohead also cut a handful of songs to be issued as b-sides to single releases from *The Bends*. One of these, 'Talk Show Host,' gives an indication of the kind of sound Radiohead would soon be aiming for. As impressive as *The Bends* is, it is clearly in debt to the likes of R.E.M. and U2. Built on sparse electric piano and a hypnotic, Krautrock rhythm, 'Talk Show Host' is the sound of a band preparing to head into uncharted waters.

Radiohead's September 1995 recordings were produced by Nigel Godrich, a relatively inexperienced studio engineer who had got his break on *The Bends*. Impressed at how well they worked together, the group asked Godrich to seek out the necessary equipment to record their third full-length album. After touring in support of *The Bends*, Radiohead started work with Godrich on *OK Computer* in a remote English mansion owned by the actress Jane Seymour. The group spent most of the latter half of 1996 working on the album, cutting most of the basic tracks live in the house's large dining-room late at night.

The resulting album is a staggering leap forward from the arena rock of its predecessor, totally redefining what a rock band could achieve. *OK Computer*'s songs shift in time signature and dynamics at the drop of a hat, taking in elements of recordings by artists as wide-ranging as Ennio Morricone, Miles Davis, DJ Shadow, and Pink Floyd. Lyrically, the album is also a huge improvement on its predecessors. Before, Thom Yorke's songs tended toward miserable introspection, but on *OK Computer* his scope widens to include urban decay and alienation in a world overrun by technology, neatly capturing the tense, pre-millennial zeitgeist and dovetailing effectively with the futuristic-sounding musical backdrop.

OK Computer was preceded by the release of the six-minute single 'Paranoid Android,' memorably described at the time as "the 'Bohemian Rhapsody' of the 1990s." This multipart epic opens with descending acoustic-guitar chords, brushed percussion, and chiming lead guitar before erupting abruptly into an electrified section reminiscent of The Pixies at their most aggressive; a mournful choral part follows before Jonny Greenwood ends the song with another deft, economical guitar solo. One of the most ambitious singles of recent times, 'Paranoid Android' is essentially *OK Computer* in microcosm. The album's remaining 11 tracks span the cut-up hip-hop drum loops of the opening 'Airbag,' the claustrophobic, dissonant string arrangements of 'Climbing Up The Walls,' and the glockenspiel-led lament 'No Surprises.'

OK Computer was immediately hailed as a modern classic, topping the U.K. albums chart and reaching Number 21 in the U.S.A. A mere six months after its release, the album was chosen as the greatest of all time by readers of *Q* magazine. In addition to 'Paranoid Android,' *OK Computer* spawned the U.K. hit singles 'Karma Police' – which borrows a chord progression from The Beatles' 'Sexy Sadie' – and 'No Surprises.' With worldwide sales of over six million, *OK Computer* has proven inspirational to a host of other guitar bands, most notably Travis and Coldplay.

The Fat Of The Land **The Prodigy**

Geffen 46606 (U.S.A.) / XL XLS80 (U.K.)
Released July 1997

**The biggest-selling electronica
album of the 1990s, *The Fat Of
The Land* is also one of a select
few British albums to enter the
U.S. chart at Number One.**

Arriving at the height of early-1990s
rave culture, The Prodigy established
themselves as one the most
commercially viable electronic acts in
the U.K. with the albums *Experience*
(1992) and *Music For The Jilted
Generation* (1995) and a stream of Top
20 chart singles. Much of The Prodigy's
early recordings – which merged hardcore breakbeats with euphoric dance-
music samples – were made in producer Keith Howlett's bedroom studio. In
1996 the group topped the U.K. chart with the controversial 'Firestarter,' a
frantic, visceral single built on a nagging guitar riff and the demonic, chanted
vocal of Keith Flint, formerly one of The Prodigy's on-stage dancers.

The success of 'Firestarter' and its follow-up, 'Breathe,' considerably raised
expectations for The Prodigy's third full-length album, which was delayed
several times as the perfectionist Howlett tinkered with the final mix. Both
singles were eventually included on *The Fat Of The Land*, which also
features vocal contributions from highly regarded rapper Kool Keith and
Crispian Mills of the short-lived psychedelia-revival group Kula Shaker. The
album was successful enough that Howlett received invitations to work with
Madonna, U2, and David Bowie. He turned them all down.

Urban Hymns **The Verve**

Virgin / Hut 44913 (U.S.A. & U.K.)
Released September 1997

Ladies And Gentlemen We Are Floating In Space
Spiritualized

Arista 18974 (U.S.A.) / Dedicated DED034 (U.K.)
Released June 1997

**Two of the finest British guitar-based albums of the later 1990s
emerged within two months of each other in 1997, each of them
inspired by the same woman.**

The upbeat, euphoric songs on The Verve's *Urban Hymns* were informed by
frontman Richard Ashcroft's new marriage to Kate Radley, the former
musical and romantic partner of Spiritualized leader Jason Pierce, whose
Ladies And Gentlemen drew on quite the opposite set of emotions.

Urban Hymms was The Verve's third album, and was recorded after a year-long
split instigated by the tempestuous relationship between Ashcroft and guitarist
Nick McCabe. It was preceded by the majestic, orchestral single 'Bittersweet
Symphony,' which reached Number Two in the U.K. in the week that Radiohead's
OK Computer topped the albums chart, effectively bringing to an end the

waning Brit-pop era and replacing it with something more serious and
substantial. The single did, however, cause legal problems for the group, as it
contained a small sample from an orchestral reworking of The Rolling Stones'
'The Last Time' by their former manager Andrew Loog Oldham. The Verve had to
surrender 100 per cent of the royalties on the song to The Stones' publishing
company, ABKCO, while 'Bittersweet Symphony' was rather bizarrely re-credited
to Jagger & Richards. Despite this setback, the single's success propelled
Urban Hymns, released two months later, to the top of the U.K. chart and
widened the group's exposure in the U.S.A., where the album reached Number
23. The Verve had split again within a year, however, and this time for good.

Ladies And Gentlemen, meanwhile, was the third full-length effort from
Spiritualized, the group formed for the ashes of the cult garage-rock group
Spacemen 3. Housed in an elaborate, CD-sized reproduction of a
prescription pill packet, the album was an expansive, psychedelic meditation
on love, religion, and chemical dependency, and a minor U.K. hit.

Zaireeka **The Flaming Lips**

Warners 9362 46804 (U.S.A. & U.K.)
Released October 1997

**A set of four CDs designed to be
played simultaneously, The
Flaming Lips' *Zaireeka* might have
been written off as an eccentric
oddity had it not also contained
some of the best psychedelic rock
recorded in years.**

Bandleader Wayne Coyne had started
to toy with the idea of music for
multiple stereo systems in 1995,
when he held his first 'boom box
experiment.' He called together
groups of his friends and gave each
of them one of a set of tapes to play, on cue, on either their car stereos or
on portable tape machines. *Zaireeka* is a similarly interactive experience,
requiring four CD players to gain the full effect of the music. Each of the
four disks contains different mixes of the same eight songs. Depending on
the song, Disk One might highlight the rhythm section, Disk Two a choral
part, Disk Three guitars and strings, Disk Four piano and vocals. Part of the
fun of listening to the album is the different combinations of sounds that
form if disks are out of sync with each other.

Given its unusual format, *Zaireeka* didn't sell well, but The Flaming Lips did
begin to edge toward mainstream success two years later with *The Soft
Bulletin*, the group's tenth album. A critical smash, it shared many stylistic
similarities – widescreen, string-drenched arrangements; frail, Neil Young-
style vocals – and a producer, Dave Fridmann, with the equally acclaimed
Deserter's Songs by Mercury Rev, the band led by one-time Lips guitarist
Jonathan Donahue.

■ **Below: Wayne Coyne (center) conducts a 'boom box experiment' at the
Forum, London, on May 16th 1998.**

1998

Moon Safari **Air**

Caroline CAR6644 (U.S.A.) / Source-Virgin V2848 (U.K.)
Released January 1998

In the late 1990s Air was one of several French groups to achieve unexpected international success.

Historically, French music has been largely ignored – at least by sneering Anglophone critics – outside its homeland and Francophone Canada, aside from a few notable exceptions such as the enduring lothario Serge Gainsbourg and child star Vanessa Paradis. This can be attributed as much to snooty post-war attitudes toward France as to the quality of the nation's music. The first rumblings of a French pop renaissance came with the release of the compilation album *Super Discount*, which featured Air among other less well-known French acts. Techno-pop duo Daft Punk then topped the U.K. chart with the single 'Da Funk' and had a minor U.S. hit with 'Around The World.' Both singles were included on Daft Punk's debut album *Homework* (1997).

With worldwide audiences suddenly able to accept that French music could be cool, the stage was perfectly set for Air's full-length debut *Moon Safari*. The duo of Nicolas Godin and Jean-Benoit Dunckel recorded the album in their own home studio on the outskirts of Paris, making pronounced use of vintage synthesizers, particularly the Mini Moog. *Moon Safari* has an easy, seductive sound, full of soft, hypnotic drum machines, rich synthesizer strings, and echoing electric pianos. The album draws on artists as diverse as Claude Debussy, The Beach Boys, and ELO, which somehow combine toward an impossibly cool end product. *Moon Safari* reached Number Six in the U.K., where it provided Air with the memorable hit singles 'Sexy Boy' and 'Kelly Watch The Stars.'

You've Come A Long Way, Baby **Fatboy Slim**

Astralwerks ASW 66247 (U.S.A.) / Skint BRASSIC 11 (U.K.)
Released October 1998

Fatboy Slim – aka Norman Cook, under which name he had recorded with The Housemartins – was the key figure in British dance music in the late 1990s.

He had scored numerous hits throughout the decade under a variety of pseudonyms, including topping the U.K. singles chart with 'Dub Be Good To Me' (1990) as Beats International. After working as both Freak Power and Pizzaman in the mid 1990s, he settled on the name Fatboy Slim in 1996 and made the critically acclaimed *Better Living Through Chemistry*. Alongside The Chemical Brothers, Fatboy Slim typified the 'Big Beat' style that had begun to dominate the U.K. club scene. Big Beat essentially meant hard, rocky beats served with deep bass lines and catchy, repetitive vocal samples.

You've Come A Long Way, Baby is a more refined, hook-laden update of its predecessor, and was the album that made Fatboy Slim a star. It's not hard to see why. Cook's energy and enthusiasm never lets up, and each of the 11 songs sounds like a ready-made hit. In the end, four songs from the album

reached the Top Ten of the U.K. singles chart, including the relentless 'Right Here, Right Now' and the gospel-tinged 'Praise You,' while the album itself debuted at Number One. Significantly, it was also a hit in the U.S.A. Following The Prodigy's recent success there with *The Fat Of The Land*, electronica seemed finally to have broken out of the underground club scene and into the pop charts, but the genre's popularity ultimately proved to be fleeting.

Ray Of Light **Madonna**

Maverick-Sire 9362 46847 (U.S.A.) / Maverick-Warners 9362 46847 (U.K.)
Released March 1998

Ray Of Light **re-established Madonna as the most important female solo performer of the late 20th century.**

Up to that point, her work in the 1990s had been inconsistent: the forced sexuality of *Erotica* (1992) and *Bedtime Stories* (1994) had seemed pale in comparison with her best work and both were relatively poor sellers.

In 1996 Madonna revived her fortunes with a star turn in the movie adaptation of the musical *Evita*. Later the same year she gave birth to her first daughter, Lourdes. This led to a creative rebirth for Madonna, who sought out the dance producer William Orbit as her main collaborator on *Ray Of Light*. Orbit's productions draw on the best elements of 1990s electronica, taking in low-key, ambient ballads, unfussy trip-hop rhythms, and euphoric dance pop. Madonna turns in the strongest and most assured vocal performances of her career, the result of singing lessons taken prior to the filming of *Evita*.

Ray Of Light quickly became Madonna's most successful album since *Like A Prayer* (1989), selling 15 million copies. The gothic ballad 'Frozen,' 'The Power Of Goodbye,' and the title track were all huge international hit singles. No longer in thrall to controversy, she became a universal, pan-generational megastar. 'Ray Of Light' did land Madonna in a spot of legal hot water, however, when it was found that the song was based on an early-1970s composition, 'Sepheryn,' by Curtis Muldoon and Dave Curtis. Both were granted a significant portion of the song's royalties.

Painted From Memory
Elvis Costello And Burt Bacharach

Mercury 538002 (U.S.A. & U.K.)
Released September 1998

Elvis Costello began his career in the midst of the U.K. punk explosion of 1977 as a cynical new-wave singer-songwriter and continued to record hit albums through the 1980s.

By the start of the 1990s, however, Costello was fast approaching his 40s and could no longer play the angry-young-man role, so he began to turn to more challenging, 'mature' projects. The highest-profile of these was *Painted From Memory*, a collaboration with the legendary popular composer Burt Bacharach, writer of countless hits since the 1960s for artists including Aretha Franklin, Dionne Warwick, Tom Jones, and Dusty Springfield.

Costello and Bacharach first worked together in 1996 on 'God Give Me Strength,' written for the soundtrack to *Grace Of My Heart*. The song won a Grammy Award, prompting its composers to commence work on a full album together the following year. The result was the best work from either party for some time. There is none of the cloying schmaltziness of Bacharach's lesser work, while Costello manages to avoid the wordiness and over-complex song structures that marred some of his 1990s output. Many of the songs are arranged for full orchestra, giving them a timeless feel, to which Costello responds with some of his strongest ever vocal performances.

Painted From Memory was heaped with critical praise in Britain and the U.S.A., and became a minor chart hit in both countries. One of the album's standout tracks, 'I Still Have That Other Girl,' earned the pair a second Grammy, this time for Best Pop Collaboration.

Vol. 2: Hard Knock Life Jay-Z

Roc-a-fella 558902 (U.S.A.) / Northwest-Arista 74321 63533 (U.K.)
Released October 1998 (U.S.A.) / January 1999 (U.K.)

In the late 1990s and early 2000s, Jay-Z – real name Shawn Carter – was like a hip-hop barometer. He worked with the coolest producers – Timbaland, The Neptunes, Kanye West – and the hottest rappers, including DMX, Ja Rule, and Missy Elliott.

He also founded the Roc-A-Fella record label, which later expanded to take in a clothing line and movie production company, and even found time to date Beyoncé Knowles, the sometime Destiny's Child vocalist and solo performer.

Despite all his extra-curricular activities, Jay-Z worked at a prodigious rate, recording ten albums between 1996 and 2003. *Vol. 2: Hard Knock Life* – actually his third album – was his commercial breakthrough and contains

the first traces of the pop-rap hybrid sound that would serve him so well across the next half-decade. Most notable is the title song, which has an unforgettable chorus sampled from the musical *Annie*. 'Hard Knock Life' was a huge hit when issued as a single, reaching Number Two in the U.K. and Number 15 in the U.S.A. Some of the songs on *Vol. 2: Hard Knock Life* are in a harder, gangsta-rap vein, as was much of the earlier *In My Lifetime* (1997). By the time of his next full-length set, *Vol. 3: The Life And Times Of S. Carter* (2000), Jay-Z had curbed this side of his personality completely in an effort to create a more wholesome mainstream image.

Jay-Z's profile continued to rise in the early 21st century with the release of albums including *The Blueprint* (2001), *The Black Album* (2003), and an MTV *Unplugged* set.

Follow The Leader Korn

Immortal/Epic 69001 (U.S.A. & U.K.)
Released August 1998

On its third outing, Southern California alt-metal outfit Korn made it very big with *Follow The Leader*.

The album became the band's biggest-selling record to date – eventually reaching the five-million mark – as well as "one of the most essential alternative albums of the '90s," according to *Rolling Stone*.

In many ways *Follow The Leader* was the ultimate expression of alt-metal as a genre during the late 1990s, which, unlike grunge, was less about song form than song sound. In the hands of lesser artists – and there were plenty of them – the droning guitars, scratching bass, and unrelenting psychobabble could get tedious in a very sort time, but somehow Korn made it work on a commercial level, no doubt owing to the tenacity of its lead singer, Jonathan Davis, as well as the instrumental prowess of guitarists James 'Munky' Shaffer and Brian 'Head' Welch.

While the band's two previous efforts – *Korn* (1994) and *Life Is Peachy* (1996) – had offered glimmers of studio craft, on *Follow The Leader* the sound is completely focused throughout, Davis's visceral gibberish notwithstanding, and the controlled sonic attack presented within served as a blueprint for up-and-coming metal artists in the years that followed. Not that this makes for easy listening by any stretch: on *Follow The Leader* Davis's decidedly dark lyrical content includes grisly tales of childhood ('Dead Bodies Everywhere'), and suicide ('BBK'), capped by a particularly gruesome 'love song' to his girlfriend ('My Gift To You').

While lite raps by guests Fred Durst and Ice Cube and the presence of veteran cut-ups Cheech & Chong – heard on a cover of the 1970s send-up 'Earache My Eye' – offer some comic relief, Davis's resentment looms large throughout. That the hit 'Freak On A Leash,' which reached the Top Ten and still receives regular airplay, was both radio friendly and supremely unnerving is testament to Korn's underlying talent.

A large degree of credit should go to 1990s studio wunderkind Brendan O'Brien – producer for Stone Temple Pilots, Rage Against The Machine, Michael Penn, and others – whose supreme effort in mixing *Follow The Leader* helped bring out the best in Korn's capable rhythm section. An obviously impressed Korn retained O'Brien as producer for the follow-up, 1999's *Issues*, as O'Brien expanded his nu-metal and rap-rock credentials to include the likes of Limp Bizkit and Papa Roach.

Wide Open Spaces Dixie Chicks

Monument 68195 (U.S.A.) / Epic 489482 (U.K.)
Released January 1998 (U.S.A.) / September 1998 (U.K.)

Blending bluegrass, rockabilly, and country rock with infectious pop hooks, The Dixie Chicks' major label debut, *Wide Open Spaces*, was an unexpected international hit, selling 12 million copies worldwide.

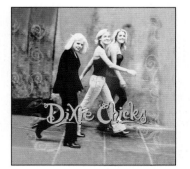

Dixie Chicks was formed by sisters Martie Seidel (fiddle) and Emily Erwin (banjo) in 1989. The group issued three albums of fairly traditional country on independent labels between 1990 and 1993, after which the sisters ousted vocalist Laura Lynch, allegedly because she didn't fit the youthful image they wanted. Her replacement, Natalie Maines, was younger and more glamorous and the daughter of noted pedal-steel guitarist Lloyd Maines. The trio signed to the Sony subsidiary Monument in 1995 and began working the following year on a new album, one that would have a much more contemporary sound, ripe for an assault on the mainstream.

Wide Open Spaces does, however, keep a firm footing in country music. Unlike Shania Twain, then in the midst of a similar transformation from country performer to pop star, the group sticks to its musical heritage, albeit with the addition of more pop savvy than before. The fiddles, dobro guitar, and pedal steel remain an integral part of the trio's sound rather than just being a gimmick for the pop charts. The songs are light and breezy unchallenging country, and on that basis – given the perceived political stance of the world of C&W – it may surprise some that, a few years later, Dixie Chicks would be one of the first U.S. groups to date to criticize the second Iraq war. They were encouraged to apologize.

Car Wheels On A Gravel Road Lucinda Williams

Mercury 558338 (U.S.A. & U.K.)
Released July 1998

Lucinda Williams is one of the most feted female singer-songwriters of recent times, whose work blends country, blues, and rustic folk. Always a critical favorite, she found a wider audience at a time of growing enthusiasm for Americana in the late 1990s.

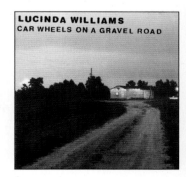

Car Wheels On A Gravel Road had a troubled gestation. Interest in Williams's work had begun to rise following the widespread acclaim for her *Sweet Old World* (1992) and covers of her songs by artists including Emmylou Harris and Tom Petty. In 1994 she signed to Rick Rubin's American label and started work on her fifth album. The initial sessions were produced by Gurf Morlix, with whom Williams had worked since the late 1980s. Deciding that these recordings didn't do justice to her songs, she moved to Nashville the following year and started recording afresh with Steve Earle, but this time she felt the results were too polished and upped sticks again. Now in Los Angeles, she worked with tireless perfectionism on overdubbing the Nashville sessions with former E Street Band member Roy Bittan. Eventually, in 1997, she handed over the tapes for mixing to Rubin, who was in the process of selling American Recordings to Mercury, meaning Williams had to renegotiate her deal with a new label.

Car Wheels On A Gravel Road was finally issued in 1998 to pretty much unanimous critical praise. It topped many an albums-of-the-year poll and was named Best Contemporary Folk Album at the Grammys. Williams followed it in 2001 with her most commercially successful album, *Essence*.

1999

Play **Moby**

V2 27049 (U.S.A.) / Mute STUMM172 (U.K.)
Released May 1999

A staggering example of how a home-recorded album could become a huge international hit, *Play* sold over ten million copies worldwide after its creator allowed over 200 companies to license its songs for use in television advertisements.

Taking his name from his ancestor Herman Melville's classic novel *Moby Dick*, Moby had an early U.K. hit with the single 'Go' in 1991, which melded a memorable piano sample from the soundtrack to *Twin Peaks* with an unrelenting techno beat. While much of his subsequent work failed to chart, Moby continued to work at quite a pace throughout the 1990s. After two albums of hard techno, Moby issued 'Thousand,' which is notable for being, at 1,000 bpm, the fastest single ever released. The first phase of Moby's career, which included remix work for the likes of Michael Jackson and Depeche Mode, ended with the release, in 1993, of three collections of his early recordings.

In 1994 he signed to Elektra in the U.S.A. and Mute in the U.K., where he had two minor hit singles, 'Hymn' and 'Feeling So Real.' *Everything Is Wrong* (1995) was the first Moby album to gain any kind of exposure in the U.S.A.,

but still failed to chart. Many expected his commercial breakthrough to follow, but Moby confounded all but his most devoted listeners with the political, hardcore guitar rock of *Animal Rights* (1996), which made explicit the singer's militant vegan attitudes. In late 1997 Moby scored a U.K. Top Ten hit with the James Bond theme 'Tomorrow Never Dies,' but the instrumental album *I Like To Score* was a commercial failure.

Animal Rights aside, an important thread throughout Moby's work is that he has always worked alone in a small home studio. One of the prevailing trends to develop during the 1990s and into the early 21st century is the galloping progress in computer-based music production. An earlier revolution in music production had occurred in the 1970s with the introduction of the first budget 4-track cassette recorders for home use, but they still required a full band to be present and often gave poor-quality sound recordings. With the arrival in the mid 1980s of the first samplers and cheap synthesizer modules and then the widespread availability of computer-based recording methods in the 1990s, musicians could make high quality recordings alone and on a fairly small budget. Software programs such as Pro Tools and Cubase allow amateur and professional musicians alike to put together songs in a virtual multitrack environment that requires no bulky, expensive mixing boards. In the late 1990s it also became possible to record CD-quality sound direct on to the hard drive of a computer, eliminating the need for tape machines in home studios. This way of working soon became so widespread that by 2004 all Apple Mac computers were packaged with GarageBand, a basic music-production program.

An early advocate of these new technologies, Moby wrote, recorded, produced, and mixed *Play* in its entirety on his own in a small bedroom studio in his New York apartment in 1997 and 1998. The album's 18 tracks were whittled down from around 200 recorded over the period. Overall, the album has a more restrained, downbeat feel when compared with his earlier, abrasive techno, though some songs – the meaty, beaty 'Bodyrock,' for example – still had the potential to be dance-club hits. The key ingredient of *Play*, however, is Moby's clever use of vocal samples from early blues recordings, all old enough to be out of copyright, and therefore royalty free. On almost half of the album's songs he lays these spare, soulful vocal tracks over fragmented, melancholy beats, light synth strings and the

1999

occasional flourish of piano. He also provides vocals of his own on some of the album. While not a technically strong singer, Moby is aware of the limitations of his voice, so doesn't overuse it, instead adding subtle, touching melodies to a number of songs, including 'Porcelain.'

Play was not greeted with particular interest or enthusiasm on its release. If anything, many earlier Moby supporters considered it to be a transparent attempt at a more commercial sound. The album and the first two singles to be taken from it, 'Run On' and 'Bodyrock,' entered the lower reaches of the U.K. charts but made little or no impact in the U.S.A. Gradually, however, advertising executives became aware of the album and began to use the songs from *Play* as the sonic backdrop to numerous television commercials. Unlike a lot of other indie acts, Moby had few reservations about licensing his music for commercials, though he did draw the line at anything involving animal cruelty, cosmetics, or petrochemicals – but not, strangely, cars. Moby's songs also became a regular fixture on movie soundtracks, including *The Next Best Thing*, *The Beach*, and *Any Given Sunday*.

During the course of 1999 and 2000, every single track from *Play* was used as background music for something, many of them repeatedly. It has been claimed that Moby has earned over ten million dollars from licensing tracks from the album, which led to much criticism of him and his principles from some of his peers and various sections of the media. He has since informed his detractors that he has donated a chunk of the proceeds to humanitarian and animal charities. Many are still suspicious of his motives, however, and the ubiquity of the songs from *Play* in advertisements has blurred the line between whether, in such cases, the song is selling the product, or the product is selling the song.

What is undeniable is that this wide-ranging, often subliminal exposure of *Play* is what eventually propelled sales of the album toward the ten million mark after its slow start. In 2000 *Play* gradually rose to the top of the U.K. chart – providing Moby with three U.K. hit singles in 2000, 'Why Does My Heart Feel So Bad,' 'Porcelain,' and 'Natural Blues' along he way – and reached Number 38 in the U.S.A., where none of his releases, albums or singles, had ever charted before. The album *Play* was still selling strongly in 2001, when Moby had his first U.S. hit single with a reworked version of the track 'Southside,' featuring guest vocals by No Doubt's Gwen Stefani. By this stage the German record label Wrasse had capitalized on the success of *Play* by releasing *Natural Blues Vol. 1*, a compilation album that included the original recordings of a number of the songs Moby had sampled on *Play* alongside other early blues recordings.

. . . Baby One More Time Britney Spears

Jive 42545 (U.S.A.) / 052169-4 (U.K.)
Released March 1999

Britney Spears emerged with this, her debut album, at the tail end of the 20th century, and has since become the most recognizable pop starlet of the new millennium.

In 1993, at the age of 11, Spears was a regular performer on *The New Mickey Mouse Club* alongside a number of other future pop stars, including boyfriend-to-be Justin Timberlake and Christina Aguilera. In 1997 she signed a deal with the large independent label Jive and began work the following year on her debut album with a host of big-name writers and producers. These included Eric Foster White – best known for his work with Whitney Houston – and Swedish pop supremo Max Martin, who had already produced big records for Ace Of Base and The Backstreet Boys, and would, between 1999 and 2000, write huge global hits for Celine Dion, Bryan Adams, Bon Jovi, and *Nsync as well as Spears herself.

Spears's debut single, '. . . Baby One More Time,' topped the U.S. chart in November 1998 and rose to Number One across Europe in early 1999. A key part of the single's success was Spear's image: despite making it known that she intended to remain a virgin until she married, the 17-year-old cultivated a coy, Lolita-like sexuality by way of her ambiguously suggestive lyrics and the skimpy school uniform she wore in her debut video. The album capitalized on the success of the title track in the singles market, topping the charts in over 20 countries and selling over 25 million copies worldwide, and shifting many more records than any of the other U.S. teen-pop acts that flooded the charts in the late 1990s and early 2000s.

Several months after the release of . . . *Baby One More Time*, Spears's former *Mickey Mouse Club* co-star Aguilera topped the charts at home and abroad with the single 'Genie In A Bottle' and her eponymous debut album, which sold eight million copies in the U.S.A. alone.

Supernatural Santana

Arista 07822 19080 (U.S.A. & U.K.)
Released June 1999

One of the leading jazz-rock fusion guitarists of the late 1960s and 1970s, Carlos Santana scored a huge international hit with *Supernatural* in the late 1990s after years of relative obscurity.

The album is notable for the number of high-profile guest performers it features, among them Eric Clapton, Lauryn Hill, and Rob Thomas of the group Matchbox Twenty. *Supernatural* also equaled the record held by Michael Jackson's *Thriller* by winning eight Grammy Awards, and sold over ten million copies, making it far and away the biggest commercial success of Santana's career.

Until the release of *Supernatural*, Santana was probably best known for his hit cover of Fleetwood Mac's 'Black Magic Woman,' as featured on the classic album *Abraxas* (1970). In the ensuing decades his most notable releases were *Illuminations* (1974), a collaboration with Alice Coltrane, *The Swing Of Delight* (1980), recorded with the 1960s line-up of The Miles Davis Quintet (minus Davis himself), and the U.S. hit album *Zebop!* (1981).

Santana hadn't recorded much of note during the remaining years of the 1980s or the 1990s, but was offered a new deal by Clive Davis of Arista Records in 1997. Davis had been responsible for signing Santana to his very first recording contract in 1969 in his capacity as an A&R man for Columbia. He hoped Santana could make a similar comeback to those made by other rock veterans in the late 1990s, including Bob Dylan, who had recently issued *Time Out Of Mind* (1997), his best work since the mid 1970s.

> ## "*SUPERNATURAL* IS A BEAUTIFUL EXAMPLE OF SYNCHRONICITY. EVERYONE WHO PARTICIPATED WAS ON THE SAME WAVELENGTH AND ARTISTIC ENERGY AS I WAS."
>
> *CARLOS SANTANA*

Davis and Santana hatched the idea of an album that would allow the guitarist to work with a number of younger stars, in the hope that this would introduce Santana to a new generation of fans while also appealing to older fans nostalgic for rock's golden age. To that end, most of the songs on *Supernatural* feature the vocal talents of a modern pop or rock singer, but also afford Santana space to showcase his silky-smooth guitar playing. Eric Clapton was the only guest on the album from the 1960s or 1970s, aside from some of the session musicians in the band. 'Do You Like The Way' was sung by former Fugees vocalist Lauryn Hill, and 'Love Of My Life' featured Dave Matthews, who had recently achieved huge popularity in the U.S.A. with the albums *Crash* (1996) and *Before These Crowded Streets* (1998).

The most successful collaboration, however, was 'Smooth,' fronted by Rob Thomas. His group Matchbox Twenty were not particularly well known outside the U.S.A., but had scored a big U.S. hit in 1997 with the album *Yourself Or Someone Like You*. 'Smooth' topped the U.S. singles chart, as did 'Maria Maria,' which featured another former member of The Fugees, Wyclef Jean. Both were Top Ten hits in the U.K., while *Supernatural* itself was a Number One entry there and in the U.S.A. The album's biggest success, though, was at the 1999 Grammy Awards, where it won in eight of 11 categories in which it was nominated, including Record Of The Year and Album Of The Year.

Enema Of The State Blink-182

MCA 111950 (U.S.A.) / 11950 (U.K.)
Released June 1999

Blink-182 was the latest in a long line of groups to take the three-chord exuberance and anti-social attitudes of classic punk and turn it into something much more commercially viable.

The likes of Blink-182 – and similar acts from earlier in the 1990s, Green Day and The Offspring – were able to achieve far more fame and fortune than The Sex Pistols or The Ramones despite paling somewhat in comparison with their 1970s forebears. The band was formed in 1993 by guitarist-singer Tom Delonge and bassist Mark Hoppus. Drummer Travis Barker didn't arrive until after the albums *Buddha* (1994), *Cheshire Cat* (1996), and *Dude Ranch* (1997), joining just before the group signed a deal with MCA in 1998. Despite graduating to a major label, the group saw no reason to deviate from the childish humor of its first three albums on *Enema Of The State*.

The album's content is summed up by the cover image – a porn starlet dressed in nurse's uniform preparing to administer said enema – and the song titles, which include 'Dysentery Gary' and 'Dumpweed.' The songs themselves rarely depart from neat, upbeat two-minute punk anthems, albeit punk that has been expertly crafted by producer Jerry Finn. (Finn had previously worked with a host of other punk revivalists in the 1990s, including Pennywise and Rancid.) *Enema Of The State* was hugely popular in the U.S.A. and across Europe, shifting seven million copies worldwide, and spawned a U.S. and British Top Ten hit single, 'All The Small Things.'

Human Clay Creed

Wind Up-Epic 13053 (U.S.A.) / 495027 (U.K.)
Released September 1999

Human Clay was a huge success in the U.S.A. at a time when most grunge-influenced groups there were being supplanted by the rock-rap crossovers of Limp Bizkit, Korn, and their ilk.

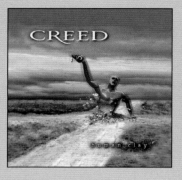

Creed was initially labeled a Christian rock band on the basis of the religious themes of the many of the group's songs. If anything, however, Creed was an act of rebellion for vocalist Scott Stapp against his Pentecostal minister father rather than an attempt to follow in his footsteps as a rock'n'roll preacher.

Creed's debut, *My Own Prison* (1996), sold five million copies despite little interest from the mainstream media and provided the first four of a record-breaking run of seven Number One entries on *Billboard*'s rock-radio charts. In the late 1990s many alternative rock groups tended to disappear after one hit album. *Human Clay* did more than just buck that trend, it topped the U.S. albums chart and sold ten million copies in the U.S.A.

Like its predecessor, *Human Clay* was produced by John Kurzweg, and features a sound highly reminiscent of Pearl Jam. 'Higher,' 'What If,' and 'With Arms Wide Open' dominated U.S. rock radio for the next year, while the latter cut was named Best Rock Song at the 2000 Grammy Awards. Creed's third album, *Weathered* (2001), was equally successful, and holds the record for most consecutive weeks spent at Number One by an album that debuted at the top of the chart. During those eight weeks alone it sold five million copies.

Hours . . . David Bowie

Virgin 48157 (U.S.A.) / V2900 (U.K.)
Released October 1999

Still innovating in his 50s, David Bowie made pioneering use of the internet as a promotional device with Hours . . .

As with every album Bowie recorded in the 1990s, *Hours . . .* was greeted as his best work since *Scary Monsters* (1980). While the album contains a clutch of strong songs, in particular the singles 'Thursday's Child' and 'Seven,' it is not one of Bowie's most sonically interesting recordings. It is notable, however, for the way he made use of the internet in both its conception and promotion. Apparently stuck when it came to writing the lyrics to 'What's Really Happening,' Bowie set up a contest via his Bowienet website in which entrants could listen online to an instrumental version of the song and then had to come up with a suitable set of lyrics. The winner received a $5,000 publishing contract and the honor of being part of Bowie's new album.

As the release of *Hours . . .* neared, Bowie announced that internet users would be able to preview the album in its entirety in the weeks leading up to its on-sale date. Such a move was unprecedented and came at a time when most musical acts were in a state of panic about how internet downloads could harm their earnings. The move clearly helped Bowie, however, as *Hours . . .* became his strongest-selling album in a decade, reaching Number 47 in the U.S.A. and Number Five in the U.K.

2000

The Marshall Mathers LP
Eminem

Interscope 490629 (U.S.A. & U.K.)
Released May 2000

The best-selling and most controversial rapper of the new millennium, Eminem made his mainstream breakthrough with *The Marshall Mathers LP*.

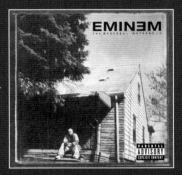

As with its predecessor, *The Slim Shady LP*, the album's lyrical content provoked accusations of homophobia and misogyny, but didn't stop *The Marshall Mathers LP* becoming the fastest-selling rap album of all time, selling two million copies in its first week.

Eminem had made his recording debut with the independently issued *Infinite* in 1996 before finishing in second place at the 1997 Rap Olympics in Los Angeles. This drew the interest of Interscope Records boss Jimmy Iovine, who paired Eminem – born Marshall Bruce Mathers III in 1972 – with the highly regarded hip-hop producer Dr Dre, a former member of NWA who had also worked with the likes of Snoop Doggy Dogg and 2Pac Shakur. Legend states that Eminem and Dre had created the basic elements of 'My Name Is' – soon to become the rapper's first hit single – within an hour of their first meeting. *The Slim Shady LP* followed shortly thereafter, reaching Number Two on the U.S. charts. Eminem's raps, delivered in his scattershot, nasal style, brought him instant notoriety in the U.S.A. He rails against a litany of targets on *The Slim Shady LP*, most famously his mother – dismissed as a bad parent and drug addict – and his new wife Kim, whom he gleefully imagines murdering on ''97 Bonnie And Clyde.'

At the outset of his career, Eminem made repeated claims that his skin color made it difficult for him to gain any respect in the rap world, given that his most famous white predecessor, Vanilla Ice, was seen by many as a lame caricature, a white performer attempting to capitalize on a predominantly black style of music. While that may be true, once he earned a record deal, Eminem's Caucasian skin tone helped him burst through so many more doors than had previously been opened to black rappers. He became a regular fixture on daytime MTV, on popular alternative-rock radio stations, and on the covers of such magazines as *Rolling Stone* and *Entertainment Weekly*. Eminem provided a voice that young, white, suburban hip-hop fans could relate to, further boosting both his mainstream appeal and the controversy surrounding his bad-tempered, foul-mouthed records. With the emergence of Eminem, out-of-touch critics could no longer ghettoize rap as the music of a black underclass. For his part, despite attacking virtually all other minority groups – in what he claims is the voice of an exaggerated character, and one who does not always represent his own views – Eminem appears to be very careful not to say anything in his songs that could lead to him being branded a racist. He is also keenly aware of his debt to his predecessors in the rap world. On the single 'Without Me' (2002) he describes himself as "... the worst thing since Elvis Presley / To use black music so selfishly."

Some critics expected Eminem's anger to subside on his second album – after all, much of the dissatisfaction on *The Slim Shady LP* seemed to stem from his poverty-stricken upbringing in a run-down part of Detroit, and he could hardly continue on that track now that he had become a big international star. If anything, however, *The Marshall Mathers LP* ups the ante further. Recorded in late 1999 and early 2000, again with Dr Dre at the helm, this is an even darker journey through Eminem's twisted psyche, full once again of profanity-ridden tales of rape, murder, and drug abuse.

Though the focus of interest and debate with Eminem is inevitably the album's lyrical content, *The Marshall Mathers LP* is highly accomplished musically. The songs are set on a foundation of sparse, staccato drum loops and smooth, liquid bass lines, with additional instrumental flourishes where necessary, be it the synthesized guitar on 'Kill You' or the foreboding bells on 'The Way I Am.'

The Marshall Mathers LP easily surpassed the success of its predecessor, chalking up two million sales in its first week in the U.S.A. alone and topping the charts there and in the U.K. The album was trailed by the single 'The Real Slim Shady,' on which Eminem decries the sudden surge of white rappers to have emerged in the wake of his success before suggesting that he caught a venereal disease from pop singer Christina Aguilera. She is just one of a number of pop and rock stars at whom Eminem takes aim on *The Marshall Mathers LP*: others include Britney Spears, Limp Bizkit's Fred Durst, and one of his white rap forebears, Marky Mark.

As on his first record, Eminem treats all comers with a violent disdain, particularly women and homosexuals. His insult of choice on *The Marshall Mathers LP* is "faggot," regardless of the sexual orientation of his victim. On one of the album's most infamous cuts, 'Criminal,' Eminem announces "my words are like a dagger with a jagged edge that'll stab you in the heart whether you're a fag or a les." This, as well as many other examples of apparently homophobic lyrics, provoked a strong reaction from The Gay And Lesbian Alliance Against Defamation (GLAAD), who began to picket Eminem's concerts and organized a protest outside the 2000 MTV Music Awards, at which the rapper performed and won in several categories. Eminem took some of the wind out of their criticisms at the 2001 Grammy Awards, where he dueted with Elton John on an impressive rendition of the U.K. Number One hit single 'Stan.'

'Stan' was the song that elevated *The Marshall Mathers LP* beyond being merely a huge-selling rap album toward its status as one of the biggest and most important albums of the early 21st century. The track makes use of the melodic chorus from the then unknown British soft-rock singer Dido's 'Thank You,' before Eminem embarks on an epic, cinematic lyric about the title character, a devoted fan who takes his own life after being shunned by the rapper. The single shows off a thoughtful, sensitive side of Eminem rarely seen on his early albums. Just as importantly, however, it provides a pop hook that even non-rap fans could grab hold of. ('Stan' also helped launch the career of Dido, whose 1999 debut album, *No Angel*, became a big international hit.)

The Marshall Mathers LP arrived in by far the most turbulent year of Eminem's life to date. He faced legal action from his mother, suing for defamation of character, and a Detroit clubber, allegedly beaten by Eminem after kissing the rapper's wife. Kim Mathers attempted suicide after hearing the songs 'Kim' and 'Kill You,' in which Eminem again fantasizes about the violent murder of his wife. They divorced in 2002. The net result of all this controversy, however, was more publicity for Eminem and more sales for *The Marshall Mathers LP*, which has to date sold over 15 million copies. Eminem's next release was another global chart topper, *The Eminem Show*, after which he starred in the autobiographical movie *8 Mile*. His success has inspired a host of other white rappers, but none has come close to his talent or staying power.

Metallica vs. Napster

At the turn of the 21st century a technological revolution began that changed the way we listen to and acquire music.

It began with the peer-to-peer file-trading software program Napster, which allowed registered users to swap songs stored in the digital MP3 format on each other's computers. Inevitably, the recording industry was furious that its products were being shared for free online, and reacted with a fervor reminiscent of the 1980s, when it had decided that "home taping is killing music."

Some commentators were calmer in their assessments of the effects of Napster, however, and saw file-sharing as a way for music fans to hear new bands and artists, whose albums they would invariably then buy on CD. They pointed to the fact that, as downloading grew in popularity in 2000, Eminem's *The Marshall Mathers LP* was regularly swapped on file-sharing programs before its release, but still sold two million copies in its first week on sale.

The attitudes of bands and musicians were equally diverse. Some – Radiohead and David Bowie, for example, and more recently U2 – embraced the new technology and looked for ways to integrate themselves and their music with it. Others made pseudo-liberal pronouncements that they made their music "for the people man," and didn't mind if their fans were no longer paying for it. However, many musicians were justifiably worried about the effect that illegal file sharing could have on them and their earning power. The most vocal opponent of Napster and its users was the hard-rock act Metallica, and in particular the group's drummer, Lars Ulrich. The group was incensed when, in 1999, it found that its entire discography was being shared online, for free, without any consideration for the records' copyright and the group's intellectual property.

By early 2000 the Recording Industry Association Of America (RIAA) had instigated legal action against Napster and various U.S. colleges, who, the organization claimed, did nothing to stop their students using the file-sharing program. Metallica made the battle personal when, on May 3rd 2000, Ulrich handed over a list of 300,000 Napster users who, he claimed, were using the software to share illegally the group's music. All 300,000 were banned from using Napster, as were a similar number of culprits named on another list offered up by Ulrich later the same month.

A backlash soon started against Metallica and Ulrich, who was painted in many sections of the media as a poster boy for greedy, corporate rock stars. Many of the Metallica fans now banned from Napster claimed to own most or all of the music they were sharing through the program on CD or vinyl, so were not doing anything to affect the group's financial viability; others maintained that they only traded live recordings of the group, and pointed to the fact that Metallica had always allowed – and encouraged – fans to tape its concerts. It also didn't help Ulrich's cause that, regardless of the legalities involved, he was one quarter of one of the biggest-selling rock groups of all time, so hardly needed the money.

By mid 2001 the RIAA had succeeded in shutting Napster down. Numerous other file-sharing programs soon sprung up in its place, however, including Soulseek, Kazaa, and Gnutella. Many had the advantage – for the file sharers – over Napster that they were completely anonymous and that it was no longer possible to trace who was downloading what.

Ironically, for a program that was once the scourge of the music industry, Napster was relaunched as a legal download site, with the full co-operation of countless international record labels in 2004. To date, however, no Metallica material is for sale on the site.

2000

Kid A Radiohead

Capitol 2435 27753 (U.S.A.) / Parlophone 2435 27753 (U.K.)
Released October 2000

After reinvigorating rock music with *The Bends* and *OK Computer*, Radiohead made their 'difficult' fourth album, *Kid A*, notable for the unorthodox promotional campaign that trailed it.

Radiohead found themselves at a creative impasse after *OK Computer*, with frontman Thom Yorke adamant that the group could not continue with the guitar-based sound that had brought so much fame and acclaim – in part because he felt it had been devalued by the emergence of similar groups such as Coldplay, Muse, and Travis. Following fruitless recording sessions in Paris and Copenhagen in early 1999, Radiohead started work afresh in September at their own newly built studio complex just outside Oxford, England, with *OK Computer* producer Nigel Godrich, where they remained until midway through the following year.

Kid A leaves behind the guitar heroics of *OK Computer*, replacing them with an uncompromising computer-manipulated sound, drawing on influences as diverse as Aphex Twin and Charles Mingus. The album's ten songs span the moody electric piano and cut-up vocals of 'Everything In Its Right Place,' the breakbeat-driven 'Idioteque,' and the free-jazz cacophony of 'The National Anthem.'

Refusing to issue any singles or videos from the album, and giving few interviews, Radiohead instead created a number of 30-second blips – short animated clips that were broadcast over the internet. Prior to the album's release, Radiohead had kept their internet-savvy fan base informed of their progress with several webcasts from their studio, during which they debuted songs from *Kid A* and its successor *Amnesiac*.

Despite the group's unusual methods of production and the album's unconventional sound, *Kid A* topped the charts in both the U.S.A. and the U.K.

■ *Radiohead premiered material from* **Kid A** *on their summer 2000 tour of outdoor European venues. Bootleg recordings appeared on the internet mere hours after each performance; the band was bemused to find that large sections of the audience knew the words to the new, unreleased songs within a few dates of the the tour.*

Hybrid Theory **Linkin Park**

Warner Bros 9362 47755 (U.S.A. & U.K.)
Released April 2000 (U.S.A.) / October 2000 (U.K.)

Often lumped together with the numerous rap-metal and nu-metal acts of the late 1990s and early 2000s, Linkin Park is, in fact, a more musically inventive group than many of its peers.

As well as the stock influences of Korn and Rage Against The Machine, the sextet draws on The Roots' hip-hop polyrhythms and Aphex Twin's nightmarish electronica.

Formed by a group of early 20-somethings in 1999, Linkin Park had earned a recording contract with Warner Bros within a year. The group has two vocalists: Chester Bennington is the more traditional alternative-rock singer, while Mike Shinoda is a hip-hop style MC. As well as the usual drums, bass, and guitar, Linkin Park has a permanent turntablist in its ranks. Most members of the multitalented group also dabbled with electronic production techniques during the making of *Hybrid Theory*.

The album was recorded at NRG Recordings in North Hollywood, California, and produced by Don Gilmore, engineer of Pearl Jam's landmark *Ten* (1991). The title *Hybrid Theory*, of course, refers to the fusion of rap and metal contained within, but the album is a subtle work in places, even if, lyrically, it tends toward alt-rock clichés – "Crawling in my skin / These wounds, they will not heal." 'One Step Closer,' 'Crawling,' and 'In The End' were hit singles both in the U.S.A. and the U.K., while *Hybrid Theory* itself has sold in excess of 15 million copies worldwide, making it one of the biggest successes of the early 21st century.

Rated R **Queens Of The Stone Age**

Interscope Records 10007 (U.S.A.) / 490683-2 (U.K.)
Released June 2000

After 45 years of guitars and drums, can anyone make a great rock record? Queens Of The Stone Age proved you could, with the right blend of humor, aggression, lyricism, and mania, channeled into a hook-ridden collection of songs.

Rated R is, by turns, loud, hip, poetic, funny, trashy, dignified, and unexpected. It is 42 minutes of the most varied rock imaginable that comes roaring in with the jump-around-the-room buzz of the ironically titled 'Feel Good Hit Of The Summer,' whose lyric consists mostly of the names of six drugs sung over a backing that resembles a head-on collision between Nirvana and The MC5. It segues straight into the bells'n'riff combination of 'The Lost Art Of Keeping A Secret' with its gently sung vocal over an ultra-grunge chorus. 'Leg Of Lamb' is as quirky as early Roxy Music, 'Auto Pilot' is a 21st-century fuzz-guitar minor blues, 'Monsters In The Parasol' is a hipper ZZ Top boogie, and the 1:42 of 'Quick And To The Pointless' puts a manically hormonal vocal over a neo-T. Rex riff, handclaps, and the "yeah, yeah, yeah, yeahs" of the female backing singers.

The masterpiece of arrangement is 'Better Living Through Chemistry,' where the band pull the amazing stunt of stopping the song at just over 90 seconds, letting a chord drift in low-level feedback for almost 40 seconds, and resuming with a guitar solo, which in turn is pushed aside at the three-minute mark by vocal harmonies, as though CSN&Y had gate-crashed a Soundgarden session.

Parachutes **Coldplay**

Capitol 30162 (U.S.A.) / Parlophone 527783 (U.K.)
Released December 2000 (U.S.A.) / July 2000 (U.K.)

Coldplay became the most successful of a number of British groups that emerged around the turn of the millennium with a sound reminiscent of the anthemic, melancholic guitar rock of Radiohead, The Verve, and Jeff Buckley.

Coldplay was formed in 1998 by pianist-guitarist-vocalist Chris Martin and Phil Harvey – who stepped back from performing and recording to become the group's manager – with the addition of guitarist Jon Buckland, bassist Guy Berryman, and drummer Will Champion. The group issued the independent 'The Safety EP' (1998) and 'Brothers And Sisters' (1999) before signing to Parlophone. After issuing another EP, 'Blue Room,' the group started work on its full-length debut with producer Ken Thomas in November 1999 at Parr Street in Liverpool and Rockfield Studios in Wales.

These sporadic sessions lasted until May 2000, at which point Coldplay emerged with a well-rounded debut that took in wistful acoustic ballads, dissonant – but never tuneless – rock, and the occasional subtle hint of psychedelia. Coldplay cleverly positioned themselves in the middle ground between Radiohead (too arty) and Oasis (too arrogant), the two most feted British groups of the 1990s. *Parachutes* became the biggest album of the year in the U.K. on the strength of two exemplary singles – 'Yellow' and the soulful, piano-led 'Trouble' – and was a minor U.S. hit when released there in late 2000. The group rose to bona fide superstar status with *A Rush Of Blood To The Head* (2002), which has a more epic feel that draws on U2 and Echo And The Bunnymen.

Sing When You're Winning **Robbie Williams**

Capitol 29024 (U.S.A.) / Chrysalis 528125 (U.K.)
Released August 2000

Robbie Williams was the cheeky, chirpy face of British pop in the 1990s and early 2000s, first as a member of Take That, and then as a solo performer.

When Take That, the most popular British teen group since the 1960s, split in 1996, songwriters Gary Barlow and Mark Owen were deemed most likely to achieve solo success. After a shaky start, however, it was Williams who went on to become the defining face of British pop at the turn of the millennium.

His first few solo singles were fairly lightweight, but Williams stamped himself on the national consciousness with the heartfelt ballad 'Angels' and the Kiss-aping rock showmanship of 'Let Me Entertain You.' Williams's third full-length effort, *Sing When You're Winning*, doesn't deviate far from the pattern set by its predecessors, *Life Thru A Lens* (1997) and *I've Been Expecting You* (1998). The album was co-written and produced by his regular collaborator Guy Chambers, who again offers Williams the perfect backdrop to showcase both the roguish bad-boy and the sensitive new man in him. Williams's third consecutive chart topper in the U.K., the album provided four Top Ten hit singles, including the 1980s pop of 'Rock DJ' and a duet with Kylie Minogue on 'Kids.' Try as he might, transatlantic success has continued to elude Williams, even though his next album, *Swing When You're Winning* (2001), was a tribute to The Rat Pack. It did, however, give him a fourth solo U.K. Number One hit single, a duet with Nicole Kidman on the Frank and Nancy Sinatra classic 'Somethin' Stupid.'

Beyond CD

The big question in audio today is what will replace CD. The aging digital format has always had its critics among audio enthusiasts, though the bulk of the population appears happy with it. Indeed, it is a very real question whether there is a long-term future for any physical delivery system for home music.

For many, especially the young, music involves collecting digital music from legal or illegal sources and then storing it on portable devices. With the iPod and similar players now beginning to take on the role of providing music in the home, through players with built-in speakers or simply plugging one into a stereo system, the future of the plastic disk is possibly in the balance.

That has not stopped the electronics giants from conjuring up new hi-tech paths for us all to follow, promising improved sound – even though CDs' promise of "perfect sound forever" still lingers in the memory of many consumers – and, once again, they have managed to introduce competing and incompatible formats. Two systems are currently being promoted: Super Audio CD (SACD) and DVD-Audio. Both use the same plastic disk as DVD video, but there the similarities end.

SACD, introduced by Sony and Philips in 1999 as a replacement for CD, boasts a greatly improved system for digitizing sound – known as Direct Stream Digital or DSD – the capacity for six-channel 5.1 sound, and an inbuilt CD track that gives it total compatibility with the older system: you can play SACD disks on your old system as well as old disks on your new SACD player, without, of course, getting any of the benefits. But SACD remains strictly an audio product, without on-screen graphics or video.

When DVD video was introduced in 1996 it had to cope with carrying two hours of moving pictures and a 5.1 soundtrack on a single disk. That meant compromises, with sound being compressed to the point that its quality fell below that of standard CD. That didn't much matter, since DVD customers were watching television rather than concentrating on the sound, but it did mean that a new format needed to be devised and negotiated if DVD was to be used as a high-quality sound medium. The answer was DVD-Audio, and it arrived in 1999. This provides for the usual 5.1 channels of high-quality sound, though these do not have the theoretical advantages of SACD's DSD system, being effectively an update of the CD system. Where DVD-Audio scores is in having the ability to carry visual program material – namely lyrics, photographs, and short videos – as well as sound. Where it falls down, however, is in being entirely incompatible with CD, though it will play on DVD-Video players.

This incompatibility has become a cause of great concern for DVD-Audio makers, and recently considerable efforts have gone into making a format in which a standard CD is placed on the reverse side of the DVD-Audio disk. The current front-runner is called DVDPlus, but its CD side is not technically compatible with the Philips standard, and some equipment manufacturers have warned that their players won't play it. Nonetheless, as things stand at the time of writing, many of the major labels showed signs of adopting it.

While both formats have their fans, there is a general admission that the improvements in quality are not significant enough to persuade ordinary music-lovers to shell out either on new equipment or premium-priced disks. The multichannel aspect may appeal more to some, especially as increasing numbers of people use home cinema equipment, but for portable or car use the improvements would hardly seem to represent great value for money. And, as things stand, even six years after the announcement of the new systems, there is little music available to encourage buyers to invest. SACD seems to be slightly ahead, but neither system appears to be gaining much in the way of momentum.

What little enthusiasm the record companies can muster for these formats, however, has more to do with their continued battle against copying. Most CDs can be copied easily on any modern computer. In consequence, record companies have recently started introducing locked CDs. Both SACD and DVD-Audio are designed with copy-protection built in – an example of the manufacturers trying to bolt the stable door

Continued on page 300

2001

Celebrity *Nsync

Jive 41758 (U.S.A. & U.K.)
Released July 2001

***Celebrity* marks the culmination of a period of teen-pop dominance on the U.S. charts – which also included Britney Spears, Christina Aguilera, and Destiny's Child.**

The album sold over two million copies in its first week in the U.S.A., falling just short of the sales record of 2.4 million *Nsync had set with the previous year's *No Strings Attached*. The group split shortly after the release of *Celebrity*, however, leaving frontman Justin Timberlake to pursue a career as a more mature solo artist.

One distinct change in pop music in the early 21st century, as online downloads began to rip the heart out of the singles market, is that the likes of *Nsync began to make more of an effort to create stronger, more cohesive albums than the traditional two-good-singles-and-a-load-of-filler variety. Recruiting the cream of contemporary writers and producers was nothing new, but *Nsync took the idea to its logical conclusion, deploying a different team on almost every song on *Celebrity*. The net result is a diverse, kinetic collection of cutting-edge pop. British dance producer BT provides a skittering electronic backdrop for the opening song and lead single 'Pop,' while the slick title track is the work of R&B hitmaker Rodney Jerkins, best known for his collaborations with Whitney Houston and Jennifer Lopez. *Celebrity*'s finest cut is the sultry, smooth single 'Girlfriend,' produced by The Neptunes and featuring a guest vocal from rising rap star Nelly. Timberlake himself also co-produced several songs, while other contributors to the project include Max Martin, writer of Britney Spears's breakout hit '. . . Baby One More Time.'

In Search Of . . . NERD

Virgin Records 11521 (U.S.A.) / 8100972 (U.K.)
Released March 2002 (U.S.A.) / August 2001 (U.K.)

Better known as The Neptunes, Pharrell Williams and Chad Hugo became the hottest producers in commercial rap and R&B around the end of the century, working their magic on hits by the likes of Ol' Dirty Bastard, LL Cool J, Jay-Z, and Britney Spears.

The duo issued their debut, *In Search Of . . .*, across Europe in the summer of 2001, under the name NERD (an acronym for No one Ever Really Dies), just as the single 'Lapdance' had begun climbing up the U.S. chart. The album met with a lukewarm critical response, however, prompting NERD to delay its U.S. release.

Deciding they were unhappy with the sound of the album, as well as taking note of the way it had been received in Europe, Williams and Hugo returned to The Record Plant in Los Angeles to make alterations. The duo removed much of the electronic, programmed rhythm sections, replacing them with taut live guitar and drum parts that at times resemble the nu-metal of Linkin Park or Limp Bizkit. Despite these surface changes, the songs themselves remain much the same,

and are in keeping with the vibrant, funky, modern-pop hybrids with which The Neptunes had made their name. The album also reveals Williams as a talented vocalist, with his smooth falsetto providing the focus of most of the songs.

The re-recorded *In Search Of . . .* earned much more positive reviews than the original version, but fell well short of the commercial success of many of the duo's productions as The Neptunes, stalling at Number 56 on the U.S. chart.

Miss E . . . So Addictive
Missy 'Misdemeanor' Elliott

East West 7559 62639 (U.S.A.) / Elektra 7559 62639 (U.K.)
Released May 2001

Alongside her mentor and regular co-producer Timbaland, Missy Elliott was one of the most influential and respected figures in hip-hop in the late 1990s and early 21st century.

Elliott's early work includes two U.S. Top Ten solo albums, *Supa Dupa Fly* and *Da Real World*, and collaborations with the likes of Aaliyah and Spice Girl Mel B. She began 2001 by producing the U.S. and U.K. Number One hit single 'Lady Marmalade,' a cover of the 1975 LaBelle hit by Pink, Christina Aguilera, Lil' Kim, and Maiya for the *Moulin Rouge* soundtrack. Elliott then unleashed her landmark single 'Get Ur Freak On,' a breathtaking collision of slick breakbeats, Middle Eastern instrumentation, and ultra-cool vocals. *Miss E . . . So Addictive* followed shortly thereafter and, like the single, confidently bridges the gap between cutting-edge dance music and smooth hip-hop. The album also confirms that, as well as being one of the hottest producers around, Elliott is also pretty faultless as a rapper. *Miss E . . . So Addictive* reached Number Two in the U.S.A. and became Elliott's first big hit in the U.K., charting at Number Ten.

Elliott scored further international hits with the album tracks '4 My People' and 'One Minute Man,' which features a cameo from the rapper Ludacris.

The sly line "I'm copywritten, so don't copy me," from 'Get Ur Freak On,' anticipated a rash of rap and hip-hop releases over the next year that were highly derivative of Elliott's and Timbaland's work. Not content to rest on her laurels, Elliott issued the equally impressive *Under Construction* barely a year later.

Songs In A Minor Alicia Keys

J Records / Arista 80813 20002 (U.S.A. & U.K.)
Released June 2001

A prodigiously talented vocalist and pianist, Keys studied briefly at Columbia University before signing a deal with Clive Davis at Arista.

So sure was Davis that Keys was a major new talent that, when Davis formed his own J Records in 1999, he insisted she follow him as one of the new label's flagship artists. Keys began work on her debut album early the following year in her native New York with producer Kerry 'Krucial' Brothers. The album was recorded with a host of talented session players as well as a handful of established stars, most impressively Isaac Hayes, who adds an electric piano part to 'Rock Wit U,' which was also included on the soundtrack to the remake of the movie *Shaft* (2000).

Songs In A Minor is a highly accomplished debut for a 19 year old, drawing equally on smooth 1970s soul, Prince's funky erotica, and the mid-1990s hip-hop of 2Pac Shakur and The Notorious B.I.G. Keys is clearly a talented singer, and manages to rein in the kind of vocal excesses that blight the recordings o so many of her contemporaries. She was immediately tagged as an important new star, the latest in a line of classic singer-songwriters. *Rolling Stone* magazine concluded that "many young female artists court the tweenie marke by exaggerating their girlish charms, but Alicia Keys sings for adults . . . we're only beginning to see the depth of her talent." *Songs In A Minor* has since sold over ten million copies worldwide, winning Keys three Grammy Awards and providing her with the international hit single 'Fallin'.'

■ *Main picture: Missy Elliott. Below: her regular co-producer, Timbaland.*

Continued from page 298

long after the file-sharing horse has bolted. It may be that they eventually persuade record buyers to move to the new medium, but the whole back catalog of recorded music history will still be readily available to anyone with a portable MP3 player.

The name MP3 is now applied generically to any compressed digital music file or system, but it really belongs to the original 'codec' – compression-decompression system – developed by Karlheinz Brandenburg and others at the Frauenhofer Institute in Germany. In 1977 Brandenburg joined a project that was looking at ways of compressing sound so that high-quality music could be sent down a telephone line. Their solution was to remove portions of the sound that are inaudible. (Brandenburg used quiet tracks, such as Suzanne Vega's 'Tom's Diner,' as test material, because flaws would be more apparent.) In 1989 Brandenburg was awarded a German patent for MP3 – the U.S. patent followed in 1996 – and set about developing playback software, though with no great success.

That came in 1997 when Tomislav Uzelac of Advanced Multimedia Products developed the AMP MP3 Playback Engine. Two university students, Justin Frankel and Dmitry Boldyrev, then ported AMP to Windows and created Winamp, which soon became widely available free over the internet. The business of 'ripping' and swapping tracks had begun, though it took the arrival of file-sharing software such as Napster before it really took off and the record industry belatedly woke up to what they saw as the threat of their own extinction.

Today, other compression systems are in use, including AAC/MP4 – The Frauenhofer Institute's own replacement for MP3 and Apple's choice for the iPod – and WMA, Microsoft's format intended for use with its Windows Media Player. What these new formats have in common – at the insistence, once again, of the record companies – is 'Digital Rights Management,' allowing the copyright owners to control how the files are used. Files downloaded from Apple's legal iTunes Music Store, for instance, have a built-in limit on the number of times they can be copied, and can only be used on five computers registered with Apple. Despite this, Apple had sold over 500 million songs by July 2005 – just 27 months after opening the first iTunes Music Store.

Much ink has been wasted on the change from physical music delivery to electronic delivery. The change is already being felt in two ways. In the first place, packaging ceases to be of consequence, but then many felt that the jacket died as an art form when the LP gave way to the nasty CD jewel-box. The second result is that artists can no longer lay down a default running order for their music and expect listeners to follow it. Though the iPod and other players will play music in the correct album order, they also shuffle and randomize playback at the touch of a button. Many listeners to digital files enjoy the serendipity that comes when your music is randomly selected from several thousand tracks you know you already like.

Perhaps this method of delivering music has a lot of advantages for pop. It throws attention back to the individual song, the individual track, for the first time since the 1960s. And that may be no bad thing, with Brian Wilson's stated ambition with *Pet Sounds* to create "an album with all good tracks" remaining an elusive goal for many artists.

2001

Gorillaz **Gorillaz**

Virgin 33748 (U.S.A.) / Parlophone 531138 (U.K.)
Released June 2001 (U.S.A.) / March 2001 (U.K.)

The brainchild of Blur's Damon Albarn, Gorillaz was the world's first cartoon hip-hop pop group.

After recording four U.K. Number One hit albums with Blur in the 1990s, Albarn conceived the idea of Gorillaz in 1999 with cartoonist Jamie Hewitt, best known for the cult comic-book series *Tank Girl*. While Hewitt created the four-piece animated group, Albarn sought out a team of musical collaborators, the nucleus of which consisted of producer Dan 'The Automator' Nakamura, DJ Kid Koala, and rapper Del Tha Funky Homosapien, who had all previously worked together – with Albarn – as Deltron 3030. The album also features contributions from former Talking Heads Tina Weymouth and Chris Frantz.

Sonically, *Gorillaz* builds on the futuristic hip-hop of Deltron 3030's eponymous debut (2000), adding elements of dub, 2-Tone, and Albarn's knack for a catchy pop hook. The album reached the Top 20 on both sides of the Atlantic – giving Albarn his first true taste of mainstream success in the U.S.A. – while 'Clint Eastwood,' '19-2000,' and 'Rock The House' were all U.K. hit singles.

The musicians involved originally attempted to keep their identities a secret, but the music press soon got wind of who was involved. That didn't stop the group performing live behind a large screen, on to which their animated alter egos were projected. Albarn next refocused his energies on Blur – who issued their strongest album to date, *Think Tank*, in 2003 – before recording a second Gorillaz album, *Demon Days*, in 2005.

■ *Gorillaz perform live at the 2002 Brit Awards at Earls Court, in London, England. The musicians played behind screens, on to which images of the cartoon band were projected.*

White Blood Cells The White Stripes

Sympathy For The Record Industry SFTRI 660 (U.S.A. & U.K.)
Released July 2001

The White Stripes were at the forefront of a new wave of pared-down, retro rock groups charged with reinvigorating guitar-based music in the early 2000s.

The group, unusually, is a blues-based, bass-less duo, made up of guitarist-vocalist Jack White and drummer Meg White, both of whom stick to a strict dress code of red, white, and black. Adding to their quirky appeal was the pair's initial claim to be siblings, though the *Detroit Free Press* soon discovered that they are, in fact, a divorced couple, and that Jack had taken Meg's surname. (Despite this, he still introduces his ex-wife on stage as "my big sister.")

The White Stripes' sound is an electrified update of the early blues of Blind Willie McTell or Robert Johnson, with a hint of late-1960s psychedelia. *White Blood Cells* was the group's third album, and was cut in the winter of 2001 at Easley-McCain Recording in Memphis. With its ancient tube amplifiers, vintage microphones, and clunky, analog tape machines, Easley-McCain was the perfect venue for Jack to indulge his love of pre-digital recording equipment. While a White Stripes on-stage performance is the picture of minimalism, *White Blood Cells* does make some concessions to modern, multitrack recording, as several songs are underpinned by Hammond organ, while others are embellished by piano and over-dubbed vocal harmonies. Though never a huge chart hit, *White Blood Cells* caused quite a stir on its release in the U.K., with some critics going so far as to say that Jack White was the greatest guitarist since Jimi Hendrix. A single, 'Hotel Yorba,' reached the U.K. Top 30.

Is This It The Strokes

RCA 68101 (U.S.A.) / Rough Trade RTRADE CD/LP 30 (U.K.)
Released September 2001

The Strokes were the most successful of a new wave of garage-rock groups to emerge during the early 2000s.

Vocalist and songwriter Julian Casablancas – son of the Elite modeling agency CEO John Casablancas – guitarist Nick Valensi, and drummer Fab Moretti started playing together in 1998 after meeting at the exclusive Dwight School in Manhattan. Bassist Nikolai Fraiture and guitarist Albert Hammond Jr – whose singer-songwriter father, also named Albert, penned the hits 'It Never Rains In Southern California' and 'The Air That I Breathe' – joined in 1999.

In 2001 the *New Musical Express* (U.K.) placed The Strokes at the head of its "new rock revolution," alongside a number of other New York groups and Detroit duo The White Stripes. While they did succeed in making their home city the epicenter of cool guitar-based music for the next few years, The Strokes lacked the musical innovations of their forebears, notably The Velvet Underground and Television, to whom their sound was so indebted. Given a spacious, uncluttered sheen by producer Gordon Raphael, *Is This It* reached Number Two in the U.K. – where The Strokes became the most hyped new band since Oasis in the mid 1990s – and spawned a pair of British hit singles, 'Hard To Explain' and 'Last Nite.' The album was less successful in the U.S.A., where it stalled at Number 74. Issued in the aftermath of the World Trade Center terrorist attacks, the U.S. edition of *Is This It* omits the scathing 'New York City Cops,' and opts for an abstract, psychedelic cover instead of the mildly controversial gloved-hand-on-naked-buttock U.K. edition.

2002

Original Pirate Material The Streets

Atlantic 93181 (U.S.A.) / Locked On 0927 43568 (U.K.)
Released October 2002 (U.S.A.) / March 2002 (U.K.)

Boy In Da Corner Dizzee Rascal

Matador Records OLE600 (U.S.A.) / XL Recordings XL150 (U.K.)
Released July 2003

While U.S. rap and hip-hop has sold strongly in Britain since the late 1980s, there was no viable homegrown response until the emergence of the U.K. garage scene in the early 2000s.

U.K. garage is a loose term to describe sped-up drum & bass rhythms overlaid with spoken or sung vocals. After a clutch of hit singles by other artists, The Streets' *Original Pirate Material* became the genre's first big critical and commercial success in the albums market.

The Streets is the recording pseudonym of Mike Skinner, a native of Birmingham, England, a city not particularly well known for its hip-hop stars. Recorded, like all of his music, on a home computer, *Original Pirate Material* builds on the musical template of fast, stuttering U.K.-garage beats by adding elements of the likes The Specials and Blur.

Where his predecessors So Solid Crew's gritty, inner-city caricatures suggested they had listened to too much mid-1990s gangsta rap, *Original Pirate Material* provides a more realistic snapshot of urban British life in the early 21st century. Skinner's half-spoken, half-rapped lyrics reveal all manner of seemingly mundane but captivating details, from drunkenly playing computer games to going out for Indian takeout food, while on 'The Irony Of It All' Skinner and a friend debate the relative merits of alcohol over cannabis. The Streets earned a mainstream following in the U.K. with the successful singles 'Let's Push Things Forward' and 'Don't Mug Yourself,' while the album was a cult hit in the U.S.A.

Several months after the release of *Original Pirate Material* came 'I Luv U,' the debut single by the 17-year-old Dizzee Rascal (aka Dylan Mills). Like Skinner, the London-born MC and producer recorded the single and the following year's full-length album *Boy In Da Corner* on his home computer, utilizing skills picked up at a community music project. *Boy In Da Corner* is a much more volatile, moody album than The Streets' debut, and has a sparser, grittier production highly evocative of its gestation. Dizzee's vocal style has more in common with traditional rap than Skinner's, but still has a distinct Britishness to it.

Dizzee Rascal had a U.K. chart hit with the single 'Fix Up Look Sharp' from the album, which won the 2003 Mercury Music Prize. Not only is he far and away the youngest recipient of the award to date, his is also the most outré, cutting-edge album to win it, making his victory all the more impressive. In 2004 *Boy In Da Corner* was licensed by Matador Records for release in the U.S.A., where it has received positive reviews but failed to make any great waves commercially.

2002

Come Away With Me **Norah Jones**

Blue Note 32088 (U.S.A.) / Parlophone 5386092 (U.K.)
Released February 2002

Norah Jones was one of the most startling breakout successes of the early 2000s, scoring a huge international hit and countless Grammys with her debut.

Come Away With Me is an effortless blend of folk, jazz, and blues, accentuated by Jones's cool vocal delivery – which drew comparisons with Nina Simone and Billie Holiday – and a flair for concise, catchy melodies.

Jones is the daughter of the world's most famous sitar player, Ravi Shankar, but was brought up by her mother in Texas. She studied jazz piano at the University Of North Texas for two years before moving to New York in 1999 at the age of 20. She originally intended only to stay for the summer, but soon got hooked on the city's musical nightlife, playing in folksy coffee houses and jazz clubs. A demo tape of songs written with guitarist Jesse Harris and bassist Lee Alexander caught the attention of the famous jazz label Blue Note, who signed Jones in early 2001. She spent the first half of the year honing her songwriting and performing talents before commencing work on her debut album at Sorcerer Sound and Allaire Studios in New York. Production duties were split between Craig Street and the legendary Arif Mardin, who had previously worked with a galaxy of stars, including Dusty Springfield and Aretha Franklin. There are also a number of impressive guest musicians – particularly given that the album is Jones's debut – including jazz guitarist Bill Frisell and drummer Brian Blade.

Come Away With Me is a remarkably assured first effort. Though the overall feel is one of gentle, acoustic-guitar pop, there are elements of jazz, folk, soul, blues, and country within the songs. Unlike the equally prodigious Alicia Keys, Jones eschews contemporary pop production in favor of a self-contained, timeless sound. The songs are split between covers – notably an arresting rendition of Hank Williams's 'Cold Cold Heart' – and original material written by Jones with Harris and Alexander. These include

the moody, subtle title track and the lighter, languid 'Don't Know Why,' a Top 30 hit in the U.S.A. and Britain.

Audiences took to Jones's album almost immediately, confounding all expectations of what was assumed might be a modest crossover success, not a worldwide smash hit. *Come Away With Me* topped the charts across Europe and in the U.S.A., and has sold over 18 million copies. Jones cleaned up at the 2002 Grammy Awards, taking home six trophies including Record, Song, and Album Of The Year.

Jones's success opened the doors for a number of other performers with a similar cross-genre sound. Perhaps surprisingly, they have tended mostly to hail from Britain. Most notable of this new breed of jazz-based youngsters is Jamie Cullum, who rose to fame in 2003 on the back of his *Twentysomething* debut. Among the others were Katie Melua, Amy Winehouse, and Joss Stone, the latter of whom emerged at the age of 16 in 2004 with an astoundingly mature voice and an acclaimed album, *Mind, Body And Soul*.

Yankee Hotel Foxtrot Wilco

Nonesuch 7559-79669 (U.S.A. & U.K.)
Released April 2002

The fourth Wilco album was much more than just a triumph over the difficult circumstances surrounding its creation and release: it was the metamorphosis of the rootsy Americana alt.country genre from caterpillar into butterfly.

Wilco's lynchpin, Jeff Tweedy, first attracted attention as a member of Uncle Tupelo, a Belleville, Illinois, high-school band dedicated to the notion of blending their love of punk rock with their equal affection for traditional American roots music. After four acclaimed but financially unrewarding albums, Uncle Tupelo splintered, with various other members going on to become guiding lights in such bands as Son Volt, Bottle Rockets, and The Gourds, while Tweedy formed Wilco. Wilco's 1995 debut, *AM*, was unimpressive but, by the time of 1999's *Summer Teeth*, they had quantum-leaped to an album that skillfully combined elements of classic country with the worlds of avant-garde, ambient, and psychedelic music.

> **"THE RECORD NAMED ITSELF. ONE THING THAT INTRIGUED ME ABOUT THE STATIONS THAT BROADCAST IN CODE WAS THE RANDOMNESS OF COMMUNICATION, THE SAME THING THAT ALWAYS INTRIGUED ME ABOUT MUSIC AND PUTTING OUT RECORDS."**
>
> *JEFF TWEEDY*

Work on *Yankee Hotel Foxtrot* started optimistically in Chicago, on a Reprise Records budget of $85,000, but Tweedy's ongoing search for new avenues of musical expression led to conflicts with multi-instrumentalist Jay Bennet and drummer Ken Coomer, both of whom quit during recording. The kind of ideas that disturbed the more traditionally inclined Bennet would probably have been the decision, during the recording of 'Poor Places,' to set up instruments that could play themselves – including a drum machine, a keyboard with several keys taped down, and a guitar strummed by an electric fan – and then just let them roll. The song ends with a disembodied sample from a short-wave radio transmission of a woman reciting the phonetic code-words "yankee hotel foxtrot," which gave the album its title.

Tweedy has revealed that another technique involved recording songs with standard band arrangements and then, "just to see how sturdy the melody was," breaking them down and rebuilding them, sometimes adding totally random noises. "We worked along film-editing lines," he explains, "trying to think about pacing and the overall shape, trying to make something that started one place and ended in another."

The album was scheduled for release during September of 2001, and an excited media buzz was already building when suddenly everything changed. "Initially there seemed to be some excitement about the songs we were sending in," remembers Tweedy, "but once we got serious about making the record and shaping it into what it became, one of the comments from them was, 'It keeps getting worse and worse.'" Essentially, the record company couldn't hear any hits and demanded changes. Instead, the band stuck to its guns and negotiated a release from the Reprise contract, which included buying the rights to the album. Shortly afterward it became available on Wilco's website, and rapidly notched up 30,000 hits.

Several companies, Reprise among them, were now clamoring to sign the band. The eventual winners were Nonesuch, and on release the album drew rave reviews and debuted at Number 13 with an immediate sale of 56,000 copies. Since then it has earned two Grammies, much to the chagrin of Reprise, which is, like Nonesuch, a division of the Time-Warner group. Tweedy takes understandable delight in pointing out to interviewers that this means Time-Warner has paid for *Yankee Hotel Foxtrot* twice.

Best Of Both Worlds R Kelly And Jay-Z

Universal 586783 (U.S.A.) / Jive 9223512 (U.K.)
Released March 2002

Expectations were high for *Best Of Both Worlds*, a collaboration between two of the most successful urban-music performers of recent times.

The two stars first collaborated in 2000, when Jay-Z guested on a remix of Kelly's 'Fiesta.' It was a hit, and prompted them to start work on a full album together the following year. *Best Of Both Worlds* finds a pretty formulaic middle ground between both artists' work: Jay-Z raps the verses, Kelly sings the choruses. Though at times the performances sound half-hearted, where the album works Jay-Z and Kelly are a perfect match, particularly on the single 'Get This Money.' Both had hopes that it might end up as the biggest-selling hip-hop album ever made. In the event, *Best Of Both Worlds* didn't reach its potential and falls well short of either Kelly's or Jay-Z's best work.

The release of the album was overshadowed by a string of allegations about Kelly's sexual relationships with a number of underage girls. Radio stations banned his songs and some former fans organized protests against him, which did little to help the album's commercial performance. It debuted at Number Two in the U.S.A., but quickly fell out of the charts. Undeterred by its poor performance, which in no way equals the multiplatinum successes of either artist's solo work, Jay-Z and Kelly reconvened for *Unfinished Business* in 2004. That, too, failed both critically and commercially, while Kelly left a co-headlining tour amid rumors of bad blood between the duo.

■ *Below: a still from I Am Trying To Break Your Heart, Sam Jones's documentary movie about the making of Wilco's Yankee Hotel Foxtrot. Inset: the cover of the DVD edition.*

2002

Justified **Justin Timberlake**

Jive 41823 (U.S.A.) / 9224632 (U.K.)
Released November 2002

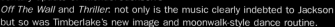

After recording the two fastest-selling albums ever in the U.S.A. as a member of *Nsync, there was perhaps little left for Justin Timberlake to prove. Nonetheless, 18 months after the release of *Celebrity* he launched his solo career with a more mature sound and image.

Justified was recorded in the main with production wizards The Neptunes. It is, essentially, a 21st-century update of Michael Jackson's *Off The Wall* and *Thriller*: not only is the music clearly indebted to Jackson but so was Timberlake's new image and moonwalk-style dance routine.

Thematically, the album has a 'before and after the breakup' air, which most commentators assumed must surely allude to the end of Timberlake's romantic relationship with fellow pop starlet Britney Spears, with whom he had starred in *The New Mickey Mouse Club* a decade earlier. Such suspicions were confirmed when the promo video for the single 'Cry Me A River' featured Timberlake singing to a Britney look-alike.

Regardless, this was the album that made Timberlake a star in his own right rather than just being Britney's ex or the guy from *Nsync. *Justified* peaked at Number Two on the U.S. chart and provided three further hit singles: 'Like I Love You,' 'Rock Your Body,' and 'Senorita.' It also won a Grammy for Best Pop Vocal Album.

Timberlake's former bandmates fared less well as solo performers. JC Chasez's *Schizophrenic* was a U.S. hit, but paled in comparison with *Justified* both in terms of sales and artistic merit.

2003

Dangerously In Love **Beyoncé**

Sony 86386 (U.S.A.) / Columbia 5093952 (U.K.)
Released May 2003

Like Justin Timberlake the year before, in 2003 Beyoncé Knowles, formerly of Destiny's Child, made the successful transition from teen-pop group member to solo star.

Destiny's Child had been one of the most commercially successful female pop acts of the late 1990s and early 2000s. *The Writing's On The Wall* (1999) and *Survivor* (2001) both sold in extraordinary quantities, while the group had a string of international hit singles including 'Bills, Bills, Bills,' 'Independent Women Part 1,' and 'Bootylicious.' In 2002 the three group members announced a desire to pursue solo careers. Always the focal point of the band, Beyoncé's has been by far the most successful.

Dangerously In Love keeps to pretty much the same formula as *Survivor*, but the songs sound less throwaway. Smooth soul ballads vie for space with 1970s-style disco-inflected dance tracks, provided by an impressive think tank of contemporary producers, including Missy Elliott and OutKast's Big Boi. The album topped the charts in the U.S.A. and the U.K. and provided a huge international hit single, 'Crazy In Love,' on which Beyoncé duets with her beau, the rapper Jay-Z. (The pair had previously collaborated on his ''03 Bonnie and Clyde.') A year later Beyoncé reunited with Destiny's Child for what is presumably the group's swansong, *Destiny Fulfilled*. It has been alleged that the group's other two members drafted an agreement to ensure that Beyoncé didn't stand centerstage in any press photographs during the promotion of the album, suggesting that this might not have been the most amicable of reunions.

Speakerboxxx / The Love Below **OutKast**

La Face 53022 (U.S.A.) / Arista 82976 52905 2 (U.K.)
Released September 2003

Essentially a pair of solo albums by the group's two members, *Speakerboxxx / The Love Below* contains some of the most innovative and forward-thinking hip-hop of recent years.

Big Boi's *Speakerboxxx* pushes out the boundaries of contemporary rap with hard-edged techno production, while Andre 3000's *The Love Below* is in a melting pot of soul, funk, rock, jazz, and hip-hop.

After recording a trio of acclaimed albums in the 1990s, OutKast became a bona fide pop phenomenon with the release of *Stankonia* (2000) and its resplendent singles 'BOB' and 'Ms Jackson,' a U.S. Number One hit. (The Ms Jackson in question is actually the mother of the singer Erykah Badu, with whom Andre 3000 had a child in 1997.) The retrospective compilation album *Big Boi And Dre Present . . . OutKast* (2001) effectively drew a line under the first phase of the group's career, as it was subsequently announced that the duo was working separately on what were perceived to be solo albums.

In fact, the pair decided to issue these two very different albums in one package, under the unifying OutKast banner. Big Boi's *Speakerboxxx* is the more conventional of the two, but is still leaps and bounds ahead of most of his rap contemporaries. Musically, the album is built around a blend of retro drum-machine sounds and cutting-edge electronic rhythms, overlaid with deep bass pulses and funky guitar flourishes. For the most part, the songs retain an upbeat, post-disco feel, though in 'War' the album does contain a rare criticism from an American artist of the Bush administration's War On Terror: "Operation Anaconda: ask yourself, was it full of bleeps and blunders? / Did they ever find Osama? And why the fuck did Daniel Pearl have to pay the price of his life?" *Speakerboxxx* also contains the only direct collaboration between Big Boi and Andre 3000, 'Ghetto Musick.'

The album's other disk is a completely different animal, and one that makes a mockery of genre categorization. *The Love Below* begins with a sweeping orchestral title track, before 'Love Hater' somehow bridges the gap between psychedelic funk and swinging 1950s jazz. Unusually for a supposed hip-hop album, *The Love Below* is laced with acoustic guitars and warm, vintage synthesizer parts. The rest of the album takes in soulful electro-pop ('She Lives In My Lap'), a touching, piano-led tribute to Andre's mother ('She's Alive'), a fuzz bass-led duet with the equally eccentric Kelis ('Dracula's Wedding'), and a restrained collaboration with Norah Jones ('Take Off Your Cool'). *The Love Below* also featured one of the best and most recognizable singles of 2003, 'Hey Ya!'

Speakerboxxx / The Love Below was the first OutKast album to top the U.S. albums chart – the group's three previous efforts all stalled at Number Two – and reached the Top Ten in the U.K. The album provided four international hit singles, the aforementioned 'Ghetto Musick' and 'Hey Ya!' plus Big Boi's 'The Way You Move' and Andre's 'Roses.' The album also won the duo three Grammys, including Album Of The Year.

■ **Main picture: Beyoncé struts her stuff on stage in 2003. Inset: Big Boi (left) and Andre 3000 of OutKast.**

2003

Permission To Land The Darkness

Atlantic 60817 (U.S.A.) / Must Destory 5046 67452 (U.K.)
Released July 2003

Out of nowhere, The Darkness made the oft-derided sound and image of late-1970s hard rock fashionable again.

Written off at first as a novelty act, The Darkness began to look more and more like the real thing as *Permission To Land* climbed to the top of the British charts and became a cult hit in the U.S.A.

The Darkness formed on New Year's Eve 1999 in Lowestoft, England – a small coastal town not exactly known for its musical heritage – by vocalist-guitarist Justin Hawkins and his guitar-playing younger brother Dan. Adding bassist Frankie Poullain and drummer Ed Graham, the group built up a reputation as a highly entertaining live act. The Darkness drew unapologetically on the big hair, spandex, falsetto vocals, and wild guitar soloing of Queen and Aerosmith, and soon signed a deal with the independent label Must Destroy. The group was often pilloried by a picky music press, but won over huge swathes of the British public with the singles 'I Believe In A Thing Called Love' and 'Get Your Hands Off My Woman.'

After a triumphant, televised performance at the *Glastonbury Festival*, *Permission To Land* topped the U.K. albums chart and stayed in its upper reaches for much of the next year. While some elements might have been included self-consciously for entertainment purposes, the album is underpinned by fine musicianship and catchy songwriting. *Permission To Land* became harder to write off as a joke when it entered the U.S. Top 40 in early 2004.

Elephant The White Stripes

V2 27184 (U.S.A. & U.K.)
Released April 2003

Rock history is littered with bands who disappeared into 48-track high-tech studios for years of overdubbing, only to end up with a record that couldn't match its predecessor cut in a fortnight on 16-track.

The White Stripes didn't fall into that trap, however. Instead the duo recorded the follow-up to their breakthrough album *White Blood Cells* in ten days in the sparse, retro environment of Toe Rag Studios in east London, England. As Jack White put it: "Having a huge budget or unlimited time or tracks to make an album, all that opportunity robs you of a lot of creativity, because you're not focused or confined. We purposefully confined ourselves to help us be more focused."

Elephant doesn't deviate much from the template of *White Blood Cells*, but then it doesn't need to. Each of the 14 songs is dispatched in The White Stripes' trademark economical garage-blues style. The only surprise element is the multitracked vocal part on 'There's No Home For You Here,' which brings to mind Queen's 'Bohemian Rhapsody.' 'Seven Nation Army' opens the set with what sounds like a bass, but is actually just Jack White's guitar played through an octave pedal. The album also includes the primal, staccato 'Hardest Button To Button' and 'It's True That We Love One Another,' a duet with cult British singer Holly Golightly on which Jack mocks the endless media speculation about the group.

Elephant topped the U.K. albums chart and provided The White Stripes with their first widespread success in the U.S.A., where it peaked at Number Six. It was named Best Alternative Music Album at the 2003 Grammy Awards, while 'Seven Nation Army' was chosen as the year's Best Rock Song.

2004

Smile **Brian Wilson**

Nonesuch 79846 (U.S.A. & U.K.)
Released September 2004

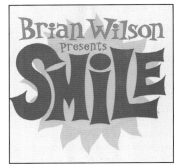

Brian Wilson's *Smile* – a "teenage symphony to God" conceived in 1966, but not completed or issued until 2004 – had by far the longest gestation of any popular-music album.

For decades it was *the* great lost work of the rock era, a supposed masterpiece that might have surpassed even The Beatles' *Sgt Pepper* had Wilson's group, The Beach Boys, released it on schedule in 1967.

Wilson sought out a lyricist to collaborate with him and help him realize his ideas for *Smile*, as he had done for *Pet Sounds* in 1966. He chose Van Dyke Parks, a songwriter and producer who, like Wilson, was considered to be something of a musical prodigy. He and Parks started to write together in May 1966 at the piano Wilson had situated in an indoor sandbox at his Los Angeles home – installed to evoke the feeling of being at the beach. The songs they wrote were intended to represent a journey through the history and musical heritage of the U.S.A.

The prototype for *Smile* was 'Good Vibrations,' Wilson's first "pocket symphony" – as he called it – recorded during the late spring and summer of 1966. Wilson had pioneered his 'modular' recording technique on 'Good Vibrations,' taping the different parts of the song separately before piecing the various sections together into a seamless whole. He intended to take this methodology a step further with *Smile*, and create an entire album out of repeated musical themes and song fragments, in a manner that often evoked his favorite piece of music, Gershwin's 'Rhapsody In Blue.'

After completing 'Good Vibrations' Wilson started work on *Smile* in July at Gold Star Studios and Sunset Sound in Los Angeles. He spent the rest of the year and the first few months of 1967 working through such songs as 'Wind Chimes,' 'Our Prayer,' and 'Wonderful' with a cast of talented session players and, occasionally, the other Beach Boys.

The wider world got its first taste of *Smile* on April 25th 1967 when a staggering solo piano performance of 'Surf's Up' by Wilson aired as part of the CBS documentary *Inside Pop: The Rock Revolution*. By this stage, however, *Smile* had begun to fall apart at the seams. Obsessed with the idea of creating the perfect pop album before The Beatles got there, Wilson scrapped and restarted songs repeatedly. Deadlines came and went. Much of the album had been recorded, but still lay in the form of isolated fragments.

On May 19th, after ten months of sessions, Wilson stopped working on *Smile*. Rock historians have long since discussed his reasons. What is clear is that Wilson suffered some kind of mental breakdown, likely aggravated by his intake of hallucinogenic drugs. Notoriously thin-skinned, he was also wounded by the reluctance of the other Beach Boys, in particular Mike Love, to engage fully with a project they found too weird and avant-garde. A major sticking point was the 'Fire' section of 'Mrs O'Leary's Cow.' Recording that wonderfully evocative piece, Wilson insisted the musicians wear firemen's helmets as they played. Such was his mental state at the time that, on hearing that fires had broken out nearby, he scrapped the tapes, fearing that his music had the power to burn down buildings.

On June 1st The Beatles issued the epochal *Sgt Pepper*, and Brian was defeated. He would never again attempt to record music of such complexity or magnitude as *Smile* with The Beach Boys. Instead, the group released *Smiley Smile* in September, a hastily re-recorded, watered-down version of the album. Beset by manic depression and substance abuse, Wilson began to withdraw from The Beach Boys and led a life of semi-seclusion for much of the next three decades.

Over the years, several more *Smile*-era songs found release on The Beach Boys albums *20/20* (1969) and *Surf's Up* (1971), and bootleg recordings of others began to surface, further fueling the mythology surrounding Wilson's lost masterpiece. The 1993 boxed set *Good Vibrations: Thirty Years Of The Beach Boys* included 30 minutes of previously unheard *Smile* recordings that offer tantalizing glimpses of what might have been.

In 1998, to the surprise of many, a rehabilitated Wilson embarked on his first regular live performances since 1965. His 2001 tour centered on a rapturously received live replication of *Pet Sounds*. Two years later he announced an even more surprising project: a live *Smile*. Few would have predicted that Wilson could ever revisit the unfinished album that, it seemed, had caused him so much emotional turmoil. For years he refused to speak about *Smile* and had often denied that any tapes of the sessions still existed. In the spring of 2003, however, he began to reassemble the songs into a cohesive whole with the help of Darian Sahanaja, keyboardist in his current band, and Van Dyke Parks, who provided new lyrics to the incomplete sections.

The live *Smile* premiered at the Royal Festival Hall in London in February 2004 and was met with unanimous awe. Two months later Wilson and his band finally recorded *Smile* at Sunset Sound, the studio he had used in the 1960s to create numerous Beach Boys classics. This time the songs were completed in five days, between April 13th and 17th. The album was recorded and mixed by Wilson, Sahanaja, and Mark Linett, who had previously been responsible for compiling the 1966–7 tapes for the *Good Vibrations* boxed set.

Above all else, the release of *Smile* marks a personal triumph for Wilson, after 38 years able to complete his masterwork. Inevitably it lacks the zeitgeist in which it was originally conceived, as the world is a very different place today than it was in that departed decade. However, if it is not quite the album it might have been – Wilson's voice, at 62, is not what it was at 24, and the other vocalists can't match the uncanny harmonic cohesion of The Beach Boys – it does contain note-perfect renditions of some of the finest compositions by the man many consider to be one of the greatest songwriters of the 20th century. For that alone, and given its rich history, *Smile* is an important entry into the canon of popular-music albums. It remains a flawed masterpiece, as it likely would have been had it seen release in 1967.

■ **Brian Wilson gives Smile** *its first public airing at the Royal Festival Hall in London, England, on February 20th 2004.*

2004

How To Dismantle An Atomic Bomb **U2**

Interscope Records 000361302 (U.S.A.) / Island CIDU214 (U.K.)
Released November 2004

U2's 11th album, *How To Dismantle An Atomic Bomb*, was accompanied by more promotional gimmicks than any album before it.

Capitalizing on the growing popularity of MP3 technology, the group and Apple Computer, Inc. launched a special edition U2 iPod to coincide with the album's release. The record itself was also made available in a variety of formats, including a deluxe boxed-set edition.

Musically, *How To Dismantle An Atomic Bomb* shares the back-to-basics sound of its predecessor, the multiple Grammy Award-winning *All That You Can't Leave Behind* (2000). U2 had spent the 1990s experimenting with cutting-edge production techniques and dance-music rhythms, resulting in a sequence of uneven and less commercially viable albums. However, in 2000 the band returned to the stripped-down, guitar-led sound that had served the group so well during the 1980s, resulting in sales of more than 11 million copies of *All That You Can't Leave Behind*.

U2 consolidated its position as "biggest band in the world" with *How To Dismantle An Atomic Bomb*, a British and U.S. chart topper. The album is

U2's sparsest sounding since the early 1980s, but is given a sharp, polished sound by a mouthwatering assortment of producers, including Brian Eno, Flood, Nellee Hooper, Steve Lillywhite, Chris Thomas, and Daniel Lanois, who also plays pedal steel and mandolin. Given the presence of six very different producers, the album is never allowed to become repetitive, and just about manages to hang together as a cohesive unit. Its highlights include the raw, post-punk of lead-off single 'Vertigo' and 'Sometimes You Can't Make It On Your Own,' Bono's heartfelt tribute to his recently deceased father. On other songs, however, his well-meaning if somewhat glib political rhetoric can begin to grate, particularly on 'Love And Peace Or Else.'

On its release in November 2004 *How To Dismantle An Atomic Bomb* was made available in four different physical formats, in addition to the digital download. Alongside the standard CD and vinyl copies were a limited-edition CD plus DVD version and a special boxed set. The DVD – also included in the boxed set – features studio footage of the making of the album and live performances of four songs. For the U2 completist, the boxed set, which sold for three times the price of a normal CD, is packaged as a lavish, hardcover book, complete with drawings and paintings by the band members and illustrated lyrics.

U2 wasn't the first group to present an album in this format – notable antecedents include Pearl Jam's *Vitalogy* (1994), which included extracts from old medical texts, and Radiohead's *Amnesiac* (2001), made to look like an old library book – but was certainly the first, and, to date, only, group to have its own special-edition iPod. More expensive than a standard iPod, though with the same hard-disk capacity, the U2 model is housed in a distinctive black case with red controls, in striking contrast to the familiar all-white finish.

The group also made available its complete discography – 446 songs – as a digital boxed set through the iTunes Music Store.

Scissor Sisters **Scissor Sisters**

Universal 000277202 (U.S.A.) / Polydor 9866058 (U.K.)
Released February 2004

Something strange happened in the mid 2000s: modern groups began to achieve considerable success by mining music from the 1970s and 1980s in a way that would, a few years previously, have been met with derision.

First came the British group The Darkness, which drew on the flamboyance of late-1970s heavy rock. Then Scissor Sisters emerged from the other side of the Atlantic a year later, with an Elton John-inspired sound that wouldn't have been out of place in a 1970s New York gay club.

Fronted by vocalists Jake Shears and Ana Mantronic, the group's early live performances resembled drag shows. Aside from a cover of Pink Floyd's 'Comfortably Numb,' all of the songs on the group's self-produced eponymous debut are originals, though most sound as though they could have been released in the 1970s or early 1980s. Along the way Elton, The Bee Gees, Frankie Goes To Hollywood, and George Michael are referenced as *Scissor Sisters* veers from epic rock balladry to shimmering disco pop. Perhaps the album's strongest quality is its unstinting enthusiasm: the group's energy and total lack of cynicism shines through each of the 11 tracks. *Scissor Sisters* spent the best part of 2004 in the upper reaches of the U.K. albums chart, while 'Mary,' 'Take Your Mama,' and 'Filthy / Gorgeous' were all British hits.

Sweat **Nelly**

Universal 33140 (U.S.A.) / Mercury 9863935 (U.K.)
Released September 2004

Suit **Nelly**

Universal 33160 (U.S.A.) / Mercury 9863936 (U.K.)
Released September 2004

Abattoir Blues / The Lyre Of Orpheus
Nick Cave & The Bad Seeds

Anti 86729 (U.S.A.) / Mute STUMM233 (U.K.)
Released October 2004

In the fall of 2004 two very different artists released two-album sets that demonstrate different sides of their musical personalities.

Nick Cave's *Abattoir Blues* and *The Lyre Of Orpheus* were packaged together for the price of a single disk, while Nelly's *Sweat* and *Suit* were sold separately. Both are, in essence, an extension of the double album, which, in rock music, has traditionally symbolized a big artistic statement by an 'important' band. In the mid 2000s it became a similar signifier in hip-hop, with acts such as OutKast and R Kelly opting to release expansive, two-disk sets. Nelly took the process a step further, issuing a pair of albums on the same day in 2004. He had risen to prominence several years earlier with the albums *Country*

Dear Heather Leonard Cohen

Columbia 92891 (U.S.A.) / 5147682 (U.K.)
Released October 2004

When Leonard Cohen's debut album appeared in 1967 no one would have predicted that the soberly dressed 30-something would be in for the long haul.

Already an established poet and novelist, surely this was at best a flirtation with song, at worst a vanity project? Yet here he is, nearly 40 years later, one of the few performers of his generation still sufficiently vibrant artistically to attract new listeners.

On *Dear Heather* Cohen ruminates on his familiar themes of sex, mortality, and religion in a voice reduced to a husky bass growl by decades of red wine and cigarettes. Often he just speaks the lyrics, leaving the singing to the handful of women who co-wrote and produced the album with him. At times he rouses himself to a few grizzled notes, his sense of melody still sufficiently sharp that even with such limited vocal resources he is able to fashion some memorable tunes.

By the mid 1980s, on *I'm Your Man*, Cohen had set aside his familiar nylon-string guitar to embrace synthesizer technology. *Dear Heather* finds him integrating the two approaches into a warm, seasoned sound that makes an unobtrusive backdrop for what everyone who buys a Cohen album really wants to hear: that fathoms-deep voice gravely intoning some of the best lyrics in pop music.

The lazy stereotype of Cohen's music is that it's depressing, but that's simply not true. Serious, maybe, but it's seriousness with a glint in the eye, shot through with many a droll aside.

The College Dropout Kanye West

Roc-A-Fella 20300 (U.S.A.) / 9862061 (U.K.)
Released February 2004

Before launching his solo career as a rapper, Kanye West was – and remains – one of the most sought-after hip-hop producers of the early 2000s.

West has to date been responsible for hits by the likes of Jay-Z ('Izzo (HOVA)' and ''03 Bonnie And Clyde'), Ludacris ('Stand Up'), and Alicia Keys ('You Don't Know My Name'). Stylistically, West's production owes a debt to the likes of Run-DMC in the way that he creates new beats out of snatches of recognizable songs, from The Doors to The Jackson 5. West's own solo career was repeatedly stalled by the success of his work as a producer and by a near-fatal car accident in October 2002. West reflects on this incident on his first solo single, 'Through The Wire,' a big hit on U.S. radio in late 2003.

West finally unleashed his long-awaited, self-produced debut album early the following year. His productions had by this point become ubiquitous on the U.S. charts, which lent a useful familiarity to his solo work and helped send *The College Dropout* straight in at Number Two in the U.S. albums chart. Unlike many of his rap peers, West does not draw on – or, in the case of some, invent – a past of poverty and violence, instead imbuing his songs with an Everyman charm and a cheery sense of humor. (How many other hip-hop artists would wear a bear suit on the cover of their debut album?) Issued on Jay-Z's Roc-A-Fella label, the album includes the hits 'Jesus Walks' and 'All Fall Down.'

Grammar and *Nellyville*, with its huge international hit single 'Hot In Herre.' Unlike many of his more aggressive rap contemporaries, Nelly's vocal delivery is smooth and laidback, as, generally speaking, is his music, which helped him develop a strong mainstream pop following. Aware of his cross-genre appeal, Nelly opted to divide his new material into two themed albums in 2004. *Sweat* is the more up-tempo of the two, containing 13 songs ripe for club play. *Suit*, meanwhile, is a slowed down, sensual collection. Across both albums Nelly collaborates with some of the biggest stars of pop and rap, from Snoop Dogg and Missy Elliott to Christina Aguilera and The Neptunes. While from an artistic standpoint it could be argued that Nelly might have been better advised to put together one single, concise, yet more diverse set out of these two, the commercial sense of issuing simultaneous albums is hard to fault: *Suit* and *Sweat* entered the U.S. albums chart at Numbers One and Two respectively.

Nick Cave's *Abattoir Blues* and *The Lyre Of Orpheus*, recorded with his longtime backing group The Bad Seeds, are similarly split between two different musical styles. Both albums were recorded in 16 days in April 2004 with producer Nick Launay at Studio Ferber in Paris. The latter set is a more sedate affair, dominated by the piano balladry to which Cave had begun to turn in the mid 1990s on albums such as *The Boatman's Call* (1997). Its doomy elegance recalls Leonard Cohen in places, and it is embellished by subtle touches of flute, violin, and mandolin. By contrast, *Abattoir Blues* recalls the apocalyptic rock of the early part of Cave's career, from his work with The Birthday Party in the 1980s to the acclaimed albums *The Good Son* (1990) and *Henry's Dream* (1992). From the opening 'Get Ready For Love' through to 'There She Goes, My Beautiful World' and the title track, *Abattoir Blues* sounds like it could self-destruct at any moment, while The London Community Gospel Choir feature on several of the songs. Taken together, *Abattoir Blues* and *The Lyre Of Orpheus* provide a fitting encapsulation of the two sides of Cave's musical career.

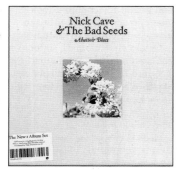

Franz Ferdinand **Franz Ferdinand**

Sony 92441 (U.S.A.) / Domino WIG 136 (U.K.)
Released February 2004

Hot Fuss **The Killers**

Island 000246802 (U.S.A.) / Lizard King LIZARD011 (U.K.)
Released June 2004

Silent Alarm **Bloc Party**

V2 205 (U.S.A.) / Wichita WEBB075 (U.K.)
Released January 2005

In the early 2000s, guitar-based rock was revitalized first by The Strokes and The White Stripes and then by a slew of bands that drew on the post-punk and new-wave scenes of the late 1970s and early 1980s.

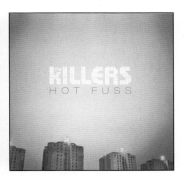

In the U.K., the charge was led by Franz Ferdinand, the group formed in Glasgow in 2001 by a trio of art students and a life-model-turned-drummer. The group signed to Domino in 2003 and became overnight sensations in their homeland with the release of their second single, 'Take Me Out,' which mixed wiry guitars with a disco backbeat and euphoric, chanted vocals. Issued later the same year, *Franz Ferdinand* kept to much the same template. It topped the U.K. albums chart and won the 2004 Mercury Music Prize.

Hailing from the Nevada desert, the Las Vegas quartet The Killers arrived fully formed in the summer of 2004 with a sound derived equally from the angular art rock of Television and the synthesized new-wave pop of early-1980s Duran Duran. The Killers' debut, *Hot Fuss*, was an instant hit in the U.K., where sales were buoyed by the success of the singles 'Mr Brightside' and 'Somebody Told Me,' but struggled to have the same impact back home.

Back in Britain, the London foursome Bloc Party first caught the attention of the U.K. music press with the singles 'She's Hearing Voices' and 'Banquet' (2004), which sounded like Gang Of Four by way of Sonic Youth. Released early the following

year, *Silent Alarm* was immediately hailed as one of the more promising debuts of recent years. The album makes use of a much wider sonic palette than most of the group's peers' work, taking in windswept ballads and politically aware pop as well as the de rigueur arty punk.

Arular **M.I.A.**

XL 186 (U.S.A. & U.K.)
Released March 2005

An intoxicating mix of Eastern and Western musical influences, held together with cutting-edge beats and chart-friendly hooks, *Arular* is one the most forward-thinking pop records of recent times.

The album was preceded by the release of a 'mix-tape,' *Piracy Funds Terrorism*, which gave a strong indication of the multicultural mishmash of musical styles that would appear on M.I.A.'s debut album proper. Its title also hints at the revolutionary political aspect to the lyrics of many of her songs. These clearly bear the influence of the singer's upbringing: her Sri Lankan father was a prominent activist in the country's civil war.

Born Maya Arulpragasam, M.I.A. spent her childhood in Sri Lanka, before returning to London, England, the city of her birth, in her teens to study art. There she became acquainted with former Elastica vocalist Justine Frischmann, who co-wrote *Arular*'s closing track, 'Galang.' Issued as a single in 2004, the electro-dancehall-hip-hop hybrid of 'Galang' gave M.I.A. an instant U.K. club hit, and brought anticipation for her full-length debut to fever pitch.

She didn't disappoint: *Arular* – which leaked on to the internet months before its official release, serving only to increase the hype around it – is positively overflowing with memorable songs that recall Dizzee Rascal or Missy Elliott at their most euphoric. M.I.A.'s vocals are delivered in a mix of London street slang and Sri Lankan patois, while the non-standard musical elements – the steel drums on 'Bingo,' the Brazilian trumpets on 'Bucky Done Gun' – are integral to the songs rather than sounding like artificial afterthoughts. The album makes canny use of an intriguing assortment of producers and co-writers, from former Pulp bassist Steve Mackey to U.K. chart-pop mastermind Richard X.

Be **Common**

Geffen 004670 (U.S.A.) / Island 9882497 (U.K.)
Released May 2005

Hip-hop in the early 21st century had begun to resemble rock music in the 1970s, with too many acts opting to punish their listeners with bloated, unfocused double-disk concept albums. *Be* is a rare beast: a short, punchy masterpiece of modern rap, all killer and no filler.

Born Lonnie Rashied Lynn, Common produced some of the best underground hip-hop of the 1990s, on such albums as *Resurrection* (1994, under the name Common Sense) and *One Day It'll Make Sense* (1997). He began to attract wider mainstream attention with his first major-label effort, 2000's *Like Water For Chocolate*, but misfired on the sprawling, psychedelic *Electric Circus* (2002), intended as a hip-hop update of Jimi Hendrix's *Electric Ladyland*.

On *Be*, Common reined in his talents to produce a concise, 40-minute set of

refined, thought-provoking songs. Some long-term fans were dubious about his decision to place pop-rap producer Kanye West behind the board for the bulk of *Be*'s 12 songs, fearing that Common was planning to move towards a slick, commercial sound. But *Be* is nothing of the sort. Instead, it draws on the effortless funk and murky textures of Sly & The Family Stone and Curtis Mayfield. The album was Common's most popular to date, peaking at Number Two in the U.S.A. and drawing near-unanimous critical plaudits.

In Your Honor **Foo Fighters**

Roswell/RCA 68038 (U.S.A.) / 82876701932 (U.K.)
Released June 2005

Foo Fighters' defining work, the two-disk set *In Your Honor* is split equally between electric and acoustic rock.

The bulk of the songs on *In Your Honor* were inspired by people who frontman Dave Grohl met on John Kerry's 2004 Presidential Election campaign trail. Kerry might have lost out to George W. Bush, but Grohl stuck with the songs, molding them into this sweeping double album.

Grohl was, of course, the drummer in Nirvana, until Kurt Cobain's suicide brought the band to a sudden end. By the end of the 1990s, however, he had established Foo Fighters as an important band in its own right, by way of a 1995 self-titled debut (much of which Grohl had recorded alone, at home, while still in Nirvana), *The Color And The Shape* (1997), and *There Is Nothing Left To Lose* (1999). The post-grunge formula had grown stale by the time of *One By One* (2002), leading Grohl and his current crop of bandmates – bassist Nate Mendel, drummer Taylor Hawkins, and guitarist Chris Shiflett – to try something new with *In Your Honor*.

The album devotes one whole disk to each of the two sides of Foo Fighters' musical personality, and in doing so affords the group room to diversify. Grohl sings through a wall of distortion on the punishing title track, and sounds angrier than ever before on the short sharp shock of 'Hell.' The second disk is much more reflective, however, and even finds room for an unexpectedly gentle duet with Norah Jones. Former Led Zeppelin bassist John Paul Jones appears on the acoustic disk, too, as does John Homme of Queens Of The Stone Age (Grohl had previously starred as guest drummer on the latter group's *Songs From The Deaf*). *In Your Honor* continued Foo Fighters' unbroken run of commercial success, peaking at Number Two in the U.S.A. and the U.K, while 'Best Of You' was a transatlantic hit single.

Recording The Future

Has the evolution of recording technology helped or hindered the art of music during the last 50 years?

Naturally there are many different opinions. One can only imagine what Duke Ellington would have thought about a device like Pitch 'n Time, a studio processor that automatically corrects an out-of-tune vocal, or how many choice expletives Buddy Rich would have used to describe Roland's V-Drums, an electronic percussion kit that comes complete with rubber cymbals. It's quite clear, however, that with the passing of time – and the advent of affordable, professional-grade home-studio equipment – that the business of recording has increasingly become a one-dimensional affair. By and large, popular genres such as hip-hop and techno have had little use for big-studio acoustics. Automation and sophisticated do-it-yourself recording machinery have all but taken the professional studio out of the equation. Today, what once took an army of trained musicians and a roomful of songwriters now only takes a single producer and a modest amount of gear.

Consequently, the recording business, like many other industries, now finds itself in a perpetual state of consolidation. In 2005 three of the most respected recording studios – New York's Hit Factory, Alabama's Muscle Shoals Sound Studio, and Cello Studios in Los Angeles (formerly the renowned Western Studios) – ceased operations within weeks of each other. Observers claim that the demise of these and other legendary facilities is due in large part to the DIY trend. "People can easily have a studio in their home if they want," remarked a Hit Factory employee. "This is an expensive building to run." Meanwhile automation, which helped seal the fate of studio house bands – the likes of Motown's Funk Brothers and Hollywood's Wrecking Crew – during the 1970s and 1980s, has made it increasingly difficult for those hoping to launch a brilliant career as a session player in today's music market.

And yet the proliferation of home-studio digital technology, combined with a growing internet-based independent music movement, has been a godsend for countless up-and-coming musicians looking for a way to bust into the business. Unlike their predecessors, who were forced to borrow large sums of cash to make a decent demo or make knee-marks on the rug of some record executive's office, for only a few hundred dollars today's musical wannabe can create a studio-quality multitrack production using little more than a guitar, an entry-level digital recorder, and a CD burner. Such functions as drag-and-drop editing and motorized faders have become standard issue on many digital audio workstations, and this kind of micro-ingenuity has given basement dwellers a fighting chance against the forces of evil in the big, bad world of music.

"In reality, maybe one-third of the hits I've done have originated in the home or home-type studio," says R&B engineer Dave 'Hard Drive' Pensado, who prepared Pink's 2001 multiplatinum effort *M!ssundaztood*, recorded mainly in the home studio of Pink's producer Linda Perry. "While there are definitely some sonic improvements to be made, in many ways there are a lot of things the home guys do that are in fact better than the recordings that come from a big facility. That's because, in general, the creativity that emerges from a home studio almost always surpasses that of an expensive studio. Never mind the sound quality; personally, I'd rather start with the kind of feeling, emotion, and creativity you get on a homemade record like Pink's. That's the main thing."

Hear Today, Gone Tomorrow

One thing's for certain: the tremendous technological wave that swept over the music business during the 1990s has irrevocably altered the way we receive our music. The recent popularity of downloadable music sites such as Apple's iTunes and Napster's subscription service is living proof that music is no longer the tactile commodity it once was. Of course, this is nothing new: the fragile plastic and cramped cover space of the Compact Disc long ago diminished the visual aspect of the vinyl LP, while the ability for listeners to compile, burn, and shuffle tracks at will has rendered the age-old art of Side-One-Side-Two song sequencing obsolete.

Still, there's no denying the many benefits of digital portability. In a world where laptops outnumber desktops and cell phones are fast replacing landlines, being able

Continued on page 313

2005

X&Y **Coldplay**

Capitol 74786 (U.S.A.) / Parlophone 72434747862 (U.K.)
Released June 2005

A transatlantic Number One hit, Coldplay's third album cemented the group's position as the biggest new band of the 2000s.

X&Y was one of the most eagerly anticipated album releases of recent times, to the extent that, when it was announced that Coldplay would be unable to deliver the album by March 2005 (and thus the end of the financial year), shares in EMI – the parent label of Capitol and Parlophone – fell by 18 percent.

Sessions for *X&Y* began in January 2004, and lasted into the early months of the following year. As on its predecessor, *A Rush Of Blood To The Head* (2002), production duties were split between Danton Supple, Ken Nelson, and Coldplay themselves. There had been much speculation prior to the release of *X&Y* that its long gestation was the result of the band's attempts to redefine its sound. Ultimately, though, the furthest they stray from the melodic, anthemic rock of their earlier work is on the lead-off track, 'Square One,' which begins with vocalist Chris Martin intoning 'You're in control / Is there anywhere you wanna go?' over soothing synthesizer chords and a funky backbeat from drummer Will Champion, but is reined back into familiar territory by Jonny Buckland's chiming guitar-playing.

The next three songs – 'What If,' 'White Shadows,' and 'Fix You' – stick to a template easily recognizable from earlier Coldplay albums. Each begins with Martin crouched over his piano or organ, before slowly building into an epic, string-laden chorus. It's a measure of their success that the group have already achieved such a distinctive signature sound; even the much talked-about 'Talk,' which appropriates a riff from 'Computer Love' by the pioneering electronic group Kraftwerk, sounds like nothing so much as it does Coldplay.

The second half of *X&Y* continues in much the same vein, alternating between epic, widescreen ballads and rock tracks that sound like a gentler U2. 'Low' features a guest appearance from Brian Eno, whose synthesizer parts are subtly reminiscent of his work in the late 1970s with David Bowie. Martin originally wrote the unlisted closing track, 'Til Kingdom Come,' for Johnny Cash, but the legendary country singer died before he could record it.

X&Y's centerpiece, 'Speed Of Sound,' was the first song by a British group to go straight into the Top Ten of the U.S. singles chart since The Beatles' 'Hey Jude' in 1968. The album itself was only the ninth in chart history to simultaneously debut at Number One in both the U.S.A. and the U.K. (the last was Radiohead's *Kid A* in 2000). It is also the second fastest-selling album of all time in the U.K., after *Be Here Now* (1997) by Oasis, having shifted close to 500,000 copies in its first week on sale.

Continued from page 311

Devils & Dust Bruce Springsteen

Sony 93900 (U.S.A.) / Columbia 5200002 (U.K.)
Released April 2005

On *Devils & Dust*, his 13th studio album, Bruce Springsteen ditched the E Street Band (again) in favor of a sparse, intimate sound pitched somewhere between *Nebraska* (1982) and *The Ghost Of Tom Joad* (1995).

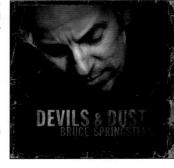

Springsteen's previous full-band set, the 9/11-themed *The Rising*, seemed almost obligatory in places, as though Springsteen – as one of the great American rock'n'roll heroes of the past three decades – felt compelled to reflect on a national tragedy. *Devils & Dust*, on the other hand, feels more like an album he wanted to make rather than one he felt he had to.

On the opening title track, Springsteen asks: "What would you do to survive? / Kill the things you love / Fear's a powerful thing." This theme of facing demons crops up time and again on the 12 narrative tales of *Devils & Dust*. Springsteen sings from the perspective of a range of troubled but essentially well-intentioned characters, from errant husbands to Nevada prostitutes. The already infamous lyrics to the song 'Reno' – "$200 straight in / Two-fifty up the ass" – earned Springsteen the first 'Parental Advisory' sticker of his career. Sonically, the album is brighter than either *Nebraska* or *The Ghost Of Tom Joad*, and in places producer Brendan O'Brien's overdubbed parts – be they strings, organ, or pedal steel – are a touch obtrusive. *Devils & Dust* works best at its starkest, such as on the closing 'Matamoras Banks.'

In the early 2000s no big album release was complete without a deluxe, audio-visual 'special edition,' and *Devils & Dust* is no exception. For a few dollars more you get the album itself plus a DVD of Springsteen performing solo-acoustic versions of five of the songs. *Devils & Dust* was well received by critics – *Rolling Stone* magazine concluded that it "sparkles in the right places like stars in a clear Plains sky" – and entered the U.S. *Billboard* chart at Number One.

to cart your entire record collection around on an MP3 player the size of your shirt pocket is enormously attractive. Above all, the transformation of music from a physical medium to a bunch of bits and bytes on your computer – as well as the seemingly infinite selection offered by most internet music libraries – has had the effect of making music increasingly disposable as listeners grow accustomed to downloading and listening, then quickly deleting and repeating.

"I've watched my kids buy a CD, and once they'd rip it, they could roller-skate over the original if they wanted to," says Napster's Chris Gorog. "It didn't matter, because at that point they didn't value it. What I believe is happening is an absolute paradigm shift in all media, but in music in particular, where people will clamor for instantaneous access to everything, any time, anywhere. That's what they'll pay for and that's what they'll really value. Let's face it, if you were a record collector, you spent years dragging around all those albums and CDs from place to place, listening to only a small percentage of them while all the rest gathered dust. But in this new environment, the idea of owning a CD, or a set of music files, or whatever, will become less essential. And, in time, the whole concept of how we value our music will change for good."

The question remains: are we better off today than we were 50 years ago when Frank Sinatra issued *In the Wee Small Hours*, proving once and for all the artistic merits of the long-playing album? Analog enthusiasts might argue that, even now, a mint-condition copy of the 1955 classic would still sound 'warmer' than its CD update; proponents of digital technology could counter that the luxury of downloading Ol' Blue Eyes' whole catalog in a matter of minutes is well worth any negligible loss of sound quality.

And yet rather than one medium proving its superiority over the other, within the past few years analog and digital have in many ways formed a mutually beneficial alliance. In the studio, recording artists seeking that 'classic' sound still cut their tracks using old-fashioned tape machines, then transfer the music on to digital equipment in order to edit and manipulate. At home, an array of user-friendly software packages make it possible for listeners to copy their favorite old vinyl selections on to the computer, removing crackles, pops and other annoyances along the way. In some respects, the merging of the two disparate cultures has helped bring the entire process full circle. Somewhere tonight, a traditionalist baby-boomer perusing Napster for the first time will stumble upon some long-lost classic album, download the tracks in seconds, and will be hooked instantly; while in the next room, his teenage offspring will carefully drop a needle on to his dad's pristine vinyl copy of *The White Album,* then sit transfixed at the sound of Paul McCartney's piano and the sight of that hypnotic rotating green apple.

2006

Whatever People Say I Am, That's What I'm Not
Arctic Monkeys

Domino WIG 162 (U.S.A. & U.K.)
Released January 2006

The fastest-selling debut album of all time in the U.K., *Whatever People Say I Am ...* served as a powerful statement of intent by one of the most promising British bands of recent times.

Arctic Monkeys formed at school in Sheffield, England, in 2003. All four bandmembers were still in their teens when 'I Bet You Look Good On The Dancefloor,' the group's first proper single, topped the U.K. singles chart in October 2005. While to some observers it appeared that Arctic Monkeys had appeared out of nowhere, the band had, in fact, built up a devoted following on the strength of fan-made demos and song files shared online, thus calling into question the traditional methods of marketing and promoting new musical acts.

In early 2007 the band's second single, 'When The Sun Goes Down,' a gritty tale of prostitution in one of Sheffield's poorest areas, gave the group a second U.K. Number 1. Like 'Dancefloor,' it drew praise not just for its catchy, punky sound but also for frontman Alex Turner's lyrics, which drew comparisons with the social-realist style of Morrissey and Jarvis Cocker.

▨ *Below: Arctic Monkeys made their live TV debut on* Later With Jools Holland *in the week that 'Dancefloor' topped the U.K. singles chart.*

The success of both singles considerably raised expectations for Arctic Monkeys' debut, but *Whatever People Say I Am* didn't disappoint. The album's title comes from a line spoken by Albert Finney in the 1960 movie *Saturday Night And Sunday Morning*. Turner later revealed that the movie had inspired several of the songs on the album, which when taken as a whole paint a vivid picture of early 21st century life in Northern Britain. Hailed by critics as a modern classic, *Whatever People Say I Am* provoked the kind of sales not seen for a guitar band in the U.K. since the Britpop boom of the mid 1990s, selling more copies in its first week than the rest of the Top 20 combined. The album sold respectably, if not quite so exceptionally, in the U.S.A., too, peaking at Number 24 on *Billboard* – no mean feat for a new British group – while its critical standing was confirmed when it won the Mercury Music Prize.

Modern Times Bob Dylan

Columbia 87606 (U.S.A. & U.K.)
Released August 2006

The 32nd studio album of Bob Dylan's career continued his latter day renaissance at a time when he seemed to be as popular as he'd ever been.

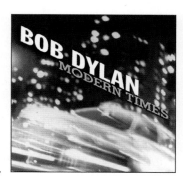

Given that there now tends to be an appreciable gap between them, Bob Dylan albums, and the release thereof, have become something of an event. *Modern Times* was no exception. As is customary, its arrival was preceded by frenzied speculation, and then followed by the kind of detailed contextual analysis usually reserved for newly discovered works by the great masters of literature and poetry.

Modern Times was released during a period when Dylan was hard to avoid. The first of three planned volumes of autobiography, *Chronicles Volume One*,

had not long ago been issued in paperback; two high-profile documentaries, *Masked And Anonymous* and *No Direction Home* – the latter directed by Martin Scorsese – had recently been released; and Dylan himself had taken advantage of a short break in his seemingly never-ending touring schedule to star in a commercial for Victoria's Secret. In May 2006 he also started hosting a weekly radio show for XM Satellite Radio. Each week's *Theme Time Radio Hour* contains a selection of songs, chosen by Dylan, on a common theme – anything from 'Shoes' to 'Divorce.'

Modern Times is similar in sound to its predecessor, *Love And Theft*. Although it was recorded digitally, using Protools, its main musical antecedents are to be found in the jazz and blues of the 1930s and '40s. This produces an interesting distinction. The recordings are so clean and precise that they could only have been made, as the album's title suggests, in the present day. But the songs themselves sound as though they could have been written at any point in the last hundred years; the album's only direct reference to 'modern times' is a slightly awkward passing mention of the contemporary R&B singer Alicia Keys at the start of the second verse of 'Thunder On The Mountain.'

Despite this apparent lack of contemporary relevance, *Modern Times* certainly struck a chord with the 21st century record-buying public, to the extent that it was Dylan's first *Billboard* chart-topper for 30 years. Its release was not, however, without controversy. Despite the fact that Dylan is credited with having written all ten of its songs, quite a few them seemed to be rooted significantly in old and not particularly obscure standards.

The most obvious example is 'Rollin' And Tumblin',' which shares its name and much of its arrangement with an old Muddy Waters hit, but there are plenty more. But while some critics were troubled by this discovery, and by the fact that Dylan had made no effort to reveal his sources, others felt that he was simply working in the old folk tradition of borrowing and collecting songs and letting them evolve on their own.

Alright, Still **Lily Allen**

Capitol 74566 (U.S.A.) / EMI/Regal 094636702827 (U.K.)
Released July 2006

Back To Black **Amy Winehouse**

Republic 08555 (U.S.A.) / Island 1734128 (U.K.)
Released October 2006

Introducing **Joss Stone**

Virgin 76268 (U.S.A.) / Relentless CDREL 13 (U.K.)
Released March 2007

Bold, brash, and frequently brilliant, Lily Allen, Amy Winehouse, and Joss Stone provided a much-needed antidote to a British pop scene dominated by the lightweight stars of reality television.

Like the Arctic Monkeys before her, Lily Allen (the daughter of comic actor Keith Allen) was very much a product of the internet age. During the early months of 2006 she became the first break-out star of MySpace, the social-networking website on which she had posted snippets of her songs, notably 'LDN.' The buzz around her grew so quickly that the British newspaper *The Observer* put her on the cover of its *Music Monthly* magazine supplement even before she had released a record.

Allen's first single, the deceptively breezy 'Smile,' went straight to Number 1 in the U.K., where it became the most unavoidable song of the summer (by 2007, Allen herself admitted to being "so sick" of it). *Alright, Still* followed shortly thereafter and drew rave reviews for its laid-back blend of pop and ska and its sharp, literate lyrics, which sometimes recall the biting social commentary of The Streets. Just as important to the album's success was Allen's personality. She's confident, outspoken, and, by comparison to her pop-puppet rivals, very much her own woman.

So, too, is Amy Winehouse, despite her repeated public acts of attempted self-destruction. *Back To Black* was her second album, but might as well have been her first. She first emerged in 2003 with the rather more stage-managed *Frank*, an album of pleasant jazz-soul songs that only occasionally hinted at the real Winehouse. The album received largely positive reviews and sold well, but its author was quick to dismiss it.

Winehouse seemed almost to disappear after the release of *Frank* amid frequent newspaper stories about her battles with drugs, alcohol, and eating disorders. Then, three years on from her debut, came 'Rehab,' a stirring instant-classic that seemed at once to confirm and shrug off the newspaper reports about her lifestyle. Both the single and the subsequent *Back To Black* were given a superb, modern-day Motown polish by the producer Mark Ronson (who also had a hand in *Alright, Still*, and in 2007 released a star-studded covers album, *Version*, which features guest vocals by Winehouse, Allen, and a host of other singers, among them Robbie Williams).

Ronson's excellent production aside, *Back To Black*'s core strength is the quality of Winehouse's songwriting. Few contemporary singers have voices as good as Winehouse's; on this evidence, even fewer can write songs as good as hers. 'Rehab,' 'You Know I'm No Good,' and the Beach Boys-like 'Love Is A Losing Game' are about as good as modern pop gets.

By the end of 2006, Allen and Winehouse had both topped the single and album charts in the U.K. and found themselves at the pinnacle of the British pop scene. In 2007, both made the breakthrough in the U.S.A., too. *Back To Black* was particularly successful – despite the fact that Winehouse's year was dominated by increasingly lurid reports about the state of her health – hitting Number 6 on the *Billboard* Top 200. (Allen's *Alright, Still* peaked a more modest Number 20.)

It was, all in all, a good year for British women on the U.S. charts. A few weeks later, another U.K. soul diva, Joss Stone, hit Number 2 with *Introducing* – the highest ever *Billboard* chart entry by a British female artist. While its title might suggest it to be a debut, *Introducing* was in fact Stone's third album. The precocious singer-songwriter had released her first album, *The Soul Sessions*, a couple of months after her 16th birthday in 2003, and followed it a year later with the more contemporary-sounding *Mind, Body & Soul*.

Having subsequently signed to Virgin, she spent the next couple of years out of the limelight, but seemingly being groomed for superstardom. *Introducing*, which Stone claims is the first of her albums to be "truly me," features an impressive array of guest stars including Lauryn Hill, Common, and hip-hop producer Raphael Saadiq (whose previous credits include albums and singles by Mary J. Blige, Snoop Dogg, and Macy Gray). Stone and her cohorts spent over a year working on the album at a range of famous recording facilities such as Compass Point in the Bahamas and New York's Electric Lady Studios.

With her sound suitably updated to reflect the influence of 1970s R&B and modern hip-hop, Stone was also given a striking new image – for which she even adopted a rather baffling faux-American accent. But while this clearly helped consolidate her appeal in the U.S.A., the response back home in Britain was decidedly lukewarm. Whereas *Mind, Body & Soul* spent several weeks at the top of the charts and sold over a million copies in the U.K. alone (as did *The Soul Sessions*), *Introducing* stalled at Number 12 and didn't look like coming close to matching the success of its predecessors.

2006

Ys Joanna Newsom

Drag City 303 (U.S.A. & U.K.)
Released November 2006

The pinnacle of the mid-2000s free-folk scene, Joanna Newsom's Ys is one of the most original, otherworldly albums of recent times.

Newsom grew up in Nevada City, California, as the youngest member of a distinctly musical family. But where the rest of the Newsoms took up conventional instruments – her mother plays the piano, her father the guitar, her brother the drums, and her sister the cello – she opted, at the age of seven, for the harp. She has stuck with it ever since, fashioning songs arranged for harp and voice that take in everything from Appalachian folk and jazz to avant-garde composition and West African classical music.

At 22 she released *The Milk-Eyed Mender* (2004), a striking collection of gentle ballads and whimsical introspection. The album was well received by critics, even if some found Newsom's voice rather too cloying (more than one reviewer compared it to Lisa Simpson's). Songs such as 'Sprout & The Bean' and 'This Side Of The Blue' were certainly a cut above the average, and belied comparison with any other indie-rock act of the time.

On the strength of *The Milk-Eyed Mender*, Newsom was able to call in an impressive array of collaborators for *Ys*, which goes several steps further than its predecessor's unconventional arrangements and quirky melodies. The initial harp-and-vocal tracks – five expansive songs of which only one is less than nine minutes long – were recorded by alt-rock luminary Steve Albini; Newsom then collaborated with Van Dyke Parks on a series of sweeping orchestral arrangements before inviting Jim O'Rourke to mix the record. The result is an album about as demanding as one might care to listen to, but also one that is full of charming and surprising hooks, harmonies, and complex, richly poetic lyrics, which even go so far as to explain the difference between meteors and meteorites.

High School Musical (Original Soundtrack)

Disney 861246 (U.S.A.) / Disney 3654622 (U.K.)
Released January 2006

In a year that seemed to lack a common musical theme, it was perhaps fitting that the biggest selling album of 2006 in the U.S.A. was the soundtrack to a made-for-TV Disney movie.

Based loosely on the themes and ideas of *Romeo And Juliet*, the *High School Musical* movie tells the story of two students, played by Zac Efron and Vanessa Hudgens, who discover a shared love, first of karaoke and then of musicals. In auditioning for a big school production, they inadvertently bring to a head divisions between their rival social circles. While the plot might not be particularly revolutionary, the movie had just the right mix of song, dance, and drama for its audience, which made it Disney's most-watched TV broadcast when it first aired on January 20th, 2006.

The accompanying soundtrack was recorded in five days by producers Kenny Ortega, Bill Borden, and Barry Rosenbush, with each of the main cast-members reprising their roles – and songs – from the movie. The material is split, as one might expect, between upbeat, empowering pop ('Get'cha Head In The Game,' 'Stick To The Status Quo') and heartfelt balladry ('When There Was Me And You,' 'Breaking Free').

Released ten days prior to the movie's cable-TV debut, the album sold slowly to begin with, shifting less than 7,000 copies in its first week and entering the *Billboard* charts at a lowly Number 143. Within a few months, however, *High School Musical* had become something of a nationwide phenomenon. By March, the album had risen to the top of the charts, making it the first TV soundtrack album to reach Number 1 in the U.S.A. since *Miami Vice* in 1985. Widespread international success quickly followed for both the movie and its soundtrack, which has since topped the charts in Britain, Australia, and a number of South American nations and sold over seven million copies worldwide. In addition, nine of the album's 11 tracks have appeared on *Billboard*'s Hot 100 singles chart.

Disney has since produced *Sing-Along* and *Dance-Along* versions of *High School Musical* and all manner of additional merchandise, including a video game. The August 2007 premiere of *High School Musical 2* on the Disney Channel pulled in 17.2 million viewers, making it the highest rated cable-TV broadcast in U.S. history. A third movie is planned for 2008.

■ *Left: Joanna Newsom performing the tongue-twisting 'Clam, Crab, Cockle, Cowrie' on television in May 2007.*

2007

In Rainbows **Radiohead**

www.inrainbows.com
Released October 2007

In 2007, Radiohead returned after a four-year hiatus to reclaim their position as one of the world's finest bands – not to mention one of its canniest.

Few bands have so fully embraced the possibilities of the internet as have Radiohead. The five-piece group from Oxford, England, was one of the first major-label acts to explore ways of utilizing the web as a means of maintaining a dialogue with fans, promoting new releases, and generally avoiding going about the business of being a band in a conventional fashion. There was a certain inevitability, then, about the band's decision to release *In Rainbows*, their seventh studio album, as a bunch of bits and bytes via radiohead.com.

The band's contract with EMI/Capitol expired after the release of the patchy *Hail To The Thief* in 2003, and they seemed in no hurry to renew it. In the intervening period, Radiohead toured the world as a completely independent entity, while frontman Thom Yorke licensed his solo debut, *The Eraser*, to a relatively small British label, XL, rather than his friends at EMI-Time Warner.

What came as more of a surprise, and provoked furious debate among musicians and financiers alike, was the band's decision to offer *In Rainbows* for sale at a price of the buyer's choosing. Upon logging on to the Radiohead web site, visitors were told "It's up to you," and allowed to pick a price between £0.00 and £99.99, the upshot of which was a chorus of opinion pieces about the (latest) death of the music industry in publications as diverse as the *New Musical Express* and the *Wall Street Journal*. But while listeners could, if they wanted, get the album for free, unofficial figures suggested Radiohead fans to be a fairly honest bunch. Over a million copies were 'sold' on the first day, for a reported average price of around £4.00 (approximately $8.20 at the time of writing).

While some commentators praised *In Rainbows* as a bold, egalitarian move, others were quick to point out that, without a middle-man, Radiohead stood to earn a lot more per-copy for downloads of the album than they would have had they issued it is as a conventional, major-label disc. (In any case, the band plans to release the album on CD in early 2008, while their most devoted fans were given the option of pre-ordering a two CD 'discbox' set of *In Rainbows* for a hefty £40.)

Amid all the discussion of the ramifications of Radiohead's download experiment, the actual musical content of *In Rainbows* seemed to become a secondary concern – which is a shame, because a lot of it is actually very good. While one or two songs, such as the lumpen 'Bodysnatchers,' suggest a slow slide into musical middle-age, others – notably the hypnotic 'Weird Fishes/Arpeggi' and 'All I Need' – are up there with the band's best work. And where parts of their previous albums gave the impression that Radiohead were trying desperately to break free from self-imposed shackles, the restrained arrangements of 'Nude,' 'Faust Arp,' and 'Videotape' can be taken as evidence of a band totally comfortable in its own skin. *In Rainbows* isn't Radiohead's best album, but it is at least as coherent and cohesive a listen as their twin masterpieces, *OK Computer* and *Kid A*.

■ *Below: Before completing the recording of* **In Rainbows***, Radiohead premiered most of the songs from it on their 2006 world tour.*

2007

Neon Bible **Arcade Fire**

Merge 285 (U.S.A.) / Sonovox 1724447 (U.K.)
Released March 2007

With *Neon Bible*, Arcade Fire consolidated their status as one of the most promising new bands of the early 2000s and established genuine mainstream success for the first time.

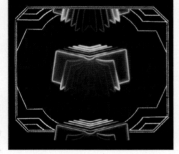

Arcade Fire formed in 2003 in Montreal, Quebec, Canada, around a nucleus of Win Butler, his wife Régine Chassagne, and Win's brother William as more of a collective than a traditional band, with an ever-changing membership that sometimes swells into double figures. After self-releasing an eponymous EP, the group signed to Merge for the release of *Funeral* (2004), which sounds less like a debut album than the work of a band at the peak of its powers. Its quality of songwriting and rich arrangements – which make use of unconventional instruments such as hurdy gurdy, harp, and mandolin alongside the expected guitar, bass, and drums – drew widespread acclaim and even got "Canada's most intriguing rock band" on the cover of *Time* magazine.

Neon Bible is essentially a more polished, assured take on the musical themes of *Funeral*. Many of the songs are underpinned by pipe organ, while a Hungarian orchestra and a military choir also feature. The overall effect is that of a 21st century update of rock at its most epic. Where *Funeral* was a rather insular record, with much of its mood dictated by the deaths of relatives of several bandmembers during the recording sessions, *Neon Bible* looks out at the world at large, albeit with a similarly bleak mindset.

The album's release was trailed by a well-thought-out publicity campaign that included a faux-religious pamphlet, a *Neon Bible* hotline, and a series of intriguing videos posted both on the band's website and on YouTube. The cumulative effect of these efforts was that *Neon Bible* hit Number 2 on both the U.S. and U.K. album charts, a marked improvement on the sleeper success of its predecessor.

Shock Value **Timbaland**

Blackground/Interscope 8594 (U.S.A.) / Polydor 1726606 (U.K.)
Released April 2007

On *Shock Value*, the 21st century's most notable record producer became a bona fide solo star in his own right.

Timbaland first rose to prominence in his mid 20s after working on acclaimed albums and singles by Missy Elliott, Aaliyah, and Ginuwine. By the turn of the millennium he had established himself as one of the most sought-after producers and mixers around and over the next few years worked with everybody from Beck and Bubba Sparxxx to Lil' Kim and Limp Bizkit. One thing he seemed to lack, however, was any meaningful success in his own right.

The comparative failure of his debut album, *Tim's Bio: Life From Da Basement*, in 1998 seemed to have put Timbaland off the idea of a solo career for good. But then, in 2006, he gave himself a guest spot on two of his biggest productions yet, the U.S. Number 1 hits 'Promiscuous' by Nelly Furtado and 'SexyBack' by Justin Timberlake, and was encouraged by the response, so set about having another crack at a career outside the recording studio.

The resulting *Shock Value* is a star-studded and sometimes baffling collection of the kind of futuristic R&B-pop hybrids for which Timbaland is famous. At its best, such as on the singles 'Give It To Me' and 'The Way I Are,' *Shock Value* is as good as Timbaland gets, but elsewhere he seems to try to too hard to assert his 'street' credentials instead of concentrating on what he does best: that is, fashioning some of modern music's most groundbreaking sounds. Overall, *Shock Value* is simply too confusingly eclectic for its own good. Collaborations with rock bands The Hives and Fall Out Boy don't quite work, while '2 Man Show,' on which Timbaland's main vocal contribution consists mostly of a series of spoken instructions to guest piano-man Elton John, is just plain bizarre.

Graduation **Kanye West**

Rock-A-Fella/Def Jam 009541 (U.S.A.) / Mercury 1745502 (U.K.)
Released September 2007

Curtis **50 Cent**

Shady/Aftermath/Interscope 008931 (U.S.A.) / Polydor 1746491 (U.K.)
Released September 2007

When the two biggest hip-hop albums of the year were scheduled for release on the same day it confirmed that nothing boosts sales better than a race to the top of the charts.

 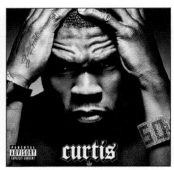

Rap music found itself in a curious position in the mid 2000s. After a decade during which artists such as Eminem and OutKast routinely dominated the charts and outsold all comers, it seemed to have hit something of a slump. Thankfully for all concerned, the fall of 2007 marked the return of two of the hip-hop world's biggest hitters. And when Kanye West moved the release of his *Graduation* back to the same day that 50 Cent's *Curtis* was set to drop, the hype machine went into overdrive.

It's not entirely clear whether West had a battle for the Number 1 spot in mind when he rescheduled *Graduation*, but that's certainly what he got, particularly after 50 Cent upped the ante by announcing that he would 'retire' as a solo artist if *Curtis* didn't win the race.

Perhaps inevitably, *Graduation* won out – in the end by quite a considerable margin (West's album sold a little under a million copies in its first week on sale in the U.S.A.; *Curtis* managed a mere 691,000). From a strictly musical perspective, it seemed as though the best man won. While *Graduation* doesn't quite hit the peaks of West's two previous albums, *The College Graduate* and *Late Registration*, it is certainly an engaging listen from start to finish, demonstrating once again West's magpie-like ear for interesting source material. Among the surprising assortment of artists sampled on the album are Laura Nyro, Steely Dan, Daft Punk, and the pioneering German group Can, while 'Homecoming' was co-written by Coldplay's Chris Martin.

Curtis, on the other hand, doesn't show much of a progression from 50 Cent's previous albums, *Get Rich Or Die Tryin'* and *The Massacre*, but tracks such as 'I Get Money' and 'Ayo Technology' (a duet with Justin Timberlake) are as catchy as ever. Since coming in a distant second on the *Billboard* Hot 100, 50 Cent has played down his threat to quit the rap game, although he has suggested that his next album, *Before I Self Destruct*, set for release in early 2008, might really be his last.

In the end, despite losing out in the race to the top of the charts, 50 Cent was canny enough to realize that the whole enterprise had been beneficial to both himself and West. "This marks a great moment for hip-hop music," he told the *Associated Press*, "one that will go down in history." And he was probably right. Only once before, when Guns N' Roses issued *Use Your Illusion I* and *II* simultaneously, had a pair of albums each sold more than 600,000 copies during the same week, suggesting that, actually, hip-hop was in a much healthier state than was previously thought.

Blackout **Britney Spears**

Jive 19073 (U.S.A.) / Jive 88697190732 (U.K.)
Released October 2007

At the end of so cataclysmic a 2007, few would have expected Britney Spears to make the best album of her career. But that's exactly what she did.

Pop music is a fickle, fast-moving business, in which the stars of one year are often forgotten the next. By the usual standards, then, the fact that Britney Spears's profile was so high in 2007 when she hadn't released an album of new material for four years is nothing short of astounding. Not that there wasn't plenty to keep the press occupied in the intervening period.

Divorced (for the second time), shaven headed, and separated from her children – all before her 26th birthday – Spears reached her lowest ebb in the fall of 2007. But somehow, barely a few weeks after losing custody of her two young sons, she was still able to re-emerge with the best and most cohesive album of her career. How much she had to do with the making of it is open to debate: her voice is often mangled, digitally, almost beyond recognition, while a whole host of modern pop's finest producers are listed on the credits, among them Timbaland's right-hand man, Nate 'Danja' Hills; The Neptunes; and Bloodshy & Avant, most famous for their work on Spears's 2004 mega-hit 'Toxic.'

Despite the wide range of collaborators involved in recording them, each of *Blackout*'s hot, sticky songs fits, sonically and thematically, with the rest. 'Gimme More,' 'Get Naked (I Got A Plan),' and 'Freakshow' are up there with the best of Britney's back catalogue, even if one can't quite imagine them having as wide an appeal as her earlier sugary pop.

The only major disappointment comes in the form of the lyrics. One might have expected Spears to have a thing or two to say about the past few years, but the closest she gets to that is to complain about "pictures of my derriere in the magazines" in 'Piece Of Me' – to which the obvious response might be to suggest she stops going out without wearing any underwear.

CLASSIC TRACKS

BACK TO BACK

ALBUMS